June 18–22, 2018
Ithaca, NY, USA

Association for
Computing Machinery

*Advancing Computing as a Science & Profession*

# ACM EC'18

## Proceedings of the 2018 ACM Conference on Economics and Computation

*Sponsored by:*

***ACM SIGecom***

*Supported by:*

***Facebook, Lyft, Microsoft, Uber, Cornell University, & Google***

Association for
Computing Machinery

*Advancing Computing as a Science & Profession*

**The Association for Computing Machinery**
**2 Penn Plaza, Suite 701**
**New York, New York 10121-0701**



**ISBN:** 978-1-4503-5829-3 (Digital)

**ISBN:** 978-1-4503-6148-4 (Print)

Additional copies may b**ISBN:** l prepaid from:
**ACM Order Department**
PO Box 30777
New York, NY 10087-0777, USA

Phone: 1-800-342-6626 (USA and Canada)
+1-212-626-0500 (Global)
Fax: +1-212-944-1318
E-mail: acmhelp@acm.org
Hours of Operation: 8:30 am – 4:30 pm ET

# EC 2018 Foreword

The papers in these Proceedings were presented at the Nineteenth ACM Conference on Economics and Computation (EC'18), held between June 18 and 22, 2018, at Cornell University in Ithaca, New York, USA. Since 1999 the ACM Special Interest Group on Electronic Commerce (SIGecom) has sponsored EC, the leading scientific conference on advances in theory, systems, and applications at the interface of economics and computation, including applications to electronic commerce.

The program committee selected 70 papers from among 269 submissions that were received by February 15, 2018. Papers were invited in the following three non-exclusive focus areas:

- TF: Theory and Foundations
- AI: Artificial Intelligence and Applied Game Theory
- EEA: Experimental, Empirical, and Applications

Each paper was reviewed by at least three program committee members and two senior program committee members on the basis of significance, scientific novelty, technical quality, readability, and relevance to the conference. Following the tradition of recent iterations of the conference, the authors were asked to align their submission with one or two of the tracks. The next table summarizes the number of submissions and the number of accepted papers for each possible combination of tracks.

| Tracks | Submissions | Accepted |
|---|---|---|
| TF | 166 | 46 |
| AI | 37 | 9 |
| TF+AI | 27 | 7 |
| EEA | 28 | 7 |
| TF+EEA | 5 | 1 |
| AI+EEA | 6 | 0 |
| **Total** | **269** | **70** |

Of the 70 accepted papers, 36 are published in these Proceedings. The remaining 34, at the authors' request, are included as abstracts with pointers to full working papers that the authors guarantee to be reliable for at least two years. This option accommodates the practices of fields outside of computer science in which conference publishing can preclude journal publishing. We expect that many of the papers in these Proceedings will appear at a later date in a more polished and complete form in scientific journals.

Papers were presented in two parallel sessions. To emphasize commonalities among the problems studied at EC, and to encourage discussion at the conference, sessions were organized by topic rather than by focus area, and no indication of a paper's focus area(s) was given at the conference or appears in these proceedings.

EC'18 featured the following invited plenary talks:

- *Will the Market Fix the Market?,* by Eric Budish (Chicago Booth)
- *Algorithmic Fairness and the Social Welfare Function,* by Sendhil Mullainathan (Harvard)

- *ACM SIGecom Test of Time Award: First Analyses of the Generalized Second Price Auction (GSP) for Sponsored Search,* awarded jointly to three papers:
    - Gagan Aggarwal, Ashish Goel, and Rajeev Motwani. "Truthful auctions for pricing search keywords." Proceedings of the 7th ACM Conference on Electronic Commerce. ACM, 2006.
    - Benjamin Edelman, Michael Ostrovsky, and Michael Schwarz. "Internet advertising and the generalized second-price auction: Selling billions of dollars worth of keywords." American Economic Review 97.1 (2007): 242-259
    - Hal R. Varian, "Position auctions." International Journal of Industrial Organization 25.6 (2007): 1163-1178
- *SIGecom Doctoral Dissertation Award,* by Aviad Rubinstein

The conference program also included an informal evening talk by Vitalik Buterin (Ethereum), and a Women in EC breakfast.

The following five papers were shortlisted for the best paper award:

- Mohammad Akbarpour and Shengwu Li. "Credible Mechanisms"
- Martin Lackner and Piotr Skowron. "Consistent Approval-Based Multi-Winner Rules"
- Yiling Chen, Chara Podimata, Ariel Procaccia and Nisarg Shah. "Strategyproof Linear Regression in High Dimensions"
- Omar Besbes and Amine Allouah. "Prior-Independent Optimal Auctions"
- Mark Braverman, Jieming Mao, Jon Schneider and Matthew Weinberg. "Selling to a No-Regret Buyer"

The winner of the best paper award was "Credible Mechanisms" by Akbarpour and Li. The best full paper award was given to "Selling to a No-Regret Buyer", by Braverman, Mao, Schneider and Weinberg.

In addition to the main technical program, EC'18 also featured six tutorials:

- *Emerging Research Directions Regarding Incentives and Cryptocurrencies,* presented by Jacob Leshno, Arvind Narayanan, Georgios Piliouras, Alex Psomas and Matt Weinberg
- *The Menu-Size of Precise and Approximate Revenue Maximizing Auctions,* presented by Kira Goldner and Yannai Gonczarowski
- *Information, Persuasion, and Decision Making,* presented by Bo Waggoner and Haifeng Xu
- *Algorithmic Fairness,* presented by Sam Corbett-Davies, Rachel Cummings, Sharad Goel and Jamie Morgenstern
- *Industrial Organization,* presented by Michael Dinerstein, Greg Lewis and Tom Wollmann
- *Gross Substitutes: Combinatorial Structure and Algorithms,* presented by Renato Paes Leme and Inbal Talgam-Cohen,

three technical workshops:

- *Frontiers of Market Design.* Organizers: Alex Teytelboym and Mohammad Akbarpour

- *Workshop on Opinion Aggregation, Dynamics, and Elicitation.* Organizers: Yiling Chen, Vincent Conitzer, Ashish Goel, Kamesh Munagala
- *2nd Workshop on Mechanism Design for Social Good.* Organizers: Rediet Abebe and Kira Goldner,

a mentoring workshop organized by Nicole Immorlica, Ruta Mehta, and Matt Weinberg, as well as a poster session in which 25 posters were presented.

We thank the Workshop Chairs, Scott Duke Kominers and Jenn Wortman Vaughan, and Tutorial Chairs, Itai Ashlagi and Katrina Ligett, for assembling the workshop and tutorial programs.

We hope that you find this conference program interesting and thought provoking and that the conference furnished a valuable opportunity to share ideas with other researchers from institutions around the world.

We are very grateful to the SIGecom chair Kevin Leyton-Brown, for his help in organizing the conference. Our thanks to Robert Kleinberg and David Easley for serving as the Local Arrangements Chairs and Ayush Sekhari and Makis Arsenis for maintaining the conference website. We also want to acknowledge EasyChair for the facilities provided to support the submission and review of the papers. We thank Lisa Tolles for her professional work in the production of the conference proceedings. We are very grateful to Scott Duke Kominers for shepherding us through the publication process. Cornell University was kind enough to provide the facilities for hosting the conference. The generosity of our sponsors is gratefully acknowledged: Facebook, Lyft, Microsoft Research, Uber, SIGecom, the Economics and Computer Science Departments at Cornell, and Google.

Listed on a separate page are the members of our community who yielded that scarcest of resources, time to assist in assessing the merits of the submissions. Last, but not least, our thanks to the Program Committee and the Senior Program Committee for their insight and industry.

| **Edith Elkind** | **Rakesh Vohra** | **Eva Tardos** |
|---|---|---|
| *EC'18 Program Chair* | *EC'18 Program Chair* | *EC'18 General Chair* |
| *University of Oxford, UK* | *University of Pennsylvania, UK* | *Cornell, USA* |

# Table of Contents

## Session 4b: Information Acquisition and Rationality



## Session Invited Talk



## Session 5a: Matching



## Session 5b: Prophet Inequalities

## Session 6a: Equilibrium Dynamics



## Session 6b: Mechanism Design II



## Session 7a: Equilibrium Analysis



## Session 7b: Mechanism Design III

# EC 2018 Conference Organization

**General Chair:** Eva Tardos, Cornell University, USA

**Program Chairs:** Edith Elkind, University of Oxford, UK
Rakesh Vohra, University of Pennsylvania, USA

**Workshop Chairs:** Scott Duke Kominers, Harvard Business School, USA
Jenn Wortman Vaughan, Microsoft Research, USA

**Tutorial Chairs:** Itai Ashlagi, Stanford University, USA
Katrina Ligett, Hebrew University of Jerusalem, Israel

**Local Arrangement Chairs:** Robert Kleinberg, Cornell University, USA
David Easley, Cornell University, USA

**SIGecom Executive Committee:** Kevin Leyton-Brown, University of British Columbia, Canada
Michal Feldman, Tel Aviv University, Israel
Jennifer Wortman Vaughan, Microsoft Research, USA

**Webmasters:** Ayush Sekhari, Cornell University, USA
Makis Arsenis, Cornell University, USA

## Senior Program Committee

**Theory & Foundations SPC:** Eduardo Azevedo, University of Pennsylvania, USA
Moshe Babaioff, Microsoft Research, USA
Ozan Candogan, University of Chicago, USA
Michal Feldman, Tel Aviv University, Israel
Ben Golub, Harvard University, USA
Martin Hoefer, Goethe University Frankfurt, Germany
Nicole Immorlica, Microsoft Research, USA
Ramesh Johari, Stanford University, USA
David Kempe, University of Southern California, USA
Katrina Ligett, Hebrew University, Israel
Brendan Lucier, Microsoft Research, USA
Mohammad Mahdian, Google Research, USA
Azarakhsh Malekian, University of Toronto, Canada
Debasis Mishra, Indian Statistical Institute, India
Thanh Nguyen, Purdue University, USA
Grant Schoenebeck, University of Michigan, USA
Jay Sethuraman, Columbia University, USA
Yaron Singer, Harvard University, USA
Aleksandrs Slivkins, Microsoft Research, USA
Adrian Vetta, McGill University, Canada
Adam Wierman, California Institute of Technology, USA

**Artificial Intelligence and Applied Game Theory SPC:**
Haris Aziz, Data61, Australia
Ioannis Caragiannis, University of Patras, Greece
Vincent Conitzer, Duke University, USA
Sanmay Das, Washington University in St. Louis, USA
Sebastien Lahaie, Google Research, USA
Evangelos Markakis, Athens University of Economics and Business, Greece
Tuomas Sandholm, Carnegie Mellon University, USA
Sven Seuken, University of Zurich, Switzerland
Maria Polukarov, King's College London, UK

**Experimental, Empirical and Applications SPC:**
Michael Bailey, Facebook Research, USA
Craig Boutilier, Google Research, USA
Eric Budish, University of Chicago, USA
Sharad Goel, Stanford University, USA
David Manlove, University of Glasgow, UK
Denis Nekipelov, University of Virginia, USA
David Rothschild, Microsoft Research, USA
Nicolas Stier, Facebook Research, USA

**Program Committee:**
Saeed Alaei, Google, USA
Georgios Amanatidis, CWI Amsterdam, USA
Elliot Anshelevich, Rensselaer Polytechnic Institute, USA
Nick Arnosti, Columbia University, USA
Itai Ashlagi, Stanford University, USA
Yossi Azar, Tel Aviv University, Israel
Yakov Babichenko, Technion, Israel
Ashwinkumar Badanidiyuru, Google, USA
Siddhartha Banerjee, Cornell University, USA
Oleg Baranov, University of Colorado Boulder, USA
Siddharth Barman, Indian Institute of Science, India
Pathikrit Basu, California Institute of Technology, USA
Xiaohui Bei, Nanyang Technological University, Singapore
Umang Bhaskar, Tata Institute of Fundamental Research, India
Martin Bichler, Technical University of Munich, Germany
Vittorio Bilò, University of Salento, Italy
Kostas Bimpikis, Stanford University, USA
Peter Biro, Hungarian Academy of Sciences, Hungary
Tom Blake, A9, USA
Liad Blumrosen, Hebrew University of Jerusalem, Israel
Simina Branzei, Purdue University, USA
Yang Cai, McGill University, Canada
Juan Carlos Carbajal, UNSW, Australia
Augustin Chaintreau, Columbia University, USA

**Program Committee (continued):**

Krishnamurthy Iyer, Cornell University, USA
Yash Kanoria, Columbia University, USA
Ian Kash, University of Illinois at Chicago, USA
Telikepalli Kavitha, Tata Institute of Fundamental Research, India
Bart de Keijzer, University of Liverpool, UK
Thomas Kesselheim, Technische Universitat Dortmund, Germany
Sanjeev Khanna, University of Pennsylvania, USA
Christopher Kiekintveld, University of Texas at El Paso, USA
Max Klimm, Humboldt University, Germany
Dan Knoepfle, Uber Technologies, Inc., USA
Jochen Koenemann, University of Waterloo, Canada
Maria Kyropoulou, University of Essex, UK
Kate Larson, University of Waterloo, Canada
Silvio Lattanzi, Google, USA
Ron Lavi, Technion, Israel
Randall Lewis, Netflix, USA
Yunan Li, City University of Hong Kong, Hong Kong
Annie Liang, University of Pennsylvania, USA
Ilan Lobel, New York University, USA
Pinyan Lu, Shanghai University of Finance and Economics, China
Benjamin Lubin, Boston University, USA
Vahideh Manshadi, Yale University, USA
Ruta Mehta, UIUC, USA
Reshef Meir, Technion, Israel
Vahab Mirrokni, Google, USA
Gianpiero Monaco, University of L'Aquila, Italy
Jamie Morgenstern, Georgia Institute of Technology, USA
Sarah Moshary, University of Pennsylvania, USA
Kamesh Munagala, Duke University, USA
Swaprava Nath, IIT Kanpur, India
Rad Niazadeh, Stanford University, USA
Alexandru Nichifor, University of Melbourne, Australia
Evdokia Nikolova, University of Texas at Austin, USA
Sigal Oren, Ben Gurion University, Israel
Renato Paes Leme, Google, USA
Mallesh Pai, Rice University, USA
Debmalya Panigrahi, Duke University, USA
David Pennock, Microsoft, USA
Alexander Peysakhovich, Facebook, USA
Georgios Piliouras, Singapore University of Technology and Design, Singapore
Emmanouil Pountourakis, Northwestern University, USA
Christos-Alexandros Psomas, Carnegie Mellon University, USA
Goran Radanovic, Harvard University, USA

**Program Committee (continued):** Baharak Rastegari, University of Bristol, UK
Assaf Romm, Hebrew University of Jerusalem, Israel
Aaron Roth, University of Pennsylvania, USA
Aviad Rubinstein, Harvard University, USA
Christopher Ryan, University of Chicago, USA
Daniela Saban, Stanford University, USA
Evan Sadler, Harvard University, USA
Tuomas Sandholm, Carnegie Mellon University, USA
Marco Scarsini, LUISS, Italy
Guido Schaefer, CWI Amsterdam, The Netherlands
Karl Schmedders, University of Zurich, Switzerland
Lior Seeman, Uber Technologies, Inc., USA
Nisarg Shah, University of Toronto, Canada
Ran Shorrer, Pennsylvania State University, USA
Balasubramanian Sivan, Google, USA
Piotr Skowron, University of Warsaw, Poland
Rann Smorodinsky, Technion, Israel
Eric Sodomka, Facebook, USA
Bernhard von Stengel, London School of Economics, UK
Vijay Subramanian, University of Michigan, USA
Vasilis Syrgkanis, Microsoft, USA
Samuel Taggart, Oberlin College, USA
Inbal Talgam-Cohen, Hebrew University of Jerusalem, Israel
Omer Tamuz, California Institute of Technology, USA
Pingzhong Tang, Tsinghua University, China
Christos Tzamos, Massachusetts Institute of Technology, USA
Johan Ugander, Stanford University, USA
Shai Vardi, California Institute of Technology, USA
Sergei Vassilvitskii, Google, USA
Laszlo Vegh, London School of Economics, UK
Carmine Ventre, University of Essex, UK
Yevgeniy Vorobeychik, Vanderbilt University, USA
Bo Waggoner, University of Pennsylvania, USA
S. Matthew Weinberg, Massachusetts Institute of Technology, USA
Udi Weinsberg, Facebook, USA
Alexander Westkamp, University of Cologne, Germany
E. Glen Weyl, Microsoft, USA
Christopher Wilkens, Facebook, USA
James Wright, Microsoft, USA
Steven Wu, Microsoft Research, SA
Lirong Xia, Rensselaer Polytechnic Institute, USA
Georgios Zervas, Boston University School of Management, USA
Yair Zick, National University of Singapore, Singapore
Aviv Zohar, Hebrew University of Jerusalem, Israel

**Additional reviewers:** Arpit Agarwal, University of Pennsylvania, USA
Michael Albert, Duke University, USA
Itai Arieli, Technion, Israel
Ramnik Arora, Facebook, USA
Imanol Arrieta Ibarra, Stanford University, USA
Sepehr Assadi, University of Pennsylvania, USA
Eric Balkanski, Harvard University, USA
Amir Ban, Tel Aviv University, Israel
Shrabastee Banerjee, Boston University, USA
Anjon Basak, University of Texas at el Paso, USA
Soumya Basu, University of Texas at Austin, USA
Soheil Behnezhad, University of Maryland, USA
Nawal Benabbou, National University of Singapore, Singapore
Hedyeh Beyhaghi, Cornell University, USA
Georgios Birmpas, Athens University of Economic and Business, Greece
Vitor Bosshard, University of Zurich, Switzerland
Maximilien Burq, Massachusetts Institute of Technology, USA
Moinul Morshed Porag Chowdhury, University of Texas at El Paso, USA
Gal Cohensius, Technion, Israel
Ágnes Cseh, Hungarian Academy of Sciences, Hungary
Argyrios Deligkas, Technion, Israel
Antoine Desir, Columbia University, USA
Jinshuo Dong, University of Pennsylvania, USA
Songzi Du, Simon Frazer University, Canada
Soheil Ehasani, University of Maryland, USA
Hadi Elzayn, University of Pennsylvania, USA
Markos Epitropou, University of Pennsylvania, USA
Yifan Feng, Chicago Booth, USA
Marcelo Fernandez, California Institute of Technology, USA
Abheek Ghosh, Tata Institute for Fundamental Research, India
Marek Grzes, University of Kent, UK
Roch Guerin, Washington University in St. Louis, USA
Marcus Gutierrez, University of Texas at El Paso, USA
Chen Hajaj, Vanderbilt University, USA
Wade Hann-Caruthers, California Institute of Technology, USA
Yinghua He, Rice University, USA
Stratis Ioannidis, Northeastern University, USA
Shahin Jabbari, University of Pennsylvania, USA
Matthew Joseph, University of Pennsylvania, USA
Anson Kahng, Carnegie Mellon University, USA
Karam Kang, Carnegie Mellon University, USA
Ali Khodabakhsh, University of Texas at Austin, USA
Anilesh Krishnaswamy, Stanford University, USA

**Additional reviewers (continued):**

Rucha Kulkarni, UIUC, USA
Wanyi Li, Stanford University, USA
Thanasis Lianeas, National Technical University of Athens, Greece
David Lingenbrink, Cornell University, USA
Siqi Liu, UC Berkeley, USA
Phani Raj Lolakapuri, Tata Institute of Fundamental Research, India
Jian Lou, Vanderbilt University, USA
Jiaqi Lu, Columbia University, USA
Gregory Macnamara, Stanford University, USA
Ali Makhdoumi, Massachusetts Institute of Technology, USA
Marco Manna, University of Calabria, Italy
Jieming Mao, Princeton University, USA
Francisco Javier Marmolejo Cossio, University of Oxford, UK
Peter McGlaughlin, UIUC, USA
Vijay Menon, University of Waterloo, Canada
Sujan Miah, University of Texas at El Paso, USA
Benjamin Miller, University of Wisconsin-Madison, USA
Barnabé Monnot, Singapore University of Technology and Design, Singapore
Ayan Mukhopadhyay, Vanderbildt University, USA
Paresh Nakhe, Goethe University Frankfurt, Germany
Afshin Nikzad, Stanford University, USA
Erhun Ozkan, University of Southern California, USA
Swetasudha Panda, Vanderbilt University, USA
Orestis Papadigenopoulos, University of Texas at Austin, USA
Yakym Pirozhenko, Rice University, USA
Benjamin Plaut, Stanford University, USA
Kirk Pruhs, University of Pittsburgh, USA
Pengyu Qian, Columbia University, USA
Stephen Ragain, Stanford University, USA
Ignacio Rios, Stanford University, USA
William Sandholm, University of Wisconsin-Madison, USA
Karthik Abinav Sankararaman, University of Maryland, USA
Francesco Scarcello, University of Calabria, Italy
Kevin Schewior, Universidad de Chile, Chile
Jon Schneider, Princeton University, USA
Okke Schrijvers, Stanford University, USA
Zachary Schutzman, University of Pennsylvania, USA
Ariel Schvartzman, Princeton University, USA
Saeed Seddighin, University of Maryland, USA
Weiran Shen, Tsinghua University, China

## EC'18 Sponsor and Supporters

**Sponsor:** sigecom — ACM Special Interest Group on E-commerce

**Supporters:**

facebook

lyft

Microsoft

UBER

Cornell University Department of Computer Science

Cornell University Department of Economics

Google

# Algorithmic Fairness and the Social Welfare Function*

SENDHIL MULLAINATHAN, University of Chicago

Social scientists have long been interested in discrimination and other inherent social inequities; and as such have developed models to evaluate policies through the dual lenses of efficiency and equity. More recently, computer scientists have illustrated that algorithms in many domains inherit and (sometimes inadvertently) bake in these same human biases and inequities. In this talk, I attempt to bring these two strands together: I embed concerns about algorithmic bias within a broader welfare economics framework. Instead of viewing the data as given, it begins with a model of the underlying social phenomena and their accompanying inequities. It then posits a social welfare function, where the social planner cares both about efficiency and equity. In particular, she places greater weight on equity than individual algorithm designers (firms or citizens) do. Intrinsic to this approach is that the social planner's preferences imply desired properties of the algorithm: the fairness of a given algorithm is not a primitive; instead, it is derived from the welfare of the outcomes it embodies. Several pieces of conventional wisdom do not hold true in this framework. For example, "blinding the algorithm" to variables such as race generally reduces welfare, even for the disadvantaged group. At the other extreme, I characterize situations where apparently fair algorithms can drastically increase inequities. Overall, I argue that it would be beneficial to model fairness and algorithmic bias more holistically, including both a generative model of the underlying social phenomena and a description of a global welfare function.

**Keywords:** Machine Learning; Algorithmic Bias; Fairness; Welfare Economics; Racial Bias; Prediction Policy

**ACM Reference Format**

Sendhil Mullainathan. 2018. Algorithmic Fairness and the Social Welfare Function *In ACM EC'18: Proceedings of the 2018 ACM Conference on Economics and Computation,* June 18-22, Ithaca, NY. ACM, NY, NY. 2 pages. DOI: https://doi.org/10.1145/3219166.3219236

*This talk summarizes several papers which involves as coauthors in different combinations: Jon Kleinberg, Jens Ludwig, Ziad Obermeyer and Ashesh Rambachan.



*ACM EC'18, June 18–22, 2018, Ithaca, NY, USA.*



ACM ISBN 978-1-4503-5829-3/18/06. https://doi.org/10.1145/3219166.3219236

# Surge Pricing Moves Uber's Driver-Partners

ALICE LU, Uber, Inc., USA
PETER I. FRAZIER, Uber, Inc., School of Operations Research and Information Engineering, Cornell University, USA
OREN KISLEV, Uber, Inc., USA

We study the impact of dynamic pricing (so-called "surge pricing") on relocation decisions by Uber's driver-partners and the corresponding revenue they collected. Using a natural experiment arising from an outage in the system that produces the surge pricing heatmap for a portion of Uber's driver-partners over 10 major cities, and a difference-in-differences approach, we study the short-run effect that visibility of the surge heatmap has on 1) drivers' decisions to relocate to areas with higher or lower prices and 2) drivers' revenue. We demonstrate that the ability to see the surge heatmap has a statistically significant impact on both outcomes. Ability to see the surge heatmap explains 10%-60% of Uber drivers' self-positioning decisions, attracts drivers toward areas with higher surge prices, and increases drivers' revenue on surged trips by up to 70%. This suggests that dynamic pricing helps drivers move to where riders' demand is largest, and that the resulting reduction in spatial search friction and spatial mismatch improves waiting times and welfare for both riders and drivers.

Full Paper: http://ssrn.com/abstract=3180246

CCS Concepts: • **Applied computing** → **Consumer products**; **Economics**;

Additional Key Words and Phrases: Dynamic Pricing, Ride Sharing Economy, Labor Economics

We would like to thank Chris Wilkins, Robert L. Phillips, and Jonathan Hall for their comments.

Authors' addresses: Alice Lu, Uber, Inc. 1455 Market Street, San Francisco, CA, 94103, USA, alicelu@uber.com; Peter I. Frazier, Uber, Inc., School of Operations Research and Information Engineering, Cornell University, Street Address, Ithaca, NY, 14850, USA, pf98@cornell.edu; Oren Kislev, Uber, Inc. 1455 Market Street, San Francisco, CA, 94103, USA, ok@uber.com.


*ACM EC'18, June 18–22, 2018, Ithaca, NY, USA.* ACM ISBN 978-1-4503-5829-3/18/06.
https://doi.org/10.1145/3219166.3219192

# The Sharing Economy and Housing Affordability: Evidence from Airbnb

KYLE BARRON, National Bureau of Economic Research
EDWARD KUNG, University of California Los Angeles
DAVIDE PROSERPIO, University of Southern California

We assess the impact of home-sharing on residential house prices and rental rates. Using a comprehensive dataset comprised of Airbnb listings from the entire United States, we regress zipcode level house prices and rental rates on the number of Airbnb listings, using fixed effects to control for permanent differences across zipcodes as well as arbitrary CBSA level time trends, and using an instrumental variable based on Google search interest for Airbnb to control for any remaining endogeneity. We find that a 10% increase in Airbnb listings leads to a 0.42% increase in rents and a 0.76% increase in house prices. Moreover, we find that the effect of Airbnb is smaller in zipcodes with a larger share of owner-occupiers, a result consistent with absentee landlords taking their homes away from the long-term rental market and listing them on Airbnb. We present a simple model that rationalizes these findings.

Full paper avaialable at: https://papers.ssrn.com/sol3/papers.cfm?abstract_id=3006832

CCS Concepts: • **Applied computing** → *Economics*;

**ACM Reference Format:**
Kyle Barron, Edward Kung, and Davide Proserpio. The Sharing Economy and Housing Affordability: Evidence from Airbnb. *ACM EC '18: 2018 ACM Conference on Economics and Computation (ACM EC '18), June 18–22, 2018, Ithaca, NY, USA*, 1 page. https://doi.org/10.1145/3219166.3219180

Authors' addresses: Kyle Barron, National Bureau of Economic Research, barronk@nber.org; Edward Kung, University of California Los Angeles, ekung@econ.ucla.edu; Davide Proserpio, University of Southern California, proserpi@marshall.usc.edu.


*ACM EC'18, June 18–22, 2018, Ithaca, NY, USA*. ACM ISBN 978-1-4503-5829-3/18/06.
https://doi.org/10.1145/3219166.3219180

# Advertising Strategy in the Presence of Reviews: An Empirical Analysis

BRETT HOLLENBECK, University of California Los Angeles
SRIDHAR MOORTHY, University of Toronto
DAVIDE PROSERPIO, University of Southern California

Over the last fifteen years, one of the major developments online has been the growth and proliferation of review websites such as TripAdvisor. The ready availability of independent information from past users poses interesting questions for marketing strategy. What role does advertising play in the new environment? How should firms adjust their advertising strategy to the presence of reviews? In this paper we address these questions in the context of the hotel industry. Using a data set of TripAdvisor hotel reviews and another describing hotels' advertising expenditures, we show, first, that overall ad spending decreased from 2002 to 2015, suggesting that online reviews have had the effect of displacing advertising. Second, there is a negative causal relationship between TripAdvisor ratings and advertising spending in the cross-section: hotels with higher ratings spend less. This suggests that user ratings and advertising are substitutes, not complements. Third, this relationship is stronger for independent hotels than for chains, and stronger in competitive markets than in noncompetitive markets. The former suggests that a strong brand name provides some immunity to reviews, and the latter suggests that when ratings are pivotal, the advertising response might be particularly strong. Finally, we show that the relationship between user ratings and advertising has strengthened over time, as websites such as TripAdvisor have become more influential. This provides further confirmation that the effect of online ratings on advertising operates through the demand side, and not the supply side. Hotels seem to react to reviews if and only if consumers react to them.

Full paper avaialable at: https://papers.ssrn.com/sol3/papers.cfm?abstract_id=3076239

CCS Concepts: • **Applied computing** → *Economics*;

**ACM Reference Format:**
Brett Hollenbeck, Sridhar Moorthy, and Davide Proserpio. Advertising Strategy in the Presence of Reviews: An Empirical Analysis. *In the Proceedings of 2018 ACM Conference on Economics and Computation (ACM EC '18), June 18–22, 2018, Ithaca, NY, USA*, 1 page. https://doi.org/10.1145/3219166.3219181

Authors' addresses: Brett Hollenbeck, University of California Los Angeles, brett.hollenbeck@anderson.ucla.edu; Sridhar Moorthy, University of Toronto, Moorthy@rotman.utoronto.ca; Davide Proserpio, University of Southern California, proserpi@marshall.usc.edu.


*ACM EC'18, June 18–22, 2018, Ithaca, NY, USA*. ACM ISBN 978-1-4503-5829-3/18/06.
https://doi.org/10.1145/3219166.3219181

# Strategyproof Linear Regression in High Dimensions

YILING CHEN, Harvard University, USA
CHARA PODIMATA, Harvard University, USA
ARIEL D. PROCACCIA, Carnegie Mellon University, USA
NISARG SHAH, University of Toronto, Canada

This paper is part of an emerging line of work at the intersection of machine learning and mechanism design, which aims to avoid noise in training data by correctly aligning the incentives of data sources. Specifically, we focus on the ubiquitous problem of *linear regression*, where *strategyproof* mechanisms have previously been identified in two dimensions. In our setting, agents have single-peaked preferences and can manipulate only their response variables. Our main contribution is the discovery of a family of *group strategyproof* linear regression mechanisms in any number of dimensions, which we call *generalized resistant hyperplane* mechanisms. The game-theoretic properties of these mechanisms — and, in fact, their very existence — are established through a connection to a discrete version of the Ham Sandwich Theorem.

## 1 INTRODUCTION

Designing machine learning algorithms that are robust to noise in training data is a topic of intense research. A large body of work addresses stochastic noise [20, 29]. On the other extreme, another branch of the literature focuses on adversarial noise [6, 12, 25], that is, errors are introduced by an adversary with the explicit purpose of sabotaging the algorithm. The latter approach is often too pessimistic, and generally leads to negative results.

More recently, some researchers have taken a game-theoretic viewpoint; it suggests a model of *strategic noise* that can be seen as occupying the middle ground of noise models. Specifically, training data is provided by strategic sources — hereinafter *agents* — that may intentionally introduce errors *to maximize their own benefit*. Compared to adversarial noise, the advantage of this model (when its underlying assumptions hold true) is that, if we aligned the agents' incentives correctly, it would be possible to obtain uncontaminated data. From this viewpoint, the ideal is the design of learning algorithms that in addition to being statistically efficient, are *strategyproof*, i.e., where supplying pristine data is a dominant strategy for each agent.

We subscribe to this agenda, and advance it in the context of the ubiquitous problem of linear regression, i.e., fitting a hyperplane through given data. We consider agents who can manipulate

This work was partially supported by the National Science Foundation under grants CCF-1718549, IIS-1350598, IIS-1714140, CCF-1525932, and CCF-1733556; by the Office of Naval Research under grants N00014-16-1-3075 and N00014-17-1-2428; by a Sloan Research Fellowship and a Guggenheim Fellowship; and by the Natural Sciences and Engineering Research Council of Canada (NSERC) under the Discovery Grants program.
Authors' addresses: Yiling Chen, Harvard University, Cambridge, MA, 02138, USA, yiling@seas.harvard.edu; Chara Podimata, Harvard University, Cambridge, MA, 02138, USA, podimata@g.harvard.edu; Ariel D. Procaccia, Carnegie Mellon University, Pittsburgh, PA, 15213, USA, arielpro@cs.cmu.edu; Nisarg Shah, University of Toronto, Toronto, ON, M5S 3G8, Canada, nisarg@cs.toronto.edu.


*ACM EC'18, June 18–22, 2018, Ithaca, NY, USA.* ACM ISBN 978-1-4503-5829-3/18/06...$15.00
https://doi.org/10.1145/3219166.3219175

their dependent variables in order to minimize their vertical distance from the output hyperplane, and design strategyproof regression mechanisms without payments.

When does this type of strategic regression problem arise? Dekel et al. [15] give the real-world example of the global fashion chain Zara, whose distribution process relies on regression [9]. Specifically, the demand for each product at each store is predicted based on historical data, as well as information provided by store managers. Since the supply of popular items is limited, store managers may strategically manipulate requested quantities so that the output of the regression process would better fit their needs, and, indeed, there is ample evidence that many of them have done so [10]. More generally, as discussed in detail by Perote and Perote-Peña [36], this type of setting is relevant whenever "data could come from surveys composed by agents interested in not being perceived as real outliers if the estimation results could be used in the future to change the economic situation of the agents that generate the sample."

## 1.1 Our Model and Results

A bit more formally, we study a linear regression setting in which the task is to fit a hyperplane through data points $(\boldsymbol{x}_i, y_i)$ for $i \in \{1, \ldots, n\}$, where $\boldsymbol{x}_i \in \mathbb{R}^d$ are the independent variables and $y_i \in \mathbb{R}$ is the dependent variable. Following Dekel et al. [15] and Perote and Perote-Peña [36], we assume that the independent variables are public information, but dependent variable $y_i$ is held privately by agent $i$. A mechanism elicits the private information of the agents, and returns a hyperplane represented by vector $\boldsymbol{\beta} = (\boldsymbol{\beta}_1, \beta_0) \in \mathbb{R}^{d+1}$. Under this outcome, the residual for agent $i$ is $r_i = y_i - \boldsymbol{\beta}_1^T \boldsymbol{x}_i - \beta_0$, and, loosely speaking, agents wish to minimize $|r_i|$ (see Section 2 for a precise description of agent preferences).

Our starting point is the work of Dekel et al. [15], who show that empirical risk minimization (ERM) with the $L_1$ loss (in short, $L_1$-ERM), coupled with a specific tie-breaking rule, is group strategyproof, that is, no coalition of agents can be weakly better off by misreporting. We extend this result and show that replacing the $L_1$ loss by a weighted $L_1$ loss and adding convex regularization to the risk function preserves group strategyproofness. But this still gives a relatively restricted family of strategyproof mechanisms, and we seek a broader understanding of what is possible in our setting.

To that end, we look to the work of Perote and Perote-Peña [36], who focus on the two-dimensional case (known as *simple linear regression*), i.e., fitting a line through points on a plane. They propose a wide family of strategyproof mechanisms, which they call *clockwise repeated median* (CRM) mechanisms. These mechanisms are parametrized by two subsets of agents $S$ and $S'$. Perote and Perote-Peña [36] establish conditions on $S$ and $S'$ under which they claim that CRM mechanisms are strategyproof. We identify a mistake in this result, present counterexamples showing violation of strategyproofness under their conditions, and identify three stricter conditions under which we can recover strategyproofness — in fact, we prove group strategyproofness. Under one of our conditions, CRM mechanisms coincide with a family of mechanisms from the statistics literature known as *resistant line mechanisms* [24]. Our work therefore establishes the group strategyproofness of these mechanisms.

Our main result is that we generalize the CRM family to higher dimensions, thereby justifying the title of this paper. We introduce the family of *generalized resistant hyperplane* (GRH) mechanisms, which, to the best of our knowledge, is the first extension of resistant line mechanisms beyond the plane. In $d + 1$ dimensions, GRH mechanisms are parametrized by $d + 1$ subsets of agents. Through a surprising connection to the literature on the Ham Sandwich Theorem, we find a condition on the subsets under which GRH mechanisms are group strategyproof. Strikingly, our proof of this general *group strategyproofness* result in *any number* of dimensions is much shorter than the (incorrect) proof of Perote and Perote-Peña [36] for the *strategyproofness* of CRM mechanisms in *two dimensions*.

We also study a property called impartiality, which is stricter than strategyproofness. We establish the existence of a wide family of impartial mechanisms, which, unlike our generalized $L_1$-ERM and generalized resistant hyperplane mechanisms, are strategyproof but not group strategyproof (except for constant functions). Building upon the work of Moulin [33], we also provide two non-constructive characterizations of strategyproof mechanisms for linear regression.

Strategyproofness is not the sole desideratum; constant functions (e.g., the flat hyperplane $y = 0$) are strategyproof but not necessarily desirable. We would also like the mechanism to have good statistical efficiency. For that, we compare (families of) strategyproof mechanisms in terms of their approximation of the optimal squared loss, leveraging our characterization. Most importantly, we establish a lower bound of 2 on the approximation ratio of any strategyproof mechanism, which means that any mechanism that is even close to *ordinary least squares* regression must be manipulable.

### 1.2 Related Work

As discussed above, our work is most closely related to that of Perote and Perote-Peña [36] and Dekel et al. [15]. Here we try to give a broader picture of the state of research on machine learning algorithms that are robust to strategic noise. This research can be categorized using three key axes: (i) manipulable information, (ii) goal of the agents, and (iii) use of payments and incentive guarantees.

On the first axis, like us, most papers assume that independent variables (or *feature vectors* in the language of classification) are public information, and dependent variables (labels) are private, manipulable information [15, 32, 35, 36], though some papers also design algorithms robust to strategic feature vectors [16, 21]. Meir et al. [32] provide strong positive results for designing strategyproof classifiers when there are either only two classifiers, or the agents are interested in a shared set of input points. On the other hand, Hardt et al. [21] study the problem of constructing classifiers that are robust to agents strategically misreporting their *feature vector*, in order to trick the algorithm into misclassifying them. Their setting is modeled as a one-shot Stackelberg game. The more recent work of Dong et al. [16] models the same problem in an online setting; they provide guarantees that ensure that the problem is convex, and, therefore, they are able to derive a computationally efficient learning algorithm that has diminishing *Stackelberg regret*.

On the second axis, one line of research focuses on agents motivated by privacy concerns, with a tradeoff between accuracy and privacy [7, 13]; another focuses on agents who want the algorithm to make accurate assessment on their own sample, even if this reduces the overall accuracy. This form of strategic manipulation has been studied for estimation [8], classification [30–32], and regression [15, 36] problems. Our problem falls squarely into the second category.

Finally, on the third axis, various papers differ on whether monetary payments to agents are allowed [7], and on how strongly to guarantee truthful reporting: the stronger strategyproofness requirement [32, 35, 36] versus the weaker Bayes-Nash incentive compatibility [13, 23]. Our work falls into the literature of mechanism design without money; we study linear regression mechanisms that enforce strategyproofness without paying the agents, or asking the agents to pay.

## 2 MODEL

Let $[k] \triangleq \{1, \ldots, k\}$ be the set of first $k$ natural numbers, and $\overline{\mathbb{R}} = \mathbb{R} \cup \{-\infty, \infty\}$ be the extended real line. Given numbers $t_1, \ldots, t_k \in \overline{\mathbb{R}}$, let $\min(t_1, \ldots, t_k)$ denote the smallest value, and $\min^j(t_1, \ldots, t_k)$ denote the $j^{\text{th}}$ smallest value. Let $\text{med}(t_1, \ldots, t_k)$ denote their median: when $k$ is odd, this is equal to

$\min^{(k+1)/2}(t_1, \ldots, t_k)$, but when $k$ is even, this could be either $\min^{k/2}(t_1, \ldots, t_k)$ (the "left median") or $\min^{k/2+1}(t_1, \ldots, t_k)$ (the "right median").[1]

Our work focuses on the problem of linear regression, i.e., fitting a hyperplane through given data. Let $N = [n]$. We are given a collection of data points $\mathcal{D} = (\boldsymbol{x}_i, y_i)_{i \in N}$, where $\boldsymbol{x}_i \in \mathbb{R}^d$ and $y_i \in \mathbb{R}$ are called the *independent* and *dependent* variables of point $i$, respectively. Let $\overline{\boldsymbol{x}_i} = (\boldsymbol{x}_i, 1)$. Our goal is to find a vector $\boldsymbol{\beta} = (\boldsymbol{\beta}_1, \beta_0) \in \mathbb{R}^{d+1}$ such that $\boldsymbol{\beta}^T \overline{\boldsymbol{x}_i} = \boldsymbol{\beta}_1^T \boldsymbol{x}_i + \beta_0$ is a good approximation of $y_i$ for each $i \in N$. The quantity $r_i = y_i - \boldsymbol{\beta}^T \overline{\boldsymbol{x}_i}$ is called the residual of point $i$.

*Strategic setting.* We study a setting in which each data point $p_i = (\boldsymbol{x}_i, y_i)$ is provided by a strategic agent $i$. We also denote the set of agents by $N$. Following Perote and Perote-Peña [36] and Dekel et al. [15], we assume that the independent variables $\boldsymbol{x} = (\boldsymbol{x}_i)_{i \in N}$ constitute *public* information, which the agents cannot manipulate. Each agent $i$ holds the dependent variable $y_i$ as private information, and may report a different value $\widetilde{y}_i$ in order to receive a more preferred outcome. Thus, the principal observes the reported data points $\widetilde{\mathcal{D}} = (\boldsymbol{x}_i, \widetilde{y}_i)_{i \in N}$. Let us denote $\boldsymbol{y} = (y_i)_{i \in N}$ and $\widetilde{\boldsymbol{y}} = (\widetilde{y}_i)_{i \in N}$.

*Mechanisms.* Because the agents cannot change $\boldsymbol{x}$, we can effectively treat it as fixed. A mechanism for linear regression $M^{\boldsymbol{x}}$ is therefore defined for given public information $\boldsymbol{x}$, takes as input reported private information $\widetilde{\boldsymbol{y}}$, and returns a vector $\boldsymbol{\beta}$. We omit $\boldsymbol{x}$ when it is clear from the context.

*Agent preferences.* When a mechanism returns $\boldsymbol{\beta}$, we say that the outcome for agent $i$ is $\widehat{y}_i(\boldsymbol{\beta}) = \boldsymbol{\beta}^T \boldsymbol{x}_i$. We omit $\boldsymbol{\beta}$ when it is clear from the context. The agent only cares about her own outcome $\widehat{y}_i$, and would like it to be as close to $y_i$ as possible. Formally, we assume that agent $i$ has *single-peaked preferences* [3, 33] over $\widehat{y}_i$ with peak at $y_i$. We represent the weak preference relation by $\succcurlyeq_i$ and the strict preference relation by $\succ_i$. Formally, for all $a, b \in \mathbb{R}$, $y_i > a \geq b$ or $y_i < a \leq b$ must imply $y_i \succ_i a \succcurlyeq_i b$.

*Game-theoretic desiderata.* Our goal is to prevent agents from misreporting their private information. The game theory literature offers a strong desideratum under which agents have no incentive to misreport even if they have know what the other agents would report.

*Definition 2.1 (Strategyproofness).* A mechanism $M^{\boldsymbol{x}}$ is called *strategyproof* (SP) if each agent weakly prefers truthfully reporting her private information to misreporting it, regardless of the reports of the other agents. Formally, for each $i \in N$, $y_i \in \mathbb{R}$, and $\widetilde{\boldsymbol{y}} \in \mathbb{R}^n$, we need $\widehat{y}_i(M^{\boldsymbol{x}}(y_i, \widetilde{\boldsymbol{y}}_{-i})) \succcurlyeq_i \widehat{y}_i(M^{\boldsymbol{x}}(\widetilde{\boldsymbol{y}}))$. Note that this must hold for any possible single-peaked preferences the agent may have.

While no individual agent can benefit from misreporting under a strategyproof mechanism, a group of agents may still be able to collude, and benefit by simultaneously misreporting. This can be prevented by imposing a stronger desideratum.

*Definition 2.2 (Group Strategyproofness).* A mechanism $M^{\boldsymbol{x}}$ is called *group strategyproof* (GSP) if no coalition of agents can simultaneously misreport in a way that no agent in the coalition is strictly worse off and some agent in the coalition is strictly better off, irrespective of the reports of the other agents. Formally, for each $S \subseteq N$, $\boldsymbol{y}_S = (y_i)_{i \in S} \in \mathbb{R}^{|S|}$, and $\widetilde{\boldsymbol{y}} \in \mathbb{R}^n$, it should not be the case that $\widehat{y}_i(M^{\boldsymbol{x}}(\widetilde{\boldsymbol{y}})) \succcurlyeq_i \widehat{y}_i(M^{\boldsymbol{x}}(\boldsymbol{y}_S, \widetilde{\boldsymbol{y}}_{N \setminus S}))$ for every $i \in S$, and the preference is strict for at least one $i \in S$.

[1]This is different from the standard definition, which takes the average of the left and right medians, but necessary to ensure incentive guarantees.

The game theory literature also considers a weaker notion of group strategyproofness in which not all the agents in a manipulating coalition should be strictly better off. We do not consider this notion because our group strategyproof mechanisms are able to satisfy the stronger notion.

Note that we do not assume that the data points are generated by an underlying statistical process. Our results are independent of how the data points were generated.

## 3 FAMILIES OF STRATEGYPROOF MECHANISMS

In this section, we analyze families of (group) strategyproof mechanisms for linear regression. Our results generalize existing families of mechanisms, and propose novel families.

### 3.1 Empirical Risk Minimization with the $L_1$ Loss

Consider a single dimensional setting, in which each agent $i$ has a private value $y_i$, reports a possibly different value $\widetilde{y}_i$, and the mechanism returns a single value $\widehat{y}$. Each agent $i$ has single-peaked preferences over $\widehat{y}$ with peak at $y_i$. This corresponds to the special case of our setting in which $\boldsymbol{x}_i = \boldsymbol{x}_j$ for all $i, j \in N$, or alternatively, the dimension $d = 0$. In this setting, it has long been known that choosing the *median* of the reported values achieves group strategyproofness [17]. It can be shown that the median minimizes the sum of absolute ($L_1$) losses with respect to the reports, i.e., given $\boldsymbol{y}$, it chooses $\arg\min_{y \in \mathbb{R}} \sum_{i=1}^{n} |y - y_i|$, with an appropriate tie-breaking when $n$ is even. In the machine learning terminology, the median is the empirical risk minimizer (ERM) with the $L_1$ loss.

Inspired by this, Dekel et al. [15] study ERM with the $L_1$ loss in a more general regression setting, and show that it remains group strategyproof. Specifically, they focus on finding a (potentially non-linear) regression function $f : \mathbb{R}^d \to \mathbb{R}$ from a given convex set $\mathcal{F}$. Given $\mathcal{D} = (\boldsymbol{x}_i, y_i)_{i \in N}$, define the empirical $L_1$ risk of a regression function $f \in \mathcal{F}$ as $\widehat{R}(f, \mathcal{D}) = \sum_{i \in N} |y_i - f(\boldsymbol{x}_i)|$. Let $\|\cdot\| : \mathcal{F} \to \mathbb{R}$ be a strictly convex function. They show that minimizing the empirical $L_1$ risk, and breaking ties among the optimal solutions by minimizing $\|\cdot\|$ is group strategyproof. We refer to this mechanism by $L_1$-ERM [2]. For linear regression, this approach is known by various names in the literature, such as Least Absolute Deviations (LAD), Minimum Sum of Absolute Errors (MSAE), or Least Absolute Value (LAV). The tie-breaking step is crucially required because the empirical $L_1$ risk may have multiple minimizers.

We present a generalization of their mechanism while retaining group strategyproofness. In particular, we extend the objective function $\widehat{R}$ in two ways: i) we allow a weighted $L_1$ loss, in which the loss of each agent $i$ is multiplied by a weight $w_i^{\boldsymbol{x}}$, and ii) we allow adding a convex regularizer $h : \mathcal{F} \to \mathbb{R}$. Note that regularization is widely used in machine learning to prevent ERM from overfitting. Our generalization, which we term *generalized $L_1$-ERM*, is presented as Algorithm 1. While we are only interested in linear regression, we note that generalized $L_1$-ERM works for the general regression setting of Dekel et al. [15].

**ALGORITHM 1:** Generalized $L_1$-ERM (Regularized ERM with a weighted $L_1$ loss)

**Input:** Data points $\mathcal{D} = (\boldsymbol{x}_i, y_i)_{i \in N}$, convex hypothesis space $\mathcal{F}$, constants $(w_i^{\boldsymbol{x}})_{i \in N}$, convex regularizer $h : \mathcal{F} \to \mathbb{R}$, strictly convex function $\|\cdot\| : \mathcal{F} \to \mathbb{R}$.

**Output:** Function $f^* \in \mathcal{F}$.

$\forall f \in \mathcal{F},\ \widehat{R}(f, \mathcal{D}) \triangleq \sum_{i \in N} w_i^{\boldsymbol{x}} \cdot |y_i - f(\boldsymbol{x}_i)| + h(f)$;

$r^* \leftarrow \inf_{f \in \mathcal{F}} \widehat{R}(f, \mathcal{D})$;

**return** $f^* \leftarrow \arg\min_{f \in \mathcal{F} : \widehat{R}(f, \mathcal{D}) = r^*} \|f\|$;

[2]For a formal description of the algorithm, we refer the interested reader to the full version of our paper (available on the authors' webpages).

Theorem 3.1. *Generalized $L_1$-ERM is a group strategyproof regression mechanism.*

Our proof, presented in the full version for completeness, essentially mirrors the proof of Dekel et al. [15]; we identify three steps in their proof where they use the structure of the risk function $\widehat{R}$, and observe that these steps follow through with our more general risk function.

There are several potential advantages of generalized $L_1$-ERM over the vanilla $L_1$-ERM. First, generalized $L_1$-ERM allows eliminating the tie-breaking step if the new risk function is guaranteed to have a unique minimizer. For instance, adding a *strictly convex* regularizer would achieve this.

Second, for the aforementioned single dimensional setting, Moulin [33] proved that every strategyproof[3] and anonymous[4] mechanism is a *generalized median*: for every $\alpha_1, \ldots, \alpha_{n+1} \in \overline{\mathbb{R}}$, the corresponding generalized median returns $\text{med}\{y_1, \ldots, y_n, \alpha_1, \ldots, \alpha_{n+1}\}$. Here, $\{\alpha_j\}_{j \in [n+1]}$ are called "phantoms". We can alternatively view this as returning $\arg\min_{y \in \mathbb{R}} \sum_{i \in [n]} |y - y_i| + h(y)$, where $h(y) = \sum_{j \in [n+1] \text{ s.t. } \alpha_j \in \mathbb{R}} |y - \alpha_j| + (k_{-\infty} - k_{\infty}) \cdot y$, and for $t \in \{-\infty, \infty\}$, $k_t = |\{j : \alpha_j = t\}|$.[5] Since $h(y)$ is a convex function, we can view it as a regularizer in our generalized $L_1$-ERM. Hence, for the single dimensional setting, generalized $L_1$-ERM covers all generalized medians. In contrast, $L_1$-ERM reduces to a specific mechanism in this family, the median.

Finally, algorithms that add convex regularization to $L_1$-ERM have been studied in the machine learning literature [41, 42]; our generalization establishes group strategyproofness of these algorithms.

We also note that in the statistics literature, the vanilla $L_1$-ERM is treated as a member of the more general family of *quantile regression* mechanisms [27], which, given $q \in [0, 1]$, minimize the following empirical risk function:

$$\widehat{R}_q(f, \mathcal{D}) = \sum_{i \in N : y_i \geq f(\boldsymbol{x}_i)} q \cdot |y_i - f(\boldsymbol{x}_i)| + \sum_{i \in N : y_i < f(\boldsymbol{x}_i)} (1 - q) \cdot |y_i - f(\boldsymbol{x}_i)|. \tag{1}$$

$L_1$-ERM corresponds to the choice of $q = 0.5$. In the one-dimensional setting, other values of $q$ correspond to different quantiles (i.e., correspond to $\min^k$ for various $k$), and thus induce strategyproof mechanisms. One might wonder if quantile regression remains strategyproof in higher dimensions. We answer this *negatively* by providing an example in the full version, in which the quantile regression mechanism for $q = 0.4$ is shown to violate strategyproofness. It is an interesting question to discover a strategyproof version of quantiles for linear regression.

### 3.2 Generalized Resistant Hyperplane Mechanisms

In this section, we introduce a novel family of strategyproof mechanisms for linear regression. Our family extends the known family of resistant line mechanisms from the statistics literature [24], which were only defined for simple linear regression ($d = 1$), to higher dimensions. We first take a slight detour through a previous approach in the literature.

*3.2.1 A Detour Through Clockwise Repeated Median Mechanisms.* Perote and Perote-Peña [36] introduced a novel family of mechanisms, which they termed *Clockwise Repeated Median* (CRM) mechanisms. CRM mechanisms are only defined for the special case of *simple linear regression*, i.e., for fitting a straight line through a set of points on a plane. In describing these mechanisms, we use scalar notations where possible. For instance, we use $x_i$ to denote the x-coordinate of agent $i$, and

[3]Moulin [33] shows that for the single dimensional setting, strategyproofness is equivalent to group strategyproofness.

[4]A mechanism is anonymous if permuting the reports of the agents does not change the output of the mechanism. This is a reasonable desideratum in the single dimensional setting due to the absence of public information that distinguishes agents naturally.

[5]When all phantoms are finite, $h(y) = \sum_{j \in [n+1]} |y - \alpha_j|$. The term $|y - \alpha_j|$ has derivative 1 when $y > \alpha_j$, and $-1$ when $y < \alpha_j$. For $\alpha_j = -\infty$ (resp. $\infty$), we can mimic this effect by adding a different term whose derivative is always $-1$ (resp. 1).

$\beta_1$ to denote the slope of the regression line. For CRM mechanisms to be well defined, we also need to assume that the set of points is "admissible".

*Definition 3.2 (Admissible Set).* A collection of data points $\mathcal{D} = (x_i, y_i)_{i \in N}$ is called *admissible* if $x_i \neq x_j$ for all distinct $i, j \in N$.

The CRM family is parametrized by two subsets of agents, $S, S' \subseteq N$. These subsets must be chosen based on the public information $\boldsymbol{x}$, and therefore can be treated as fixed. Informally, given $S, S' \subseteq N$, the $(S, S')$-CRM mechanism first computes the median *clockwise angle* (CWA), defined below, from each point $i \in S$ to points in $S'$. Then, it chooses the point $i^* \in S$ whose median CWA is the median of the median CWAs from all points in $S$. If the median CWA from point $i^*$ is towards point $j^* \in S'$, then the mechanism returns the straight line passing through points $i^*$ and $j^*$. Formally, the mechanism is defined as follows. Perote and Perote-Peña [36] established the equivalence of this formal definition and the aforementioned informal description.

*Definition 3.3 (CRM Mechanisms).* Define the *clockwise angle* (CWA) from $(x_i, y_i)$ to $(x_j, y_j)$ as:

$$\mathrm{CWA}((x_i, y_i), (x_j, y_j)) = \pi + \mathrm{sign}(x_j - x_i) \cdot \frac{\pi}{2} + \mathrm{sign}\left(\frac{y_j - y_i}{x_j - x_i}\right) \left|\arctan\left(\frac{y_j - y_i}{x_j - x_i}\right)\right|. \tag{2}$$

Given $\mathcal{D} = (x_i, y_i)_{i \in N}$ and $S, S' \subseteq N$, let the *directing angle* be defined as:

$$\mathrm{DA}(S, S') = \underset{i \in S}{\mathrm{med}} \ \underset{j \in S' : j \neq i}{\mathrm{med}} \ \mathrm{CWA}((x_i, y_i), (x_j, y_j)). \tag{3}$$

Then, the $(S, S')$-CRM mechanism returns the line $\boldsymbol{\beta} = (\beta_1, \beta_0)$ given by:

$$\begin{aligned} \beta_1 &= \tan\left[\mathrm{DA}(S, S') - \pi - \frac{\pi}{2} \cdot \mathrm{sign}\left(\mathrm{DA}(S, S') - \pi\right)\right], \\ \beta_0 &= \underset{i \in S}{\mathrm{med}} \ (y_i - \beta_1 \cdot x_i). \end{aligned} \tag{4}$$

First, we notice that the definition of the CRM family uses three medians: two to define the directing angle $DA(S, S')$, and one to define the $y$-intercept $\beta_0$. Each median, when taken over an even number of values, can be the left median or the right median. While Perote and Perote-Peña [36] do not mention how these choices should be made, it is easy to check that in order to achieve the desired incentive properties, these choices cannot be made independently of each other. Later, we present a generalization which captures the different feasible choices in a simpler form.

Perote and Perote-Peña [36] claimed that the $(S, S')$-CRM mechanism is strategyproof when $S \subseteq S'$ or $S \cap S' = \emptyset$, and provided an involved, geometric proof. However, we have identified a mistake in their proof. In fact, we have found two counterexamples, one with $S \subseteq S'$ and one with $S \cap S' = \emptyset$, for which the corresponding $(S, S')$-CRM mechanisms violate strategyproofness, thus disproving their claim. These counterexamples are presented in Figure 1,

*Example 3.4 (Example with $S \cap S' = \emptyset$.).* This example is shown in Figure 1a. Points in filled dots are in $S$, while points in empty dots are in $S'$. The coordinates of these points are as follows.

$$S = \{(1, 0), (3, 1), (5, 1.9)\}, S' = \{(0, 1), (2, 2), (4, 3)\}.$$

Notice that $S \cap S' = \emptyset$. Also, $|S|$ and $|S'|$ are odd, alleviating the need to choose between left and right medians in the CRM definition.

When the agents truthfully report, one can check that CRM returns the line connecting points $(3, 1)$ from $S$ and $(0, 1)$ from $S'$. This line is given by the equation $y = 1$.

Suppose that the agent $i$ controlling the point at $x = 4$ misreports $\widetilde{y}_i = 1.8$ instead of $y_i = 3$. The new point is depicted with a cross. One can check that this causes the CRM mechanism to switch to the dashed line ($y = 0.1 \cdot x + 1.4$), which makes agent $i$ strictly better off, and violates strategyproofness.

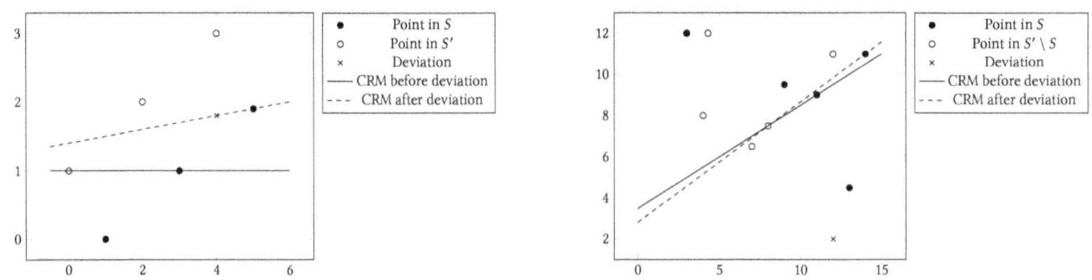


(a) $S \cap S' = \emptyset$ (b) $S \subsetneq S'$

Fig. 1. Counterexamples showing violation of strategyproofness of $(S, S')$-CRM mechanisms. Figure 1a shows a case with $S \cap S' = \emptyset$, while Figure 1b shows a case with $S \subsetneq S'$.

*Example 3.5 (Example with $S \subsetneq S'$.).* This example is shown in Figure 1b. Points in $S$ (thus also in $S'$) are depicted with filled dots, while points in $S' \setminus S$ are depicted with empty dots. The coordinates of these points are as follows.

$$S = \{(3,12), (9,9.5), (11,9), (13,4.5), (14,11)\}, S' = S \cup \{(4,8), (4.3,12), (7,6.5), (8,7.5), (12,11)\}.$$

Notice that $S \subsetneq S'$. Further, $|S|$ is odd, and $|S'|$ is even (thus, for each $i \in S$, $|S' \setminus \{i\}|$ is odd), once again eliminating the need to choose between the left and the right medians in the CRM definition.

When all points are reported truthfully, one can check that the CRM mechanism chooses the solid line ($3y = 2x + 8$). Suppose now that agent $i$ with point $(12, 11)$ reports $\widetilde{y}_i = 0$, instead of $y_i = 11$. Then, the CRM mechanism chooses the dashed line, which makes agent $i$ strictly better off, again violating strategyproofness.

Nevertheless, we have been able to identify a subset of the CRM family, for which we can establish strategyproofness (in fact, group strategyproofness). In particular, we replace $S \subsetneq S'$ with the more restrictive condition $S = S'$, and for $S \cap S' = \emptyset$, we either add $|S| = 1$ or $|S'| = 1$, or replace it with a stricter condition that we define below.

*Definition 3.6 (Separable Sets of Points in a Plane).* Let $S, S'$ be two sets of points in $\mathbb{R}^2$. We say that $S$ and $S'$ are *separable* if $\max_{i \in S} x_i < \min_{j \in S'} x_j$ or $\max_{j \in S'} x_j < \min_{i \in S} x_i$. In other words, it should be possible to separate them by a vertical line.

Note that separability of $S$ and $S'$ implies $S \cap S' = \emptyset$. We now present a corrected version of the result of Perote and Perote-Peña [36], and claim the stronger guarantee of group strategyproofness. We do not present a proof as we later introduce a much broader family of mechanisms, and prove their group strategyproofness directly.

Theorem 3.7. *Given $S, S' \subseteq N$, the $(S, S')$-CRM mechanism is group strategyproof if one of the following conditions holds.*

*(1) $S = S'$.*
*(2) $S$ and $S'$ are separable.*
*(3) $S \cap S' = \emptyset$ and $\min(|S|, |S'|) = 1$.*

The third condition partially resembles dictatorship as the agent in the singleton set is guaranteed to have zero residual (i.e., be on the regression line).

3.2.2 *Generalized Resistant Line Mechanisms on a Plane.* In this section, our goal is to introduce a novel family of group strategyproof mechanisms that include, as special cases, the mechanisms covered in the three cases of Theorem 3.7. Our starting point is the family of *resistant line* (RL) mechanisms from the statistics literature [24], which Perote and Perote-Peña [36] showed to be equivalent to the case of separable $S$ and $S'$.

The standard formulation of the RL mechanism involves three sets $L, M, R \subseteq N$ such that $\max_{i \in L} x_i < \min_{i \in M} x_i$ and $\max_{i \in M} x_i < \min_{i \in R} x_i$, and returns a line $\boldsymbol{\beta} = (\beta_1, \beta_0)$ given by

$$\text{med}_{i \in L}\, y_i - \beta_1 \cdot x_i - \beta_0 = \text{med}_{i \in R}\, y_i - \beta_1 \cdot x_i - \beta_0 = 0.$$

That is, the line makes the median residuals in $L$ and $R$ zero. It is known that this equation yields a unique solution [24]. Perote and Perote-Peña [36] showed that this is identical to the $(L, R)$-CRM mechanism. Indeed, separability of $L$ and $R$ makes clockwise angles from points in $L$ to points in $R$ monotonic in (and thus replaceable by) slopes, yielding the following formulation for the $(L, R)$-CRM mechanism.

$$\beta_1 = \text{med}_{i \in L}\, \text{med}_{j \in R}\, \frac{y_j - y_i}{x_j - x_i},$$
$$\beta_0 = \text{med}_{i \in L}\, y_i - \beta_1 x_i = \text{med}_{j \in R}\, y_j - \beta_1 x_j.$$

The alternative definition of $\beta_0 = \text{med}_{j \in R}(y_j - \beta_1 \cdot x_j)$ follows from the fact that if the line passes through $i^* \in L$, it is directed towards the point in $R$ which is at the median angle or slope, and thus bisects $R$ in addition to bisecting $L$.

Along with Theorem 3.7, this observation establishes group strategyproofness of all resistant line mechanisms. Two popular mechanisms from this family are the Brown-Mood mechanism [5], in which $L$ and $R$ each contain half of the points while $M$ is empty, and the Tukey mechanism [40], in which $L$, $M$, and $R$ each contain a third of the points.

Our next step is to extend this family. A natural idea is that instead of making the *median* residuals from $S$ and $S'$ zero, we make the $k^{\text{th}}$ smallest residual in $S$ and the $(k')^{\text{th}}$ smallest residual in $S'$ zero, for fixed $k \in [|S|]$ and $k' \in [|S'|]$.

*Definition 3.8 (Generalized Resistant Line (GRL) Mechanisms).* Given separable sets $S, S' \subseteq N$, $k \in [|S|]$, and $k' \in [|S'|]$, the $(S, S', k, k')$-generalized resistant line (GRL) mechanism returns the line $\boldsymbol{\beta} = (\beta_1, \beta_0)$ given by

$$\min^k_{i \in S} y_i - \beta_1 x_i - \beta_0 = \min^{k'}_{j \in S'} y_j - \beta_1 x_j - \beta_0 = 0. \tag{5}$$

We show that these mechanisms are well defined (i.e., there is a unique solution to Equation (5)), and they are group strategyproof. Once again, we omit the proof because we later introduce an even broader family of mechanisms, for which we prove these results directly.

THEOREM 3.9. *For separable sets $S, S' \subseteq N$, $k \in [|S|]$ and $k' \in [|S'|]$, the $(S, S', k, k')$-generalized resistant line mechanism is well defined and group strategyproof.*

While it is clear that generalized resistant line mechanisms cover the second case of Theorem 3.7 (i.e., separable $S$ and $S'$), we surprisingly find that they also cover the first case ($S = S'$) and the third case ($S \cap S' = \emptyset$ and $\min(|S|, |S'|) = 1$). That is, Theorem 3.9 strictly generalizes Theorem 3.7. The proof of the next result is in the full version.

LEMMA 3.10. *The $(S, S')$-CRM mechanism is a generalized resistant line mechanism when (1) $S = S'$, (2) $S$ and $S'$ are separable, or (3) $S \cap S' = \emptyset$ and* $\min(|S|, |S'|) = 1$.

*3.2.3 Generalized Resistant Hyperplane Mechanisms in High Dimensions.* Surprisingly, the statistics literature does not offer an extension of resistant line mechanisms to higher dimensions. In our efforts to do so, we quickly realized that this is a non-trivial task. In two dimensions, a generalized resistant line mechanism takes two subsets of data points separable by a vertical line, and returns the regression line which makes prescribed percentiles of residuals in each set zero.

In $d + 1$ dimensions (recall that $\boldsymbol{x}_i \in \mathbb{R}^d$ and $y_i \in \mathbb{R}$), it seems natural to take $d + 1$ "separable" subsets of data points, and return the regression hyperplane which makes prescribed percentiles of residuals in each set zero. However, the separability condition must now ensure existence of a unique hyperplane with this property, even if we ignore our game-theoretic desiderata.

In resolving this issue, we make a connection to the literature on the *Ham Sandwich Theorem* and its generalizations. Hereinafter, given a hyperplane $H$, we denote by $H^+$ and $H^-$ its positive and negative closed half-spaces, respectively. A basic version of the ham sandwich theorem due to Stone and Tukey [38] states that given $k$ continuous measures $\mu_1, \ldots, \mu_k$ on $\mathbb{R}^k$, there exists a hyperplane $H$ such that $\mu_i(H^+) = 1/2$ for each $i \in [k]$. A discrete version of this result due to Elton and Hill [18] states that given $k$ finite sets $S_1, \ldots, S_k \subseteq \mathbb{R}^k$, there exists a hyperplane $H$ such that for each $i \in [k]$, $H$ "bisects" $S_i$ and $H \cap S_i \neq \emptyset$. Here, we say that a hyperplane $H$ bisects a set of points $S$ if each *closed* half-space of $H$ contains at least $\lceil |S|/2 \rceil$ points.

For linear regression, this implies that given $S_1, \ldots, S_{d+1} \subseteq \mathcal{D}$, there exists a "resistant hyperplane" which makes the median residual from $S_t$ zero, for each $t \in [d + 1]$. While this seems like a natural generalization of resistant line mechanisms, it is easy to check that such a hyperplane is not always unique, even in two dimensions. Further, if the median is replaced by other percentiles, the existence is no longer guaranteed.[6]

Steiger and Zhao [37] provide a generalization that *almost* perfectly fits our needs. They show that under certain conditions on $S_1, \ldots, S_{d+1}$, there exists a unique hyperplane $H$ which contains a given number of points from each set in its negative closed half-space. This discrete result builds upon previous continuous variants [1, 4]. We first define a condition they require, which also plays a key role in our result.

*Definition 3.11 (Well Separable Sets [26]).* Given $t \in [k + 1]$, finite sets $S_1, \ldots, S_t$ of points in $\mathbb{R}^k$ are called *well separable* if for all disjoint $I, J \subseteq [t]$, there exists a hyperplane $H$ such that $S_i \subset H^+ \setminus H$ for each $i \in I$ and $S_j \subset H^- \setminus H$ for each $j \in J$, i.e., $H$ separates $\cup_{i \in I} S_i$ from $\cup_{j \in J} S_j$ by putting them in different *open* half-spaces.

Well separable sets are sometimes called *affinely independent* sets [4]. Well separability is equivalent to various other conditions [4, 37]. In what follows, $\mathrm{Conv}(\cdot)$ denotes the convex hull.

Proposition 3.12. *For $t \in [k + 1]$, finite sets $S_1, \ldots, S_t \subset \mathbb{R}^k$ are well separable if and only if:*

*(1) For all choices of $(x_i \in \mathrm{Conv}(S_i))_{i \in [t]}$, the affine hull of $x_1, \ldots, x_t$ is a $(t-1)$-dimensional flat.*
*(2) No $(t-2)$-dimensional flat has a nonempty intersection with $\mathrm{Conv}(S_i)$ for each $i \in [t]$.*
*(3) $\mathrm{Conv}(S_1), \ldots, \mathrm{Conv}(S_t)$ are well separable.*

Steiger and Zhao [37] impose an additional condition, which we eliminate in our work.

*Definition 3.13 (Weak General Position).* Finite sets $S_1, \ldots, S_k \subset \mathbb{R}^k$ are said to have *weak general position* if for every choice of $(x_i \in S_i)_{i \in [k]}$, the affine hull of $x_1, \ldots, x_k$ is a $(k-1)$-dimensional flat which contains no other point of $\cup_{i \in [k]} S_i$.

Theorem 3.14 ([37]). *If finite sets $S_1, \ldots, S_k \subset \mathbb{R}^k$ are well separable and have weak general position, then given any choice of $k_i \in [|S_i|]$ for $i \in [k]$, there exists a unique hyperplane $H$ such that for each $i \in [k]$, $H \cap S_i \neq \emptyset$ and $|H^- \cap S_i| = k_i$.*

This result gives us *almost* what we want for linear regression in $\mathbb{R}^{d+1}$. Given a family of sets $S_1, \ldots, S_{d+1} \subseteq \mathcal{D}$ that are well separable and have weak general position, and $k_t \in [|S_t|]$ for $t \in [d + 1]$, it ensures the existence of a unique hyperplane which makes the $k_t^{\text{th}}$ smallest residual in each set $S_t$ zero. However, it falls short of our requirements in two key aspects.

[6]Recall that even in two dimensions, we needed an additional condition on the sets $S$ and $S'$: separability by a vertical line.

- Theorem 3.14 allows the assignment of points in $\mathcal{D}$ to sets $S_1, \ldots, S_{d+1}$ to depend on the private information $\boldsymbol{y}$. For strategyproofness, we need this assignment to be based solely on the public information $\boldsymbol{x}$. Recall that in two dimensions, we required sets $S$ and $S'$ to be separable by a *vertical* line. We choose the $d+1$ sets so that they are well separable in the $d$-dimensional public information space,[7] and establish group strategyproofness using a technical lemma, which may be of independent interest.
- While we only want to make the $k_t^{\text{th}}$ smallest residual in each $S_t$ zero, Steiger and Zhao [37] aim for something stronger: they want the number of points from each $S_t$ in the negative closed halfspace to be exactly $k_t$. This necessitates their weak general position assumption, which we relax.

We are now ready to present our results. They closely mirror, but do not make use of, the results of Steiger and Zhao [37]. We revert to using notation of our linear regression setting. Recall that a hyperplane $\boldsymbol{\beta} = (\boldsymbol{\beta}_1, \beta_0)$ passes through $(\boldsymbol{x}_i, \boldsymbol{\beta}^T\,\overline{\boldsymbol{x}_i})$ for each $i \in N$, where $\overline{\boldsymbol{x}_i} = (\boldsymbol{x}_i, 1)$.

*Definition 3.15.* Given a family $\mathcal{S} = (S_1, \ldots, S_k)$ of nonempty, pairwise disjoint subsets of $N$, and a set of points $P = (p_i)_{i \in N}$, define the partition function $\mathcal{P}(P, \mathcal{S}) = (P_t)_{t \in [k]}$, where $P_t = (p_i)_{i \in S_t}$ for each $t \in [k]$. That is, $\mathcal{P}(P, \mathcal{S})$ partitions the set of points $P$ based on index sets from $\mathcal{S}$.

*Definition 3.16 (Publicly Separable Sets of Agents).* We say that a family $\mathcal{S} = (S_1, \ldots, S_{d+1})$ of nonempty, pairwise disjoint subsets of $N$ is *publicly separable* if $\mathcal{P}(\boldsymbol{x}, \mathcal{S})$ is well separable.

*Definition 3.17 (Generalized Resistant Hyperplane (GRH) Mechanisms).* Given a family $\mathcal{S} = (S_1, \ldots, S_{d+1})$ of publicly separable sets of agents, and $\boldsymbol{k} = (k_1, \ldots, k_{d+1})$ with $k_t \in [|S_t|]$ for $t \in [d+1]$, the $(\mathcal{S}, \boldsymbol{k})$-generalized resistant hyperplane (GRH) mechanism returns a hyperplane $\boldsymbol{\beta}$ such that $\min^{k_t}_{i \in S_t} (r_i \triangleq y_i - \boldsymbol{\beta}^T\,\overline{\boldsymbol{x}_i}) = 0$ for each $t \in [d+1]$. That is, it makes the $k_t^{\text{th}}$ smallest residual from every set $S_t \in \mathcal{S}$ zero.

We first need to establish that the GRH mechanisms are well defined, i.e., the hyperplane they seek is guaranteed to exist and be unique. To that end, we prove a useful technical lemma, which may be of independent interest.

Lemma 3.18 (Hyperplane Comparison Lemma). *Given a family $\mathcal{S} = (S_1, \ldots, S_{d+1})$ of publicly separable sets of agents, and two distinct hyperplanes $\boldsymbol{\beta}^1$ and $\boldsymbol{\beta}^2$ in $\mathbb{R}^{d+1}$, there exists a set $S_t \in \mathcal{S}$ such that either $(\boldsymbol{\beta}^1)^T\,\overline{\boldsymbol{x}_i} < (\boldsymbol{\beta}^2)^T\,\overline{\boldsymbol{x}_i}$ for all $i \in S_t$, or $(\boldsymbol{\beta}^1)^T\,\overline{\boldsymbol{x}_i} > (\boldsymbol{\beta}^2)^T\,\overline{\boldsymbol{x}_i}$ for all $i \in S_t$.*

Proof. Consider the intersection of the two hyperplanes in $\mathbb{R}^{d+1}$, and let $W$ be its projection on $\mathbb{R}^d$ (the public information space). Note that $W$ is a $(d-1)$-dimensional hyperplane in $\mathbb{R}^d$. Given an *open* half-space of $W$ (say $W^+$), let $Z$ be the set of points $\mathbb{R}^{d+1}$ whose projection on $\mathbb{R}^d$ lies in $W^+$. Then, either $(\boldsymbol{\beta}^1)^T\,\overline{\boldsymbol{p}} > (\boldsymbol{\beta}^2)^T\,\overline{\boldsymbol{p}}$ for all $\boldsymbol{p} \in Z$, or $(\boldsymbol{\beta}^1)^T\,\overline{\boldsymbol{p}} < (\boldsymbol{\beta}^2)^T\,\overline{\boldsymbol{p}}$ for all $\boldsymbol{p} \in Z$, where $\overline{\boldsymbol{p}} = (\boldsymbol{p}, 1)$.

Let $\mathcal{P}(\boldsymbol{x}, \mathcal{S}) = (X_1, \ldots, X_{d+1})$. Because $\mathcal{S}$ is publicly separable, $X_1, \ldots, X_{d+1}$ are well separable. By Proposition 3.12, no $(d-1)$-dimensional flat has a nonempty intersection with $\text{Conv}(X_t)$ for each $t \in [d+1]$. Because $W$ is a $(d-1)$-dimensional flat, there exists $t \in [d+1]$ such that $W$ does not intersect $\text{Conv}(X_t)$, i.e., $X_t$ lies entirely in an *open* half-space of $W$. Using the previous argument, either $(\boldsymbol{\beta}^1)^T\,\overline{\boldsymbol{x}_i} < (\boldsymbol{\beta}^2)^T\,\overline{\boldsymbol{x}_i}$ for all $i \in S_t$, or $(\boldsymbol{\beta}^1)^T\,\overline{\boldsymbol{x}_i} > (\boldsymbol{\beta}^2)^T\,\overline{\boldsymbol{x}_i}$ for all $i \in S_t$. ■

Proposition 3.19. *Generalized resistant hyperplane mechanisms are well defined. That is, given a family $\mathcal{S} = (S_1, \ldots, S_{d+1})$ of publicly separable sets of agents, and $\boldsymbol{k} = (k_1, \ldots, k_{d+1})$ with $k_t \in [|S_t|]$ for $t \in [d+1]$, there exists a unique hyperplane $\boldsymbol{\beta}$ for which $\min^{k_t}_{i \in S_t} y_i - \boldsymbol{\beta}^T\,\overline{\boldsymbol{x}_i} = 0$ for each $t \in [d+1]$.*

[7] While Theorem 3.14 uses $d+1$ well separable sets in $\mathbb{R}^{d+1}$, even $\mathbb{R}^d$ allows up to $d+1$ well separable sets.

Proof. First, we show that *if* such a hyperplane exists, it must be unique. Suppose for contradiction that there are two distinct hyperplanes $\boldsymbol{\beta}^1$ and $\boldsymbol{\beta}^2$ which make the $k_t^{\text{th}}$ smallest residual from every $S_t \in \mathcal{S}$ zero. By the hyperplane comparison lemma (Lemma 3.18), there exists $S_t \in \mathcal{S}$ such that either $(\boldsymbol{\beta}^1)^T\,\overline{\boldsymbol{x}_i} < (\boldsymbol{\beta}^2)^T\,\overline{\boldsymbol{x}_i}$ for all $i \in S_t$, or $(\boldsymbol{\beta}^1)^T\,\overline{\boldsymbol{x}_i} > (\boldsymbol{\beta}^2)^T\,\overline{\boldsymbol{x}_i}$ for all $i \in S_t$. Without loss of generality, suppose it is the former. Then, at least $k_t$ points in $S_t$ which have a non-positive residual under $\boldsymbol{\beta}^2$ have a negative residual under $\boldsymbol{\beta}^1$, contradicting the fact that $\boldsymbol{\beta}^1$ makes the $k_t^{\text{th}}$ smallest residual from $S_t$ zero.

For proving existence, we use a counting technique. Create two bipartite graphs $G = (V \cup W, E)$ and $G' = (V' \cup W, E')$. Let $V$ (resp. $V'$) contain a vertex $v_{\boldsymbol{k}}$ (resp. $v'_{\boldsymbol{k}}$) corresponding to each $\boldsymbol{k} = (k_1, \ldots, k_{d+1})$ such that $k_t \in [|S_t|]$ for each $t \in [d+1]$. Thus, $|V| = |V'| = \prod_{t=1}^{d+1} |S_t|$. Let $W$ contain a vertex $w_{\boldsymbol{\beta}}$ corresponding to every *traversal* hyperplane $\boldsymbol{\beta}$, i.e., every hyperplane that passes through at least one point from each set $S_t \in \mathcal{S}$.

In graph $G$, we draw an edge between $v_{\boldsymbol{k}}$ and $w_{\boldsymbol{\beta}}$ if $\boldsymbol{\beta}$ makes the $k_t^{\text{th}}$ smallest residual zero in each $S_t \in \mathcal{S}$. For constructing graph $G'$, we fix an arbitrary ordering of points in each set, so that we can write $S_t = \{i_1^t, \ldots, i_{|S_t|}^t\}$. Then, we draw an edge in $G'$ between $v'_{\boldsymbol{k}}$ and $w_{\boldsymbol{\beta}}$ if $\boldsymbol{\beta}$ passes through point $i_{k_t}^t$ for each $t \in [d+1]$.

Our goal is to show that each vertex $v_{\boldsymbol{k}} \in V$ has exactly one incident edge in graph $G$. We prove this through a sequence of claims. First, we argue that each vertex $v'_{\boldsymbol{k}} \in V'$ has exactly one incident edge in graph $G'$. The fact that it has *at least* one incident edge follows from the fact that any set of $d+1$ points in $\mathbb{R}^{d+1}$ (in particular, $T = \{i_{k_t}^t\}_{t\in[d+1]}$) lie on a hyperplane. If $v'_{\boldsymbol{k}}$ has two or more incident edges, then there exist two distinct hyperplanes $\boldsymbol{\beta}^1$ and $\boldsymbol{\beta}^2$ which pass through all points in $T$. Then, their intersection $\boldsymbol{\beta}^*$, which is a $(d-1)$-dimensional flat in $\mathbb{R}^{d+1}$, must also pass through all points in $T$. Let $\mathcal{P}(\boldsymbol{x}, \mathcal{S}) = (X_1, \ldots, X_{d+1})$. Then, the projection of $\boldsymbol{\beta}^*$ on the public information space $\mathbb{R}^d$ is a $(d-1)$-dimensional hyperplane in $\mathbb{R}^d$ which intersects each $X_t$ (and thus each $\text{Conv}(X_t)$). However, $\mathcal{S}$ is a publicly separable family, i.e., $X_1, \ldots, X_{d+1}$ are well separable in $\mathbb{R}^d$. This violates the first condition of Proposition 3.12.

Since each vertex in $V'$ has exactly one incident edge, we have $|E'| = |V'| = \prod_{t=1}^{d+1} |S_t|$. We next argue that $|E| = |E'|$. Take a vertex $w_{\boldsymbol{\beta}} \in W$. Note that if hyperplane $\boldsymbol{\beta}$ passes through $a_t$ points from each $S_t \in \mathcal{S}$, then it has degree $\prod_{t=1}^{d+1} a_t$ in both $G$ and $G'$. Since each vertex in $W$ has the same degree in both graphs, we have $|E| = |E'| = |V'| = |V|$.

Finally, we already established that if there is a hyperplane which makes the $k_t^{\text{th}}$ smallest residual in each $S_t$ zero, then it must be unique. Thus, each vertex in $V$ has *at most* one incident edge in $G$. Together with $|E| = |V|$, this implies that each vertex in $V$ has *exactly* one incident edge in $G$. ∎

We are now ready to present our main contribution.

Theorem 3.20. *Every generalized resistant hyperplane mechanism is group strategyproof.*

Proof. Consider an $(\mathcal{S}, \boldsymbol{k})$-generalized resistant hyperplane mechanism. Consider a set of data points $\mathcal{D} = (\boldsymbol{x}_i, y_i)_{i\in N}$. Suppose a coalition $S \subseteq N$ of agents changes their report to $(\widetilde{y}_i)_{i\in S}$, and changes the resulting hyperplane from $\boldsymbol{\beta}$ to $\widetilde{\boldsymbol{\beta}}$. Set $\widetilde{y}_i = y_i$ for $i \in N \setminus S$, and let $\widetilde{\mathcal{D}} = (\boldsymbol{x}_i, \widetilde{y}_i)_{i\in N}$.

By the hyperplane comparison lemma (Lemma 3.18), there exists $S_t \in \mathcal{S}$ such that either $\boldsymbol{\beta}^T\,\overline{\boldsymbol{x}_i} < \widetilde{\boldsymbol{\beta}}^T\,\overline{\boldsymbol{x}_i}$ for all $i \in S_t$, or $\boldsymbol{\beta}^T\,\overline{\boldsymbol{x}_i} > \widetilde{\boldsymbol{\beta}}^T\,\overline{\boldsymbol{x}_i}$ for all $i \in S_t$.

Without loss of generality, suppose it is the former. The $k_t^{\text{th}}$ smallest residual from $S_t$ is zero under $\boldsymbol{\beta}$ in $\mathcal{D}$, and under $\widetilde{\boldsymbol{\beta}}$ in $\widetilde{\mathcal{D}}$. If $S \cap S_t = \emptyset$, or if every manipulator in $S \cap S_t$ has a positive residual under $\boldsymbol{\beta}$ in $\mathcal{D}$, then at least $k_t$ non-manipulators in $N \setminus S$ have a non-positive residual under $\boldsymbol{\beta}$ in $\mathcal{D}$, and thus a strictly negative residual under $\widetilde{\boldsymbol{\beta}}$ in $\widetilde{\mathcal{D}}$, which contradicts the fact that $\widetilde{\boldsymbol{\beta}}$ makes the $k_t^{\text{th}}$ smallest residual in $S_t$ zero in $\widetilde{\mathcal{D}}$.

In other words, there must exist a manipulator $i \in S \cap S_t$ who has a non-positive residual under $\boldsymbol{\beta}$ in $\mathcal{D}$. Thus, $\widetilde{\boldsymbol{\beta}}^T\ \overline{x_i} > \boldsymbol{\beta}^T\ \overline{x_i} \geq y_i$, implying that the manipulator is strictly worse off after the manipulation. Hence, the mechanism is group strategyproof. ■

For two dimensions ($d = 1$), we already argued that our sub-family of group strategyproof CRM mechanisms given by Theorem 3.7 is part of the larger family of GRL mechanisms (Lemma 3.10). It is easy to see that GRL mechanisms are precisely GRH mechanisms in two dimensions. Indeed, GRH mechanisms would require two subsets of agents $S_1, S_2$ that are publicly separable, i.e., well separable on the $x$-axis. Note that this coincides with the separability definition used by GRL mechanisms (Definition 3.6). Hence, the $(S, S', k, k')$-GRL mechanism is precisely the $(\mathcal{S}, \boldsymbol{k})$-GRH mechanism with $\mathcal{S} = (S, S')$ and $\boldsymbol{k} = (k, k')$. In three or more dimensions, we do not know if, given $\boldsymbol{x}$, one can always construct a family $\mathcal{S}$ of publicly separable sets of agents such that each set $S_t \in \mathcal{S}$ contains at least a constant fraction of the agents.

### 3.3 Strategyproofness vs Group Strategyproofness

In the single dimensional setting ($d = 0$), Moulin [33] proved that all strategyproof mechanisms are also group strategyproof. This alternatively follows from a result by Barberà et al. [2], who gave a sufficient condition on the underlying domain for the sets of strategyproof and group strategyproof mechanisms to coincide.

Interestingly, all known strategyproof mechanisms for the multidimensional linear regression setting (including generalized $L_1$-ERM and generalized resistant hyperplane mechanisms) are group strategyproof as well. However, it is easy to check that the linear regression setting does not satisfy the sufficient condition of Barberà et al. [2]. Is it still true that all strategyproof mechanisms for linear regression are also group strategyproof? We answer this question *negatively.*

*Example 3.21.* Consider the simple linear regression setting ($d = 1$) with $n = 2$ agents. Fix the public information $\boldsymbol{x} = (x_1, x_2) \in \mathbb{R}^2$, and consider the mechanism $M$ that, on input $\boldsymbol{y} = (y_1, y_2)$, returns the line passing through points $(x_1, y_2)$ and $(x_2, y_1)$. Under this mechanism, the outcome for each agent is independent of the agent's report: indeed, the outcome for agent 1 (resp. agent 2) is $\widehat{y}_1 = y_2$ (resp. $\widehat{y}_2 = y_1$). Hence, the mechanism is clearly strategyproof. However, group strategyproofness is violated because when $y_1 \neq y_2$, the two agents can collude, and report $\widetilde{\boldsymbol{y}} = (y_2, y_1)$. This makes the resulting line pass through both agents, making both strictly better off.

The requirement that the outcome for each agent be independent of the agent's report, called *impartiality* in mechanism design, is stricter than (i.e., logically implies) strategyproofness, and has been studied for aggregating opinions or dividing rewards [14, 19, 22, 28, 39].

*Definition 3.22 (Impartial Mechanisms).* A mechanism $M$ is called *impartial* if the outcome for each agent is independent of the agent's report. Formally, for every agent $i \in N$, reports $\boldsymbol{y}$, and alternative report $y_i'$ by agent $i$, we require that $\widehat{y}_i(M(\boldsymbol{y})) = \widehat{y}_i(M(y_i', \boldsymbol{y}_{-i}))$.

In linear regression, when the number of agents is $n = d + 1$, we can easily characterize all impartial mechanisms because we can set $\widehat{y}_i$ to be an arbitrary function of $\boldsymbol{y}_{-i}$, and return a hyperplane passing through the resulting $d + 1$ points $(\boldsymbol{x}_i, \widehat{y}_i)_{i \in N}$.

PROPOSITION 3.23. *For $n = d + 1$, mechanism $M$ is impartial if and only if there exist functions $f_1, \ldots, f_n : \mathbb{R}^{n-1} \to \mathbb{R}$ such that given $\boldsymbol{y}$, $M$ returns a hyperplane passing through $(\boldsymbol{x}_i, f_i(\boldsymbol{y}_{-i}))_{i \in N}$.*

Note that functions $f_i$ can even be discontinuous, which can make the regression hyperplane discontinuous in the input $\boldsymbol{y}$. However, we later show (Theorem 4.3) that under any strategyproof mechanism, the outcome $\widehat{y}_i$ for agent $i$ must be a continuous function of $y_i$ (it is a constant function of $y_i$ in case of impartial mechanisms).

With $n > d + 1$ points, the question of whether impartial mechanisms even exist is non-trivial. While we still need to set each $\widehat{y}_i$ as a function of $\boldsymbol{y}_{-i}$, it cannot be done arbitrarily as the resulting points $(\boldsymbol{x}_i, \widehat{y}_i)_{i \in N}$ may no longer lie on a hyperplane. In other words, setting $\widehat{y}_i$ as a function of $\boldsymbol{y}_{-i}$ for $d + 1$ agents already determines the hyperplane, and thus $\widehat{y}_j$ for all remaining agents $j$. The mechanism must ensure that these $\widehat{y}_j$ are also independent of $y_j$. At first glance, this may seem impossible, except in the trivial case where a constant hyperplane is returned regardless of $\boldsymbol{y}$.

Nonetheless, we show that there exists a wide family of non-trivial impartial mechanisms for linear regression. Our family provides a full characterization of impartial mechanisms for $d = 1$ (i.e., for simple linear regression). In the result below, we use the notation $\langle \boldsymbol{a}, \boldsymbol{b} \rangle$ instead of $\boldsymbol{a}^T \boldsymbol{b}$ for the sake of simplicity. Its proof is in the full version.

THEOREM 3.24. *Given* $\boldsymbol{x}$, *mechanism* $M^{\boldsymbol{x}}$ *for linear regression is impartial if there exist functions* $\{g_i^{\boldsymbol{x}} : \mathbb{R} \to \mathbb{R}^d\}_{i \in N}$ *and constant* $c^{\boldsymbol{x}} \in \mathbb{R}$ *such that for all* $\boldsymbol{y}$, *we have* $M^{\boldsymbol{x}}(\boldsymbol{y}) = \boldsymbol{\beta} = (\boldsymbol{\beta}_1, \beta_0)$, *where*

$$\boldsymbol{\beta}_1 = \sum_{i \in N} g_i^{\boldsymbol{x}}(y_i), \quad \beta_0 = c^{\boldsymbol{x}} - \sum_{i \in N} \left\langle g_i^{\boldsymbol{x}}(y_i), \boldsymbol{x}_i \right\rangle. \tag{6}$$

*For* $d = 1$ *and an admissible set of points, this characterizes all impartial mechanisms.*

Impartial mechanisms are not compelling from a statistical viewpoint. For instance, in the standard two-dimensional stochastic model where the data points are assumed to be generated by taking points on an underlying line and introducing i.i.d. errors in the dependent variables, it is easy to show that no impartial mechanism can produce an unbiased estimator of the underlying line. Nonetheless, impartial mechanisms help us establish the existence of a rather wide family of strategyproof mechanisms that are *not* group strategyproof. In fact, the next result shows that almost all impartial mechanisms violate group strategyproofness; its proof is in the full version.

PROPOSITION 3.25. *For simple linear regression* ($d = 1$) *with an admissible set of points, an impartial mechanism is group strategyproof if and only if it is a constant function (i.e., it returns a fixed regression line regardless of its input).*

## 4 CHARACTERIZING STRATEGYPROOF MECHANISMS

As mentioned in Section 3.1, Moulin [33] studied the one-dimensional setting ($d = 0$), and analytically characterized all strategyproof mechanisms for $n$ agents. While we are unable to provide an analytical characterization for multidimensional linear regression, we provide two non-constructive characterizations, and discuss their implications.

Interestingly, to characterize strategyproof mechanisms for linear regression with $n$ agents, we use the characterization of strategyproof mechanisms for the one-dimensional setting with a single agent. In this case, Moulin [33] shows that a mechanism is strategyproof if and only if there exist constants $\alpha^1, \alpha^2 \in \overline{\mathbb{R}}$ such that when the agent reports $y$, the mechanism returns $\widehat{y} = \text{med}(y, \alpha^1, \alpha^2)$. Constants $\alpha^1$ and $\alpha^2$ are called *phantoms*. First, we extend this result by providing an alternative characterization, which uses the following definition. The proof of the next result is in the full version.

*Definition 4.1 (Locally Constant Function).* For $A, B \subseteq \mathbb{R}$, function $f : A \to B$ is called locally constant at $x \in A$ if there exists $\epsilon > 0$ such that for all $x' \in [x - \epsilon, x + \epsilon]$, $f(x') = f(x)$.

LEMMA 4.2. *Suppose mechanism* $\pi : \mathbb{R} \to \mathbb{R}$ *for the one-dimensional setting with a single agent elicits private value* $y$ *from the agent and returns* $\pi(y)$. *Then,* $\pi$ *being strategyproof is equivalent to each of the following conditions.*

(a) *There exist constants* $\alpha^1, \alpha^2 \in \overline{\mathbb{R}} \triangleq \mathbb{R} \cup \{-\infty, \infty\}$ *such that for all* $y \in \mathbb{R}$, $\pi(y) = \text{med}(y, \alpha^1, \alpha^2)$.

(b) $\pi$ *is continuous, and for every* $y \in \mathbb{R}$, *either* $\pi(y) = y$ *or* $\pi$ *is locally constant at* $y$.

In the one-dimensional setting, Moulin [33] observed that a mechanism is strategyproof if and only if its outcome is strategyproof in the report of each individual agent when other agents' reports are fixed. That is, a mechanism $\pi : \mathbb{R}^n \to \mathbb{R}$ for $n$ agents is strategyproof if and only if

$$\forall i \in [n],\ \exists \alpha_i^1, \alpha_i^2 \in \overline{\mathbb{R}} \text{ independent of } y_i \text{ s.t. } \pi(y_1, \dots, y_n) = \text{med}(y_i, \alpha_i^1, \alpha_i^2). \tag{7}$$

Moulin [33] solved Equation (7) to derive an elegant analytical expression for $\pi$ in terms of $\{y_i\}_{i\in[n]}$. Note that in this equation, the outcome $\widehat{y} = \pi(y_1, \dots, y_n)$ is common to all agents.

In contrast, in linear regression each agent $i$ has a potentially different outcome $\widehat{y}_i$. Like before, strategyproofness requires that each $\widehat{y}_i$ obey the conditions in Lemma 4.2, when seen as a function of $y_i$, when other agents' reports are fixed. However, the outcomes for different agents are now constrained so that $(\boldsymbol{x}_i, \widehat{y}_i)_{i\in N}$ lie on a hyperplane. This added complexity prevented us from solving the equations to derive an analytical characterization, despite significant effort. The only exception was the special case of *impartial* mechanisms, where we further restrict $\widehat{y}_i$ to be independent of $y_i$ (Theorem 3.24). This corresponds to the case where $\alpha_i^1 = \alpha_i^2$ for each agent $i$. Nonetheless, by simply applying Lemma 4.2 for every agent $i$, we obtain the following non-constructive characterization of strategyproof mechanisms for linear regression.

Theorem 4.3. *Given public information $\boldsymbol{x}$, mechanism $M^{\boldsymbol{x}}$ for linear regression being strategyproof is equivalent to each of the following conditions.*

*(a) For every $\boldsymbol{y}_{-i} \in \mathbb{R}^{n-1}$ and $i \in N$, there exist $\ell_i, h_i \in \overline{\mathbb{R}}$ such that $\widehat{y}_i(M^{\boldsymbol{x}}(\boldsymbol{y})) = \text{med}(y_i, \ell_i, h_i)$ for all $y_i \in \mathbb{R}$;*

*(b) For every $\boldsymbol{y}_{-i} \in \mathbb{R}^{n-1}$ and $i \in N$, function $f_i(\cdot) = \widehat{y}_i(M(\cdot, \boldsymbol{y}_{-i}))$ is continuous, and for every $y_i \in \mathbb{R}$, either $f_i(y_i) = y_i$ or $f_i$ is locally constant at $y_i$.*

The first condition provides an analytical form of $\widehat{y}_i$ in terms of $y_i$, and is perhaps the more useful characterization. For instance, we crucially use this characterization in the next section to give a lower bound on the efficiency of strategyproof mechanisms. Our earlier (more complex) proof of group strategyproofness of GRH mechanisms (Theorem 3.20) was also based on this condition, and identified the precise $\ell_i$ and $h_i$ for each agent $i$.

Note that for fixed $\boldsymbol{y}_{-i}$, we have $\widehat{y}_i = y_i$ when $y_i \in [\ell_i, h_i]$. For $y_i \le \ell_i$, $\widehat{y}_i = \ell_i$ is fixed, and for $y_i \ge h_i$, $\widehat{y}_i = h_i$ is fixed. We therefore say that agent $i$ is *influential* over the interval $(\ell_i, h_i)$, and call $\ell_i$ and $h_i$ the *lower* and *upper influence bounds*, respectively. Analysis of influence bounds has received attention in the statistics literature, where it is called *sensitivity analysis*. For instance, Narula and Wellington [34] observed that under $L_1$-ERM, the regression hyperplane is unaffected when the dependent variable of a point is changed so that the point still lies on the same side of the hyperplane as before. From Theorem 4.3, we can see that for every strategyproof mechanism, doing so should at least keep the outcome for agent $i$ unchanged. Narula and Wellington [34] also focused on computing the influence bounds. Theorem 4.3 lends a simple algorithm to compute influence bounds (see the full version). Finally, note that while $\widehat{y}_i$ must be continuous in $y_i$, it need not be continuous in $\boldsymbol{y}$ (see our discussion on Proposition 3.23).

## 5 EFFICIENCY OF STRATEGYPROOF MECHANISMS

Insofar, we studied families of strategyproof mechanisms for linear regression. In the absence of strategic considerations, a popular mechanism for linear regression is the OLS (ordinary least squares), which is the empirical risk minimizer for the squared loss. Under this loss function, which is also called the *residual sum of squares* (RSS), the loss when choosing hyperplane $\boldsymbol{\beta}$ given data points $\mathcal{D}$ is $\text{RSS}(\mathcal{D}, \boldsymbol{\beta}) = \sum_{i\in N} \left(y_i - \boldsymbol{\beta}^T \overline{\boldsymbol{x}_i}\right)^2$. A classic justification for the OLS is due to the Gauss-Markov theorem, which states that when the errors (deviations of data points from an underlying hyperplane we wish to identify) are stochastic, zero in expectation, uncorrelated, and of equal variance, the OLS is the *best linear unbiased estimator.*

However, in our strategic setting, the OLS is not strategyproof [15]. This raises an important question: *Is there a strategyproof mechanism that is close to the OLS?* We assess this by the worst-case approximation ratio of a mechanism for the optimal squared loss.

*Definition 5.1 (Efficiency).* Given $\boldsymbol{x}$, we say that mechanism $M^{\boldsymbol{x}}$ for linear regression is $c$-efficient if for every $\mathcal{D} = (\boldsymbol{x}_i, y_i)_{i \in N}$, we have $\text{RSS}(\mathcal{D}, M^{\boldsymbol{x}}(\boldsymbol{y})) \leq c \cdot \inf_{\boldsymbol{\beta}} \text{RSS}(\mathcal{D}, \boldsymbol{\beta})$.

We show that no strategyproof mechanism that is too close to the OLS can be strategyproof. The proof of the next result leverages our characterization of strategyproof mechanisms (Theorem 4.3).

Theorem 5.2. *For $n \geq 4$, there exist $\boldsymbol{x}$ for which no strategyproof mechanism is $(2-\epsilon)$-efficient for any $\epsilon > 0$.*

Proof. For simplicity of notation, we use $n+1$ agents instead of $n$ agents (and assume $n+1 \geq 4$, i.e., $n \geq 3$). We also consider simple linear regression ($d = 1$); the proof easily extends to higher dimensions by simply setting all other coordinates to zero. Fix $n \geq 3$. Consider a setting with $n+1$ agents where $x_i = i$ for $i \in [n]$, and $x_{n+1} = X$, where $X$ is the solution of the following equation:

$$\frac{n^3 - n}{2(1 + 3n + 2n^2 + 6X^2 - 6Xn - 6X)} = 1. \tag{8}$$

Interested readers may note that $X = \Theta(n^{1.5})$. Let $T$ denote the LHS in Equation (8).

Consider a strategyproof mechanism $M^{\boldsymbol{x}}$. Suppose $M^{\boldsymbol{x}}$ is $c$-efficient. We want to show that $c \geq 2$. We consider a family of inputs $\boldsymbol{y}$, in which we fix $y_i = 0$ for $i \in [n]$, and vary $y_{n+1} = Y$. First, we note that the optimal RSS, as a function of $Y$, is given by

$$f_0(Y) = Y^2 \cdot \frac{n^3 - n}{2 + 5n + 4n^2 + n^3 - 12X - 12nX + 12X^2} = Y^2 \cdot \frac{T}{T+1} = \frac{Y^2}{2},$$

where the first transition is obtained by minimizing $(Y - X \cdot \beta_1 - \beta_0)^2 + \sum_{i=1}^n (i \cdot \beta_1 + \beta_0)^2$ over all $(\beta_1, \beta_0)$, the second transition follows through simple algebra, and the final transition follows from Equation (8).

Recall that we fixed $y_i$ for $i \in [n]$. Due to our characterization result (Theorem 4.3), there exist $\ell, h \in \overline{\mathbb{R}}$ with $\ell \leq h$ such that the line returned by the mechanism passes through $(X, \text{med}(Y, \ell, h))$ for all $Y$. We take two cases.

*Case 1: $h > 0$.* Set $Y = h$. Then, the line returned by the mechanism passes through $(X, h)$. In this case, we can show that the RSS of the mechanism is at least

$$f_1 = h^2 \cdot \frac{n^3 - n}{2(1 + 3n + 2n^2 + 6X^2 - 6Xn - 6X)} = h^2 \cdot T = h^2,$$

where the first transition is obtained by minimizing $(Y - \beta_1 \cdot X - \beta_0)^2 + \sum_{i=1}^n (\beta_1 \cdot i + \beta_0)^2$ over all $(\beta_1, \beta_0)$ which satisfy $\beta_1 \cdot X + \beta_0 = Y$, and the rest follows from Equation (8). This implies $c \geq f_1 / f_0(h) = 2$.

*Case 2: $h \leq 0$.* Set $Y = 1$. Then, the line returned by the mechanism passes through $(X, h)$. In this case, the RSS of the mechanism is at least $f_2 = 1$ because agent $n+1$ contributes $(1-h)^2 \geq 1$ to the squared loss. Once again, we have $c \geq f_2 / f_0(1) = 2$.

The proof is complete as we have $c \geq 2$ in each case. ∎

For $n = 2$ agents (or $n = d + 1$ agents in $d + 1$ dimensions), there is an obvious 1-efficient strategyproof mechanism which returns a hyperplane passing through all input points. Theorem 4.3 leaves open the case of $n = 3$ in two dimensions.

## 6 DISCUSSION

Our work leaves several open questions. Perhaps the most ambitious one is to find a constructive characterization of all strategyproof or group strategyproof mechanisms for linear regression, which may allow us to pinpoint the most efficient strategyproof mechanism; Caragiannis et al. [8] provide a similar analysis in the one-dimensional setting. It is easy to show that $L_1$-ERM is $n$-efficient (see the full version). Does there exist a more efficient strategyproof mechanism? It would also be interesting to analyze efficiency in a stochastic setting where the data points are drawn from an underlying distribution.

The characterization result of Moulin [33] for strategyproof and anonymous mechanisms in the one-dimensional setting extends the median to generalized medians by adding fixed phantom values, and then taking the median. It is also shown that adding $n + 1$ phantoms is sufficient to obtain full generality. We can extend all our proposed families of mechanisms by adding a certain number of "phantom points" in $\mathbb{R}^{d+1}$, and then applying the mechanisms to the union of data points and phantom points. The resulting mechanism retains the incentive guarantees.[8] Given $n$ data points, how many phantoms are sufficient to obtain full generality? Do the phantoms play a role in obtaining the elusive constructive characterization?

Another interesting observation is that our generalized resistant hyperplane mechanisms are guaranteed pass through $d + 1$ input points in $d + 1$ dimensions. It is known that at least one minimizer of the $L1$ loss also has this property. It would be interesting to identify a generic family of conditions, which, when imposed in addition to the requirement of making $d + 1$ residuals zero, yield group strategyproofness.

Finally, Dekel et al. [15] study a regression setting in which a single agent may control multiple data points, show that $L_1$-ERM is no longer strategyproof, and provide novel strategyproof mechanisms. It would be useful to see if our ideas can be used to design additional strategyproof mechanisms in this model. Another interesting variant is when only a small number of data points are held by strategic agents, but the mechanism does not know which ones. A similar setting was studied by Charikar et al. [11], but for classification and with adversarial manipulations. On a high level, we view our work as a stepping stone to studying incentives in more realistic machine learning environments.

## REFERENCES


[1] I. Bárány, A. Hubard, and J. Jerónimo. 2008. Slicing convex sets and measures by a hyperplane. *Discrete & Computational Geometry* 39, 1-3 (2008), 67–75.

[2] S. Barberà, D. Berga, and B. Moreno. 2010. Individual versus group strategy-proofness: When do they coincide? *Journal of Economic Theory* 145, 5 (2010), 1648–1674.

[3] D. Black. 1958. *Theory of Committees and Elections.* Cambridge University Press.

[4] F. Breuer. 2010. Uneven splitting of ham sandwiches. *Discrete & Computational Geometry* 43, 4 (2010), 876–892.

[5] G. W. Brown and A. M. Mood. 1951. On Median Tests for Linear Hypotheses. In *Proceedings of the 2nd Berkeley Symposium on Mathematical Statistics and Probability.* 159–166.

[6] N. H. Bshouty, N. Eiron, and E. Kushilevitz. 2002. PAC Learning with Nasty Noise. *Theoretical Computer Science* 288, 2 (2002), 255–275.

[7] Y. Cai, C. Daskalakis, and C. H. Papadimitriou. 2015. Optimum Statistical Estimation with Strategic Data Sources. In *Proceedings of the 28th Conference on Computational Learning Theory (COLT).* 280–296.

[8] I. Caragiannis, A. D. Procaccia, and N. Shah. 2016. Truthful Univariate Estimators. In *Proceedings of the 33rd International Conference on Machine Learning (ICML).* 127–135.

[9] F. Caro and J. Gallien. 2010. Inventory Management of a Fast-Fashion Retail Network. *Operations Research* 58, 2 (2010), 257–273.


[8] We also considered adding phantom values directly in the equations where a median is used. However, most such attempts violated strategyproofness.

[10] F. Caro, J. Gallien, M. D. Miranda, J. C. Torralbo, J. M. C. Corras, M. M. Vazquez, J. A. R. Calamonte, and J. Correa. 2010. Zara Uses Operations Research to Reengineer its Global Distribution Process. *Interfaces* 40, 1 (2010), 71–84.

[11] M. Charikar, J. Steinhardt, and G. Valiant. 2017. Learning from untrusted data. In *Proceedings of the 49th Annual ACM Symposium on Theory of Computing (STOC)*. 47–60.

[12] Yudong Chen, Constantine Caramanis, and Shie Mannor. 2013. Robust sparse regression under adversarial corruption. In *International Conference on Machine Learning*. 774–782.

[13] R. Cummings, S. Ioannidis, and K. Ligett. 2015. Truthful Linear Regression. In *Proceedings of the 28th Conference on Computational Learning Theory (COLT)*. 448âĂŞ–483.

[14] G. de Clippel, H. Moulin, and N. Tideman. 2008. Impartial division of a dollar. *Journal of Economic Theory* 139 (2008), 176–191.

[15] O. Dekel, F. Fischer, and A. D. Procaccia. 2010. Incentive Compatible Regression Learning. *J. Comput. System Sci.* 76, 8 (2010), 759–777.

[16] J. Dong, A. Roth, Z. Schutzman, B. Waggoner, and Z. S. Wu. 2017. Strategic Classification from Revealed Preferences. arXiv:1710.07887. (2017).

[17] M. Dummett and R. Farquharson. 1961. Stability in voting. *Econometrica* 29, 1 (1961), 33–43.

[18] J. H. Elton and T. P. Hill. 2011. A stronger conclusion to the classical ham sandwich theorem. *European Journal of Combinatorics* 32, 5 (2011), 657–661.

[19] F. Fischer and M. Klimm. 2015. Optimal impartial selection. *SIAM J. Comput.* 44, 5 (2015), 1263–1285.

[20] S. A. Goldman and R. H. Sloan. 1995. Can PAC Learning Algorithms Tolerate Random Attribute Noise? *Algorithmica* 14, 1 (1995), 70–84.

[21] M. Hardt, N. Megiddo, C. H. Papadimitriou, and M. Wootters. 2016. Strategic Classification. In *Proceedings of the 7th Innovations in Theoretical Computer Science Conference (ITCS)*. 111–122.

[22] R. Holzman and H. Moulin. 2013. Impartial nominations for a prize. *Econometrica* 81, 1 (2013), 173–196.

[23] S. Ioannidis and P. Loiseau. 2013. Linear regression as a non-cooperative game. In *Proceedings of the 9th Conference on Web and Internet Economics (WINE)*. 277–290.

[24] I. M. Johnstone and P. F. Velleman. 1985. The resistant line and related regression methods. *J. Amer. Statist. Assoc.* 80, 392 (1985), 1041–1054.

[25] M. Kearns and M. Li. 1993. Learning in the Presence of Malicious Errors. *SIAM J. Comput.* 22, 4 (1993), 807–837.

[26] H. Kermer and A. B. Németh. 1973. Supporting spheres for families of independent convex sets. *Archiv der Mathematik* 24, 1 (1973), 91–96.

[27] R. Koenker and Gilbert Bassett, Jr. 1978. Regression quantiles. *Econometrica* 46, 1 (1978), 33–50.

[28] D. Kurokawa, O. Lev, J. Morgenstern, and A. D. Procaccia. 2015. Impartial Peer Review.. In *Proceedings of the 24th International Joint Conference on Artificial Intelligence (IJCAI)*. 582–588.

[29] N. Littlestone. 1991. Redundant noisy attributes, attribute errors, and linear-threshold learning using winnow. In *Proceedings of the 4th Conference on Computational Learning Theory (COLT)*. 147–156.

[30] R. Meir, S. Almagor, A. Michaely, and J. S. Rosenschein. 2011. Tight bounds for strategyproof classification. In *Proceedings of the 10th International Conference on Autonomous Agents and Multi-Agent Systems (AAMAS)*. 319–326.

[31] R. Meir, A. D. Procaccia, and J. S. Rosenschein. 2010. On the limits of dictatorial classification. In *Proceedings of the 9th International Conference on Autonomous Agents and Multi-Agent Systems (AAMAS)*. 609–616.

[32] R. Meir, A. D. Procaccia, and J. S. Rosenschein. 2012. Algorithms for Strategyproof Classification. *Artificial Intelligence* 186 (2012), 123–156.

[33] H. Moulin. 1980. On strategy-proofness and single-peakedness. *Public Choice* 35 (1980), 437–455.

[34] S. C. Narula and J. F. Wellington. 1985. Interior analysis for the minimum sum of absolute errors regression. *Technometrics* 27, 2 (1985), 181–188.

[35] J. Perote and J. Perote-Peña. 2003. The impossibility of strategy-proof clustering. *Economics Bulletin* 4, 23 (2003), 1–9.

[36] J. Perote and J. Perote-Peña. 2004. Strategy-proof estimators for simple regression. *Mathematical Social Sciences* 47 (2004), 153–176.

[37] W. Steiger and J. Zhao. 2010. Generalized ham-sandwich cuts. *Discrete & Computational Geometry* 44, 3 (2010), 535–545.

[38] A. H. Stone and J. W. Tukey. 1942. Generalized "sandwich" theorems. *Duke Mathematical Journal* 9, 2 (1942), 356–359.

[39] S. Tamura and S. Ohseto. 2014. Impartial nomination correspondences. *Social Choice and Welfare* 43 (2014), 47–54.

[40] J. W. Tukey. 1977. *Exploratory Data Analysis*. Addison-Wesley.

[41] L. Wang. 2013. The L1 penalized LAD estimator for high dimensional linear regression. *Journal of Multivariate Analysis* 120 (2013), 135–151.

[42] L. Wang, M. D. Gordon, and J. Zhu. 2006. Regularized least absolute deviations regression and an efficient algorithm for parameter tuning. In *Proceedings of the 6th IEEE International Conference on Data Mining (ICDM)*. 690–700.

# Optimal Data Acquisition for Statistical Estimation

YILING CHEN, Harvard University, USA
NICOLE IMMORLICA, Microsoft Research New England, USA
BRENDAN LUCIER, Microsoft Research New England, USA
VASILIS SYRGKANIS, Microsoft Research New England, USA
JUBA ZIANI, California Institute of Technology, USA

We consider a data analyst's problem of purchasing data from strategic agents to compute an unbiased estimate of a statistic of interest. Agents incur private costs to reveal their data and the costs can be *arbitrarily correlated* with their data. Once revealed, data are verifiable. This paper focuses on *linear* unbiased estimators. We design an individually rational and incentive compatible mechanism that optimizes the worst-case mean-squared error of the estimation, where the worst-case is over the unknown correlation between costs and data, subject to a budget constraint in expectation. We characterize the form of the optimal mechanism in closed-form. We further extend our results to acquiring data for estimating a parameter in regression analysis, where private costs can correlate with the values of the dependent variable but not with the values of the independent variables.

Full Paper: https://arxiv.org/abs/1711.01295

CCS Concepts: • **Theory of computation → Algorithmic mechanism design**;

Additional Key Words and Phrases: buying data; budget-feasible mechanism design; statistical estimation; optimization

## 1 INTRODUCTION

In the age of automation, data is king. The statistics and machine learning algorithms that help curate our online content, diagnose our diseases, and drive our cars, among other things, are all fueled by data. Typically, this data is mined by happenstance: as we click around on the internet, seek medical treatment, or drive "smart" vehicles, we leave a trail of data. This data is recorded and used to make estimates and train machine learning algorithms. So long as representative data is readily abundant, this approach may be sufficient. But some data is sensitive and therefore inaccurate, rare, or lacking detail in observable data traces. In such cases, it is more expedient to buy the necessary data directly from the population.

Consider, for example, the problem a public health administration faces in trying to learn the average weight of a population, perhaps as an input to estimating the risk of heart disease. Weight

Yiling Chen was partially supported by NSF grant CCF-1718549. Juba Ziani was supported by NSF grants CNS-1331343 and CNS-1518941, and the US-Israel Binational Science Foundation grant 2012348. Part of the work was done while Yiling Chen and Juba Ziani were at Microsoft Research New England.
Authors' addresses: Yiling Chen, Harvard University, Cambridge, MA, USA, yiling@seas.harvard.edu; Nicole Immorlica, Microsoft Research New England, Cambridge, MA, USA, nicimm@microsoft.com; Brendan Lucier, Microsoft Research New England, Cambridge, MA, USA, brlucier@microsoft.com; Vasilis Syrgkanis, Microsoft Research New England, Cambridge, MA, USA, vasy@microsoft.com; Juba Ziani, California Institute of Technology, Pasadena, CA, USA, jziani@caltech.edu.


*ACM EC'18, June 18–22, 2018, Ithaca, NY, USA.* ACM ISBN 978-1-4503-4529-3/18/06...$15.00
https://doi.org/10.1145/3219166.3219195

is a sensitive personal characteristic, and people may be loath to disclose it. It is also variable over time, and so must be collected close to the time of the average weight estimate in order to be accurate. Thus, while other characteristics, like height, age, and gender, are fairly accurately recorded in, for example, driver's license databases, weight is not. The public health administration may try surveying the public to get estimates of the average weight, but these surveys are likely to have low response rates and be biased towards healthier low-weight samples.

In this paper, we propose a mechanism for buying verifiable data from a population in order to estimate a statistic of interest, such as the expected value of some function of the underlying data. We assume each individual has a private cost, or disutility, for revealing his or her sensitive data to the analyst. Importantly, this cost may be correlated with the private data. For example, overweight or underweight individuals to have a higher cost of revealing their data than people of a healthy weight. Individuals wish to maximize their expected utility, which is the expected payment they receive for their data minus their expected cost. The analyst has a fixed budget for buying data. The analyst does not know the distribution of the data: properties of the distribution is what she is trying to learn from the data samples, therefore it is important that she uses the data she collects to learn it rather than using an inaccurate prior distribution (for example, the analyst may have a prior on weight distribution within a population from DMV records or previous surveys, but such a prior may be erroneous if people do not accurately report their weights). However, we do assume the analyst has a prior for the marginal distribution of costs, and that she estimates how much a survey may cost her as a function of said prior.[1]

The analyst would like to buy data subject to her budget, then use that data to obtain an unbiased estimator for the statistic of interest. To this end, the analyst posts a menu of probability-price pairs. Each individual $i$ with cost $c$ selects a pair $(A, P)$ from the menu, at which point the analyst buys the data with probability $A$ at price $P$. The expected utility of the individual is thus $(P - c)A$.[2] To form an estimate based on this collected data, we assume the analyst uses *inverse propensity scoring*, pioneered by Horvitz and Thompson [13]. This is the unique unbiased linear estimator; it works by upweighting the data from individual $i$ by the inverse of his/her selection probability, $1/A$.

The Horvitz-Thompson estimator always generates an unbiased estimate of the statistic being measured, regardless of the price menu. However, the precision of the estimator, as measured by the variance or mean-squared error of the estimate, depends on the menu of probability-price pairs offered to each individual. For example, offering a high price would generate data samples with low bias (since many individuals would accept such an offer), but the budget would limit the number of samples. Offering low prices allows the mechanism to collect more samples, but these would be more heavily biased, requiring more aggressive correction which introduces additional noise. The goal of the analyst is to strike a balance between these forces and post a menu that minimizes the variance of her estimate in the worst-case over all possible joint distributions of the data and cost consistent with the cost prior. We note that this problem setting was first studied by Roth and Schonebeck [21], who characterized an approximately optimal mechanism for moment estimation.

### 1.1 Summary of results and techniques

Our main contribution comes in the form of an exact solution for the optimal menu, as discussed in Section 3. As one would expect, if the budget is large, the optimal menu offers to buy, with probability 1, all data at a cost equal to the maximum cost in the population. If the budget is

[1]This prior could come from similar past exercises. Alternatively, when no prior is known, the analyst can allocate a fraction of his budget to buying data for the sake of learning this distribution of costs. In this paper, we follow prior work (e.g., Roth and Schoenebeck [21]) and assume that a prior distribution is known, instead of focusing on how one might learn the distribution of costs.

[2]As we show, this menu-based formulation is fully general and captures arbitrary data-collection mechanisms.

small, the optimal menu buys data from an individual with probability inversely proportional to the square root of their cost.[3] Interestingly, in intermediate regimes, we show the optimal menu employs pooling: for all individuals with sufficiently low private cost, it buys their data with equal probability; for the remaining high cost agents, it buys their data with probability inversely proportional to the square root of their costs. Revisiting the example of estimating the weight of a population of size $n$, our scheme suggests the following solution. Imagine the costs are $0, 4, 8$ with probability $\frac{1}{2}, \frac{1}{4}, \frac{1}{4}$, and the total budget of the analyst is $B = 7n$. The analyst brings a scale to a public location and posts the following menu of pairs of allocation probability and price: $\{(1, \frac{36}{5}), (\frac{4}{5}, 8)\}$. A simple calculation shows that individuals with cost 0 or 4 will pick the first menu option: stepping on the scale and having their weight recorded with probability 1, and receiving a payment of $\frac{36}{5}$ dollars. Individuals with cost 8 will pick the second menu option; if they are selected to step on the scale, which happens with probability $\frac{4}{5}$, the analyst records their weight scaled by a factor of $\frac{5}{4}$. This scaling is precisely the upweighting from inverse propensity scoring. In expectation over the population, the analyst spends exactly his budget $7n$. The estimate is the average of the scaled weights.

We show how to extend our approach in multiple directions. First, our characterization of the optimal mechanism holds even when the quantity to be estimated is the expected value of a $d$-dimensional moment function of the data. Second, we extend our techniques beyond moment estimation to the common task of multi-dimensional linear regression. In this regression problem, an individual's data includes both features (which are assumed to be insensitive or publicly available) and outcomes (which may be sensitive). The analyst's goal is to estimate the linear regression coefficients that relate the outcomes to the features. We make the assumption that an individual's cost is independent of her features, but may be arbitrarily correlated with her outcome. For example, the goal might be to regress a health outcome (such as severity of a disease) on demographic information. In this case, we might imagine that an agent incurs no cost for reporting his age, height or gender, but his cost might be highly correlated with his realized health outcome. In such a setting, we show that the asymptotically optimal allocation rule, given a fixed average budget per agent as the number of agent grows large, can be calculated efficiently and exhibits a pooling region as before. However, unlike for moment estimation, agents with intermediate costs can also be pooled together. We further show that our results extend to non-linear regression in the full version of the paper, under mild additional conditions on the regression function.

Our techniques rely on i) reducing the mechanism design problem to an optimization problem through the classical notion of virtual costs, then ii) reducing the problem of optimizing the worst-case variance to that of finding an equilibrium of a zero-sum game between the analyst and an adversary. The adversary's goal is to pick a distribution of data, conditional on agents' costs, that maximizes the variance of the analyst's estimator. We then characterize such an equilibrium through the optimality conditions for convex optimization described in [2].

## 1.2 Related work

A growing amount of attention has been placed on understanding interactions between the strategic nature of data holders and the statistical inference and learning tasks that use data collected from these holders. The work on this topic can be roughly divided into two categories according to whether money is used for incentive alignment.

[3] Of course, the individual is him/herself selecting the menu option and so the use of an active verb in this context is perhaps a bit misleading. What we mean here is that, given his/her incentives based on his/her private cost, the choice the individual selects is one that buys his/her data with probability inversely proportional to the square root of his/her cost.

In the first category, individuals as data holders do not directly derive utility from the accuracy of the inference or learning outcome, but in some cases may incur a privacy cost if the outcome leaks their private information. The analyst uses monetary payments to incentivize agents to reveal their data. Our work falls into this category. Prior papers by Roth and Schoenebeck [21] and Abernethy et al. [1] are closest to our setting. Similarly to our work, both Roth and Schoenebeck [21] and Abernethy et al. [1] consider an analyst's problem of purchasing data from individuals with private costs subject to a budget constraint, allow the cost to be correlated with the value of data, and assume that individuals cannot fabricate their data. Roth and Schoenebeck [21] aim at obtaining an optimal unbiased estimator with minimum worst-case variance for population mean, while their mechanism achieves optimality only approximately: instead of the actual worst-case variance, a bound on the worst-case variance is minimized. While our setting is identical to that of [21], our work precisely minimizes worst-case variance (under a regularity assumption on the cost distribution), and our main contribution is to exhibit the structure of the optimal mechanism, as well as to extend our results to broader classes of statistical inference, moment estimation and linear regression. In particular, compared to [21], our solution exhibits new structure in the form of a pooling region for low cost agents; i.e., the optimal mechanism pools agents with the lowest costs together and treats them identically. Such structure does not arise in [21] under a regularity assumption on the cost distribution. Abernethy at al. [1] consider general supervised learning. They do not seek to achieve a notion of optimality; instead, they take a learning-theoretic approach and design mechanisms to obtain learning guarantees (risk bounds).

Several papers consider data acquisition models with different objectives under the assumptions that (a) individuals do not fabricate their data, and (b) private costs and value of data are uncorrelated. For example, in the work of Cummings et al. [6], the analyst can decide the level of accuracy for data purchased from each individual, and wishes to guarantee a certain desired level of accuracy of the aggregated information while minimizing the total privacy cost incurred by the agents. Cai et al. [3] focus on incentivizing individuals to exert effort to obtain high-quality data for the purpose of linear regression. Another line of research in the first category examines the data acquisition problem under the lens of differential privacy [5, 9–11, 18]. The mechanism designer then uses payments to balance the trade-off between privacy and accuracy.

In the second category, individuals' utilities directly depend on the inference or learning outcome (e.g. they want a regression line to be as close to their own data point as possible) and hence they have incentives to manipulate their reported data to influence the outcome. There often is no cost for reporting one's data. The data analyst, without using monetary payments, attempts to design or identify inference or learning processes so that they are robust to potential data manipulations. Most papers in this category assume that independent variables (feature vectors) are unmanipulable public information and dependent variables are manipulable private information [7, 14, 15, 19], though some papers consider strategic manipulation of feature vectors [8, 12]. Such strategic data manipulations have been studied for estimation [4], classification [12, 14, 15], online classification [8], regression [7, 20], and clustering [19]. Work in this category is closer to mechanism design without money in the sense that they focus on incentive alignment in acquiring data (e.g., strategy-proof algorithms) but often do not evaluate the performance of the inference or learning, with a few notable exceptions [8, 12].

## 2 MODEL AND PRELIMINARIES

*Survey Mechanisms.* There is a population of $n$ agents. Each agent $i$ has a private pair $(z_i, c_i)$, where $z_i \in \mathcal{Z}$ is a data point and $c_i > 0$ is a cost. We think of $c_i$ as the disutility agent $i$ incurs by releasing her data $z_i$. The pair is drawn from a distribution $\mathcal{D}$, unknown to the mechanism designer.

We denote with $\mathcal{F}$ the CDF of the marginal distribution of costs,[4] supported on a set $C$. We assume that $\mathcal{F}$ and the support of the data points, $\mathcal{Z}$, are known. However, the joint distribution $\mathcal{D}$ of data and costs is unknown.

A *survey mechanism* is defined by an allocation rule $A : C \longrightarrow [0, 1]$ and a payment rule $P : C \longrightarrow \mathbb{R}$, and works as follows. Each agent $i$ arrives at the mechanism in sequence and reports a cost $\hat{c}_i$. The mechanism chooses to buy the agent's data with probability $A(\hat{c}_i)$. If the mechanism buys the data, then it learns the value of $z_i$ (i.e., agents cannot misreport their data) and pays the agent $P(\hat{c}_i)$. Otherwise the data point is not learned and no payment is made.

We assume agents have quasi-linear utilities, so that the utility enjoyed by agent $i$ when reporting $\hat{c}_i$ is

$$u(\hat{c}_i; c_i) = (P(\hat{c}_i) - c_i) \cdot A(\hat{c}_i) \tag{1}$$

We will restrict attention to survey mechanisms that are truthful and individually rational.

Definition 1 (Truthful and Individually Rational - TIR). *A survey mechanism is truthful if for any cost c it is in the agent's best interest to report their true cost, i.e. for any report $\hat{c}$:*

$$u(c; c) \geq u(\hat{c}; c) \tag{2}$$

*It is individually rational if, e. for any cost $c \in C$, $P(c) \geq c$.*

We assume that the mechanism is constrained in the amount of payment it can make to the agents. We will formally define this as an expected budget constraint for the survey mechanism.

Definition 2 (Expected Budget Constraint). *A mechanism respects a budget constraint B if:*

$$n \cdot \mathbb{E}_{c\sim\mathcal{F}}[P(c) \cdot A(c)] \leq B \tag{3}$$

*Estimators.* The designer (or *data analyst*) wishes to use the survey mechanism to estimate some parameter $\theta \in \mathbb{R}$ of the marginal distribution of data points.[5] For example, it might be that $\mathcal{Z} = \mathbb{R}$ and $\theta$ is the mean of the distribution over data points in the population. To this end, the designer will apply an *estimator* to the collection of data points $S$ elicited by the survey mechanism. We will write $\hat{\theta}_S$ for the estimator used. Note that the value of the estimator $\hat{\theta}_S$ depends on the sample $S$, but might also depend on the distribution of costs $\mathcal{F}$ and the survey mechanism. Due to the randomness inherent in the survey mechanism (both in the choice of data points sampled and the values of those samples), we think of $\hat{\theta}_S$ as a random variable, drawn from a distribution $\mathcal{T}(\mathcal{D}, A)$. We will focus exclusively on *unbiased* estimators.

Definition 3 (Unbiased Estimator). *Given an allocation function A, an estimator $\hat{\theta}_S$ for $\theta$ is* unbiased *if for any instantiation of the true distribution $\mathcal{D}$ its expected value is equal to $\theta$:*

$$\mathbb{E}_{\hat{\theta}_S\sim\mathcal{T}(\mathcal{D},A)}\left[\hat{\theta}_S\right] = \theta. \tag{4}$$

Given a fixed choice of estimator, the mechanism designer wants to construct the survey mechanism to minimize the variance (finite sample or asymptotic as the population grows) of that estimator. Since the designer does not know the distribution $\mathcal{D}$, we will work with the worst-case variance over all instantiations of $\mathcal{D}$ that are consistent with the cost marginal $\mathcal{F}$.

Definition 4 (Worst-Case Variance). *Given an allocation function A and an instance of the true distribution $\mathcal{D}$, the* variance *of an estimator $\hat{\theta}_S$ is defined as:*

$$\mathbb{V}(\hat{\theta}_S; \mathcal{D}, A) = \mathbb{E}_{\hat{\theta}_S\sim\mathcal{T}(\mathcal{D},A)}\left[\left(\hat{\theta}_S - \mathbb{E}\left[\hat{\theta}_S\right]\right)^2\right] \tag{5}$$

[4]Throughout the text we will use the CDF to refer to the distribution itself.

[5]We also extend our results to multi-dimensional parameters; see Section 4.

*The* worst-case variance *of* $\hat{\theta}_S$ *is*

$$\mathbb{V}^*(\hat{\theta}_S; \mathcal{F}, A) = \sup_{\mathcal{D} \text{ consistent with } \mathcal{F}} \mathbb{V}(\hat{\theta}_S; \mathcal{D}, A). \tag{6}$$

We are now ready to formally define the mechanism design problem faced by the data analyst.

Definition 5 (Analyst's Mechanism Design Problem). *Given an estimator $\hat{\theta}_S$ and cost distribution $\mathcal{F}$, the goal of the designer is to design an allocation rule $A$ and payment rule $P$ so as to minimize worst-case variance subject to the truthfulness, individual rationality and budget constraints:*

$$\begin{aligned} &\inf_{A,P} \ \mathbb{V}^*(\hat{\theta}_S; \mathcal{F}, A) \\ &\text{s.t. } n \cdot \mathbb{E}_{c\sim\mathcal{F}}[P(c) \cdot A(c)] \leq B \\ &\qquad A, P \text{ define a TIR mechanism} \end{aligned} \tag{7}$$

*Implementing Surveys as Posted Menus.* The formulation above describes surveys as direct-revelation mechanisms, where agents report costs. We note that an equivalent indirect implementation might be more natural: a *posted menu survey* offers each agent a menu of (price, probability) pairs $(p_1, A_1), \ldots, (p_k, A_k)$. If the agent chooses $(p_m, A_m)$ then their data is elicited with probability $A_m$, in which case they are paid $p_m$. Each agent can choose the item that maximizes their expected utility, i.e., $\text{argmax}_{m\in[k]} (p_m - c) \cdot A_m$. By the well-known *taxation principle*, any survey mechanism can be implemented as a posted menu survey, and the number of menu items required is at most the size of the support of the cost distribution.

## 2.1 Reducing Mechanism Design to Optimization

We begin by reducing the mechanism design problem to a simpler full-information optimization problem where the designer knows the private cost of each player and can acquire their data by paying them exactly that cost. However, the designer is constrained to using *monotone* allocation rules, in which players with higher costs have weakly lower probability of being chosen.

Definition 6 (Analyst's Optimization Problem). *Given an estimator $\hat{\theta}_S$ and cost distribution $\mathcal{F}$, the optimization version of the designer's problem is to find a non-increasing allocation rule $A$ that minimizes worst-case variance subject to the budget constraint, assuming agents are paid their cost:*

$$\begin{aligned} &\inf_{A} \ \mathbb{V}^*(\hat{\theta}_S; \mathcal{F}, A) \\ &\text{s.t. } n \cdot \mathbb{E}_{c\sim\mathcal{F}}[c \cdot A(c)] \leq B \\ &\qquad A \text{ is monotone non-increasing} \end{aligned} \tag{8}$$

The mechanism design problem in Definition 5 reduces to the optimization problem given by Definition 6, albeit with a transformation of costs to *virtual cost.*

Definition 7 (Virtual Costs and Regular Distributions). *If $\mathcal{F}$ is continuous and admits a density $f$ then define the virtual cost function as $\phi(c) = c + \frac{\mathcal{F}(c)}{f(c)}$. If $\mathcal{F}$ is discrete with support $C = \{c_1, \ldots, c_{|C|}\}$ and PDF $f$, then define the virtual cost function as: $\phi(c_t) = c_t + \frac{c_t - c_{t-1}}{f(c_t)} \mathcal{F}(c_{t-1})$, with $c_0 = 0$. We also denote with $\phi(\mathcal{F})$ the distribution of virtual costs; i.e., the distribution created by first drawing $c$ from $\mathcal{F}$ and then mapping it to $\phi(c)$. A distribution $\mathcal{F}$ is regular if the virtual cost function is increasing.*

When $\mathcal{F}$ is twice-continuously differentiable, $\mathcal{F}$ is regular if and only if $\mathcal{F}(c)f'(c) < 2f(c)^2$ for all $c \in C$. Importantly, in this case, the allocation rule of Roth and Schoenebeck [21] is monotone strictly decreasing in $c$ and does not exhibit a pooling region at low-cost as our solution does.

The following is an analogue of Myerson's [16] reduction of mechanism design to virtual welfare maximization, adapted to the survey design setting.

LEMMA 2.1. *If the distribution of costs $\mathcal{F}$ is regular, then solving the Analyst's Mechanism Design Problem reduces to solving the Analyst's Optimization Problem for distribution of costs $\phi(\mathcal{F})$.*

PROOF. The proof is given in the full version of the paper. □

## 2.2 Unbiased Estimation and Inverse Propensity Scoring

We now describe a class of estimators $\hat{\theta}_S$ that we will focus on for the remainder of the paper. Note that simply calculating the quantity of interest, $\theta$, on the sampled data points can lead to bias, due to the potential correlation between costs and data. For instance, suppose that $z \in \mathbb{R}$ and the goal is to estimate the mean of the distribution of $z$. A natural estimator is the average of the collected data: $\hat{\theta}_S = \frac{1}{|S|}\sum_{i\in S} z_i$. However, if players with lower $z$ tend to have lower cost, and are therefore selected with higher probability by the analyst, then this estimator will consistently underestimate the true mean.

This problem can be addressed using *inverse propensity scoring* (IPS), pioneered by Horvitz and Thompson [13]. The idea is to recover unbiasedness by weighting each data point by the inverse of the probability of observing it. This IPS approach can be applied to any parameter estimation problem where the parameter of interest is the expected value of an arbitrary *moment function* $m : \mathcal{Z} \to \mathbb{R}$.

DEFINITION 8 (HORVITZ-THOMPSON ESTIMATOR). *The Horvitz-Thompson estimator for the case when the parameter of interest is the expected value of a (moment) function $m : \mathcal{Z} \to \mathbb{R}$ is defined as:*

$$\hat{\theta}_S = \frac{1}{n}\sum_{i\in[n]} \frac{m(z_i)\cdot 1\{i \in S\}}{A(c_i)} \tag{9}$$

The Horvitz-Thompson estimator is the unique unbiased estimator that is a linear function of the observations $m(z_i)$ [21]. It is therefore without loss of generality to focus on this estimator if one restricts to unbiased linear estimators.[6]

*IPS beyond moment estimation.* We defined the Horvitz-Thompson estimator with respect to moment estimation problems, $\theta = \mathbb{E}[m(z)]$. As it turns out, this approach to unbiased estimation extends even beyond the moment estimation problem to parameter estimation problems defined as the solution to a system of moment equations $\mathbb{E}[m(z;\theta)] = 0$ or parameters defined as the minima of a moment function $\operatorname{argmin}_\theta \mathbb{E}[m(z;\theta)]$. We defer this discussion to Section 5.

# 3 ESTIMATING MOMENTS OF THE DATA DISTRIBUTION

In this section we consider the case where the analyst's goal is to estimate the mean of a given moment function of the distribution. That is, there is some function $m : C \to [0, 1]$ such that both 0 and 1 are in the support of random variable $m(z)$, and the goal of the analyst is to estimate $\theta = \mathbb{E}[m(z)]$.[7] We assume that $\hat{\theta}_S$, the estimator being applied, is the Horvitz-Thompson estimator given in Definition 8.

For convenience we will assume that the cost distribution $\mathcal{F}$ has finite support, say $C = \{c_1, \ldots, c_{|C|}\}$ with $c_1 < \ldots < c_{|C|}$. (We relax the finite support assumption in Section 3.2.) Write

[6]We note that we have assumed, for convenience, that $A(c_i) > 0$ for all $i \in [n]$ in the expression of this estimator, for it to be unbiased and well-defined. It is easy to see from the expression for the variance given in Section 3 that the variance-minimizing allocation rule will indeed be non-zero for each cost.

[7]Observe that it is easy to deal with the more general case of $m(z) \in [a, b]$ by a simple linear translation, i.e., estimate $\tilde{m}(z) = \frac{m(z)-a}{b-a}$ instead, which is in [0, 1] and then translate the estimator back to recover $m(z)$.

$\pi_t = f(c_t)$ for the probability of cost $c_t$ in $\mathcal{F}$. Also, for a given allocation rule $A$, we will write $A_t = A(c_t)$ for convenience. That is, we can interpret an allocation rule $A$ as a vector of $|C|$ values $A_1, \ldots, A_{|C|}$. For further convenience, we will write $q_t = \Pr[m(z) = 1|c_t]$. This is the probability that the moment takes on its maximum value when the cost is $c_t$. Finally, we will assume that the distribution of costs is regular.

Our goal is to address the analyst's mechanism design problem for this restricted setting. By Lemma 2.1 it suffices to solve the analyst's optimization problem. We start by characterizing the worst-case variance for this setting.

Lemma 3.1. *The worst-case variance of the Horvitz-Thompson estimator of a moment $m : C \rightarrow [0, 1]$, given cost distribution $\mathcal{F}$ and allocation rule $A$, is:*

$$n \cdot \mathbb{V}^*(\hat{\theta}_S; \mathcal{F}, A) = \sup_{q \in [0,1]^{|C|}} \sum_{t=1}^{|C|} \pi_t \cdot \frac{q_t}{A_t} - \left( \sum_{t=1}^{|C|} \pi_t \cdot q_t \right)^2 \tag{10}$$

Proof. For any distribution $\mathcal{D}$, observe that the Horvitz-Thompson estimator can be written as the sum of $n$ i.i.d. random variables each with a variance:

$$\sigma^2 = \mathbb{E}\left[\left(\frac{m(z_i) \cdot 1\{i \in S\}}{A(c_i)}\right)^2\right] - \mathbb{E}\left[\frac{m(z_i) \cdot 1\{i \in S\}}{A(c_i)}\right]^2 = \sum_{t=1}^{|C|} \pi_t \cdot \frac{\mathbb{E}\left[m(z)^2|c_t\right]}{A_t} - \mathbb{E}[m(z)]^2$$

Hence, the variance of the estimator is $\sigma^2/n$. Observe that conditional on any value $c$, the worst-case distribution $\mathcal{D}$, will assign positive mass only to values $z \in \mathcal{Z}$ such that $m(z) \in \{0, 1\}$. This is because any other conditional distribution can be altered by a mean-preserving spread, pushing all the mass on these values, while preserving the conditional mean $\mathbb{E}[m(z)|c]$. This would strictly increase the latter variance. Thus we can assume without loss of generality that $m(z) \in \{0, 1\}$, in which case $m(z)^2 = m(z)$ and $\mathbb{E}[m(z)|c] = \Pr[m(z) = 1|c]$. Recall that $q_t = \Pr[m(z) = 1|c_t]$. Then we can simplify the variance as:

$$n \cdot \mathbb{V}(\hat{\theta}_S; \mathcal{D}, A) = \sum_{t=1}^{|C|} \pi_t \cdot \frac{\mathbb{E}[m(z)|c_t]}{A_t} - \mathbb{E}[m(z)]^2 = \sum_{t=1}^{|C|} \pi_t \cdot \frac{q_t}{A_t} - \left( \sum_{t=1}^{|C|} \pi_t \cdot q_t \right)^2$$

The theorem follows since the worst-case variance is a supremum over all possible consistent distributions, hence equivalently a supremum over conditional probabilities $q : [0, 1]^{|C|}$. □

Given the above characterization of the variance of the estimator, we can greatly simplify the analyst's optimization problem for this setting. Indeed, it suffices to find the allocation rule $A \in (0, 1]^{|C|}$ that minimizes (10), subject to $A$ being monotone non-decreasing and satisfying the expected budget constraint.

### 3.1 Characterization of the Optimal Allocation Rule

We are now ready to solve the analyst's optimization problem for moment estimation. In this and all following sections, we denote $\bar{B} = \frac{B}{n}$ for simplicity of notations, and refer to $\bar{B}$ as the "average budget per agent". Note that different agents with different costs may be allocated different fractions of the total budget $B$ that in general do not coincide with $\bar{B}$. We remark that if $\bar{B}$ is larger than the expected cost of an agent, then it is feasible (and hence optimal) for the analyst to set the allocation rule to pick any type with probability 1. We therefore assume without loss of generality that $\mathbb{E}[c] > \bar{B}$.

Our analysis is based on an equilibrium characterization, where we view the analyst choosing $A$ and the adversary choosing $z$ as playing a zero-sum game and solve for its equilibria. We first present the characterization and some qualitative implications and then present an outline of our proof. We defer the full details of the proof to the full version of the paper.

THEOREM 3.2 (OPTIMAL ALLOCATION FOR MOMENT ESTIMATION). *The optimal allocation rule $A$ is determined by two constants $\bar{A}$ and $t^* \in \{0, \ldots, |C|\}$ such that:*

$$A_t = \begin{cases} \bar{A} & if\, t \leq t^* \\ \frac{\alpha}{\sqrt{c_t}} & o.w. \end{cases} \tag{11}$$

*with $\alpha$ uniquely determined such that the budget constraint is binding.*[8] *Moreover, the parameters $\bar{A}$ and $t^*$ can be computed in time $O(\log(|C|))$.*

The parameters $\bar{A}$ and $t^*$ in Theorem 3.2 are explicitly derived in closed form in the full version of the paper. For instance, when $\bar{B} \geq \frac{c_{|C|}}{2}$, then $t^* = |C|$ and $A_t = \bar{A} = \min\{1, \bar{B}/\mathbb{E}[c]\}$ for all $t$. When $\bar{B} \leq \frac{\sqrt{c_1}\,\mathbb{E}[\sqrt{c}]}{2}$ then $t^* = 0$ and $A_t = \frac{\bar{B}}{\sqrt{c_t}\,\mathbb{E}[\sqrt{c}]}$. In fact, it can be shown (see full version) that in this latter case, the worst-case distribution is given by $q = 1$. In particular, in this restricted case, the approximation of Roth and Schoenebeck [21] is in fact optimal, and indeed our allocation rule is expressing the solution of Roth and Schoenebeck [21] as a posted menu for a discrete, regular distribution of costs. In every other case, $q \neq 1$ and our solution differs from that of Roth and Schoenebeck [21], exhibiting a pooling region for low-cost agents. More generally, the computational part of Theorem 3.2 follows by performing binary search over the support of $\mathcal{F}$, which can be done in $O(\log(|C|))$ time.

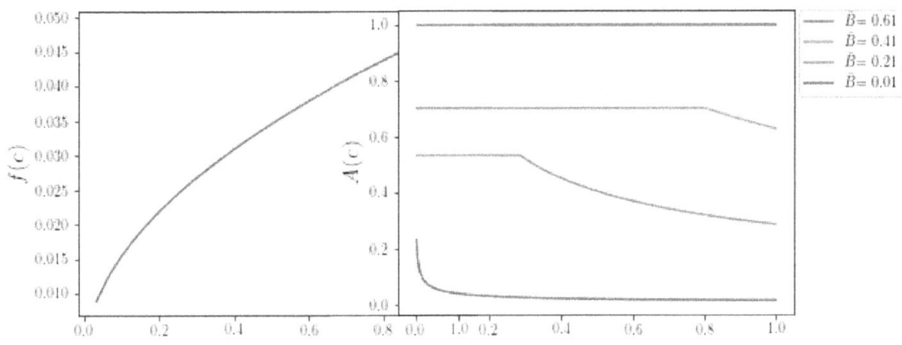


Fig. 1. The pdf (left) of a distribution of costs and the corresponding optimal allocation rule for varying levels of per-agent budget (right). Note that for sufficiently large budgets, a flat pooling region forms for agents with low costs.

We note that the optimal rule essentially allocates to each agent inversely proportionally to the square root of their cost, but may also "pool" the allocation probability for agents at the lower end of the cost distribution. See Figure 1 for examples of optimal solutions.

The proof of Theorem 3.2 appears in the full version of the paper. The main idea is to view the optimization problem as a zero-sum game between the analyst who designs the allocation rule $A$, and an adversary who designs $q$ so as to maximize the variance of the estimate. We show how to compute an equilibrium $(A^*, z^*)$ of this zero-sum game via Lagrangian and KKT conditions, and then note that the obtained $A^*$ must in fact be an optimal allocation rule for worst-case variance.

[8] The explicit form of this is $\alpha = \frac{\bar{B} - \bar{A}\,\mathbb{E}[c \cdot 1\{c \leq c_{t^*}\}]}{\mathbb{E}[\sqrt{c} \cdot 1\{c > c_{t^*}\}]}$.

The analysis above applied to a discrete cost distribution over a finite support of possible costs. We show how to extend this analysis to a continuous distribution below, noting that the continuous variant of the Optimization Problem for Moment Estimation can be derived by taking the limit over finer and finer discrete approximations of the cost distribution.

### 3.2 Continuous Costs for Moment Estimation

DEFINITION 9 (CONTINUOUS OPTIMIZATION PROBLEM FOR MOMENT ESTIMATION). *When costs are supported on $C = [0, 1]$, the analyst's optimization problem for the moment estimation problem based on the Horvitz-Thompson estimator can be written as:*

$$\begin{aligned} \inf_{A:(0,1]\to[0,1]} \sup_{x:[0,1]\to[0,1]} & \int_0^1 \frac{x(c)}{A(c)}\, d\mathcal{F}(c) - \left(\int_0^1 x(c)\, d\mathcal{F}(c)\right)^2 \\ \text{s.t.} & \int_0^1 c \cdot A(c)\, d\mathcal{F}(c) \le \bar{B} \\ & A \text{ is monotone non-increasing} \end{aligned} \tag{12}$$

We can now establish the following continuous variant of Theorem 3.2, which describes the optimal survey mechanism for continuous cost distributions.

THEOREM 3.3 (CONTINUOUS LIMIT OF OPTIMAL ALLOCATION). *If the distribution of costs is atomless and supported in $(0, 1]$, then the optimal allocation rule $A$ is determined by two constants $\bar{A}$ and $x^* \in \mathbb{R}$ such that:*

$$A(c) = \begin{cases} \bar{A} & \text{if } c \le x^* \\ \frac{\alpha}{\sqrt{c}} & \text{o.w.} \end{cases} \tag{13}$$

*with $\alpha$ uniquely determined such that the budget constraint is binding.*[9]. *The quantities $\bar{A}$ and $x^*$ are defined as follows: for any $x \in \mathbb{R}$ let*

$$Q_\infty(x) = \mathbb{E}_{c\sim\mathcal{F}}[\min\{c, \sqrt{cx}\}] \qquad R_\infty(x) = 2\,\mathbb{E}_{c\sim\mathcal{F}}\left[\min\left\{\frac{c}{x}, 1\right\}\right] \qquad G(x) = \frac{Q_\infty(x)}{\max(1, R_\infty(x))}$$

*Then $x^* = \min\{1, G^{-1}(\bar{B})\}$ and $\bar{A} = \frac{1}{\max(1, R_\infty(x^*))}$ (see Figure 2).*[10]

PROOF. See full version. □

Let us give some intuition behind the form of the allocation rule described in Theorem 3.3. As in Theorem 3.2, the allocation rule will pool agents with low costs (i.e., less than some threshold $x^*$), then allocate to higher-cost agents inversely proportional to the square root of their costs. In the definition of $x^*$ and $\bar{A}$, note that $Q_\infty$ is non-decreasing and $R_\infty$ is non-increasing, so $G$ is non-decreasing. We therefore have that $x^*$, the boundary of the pooling region, increases with $\bar{B}$ up to a maximum value of 1 (at which point all agents are pooled).

Let's restrict attention to the case where the mean of the distribution is at least as large as half of the maximum value of the support, i.e. $\mathbb{E}[c] \ge 1/2$. In this setting, we see that $R_\infty(x) \le 1$ for all $x \in [0, 1]$, so

$$G(x) = \frac{Q_\infty(x)}{R_\infty(x)} = \frac{x}{2} \cdot \frac{\mathbb{E}_{c\sim\mathcal{F}}[\min\{c, \sqrt{cx}\}]}{\mathbb{E}_{c\sim\mathcal{F}}[\min\{c, x\}]} \approx \frac{x}{2} \qquad \text{(see Figure 2)}$$

So the optimal allocation sets $x^* \approx 2\bar{B}$. Moreover, the allocation for the pooling region is $\bar{A} = \frac{1}{R_\infty(x^*)} \approx \frac{\bar{B}}{\mathbb{E}[\min\{c, 2\bar{B}\}]}$. So the optimal mechanism takes the following intuitive form: first, assign

[9]The explicit form of this is $\alpha = \frac{\bar{B} - \bar{A}\,\mathbb{E}[c\cdot 1\{c \le x^*\}]}{\mathbb{E}[\sqrt{c}\cdot 1\{c > x^*\}]}$.

[10]We take the convention that if $\bar{B}$ lies above the range of $G$, then $G^{-1}(\bar{B}) = +\infty$.

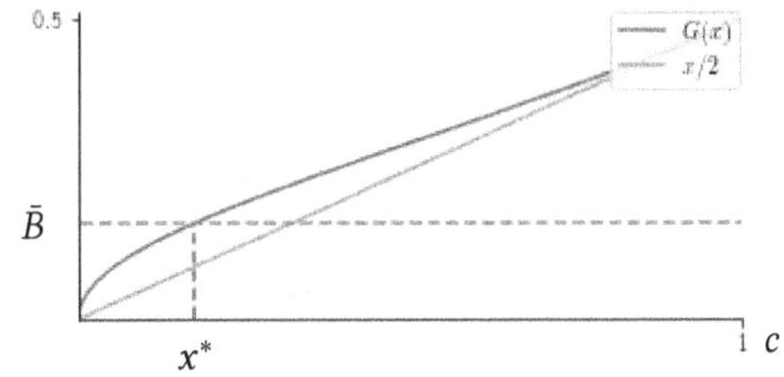


Fig. 2. Pictorial representation of the function $G(x)$ which defines the optimal threshold $x^*$, portraying its close approximation by the function $x/2$.

each agent an allocation probability $\bar{A}$ that would, in an alternate world where costs are capped at $2\bar{B}$, precisely exhaust the budget. Since costs can actually be greater than $2\bar{B}$, this flat allocation goes over-budget. So, for agents whose costs are greater than $2\bar{B}$, we remove allocation probability so that (a) the budget becomes balanced, and (b) the remaining probability of allocation is inversely proportional to the square root of the costs.

## 4 MULTI-DIMENSIONAL PARAMETERS FOR MOMENT ESTIMATION

Section 3 focused on the case of estimating a single-dimensional parameter of the data distribution. In this section we note that our characterization of the optimal mechanism extends to multi-dimensional moment estimation as well. In multi-dimensional moment estimation, there is a function $m\colon C \to [0,1]^d$, and our goal is to estimate $\theta = \mathbb{E}[m(z)] \in [0,1]^d$. Here $d$ is the dimension of the estimation problem, which we assume to be a fixed constant.

As before, we will estimate $\theta$ by applying an estimator $\hat{\theta}$ to the data collected from a survey mechanism. To evaluate an estimator, we must extend our definition of variance to the $d$-dimensional setting, as follows.

Definition 10 (Worst-Case Mean Squared Error - Risk). *Given allocation function $A$ and distribution $\mathcal{D}$, the expected mean squared error (or* risk*) of an estimator $\hat{\theta}$ is*

$$\mathcal{R}(\hat{\theta}_S; \mathcal{D}, A) = \mathbb{E}_{\hat{\theta}_S \sim \mathcal{T}(\mathcal{D}, A)}\left[\left\|\hat{\theta}_S - \theta_0\right\|_2^2\right] \tag{14}$$

*and the worst-case variance of $\hat{\theta}$ is*

$$\mathcal{R}^*(\hat{\theta}_S; \mathcal{F}, A) = \sup_{\mathcal{D} \text{ consistent with } \mathcal{F}} \mathcal{R}(\hat{\theta}_S; \mathcal{D}, A). \tag{15}$$

When $\hat{\theta}$ is unbiased, the risk has a natural interpretation: it is simply the sum of variances of each coordinate of $\theta$, considered separately.

Claim 1 (Risk of Unbiased Estimators). *The risk of any unbiased estimator is equal to the sum of variances of every coordinate:*

$$\mathcal{R}(\hat{\theta}_S; \mathcal{D}, A) = \mathbb{E}_{\hat{\theta}_S \sim \mathcal{T}(\mathcal{D}, A)}\left[\sum_{r=1}^{d} (\hat{\theta}_{S,r} - \mathbb{E}[\hat{\theta}_{S,r}])^2\right] = \sum_{r=1}^{d} \mathbb{V}(\hat{\theta}_{S,r}). \tag{16}$$

As in the single-dimensional case, the analyst obtains an estimate through the Horvitz-Thompson estimator, which is defined as follows for parameters in $\mathbb{R}^d$. Also as in the single-dimensional case, The Horvitz-Thompson estimator is an unbiased estimator of $\mathbb{E}[m(z)]$.

Definition 11 (Horvitz-Thompson Estimator for Multi-dimensional Moment Estimation). *The Horvitz-Thompson estimator for the case when the parameter of interest is the expected value of a vector of moments $m : \mathcal{Z} \to \mathbb{R}^d$ is defined as:*

$$\hat{\theta}_S = \frac{1}{n} \sum_{i \in [n]} \frac{1\{i \in S\}}{A(c_i)} \cdot m(z_i) \tag{17}$$

For our characterization of worst-case risk, we will assume that the moment function $m$ can take on the extreme points of the hypercube $[0, 1]^d$.

Assumption 1. *$\mathcal{D}$ is such that the induced distribution of $m(z)$ is supported on every extreme point of the $[0, 1]^d$ hypercube.*

Lemma 4.1. *Under Assumption 1, the worst-case risk of the Horvitz-Thompson estimator of moment $m : C \to [0, 1]$ is*

$$\frac{n}{d} \cdot \mathcal{R}^*(\hat{\theta}_S; \mathcal{F}, A) = \sup_{q \in [0,1]^{|C|}} \sum_{t=1}^{|C|} \pi_t \cdot \frac{q_t}{A_t} - \left( \sum_{t=1}^{|C|} \pi_t \cdot q_t \right)^2. \tag{18}$$

Proof. See full version. □

Lemma 4.1 implies that the optimal survey design problem in the $d$-dimensional case is, in fact, identical to the problem considered in the single-dimensional case. We can conclude that Theorems 3.2 and 3.3, which characterized the optimal survey mechanisms for discrete and continuous single-parameter settings, respectively, also apply to the multi-dimensional setting without change.

## 5 MULTI-DIMENSIONAL PARAMETER ESTIMATION VIA LINEAR REGRESSION

In this section, we extend beyond moment estimation to a multi-dimensional linear regression task (we discuss the non-linear case in the full version). For this setting we will impose additional structure on the data held by each agent. Each agent's private information consists of a feature vector $x_i \in \mathbb{R}$, an outcome value $y_i \in \mathbb{R}$, and a residual value $\epsilon_i \in \mathbb{R}$, that are i.i.d among agents. Each agent also has a cost $c_i$. The data is generated in the following way: first, $x_i$ is drawn from an unknown distribution $\mathcal{X}$. Then, independently from $x_i$, the pair $(c_i, \epsilon_i)$ is drawn from a joint distribution $\mathcal{D}$ over $\mathbb{R}^2$. The marginal distribution over costs, $\mathcal{D}_c$, is known to the designer, but not the full joint distribution $\mathcal{D}$. Then $y_i$ is defined to be

$$y_i = x_i^\top \theta^* + \epsilon_i \tag{19}$$

where $\theta^* \in \Theta$ with $\Theta$ a compact subset of $\mathbb{R}^d$. We further require that $\theta^*$ is in the interior of $\Theta$. We write $\mathcal{D}_\epsilon$ for the marginal distribution over $\epsilon_i$, which is supported on some bounded range $[L, U]$, and has expected value 0. (So, in particular, $L \leq 0 \leq U$.)

When a survey mechanism buys data from agent $i$, the pair $(x_i, y_i)$ is revealed. Crucially, the value of $\epsilon_i$ is not revealed to the survey mechanism. The goal of the designer is to estimate the parameter vector $\theta^*$.

Note that the single-dimensional moment estimation problem from Section 3 is a special case of linear regression. Indeed, consider setting $d = 1$, $\epsilon_i = m(z_i) - \mathbb{E}[m(z_i)]$ for each $i$, $\theta^* = \mathbb{E}[m(z_i)]$, and $x_i$ to be the constant $-1$. Then, when the survey mechanism purchases data from agent $i$, it learns $y_i = m(z_i)$, and estimating $\theta^*$ is equivalent to estimating the expected value of $m(z_i)$.

More generally, one can interpret $x_i$ as a vector of publicly-verifiable information about agent $i$, which might influence a (possibly sensitive) outcome $y_i$. For example, $x_i$ might consist of demographic information, and $y_i$ might indicate the severity of a medical condition. The coefficient vector $\theta^*$ describes the average effect of each feature on the outcome, over the entire population.

Under this interpretation, $\epsilon_i$ is the residual agent-specific component of the outcome, beyond what can be accounted for by the agent's features. We can interpret the independence of $x_i$ from $(c_i, \epsilon_i)$ as meaning that each agent's cost to reveal information is potentially correlated with their (private) residual data, but is independent of the agent's features.

As in Section 3, the analyst wants to design a survey mechanism to buy from the agents, obtain data from the set $S$ of elicited agents, then compute an estimate $\hat{\theta}_S$ of $\theta$. The expected average payment to each of the n agents should be no more than $\bar{B}$. As in Section 2.1, we note that the problem of designing a survey mechanism in fact reduces to that of designing an allocation rule $A$ that minimizes said variance and satisfies a budget constraint in which the prices are replaced by known virtual costs. To this end, the analyst designs an allocation rule $A$ and a pricing rule $P$ so as to minimize the $\sqrt{n}$-normalized worst-case asymptotic mean-squared error of $\hat{\theta}_S$ as the population size goes to infinity. Our mechanism will essentially be optimizing the coefficient in front of the leading $1/n$ term in the mean squared error, ignoring potential finite sample deviations that decay at a faster rate than $1/n$. Note that we will design allocation and pricing rules to be independent of the population size $n$; hence, the analyst can use the designed mechanism even if the exact population size in unknown.

## 5.1 Estimators for Regression

Let $S$ be the set of data points elicited by a survey mechanism. The analyst's estimate will then be the value $\hat{\theta}_S$ that minimizes the Horvitz-Thompson mean-squared error $\mathbb{E}[(y_i - x_i^\top \theta^*)^2]$, i.e.,

$$\hat{\theta}_S = \operatorname*{argmin}_{\theta \in \Theta} \sum_i \frac{1\{i \in S\}}{A(c_i)} (y_i - x_i^\top \theta)^2. \tag{20}$$

Further, we make the following assumptions on the distribution of data points:

Assumption 2 (Assumption on the distribution of features). *$E[x_i x_i^\top]$ is finite and positive-definite, and hence invertible.*

Finite expectation is a property one may expect real data such has age, height, weight, etc. to exhibit. The second part of the assumption is satisfied by common classes of distributions, such as multivariate normals. We first show that $\hat{\theta}_S$ is a consistent estimator of $\theta$.

Lemma 5.1. *Under Assumption 2, for any allocation rule $A > 0$ that does not depend on n, $\hat{\theta}_S$ is a consistent estimator of $\theta^*$.*

Proof of Lemma 5.1. Let $m(\theta; x, y) = (y - x^\top \theta)^2$, and let $w_i = 1\{i \in S\}$ for simplicity. The following holds:

(1) First, we note that $\theta^*$ is the unique parameter that minimizes $\mathbb{E}[(y_i - x_i^\top \theta)^2]$; indeed, take any $\theta \neq \theta^*$, we have that

$$\begin{aligned}\mathbb{E}[(y_i - \theta^\top x_i)^2] &= \mathbb{E}\left[(y_i - x_i^\top \theta^* + x_i^\top(\theta^* - \theta))^2)\right] \\ &= \mathbb{E}\left[\left(y_i - x_i^\top \theta^*\right)^2\right] + \mathbb{E}\left[\left(x_i^\top(\theta^* - \theta)\right)^2\right] + 2\,\mathbb{E}\left[\epsilon_i(\theta^* - \theta)^\top x_i\right]\end{aligned}$$

As $x$ and $\varepsilon$ are independent, $\varepsilon$ has mean 0, this simplifies to

$$\begin{aligned}\mathbb{E}[(y_i - \theta^\top x_i)^2] &= \mathbb{E}\left[\left(y_i - \theta^{*\top} x_i\right)^2\right] + (\theta^* - \theta)^\top \mathbb{E}\left[x_i x_i^\top\right](\theta^* - \theta) + 2(\theta^* - \theta)^\top \mathbb{E}\left[\epsilon_i x_i\right] \\ &= \mathbb{E}\left[\left(y_i - \theta^{*\top} x_i\right)^2\right] + (\theta^* - \theta)^\top \mathbb{E}\left[x_i x_i^\top\right](\theta^* - \theta) \\ &> \mathbb{E}\left[\left(y_i - \theta^{*\top} x_i\right)^2\right]\end{aligned}$$

where the last step follows from $\mathbb{E}[x_i x_i^\top]$ being positive-definite by Assumption 2.

(2) By definition, $\Theta$ is compact.

(3) $m(\theta; x, y)$ is continuous in $\theta$, and so is its expectation.

(4) $m(.;.)$ is also bounded (lower-bounded by 0, and upper-bounded by either $L^2$ or $U^2$), implying that $\theta \longrightarrow \frac{w_i}{A(c_i)} m(\theta; x_i, y_i)$ is continuous and bounded. Hence, by the uniform law of large number, remembering that $\frac{w_i}{A(c_i)} m(\theta; x_i, y_i)$ are i.i.d,

$$\sup_{\theta \in \Theta} \left| \frac{1}{n} \sum_{i=1}^{n} \frac{w_i}{A(c_i)} m(\theta; x_i, y_i) - \mathbb{E}\left[ \frac{w_i}{A(c_i)} m(\theta; x_i, y_i) \right] \right| \longrightarrow 0.$$

Finally, noting that conditional on $c_i$, $m(\theta; x_i, y_i)$ and $\frac{w_i}{A(c_i)}$ are independent, we have:

$$\mathbb{E}\left[ \frac{w_i}{A(c_i)} m(\theta; x_i, y_i) \right] = \mathbb{E}\left[ \mathbb{E}\left[ \frac{w_i}{A(c_i)} \,\middle|\, c_i \right] \mathbb{E}[\, m(\theta; x_i, y_i) \mid c_i \,] \right] = \mathbb{E}\left[ m(\theta; x_i, y_i) \right]$$

using $\mathbb{E}\left[ \frac{w_i}{A(c_i)} \,\middle|\, c_i \right] = 1$.

Therefore, all of the conditions of Theorem 2.1 of [17] are satisfied, which is enough to prove the result. □

Similarly to the moment estimation problem in Section 3, the goal of the analyst is to minimize the worst-case (over the distribution of data and the correlation between $c_i$'s and $\epsilon_i$'s) asymptotic mean-squared error of the estimator $\hat{\theta}_S$. Here "asymptotic" means the worst-case error as $\hat{\theta}_S$ approaches the true parameter $\theta^*$. The following theorem characterizes the asymptotic covariance matrix of $\hat{\theta}_S$. (In fact, it fully characterizes the asymptotic distribution of $\hat{\theta}_S$.)

Lemma 5.2. *Under Assumption 2, for any allocation rule $A > 0$ that does not depend on $n$, the asymptotic distribution of $\hat{\theta}_S$ is given by*

$$\sqrt{n}(\hat{\theta}_S - \theta^*) \xrightarrow{d} \mathcal{N}\left(0, \mathbb{E}[x_i x_i^\top]^{-1}\, \mathbb{E}\left[ \epsilon_i^2 \frac{\mathbb{1}\{i \in S\}}{A^2(c_i)} \right] \right)$$

*where $d$ denotes convergence in distribution and where randomness in the expectations is taken on the costs $c_i$, the set of elicited data points $S$, the features of the data $x_i$, and the noise $\epsilon_i$.*

Proof of Lemma 5.2. For simplicity, let $w_i = \mathbb{1}\{i \in S\}$ and note that the $w_i$'s are i.i.d. Let $m(\theta; x_i, y_i) = (y_i - x_i^\top \theta)^2$. First we remark that $\nabla_\theta m(\theta; x_i, y_i) \cdot \frac{w_i}{A(c_i)} = 2\frac{w_i}{A(c_i)} x_i (x_i^\top \theta - y_i)$ and $\nabla^2_{\theta\theta} m(\theta; x_i, y_i) \cdot \frac{w_i}{A(c_i)} = 2\frac{w_i}{A(c_i)} x_i x_i^\top$. We then note the following:

(1) $\theta^*$ is in the interior of $\Theta$.

(2) $\theta \longrightarrow m(\theta; x_i, y_i) \cdot \frac{w_i}{A(c_i)}$ is twice continuously differentiable for all $x_i, y_i, c_i, w_i$.

(3) $\sqrt{n}\left( \frac{1}{n} \sum_{i=1}^{n} \nabla_\theta\, m(\theta^*; x_i, y_i) \cdot \frac{w_i}{A(c_i)} \right) \longrightarrow \mathcal{N}\left(0, 4\,\mathbb{E}\left[ \frac{w_i}{A^2(c_i)} x_i x_i^\top (x_i^\top \theta^* - y_i)^2 \right]\right)$. This follows directly from applying the multivariate central limit theorem, noting that

$$\mathbb{E}\left[ \nabla_\theta m(\theta^*; x_i, y_i) \cdot \frac{w_i}{A(c_i)} \right] = \mathbb{E}\left[ \mathbb{E}[\, 2 x_i \epsilon_i \mid c_i \,] \cdot \mathbb{E}\left[ \frac{w_i}{A(c_i)} \,\middle|\, c_i \right] \right] = \mathbb{E}\left[ 2 x_i \epsilon_i \right] = 0$$

where the first step follows from conditional indepence on $c$ of $x, \epsilon$ with $A(c), S$, the second step from $\mathbb{E}\left[ \frac{w_i}{A(c_i)} \,\middle|\, c_i \right] = 1$, and the last equality follows from the fact that $x$ and $\epsilon$ are independent and $\mathbb{E}[\epsilon_i] = 0$.

(4) $\sup_{\theta\in\Theta}\left\|\mathbb{E}\left[\nabla^2_{\theta\theta}m(\theta;x_i,y_i)\cdot\frac{w_i}{A(c_i)}\right]-\frac{1}{n}\sum_i\nabla^2_{\theta\theta}m(\theta;x_i,y_i)\cdot\frac{w_i}{A(c_i)}\right\|\to 0$, applying the uniform law of large numbers as $\nabla^2_{\theta\theta}m(\theta;x_i,y_i)\cdot\frac{w_i}{A(c_i)} = 2\frac{w_i}{A(c_i)}x_ix_i^\top$ is i) continuous in $\theta$, and ii) constant in $\theta$, thus bounded coordinate-by-coordinate by $2\frac{w_i}{A(c_i)}x_ix_i^\top$ that is independent of $\theta$ and has finite expectation $2\,\mathbb{E}[x_ix_i^\top]$.

(5) $\mathbb{E}\left[\nabla^2_{\theta\theta}m(\theta;x_i,y_i)\cdot\frac{w_i}{A(c_i)}\right]=2\,\mathbb{E}[x_ix_i^\top]$ is invertible as it is positive-definite.

Therefore the sufficient conditions i)-v) in Theorem 3.1 of [17] hold, proving that the asymptotic distribution is normal with mean 0 and variance

$$\mathbb{E}[2x_ix_i^\top]^{-1}\,\mathbb{E}\left[4\frac{w_i}{A^2(c_i)}(x_i^\top\theta-y_i)^2x_ix_i^\top\right]\mathbb{E}[2x_ix_i^\top]^{-1}.$$

To conclude the proof, we remark that by independence of $x_i$ with $c_i$ and $\varepsilon_i$,

$$\mathbb{E}\left[\frac{w_i}{A^2(c_i)}(x_i^\top\theta-y_i)^2x_ix_i^\top\right]=\mathbb{E}[x_ix_i^\top]\,\mathbb{E}\left[\epsilon_i^2\frac{w_i}{A^2(c_i)}\right]$$

□

Lemma 5.2 implies that the worst-case asymptotic mean-squared error, under a budget constraint, is given by the worst-case trace of the variance matrix. That is,

$$\begin{aligned}\mathcal{R}^*(\mathcal{F},A)\triangleq\sup_{\mathcal{X}}\sup_{\mathcal{D}_\epsilon}\mathbb{E}\left[\epsilon_i^2\frac{1\{i\in S\}}{A^2(c_i)}\right]\cdot\sum_{j=1}^d\mathbb{E}[x_ix_i^\top]^{-1}_{jj}\\ \text{s.t. }\mathbb{E}[\epsilon_i]=0\end{aligned}\tag{21}$$

where recall that $\mathcal{D}_\epsilon$ is the marginal distribution over $\epsilon$ and $\mathcal{X}$ the distribution over $x$. Importantly, this can be rewritten as

$$\begin{aligned}\mathcal{R}^*(\mathcal{F},A)\triangleq\left(\sup_{\mathcal{X}}\sum_{j=1}^d\mathbb{E}[x_ix_i^\top]^{-1}_{jj}\right)\cdot\sup_{\mathcal{D}_\epsilon}\mathbb{E}\left[\epsilon_i^2\frac{1\{i\in S\}}{A^2(c_i)}\right]\\ \text{s.t. }\mathbb{E}[\epsilon_i]=0\end{aligned}\tag{22}$$

Therefore, the analyst's decision solely depend on the worst-case correlation between costs $c_i$ and noise $\epsilon_i$, and not on the worst-case distribution $\mathcal{X}$. In turn, the analyst's allocation is completely independent of and robust in $\mathcal{X}$.

### 5.2 Characterizing the Optimal Allocation Rule for Regression

As in Section 3, we assume costs are drawn from a discrete set, say $C=\{c_1,\dots,c_{|C|}\}$. We will then write $A_t$ for an allocation rule conditional on the cost being $c_t$, and $\pi_t$ the probability of the cost of an agent being $c_t$. We will assume that $\bar{B}<\sum_{t=1}^{|C|}\pi_tc_t$, meaning that it is not feasible to accept all data points, since otherwise it is trivially optimal to set $A_t=1$ for all $t$.

The following lemma describes the optimization problem faced by an analyst wanting to design an optimal survey mechanism. Recall that residual values lie in the interval $[L,H]$.

Lemma 5.3 (Optimization Problem for Parameter Estimation). *The optimization program for the analyst is given by:*

$$
\begin{aligned}
\inf_{A\in[0,1]^{|C|}} \quad & \sup_{q\in[0,1]^{|C|}} \sum_{t=1}^{l} \frac{\pi_t}{A_t}\left((1-q_t)\cdot L^2 + q_t \cdot U^2\right) \\
\text{s.t.} \quad & \sum_{t=1}^{|C|} \pi_t \left((1-q_t)\cdot L + q_t\cdot U\right) = 0 \\
& \sum_{t=1}^{|C|} \pi_t c_t A_t \leq \bar{B} \\
& A \text{ is monotone non-increasing}
\end{aligned}
\tag{23}
$$

Proof of Lemma 5.3. First we note that

$$
\begin{aligned}
\mathcal{R}^*(\mathcal{F}, A) \triangleq \left(\sup_{X} \sum_{j=1}^{d} \mathbb{E}[x_i x_i^\top]_{jj}^{-1}\right) \cdot \sup_{\mathcal{D}_\epsilon} \mathbb{E}\left[\epsilon_i^2 \frac{1\{i\in S\}}{A^2(c_i)}\right] \\
\text{s.t. } \mathbb{E}[\epsilon_i] = 0
\end{aligned}
\tag{24}
$$

We can therefore renormalize the worst-case variance by $\sup_X \sum_{i=1}^{d} \mathbb{E}[x_i x_i^\top]_{ii}^{-1}$, as it does not depend on any other parameter of the problem. The analyst's objective is now given by

$$
\begin{aligned}
\sup_{\mathcal{D}_\epsilon} \sum_{t=1}^{|C|} \pi_t \frac{\mathbb{E}[\epsilon_i^2 | c_t]}{A_t} \\
\text{s.t. } \mathbb{E}[\epsilon_i] = 0
\end{aligned}
\tag{25}
$$

The worst case distribution is reached when $\epsilon_i | c_t$ is binomial between $L$ and $U$ (and such a distribution is feasible for $\epsilon_i | c_t$), therefore letting $q_t = P[\epsilon_i = U \mid c_t]$, we obtain the lemma. □

We can now characterize the form of the optimal survey mechanism. For simplicity, we will assume that $U^2 \geq L^2$. This is without loss of generality, since the optimization program is symmetric in $L$ and $U$; if $L^2 > U^2$, the analyst can set $q_t = 1 - q_t$, $L = U$ and $U = L$ to obtain Program (23) with $U^2 > L^2$.

Theorem 5.4. *Under the assumptions described above, an optimal allocation rule A has the form*

(1) $A_t = \min\left(1, \alpha \frac{|L|}{\sqrt{c_t}}\right)$ *for* $t < t^-$
(2) $A_t = \bar{A}$ *for all* $t \in \{t^-, \dots, t^+\}$
(3) $A_t = \min\left(1, \alpha \frac{U}{\sqrt{c_t}}\right)$ *for* $t > t^+$

*for* $\bar{A}$ *and* $\alpha$ *positive constants that do not depend on n, and* $t^-$ *and* $t^+$ *integers with* $t^- \leq t^+$. *Further,* $\bar{A}$ *and* $\alpha$ *can be computed efficiently given knowledge of* $t^-, t^+$.

We remark that the allocation rule that we designed is strictly positive and independent of $n$ (as the optimization program itself does not depend on $n$), so Lemmas 5.1 and 5.2 apply. Theorem 5.4 immediately implies that an optimal allocation rule can be obtained by simply searching over the space of parameters $(t^-, t^+)$, which can be done in at most $|C|^2$ steps. For each pairs of parameters $(t^-, t^+)$, $A$ can be computed efficiently as stated in the Theorem. Then the analyst only needs to pick the allocation rule that minimizes the objective value among the obtained allocation rules that are feasible for Program (23). Further, we remark that the solution for the linear regression case exhibits a structure that is similar to the structure of the optimal allocation rule for moment estimation (see Theorem 3.2): it exhibits a pooling region in which all cost types are treated the same way, and changes in the inverse of the square root of the cost outside said pooling region. However, we note that we may now choose to pool agents together in an intermediate range of costs, instead of pooling together agents whose costs are below a given threshold.

Proof sketch. We first compute the best response $q^*$ of the adversary; we note that this best response is in fact the solution to a knapsack problem that is independent of the value taken by the allocation rule $A$. We can therefore plug the adversary's best response into the optimization problem, and reduce the minimax problem above in a simple minimization problem on $A$. We then characterize the solution as a function of the parameters $(t^-, t^+) \in [|C|]^2$ through KKT conditions. The full proof is given in the full version of this paper. □

*Non-linear regression:* We further show in the full version of the paper that our results extend to non-linear regression, i.e. when $y_i$ is generated by a process of the more general form

$$y_i = f(\theta^*, x_i) + \epsilon_i,$$

under a few additional assumptions on the distribution of $x$ and on the regression function $f$.

## REFERENCES


[1] Jacob Abernethy, Yiling Chen, Chien-Ju Ho, and Bo Waggoner. 2015. Low-Cost Learning via Active Data Procurement. In *Proceedings of the Sixteenth ACM Conference on Economics and Computation (EC '15)*. ACM, New York, NY, USA, 619–636. https://doi.org/10.1145/2764468.2764519

[2] Stephen Boyd and Lieven Vandenberghe. 2004. *Convex Optimization.* Cambridge University Press, New York, NY, USA.

[3] Y. Cai, C. Daskalakis, and C. H. Papadimitriou. 2015. Optimum Statistical Estimation with Strategic Data Sources. In *Proceedings of the 28th Conference on Learning Theory.* 280–296.

[4] Ioannis Caragiannis, Ariel D. Procaccia, and Nisarg Shah. 2016. Truthful Univariate Estimators. In *Proceedings of the 33rd International Conference on International Conference on Machine Learning - Volume 48 (ICML'16).* JMLR.org, 127–135. http://dl.acm.org/citation.cfm?id=3045390.3045405

[5] Rachel Cummings, Stratis Ioannidis, and Katrina Ligett. 2015. Truthful Linear Regression. In *Proceedings of the 28th Conference on Learning Theory.* 448–483.

[6] Rachel Cummings, Katrina Ligett, Aaron Roth, Zhiwei Steven Wu, and Juba Ziani. 2015. Accuracy for Sale: Aggregating Data with a Variance Constraint. In *Proceedings of the 2015 Conference on Innovations in Theoretical Computer Science (ITCS '15).* ACM, New York, NY, USA, 317–324. https://doi.org/10.1145/2688073.2688106

[7] O. Dekel, F. Fischer, and A. D. Procaccia. 2010. Incentive Compatible Regression Learning. *J. Comput. System Sci.* 76, 8 (2010), 759–777.

[8] Jinshuo Dong, Aaron Roth, Zachary Schutzman, Bo Waggoner, and Zhiwei Steven Wu. 2017. Strategic Classification from Revealed Preferences. (2017).

[9] Lisa Fleischer and Yu-Han Lyu. 2012. Approximately Optimal Auctions for Selling Privacy when Costs are Correlated with Data. *CoRR* abs/1204.4031 (2012). http://arxiv.org/abs/1204.4031

[10] Arpita Ghosh, Katrina Ligett, Aaron Roth, and Grant Schoenebeck. 2014. Buying Private Data without Verification. *CoRR* abs/1404.6003 (2014). http://arxiv.org/abs/1404.6003

[11] Arpita Ghosh and Aaron Roth. 2011. Selling Privacy at Auction. In *Proceedings of the 12th ACM Conference on Electronic Commerce (EC '11).* ACM, New York, NY, USA, 199–208. https://doi.org/10.1145/1993574.1993605

[12] M. Hardt, N. Megiddo, C. H. Papadimitriou, and M. Wootters. 2016. Strategic Classification. In *7th.* 111–122.

[13] D. G. Horvitz and D. J. Thompson. 1952. A Generalization of Sampling Without Replacement from a Finite Universe. *J. Amer. Statist. Assoc.* 47, 260 (1952), 663–685. https://doi.org/10.1080/01621459.1952.10483446 arXiv:http://amstat.tandfonline.com/doi/pdf/10.1080/01621459.1952.10483446

[14] R. Meir, S. Almagor, A. Michaely, and J. S. Rosenschein. 2011. Tight bounds for strategyproof classification. In *10th.* 319–326.

[15] R. Meir, A. D. Procaccia, and J. S. Rosenschein. 2012. Algorithms for Strategyproof Classification. *Artificial Intelligence* 186 (2012), 123–156.

[16] Roger B. Myerson. 1981. Optimal Auction Design. *Math. Oper. Res.* 6, 1 (Feb. 1981), 58–73. https://doi.org/10.1287/moor.6.1.58

[17] Whitney K. Newey and Daniel McFadden. 1986. Large sample estimation and hypothesis testing. In *Handbook of Econometrics*, R. F. Engle and D. McFadden (Eds.). Handbook of Econometrics, Vol. 4. Elsevier, Chapter 36, 2111–2245. https://ideas.repec.org/h/eee/ecochp/4-36.html

[18] Kobbi Nissim, Salil Vadhan, and David Xiao. 2014. Redrawing the Boundaries on Purchasing Data from Privacy-sensitive Individuals. In *Proceedings of the 5th Conference on Innovations in Theoretical Computer Science (ITCS '14)*. ACM, New York, NY, USA, 411–422. https://doi.org/10.1145/2554797.2554835

[19] J. Perote and J. Perote-Peña. 2003. The impossibility of strategy-proof clustering. *Economics Bulletin* 4, 23 (2003), 1–9.

[20] J. Perote and J. Perote-Peña. 2004. Strategy-proof estimators for simple regression. *Mathematical Social Sciences* 47 (2004), 153–176.

[21] Aaron Roth and Grant Schoenebeck. 2012. Conducting Truthful Surveys, Cheaply. In *Proceedings of the 13th ACM Conference on Electronic Commerce (EC '12)*. ACM, New York, NY, USA, 826–843. https://doi.org/10.1145/2229012.2229076

# Optimal and Myopic Information Acquisition

ANNIE LIANG, University of Pennsylvania
XIAOSHENG MU, Harvard University
VASILIS SYRGKANIS, Microsoft Research

Full Paper: https://arxiv.org/abs/1703.06367

CCS Concepts: • **Applied computing → Economics; Multi-criterion optimization and decision-making**;

Additional Key Words and Phrases: Information Acquisition; Correlation; Endogenous Attention; Myopic Choice; Robustness; Value of Information

In a classic problem of sequential information acquisition, a Bayesian decision-maker (DM) repeatedly acquires information and takes actions. His payoff depends on the sequence of actions taken, as well as on an unknown payoff-relevant state. We consider a setting in which the DM acquires information from a limited number of *flexibly correlated* information sources, and allocates a fixed number of observations across these sources each period. We assume that it is possible to learn the payoff-relevant state by observing all of the sources infinitely often, but not by observing any proper subset of sources (information is "not redundant"). The optimal strategy for information acquisition is of interest.

Neglecting dynamic considerations, a simple strategy is to acquire at each period the signal (or the set of signals) that maximally reduces uncertainty about the payoff-relevant state. We refer to this as the *myopic* (or greedy) rule, as it is the optimal rule if the DM mistakenly believes each period to be the last possible period of information acquisition.

This myopic rule turns out to possess strong optimality properties in a widely used setting. Suppose that the available signals are *jointly normal*. If signal observations are acquired in sufficiently large blocks each period, then myopic information acquisition is optimal from period 1 (Theorem 1). We provide a sufficient condition on the required size of the block; this condition depends on primitives of the informational environment but not on the payoff function. Theorem 2 characterizes a condition on the prior and signal structure, given which myopic information acquisition is optimal from period 1 for *any* block size. In both of these cases, the optimal information acquisition strategy can be exactly and simply characterized. Additionally, instead of solving for the optimal decision rule and information acquisition strategy jointly (as would otherwise be required), our results show that one can separate these two problems, and solve for the optimal decision rule in this setting as if information acquisition were exogenous.

Finally, for generic signal structures, and for any block size, the optimal strategy proceeds by myopic acquisition after finitely many periods (Theorem 3). These results hold across all payoff

---

Authors' addresses: Annie Liang, University of Pennsylvania, anliang@upenn.edu; Xiaosheng Mu, Harvard University, xiaoshengmu@fas.harvard.edu; Vasilis Syrgkanis, Microsoft Research, vasy@microsoft.com.

---


*ACM EC'18, June 18–22, 2018, Ithaca, NY, USA.* ACM ISBN 978-1-4503-5829-3/18/06...$15.00
https://doi.org/10.1145/3219166.3219214

functions (and in particular, independently of discounting); thus, myopic information acquisition is (eventually) "robustly" best.

Why does the myopic rule perform so well? The main inefficiency of myopia is that it neglects potential complementarities across signals. A signal that is individually uninformative can be very informative when paired with other signals; thus, repeated (greedy) acquisition of the best single signal need not result in the best sequence of signals. A key observation is that whether the DM perceives two signals as providing complementary information depends on his current belief over the state space. This means that complementarities across signals are not intrinsic to the underlying signal correlation structure: As the DM's beliefs about the states evolve, so too do his perceptions of the correlations across signals. It is clear that as information accumulates, the DM's beliefs become more precise about each of the unknown states. This does not itself lead to optimality of myopic information acquisition. We show that the key force comes from a second effect of information accumulation: The DM's beliefs evolve in such a way that the signals *endogenously de-correlate* from his perspective, and are eventually perceived as providing approximately independent information. At the limit in which all signals are independent, the value of any given signal can be evaluated separately of the others. The dynamic problem is thus "separable," and can be replaced with a sequence of static problems. Given sufficiently many signal observations, we have only approximate separability, which we show is sufficient for the myopic rule to be optimal.

The mechanism we identify is different from the one underlying a classic result from the experimentation literature. In "learning by experimentation" settings, myopic behavior is eventually near-optimal: in the long run, the DM's beliefs converge, so the value of exploration (i.e. learning) becomes second-order relative to the value of exploitation of the perceived best arm. In our paper, signal acquisition decisions are driven by learning concerns exclusively, as there is by design no exploitation incentive. To see this, recall that in the classic multi-armed bandit problem [1, 2], actions play the dual role of influencing the evolution of beliefs and also determining flow payoffs. In our setting (which does not fall into the multi-armed bandit framework), there is a separation between *signal choices*, which influence the evolution of beliefs, and *actions*, which determine (unobserved) payoffs. Myopic signal choices become optimal in our framework because *they maximize the speed of learning*, and not because they optimize a tradeoff between learning and payoff.

We extend our results to a multi-player setting in which individuals privately acquire information before playing a one-shot game at a random final period (thus connecting to a literature on games with Gaussian information [3–5]). We also demonstrate extensions to environments with choice of information "intensity" (the number of signals to acquire each period), to multiple payoff-relevant states (for a class of prediction problems) and to a continuous-time setting.

## REFERENCES

[1] Dirk Bergemann and Juuso Välimäki. 2008. Bandit Problems. In *The New Palgrave Dictionary of Economics*, Steven N. Durlauf and Lawrence E. Blume (Eds.). Palgrave Macmillan, Basingstoke.

[2] J. C. Gittins. 1979. Bandit processes and dynamic allocation indices. *Journal of the Royal Statistical Society, Series B* (1979), 148–177.

[3] Christian Hellwig and Laura Veldkamp. 2009. Knowing What Others Know: Coordination Motives in Information Acquisition. *The Review of Economic Studies* 76 (2009), 223–251.

[4] Nicolas Lambert, Michael Ostrovsky, and Mikhail Panov. 2018. Strategic Trading in Informationally Complex Environments. *Econometrica* (2018).

[5] David P. Myatt and Chris Wallace. 2012. Endogenous Information Acquisition in Coordination Games. *The Review of Economic Studies* 79 (2012), 340–374.

# Consistent Approval-Based Multi-Winner Rules

MARTIN LACKNER, TU Wien, Austria
PIOTR SKOWRON, University of Warsaw, Poland

This paper is an axiomatic study of consistent approval-based multi-winner rules, i.e., voting rules that select a fixed-size group of candidates based on approval ballots. We introduce the class of counting rules, provide an axiomatic characterization of this class and, in particular, show that counting rules are consistent. Building upon this result, we axiomatically characterize three important consistent multi-winner rules: Proportional Approval Voting, Multi-Winner Approval Voting and the Approval Chamberlin–Courant rule. Our results demonstrate the variety of multi-winner rules and illustrate three different, orthogonal principles that multi-winner voting rules may represent: individual excellence, diversity, and proportionality.

A *multi-winner* rule [1] selects a fixed-size set of candidates—a *committee*—based on the preferences of voters. In this paper, we look at multi-winner rules based on approval ballots [3]; an approval ballot corresponds to a subset of (approved) candidates. Consider the following simple example: There are 100 voters and 5 candidates $\{a,b,c,d,e\}$: 66 voters approve the set $\{a,b,c\}$, 33 voters approve $\{d\}$, and one voter approves $\{e\}$. Assume we want to select a committee of size three. If we follow the principle of proportionality, we could choose, e.g., $\{a,b,d\}$; this committee closely reflects the proportions of voter support. If we aim for diversity and do not consider it important to give voters more than one representative, we may choose the committee $\{a,d,e\}$; it contains one approved candidate of every voter. The principle of individual excellence aims to select the strongest candidates: $a$, $b$, and $c$ have most supporters and are thus a natural choice, although the opinions of 34 voters are essentially ignored. We see that these three intuitive principles give rise to very different committees and will explore these principles in a formal, mathematical framework.

The first main result of this paper is an axiomatic characterization of *ABC counting rules*, which are a subclass of multi-winner approval-based rules. ABC counting rules are informally defined as follows: given a real-valued function $f(x,y)$ (the so-called *counting function*), a committee $W$ receives a score of $f(x,y)$ from every voter for whom committee $W$ contains $x$ approved candidates and who approves $y$ candidates in total; the ABC counting rule implemented by $f$ ranks committees according to the sum of scores obtained from all voters. We obtain the following characterization.

THEOREM 1. *A multi-winner approval-based rule is an ABC counting rule if and only if it satisfies symmetry, consistency, weak efficiency, and continuity.*

---

For the full version of the paper we refer the reader to the technical report [2]: https://arxiv.org/abs/1704.02453.
We thank Edith Elkind, Piotr Faliszewski, Paul Harrenstein and Dominik Peters for insightful discussions. We are grateful to Marie-Louise Lackner for providing feedback on early drafts of this paper. Furthermore, we thank Itzhak Gilboa for his supportive comments on our paper. Martin Lackner was supported by the European Research Council (ERC) under grant number 639945 (ACCORD) and the Austrian Science Foundation FWF, grant P25518 and Y698. Piotr Skowron was supported by the ERC grant 639945 (ACCORD), by a Humboldt Research Fellowship for Postdoctoral Researchers, and by the Foundation for Polish Science within the Homing programme (Project title: "Normative Comparison of Multiwinner Election Rules").
Authors' addresses: Martin Lackner, TU Wien, Favoritenstraße 9, Vienna, 1040, Austria, lackner@dbai.tuwien.ac.at; Piotr Skowron, University of Warsaw, Banacha 2, Warsaw, 02-097, Poland, p.skowron@mimuw.edu.pl.

---


*ACM EC'18, June 18–22, 2018, Ithaca, NY, USA.* ACM ISBN 978-1-4503-5829-3/18/06.
https://doi.org/10.1145/3219166.3219170

The axioms used in this theorem can be intuitively described as follows: A rule is consistent if the following holds: if two disjoint societies decide on the same set of candidates and if both societies prefer committee $W_1$ to a committee $W_2$, then the union of these two societies should also prefer $W_1$ to $W_2$. This is a straightforward adaption of consistency as defined for single-winner rules by Smith [4] and Young [5]. We say that a rule is symmetric if the names of voters and candidates do not affect the result of an election. Weak efficiency informally states that candidates that no one approves cannot be "better" committee members than approved candidates. Continuity [4] is a more technical condition that states that sufficiently large majorities can dictate decisions.

Theorem 1 gives a powerful technical tool that allows to obtain further axiomatic characterizations of more specific rules. Indeed, building upon this result, we explore the space of ABC counting rules, and obtain our second main result—the axiomatic explanation of the differences between three important rules: Multi-Winner Approval Voting (AV), Proportional Approval Voting (PAV), and Approval Chamberlin–Courant (CC), which are defined by the following counting functions:

$$f_{\mathrm{AV}}(x,y) = x; \qquad f_{\mathrm{PAV}}(x,y) = \sum_{i=1}^{x} 1/i; \qquad f_{\mathrm{CC}}(x,y) = \begin{cases} 0 & \text{if } x = 0, \\ 1 & \text{if } x \geq 1. \end{cases}$$

These three well-known rules are prime examples of multi-winner systems following the principle of individual excellence, proportionality, and diversity, respectively. Our results imply that the differences between these three voting rules can be understood by studying how these rules behave when viewed as *apportionment methods*. Apportionment methods are a well-studied special case of approval-based multi-winner voting, where the set of candidates can be represented as a disjoint union of groups (intuitively, each group can be viewed as a political party), and where each voter approves all candidates within one of these groups (which can be viewed as voting for a single party). For these mathematically much simpler profiles it is easier to formalize the principles of individual excellence, proportionality and diversity:

**Disjoint equality** states that if each candidate is approved by at most one voter, then any committee consisting of approved candidates is a winning committee. One can argue that the principle of individual excellence implies disjoint equality: if every candidate is approved only once, then every approved candidate has the same support, their "quality" cannot be distinguished, and hence all approved candidates are equally well suited for selection.

**D'Hondt proportionality** defines a way in which parliamentary seats are assigned to parties in a proportional manner. The D'Hondt method (also known as Jefferson method) is one of the most commonly used methods of apportionment in parliamentary elections.

**Disjoint diversity** states that as many parties as possible should receive one seat and, if necessary, priority is given to stronger parties. In contrast to D'Hondt proportionality, there are no guarantees for strong parties to receive more than one seat.

We show that Multi-Winner Approval Voting is the only ABC counting rule satisfying disjoint equality, Proportional Approval Voting is the only ABC counting rule satisfying D'Hondt proportionality and that Approval Chamberlin–Courant is the only one satisfying disjoint diversity.

For a complete version of this paper we refer the reader to the technical report [2].

## REFERENCES

[1] P. Faliszewski, P. Skowron, A. Slinko, and N. Talmon. 2017. Multiwinner Voting: A New Challenge for Social Choice Theory. In *Trends in Computational Social Choice*, U. Endriss (Ed.). AI Access.

[2] M. Lackner and P. Skowron. 2017. *Consistent Approval-Based Multi-Winner Rules.* Technical Report arXiv:1704.02453.

[3] J.-F. Laslier and R. Sanver (Eds.). 2010. *Handbook on Approval Voting.* Springer.

[4] J. Smith. 1973. Aggregation of Preferences with Variable Electorate. *Econometrica* 41, 6 (1973), 1027–1041.

[5] H. P. Young. 1974. A Note on Preference Aggregation. *Econometrica* 42, 6 (1974), 1129–1131.

# Social Choice with Non Quasi-linear Utilities

HONGYAO MA, Harvard University, USA
RESHEF MEIR, Technion- Israel Institute of Technology, Israel
DAVID C. PARKES, Harvard University, USA

We study social choice mechanisms that aggregate individual preferences and select one among a finite set of alternatives. Our interest is in the existence of strategy-proof mechanisms under non quasi-linear utility functions. In the classical voting problem without money, the seminal Gibbard-Satterthwaite theorem states that if agents' preferences can be any ordering over the alternatives, the only deterministic, onto (i.e. every alternative can be selected) and strategy-proof mechanisms for three or more alternatives are dictatorial. On the other hand, with monetary transfers and quasi-linear utilities, the Vickrey-Clarke-Groves (VCG) mechanism maximizes social welfare in dominant strategies, and can be generalized to implement any affine maximizer of agents' values. By Roberts' theorem, with three or more alternatives, the weighted VCG mechanisms are essentially unique for the quasi-linear domain. However, quasi-linearity is a strong assumption, violated for example in domains with budget constraints, lack of liquidity, wealth effect or risk-aversion.

The main result of this paper is a tight characterization of the maximal utility domain, which we name the *largest parallel domain*, where there exist non-dictatorial mechanisms that are strategy-proof, onto, deterministic, individually rational (IR) and satisfy *no subsidy* (i.e. no positive transfers from the mechanism to the agents). These properties are those of the VCG mechanism in quasi-linear utility domains. As a special case, for utility domains that contain all quasi-linear types but do not reside within the largest parallel domain, the only mechanisms with the above properties are dictatorial. We also provide a negative result for a broader class of mechanisms: by allowing richer utility domains that still differ very slightly from quasi-linearity, we establish the impossibility of non-dictatorial mechanisms even without requiring IR or no subsidy.

A key observation is that the critical property of agents' utilities that enables non-dictatorial mechanisms is not the linear dependency on payments. We say the utility functions of an agent is of *parallel type* if for any two alternatives $a$ and $b$, within the range of interest, no matter how much the agent is charged for $b$, to achieve the same utility, the additional amount she is willing to pay for $a$ stays the same. Quasi-linear utility functions have this property, but there can also be non quasi-linear parallel types. Intuitively, a type being parallel requires that regardless of which alternative is selected, the agent's marginal cost for money is the same as long as she has the same utility level— the trade-off with money depends on how happy the agent is, not how much she is paying. A domain where all types are parallel is called a *parallel domain*, and the largest parallel domain is the set of all parallel types. Within the parallel domains, we prove a positive result, that the generalized weighted VCG mechanisms truthfully implement any affine maximizer of agents' willingness to pay. We then generalize Roberts' Theorem to parallel domains with unrestricted willingness to pay, with which we prove our main characterization and impossibility results.

Full Paper: https://arxiv.org/abs/1804.02268

Additional Key Words and Phrases: Social Choice, Strategy-proofness, Non Quasi-linear Utilities.

Thanks to Brian Baisa, Vincent Conitzer, Debasis Mishra, Aris Filos-Ratsikas, and Moshe Tennenholtz for helpful comments. Ma is supported by a Siebel scholarship. Meir is supported by the Israel Science Foundation (ISF) under Grant No. 773/16.

Authors' addresses: Hongyao Ma, Harvard University, 33 Oxford Street, Cambridge, MA, 02138, USA, hma@seas.harvard.edu; Reshef Meir, Technion- Israel Institute of Technology, Bloomfield Building, Technion City, Haifa, 3200003, Israel, reshefm@ie.technion.ac.il; David C. Parkes, Harvard University, 33 Oxford Street, Cambridge, MA, 02138, USA, parkes@eecs.harvard.edu.


*ACM EC'18, June 18–22, 2018, Ithaca, NY, USA.* ACM ISBN 978-1-4503-5829-3/18/06.
https://doi.org/10.1145/3219166.3219167

# Optimal Pricing and Introduction Timing of New Virtual Machines

IAN A. KASH, Microsoft Research, U.K.
PETER B. KEY, Microsoft Research, U.K.
SPYROS I. ZOUMPOULIS, INSEAD, France

As the quality of computer hardware increases over time, cloud service providers have the ability to offer more powerful virtual machines (VMs) and other resources to their customers. But providers face several trade-offs as they seek to make the best use of improved technology. On one hand, more powerful machines are more valuable to customers and command a higher price. On the other hand, there is a cost to develop and launch a new product. Further, the new product competes with existing products. Thus, the provider faces two questions. First, when should new classes of VMs be introduced? Second, how should they be priced, taking into account both the VM classes that currently exist and the ones that will be introduced in the future?

This decision problem, combining scheduling and pricing new product introductions, is common in a variety of settings. One aspect that is more specific to the cloud setting is that VMs are rented rather than sold. Thus existing customers can switch to a new offering, albeit with some inconvenience. There is indeed evidence of customers' aversion to upgrades in the cloud computing services market. Based on a study of Microsoft Azure, we estimate that customers who arrive after a new VM class is launched are 50% more likely to use it than existing customers, indicating that these switching costs may be substantial.

This opens up a wide range of possible policies for the cloud service provider. Our main result is that a surprisingly simple policy is close to optimal in many situations: new VM classes are introduced on a periodic[1] schedule and each is priced as if it were the only product being offered. We refer to this pricing policy as Myerson pricing, as these prices can be computed as in Myerson's classic paper [2]. This policy produces a marketplace where new customers always select the newest and best offering, while existing customers may stick with older VMs due to switching costs.

In more detail, we model product introduction as a discrete-time process over an infinite time horizon, with future rewards discounted. The provider seeks to maximize expected discounted return. At each time period, the provider decides whether or not to introduce a new VM class (at a fixed cost) and at what price. The quality of a new VM class is assumed to grow linearly with the introduction time. Customers act as simple utility maximizers, and choose the VM offering that is most valuable to them; if they are existing customers, they incur a switching cost for switching technologies. New customers arrive at each time period, and stay for a fixed number of time periods.

For our first set of results, we analyze policies which introduce VM classes on a periodic schedule and establish two key results. First, if the Myerson pricing rule is always used, then the optimal introduction schedule is in fact periodic. Second, if a periodic schedule is used, then Myerson pricing is optimal in the limit,

[1]Periodic introductions have been noticeable in the practice of cloud computing. For example, Amazon Elastic Compute Cloud (EC2) launched new classes of the m.xlarge series in October 2007, February 2010, October 2012, and June 2015, i.e., in intervals of 28 months, 32 months, and 32 months [1].

This research was partially funded through a grant from Sorbonne University.

Authors' addresses: Ian A. Kash, Microsoft Research, U.K., iankash@microsoft.com; Peter B. Key, Microsoft Research, U.K., peter.key@outlook.com; Spyros I. Zoumpoulis, INSEAD, Boulevard de Constance, Fontainebleau, Île-de-France, 77305 Cedex, France, spyros.zoumpoulis@insead.edu.


*ACM EC'18, June 18–22, 2018, Ithaca, NY, USA.* ACM ISBN 978-1-4503-5829-3/18/06.
https://doi.org/10.1145/3219166.3219209

in the sense that for introduction times sufficiently far in the future, the (undiscounted) benefit of shading prices downward from the Myerson prices goes to zero.

With our second set of results, we argue that, given arbitrary fixed introduction times, Myerson pricing is approximately optimal. Combined with our first result, this means that Myerson pricing with periodic introductions is approximately optimal. Our analysis, which assumes the distribution of customer types satisfies the monotone hazard rate condition, establishes an upper bound on the possible revenue in a single time period and characterizes prices which achieve this upper bound. We extend this bound to discriminatory policies, which are permitted to charge different prices to new and existing customers (intuitively to provide existing customers a discount to entice them to switch), and provide a bound on the competitive ratio between such policies and Myerson pricing. This bound shows that Myerson pricing is approximately optimal when switching costs are small or large.

Following our analysis, we conduct numerical simulations of our model for both regular and discriminatory pricing. Our bounds can be used to show that, for several natural distributions, gains over the Myerson policy are less than 10% even at intermediate values of the switching cost. Furthermore, when we numerically compute optimal prices, rather than using our bounds, we find that Myerson pricing is often several orders of magnitude closer to optimal than even this already good bound suggests.

Full Paper: https://papers.ssrn.com/sol3/papers.cfm?abstract_id=3137038

CCS Concepts: • **Information systems → Cloud based storage**; • **Networks → Cloud computing**; • **Computer systems organization → Cloud computing**; • **Software and its engineering → Cloud computing**; • **Social and professional topics → Pricing and resource allocation**; • **Theory of computation →** *Computational pricing and auctions*; **Approximation algorithms analysis**; • **Mathematics of computing →** *Convex optimization*;

Additional Key Words and Phrases: New product introduction; Competitive analysis.

## REFERENCES

[1] Jeff Barr. 2015. EC2 Instance History. https://aws.amazon.com/blogs/aws/ec2-instance-history/. Accessed: 2018-02-14.
[2] Roger B. Myerson. 1981. Optimal Auction Design. *Math. Oper. Res.* 6, 1 (Feb. 1981), 58–73.

# Learnability and Models of Decision Making under Uncertainty

PATHIKRIT BASU, California Institute of Technology, USA
FEDERICO ECHENIQUE, California Institute of Technology, USA

We study whether some of the most important models of decision-making under uncertainty are uniformly learnable, in the sense of PAC (probably approximately correct) learnability. Many studies in economics rely on Savage's model of (subjective) expected utility. The expected utility model is known to predict behavior that runs counter to how many agents actually make decisions (the contradiction usually takes the form of agents' choices in the Ellsberg paradox). As a consequence, economists have developed models of choice under uncertainty that seek to generalize the basic expected utility model. The resulting models are more general and therefore more flexible, and more prone to overfitting. The purpose of our paper is to understand this added flexibility better. We focus on the classical expected utility (EU) model, and its two most important generalizations: Choquet expected utility (CEU) and Max-min Expected Utility (MEU).

Our setting involves an analyst whose task is to estimate or learn an agent's preference based on data available on the agent's choices. A model of preferences is PAC learnable if the analyst can construct a learning rule to precisely learn the agent's preference with enough data. When a model is not learnable we interpret it as the model being susceptible to overfitting. PAC learnability is known to be characterized by the model's VC dimension: thus our paper takes the form of a study of the VC dimension of economic models of choice under uncertainty. We show that EU and CEU have finite VC dimension, and are consequently learnable. Morever, the sample complexity of the former is linear, and of the latter is exponential, in the number of states of uncertainty. The MEU model is learnable when there are two states but is not learnable when there are at least three states, in which case the VC dimension is infinite. Our results also exhibit a close relationship between learnability and the underlying axioms which characterise the model.

Full Paper: http://people.hss.caltech.edu/~fede/wp/learnability.pdf

CCS Concepts: • **Applied computing → Electronic commerce**; **Economics**;

Additional Key Words and Phrases: Decisions under Uncertainty; PAC Learning; Revealed Preference; Preference Recovery

---

We thank Fabio Maccheroni and Adam Wierman for comments and suggestions.

Authors' addresses: PATHIKRIT BASU, California Institute of Technology, Department of Computing and Mathematical Sciences, Pasadena, CA, 91125, USA, pathkrtb@caltech.edu; FEDERICO ECHENIQUE, California Institute of Technology, Division of the Humanities and Social Sciences , Pasadena, CA, 91125, USA, fede@hss.caltech.edu.

---


*ACM EC'18, June 18–22, 2018, Ithaca, NY, USA.* ACM ISBN 978-1-4503-4529-3/18/06.
https://doi.org/10.1145/3219166.3219223

# Strategic Classification from Revealed Preferences

JINSHUO DONG, University of Pennsylvania
AARON ROTH, University of Pennsylvania
ZACHARY SCHUTZMAN, University of Pennsylvania
BO WAGGONER, University of Pennsylvania
ZHIWEI STEVEN WU, Microsoft Research

We study an online linear classification problem in which the data is generated by strategic agents who manipulate their features in an effort to change the classification outcome. In rounds, the learner deploys a classifier, then an adversarially chosen agent arrives and possibly manipulates her features to optimally respond to the learner's choice of classifier. The learner has no knowledge of the agents' utility functions or "real" features, which may vary widely across agents. Instead, the learner is only able to observe their "revealed preferences", i.e., the manipulated feature vectors they provide. For a broad family of agent cost functions, we give a computationally efficient learning algorithm that is able to obtain diminishing "Stackelberg regret" – a form of policy regret that guarantees that the learner is realizing loss nearly as small as that of the best classifier in hindsight, even allowing for the fact that agents would have best-responded differently to the optimal classifier.

Full Paper: https://arxiv.org/abs/1710.07887

CCS Concepts: • **Applied computing → Electronic commerce**; **Economics**;

Additional Key Words and Phrases: strategic agents; online learning; Stackelberg regret; revealed preferences; strategic classification

## 1 INTRODUCTION

Machine learning is typically studied under the assumption that the data distribution a classifier is deployed on is the same as the data distribution it was trained on. However, the outputs of many classification and regression problems are used to make decisions about human beings, in settings such as determining whether an individual will receive a loan, be hired, be admitted to college, or whether their email will pass through a spam filter. In these settings, the individuals have a vested interest in the outcome, and so the data generating process is better modeled as part of a strategic game in which individuals edit their data before sending it to the classifier to increase the likelihood of a particular desired outcome. Tax evaders may carefully craft their tax returns to decrease the likelihood of an audit; home buyers may strategically sign up for more credit cards in an effort to increase their credit score; email spammers may modify their emails in order to evade existing filters. In each of these settings, the individuals have a natural objective that they want to maximize – they want to increase their probability of being (say) positively classified. However,

Authors' addresses: Jinshuo Dong, University of Pennsylvania, Philadelphia, PA, djs.pku@gmail.com; Aaron Roth, University of Pennsylvania, Philadelphia, PA, aaroth@cis.upenn.edu; Zachary Schutzman, University of Pennsylvania, Philadelphia, PA, ianzach@seas.upenn.edu; Bo Waggoner, University of Pennsylvania, Philadelphia, PA, bwag@seas.upenn.edu; Zhiwei Steven Wu, Microsoft Research, New York, NY, steven7woo@gmail.com.


*ACM EC'18, June 18–22, 2018, Ithaca, NY, USA.* ACM ISBN 978-1-4503-5829-3/18/06...$15.00
https://doi.org/10.1145/3219166.3219193

they also incur a cost from performing these manipulations (tax evaders may have to pay *some* tax to avoid an audit, and email spammers must balance their ability to evade spam filters with their original goal in crafting email text). These costs can be naturally modeled as the distance between the "true" features $x$ of the individual and the manipulated features $\hat{x}$ that he ends up sending, according to some measure. In settings of this sort, learning can be viewed as a game between a learner and the set of individuals who generate the data, and the goal of the learner is to compute an equilibrium strategy of the game that maximizes her utility.

The relevant notion of equilibrium depends on the order of information revelation in the game. Frequently, the learner will first deploy her classifier, and then the data generating players (agents) will get to craft their data with knowledge of the learner's classifier. In such settings, the learner should seek to play a classifier corresponding to a *Stackelberg equilibrium* of the game; she should deploy the classifier that minimizes her error *after* the agents are given an opportunity to best-respond to the learner's classifier. This is the approach taken by the most closely related prior work: [8] and [14]. Both of these papers consider a one-shot game and study how to compute the Stackelberg equilibria of this game. To do this, they necessarily assume that the learner has (almost) full knowledge of the agents' utility functions; in particular, it is assumed that the learner has access to the "true" distribution of agent features (before manipulation), and that the costs experienced by the agents for manipulating their data are the same for all agents and known to the learner. [1]

The primary point of departure in our work is to study the strategic classification problem when the learner does not know the utility functions of the agents: neither their true features $x$, nor the cost they experience for manipulation (which we allow to differ for each agent). In this setting, it no longer makes sense to study learning as a one-shot game; we cannot compute an equilibrium when the utility functions of the agents are unknown. Instead, we model the learning process as an iterative, online procedure. In each round $t = 1, 2, \ldots T$, the learner proposes a classifier $\beta_t$. Then, an agent arrives, with an unknown set of $d$ "true" features $x_t \in \mathbb{R}^d$, and an unknown cost function $d_t : \mathbb{R}^d \times \mathbb{R}^d \to \mathbb{R}$ for manipulation. The learner observes only the manipulated set of features $\hat{x}_t \in \mathbb{R}^d$, which represents the agent's best response to $\beta_t$. After classification, the learner observes the agent's true label $y_t$, and suffers the corresponding loss. Crucially, the learner never gets to observe either $x_t$ or $d_t$, and we do not even assume that these are drawn from a distribution (they may be adversarially chosen). The only access that the learner has to these parameters is via the *revealed preferences* of the agents — the learner gets to observe the actions of the agents, which are the result of optimizing their unknown utility functions. The learner must use this information to improve her classifier.

We measure the performance of our algorithms via a quantity that we call *Stackelberg regret*: informally, by comparing the average loss of the learner to the loss she could have experienced with the best fixed classifier in hindsight, *taking into account that the agents would have best-responded differently had she used a different classifier.* If the learner were in fact interacting with the same agent repeatedly, or if the agents $(x_t, d_t)$ were drawn from a fixed distribution, then the guarantee of diminishing Stackelberg regret would imply the convergence to a Stackelberg equilibrium of the corresponding one-shot game. However, Stackelberg regret is more general, and applies even in settings in which the agents are adversarially chosen.

We add one further twist. Previous work on strategic classification has typically assumed that all agents are strategic. However, the equilibrium solutions that result from this assumption may be undesirable. For example, in a spam classification setting, the Stackelberg-optimal classifier may

[1] Brückner and Scheffer [8] model a single data generation player who manipulates the data distribution, and experiences cost equal to the squared $\ell_2$ distance of his manipulation. Hardt et al. [14] study a model in which each agent can independently manipulate his own data point, but assume that all agents have the same separable cost function, known to the learner.

attain its optimal accuracy only if all agents, even legitimate (non-spam) senders, actively seek to manipulate their emails to avoid the spam filter. In these settings, it would be more desirable to compute a classifier that was optimal under the assumption that spammers would attempt to manipulate their emails in order to game the classifier, but that legitimate senders would not manipulate their emails. To capture this nuance, in our model, only agents whose true label $y_t = -1$ (e.g. spammers) are strategic, and agents for whom $y_t = 1$ are non-strategic.

## 1.1 Our Results and Techniques

The problem that the learner must solve is a bi-level optimization problem in which the objective of the inner layer (the agents' maximization problem) is unknown. Even with full information, bi-level optimization problems are often NP-hard. As a first step in our solution, we seek to identify conditions under which the learner's optimization problem is convex. Under these conditions, computing an optimal solution would be tractable in the full information setting. The remaining difficulty is solving the optimization problem in our limited feedback model.

We study learners who deploy *linear classifiers* $\beta_t$, and consider two natural learner loss functions: logistic loss (corresponding to logistic regression) and hinge loss (corresponding to support vector machines). The agents in our model are parameterized by target feature vectors $x_t$ and cost functions $d_t$, and will play the modified feature vector $\hat{x_t}(\beta_t)$ that maximizes their utility given $\beta_t$. We model agent utility functions as $u_t(\hat{x}, \beta) = \langle \beta, \hat{x} \rangle - d_t(x_t, \hat{x}_t)$. Using tools from convex analysis, we give general conditions on the cost functions $d_t$ that suffice to make the learner's objective convex, for both logistic and hinge loss, for all $x_t$. These conditions are satisfied by (among other classes of cost functions) any squared Mahalanobis distance and, more generally, by any norm-induced metric raised to a power greater than one.

Finally, we turn to the learner's optimization problem. Once we have derived conditions under which the learner's optimization problem is convex, we can achieve quickly diminishing Stackelberg regret with any algorithm for online bandit (i.e. zeroth order) optimization that works for adversarialy chosen loss functions. However, we observe that when some of the agents are non-strategic (e.g. the non-spammers), there is additional structure that we can exploit. In particular, on rounds for which the agent is non-strategic, the learner can also derive gradients for her loss function, in contrast to rounds on which the agent is strategic, where she only has access to zeroth-order feedback. To take advantage of this, we analyze a variant of the bandit convex optimization algorithm of [12] which can make use of both kinds of feedback. The regret bound we obtain interpolates between the bound of [12], obtained when all agents are strategic, and the regret bound of online gradient descent [24], obtained when no agents are strategic, as a function of the proportion of the observed agents which were strategic.

## 1.2 Further Related Work

In the *adversarial* or *strategic* learning literature, the most closely related works are [8] and [14], as discussed above, which also consider notions of Stackelberg equilibrium, and make other similar modelling choices. [18] also model adversarial learning as a Stackelberg game. Other works in this line model the learning problem as a purely adversarial (zero sum) game as in [11] for which the appropriate solution concept is a minmax equilibrium, study the simultaneous move equilibria of non-zero sum games as in [6, 7], and study the Bayes-Nash equilibria of incomplete information games given Bayesian priors on the player types as in [13]. Common to all of these works is the assumption that the learner either has full knowledge of the data generator's utility functions (when Nash and Stackelberg equilibria are computed), or else knowledge of a prior distribution (when Bayes-Nash equilibria are computed). The point of departure of the current paper is to assume that the learner does *not* have this knowledge, and instead only has the power to observe agent decisions in response to deployed learners.

There is a parallel literature in machine learning and algorithmic game theory focusing on the problem of *learning from revealed preferences* — which corresponds to learning from the choices that agents make when optimizing their (unknown) utility functions in response to some decision of the learner as in [4]. This literature has primarily focused on how buyers with unknown combinatorial valuation functions make purchases in response to prices. Learning problems studied in this literature include learning to predict what purchase decisions a buyer will make in response to a set of prices drawn from an unknown distribution as in [3, 23], finding prices that will maximize profit or welfare after buyers best respond as in [1, 20, 21], and generalizations of these problems as in [15]. We study the problem of strategic classification with this sort of "revealed preferences" feedback.

Finally, Stackelberg games are studied extensively in the "security games" literature: see [22] for an overview. Most closely related to this paper is the work of [2], who develop no-regret algorithms for certain kinds of security games when "attackers" arrive online, using a notion of regret that is equivalent to the "Stackelberg regret" that we consider. This work is similar in motivation to ours; its goal is to give algorithms to compute equilibrium-like strategies for the "defender" without assuming that he has an unrealistic amount of knowledge about his opponents' utility functions. Technically, the work is quite different, since we are operating in very different settings. In particular, [2] are primarily interested in information theoretic bounds, and do not give computationally efficient algorithms (since in general, solving Stackelberg security games is NP hard — see [16].)

## 2 MODEL AND PRELIMINARIES

We study a sequential binary classification problem in which a learner wishes to classify a sequence of examples over $n$ rounds. The example at each round $t$ is associated with an agent $a_t = (x_t, y_t, d_t)$, where $x_t \in \mathbb{R}^d$ is the agent's true feature vector, $y_t \in \{-1, 1\}$ is the true label and $d_t : \mathbb{R}^d \times \mathbb{R}^d \to \mathbb{R}$ is a distance function that maps pairs of feature vectors to costs. We will think of $d_t(x_t, \hat{x}_t)$ as the cost for the agent to change his feature vector $x_t$ to the feature vector $\hat{x}_t$. If the example is positive ($y_t = 1$), then we say the agent is *non-strategic*, and if the example is negative ($y_t = -1$), then we say the agent is *strategic*.

Each agent $a_t$ has a utility function $u_t(x_t, \beta_t) = \langle \beta_t, x_t \rangle - d_t(\hat{x}_t, x_t)$. In each round $t$, the interaction between the learner and the agent is the following:

(1) The learner commits to a linear classifier parameterized by $\beta_t \in K$, where $K$ is the set of feasible parameters.
(2) An adversary, oblivious to the learner's choices up to round $t$, selects an agent $a_t = (x_t, y_t, d_t)$.
(3) The agent $a_t$ sends the data point $\hat{x}_t$ to the learner:
   - If the agent is strategic ($y_t = -1$), then the agent sends the learner his best response to $\beta_t$ (ties broken arbitrarily):
$$\hat{x}_t(\beta_t) \in \arg\max_x u_t(x, \beta) \tag{1}$$
   - If the agent is non-strategic ($y_t = 1$), then the agent does not modify the feature vector, and so sends $\hat{x}_t(\beta_t) = x_t$ to the learner.
(4) The learner observes $y_t$, and experiences classification loss $c_t(\beta_t) = c(\hat{x}_t, y_t, \beta_t)$.

We focus on two standard classification loss functions $c$. The first is logistic loss, which corresponds to logistic regression:

$$c_{log}(\hat{x}_t, y_t, \beta_t) = \log(1 + e^{-y_t \cdot \langle \hat{x}_t, \beta_t \rangle})$$

The second is hinge loss, which corresponds to a support vector machine:

$$c_h(\hat{x}_t, y_t, \beta_t) = \max(0, 1 - y_t \cdot \langle \hat{x}_t, \beta_t \rangle)$$

The interaction between the learner and the agent in each strategic round can be viewed as a Stackelberg game, in which the learner as the leader plays her strategy first, and then the agent as the follower best-responds. With this observation, we define the *Stackelberg regret* to measure the performance of the learner.[2] In words, Stackelberg regret is the difference between the cumulative loss of the learner and the cumulative loss she would have experienced if she had deployed the *single best classifier in hindsight* $\beta^*$, for the same sequence of agents (who may have responded differently). More formally, for a history of play involving the $T$ agents $A = (a_1, a_2, \dots, a_T)$ and the sequence of $T$ classifiers $B = (\beta_1, \beta_2, \dots, \beta_T)$ the Stackelberg regret is defined as

$$\mathcal{R}_S(A, B) = \sum_{t=1}^{T} c(\hat{x}_t(\beta_t), y_t, \beta_t) - \min_{\beta \in K} \sum_{t=1}^{T} c(\hat{x}_t(\beta), y_t, \beta)$$

Observe that the regret-minimizing classifier $\beta^*$ is a Stackelberg equilibrium strategy for the learner in the one-shot game in which the learner first commits to a classifier $\beta^*$, then all the agents $(a_1, \dots, a_T)$ simultaneously respond with $\hat{x}_t(\beta^*)$, which results in the learner experiencing classification loss $\sum_{i=1}^{n} c(\hat{x}_i(\beta^*), y_i, \beta^*)$.

In order to derive efficient algorithms with sub-linear Stackelberg regret, we will impose some restrictions the agents' distance functions $d_t$ (formally described in Section 3), and we will assume the Euclidean norms of the original feature vectors $x_t$ are bounded by a constant $R_1$. We also assume our feasible set of classifers $K \subseteq \mathbb{R}^d$ is convex, contains the unit $\ell_2$-ball, and has Euclidean norm bounded by $R_2$, such that for any $\beta \in K$, $\|\beta\|_2 \le R_2$.

## 3 CONDITIONS FOR A CONVEX LEARNING PROBLEM

In this section, we derive general conditions under which the learner's problem can be cast as a convex minimization problem. In each round, the learner proposes some hypothesis $\beta$ and experiences a loss that depends on the agent's best-response to $\beta$. Even when the original loss function is a convex function of $\beta$ alone, holding $\hat{x}$ and $y$ fixed, it may no longer be convex when $\hat{x}$ is chosen strategically as a function of $\beta$.

Since the learner's objective is a summation of the loss over all rounds, and the sums of convex loss functions are convex, it suffices to show convexity for the loss experienced at each fixed round $t$. We omit the subscript $t$ for cleanliness of notation.

Recall that each strategic agent $a = (x, y, d)$ (with $y = -1$), when facing a classifier $\beta$, will misreport his feature vector $x$ as $\hat{x}(\beta)$ by solving a maximization problem:

$$\hat{x}(\beta) \in \arg\max_{\hat{x} \in \mathbb{R}^d} u(\hat{x}, x, \beta) = \arg\max_{\hat{x} \in \mathbb{R}^d} (\langle \hat{x}, \beta \rangle - d(\hat{x}, x))$$

where $d(\cdot, \cdot)$ is a "distance" function modeling the cost of deviating from the original feature vector $x$. We first show that both the logistic and hinge loss objective are convex if $\langle \hat{x}(\beta), \beta \rangle$ is convex in $\beta$, and then prove the convexity of $\langle \hat{x}(\beta), \beta \rangle$ when the distance has the form $d(x, x') = f(x - x')$, for $f$ satisfying reasonable assumptions (stated in Theorem 3.3). In Section 3.2, we present a large class of distance functions which satisfy our assumptions as well as examples of seemingly natural choices which either fail to satisfy the assumptions or lead to agents not having a well-defined optimization problem, demonstrating the necessity of our restrictions on $d$.

[2] The same regret notion has also appeared in the context of repeated security games [2].

As an abstraction, let $h(z)$ denote the learner's loss function where $z$ corresponds to $y\langle\hat{x}(\beta),\beta\rangle$. For example, if the learner is performing logistic regression, then $h(z) = \log(1 + e^{-z})$; and if the learner is building a support vector machine, then $h(z) = (1 - z)_+$, where $(x)_+$ denotes $\max(x, 0)$. Observe, critically, that both of these functions are non-decreasing and convex functions in $z$.

First, consider the learner's objective. She wants to minimize

$$c(x, y, \beta) = h(y\langle\hat{x}(\beta), \beta\rangle) = h(y\langle\hat{x}(\beta, x, y), \beta\rangle).$$

where

$$\hat{x}(\beta, x, y) = \begin{cases} x, & y = 1, \\ \arg\max u(\hat{x}, x, \beta), & y = -1. \end{cases}$$

Note that we are now writing $\hat{x}(\beta, x, y)$ rather than $\hat{x}(\beta)$ to make explicit the dependence on $x$ and $y$. Where $x$ and $y$ are clear from context and fixed, we continue to write $\hat{x}(\beta)$. We note that in general, $\hat{x}(\beta, x, y)$ is not necessarily a well-defined map, as when the arg max is not unique, there may be multiple choice of $\hat{x}$ which are best-responses to the learner's choice of $\beta$, or the agent's best-response may not even be finite. However, we show in Theorem 3.3 that as long as the agent's utility function obeys some very general properties, neither of these problems occur and both the agent's and learner's optimizations are well-defined.

To begin, we make the following observation from convex analysis:

Lemma 3.1 (e.g. [19], Theorem 5.1). *Let $g : \mathbb{R} \to \mathbb{R}$ be a non-increasing convex function of a single variable and $F : \mathbb{R}^d \to \mathbb{R}$ be convex. Then $g(-F(x))$ is convex in $x$.*

This implies the following:

Theorem 3.2. *Suppose, for all $(x, y)$, a strategic agent's best-response function $\hat{x}(\beta, x, y)$ satisfies the condition that the function $\beta \mapsto \langle\hat{x}(\beta), \beta\rangle$ is convex. Then logistic loss and hinge loss are convex functions of $\beta$, i.e. for all $(x, y)$, both of the following are convex:*

- *(logistic) $c(x, y, \beta) = \log\left(1 + e^{-y\langle\hat{x}(\beta),\beta\rangle}\right)$;*
- *(hinge) $c(x, y, \beta) = (1 - y\langle\hat{x}(\beta), \beta\rangle)_+$.*

Proof. For strategic agents, i.e. when $y = -1$, this follows immediately from Lemma 3.1 and the fact that both loss functions are non-increasing convex functions of the variable $z = \langle\hat{x}(\beta), \beta\rangle$. When $y = 1$, i.e. the agent is not strategic, $c(x, y, \beta) = h(\langle\beta, x\rangle) = h(-\langle\beta, -x\rangle)$. Note that $\langle\beta, -x\rangle$ is linear (and hence convex), so the lemma applies here as well. □

Therefore, in order to show the convexity of the learner's loss function $c(x, y, \beta)$ for every $x, y$, it suffices to show that for any fixed $x$ and $y$,$\langle\hat{x}(\beta, x, y), \beta\rangle$ is a convex function in $\beta$. In the next section, we give sufficient conditions for this to be the case.

### 3.1 Sufficient Conditions

Our main result of this section is the following theorem, which describes a set of sufficient conditions on an agent's utility function for his optimization problem to be well-defined and convex.

Theorem 3.3. *Let $u(\hat{x}, x, \beta) = \langle\hat{x}, \beta\rangle - d(\hat{x}, x)$ be the strategic agent's utility function. If $d$ has the form $d(\hat{x}, x) = f(\hat{x} - x)$ where $f : \mathbb{R}^d \to \mathbb{R}$ satisfies:*

- *$f(x) > 0$ for all $x \neq 0$ ;*
- *$f$ is convex over $\mathbb{R}^d$;*
- *$f$ is positive homogeneous[3] of degree $r > 1$.*

[3] A function $f : \mathbb{R}^d \to \mathbb{R}$ is *positive homogeneous of degree $k$* if for any scalar $\alpha \in \mathbb{R}$ with $\alpha > 0$ and vector $x \in \mathbb{R}^d$, we have $f(\alpha x) = \alpha^k f(x)$, where $k > 0$. Note that $k$ need not be an integer.

*then the function* $\beta \mapsto \langle \beta, \arg\max_{\hat{x}} u(\hat{x}, x, \beta)\rangle$ *is well-defined (i.e. finite and independent of the choices of maximizer) and convex.*

When these conditions hold, we can speak of the function $\beta \mapsto \langle \hat{x}(\beta), \beta\rangle$ without ambiguity even when there are multiple best responses $\hat{x}(\beta)$.

Proof. We present the proof in a series of steps, which we first outline here. The remainder of this subsection contains the formal statement and proof of each of these steps.

(1) First, we show (Corollary 3.6) that any best-response $\hat{x}(\beta)$ satisfies $\hat{x}(\beta) = x + v$, where $v$ is some subgradient of $f^*$ at $\beta$ and $f^*$ is the convex conjugate of $f$.
(2) Next, we show (Claim 2) that $f^*(\beta)$ is finite for all $\beta$.
(3) Then, we prove (Claim 3) that homogeneity of $f^*$ follows from the homogeneity of $f$.
(4) Finally, we apply a slight generalization of Euler's homogeneous function theorem, which says that if $f^*$ is homogenous and convex, there is a $k$ such that for any choice of subgradient $v \in \partial f^*(\beta)$ (the set of subgradients at $\beta$), we have $\langle v, \beta\rangle = kf^*(\beta)$. This, together with Claims 2 and 3, implies that $\langle \hat{x}(\beta), \beta\rangle = \langle x, \beta\rangle + kf^*(\beta)$ for any choice of best response $\hat{x}(\beta)$, and this function is well-defined and convex.

□

We begin with the first step. First, we rewrite the utility function:

$$u(\hat{x}, x, \beta) = \langle \hat{x}, \beta\rangle - f(\hat{x} - x).$$

We perform a change of variable from $\hat{x}$ to $w = \hat{x} - x$ and write:

$$v(w, \beta) = u(\hat{x}, x, \beta) = \langle x, \beta\rangle + \langle w, \beta\rangle - f(w).$$

The first step only relies on the convexity of $f$. Let

$$w^*(\beta) = \arg\max_{w \in \mathbb{R}^d} v(w, \beta)$$

be the set of maximizers of $v$ given $\beta$. We note that $w^*(\beta)$ is a convex set since $v(w, \beta)$ is concave in $w$ for any $\beta$. Note that if $f$ is differentiable, $w^*(\beta)$ is a singleton set.

*Definition 3.4.* The *convex conjugate* of a function $f : \mathbb{R}^d \to \mathbb{R}$ , denoted $f^* : \mathbb{R}^d \to \mathbb{R}$ is the function defined as

$$f^*(x^*) = \sup_{x \in \mathbb{R}^d} (\langle x^*, x\rangle - f(x)).$$

$f^*$ is always convex (even when $f$ is not) but is not necessarily finite. However, our positivity and homogeneity assumptions imply that it must be finite everywhere, as we will prove in Claim 2.

Claim 1. *The set* $w^*(\beta)$ *is equal to* $\partial f^*(\beta)$*, the set of subgradients of* $f^*$ *at* $\beta$*.*

Proof. Fix a $\beta$. Recall that

$$v(w, \beta) = \langle x, \beta\rangle + \langle w, \beta\rangle - f(w).$$

We can ignore $\langle x, \beta\rangle$ as it is a constant with respect to a fixed $\beta$. We have that

$$\begin{aligned} w \in w^*(\beta) &\Leftrightarrow 0 \in \partial[\langle w, \beta\rangle - f(w)] \\ &\Leftrightarrow \beta \in \partial f(w) \\ &\Leftrightarrow w \in \partial f^*(\beta). \end{aligned}$$

The first equivalence follows from the optimality of $w$. The second follows from computation. To show the last equivalence, we apply the following theorem from convex analysis:

Theorem 3.5 (Rockafellar [19], Theorem 23.5; cf Corollary 10.1.1, Theorem 7.1). *Let $f : \mathbb{R}^d \to \mathbb{R}$ be convex and finite everywhere. Then*

$$x^* \in \partial f(x) \Leftrightarrow x \in \partial f^*(x^*).$$

□

Therefore, we have

Corollary 3.6. *The Strategic agent's best-response set is*

$$\arg\max_{\hat{x} \in \mathbb{R}^d} u(\hat{x}, x, \beta) = x + w^*(\beta) = x + \partial f^*(\beta),$$

which concludes the first step of the proof of Theorem 3.3.

We now move on to the second step. We want to show that $f^*$ is always finite and that the set of best responses of the strategic agent is non-empty and bounded.

Claim 2. *Under the assumptions in Theorem 3.3, $f^*(\beta)$ is finite for all $\beta \in \mathbb{R}^d$.*

See the full version for the proof.

We now turn our attention to the set of best responses. The following theorem guarantees that the strategic agents' best response correspondence is well behaved:

Theorem 3.7 (Rockafellar [19], Theorem 23.4). *Suppose $g : \mathbb{R}^d \to \mathbb{R}$ is convex and finite everywhere. Then $\partial g(x)$ is a non-empty and compact subset of $\mathbb{R}^d$ for all $x \in \mathbb{R}^d$.*

Since we showed that $f^*$ is convex and finite everywhere, this, together with Corollary 3.6, implies:

Corollary 3.8. *Under the assumption of Theorem 3.3, the set $\arg\max_{\hat{x} \in \mathbb{R}^d} u(\hat{x}, x, \beta)$ is non-empty and bounded for all $\beta \in \mathbb{R}^d$.*

The boundedness of the set $\arg\max_{\hat{x} \in \mathbb{R}^d} u(\hat{x}, x, \beta)$ is not directly used in the proof of Theorem 3.3, but it excludes the unrealistic situation in which the strategic agent's best response can be arbitrarily far from the origin. Thus we have completed the second step of the proof of Theorem 3.3.

The third step consists of showing the following claim:

Claim 3. *If $f : \mathbb{R}^d \to \mathbb{R}$ is convex and homogeneous of degree $r > 1$, then $f^* : \mathbb{R}^d \to \mathbb{R}$ is convex and homogeneous of degree $s > 1$, where $\frac{1}{r} + \frac{1}{s} = 1$.*

Throughout the rest of the paper, $(r, s)$ (and also $(p, q)$ which we will use when discussing norms) will refer to such a pair of numbers unless stated otherwise. For the proof of Claim 3, see the full version.

Finally we move to the fourth step of the proof. First we use a slightly more general version of Euler's theorem on homogeneous functions.

Theorem 3.9 (Euler). *Assume $g$ is convex and homogeneous of degree $k > 0$, then for any $v \in \partial g(x)$, $\langle v, x \rangle = kg(x)$.*

We make two quick observations about this version of Euler's theorem. First, this is a slightly more general statement than the standard statement of Euler's theorem in that it can deal with non-differentiable functions. Secondly, the value of the inner product is independent of the choice of the subgradient, which is interesting. Curious readers may refer to the full version[4] for the proof.

[4] Available on ArXiv at https://arxiv.org/abs/1710.07887.

Combining Claim 3 and Euler's theorem, if $f$ is convex and homogeneous of degree $r > 1$, we have that

$$\langle \hat{x}(\beta), \beta \rangle = \langle x, \beta \rangle + s f^*(\beta)$$

for any $\hat{x}(\beta) \in \arg\max_{\hat{x} \in \mathbb{R}^d} u(\hat{x}, x, \beta)$. This shows that $\langle \hat{x}(\beta), \beta \rangle$ is a well-defined convex function of $\beta$. This concludes the proof of Theorem 3.3.

## 3.2 Example distance functions

In this section we provide a large class of functions $f$ that satisfy the assumptions in Theorem 3.3. (Recall that we focus on distance functions of the form $d(x, x') = f(x - x')$.) We will also see that for this class of functions, we can derive simple closed form expressions for $f^*$, which will help us determine the convergence rate of the optimization procedure we develop in Section 4. We will also see some examples that violate our assumptions, which demonstrate the necessity of those assumptions; without them, agent best responses are not necessarily well-defined.

Claim 4. *For any arbitrary norm $||\cdot||$ on $\mathbb{R}^d$ and any $r > 1$*

$$f(x) = \frac{1}{r}||x||^r$$

*satisfies the conditions of Theorem 3.3. Namely,*

- *$f(x) > 0$ for all $x \neq 0$;*
- *$f$ is convex over $\mathbb{R}^d$;*
- *$f$ is positive homogeneous of degree $r > 1$.*

*Furthermore, let $||\cdot||_*$ be the dual norm of $||\cdot||$. $f^*$ has the following form:*

$$f^*(\beta) = \frac{1}{s}||\beta||_*^s.$$

*Here $1/r + 1/s = 1$.*

The conditions can be easily checked. See the full version for the derivation of $f^*$.

Corollary 3.10. *For any norm $||\cdot||$ on $\mathbb{R}^d$, any $r > 1$ and any invertible linear transformation $A : \mathbb{R}^d \to \mathbb{R}^d$, the function*

$$f(x) = \frac{1}{r}||Ax||^r$$

*satisfies all the conditions in Theorem 3.3. In this case, $f^*$ has the following form:*

$$f^*(\beta) = \frac{1}{s}||(A^T)^{-1}\beta||_*^s.$$

Proof. Since $||A(\cdot)||$ is also a norm, the conditions follow from Claim 4. The expression for $f^*$ follows from the identity

$$\langle x, \beta \rangle - g(Ax) = \langle Ax, (A^T)^{-1}\beta \rangle - g(Ax).$$

□

In particular, if $||\cdot||_2$ is the Euclidean 2-norm and $r = s = 2$, $f(x) = \frac{1}{2}||Ax||^2$ can be viewed as a form of *Mahalanobis distance*, commonly studied in the metric learning literature [17].

Combining Corollary 3.10, Theorem 3.2, and Theorem 3.3, we can naturally extend this general form of distance functions.

Corollary 3.11. *For any norm $||\cdot||$ on $\mathbb{R}^d$, any invertible linear transformation $A : \mathbb{R}^d \to \mathbb{R}^d$, and any $r > 1$, if an agent's utility is of the form*

$$u(\hat{x}, x, \beta) = \langle \hat{x}, \beta \rangle - \frac{1}{r}||Ax - A\hat{x}||^r,$$

*then both the logistic loss and and hinge loss are convex functions of $\beta$, assuming the agent best-responds to $\beta$.*

*Norms and Non-examples.* We present two non-examples of distance functions, which illustrate the following points:

(1) There exist functions $f$ which violate the condition that $f$ is nonvanishing except at the origin, for which strategic agents might not have finite best responses, and;
(2) When we let the power $r = 1$ (violating the $r > 1$ condition), again, strategic agents might not have finite best-responses.

Our first example shows that the linear transformation $A$ we used in Corollary 3.11 must be invertible, i.e. full rank. The second example shows that $f(x) = ||x||$ where $||\cdot||$ is a norm (not raised to any power $r > 1$) also fails to constrain the agent's best-responses to be finite.

To illustrate the first point, consider a utility function of the form used in Corollary 3.11 but with $A$ having non-trivial kernel. Assume $v \in \ker A, v \neq 0$. Note that $f(v) = 0$, violating our non-degeneracy condition. When $\hat{x} = x + \lambda v$, for any $\lambda \in \mathbb{R}$, the deviation incurs no cost since $v$ is in the kernel of $A$. Whenever $\beta$ is not orthogonal to $v$, therefore, the agents have no finite best response; they can increase their utility to $+\infty$ by letting $\lambda$ go to $+\infty$ or $-\infty$. Hence, for this choice of $f$, best-responses for the agents are not even well-defined.

It is also natural to ask what happens when $f$ is a norm, rather than a norm raised to some power $r$ greater than one. After all, any norm is positive homogeneous of degree one. In this case too, agent best responses are not necessarily well defined. The issue is that norms do not exhibit *diminishing returns* to the agent as he moves $\hat{x}$ increasingly far from $x$. Thus, the agent's best response would always be either to not manipulate at all (resulting in truthfully setting $\hat{x} = x$), or else to manipulate his data arbitrarily far from $x$, with arbitrarily high reward achievable. Formally,

Claim 5. *Suppose the agent's distance function is $d(\hat{x}, x) = ||\hat{x} - x||$ for some norm $||\cdot||$, and let $||\cdot||_*$ be the dual norm. Then his best response is $\hat{x} = x$ for $||\beta||_* \le 1$; and if $||\beta||_* > 1$, his best response is undefined with arbitrarily high utility achievable.*

Proof. Let $f$ be some norm, i.e. $f(z) = ||z||$. The agent wishes to solve

$$\begin{aligned}\sup_{\hat{x}} (\langle \hat{x}, \beta \rangle - f(\hat{x} - x)) = \\ &= \langle x, \beta \rangle + \sup_{\hat{x}} (\langle \hat{x} - x, \beta \rangle - f(\hat{x} - x)) \\ &= \langle x, \beta \rangle + \sup_{x'} \langle x', \beta \rangle - f(x') \\ &= \langle x, \beta \rangle + f^*(\beta)\end{aligned}$$

where $f^*$, the conjugate of $f$, is the $(0 - \infty)$ indicator function of the unit ball in the dual norm [19], namely

$$f^*(\beta) = \begin{cases} 0 & ||\beta||_* \leqslant 1 \\ \infty & \text{otherwise.} \end{cases}$$

This implies the claim. □

## 4 REGRET MINIMIZATION

In this section, we will present an online convex optimization method that has sub-linear Stackelberg regret. Our algorithm is a slight variant of the bandit algorithm in [12], which only uses zeroth-order feedback. That is, it only observes information of the form (input, function value). In our setting, the learner always has access to zeroth-order information, as she observes the loss function at a particular choice of parameters $\beta_t$. However, when a non-strategic agent arrives, the learner can also deduce *first-order* information, that is, the subgradient of the loss evaluated at $\beta_t$. Our algorithm takes advantage of this mixture of feedback and performs a full subgradient descent update for every non-strategic round. As a result, we obtain a regret rate that depends on the fraction of strategic agents that show up.

### 4.1 Convex Optimization with Mixture Feedback

In this section, we abstract away from the particular forms of the loss function until they become relevant. At a high level, our algorithm is running (stochastic) subgradient descent to minimize a sequence of convex loss functions $c_t(\beta)$ while the learner proposes a sequence of parameters $\beta_t$. The key challenge is to obtain subgradient feedback based on the agent's data $(\hat{x}, y)$. In each non-strategic round, we can explicitly compute a subgradient in $\partial c_t(\beta_t)$. In other words, we have first-order information. In each strategic round, however, since $\hat{x}_t$ is a function of $\beta_t$, we do not have direct access to the subgradients of $c_t$, and only see the "zeroth-order" information $c_t(\beta_t)$.

To estimate a subgradient with this information, we utilize the approach of Flaxman et al. [12] and minimize a "smoothed" version of the classification loss. In particular, for any $c_t$ and parameter $\delta$, the $\delta$-smoothed version of $c_t$ is defined as:

$$\tilde{c}_t(\beta) = \mathbb{E}[c_t(\beta + \delta S)]$$

where $S$ is a random vector drawn from the uniform distribution over the unit sphere in $\mathbb{R}^d$. Notice that $\tilde{c}_t$ is both convex and differentiable. Flaxman et al. [12] provides a method to obtain an unbiased estimate for the gradient of the smoothed loss $\tilde{c}$. This is done by perturbing $\beta_t$ to get a noisy $\beta_t^+$ and then evaluating the classification loss at $\beta_t^+$. More formally:

Lemma 4.1 ([12]). *Let $\beta_t^+ = \beta_t + \delta \cdot S$ and $G_t = \frac{d}{\delta} c_t(\beta_t^+) S$, where $S$ is a random vector drawn from the uniform distribution over the unit sphere in $\mathbb{R}^d$. Then $\mathbb{E}[G_t] = \nabla \tilde{c}_t(\beta_t)$.*

Note that the perturbed point $\beta_t^+$ may fall outside of the feasible set $K$. To prevent that, we will optimize over a strict subset $K_\delta = \{(1-\delta)\beta \mid \beta \in K\}$. Then we can guarantee that for any $\beta \in K_\delta$, the $\delta$-ball centered at $\beta$ is fully contained in $K$.[5]

Let $\theta = \frac{\#\{t: y_t = -1\}}{n}$ be the fraction of rounds in which the learner interacts with a strategic agent. For simplicity, we assume for now that $\theta$ is known to the algorithm in advance, and use it to set the parameters $\eta$ and $\delta$ in our algorithm. However, as we discuss at the end of this section, any upper bound $\hat{\theta}$ on $\theta$ suffices, and can be used in its place, at the cost of only an additional additive constant to the final regret bound. We are now ready to present our main algorithm in Algorithm 1.

Now we will proceed to bound the regret rate of our algorithm. To facilitate our analysis, we will make the following well-behaved assumption on the loss function $c_t$ for all rounds $t$:

- $|c_t(\beta)| \leqslant M$ for any $\beta \in K$, and
- $c_t$ is $L$-Lipschitz (with respect to the $\ell_2$ norm) over the set $K$.

In the full version, we work out the parameters $M$ and $L$ for both logistic loss and hinge loss, along with distance function of the form $d_t(x, y) = f(A_t(x - y))$ for the strategic agents.

[5] Any $\beta_t^+ = (1-\delta)\beta + \delta v$ for some $\beta \in K$ and some unit vector $v$. We assume $K$ contains the unit ball, in particular, both $v$ and $\beta$ are $K$, and $\beta_t^+$ is a convex combination of them, so it also lies in $K$.

**ALGORITHM 1:** Convex optimization with mixture feedback

**Input:** smoothing parameter $\delta = \theta^{1/4} \cdot \sqrt{\frac{dMR}{L(R+3)}} \cdot n^{-1/4}$, subset to optimize over $K_\delta \subset K$, step size $\eta = R/\sqrt{n(\theta \cdot \frac{d^2M^2}{\delta^2} + (1-\theta)L^2)}$

**For** each round $t$:

Let $S_t$ be drawn uniformly from the unit sphere;

Let $\beta_t^+ = \beta_t + \delta \cdot S_t$;

Query at $\beta_t^+$, observe corresponding $\hat{x}_t, y_t$, and suffer loss $c_t(\beta_t^+)$;

Compute stochastic subgradient:

**If** $y_t = 1$, then set $g_t$ as a subgradient in $\partial c_t(\beta_t)$; **otherwise** set $g_t = \frac{d}{\delta} \cdot c_t(\beta_t^+) \cdot S_t$ .

**Update:** $\beta_{t+1} = \Pi_{K_\delta}(\beta_t - \eta g_t)$, where $\Pi_{K_\delta}$ is the Euclidean projection map onto the set $K_\delta$.

The following lemma allows us to bound the regret separately in non-strategic and strategic rounds, and also bounds the additional regret due to the $\delta$-smoothing of our losses.

Lemma 4.2. *Let $T_1 := \{t : y_t = 1, t = 1, 2, \ldots, n\}$ be the non-strategic rounds and $T_{-1} := \{t : y_t = -1, t = 1, 2, \ldots, n\}$ be the strategic rounds. Then for any $\beta \in K$,*

$$\mathbb{E}\left[\sum_{t=1}^{n} c_t(\beta_t^+) - c_t(\beta)\right] \leqslant \mathbb{E}\left[\sum_{t\in T_{-1}} \tilde{c}_t(\beta_t) - \tilde{c}_t(\beta)\right] + \mathbb{E}\left[\sum_{t\in T_1} c_t(\beta_t) - c_t(\beta)\right] + 3nL\delta,$$

*where the expectation is taken over the randomness of the algorithm.*

Proof. Fix any $\beta \in K_\delta$. Since the vector $S$ is drawn from the unit sphere, $|c_t(\beta + \delta S) - c_t(\beta)| \leqslant L\|\delta S\| = L\delta$. Hence by taking expectation over $S$,

$$|\tilde{c}_t(\beta) - c_t(\beta)| \leqslant L\delta. \tag{2}$$

Recall that $\beta_t^+ = \beta_t + \delta \cdot S$, by Lipschitz property again, $|c_t(\beta_t^+) - c_t(\beta_t)| \leqslant L\delta$. For any $t \in T_{-1}$, we have

$$\begin{aligned} |c_t(\beta_t^+) - \tilde{c}_t(\beta_t)| &\leqslant |c_t(\beta_t^+) - c_t(\beta_t)| + |c_t(\beta_t) - \tilde{c}_t(\beta_t)| \\ &\leqslant L\delta + L\delta = 2L\delta. \end{aligned} \tag{3}$$

Now, we want to bound the difference between the two expressions, $c_t(\beta_t^+) - c_t(\beta)$ and $\tilde{c}_t(\beta_t) - \tilde{c}_t(\beta)$. By Equation (3), we have $|c_t(\beta_t^+) - \tilde{c}_t(\beta_t)| \leq 2L\delta$, and by Equation (2), we have $|c_t(\beta) - \tilde{c}_t(\beta)| \leq L\delta$. It follows that

$$c_t(\beta_t^+) - c_t(\beta) \leqslant \tilde{c}_t(\beta_t) - \tilde{c}_t(\beta) + 3L\delta.$$

Similarly, for any $t \in T_1$, we can bound

$$c_t(\beta_t^+) - c_t(\beta) \leqslant c_t(\beta_t) - c_t(\beta) + L\delta.$$

Summing over all rounds $t$, we recover the stated bound. □

By bounding the regret separately in non-strategic and strategic rounds, we can then bound the Stackelberg regret of Algorithm 1.

Theorem 4.3. *For any sequence of agents $A = (a_1, \ldots, a_n)$, Algorithm 1 will output a sequence of classifiers $B = (\beta_1, \ldots, \beta_n)$ such that the expected Stackelberg regret satisfies*

$$\mathbb{E}\left[\mathcal{R}_S(A, B)\right] \leqslant \frac{\eta}{2}[n\theta \cdot \frac{d^2M^2}{\delta^2} + n(1-\theta)L^2] + \frac{1}{2\eta}R^2 + 3nL\delta + nLR\delta.$$

Proof. Our proof essentially follows from the standard analysis for online subgradient descent. We will first bound

$$\mathbb{E}\left[\sum_{t\in T_{-1}} \tilde{c}_t(\beta_t) - \tilde{c}_t(\beta^*)\right] + \mathbb{E}\left[\sum_{t\in T_1} c_t(\beta_t) - c_t(\beta^*)\right]$$

which then allows us to apply Lemma 4.2. By convexity, we get for any $\beta \in K$,

$$\tilde{c}_t(\beta_t) - \tilde{c}_t(\beta) \leqslant \langle \nabla\tilde{c}_t(\beta_t), \beta_t - \beta\rangle$$

and for any subgradient $G_t(\beta) \in \partial c_t(\beta_t)$,

$$c_t(\beta_t) - c_t(\beta) \leqslant \langle G_t(\beta), \beta_t - \beta\rangle.$$

$$\begin{aligned}\tilde{c}_t(\beta_t^+) - \tilde{c}_t(\beta) &= [\tilde{c}_t(\beta_t^+) - \tilde{c}_t(\beta_t)] + [\tilde{c}_t(\beta_t) - \tilde{c}_t(\beta)] \\ &\leqslant L_0\delta + \tilde{c}_t(\beta_t) - \tilde{c}_t(\beta)\end{aligned}$$

Recall that for any $t \in T_1$, $g_t \in \partial c_t(\beta_t)$, and by Lemma 4.1, we know for $t \in T_{-1}$, we can write $g_t = \nabla\tilde{c}_t(\beta_t) - \xi_t$ where $\xi_t$ is a random vector with zero mean. Let $\beta' \in \arg\min_{\beta\in K_\delta} \sum_{t=1}^n c_t(\beta)$, then

$$\sum_{t\in T_{-1}} [\tilde{c}_t(\beta_t) - \tilde{c}_t(\beta')] + \sum_{t\in T_1} [c_t(\beta_t) - c_t(\beta')] \leqslant \sum_{t=1}^n \langle g_t, \beta_t - \beta'\rangle + \sum_{t\in T_{-1}} \langle \xi_t, \beta_t - \beta'\rangle.$$

Taking the expectation, we have

$$\mathbb{E}[\sum_{t\in T_{-1}} \tilde{c}_t(\beta_t) - \tilde{c}_t(\beta')] + \mathbb{E}[\sum_{t\in T_1} c_t(\beta_t) - c_t(\beta')] \leqslant \mathbb{E}\sum_{t=1}^n \langle g_t, \beta_t - \beta'\rangle. \tag{4}$$

Now we can employ the standard cosine law trick (see e.g. [9], [5]) and get:

$$\langle g_t, \beta_t - \beta'\rangle \leqslant \frac{\eta}{2}\|g_t\|^2 + \frac{1}{2\eta}(\|\beta' - \beta_t\|^2 - \|\beta' - \beta_{t+1}\|^2)$$

Summing them up, telescoping and leaving out the negative term yields:

$$\sum_{t=1}^n \langle g_t, \beta_t - \beta'\rangle \leqslant \frac{\eta}{2}\sum_{t=1}^n \|g_t\|^2 + \frac{1}{2\eta}\|\beta' - \beta_1\|^2 \tag{5}$$

Since we have

$$\|g_t\| \leqslant \begin{cases} L, & y_t = 0, \\ \frac{d}{\delta}\cdot M, & y_t = 1, \end{cases}$$

Combining (4) and (5) and using the above bound for $g_t$, we get

$$\mathbb{E}[\sum_{t\in T_{-1}} \tilde{c}_t(\beta_t) - \tilde{c}_t(\beta')] + \mathbb{E}[\sum_{t\in T_1} c_t(\beta_t) - c_t(\beta')] \leqslant \frac{\eta}{2}[n\theta\cdot\frac{d^2M^2}{\delta^2} + n(1-\theta)L^2] + \frac{1}{2\eta}R^2. \tag{6}$$

Finally, we need bound the additional error we incur for restricting to the subset $K_\delta$. Since for any point $\beta \in K$, the closet point to $\beta$ in $K_\delta$ has $\ell_2$ distance no more than $\delta R$, by the Lipschitz property of each $c_t$, we know

$$\sum_{t=1}^n c_t(\beta') - \min_{\beta\in K}\sum_{t=1}^n c_t(\beta) \leq nLR\delta \tag{7}$$

Our regret bound then follows from Equation (6) and Equation (7). □

In Corollary 4.4, we provide a regret rate for three different regimes of $p$ (hiding dependence on $M$, $L$, and $R$).

Corollary 4.4. *For different ranges of $\theta$, we can bound the expected Stackelberg regret by*

$$\mathbb{E}\left[\mathcal{R}_S(A,B)\right] \leqslant \begin{cases} O(\sqrt{n}), & \theta = 0, \\ O(\sqrt{d}n^{3/4}), & \theta = \Omega(1), \\ O(\sqrt{d}n^{1-\frac{1+\gamma}{4}}) & \theta = O(n^{-\gamma}) \end{cases}$$

Proof. Plugging the algorithm parameter $\eta = R/\sqrt{n(\theta \cdot \frac{d^2M^2}{\delta^2} + (1-\theta)L^2)}$ into the regret bound in Theorem 4.3,

$$\mathcal{R}_S \leqslant \sqrt{\theta \cdot \frac{d^2M^2}{\delta^2} + (1-\theta)L^2} \cdot \sqrt{n} \cdot R + n\delta L(R+3).$$

Using $\sqrt{a+b} \leqslant \sqrt{a} + \sqrt{b}$, we can further simplify the bound:

$$\mathcal{R}_S \leqslant \sqrt{n\theta} \cdot \frac{dMR}{\delta} + LR\sqrt{n(1-\theta)} + n\delta L(R+3).$$

Plugging in $\delta = \theta^{1/4} \cdot \sqrt{\frac{dMR}{L(R+3)}} \cdot n^{-1/4}$ yields:

$$\mathcal{R}_S \leqslant LR\sqrt{n(1-\theta)} + n^{3/4}\sqrt{dMLR(R+3)}\theta^{1/4}.$$

The rest of the result follows by setting $\theta = 0, \Omega(1)$ or $O(n^{-\gamma})$. □

*Relaxing $\theta$ to $\hat{\theta}$.* Let $\hat{\theta}$ be an upper bound on the true fraction of strategic agents in rounds $1, 2, \ldots, n$, i.e. $\theta \leqslant \hat{\theta}$. We briefly explain why $\hat{\theta}$ can be used in place of $\theta$ in setting the parameters of Algorithm 1, and Corollary 4.4 still holds (with $\hat{\theta}$ replacing $\theta$ in the bound.) First, consider the case in which $\frac{dM}{\delta} \geqslant L$. In this case, the right hand side of the bound in Theorem 4.3 is increasing in $\theta$, so we can replace $\theta$ with $\hat{\theta}$ and still get a correct regret bound:

$$\mathbb{E}\left[\mathcal{R}_S(A,B)\right] \leqslant \frac{\eta}{2}[n\hat{\theta} \cdot \frac{d^2M^2}{\delta^2} + n(1-\hat{\theta})L^2] + \frac{1}{2\eta}R^2 + 3nL\delta + nLR\delta.$$

Thus, we can carry out the calculations from the proof of Corollary 4.4, again with $\hat{\theta}$ replacing $\theta$. Finally, it is not hard to show that when $n \geqslant (\frac{L}{dM})^2$, we are in the case in which $\frac{dM}{\delta} \geqslant L$. Since we assume $c_t(\beta) \leqslant M$, each round incurs regret at most $2M$. Therefore in the remaining case in which $n < (\frac{L}{dM})^2$, we can upper bound the regret by $2M \cdot n \leqslant 2M \cdot (\frac{L}{dM})^2$. Hence, we obtain the regret bound

$$\mathcal{R}_S \leqslant \max\left\{LR\sqrt{n(1-\hat{\theta})} + n^{3/4}\sqrt{dMLR(R+3)}\hat{\theta}^{1/4}, \frac{2L^2}{d^2M}\right\}.$$

The new (second) term in the maximum is independent of $n$, and so does not change the asymptotic bound stated in Corollary 4.4.

*Applying other tools for bandit convex optimization.* We can in fact apply other tools for bandit convex optimization to minimize regret. For example, we can use the algorithm in [10], which will achieve a Stackelberg regret rate of $\tilde{O}(d^{9.5}\sqrt{n})$ even when all the agents are strategic (that is $p = 1$). Our algorithm, which is a variant of [12], has a regret rate with a worse dependence on the time horizon, but has a milder dependence on the dimension. Furthermore, it also permits a natural interpolation between the fully strategic and fully non-strategic settings (as shown in Corollary 4.4).

*Deriving the Constants.* In the full version, we first illustrate how to determine the constants $L$ and $M$ that appear in our regret bound for general classes of cost functions $d(x, y)$, namely any abstract norm raised to some power greater than 1:

$$d(x, x') = \frac{1}{r}\|x - x'\|^r.$$

The constant $C$ in the inequality $\|x\|_2 \leqslant C\|x\|$ can be used to determine $L$ and $M$. See the full version for details.

We also give explicit expressions for $L$ and $M$ when the abstract norm is some $p$-norm with $p \geqslant 1$ in the full version.

All assumptions and the resulting fully expanded regret bound are described in the full version. We state here a noteworthy special case that has an especially mild dependence on the dimension $d$:

When $1 \leqslant p \leqslant 2$, and for any power $r > 1$, Algorithm 1 has regret bound:

$$\mathbb{E}\left[\mathcal{R}_S(A, B)\right] \leqslant \begin{cases} O(\sqrt{n}), & \theta = 0, \\ O(\sqrt{d}n^{3/4}), & \theta = \Omega(1), \\ O(\sqrt{d}n^{1-\frac{1+\gamma}{4}}), & \theta = O(n^{-\gamma}). \end{cases}$$

i.e. for $p$ norms when $1 \leqslant p \leqslant 2$, regardless of the power $r > 1$, we obtain a fixed (and mild) dependence on $d$. When $p > 2$, the situation changes: our dependence on $d$ grows with $p$, and shrinks with $r$.

## 5 DISCUSSION AND OPEN QUESTIONS

Our work suggests a number of interesting directions. Broadly speaking, these can be grouped into two thrusts: *broadening* the class of problems to which our approach can be applied, and *weakening* the assumptions that need to be made about the agents. Here we list a concrete example of each type of question.

The broad approach we take in this paper is to identify classes of utility functions for the strategic agents, that, when paired with natural cost functions for the learner, lead to a convex objective, even in the strategic setting. However, this precludes several natural utility functions for the agents: most notably, utility functions that are defined in terms of 0/1 classification loss. What can be done in the face of non-convexity? When agent cost functions $d$ are known and *separable*, [14] show that even for 0/1 loss, Stackelberg equilibria have structure that allows for their efficient computation, despite non-convexity of the learner's objective. Can similar structure be taken advantage of in the setting we consider, when agent cost functions are not known to the learner?

Next, the overarching motivation of this paper is to weaken the assumptions on the knowledge of the learner necessary to solve the strategic classification problem. We should also aim to weaken other assumptions. For example, we assume in this paper that strategic agents play exact best responses — i.e. the always exactly optimize their utility function. What if strategic agents are not perfect – i.e. they are only guaranteed to play approximate best responses (or, perhaps only *usually* guaranteed to). Is it possible to give optimization procedures with guarantees that are robust to strategic agent imperfection?

## REFERENCES

[1] Kareem Amin, Rachel Cummings, Lili Dworkin, Michael Kearns, and Aaron Roth. 2015. Online Learning and Profit Maximization from Revealed Preferences.. In *AAAI*. 770–776.

[2] Maria-Florina Balcan, Avrim Blum, Nika Haghtalab, and Ariel D. Procaccia. 2015. Commitment Without Regrets: Online Learning in Stackelberg Security Games. In *Proceedings of the Sixteenth ACM Conference on Economics and Computation, EC '15, Portland, OR, USA, June 15-19, 2015*. 61–78. https://doi.org/10.1145/2764468.2764478

[3] Maria-Florina Balcan, Amit Daniely, Ruta Mehta, Ruth Urner, and Vijay V Vazirani. 2014. Learning economic parameters from revealed preferences. In *International Conference on Web and Internet Economics*. Springer, 338–353.

[4] Eyal Beigman and Rakesh Vohra. 2006. Learning from revealed preference. In *Proceedings of the 7th ACM Conference on Electronic Commerce*. ACM, 36–42.

[5] Aharon Ben-Tal and Arkadi Nemirovski. 2001. *Lectures on modern convex optimization: analysis, algorithms, and engineering applications*. SIAM.

[6] Michael Brückner, Christian Kanzow, and Tobias Scheffer. 2012. Static prediction games for adversarial learning problems. *Journal of Machine Learning Research* 13, Sep (2012), 2617–2654.

[7] Michael Brückner and Tobias Scheffer. 2009. Nash equilibria of static prediction games. In *Advances in neural information processing systems*. 171–179.

[8] Michael Brückner and Tobias Scheffer. 2011. Stackelberg games for adversarial prediction problems. In *Proceedings of the 17th ACM SIGKDD international conference on Knowledge discovery and data mining*. ACM, 547–555.

[9] Sébastien Bubeck. 2015. Convex Optimization: Algorithms and Complexity. *Foundations and Trends in Machine Learning* 8, 3-4 (2015), 231–357. https://doi.org/10.1561/2200000050

[10] Sébastien Bubeck, Yin Tat Lee, and Ronen Eldan. 2017. Kernel-based methods for bandit convex optimization. (2017), 72–85. https://doi.org/10.1145/3055399.3055403

[11] Nilesh Dalvi, Pedro Domingos, Sumit Sanghai, and Deepak Verma. 2004. Adversarial classification. In *Proceedings of the tenth ACM SIGKDD international conference on Knowledge discovery and data mining*. ACM, 99–108.

[12] Abraham D Flaxman, Adam Tauman Kalai, and H Brendan McMahan. 2005. Online convex optimization in the bandit setting: gradient descent without a gradient. In *Proceedings of the sixteenth annual ACM-SIAM symposium on Discrete algorithms*. Society for Industrial and Applied Mathematics, 385–394.

[13] Michael Großhans, Christoph Sawade, Michael Brückner, and Tobias Scheffer. 2013. Bayesian games for adversarial regression problems. In *International Conference on Machine Learning*. 55–63.

[14] Moritz Hardt, Nimrod Megiddo, Christos Papadimitriou, and Mary Wootters. 2016. Strategic classification. In *Proceedings of the 2016 ACM Conference on Innovations in Theoretical Computer Science*. ACM, 111–122.

[15] Shahin Jabbari, Ryan M Rogers, Aaron Roth, and Steven Z Wu. 2016. Learning from rational behavior: Predicting solutions to unknown linear programs. In *Advances in Neural Information Processing Systems*. 1570–1578.

[16] Dmytro Korzhyk, Vincent Conitzer, and Ronald Parr. 2010. Complexity of Computing Optimal Stackelberg Strategies in Security Resource Allocation Games.. In *AAAI*.

[17] Brian Kulis et al. 2013. Metric learning: A survey. *Foundations and Trends® in Machine Learning* 5, 4 (2013), 287–364.

[18] Wei Liu and Sanjay Chawla. 2009. A game theoretical model for adversarial learning. In *Data Mining Workshops, 2009. ICDMW'09. IEEE International Conference on*. IEEE, 25–30.

[19] Ralph Tyrell Rockafellar. 1970. *Convex analysis*. Princeton University Press.

[20] Aaron Roth, Aleksandrs Slivkins, Jonathan Ullman, and Zhiwei Steven Wu. 2017. Multidimensional Dynamic Pricing for Welfare Maximization. In *Proceedings of the 2017 ACM Conference on Economics and Computation*. ACM, 519–536.

[21] Aaron Roth, Jonathan Ullman, and Zhiwei Steven Wu. 2016. Watch and learn: Optimizing from revealed preferences feedback. In *Proceedings of the forty-eighth annual ACM symposium on Theory of Computing*. ACM, 949–962.

[22] Milind Tambe. 2011. *Security and game theory: algorithms, deployed systems, lessons learned*. Cambridge University Press.

[23] Morteza Zadimoghaddam and Aaron Roth. 2012. Efficiently Learning from Revealed Preference.. In *WINE*. Springer, 114–127.

[24] Martin Zinkevich. 2003. Online convex programming and generalized infinitesimal gradient ascent. In *Proceedings of the 20th International Conference on Machine Learning (ICML-03)*. 928–936.

# Overabundant Information and Learning Traps

ANNIE LIANG, University of Pennsylvania
XIAOSHENG MU, Harvard University

Full Paper: https://papers.ssrn.com/sol3/papers.cfm?abstract_id=3057805

CCS Concepts: • **Applied computing → Economics; Multi-criterion optimization and decision-making;**

Additional Key Words and Phrases: Information Acquisition; Correlated Information; Social Learning; Information Aggregation

In many learning problems, agents cannot design their information in a completely flexible way. Instead, they choose from a given, finite (though often large) set of information sources. For instance, a researcher studying the genetic determinants of depression cannot, at any cost, access an arbitrarily precise signal about the magnitude of this effect. He can, however, acquire many kinds of information related to it; for example, he might obtain neurochemical and genetic data, or analyze the incidence of depression in different groups.

When information is heterogeneous in this way, the value of new information depends on its relationship to information that has already been acquired. Consequently, current information acquisitions shape future information acquisitions. For example, research on how to interpret serotonin levels increases the value of future serotonin measurements. Such externalities are particularly relevant in settings (e.g. research) in which information is passed on over time, and acquisition of new kinds of information is based on an existing body of knowledge.

This paper characterizes the consequences of these externalities for long-run aggregation of information. We show that there are two starkly different possibilities:

- *Efficient information aggregation:* Past information helps future agents identify the "best" kinds of information. At all sufficiently late periods, a social planner cannot improve on the history of acquisitions.
- *Learning traps:* Past information pushes future decision-makers to acquire information that leads to inefficiently slow learning. Early suboptimal choices propagate over time.

Our main contribution is to show that which of these long-run outcomes obtains depends on a simple property of the correlation structure across sources.

Our model is as follows. Agents are indexed by (discrete) time and sequentially choose from a large number of information sources, each identified with a signal about the payoff-relevant state. To permit flexible correlations across sources, we introduce payoff-irrelevant "confounding terms" that are common across sources. Each kind of information is a (noisy) linear combination of the payoff-relevant state and these confounding variables.

In contrast to the classic sequential learning model [1, 2, 4], we suppose that all information realizations are public. This departure permits us to focus on the externalities created by choice of

Authors' addresses: Annie Liang, University of Pennsylvania, anliang@upenn.edu; Xiaosheng Mu, Harvard University, xiaoshengmu@fas.harvard.edu.


*ACM EC'18, June 18–22, 2018, Ithaca, NY, USA.* ACM ISBN 978-1-4503-4529-3/18/06.
https://doi.org/10.1145/3219166.3219210

kind of information, as opposed to the more frequently studied frictions that emerge from inference. We assume that each agent takes an action based on all information acquired up to (and including) himself, and maximizes a private objective that depends only on his action and the payoff-relevant state. We work with normal signals, which gives the additional tractability that signal choices depend only on the history of acquisitions, but not the history of signal realizations: the information choice that maximizes payoffs for each agent will be the one that maximizes that period's reduction of uncertainty about the payoff-relevant state.

Our focus is on informationally overabundant settings, in which some kinds of information are redundant. Formally, agents can completely learn the payoff-relevant state from various (proper) subsets of signals. As a benchmark, we first derive the *optimal* long-run frequency of signal acquisitions, corresponding to the choices that maximize speed of information revelation about the payoff-relevant state.

We then show that whether society's acquisitions converge to this optimal long-run frequency depends critically on how many signals are needed to identify this state. The key intuition refers back to an observation made in Sethi and Yildiz [3]: An agent who repeatedly observes a source confounded by an unknown parameter learns *both* about the payoff-relevant state and also about the confounding term, and hence improves his interpretation of this source over time. In our setting, where a single confounding term can affect multiple sources, there is a further spillover effect: learning from one source helps agents to interpret information from all sources confounded by the same parameters.

Suppose then that there are $K$ unknowns in total (the single payoff-relevant state and $K - 1$ additional confounding terms), and agents can only recover the payoff-relevant state by observing $K$ sources. Endogenously, agents will observe some $K$ sources and learn not just the payoff-relevant state but also all confounding states. This leads them to eventually evaluate *all* sources by an "objective" asymptotic criterion, and discover the best set of sources. More formally, we obtain the following result: If $K$ sources are required to recover the payoff-relevant state, then long-run acquisitions are optimal, independently of the prior belief.

In contrast, if it is possible to learn the payoff-relevant state from fewer than $K$ sources, then inefficient long-run learning may obtain. This is because repeated observation of fewer than $K$ information sources will not reveal all of the confounding terms, leading agents to persistently undervalue sources that provide information confounded by the remaining unknowns. Our second main result says that any set of fewer than $K$ sources that recovers the payoff-relevant state is a "learning trap" under some prior beliefs. We further show that the long-run inefficiency under a learning trap—measured as the ratio of the optimal speed of learning to the achieved speed of learning—can be arbitrarily large.

## REFERENCES

[1] Abhijit Banerjee. 1992. A Simple Model of Herd Behavior. *Quaterly Journal of Economics* 107, 3 (1992), 797–817.

[2] Sushil Bikhchandani, David Hirshleifer, and Ivo Welch. 1992. A Theory of Fads, Fashion, Custom, and Cultural Change as Information Cascades. *Journal of Political Economy* 100, 5 (1992), 992–1026.

[3] Rajiv Sethi and Muhamet Yildiz. 2016. Communication with Unknown Perspectives. *Econometrica* 84, 6 (2016), 2029–2069.

[4] Lones Smith and Peter Sorenson. 2000. Pathological Outcomes of Observational Learning. *Econometrica* (2000).

# Combinatorial Auctions with Endowment Effect

MOSHE BABAIOFF, Microsoft Research, Israel
SHAHAR DOBZINSKI, Weizmann Institute of Science, Israel
SIGAL OREN, Ben-Gurion University of the Negev, Israel

We study combinatorial auctions with bidders that exhibit endowment effect. In most of the previous work on cognitive biases in algorithmic game theory (e.g., [Kleinberg and Oren, EC'14] and its follow-ups) the focus was on analyzing the implications and mitigating their negative consequences. In contrast, in this paper we show how in some cases cognitive biases can be harnessed to obtain better outcomes.

Specifically, we study Walrasian equilibria in combinatorial markets. It is well known that Walrasian equilibria exist only in limited settings, e.g., when all valuations are gross substitutes, but fails to exist in more general settings, e.g., when the valuations are submodular. We consider combinatorial settings in which bidders exhibit the *endowment effect*, that is, their value for items increases with ownership.

Our main result shows that when the valuations are submodular, even a mild degree of endowment effect is sufficient to guarantee the existence of Walrasian equilibria. In fact, we show that in contrast to Walrasian equilibria with standard utility maximizing bidders – in which the equilibrium allocation must be efficient – when bidders exhibit endowment effect any *local* optimum can be an equilibrium allocation.

Our techniques reveal interesting connections between the LP relaxation of combinatorial auctions and local maxima. We also provide lower bounds on the intensity of the endowment effect that the bidders must have in order to guarantee the existence of a Walrasian equilibrium in various settings.

## 1 INTRODUCTION

Research in algorithmic mechanism design typically assumes that bidders are utility maximizers, i.e., they maximize their value for the chosen alternative minus their payment. However, empirical evidence from behavioral economics suggests that this assumption is often inaccurate. In practice, individuals tend to exhibit different cognitive biases that are not captured by the classic model of utility maximization. For example, the price tag might affect their value for a bottle of wine (irrational value assessment); or they may attribute higher values to items once they own them (endowment effect).

A recent line of work in algorithmic game theory (Kleinberg and Oren 2014 and their follow-ups [1–3, 14, 23, 24, 33]) mathematically models and analyzes the behavior of agents that exhibit cognitive biases in planning settings. In contrast, in this paper we initiate the study of cognitive biases in the central setting of algorithmic mechanism design: combinatorial auctions.[1] Furthermore, this line of work mostly focused on analyzing the implications of cognitive biases and mitigating

[1]In the context of algorithmic mechanism design, the only paper that incorporates behavioral assumptions that we are aware of is [8]. The paper applies prospect theory to a crowdsourcing setting.

The second author was partially supported by BSF grant no. 2016192.

Authors' addresses: Moshe Babaioff, Microsoft Research, Israel, moshe@microsoft.com; Shahar Dobzinski, Weizmann Institute of Science, Israel, shahar.dobzinski@weizmann.ac.il; Sigal Oren, Ben-Gurion University of the Negev, Israel, orensi@cs.bgu.ac.il.


*ACM EC'18, June 18–22, 2018, Ithaca, NY, USA.* ACM ISBN 978-1-4503-5829-3/18/06...$15.00
https://doi.org/10.1145/3219166.3219197

their *negative* consequences. In this paper we take a different approach and show that in some settings cognitive biases can be harnessed to obtain *better* outcomes.

Walrasian equilibrium is the traditional concept of market equilibrium. Roughly speaking, a market is in Walrasian equilibrium if there exists a price for each item such that every bidder is allocated his most profitable bundle and all items are allocated. Walrasian equilibria are attractive since they are simple and since their pricing structure is easy to understand. Not only that, it is also guaranteed that any allocation of such an equilibrium must be efficient (the "First Welfare Theorem").

A major downside of Walrasian equilibria is that often they do not exist at all. In the context of combinatorial auctions it is known that a Walrasian equilibrium is guaranteed to exist when the valuations are gross substitutes [15]. This relatively small class of valuations is in a (formal) sense the maximal one guaranteeing existence [15]. In particular, a Walrasian equilibrium is not guaranteed to exist if the valuations are submodular.

In this paper we consider bidders in combinatorial auctions that exhibit an endowment effect. Our main contribution is utilizing the cognitive biases of the bidders to extend the valuations classes for which a Walrasian equilibrium exists: if bidders exhibit a mild endowment effect then a Walrasian equilibrium is guaranteed to exist even when the valuations are submodular.

Before formally presenting our model and results, we now discuss the endowment effect.

**Endowment Effect.** Do owning items makes them more valuable to us? The Nobel Laureate economist Richard Thaler coined the term endowment effect [34] to explain situations in which the mere possession of an item makes it more valuable. An experiment by Knetsch 1989 provides a stark illustration: two groups of students received goods in return for filling out a questionnaire. One group received mugs and the other chocolate bars. Next, the students were given the option to swap items. Since the items were allocated to the students randomly, we expect that about half of them would have received the less desirable item and would like to switch. In contrary to this logic, 90% of the students in each group decided to keep their endowed item.

A classic experiment by Kahneman, Knetsch and Thaler 1990 attempts to quantify the endowment effect. In this experiment half of the students in a Law and Economics class at Cornell University received a $6 mug. After examining the mug, the students who received the mug were asked at which price are they willing to sell the mug (willingness to accept). The students who did not receive the mug were asked for the price they are willing to pay for the mug (willingness to pay). As in the Knetch's experiment, one could have expected that about 50% of the mug owners could be matched with a buyer that values the mug more than they do. However, in the experiment only 20% of the mug owners sold their mug. Moreover, there was a significant gap between the median price sellers were willing to sell at ($5.25), and the median price that buyers where willing to buy at ($2.25).

The endowment effect can be thought of as a special case of the status quo bias [31], according to which individuals have a strong preference for the current state (i.e., a mug owner prefers to stay a mug owner). Kahneman et al. 1990, 1991 claim that loss aversion from prospect theory [21] is the source of the endowment effect (i.e., for a mug owner exchanging the mug for a chocolate bar entails *losing* the mug). Kőszegi and Rabin 2006 incorporate reference points and expectations into prospect theory. Their framework suggests that the endowment effect will only appear in settings in which individuals do not expect to trade.[2] Masatlioglu and Ok 2005 propose a model in which the individuals make a rational choice on a constrained set of alternatives defined according to the status quo.

[2]See [9, 28] for some experimental work supporting this prediction.

Several papers study endowment effect in auction settings (e.g., [17, 26]). However, apart from [5] that discusses the endowment effect with multiple identical goods, all considered the single item setting, leaving open the question of incorporating the endowment effect into the more general combinatorial auctions setting.

**The Model.** We consider a combinatorial auction with $n$ bidders and a set $M$ of $m$ items. Each bidder $i$ has a valuation function $v_i : 2^M \rightarrow \mathbb{R}_+$ that specifies his value for every bundle. The valuation function is non-decreasing and normalized ($v_i(\emptyset) = 0$).

Our modeling of the endowment effect is driven by the essence of this effect: an individual attributes an item a higher value after owning it; his value for items that he does not own remains the same. Formally, bidder $i$ who previously valued item $a$ at $v_i(a)$ will now value it at $\alpha_i \cdot v_i(a)$ for some $\alpha_i \geq 1$.[3] Similarly, when turning to the more general setting of combinatorial auctions we define the value of a bundle $S_i$ that bidder $i$ owns as $\alpha_i \cdot v_i(S_i)$. Note that it is insufficient to define the new value of bidder $i$ only for the bundle $S_i$, we also need to define how the value of any other bundle $T$ changes when bidder $i$ owns $S_i$. We follow a similar line of reasoning: the value of the items in $S_i \cap T$ is multiplied by $\alpha_i$, while the marginal contribution of the remaining items $T - S_i$ remains the same. Formally, we define the endowed valuation of player $i$ with $\alpha_i$ who is endowed with bundle $S_i$ to be:[4]

$$\forall T \subseteq M,\ v_i^{S_i,\alpha_i}(T) = \alpha_i \cdot v_i(S_i \cap T) + v_i(T - S_i | S_i \cap T)$$

where $v(X|Y) = v(X \cup Y) - v(Y)$ denotes the marginal contribution of the bundle $X$ given $Y$.

Recall that a Walrasian equilibrium consists of an allocation $(S_1, \ldots, S_n)$ and prices $(p_1, \ldots, p_m)$ such that:

(1) For each player $i$, $v_i(S_i) - \sum_{j \in S_i} p_j \geq v_i(T) - \sum_{j \in T} p_j$, for every bundle $T \subseteq M$.
(2) If $j \notin \cup_i S_i$ then $p_j = 0$.

Several works attempted to relax the definition of a Walrasian Equilibrium in order to ensure existence [12, 13][5]. Our approach is different; Given that the endowment effect changes the valuations anyways, we are simply interested in a Walrasian equilibrium with respect to the endowed valuations: an allocation $S$ and non-negative item prices $(p_1, \ldots, p_m)$ form an $(\alpha_1, \ldots, \alpha_n)$*-endowed equilibrium* in an instance $(v_1, \ldots, v_n)$ if they constitute a Walrasian equilibrium in the instance $(v_1^{S_1,\alpha_1}, \ldots, v_n^{S_n,\alpha_n})$.

When $\alpha = \alpha_1 = \ldots = \alpha_n$ we use the compact notation $\alpha$*-endowed equilibrium*. Let $S$ be the allocation and $(p_1, \ldots, p_m)$ be the prices of some $(\alpha_1, \ldots, \alpha_n)$-endowed equilibrium. Observe that $S$ and $(p_1, \ldots, p_m)$ also form an $(\alpha, \alpha, \ldots, \alpha)$-endowed equilibrium, for $\alpha = \max_i \alpha_i$. The reason is that when $S_i$ maximizes the profit of $v_i^{S_i,\alpha_i}$, it also maximizes the profit of $v_i^{S_i,\alpha'}$, for every $\alpha' > \alpha_i$. Thus, in the rest of the paper we let $\alpha = \max_i \alpha_i$ and focus on $\alpha$-endowed equilibria.

Note that for $\alpha = 1$ we recover the classic notion of Walrasian Equilibrium while, roughly speaking, as $\alpha$ goes to infinity the players insist more and more on keeping the bundle they were

[3]The case $0 \leq \alpha_i < 1$ is also of conceptual interest. In particular, it models situations of the type "the grass is always greener on the other side", when a person values items less once he owns them. The analysis of this case is technically simpler and is provided in in the full version.

[4]One can also give a "classic" interpretation that does not involve cognitive biases to this transformation: consider an environment with transaction costs, e.g., a company that acquires a new location might be subject to property taxes and/or have to invest in new infrastructure. Similarly, a shop that moves to a new location might have to start a costly advertising campaign to inform its costumers about the move. In all these cases after owning their resources the preference of the agents to the new status quo allocation increases.

[5]Feldman et al. 2016 use bundle prices instead of individual item prices and do not require market clearance; Fu et al. 2012 define a conditional equilibrium where each player does not wish to add any items to the bundle he was allocated. Also related are works on simultaneous first [16] and second price [7] auctions.

allocated.[6] Throughout the paper we say that $\alpha$ *supports* an allocation $S$ if there exist item prices that together with $S$ form an $\alpha$-endowed equilibrium.

**Results.** Analyzing Walrasian equilibria in the context of endowed valuations brings with it a natural question: when does an endowed equilibrium exist? The simple answer is *always*; we show that in any instance there exists an $\alpha > 1$ and an allocation for which an $\alpha$-endowed equilibrium exists. However, this answer completely misses the point as the value of $\alpha$ for which an endowed equilibrium exists might be huge. Recall that the value of $\alpha$ corresponds to the intensity of the endowment effect, thus we expect $\alpha$-endowed equilibria that arise in practice to have small value of $\alpha$ (in the experiment of [19] mentioned above, for example, it seems like $\alpha$ was about 2). This leads us to the definition of the endowment gap – the minimal value of $\alpha$ for which a Walrasian Equilibrium is guaranteed to exist. Thus, the main question that we ask in this paper is *what is the endowment gap for different valuation classes?*

Our main result shows that for submodular valuations there is always an allocation that is supported by $\alpha = 2$. That is, *in combinatorial auctions with submodular valuations the endowment gap is at most* 2.

The proof of the theorem is constructive: an allocation is a local maximum if the welfare of the allocation cannot be improved by moving a single item from one player to another. We show that in any instance of combinatorial auctions with submodular valuations *any local maximum* is supported by $\alpha = 2$. In contrast, the First Welfare Theorem asserts that the allocation in a Walrasian equilibrium is a *global* optimum. Hence, a local maximum that is not a global maximum can be part of a 2-endowed equilibrium, but cannot be a part of a Walrasian equilibrium.

Our work reveals interesting connections between the integrality gap of the linear program relaxation for combinatorial auctions and the endowment gap. Nisan and Segal 2006 show that a Walrasian equilibrium exists if and only if the integrality gap of a natural relaxation of the LP for combinatorial auctions (the "configuration LP") is 1, in other words, if and only if there is an optimal integral solution to the LP. This in turn implies that an (integral) allocation $S$ is supported by $\alpha$ if and only if it is an optimal solution of the (fractional) LP with respect to the perturbed valuations.

An equivalent geometric interpretation is the following: consider the polytope defined by a given instance of a combinatorial auction. With submodular valuations, there might not be any optimal integral solution on a vertex of the polytope. Fix some allocation and consider the change to the objective function of the LP as $\alpha$ grows (changing the corresponding endowed valuations.) As $\alpha$ grows, the direction changes, rotating towards the direction of the endowed allocation.

The allocation can be supported by the minimal value of $\alpha$ (if exists) for which the (integral) endowment allocation becomes an optimal solution to the LP. For submodular valuations, our result shows that this happens quickly: when the allocation is a local maximum then a value of $\alpha$ of only 2 suffices.

It is not hard to see that the endowment gap is at least the integrality gap. However, note that the endowment gap is typically strictly larger. More generally, by analyzing the LP we give a precise definition for the minimal value of $\alpha$ required to support a given allocation. Roughly speaking, this minimal value of $\alpha$ that supports an allocation $S$ must be bigger than some combination of the value of any fractional solution plus the "intersection" of this fractional solution with $S$. See a formal treatment in Section 3.1.

In fact, the LP point of view provides some interesting implications of our main result beyond the realm of endowed valuations: it is implicit in previous work that a local maximum in combinatorial

[6]When $\alpha$ is very large this is similar to conditional equilibrium [13] as the bidders do not want to discard any item with marginal value greater than 0.

auctions with submodular bidders provides a 2 approximation to the welfare maximizing solution. One implication of our main result is that a local maximum provides a 2 approximation even with respect to the optimal *fractional* social welfare. More generally, the equilibrium allocation in an $\alpha$-endowed equilibrium provides an $\alpha$ approximation to the optimal fractional social welfare.

We also show that our analysis of submodular valuations is tight in the following sense: there is an instance in which any local maximum requires $\alpha \geq 2$ to be supported (but there are other allocations that can be supported by a smaller value of $\alpha$). We also show that there is an instance with just 2 bidders in which *every* allocation requires $\alpha \geq 1.5$ to be supported. We thus conclude that the endowment gap for submodular valuations is between 1.5 and 2.

What about classes of valuations, like XOS or subadditive? Here we give a definite negative result: for every $\alpha > 1$ there exists an instance with just two bidders with identical XOS valuations and three identical items in which the endowment gap is $\alpha' > \alpha$.

**Open Questions.** This work models the endowment effect in combinatorial auctions and analyzes the endowment gap. Our main finding is that every local maximum can be supported by $\alpha = 2$ when the valuations are submodular and that the endowment gap for submodular valuations is at least 1.5. An obvious open question is to close this gap. A related open question is to analyze the endowment gap of subclasses of submodular valuations. For example, for budget additive valuations we are able to show that the endowment gap is also at least 1.5, but we are unable to prove that the endowment gap is strictly smaller than 2 even for this restricted class.

The focus of this paper is on characterizing the existence of $\alpha$-endowed equilibria. An interesting follow-up question is to understand the "computational endowment gap": the minimal value of $\alpha$ for which an $\alpha$-endowed equilibrium can be efficiently computed. One would hope that for submodular valuations a local maximum can be efficiently computed. Unfortunately, we show that there are both communication and computation hurdles in finding a local maximum: finding a local maximum in combinatorial auctions with submodular bidders requires an exponential number of value queries. Moreover, we present a family of succinctly represented submodular valuations for which finding a local optimum is PLS hard. On the somewhat more positive side, we do know how to find with only polynomially many value queries an allocation (not necessarily a local maximum) that can be supported by some $\alpha > 1$. However, this value of $\alpha$ is typically huge. Are there other allocations that can both be efficiently computed and supported by a small value of $\alpha$? Remarkably, we are unable to provide an answer for this question for any reasonable value of $\alpha$, not even for a restricted class like budget additive valuations. In fact, we do not know if finding a local maximum when the valuations are budget additive is computationally hard. This question might be of independent interest, regardless of the specific application to the endowment gap.

Another interesting question is to devise natural auction methods that end up with an endowed equilibrium. If the valuations are gross-substitutes, then there are natural ascending auctions that end up with a Walrasian equilibrium (e.g., [15]). Are there natural ascending auctions that end up with an endowed equilibrium when the valuations are submodular? One question that might arise while developing such ascending auctions is to understand the extent to which bidders exhibit an endowment effect with respect to items that are temporarily assigned to them during the auction and take this temporary endowment effect – if exists – into account.

Finally, a natural measure of how far the market is from equilibrium suggests itself. Recall that a valuation $v$ is $c$-approximated by a valuation $v'$ if for every bundle $S$, $\frac{v'(S)}{c} \leq v(S) \leq v'(S)$. Given valuations $v_1, \ldots, v_n$, define the "distance to equilibrium" as the minimal $c$ for which there exist $v'_1, \ldots, v'_n$ such that each $v'_i$ $c$-approximates $v_i$ and the instance $v'_1, \ldots, v'_n$ admits a Walrasian equilibrium. Since the endowment gap for submodular valuations is at most 2, this means that the distance to equilibrium of any instance with submodular valuations is at most 2. It will be interesting to see if this result can be improved, e.g., maybe by using valuations that are not endowed valuations. Similarly, what is the distance to equilibrium of instances with subadditive or XOS valuations?

## 2 THE MODEL

There are $n$ players and a set $M$ of $m$ goods, each agent $i$ has a combinatorial valuation function $v_i : 2^M \to \mathbb{R}_+$. We assume that for each player $i$, $v_i$ is monotone ($S \subseteq T$ implies $v_i(S) \leq v_i(T)$) and normalized ($v_i(\emptyset) = 0$). We use the notation $v_i(T|S)$ to denote $v_i(S \cup T) - v_i(S)$, the marginal value of $T$ given $S$.

Each player $i$ has a parameter $\alpha_i$ that measures the intensity of his endowment effect. Specifically, if player $i$ is endowed with a bundle $S_i$, then his valuation function is

$$\begin{aligned} v_i^{S_i,\alpha_i}(T) &= \alpha_i \cdot v_i(S_i \cap T) + v_i(T - S_i|S_i \cap T) \\ &= v_i(T) + (\alpha_i - 1) \cdot v_i(S_i \cap T) \end{aligned}$$

We will use both expressions interchangeably.

An allocation $S = (S_1, \ldots, S_n)$ assigns to each agent $i$ a set $S_i$ such that for every $i \neq j$, $S_i \cap S_j = \emptyset$. An allocation $(S_1, \ldots, S_n)$ and (non-negative) item prices $(p_1, \ldots, p_m)$ constitute an $(\alpha_1, \ldots, \alpha_n)$-*endowed equilibrium* if:

(1) For each player $i$, $v_i^{S_i,\alpha_i}(S_i) - \sum_{j \in S_i} p_j \geq v_i^{S_i,\alpha_i}(T) - \sum_{j \in T} p_j$, for every bundle $T \subseteq M$.
(2) If $j \notin \cup_i S_i$ then $p_j = 0$.

When $\alpha = \alpha_1 = \ldots = \alpha_n$ we shorten the name to *$\alpha$-endowed equilibrium.* Let $S$ be the allocation and $(p_1, \ldots, p_m)$ be the prices of some $(\alpha_1, \ldots, \alpha_n)$-endowed equilibrium. Observe that $S$ and $(p_1, \ldots, p_m)$ also form an $(\alpha, \alpha, \ldots, \alpha)$-endowed equilibrium, for $\alpha = \max_i \alpha_i$. The reason for this is that when $S_i$ maximizes the profit of $v_i^{S_i,\alpha_i}$, it also maximizes the profit of $v_i^{S_i,\alpha'}$, for every $\alpha' > \alpha_i$. Thus, from this point onwards we let $\alpha = \max_i \alpha_i$ and focus on $\alpha$-endowed equilibrium.

An allocation $(S_1, \ldots, S_n)$ is *supported by $\alpha$* if there exist prices $(p_1, \ldots, p_m)$ such that the prices and the allocation form an $\alpha$-endowed equilibrium. In particular, in every instance in which a Walrasian equilibrium exists (e.g., every instance in which the valuation functions are gross substitutes), we obviously have an endowed equilibrium supported by $\alpha = 1$. In instances where a Walrasian equilibrium does not necessarily exist, we will be looking for the minimal value of $\alpha$ for which an $\alpha$-endowed equilibrium exists.

The conceptually and technically interesting regime is when $\alpha > 1$, that is, a player assigns higher value for items in their endowment, but see the full version for the regime $0 \leq \alpha < 1$.

In this work we are interested in the following valuations classes (each class is contained in its successor in the list):

- *Additive valuations:* A valuation $v$ is additive if for every $S$, $v(S) = \sum_{j \in S} v(\{j\})$.
- *Budget additive valuations:* A valuation $v$ is budget additive if there exists $b$ such that for every $S$, $v(S) = \min\{b, \sum_{j \in S} v(\{j\})\}$.
- *Submodular valuations:* a valuation $v$ is submodular if for every $S, T$, $v(S) + v(T) \geq v(S \cup T) + v(S \cap T)$.
- *XOS valuations:* a valuation is XOS if there exists additive valuations $\{a_1, \ldots, a_l\}$ such that for every bundle $S$, $v(S) = \max_{1 \leq k \leq l} a_k(S)$.
- Subadditive valuations: a valuation $v$ is subadditive if for every $S, T$, $v(S) + v(T) \geq v(S \cup T)$.

## 3 THE ENDOWMENT GAP

Consider some instance of a combinatorial auction with $n$ players with valuations $v_1, \ldots, v_n$ and a set $M$ of $m$ items. For a given instance, the *endowment gap* is, roughly speaking, the minimal value of $\alpha$ for which an $\alpha$-endowed equilibrium exists in that instance. We are interested in proving bounds on the value of $\alpha$ for which an $\alpha$-endowed equilibrium exists for all instances of classes of combinatorial valuations (e.g. submodular, XOS, subadditive).

*Definition 3.1.* The *endowment gap of an instance* $(v_1, \ldots, v_n)$ *with respect to an allocation* $A = (A_1, \ldots, A_n)$, denoted $\mathcal{G}^A(v_1, \ldots, v_n)$, is the infimum of the values of $\alpha$ that support $A$.

We naturally extend the definition of an endowment gap to an instance and to a class of valuations:
*Definition 3.2.*

- The *endowment gap of an instance* $(v_1, \ldots, v_n)$ is the minimum value, over every allocation $S$, of the endowment gap with respect to the allocation $S$: $\min_S \mathcal{G}^S(v_1, \ldots, v_n)$.
- The *endowment gap of a class of valuations* $\mathcal{V}$ is the supremum over the endowment gaps over all valuations profiles in which each valuation belongs to the class $\mathcal{V}$:

$$\sup_{(v_1,\ldots,v_n)\in\mathcal{V}^n} \min_S \mathcal{G}^S(v_1, \ldots, v_n)$$

Next, we provide a simple characterization that shows that any allocation $A$ that its social welfare cannot be improved by reallocating items that do not contribute to the social welfare of $A$, can be supported by some $\alpha > 1$.

*Definition 3.3.* Let $S = (S_1, \ldots, S_n)$ be some allocation. For every item define $q_j$ to be the marginal contribution of item $j$ to the allocation $S$ as follows: if there exists $i$ such that $j \in S_i$, let $q_j = v_i(j|S_i - \{j\})$ . For every item $j$ that is not allocated, let $q_j = 0$. Let $Z = \{j|q_j = 0\}$. $S$ is *maximal* if for every player $i$, $v_i(S_i \cup Z) = v_i(S_i)$.

Note that in particular, in a maximal allocation there is no bidder with zero marginal value for an item, for which some other bidder has positive marginal value given his set.

Proposition 3.4.

1. *Every maximal allocation* $S = (S_1, \ldots, S_n)$ *can be supported by some* $\alpha > 0$*. Furthermore, for a given allocation, we can find some* $\alpha$ *that supports it and the prices with* $poly(n, m)$ *value queries.*
2. *If an allocation* $S = (S_1, \ldots, S_n)$ *is not maximal then there is no* $\alpha \geq 1$ *that supports it.*

The proof can be found in the full version. In addition, in the full version of the paper we use this characterization to show that not only in every instance there is an allocation that can be supported, but there is even *some welfare maximizing allocation* that can be $\alpha$-supported by some $\alpha > 1$. The caveat is that the $\alpha$ that we guarantee might be huge. In Claim 3.8 we give the exact value of the minimal $\alpha$ that supports an allocation $S$. However, even this precise characterization might result in large values of $\alpha$. This is no coincidence: Proposition 5.1 shows that for every fixed $\alpha$ there is an instance for which the endowment gap is strictly bigger than $\alpha$. Thus in most of this paper we restrict our attention to specific classes of valuations, aiming to find bounds on the endowment gap that hold for all instances in the class and, ideally, find prominent classes of valuations for which the gap is small.

### 3.1 The Endowment Gap and the LP Relaxation

In this section we explore the connections between the endowment gap and the following linear program relaxation for combinatorial auctions:

*Maximize:* $\sum_{i=1}^{n} \sum_{S\subseteq M} x_{i,S} \cdot v_i(S)$
*Subject to:*

- For each item $j$: $\sum_{i=1}^{n} \sum_{S \subseteq M | j \in S} x_{i,S} \leq 1$.
- for each bidder $i$: $\sum_{S \subseteq M} x_{i,S} \leq 1$.
- for each $i$, $S$: $x_{i,S} \geq 0$.

This linear program is tightly connected to the notion of *Walrasian equilibrium*:

Theorem 3.5 ([30]). *For every instance $(v_1, \ldots, v_n)$, there exists a Walrasian Equilibrium in the instance $(v_1, \ldots, v_n)$ if and only if the integrality gap of the above linear program is 1. Moreover, an integral allocation is the allocation of some Walrasian Equilibrium if and only if it is an optimal solution to the LP.*

When considering endowed valuations $v_1^{A_1,\alpha}, \ldots, v_n^{A_n,\alpha}$ the theorem immediately implies an analogous result for $\alpha$-endowed equilibrium:

Corollary 3.6. *In an instance $(v_1, \ldots, v_n)$ an allocation $A = (A_1, \ldots, A_n)$ is $\alpha$-supported if and only if $A$ is an optimal solution to the LP of the instance $(v_1^{A_1,\alpha}, \ldots, v_n^{A_n,\alpha})$ (implying in particular that the integrality gap of the latter instance is 1.) Furthermore, by the first welfare theorem we get that $A$ is welfare maximizing with respect to $v_1^{A_1,\alpha}, \ldots, v_n^{A_n,\alpha}$.*

We can also relate the welfare of supported allocations to that of fractional allocations. In Subsection 4.1 we use the next corollary to improve the bounds on the welfare guaranteed by local maxima in combinatorial auctions with submodular valuations.

Corollary 3.7. *In an instance $(v_1, \ldots, v_n)$, if an allocation $A = (A_1, \ldots, A_n)$ is $\alpha$-supported then it provides an $\alpha$-approximation to the maximum* fractional *welfare of the instance $(v_1, \ldots, v_n)$.*

Proof. Let $\{x_{i,S}\}$ be some fractional solution of the LP of the instance $(v_1^{A_1,\alpha}, \ldots, v_n^{A_n,\alpha})$. As the allocation $A = (A_1, \ldots, A_n)$ is $\alpha$-supported, by Corollary 3.6 and the definition of endowed valuations we have that:

$$\alpha \sum_{i=1}^{n} v_i(A_i) \geq \sum_{i=1}^{n} \sum_{S \subseteq M} x_{i,S} \cdot v_i^{A_i,\alpha}(S) \geq \sum_{i=1}^{n} \sum_{S \subseteq M} x_{i,S} \cdot v_i(S)$$

In particular, this holds for the welfare maximizing fractional solution of the instance $(v_1, \ldots, v_n)$, implying that $A$ provides an $\alpha$-approximation to the value of that fractional allocation, as needed. □

As we will see next, the endowment gap has some interesting and useful connections to the integrality gap. For our first application, recall that Proposition 3.4 shows that an allocation can be supported by some $\alpha$ if and only if it is maximal. We now use the connection to the LP to determine the minimal value of $\alpha$ that can support a maximal allocation.

Claim 3.8. *Let $A = (A_1, ..., A_n)$ be some allocation. Given a fractional solution $\{x_{i,S}\}$ to the LP, define*

$$\psi_{A,\{x_{i,S}\}} = \sum_{i=1}^{n} \sum_{S \subseteq M} x_{i,S} \cdot v_i(S \cap A_i)$$

*Suppose that $A$ is supported by $\alpha$. Then,*

1. *For every fractional solution $\{x_{i,S}\}$, $\alpha \cdot \sum_{i=1}^{n} v_i(A_i) \geq \sum_{i=1}^{n} \sum_{S \subseteq M} x_{i,S} \cdot v_i(S) + (\alpha - 1)\psi_{A,\{x_{i,S}\}}$.*
2. *The endowment gap with respect to $A$ equals to*

$$\sup \left\{ \frac{\sum_{i=1}^{n} \sum_{S \subseteq M} x_{i,S} \cdot v_i(S) - \psi_{A,\{x_{i,S}\}}}{\sum_{i=1}^{n} v_i(A_i) - \psi_{A,\{x_{i,S}\}}} \middle| \{x_{i,S}\} \text{ s.t. } \sum_{i=1}^{n} v_i(A_i) - \psi_{A,\{x_{i,S}\}} > 0 \right\}$$

Proof. By Corollary 3.6, $A$ can be $\alpha$-supported if and only if for every fractional solution $\{x_{i,S}\}$:

$$\sum_{i=1}^{n} v_i^{A_i,\alpha}(A_i) \geq \sum_{i=1}^{n}\sum_{S\subseteq M} x_{i,S}\cdot v_i^{A_i,\alpha}(S)$$

Additionally, since for every bundle $S$, $v_i^{A_i,\alpha}(S) = v_i(S) + (\alpha-1)\cdot v_i(S\cap A_i)$, for every fractional solution $\{x_{i,S}\}$ it holds that:

$$\sum_{i=1}^{n}\sum_{S\subseteq M} x_{i,S}\cdot v_i^{A_i,\alpha}(S) = \sum_{i=1}^{n}\sum_{S\subseteq M} x_{i,S}\cdot v_i(S) + (\alpha-1)\underbrace{\sum_{i=1}^{n}\sum_{S\subseteq M} x_{i,S}\cdot v_i(S\cap A_i)}_{\psi_{A,\{x_{i,S}\}}}$$

Note that the combination of the above two facts already establishes that if $A$ is $\alpha$-supported then claim (1) holds.

We now continue to prove the second part. Rearranging, we have that $A$ is $\alpha$-supported if and only if for every fractional solution:

$$\alpha\cdot\sum_{i=1}^{n} v_i(A_i) \geq \alpha\cdot\psi_{A,\{x_{i,S}\}} + \sum_{i=1}^{n}\sum_{S\subseteq M} x_{i,S}\cdot v_i(S) - \psi_{A,\{x_{i,S}\}} \tag{1}$$

Consider the expression $\lambda_{A,\{x_{i,S}\}} = \alpha\cdot\sum_{i=1}^{n} v_i(A_i) - \alpha\cdot\psi_{A,\{x_{i,S}\}}$. Observe that $\lambda_{A,\{x_{i,S}\}} \geq 0$, simply because $\psi_{A,\{x_{i,S}\}}$ is composed of a sum of linear combinations of subsets of $A_i$, for each player $i$ (and the valuations are monotone).

If $\lambda_{A,\{x_{i,S}\}} > 0$ then obviously there is a large enough value of $\alpha$ such that inequality (1) holds. Suppose that $\lambda_{A,\{x_{i,S}\}} = 0$. Observe that $\sum_{i=1}^{n}\sum_{S\subseteq M} x_{i,S}\cdot v_i(S) \geq \psi_{A,\{x_{i,S}\}}$, simply because each term $v_i(S)$ in the LHS is replaced by $v_i(S\cap A_i)$ in the RHS and the valuations are monotone.

If $\sum_{i=1}^{n}\sum_{S\subseteq M} x_{i,S}\cdot v_i(S) > \psi_{A,\{x_{i,S}\}}$ and $\lambda_{A,\{x_{i,S}\}} = 0$, which holds for any $A$ that is not maximal, then no value of $\alpha$ makes inequality (1) hold and thus this allocation cannot be supported by any $\alpha$. However, if $\sum_{i=1}^{n}\sum_{S\subseteq M} x_{i,S}\cdot v_i(S) = \psi_{A,\{x_{i,S}\}}$ then any value of $\alpha$ makes the inequality hold.

We have thus identified that for an allocation not to be supported by any $\alpha$ it must be that there is some fractional solution $\{x_{i,S}\}$ for which $\lambda_{A,\{x_{i,S}\}} = 0$ and $\sum_{i=1}^{n}\sum_{S\subseteq M} x_{i,S}\cdot v_i(S) > \psi_{A,\{x_{i,S}\}}$. If this is not the case then by rearranging inequality (1) we can determine the minimal value of $\alpha$ that supports $A$:

$$\sup\left\{\frac{\sum_{i=1}^{n}\sum_{S\subseteq M} x_{i,S}\cdot v_i(S) - \psi_{A,\{x_{i,S}\}}}{\sum_{i=1}^{n} v_i(A_i) - \psi_{A,\{x_{i,S}\}}}\middle|\{x_{i,S}\}\ s.t.\ \sum_{i=1}^{n} v_i(A_i) - \psi_{A,\{x_{i,S}\}} > 0\right\}$$

Note that the supremum is bounded, since we assume that $A$ can be supported by some $\alpha$. □

Claim 3.8 implies that the endowment gap is at least the integrality gap: take $A$ to be any allocation and $\{x_{i,S}\}$ to be a fractional welfare maximizing solution:

$$\alpha \geq \frac{\sum_{i=1}^{n}\sum_{S\subseteq M} x_{i,S}\cdot v_i(S) - \psi_{A,\{x_{i,S}\}}}{\sum_{i=1}^{n} v_i(A_i) - \psi_{A,\{x_{i,S}\}}} \geq \frac{\sum_{i=1}^{n}\sum_{S\subseteq M} x_{i,S}\cdot v_i(S)}{\sum_{i=1}^{n} v_i(A_i)}$$

and the right hand side is obviously at least the integrality gap.

However, as we will see in the paper, the integrality gap is usually strictly larger than the endowment gap. We now show that this is generically true for every instance with subadditive valuations with an integrality gap bigger than 1. The proof can be found in the full version.

Claim 3.9. *Consider an instance with two subadditive valuations. Suppose that the integrality gap of this instance is $y > 1$. Then, for every small enough $\delta > 0$ there is an instance with integrality gap $x = y\cdot\frac{(1+\delta)}{(1+\delta y)}$ in which the endowment gap is strictly bigger than $x$.*

The claim provides a generic way of proving lower bounds on the endowment gap of subclasses of subadditive valuations: start with an instance with the maximal integrality gap in the subclass. The claim guarantees that there is an instance with an endowment gap that is strictly higher than the maximal integrality gap. A more careful look at the proof shows that the new instance belongs to the subclass as long as the subclass is closed under sum, like submodular and XOS valuations (a class of valuations $\mathcal{V}$ is closed under sum if for each $v, u \in \mathcal{V}$ we also have that $v + u \in \mathcal{V}$). We note that although the claim guarantees a generic method of proving lower bounds on the endowment gap, in the specific settings we study in this paper we are able to beat these bounds by introducing specific instances with stronger guarantees.

## 4 THE MAIN RESULT: THE ENDOWMENT GAP OF SUBMODULAR VALUATIONS IS AT MOST 2

Ö£In this section we prove our main positive result: the endowment gap for submodular valuations is at most 2. We prove this by showing that any allocation that is a "local optimum" of the social welfare function can be supported for $\alpha = 2$ with prices that are equal to the marginal value of the items for the player that receives each item. We start by defining the notion of local optimum.

*Definition 4.1.* An allocation $(O_1, \ldots, O_n)$ is a *local optimum* if $\cup_{i=1}^{n} O_i = M$, and for every pair of players $i$ and $i'$ and item $j \in O_i$ we have that $v_i(O_i) + v_{i'}(O_{i'}) \geq v_i(O_i - \{j\}) + v_{i'}(O_{i'} \cup \{j\})$.

In other words, in a local optimum every item is allocated to some player, and reallocating any single item does not improve the welfare. Note that any welfare maximizing allocation is in particular a local optimum. We are now ready to state our main positive result.

THEOREM 4.2. *Let $v_1, \ldots, v_n$ be submodular valuations. Let $O = (O_1, \ldots, O_n)$ be a local optimum. Then $O$ is supported by any $\alpha \geq 2$. As an immediate corollary, the endowment gap of every instance with submodular valuations is at most 2.*

PROOF. We explicitly construct prices that show that $O$ is supported by 2. For each item $j \in O_i$ we define its price to be $p_j = v_i(j|O_i - j)$. Using the following two claims we show that for $\alpha \geq 2$ the prices $(p_1, \ldots, p_m)$ and the allocation $(O_1, \ldots, O_n)$ form an $\alpha$-endowed equilibrium. Later we will observe that our proofs hold even for lower prices.

We start by showing that with these prices and $\alpha \geq 2$, no player can gain by discarding items from his endowment.

CLAIM 4.3. *Consider player $i$ that is allocated bundle $S_i$. Suppose that the price of each item $j \in S_i$ is $p_j = v_i(j|S_i - \{j\})$. Then, if $\alpha \geq 2$ the profit of player $i$ from every bundle $S'$ is at most the profit of $S_i \cup S'$. I.e., $v_i^{S_i,\alpha}(S') - \sum_{j \in S'} p_j \leq v_i^{S_i,\alpha}(S_i \cup S') - \sum_{j \in S_i \cup S'} p_j$.*

PROOF. We compare the profit of player $i$ from bundle $S'$:

$$v_i^{S_i,\alpha}(S') - \sum_{j \in S'} p_j = v_i(S') + (\alpha - 1) \cdot v_i(S_i \cap S') - \sum_{j \in S'} p_j$$

to his profit from the bundle $S' \cup S_i$:

$$v_i^{S_i,\alpha}(S_i \cup S') - \sum_{j \in S' \cup S_i} p_j = v_i(S' \cup S_i) + (\alpha - 1) \cdot v_i(S_i) - \sum_{j \in S' \cup S_i} p_j$$

Using the fact that $v_i(S_i) = v_i(S_i - S'|S_i \cap S') + v_i(S' \cup S_i)$ and rearranging the last expression, we get that the profit of bundle $S' \cup S_i$ equals:

$$\underbrace{v_i(S' \cup S_i) + (\alpha - 1) \cdot v_i(S_i \cap S')}_{\geq v_i^{S_i,\alpha}(S') \text{ by monotonicity}} - \sum_{j \in S'} p_j + (\alpha - 1) \cdot v_i(S_i - S'|S_i \cap S') - \sum_{j \in S_i - S'} p_j.$$

Thus, in order to show that $v_i^{S_i,\alpha}(S_i \cup S') - \sum_{j \in S' \cup S_i} p_j \geq v_i^{S_i,\alpha}(S') - \sum_{j \in S'} p_j$, it suffices to show that $(\alpha - 1) \cdot v_i(S_i - S' | S_i \cap S') - \sum_{j \in S_i - S'} p_j \geq 0$. Since $\alpha \geq 2$, it holds that $\alpha - 1 \geq 1$ and so to show this it is enough to prove that $v_i(S_i - S' | S_i \cap S') \geq \sum_{j \in S_i - S'} p_j$ for every submodular valuation. Towards this end, denote the items in $S_i - S'$ by $1, \ldots, |S_i - S'|$. With this notation we have that $v_i(S_i - S' | S_i \cap S') = \sum_{j=1}^{|S_i - S'|} v_i(j | (S_i \cap S') \cup \{1, \ldots j - 1\})$. Finally, observe that by submodularity we have that for every $1 \leq j \leq |S_i - S'|$ it holds that $p_j = v_i(j | S_i - j) \leq v_i(j | S_i \cup S' - \{j, j+1, \ldots, |S_i - S'|\}) = v_i(j | (S_i \cap S') \cup \{1, \ldots j - 1\})$. □

We next show that with these prices, an agent can never gain by adding items to his endowment.

Claim 4.4. *Let $O = (O_1, \ldots, O_n)$ be a local optimum and suppose that the price of each item $j \in O_i$ is $p_j = v_i(j | O_i - j)$. Then, for any $\alpha \geq 1$ and bundle $T$ the profit from $O_i$ is at least the profit from $O_i \cup T$.*

Proof. Assume without loss of generality that $O_i \cap T = \emptyset$. Observe that since the allocation $O$ is a local optimum we have that for any $j \in T$, $v_i(j | O_i) \leq p_j = v_k(j | O_k - j)$ for player $k$ such that $j \in O_k$. Denote the items in $T$ by $1, \ldots, |T|$. Since the valuations are submodular we have that:

$$\begin{aligned}
\alpha \cdot v_i(O_i) + v_i(T - O_i | O_i) - \sum_{j \in O_i \cup T} p_j &= \alpha \cdot v_i(O_i) - \sum_{j \in O_i} p_j + \sum_{j=1}^{|T|} v_i(j | O_i \cup \{1, \ldots, j-1\}) - \sum_{j \in T} p_j \\
&\leq \alpha \cdot v_i(O_i) - \sum_{j \in O_i} p_j + \sum_{j=1}^{|T|} v_i(j | O_i) - \sum_{j \in T} p_j \\
&\leq \alpha \cdot v_i(O_i) - \sum_{j \in O_i} p_j
\end{aligned}$$

where in the second-to-last inequality we use the submodularity of $v_i$ to claim that $v_i(j | O_i) \geq v_i(j | O_i \cup \{1, \ldots, j-1\})$.

□

We apply claims 4.3 and 4.4 to conclude the proof of the theorem. Let $O = (O_1, \ldots, O_n)$ be a local optimum, recall that in a local optimum we have that $\cup_{i=1}^n O_i = M$, and suppose that the price of each item $j \in O_i$ is $p_j = v_i(j | O_i - j)$. To complete the proof we show that any player $i$ demands the set $O_i$ at the these prices. By Claim 4.4, for $\alpha \geq 1$ for any bundle $T$:

$$v_i^{O_i,\alpha}(O_i) - \sum_{j \in O_i} p_j \geq v_i^{O_i,\alpha}(O_i \cup T) - \sum_{j \in O_i \cup T} p_j$$

and by Claim 4.3 for $\alpha \geq 2$ and any bundle $T$:

$$v_i^{O_i,\alpha}(O_i \cup T) - \sum_{j \in O_i \cup T} p_j \geq v_i^{O_i,\alpha}(T) - \sum_{j \in T} p_j$$

Combining the two inequalities we get that for any $\alpha \geq 2$ and any bundle $T$:

$$v_i^{O_i,\alpha}(O_i) - \sum_{j \in O_i} p_j \geq v_i^{O_i,\alpha}(T) - \sum_{j \in T} p_j$$

as needed. □

We note that the proof still holds even if we reduce the prices such that the price of item $j \in O_i$ is $\max_{i' \neq i} v_{i'}(j | O_{i'}) \leq p_j \leq v_i(j | O_i - \{j\})$. That is, the price $p_j$ can be reduced to the second highest marginal value for the item. The reason is simple: the profit of player $i$ from the bundle $O_i$ has increased at least as any other bundle in this reduction, so Claim 4.3 still holds. Claim 4.4 also holds, as for the proof to hold we only need the price of each item to be the second highest marginal value.

### 4.1 An Implication: The Approximation Ratio of a Local Maximum

One interesting corollary of the algorithm is not directly related to the endowment gap. In previous work it was implicit that the welfare of any local optimum is at least half of the value of the welfare maximizing *integral* solution. By a direct application of Corollary 3.7, we are able to strengthen this result and show that the welfare of any local optimum is at least half of the welfare of the welfare maximizing *fractional* solution:

Proposition 4.5. *Let $(O_1, \dots, O_n)$ be a local optimum. Let $\{x_{i,S}\}$ be some fractional solution for the LP presented in Section 3.1. Then:*

$$2 \cdot \sum_{i=1}^{n} v_i(O_i) \geq \sum_{i=1}^{n} \sum_{S \subseteq M} x_{i,S} \cdot v_i(S)$$

### 4.2 Tightness of Analysis

The following proposition shows that considering local optima (or even global ones) will not help us prove a better bound than 2 on the endowment gap for submodular valuations:

Proposition 4.6. *For any $\delta > 0$, there is an instance with submodular valuations in which every local optimum maximizes the welfare and these local optima cannot be supported by $\alpha < 2 - \delta$. In this instance there is another allocation that can be supported by $\alpha = 1.5 + \delta$.*

Proof. Consider an instance with four submodular players $(a_1, a_2, b_1, b_2)$ and $2k+1$ items ($k \geq 2$). Each of the items belongs to one of the following three sets: $X, Y, \{c\}$, where $X = \{x_1, ..., x_k\}$ and $Y = \{y_1, ..., y_k\}$. The valuations of the players are as follows:

- $a_1$ has a unit demand valuation with value $\frac{1}{k}$ for each of the items in $X$ (and 0 for the rest).
- $a_2$ has a unit demand valuation with value $\frac{1}{k}$ for each of the items in $Y$ (and 0 for the rest).
- The valuations of $b_1, b_2$ are defined as follows: given a set $T$, let $v_T$ be the budget additive valuation with budget 1 that gives value $\frac{1}{k}$ for every item in $T$ and value of 1 for item $\{c\}$. Then the valuation of $b_1$ is $b_1(S) = v_X(S) + |S| \cdot \epsilon$ and $b_2(S) = v_Y(S) + |S| \cdot \epsilon$, where $\epsilon > 0$ is small enough.

Observe that the valuations of $b_1$ and $b_2$ are submodular as they are the sum of two submodular valuations.

We next show that up to symmetry, there is only one locally optimal allocation. In every local maximum item $c$ must be allocated to either $b_1$ or $b_2$ as its marginal value for both is positive given any bundle, and $a_1, a_2$ have a value of 0 for item $c$. Without loss of generality assume it is allocated to $b_1$. Now, it is not possible that in a local optimum $b_1$ is allocated $X \cup \{c\}$ as his marginal value for each item in $X$ is only $\epsilon$, while $a_1$ values each item in $X$ at $1/k$. Thus, for $\epsilon < 1/k$ player $a_1$ must receive an item from $X$, without loss of generality item $x_1$. Now, given any subset of $X - \{x_1\}$, $b_1$ has positive value for any additional item in $X - \{x_1\}$, and is the only player with such positive value, so he must get $X \cup \{c\} - \{x_1\}$. Finally, all items in $Y$ must be allocated to $b_2$ as the marginal value of any item in $Y$ (given any subset of $Y$) is larger for $b_2$ than for any other player, in particular $a_2$.

We conclude that in a local maximum, without loss of generality, $a_1$ is allocated $\{x_1\}$, $b_1$ is allocated $X \cup \{c\} - \{x_1\}$ and $b_2$ is allocated $Y$.

Fix some value of $\alpha$ that supports this allocation. First, we observe that for any $j \in X - \{x_1\}$, $b_1(j|X \cup \{c\} - \{x_1, j\}) = \epsilon$, thus $p_j \leq \alpha \cdot \epsilon$ (otherwise the profit of $b_1$ from the bundle $X \cup \{c\} - \{x_1\} - \{j\}$ is bigger than the profit of his equilibrium allocation). Similarly, $p_c \leq \alpha \cdot (\frac{1}{k} + \epsilon)$.

Then, it must be that:

(1) $b_2$ prefers his allocation over item $c$: $(1 + k \cdot \epsilon) \cdot \alpha - \sum_{y \in Y} p_y \geq 1 + \epsilon - p_c$.
(2) $a_2$ that has zero profit in equilibrium has a non-positive profit from items in $Y$: for every $y \in Y, 0 \geq \frac{1}{k} - p_y$.

Summing up all these inequalities with $p_c \leq \alpha \cdot (\frac{1}{k} + \epsilon)$, we get that: $\alpha \cdot (1 + k \cdot \epsilon) \geq 2 + \epsilon - \alpha \cdot (\frac{1}{k} + \epsilon)$. That is, $\alpha \geq \frac{2+\epsilon}{1+k\cdot\epsilon+(\frac{1}{k}+\epsilon)}$, which approaches 2 for $k$ that approaches $\infty$ and a choice of $\epsilon = \frac{1}{k^2}$.

As for the second part of the proposition, we will now see that the allocation in which $a_1$ is allocated $\{x_1\}$, $b_1$ is allocated $X - \{x_1\} \cup \{c\}$, $b_2$ is allocated $Y - \{y_1\}$ and $a_2$ is allocated $\{y_1\}$ is supported by $1.5 + \epsilon$. To see this, we simply note that with this value of $\alpha$ the following prices constitute an equilibrium with respect to this allocation: $p_c = \frac{1}{k} + \epsilon$, $p_x = \epsilon$ (for each $x \in X$), $p_y = \frac{1}{2k} + \epsilon$ (for each $y \in Y - \{y_1\}$), and $p_{y_1} = \frac{1}{k} + \epsilon$. □

### 4.3 The Complexity of Finding a Local Optimum

Our proof that the endowment gap for submodular valuations is at most 2 starts with a local maximum (local optimum) $(O_1, \ldots, O_n)$. Can such a local optimum be efficiently found? We next show that there are both communication and computation hurdles in finding a local optimum: We first show that finding a local optimum in combinatorial auctions with submodular valuations requires exponential number of value queries. In addition, we show that there exists some family of succinctly represented submodular valuations for which finding a local optimum is PLS hard.[7] Both results hold even if there are only two players.

In light of the hardness of finding exact local optimum, one might be tempted to use an approximate local optimum instead, as it is computationally feasible to find, and hope it can be supported by a small $\alpha$. However, it is easy to provide examples in which a $(1 - \epsilon)$-approximate local optimum cannot be supported by any $\alpha$. Consider a setting with two additive bidders and two items. The first additive bidder has a value of $1 - \epsilon$ for item $a$, and $\epsilon$ for item $b$. The second bidder has a value of 0 for both items. Observe that allocating $a$ to the first bidder and $b$ to the second one is an $(1 - \epsilon)$-local optimum. However, this allocation cannot be supported by any $\alpha$: for the bundle $\{b\}$ to be in the demand of the second player, the price of item $b$ must be 0. However, the profit of the bundle $\{ab\}$ for player 1 is then strictly bigger than that of $\{a\}$. We thus leave as an open question the problem of efficiently computing an $\alpha$-endowed equilibrium for combinatorial auctions with submodular bidders for a small value of $\alpha$ (in the full version we show that it is possible to efficiently compute an allocation that is supported by some huge $\alpha \geq 1$).

We now turn to proving the hardness results for finding a local optimum (proof in the full version):

Proposition 4.7. *Finding a local optimum in a combinatorial auction with two submodular valuations requires exponentially many value queries, even with randomized algorithms.*

The proposition proves that finding a local maximum requires exponentially many value queries. The other common model for accessing the valuations is the more general communication model. That is, how many bits do the players need to exchange in order to compute a local optimum? One obstacle in proving hardness in the communication model is that the proof of Proposition 4.7 is based on the result of [32] which proves the hardness of finding a local maximum on the odd graph using value queries. An analogous result for the communication model was not known when the first version of the paper was written.

[7] We will not give a precise definition here (see [18] for a formal definition), but the PLS class intuitively captures problems which admit a local search algorithm. An example for a PLS complete problem is finding a pure Nash equilibrium in congestions games [10].

However, inspired by our work, the paper [4] studies a communication variant of local search on the odd graph. Using this result and a very similar reduction to that of Proposition 4.7, we show:

PROPOSITION 4.8. *The communication complexity of finding a local optimum in a combinatorial auction with two submodular valuations is exp(m). This results holds even for randomized protocols.*

We give a sketch of the proof in the full version.

PROPOSITION 4.9. *There exists a family of succinctly described submodular functions for which computing a value query can be done in polynomial time but finding a local optimum in a combinatorial auction with two valuations that belong to this family is PLS-hard.*

PROOF. We reduce from the PLS complete problem of finding a locally optimal cut in a graph $G$. In this problem, we are given an edge-weighted graph $G = (V, E)$, and we are looking for a partition of the vertices $(S, V - S)$ such that the (weighted) cut cannot be improved by moving any single vertex from one side of the cut to the other.

We now reduce this problem to a combinatorial auction with two identical submodular valuations. The items in the combinatorial auction are the vertices of the graph. For each set of vertices $S$, we set $v(S)$ to be the sum of the weights of all edges that touch at least one vertex in $S$. It is not hard to see that this valuation is monotone and submodular.

Consider an allocation $(S, M - S)$. Observe that the welfare of $(S, M - S)$ is exactly the sum of the weights of all edges in the graph plus the sum of edges in the cut: the weight of an edge $e = (v, u)$ is counted once if and only if both are in $S$ or if both are in $M - S$. It is counted twice if and only if $v \in S$ or $u \in M - S$ or $u \in S$ or $v \in M - S$. This implies that $(S, M - S)$ is a local optimum in the combinatorial auction if and only if $(S, V - S)$ is a locally optimal cut in the graph, as needed. □

## 5 LOWER BOUNDS ON THE ENDOWMENT GAP

We now prove some lower bounds on the endowment gap. In Section 4 we have shown that the endowment gap for submodular valuations is at most 2. What about larger classes of valuations, such as XOS or subadditive valuations? In sharp contrast to the case of submodular valuations, we show that with the larger classes, the endowment gap cannot be bounded uniformly for the entire class, even if there are only two players. Note that this does not contradict our claim that for any instance, there exists an allocation that is supported by *some* $\alpha$, as we now only show that for every *fixed* $\alpha$ there is some instance such that no allocation is supported by that value of $\alpha$.

PROPOSITION 5.1. *Fix* $\alpha > 1$. *There exists an instance that consists of only three identical items and two players with identical XOS valuations such that no allocation is supported by* $\alpha$.

PROOF. Consider an instance with two bidders and three identical items $x_1, x_2, x_3$. The valuations of the bidders are identical (since the items are identical we slightly abuse notation and use $v(x)$ to specify the value of every bundle $S$ such that $|S| = x$): $v(1) = 1, v(2) = 1 + \frac{1}{12\alpha^2}, v(3) = 1 + \frac{1}{3\alpha}$. We prove that this is indeed an XOS valuation by providing an explicit construction of the clauses of $v$: a clause $(x_j = 1)$ for every item $x_j$, a clause $(x_j = \frac{1}{2} + \frac{1}{24\alpha^2}, x_{j'} = \frac{1}{2} + \frac{1}{24\alpha^2})$, for every pair of $x_{j'}$ and $x_j, j' \neq j$, and a clause $(x_1 = \frac{1}{2}, x_2 = \frac{1}{2}, x_3 = \frac{1}{3\alpha})$.

Note that in every equilibrium allocation all items must be allocated: if item $x_j$ is unallocated, then its price is 0. However, since the valuations of the players are strictly increasing, the profit of his equilibrium allocation with $x_j$ is strictly bigger than his profit from his equilibrium allocation.

Thus, from now on we only consider allocations that allocate all items. There are two possible allocations that allocate all items (up to symmetry). We will show that both allocations are not supported by $\alpha$. In the first allocation, one player, say player 1, gets all three items. The marginal value of an item for player 1 is $\frac{1}{3\alpha} - \frac{1}{12\alpha^2} < \frac{1}{3\alpha}$. Thus the price of every item in equilibrium is at most $\alpha \cdot \frac{1}{3\alpha} = \frac{1}{3}$ (if there is an item with a higher price, the profit for player 1 of the bundle that contains the other two items is higher than the profit of the grand bundle). In this case the profit of player 2 from taking one item is positive: $1 - \frac{1}{3} = \frac{2}{3}$. A contradiction to the assumption that the empty bundle maximizes the profit of player 2.

The other allocation is when one player, say player 1, is allocated two items and player 2 receives only one item. This allocation is not supported by $\alpha$ as well: since $v(1) = 1$ and $v(2) = 1 + \frac{1}{12\alpha^2}$, the marginal value of player 1 for any item is $\frac{1}{12\alpha^2}$. Thus, taking the endowment effect into account, the price of each item that is allocated to player 1 cannot exceed $\frac{1}{12\alpha}$. But now the profit of the grand bundle for player 2 is strictly higher than its current single item allocation: the marginal value of player 2 for the two items that were allocated to player 1 is $\frac{1}{3\alpha}$, while the sum of prices of these items is at most $\frac{1}{6\alpha}$. We have reached a contradiction once again. □

For submodular valuations we can prove that the endowment gap is at least $\frac{3}{2}$. This leaves us with a small gap to the upper bound of 2.

Proposition 5.2. *There exists an instance of two players with submodular valuations where the endowment gap is at least* $\frac{3}{2}$.

Proof. Feige and Vondrak 2006 show that the integrality gap of two players with submodular valuations is at least $\frac{6}{5}$. We now show that this example shows that the endowment gap is at least $\frac{3}{2}$.

As mentioned, we have two players, call them Alice and Bob. There are 4 items, the value of each singleton is 1 the value of each bundle of three or more items is 2. The values of pairs of items are:

| | *Alice* | *Bob* |
|---|---|---|
| $\{ab\}$ | 2 | 4/3 |
| $\{cd\}$ | 2 | 4/3 |
| $\{ac\}$ | 4/3 | 2 |
| $\{bd\}$ | 4/3 | 2 |
| $\{ad\}$ | 5/3 | 5/3 |
| $\{bc\}$ | 5/3 | 5/3 |

There are 4 possible allocations of all items (up to symmetry), and we will see that none of them is supported by $\alpha < \frac{3}{2}$. We will use the fact that the value of the optimal fractional solution is 4 (Alice receives $\frac{1}{2}$ of each of the sets $\{ab\}, \{cd\}$, Bob receives $\frac{1}{2}$ of each of the sets $\{ac\}, \{bd\}$: $x_{A,\{ab\}} = x_{A,\{cd\}} = x_{B,\{ac\}} = x_{B,\{bd\}} = \frac{1}{2}$).

(1) $(\{abcd\}, \emptyset)$: The value of this allocation is 2, and since there is a fractional solution with value 4, by Claim 3.8 this allocation requires $\alpha \geq 2$ to support it.

(2) $(\{abc\}, \{d\})$: Suppose that there is an equilibrium with some $\alpha > 1$ and prices $p_a, p_b, p_c, p_d$. $v_A(c|\{ab\}) = 0$, hence $p_c = 0$ (as if $p_c > 0$ the profit of Alice from the bundle $\{ab\}$ is strictly bigger than that of $\{abc\}$.) However, this means that $v_B(c|\{d\}) - p_c = \frac{1}{3}$, thus

$$\alpha \cdot v_B(\{d\}) - p_d < \alpha \cdot v_B(\{d\}) - p_d + v_B(c|\{d\}) - p_c$$

I.e., the profit of Bob from the bundle $\{cd\}$ is strictly bigger than that of $\{d\}$. A contradiction to the assumption that there is an equilibrium.

(3) $(\{ab\}, \{cd\})$: Denote this allocation by $A$ and note that its welfare is 10/3. Observe that:

$$\psi_{A,\{x_{i,S}\}} = \sum_{i=1}^{n} \sum_{S \subseteq M} x_{i,S} \cdot v_i(S \cap A_i) = \frac{1}{2} v_A(\{ab\}) + \frac{1}{2} v_B(\{c\}) + \frac{1}{2} v_B(\{d\}) = 2$$

Thus, by Claim 3.8, to support $A$ we must have $\alpha \geq \frac{4-2}{\frac{10}{3}-2} = \frac{3}{2}$.

(4) $(\{ad\},\{bc\})$: Denote this allocation by $A$ and note that its welfare is 10/3. Observe that

$$\psi_{A,\{x_{i,S}\}} = \sum_{i=1}^{n}\sum_{S\subseteq M} x_{i,S}\cdot v_i(S\cap A_i) = \frac{1}{2}v_A(\{a\}) + \frac{1}{2}v_A(\{d\}) + \frac{1}{2}v_B(\{b\}) + \frac{1}{2}v_B(\{c\}) = 2.$$

Similarly to before, by Claim 3.8, to support $A$ we must have $\alpha \geq \frac{4-2}{\frac{10}{3}-2} = \frac{3}{2}$.

Finally, we note that the optimal integral allocation $(\{ab\},\{cd\})$ is indeed supported by $\alpha = 3/2$ by using the prices $p_a = p_b = 1, p_c = p_d = 2/3$. □

The above claim shows that if we have two players with general submodular valuations then the endowment gap is at least $\frac{3}{2}$. Next, we consider a more restricted class – budget additive valuations – and show that even in this much simpler class the endowment gap is essentially the same. However, we do need more players to show this.

Proposition 5.3. *For every $\epsilon > 0$, there exists an instance of four players with budget additive valuations in which the endowment gap is at least $\frac{3}{2+\epsilon/2}$.*

Proof. We consider a modification of the integrality gap example of Chakrabarty and Goel 2010. We have 4 players $(a_1, a_2, b_1, b_2)$ and 5 items $(x_1, x_2, y_1, y_2, c)$. $a_1, a_2$ have budget 1, $b_1, b_2$ have budget $2+\epsilon$, for some arbitrarily small $\epsilon > 0$.

To complete the definition of the valuations, we only need to specify the values of players for single items:

- Players $a_1$ and $b_1$ have value 1 for items $x_1, x_2$.
- Players $a_2$ and $b_2$ have value 1 for items $y_1, y_2$.
- Players $b_1, b_2$ value 2 for item $c$.
- The rest of the values are 0.

To analyze the endowment gap we provide several lemmas that characterize the allocations that can be supported in an endowed equilibrium. We then show that each of these allocations can be supported only by $\alpha \geq \frac{3}{2+\epsilon/2}$.

Lemma 5.4. *Without loss of generality, in an endowed equilibrium $b_1$ is assigned item $c$.*

Proof. We claim that in equilibrium item $c$ must be allocated to one of the players $b_1, b_2$. If $c$ is not allocated, then its price must be 0. The same holds if $c$ is allocated to player $a_1$ or player $a_2$, the value of both players for $c$ is 0. Now observe that each player $b_i$ has three items with positive value, and that $b_1(c|\{x_1,x_2\}) = \epsilon > 0$. Thus, when $p_c = 0$, the profit of player $b_1$ from a bundle that contains $c$ is always strictly bigger than his profit from a bundle without it. The argument for player $b_2$ is identical, and thus without loss of generality in equilibrium $b_1$ is assigned item $c$. □

Lemma 5.5. *Without loss of generality, in an endowed equilibrium player $b_2$ is assigned at least one of $y_1, y_2$.*

Proof. Observe that if player $b_1$ was not assigned any of the items $y_1, y_2$ , then his profit is 0, since he has positive value only for items $c, y_1, y_2$ and did not get any of them. The only other player with positive value for $y_1$ and $y_2$ is $a_2$. However, if $a_2$ receives the bundle $\{y_1, y_2\}$ the marginal contribution of any of these items is 0, thus the price of both of these two items is 0. In that case, the profit of player $b_2$ from the bundle $\{y_1\}$ is strictly positive and is bigger than his 0 profit in equilibrium, which is a contradiction. □

Lemma 5.6. *Without loss of generality, in an endowed equilibrium $a_1$ is assigned item $x_2$.*

Proof. We can claim that player $a_1$ is allocated at least one of $x_1, x_2$: the only other player with positive value for these items is $b_1$. Now, $b_1$ is already assigned item $c$, so the marginal contribution of the item is at most $\epsilon$ and thus the price is at most $\alpha \cdot \epsilon$. For $\epsilon < \frac{1}{\alpha}$, $\alpha \cdot \epsilon < 1$ and the bundle $\{x_1\}$ has a positive profit for player $a_1$. This profit is bigger than his 0 profit in equilibrium. □

Lemma 5.7. *Without loss of generality, in equilibrium player $b_1$ is assigned $x_1$ and $p_{x_1} < \alpha \cdot \epsilon$.*

Proof. Observe that $x_1$ can only contribute positively to players $a_1, b_1$ and that $a_1(x_1|\{x_2\}) = 0$. Thus, if $x_1$ is allocated to $a_1$ then its price must be 0, but then $b_1(x_1|\{c\}) > 0$, which implies that $b_1$ profit increases when he adds $x_1$ to his bundle. Similarly to before, this means that this is not an equilibrium allocation. Also, similarly to the previous lemma, $p_{x_1} < \alpha \cdot \epsilon$. □

This leaves us with the following two allocations that can be supported (up to symmetry):

(1) $b_1$ gets $\{c, x_1\}$, $b_2$ gets $\{y_1, y_2\}$, $a_1$ gets $x_2$: in this case we have:
  (a) $b_2$ prefers his allocation over item $c$: $2 \cdot \alpha - p_{y_1} - p_{y_2} \geq 2 - p_c$.
  (b) $a_1$ prefers his allocation over item $x_1$ (recall that $p_{x_1} \leq \alpha \cdot \epsilon$): $\alpha - p_{x_2} \geq 1 - \epsilon \cdot \alpha$.
  (c) $b_1$ prefers his allocation over $\{x_1, x_2\}$: $2 \cdot \alpha - p_c \geq 1 + \alpha - p_{x_2}$ (by rearranging $\alpha - p_c \geq 1 - p_{x_2}$).
  (d) $a_2$ that has zero profit in equilibrium has a non-positive profit from $y_1$ and $y_2$: $0 \geq 1 - p_{y_1}$, $0 \geq 1 - p_{y_2}$.

  Summing these inequalities we get that $\alpha \cdot (4 + \epsilon) \geq 6$. I.e., to support this allocation we need $\alpha \geq \frac{3}{2+\epsilon/2}$. As $\epsilon$ approaches 0 this ratio approaches $\frac{3}{2}$.

(2) $b_1$ gets $\{c, x_1\}$, $b_2$ gets $y_1$, $a_1$ gets $x_2$, $a_2$ gets $y_2$:
  (a) $b_2$ prefers his allocation over item $c$: $\alpha - p_{y_1} \geq 2 - p_c$.
  (b) $b_2$ prefers his allocation over $\{y_1, y_2\}$: $\alpha - p_{y_1} \geq \alpha + 1 - p_{y_1} - p_{y_2}$. Hence $p_{y_2} \geq 1$.
  (c) $a_1$ prefers his allocation over item $x_1$ (recall that $p_{x_1} \leq \alpha \cdot \epsilon$): $\alpha - p_{x_2} \geq 1 - \epsilon \cdot \alpha$.
  (d) $b_1$ prefers his allocation over $\{x_1, x_2\}$: $2 \cdot \alpha - p_c \geq 1 + \alpha - p_{x_2}$.
  (e) $a_2$ prefers his allocation over item $y_1$: $\alpha - p_{y_2} \geq 1 - p_{y_1}$.

  Summing these inequalities we get that $\alpha \cdot (4 + \epsilon) \geq 6$. I.e., to support this allocation we need $\alpha \geq \frac{3}{2+\epsilon/2}$. As $\epsilon$ approaches 0 this ratio approaches $\frac{3}{2}$.

□

## REFERENCES


[1] Susanne Albers and Dennis Kraft. 2016. Motivating Time-Inconsistent Agents: A Computational Approach. In *Proc. 12th Workshop on Internet and Network Economics.*

[2] Susanne Albers and Dennis Kraft. 2017. On the Value of Penalties in Time-Inconsistent Planning. In *44th International Colloquium on Automata, Languages, and Programming, ICALP 2017, July 10-14, 2017, Warsaw, Poland.* 10:1–10:12.

[3] Susanne Albers and Dennis Kraft. 2017. The Price of Uncertainty in Present-Biased Planning. In *Proc. 13th Workshop on Internet and Network Economics.*

[4] Yakov Babichenko, Shahar Dobzinski, and Noam Nisan. 2018. The Communication Complexity of Local Search. *arXiv preprint arXiv:1804.02676* (2018).

[5] Katherine Burson, David Faro, and Yuval Rottenstreich. 2013. Multiple-unit holdings yield attenuated endowment effects. *Management Science* 59, 3 (2013), 545–555.

[6] Deeparnab Chakrabarty and Gagan Goel. 2010. On the approximability of budgeted allocations and improved lower bounds for submodular welfare maximization and GAP. *SIAM J. Comput.* 39, 6 (2010), 2189–2211.

[7] George Christodoulou, Annamária Kovács, and Michael Schapira. 2008. Bayesian combinatorial auctions. In *International Colloquium on Automata, Languages, and Programming.* Springer, 820–832.

[8] David Easley and Arpita Ghosh. 2015. Behavioral Mechanism Design: Optimal Crowdsourcing Contracts and Prospect Theory.. In *Proc. 16th ACM Conference on Electronic Commerce.*

[9] Dirk Engelmann and Guillaume Hollard. 2010. Reconsidering the effect of market experience on the âĂIJendowment effectâĂİ. *Econometrica* 78, 6 (2010), 2005–2019.

[10] Alex Fabrikant, Christos Papadimitriou, and Kunal Talwar. 2004. The complexity of pure Nash equilibria. In *Proceedings of the thirty-sixth annual ACM symposium on Theory of computing.* ACM, 604–612.

[11] Uriel Feige and Jan Vondrak. 2006. Approximation algorithms for allocation problems: Improving the factor of 1-1/e. In *Foundations of Computer Science, 2006. FOCS'06. 47th Annual IEEE Symposium on.* IEEE, 667–676.

[12] Michal Feldman, Nick Gravin, and Brendan Lucier. 2016. Combinatorial walrasian equilibrium. *SIAM J. Comput.* 45, 1 (2016), 29–48.

[13] Hu Fu, Robert Kleinberg, and Ron Lavi. 2012. Conditional equilibrium outcomes via ascending price processes with applications to combinatorial auctions with item bidding.. In *ACM Conference on Electronic Commerce.*

[14] Nick Gravin, Nicole Immorlica, Brendan Lucier, and Emmanouil Pountourakis. 2016. Procrastination with Variable Present Bias. In *Proceedings of the 2016 ACM Conference on Economics and Computation (EC '16).* ACM, New York, NY, USA, 361–361.

[15] Faruk Gul and Ennio Stacchetti. 1999. Walrasian equilibrium with gross substitutes. *Journal of Economic theory* 87, 1 (1999), 95–124.

[16] Avinatan Hassidim, Haim Kaplan, Yishay Mansour, and Noam Nisan. 2011. Non-price equilibria in markets of discrete goods. In *Proceedings 12th ACM Conference on Electronic Commerce (EC-2011), San Jose, CA, USA, June 5-9, 2011.* 295–296.

[17] James E Heyman, Yesim Orhun, and Dan Ariely. 2004. Auction fever: the effect of opponents and quasi-endowment on product valuations. *Journal of Interactive Marketing* 18, 4 (2004), 7–21.

[18] David S Johnson, Christos H Papadimitriou, and Mihalis Yannakakis. 1988. How easy is local search? *Journal of computer and system sciences* 37, 1 (1988), 79–100.

[19] Daniel Kahneman, Jack L Knetsch, and Richard H Thaler. 1990. Experimental tests of the endowment effect and the Coase theorem. *Journal of political Economy* (1990), 1325–1348.

[20] Daniel Kahneman, Jack L Knetsch, and Richard H Thaler. 1991. Anomalies: The endowment effect, loss aversion, and status quo bias. *The journal of economic perspectives* 5, 1 (1991), 193–206.

[21] Daniel Kahneman and Amos Tversky. 1979. Prospect theory: An analysis of decision under risk. *Econometrica 47,2* (1979), 263–291.

[22] Jon Kleinberg and Sigal Oren. 2014. Time-inconsistent Planning: A Computational Problem in Behavioral Economics. In *Proceedings of the Fifteenth ACM Conference on Economics and Computation (EC '14).* ACM, New York, NY, USA, 547–564.

[23] Jon Kleinberg, Sigal Oren, and Manish Raghavan. 2016. Planning Problems for Sophisticated Agents with Present Bias. In *Proceedings of the 2016 ACM Conference on Economics and Computation (EC '16).* ACM, New York, NY, USA, 343–360.

[24] Jon Kleinberg, Sigal Oren, and Manish Raghavan. 2017. Planning with Multiple Biases. In *Proceedings of the 2017 ACM Conference on Economics and Computation (EC '17).* ACM, New York, NY, USA, 567–584.

[25] Jack L Knetsch. 1989. The endowment effect and evidence of nonreversible indifference curves. *The american Economic review* 79, 5 (1989), 1277–1284.

[26] Jack L Knetsch, Fang-Fang Tang, and Richard H Thaler. 2001. The endowment effect and repeated market trials: Is the Vickrey auction demand revealing? *Experimental economics* 4, 3 (2001), 257–269.

[27] Botond Kőszegi and Matthew Rabin. 2006. A model of reference-dependent preferences. *The Quarterly Journal of Economics* (2006), 1133–1165.

[28] John List. 2003. Does Market Experience Eliminate Market Anomalies? *The Quarterly Journal of Economics* 118, 1 (2003), 41–71.

[29] Yusufcan Masatlioglu and Efe A Ok. 2005. Rational choice with status quo bias. *Journal of Economic Theory* 121, 1 (2005), 1–29.

[30] Noam Nisan and Ilya Segal. 2006. The communication requirements of efficient allocations and supporting prices. *Journal of Economic Theory* 129, 1 (2006), 192–224.

[31] William Samuelson and Richard Zeckhauser. 1988. Status quo bias in decision making. *Journal of risk and uncertainty* 1, 1 (1988), 7–59.

[32] Miklos Santha and Mario Szegedy. 2004. Quantum and classical query complexities of local search are polynomially related. In *Proceedings of the thirty-sixth annual ACM symposium on Theory of computing.* ACM, 494–501.

[33] Pingzhong Tang, Yifeng Teng, Zihe Wang, Shenke Xiao, and Yichong Xu. 2014. Computational issues in time-inconsistent planning models. *arXiv preprint arXiv:1411.7472* (2014).

[34] Richard Thaler. 1980. Toward a positive theory of consumer choice. *Journal of Economic Behavior & Organization* 1, 1 (1980), 39–60.

# The Combinatorial Clock Auction: the Effects of Strategic Behaviour and the Price Increment Rule on Social Welfare

MAX DUPRE LA TOUR, Ecole Normale Superieure
ADRIAN VETTA, McGill University

We present tight bounds on the social welfare ratio of the combinatorial clock auction under the *basic price increment rule* used in practice. Specifically, under the assumption of truthful bidding, we prove that the welfare ratio is $\Theta(m^{\frac{2}{3}})$ in the case of unit-demand bidders, and $\Theta(m)$ for general bidders. We explain how changes to the price increment rule effect the welfare guarantee, and extend our results to settings with strategic bidding.

Additional Key Words and Phrases: Spectrum Auctions; Combinatorial Auction; Auction Design ; Clock Auction

## 1 INTRODUCTION

The combinatorial clock auction was introduced by Porter, Rassenti, Roopnarine and Smith [? ] in 2003. It is an ascending price auction with package bidding. In each round, every item has a individual price based upon which each agent demands a package of items. If there is excess demand[1] for an item then there is another round in which the prices of items under excess demand have risen. Since its inception, the combinatorial clock auction has become extremely important in practice. Indeed, it is now perhaps the most widely used auction mechanism for selling spectrum [? ]. These bandwidth auctions are based on a two-phase implementation of the combinatorial clock auction due to Ausubel, Cramton and Milgrom [? ]. To distinguish between these variants of the auction, we refer to the procedure of Porter et al. as the combinatorial clock (CC) mechanism and the procedure of Ausubel et al. as the combinatorial clock auction (CCA).

Despite the auction's importance, quantitative analyses of the combinatorial clock auction remained elusive until the recent work of Bousquet et al. [? ]. That paper studied the *welfare ratio*, the worst case ratio between the social welfare of the optimal allocation and the allocation output by the auction. From a practical perspective, the paper highlighted three critical factors in determining whether or not an ascending combinatorial auction can proffer good social welfare guarantees:

(1) All-Bids-Count: In some ascending auction implementations only bids from the final round can win. These implementations cannot guarantee high social welfare; it is essential that bids from earlier rounds in the auction, not just the final round, are eligible to win. Specifically, the winning set of bids should be the best disjoint set of bids over all rounds. Because of this, in this paper we will only consider *all-bids-count* auctions.

[1]There is *excess demand* if the number of agents bidding for an item strictly exceeds the supply of that item. In this paper we will assume the supply of each item is one, so excess demand arises if two or more agents demand the item. We remark that our results extend to the case of *generic lots* where the auctioneer may supply multiple copies of an item.

Author's emails: mdupre@clipper.ens.fr; adrian.vetta@mcgill.ca.


*ACM EC'18, June 18–22, 2018, Ithaca, NY, USA.* ACM ISBN 978-1-4503-5829-3/18/06...$15.00
https://doi.org/10.1145/3219166.3219230

(2) The Stopping Rule: Implicit in the description of the combinatorial clock above is that the auction terminates when there is no excess demand for any item. Thus, the final round is the first round in which the bids of the agents are disjoint. We call this the *standard stopping rule*, and this is the rule used in current CCA auctions. In contrast, the original CC mechanism of Porter et al. uses a different stopping rule which we term *enhanced*. To understand this rule, notice that if all-bids-count then a final round bid may lose. Specifically, there may be a conflict in that an item may be bid upon in the final round and yet assigned to a different bidder in the winning set of bids. Unfortunately, this possibility implies that the standard stopping rule cannot guarantee high welfare. To counteract this, if there is a conflict for an item then the CC mechanism treats this as an item under excess demand. Consequently, the mechanism increments the price of the item and holds an additional round of bidding. Therefore, under the *enhanced stopping rule*, the auction only stops when the final round bids are disjoint **and** there are no conflicts.

(3) The Price Increment Rule: We have yet to specify the formula by which prices rise during the auction. This is done via an *increment function* $\iota : \mathbb{N} \rightarrow \mathbb{N}$ and a parameter $\epsilon > 0$. Specifically, if $d_j^t$ is the total demand for item $j$ in round $t$, then we set the price in round $t+1$ to be $p_j^{t+1} := p_j^t + \epsilon \cdot \iota(d_j^t)$. The simplest increment rule, and the one currently used, satisfies $\iota(d) = 0$ if $d \in \{0, 1\}$ and $\iota(d) = 1$ if $d \geq 2$.[2] Thus the price rises by a fixed additive amount if and only if there is excess demand. We call this the *basic increment rule*. Unfortunately, again, this increment rule can lead to a poor welfare ratio; so [? ] also studied a *demand-based increment rule* where $\iota(d) = d$ for all $d$. Thus the price increase is now linear in the demand for an item.

Given an auction with $n$ bidders and $m$ items, Bousquet et al. [? ] prove:

Theorem 1 ([? ]). *Take a combinatorial clock auction using the demand-based increment rule and the enhanced stopping rule. Then, assuming truthful bidding, the auction has an $O(\kappa^2 \cdot \log n \log^2 m)$ welfare ratio, provided all the bids made are on packages of cardinality at most $\kappa$.* □

For example, this gives a poly-logarithmic welfare ratio for unit-demand auctions, where $\kappa = 1$.

However, Theorem ?? is incomplete in three aspects. First, the price increment and stopping rules required by the theorem do not correspond to the rules used in practice. Consequently, it is important to study the performance of the current rules. That we do in this paper, where we present quantitative – and tight – performance analyses for the CC mechanism and for the (first phase of the) CCA.[3] Specifically, we prove in Section ?? and Section ??:

Theorem 2. *Given truthful bidding, the welfare ratio of the combinatorial clock auction using the basic price increment rule is $\Theta(m^{\frac{2}{3}})$ for unit-demand bidders (using either the standard or the enhanced stopping rules).*

Theorem 3. *Given truthful bidding, the welfare ratio of the combinatorial clock auction using the basic price increment rule is $\Theta(m)$ for general bidders, even in the case where every bid is on packages of cardinality at most two (using either the standard or the enhanced stopping rules).*

Second, the demand-based increment rule used in [? ] is linear in demand, it is not linear in excess demand. In particular, the price of an item will rise even if there is only one agent bidding

[2]In practice, rather than a fixed additive increase the current CCA auctions use a fixed multiplicative increase; this distinction is not important to us here.

[3]For the current two-phase CCA, the first phase is viewed as a price-discovery mechanism. The actual payments and allocations are determined in the second sealed-bid phase. As such, our results do not immediately extrapolate to the two-phase CCA.

for it. This distinction may seem innocuous but it has far reaching consequences. In particular, we show in Section ?? that sub-polynomial welfare ratios cannot be achieved if price rises are tied purely to excess demand.[4]

Theorem 4. *Take any price increment rule where prices can rise only under excess demand. That is* $\iota(d) = 0$ *if* $d \in \{0, 1\}$. *Then the welfare ratio of the combinatorial clock auction is* $\Omega(\sqrt{m})$, *even in the case of unit-demand bidders.*

Thus, surprisingly, Theorem ?? even applies to the natural case of an *excess-demand-based increment rule* where $\iota(d) = d - 1$ for all $d \geq 1$.

It is worth briefly discussing what complications arise when the price increment rule is tied to excess demand. Most dramatically, in this setting the price of an item in the auction may freeze for long periods of time. In turn, the agent that is bidding for that item also becomes frozen (inactive) for long periods of time. This implies that by the time the agent become active again the auction landscape may have changed significantly. In particular, prices for some items may have risen sharply. This is problematic as ascending auctions appear to work best when agents have time to learn and react in response to slowly changing price signals. Large shifts in prices can lead to unusual bidding patterns and low social welfare. This dynamic makes analyzing the basic price increment rule extremely challenging as we will see, for example, in the proof of Theorem ??.

The third incomplete aspect of Theorem ?? is that it does not deal with the incentive aspects that arise in ascending combinatorial auctions. Specifically, it assumes that each agent bids truthfully or sincerely in every round; that is, given the item prices for that round, each agent selects its utility-maximizing package. In iterative auctions, such as the CC mechanism and the CCA, the assumption of truthful bidding is unrealistic. Moreover in spectrum auctions, for example, the bids firms make are often value-dependent rather than simply utility-dependent.[5] Consequently, we examine the welfare ratio when agents are strategic. Positive results can be obtained provided the increment rule is not constrained by $\iota(1) = 0$. Specifically, we prove in Section ??:

Theorem 5. *Take a combinatorial clock auction using the increment rule* $\iota(d) = 1$ *if* $d \geq 1$ *and a modified stopping rule. Then, given the assumptions of no-overbidding and no-early departure, the auction has a welfare ratio* $O(\sqrt{m} \cdot \log m)$ *for unit-demand bidders, even when the agents have arbitrary bidding strategies.*

We remark that Theorem ?? is extremely general. It does not require the imposition of equilibrium constraints nor prescriptions concerning the bidding strategies the agents must utilize. We are unaware of any result of this form in the literature on dynamic auctions.

## 2 THE COMBINATORIAL CLOCK AUCTION

There is a set $M = [\![1, m]\!] = \{1, 2, \ldots, m\}$ of items and a set $N = [\![1, n]\!]$ of agents. At time (round) $t$, each item $j$ has a price $p_j^t$. The corresponding price for a package $S \subseteq M$, at time $t$, is then $p^t(S) = \sum_{j \in S} p_j^t$. Agent $i$ has value $v_i(S)$ for a package $S$. So, under the assumption of quasi-linear utilities, the utility of agent $i$ for package $S$ in round $t$ is $u_i^t(S) = v_i(S) - p^t(S)$. Let agent $i$ bid for package $S_i^t$ in round $t$. Let $d_j^t$ be the total demand for item $j$ in round $t$. Then, at the start of round $t + 1$, the price of item $j$ will rise by $\epsilon \cdot \iota(d_j^t)$. Here $\iota : \mathbf{N} \to \mathbf{N}$ is the increment function and $\epsilon > 0$ is

[4] A welfare ratio is sub-polynomial if it is $o(n^\delta)$ for any constant $\delta > 0$. Of particular interest in this setting are welfare ratios that are poly-logarithmic in $m$.

[5] For example, subject to budget constraints, a bidder may be interested in maximizing the quality and quantity of the spectrum it wins. Such an objective may lead to different bidding behaviours than would arise with an objective that seeks to maximize the difference between the value and the price of the spectrum won.

a parameter. Moreover $\iota$ is non-negative and non-decreasing. Furthermore, $\iota(d) > 0$ for all $d > 2$; thus prices must rise if there is excess demand.[6]

The price increment function used in both the CC mechanism and the current CCA mechanism is:

$$\iota(d) = \begin{cases} 0 & \text{if } d \in \{0, 1\} \\ 1 & \text{if } d \geq 2 \end{cases}$$

That is, prices rise by a fixed amount if there is excess demand. If there is no excess demand then the price does not change. We call this the *basic price increment rule*. The CC mechanism and the CCA mechanism differ, however, in the choice of *stopping rule*. Specifically, the CCA uses the *standard stopping rule* where the procedure terminates when the bids are disjoint. In contrast, the CC mechanism of Porter et al. follows the *enhanced stopping rule*: the auction does not terminate once bids the bids are disjoint *unless* there is no conflict between the final round bids and the revenue maximizing allocation. In particular, every agent should win all the items in their final clock round package. If this is not the case, then the mechanism runs another round under which the prices of potentially misallocated items have been incremented.

The results in [? ] show that the choice of the *enhanced stopping rule* is better. When combined with a price increment function that is linear in demand the welfare ratio improves dramatically over the ratio proffered by the standard stopping rule. Interestingly in this paper, where the main objective is to study the basic price increment function, the choice of stopping rule turns out to be unimportant. That is, under the basic price increment rule, the welfare ratio is the same for both the standard stopping rule and the enhanced stopping rule. Now, in Section ?? and Section ?? we quantify exactly what this welfare ratio is for unit-demand bidders and general bidders, respectively.

## 3 THE WELFARE RATIO FOR UNIT-DEMAND-BIDDERS

Let the allocation output by the Combinatorial Clock Auction be $\mathcal{S} = \{S_1, S_2, \ldots, S_n\}$. Then the social welfare of the allocation is $\texttt{cca} = \sum_i v_i(S_i)$. Let $\mathcal{S}^* = \{S_1^*, S_2^*, \ldots, S_n^*\}$ be the allocation with the optimal social welfare, and let $\texttt{opt} = \sum_i v_i(S_i^*)$. The welfare ratio is then the worst case ratio $\frac{\texttt{opt}}{\texttt{cca}}$, over all auction instances. As stated, our aim is to quantify the welfare ratio for the combinatorial clock auction with the basic price increment rule. That is, $\iota(d) = 0$ if $d \in \{0, 1\}$ and $\iota(d) = 1$ if $d \geq 2$. In this section we give a tight bound for the case of unit-demand bidders. This turns out be by far the more challenging case. In Section ??, we present a tight bound for the case of general bidders.

### 3.1 An Upper Bound on The Welfare Ratio for Unit-Demand-Bidders

We begin with showing an upper bound for unit-demand bidders. Then we will present a matching lower bound.

Theorem 6. *Given truthful bidding, the welfare ratio of the combinatorial clock auction using the basic price increment rule is $O(m^{\frac{2}{3}})$ for unit-demand bidders.*

The result applies with both the standard and enhanced stopping rules. We will prove it for the standard stopping rules; with minor modifications it extends the enhanced stopping rule. To prove Theorem ??, we will evaluate the social welfare of the auction's allocation via comparisons with the following greedy algorithm that was also studied in [? ].

We begin with two trivial, but important, claims.

Claim 7. *The revenue of the combinatorial clock auction is at least the revenue from the greedy allocation.*

[6]Of course, without this assumption, the auction may never end.

**Procedure** Greedy Allocation

**Input:** $\mathcal{S} = \{(s_i^t, p_{s_i^t}^t)\}_{i,t}$ the collection of bids made in the combinatorial clock auction.

**while** $\mathcal{S} \neq \emptyset$ **do**

  Let $(s_i^t, p_{s_i^t}^t)$ be the bid with maximum price (break ties arbitrarily);

  Allocate item $s_i^t$ to bidder $i$ with price $p_{s_i^t}^t$;

  Remove every bid of bidder $i$ and remove every bid for item $s_i^t$ in $\mathcal{S}$.

**end**

Proof. Given the bids, the auction selects a revenue maximizing allocation. □

Claim 8. *The welfare of the combinatorial clock auction is at least the revenue from the combinatorial clock auction.*

Proof. The bidders are truthful. In particular, by individual rationality, each bid is most the corresponding valuation. Thus, welfare is at least revenue. □

Together, Claims **??** and **??** imply that we can lower bound the performance of the combinatorial clock auction by quantifying the revenue of the greedy allocation.

Recall that the fundamental problem we face is that bidders may become inactive (as the price of an item it is bidding for is frozen) for long periods of the auction. Specifically, an agent may make a low bid for an item that it values highly. Then as the price of that first item rises, the agent changes strategy and makes a low bid for a second item whose price subsequently freezes. Whilst the agent is inactive, the price of the original item may increase dramatically so the agent will never again bid on that item. This process may then iterate, causing the agent to make low bids throughout the auction. On termination, even if the agent wins an item it will be for a low price and perhaps of low value. This is problematic because there are items that the agent does value highly. If this dynamic occurs and if it can simultaneously effect a large number of agents then the welfare ratio of the combinatorial clock auction could be very poor. Unfortunately, as we will see this can indeed happen. In the case of unit demand bidders, we can show that, whilst this phenomenon still arises and its detrimental effects are considerable, the consequences are much less drastic than in the case of general bidders. Before showing this, let's give some intuition behind our approach to proving Theorem **??**. First suppose there is a set $\mathcal{F}$ of agents who provide at least half of the social welfare in the optimal allocation but who make only low bids throughout the auction; here we define a low bid to be a bid of value at most $\frac{1}{\epsilon m^{\frac{2}{3}}} \cdot \mathtt{cca}$. Observe that, because these bidders receive high value in the optimal allocation, the sum of their utilities must be high at the beginning of the auction. If the sum of their utilities is still high when the auction ends then the welfare of the combinatorial clock auction is high. Therefore, we may assume that the sum of their utilities has decreased by $\Theta(\mathtt{opt})$. The next step is to show that $\Theta(\mathtt{opt})$ bids were made while the agents in $\mathcal{F}$ were active (i.e. during a round where the price of at least one item on which a agent in $\mathcal{F}$ bids rises). By definition, the players in $\mathcal{F}$ are active for at most $m^{\frac{1}{3}} \cdot \frac{\mathtt{cca}}{\epsilon}$ rounds, otherwise they would have made some high bids. The final step is to show that a constant fraction of the aforementioned $\Theta(\mathtt{opt})$ bids were made by agents belonging to a group of cardinality $m^{\frac{1}{3}}$. Putting everything together, we conclude that $m^{\frac{2}{3}} \cdot \mathtt{cca} \geq \Omega(\mathtt{opt})$.

We are now ready to present the formal argument. Towards this goal, we require the following notation. Let $v_i(j)$ be the valuation of agent $i$ for item $j$. Let $\mathcal{T}$ be the last round of the auction and let $b_i(j)$ be the maximum bid of agent $i$ for item $j$ during the course of the auction. It will be convenient to define $b_i(j) = 0$ if $i = 0$ or $i > n$ or if $j = 0$, and similarly for $v_i(j)$. Without loss of generality, if item $j$ is allocated by the greedy procedure then we may assume that agent $j$ wins it. Furthermore, we may reorder the items such that $j \mapsto b_j(j)$ is a decreasing function. Observe that the revenue of the greedy procedure is exactly $\sum_{j=1}^{m} b_j(j)$.

Next consider the allocation of maximum social welfare. Denote by $a_j$ the winner of item $j$ in the optimal allocation. If $j$ has no winner in this allocation, we set $a_j = 0$. Observe that the social welfare of the optimal allocation is exactly $\sum_{j=1}^{m} v_{a_j}(j)$. Consequently, Theorem **??** will follow if we can show that $\sum_{j=1}^{m} v_{a_j}(j) = O\left(m^{\frac{2}{3}} \cdot \sum_{j=1}^{m} b_j(j)\right)$. We will prove that either this is the case or that the sum of the utilities of the agents is sufficient to give the welfare guarantee. To prove this we will use the following two technical lemmas.

Lemma 9. *Given functions $f, g : M \to \mathbf{N}$ and $k \in \mathbf{R}^+$ such that $\frac{2m}{k} \in \mathbb{Z}$ and $\sum_{j=1}^{m} f(j) \le \frac{\sum_{j=1}^{m} g(j)}{k}$. If $f$ is decreasing then*

$$\sum_{j=1}^{m} \left(g(j) - f(\frac{2m}{k})\right)^+ \;\ge\; \frac{1}{2} \cdot \sum_{j=1}^{m} g(j)$$

Proof. Set $c := f(\frac{2m}{k})$. Then, as $f$ is decreasing,

$$\sum_{j=1}^{m} f(j) \;\ge\; \sum_{j=1}^{\frac{2m}{k}} f(j) \;\ge\; \frac{2m}{k} \cdot c \tag{1}$$

By assumption, $\sum_{j=1}^{m} g(j) \ge k \cdot \sum_{j=1}^{m} f(j)$. Thus, applying Inequality (??) gives $\frac{1}{2} \cdot \sum_{j=1}^{m} g(j) \ge mc$. Furthermore,

$$\sum_{j=1}^{m} g(j) = \sum_{j=1}^{m} c + (g(j) - c) \le \sum_{j=1}^{m} c + (g(j) - c)^+ = mc + \sum_{j=1}^{m} (g(j) - c)^+ \le \frac{1}{2} \cdot \sum_{j=1}^{m} g(j) + \sum_{j=1}^{m} (g(j) - c)^+$$

Rearranging, we obtain

$$\sum_{j=1}^{m} (g(j) - c)^+ \;\ge\; \frac{1}{2} \cdot \sum_{j=1}^{m} g(j)$$

The lemma follows by plugging back in $c := f(\frac{2m}{k})$. □

Lemma 10. *Given functions $f, g : M \to \mathbf{N}$ and $k \in \mathbf{R}^+$ such that $\frac{2m}{k} \in \mathbb{Z}$ and $\sum_{j=1}^{m} f(j) \le \frac{\sum_{j=1}^{m} g(j)}{k}$. Set $\mathcal{F} := \{j \in [\![1, m]\!] : f(j) < \frac{2max(g)}{k}, g(j) > 0\}$. Then*

$$\sum_{j \in \mathcal{F}} g(j) \;\ge\; \frac{1}{2} \cdot \sum_{j=1}^{m} g(j)$$

Proof. Let $\bar{g} = \max_j g(j)$. Then

$$\sum_{j=1}^{m} g(j) \;=\; \sum_{j \notin \mathcal{F}} g(j) + \sum_{j \in \mathcal{F}} g(j) \;\le\; \bar{g} \cdot (supp(g) - |\mathcal{F}|) + \sum_{j \in \mathcal{F}} g(j)$$

Rearranging gives

$$\sum_{j \in \mathcal{F}} g(j) \;\ge\; \sum_{j=1}^{m} g(j) - \bar{g} \cdot (supp(g) - |\mathcal{F}|) \tag{2}$$

Next, by definition, for $j \notin \mathcal{F}$, we have $f(j) \geq \frac{2\bar{g}}{k}$. Therefore

$$\sum_{j=1}^{m} f(j) \;\geq\; \sum_{j \notin \mathcal{F}} f(j) \;\geq\; \frac{2\bar{g}}{k} \cdot (supp(g) - |\mathcal{F}|) \tag{3}$$

By assumption, $\sum_{j=1}^{m} g(j) \geq k \cdot \sum_{j=1}^{m} f(j)$. Thus Inequalities (??) and (??) imply that

$$\bar{g} \cdot (supp(g) - |\mathcal{F}|) + \sum_{j \in \mathcal{F}} g(j) \;\geq\; 2\bar{g} \cdot (supp(g) - |\mathcal{F}|)$$

In particular

$$\sum_{j \in \mathcal{F}} g(j) \;\geq\; \bar{g} \cdot (supp(g) - |\mathcal{F}|) \tag{4}$$

Thus summing (??) and (??) gives $2 \cdot \sum_{j \in \mathcal{F}} g(j) \;\geq\; \sum_{j=1}^{m} g(j)$ as desired. □

We may assume that $\sum_{j=1}^{m} b_j(j) \leq \frac{\sum_{j=1}^{m} v_{a_j}(j)}{m^{\frac{2}{3}}}$, otherwise we are done.

Corollary 11. *Set* $\mathcal{F} := \{j \in [\![1, m]\!] : b_{a_j}(a_j) < \frac{2max_\ell v_{a_\ell}(\ell)}{m^{\frac{2}{3}}}, v_{a_j}(j) > 0\}$. *We have*

$$\sum_{j \in \mathcal{F}} v_{a_j}(j) \geq \frac{1}{2} \cdot \sum_{j=1}^{m} v_{a_j}(j)$$

Proof. Simply set $f(j) = b_{a_j}(a_j)$, $g(j) = v_{a_j}(j)$ and $k = m^{\frac{2}{3}}$. If $\sum_{j=1}^{m} b_j(j) \leq \frac{\sum_{j=1}^{m} v_{a_j}(j)}{m^{\frac{2}{3}}}$ then we may apply Lemma ?? and $\sum_{j \in \mathcal{F}} v_{a_j}(j) \geq \frac{\sum_{j=1}^{m} v_{a_j}(j)}{2}$ follows immediately. □

We are almost ready to prove Theorem ??. First, we require another set of definitions. Let $u_i^t(j)$ be the utility of player $i$ for item $j$ in round $t$; thus, as the utility functions are *quasi-linear*, we have $u_i^t(j) := v_i(j) - p_j^t$. Define $U_i^t := \max_{j \in M}(u_i^t(j))$ for all $i \in N$, $j \in M$, $t \in [\![0, \mathcal{T}]\!]$. If $i = 0$, we set for all $j \in M$, $t \in [\![0, \mathcal{T}]\!]$, $U_i^t = u_i^t(j) = 0$. Denote by $S_i^t$ the item agent $i$ bids on in round $t$. As agent $i$ bids truthfully, it follows that $S_i^t \in \text{argmax}_{j \in M}(u_i^t(j))$ and item $S_i^t$ provides utility $U_i^t$ for agent $i$ in round $t$. This leads to the following trivial lower bound on the welfare of the auction.

Observation 12. *The social welfare of the combinatorial clock auction is at least* $\sum_{i \in N} U_i^{\mathcal{T}}$.

Proof. The social welfare of the combinatorial clock auction is exactly

$$\sum_{i \in N} v_i(S_i^{\mathcal{T}}) \;\geq\; \sum_{i \in N} \left(v_i(S_i^{\mathcal{T}}) - p_{S_i^{\mathcal{T}}}^{\mathcal{T}}\right) \;=\; \sum_{i \in N} U_i^{\mathcal{T}}$$

where the inequality holds because prices are non-negative. □

Thus we may assume that $\sum_{j=1}^{m} U_{a_j}^{\mathcal{T}} \leq \frac{\sum_{j=1}^{m} v_{a_j}(j)}{m^{\frac{2}{3}}}$.

Corollary 13. *With* $\mathcal{F}$ *defined as in Corollary ??, we have*

$$\sum_{j \in \mathcal{F}} \left(v_{a_j}(j) - U_{a_j}^{\mathcal{T}}\right) \;\geq\; \frac{1}{3} \cdot \sum_{j=1}^{m} v_{a_j}(j)$$

Proof. We have

$$\sum_{j \in \mathcal{F}} \left(v_{a_j}(j) - u_{a_j}^{\mathcal{T}}\right) \;=\; \sum_{j \in \mathcal{F}} v_{a_j}(j) - \sum_{j \in \mathcal{F}} u_{a_j}^{\mathcal{T}} \;\geq\; \frac{1}{2} \cdot \sum_{j=1}^{m} v_{a_j}(j) - \sum_{j \in \mathcal{F}} u_{a_j}^{\mathcal{T}} \;\geq\; \frac{1}{2} \cdot \sum_{j=1}^{m} v_{a_j}(j) - \sum_{j=1}^{m} u_{a_j}^{\mathcal{T}}$$

To see this, note that the first inequality follows from Corollary ??. Then, by assumption, we obtain

$$\sum_{j\in\mathcal{F}}\left(v_{a_j}(j)-u_{a_j}^{\mathcal{T}}\right) \;\geq\; \frac{1}{2}\cdot\sum_{j=1}^{m}v_{a_j}(j)-\frac{1}{m^{\frac{2}{3}}}\cdot\sum_{j=1}^{m}v_{a_j}(j) \;\geq\; \frac{1}{3}\cdot\sum_{j=1}^{m}v_{a_j}(j) \qquad \square$$

Next define, for all $j \in \mathcal{F}$, a sequence $(\omega_j^t)$, $t \in [\![0, \mathcal{T}]\!]$. Again, here $\mathcal{F}$ defined as in Corollary ??. To initialize each sequence, set $\omega_j^0 := j$. Next, take $t > 0$. If for every pair $j, j' \in \mathcal{F}$ we have $S_{a_j}^t \neq S_{a_{j'}}^t$ then set $\omega_j^t := S_{a_j}^t$. Otherwise set $\omega_j^t := \omega_j^{t-1}$. A key observation is that $\omega^t$ is an injection.

Lemma 14.

$$\sum_{j\in\mathcal{F}}\sum_{t=0}^{\mathcal{T}-1}\left(p_{\omega_j^t}^{t+1}-p_{\omega_j^t}^{t}\right) \;\geq\; \frac{1}{3}\cdot\sum_{j=1}^{m}v_{a_j}(j)$$

Proof. Thus, by definition, we have $u_{a_j}^0(\omega_j^0) = v_{a_j}(j)$, for all $j \in \mathcal{F}$. Furthermore, $u_{a_j}^t(\omega_j^t) \leq U_{a_j}^t$, for all $t \in [\![1, \mathcal{T}]\!]$ and $j \in \mathcal{F}$. This inequality follows trivially from the definition of $U_{a_j}^t$. Combining these inequalities with Corollary ??, we obtain

$$\frac{1}{3}\cdot\sum_{j=1}^{m}v_{a_j}(j) \leq \sum_{j\in\mathcal{F}}\left(v_{a_j}(j)-U_{a_j}^{\mathcal{T}}\right) \leq \sum_{j\in\mathcal{F}}\left(u_{a_j}^0(\omega_j^0)-u_{a_j}^{\mathcal{T}}(\omega_j^{\mathcal{T}})\right) = \sum_{j\in\mathcal{F}}\sum_{t=0}^{\mathcal{T}-1}\left(u_{a_j}^t(\omega_j^t)-u_{a_j}^{t+1}(\omega_j^{t+1})\right) \tag{5}$$

Here, the last equality follows by telescoping. Moreover, $u_{a_j}^t(\omega_j^{t-1}) \leq u_{a_j}^t(\omega_j^t) \leq U_{a_j}^t$, for all $t \in [\![1, \mathcal{T}]\!]$ and $j \in \mathcal{F}$. To see this, observe that if $\omega_j^{t+1} \neq \omega_j^t$ then $\omega_j^{t+1} := S_{a_j}^{t+1}$; thus, by truthfulness, we have $u_{a_j}^t(\omega_j^t) \leq u_{a_j}^t(\omega_j^{t+1})$. Hence

$$\sum_{j\in\mathcal{F}}\sum_{t=0}^{\mathcal{T}-1}\left(u_{a_j}^t(\omega_j^t)-u_{a_j}^{t+1}(\omega_j^{t+1})\right) \leq \sum_{j\in\mathcal{F}}\sum_{t=0}^{\mathcal{T}-1}\left(u_{a_j}^t(\omega_j^t)-u_{a_j}^{t+1}(\omega_j^t)\right) = \sum_{j\in\mathcal{F}}\sum_{t=0}^{\mathcal{T}-1}\left(p_{\omega_j^t}^{t+1}-p_{\omega_j^t}^{t}\right) \tag{6}$$

The equality arises because the difference in utility an agent derives from a good at two distinct points in time is equal to the difference in prices of the good at those two points in time. Putting together (??) and (??) completes the proof of the lemma. □

Proof of Theorem ??. To further understand how prices change during the auction, we apply our technical lemmas to a new function $g : M \to \mathbf{N}$. For each $i \in M$, set

$$g(i) \;:=\; \epsilon\cdot\left|\{t \in [\![0,\mathcal{T}]\!] \;:\; \exists j \in \mathcal{F} \text{ such that } \omega_j^t = i, \text{ and } p_{\omega_j^t}^{t+1} - p_{\omega_j^t}^{t} = \epsilon\}\right|$$

Because $j \mapsto \omega_j^t$ is injective, for all $t \in [\![0, \mathcal{T}]\!]$, we have that

$$\sum_{i=1}^{m}g(i) \;=\; \sum_{t=0}^{\mathcal{T}-1}\sum_{j\in\mathcal{F}}(p_{\omega_j^t}^{t+1}-p_{\omega_j^t}^{t}) \tag{7}$$

By (??) and Lemma ??, we immediately obtain

Corollary 15. $\sum_{i=1}^m g(i) \;\geq\; \frac{1}{3}\cdot\sum_{j=1}^m v_{a_j}(j)$ □

In addition, for any $t \in [\![0, \mathcal{T}-1]\!]$, if $(S_{a_j}^t, p_{S_{a_j}^t}^t)_{j\in F} = (S_{a_j}^{t+1}, p_{S_{a_j}^{t+1}}^{t+1})_{j\in F}$ then $S_{a_j}^t = \omega_j^t$, for all $j \in \mathcal{F}$. This follows as the price of an item rises if it is demanded by more than one agent in round $t$. So if agent $a_j$ demand the same item in round s $t$ and $t + 1$ **and** the price if this item is unchanged, then $a_j$ was the only agent who demanded that item. Consequently, for evry pair $j, j' \in \mathcal{F}$ we have $S_{a_j}^t \neq S_{a_{j'}}^t$ and this causes us to set $\omega_j^t := S_{a_j}^t$. In this case, $\sum_{j\in\mathcal{F}}(p_{\omega_j^t}^{t+1} - p_{\omega_j^t}^t) = 0$. This implies that the bids that cause the price of item $\omega_j^t$ to rise are made when $(S_{a_j}^t, P_{a_j}^t)_{j\in F} \neq (S_{a_j}^{t+1}, P_{a_j}^{t+1})_{j\in F}$. We define $\tau := \{t \in [\![0, \mathcal{T}-1]\!] : (S_{a_j}^t, P_{a_j}^t)_{j\in F} \neq (S_{a_j}^{t+1}, P_{a_j}^{t+1})_{j\in F}\}$.

We now apply the technical Lemma ?? to $g$. To do so we again set $f(j) = b_j(a_j)$ and also set $k = \frac{m^{\frac{2}{3}}}{3}$. The conditions of the lemma hold. To see this first note that, by construction, $b_j(a_j)$ is decreasing. Second, we may assume that $\sum_{j=1}^m b_j(j) \leq \frac{\sum_{j=1}^m v_{a_j}(j)}{m^{\frac{2}{3}}}$, otherwise we are done. Thus

$$\sum_{j=1}^m b_j(j) \leq \frac{\sum_{j=1}^m v_{a_j}(j)}{m^{\frac{2}{3}}} \leq \frac{3}{m^{\frac{2}{3}}} \cdot \sum_{j\in\mathcal{F}} \sum_{t=0}^{\mathcal{T}-1} \left(p_{\omega_j^t}^{t+1} - p_{\omega_j^t}^t\right) = \frac{1}{k} \cdot \sum_{j\in\mathcal{F}} \sum_{t=0}^{\mathcal{T}-1} \left(p_{\omega_j^t}^{t+1} - p_{\omega_j^t}^t\right) = \frac{1}{k} \cdot \sum_{j=1}^m g(j) \quad (8)$$

Note that (??) implies the final condition of the Lemma ?? holds. So, we obtain that

$$\sum_{j=1}^m (g(j) - c)^+ \geq \frac{\sum_{j=1}^m g(j)}{2} \quad (9)$$

We proceed by applying some counting arguments. Take an item $j$ such that $g(j) > \max(b_j(j), c)$. Observe that the price of item $j$ has increased $\frac{g(j)}{\epsilon}$ times during the time periods in $\tau$. Furthermore, at least $\frac{g(j)-\max(b_j(j),c)-\epsilon}{\epsilon}$ of the bids causing the price rises were bids with value strictly above $\max(b_j(j), c)$. An agent who made a bid above $\max(b_j(j), c)$ on item $j$ must have won an item with a price greater than $c$ or he would have won item $j$ instead of bidder $j$ in the greedy allocation. Therefore, by definition of $c$ in the Lemma ??, the agents who can bid above $\max(b_j(j), c)$ on item $j$ belong to the set $\{i \in N, i < 6m^{\frac{1}{3}}\}$. So we must have that

$$6m^{\frac{1}{3}}|\tau| \geq \sum_{j=1}^m \frac{(g(j) - \max(b_j(j), c) - \epsilon)^+}{\epsilon} \geq \frac{\sum_{j=1}^m (g(j) - c)^+ - \sum_{j=1}^m b_j(j)}{\epsilon} - m \quad (10)$$

We must now bound $\tau$. To do this, we need to bound the number of different bids players in $\{a_j, j \in \mathcal{F}\}$ can make. Take $j \in \mathcal{F}$ and $i \in M$. If $b_i(i) \geq b_{a_j}(a_j)$ then the maximum bid of $a_j$ on $i$ is at most $b_i(i)$. Otherwise, the greedy procedure would have selected agent $a_j$ to win item $i$ rather than agent $i$. If $b_i(i) < b_{a_j}(a_j)$ then the maximum bid of $a_j$ on $i$ is at most $b_{a_j}(a_j)$. Otherwise, again, the greedy procedure would have selected agent $a_j$ to win item $i$ rather than agent $i$. By definition of $\mathcal{F}$, we have $b_{a_j}(a_j) \leq \frac{2\max_\ell v_{a_\ell}(\ell)}{m^{\frac{2}{3}}}$. Consequently, for any item $i \in M$ all the bids of the players in $\{a_j, j \in \mathcal{F}\}$ on $i$ are below $\max(\frac{2\max_\ell v_{a_\ell}(\ell)}{m^{\frac{2}{3}}}, b_i(i))$. Therefore, by definition of $\tau$, we have $|\tau| \leq \frac{\sum_{i=1}^m \max(\frac{2\max_\ell v_{a_\ell}(\ell)}{m^{\frac{2}{3}}}, b_i(i))}{\epsilon} + m$.

Claim 16. $\max_\ell v_{a_\ell}(\ell) \leq \sum_{i=1}^m b_i(i) + \sum_{i\in N} U_i^{\mathcal{T}}$

Proof. Let $j \in \operatorname{argmax}_\ell v_{a_\ell}(\ell)$, let $i$ be the bidder who have made the maximal bid on $j$. We have $v_{a_j}(j) \leq b_i(j) + u_{a_j}^{\mathcal{T}}(j) \leq b_i(i) + U_{a_j}^{\mathcal{T}} \leq \sum_{i=1}^m b_i(i) + \sum_{i\in N} U_i^{\mathcal{T}}$. □

Therefore,

$$\epsilon \cdot |\tau| \leq m\epsilon + \sum_{i=1}^m \max\left(\frac{2\max_\ell v_{a_\ell}(\ell)}{m^{\frac{2}{3}}}, b_i(i)\right) \leq m\epsilon + \sum_{i=1}^m \frac{2\max_\ell v_{a_\ell}(\ell)}{m^{\frac{2}{3}}} + \sum_{i=1}^m b_i(i) \quad (11)$$

$$\leq m\epsilon + 2m \cdot \frac{\sum_{i=1}^m b_i(i) + \sum_{i\in N} U_i^{\mathcal{T}}}{m^{\frac{2}{3}}} + \sum_{i=1}^m b_i(i) \leq m\epsilon + (2m^{\frac{1}{3}} + 1)\sum_{i=1}^m b_i(i) + 2m^{\frac{1}{3}} \cdot \sum_{i\in N} U_i^{\mathcal{T}}$$

Combining (??) and (??) gives

$$6m^{\frac{1}{3}} \cdot \frac{m\epsilon + (2m^{\frac{1}{3}}+1)\sum_{i=1}^m b_i(i) + 2m^{\frac{1}{3}}\sum_{i\in N} U_i^{\mathcal{T}}}{\epsilon} \geq \frac{\sum_{j=1}^m (g(j)-c)^+ - \sum_{j=1}^m b_j(j)}{\epsilon} - m$$

Simplifying this gives

$$(12m^{\frac{2}{3}} + 6m^{\frac{1}{3}} + 1) \cdot \sum_{i=1}^m b_i(i) + 12\sum_{i\in N} U_i^{\mathcal{T}} \geq \sum_{j=1}^m (g(j)-c)^+ - m\epsilon - 6m^{\frac{4}{3}}\epsilon \tag{12}$$

Finally, assuming $m \gg 1$ and $\epsilon \ll \frac{\sum_{i=1}^m b_i(i)}{m^{\frac{4}{3}}}$, we obtain from (??) that

$$13m^{\frac{2}{3}} \cdot \sum_{i=1}^m b_i(i) + 12m^{\frac{2}{3}} \cdot \sum_{i\in N} U_i^{\mathcal{T}} \geq \sum_{j=1}^m (g(j)-c)^+ \geq \frac{\sum_{j=1}^m g(j)}{2} \geq \frac{\sum_{j=1}^m v_{a_j}(j)}{6}$$

Here the second inequality follows directly from Inequality (??). The final inequality follows from Corollary ??. Therefore, either

$$13m^{\frac{2}{3}} \cdot \sum_{i=1}^m b_i(i) \geq \frac{\sum_{j=1}^m v_{a_j}(j)}{12} \quad \text{or} \quad 12m^{\frac{2}{3}} \cdot \sum_{i\in N} U_i^{\mathcal{T}} \geq \frac{\sum_{j=1}^m v_{a_j}(j)}{12}$$

In both cases, the welfare ratio is $O(m^{\frac{2}{3}})$. This completes the proof of the theorem. □

As stated, the above proof of Theorem ?? is for the standard stopping rule. However, the counting arguments used in the proof also apply for the enhanced stopping rule; this is because there an item price can still only rise in the final round if some agent was bidding for the item (and there is a conflict with the revenue maximizing allocation).

### 3.2 A Lower Bound on The Welfare Ratio for Unit-Demand-Bidders

Surprisingly, the $m^{\frac{2}{3}}$ bound is tight. Due to space constraints, the proof of this lower bound theorem is given the full version of the paper.

Theorem 17. *Given truthful bidding, there is a unit-demand instance of the combinatorial clock auction using the basic price increment rule with welfare ratio $\Omega(m^{\frac{2}{3}})$.*

## 4 THE WELFARE RATIO FOR GENERAL BIDDERS

We now proceed to the case of general bidders. Again, we consider the standard price increment rule when prices increase by a fixed amount under excess demand, that is $\iota(0) = \iota(1) = 0$, and $\iota(i) = 1$ if $i \geq 2$. First we present a simple upper bound on the welfare ratio.

Theorem 18. *Given truthful bidding, the welfare ratio of the combinatorial clock auction is $O(m)$.*

Proof. Take an instance with $n$ agents and $m \geq n$ items. Let $\mathcal{S}^* = \{S_1^*, S_2^*, \ldots, S_n^*\}$ be the optimal allocation with welfare $\texttt{opt} = \sum_{i=1}^n v_i(S_i^*)$. Let $\mathcal{F}$ be the set of bidders who get at least one item in the optimal allocation. That is, $\mathcal{F} := \{i \in [\![1,n]\!] : S_i^* \neq \emptyset\}$. Note that we clearly have $|\mathcal{F}| \leq m$. Now let $p_j^{\mathcal{T}}$ be the price of item $j$ at the end of the combinatorial clock auction. Suppose there is an agent $i$ such that $\sum_{j\in S_i^*} p_j^{\mathcal{T}} \leq v_i(S_i^*) - \frac{\texttt{opt}}{2m}$. Then agent $i$ has utility at least $\frac{\texttt{opt}}{2m}$ in the combinatorial clock auction. Hence $\texttt{cca} \geq \frac{\texttt{opt}}{2m}$ as required. If no such agent exists, then we have

$$\sum_{j=1}^m p_j^{\mathcal{T}} \geq \sum_{i\in\mathcal{F}}\sum_{j\in S_i^*} p_j^{\mathcal{T}} \geq \sum_{i\in\mathcal{F}}\left(v_i(S_i^*) - \frac{\texttt{opt}}{2m}\right) = \sum_{i\in\mathcal{F}} v_i(S_i^*) - \frac{|\mathcal{F}|}{2m}\cdot\texttt{opt} \geq \frac{1}{2}\cdot\texttt{opt}$$

Consequently, there is an item $j$ with price $p_j^{\mathcal{T}} \geq \frac{1}{2m} \cdot \texttt{opt}$. Therefore there must have been a bid during the auction for a package $S$ containing item $j$ at a price at least $\frac{1}{2m} \cdot \texttt{opt} - \epsilon$. Thus, in this case $\texttt{cca} \geq \frac{\texttt{opt}}{2m} - \epsilon$ and the result follows. □

A simple example was given in [? ] that has a matching lower bound. We repeat this result as the exemple is informative.

Theorem 19 ([? ]). *Given truthful bidding, the welfare ratio of the combinatorial clock auction is at least* $\Omega(m)$.

Proof. Take a set $[\![0, l]\!]$ of items and a set $[\![1, 2l]\!]$ of agents. (We may also add dummy items to match the assumption in the proof of the upper bound that $m \geq n$.) For $i \in [\![1, l]\!]$ the valuation function of agent $2i$ and agent $2i - 1$ are identical. We denote this function by $v_i$ and define it as:

$$v_i(S) = \begin{cases} 2V \text{ if } S = \{0, i\} \\ V \text{ if } S = \{i\} \\ 0 \text{ otherwise} \end{cases}$$

Here we assume that $V$ is a large multiple of $\epsilon$. We assume, in the case of a tie that the pair $\{0, i\}$ is chosen by player $2i$ and $2i - 1$ over the singleton $\{i\}$. This can be done by perturbing the valuation function. It is easy to see that, for all $i \in [\![1, l]\!]$, agents $2i$ and $2i - 1$ will bid every round on the pair $\{0, i\}$ until the price of every item is $V + \epsilon$. No bids will then occur and the auction will then terminate. Because every bid submitted contains the item 0, the auction can only accept one bid. Thus the social welfare of this allocation is $V$. The welfare of the optimal allocation is clearly $l \cdot V$. So the welfare ratio of the combinatorial clock auction is at least $\Omega(m)$. □

Notice that the above example consists of bidders who desire packages of cardinality at most 2. It follows that there is no hope of obtaining a sub-linear welfare ratio even in the basic case where all the agents bid on sets of size at most two. Therefore, sub-linear welfare ratios apply only for unit-demand bidders. We also remark that this lower bound (and the others in this paper) extend to the case of generic lots where item supply can be greater than one. This is easy to show by making identical copies of appropriately chosen bidders.

## 5 THE IMPOSSIBILITY OF GENERATING HIGH WELFARE WHILST INCREMENTING PRICES WITH RESPECT TO EXCESS DEMAND

Recall that Theorem **??** states that if the price increment function is a linear function of demand then the combinatorial clock auction always performs very well in that the welfare ratio is polylogarithmic in the number of agents and items. Specifically, under truthful bidding, the price increment rule $\iota(i) = i$ gives an $O(\kappa^2 \log n \log^2 m)$ welfare ratio if the agents only bid on packages with cardinality at most $\kappa$.

There are two major issues of concern that arise with such a price increment rule, one theoretic and one practical. First, on the theory side, aesthetically it is much more natural if prices rise only under excess demand. For example, the affine function $\iota(i) = i - 1$ is preferable to the linear function. In particular, we may want to impose the constraint that $\iota(1) = 0$ and $\iota(2) > 0$. As we have seen, that is indeed the current practice. However, we will show in this section that this constraint is very undesirable: its usage guarantees a polynomial welfare ratio, even in the case of unit-demand bidders.

The second concern is more practical. *Demand reduction* is the strategic behaviour where agents artificially reduce demand to limit price rises during the auction. We remark that this behaviour can arise in combinatorial clock spectrum auctions where $\iota(1) = 0$. But, when $\iota(1) > 0$ the issue is even more pressing. There is an apparent contradiction between the aim of truthful bidding and the property of essentially continuous price rises. In this situation, an agent faces the dilemma of risking losing an item by dropping out of the bidding or potentially watching its profits evaporate by staying in the auction as the prices rise simply by its own presence. We will examine this issue in detail in Section ?? when we study strategic bidding. In this section, though, we return to the theoretic concern and show why restricting the price increment function to be a function of excess demand is theoretically problematic.

THEOREM 20. *Take any increment rule $\iota : N \to \mathbf{N}$ with $\iota(0) = \iota(1) = 0$. Then, for all $\mathcal{N}, \mathcal{M}$, there exists an auction with $n \geq \mathcal{N}$ unit-demand bidders and $m \geq \mathcal{M}$ items, where the welfare ratio is $\Omega(n) = \Omega(\sqrt{m})$.*

PROOF. Take any price increment function where a price can only rise with excess demand. Thus $\iota(0) = \iota(1) = 0$. Furthermore, we must $\iota(2) > 0$ otherwise the combinatorial clock auction may never terminate. In the auction we construct, no more than three agents will ever bid on the same item. Hence, we are only concerned with $\iota(2)$ and $\iota(3)$. By the monotonicity of $\iota$ we have $\iota(2) \leq \iota(3)$. Without loss of generality, we may also assume that $\epsilon\iota(3) \ll 1$ and that $\iota(3)$ divide 1. We take $n = max(\mathcal{N}, \sqrt{\mathcal{M}})$. We construct a unit-demand auction with $n + 2$ agents labelled $\{0, 0', 1, \dots, n\}$, and $n^2$ items labelled $\{a_{i,j}, 1 \leq i, j \leq n\}$. For each bidder $i' \in \{1, \dots, n\}$, we set

$$v_{i'}(a_{i,j}) = \begin{cases} n + 1 - j & \text{if } i = i' \\ 0 & \text{if } i \neq i' \end{cases}$$

Given a tie in the utility, we assume agent $i'$ bids on the item with the highest value. We then have two additional bidders. The valuation function of agent 0 is $v_0(a_{i,j}) = 3(n + 1 - j)$ for all $1 \leq i, j \leq n$. The valuation function of agent $0'$ is identical. To complete the proof we need the following claim:

CLAIM 21. *Let $k \in [\![0, n]\!]$. Let $t_k$ be the first round where the utility of 0 and $0'$ is $3n - 3k$. Then at round $t_k$:*

- *For any $i, j \in [\![1, n]\!]$ with $j > k$, the price of item $a_{i,j}$ is 0.*
- *For any $i, j \in [\![1, n]\!]$ with $j \leq k$, the price of item $a_{i,j}$ is in $[3(k + 1 - j), 3(k + 1 - j) + \iota(2)]$.*
- *For any $i, j \in [\![1, n]\!]$ with $j \leq k$, the maximum bid of agent $i$ on item $a_{j,k}$ is 1.*

PROOF. We begin with some observations. First, because 0 and $0'$ have the same valuation function, they will stay in the auction until their utility becomes 0. Thus $t_k$ exists for all $k \in [\![0, n]\!]$. Second, for distinct $i, i' \in [\![1, n]\!]$, the supports of $v_i$ and $v_{i'}$ are disjoint. That is, agents $i$ and $i'$ want completely different items. This means that only one item can have a price rise in each round, and that is the item that agents 0 and $0'$ bid for. Indeed this is why at most three agents will ever bid for the same item. These observations imply that the price on any item at time $t_k$ is the lowest such that the utility of 0 and $0'$ for this item is lower than $3n - 3k$. The first two bullets in the claim follow immediately. We prove the third bullet of the claim by induction on $k$. For the base case, at the start of the auction, the statement holds for $k = 0$. Take $k, i \in [\![1, n]\!]$. By the induction hypothesis, we have that for any $j \in [\![1, n]\!]$ with $j \leq k - 1$, the maximum bid of agent $i$ at time $t_{k-1}$ on $a_{j,k}$ is 1. At time $t_{k-1}$, the utility of agent $i$ for item $a_{i,k}$ is $n + 1 - k$ and the utility for item $a_{i,k+1}$ is at most $n - k$. On the other hand, the utility of agent $i$ for an item $a_{i,j}$ with $j < k$ is at most

$$(n + 1 - j) - p_{a_{i,j}}^{t_{k-1}} \leq (n + 1 - j) - 3 \cdot ((k - 1) + 1 - j) = n + 1 + 2j - 3k \leq n - k - 1$$

It follows that between $t_{k-1}$ and $t_k$, agent $i$ will bid on $a_{i,k}$ until its price has risen by $1 + \iota(3)$, then $i$ will bid on $a_{i,k+1}$. Therefore, between $t_{k-1}$ and $t_k$, its maximum bid on $a_{i,k}$ is 1. Its maximum bid on $a_{i,k+1}$ is 0 as by the first bullet the price of $a_{i,k+1}$ is 0 until $t_k$. □

Now consider the allocation where agent $i \in [\![1, n]\!]$ recieves the item $a_{i,n}$, agent 0 gets item $a_{1,1}$, and agent 0′ gets item $a_{2,1}$. By Claim ??, this is a revenue maximizing allocation and thus can be output by the combinatorial clock auction. In this case, we have $\mathsf{cca} = 2 \cdot (3n) + n = 7n$. The welfare of the optimal allocation is clearly $\mathsf{opt} = n^2 + 6n - 2$. Because the number of items is $n^2$, the claimed welfare ratios arise. □

## 6 THE WELFARE RATIO WITH STRATEGIC BIDDING

Theorem ?? tells us the combinatorial clock auction may perform extremely poorly if the price increment rule is a function of excess demand. In contrast, Theorem ?? tells us that, in theory, the combinatorial clock auction will perform well if the price increment rule is simply a function of demand. But, as discussed, the use of a price increment rule with the property $\iota(1) > 0$ necessitates that we study strategic bidding. Ergo, in this section, we study non-truthful bidding in the combinatorial clock auction.

To do this, we compare the basic price increment rule with the corresponding price increment rule with the property that $\iota(1) = 1$. Specifically, recall the standard price increment function is

$$\iota(d) = \begin{cases} 0 & \text{if } d \in \{0, 1\} \\ 1 & \text{if } d \geq 2 \end{cases}$$

In this section, we allow for non-truthful bidding given the price increment function

$$\hat{\iota}(d) = \begin{cases} 0 & \text{if } d = 0 \\ 1 & \text{if } d \geq 1 \end{cases}$$

We consider unit-demand bidders and show that non-truthful bidding in the latter case leads to a strictly better welfare ratio than the ratio obtained under truthful bidding in the former case. We emphasize that this is an extremely strong result. It requires only trivial assumptions and then applies to any form of non-truthful bidding. In particular, it does does not require any equilibrium conditions nor any form of non-myopic optimization on behalf of the agents. Specifically, the agents may apply any bidding strategy they want provided that (i) they never bid for an item above its valuation, and (ii) they cannot drop out of the auction when the price of the items they desire is relatively close to zero. Formally, these two assumptions are:

**(Assumption I) No Overbidding:** An agent may not bid for an item at a price higher than its value of the item.

**(Assumption II) No Early-Departure:** Let $v_i^*$ be the value agent $i$ obtains in the optimal allocation. Then, for some small constant $\lambda > 0$, agent $i$ will not quit the auction in any round where its utility is greater than $(1 - \lambda) \cdot v_i^*$.

We remark that the no-overbidding assumption is standard in the auction literature. Furthermore, the no-early departure is very benign. In these auctions, if an agent does not bid in a round then they cannot bid in subsequent rounds. Thus, it is risky for an agent to stop bidding ("depart the auction") if prices are currently very low and its utility is currently high. If it does then, given prices are low, the agent may be subsequently outbid leading it to win nothing despite the fact it was will to pay a much higher price. For small $\mu$, it is extremely hard to envisage this assumption being violating in important auctions, such as spectrum auctions. With these two assumptions, we have the following theorem.

THEOREM 22. *Given Assumption I and II and price increment function $\hat{\iota}$, the welfare ratio of the combinatorial clock auction is $O(\frac{1}{\lambda} \cdot \sqrt{m \cdot \log m})$ for unit-demand auctions.*

Before proving the theorem, it will be useful to make a few observations. First, the bound in Theorem ?? is almost tight; we can find an auction instance where the welfare $\Omega(\frac{1}{\lambda} \cdot \sqrt{m})$. Second, both assumptions are required – without either of them extremely poor outcomes may arise. Thirdly, the theorem does not extend to the case of the basic price increment rule $\iota$; consequently, the price increment rule $\hat{\iota}$ may be more resilient against strategic behaviours than the basic price increment rule.

In order to prove Theorem ??, we will first prove a weaker, but related, result.

THEOREM 23. *Given Assumptions I and price increment function $\hat{\iota}$. Assume the agents must bid if their utility is positive. Then the welfare ratio of the combinatorial clock auction is $O(\sqrt{m \cdot \log m})$ for unit-demand auctions.*

In order to prove this theorem, we require the following two lemmas.

LEMMA 24. *For any $f : [\![1, m]\!] \to \mathbb{N}$, there exists $v^* \in \mathbb{N}$ such that*

$$\sum_{v^* \leq f(j) < 2v*} f(j) \geq \frac{\sum_{j=1}^{m} f(j)}{3 \cdot \log(|supp(f)|)}$$

PROOF. The proof is standard. See [? ] for the proof of a slightly simpler result. □

LEMMA 25. *Take any $f, g : [\![1, m]\!] \to \mathbb{N}$ where $f$ is decreasing and $\sum_{j=1}^{m} f(j) \leq \frac{1}{8} \cdot \sum_{j=1}^{m} g(j)$. Then there exists $(\gamma, c) \in [\![1, m]\!] \times \mathbb{N}$ such that $f(\gamma) \leq c$ and*

$$\sum_{j=\gamma}^{m} (g(j) - c)^+ \geq \frac{1}{384 \log m} \cdot \sum_{j=1}^{m} g(j)$$

PROOF. Set $h : j \mapsto f(j) + \frac{g(j)}{8}$. Then, by the conditions of the lemma, it follows that

$$4 \cdot \sum_{j=1}^{m} h(j) \leq \sum_{j=1}^{m} g(j) \tag{13}$$

Furthermore,

$$\sum_{j:g(j)<3h(j)} g(j) \leq \sum_{j:g(j)<3h(j)} 3h(j) \leq 3 \cdot \sum_{j=1}^{m} h(j) \tag{14}$$

Together, Inequalities (??) and (??) imply that

$$\sum_{j:g(j)\geq 3h(j)} g(j) \geq \sum_{j=1}^{m} h(j) \tag{15}$$

Inequality (??), in turn, implies that

$$\sum_{j:g(j)\geq 3h(j)} h(j) \geq \sum_{j:g(j)\geq 3h(j)} \frac{g(j)}{8} \geq \frac{1}{8} \sum_{j=1}^{m} h(j) \tag{16}$$

Now apply Proposition ?? to the function $h$. Thus, there exists $v^* \in \mathbb{N}$ such that

$$\sum_{j:v^* \leq h(j) < 2v^*} h(j) \geq \frac{1}{3 \log m} \cdot \sum_{j=1}^{m} h(j),$$

Hence by (??), we obtain that

$$\frac{1}{24\log m}\cdot\sum_{j=1}^{m}h(j) \le \sum_{\substack{j:g(j)\ge 3h(j),\\ v^*\le h(j)<2v^*}} h(j) \le \sum_{\substack{j:g(j)\ge 3h(j),\\ v^*\le h(j)<2v^*}} 2v^* \tag{17}$$

We then have

$$\sum_{\substack{j:g(j)\ge 3h(j),\\ v^*\le h(j)<2v^*}} (g(j)-2v^*) \ge \sum_{\substack{j:g(j)\ge 3h(j),\\ v*\le h(j)<2v^*}} v^* \ge \frac{1}{48\log m}\cdot\sum_{j=1}^{m}h(j) \tag{18}$$

Here the first inequality arises as the summation is over $j$ such that $g(j)\ge 3v^*$. The second inequality follows immediately from (??). Next set $c := 2v^*$ and set

$$\gamma := \min\{j\in[\![1,m]\!] : g(j)\ge 3h(j) \text{ and } v^*\le h(j)<2v^*\}$$

Observe that $c\ge h(\gamma)$. Furthermore $h(\gamma)\ge f(\gamma)$, by definition. Now,

$$\sum_{j=\gamma}^{m}(g(j)-c)^+ \ge \sum_{j=\gamma}^{m}(g(j)-2v^*) \ge \sum_{\substack{j:g(j)\ge 3h(j)\\ v^*\le h(j)<2v^*}} g(j)-2v^* \ge \frac{1}{48\log m}\cdot\sum_{j=1}^{m}h(j) \ge \frac{1}{384\log m}\cdot\sum_{j=1}^{m}g(j)$$

Here, the third inequality follows immediately from (??). The last inequality holds because, by definition, $h(j)\ge\frac{g(j)}{8}$ for all $j$. This completes the proof of the lemma. □

We will also need the following technical lemma.

Lemma 26. *Given functions $f,g:[\![1,m]\!]\to\mathbb{N}$ and $k\in\mathbb{N}$. If $f$ is decreasing and $\sum_{j=1}^{m}f(j)\le\frac{\sum_{j=1}^{m}g(j)}{16k}$ then there exists $(\gamma,c)\in[\![1,m]\!]\times\mathbb{N}$ such that*

$$f(\gamma) \le c \tag{19}$$

$$\gamma_c := |\{j\in[\![1,m]\!] : f(j)>c\}| \le \frac{m}{8k} \tag{20}$$

$$f(\gamma)\cdot\gamma_c \le \frac{\sum_{j=1}^{m}f(j)}{k} \tag{21}$$

$$\sum_{j=\gamma}^{m}(g(j)-c)^+ \ge \frac{1}{768\log m}\cdot\sum_{j=1}^{m}g(j) \tag{22}$$

Proof. Set $c' := f(\frac{m}{8k})$. Then, by Lemma ??, we have

$$\sum_{j=1}^{m}(g(j)-c')^+ \ge \frac{1}{2}\cdot\sum_{j=1}^{m}g(j) \ge 8k\cdot\sum_{j=1}^{m}f(j)$$

We now apply Lemma ?? with $j\mapsto kf(j)$ and $j\mapsto(g(j)-c')^+$. So there exists $(\gamma,c'')$ such that $k\cdot f(\gamma)\le c''$ and

$$\sum_{j=\gamma}^{m}(g(j)-c')^+-c'')^+ \ge \frac{1}{768\log m}\cdot\sum_{j=1}^{m}g(j)$$

Setting $c := c'+c''$, we derive (??). We proceed to prove (??)-(??). For (??), observe that

$$f(\gamma) \le \frac{c''}{k} \le c'' \le c$$

Next, by definition, $\gamma_c := |\{j \in [\![1, m]\!] : f(j) > c\}|$. Thus $\gamma_c \leq \gamma_{c'}$ because $c \geq c'$. Therefore, we now obtain (??) as $\gamma_c \leq \frac{m}{8k}$. On the other hand, we have $k \cdot f(\gamma) \leq c'' \leq c$ and $\gamma_c \leq \gamma_{c''}$. We can now derive (??) as follows:

$$\gamma_c \cdot f(\gamma) \leq \gamma_{c''} \cdot \frac{c''}{k} \leq \frac{\sum_{j=1}^{m} f(j)}{k}$$

Here the second inequality holds because trivially $\gamma_{c''} \cdot |\{j \in [\![1, m]\!] : f(j) > c''\}| \leq \sum_{j=1}^{m} f(j)$. □

We are now ready to prove Theorem ??.

Proof of Theorem ??. Again we make a comparisons via the greedy algorithm used in the proof of Theorem ??. Let $b_i(j)$ be the maximal bid of player $i$ for item $j$; we set $b_i(j) = 0$ if $i = 0$ or $j = 0$. Let $a_j$ be the winner of item $j$ in the optimal allocation; if $j$ has no winner in the optimal allocation, then set $a_j = 0$. Thus social welfare of the optimal allocation is $\sum_{j=1}^{m} v_{a_j}(j)$. Again, if some agent wins item $j$ in the greedy procedure then we may assume it is agent $j$. We may also assume that $f : j \mapsto b_{a_j}(a_j) + b_j(j)$ is decreasing. Note that the social welfare of the greedy procedure is $\sum_{j=1}^{m} v_j(j) \geq \sum_{j=1}^{m} b_j(j)$. We then have the following claim.

Claim 27. $\sum_{j=1}^{m} b_j(j) \leq \sum_{j=1}^{m} f(j) \leq 2 \cdot \sum_{j=1}^{m} b_j(j)$

Proof. By definition, we have

$$\sum_{j=1}^{m} f(j) = \sum_{j=1}^{m} \left(b_{a_j}(a_j) + b_j(j)\right) \geq \sum_{j=1}^{m} b_j(j)$$

So the lower bound holds trivially. On the other hand,

$$\sum_{j=1}^{m} f(j) = \sum_{j=1}^{m} b_{a_j}(a_j) + \sum_{j=1}^{m} b_j(j) \leq \sum_{j=1}^{m} b_j(j) + \sum_{j=1}^{m} b_j(j) = 2 \cdot \sum_{j=1}^{m} b_j(j)$$

To see the inequality, observe that if $a_j = a_{j'}$, then we must have either $j = j'$ or $a_j = 0$. □

Next we may assume that $\sum_{j=1}^{m} f(j) \leq \frac{\sum_{j=1}^{m} v_{a_j}(j)}{16 \cdot \sqrt{m \log m}}$. Thus we can apply the technical Lemma ?? with $j \mapsto f(j)$, $j \mapsto v_{a_j}(j)$ and $k = \sqrt{m \log m}$. Now, recall the definition of $\gamma$. Take $j \geq \gamma$ such that $v_{a_j}(j) > c = 2v^*$. Now $f(\gamma) \leq c$; thus, $f(j) = b_{a_j}(a_j) + b_j(j) \leq c$ because $f$ is decreasing. From this, can deduce that agent $a_j$ did not bid above $c$ on item $j$. Otherwise, because $b_{a_j}(a_j) \leq c$ and $b_j(j) \leq c$, the greedy algorithm with have selected agent $a_j$ to win item $j$. Furthermore, the maximum bid during the auction for item $j$ must be at least $v_{a_j}(j)$, as we assumed that each bidder remains in the auction whilst any positive utility item is available to it. Consequently, the price gap between $c$ and $v_{a_j}(j)$ for item $j$ must have been filled by other agents whilst agent $a_j$ was bidding elsewhere.

We now apply a counting argument to determine how many rounds agent $a_j$ can stay active in during the auction. Let $i \in [\![1, m]\!]$ be another item. If $b_i(i) \geq b_{a_j}(a_j)$ then the maximum bid of $a_j$ on $i$ is at most $b_i(i)$. Otherwise, the greedy procedure would have selected agent $a_j$ to win item $i$ rather than agent $i$. If $b_i(i) < b_{a_j}(a_j)$ then the maximum bid of $a_j$ on $i$ is at most $b_{a_j}(a_j)$. Otherwise, again, the greedy procedure would have selected agent $a_j$ to win item $i$ rather than agent $i$. In both cases we deduce that $b_{a_j}(i) \leq \max(b_{a_j}(a_j), b_i(i))$. Summing this inequality over all items gives $\sum_{i=1}^{m} b_{a_j}(i) \leq \sum_{i=1}^{m} \max(b_{a_j}(a_j), b_i(i))$. This implies that agent $a_j$ stops bidding after at most $\sum_{i=1}^{m} \max(b_{a_j}(a_j), b_i(i))$ rounds. We bound this sum as follows

$$\sum_{i=1}^{m} \max(b_{a_j}(a_j), b_i(i)) \leq \sum_{i=1}^{m} \left(b_{a_j}(a_j) + b_i(i)\right) \leq \sum_{i=1}^{m} f(j) + \sum_{i=1}^{m} b_i(i) \leq m \cdot f(\gamma) + \sum_{i=1}^{m} f(i) \quad (23)$$

Here, the second inequality arises because by definition, $f(j) \geq b_j(a_j)$. The third inequality arises because $f(\gamma) \leq c$ and $f$ is decreasing. The last inequality holds because, by definition, $f(i) \geq b_i(i)$, for all $i$. So which agents can fill the aforementioned price gap on item $j$? If agent $i \in [\![1, n]\!]$ bids over $c$ for the item $j$, then $b_i(i) > c$. If not, agent $i$ would have won item $j$ because $c \geq f(\gamma) \geq b_j(j)$. Therefore, the set of agents that can feasibly bid over $c$ for item $j$ is $\{i \in [\![1, n]\!] : b_i(i) > c\}$.
It follows that the total sum of the prices gaps $\sum_{j=\gamma}^{m} (v_{a_j}(j) - c)^+$ must be filled by agents in $\{i \in [\![1, n]\!] : b_i(i) > c\}$. Observe that the cardinality of this set at most $\gamma_c := |\{j \in [\![1, m]\!] : f(j) > c\}|$. Moreover, because we are using a constant price increment rule, the gaps must be closed in at most $mf(\gamma) + \sum_{i=1}^{m} f(i)$ rounds, by Inequality (??). This produces the constraint that

$$\sum_{j=\gamma}^{m} (v_{a_j}(j) - c)^+ \;\leq\; \gamma_c \cdot \left( mf(\gamma) + \sum_{j=1}^{m} f(j) \right) \tag{24}$$

We now apply (??) to obtain

$$\sum_{j=\gamma}^{m} (v_{a_j}(j) - c)^+ \;\geq\; \frac{\sum_{j=1}^{m} v_{a_j}(j)}{768 \log m} \tag{25}$$

Moreover, (??) and (??) imply

$$\begin{aligned} \gamma_c \cdot \left( mf(\gamma) + \sum_{j=1}^{m} f(j) \right) \;&=\; m \cdot f(\gamma) \cdot \gamma_c + \gamma_c \cdot \sum_{j=1}^{m} f(j) \;\leq\; \left( \frac{m}{k} + \gamma_c \right) \cdot \sum_{j=1}^{m} f(j) \\ &\leq\; \left( \frac{m}{k} + \frac{2m}{k} \right) \cdot \sum_{j=1}^{m} f(j) \;=\; \frac{3\sqrt{m} \cdot \sum_{j=1}^{m} f(j)}{\sqrt{\log m}} \end{aligned} \tag{26}$$

The last equality follows as $k = \sqrt{m \log m}$. Combining (??), (??) and (??) then gives

$$\frac{3\sqrt{m} \cdot \sum_{j=1}^{m} f(j)}{\sqrt{\log m}} \;\geq\; \frac{\sum_{j=1}^{m} v_{a_j}(j)}{768 \log m}$$

Equivalently,

$$\sum_{j=1}^{m} f(j) \;\geq\; \frac{\sum_{j=1}^{m} v_{a_j}(j)}{2304\sqrt{m \log m}}$$

Therefore, by Claim ??, we have

$$\sum_{j=1}^{m} b_j(j) \;\geq\; \frac{1}{4608\sqrt{m \log m}} \cdot \sum_{j=1}^{m} v_{a_j}(j)$$

Therefore the welfare ratio is $O(\sqrt{m \log m})$. □

Finally, Theorem ?? now follows.

Proof of Theorem ??. We use the following notation. Recall, for any $i \in N$ and any $j \in M$, that $v_i(j)$ is the value of agent $i$ for item $j$. In addition, let $t_i$ be the round where agent $i$ drops out of the auction, and let $u(i)$ be the utility agent $i$ could have obtained in the round $t_i$. Let $v(i)$ be the value agent $i$ gets in the CCA procedure and let $v^*(i)$ be the value $i$ gets in the optimal allocation. Observe for any $i \in N$, and any $j \in M$, that $p^{t_i}(j) \geq v_i(j) - u(i)$.

We now define a new valuation function. For all $i \in N$ and $j \in M$, set $\hat{v}_i(j) := \min(p^{t_i}(j), v_i(j))$. We deduce from the previous observation that $\hat{v}_i(j) \geq v_i(j) - u(i)$. Let $\hat{v}^*(i)$ be the value $i$ gets in the optimal allocation where every agent has these new valuation functions. The two conditions of Theorem ?? are true for this new valuation function. First, each agent remains in the auction as long as it has a bid of positive utility. Second, no agent overbids so the procedure stops when no agent has a profitable bid. We set $\beta := \frac{1}{4608}$. Hence, we have

$$\sum_{i=1}^{n} v(i) \geq \frac{\beta}{\sqrt{m \log m}} \cdot \sum_{i=1}^{n} \hat{v}^*(i)$$

Finally, assume that $u(i) \leq (1 - \lambda) \cdot v^*(i)$, for all $i \in N$. Then we have that

$$\sum_{i=1}^{n} \hat{v}^*(i) \geq \sum_{i=1}^{n} (v^*(i) - u(i)) \geq \sum_{i=1}^{n} \lambda \cdot v^*(i)$$

so

$$\sum_{i=1}^{n} v(i) \geq \frac{\beta \cdot \lambda}{\sqrt{m \log m}} \cdot \sum_{i=1}^{n} v^*(i)$$

Therefore the welfare ratio is $O(\frac{\sqrt{m \log m}}{\lambda})$. □

## 7 CONCLUSION

Numerous open problems remain. For example, assuming truthful bidding, what is the optimal choice of price increment function? In terms of strategic bidding, it would be interesting to study whether additional restrictions, such as equilibrium constraints, on the bidding behaviours of the agents allow for better welfare guarantees. For example, are good price of anarchy bounds obtainable when the price increment function is linear in demand?

## ACKNOWLEDGMENTS

We thank the referees for numerous comments and suggestions that improved this paper. This research was supported by a Trottier Fellowship in Science and Public Policy and by NSERC.

## REFERENCES

[1] L. Ausubel and O. Baranov, "Market design and the evolution of the combinatorial clock auction", *American Economic Review*, **104(5)**, pp446–451, 2014.

[2] L. Ausubel and O. Baranov, "A practical guide to the combinatorial clock auction", to appear in *Economic Journal*, 2018.

[3] L. Ausubel and P. Cramton, "Auctioning many divisible goods", *Journal of the European Economic Association*, **2**, pp480–493, 2004.

[4] L. Ausubel, P. Cramton and P. Milgrom, "The clock-proxy auction: a practical combinatorial auction design", in P. Cramton, Y. Shoham and R. Steinberg (eds.), *Combinatorial Auctions*, pp115–138, MIT Press, 2006.

[5] M. Bichler, P. Shabalin and G. Zeigler, "Efficiency with linear prices? A theoretical and experimental analysis of the combinatorial clock auction", *INFORMS Information System Research*, **24**, 394–417, 2013.

[6] M. Bichler, J. Georee, S. Mayer and P. Shabalin, "Spectrum auction design: simple auctions for complex sales", *Telecommunications Policy*, **38(7)**, pp613-622, 2014.

[7] N. Bousquet, Y. Cai and C. Hunkenschröder and A. Vetta, "The economic efficiency of the combinatorial clock auction", *Proceedings of 27th Symposium on Discrete Algorithms (SODA)*, pp1407-1423, 2016.

[8] P. Cramton, "Simultaneous ascending auctions", in P. Cramton, Y. Shoham and R. Steinberg (eds.), *Combinatorial Auctions*, pp99–114, MIT Press, 2006.

[9] P. Cramton, "Spectrum auction design", *Review of Industrial Organization*, **42(2)**, pp161–190, 2013.

[10] P. Klemperer, *Auctions: Theory and Practice*, Princeton University Press, 2004.

[11] J. Levin and A. Skrzypacz, "Properties of the Combinatorial Clock Auction", *American Economic Review*, **106(9)**, pp2528–2551, 2016.

[12] P. Milgrom, *Putting Auction Theory to Work*, Cambridge University Press, 2004.

[13] D. Porter, S. Rassenti, A. Roopnarine and V. Smith, "Combinatorial auction design", *Proceedings of the National Academy of Sciences of the United States of America*, **100(19)**, pp11153-11157, 2003.

# Designing Core-selecting Payment Rules: A Computational Search Approach

BENEDIKT BÜNZ, Stanford University, USA†
BENJAMIN LUBIN, Boston University, USA‡
SVEN SEUKEN, University of Zurich, Switzerland

We study the design of core-selecting payment rules for combinatorial auctions (CAs), a challenging setting where no strategyproof rules exist. Unfortunately, under the rule most commonly used in practice, the *Quadratic* rule [1], the Bayes-Nash equilibrium strategies are untruthful enough such that truthful play may be an implausible model of bidder behavior, which also raises concerns about revenue and efficiency. In this paper, we present a computational approach for finding good core-selecting payment rules. We present a parametrized payment rule we call FRACTIONAL* that takes three parameters (reference point, weights, and amplification) as inputs. This way, we construct and analyze 366 rules across 29 different domains. To evaluate each rule in each domain, we employ a computational Bayes-Nash equilibrium solver. We first use our approach to study the well-known Local-Local-Global domain in detail, and identify a set of 20 "all-rounder rules" which beat Quadratic by a significant margin on efficiency, incentives, and revenue in all, or almost all domains. To demonstrate robustness of our findings, we take four of these all-rounder rules and evaluate them in the significantly larger LLLLGG domain (with six bidders and eight goods), where we show that all four rules also beat Quadratic. This suggests that, in practice, auctioneers may want to consider using alternative core-selecting payment rules because of the large improvements over Quadratic that may be available. Overall, our results demonstrate the power of a computational search approach in a properly parametrized mechanism design space.

The full version of this paper is available at http://ssrn.com/abstract=3178454.

CCS Concepts: • **Theory of computation → Computational pricing and auctions**; *Algorithmic mechanism design; Exact and approximate computation of equilibria*;

Additional Key Words and Phrases: Combinatorial Auctions, Payment Rules, Core

## REFERENCES

[1] Robert W. Day and Peter Cramton. 2012. Quadratic Core-Selecting Payment Rules for Combinatorial Auctions. *Operations Research* 60, 3 (2012), 588–603.

†Authors listed in alphabetical order. All authors contributed equally to this paper. ‡Corresponding Author.
Authors' addresses: Benedikt Bünz, Stanford University, 353 Serra Mall, Palo Alto, CA, 94305, USA, buenz@stanford.edu; Benjamin Lubin, Boston University, 595 Commonwealth Ave, Boston, MA, 02215, USA, blubin@bu.edu; Sven Seuken, University of Zurich, Binzmühlestrasse 14, Zürich, CH, 8050, Switzerland, seuken@ifi.uzh.ch.


*ACM EC'18, June 18–22, 2018, Ithaca, NY, USA.* ACM ISBN 978-1-4503-4529-3/18/06.
https://doi.org/10.1145/3219166.3219206

# Fast Core Pricing for Rich Advertising Auctions

JASON HARTLINE, Electrical Engineering and Computer Science Department, Northwestern University.
NICOLE IMMORLICA, Microsoft Research, New England.
MOHAMMAD REZA KHANI, Microsoft, Redmond.
BRENDAN LUCIER, Microsoft Research, New England.
RAD NIAZADEH, Department of Computer Science, Stanford University.

Full Paper: https://arxiv.org/pdf/1610.03564.pdf

CCS Concepts: • **Theory of computation → Algorithmic mechanism design; Computational pricing and auctions; Computational advertising theory;** • **Applied computing → Operations research;**

Additional Key Words and Phrases: Core selecting auctions, Sale of ad-space, Core Constraint Generation (CCG), VCG auction, GSP auction.

As online ad offerings become increasingly complex, with multiple size configurations and layouts available to advertisers, the sale of web advertising space increasingly resembles a combinatorial auction with complementarities. Standard ad auction formats do not immediately extend to these settings, and truthful combinatorial auctions, such as the Vickrey-Clarke-Groves auction, can yield unacceptably low revenue. Core selecting auctions, which apply to combinatorial markets, boost revenue by setting prices so that no group of agents, including the auctioneer, can jointly improve their utilities by switching to a different allocation and payments. Among outcomes in the core, bidder-optimal core points have been the most widely studied due to their incentive properties, such as being implementable at natural equilibria [2, 3].

Prior work in economics has studied heuristics and algorithms for computing approximate bidder-optimal core points, given oracle access to the welfare optimization problem [1, 3]. Relative to prior work, our goal is to develop an algorithm with asymptotically fewer oracle calls while maintaining theoretical performance guarantees. Our main result is a combinatorial algorithm that finds an approximate bidder-optimal core point with almost linear number of calls to the welfare maximization oracle. Our algorithm is faster than previously-proposed heuristics, it has theoretical guarantees, and it reveals some useful structural properties of the core polytope.

We take a two-pronged approach to evaluating our core-pricing method. We first consider a theoretical treatment of the problem of finding a bidder-optimal core point in a general combinatorial auction setting. We then consider an experimental treatment of deploying our algorithm in a highly time-sensitive advertising auction platforms.

Authors' addresses: Jason Hartline, Electrical Engineering and Computer Science Department, Northwestern University. hartline@eecs.northwestern.edu; Nicole Immorlica, Microsoft Research, New England. nicimm@microsoft.com; Mohammad Reza Khani, Microsoft, Redmond. rezak@microsoft.com; Brendan Lucier, Microsoft Research, New England. brlucier@microsoft.com; Rad Niazadeh, Department of Computer Science, Stanford University. rad@cs.stanford.edu.


*ACM EC'18, June 18–22, 2018, Ithaca, NY, USA.* ACM ISBN 978-1-4503-5829-3/18/06.
https://doi.org/10.1145/3219166.3219231

***Theoretical results.*** Our main result is a quasi-linear time deterministic algorithm for computing bidder-optimal core payments in combinatorial auctions. Our algorithm requires access to an oracle that finds a welfare-optimal allocation for a given profile of (possibly truncated) buyer valuations. In a truncated valuation, the buyer's value for each bundle is reduced by an additive constant; if this causes the value of any bundle to become negative, it is instead set to zero.

**Theorem (informal):** *Given oracle access to a welfare-optimization algorithm (for truncated values), there exists a deterministic algorithm that computes an $\epsilon$-approximate bidder optimal core point using $O(n \log(n/\epsilon))$ oracle evaluations and additional time $O(n^2 \log(n/\epsilon))$.*

Our algorithm searches for a buyer-optimal profile of utilities achievable by an outcome in the core. The set of all such core utilities is a polytope, determined by the (exponentially many) constraints that no subset of bidders can simultaneously improve their utilities. Intuitively, the algorithm proceeds by exploring this polytope. Starting from an arbitrary point in the core, the algorithm attempts to increase bidder utilities, which corresponds geometrically to following a positively-oriented ray until hitting a facet of the polytope. It then determines whether there exists a subset of the bidders whose utilities can be increased while remaining in the core, and if so continues to follow an appropriate ray. This process repeats until a bidder-optimal core point is reached.

This geometric intuition corresponds to a water-filling algorithm, in which the utilities of agents are simultaneously increased and frozen as constraints become tight. Implementing this approach requires an efficient test for inclusion in the core polytope, as well as a method for determining which bidders are involved in a tight core constraint. It turns out that both questions can be expressed as queries to the welfare-optimization oracle, with appropriately truncated valuation profiles. This result is the most technical contribution of the paper, and involves an analysis of the geometry of the core constraints. Given these tests, finding a tight core constraint can be done using binary search (which is what generates the logarithmic factors in our runtime). The algorithm terminates after at most $n$ iterations, since each iteration will freeze the payment of at least one bidder.

***Experimental results.*** We test the performance of our core auction on text ads using the Microsoft Bing search engine. Our dataset consists of around 20, 000 auctions, each containing at most 23 advertisers, with ad sizes ranging from the basic three lines up to fourteen lines. We compare the performance of our core auction against VCG and GSP. Since GSP is technically ill-defined in such combinatorial settings, we consider an implementation of GSP that generates the optimal allocation and charges each ad a price equal to the bid of the next ad in the ordering. Our results show that, due to the complementarity induced by variable length ads, VCG and GSP can lead to significantly lower revenue than core auctions. Our bidder optimal core outcome leads to almost 100% more revenue than VCG and almost 20% more revenue than GSP in our dataset, on average. In our setting, we can implement an optimal welfare oracle with runtime polynomial in the number of ads and the total number of lines of advertising space. We ran our experiments using 20 lines of advertising space. Our algorithm, which makes $\tilde{O}(n)$ calls to the welfare oracle, ran in under 55 milliseconds per auction, compared to 11 milliseconds for VCG (which makes $n + 1$ calls to the oracle) and 3 milliseconds for GSP (which makes a single call to the oracle). While being slower than GSP and VCG, our auction still is faster than blackbox linear programming or running sophisticated iterative heuristics, and it is still in the acceptable speed range for ad-auctions.

## REFERENCES

[1] Benedikt Bünz, Sven Seuken, and Benjamin Lubin. 2015. A faster core constraint generation algorithm for combinatorial auctions. In *Proceedings of the Twenty-Ninth AAAI Conference on Artificial Intelligence.* AAAI Press, 827–834.

[2] Robert W Day and Paul Milgrom. 2008. Core-selecting package auctions. *international Journal of game Theory* 36, 3-4 (2008), 393–407.

[3] Robert W Day and Subramanian Raghavan. 2007. Fair payments for efficient allocations in public sector combinatorial auctions. *Management Science* 53, 9 (2007), 1389–1406.

# Computational Complexity of Proper Equilibrium

KRISTOFFER ARNSFELT HANSEN, Aarhus University
TROELS BJERRE LUND, IT-University of Copenhagen

We study the computational complexity of proper equilibrium in finite games and prove the following results. First, for two-player games in strategic form we show that the task of simply verifying the proper equilibrium conditions of a given pure Nash equilibrium is NP-complete. Next, for $n$-player games in strategic form we show that the task of computing an approximation of a proper equilibrium is $\text{FIXP}_a$-complete. Finally, for $n$-player polymatrix games we show that the task of computing a symbolic proper equilibrium is PPAD-complete.

CCS Concepts: • **Theory of computation → Problems, reductions and completeness**; **Exact and approximate computation of equilibria**;

## 1 INTRODUCTION

We study the Nash equilibrium *refinement* of proper equilibrium due to Myerson [24] and obtain new results concerning the tasks of verification, approximation, and computation. Several recent works have been concerned with the complexity of such tasks for Nash equilibrium refinements in general, including proper equilibrium.

The task of verifying the conditions of a given Nash equilibrium of a game in strategic form is computationally a trivial task. On the other hand Hansen et al. [17] showed NP-hardness and Sqrt-Sum-hardness for verifying the conditions of standard Nash equilibrium refinements in $n$-player games for $n \geq 3$, including proper equilibrium. Recently Hansen [16] showed that the problems are in fact complete for $\exists\mathbb{R}$, meaning that they are computationally equivalent to the decision problem of the existential theory of the reals.

For two-player games, similar results have so far been positive. For games in strategic form, trembling hand perfect equilibrium coincide with admissible equilibrium and can be verified in polynomial time using linear programming [28]. For games in extensive form with perfect recall, Gatti and Panozzo [15] showed that quasi-perfect equilibrium can be verified in polynomial time and Gatti et al. [14] obtained the same for the strategy part of sequential equilibrium. Determining the computational complexity of verifying a proper equilibrium was explicitly stated as an open problem by Hansen et al. [17] and Gatti and Panozzo [15]. Given the equivalence between the verification problems in $n$-player games and the positive results so far one may expect that proper equilibrium in two-player games can be verified in polynomial time as well. As our first result we show, perhaps surprisingly, that the problem is NP-complete. To the best of our knowledge, this is the first instance of NP-hardness for verifying whether a fully specified two player strategy profile satisfies the conditions of an equilibrium refinement. We note that Gatti and Panozzo [15] showed that it is NP-complete to verify whether a two player strategy profile given as a *realization plan* is subgame perfect or part of a sequential equilibrium, but this crucially relies on the strategy not

Authors' addresses: Kristoffer Arnsfelt Hansen, Aarhus University, arnsfelt@cs.au.dk; Troels Bjerre Lund, IT-University of Copenhagen, trbj@itu.dk.


*ACM EC'18, June 18–22, 2018, Ithaca, NY, USA.* ACM ISBN 978-1-4503-4529-3/18/06...$15.00
https://doi.org/10.1145/3219166.3219199

being specified in the subgame. If the full strategy profile is specified, the verification can be done in polynomial time [14].

In seminal work Daskalakis et al. [8] and Chen and Deng [3] showed that computing a Nash equilibrium in a two-player game is PPAD-complete and Etessami and Yannakakis [11] showed that computing a Nash equilibrium in a $n$-player game is FIXP-complete, when $n \geq 3$. Thus containment in PPAD and FIXP are best possible results for computing equilibrium refinements, and such results show that computing the equilibrium refinements is polynomial time *equivalent* to computing *any* Nash equilibrium.

For two-player games in strategic form, computing a *symbolic* proper equilibrium was shown to be in PPAD by Sørensen [26]. For two-player games in extensive form with perfect recall, computing a quasi-perfect equilibrium was shown to be in PPAD by Miltersen and Sørensen [23], and computing a trembling hand perfect equilibrium was shown to be in PPAD by Farina and Gatti [12]. It was asked by Sørensen [26] whether computing a proper equilibrium by itself belongs to PPAD. The obstacle here was that it was not clear how to efficiently verify a proper equilibrium. Our NP-hardness result shows that this is not likely to be possible and underlines the importance and usefulness of computing a *symbolic* proper equilibrium rather than just a proper equilibrium by itself, since the former is straightforward to verify efficiently.

For $n$-player games in strategic form, computing an approximation to a trembling hand perfect equilibrium was shown to be in $\text{FIXP}_a$ by Etessami et al. [10]. For $n$-player games in extensive form with perfect recall, Etessami [9] proved membership in $\text{FIXP}_a$ for approximating a quasi-perfect equilibrium and for approximating trembling hand perfect equilibrium. It was stated as an explicit open problem by Etessami [9] whether the task of computing a proper equilibrium of a $n$-player game in strategic form is in $\text{FIXP}_a$. As our second result we give an affirmative answer to this question. Thus, in strategic form games, computing an approximating to a proper equilibrium is polynomial time equivalent to approximating any Nash equilibrium. The original proof of existence of a proper equilibrium in every finite strategic form game by Myerson [24] was based on the powerful Kakutani fixed point theorem. Our result provides an alternative proof of existence based on the Brouwer fixed point theorem.

Our final result is that in $n$-player *polymatrix* games the task of computing a symbolic proper equilibrium belongs to PPAD. Thus, in polymatrix games, computing an a symbolic proper equilibrium is polynomial time equivalent to computing any Nash equilibrium. This significantly strengthens the result of Sørensen [26].

## 2 PRELIMINARIES

### 2.1 Games in Strategic Form

A finite game $\Gamma$ with $n$ players in strategic form is specified as follows. Player $i$ has a set $S_i$ of $m_i$ pure strategies which may be identified with the set $\{1, \ldots, m_i\}$ when needed. We denote by $\Delta(S_i) = \Delta_{m_i}$ the set of mixed strategies for Player $i$. That is, $\Delta_{m_i} = \{y \in \mathbb{R}^{m_i} \mid \|y\|_1 = 1; \forall j : y_j \geq 0\}$. We denote by $\Delta^o(S_i) = \Delta^o_{m_i}$ the set of fully-mixed strategies for Player $i$. That is, $\Delta^o m_i = \{y \in \mathbb{R}^{m_i} \mid \|y\|_1 = 1; \forall j : y_j > 0\}$. We let $D_\Gamma = \prod_{i=1}^n \Delta_{m_i}$ be the set of all mixed strategy profiles for $\Gamma$ and $D^o_\Gamma = \prod_{i=1}^n \Delta^o_{m_i}$ the set of all fully mixed strategy profiles. Each combination $(a_1, \ldots, a_n)$ of pure strategies specifies a payoff $U_i(a_1, \ldots, a_n)$ to Player $i$, for every $i$. The *utility functions* $U_i$ are extended to $D_\Gamma$ in the natural way. For a *strategy profile* $x = (x_1, \ldots, x_n) \in D_\Gamma$ and a pure strategy $k$ for Player $i$, we denote by $(x_{-i}; k)$ the strategy profile where Player $i$ uses the pure strategy $k$ and Player $j$ uses the mixed strategy $x_j$, for every $j \neq i$.

## 2.2 Proper Equilibrium

The definition below of proper equilibrium is due to Myerson [24]. Every finite game $\Gamma$ has a proper equilibrium and every proper equilibrium is in particular a Nash equilibrium.

*Definition 2.1.* Given $\varepsilon > 0$, a mixed strategy profile $x$ is an $\varepsilon$-proper equilibrium if it is fully mixed and satisfies $x_{ik} \le \varepsilon x_{i\ell}$ whenever $U_i(x_{-i};k) < U_i(x_{-i};\ell)$, for all $i \in \{1,\dots,n\}$ and $k,\ell \in S_i$.

*Definition 2.2.* A mixed strategy profile $x$ is a proper equilibrium if it is the limit point of a sequence $\{x^{\varepsilon_k}\}$ of $\varepsilon_k$-proper equilibria where $\varepsilon_k \to 0^+$ for $k \to \infty$.

*Definition 2.3.* A symbolic proper equilibrium is a collection of polynomials $P_{ij}(\varepsilon)$ in the formal variable $\varepsilon$, such that the strategy profile $x_\varepsilon$ given by $(x_\varepsilon)_{ij} = P_{ij}(\varepsilon)/\sum_{k\in S_i} P_{ik}(\varepsilon)$ is an $\varepsilon$-proper equilibrium for every sufficiently small $\varepsilon > 0$.

## 2.3 Complexity Classes

Our main results are concerned with the complexity classes NP, PPAD, and FIXP$_a$. We give a brief description of the classes PPAD and FIXP and refer to Papadimitriou [25] and Etessami and Yannakakis [11] for detailed definitions of the two classes.

PPAD is a class of discrete total search problems, whose totality is guaranteed based on a parity argument on a directed graph. More formally PPAD is defined by a canonical complete problem EndOfTheLine. Here a directed graph is given implicitly by predecessor and successor circuits, and the search problem is to find a degree 1 node different from a given degree 1 node.

FIXP is the class of real-valued total search problems that can be cast as Brouwer fixed points of functions represented by $\{+,-,*,/,\max,\min\}$-circuits computing a function mapping a convex polytope described by a set of linear inequalities to itself. The class FIXP$_a$ is the class of *discrete* total search problems that reduce to *approximate* Brouwer fixed points.

# 3 VERIFICATION OF PROPER EQUILIBRIUM IN BIMATRIX GAMES

In this section we show that deciding whether a given pure Nash equilibrium is a proper equilibrium in a given 2-player game in strategic form is NP-hard. Our reduction is based on a modification of a game construction used by Conitzer and Sandholm [5] to show that determining existence of Nash equilibria with several natural properties in 2-player games in strategic form is NP-complete.

The game construction by Conitzer and Sandholm [5] takes any CNF formula $\Phi$ and produces a 2-player game in strategic form $G_{CS}(\Phi)$ in which, except for a special Nash equilibrium, there is a one-to-one correspondence between satisfying assignments to $\Phi$ and Nash equilibria of $G_{CS}(\Phi)$. We will actually describe the construction from the conference version by Conitzer and Sandholm [4], which is slightly simpler to use for our purpose. Also for simplicity, and since this is sufficient, we shall also define the game only for 3CNF formulas $\Phi$.

Let $V = \{x_1,\dots,x_n\}$ be a set of $n$ Boolean variables. It is convenient to have explicit signs on literals. Thus, a variable $x_i$ gives rise to the positive literal $+x_i$ and the negative literal $-x_i$. Thus define $L = \{+x_1,-x_1,\dots,+x_n,-x_n\}$ to be the set of literals given by $V$. We say that $+x_i$ and $-x_i$ are opposite of each other and for $\ell \in L$ we denote by $-\ell$ the opposite of $\ell$. Define $v : L \to V$ by $v(+x_i) = v(-x_i) = x_i$. We may now identify the clauses with subsets of $L$, and a CNF formula $\Phi$ is thus a set of clauses $C = \{c_1,\dots,c_m\}$. Similarly, a truth assignment to variables $V$ is identified with a subset $T \subseteq L$ such that for all $i$, exactly one of $+x_i$ and $-x_i$ belong to $T$. We then have that $T$ is a satisfying assignment for $\Phi$ if and only if $c_i \cap T \neq \emptyset$, for all $i$.

The game $G_{CS}(\Phi)$ is a symmetric game where the players have the set of strategies $S = L \cup V \cup C \cup \{f\}$. The payoffs are given as listed in table 1a given $\ell,\ell' \in L$, $x,x' \in V$, and $c,c' \in C$. Clearly $(f,f)$ is a pure Nash equilibrium in $G_{CS}(\Phi)$. Conitzer and Sandholm show that a satisfying assignment

| | $\ell'$ | $x'$ | $c'$ | $f$ |
|---|---|---|---|---|
| $\ell$ | $1$ if $\ell \neq -\ell'$<br>$-2$ if $\ell = -\ell'$ | $-2$ | $-2$ | $-2$ |
| $x$ | $2$ if $v(\ell') \neq x$<br>$2-n$ if $v(\ell') = x$ | $-2$ | $-2$ | $-2$ |
| $c$ | $2$ if $\ell' \notin c$<br>$2-n$ if $\ell' \in c$ | $-2$ | $-2$ | $-2$ |
| $f$ | $1$ | $1$ | $1$ | $0$ |

(a) $G_{\mathrm{CS}}(\Phi)$

| | $\ell'$ | $x'$ | $c'$ | $f$ |
|---|---|---|---|---|
| $\ell$ | $1$ if $\ell \neq -\ell'$<br>$-4n$ if $\ell = -\ell'$ | $-2$ | $-2$ | $-2$ |
| $x$ | $2$ if $v(\ell') \neq x$<br>$2-n$ if $v(\ell') = x$ | $-2$ | $-2$ | $-2$ |
| $c$ | $2$ if $\ell' \notin c$<br>$2-n$ if $\ell' \in c$ | $-2$ | $-2$ | $-2$ |
| $f$ | $1/2$ | $1/2$ | $1/2$ | $2$ |

(b) $\widetilde{G_{\mathrm{CS}}}(\Phi)$

Table 1. The Conitzer-Sandholm game $G_{\mathrm{CS}}(\Phi)$, with payoffs to the row player, and its robust variation $\widetilde{G_{\mathrm{CS}}}(\Phi)$

$A$ to $\Phi$ gives a Nash equilibrium where each true literal $\ell \in A$ is played with probability $\frac{1}{n}$, and that these are the only Nash equilibria, other than $(f, f)$. These equilibria are however not very robust, since the pure strategy $f$ weakly dominates all $\ell \in L$. In addition, should the other player make a tremble, it would be better to play $f$. Thus the only trembling hand perfect equilibrium of $G_{\mathrm{CS}}(\Phi)$ is $(f, f)$. The first step of our construction is to change $G_{\mathrm{CS}}(\Phi)$ into a more robust game $\widetilde{G_{\mathrm{CS}}}(\Phi)$ in which satisfying assignments will correspond to proper equilibria. We obtain robustness by decreasing the payoff of $(f, a)$ to $\frac{1}{2}$ for all $a \in S \setminus \{f\}$. To make up for this in the analysis we increase the penalty to the players for playing opposite literals from $-2$ to $-4n$. A final change, not done for robustness but for use in the final construction is to change the payoff for $(f, f)$ from 0 to 2. Clearly $(f, f)$ remains a pure Nash equilibrium. The next lemma shows that every other Nash equilibrium identifies a unique satisfying assignment of $\Phi$.

Lemma 3.1. *Let $\Phi$ be a 3CNF formula. Every Nash equilibrium $(\sigma_1, \sigma_2)$ in $\widetilde{G_{\mathrm{CS}}}(\Phi)$ different from $(f, f)$ corresponds to a satisfying assignment of $\Phi$.*

Proof. For a Nash equilibrium $(\sigma_1, \sigma_2)$ we have that $\Pr_{\sigma_2}[f] = 1$ implies that $\Pr_{\sigma_1}[f] = 1$, since $f$ is the unique best reply to $f$. Likewise, $\Pr_{\sigma_1}[f] = 1$ implies that $\Pr_{\sigma_2}[f] = 1$. Since $(\sigma_1, \sigma_2) \neq (f, f)$ it follows that $\Pr_{\sigma_1}[f] < 1$ and $\Pr_{\sigma_2}[f] < 1$. We next show that significant probability mass must be placed on $L$. We have that $\mathrm{E}_{b\sim\sigma_2}[u_1(a, b) \mid b \neq f] \geq \frac{1}{2}$ for all $a \in \mathrm{supp}(\sigma_1) \setminus \{f\}$, since otherwise $f$ would be a strictly better reply to $\sigma_2$ than $a$. Likewise $\mathrm{E}_{a\sim\sigma_1}[u_2(a, b) \mid a \neq f] \geq \frac{1}{2}$ for all $b \in \mathrm{supp}(\sigma_2) \setminus \{f\}$. Thus for $a \in \mathrm{supp}(\sigma_1) \setminus \{f\}$ we have

$$
\begin{aligned}
\frac{1}{2} &\leq \mathop{\mathrm{E}}_{b\sim\sigma_2}[u_1(a,b)|b \in L]\Pr_{\sigma_2}[L \mid (S \setminus \{f\})] + \mathop{\mathrm{E}}_{b\sim\sigma_2}[u_1(a,b)|b \in V \cup C)]\Pr_{\sigma_2}[V \cup C \mid (S \setminus \{f\})] \\
&\leq 2\Pr_{\sigma_2}[L \mid (S \setminus \{f\})] - 2\Pr_{\sigma_2}[V \cup C \mid (S \setminus \{f\})] \\
&= 2\Pr_{\sigma_2}[L \mid (S \setminus \{f\})] - 2\left(1 - \Pr_{\sigma_2}[L \mid (S \setminus \{f\})]\right) \\
&= 4\Pr_{\sigma_2}[L \mid (S \setminus \{f\})] - 2 \ ,
\end{aligned}
$$

and it follows that $\Pr_{\sigma_2}[L \mid S \setminus \{f\}] \geq (\frac{1}{2} + 2)/4 = \frac{5}{8}$. Likewise $\Pr_{\sigma_1}[L \mid S \setminus \{f\}] \geq \frac{5}{8}$. We next show that the probability mass placed on $L$ must be evenly distributed on literal pairs. Let $i \in \{1, \ldots, n\}$.

Clearly $\mathrm{E}_{b\sim\sigma_2}[u_1(a,b) \mid b \in L] \leq 1$ for all $a \in L$. Since

$$\mathop{\mathrm{E}}_{b\sim\sigma_2}[u_1(x_i,b) \mid b \in L] = 2 - n \Pr_{\sigma_2}[\{+x_i, -x_i\} \mid L] \ ,$$

it follows that $2 - n \Pr_{\sigma_2}[\{+x_i,-x_i\} \mid L] \leq 1$, since otherwise no $a \in L$ can be a best reply to $\sigma_2$. Hence $\Pr_{\sigma_2}[\{+x_i,-x_i\} \mid L] \geq \frac{1}{n}$ and we can conclude that $\Pr_{\sigma_2}[\{+x_i,-x_i\} \mid L] = \frac{1}{n}$ for all $i$. Likewise, $\Pr_{\sigma_1}[\{+x_i,-x_i\} \mid L] = \frac{1}{n}$ for all $i$.

We now show that for each literal pair, the players must both favor either the positive or the negative literal. Consider any $i \in \{1,\ldots,n\}$. Let $\ell \in \{+x_i,-x_i\}$ and suppose that $\Pr_{\sigma_2}[\ell \mid L] \geq \frac{1}{4n}$. We then have

$$\mathop{\mathrm{E}}_{b\sim\sigma_2}[u_1(-\ell,b) \mid b \neq f] \leq 1 - 4n \Pr_{\sigma_2}[\ell \mid L] \Pr_{\sigma_2}[L \mid S \setminus \{f\}]$$
$$\leq 1 - 4n\frac{1}{4n}\frac{5}{8} = \frac{3}{8} < \frac{1}{2} \ ,$$

and we must have $\Pr_{\sigma_1}[-\ell] = 0$. Likewise, if $\Pr_{\sigma_1}[\ell \mid L] \geq \frac{1}{4n}$ we must have $\Pr_{\sigma_2}[-\ell] = 0$.

We now established that the strategy profile identifies a truth assignment $A$ to the variables. Namely for each $i \in \{1,\ldots,n\}$ there is $\ell \in \{+x_i,-x_i\}$ with $\Pr_{\sigma_1}[\ell \mid L] = \Pr_{\sigma_2}[\ell \mid L] = \frac{1}{n}$ and $\Pr_{\sigma_1}[-\ell \mid L] = \Pr_{\sigma_2}[-\ell \mid L] = 0$, and we define $A$ to be the set of these $\ell$. We will finally show that $A$ satisfies all clauses. Let $c = \{\ell_1,\ell_2,\ell_3\}$ be a clause. Note that

$$\mathop{\mathrm{E}}_{b\sim\sigma_2}[u_1(c,b) \mid b \in L] = 2 - n \Pr_{\sigma_2}[\{\ell_1,\ell_2,\ell_3\} \mid L] \ ,$$

We must have $2 - n \Pr_{\sigma_2}[\{\ell_1,\ell_2,\ell_3\} \mid L] \leq 1$, since otherwise no $a \in L$ can be a best reply to $\sigma_2$. It follows that $\Pr_{\sigma_2}[\{\ell_1,\ell_2,\ell_3\} \mid L] \geq \frac{1}{n}$, and there must then be $j \in \{1,2,3\}$ for which $\Pr_{\sigma_2}[\ell_j \mid L] \geq \frac{1}{3n}$, which means that $\ell_j \in A$. □

We are now ready to define final game $G_{\mathrm{Prop}}(\Phi)$ for any 3CNF formula $\Phi$. The game $G_{\mathrm{Prop}}(\Phi)$ is simply obtained from $\widetilde{G_{\mathrm{CS}}}(\Phi)$ by giving each player an additional pure strategy $g$. By playing the new strategy $g$ both players are able to fix the payoff to 1, and otherwise the payoffs are unchanged. The resulting game is shown in table 2.

| | $\ell'$ | $x'$ | $c'$ | $f$ | $g$ |
|---|---|---|---|---|---|
| $\ell$ | $1$ if $\ell \neq -\ell'$<br>$-4n$ if $\ell = -\ell'$ | $-2$ | $-2$ | $-2$ | $1$ |
| $x$ | $2$ if $v(\ell') \neq x$<br>$2-n$ if $v(\ell') = x$ | $-2$ | $-2$ | $-2$ | $1$ |
| $c$ | $2$ if $\ell' \notin c$<br>$2-n$ if $\ell' \in c$ | $-2$ | $-2$ | $-2$ | $1$ |
| $f$ | $1/2$ | $1/2$ | $1/2$ | $2$ | $1$ |
| $g$ | $1$ | $1$ | $1$ | $1$ | $1$ |

Table 2. $G_{\mathrm{Prop}}(\Phi)$.

Lemma 3.2. *Let $\Phi$ be a 3CNF formula. If $\Phi$ has a satisfying assignment then $(g,g)$ is a proper Nash equilibrium of $G_{\mathrm{Prop}}(\Phi)$.*

Proof. Let $\varepsilon > 0$ be arbitrary and suppose $t_i \in \{+\ell_i, -\ell_i\}$ such that $A = \{(t_1, \ldots, t_n\}$ is a satisfying assignment of $\Phi$. Write $C = C_1 \cup C_2 \cup C_3$, where $C_k$ is the set of clauses containing $k$ literals from $A$.

Define $\sigma^\varepsilon$ according to table 3, where $x \in V$, $c_1 \in C_1$, $c_2 \in C_2$, $c_3 \in C_3$, and we let $N = 1 + n\varepsilon + n\varepsilon^2 + |C_1|\varepsilon^3 + \varepsilon^4 + |C_2|\varepsilon^5 + |C_3|\varepsilon^6 + n\varepsilon^7$ be a normalizing factor.

| $i$ | $g$ | $t_i$ | $x$ | $c_1$ | $f$ | $c_2$ | $c_3$ | $-t_i$ |
|---|---|---|---|---|---|---|---|---|
| $\sigma^\varepsilon(i)N$ | 1 | $\varepsilon$ | $\varepsilon^2$ | $\varepsilon^3$ | $\varepsilon^4$ | $\varepsilon^5$ | $\varepsilon^6$ | $\varepsilon^7$ |

Table 3. An $\varepsilon$-proper equilibrium of $G_{\text{Prop}}(\Phi)$.

By construction we have that $\sigma^\varepsilon$ is a fully mixed strategy. We claim that $(\sigma^\varepsilon, \sigma^\varepsilon)$ is an $\varepsilon$-proper equilibrium. In order to verify this we compute the payoffs for all pure strategies played against $\sigma^\varepsilon$. Clearly $u_1(g, \sigma^\varepsilon) = 1$. Next we have that $u_1(a, \sigma^\varepsilon)$ for $a \in A \cup V \cup C_1$ are all exactly equal and have value of the form[1] $1 + O(\varepsilon^2)$. For instance we have

$$\begin{aligned} u_1(x, \sigma^\varepsilon)N &= 1 + (n-1)2\varepsilon + (2-n)\varepsilon \\ &\quad - 2(n\varepsilon^2 + |C_1|\varepsilon^3 + \varepsilon^4 + |C_2|\varepsilon^5 + |C_3|\varepsilon^6) - n\varepsilon^7 \\ &= 1 + n\varepsilon - 2(n\varepsilon^2 + |C_1|\varepsilon^3 + \varepsilon^4 + |C_2|\varepsilon^5 + |C_3|\varepsilon^6) - n\varepsilon^7 \\ &= 1 + n\varepsilon + O(\varepsilon^2) \ , \end{aligned}$$

from which the stated bound follows using $1/N = 1 - n\varepsilon + O(\varepsilon^2)$.

Similarly we obtain $u_1(f, \sigma^\varepsilon) = 1 - n\varepsilon/2 + O(\varepsilon^2)$, $u_1(c_2, \sigma^\varepsilon) = 1 - n\varepsilon + O(\varepsilon^2)$, $u_1(c_3, \sigma^\varepsilon) = 1 - 2n\varepsilon + O(\varepsilon^2)$, and $u_1(-t_i, \sigma^\varepsilon) = 1 - n(4n+1)\varepsilon + O(\varepsilon^2)$. With these computed it is now straightforward to observe that $(\sigma^\varepsilon, \sigma^\varepsilon)$ is an $\varepsilon$-proper equilibrium for all sufficiently small $\varepsilon > 0$. Since $(\sigma^\varepsilon, \sigma^\varepsilon) \to (g, g)$ for $\varepsilon \to 0^+$, it follows that $(g, g)$ is a proper equilibrium. □

Lemma 3.3. *Let $\Phi$ be a 3CNF formula. If $(g, g)$ is a proper Nash equilibrium of $G_{\text{Prop}}(\Phi)$ then $\Phi$ has a satisfying assignment.*

Proof. By definition of $(g, g)$ being a proper equilibrium there exist a sequence $(\sigma_1^\varepsilon, \sigma_2^\varepsilon)$ of $\varepsilon$-proper equilibrium with $(\sigma_1^\varepsilon, \sigma_2^\varepsilon) \to (g, g)$ for $\varepsilon \to 0^+$. Assume $\varepsilon \le \frac{1}{2}$, $\Pr_{\sigma_1^\varepsilon}[g] \ge \frac{1}{2}$, and $\Pr_{\sigma_2^\varepsilon}[g] \ge \frac{1}{2}$. Then $g$ is a best reply to $\sigma_1^\varepsilon$ and $\sigma_2^\varepsilon$. This means in particular that $\mathrm{E}_{b \sim \sigma_2^\varepsilon}[u_1(a, b) \mid b \ne g] \le 1$ for all $a \in S$. Likewise $\mathrm{E}_{a \sim \sigma_1^\varepsilon}[u_2(a, b) \mid a \ne g] \le 1$ for all $b \in S$.

Define the conditional strategies $\tau_1^\varepsilon = \sigma_1^\varepsilon \mid (S \setminus \{g\})$ and $\tau_2^\varepsilon = \sigma_2^\varepsilon \mid (S \setminus \{g\})$. By our construction of the game $G_{\text{Prop}}(\Phi)$ we have that $\mathrm{E}_{b \sim \tau_2^\varepsilon}[u_1(a, b)] < \mathrm{E}_{b \sim \tau_2^\varepsilon}[u_1(a', b)]$ if and only if $\mathrm{E}_{b \sim \sigma_2^\varepsilon}[u_1(a, b)] < \mathrm{E}_{b \sim \sigma_2^\varepsilon}[u_1(a', b)]$ for all $a, a' \in S$. Likewise $\mathrm{E}_{a \sim \tau_1^\varepsilon}[u_2(a, b)] < \mathrm{E}_{a \sim \tau_1^\varepsilon}[u_2(a, b')]$ if and only if $\mathrm{E}_{a \sim \sigma_1^\varepsilon}[u_2(a, b)] < \mathrm{E}_{a \sim \sigma_1^\varepsilon}[u_2(a, b')]$ for all $b, b' \in S$.

Also $\Pr_{\tau_1^\varepsilon}[a] \le \varepsilon \Pr_{\tau_1^\varepsilon}[a']$ if and only if $\Pr_{\sigma_1^\varepsilon}[a] \le \varepsilon \Pr_{\sigma_1^\varepsilon}[a']$ for all $a, a' \in S \setminus \{g\}$, and likewise $\Pr_{\tau_2^\varepsilon}[b] \le \varepsilon \Pr_{\tau_2^\varepsilon}[b']$ if and only if $\Pr_{\sigma_2^\varepsilon}[b] \le \varepsilon \Pr_{\sigma_2^\varepsilon}[b']$ for all $b, b' \in S \setminus \{g\}$. It follows that $(\tau_1^\varepsilon, \tau_2^\varepsilon)$ is an $\varepsilon$-proper equilibrium in $\widetilde{G_{\text{CS}}}(\Phi)$.

By the Bolzano-Weierstrass Theorem the sequence $(\tau_1^\varepsilon, \tau_2^\varepsilon)$ has a limit point $(\tau_1, \tau_2)$ which then by definition is a proper equilibrium of $\widetilde{G_{\text{CS}}}(\Phi)$. In particular is $(\tau_1, \tau_2)$ a Nash equilibrium. As observed $\mathrm{E}_{b \sim \tau_2^\varepsilon}[u_1(a, b)] \le 1$ for all $a \in S \setminus \{g\}$. It follows that also $\mathrm{E}_{b \sim \tau_2}[u_1(a, b)] \le 1$ for all $a \in S \setminus \{g\}$, and in particular $\mathrm{E}_{a \sim \tau_1, b \sim \tau_2}[u_1(a, b)] \le 1$. Likewise we obtain that $\mathrm{E}_{a \sim \tau_1, b \sim \tau_2}[u_2(a, b)] \le 1$. This rules out

[1]Here and below we use $O(g(\varepsilon))$ to denote a function $f$ satisfying $|f(\varepsilon)| \le M|g(\varepsilon)|$ for every $0 < \varepsilon < \varepsilon_0$ given some $M, \varepsilon_0 > 0$. The actual value of $u_1(a, \sigma^\varepsilon)$ is strictly less than 1.

the possibility that $(\tau_1, \tau_2) = (f, f)$, and it follows from Lemma 3.1 that $(\tau_1, \tau_2)$ identifies a satisfying assignment of $\Phi$. □

Theorem 3.4. *It is* NP*-complete to decide if a given pure Nash equilibrium of a two-player game in strategic form is a proper equilibrium.*

Proof. Combining Lemma 3.2 and Lemma 3.3 we have a reduction from 3SAT to the problem of verifying that a given pure Nash equilibrium is a proper equilibrium, which establishes NP-hardness. We next sketch the proof of containment in NP. For a given pure Nash equilibrium that is a proper equilibrium also a symbolic proper Nash equilibrium with coefficients of polynomial bitsize. Given such a proposed symbolic proper Nash equilibrium it may be checked in polynomial time that it does define a sequence of $\varepsilon$-proper equilibria for all sufficiently small $\varepsilon$. □

The result directly translates to extensive form as well, so the following corollary follows from the standard reduction from strategic form to extensive form.

Corollary 3.5. *It is* NP*-hard to decide if a given pure Nash equilibrium of a two-player game in extensive form is an extensive form proper equilibrium.*

## 4 APPROXIMATING A PROPER EQUILIBRIUM IN STRATEGIC FORM GAMES

In this section we show that approximating a proper equilibrium for a finite game in strategic form with $n \geq 3$ players is $\text{FIXP}_a$-complete. On a high level, our proof strategy is similar to previous work of Etessami et al. [10] who proved the analogous result for approximating (trembling hand) perfect equilibrium as well as the follow-up work of Etessami [9] who proved several analogous results for approximating refinements of Nash equilibrium in *extensive form* games of perfect recall. As shown by Etessami and Yannakakis [11] computing a Nash equilibrium for a finite game in strategic form with $n \geq 3$ is FIXP-complete and as an immediate consequence of that it is $\text{FIXP}_a$-complete to approximate a Nash equilibrium. This directly implies $\text{FIXP}_a$-hardness for approximating refinements of Nash equilibrium the nontrivial task is to prove containment in $\text{FIXP}_a$. Like proper equilibrium, a perfect equilibrium is defined as a limit point of so-called $\varepsilon$-perfect equilibrium. Etessami et al. [10] showed that in the perturbed game, where each strategy must be played with probability at least $\varepsilon$, computing an $\varepsilon$-perfect equilibrium is in FIXP. It is then shown that for $\varepsilon$ sufficiently small relative to a given $\delta > 0$, any $\varepsilon$-perfect equilibrium is $\delta$-close to an actual perfect equilibrium, and furthermore that such an $\varepsilon$ may be computed from $\delta$ by means of repeated squaring, thereby leading to the result.

Given this, it would be natural to try to analogously prove $\text{FIXP}_a$-completeness for approximating a proper equilibrium by showing that computing an $\varepsilon$-proper equilibrium (for a perturbed game) is in FIXP. Whether this is possible remains an open problem; on the other hand we show how to *approximate* an $\varepsilon$-proper equilibrium, and by doing so also approximate an actual proper equilibrium. This result is obtained by showing that computing a so-called $\delta$-almost $\varepsilon$-proper equilibrium (in a perturbed game) is in FIXP. The definition of a $\delta$-almost $\varepsilon$-proper equilibrium was suggested by Etessami [9] as a possible way to define a relaxation of proper equilibrium computable in PPAD, analogously to other relaxations defined by Etessami [9]. Whether this turns out to be the case remains to be seen. But the notion does turns out to be the right technical definition for our purposes.

Let in the following $\Gamma$ be a fixed finite game in strategic form with $n$ players and with Player $i$ having $m_i$ pure strategies.

*Definition 4.1.* Given $\varepsilon > 0$ and $\delta > 0$, a mixed strategy profile $x$ is a $\delta$-almost $\varepsilon$-proper equilibrium if it is fully mixed and satisfies $x_{ik} \leq \varepsilon x_{i\ell}$ whenever $U_i(x_{-i}; k) + \delta \leq U_i(x_{-i}; \ell)$, for all $i \in \{1, \ldots, n\}$ and $k, \ell \in S_i$.

### 4.1 Uniform Approximation

Note that an $\varepsilon$-proper equilibrium is a $\delta$-almost $\varepsilon$-proper equilibrium for all $\delta > 0$. We will show that a proper equilibrium can be approximated by a $\varepsilon$-proper equilibrium, for sufficiently small $\varepsilon$, which in turn can be approximated by a $\delta$-almost $\varepsilon$-proper equilibrium, for sufficiently small $\delta$. This is done by invoking the powerful "almost implies near" paradigm of Anderson [1] twice. First we show that any proper equilibrium may be uniformly approximated by an $\varepsilon$-proper equilibrium.

Lemma 4.2. *For any fixed strategic form game $\Gamma$, and any $\gamma > 0$, there is an $\varepsilon > 0$, so that any $\varepsilon$-proper equilibrium of $\Gamma$ has $\ell_\infty$-distance at most $\gamma$ to some proper equilibrium of $\Gamma$.*

Proof. Suppose to the contrary there is a game $\Gamma$ and $\gamma > 0$ so that for all $\varepsilon > 0$ there is an $\varepsilon$-proper equilibrium $x_\varepsilon$ of $\Gamma$ so that there is no proper equilibrium in a $\gamma$-neighborhood (with respect to the $\ell_\infty$ norm) of $x_\varepsilon$. Consider the sequence $(x_{1/n})_{n\in\mathbb{N}}$. Since this is a sequence in a compact space, by the Bolzano-Weierstrass Theorem it has a limit point, $x^*$, which is a proper equilibrium of $\Gamma$ by definition. But this contradicts the statement that there is no proper equilibrium in a $\gamma$-neighborhood of any of the strategy profiles $x_{1/n}$. □

We shall next consider a *perturbed* version of $\Gamma$. Let $\varepsilon > 0$ be given and define $\eta_i(\varepsilon) = \varepsilon^{m_i}/m_i$ for $i \in \{1, \ldots, n\}$. When $\varepsilon$ is understood from the context we shall simply denote $\eta_i(\varepsilon)$ by $\eta_i$. We denote by $\Delta_{m_i}^{\eta_i}$ the set of $\eta_i$-perturbed mixed strategies for Player $i$, meaning that each pure strategy is played with probability at least $\eta_i$. Thus $\Delta_{m_i}^{\eta_i} = \{y \in \mathbb{R}^m \mid \|y\|_1 = 1; \forall j : y_j \geq \eta_i\}$. Let $\eta = (\eta_1, \ldots, \eta_n)$, and define $D_\Gamma^\eta = \prod_{i=1}^n \Delta_{m_i}^{\eta_i}$ to be the set of all $\eta$-perturbed mixed strategy profiles for $\Gamma$. Clearly $D_\Gamma^\eta \subset D_\Gamma^o \subset D_\Gamma$. The $\eta$-perturbed game $\Gamma_\eta$ restricts the set of mixed strategy profiles to the set of $\eta$-perturbed mixed strategy profiles. The game $\Gamma_\eta$ was used also by Myerson [24] in his existence proof of proper equilibrium. One of the important properties of $\Gamma_\eta$ is that any limit point of a sequence of strategy profiles is fully mixed, which is used in the following proof that any $\varepsilon$-proper equilibrium may be uniformly approximated by a $\delta$-almost $\varepsilon$-proper equilibrium.

Lemma 4.3. *For any fixed strategic form game $\Gamma$, any $\varepsilon > 0$ and any $\gamma > 0$, there is an $\delta > 0$, so that any $\delta$-almost $\varepsilon$-proper equilibrium of $\Gamma$ in $D_\Gamma^\eta$ has $\ell_\infty$-distance at most $\gamma$ to some $\varepsilon$-proper equilibrium of $\Gamma$ in $D_\Gamma^\eta$.*

Proof. Suppose to the contrary there is a game $\Gamma$, $\varepsilon > 0$, and $\gamma > 0$ so that for all $\delta > 0$ there is a $\delta$-almost $\varepsilon$-proper equilibrium $x_\delta$ of $\Gamma$ in $D_\Gamma^\eta$ so that there is no $\varepsilon$-proper equilibrium in $D_\Gamma^\eta$ and in a $\gamma$-neighborhood (with respect to the $\ell_\infty$ norm) of $x_\delta$. Consider the sequence $(x_{1/n})_{n\in\mathbb{N}}$. Since this is a sequence in a compact space, by the Bolzano-Weierstrass Theorem is has a convergent subsequence $(x_{1/n_r})_{r\in\mathbb{N}}$. Let $x^* = \lim_{r\to\infty} x_{1/n_r}$. We now claim that $x^*$ is an $\varepsilon$-proper equilibrium, which will contradict the statement that there is no $\varepsilon$-proper equilibrium in a $\gamma$-neighborhood of any of the strategy profiles $x_{1/n}$.

First, since $x_{1/n_r} \in D_\Gamma^\eta$ for all $n$ we also have $x^* \in D_\Gamma^\eta$, and in particular is $x^*$ fully mixed. Define $\nu > 0$ by

$$\nu = \min_{i,k,\ell} \left\{ U_i(x_{-i}^*; \ell) - U_i(x_{-i}^*; k) \mid U_i(x_{-i}^*; k) < U_i(x_{-i}^*; \ell) \right\} .$$

By continuity of the functions $U_i$ we have

$$\lim_{r\to\infty} U_i\left((x_{1/n_r})_{-i}; k\right) = U_i(x_{-i}^*; k) ,$$

for all $i$ and $k$. Thus let $N$ be an integer such that

$$|U_i\left((x_{1/n_r})_{-i}; k\right) - U_i(x_{-i}^*; k)| \leq \nu/3 ,$$

and such that $1/n_r \leq \nu/3$, for all $i$,$k$, and $r \geq N$.

Consider now $k$ and $\ell$ such that $U_i(x^*_{-i};k) < U_i(x^*_{-i};\ell)$. By construction, for any $r \geq N$ we also have $U_i((x_{1/n_r})_{-i};k) + 1/n_r \leq U_i((x_{1/n_r})_{-i};\ell)$. Since $x_{1/n_r}$ is a $(1/n_r)$-almost $\varepsilon$-proper equilibrium it follows that $(x_{1/n_r})_{ik} \leq \varepsilon (x_{1/n_r})_{i\ell}$. Taking the limit $r \to \infty$ we also have $x^*_{ik} \leq \varepsilon x^*_{i\ell}$, which shows that $x^*$ is a $\varepsilon$-proper equilibrium as claimed. □

## 4.2 Approximate Selection and Fixed Points

We shall now work toward a fixed point characterization of $\delta$-almost $\varepsilon$-proper equilibrium in $\Gamma_\eta$. We shall first generalize the property defining a $\delta$-almost $\varepsilon$-proper equilibrium in two ways. First, the definition applies to all scalar multiples of mixed strategies. Secondly, the definition incorporates a notion of *action valuation* which take the place of the utilities $U_i(x_{-i};k)$.

*Definition 4.4.* An action valuation for Player $i$ is an assignment $v_i \in \mathbb{R}^{m_i}$ of valuations to actions. We say that $x_i \in \mathbb{R}^{m_i}_+$ satisfies the $\delta$-almost $\varepsilon$-proper property with respect to action valuation $v_i$ if and only if $x_{ik} \leq \varepsilon x_{i\ell}$ whenever $v_{ik} + \delta \leq v_{i\ell}$, for all $k, \ell \in S_i$.

Note that while we do not require that $x_i \in \Delta^o_{m_i}$ we have that $x_i$ satisfies the $\delta$-almost $\varepsilon$-proper property with respect to action valuation $v_i$ if and only if $x_i/\|x_i\|_1$ does as well.

There is a discontinuity in the $\delta$-almost $\varepsilon$-proper property on the upper bounds imposed on the individual coordinates of $x_i$ as a function of the action valuation $v_i$. For $\delta = 0$ this discontinuity is inherent, but for $\delta > 0$ we can resolve it by defining a notion of $\delta$-approximate selection that linearly interpolates between two values $x$ and $y$ in an interval of length $\delta$ on the right side of a selection point 0.

*Definition 4.5.* For given $\delta > 0$, the $\delta$-approximate selection function $\mathrm{Sel}_\delta$ is defined by

$$\mathrm{Sel}_\delta(x,y,z) = \begin{cases} x & \text{if } z \leq 0 \\ (1 - z/\delta)x + (z/\delta)y & \text{if } 0 \leq z \leq \delta \\ y & \text{if } \delta \leq z \end{cases}$$

We next incorporate the $\delta$-approximate selection function into a function $P_{i,\varepsilon}$ that captures the upper bounds imposed on the individual coordinates of $x_i$.

*Definition 4.6.* Define the function $P_{i,\varepsilon} : \mathbb{R}^{m_i}_+ \times \mathbb{R}^{m_i} \to \mathbb{R}^{m_i}_+$ by

$$(P_{i,\varepsilon}(x_i, v_i))_k = \min_\ell \{\mathrm{Sel}_\delta(x_{ik}, \varepsilon x_{i\ell}, v_{i\ell} - v_{ik})\}$$

For a fixed action valuation $v_i$ we obtain an operator $P^{v_i}_{i,\varepsilon} : \mathbb{R}^{m_i}_+ \to \mathbb{R}^{m_i}_+$ in the natural way.

*Definition 4.7.* Let $v_i$ be an action valuation. Then the operator $P^{v_i}_{i,\varepsilon} : \mathbb{R}^{m_i}_+ \to \mathbb{R}^{m_i}_+$ is defined by

$$P^{v_i}_{i,\varepsilon}(x_i) = P_{i,\varepsilon}(x_i, v_i) \ .$$

A simple but important property of the operator $P^{v_i}_{i,\varepsilon}$ is that it is *monotone*.

Lemma 4.8. *For any $x_i \in R^{m_i}_+$ and $v \in \mathbb{R}^{m_i}$ we have $P_{i,\varepsilon}(x_i, v_i) \leq x_i$.*

Proof. This follows from the definition of $P_{i,\varepsilon}$ since $\mathrm{Sel}_\delta(x_{ik}, \varepsilon x_{i\ell}, v_{i\ell} - v_{ik}) = x_{ik}$ for $k = \ell$. □

An immediate consequence is that fixed points of the operator are exactly the points whose $L^1$-norm is preserved by the operator.

Corollary 4.9. *Let $x_i \in \Delta^o_{m_i}$. Then $x_i$ is a fixed point of $P^{v_i}_{i,\varepsilon}$ if and only if $\|P_{i,\varepsilon}(x_i, v_i)\|_1 = 1$.*

The operator was defined precisely for the purpose that fixed points will satisfy the $\delta$-almost $\varepsilon$-proper property. This is easy to verify.

Lemma 4.10. *Suppose $x_i \in \mathbb{R}_+^{m_i}$ is a fixed point of $P_{i,\varepsilon}^{v_i}$. Then $x_i$ satisfies the $\delta$-almost $\varepsilon$-proper property with respect to $v_i$.*

Proof. Suppose that $v_{ik} + \delta \leq v_{i\ell}$. Then $v_{i\ell} - v_{ik} \geq \delta$, and since $x_i$ is a fixed point of $P_{i,\varepsilon}^{v_i}$ we must have $x_{ik} = (P_{i,\varepsilon}(x_i, v_i))_k \leq \mathrm{Sel}_\delta(x_{ik}, \varepsilon x_{i\ell}, v_{i\ell} - v_{ik}) = \varepsilon x_{i\ell}$. □

The operator $P_{i,\varepsilon}^{v_i}$ is by itself not useful for expressing $\delta$-almost $\varepsilon$-proper equilibrium as fixed points precisely for the reason that it is monotone and hence only preserves that $L^1$ norm at fixed points. We will instead be able to use it for actually computing a mixed strategy that satisfy the $\delta$-almost $\varepsilon$-proper property with respect to $v_i$, for a given action valuation $v_i$. We will see that iterating the $P_{i,\varepsilon}^{v_i}$ operator on the uniform distribution will work for this purpose.

### 4.3 Computing a $\delta$-almost $\varepsilon$-proper Mixed Strategy

Let $\tau_{m_i} \in \Delta_{m_i}$ be the uniform distribution over the pure strategies of Player $i$, i.e. $\tau_{m_i k} = 1/m_i$ for $k = 1, \ldots, m_i$. For a fixed action valuation $v_i$, let $(P_{i,\varepsilon}^{v_i})^{\circ j}$ denote the $j$-th iteration of the operator $P_{i,\varepsilon}^{v_i}$. That is we let $(P_{i,\varepsilon}^{v_i})^{\circ 0}$ simply denote the identity function on $\mathbb{R}_+^{m_i}$ and define $(P_{i,\varepsilon}^{v_i})^{\circ(j+1)} := P_{i,\varepsilon}^{v_i} \circ (P_{i,\varepsilon}^{v_i})^{\circ j}$. Define for all $j \geq 0$ the vectors $\tau_{m_i}^{(j)} = (P_{i,\varepsilon}^{v_i})^{(j)}(\tau_{m_i})$. Starting the iteration of $P_{i,\varepsilon}^{v_i}$ on the uniform distribution means that individual coordinates can not become very small.

Lemma 4.11. *For all $j \geq 0$ and $k$ we have $\tau_{m_i k}^{(j)} \geq \varepsilon^{m_i - 1}/m_i$.*

Proof. By possibly reordering coordinates, we may without loss of generality assume that $v_1 \geq \cdots \geq v_{m_i}$. Note then that $\mathrm{Sel}_\delta(x, y, v_{i\ell} - v_{ik}) = x$ for all $\ell \geq k$. We shall then show by induction in $k$ that $\tau_{m_i k}^{(j)} \geq \varepsilon^{k-1}/m_i$ for all $j$. For the base case of $k = 1$, by the above we have $\mathrm{Sel}_\delta(\tau_{m_i k}^{(j)}, \varepsilon\tau_{m_i \ell}^{(j)}, v_{i\ell} - v_{ik}) = \tau_{m_i k}^{(j)}$ for all $j$ and $\ell$, and hence $\tau_{m_i k}^{(j)} = \tau_{m_i k} = 1/m_i$ for all $j$. Consider now a general $k \geq 2$. We get $\mathrm{Sel}_\delta(\tau_{m_i k}^{(j)}, \varepsilon\tau_{m_i \ell}^{(j)}, v_{i\ell} - v_{ik}) \geq \min\{\tau_{m_i k}^{(j)}, \varepsilon^{\ell-1}/m_i\}$ for all $j$ and $\ell < k$ and $\mathrm{Sel}_\delta(\tau_{m_i k}^{(j)}, \varepsilon\tau_{m_i \ell}^{(j)}, v_{i\ell} - v_{ik}) = \tau_{m_i k}^{(j)}$ for all $j$ and $\ell \geq k$, from which the result follows. □

Note that by the above lemmas as $j$ tends to infinity the sequence $\tau_{m_i}^{(j)}$ converges to a limit point $\tau^*$ that satisfies the $\delta$-almost $\epsilon$-proper property and furthermore satisfies $\tau_k^* \geq \varepsilon^{m_i-1}/m_i$ for all $k$. It follows that $\tau^*/\|\tau^*\|_1 \in \Delta_{m_i}^{\eta_i}$ and satisfies the $\delta$-almost $\epsilon$-proper property as well. Of course we will only be able to iterate $P_{i,\varepsilon}^{v_i}$ polynomially many times. We will next show that this is sufficient for our purposes.

Lemma 4.12. *For a given $k$ suppose that for every $\ell$ with $v_{i\ell} \geq v_{ik}$ we have that $\tau_{m_i \ell}^{(j+1)} \geq \sqrt{\varepsilon}\tau_{m_i \ell}^{(j)}$. Then $\tau_{m_i k}^{(j+2)} \geq \sqrt{\varepsilon}\tau_{m_i k}^{(j+1)}$.*

Proof. By assumption, if $v_{i\ell} \geq v_{ik}$ we have

$$\begin{aligned}\mathrm{Sel}_\delta(\tau_{m_i k}^{(j+1)}, \varepsilon\tau_{m_i \ell}^{(j+1)}, v_{i\ell} - v_{ik}) &\geq \mathrm{Sel}_\delta(\sqrt{\varepsilon}\tau_{m_i k}^{(j)}, \varepsilon\sqrt{\varepsilon}\tau_{m_i \ell}^{(j)}, v_{i\ell} - v_{ik}) \\ &= \sqrt{\varepsilon}\,\mathrm{Sel}_\delta(\tau_{m_i k}^{(j)}, \varepsilon\tau_{m_i \ell}^{(j)}, v_{i\ell} - v_{ik})\end{aligned},$$

and by since by definition of $\mathrm{Sel}_\delta$, if $v_{i\ell} \leq v_{ik}$ we have $\mathrm{Sel}_\delta(x, y, v_{i\ell} - v_{ik}) = x$ it follows that

$$\tau_{m_i k}^{(j+2)} = \min_\ell \left\{\mathrm{Sel}_\delta(\tau_{m_i k}^{(j+1)}, \varepsilon\tau_{m_i \ell}^{(j+1)}, v_{i\ell} - v_{ik})\right\}$$

$$\begin{aligned}&= \sqrt{\varepsilon}\min_\ell \left\{\mathrm{Sel}_\delta(\tau_{m_i k}^{(j)}, \varepsilon\tau_{m_i \ell}^{(j)}, v_{i\ell} - v_{ik})\right\} \\ &= \sqrt{\varepsilon}\tau_{m_i k}^{(j+1)}\ .\end{aligned}$$

□

Thus, as soon $\tau^{(j)}_{m_i\ell}$ decreases by a factor at no less than $\sqrt{\varepsilon}$ with each application of $P^{v_i}_{i,\varepsilon}$, for all $\ell$ such that $v_{i\ell} \geq v_{ik}$, the same will be true for $\tau_{m_ik}$. Since each $\tau^{(j)}_{m_ik}$ is bounded from below by $\varepsilon^{m_i-1}/m_i$ they must each decrease by a factor no less than $\sqrt{\varepsilon}$ after polynomially many iterations. More precisely we have the following precise bound.

Corollary 4.13. *If $\varepsilon \leq 1/m_i$ and $j \geq 2m_i^2$ then $\tau^{(j+1)}_{m_ik} \geq \sqrt{\varepsilon}\tau^{(j)}_{m_ik}$ for all $k$.*

Proof. Since $\varepsilon \leq 1/m_i$ we have $\tau^{(j)}_{m_ik} \geq \varepsilon^{m_i}$ for all $k$ and $j \geq 0$. Thus every $\tau^{(j)}_{m_ik}$ can decrease by a factor less than $\sqrt{\varepsilon}$ at most $2m_i$ times. By possibly reordering coordinates, we may without loss of generality assume that $v_1 \geq \cdots \geq v_{m_i}$. By induction in $k$ follows that for every $\ell \leq k$ we have that $\tau^{(j+1)}_{m_i\ell} \geq \sqrt{\varepsilon}\tau^{(j)}_{m_i\ell}$ whenever $j \geq 2m_ik$ by the previous lemma. □

We next show that $\tau^{(j)}_{m_i}$ for our purposes will be essentially as useful as the limit point $\tau^*$ for $j \geq 2m_i^2$. First we need another simple observation about the operator $P^{v_i}_{i,\varepsilon}$.

Lemma 4.14. *Suppose $k$ and $\ell$ are such that $v_{ik} + \delta \leq v_{i\ell}$. For $x_i \in \mathbb{R}^{m_i}_+$ and $x'_i = P^{v_i}_{i,\varepsilon}(x_i)$. If $x'_{ik} > \sqrt{\epsilon}x'_{i\ell}$ it follows that $x'_{i\ell} < \sqrt{\epsilon}x_{i\ell}$.*

Proof. By the assumptions and the definition of $P^{v_i}_{i,\varepsilon}$ we have $x'_{ik} \leq \epsilon x_{i\ell}$. Thus we have $x'_{i\ell} < 1/\sqrt{\epsilon}x'_{ik} \leq \sqrt{\epsilon}x_{i\ell}$ as stated. □

We can now finally state our conclusion about $\tau^{(j)}_{m_i}$, which follows directly from the above statements.

Proposition 4.15. *Let $\varepsilon \leq 1/m_i$. Then $\tau^{(j)}_{m_i}$ satisfy the $\delta$-almost $\sqrt{\varepsilon}$-proper property for all $j \geq 2m_i^2$.*

## 4.4 Fixed Point Characterization

We are now finally in position to give a fixed point characterization of $\delta$-almost $\varepsilon$-proper equilibrium. For this we define a function $F^{\varepsilon,\delta}_\Gamma : D^{\eta(\varepsilon^2)}_\Gamma \to D^{\eta(\varepsilon^2)}_\Gamma$ such that every fixed point of $F^{\varepsilon,\delta}_\Gamma$ is a $\delta$-almost $\varepsilon$-proper equilibrium of $\Gamma$. Let $x \in D^{\eta(\varepsilon^2)}_\Gamma$ be given and define the following for all $i$ and all $k \in S_i$:

(1) $v_{ik} = U_i(x_{-1}; k)$.
(2) $y_i = (P^{v_i}_{i,\varepsilon^2})^{\circ(2m_i^2)}(\tau_{m_i})$.

We now simply define $(F^{\varepsilon,\delta}_\Gamma(x))_i = y_i/\|y_i\|_1$. Note that by Lemma 4.11 we have that $y_i \in \Delta^{\eta_i(\varepsilon^2)}_{m_i}$ for all $i$. Hence $(F^{\varepsilon,\delta}_\Gamma(x)) \in D^{\eta(\varepsilon^2)}_\Gamma$ thereby making $F^{\varepsilon,\delta}_\Gamma$ well defined. We next consider the fixed points of $F^{\varepsilon,\delta}_\Gamma$.

Proposition 4.16. *Let $\delta > 0$ and $0 < \varepsilon < 1$. Then every fixed point $x \in D^{\eta(\varepsilon^2)}_\Gamma$ is a $\delta$-almost $\varepsilon$-proper equilibrium of $\Gamma$.*

Proof. Suppose that $x$ is a fixed point of $F^{\varepsilon,\delta}_\Gamma(x)$. For each $i$ we then have that $x_i = y_i/\|y_i\|_1$. By Proposition 4.15 we have that $y_i$ satisfies the $\delta$-almost $\varepsilon$-proper property with respect to action valuation $v_i$ by construction. This implies that $x_i$ satisfies the $\delta$-almost $\varepsilon$-proper property with respect to action valuation $v_i$ as well. Since this holds for each $i$, we conclude that $x$ is a $\delta$-almost $\varepsilon$-proper equilibrium. □

From the above description it is easy to construct in polynomial time a $\{+, -, *, /, \max, \min\}$-circuit computing $F_\Gamma^{\varepsilon,\delta}(x)$, where $x$, $\varepsilon$, and $\delta$ are inputs of the circuit. The function $\mathrm{Sel}_\delta$ is computable by the formula $\mathrm{Sel}_\delta(x, y, z) = (1 - \max(\min(z, \delta), 0)/\delta)x + (\max(\min(z, \delta), 0)/\delta)y$. The operator $P_{i,\varepsilon}^{v_i}$ was already defined in the required form, and the description of $F_\Gamma^{\varepsilon,\delta}(x)$ above consists mainly of polynomially many such functions composed with each other.

Theorem 4.17. *There exist a function $F_\Gamma^{\varepsilon,\delta} : D_\Gamma^{\eta(\varepsilon^2)} \to D_\Gamma^{\eta(\varepsilon^2)}$ given by a $\{+, -, *, /, \max, \min\}$-circuit computable in polynomial time from $\Gamma$, with the circuit having inputs $x$,$\varepsilon > 0$, and $\delta > 0$ as inputs, such that for all fixed $0 < \varepsilon < 1$ and $\delta > 0$, every fixed point of $F_\Gamma^{\varepsilon,\delta}$ is a $\delta$-almost $\varepsilon$-proper equilibrium of $\Gamma$. In particular is the problem of computing a $\delta$-almost $\varepsilon$-proper equilibrium of a finite game with $n$ players in strategic form in* FIXP.

## 4.5 Approximating Proper Equilibrium

We have now established that proper equilibrium may be approximated by a $\varepsilon$-proper equilibrium which in turn may be approximated by a $\delta$-almost $\varepsilon$-proper equilibrium which in turn can be computed in FIXP. What remains for proving that approximating a proper equilibrium can be done in $\mathrm{FIXP}_a$ are effective bounds on how small $\varepsilon$ and $\delta$ need to be in order to guarantee a good approximation.

We can obtain such bounds in a generic way using the general machinery of real algebraic geometry, cf. Basu et al. [2]. We shall here just outline how this is done and refer to Etessami et al. [10] for full details of an analogous derivation given for trembling hand perfect equilibrium. The main idea is to formalize the "almost implies near" statements of Lemma 4.2 and Lemma 4.3 as formulas in the first order theory of the reals. For Lemma 4.2 a first-order formula is constructed from $\Gamma$ and $\gamma$ with a single free variable $\varepsilon$, expressing that $\varepsilon$ satisfies the conclusion of the lemma. Applying quantifier elimination to that formula and employing known bounds on the result of this we obtain the following statement.

Lemma 4.18. *There is a constant $c_1$, such that for all integers $n$,$m$, and $B$ and every $\gamma > 0$, the following holds for every $\varepsilon \leq min(\gamma, 1/B)^{n^{c_1 m^3}}$. For any finite game $\Gamma$ with $n$ players having a total of at most $m$ pure strategies, and with integer payoffs of absolute value at most $B$, any $\varepsilon$-proper equilibrium of $\Gamma$ has $L^\infty$-distance at most $\gamma$ to some proper equilibrium of $\Gamma$.*

Similarly, for Lemma 4.3 a first-order formula is constructed from $\Gamma$, $\gamma$ *and* $\varepsilon$ with a single free variable $\delta$, expressing that $\delta$ satisfies the conclusion of the lemma. Again applying quantifier elimination to that formula and employing known bounds on the result of this we obtain the following statement.

Lemma 4.19. *There is a constant $c_2$, such that for all integers $n$,$m$, and $B$, every $\gamma > 0$ and every $\varepsilon > 0$, the following holds for every $\delta \leq min(\gamma, \varepsilon, 1/B)^{n^{c_2 m^2}}$. For any finite game $\Gamma$ with $n$ players having a total of at most $m$ pure strategies, and with integer payoffs of absolute value at most $B$, any $\delta$-almost $\varepsilon$-proper equilibrium of $\Gamma$ has $L^\infty$-distance at most $\gamma$ to some $\varepsilon$-proper equilibrium of $\Gamma$.*

We can now finally state the main theorem of this section. The proof is again analogous to a corresponding proof for trembling hand perfect equilibrium by Etessami et al. [10] except that we here construct *two* virtual infinitesimals $\delta \ll \varepsilon$ by means of repeated squaring instead of a single such virtual infinitesimal.

Theorem 4.20. *Given as input a finite game $\Gamma$ with $n$ players in strategic form having integer payoffs and a rational $\gamma > 0$, the problem of computing a strategy profile $x'$ such that there is a proper equilibrium $x$ of $\Gamma$ with $\|x' - x\|_\infty < \gamma$ is $\mathrm{FIXP}_a$-complete.*

Proof. Let $m = \sum_{i=1}^{n} m_i$ be the total number of pure strategies for the players. Let $B$ be the largest magnitude of a payoff in $\Gamma$. By definition of $\text{FIXP}_a$ our task is to given $\gamma > 0$ construct a polytope $P$, a circuit $C$ computing a function $F : P \to P$, and a number $\gamma'$, such that $\gamma'$-approximations to fixed points of $F$ can be efficiently transformed into $\gamma$-approximations of proper equilibrium of $\Gamma$. We simply let $\gamma' = \gamma/2$ and ensure that fixed points of $F$ are themselves $\gamma$-approximations of proper equilibrium of $\Gamma$. The polytope $P$ is just the polytope $D_\Gamma$ of all strategy profiles of $\Gamma$, whose defining inequalities can clearly be computed in polynomial time. We next describe the circuit $C$. First a suitable $\varepsilon > 0$ satisfying the conditions of Lemma 4.18 is computed by repeated squaring of the number $\min(\gamma/4, 1/B)$ exactly $\lceil c_1 m^3 \lg n \rceil$ times. Next a suitable $\delta > 0$ satisfying the conditions of Lemma 4.19 is computed by repeated squaring of the number $\min(\gamma/4, \varepsilon, 1/B)$ exactly $\lceil c_2 m^2 \lg n \rceil$ times. Next the input $x \in D_\Gamma$ is mapped to $D_\Gamma^{\eta(\varepsilon^2)}$ by any mapping that is the identity function on $D_\Gamma^{\eta(\varepsilon^2)}$. This may be done by computing for each $i$ a number $t_i$ such that $\sum_{j=1}^{m_i} \max(x_{ij} - t_i, \eta_i(\varepsilon^2)) = 1$ using a sorting network like Etessami and Yannakakis [11] and then mapping each $x_{ij}$ to $\max(x_{ij} - t_i, \eta_i(\varepsilon^2))$. Next we compute the function $F_\Gamma^{\varepsilon,\delta}$ on the transformed input with the constructed $\varepsilon$ and $\delta$, and let this be the output of $C$. By Theorem 4.17, any fixed point of $F$ is a $\delta$-almost $\varepsilon$-proper equilibrium of $\Gamma$. By Lemma 4.19 this is a $\gamma/4$-approximation to an $\varepsilon$-proper equilibrium, which in turn by Lemma 4.18 is a $\gamma/4$-approximation to a proper equilibrium of $\Gamma$. Finally, by the triangle inequality, any $\gamma' = \gamma/2$-approximation to a fixed point of $F$ is a $\gamma/2 + \gamma/4 + \gamma/4 = \gamma$-approximation of a proper equilibrium of $\Gamma$. This completes the proof. □

## 5 COMPUTING PROPER EQUILIBRIUM IN POLYMATRIX GAMES

In this section, we show that computing a proper equilibrium can be done in PPAD for some multiplayer games. Specifically, we provide a PPAD algorithm for computing a proper equilibrium of a polymatrix game. We do this by observing that the strategy constraints from Sørensen [26], which gives a symbolic $\varepsilon$-proper equilibrium, can be incorporated into the LCP formulation of Howson [18] for equilibria of polymatrix games. Lemke's algorithm is then shown to always find a solution to the LCP, which thus yields a PPAD algorithm for computing a symbolic $\varepsilon$-proper equilibrium of the given polymatrix game. The symbolic $\varepsilon$-proper equilibrium serves both as a representation of the proper equilibrium (by letting $\varepsilon \to 0^+$), but also as a witness that the equilibrium is indeed proper, thereby circumventing the hardness of recognizing a solution that is given only as standard probabilities.

A polymatrix game $G$ is an $n$-player game, where the utility of each player can be separated into independent terms for each opponent. Each player plays their chosen strategy pairwise against all other players in independent bimatrix games, and receives the sum as the combined utility. As with strategic form games, player $i$ has $m_i$ pure strategies. The game is specified by a collection of matrices, one matrix $A_{ij} \in \mathbb{R}^{m_i \times m_j}$ for each ordered pair of players $(i, j)$. If each player $i$ plays mixed strategies $x_i \in \Delta_{m_i}$, the expected utility for player $i$ is $U_i(x_1, \ldots, x_n) = \sum_{j \neq i} x_i^\top A_{ij} x_j$.

These games can be formulated as symmetric bilinear games [13, 22]. While bilinear games is a useful abstraction that would allow us to add the needed strategy constraints, that formulation is not suitable for our purpose for two reasons. First, it needlessly doubles the dimension of the LCP, which is a bad idea, since the running time for solving LCP is in general exponential in the dimension. This would not be a problem in itself, if one only cares about the complexity class. However, secondly, it adds the requirement on the solution to the LCP that it must correspond to a symmetric equilibrium, and not just any equilibrium. This either adds even more constraints to the LCP, or requires using a non-standard LCP solver. We therefore stick closer to the original formulation of Howson [18].

The approach of Howson [18] can be understood as reformulating the $n$-player polymatrix game into a form where a single meta-player specifies the strategy for all players. For conciseness, we pack all the payoff matrices $A_{ij}$ into one matrix $A$ and the strategy vectors $x_i$ into one vector $x$ in the following way:

$$A = \begin{bmatrix} 0 & A_{12} & \dots & A_{1n} \\ A_{21} & 0 & \dots & A_{2n} \\ \vdots & \vdots & \ddots & \vdots \\ A_{n1} & A_{n2} & \dots & 0 \end{bmatrix} \qquad x = \begin{pmatrix} x_1 \\ x_2 \\ \vdots \\ x_n \end{pmatrix}$$

With this representation, the sum of utilities for all players, when they combined play strategy $x$, is given by $x^\top Ax$. A strategy profile $x$ is then an equilibrium exactly when $x^\top Ax = \max_y y^\top Ax$.

We now need a brief aside to introduce the strategy constraints from Sørensen [26] that will ensure the $\varepsilon$-proper equilibria. The constraints are built on a proof of existence of proper equilibria from Kohlberg and Mertens [19, Prop. 5]. While Sørensen only applies the construction to two-player games, the proof of Kohlberg and Mertens works for any number of players. In their proof, an auxiliary game $G'$ is constructed where the $m_i$ strategies of player $i$ are replaced by $m_i!$ pure strategies, one for each of the ways that $m_i$ first powers of $\varepsilon$ can be assigned to the $m_i$ pure strategies of the original game $G$. Equilibria of $G'$ are proved to be $\varepsilon$-proper of the original game. The construction by Sørensen allows for representing the mixed strategies of $G'$ directly as a restriction of the strategy space of $G$, thus avoiding an exponential blowup in size. Specifically, for any number of pure strategies $m_i$, it gives strategy constraints $E_{m_i}x = e_{m_x}$, with all entries of $E_{m_i}$ being integers and all entries of $e_{m_x}$ being either 0 or a power of $\varepsilon$. In the full construction, the constraints also include inequalities, but standard LP tricks lets us express everything as equalities for brevity, e.g., by using auxiliary variables. In our construction, we will pack these constraints into one constraint matrix and vector as follows:

$$E = \begin{bmatrix} E_{m_1} & 0 & \dots & 0 \\ 0 & E_{m_2} & \dots & 0 \\ \vdots & \vdots & \ddots & \vdots \\ 0 & 0 & \dots & E_{m_n} \end{bmatrix} \qquad e = \begin{pmatrix} e_{m_1} \\ e_{m_2} \\ \vdots \\ e_{m_n} \end{pmatrix}$$

With this, $Ex = e$ will restrict the strategy profile $x$ such that each player of the polymatrix game to play within the $\varepsilon$-permutahedron as defined by Sørensen.

The following derivation will stay fairly closely to that of Koller et al. [20] for the sequence form, since their proofs of correctness almost directly works for our case as well. In fact, the following derivation is almost identical, except that it is specialized to finding an $x$ that is a best response to itself instead of an $(x, y)$ pair that are mutual best responses.

Given a strategy profile $y$, the task of computing a best response within the strategy constraints is captured by the following LP in the left and its dual on the right

$$\begin{aligned} \underset{x}{\text{maximize}} \quad & x^\top(Ay) \\ \text{subject to} \quad & x^\top E^\top = e^\top \\ & x \geq 0 \end{aligned} \qquad\qquad \begin{aligned} \underset{p}{\text{minimize}} \quad & e^\top p \\ \text{subject to} \quad & E^\top p \geq Ay \end{aligned} \tag{1}$$

By complementary slackness, $x$ is a best response to $y$ whenever

$$x^\top(-Ay + E^\top p) = 0 \tag{2}$$

This also holds true for $y = x$, so replacing $y$ with $x$ and constraining $x$ to the desired strategy space, we get

$$\begin{aligned} x^\top(-Ax + E^\top p) &= 0 \\ Ex &= e \\ x &\geq 0 \end{aligned} \tag{3}$$

An LCP in standard form is specified by a pair $(b, M)$ with $b \in \mathbb{R}^n$ and $M \in \mathbb{R}^{n\times n}$. The problem is to find $z \in \mathbb{R}^n$ such that

$$\begin{aligned} b + Mz &\geq 0 \\ z^\top(b + Mz) &= 0 \\ z &\geq 0 \end{aligned} \tag{4}$$

The constraints specified in this section can be packed into an LCP in standard form in the following way. If we let $z = (x, p', p'')^\top$, where $p = p' - p''$, and

$$M = \begin{pmatrix} -A & E^\top & -E^\top \\ -E & 0 & 0 \\ E & 0 & 0 \end{pmatrix} \quad \text{and} \quad b = \begin{pmatrix} 0 \\ e \\ -e \end{pmatrix}. \tag{5}$$

then the LCP standard form of (4) gives us exactly the desired constraints. This means that in a solution to the LCP, the strategy profile $x$ is a best response to itself within the restricted strategy space, and therefore an equilibrium of the auxiliary game, and therefore an $\varepsilon$-proper equilibrium of the given polymatrix game.

It is worth making two observations here. First, the above construction generalizes that of Sørensen, since a bimatrix game is the special case of polymatrix games with only two players. This generalization is direct in that if a bimatrix game is seen as a polymatrix game, the above construction will yield exactly the LCP of Sørensen. Secondly, the derivation above is the same for many other strategy constraints. In fact, if we just restrict the strategies to be the normal strategies of polymatrix games, we get exactly the original LCP of Howson.

### 5.1 Solving the LCP with Lemke's algorithm

The standard algorithm for solving LCPs in standard form is the one provided by Lemke [21]. The algorithm performs a sequence of *complementary pivots* on a relaxation of the LCP, maintaining the complementarity condition $z^\top(b+Mz) = 0$ while searching for a basic solution where the relaxation disappears. The pivots are similar to those of the simplex method [7] for linear programming, but the complementarity condition specifies the entering and leaving variables (for non-degenerate LCPs). Pivoting continues until the variable introduced by the relaxation can leave the basis and become 0. If this happens, the current solution to the relaxed problem is also a solution to the original problem. For a thorough exposition of Lemke's algorithm, see the monograph by Cottle et al. [6].

When applying Lemke's algorithm to find a solution to an LCP, there are two pitfalls that must be avoided. The first was hinted at in the above; an LCP can be degenerate, in which case the complementarity condition is not enough to specify the next pivot. This is typically handled by slightly perturbing $b$ with different powers of an indeterminate infinitesimal $\varepsilon$, which is ignored when reading off the solution at the end. Just like for Sørensen [26], this perturbation of the $b$ vector can also give an way of keeping the powers of $\varepsilon$ needed for the $\varepsilon$-permutahedra in the strategy constraints. Those $\varepsilon$ end up in the $b$ vector of the LCP, so they can serve a dual purpose. Any implementation of Lemke's algorithm using the perturbation trick can easily output the solution with these perturbations intact.

The second, and more troublesome pitfall, is an alternative undesirable way to terminate: the current entering variable might not be restricted by a basic variable. This is known as ray termination. To prove that the algorithm works for our case, we must prove that ray termination cannot happen. To do this, we use the following theorem by Koller et al. [20]

Theorem 5.1 (Koller et.al.'96). *If (i) $z^\top Mz \geq 0$ for all $z \geq 0$, and (ii) $z \geq 0$, $Mz \geq 0$ and $z^\top Mz = 0$ imply $z^\top b \geq 0$, then Lemke's algorithm computes a solution of the LCP (2.9) and does not terminate with a secondary ray.*

Our application of the theorem is similar to that of Koller et al., and we need a similar set of lemmas.

Lemma 5.2. *The only non-negative solution $x$ to $Ex = 0$ is $x = 0$.*

Proof. Observe that the constraint $Ex = 0$ unfolds into independent constraints $E_{m_1}x_1 = e_{m_1}$, $E_{m_2}x_2 = e_{m_2}, \ldots, E_{m_n}x_n = e_{m_n}$. By Lemma 5.2 of Sørensen [26], the statement holds true for each of those individually, and therefore also for the combined constraint. □

Lemma 5.3. *If $E^\top p \geq 0$, then $e^\top p \geq 0$.*

Proof. Consider the LP for finding any feasible strategy profile, (and it's dual on the right):

$$\begin{aligned} \underset{x}{\text{maximize}} \quad & 0 \\ \text{subject to} \quad & Ex = e \\ & x \geq 0 \end{aligned} \qquad\qquad \begin{aligned} \underset{p}{\text{minimize}} \quad & e^\top p \\ \text{subject to} \quad & E^\top p \geq 0 \end{aligned} \tag{6}$$

Since the primal is feasible and has value 0, by weak duality the objective function of the dual is lower bounded by 0, i.e., $e^\top p \geq 0$. □

Theorem 5.4. *If $A \leq 0$, then $M$ and $b$ in (5) satisfy all assumptions of Theorem 5.1.*

Proof. Let $z = (x, p', p'')^\top \geq 0$ and $p = p' - p''$. Then we have that $z^\top Mz = -x^\top Ax \geq 0$, satisfying condition (i) of Theorem 5.1. Furthermore, $Mz \geq 0$ implies $-Ax + E^\top p \geq 0$ and $Ex = 0$. Combining the latter with non-negativity of $x$, Lemma 5.2 implies that $x = 0$. Combining this with the first, we get $E^\top p \geq 0$. By Lemma 5.3, this implies that $e^\top p \geq 0$. Finally, $z^\top b = e^\top p \geq 0$, showing that we satisfy condition (ii) of Theorem 5.1. □

The condition $A \leq 0$ can be ensured by subtracting a suitably large constant from the payoff of all players. This does not change the set of proper equilibria, as the value of best replies are shifted by the same amount. Thus, ray termination is not a possibility, and Lemke's algorithm will terminate with an equilibrium of $G'$. The solution can be read of with the values being formal polynomials in $\varepsilon$, with $\varepsilon$ itself being an indeterminate infinitesimal. For all sufficiently small values of $\varepsilon$, this solution is an $\varepsilon$-proper equilibrium of the original polymatrix game. The limit point for $\varepsilon \to 0^+$ is simply the 0-th order terms of the polynomials. Thus the solution provides both a proper equilibrium, and a witness of this in the form of a symbolic sequence of $\varepsilon$-proper equilibria.

All of this combined allows us to strengthen the main result of Sørensen [26] from bimatrix games to polymatrix games:

THEOREM 5.5. *A symbolic $\varepsilon$-proper equilibrium for a given polymatrix game can be computed by applying Lemke's algorithm to an LCP of polynomial size.*

The last step of the way to PPAD is by using an orientation [27] of Lemke's algorithm, thus again strengthening the matching corollary of Sørensen [26]

COROLLARY 5.6. *The refinement of proper equilibria, corresponding to Kohlberg and Mertens' proof of existence, is* PPAD*-complete to compute for a given polymatrix game.*

## REFERENCES


[1] R. M. Anderson. 1986. "Almost" Implies "Near". *Trans. Amer. Math. Soc.* 296, 1 (1986), 229–237.

[2] S. Basu, R. Pollack, and M. Roy. 2008. *Algorithms in Real Algebraic Geometry* (second ed.). Springer.

[3] Xi Chen and Xiaotie Deng. 2006. Settling the Complexity of Two-Player Nash Equilibrium. In *47th Annual IEEE Symposium on Foundations of Computer Science (FOCS 2006)*. IEEE Computer Society Press, 261–272.

[4] Vincent Conitzer and Tuomas Sandholm. 2003. Complexity Results about Nash Equilibria. In *Proceedings of the Eighteenth International Joint Conference on Artificial Intelligence*, Georg Gottlob and Toby Walsh (Eds.). Morgan Kaufmann, 765–771.

[5] Vincent Conitzer and Tuomas Sandholm. 2008. New complexity results about Nash equilibria. *Games and Economic Behavior* 63, 2 (2008), 621–641.

[6] Richard W. Cottle, Jong-Shi Pang, and Richard E. Stone. 2009. *The Linear Complementarity Problem*. SIAM.

[7] G.B. Dantzig, A. Orden, and P. Wolfe. 1955. The generalized simplex method for minimizing a linear form under linear inequality restraints. *Pacific J. Math.* 5 (1955), 183–195.

[8] Constantinos Daskalakis, Paul W. Goldberg, and Christos H. Papadimitriou. 2009. The Complexity of Computing a Nash Equilibrium. *SIAM J. Comput.* 39, 1 (2009), 195–259.

[9] Kousha Etessami. 2014. The complexity of computing a (perfect) equilibrium for an n-player extensive form game of perfect recall. (2014). CoRR, abs/1408.1233.

[10] Kousha Etessami, Kristoffer Arnsfelt Hansen, Peter Bro Miltersen, and Troels Bjerre Sørensen. 2014. The Complexity of Approximating a Trembling Hand Perfect Equilibrium of a Multi-player Game in Strategic Form. In *SAGT 2014 (LNCS)*, Ron Lavi (Ed.), Vol. 8768. Springer, 231–243.

[11] Kousha Etessami and Mihalis Yannakakis. 2010. On the complexity of Nash equilibria and other fixed points. *SIAM J. Comput.* 39, 6 (2010), 2531–2597.

[12] Gabriele Farina and Nicola Gatti. 2017. Extensive-Form Perfect Equilibrium Computation in Two-Player Games. In *Proceedings of the Thirty-First AAAI Conference on Artificial Intelligence*, Satinder P. Singh and Shaul Markovitch (Eds.). AAAI Press, 502–508.

[13] Jugal Garg, Albert Xin Jiang, and Ruta Mehta. 2011. Bilinear games: Polynomial time algorithms for rank based subclasses. In *International Workshop on Internet and Network Economics*. Springer, 399–407.

[14] Nicola Gatti, Mario Gilli, and Fabio Panozzo. 2016. *Further results on verification problems in extensive-form games*. Working Papers 347. University of Milano-Bicocca, Department of Economics.

[15] Nicola Gatti and Fabio Panozzo. 2012. New Results on the Verification of Nash Refinements for Extensive-form Games. In *Proceedings of the 11th International Conference on Autonomous Agents and Multiagent Systems (AAMAS 2012)*. International Foundation for Autonomous Agents and Multiagent Systems, 813–820.

[16] Kristoffer Arnsfelt Hansen. 2017. The Real Computational Complexity of Minmax Value and Equilibrium Refinements in Multi-player Games. In *SAGT 2017 (LNCS)*, Vittorio Bilò and Michele Flammini (Eds.), Vol. 10504. Springer, 119–130.

[17] Kristoffer Arnsfelt Hansen, Peter Bro Miltersen, and Troels Bjerre Sørensen. 2010. The Computational Complexity of Trembling Hand Perfection and Other Equilibrium Refinements. In *SAGT 2010 (LNCS)*, Spyros C. Kontogiannis, Elias Koutsoupias, and Paul G. Spirakis (Eds.), Vol. 6386. Springer, 198–209.

[18] Joseph T Howson. 1972. Equilibria of polymatrix games. *Management Science* 18, 5-part-1 (1972), 312–318.

[19] Elon Kohlberg and Jean-Francois Mertens. 1986. On the Strategic Stability of Equilibria. *Econometrica* 54 (1986), 1003–1037.

[20] Daphne Koller, Nimrod Megiddo, and Bernhard Von Stengel. 1996. Efficient computation of equilibria for extensive two-person games. *Games and economic behavior* 14, 2 (1996), 247–259.

[21] C.E. Lemke. 1965. Bimatrix equilibrium points and mathematical programming. *Management Science* 11 (1965), 681–689.

[22] Ruta Mehta. 2012. *Nash Equilibrium Computation in Various Games.* Ph.D. Dissertation. Indian Institute of Technology Bombay.

[23] Peter Bro Miltersen and Troels Bjerre Sørensen. 2010. Computing a quasi-perfect equilibrium of a two-player game. *Economic Theory* 42, 1 (2010), 175–192.

[24] R. B. Myerson. 1978. Refinements of the Nash Equilibrium Concept. *International Journal of Game Theory* 15 (1978), 133–154.

[25] Christos H. Papadimitriou. 1994. On the Complexity of the Parity Argument and Other Inefficient Proofs of Existence. *J. Comput. System Sci.* 48, 3 (1994), 498–532.

[26] Troels Bjerre Sørensen. 2012. Computing a proper equilibrium of a bimatrix game. In *ACM Conference on Electronic Commerce, EC '12*, Boi Faltings, Kevin Leyton-Brown, and Panos Ipeirotis (Eds.). ACM, 916–928.

[27] Michael J. Todd. 1976. Orientation in Complementary Pivot Algorithms. *Mathematics of Operations Research* 1, 1 (1976), pp. 54–66. http://www.jstor.org/stable/3689663

[28] Eric van Damme. 1991. *Stability and perfection of Nash equilibria* (2nd ed.). Springer.

# Computing a Subgame Perfect Equilibrium of a Sequential Matching Game

YASUSHI KAWASE, Tokyo Institute of Technology and RIKEN AIP Center
YUTARO YAMAGUCHI, Osaka University and RIKEN AIP Center
YU YOKOI, National Institute of Informatics

We study a decentralized matching market in which each firm sequentially makes offers to potential workers. For each offer, the worker can choose "accept" or "reject," but the decision is irrevocable. The acceptance of an offer guarantees her job at the firm, but it may also eliminate chances of better offers from other firms in the future. We formulate this market as a perfect-information extensive-form game played by the workers. Each instance of this game has a unique subgame perfect equilibrium (SPE), which does not necessarily lead to a stable matching and has some perplexing properties. Our aim is to establish the complexity of computing the SPE, or more precisely, deciding whether each offer is accepted in the SPE. We show that the tractability of this problem drastically changes according to the number of potential offers related to each firm and worker. If each firm makes offers to at most two workers (or each worker receives offers from at most two firms), then the problem is efficiently solved by a variant of the deferred acceptance algorithm. In contrast, the problem is PSPACE-hard even if both firms and workers are related to at most three offers.

CCS Concepts: •**Theory of computation → Exact and approximate computation of equilibria;** *Algorithmic game theory;* Solution concepts in game theory; Market equilibria;

Additional Key Words and Phrases: Subgame Perfect Equilibrium; Stable Matching; PSPACE-completeness

## 1 INTRODUCTION

Imagine a decentralized job market consisting of firms and workers. Each firm has one position to fill and has a preference ordering over potential workers. Additionally, each worker has a preference on positions. To fill a position, each firm first makes an offer to its favorite worker, and if the offer is rejected, then the next offer is made to the second best worker, and so on. The offers of the firms are not synchronized with each other. That is, firms act as if they simulate an asynchronous version of the firm-oriented deferred acceptance algorithm [18, 19], which is known to find the position-optimal *stable matching* just like the original synchronous version [8]. In contrast to these algorithms, in which each worker can keep a tentative contract and decline it when she gets a better offer, the current market does not allow tentative contracts. Once a worker receives an offer from some firm, she should decide immediately whether to accept or not and cannot change the decision later. Thus, the acceptance of an offer guarantees her job at that position, but it may also eliminate

The full version of this paper can be found in [12]. The authors thank anonymous reviewers of EC'18 for their valuable comments. This work was supported by JSPS KAKENHI Grant Numbers JP16K16005, JP16H06931, and JP18K18004, and by JST ACT-I Grant Number JPMJPR17U7.


*ACM EC'18, June 18–22, 2018, Ithaca, NY, USA.*
 ACM ISBN 978-1-4503-5829-3/18/06...$15.00.
https://doi.org/10.1145/3219166.3219200

chances of better offers from other firms in the future. It is assumed that the offers are made in accordance with a prescribed schedule, i.e., there is a linear order on the set of all possible offers. All the workers know this order, but whether a worker will get each scheduled offer from each firm or not depends on the actions of other workers. Thus, this market has a sequential structure of decision problems encountered by the strategic workers.

Our model deals with any order of offers that is consistent with every firm's preference. In particular, we call a market *position-ordered* if all the offers by the same firm are successively placed in the order, i.e., there is a linear order on the set of firms according to which each firm makes all its offers. This case represents, for instance, an academic job market in which different positions have different hiring seasons. Job-seeking researchers know these seasons, and they can guess each position's preference ordering over the candidate researchers. Once a researcher accepts an offer, she cannot decline it because rescinding a contract unilaterally damages her reputation and adversely affects her future career. The position-ordered case can also be interpreted as a job market in which institutes have public invitations in different seasons and researchers strategically decide whether to apply or not for each invitation.

We formulate this market as a perfect-information extensive-form game among the workers, which we call the *sequential matching game* (a formal definition will be given in Section 2.1). Each round of the game corresponds to an offer from a firm. The offers are made in some fixed order. In each round, the worker who receives the offer is the player who takes an action, where the possible actions are ACCEPT and REJECT. If the worker chooses ACCEPT, then the firm and the worker are matched and leave the market, and we move to a subgame in which they are removed. If the worker chooses REJECT, then they stay in the market, and we move to a subgame in which that worker is eliminated from the preference list of the firm. The game ends if there is no firm with a nonempty list. Each strategy profile uniquely defines a matching, or an assignment obtained at the end of the game. Each worker's preference over outcome matchings depends only on her own assignment.

This paper investigates a subgame perfect equilibrium (SPE) of this sequential matching game, i.e., an action profile that represents the best actions of the workers in all rounds under the assumption that all the other workers will take their best actions in the future. For every offer, different actions result in different outcomes for the worker: by rejecting an offer, it is impossible to obtain the same assignment afterwards. Hence, the best action is defined uniquely at each round by backward induction. Therefore, any instance of the sequential matching game has a unique subgame perfect equilibrium. To clarify the setting, we provide a small example here.

*Example 1.1.* There are three research institutes $p_1$, $p_2$, and $p_3$ each of which has one position to fill. Three job-seeking researchers $q_1$, $q_2$, and $q_3$ are awaiting offers. The institutes have preferences on acceptable candidates and researchers have preferences on possible institutes as follows.

$$p_1 : q_1 \qquad\qquad q_1 : p_2 \succ_{q_1} p_1$$
$$p_2 : q_2 \succ_{p_2} q_1 \succ_{p_2} q_3 \qquad\qquad q_2 : p_3 \succ_{q_2} p_2$$
$$p_3 : q_3 \succ_{p_3} q_2 \qquad\qquad q_3 : p_2 \succ_{q_3} p_3.$$

Each researcher prefers being matched (with an acceptable institute) to being unmatched. The institute $p_1$ starts scouting first, and then $p_2$ and $p_3$ follow in order. Thus, the following order is defined on the offers.

$$\text{The offering order} : (p_1, q_1), (p_2, q_2), (p_2, q_1), (p_2, q_3), (p_3, q_3), (p_3, q_2),$$

where offers related to previously matched institutes or researchers are skipped.

When the first offer $(p_1, q_1)$ is made, $q_1$ has two possible actions. If she selects ACCEPT, then she is assigned to $p_1$ in the outcome matching. If she selects REJECT, she has to anticipate what happens

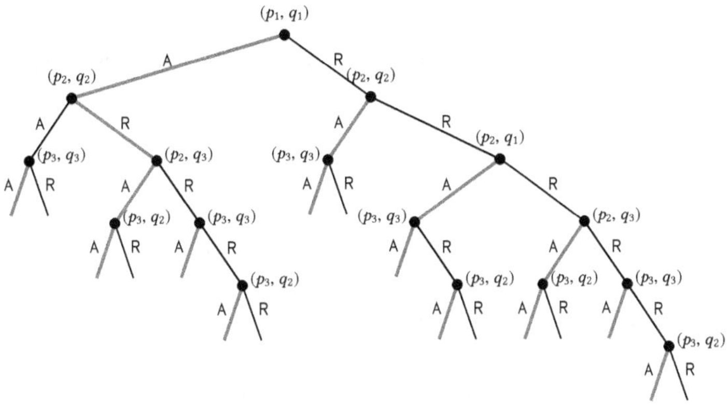


Fig. 1. The tree representation of the game. The bold red edges indicate SPE.

after the rejection. After $q_1$'s rejection, $p_1$ leaves the market because it has no other candidate. Then $p_2$ makes an offer to $q_2$ and $q_2$ may accept or reject. Under the assumption that all workers similarly take the best actions by anticipating other workers' future actions, it is concluded that $q_1$ would be unmatched in the outcome if she rejects $(p_1, q_1)$. Thus, ACCEPT is her best action in the first round. In this manner, we can define the best action for each round. Fig. 1 shows all possible rounds, and red edges represent the best actions. The SPE of this instance then results in an assignment that matches pairs $\{(p_1, q_1), (p_2, q_3), (p_3, q_2)\}$. Note that this does not coincide with a unique stable matching $\{(p_1, q_1), (p_2, q_2), (p_3, q_3)\}$ of this preference profile.

Recently, the sequential matching game has been studied actively under various settings. In many of those settings, it has been shown that the SPE leads to the proposed-side optimal stable matching. This fact implies that each player can efficiently compute her best strategy by just computing the optimal stable matching. However, such a characterization of the SPE does not hold in our setting. Indeed, the outcome matching of the above example is unstable. Furthermore, unlike many other models, the SPE outcome changes drastically depending on the order of offers in our model. These distinctive features indicate the difficulty in capturing SPEs in our model.

In this paper, we consider the complexity of computing an SPE. Note that representing an SPE itself obviously requires exponential time since the tree representation has exponential size. Therefore, it is more reasonable to consider the following decision problem: given an instance and a history (a possible sequence of actions), decide whether the next player selects ACCEPT in the SPE. Note that each subgame of a given instance is again a sequential matching game instance. Then, we would rather consider the following equivalent problem.

**Problem 1.2** (SPEM)**.** Given an instance of the sequential matching game, decide whether the first offered worker selects ACCEPT or not in the SPE.

We call this decision problem SPEM. Note that the outcome matching of the SPE, which we call *the SPE matching*, can be obtained by solving SPEM repeatedly. Conversely, SPEM is solved if we can compute the SPE matching. We classify subclasses of SPEM by the maximum length of the preference lists of firms and workers. For positive integers $s$ and $t$, the problem $(s, t)$-SPEM is the restriction of SPEM in which the preference list of each firm and worker has at most $s$ and $t$ entries, respectively. Moreover, $(s, \infty)$-SPEM and $(\infty, t)$-SPEM denote the restrictions in which only one side has a limitation on the list length.

### Contributions

This paper provides the following dichotomy theorem that completely characterizes the computational complexity of $(s, t)$-SPEM for all $s$ and $t$.

THEOREM 1.3. *The problem $(s, t)$-SPEM can be solved in polynomial time if $s \leq 2$ or $t \leq 2$. Otherwise, it is NP-hard, and furthermore PSPACE-hard.*

For the above theorem, we show the tractability of $(2, \infty)$-SPEM and $(\infty, 2)$-SPEM in Section 3 and the PSPACE-completeness of $(3, 3)$-SPEM in Section 4.

We will first show that both $(2, \infty)$-SPEM and $(\infty, 2)$-SPEM are in the complexity class P by providing an efficient algorithm to compute the SPE matching. As we have observed in the above example, the SPE matching of an $(\infty, 2)$-SPEM instance is not necessarily stable. However, fortunately, we can compute it by a variant of the deferred acceptance algorithm, which we call the *sequentially fixing deferred acceptance algorithm* (SFDA). This algorithm repeatedly computes the worker optimal stable matching and removes the matched pair that appears first in the offering order. The correctness of SFDA implies that, whenever a worker receives an offer from some firm, her best action is ACCEPT if and only if she is assigned to that firm in the worker-optimal stable matching of the "current" subgame, rather than of the original instance. SFDA also works for $(2, \infty)$-SPEM, i.e., it outputs the SPE matching. Furthermore, we can show that for $(2, \infty)$-SPEM, the output of SFDA coincides with the worker-optimal stable matching independently of the offering order. Hence, for $(2, \infty)$-SPEM, the SPE matching is exactly the worker-optimal stable matching.

In contrast to the above tractable cases, the problem $(3, 3)$-SPEM is far from tractable. Actually, it is PSPACE-complete, which means that there exists no polynomial-time algorithm to solve it unless P=PSPACE.

As we will see in Section 2.3, the sequential matching game has strange but interesting properties. First, as shown in Example 2.5 (Section 2.1), the SPE matching may differ according to offering orders, and hence the set of SPE matchings for the same preference profile with different offering orders may contain multiple matchings. Furthermore, these matchings do not satisfy a "rural hospital theorem"-like property, i.e., the set of matched positions and workers in the SPE matching may differ among these matchings. Moreover, the SPE matching is unstable in not only the standard sense but also some stronger senses such as *vNM-stability* [7] and *essential stability* [14]. Thus, SPE matchings for the general SPEM seem inexplicable by existing notions, while the above tractable cases can be clearly explained by the well-known stability notions.

### Related Work

The complexity of finding a Nash equilibrium in normal form games has been well studied in the context of algorithmic game theory [20]. However, little work has been done on a subgame perfect equilibrium in extensive-form games. It is known that computing an SPE is PSPACE-complete for the sequential versions of unrelated machine scheduling, congestion games [16], and cost sharing games [4].

In the context of economics, the outcomes generated by decentralized matching markets have been studied under various conditions [1–3, 11, 21, 23, 24]. Most existing studies have analyzed when a decentralized market will yield a stable matching. [11] considered a similar setting to ours: in each stage, each firm offers a position to a worker, and then each worker irrevocably chooses whether to accept one of the received offers or to reject all of them. Roughly speaking, their game is based on a synchronous version of deferred acceptance algorithm, while our game is based on an asynchronous version. They claimed that, when workers sequentially decide their actions in each stage, every SPE results in the worker-optimal stable matching [11, Theorem 2], but this claim has been proven not true in the present study (see Remark 2.6 for details).

## 2 PRELIMINARIES

### 2.1 Model

In this section, we give a formal definition of the sequential matching game. The sequential matching game is played by a sequential process of acceptance/rejection for offers in a stable matching instance, which is formulated as a perfect-information extensive-form game.

A matching instance is a tuple $I = (P, Q, E, \succ)$, where each component is defined as follows. There are a finite set of firms $P = \{p_1, \ldots, p_n\}$ and a finite set of workers $Q = \{q_1, \ldots, q_m\}$. Each firm has one position, and we often identify each firm with its position. The set of acceptable pairs is denoted by $E \subseteq P \times Q$. For $e = (p, q) \in E$, let us denote $\partial_P(e) := p$ and $\partial_Q(e) := q$. For each firm $p \in P$ and each worker $q \in Q$, the acceptable partner sets are denoted by $\Gamma_I(p) := \{q \in Q \mid (p, q) \in E\}$ and by $\Gamma_I(q) := \{p \in P \mid (p, q) \in E\}$, respectively. The set of acceptable pairs that contain $p \in P$ and $q \in Q$ are denoted by $\delta_I(p) := \{e \in E \mid \partial_P(e) = p\}$ and $\delta_I(q) := \{e \in E \mid \partial_Q(e) = q\}$, respectively. There is a strict ordinal preference $\succ_r$ for each $r \in P \cup Q$ over $\Gamma_I(r)$, and $\succ$ denotes the profile $(\succ_r)_{r \in P \cup Q}$. We sometimes write $q \succ_p q'$ to denote $(p, q) \succ_p (p, q')$ for $p \in P$.

A mapping $\mu\colon P \cup Q \to P \cup Q$ is called a matching in $I = (P, Q, E, \succ)$ if $\mu(r) \in \Gamma_I(r) \cup \{r\}$ and $\mu(\mu(r)) = r$ for every $r \in P \cup Q$. A firm or worker $r \in P \cup Q$ is said to be matched to $\mu(r)$ if $\mu(r) \neq r$, and to be unmatched if $\mu(r) = r$. For each $r \in P \cup Q$ and two matchings $\mu_1$ and $\mu_2$, we write $\mu_1 \succ_r \mu_2$ if $\mu_1(r) \succ_r \mu_2(r)$, where we suppose that $r$ is virtually added to the bottom of the preference $\succ_r$ over $\Gamma_I(r)$ (i.e., each $r$ prefers to be matched to an acceptable partner rather than to be unmatched). A matching $\mu$ in $I$ is often referred to as the corresponding set of acceptable pairs $\{(p, \mu(p)) \mid p \in P,\ \mu(p) \neq p\} = \{(\mu(q), q) \mid q \in Q,\ \mu(q) \neq q\}$.

A sequential matching game is defined by a pair of a matching instance $I = (P, Q, E, \succ)$ and an order $\sigma$ over $E$, which is a bijection from $\{1, \ldots, |E|\}$ to $E$. We assume that $\sigma$ is consistent with $(\succ_p)_{p \in P}$, i.e., if $\sigma(i), \sigma(j) \in \delta_I(p)$ and $i < j$ then $\sigma(i) \succ_p \sigma(j)$. We say that $\sigma$ (or the game $(I, \sigma)$) is *position-ordered* if all the pairs relevant to the same firm appear in a row, i.e., for every $p \in P$ and every $i$, $j$, and $k$ with $i \leq j \leq k$ and $\sigma(i), \sigma(k) \in \delta_I(p)$, we have $\sigma(j) \in \delta_I(p)$.

We introduce two fundamental operations on a sequential matching game. For a set $X$ and an element $e \in X$, we simply denote $X \setminus \{e\}$ by $X - e$.

*Definition 2.1 (Deletion).* For a matching instance $I = (P, Q, E, \succ)$ and a pair $e \in E$, the *deletion* of $e$ from $I$ is defined as $I \backslash e := (P, Q, E - e, \succ')$, where $\succ'_r$ is the preference over $\Gamma_{I \backslash e}(r)$ that is consistent with $\succ_r$ for each $r \in P \cup Q$, i.e., $s \succ'_r t$ if and only if $s \succ_r t$ for every $s, t \in \Gamma_{I \backslash e}(r)$. For an order $\sigma$ over $E$, the *deletion* of $e$ from $\sigma$ is an order $\sigma \backslash e$ over $E - e$ that is consistent with $\sigma$, i.e., $(\sigma \backslash e)^{-1}(e_1) < (\sigma \backslash e)^{-1}(e_2)$ if and only if $\sigma^{-1}(e_1) < \sigma^{-1}(e_2)$ for every $e_1, e_2 \in E - e$.

*Definition 2.2 (Contraction).* For a matching instance $I = (P, Q, E, \succ)$ and a pair $e = (p, q) \in E$, the *contraction* of $I$ by $e = (p, q)$ is defined as $I/e := (P - p, Q - q, E/e, \succ')$, where $E/e := E \backslash (\delta_I(p) \cup \delta_I(q))$, and $\succ'_r$ is the preference over $\Gamma_{I/e}(r)$ that is consistent with $\succ_r$ for each $r \in (P - p) \cup (Q - q)$. For an order $\sigma$ over $E$, the *contraction* of $\sigma$ by $e$ is an order $\sigma/e$ over $E/e$ that is consistent to $\sigma$.

Observation 2.3. *Deletion and contraction are commutative. That is, for any two disjoint pairs $e_1, e_2 \in E$, we have $(I/e_1) \backslash e_2 = (I \backslash e_2)/e_1$.*

Let $e = (p, q) \in E$. For a matching $\mu'$ in $I/e$, $\mu' + e$ denotes the matching $\mu$ in $I$ such that $\mu(p) = q$, $\mu(q) = p$, and $\mu(r) = \mu'(r)$ for every $r \in (P - p) \cup (Q - q)$. Conversely, for a matching $\mu$ in $I$ with $\mu(p) = q$ and $\mu(q) = p$, $\mu - e$ denotes the matching $\mu'$ in $I/e$ such that $\mu'(r) = \mu(r)$ for every $r \in (P - p) \cup (Q - q)$.

The game $(I, \sigma)$ is recursively defined as follows. Let $\sigma(1) = e = (p, q)$. In the first round, $p$ offers to $q$, and $q$ chooses ACCEPT or REJECT for the offer. If $q$ chooses ACCEPT, then $p$ and $q$ are matched irrevocably, and then $(I/e, \sigma/e)$ is played (i.e., the outcome is $\mu' + e$ for some matching $\mu'$ in $I/e$). If $q$ chooses REJECT, then $p$ and $q$ are unmatched irrevocably, and then $(I \backslash e, \sigma \backslash e)$ is played (i.e., the outcome is some matching in $I \backslash e$). As we have already seen in Fig. 1, this process can be represented by a rooted tree, where the root corresponds to the first round of the game $(I, \sigma)$, and each node (except the leaves) corresponds to a game $(I', \sigma')$ and has two children corresponding to the two subgames $(I'/\sigma'(1), \sigma'/\sigma'(1))$ and $(I' \backslash \sigma'(1), \sigma' \backslash \sigma'(1))$. We call this tree the tree representation of the game $(I, \sigma)$.

We consider a *subgame perfect equilibrium* (SPE) of the sequential matching game. A strategy profile is a subgame perfect equilibrium if it is a Nash equilibrium of every subgame of the original game. In every round of the game, the two actions ACCEPT and REJECT for an offer $(p, q)$ result in different outcome matchings, say $\mu_1$ and $\mu_2$, respectively. One of them is preferred to the other by the worker $q$, because $\mu_1(q) = p \neq \mu_2(q)$. Hence, the optimal strategy is uniquely defined in each subgame by backward induction, and every game admits a unique SPE. The outcome matching according to the SPE of a game $(I, \sigma)$ is called the SPE matching of $(I, \sigma)$, which is denoted by $\mathrm{SPE}(I, \sigma)$. The next property immediately follows from the above definitions.

Proposition 2.4. *For $e = (p, q) = \sigma(1)$, we have the following:*

- **(a)** *If $\mathrm{SPE}(I \backslash e, \sigma \backslash e)(q) >_q p$, then $\mathrm{SPE}(I, \sigma) = \mathrm{SPE}(I \backslash e, \sigma \backslash e)$*
- **(b)** *If $\mathrm{SPE}(I \backslash e, \sigma \backslash e)(q) <_q p$, then $\mathrm{SPE}(I, \sigma) = \mathrm{SPE}(I/e, \sigma/e) + (p, q)$.*

*Example 2.5.* Let us formulate Example 1.1 as a sequential matching game $(I, \sigma)$ with $I = (P, Q, E, >)$. The firm set is $P = \{p_1, p_2, p_3\}$ and the worker set is $Q = \{q_1, q_2, q_3\}$. The set of acceptable pairs is

$$E = \{(p_1, q_1), (p_2, q_1), (p_2, q_2), (p_2, q_3), (p_3, q_2), (p_3, q_3)\}.$$

The preferences $>$ are the same, i.e.,

$$\begin{aligned} &p_1 : q_1 && q_1 : p_2 >_{q_1} p_1 \\ &p_2 : q_2 >_{p_2} q_1 >_{p_2} q_3 && q_2 : p_3 >_{q_2} p_2 \\ &p_3 : q_3 >_{p_3} q_2 && q_3 : p_2 >_{q_3} p_3. \end{aligned}$$

The order of offers $\sigma \colon \{1, 2, \ldots, 6\} \to E$ is

$$(\sigma(1), \sigma(2), \ldots, \sigma(6)) = ((p_1, q_1), (p_2, q_2), (p_2, q_1), (p_2, q_3), (p_3, q_3), (p_3, q_2)).$$

We can also see that $\sigma$ is induced by a firm order $\pi \colon \{1, 2, 3\} \to P$ such that $(\pi(1), \pi(2), \pi(3)) = (p_1, p_2, p_3)$. As seen in Example 1.1 (see the tree representation in Fig. 1), the SPE matching is

$$\mathrm{SPE}(I, \sigma) = \{(p_1, q_1), (p_2, q_3), (p_3, q_2)\}.$$

Let us examine whether that different order of offers result in different SPE matchings even if the matching instance is exactly same. Consider the above instance $I$, and let $\sigma'$ be an order over $E$ such that

$$(\sigma'(1), \sigma'(2), \ldots, \sigma'(6)) = ((p_2, q_2), (p_2, q_1), (p_2, q_3), (p_3, q_3), (p_3, q_2), (p_1, q_1)).$$

Note that this $\sigma'$ is also position-ordered (induced by a firm order $\pi'$ with $(\pi'(1), \pi'(2), \pi'(3)) = (p_2, p_3, p_1)$). The tree representation of $(I, \sigma')$ is shown in Fig. 2, and the SPE matching is

$$\mathrm{SPE}(I, \sigma') = \{(p_1, q_1), (p_2, q_2), (p_3, q_3)\}.$$

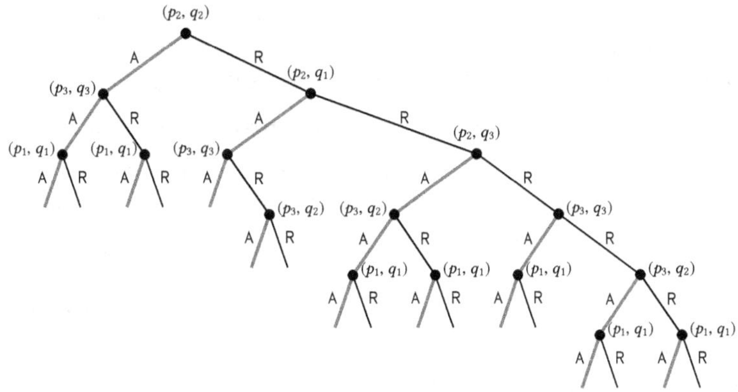

Fig. 2. The tree representation of $(I, \sigma')$. The bold red edges indicate SPE.

For any sequential matching game, a unique SPE can be computed by the backward induction algorithm. However, the algorithm requires exponential time because the tree representation has exponential size.

In this paper, we consider the decision problem of whether $\partial_Q(\sigma(1))$ selects ACCEPT in the first round. We call this problem SPEM as defined in Problem 1.2. The restriction of SPEM in which the numbers of acceptable partners of each firm and of each worker are at most $s$ and $t$, respectively, is denoted by $(s,t)$-SPEM.

**Remark 2.6.** In [11], similar sequential matching games were considered, and there are several differences between their models and ours. The most similar setting was studied in [11, Section 4], where the only difference is that, after all firms have offered (where each firm offers to the most preferred worker among the workers to whom it has never offered), the workers choose their actions (either to accept exactly one offer and reject the rest or to reject all offers) sequentially in a prespecified order.

Let us consider the matching instance $I$ in Example 2.5. In the first stage, each firm $p_i$ offers to $q_i$ $(i = 1, 2, 3)$. Suppose the first decision-maker is $q_1$. If $q_1$ rejects $p_1$'s offer, then $q_2$ and $q_3$ should accept the offers they received because, otherwise, they will be unmatched. In this case, $q_1$ will be unmatched (no other firm will offer to $q_1$), and hence $q_1$ should conclude to accept $p_1$'s offer. Then, $q_2$ and $q_3$ can reject the offers from $p_2$ and $p_3$, respectively, and they subsequently receive offers from $p_3$ and $p_2$, which are, respectively, their preferred firms, in the second stage. Thus the SPE of this game yields a matching $\{(p_1, q_1), (p_2, q_3), (p_3, q_2)\}$, which is the same as SPE$(I, \sigma)$ in Example 2.5.

[11, Theorem 2] claimed that such a game enjoys a unique SPE, and it results in the worker-optimal stable matching (which is formally defined in the next section). However, this claim is not true, as evidenced by the above example, in which the worker-optimal stable matching in $I$ is $\{(p_1, q_1), (p_2, q_2), (p_3, q_3)\}$.

## 2.2 Stability and Deferred Acceptance Algorithm

In this section, we briefly overview the stability and deferred acceptance algorithm (see [10, 15, 17, 22] for more details).

Let $I = (P, Q, E, \succ)$ be a matching instance, and $\mathcal{M}$ be the set of all matchings in $I$.

*Definition 2.7 (Stability [8]).* For a matching $\mu \in \mathcal{M}$, an acceptable pair $e = (p, q) \in E$ is called a *blocking pair* if $q \succ_p \mu(p)$ and $p \succ_q \mu(q)$ (where recall that each $r \in P \cup Q$ is regarded as the bottom of the preference $\succ_r$). A matching $\mu \in \mathcal{M}$ is said to be *stable* if there exists no blocking pair for $\mu$.

The sets of matched workers and firms are invariant across all stable matchings.

Theorem 2.8 ([18]). *If there exists a stable matching in $I$ under which $r \in P \cup Q$ is matched (resp., unmatched), then $r$ is matched (resp., unmatched) under every stable matching in $I$.*

A many-to-one generalization of this theorem is well known as the *rural hospital theorem*.

For distinct $\mu, \mu' \in \mathcal{M}$, we define $\mu \succ_Q \mu'$ if $\mu(q) \succeq_q \mu'(q)$ ($\forall q \in Q$). It is easy to observe that $\succ_Q$ is a partial order over $\mathcal{M}$. A maximal (minimal) element with respect to this partial order is unique.

*Definition 2.9 (Optimality [15] (attributed to J. H. Conway)).* The set of all stable matchings in $I$ forms a distributive lattice with respect to the partial order $\succ_Q$. A unique maximal element in this distributive lattice is said to be *worker-optimal* or *Q-optimal*, and denoted by QOPT($I$). That is, QOPT($I$)($q$) $\succeq_q \mu(q)$ for any stable matching $\mu$ in $I$ and any worker $q \in Q$.

The worker-optimal stable matching can be computed by Algorithm 1. Through the algorithm, the proposal with respect to each pair $e = (p, q) \in E$ and its rejection occur at most once in Lines 4 and 7, respectively, and the number of comparisons with respect to $\succ_p$ in Line 6 is equal to the number of workers rejected by $p$ in Line 7. Hence, the algorithm requires $O(|E|)$ time in total.

**Algorithm 1:** $Q$-oriented DA [8]

**input:** A matching instance $I = (P, Q, E, \succ)$

**output:** The $Q$-optimal stable matching QOPT($I$)

1 Set $\hat{I} \leftarrow I$ and $\mu(r) \leftarrow r$ for each $r \in P \cup Q$;

2 **while** $\exists q \in Q$ *such that* $\mu(q) = q$ *and* $\Gamma_I(q) \neq \emptyset$ **do**

3     **for** *each* $q \in Q$ *such that* $\mu(q) = q$ *and* $\Gamma_{\hat{I}}(q) \neq \emptyset$ **do**

4         Set to $\mu(q)$ the most preferred firm in $\Gamma_{\hat{I}}(q)$ ($q$ proposes to $\mu(q) \in P$);

5     **for** *each* $p \in P$ *such that* $\exists q \in Q$ *with* $\mu(q) = p$ **do**

6         Set to $\mu(p)$ the most preferred worker in $\{q \in Q \mid \mu(q) = p\}$ (among the workers who propose to $p$);

7         $\mu(q) \leftarrow q$ and $\hat{I} \leftarrow \hat{I} \backslash (p, q)$ for each $q \in Q$ such that $\mu(q) = p$ and $\mu(p) \neq q$ ($p$ irrevocably rejects $q$'s proposal);

8 **return** $\mu$;

We here show several properties on the worker-optimal stable matchings, which will be utilized in Section 3.

Claim 2.10. *If $q$ is on the top of $p$'s list, then* QOPT($I$)($q$) $\succeq_q p$.

Proof. Suppose to the contrary that QOPT($I$)($q$) $\prec_q p$. We then have QOPT($I$)($p$) $\prec_p q$ as QOPT($I$)($p$) $\neq q$, and hence $(p, q)$ is a blocking pair, contradicting the stability of QOPT($I$). □

Claim 2.11. *For $e = (p, q) \in E$, if* QOPT($I$)($q$) $= p$, *then* QOPT($I$)($q$) $\succ_q$ QOPT($I \backslash e$)($q$).

Proof. Suppose to the contrary that QOPT($I \backslash e$)($q$) $\succ_q$ QOPT($I$)($q$) $= p$. Since QOPT($I \backslash e$) is a stable matching in $I \backslash e$, any $e' \in E - e$ is not a blocking pair. Then, QOPT($I \backslash e$) is also a stable matching in $I$, because $e$ cannot be a blocking pair (due to QOPT($I \backslash e$)($q$) $\succ_q p$). This contradicts the $Q$-optimality of QOPT($I$). □

Claim 2.12. *For* $e = (p, q) \in E$, *if* $\mathrm{QOPT}(I)(q) = p$, *then* $\mathrm{QOPT}(I/e) + (p, q) \succeq_Q \mathrm{QOPT}(I)$.

Proof. Let $\mu := \mathrm{QOPT}(I) - e$. Since $\mathrm{QOPT}(I)$ is stable in $I$, there is no pair $e' = (p', q') \in E/e$ such that $q' \succ_{p'} \mu(p')$ and $p' \succ_{q'} \mu(q')$, which implies that $\mu$ is stable in $I/e$. By $Q$-optimality, we have $\mathrm{QOPT}(I/e) \succeq_{Q-q} \mu$, and hence $\mathrm{QOPT}(I/e) + (p, q) \succeq_Q \mu + (p, q) = \mathrm{QOPT}(I)$. □

Claim 2.13. *For* $e = (p, q) \in E$, *if* $\mathrm{QOPT}(I)(q) \succ_q p$, *then* $\mathrm{QOPT}(I) = \mathrm{QOPT}(I \backslash e)$.

Proof. Since $\mathrm{QOPT}(I)$ is stable in $I \backslash e$, we have $\mathrm{QOPT}(I) \preceq_Q \mathrm{QOPT}(I \backslash e)$ by $Q$-optimality. Then, $p \prec_q \mathrm{QOPT}(I)(q) \preceq_q \mathrm{QOPT}(I \backslash e)(q)$, and hence $e = (p, q)$ cannot be a blocking pair for $\mathrm{QOPT}(I \backslash e)$. Thus $\mathrm{QOPT}(I \backslash e)$ is also stable in $I$, and hence $\mathrm{QOPT}(I) \succeq_Q \mathrm{QOPT}(I \backslash e)$ by $Q$-optimality. □

We also consider another (weaker) concept of stability. For $\mu, \mu' \in \mathcal{M}$, we say that $\mu$ dominates $\mu'$ if there exists a pair $(p, q) \in E$ such that (i) $p \succ_q \mu'(q)$ and $q \succ_p \mu'(p)$, and (ii) $\mu(p) = q$.

*Definition 2.14 (von Neumann–Morgenstern (vNM) stability [7]).* A nonempty set of matchings $V \subseteq \mathcal{M}$ is called *vNM-stable set* if it satisfies the following two properties: (internal stability) any $\mu \in V$ does not dominate another $\mu' \in V$; (external stability) any $\mu' \in \mathcal{M} \setminus V$ is dominated by some $\mu \in V$. It is known that $V$ is uniquely determined [7, 26]. We say that $\mu \in \mathcal{M}$ is a *vNM-stable matching* or satisfies *vNM-stability* if $\mu \in V$.

The vNM-stable set also forms a distributive lattice, which includes all stable matchings. Hence, the worker-optimal vNM-stable matching is defined, and is a Pareto-efficient matching for the workers which all workers weakly prefer over the worker-optimal stable matching.

### 2.3 Basic Observations

In this section, we provide some basic properties of the sequential matching game. This section can be skipped if the reader is only interested in our main results.

We first observe that top-top pairs are matched in the SPE matching.

Proposition 2.15. *For a sequential matching game* $(I, \sigma)$, *let* $e = (p, q)$ *be an acceptable pair such that each of them is the most preferred partner of the other. Then,* $\mathrm{SPE}(I, \sigma) = \mathrm{SPE}(I/e, \sigma/e) + (p, q)$.

Proof. We prove the proposition by induction on $\sigma^{-1}(e)$. For the base case $\sigma^{-1}(e) = 1$, the worker $q$ selects ACCEPT because $p$ is the best position for her. Hence $\mathrm{SPE}(I, \sigma) = \mathrm{SPE}(I/e, \sigma/e) + (p, q)$. Suppose that $\sigma^{-1}(e) > 1$. Let $\sigma(1) = e' = (p', q')$. Note that $p' \neq p$ since $q$ is most preferred by $p$. By induction and Proposition 2.4, we have (i) $\mathrm{SPE}(I, \sigma) = \mathrm{SPE}(I \backslash e', \sigma \backslash e') = \mathrm{SPE}((I \backslash e')/e, (\sigma \backslash e')/e) + (p, q) = \mathrm{SPE}(I/e, \sigma/e) + (p, q)$ if $\mathrm{SPE}(I \backslash e', \sigma \backslash e')(q') \succ_{q'} p'$ and (ii) $\mathrm{SPE}(I, \sigma) = \mathrm{SPE}(I/e', \sigma/e') + (p', q') = \mathrm{SPE}(I/e'/e, \sigma/e'/e) + (p', q') + (p, q) = \mathrm{SPE}(I/e, \sigma/e) + (p, q)$ if $\mathrm{SPE}(I \backslash e', \sigma \backslash e')(q') \prec_{q'} p'$. Hence, the proposition holds. □

This proposition implies that, if an instance of the game satisfies the *Eeckhout condition*[1], the SPE matching coincides with the unique stable matching.

Next, we see that an SPE matching may have a blocking pair but it only admits a certain type.

Proposition 2.16. *For a sequential matching game* $(I, \sigma)$, *let* $\mu$ *be the SPE matching. Then* $q \succ_p \mu(p)$ *and* $p \succ_q \mu(p)$ *hold only if* $\sigma^{-1}((p, q)) > \sigma^{-1}((\mu(q), q))$.

[1] The Eeckhout condition is a sufficient condition for the existence of a unique stable matching. We say that a matching instance $I = (P, Q, E, \succ)$ satisfies the Eeckhout condition if it is possible to rearrange firms and workers so that (i) for any firm $p_i \in P$, $q_i \succ_{p_i} q_j$ for all $j > i$; (ii) for any worker $q_i \in Q$, $p_i \succ_{q_i} p_j$ for all $j > i$ [6].

Proof. We prove the proposition by contradiction. Suppose that $q \succ_p \mu(p)$, $p \succ_q \mu(p)$, and $\sigma^{-1}((p,q)) < \sigma^{-1}((\mu(q),q))$. Let us consider the subgame $(I',\sigma')$ that is reached in the SPE where $\sigma'(1) = (p,q)$. Here, the subgame $(I',\sigma')$ exists because $p$ and $q$ are not matched by $q \succ_p \mu(p)$ and $\sigma^{-1}((p,q)) < \sigma^{-1}((\mu(q),q))$. The optimal strategy of $q$ at $(I',\sigma')$ is ACCEPT since $p \succ_q \mu(p)$; however, $q$ selects REJECT in the SPE, which is a contradiction. □

Finally, we present two strange properties of the sequential matching game. The former shows that the game does not satisfy a "rural hospital theorem"-like property, and the latter shows that the SPE matchings may be unstable in not only the standard sense but also stronger senses. See the full version [12] for the detail, which includes specific examples to show them.

Proposition 2.17. *There exists a matching instance such that the set of matched firms and workers in the SPE matching changes according to the order of offers.*

Proposition 2.18. *There is an SPE matching that is neither vNM-stable nor essentially stable.*

## 3 ALGORITHM FOR TRACTABLE CASES

As one side of our main dichotomy result Theorem 1.3, we show the following theorem. Recall that $(2,\infty)$-SPEM (resp., $(\infty,2)$-SPEM) is the restriction of SPEM in which the length of each firm's (resp., worker's) preference list is at most two.

Theorem 3.1. *The problems* $(2,\infty)$-SPEM *and* $(\infty,2)$-SPEM *are polynomially solvable.*

Note that, for an instance $(I,\sigma)$, we can solve SPEM efficiently if we can compute $\mathrm{SPE}(I,\sigma)$ efficiently, because whether $\partial_P(\sigma(1))$ selects ACCEPT at the first round or not corresponds to whether $\sigma(1) \in \mathrm{SPE}(I,\sigma)$ holds or not. Therefore, to show Theorem 3.1, it suffices to prove the following theorem, which is the purpose of this section.

Theorem 3.2. *For any* $(2,\infty)$-SPEM *or* $(\infty,2)$-SPEM *instance* $(I,\sigma)$*, we can compute the SPE matching* $\mathrm{SPE}(I,\sigma)$ *in polynomial time.*

We show Theorem 3.2 in the following way. In Section 3.1, we introduce an efficient algorithm, which we call the ($Q$-oriented) *sequentially fixing deferred acceptance algorithm* (SFDA) and provide its properties. Then, Section 3.2 shows that the output of SFDA for $(I,\sigma)$ coincides with $\mathrm{SPE}(I,\sigma)$ if $(I,\sigma)$ is a $(2,\infty)$- or $(\infty,2)$-SPEM instance.

### 3.1 Sequentially Fixing Deferred Acceptance Algorithm

This section introduces the ($Q$-oriented) *sequentially fixing deferred acceptance algorithm* (SFDA), which is sketched as follows: given an instance $(I,\sigma)$, the algorithm repeatedly computes the $Q$-optimal stable matching and updates the instance by removing the firm-worker pair that appears first in the offering order among all the matched pairs. The algorithm stops the repetition when there is no acceptable pair, and then outputs the matching that consists of all the pairs removed so far. We denote the output matching by $\mathrm{SFDA}(I,\sigma)$. The formal description of SFDA is given in Algorithm 2. Recall that $\mathrm{QOPT}(I)$ in the description denotes the $Q$-optimal stable matching of a matching instance $I$.

It is worth mentioning that the algorithm SFDA is closely related to the ($Q$-oriented) efficiency adjusted deferred acceptance algorithm (EADA), which is introduced by [13] and simplified by [5] and [25]. EADA iteratively fixes a last proposer[2] under DA while SFDA fixes the minimum pair in the predetermined order $\sigma$. EADA produces the worker-optimal vNM-stable matching, and hence SFDA also produces it if the order $\sigma$ is consistent with the fixing order in EADA.

[2]This is a modified version of the algorithm EADA in [5]. In his version, the set of last proposers are fixed at a time, while, in this version, only one of them is fixed. Fortunately, this modification does not change the outcome.

**Algorithm 2:** $Q$-oriented SFDA

**input:** An instance $(I, \sigma)$, where $I = (P, Q, E, >)$
**output:** A matching SFDA$(I, \sigma)$

1 Set $(\hat{I}, \hat{\sigma}) \leftarrow (I, \sigma)$ and let $\mu(r) \leftarrow r$ for every $r \in P \cup Q$;
2 **while** *there is some acceptable pair in* $\hat{I}$ **do**
3     Let $e = (p, q)$ be the pair that minimizes $\sigma^{-1}(e)$ subject to $e \in \mathrm{QOPT}(\hat{I})$;
4     $(\hat{I}, \hat{\sigma}) \leftarrow (\hat{I}/e, \hat{\sigma}/e)$;
5     $\mu(p) \leftarrow q$ and $\mu(q) \leftarrow p$;
6 **return** $\mu$;

For any instance $(I, \sigma)$ of the sequential matching game, SFDA$(I, \sigma)$ has the following properties.

Claim 3.3. SFDA$(I, \sigma) \succeq_Q$ QOPT$(I)$.

Proof. We use induction on subgames. Let $e = (p, q)$ be the first pair chosen at Line 3 of SFDA. By the algorithm, SFDA$(I, \sigma)$ = SFDA$(I/e, \sigma/e) + (p, q)$. Since SFDA$(I/e, \sigma/e) \succeq_Q$ QOPT$(I/e)$ by induction, then SFDA$(I, \sigma)$ = SFDA$(I/e, \sigma/e) + (p, q) \succeq_Q$ QOPT$(I/e) + (p, q) \succeq_Q$ QOPT$(I)$, where the last relation follows from Claim 2.12. □

Claim 3.4. *For $e = (p, q) = \sigma(1)$, we have the following:*

**(a)** *If* QOPT$(I)(q) \neq p$, *then* SFDA$(I, \sigma)$ = SFDA$(I \backslash e, \sigma \backslash e)$.
**(b)** *If* QOPT$(I)(q) = p$, *then* SFDA$(I, \sigma)$ = SFDA$(I/e, \sigma/e) + (p, q)$.

Proof. By the algorithm, (b) is clear: since $e = (p, q) = \sigma(1)$, the condition QOPT$(I)(q) = p$ means that $e$ is the first pair chosen at Line 3, and hence SFDA$(I, \sigma)$ = SFDA$(I/e, \sigma/e) + (p, q)$.

We show (a) by induction on subgames. Since $e = (p, q) = \sigma(1)$, Claim 2.10 and QOPT$(I)(q) \neq p$ imply QOPT$(I)(q) \succ_q p$. Then Claim 2.13 implies QOPT$(I)$ = QOPT$(I \backslash e)$. Let $e^* = (p^*, q^*)$ be the first pair chosen at Line 3. As QOPT$(I)$ = QOPT$(I \backslash e)$, SFDA also chooses $e^*$ when the input is $(I \backslash e, \sigma \backslash e)$. By the algorithm, SFDA$(I, \sigma)$ = SFDA$(I/e^*, \sigma/e^*) + (p^*, q^*)$ and SFDA$(I \backslash e, \sigma \backslash e)$ = SFDA$((I \backslash e)/e^*, (\sigma \backslash e)/e^*) + (p^*, q^*)$ = SFDA$((I/e^*) \backslash e, (\sigma/e^*) \backslash e) + (p^*, q^*)$. Note that Claim 2.12 implies QOPT$(I/e^*)(q) \succeq_q$ QOPT$(I)(q) \succ_q p$, and hence SFDA$(I/e^*, \sigma/e^*)$ = SFDA$((I/e^*) \backslash e, (\sigma/e^*) \backslash e)$ by induction. Thus, we obtain SFDA$(I, \sigma)$ = SFDA$(I \backslash e, \sigma \backslash e)$. □

The output of SFDA depends on the order $\sigma$, i.e., we may have SFDA$(I, \sigma) \neq$ SFDA$(I, \sigma')$ if $\sigma \neq \sigma'$. However, the set of firms and workers matched in SFDA$(I, \sigma)$ coincides with that of QOPT$(I)$ independently from $\sigma$, i.e., the following claim holds.

Claim 3.5. *For any $r \in P \cup Q$, we have* SFDA$(I, \sigma)(r) = r$ *if and only if* QOPT$(I)(r) = r$.

Proof. We use induction on subgames. Let $e = (p, q)$ be the first pair chosen at Line 3 of SFDA. Clearly, $p$ and $q$ are matched in both SFDA$(I, \sigma)$ and QOPT$(I)$. For each $r \in (P - p) \cup (Q - q)$, we have SFDA$(I, \sigma)(r)$ = SFDA$(I/e, \sigma/e)(r)$ by the algorithm. Also, by the induction, we have SFDA$(I/e, \sigma/e)(r) = r$ if and only if QOPT$(I/e)(r) = r$. Note that QOPT$(I) - (p, q)$ is a stable matching in $I/e$ by the definition of the stability. Then Theorem 2.8 implies that, for each $r \in (P - p) \cup (Q - q)$, QOPT$(I/e)(r) = r$ if and only if QOPT$(I)(r) = r$. Combining these, we obtain that, for every $r \in P \cup Q$, we have SFDA$(I, \sigma)(r) = r$ if and only if QOPT$(I)(r) = r$. □

Finally we analyze the time complexity of SFDA. The algorithm repeats finding the $Q$-optimal stable matching of each updated instance, which requires $O(|E|)$ as mentioned in Section 2.2.

Because one pair is fixed at each iteration stage, the number of iteration is at most $\min\{|P|, |Q|\}$. Thus, the algorithm SFDA runs in $O(|E| \cdot \min\{|P|, |Q|\})$.

Claim 3.6. *The matching* $\mathrm{SFDA}(I, \sigma)$ *can be computed in polynomial time.*

### 3.2 Proof of the Tractability

This part is devoted to show the following theorem, which completes the proof of Theorem 3.2, and hence of Theorem 3.1.

Theorem 3.7. $\mathrm{SFDA}(I, \sigma) = \mathrm{SPE}(I, \sigma)$ *for any* $(2, \infty)$*- or* $(\infty, 2)$*-*SPEM *instance* $(I, \sigma)$.

We prove Theorem 3.7 by induction on subgames linking Claim 3.4 and Proposition 2.4, the inductive properties of $\mathrm{SFDA}(I, \sigma)$ and $\mathrm{SPE}(I, \sigma)$, respectively. For this purpose, we provide the following special properties of $(2, \infty)$- and $(\infty, 2)$-SPEM instances.

Claim 3.8. $\mathrm{SFDA}(I, \sigma) = \mathrm{QOPT}(I)$ *for any* $(2, \infty)$*-*SPEM *instance* $(I, \sigma)$.

Proof. We use induction on subgames. Let $e = (p, q) = \sigma(1)$. There are two cases.

If $\mathrm{QOPT}(I)(q) \neq p$, then Claim 3.4 (a) implies $\mathrm{SFDA}(I, \sigma) = \mathrm{SFDA}(I \backslash e, \sigma \backslash e)$ and Claims 2.10 and 2.13 imply $\mathrm{QOPT}(I) = \mathrm{QOPT}(I \backslash e)$. Since $\mathrm{QOPT}(I \backslash e) = \mathrm{SFDA}(I \backslash e, \sigma \backslash e)$ by induction, we obtain $\mathrm{QOPT}(I) = \mathrm{SFDA}(I, \sigma)$.

If $\mathrm{QOPT}(I)(q) = p$, then Claim 3.4 (b) implies $\mathrm{SFDA}(I, \sigma) = \mathrm{SFDA}(I/e, \sigma/e) + (p, q)$, which equals $\mathrm{QOPT}(I/e) + (p, q)$ by induction. Then it suffices to show $\mathrm{QOPT}(I) = \mathrm{QOPT}(I/e) + (p, q)$. Suppose, to the contrary, this equality fails. As we have $\mathrm{QOPT}(I/e) + (p, q) \succeq_Q \mathrm{QOPT}(I)$ by Claim 2.12, the $Q$-optimality of $\mathrm{QOPT}(I)$ implies that $\mu := \mathrm{QOPT}(I/e) + (p, q)$ is unstable in $I$, i.e., there is $(p', q') \in E$ with $q' \succ_{p'} \mu(p')$ and $p' \succ_{q'} \mu(q')$. Since $\mathrm{QOPT}(I/e)$ is stable in $I/e$, we have $(p', q') \notin E/e := E \backslash (\delta_I(p) \cup \delta_I(q))$. Hence, $p' = p$ or $q' = q$ holds. If $p' = p$, then $q' \succ_p \mu(p) = q = \mathrm{QOPT}(I)(p)$ and $p \succ_{q'} \mu(q') \succeq_{q'} \mathrm{QOPT}(I)(q')$, and hence $(p, q')$ blocks $\mathrm{QOPT}(I)$, a contradiction. Therefore, we have $q' = q$ and $p' \neq p$, from which $q \succ_{p'} \mu(p')$ and $p' \succ_q \mu(q) = p = \mathrm{QOPT}(I)(q)$ follow. Since $\mathrm{QOPT}(I)$ is not blocked by $(p', q')$ $(= (p', q))$, the latter condition implies $\mathrm{QOPT}(I)(p') \succeq_{p'} q$. As we have $\mathrm{QOPT}(I)(p') \neq \mathrm{QOPT}(I)(p) = q$, we obtain $\mathrm{QOPT}(I)(p') \succ_{p'} q \succ_{p'} \mu(p')$. Note that both $\mathrm{QOPT}(I) - (p, q)$ and $\mu - (p, q)$ are stable in $I/e$. By Theorem 2.8, $\mathrm{QOPT}(I)(p') \neq p'$ implies $\mu(p') \neq p'$. Thus, $\mathrm{QOPT}(I)(p'), q, \mu(p') \in Q$ are three different entries of the preference list of $p'$, which contradicts the fact that the list of $p'$ has at most 2 entries. □

Claim 3.9. *For any* $(2, \infty)$*- or* $(\infty, 2)$*-*SPEM *instance* $(I, \sigma)$ *and any* $e = (p, q) \in E$*, the condition* $\mathrm{QOPT}(I)(q) = p$ *implies* $p \succ_q \mathrm{SFDA}(I \backslash e, \sigma \backslash e)(q)$.

Proof. In the case of $(2, \infty)$-SPEM, the subgame $(I \backslash e, \sigma \backslash e)$ is also a $(2, \infty)$-SPEM instance, and hence $\mathrm{QOPT}(I \backslash e) = \mathrm{SFDA}(I \backslash e, \sigma \backslash e)$ by Claim 3.8. Then $p \succ_q \mathrm{QOPT}(I \backslash e)(q) = \mathrm{SFDA}(I \backslash e, \sigma \backslash e)(q)$ follows from Claim 2.11.

In the case of $(\infty, 2)$-SPEM, since $q$'s preference list is of length at most 2, $p$ is on the top or the bottom of the list. If $p$ is on the top, clearly $p \succ_q \mathrm{SFDA}(I \backslash e, \sigma \backslash e)(q)$. If $p$ is on the bottom, by Claim 2.11, $p = \mathrm{QOPT}(I)(q) \succ_q \mathrm{QOPT}(I \backslash e)(q) = q$. By Claim 3.5, this implies $\mathrm{SFDA}(I \backslash e, \sigma \backslash e)(q) = q$. Thus, we have $p \succ_q q = \mathrm{SFDA}(I \backslash e, \sigma \backslash e)(q)$. □

Now we are ready to show Theorem 3.7, which states that the output of SFDA coincides with the SPE matching for a $(2, \infty)$- or $(\infty, 2)$-SPEM instance.

Proof of Theorem 3.7. We show $\mathrm{SFDA}(I, \sigma) = \mathrm{SPE}(I, \sigma)$ by induction on subgames. Let $e = (p, q) = \sigma(1)$. Note that for a $(2, \infty)$-SPEM (resp., $(\infty, 2)$-SPEM) instance $(I, \sigma)$, the subgames $(I \backslash e, \sigma \backslash e)$

and $(I/e, \sigma/e)$ are also $(2,\infty)$-SPEM (resp., $(\infty,2)$-SPEM) instances. Therefore, by induction we have $\text{SFDA}(I/e,\sigma/e) = \text{SPE}(I/e,\sigma/e)$ and $\text{SFDA}(I\backslash e,\sigma\backslash e) = \text{SPE}(I\backslash e,\sigma\backslash e)$. We consider two cases: $\text{QOPT}(I)(q) \neq p$ and $\text{QOPT}(I)(q) = p$.

In the case $\text{QOPT}(I)(q) \neq p$, Claims 2.10 and 3.3 imply $\text{SFDA}(I,\sigma)(q) \succeq_q \text{QOPT}(I)(q) \succ_q p$. Also, Claim 3.4 (a) implies $\text{SFDA}(I,\sigma) = \text{SFDA}(I\backslash e,\sigma\backslash e) = \text{SPE}(I\backslash e,\sigma\backslash e)$. Then $\text{SPE}(I\backslash e,\sigma\backslash e)(q) \succ_q p$. By Proposition 2.4 (a), $\text{SPE}(I,\sigma) = \text{SPE}(I\backslash e,\sigma\backslash e) = \text{SFDA}(I,\sigma)$.

In the case $\text{QOPT}(I)(q) = p$, Claim 3.4 (b) implies $\text{SFDA}(I,\sigma) = \text{SFDA}(I/e,\sigma/e) + (p,q) = \text{SPE}(I/e,\sigma/e) + (p,q)$. Since $(I/e,\sigma/e)$ is a $(2,\infty)$- or $(\infty,2)$-SPEM instance, by Claims 3.9, we have $p \succ_q \text{SFDA}(I\backslash e,\sigma\backslash e)(q) = \text{SPE}(I\backslash e,\sigma\backslash e)(q)$. By Proposition 2.4 (b), then $\text{SPE}(I,\sigma) = \text{SPE}(I/e,\sigma/e) + (p,q) = \text{SFDA}(I,\sigma)$. □

In particular, for $(2,\infty)$-SPEM, combining Theorem 3.7 and Claim 3.8 gives the following corollary.

COROLLARY 3.10. $\text{SPE}(I,\sigma) = \text{QOPT}(I)$ *for any* $(2,\infty)$-SPEM *instance* $(I,\sigma)$.

Thanks to Theorem 3.7, for any $(2,\infty)$-SPEM or $(\infty,2)$-SPEM instance, we can compute the SPE matching of a given instance by the algorithm SFDA. (In particular, for $(2,\infty)$-SPEM, we can compute it by DA by Corollary 3.10.) Because SFDA runs in polynomial time as shown in Claim 3.6, Theorem 3.7 immediately implies Theorem 3.2. Then Theorem 3.1 also follows.

## 4 HARDNESS OF THE SPEM PROBLEM

In this section, we show PSPACE-completeness of computing the SPE for the sequential matching problem even if the length of each firm's and worker's preference list is at most three and the ordering is restricted to position-ordered. Formally, we prove the following theorem.

THEOREM 4.1. $(3,3)$-SPEM *is PSPACE-complete even if the problem is restricted to position-ordered.*

First of all, we can solve SPEM in polynomial space by implementing backward induction as a depth-first search of the game tree. Thus, the problem is in class PSPACE.

In what follows, we prove the hardness by giving a reduction from QUANTIFIED 3SAT, which is a PSPACE-hard problem [9]. Let $V = \{v_1,\dots,v_n\}$ be the set of variables and $(\mathcal{Q}_1 v_1)(\mathcal{Q}_2 v_2)\cdots(\mathcal{Q}_n v_n)$ $\varphi(v_1,\dots,v_n)$ be a quantified Boolean formula. Here, $\mathcal{Q}_i$ is either $\forall$ or $\exists$ for $i = 1,\dots,n$ and $\varphi(v_1,\dots,v_n)$ is a Boolean expression in 3-CNF. QUANTIFIED 3SAT asks whether the given quantified Boolean formula is true or not. Let $J^{\exists} = \{i \mid \mathcal{Q}_i = \exists\}$ and $J^{\forall} = \{i \mid \mathcal{Q}_i = \forall\}$.

In our reduction, we create a position-ordered $(3,3)$-SPEM instance $(I,\sigma)$ with $I = (P,Q,E,\prec)$ that consists of three phases—assignment, evaluation, and output—as shown in Fig. 3.

In the assignment phase, for each Boolean variable $v_i \in V$, we create two workers $x_i$ and $\bar{x}_i$, whose actions correspond to an assignment of TRUE or FALSE to $v_i$. Each $x_i$ has exactly two acceptable firms $s_i$ and $t_i$ with $t_i \succ_{x_i} s_i$. Suppose that $x_i$ is the best and the worst choice for $s_i$ and $t_i$, respectively. Thus, $x_i$ must be matched at least to $s_i$ in the SPE matching $\text{SPE}(I,\sigma)$. In addition, suppose that the best choice for $\bar{x}_i$ is $s_i$ and the second choice for $s_i$ is $\bar{x}_i$. Then, in the SPE matching $\text{SPE}(I,\sigma)$, $\bar{x}_i$ matches to $s_i$ if $x_i$ does not match to $s_i$.

Let $\pi$ be the position order that induces $\sigma$, such that it starts with $s_1,\dots,s_n$ and ends with $t_1,\dots,t_n$. Let $a_i \in \{\text{TRUE},\text{FALSE}\}$ for each $i = 1,\dots,n$. For each $0 \le k \le n$, let us denote by $(I,\sigma)_{[a_1,\dots,a_k]}$ the subgame of $(I,\sigma)$ just after $s_1,\dots,s_k$ have finished their offers in which, for each $i = 1,\dots,k$, the contraction of $(s_i,x_i)$ has occurred (i.e., $x_i$ has accepted $s_i$'s offer) if $a_i = \text{TRUE}$ and the contraction of $(s_i,\bar{x}_i)$ has occurred (i.e., $x_i$ has rejected $s_i$'s offer and then $\bar{x}_i$ has accepted) if $a_i = \text{FALSE}$. Note that the subgames $(I,\sigma)_{[a_1,\dots,a_n]}$ correspond to the assignments to the variables $v_1,\dots,v_n$ in a one-to-one manner.

In the evaluation phase, for each Boolean variable $v_i \in V$, we create a firm $r_i$ and a worker $z_i$ with $(r_i, z_i) \in E$. We will design the evaluation phase so that it correctly evaluate the value of $\varphi(a_1, \dots, a_n)$ for every assignment $(a_1, \dots, a_n) \in \{\text{TRUE}, \text{FALSE}\}^n$ by the SPE of the corresponding subgame $(I, \sigma)_{[a_1,\dots,a_n]}$. Formally, we prove the following claim.

CLAIM 4.2. *One can design the evaluation phase in Fig. 3 so that, for any assignment* $(a_1, \dots, a_n) \in \{\text{TRUE}, \text{FALSE}\}^n$ *with the corresponding subgame* $(I', \sigma') := (I, \sigma)_{[a_1,\dots,a_n]}$, *the following holds:*

(i) *for any* $i \in J^{\exists}$, *we have* $(r_i, z_i) \in \text{SPE}(I', \sigma') \iff \varphi(a_1, \dots, a_n) = \text{TRUE}$, *and*
(ii) *for any* $i \in J^{\forall}$, *we have* $(r_i, z_i) \in \text{SPE}(I', \sigma') \iff \varphi(a_1, \dots, a_n) = \text{FALSE}$.

We postpone proving Claim 4.2, and suppose that we use the evaluation phase designed so. The following claim shows whether each worker $x_i$ should accept $s_i$'s offer or not.

CLAIM 4.3. *For any* $1 \le i \le n$ *and any partial assignment* $(a_1, \dots, a_{i-1}) \in \{\text{TRUE}, \text{FALSE}\}^{i-1}$, *define*

$$\varphi' := (\mathcal{Q}_{i+1} v_{i+1}) \cdots (\mathcal{Q}_n v_n)\, \varphi(a_1, \dots, a_{i-1}, \text{FALSE}, v_{i+1}, \dots, v_n).$$

*Then, in the corresponding subgame* $(I', \sigma') := (I, \sigma)_{[a_1,\dots,a_{i-1}]}$,

(i) *if* $i \in J^{\exists}$, *we have* $(s_i, \bar{x}_i) \in \text{SPE}(I', \sigma') \iff \varphi' = \text{TRUE}$, *and*
(ii) *if* $i \in J^{\forall}$, *we have* $(s_i, \bar{x}_i) \in \text{SPE}(I', \sigma') \iff \varphi' = \text{FALSE}$.

PROOF. We prove this by backward induction on $i$. The base case $i = n$ holds by Claim 4.2 because $x_n$ will be offered from $t_n$ ($\succ_{x_n} s_n$) if and only if $(\mathcal{Q}_n, \varphi') = (\exists, \text{TRUE})$ or $(\forall, \text{FALSE})$. For a given $1 \le i < n$, suppose that the claim holds for $j \ge i + 1$. By the induction hypothesis and Claim 4.2, if $x_i$ rejects $s_i$'s offer (note that then $\bar{x}_i$ must accept $s_i$'s offer), then $x_i$ will be offered from $t_i$ ($\succ_{x_i} s_i$) if and only if $(\mathcal{Q}_i, \varphi') = (\exists, \text{TRUE})$ or $(\forall, \text{FALSE})$. Thus, the claim holds. □

Without loss of generality, we may assume that $\mathcal{Q}_1 = \exists$ and $v_1$ does not appear in the 3-CNF. Then, $x_1$ rejects $s_1$'s offer in the SPE if and only if the given QUANTIFIED 3SAT is an yes-instance. Hence, deciding whether the first edge $\sigma(1) = (s_1, x_1)$ is accepted in the SPE of $(I, \sigma)$ is PSPACE-complete.

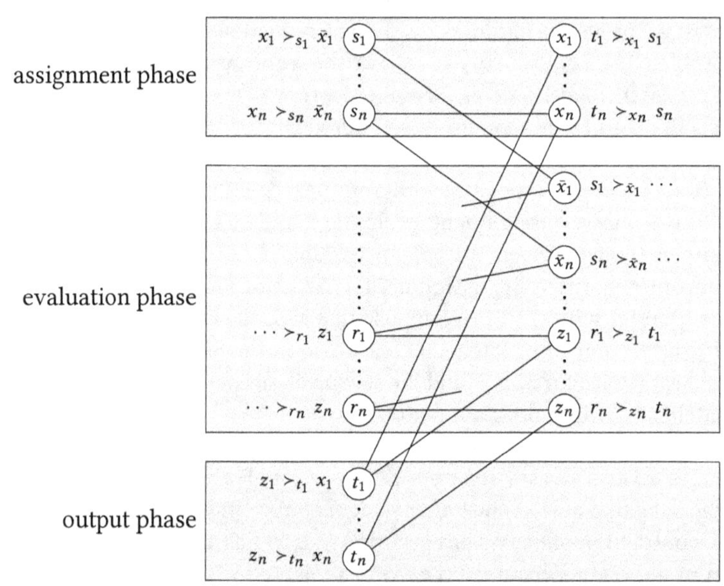


Fig. 3. Framework of the reduction

It remains to explain the details of the evaluation phase. Before the proof of Claim 4.2, we prepare several gadgets as follows. We use gadgets to simulate OR, AND, and NOT-gates (see Figs. 4, 5, and 6). Also, we use a gadget for branching, i.e., to make a copy of each value (see Fig. 7). For each gadget, we put an index $u$ to distinguish individuals.

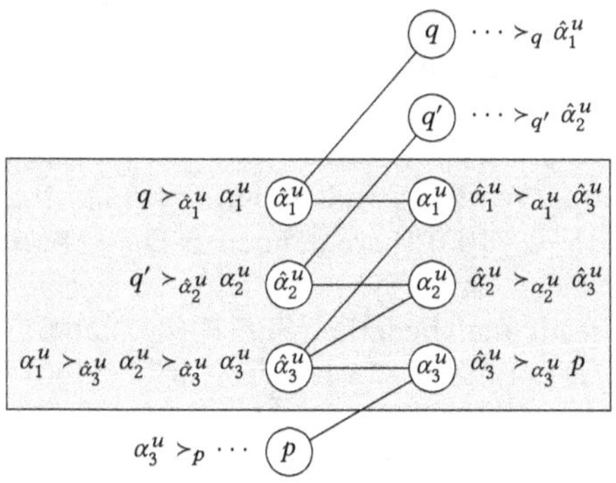


Fig. 4. OR-gate simulator $\mathsf{OR}^u$

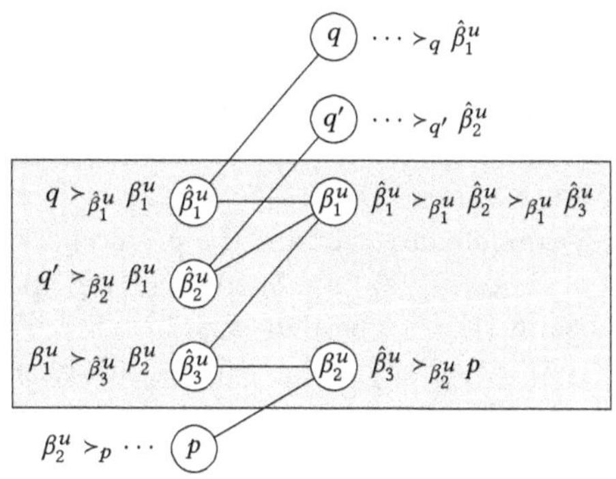


Fig. 5. AND-gate simulator $\mathsf{AND}^u$

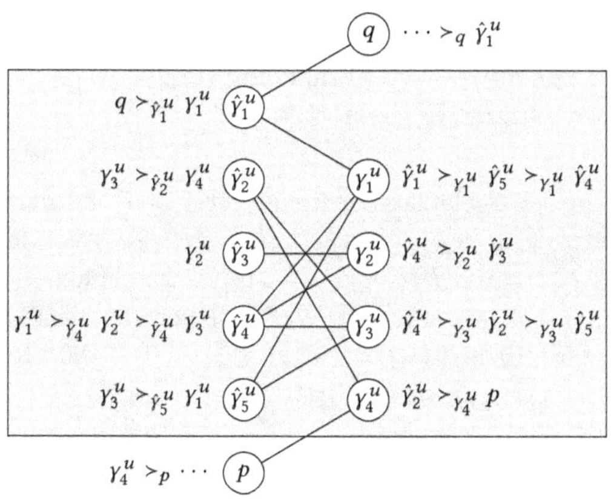


Fig. 6. NOT-gate simulator $\mathsf{NOT}^u$

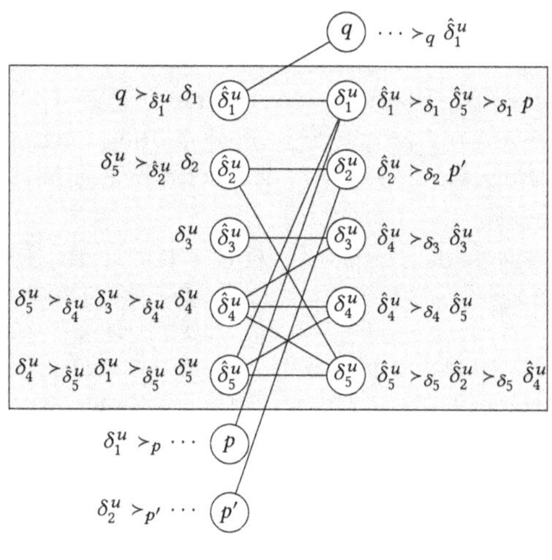


Fig. 7. Branching simulator $\mathsf{BRANCHING}^u$

$\mathsf{OR}^u$ is a piece of a sequential matching game which consists of three firms $P[\mathsf{OR}^u] = \{\hat{\alpha}_1^u, \hat{\alpha}_2^u, \hat{\alpha}_3^u\}$ and three workers $Q[\mathsf{OR}^u] = \{\alpha_1^u, \alpha_2^u, \alpha_3^u\}$ with two input workers $q, q'$ and one output firm $p$. The set of edges related to $\mathsf{OR}^u$ and the preferences of $P[\mathsf{OR}^u] \cup Q[\mathsf{OR}^u]$ are defined as Fig. 4. Assume that $\arg\max\{\sigma^{-1}(e) \mid e \in \delta_I(q)\} = (\hat{\alpha}_1^u, q)$, $\arg\max\{\sigma^{-1}(e) \mid e \in \delta_I(q')\} = (\hat{\alpha}_2^u, q)$, and $\pi^{-1}(\hat{\alpha}_1^u) < \pi^{-1}(\hat{\alpha}_2^u) < \pi^{-1}(\hat{\alpha}_3^u) < \pi^{-1}(p)$. Let us consider a subgame where the first firm is $\hat{\alpha}_1^u$. If $q$ and $q'$ are already matched, then in the SPE matching for this subgame, $(\hat{\alpha}_1^u, \alpha_1^u), (\hat{\alpha}_2^u, \alpha_2^u), (\hat{\alpha}_3^u, \alpha_3^u)$ are matched and hence $p$ is not matched with $\alpha_3^u$. On the other hand, if $q$ or $q'$ is not matched yet, then $p$ is matched with $\alpha_3^u$ in the SPE matching for this subgame. Thus, we can see $\mathsf{OR}^u$ as an OR-gate simulator.

$\mathsf{AND}^u$ is a piece of a sequential matching game which consists of three firms $P[\mathsf{AND}^u] = \{\hat{\beta}_1^u, \hat{\beta}_2^u, \hat{\beta}_3^u\}$ and two workers $Q[\mathsf{AND}^u] = \{\beta_1^u, \beta_2^u\}$ with two input workers $q, q'$ and one output firm $p$. The set of edges related to $\mathsf{AND}^u$ and the preferences of $P[\mathsf{AND}^u] \cup Q[\mathsf{AND}^u]$ are defined as Fig. 5. Assume that $\arg\max\{\sigma^{-1}(e) \mid e \in \delta_I(q)\} = (\hat{\beta}_1^u, q)$, $\arg\max\{\sigma^{-1}(e) \mid e \in \delta_I(q')\} = (\hat{\beta}_2^u, q)$, and $\pi^{-1}(\hat{\beta}_1^u) < \pi^{-1}(\hat{\beta}_2^u) < \pi^{-1}(\hat{\beta}_3^u) < \pi^{-1}(p)$. Let us consider a subgame where the first firm is $\hat{\beta}_1^u$. If $q$ or $q'$ is already matched, then in the SPE matching for this subgame, $\beta_1^u$ is matched with $\hat{\beta}_1^u$ or $\hat{\beta}_2^u$, and $\beta_2^u$ is matched with $\hat{\beta}_3^u$. Hence $p$ is not matched with $\beta_2^u$. On the other hand, if $q$ and $q'$ are not matched yet, then the SPE matching for this subgame contains $\{(\hat{\beta}_3^u, \beta_1^u), (p, \beta_2^u)\}$. Thus, we can see $\mathsf{AND}^u$ as an AND-gate simulator.

$\mathsf{NOT}^u$ is a piece of a sequential matching game which consists of five firms $P[\mathsf{NOT}^u] = \{\hat{\gamma}_1^u, \dots, \hat{\gamma}_5^u\}$ and three workers $Q[\mathsf{NOT}^u] = \{\gamma_1^u, \dots, \gamma_4^u\}$ with an input worker $q$ and an output firm $p$. The set of edges related to $\mathsf{NOT}^u$ and the preferences of $P[\mathsf{NOT}^u] \cup Q[\mathsf{NOT}^u]$ are defined as Fig. 6. Assume that $\arg\max\{\sigma^{-1}(e) \mid e \in \delta_I(q)\} = (\hat{\gamma}_1^u, q)$ and $\pi^{-1}(\hat{\gamma}_1^u) < \dots < \pi^{-1}(\hat{\gamma}_5^u) < \pi^{-1}(p)$. Let us consider a subgame $(I', \sigma')$ where the first firm is $\hat{\gamma}_1^u$. If $q$ is already matched, then $\mathrm{SPE}(I', \sigma') \cap E[\mathsf{NOT}^u] = \{(\hat{\gamma}_1^u, \gamma_1^u), (\hat{\gamma}_2^u, \gamma_3^u), (\hat{\gamma}_4^u, \gamma_2^u), (p, \gamma_4^u)\}$. Otherwise, i.e., $q$ is not matched yet, $\mathrm{SPE}(I', \sigma') \cap E[\mathsf{NOT}^u] = \{(\hat{\gamma}_1^u, q), (\hat{\gamma}_2^u, \gamma_4^u), (\hat{\gamma}_3^u, \gamma_2^u), (\hat{\gamma}_4^u, \gamma_3^u), (\hat{\gamma}_5^u, \gamma_1^u)\}$. Thus, we can see $\mathsf{NOT}^u$ as a NOT-gate simulator.

$\mathsf{BRANCHING}^u$ is a piece of a sequential matching game which consists of five firms $P[\mathsf{BRANCHING}^u] = \{\hat{\delta}_1^u, \dots, \hat{\delta}_5^u\}$ and five workers $Q[\mathsf{BRANCHING}^u] = \{\delta_1^u, \dots, \delta_5^u\}$ with one input worker $q$ and two output firms $p, p'$. The set of edges related to $\mathsf{BRANCHING}^u$ and the preferences of $P[\mathsf{BRANCHING}^u] \cup Q[\mathsf{BRANCHING}^u]$ are defined as Fig. 7. Assume that $\arg\max\{\sigma^{-1}(e) \mid e \in \delta_I(q)\} = (\hat{\delta}_1^u, q)$ and $\pi^{-1}(\hat{\delta}_1^u) < \dots < \pi^{-1}(\hat{\delta}_5^u) < \pi^{-1}(p) < \pi^{-1}(p')$. Let us consider a subgame $(I', \sigma')$ where the first firm is $\hat{\delta}_1^u$. If $q$ is already matched, then $\mathrm{SPE}(I', \sigma') \cap E[\mathsf{BRANCHING}^u] = \{(\hat{\delta}_1^u, \delta_1^u), (\hat{\delta}_2^u, \delta_2^u), (\hat{\delta}_3^u, \delta_3^u), (\hat{\delta}_4^u, \delta_4^u), (\hat{\delta}_5^u, \delta_5^u)\}$. Otherwise, i.e., $q$ is not matched yet, $\mathrm{SPE}(I', \sigma') \cap E[\mathsf{BRANCHING}^u] = \{(\hat{\delta}_1^u, p), (\hat{\delta}_2^u, \delta_5^u), (\hat{\delta}_4^u, \delta_3^u), (\hat{\delta}_5^u, \delta_4^u), (p, \delta_1^u), (p', \delta_2^u)\}$. Thus, we can see $\mathsf{BRANCHING}^u$ as a branching simulator.

Now, we are ready to design the evaluation phase required in Claim 4.2.

Proof of Claim 4.2. Let $C = \{C_1, \dots, C_m\}$ be the set of clauses for the given 3-CNF. For each clause $C_j \in C$, let $C_j = \ell_{j,1} \vee \ell_{j,2} \vee \ell_{j,3}$ such that $\ell_{j,k} \in \{x_{\lambda(j,k)}, \bar{x}_{\lambda(j,k)}\}$ $(k = 1, 2, 3)$. Also, let $N^+ = \{(j,k) \mid \ell_{j,k} = x_{\lambda(j,k)},\ k \in \{1,2,3\}\}$ and $N^- = \{(j,k) \mid \ell_{j,k} = \bar{x}_{\lambda(j,k)},\ k \in \{1,2,3\}\}$. Without loss of generality, we may assume that $\lambda(j,1) < \lambda(j,2) < \lambda(j,3)$. We construct a (3, 3)-SPEM instance $(I, \sigma)$ as follows. In the instance, we use $\mathsf{OR}^u$ for $u \in U_{\mathsf{OR}} := \bigcup_{j=1}^m \{(j,1), (j,2)\}$, $\mathsf{AND}^u$ for $u \in U_{\mathsf{AND}} := \{1, \dots, m\}$, $\mathsf{NOT}^u$ for $u \in U_{\mathsf{NOT}} := N^- \cup J^3$, and $\mathsf{BRANCHING}^u$ for $u \in U_{\mathsf{BRANCHING}} := \bigcup_{j=1}^{m-1} \{(1,j), \dots, (n,j)\} \cup \{1, \dots, n-1\}$. The set of firms and workers are respectively defined as

$$P := \{s_1, \dots, s_n, t_1, \dots, t_n, r_1, \dots, r_n, \hat{c}_1, \dots, \hat{c}_m\} \cup \bigcup_{i=1}^n \bigcup_{j=1}^m \{\hat{y}_{i,j}\} \cup \bigcup_{j=1}^m \{\hat{\ell}_{j,1}, \hat{\ell}_{j,2}, \hat{\ell}_{j,3}\}$$
$$\cup \bigcup_{u \in U_{\mathsf{OR}}} P[\mathsf{OR}^u] \cup \bigcup_{u \in U_{\mathsf{AND}}} P[\mathsf{AND}^u] \cup \bigcup_{u \in U_{\mathsf{NOT}}} P[\mathsf{NOT}^u] \cup \bigcup_{u \in U_{\mathsf{BRANCHING}}} P[\mathsf{BRANCHING}^u]$$

and

$$Q := \{x_1, \dots, x_n, \bar{x}_1, \dots, \bar{x}_n, z_1, \dots, z_n, c_1, \dots, c_m\} \cup \bigcup_{i=1}^n \bigcup_{j=1}^m \{y_{i,j}\} \cup \bigcup_{j=1}^m \{\ell_{j,1}, \ell_{j,2}, \ell_{j,3}\}$$
$$\cup \bigcup_{u \in U_{\mathsf{OR}}} Q[\mathsf{OR}^u] \cup \bigcup_{u \in U_{\mathsf{AND}}} Q[\mathsf{AND}^u] \cup \bigcup_{u \in U_{\mathsf{NOT}}} Q[\mathsf{NOT}^u] \cup \bigcup_{u \in U_{\mathsf{BRANCHING}}} Q[\mathsf{BRANCHING}^u]$$

The input and output of each gadget are given as shown in Table 1.

Table 1. The input and output of the gadgets.

| | Input | Output |
|---|---|---|
| $\mathtt{BRANCHING}^{(i,1)}$ $(i=1,\dots,n)$ | $\bar{x}_i$ | $\hat{y}_{i,1}, \hat{\delta}_1^{(i,2)}$ |
| $\mathtt{BRANCHING}^{(i,j)}$ $(^{i=1,\dots,n}_{j=2,\dots,m-2})$ | $\delta_2^{(i,j-1)}$ | $\hat{y}_{i,j}, \hat{\delta}_1^{(i,j+1)}$ |
| $\mathtt{BRANCHING}^{(i,m-1)}$ $(i=1,\dots,n)$ | $\delta_2^{(i,m-2)}$ | $\hat{y}_{i,m-1}, \hat{y}_{i,m}$ |
| $\mathtt{NOT}^{(j,k)}$ $((j,k)\in N^-)$ | $y_{\lambda(j,1),j}$ | $\ell_{j,k}$ |
| $\mathtt{OR}^{(j,1)}$ $(j=1,\dots,m)$ | $\ell_{j,1}, \ell_{j,2}$ | $\hat{\alpha}_1^{(j,2)}$ |
| $\mathtt{OR}^{(j,2)}$ $(j=1,\dots,m)$ | $\alpha_3^{(j,1)}, \ell_{j,3}$ | $\hat{\alpha}_1^{(j,2)}$ |
| $\mathtt{AND}^1$ | $c_1, c_2$ | $\hat{\beta}_1^2$ |
| $\mathtt{AND}^j$ $(j=2,\dots,m-2)$ | $\beta_2^{j-1}, c_{j+1}$ | $\hat{\beta}_1^{j+1}$ |
| $\mathtt{AND}^{m-1}$ | $\beta_2^{m-2}, c_m$ | $\hat{\delta}_1^1$ |
| $\mathtt{BRANCHING}^1$ | $\beta_2^{m-1}$ | $\begin{cases}\hat{\gamma}_1^1 & (\text{if } 1\in A)\\ r_1 & (\text{if } 1\notin A)\end{cases}, \hat{\delta}_1^2$ |
| $\mathtt{BRANCHING}^i$ $(i=2,\dots,n-2)$ | $\delta_2^{i-1}$ | $\begin{cases}\hat{\gamma}_1^i & (\text{if } i\in A)\\ r_i & (\text{if } i\notin A)\end{cases}, \hat{\delta}_1^{i+1}$ |
| $\mathtt{BRANCHING}^{n-1}$ | $\delta_2^{n-2}$ | $\begin{cases}\hat{\gamma}_1^{n-1} & (\text{if } n-1\in A)\\ r_{n-1} & (\text{if } n-1\notin A)\end{cases}, \begin{cases}\hat{\gamma}_1^n & (\text{if } n\in J^\exists)\\ r_m & (\text{if } n\in J^\forall)\end{cases}$ |
| $\mathtt{NOT}^i$ $(i\in J^\exists)$ | $\begin{cases}\delta_1^i & (\text{if } i<n)\\ \delta_2^{n-1} & (\text{if } i=n)\end{cases}$ | $r_i$ |

Moreover, the preferences of the other firms and workers are given as;

$s_i\colon\ x_i \succ_{s_i} \bar{x}_i\ (i=1,\dots,n)$,
$\hat{\ell}_{j,k}\colon\ y_{\lambda(j,k),j} \succ_{\hat{\ell}_{j,k}} \ell_{j,k}\ ((j,k)\in N^+)$,
$\hat{\ell}_{j,k}\colon\ \gamma_4^{(j,k)} \succ_{\hat{\ell}_{j,k}} \ell_{j,k}\ ((j,k)\in N^-)$,
$\hat{y}_{i,j}\colon\ \delta_1^{(i,j)} \succ_{\hat{y}_{i,j}} y_{i,j}\ (^{i=1,\dots,n}_{j=1,\dots,m-1})$,
$\hat{y}_{i,m}\colon\ \delta_2^{(i,m-1)} \succ_{\hat{y}_{i,m}} y_{i,m}\ (i=1,\dots,n)$,
$\hat{c}_j\colon\ \alpha_3^{(j,2)} \succ_{\hat{c}_j} c_j\ (j=1,\dots,m)$,
$r_i\colon\ \hat{\delta}_1^i \succ_{r_i} z_i\ (i=1,\dots,n-1)$,
$r_n\colon\ \hat{\delta}_2^{n-1} \succ_{r_i} z_n$,
$t_i\colon\ z_i \succ_{t_i} x_i\ (i=1,\dots,n)$,

$x_i\colon\ t_i \succ_{x_i} s_i\ (i=1,\dots,n)$,
$\bar{x}_i\colon\ s_i \succ_{\bar{x}_i} \hat{\delta}_1^{(i,1)}\ (i=1,\dots,n)$,

$$y_{i,j}\colon\ \begin{cases}\hat{y}_{i,j} \succ_{y_{i,j}} \hat{\ell}_{j,k} & (\text{if } \ell_{j,k}=x_i),\\ \hat{y}_{i,j} \succ_{y_{i,j}} \hat{\gamma}_1^{(j,k)} & (\text{if } \ell_{j,k}=\bar{x}_i),\\ \hat{y}_{i,j} & (\text{otherwise}),\end{cases}$$

$c_1\colon\ \hat{c}_1 \succ_{c_1} \hat{\beta}_1^1$,
$c_j\colon\ \hat{c}_j \succ_{c_j} \hat{\beta}_2^{j-1}\ (j=2,\dots,m)$,
$z_i\colon\ r_i \succ_{z_i} t_i\ (i=1,\dots,n)$.

We define $E$ and $\succ$ according to the above. Then, it is easy to check that the degree of each firm or worker is at most 3.

Let $\pi$ be a position order that satisfies the conditions of ordering in each gadget and

$$\{s_1\}\to\cdots\to\{s_n\}\to\bigcup_{i=1}^{n}\bigcup_{j=1}^{m-1}P[\mathtt{BRANCHING}^{(i,j)}]\to\bigcup_{i=1}^{n}\bigcup_{j=1}^{m}\hat{y}_{i,j}$$

$$\to\bigcup_{(j,k)\in N^-}P[\mathtt{NOT}^{(j,k)}]\to\bigcup_{j=1}^{m}\{\hat{\ell}_{j,1},\hat{\ell}_{j,2},\hat{\ell}_{j,3}\}\to\bigcup_{j=1}^{m}P[\mathtt{OR}^{(j,1)}]\to\bigcup_{j=1}^{m}P[\mathtt{OR}^{(j,2)}]\to\{\hat{c}_1,\dots,\hat{c}_m\}$$

$$\to\bigcup_{j=1}^{m}P[\mathtt{AND}^j]\to\bigcup_{j=1}^{m-1}P[\mathtt{BRANCHING}^j]\to\bigcup_{i\in J^\exists}P[\mathtt{NOT}^i]\to\{r_1,\dots,r_n\}\to\{t_1\}\to\cdots\to\{t_n\}$$

where $X\to Y$ represents that $\pi^{-1}(x)<\pi^{-1}(y)$ for any $x\in X$ and $y\in Y$. Let $\sigma$ be the order over $E$ that is induced by $\pi$.

Then, $y_{i,j}$ is matched with $\hat{y}_{i,j}$ if and only if $\bar{x}_i$ is matched with $s_i$, i.e., $v_i$ is assigned FALSE. Also, $\ell_i$ is matched with $\hat{\ell}_i$ if and only if $\ell_i$ corresponds to FALSE and $c_j$ is matched with $\hat{c}_j$ if and only if $C_j$ is unsatisfied. In addition, $\beta_2^{m-1}$ is matched with $\hat{\delta}_1^1$ if and only if $\varphi$ is satisfied. For intuitive understanding, see Figs. 8–10 in the full version [12]. Therefore, we conclude that the constructed evaluation phase satisfies the desired condition. □

Thus we have completed the proof of Theorem 4.1.

## REFERENCES


[1] J. Alcalde, D. J. Pérez-Castrillo, and A. Romero-Medina. 1998. Hiring procedures to implement stable allocations. *Journal of Economic Theory* 82, 2 (1998), 469–480.

[2] J. Alcalde and A. Romero-Medina. 2000. Simple mechanisms to implement the core of college admissions problems. *Games and Economic Behavior* 31, 2 (2000), 294–302.

[3] J. Alcalde and A. Romero-Medina. 2005. Sequential decisions in the college admissions problem. *Economics Letters* 86, 2 (2005), 153–158.

[4] G. Avni, T. A. Henzinger, and O. Kupferman. 2016. Dynamic resource allocation games. In *International Symposium on Algorithmic Game Theory*. Springer, Berlin, Heidelberg, 153–166.

[5] K. Bando. 2014. On the existence of a strictly strong Nash equilibrium under the student-optimal deferred acceptance algorithm. *Games and Economic Behavior* 87 (2014), 269–287.

[6] J. Eeckhout. 2000. On the uniqueness of stable marriage matchings. *Economics Letters* 69, 1 (2000), 1–8.

[7] L. Ehlers. 2007. Von Neumann–Morgenstern stable sets in matching problems. *Journal of Economic Theory* 134, 1 (2007), 537–547.

[8] D. Gale and L. S. Shapley. 1962. College admissions and the stability of marriage. *Amer. Math. Monthly* 69, 1 (1962), 9–15.

[9] M. R. Garey and D. S. Johnson. 1979. *Computers and Intractability: A Guide to the Theory of NP-Completeness*. Freeman New York, New York.

[10] D. Gusfield and R. W. Irving. 1989. *The Stable Marriage Problem: Structure and Algorithms*. MIT Press, Boston.

[11] G. Haeringer and M. Wooders. 2011. Decentralized job matching. *International Journal of Game Theory* 40, 1 (2011), 1–28.

[12] Y. Kawase, Y. Yamaguchi, and Y. Yokoi. 2018. Computing a subgame perfect equilibrium of a sequential matching game. (2018). arXiv:1804.10353

[13] O. Kesten. 2010. School choice with consent. *The Quarterly Journal of Economics* 125, 3 (2010), 1297–1348.

[14] A. Kloosterman and P. Troyan. 2016. Efficient and essentially stable assignments. Mimeo. (2016).

[15] D. E. Knuth. 1976. *Marriage Stables*. Montréal: Les Presses de l'Université de Montréal.

[16] R. P. Leme, V. Syrgkanis, and É. Tardos. 2012. The curse of simultaneity. In *Proceedings of the 3rd Innovations in Theoretical Computer Science Conference*. ACM, New York, 60–67.

[17] D. F. Manlove. 2013. *Algorithmics of Matching under Preferences*. World Scientific.

[18] D. G. McVitie and L. B. Wilson. 1970. Stable marriage assignment for unequal sets. *BIT Numerical Mathematics* 10, 3 (1970), 295–309.

[19] D. G. McVitie and L. B. Wilson. 1971. The stable marriage problem. *Commun. ACM* 14, 7 (1971), 486–490.

[20] N. Nisan, T. Roughgarden, É. Tardos, and V. V. Vazirani. 2007. *Algorithmic Game Theory*. Cambridge University Press, Cambridge.

[21] J. Pais. 2008. Incentives in decentralized random matching markets. *Games and Economic Behavior* 64, 2 (2008), 632–649.

[22] A. E. Roth and M. Sotomayor. 1991. *Two-sided Matching: A Study in Game-Theoretic Modeling and Analysis*. Cambridge University Press, Cambridge.

[23] A. E. Roth and J. H. Vande Vate. 1991. Incentives in two-sided matching with random stable mechanisms. *Economic theory* 1, 1 (1991), 31–44.

[24] S. Suh and Q. Wen. 2008. Subgame perfect implementation of stable matchings in marriage problems. *Social Choice and Welfare* 31, 1 (2008), 163–174.

[25] Q. Tang and J. Yu. 2014. A new perspective on Kesten's school choice with consent idea. *Journal of Economic Theory* 154 (2014), 543–561.

[26] J. Wako. 2010. A polynomial-time algorithm to find von Neumann-Morgenstern stable matchings in marriage games. *Algorithmica* 58, 1 (2010), 188–220.

# The Big Match with a Clock and a Bit of Memory

KRISTOFFER ARNSFELT HANSEN, Aarhus University
RASMUS IBSEN-JENSEN, IST Austria
ABRAHAM NEYMAN, Hebrew University

The Big Match is a multi-stage two-player game. In each stage Player 1 hides one or two pebbles in his hand, and his opponent has to guess that number; Player 1 loses a point if Player 2 is correct, and otherwise he wins a point. As soon as Player 1 hides one pebble, the players cannot change their choices in any future stage.

Blackwell and Ferguson (1968) give an $\varepsilon$-optimal strategy for Player 1 that hides, in each stage, one pebble with a probability that depends on the entire past history. Any strategy that depends just on the clock *or* on a finite memory is worthless. The long-standing natural open problem has been whether every strategy that depends just on the clock *and* a finite memory is worthless. We prove that there is such a strategy that is $\varepsilon$-optimal. In fact, we show that just two states of memory are sufficient.

Full Paper: https://ideas.repec.org/p/huj/dispap/dp716.html

CCS Concepts: • **Mathematics of computing → Stochastic processes**; • **Applied computing → Economics**;

Additional Key Words and Phrases: Stochastic Games; Markov Strategies; Bounded memory

The Big Match is a multi-stage two-player game. In each stage Player 1 hides one or two pebbles in his hand, and his opponent has to guess that number; Player 1 loses a point if Player 2 is correct, and otherwise he wins a point. As soon as Player 1 hides one pebble, the players cannot change their choices in any future stage.

The Big Match was introduced by Gillette [2] and has been much studied, in part due to its arguably being the most basic game model that illustrates the difficulty of balancing the trade-off between short- and long-term strategic considerations.

In the Big Match, Player 2 can guarantee that Player 1 gets zero points on average, independently of the number of stages, by guessing odd or even with equal probability and independently in each stage. Executing such a strategy does not require that Player 2 know past history, the number of stages, or the stage number. However, the situation of Player 1 is completely different! Henceforth, unless otherwise mentioned, a strategy refers to a strategy of Player 1.

If Player 1 knows the number of stages, $n$, in advance, he can guarantee that he gets (at least) zero points on average. To guarantee this, he *must* hide one pebble with probability $\frac{1}{k+1}$ when $k$ stages remain. Thus, for example, in the last stage he hides one or two pebbles with equal probability, and in the first stage he hides one pebble with probability $\frac{1}{n+1}$. Executing such a strategy requires that Player 1 know the stage number and the number of stages, but it does not require that Player 1 know past history.

It follows from the above that if Player 1 does not know the number of stages $n$ in advance, then he has no way of guaranteeing (at least) zero points (per stage) on average. This has led researchers

Authors' addresses: Kristoffer Arnsfelt Hansen, Aarhus University, arnsfelt@cs.au.dk; Rasmus Ibsen-Jensen, IST Austria, ribsen@ist.ac.at; Abraham Neyman, Hebrew University, aneyman@huji.ac.il.


*ACM EC'18, June 18–22, 2018, Ithaca, NY, USA.* ACM ISBN 978-1-4503-4529-3/18/06.
https://doi.org/10.1145/3219166.3219198

to look for strategies that guarantee close to zero per stage on average in all sufficiently long Big Match games.

Any strategy in the Big Match has to decide on the stopping stage. A natural possibility is just to specify in advance the probability of each stage being the stopping stage. Such a strategy is called a Markov strategy. It has long been known, and it is easy to verify, that any Markov strategy in the Big Match is *worthless*; i.e., for any $\varepsilon > 0$ it does not guarantee more than $-1 + \varepsilon$ points (per stage) on average in any sufficiently long Big Match game.

The principle of sunk cost seems to imply that optimizing from any point onwards should be independent of the past, and hence any optimization of the long-run average of the rewards can be achieved by a Markov strategy. Since any Markov strategy is worthless, one may erroneously conclude that any strategy is worthless.

However, this is not the case! Blackwell and Ferguson [1] introduced worthy (i.e., not worthless) strategies that prescribe the choice in each stage as a function of past history. Moreover, Blackwell and Ferguson introduced, for every $\varepsilon > 0$, a strategy that is *$\varepsilon$-optimal*; namely, it guarantees at least $-\varepsilon$ points (per stage) on average in all sufficiently long games.

The question that arises is how much dependence on past history is needed for an $\varepsilon$-optimal strategy, or even a worthy one. This dependence is formalized using the following concept.

A *memory-based* strategy in the Big Match is a strategy in which the conditional probability of hiding one pebble depends on the current memory state and the clock (i.e, the stage number). The memory state is updated as a stochastic function of the current memory and of the guess of Player 2 in the previous stage, as well as of the clock.

The $\varepsilon$-optimal strategies introduced by Blackwell and Ferguson [1, Theorem 1 and Theorem 2] are memory-based, and the first of these is clock-independent; i.e., the hiding and memory updating do not depend on the clock. The memory state is simply the difference between the number of odd and even guesses; hence, up to stage $n$ it takes integer values in the interval $[-n, n]$.

The $\varepsilon$-optimal strategy by Hansen, Ibsen-Jensen, and Koucký [3] is memory-based and clock-independent. The memory state can be encoded so that, with high probability, up to stage $n$ it takes integer values in $[0, \ln^c n]$, for some constant $c$ (and $n > 3$).

On the other hand, all memory-based strategies that have a finite set of memory states and either are clock-independent (see, e.g., [4]) or have a deterministic memory update function [3] are worthless in the Big Match.

It has been a long-standing natural open problem whether there exists a worthy memory-based strategy that has a finite set of memory states.

We answers this question positively. We show that, for every $\varepsilon > 0$, there is such a strategy that is $\varepsilon$-optimal. Moreover, it is a two-memory strategy; namely, it has a two-element memory set.

Our positive result applies to the infinite game as well. In the infinite game, the average win per stage need not be well defined, as the average number of wins over the first $n$ stages need not converge. Nonetheless, our result is as strong as possible given that the strategy's $\varepsilon$-optimality in the infinite game is for the limit inferior.

## REFERENCES

[1] David Blackwell and T. S. Ferguson. 1968. The Big Match. *The Annals of Mathematical Statistics* 39, 1 (1968), 159–163.

[2] Dean Gillette. 1957. Stochastic games with zero stop probabilities. In *Contributions to the Theory of Games III.* Ann. Math. Studies, Vol. 39. Princeton University Press, 179–187.

[3] Kristoffer Arnsfelt Hansen, Rasmus Ibsen-Jensen, and Michal Koucký. 2016. The Big Match in Small Space - (Extended Abstract). In *Proceedings of 9th International Symposium on Algorithmic Game Theory, SAGT 2016 (Lecture Notes in Computer Science),* Martin Gairing and Rahul Savani (Eds.), Vol. 9928. Springer, 64–76.

[4] Sylvain Sorin. 2002. *A First Course on Zero Sum Repeated Games.* Springer.

# Incremental Strategy Generation for Stackelberg Equilibria in Extensive-Form Games

JAKUB ČERNÝ, Czech Technical University in Prague, Czech Republic
BRANISLAV BOŠANSKÝ, Czech Technical University in Prague, Czech Republic
CHRISTOPHER KIEKINTVELD, University of Texas at El Paso, USA

Dynamic interaction appears in many real-world scenarios where players are able to observe (perhaps imperfectly) the actions of another player and react accordingly. We consider the baseline representation of dynamic games—the extensive form—and focus on computing Stackelberg equilibrium (SE), where the leader commits to a strategy to which the follower plays a best response. For one-shot games (e.g., security games), strategy-generation (SG) algorithms offer dramatic speed-up by incrementally expanding the strategy spaces. However, a direct application of SG to extensive-form games (EFGs) does not bring a similar speed-up since it typically results in a nearly-complete strategy space. Our contributions are twofold: (1) for the first time we introduce an algorithm that allows us to incrementally expand the strategy space to find a SE in EFGs; (2) we introduce a heuristic variant of the algorithm that is theoretically incomplete, but in practice allows us to find exact (or close-to optimal) Stackelberg equilibrium by constructing a significantly smaller strategy space. Our experimental evaluation confirms that we are able to compute SE by considering only a fraction of the strategy space that often leads to a significant speed-up in computation times.

CCS Concepts: • **Theory of computation → Algorithmic game theory; Exact and approximate computation of equilibria;**

Additional Key Words and Phrases: Extensive-form games; strong Stackelberg equilibrium; correlated equilibrium; strategy generation

## 1 INTRODUCTION

Many game-theoretic models inspired by real-world scenarios are dynamic, in that they model sequences of interacting moves and observations by the players. The players may have

This research was sponsored by the Army Research Laboratory and was accomplished under Cooperative Agreement Number W911NF-13-2-0045 (ARL Cyber Security CRA). The views and conclusions contained in this document are those of the authors and should not be interpreted as representing the official policies, either expressed or implied, of the Army Research Laboratory or the U.S. Government. The U.S. Government is authorized to reproduce and distribute reprints for Government purposes not with standing any copyright notation here on.
Access to computing and storage facilities owned by parties and projects contributing to the National Grid Infrastructure MetaCentrum provided under the programme "Projects of Large Research, Development, and Innovations Infrastructures" (CESNET LM2015042), is greatly appreciated.

Authors' addresses: Jakub Černý, Czech Technical University in Prague, Technická 2, Prague, 16627, Czech Republic, jakub.cerny@agents.fel.cvut.cz; Branislav Bošanský, Czech Technical University in Prague, Technická 2, Prague, 16627, Czech Republic, bosansky@fel.cvut.cz; Christopher Kiekintveld, University of Texas at El Paso, 500 West University Ave. El Paso, Texas, 79968-0518, USA, cdkiekintveld@utep.edu.


*ACM EC'18, June 18–22, 2018, Ithaca, NY, USA.* ACM ISBN 978-1-4503-5829-3/18/06...$15.00
https://doi.org/10.1145/3219166.3219219

uncertainty about the effects of actions and may receive only imperfect observations of the actions chosen by other players. The baseline formalism for reasoning about dynamic games with a limited horizon is *extensive form games* (EFGs), which can be represented using game trees. Many scenarios can be modeled as EFG, including card games like poker [5, 15], security games with patrols (e.g., examples in [4, 11]), computer network attacks [6, 7], and synthetic biology games in medicine [16].

The roles of the players in many real-world games are asymmetric. One player (*the leader*) has the power to commit to a strategy and the other player (*the follower*) plays a best response. For example, the leader can correspond to a market leader with the power to set the price for items or services, or a defense agency committing to a security protocol to protect critical facilities. Optimal strategies for the players in such situations are described by the Stackelberg Equilibrium (SE) [12, 22]. We follow the common assumption in the literature that the follower break ties in favor of the leader; hence, we compute a Strong Stackelberg Equilibrium (SSE)[1].

The problem of computing SSE in EFGs is known to be NP-complete [4, 13]. There are several existing algorithms for computing SSE in EFGs. Bošanský and Čermák [4] introduced a mixed-integer linear program (MILP) that extends the sequence form linear program for computing NE in EFGs to SSE [10, 20]. The scalability of this approach was improved by first computing a correlated version of the SSE (called Stackelberg Extensive-Form Correlated Equilibrium, SEFCE) and then using a search to refine the SEFCE into a SSE [19]. Finally, Kroer et al. [11] introduced a novel MILP formulation that incorporates interval uncertainty in the utility of the follower, as well as a limited lookahead approach assuming that the follower is not perfectly rational and can only reason to a limited depth.

We introduce a novel strategy-generation (SG) technique that starts from a small restricted game and incrementally expands the game tree of a two-player extensive-form game to compute SSE. The inspiration for the algorithm is based on previous algorithms that have been very successful for one-shot games (e.g., many types of security games [8, 9, 23]), as well as for zero-sum sequential [2, 14, 18] and EFGs [3]. However, none of these previous SG approaches translates directly to a practical algorithm for EFGs. In the first case, the main step in each iteration is to add sequences of actions of the leader that can potentially increase the objective of a (MI)LP. This is done by computing the reduced costs for variables that are not included in the program yet [8]. We investigate this approach for EFG in Section 3, but encounter a fundamental problem in that this approach adds many unnecessary sequences, leading to "reduced" games that are comparable in size to the original. The SG algorithm for zero-sum EFGs relies heavily on the zero-sum assumption and expands the game tree by adding best-response sequences into the game tree. Unfortunately, this approach does not converge to SSE in a general sum EFG.

We can now state the two main challenges we must solve to develop an effective SG algorithm for computing SSE in EFGs: *(1) What is the representation of the restricted game, and in particular, the abstracted parts of the game tree? (2) What is the methodology for expanding the restricted game?* We address both of these challenges and show that (1) the abstracted parts of the game tree can be effectively represented using a subset of pareto-optimal outcomes; (2) the expansion can be done when an outcome from the abstracted part of the game tree is used in the current solution of the restricted game. Our technique is independent and can be combined with any of the existing algorithms

[1] We expect that our general approach would be applicable for computing other variations of Stackelberg equilibrium, but leave this to future work.

for computing SSE. We use the SEFCE-based algorithm [19] since it has the best-known scalability. The LP for computing SEFCE is quadratic in the size of the game tree, so constructing a smaller game tree should also have a significant performance benefit. In addition to an exact algorithm, we also introduce heuristic variants that lose theoretical guarantees on convergence in exchange for much smaller games; our experimental results show that the heuristic variant can compute exact Stackelberg equilibrium of games with more than $10^7$ states by constructing only 8% of the original SEFCE LP. More aggressive heuristics are able to find near-optimal solutions considering only 3% of the LP, while the outcome for the leader is on 6.38% worse compared to the optimum. Often, such a dramatic reduction in the size of the LP leads to significant speed-up in computation times.

## 2 EXTENSIVE-FORM GAMES AND STACKELBERG SOLUTION CONCEPTS

Extensive-form games model sequential interactions between players and can be visually represented as game trees. Formally, a two-player EFG is defined as a tuple $G = (\mathcal{N}, \mathcal{H}, \mathcal{Z}, \mathcal{A}, u, \mathcal{C}, \mathcal{I})$: $\mathcal{N} = \{l, f\}$ is a set of players, the leader and the follower. We use $i$ to refer to one of the players, and $-i$ to refer to his opponent. $\mathcal{H}$ denotes a finite set of *nodes* in the game tree. Each node corresponds to a unique *history* of actions taken by all players and chance from the root of the game; hence, we use the terms history and node interchangeably. We say that $h$ is a *prefix* of $h'$ ($h \sqsubseteq h'$) if $h$ lies on a path from the root of the game tree to $h'$. $\mathcal{A}$ denotes the set of all actions. $\mathcal{Z} \subseteq \mathcal{H}$ is the set of all *terminal nodes* of the game. For each $z \in \mathcal{Z}$ we define a *utility function* for each player $i$ ($u_i : \mathcal{Z} \to \mathbb{R}$). A chance player selects actions based on a fixed probability distribution known to all players. Function $\mathcal{C} : \mathcal{H} \to [0, 1]$ denotes the probability of reaching node $h$ due to chance; $\mathcal{C}(h)$ is the product of chance probabilities of all actions in history $h$.

Imperfect observation of player $i$ is modeled via *information sets* $\mathcal{I}_i$ that form a partition over $h \in \mathcal{H}$ where $i$ takes action. Player $i$ cannot distinguish between nodes in any information set $I \in \mathcal{I}_i$. We overload the notation and use $A(I_i)$ to denote possible actions available in each node from an information set $I_i$. We assume that action $a$ uniquely identifies the information set where it is available. We assume *perfect recall*, which means that players remember the history of their own actions and all information gained during the course of the game. As a consequence, all nodes in any information set $I_i$ have the same history of actions for player $i$.

*Pure strategies* $\Pi_i$ assign one action for each $I \in \mathcal{I}_i$. A more efficient representation in the form of *reduced pure strategies* $\Pi_i^*$ assigns one action for each $I \in \mathcal{I}_i$ reachable while playing according to this strategy. A *mixed strategy* $\delta_i \in \Delta_i$ is a probability distribution over $\Pi_i$. For any pair of strategies $\delta \in \Delta = (\Delta_l, \Delta_f)$ we use $u_i(\delta) = u_i(\delta_i, \delta_{-i})$ for the expected outcome of the game for player $i$ when players follow strategies $\delta$. A *best response* of player $i$ to the opponent's strategy $\delta_{-i}$ is a strategy $\delta_i^{BR} \in BR_i(\delta_{-i})$, where $u_i(\delta_i^{BR}, \delta_{-i}) \geq u_i(\delta_i', \delta_{-i})$ for all $\delta_i' \in \Delta_i$.

Strategies in EFGs with perfect recall can be compactly represented by using the sequence form [10]. A *sequence* $\sigma_i \in \Sigma_i$ is an ordered list of actions taken by a single player $i$ in history $h$. $\emptyset$ stands for the empty sequence (i.e., a sequence with no actions). A sequence $\sigma_i \in \Sigma_i$ can be extended by a single valid action $a$ taken by player $i$, written as $\sigma_i a = \sigma_i'$. We say that $\sigma_i$ is a *prefix* of $\sigma_i'$ ($\sigma_i \sqsubseteq \sigma_i'$) if $\sigma_i'$ is obtained by finite number (possibly zero) of extensions of $\sigma_i$. We use $seq_i(I_i)$ and $seq_i(h)$ to denote the sequence of $i$ leading to $I_i$ and $h$, respectively. We use the function $inf_i(\sigma_i')$ to obtain the information set in which the last action of the sequence $\sigma_i'$ is taken. For an empty sequence, function $inf_i(\emptyset)$ returns the information set of the root node. A mixed strategy of a player can now be represented as a *realization plan* ($r_i : \Sigma_i \to \mathbb{R}$). A realization plan for a sequence $\sigma_i$ is the probability that player $i$ will play $\sigma_i$ under the assumption that the opponent plays to allow the actions specified in $\sigma_i$ to be played. By $g_i : \Sigma_l \times \Sigma_f \to \mathbb{R}$ we denote the *extended utility function*, $g_i(\sigma_l, \sigma_f) = \sum_{z \in \mathcal{Z} | seq_l(z) = \sigma_l \wedge seq_f(z) = \sigma_f} u_i(z) C(z)$. If no leaf is reachable with a pair of sequences $\sigma$, the value of $g_i$ is 0.

***Stackelberg Solution Concepts in EFGs.*** We provide a formal definition of Strong Stackelberg Equilibrium (SSE) (e.g., in [12]) and Stackelberg Extensive-Form Correlated Equilibrium (SEFCE) [1, 13] and give the intuition on an example game.

*Definition 2.1.* A strategy profile $\delta = (\delta_l, \delta_f)$ is a *Strong Stackelberg Equilibrium* if $\delta_l$ is an optimal strategy of the leader given that the follower best-responds. Formally:

$$(\delta_l, \delta_f) = \underset{\delta'_l \in \Delta_l, \delta'_f \in BR_i(\delta'_l)}{\arg\max} \; u_l(\delta'_l, \delta'_f). \tag{1}$$

The SSE of the game in Figure 1[2] (the first utility in every leaf is for the leader, second for the follower) prescribes the leader to commit to playing actions $b_7$ and $b_{10}$ in the information sets in the left subtree and $b_{11}$ in the right subtree. The strategy of the follower is then to play $b_1$ in the root of the game and $b_4$ in the left subtree, leading to the expected utility of 1 for the leader.

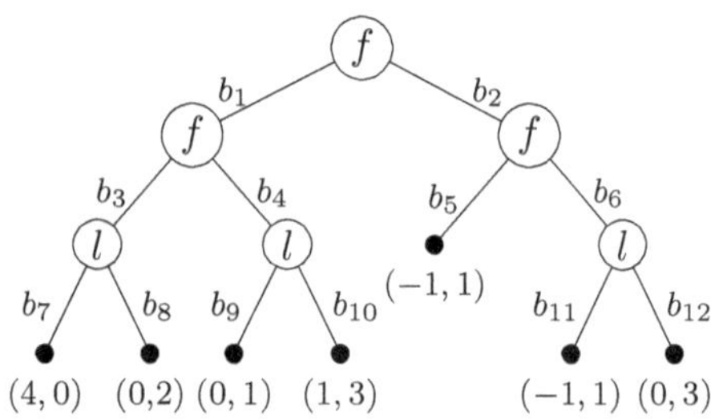


| | $\{b_1, b_3\}$ | $\{b_1, b_4\}$ | $\{b_2, b_5\}$ | $\{b_2, b_6\}$ |
|---|---|---|---|---|
| $\{b_7, b_9, b_{11}\}$ | 0.25 | 0 | 0 | 0 |
| $\{b_7, b_9, b_{12}\}$ | 0 | 0 | 0 | 0 |
| $\{b_7, b_{10}, b_{11}\}$ | 0 | 0.5 | 0 | 0 |
| $\{b_7, b_{10}, b_{12}\}$ | 0 | 0 | 0 | 0 |
| $\{b_8, b_9, b_{11}\}$ | 0.25 | 0 | 0 | 0 |
| $\{b_8, b_9, b_{12}\}$ | 0 | 0 | 0 | 0 |
| $\{b_8, b_{10}, b_{11}\}$ | 0 | 0 | 0 | 0 |
| $\{b_8, b_{10}, b_{12}\}$ | 0 | 0 | 0 | 0 |

| | $\emptyset$ | $b_7$ | $b_8$ | $b_9$ | $b_{10}$ | $b_{11}$ | $b_{12}$ |
|---|---|---|---|---|---|---|---|
| $\emptyset$ | 1 | 1 | 0 | 0.5 | 0.5 | 0 | 0 |
| $b_1$ | 0.75 | 0.75 | 0 | 0.25 | 0.5 | - | - |
| $b_2$ | 0.25 | 0.25 | 0 | 0.25 | 0 | - | - |
| $b_1b_3$ | 0.5 | 0.5 | 0 | 0.5 | 0 | - | - |
| $b_1b_4$ | 0.5 | 0.5 | 0 | 0 | 0.5 | - | - |
| $b_2b_5$ | 1 | 1 | 0 | - | - | 0 | 0 |
| $b_2b_6$ | 0 | 0 | 0 | - | - | 0 | 0 |

Fig. 1. (Left) An EFG with different SEFCE and SSE. Each internal node is labeled by a player who acts in this node, while under every terminal node is a tuple of utilities obtained by the first player and the second player, respectively. Every edge is labeled by an action performed on a way from the node above to the node below. The direction of the edges is omitted, but the tree is assumed to be traversed from top to bottom. (Right Up) The SEFCE distribution over $\Pi^*$. (Right Down) The SEFCE correlation plan.

In SEFCE we allow the leader to send signals to the follower and condition his strategy on sent signals. More specifically, the leader chooses $\pi^*_f \in \Pi^*_f$ as the recommendations for the follower according to SEFCE before the game starts. The actual recommendation to play some action $a \in A(I_f)$ is revealed to the follower only after he reaches $I_f$. Therefore, the follower only knows the past and current recommendations, and the probability distribution from which the recommendations are drawn in the future.

[2]The example is from [19].

*Definition 2.2.* A probability distribution $\lambda$ on reduced pure strategy profiles $\Pi^*$ is called a *Stackelberg Extensive-Form Correlated Equilibrium* if it maximizes the leader's utility subject to the constraint that whenever play reaches an information set $I$ where the follower can act, the follower is recommended an action $\tilde{a}$ according to $\lambda$ such that the follower cannot gain by unilaterally deviating from $\tilde{a}$ in $I$ and possibly in all succeeding information sets given the posterior on the probability distribution of the strategy of the leader, defined by the actions taken by the leader so far.

SEFCE of the EFG in Figure 1 is shown in the top table, with the rows being labeled by the leader's strategies $\Pi_l^*$ and the columns by the follower's strategies $\Pi_f^*$). At the beginning of the game, the leader decides to send either $\{b_1, b_3\}$ or $\{b_1, b_4\}$ as a recommendation to the follower according to the probabilities in the table. In both cases, the follower commits to playing action $b_{11}$ in order to incentivize the follower to play $b_1$. If the follower receives $b_3$, the leader plays action $b_9$ and mixes uniformly between $b_7$ and $b_8$ in his right-most information set. If the follower is recommended $b_4$, the leader commits to playing $b_7$ and $b_{10}$. The expected utility of the leader in this equilibrium is 1.5, which is strictly better than in the SSE.

***Using SEFCE for computing SSE.*** The correlated variant of the Stackelberg equilibrium can be used for computing SSE. The main idea is to find SEFCE and then iteratively add constraints so the recommendations for the follower are such that in each information set, the follower can receive only a single action to be played as a recommendation. In that case, the follower is playing a pure best response and the strategy of the leader is the same as in the SSE.

We now describe the linear program for computing SEFCE. In this linear program, the strategies of the players are represented using a correlation plan for relevant sequences. The sequences are termed *relevant* when decisions at the information sets reachable by one of the sequences can affect the decisions at the information sets reachable by the other sequence.

*Definition 2.3 (Relevant sequences [21]).* A pair of sequences $(\sigma_1, \sigma_2)$ is termed *relevant* if and only if $\exists i \in \{1,2\}$ either $\sigma_i = \emptyset$ or $\exists h, h' \in H, h' \sqsubseteq h; \sigma_i = seq_i(h) \wedge \sigma_{-i} = seq_{-i}(h')$.

The set of sequences of player $-i$ which form a relevant pair with $\sigma_i$ is denoted $rel(\sigma_i)$. For the EFG depicted in Figure 1 $rel(b_1) = rel(b_2) = \Sigma_l$, $rel(b_2b_5) = rel(b_2b_6) = \{\emptyset, b_{11}, b_{12}\}$, and $rel(b_1b_3) = rel(b_1b_4) = \{\emptyset, b_7, b_8, b_9, b_{10}\}$. Now it is possible to define a generalization of a realization plan suitable for joint probabilities of pairs of sequences, called a *correlation plan.* We have to ensure that in mutually relevant information sets the consistency of recommendations cannot be violated.

*Definition 2.4 (A correlation plan [21]).* A partial function $p : \Sigma_1 \times \Sigma_2 \to \mathbb{R}$ is a correlation plan if there is a probability distribution $\lambda$ on the set of reduced strategy profiles $\Pi^*$ so that for each relevant sequence pair $(\sigma_1, \sigma_2)$, the term $p(\sigma_1, \sigma_2)$ equals to $p(\sigma_1, \sigma_2) = \sum_{(\pi_1,\pi_2)\in\Pi^*} \lambda(\pi_1, \pi_2)$ where $\pi_1, \pi_2$ prescribe playing all of the actions in $\sigma_1$ and $\sigma_2$, respectively.

The correlation plans describe a joint realization probability $p(\sigma_l, \sigma_f)$ that a sequence $\sigma_f$ is recommended to the follower, in case the leader plays sequence $\sigma_l$. The bottom table of Figure 1 represents the correlation plan of the SEFCE strategies. The rows of the table are labeled by $\Sigma_f$, while columns are labeled by $\Sigma_l$. In every row identified by $\sigma_f$ is depicted the probability of the leader playing the corresponding column sequence in case the follower is recommended the sequence $\sigma_f$ and follows his recommendations. The irrelevant pairs of sequences are denoted '-'. The correlation plan of every relevant pair $(\sigma_l, \sigma_f)$ is the sum of all probabilities of pure strategies containing actions from $\sigma_l$ and $\sigma_f$ in the top table.

In [21] the authors proved that correlation plans are sufficient to characterize the set of extensive-form correlated equilibrium (EFCE) in two-player games with no chance nodes. In [19] the authors used this characterization to formulate the following linear program computing SEFCE.

THEOREM 2.5 (STACKELBERG EXTENSIVE-FORM CORRELATED EQUILIBRIUM IN TWO–PLAYER GAME WITHOUT CHANCE MOVES [19]). *The distribution $\lambda$ on $\Pi^*$ defines a SEFCE if and only if $\lambda$ is a solution of the following linear program that maximizes leader's expected utility*

$$\max_{p,v} \sum_{\sigma_l \in \Sigma_l} \sum_{\sigma_f \in \Sigma_f} p(\sigma_l, \sigma_f) g_l(\sigma_l, \sigma_f) \tag{2}$$

*and the respective correlation plan $p$ satisfies*

$$p(\emptyset, \emptyset) = 1; \quad 0 \leq p(\sigma_l, \sigma_f) \leq 1 \tag{3}$$

$$p(seq_l(I), \sigma_f) = \sum_{a \in A(I)} p(seq_l(I)a, \sigma_f) \quad \forall I \in \mathcal{I}_l, \forall \sigma_f \in rel(\sigma_l) \tag{4}$$

$$p(\sigma_l, seq_f(I)) = \sum_{a \in A(I)} p(\sigma_l, seq_f(I)a) \quad \forall I \in \mathcal{I}_f, \forall \sigma_l \in rel(\sigma_f) \tag{5}$$

$$\begin{aligned} v(\sigma_f) = \sum_{\sigma_l \in rel(\sigma_f)} p(\sigma_l, \sigma_f) g_f(\sigma_l, \sigma_f) + \\ + \sum_{I \in \mathcal{I}_f;\ seq_f(I) = \sigma_f} \sum_{a \in A_f(I)} v(\sigma_f a) \quad \forall \sigma_f \in \Sigma_f \end{aligned} \tag{6}$$

$$\begin{aligned} v(I, \sigma_f) \geq \sum_{\sigma_l \in rel(\sigma_f)} p(\sigma_l, \sigma_f) g_f(\sigma_l, seq_f(I)a) + \sum_{I' \in \mathcal{I}_f;\ seq_f(I') = seq_f(I)a} v(I', \sigma_f) \\ \forall I \in \mathcal{I}_f, \forall \sigma_f \in \bigcup_{h \in I} rel(seq_l(h)), \forall a \in A(I) \end{aligned} \tag{7}$$

$$v(seq_f(I)a) = v(I, seq_f(I)a) \qquad \forall I \in \mathcal{I}_f, \forall a \in A(I) \tag{8}$$

The first three constraints enforce the consistency of the correlation plan. The following constraint ensures that $v_{\sigma_f}$ is a representation of an expected payoff of the follower when he plays $\sigma_f$, assuming he follows his recommendations. The constraint consists of two parts – the first sum computes the expected utility of the leafs reached by playing according to $\sigma_l$ and $\sigma_f$, the second sum adds the contribution of the expected utility of information sets reachable by all the extensions of $\sigma_f$. The next constraint guarantees that the expected payoff $v(I, \sigma_f)$ is the maximum over all possible sequences leaving the information set $I$ (denoted as $seq_f(I)a$ for all possible actions $a \in A(I)$) after the follower is recommended to play $\sigma_f$. Finally, the last constraint forces the move which is recommended to the follower in the information set $I$ to be optimal. The value of SEFCE is always greater or equal than the value of SSE.

THEOREM 2.6 ([19]). *Assume a solution of the LP as described in Theorem 2.5. The objective value is greater than or equal to the expected utility of the leader in SSE.*

As stated before, SSE can be reached by a branch-and-bound algorithm [19] so that the recommendations for the follower are unique – the authors define *inconsistent recommendations* that are then fixed by a branch-and-bound type of search algorithm (BnB).

*Definition 2.7 (Inconsistent recommendations [19]).* We say that $p$ uses *inconsistent recommendation* in $I \in \mathcal{I}_f$ if and only if $p$ defines two different recommendations for the follower in $I$. Formally, $\exists a, a' \in A(I), a \neq a', \exists \sigma_l, \sigma_l' \in \bigcup_{h \in I} seq_l(h)\ p(\sigma_l, seq_f(I)a) > 0 \wedge p(\sigma_l', seq_f(I)a') > 0$. If there exists no such information set we say that $p$ uses only *consistent recommendations.*

**ALGORITHM 1:** BnB-Based Algorithm for computing SSE.

```
Input: An UB-SSE-LP P
Output: leader's expected utility and strategy profile in SSE
M ← {(∞, ∅)}; LB ← −∞; p_c ← ∅
while M ≠ ∅ do
    (UB, m) ← max(M)
    if UB < LB then
        return (LB, p_c)
    apply(m, P)
    if feasible(P) then
        (value, p) ← solve(P)
        I_in ← inconsistentRecommendations(p)
        if I_in = ∅ then
            if value > LB then LB ← value; p_c ← p
        else addRestrictions((UB, m), M, I_in, value)
    revert(m, P)
return (LB, p_c)
```

The Algorithm 1 can be decomposed into iterative applications of the following steps: (1) solve an LP $P$ in line 2, (2) find the set of information sets of the follower with inconsistent recommendations $\mathcal{I}_{in}$ in line 1, and (3) restrict the leader's strategy to use only consistent recommendations in $\mathcal{I}_{in}$ by adding new constraints $m$ to the LP $P$ in line 1. The restrictions are added recursively until a restricted LP for SEFCE uses only consistent correlation plan $p$. At the beginning, the algorithm is initiated with an LP computing SEFCE.

## 3 CHALLENGES IN STRATEGY GENERATION FOR COMPUTING SSE IN EFGS

We now describe the general framework of a strategy generation (SG) technique for computing a Strong Stackelberg Equilibrium (SSE) in extensive-form games (EFGs). We formally define a restricted game as a subgraph of the original game tree and describe the baseline SG algorithm that extends the algorithm for one-shot games [8]. However, we show on a simple example that such a direct adaptation can easily generate the full game tree.

### 3.1 Strategy Generation for SSE Using Reduced Costs

The main idea of the previous approach [8] is to decompose the mathematical program for computing SSE into a master problem and a slave problem. In the master problem, we solve for SSE of a smaller restricted game (RG), where the RG is a subset of the original unrestricted game. In the slave problem, we search for such strategies of the leader to be added into the RG which have the largest positive impact on the objective, given the solution of the master problem. The impact is measured using *reduced costs*, calculated from the dual solution.

We translate this idea for computing SSE in EFGs while exploiting SEFCE solution concept. Therefore, our master program corresponds to the LP formulation of SEFCE (LP in Theorem 2.5) and the slave problem identifies which strategies of the leader should be added to the restricted game.

After the SEFCE is found, the BnB algorithm is called in order to compute SSE. The only change from the original version depicted in Algortihm 1 is that it solves for SEFCE in the restricted game and after adding every restriction, the algorithm checks whether the RG should be expanded.

***Iterative Construction of SEFCE LP.*** We now detail how we translate this idea for computing SSE in EFGs. First, our master program – the LP formulation of SEFCE – will be solved for a restricted game that can be fully specified by the subset of sequences of the leader (called *allowed sequences*). Similarly to [3], we define the sets of nodes, actions, and information sets as subsets of the original unrestricted sets based on the allowed sequences. The RG is denoted as $G' = (\mathcal{N}, \mathcal{H}', \mathcal{Z}', \mathcal{A}', u, \mathcal{C}, \mathcal{I}')$ and the set of all sequences in the RG is denoted $\Sigma'$.

We assume the RG is always closed on prefixes of leader's sequences, such that for any leader's sequence in RG, all follower's relevant sequences are in RG. The leader's sequences hence fully define the RG. The set $\mathcal{H}'$ can be derived as

$$\mathcal{H}' \leftarrow \{h \in \mathcal{H} : \forall i \in \mathcal{N}\ seq_i(h) \in \Sigma'\}, \tag{9}$$

and the restriction $\mathcal{A}'$ of $\mathcal{A}$ to the sequences in the RG is constructed as

$$\mathcal{A}'(h) \leftarrow \{a \in \mathcal{A}(h) : ha \in \mathcal{H}'\} \quad \forall h \in \mathcal{H}'. \tag{10}$$

The leafs in the RG are $\mathcal{Z}' = \mathcal{Z} \cap \mathcal{H}'$. Finally, the information sets of the RG are derived as

$$\mathcal{I}'_i \leftarrow \{I_i \in \mathcal{I}_i : \exists h \in \mathcal{H}' \cap I_i\} \quad \forall i \in \mathcal{N}. \tag{11}$$

In the slave problem, we search for the leader's sequences not contained in the RG. The dual solution as for computing the reduced costs follows:

$$rc(\sigma_l) = \max_{\sigma_f \in rel(\sigma_l)} rc(p(\sigma_l, \sigma_f)), \tag{12}$$

where

$$\begin{aligned} rc(p(\sigma_l, \sigma_f)) &= g_l(\sigma_l, \sigma_f) - \sum_{I_l \in \mathcal{I}'_l : seq(I_l) = \sigma_l} d_4(I_l, \sigma_f) + d_4(inf(\sigma_l), \sigma_f) - \\ &- \sum_{I_f \in \mathcal{I}'_f : seq(I_f) = \sigma_f} d_5(I_f, \sigma_l) + d_5(inf(\sigma_f), \sigma_l) - d_6(\sigma_f) + \\ &+ \sum_{I_f \in \mathcal{I}'_f : \sigma_f \in \bigcup_{h \in I} rel(seq_l(h))} \sum_{a \in \mathcal{A}'(I_f)} g_f(\sigma_l, seq_f(I_f)a) d_7(I_f, \sigma_f, a), \end{aligned} \tag{13}$$

and the $d_j(\ldots)$, $j \in \{4, 5, 6, 7\}$, are the dual values of the constraints 4, 5, 6 and 7 in the current solution of the LP computing SEFCE. In order for the algorithm to guarantee a convergence to an optimum, the RG does not contain any temporary leafs, in contrast to [3]. After enumerating the costs for all leader's sequences outside the RG, the sequences with the positive reduced costs $\hat{\Sigma}$ are added to the RG. Simultaneously, we include also all relevant sequences for the follower. The sequences $\Sigma'$ hence change as

$$\Sigma' \leftarrow \Sigma' \cup \hat{\Sigma} \cup rel\left(\hat{\Sigma}\right). \tag{14}$$

The LP for the restricted game is then extended by generating new correlation plan constraints 4 and 5; and constraints 6, 7 and 8 in case a new follower's sequence enter the RG. The new correlation pairs $p(\sigma_l, \sigma_f)$ are added into the already existing constraints and to the objective.

At the beginning of the algorithm, the initial restricted game is constructed using the sequences forming an arbitrary reduced pure strategy of the leader. In practice, we started from the left-most branch of the game tree and continued adding the sequences of the leader until we arrived to the full reduced pure strategy. The process of solving the master problem and the slave problems is then repeated until all remaining leader sequences out of the RG have a non-positive cost.

### 3.2 Limitations of Reduced Costs for SSE in EFGs

However, the practical experiments with reduced costs show that the final sizes of the RGs often reach the size of the original game.

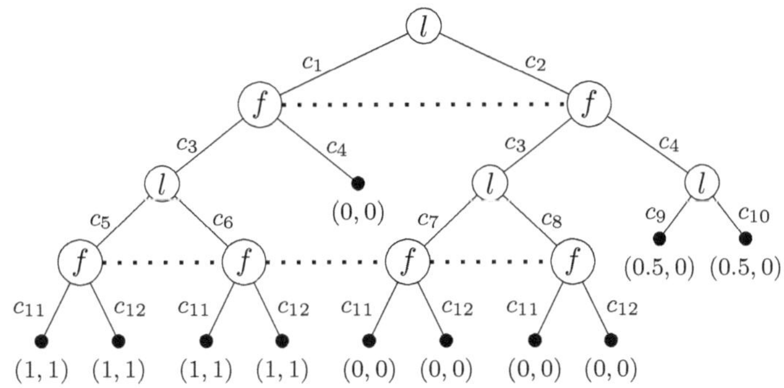


Fig. 2. An example of an EFG where the final RG for the strategy generation with reduced costs is equal to the complete game. The nodes which belong to the same information set are connected by a dashed line. Otherwise, the figure follows a standard denotation of an extensive-form game.

*Example 3.1.* As an example, consider an EFG depicted in Figure 2. At the beginning, the RG is initialized as

$$\Sigma' \leftarrow \{\emptyset, c_1, c_1c_5, c_3, c_4, c_{11}, c_{12}\}. \tag{15}$$

Note that $\Sigma'$ already describes a SEFCE in this game. After the first iteration, the sequences $\hat{\Sigma} = \{c_1c_6, c_2, c_2c_9, c_2c_{10}\}$ are added into the RG. $c_1c_6, c_2c_9$ and $c_2c_{10}$ are included, because they lead to the leafs with the positive utility and no dual variable is able to induce a non-positive reduced cost. The sequence $c_2$ is added because of the positive value of the dual variable $(4)(inf(c_2), \emptyset)$ used in computing $rc(p(c_2, \emptyset))$. The RG is hence extended into

$$\begin{aligned}\Sigma' \leftarrow \{&\emptyset, c_1, c_1c_5, c_1c_6, c_2, c_2c_9, c_2c_{10},\\ &c_3, c_3c_{11}, c_3c_{12}, c_4, c_{11}, c_{12}\}.\end{aligned} \tag{16}$$

In the second iteration, the positive value of the dual variable $(4)(inf(c_2c_7), c_4)$ enforces adding also sequences $c_2c_7, c_2c_8$ and $\Sigma = \Sigma'$, i.e. the RG in equal to the complete game.

The algorithm based on reduced costs expands the whole game tree, even though the SSE is clearly located in the left subtree. Our experiments gave comparable results even when the algorithm was modified to add only the sequences with the highest costs, or by initializing the restricted game using either a leaf with the highest utility for the leader, or a Nash equilibrium in the zero-sum variant of the games where the follower's utilities are set to be complementary to the leader's utilities.

**ALGORITHM 2:** Gadget-Based Algorithm for computing SEFCE.

```
Input: An EFG G
Output: leader's expected utility and strategy profile in SEFCE
(M, Σ') ← expand(root(G), ∅)
expansionNeeded ← size(M) > 0
while expansionNeeded do
    for state h in M do
        Σ' ← Σ' ∪ createGadget(h)
    (value, p) ← solve(Σ')
    M ← ∅, E ← getGadgetsToExpand(p)
    expansionNeeded ← False
    for state h in E do
        (M', Σ') ← expand(h, Σ')
        M ← M ∪ M'
        if size(M') > 0 then expansionNeeded ← True
return (value, p)
```

The main problem of this approach is in the inability of the reduced costs to evaluate the true impact of a sequence because the utilities are located only in the leafs. In order to design more effective strategy-generation methods, it is necessary to introduce generalized temporary leafs with utilities for non-terminal sequences. When designing the temporary leafs in the Stackelberg setting, we have to keep in mind that the leader can use the individual leafs to create threats against the follower. He can either intentionally lure the follower into a specific subtree or to punish him in another. In contrast to the double-oracle methods, the temporary leafs have to consist of more complex tree structures than just the single game states.

## 4 GADGET-BASED STRATEGY GENERATION FOR EFGS

We introduce a novel strategy-generation algorithm that follows the intuition and avoids adding complete sequences into the game tree by abstracting selected parts of the game tree. We term these abstractions as *gadgets*: a multi-level subtree is replaced with a gadget consisting of a node of the leader and actions leading directly to leafs that correspond to a subset of leafs of the original subtree. The overall structure of the algorithm is the same as in Section 3. In the master problem, we solve for SEFCE in the RG with the gadgets acting as the temporary leafs while ensuring that the gadget-based restricted game always provides an upper bound on SEFCE of the original game. In the slave problem, we identify reachable gadgets and expand the RG. If no gadget is reachable by a current strategy, we reached the equilibrium and it follows that the subtrees rooted in gadgets are not a part of the equilibrium. Algorithm 2 depicts the main steps of the algorithm. We now describe these steps in more details.

***Construction of Gadgets.*** We explain how gadgets are constructed. Let $h$ be the state of the leader which should serve as the root of the gadget. We find all leafs $Z_h$ reachable from $h$. The leafs can be visualized as points in a two-dimensional space where one dimension correspond to the utility of the leader and the second one corresponds to the utility of the follower (see Figure 4 for an example of this visualization). Since these points represent possible outcomes in the abstracted game tree and the goal is to maximize the utility for the leader, it is sufficient to keep only a subset of $Z_h$ that correspond to the upper convex hull of these points – for each reachable utility of the follower we seek maximal utility of the leader. We add new sequences, such that every gadget leaf is reachable from $h$ by one leader's action. Note that once we add these new sequences to the set of sequences in the RG $\Sigma'$, by the definition of information set, $h$ is no longer a part of the same information set as in the original unrestricted game.

**ALGORITHM 3:** Creating the gadget.

**Input:** A state $h$
**Output:** sequences added to RG
$\hat{\Sigma} \leftarrow \emptyset$
$Z_h \leftarrow$ getLeafsUnder($h$)
$Z_h \leftarrow$ getUpperConvexHull($Z_h$)
**for** *state* $z$ *in* $Z_h$ **do**
  $a_{z,h} \leftarrow$ createNewAction($z$, $h$)
  $\hat{\Sigma} \leftarrow \hat{\Sigma} \cup seq_l(h)a_{z,h}$
**return** $\hat{\Sigma}$

**ALGORITHM 4:** Expanding the gadget.

**Input:** A gadget root $h$, a set of sequences $\Sigma'$
**Output:** new gadget roots, updated set $\Sigma'$
$\Sigma' \leftarrow \Sigma' \backslash \{\sigma \in \Sigma' : \exists z \; \sigma = seq_l(h)a_{z,h}\}$
$H_h \leftarrow$ getShallowestLeaderStates($h$)
**for** *state* $g$ *in* $H_h$ **do**
  $\hat{\Sigma}_l \leftarrow \{\sigma \in \Sigma_l : \sigma \sqsubseteq \sigma_l(g)\}$
  $\hat{\Sigma}_f \leftarrow \{\sigma \in \Sigma_f : \sigma \sqsubseteq \sigma_f(g)\}$
  $\Sigma' \leftarrow \Sigma' \cup \hat{\Sigma}_f \cup \hat{\Sigma}_l$
**return** ($H_h$, $\Sigma'$)

***Expansion of Gadgets.*** Now we describe the expansion of the RG. Let $h$ be the state of the leader which should be expanded and $\Sigma'$ the current set of sequences in the RG. In case $h$ is a root of the gadget, we first delete from $\Sigma'$ all gadget sequences associated with $h$. We search the subtree in the unrestricted game under $h$ and find the set $H_h$ of the shallowest leader's states in each branch, as

$$H_h \leftarrow \{g \in \mathcal{H}_l : \sigma(h) \sqsubseteq seq(g); \nexists g' \in \mathcal{H}_l \; \sigma(h) \sqsubseteq seq(g') \sqsubseteq seq(g)\} \tag{17}$$

For each state $g$ in $H_h$ we add to $\Sigma'$ all prefixes of $seq_l(g)$ and $seq_f(g)$. Finally, all states in $H_h$ are identified as the new gadget roots.

It remains to explain which gadgets have to be expanded, based on the correlation plan $p$ of the current solution. First, we find the set $R$ of all gadgets reachable by $p$ as

$$R \leftarrow \{h \in \mathcal{H}_l : \exists z \; \exists \sigma_f \; p(seq_l(h)a_{z,h}, \sigma_f) > 0\}. \tag{18}$$

We have to ensure the gadgets provide an upper bound on SEFCE. To ensure that, the RG has to be *closed on the information sets of the follower* – whenever a node $h$ where the follower acts is added into the restricted game, all nodes from the information set $I$, such that $h$ belongs to this information set, also have to be added to the restricted game.

LEMMA 4.1. *Let $G'$ be a RG closed on the information sets of the follower. Then for the utility of the leader in SEFCE of $G'$ (denoted as $SEFCE(G')$) it holds that $SEFCE(G') \geq SEFCE(G)$, where $G$ is the complete game.*

PROOF. Because $G'$ is closed on the information sets of the follower, the belief of the follower that he is located in a given state of his information set in RG is fully determined by the strategy of the leader in the RG. Therefore, the strategy of the follower in this information set cannot be affected by any strategy of the leader in the subtrees rooted in the gadgets. Because gadgets assume that leader can always obtain any outcome in the subtree under the gadget, the abstraction represented by a gadget overestimates leader's strategizing ability in the subtree, hence providing an upper bound on $SEFCE(G)$. □

The gadgets which have to be expanded in the current iteration of the algorithm are hence both all the reachable gadgets and also the minimum set of gadgets which will retain the property of the RG being closed on the information sets, given that all gadgets in $R$ are expanded.

The gadget algorithm creates a restricted game similarly to the strategy-generation with the reduced costs. The RG is again fully defined by the sequences of the leader. However, the set $\Sigma'$ is now updated in a more complex manner, as described in the previous paragraphs about creating the gadgets and expanding the gadgets. Let $\tilde{\Sigma} = \Sigma' \backslash \Sigma$. The sets $\mathcal{H}', \mathcal{Z}', \mathcal{A}'$ and $\mathcal{I}'$ can be derived as follows:

$$\mathcal{H}' \leftarrow \{h \in \mathcal{H} : \forall i \in \mathcal{N}\ seq_i(h) \in \Sigma'\} \cup \{z : \exists h\ seq_l(h)a_{z,h} \in \tilde{\Sigma}\} \tag{19}$$

$$\mathcal{Z}' \leftarrow \mathcal{H}' \cap \mathcal{Z} \tag{20}$$

$$\mathcal{A}'(h) \leftarrow \{a \in \mathcal{A}(h) : ha \in \mathcal{H}'\} \cup \{a_{z,h} : \exists z\ seq_l(h)a_{z,h} \in \tilde{\Sigma}\} \quad \forall h \in \mathcal{H}' \tag{21}$$

$$\mathcal{I}'_i \leftarrow \{I_i \in \mathcal{I}_i : \exists h \in \mathcal{H}' \cap I_i; \nexists z\ seq_l(h)a_{z,h} \in \tilde{\Sigma}\} \cup \{I_h : \exists z\ seq_l(h)a_{z,h} \in \tilde{\Sigma}\} \quad \forall i \in \mathcal{N}. \tag{22}$$

The LP for computing SEFCE is altered according to the current set $\Sigma'$.

LEMMA 4.2. *Let $\hat{G}$ be a modified game constructed from the original game $G$ by forbidding some actions of the leader. Then $SEFCE(\hat{G}) \leq SEFCE(G)$.*

PROOF. Because some actions of the leader are forbidden, the set of strategies available to the leader is restricted, while the set of strategies of the follower remains unconstrained. In case the excluded strategies are not a part of the SEFCE support in $G$, then $SEFCE(\hat{G}) = SEFCE(G)$. Otherwise some leafs of SEFCE become unreachable, the commitment advantage of the leader is hence reduced, resulting in a worse strategy for the leader and $SEFCE(\hat{G}) \leq SEFCE(G)$. □

Now we are ready to prove the algorithm converges to SEFCE.

THEOREM 4.3. *Assume a solution $p$ of Algorithm 2. Then $p$ is a correlation plan of a SEFCE in the original unrestricted game. Algorithm 2 terminates in a finite time.*

PROOF. Since every EFG is finite, there is a finite number of gadgets which can be created. Once a gadget is expanded, it can never be created again, because the game tree is expanded top to bottom. Therefore, there is a finite number of LPs to solve. Algorithm 2 hence terminates in a finite time.

In every iteration, Algorithm 2 finds SEFCE in the current RG, such that the utility of the leader is maximal. In the worst case, the restricted game equals the complete game and it cannot be extended any further and the algorithm terminates, returning a SEFCE. Otherwise, there are states in the complete game, which are not a part of the final RG $G'$. Algorithm 2 terminates once no gadget is reachable by $p$ in the current solution. $G'$ can be hence seen as a modified game in which some actions (those not added to the RG) are forbidden. Therefore, by Lemma 4.2 it holds that $SEFCE(G') \leq SEFCE(G)$. Because RG is closed on the information sets of the follower, by Lemma 4.1 $SEFCE(G') \geq SEFCE(G)$. The SEFCE in the RG is hence a SEFCE in the original unrestricted game. □

### 4.1 Heuristic Gadget-Based Strategy Generation for EFGs

The effectiveness of the complete algorithm described in the previous section is still limited. However, at the cost of losing theoretical guarantees, the algorithm can be turned into a heuristic one and its performance can be measured experimentally. To this end, we introduce three main heuristics: (1) we relax the requirement that the restricted game (RG) has to be closed on the information sets of the follower; (2) the upper convex hull of points in a gadget can be approximated using fewer points; (3) the leader utility can be artificially decreased in order to compensate for the overestimation caused by the fact that the maximum-value leafs are rarely reached if the follower plays the best response. We applied all these heuristics and we now describe each of the heuristics in more detail:

***Restricted Game Not Closed on Information Sets of the Follower.*** In order to guarantee the convergence to the equilibrium, the requirement for the RG to be closed on follower's information sets is necessary. Consider a variant of our algorithm, where we relax the condition for maintaining the closed RG on the information sets of the follower and we expand only those gadgets that are reachable in the current solution. The following example shows a game where such a modification leads to a suboptimal solution.

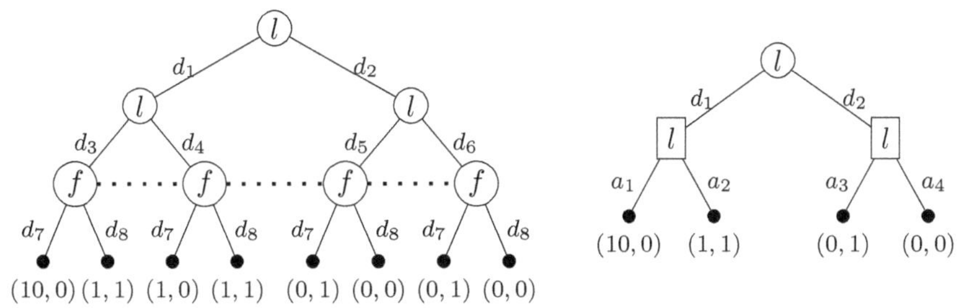


Fig. 3. (Left) An example of EFG where the heuristic algorithms does not converge. The figure follows a standard denotation of an extensive-form game. (Right) An initial RG of the gadget algorithm. By rectangles are denoted the roots of the gadgets. The full gadget algorithm would expand both gadgets after the first iteration. The heuristic gadget algorithm expands only the left gadget.

*Example 4.4.* Consider the game depicted in Figure 3, where SEFCE (which is the same as the SSE) is as follows: the leader commits to playing actions $d_1$ and $d_2$ with the same probability 0.5 and actions $d_3$ and $d_5$ in his lower information sets. The follower is, therefore, indifferent between $d_7$ and $d_8$ and by the definition of SEFCE plays $d_7$. The follower's strategy guarantees the leader the expected utility of 5.0 in the equilibrium. The right part of Figure 3 shows the initial RG of the heuristic gadget algorithm with gadget actions $a_1, a_2, a_3$ and $a_4$. Because the optimal strategy of the leader is to move into the left gadget, it is expanded into the full subtree. In the second iteration, the leader has no intention of playing $d_2$ neither, because his utility is strictly greater in the left subtree. The algorithm therefore terminates. Because the RG is not closed on the follower's information sets, the leader is unaware of the possibility to make the follower indifferent and the optimum is not reached.

***Approximation of Upper Convex Hulls.*** This approximation addresses the problem of creating gadgets for subtrees with large upper convex hull of leafs. Assume that there are $m$ sequences of the follower and $n$ sequences of the leader in the subtree. The number of leafs is hence upper bounded by $m \times n$. If the number of leafs added to the gadget is close to this bound and $mn > m + n$, the number of the sequences which are added into the RG is even larger then number of sequences in the whole subtree and the corresponding LP can be prohibitively large. We solve this issue by excluding from the upper convex hull those leafs, which do not provide a significant increase in the leader's utility when compared with

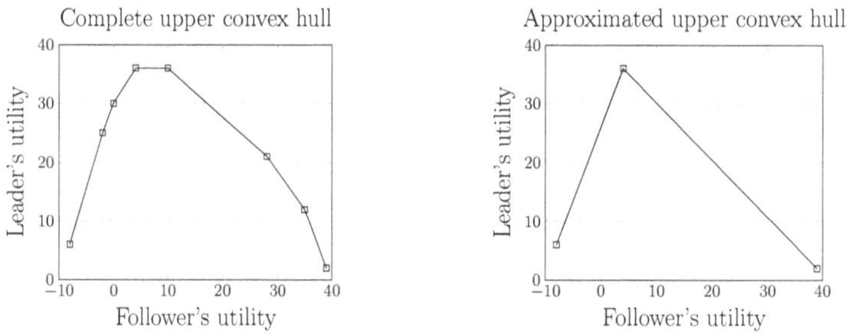


Fig. 4. An example of upper convex hull approximation. (Left) The complete upper convex hull, which is used in the full gadget algorithm. (Right) The approximated upper convex hull with parameter $\delta = 0.4$.

the affine combination of the neighboring leafs. Formally, we delete a leaf $z = (u_l, u_f)$ in between the leafs $z^1 = (u_l^1, u_f^1)$ and $z^2 = (u_l^2, u_f^2)$ in case that

$$\left| u_l^1 + \frac{(u_l^1 - u_l^2)(u_f - u_f^1)}{u_f^1 - u_f^2} - u_l \right| < \delta u_l, \tag{23}$$

where the greater the $\delta > 0$ gets, the more strict the approximation is.

***Penalization of Leader's Utilities.*** Finally, we penalize the leader's utility in order to compensate the optimism when the upper convex hull is created from the leafs directly. Also, during the iterations, there might be several SEFCE with the same optimum, but with different support. In case the solution returned from the LP solver uses the gadgets even though the same optimum can be reached with sequences leading to the ordinary leafs in the RG, the algorithm makes unnecessary iterations. Consequently, both the size of the final RG and the computational time are unnecessarily increased. To speed up the convergence of the algorithm we subtract $\epsilon|maxUtility_l|$, where $\epsilon > 0$, from all leader's utilities in leafs in the gadgets in order to enforce the LP solver into not using the gadgets if not necessary.

## 5 EXPERIMENTS

We performed experiments to evaluate the performance of our heuristic algorithm using strategy generation to compute SSE in EFGs. For comparison, we use the state-of-the-art SEFCE-based algorithm [19], which we refer to as FULL since it uses the full strategy space. All algorithms were implemented in Java 1.8 and all LP computations were completed by a single-threaded IBM CPLEX 12.8 solver using the barrier method. Based on an initial exploration of the parameter space we set the parameter $\delta$ that controls the approximation of the upper convex hulls to value $\delta = 0.3$ since it gave the best results. However, we note that the difference in performance between different values of $\delta$ was relatively small.

***Flip It Games.*** The domain we used for the experiments is the "Flip It" game [17]. This game is motivated by a cybersecurity scenario where an attacker can perform a stealthy attack to gain control of a resource (e.g., install malware on a host or steal a password) that may not be immediately detected by the defender. However, the defender can take actions to restore control to the defender (e.g., performing a virus scan or resetting a password). Flip It can be viewed as a general model of players competing over resources, and many variations have been proposed in the literature. We use it for evaluation here because it has a symmetric structure that makes it particularly difficult to compute SSE; specifically, the vast majority of follower strategies are best responses to some strategy for the leader. This makes it a particularly challenging test for our approach since strategy generation methods would perform even better in games with many irrelevant strategies.

A two-player Flip It game is defined as a tuple $F = (V, E, t, \rho, \gamma)$. The game is played by a defender and an attacker on a directed graph $(V, E)$ for a finite number of simultaneous rounds $t$. The graph represents a typical structure for a computer network where not all nodes are publicly accessible and an attacker may need to move deeper into the network. There is a positive reward $\rho : V \to \mathbb{R}^+$ and a positive cost $\gamma : V \to \mathbb{R}^+$associated with each node $v \in V$. At the beginning of the game, the defender controls all of the nodes. In each round, each player selects one node to flip, i.e to attempt to gain control of. The flipping action is successful when two conditions are met. First, the current owner of the node does not also flip it; and second, the player has control over at least one predecessor of the node. We assume that the source nodes in $(V, E)$ can be flipped in any round (i.e., they are public nodes). For every flipping action, the players pay the cost assigned to the node. At the end of every round the players collect the total rewards from all nodes they control:

$$u_j^i(V_j^i) \leftarrow -\gamma(v_j^i) + \sum_{v \in V_j^i} \rho(v) \quad \forall i \in \mathcal{N}, \tag{24}$$

where $V_j^i$ are the nodes the player $i$ owns after round $j$. After $t$ rounds the game ends and the final utilities are the sum of the rewards collected in the individual rounds. We consider two versions of the game with different amounts of information provided to the players. In the All-Points (AP) version the players learn whether their action succeeded and how many points they have in total after each round. In the No-Info (NI) version the only information the players observe is the sequence of actions they play. Moreover, we assume that the graph can also contain a single disconnected *pass* node with zero reward and zero cost, simulating a pass action. The directed graphs used in the experiments are depicted in Figure 5. All of them include the pass node, which is not depicted in the figure.

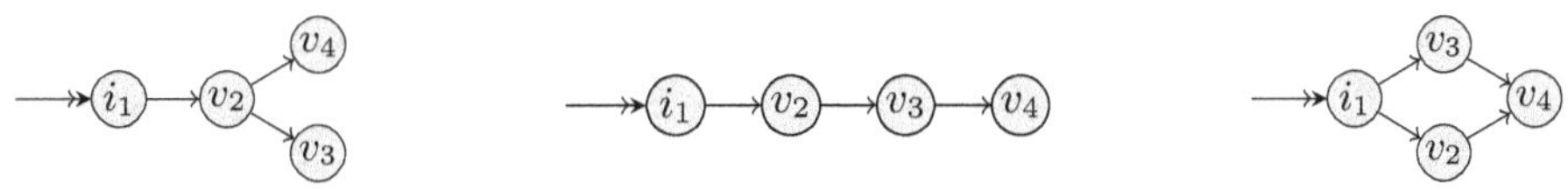


(a) Graph 4a (b) Graph 4b (c) Graph 4c

Fig. 5. Graphs used in the experiments with the Flip It game.

We assume the defender acts as a leader in this game, while the attacker assumes the role of the follower. For graphs 4a and 4c in Figure 5 we solved 40 instances of the Flip It games: 20 All-Points games and 20 No-Info games. For graphs 4b we computed 60 instances: 30 All-Points games and 30 No-Info games. Each node in the graph was randomly assigned to one of the following types: (1) high reward, high cost, (2) high reward, low cost, (3) low reward, high cost, and (4) low reward, low cost. The reward and cost were generated uniformly randomly from the intervals depicted in Table 6 to generate representative instances of Flip It games.

The number of rounds was fixed at $t = 5$, so the number of nodes in the EFG representation of the Flip It game is approximately $11 \times 10^6$. Since the SI-LP variant of FULL algorithm was reported to be fastest in [19], we use this variant as a baseline algorithm for computing SSE in Flip It games.

| Interval\Type | (1) | (2) | (3) | (4) |
|---|---|---|---|---|
| Reward interval | 6..10 | 6..10 | 3..6 | 1..4 |
| Cost interval | 6..10 | 3..6 | 5..9 | 1..4 |

Fig. 6. The intervals from which the rewards and costs were generated for individual types of nodes.

## 5.1 Results

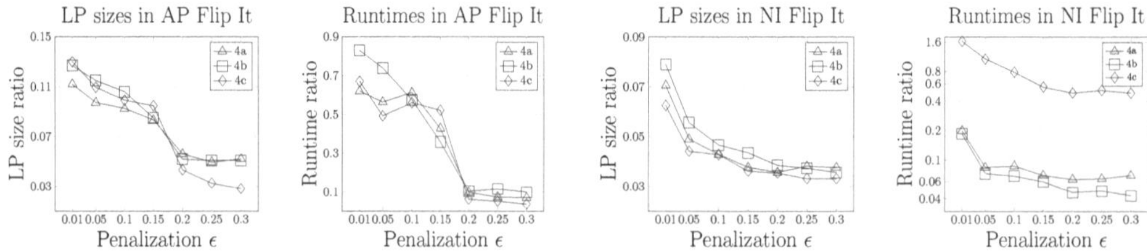


Fig. 7. The median LP sizes and median runtimes in both variants of Flip It for different values of $\epsilon$.

The sizes of the LPs generated for the final restricted games (RG) in the All-Points version of the Flip It games are presented in the leftmost graph of Figure 7. The x-axis shows the penalization parameter $\epsilon$, while the y-axis depicts the ratio of the number of coefficients in the LP describing SSE in the final RG to the number of coefficients in the complete LP used in FULL. Every point in the graph corresponds to the median ratio over the sampled instances. The results show that even with small $\epsilon$, the final LPs are more than eight times smaller than in FULL. As the $\epsilon$ is set higher, the final RGs become even smaller. For the graph 4*c* and $\epsilon = 0.3$, the final LP reaches a size of less than 3% of the full LP. The runtime results for the All-Points version are depicted in the second graph of Figure 7. The x-axis varies the penalization parameter and the y-axis shows the median speedup, which we calculate as the runtime of the heuristic gadget algorithm divided by the runtime of the FULL algorithm.

In the same Figure 7, we present also the results for the final LP sizes and runtimes on the No-Info version of the Flip It game. The graphs follow the same format as the graphs for the All-Points version. Interestingly, when given no information about the progression of the game, the more complex structure of the graph 4*c* slows down the convergence of the heuristic algorithm. The reason is that with larger information sets than in the All-Points version, the upper convex hulls are also larger and contain similar leafs. The algorithm expands only a few gadgets in every iteration and the number of LP invocations is greater. Note that even though the speedup is not that impressive, the sizes of final LPs of all graphs are still less than 4% for the largest value of the parameter $\epsilon$.

Finally, in Table 8 we present the median deviations from the optimum solution achieved by the gadget algorithm. The deviations are measured as the absolute difference in the game values computed by FULL and the heuristic gadget algorithm divided by the SSE game value. We see in the results that the heuristic gadget algorithm achieves nearly optimal results even with higher values of the penalization parameter $\epsilon$. For example, for the graph 4*c* the deviation is 6.38%, with the size of the final LP only 2.8% in the All-Points version, and 1.75% with the size of the final LP 3.3% in the No-Info version.

| Instance \ $\epsilon$ | 0.01 | 0.05 | 0.1 | 0.15 | 0.2 | 0.25 | 0.3 |
|---|---|---|---|---|---|---|---|
| 4a All-Points | 0% | 0% | 0% | 0.9% | 2.42% | 3.01% | 3.23% |
| 4a No-Info | 0% | 0.35% | 0.72% | 1.29% | 1.77% | 2.5% | 2.55% |
| 4b All-Points | 0% | 0% | 0% | 0.56% | 0.8% | 2.39% | 2.48% |
| 4b No-Info | 0% | 0.16% | 0.67% | 1.27% | 2.15% | 2.42% | 2.86% |
| 4c All-Points | 0% | 0% | 0.033% | 0.79% | 3.47% | 4.8% | 6.38% |
| 4c No-Info | 0% | 0.24% | 0.89% | 1.75% | 1.75% | 1.75% | 1.75% |

Fig. 8. The deviations achieved with the heuristic gadget algorithm under different setting of the penalization parameter $\epsilon$.

## 6 CONCLUSION

In this paper, we introduce the first algorithm that successfully exploits the ideas of incremental strategy generation for computing Stackelberg equilibria in extensive-form games. Our algorithm is based on a novel way of representing abstracted parts of the game tree, as well methods for expanding the representation systematically to compute Stackelberg equilibrium. An advantage of our representation is that it leads to three different heuristic approaches that trade off theoretical guarantees for greatly improved practical performance. The heuristic methods can compute exact (or near-optimal) outcomes in practice while constructing only 3% of the original linear program compared to the current state-of-the-art algorithm, often achieving significant speed-up in computation times even in a very challenging class of games.

The current experimental results show that even in a game that is structurally difficult for strategy generation and the Stackelberg solution concept, it is not necessary to consider the whole game tree and all the possibilities. Our algorithm suggests additional directions towards more scalable and approximate algorithms for computing (approximate) Stackelberg equilibrium in large extensive-form games, and it would be interesting to explore other types of games that may have more favorable structure.

## REFERENCES

[1] Branislav Bošanský, Simina Brânzei, Kristoffer Arnsfelt Hansen, Troels Bjerre Lund, and Peter Bro Miltersen. 2017. Computation of Stackelberg Equilibria of Finite Sequential Games. *ACM Transactions on Economics and Computation* 5, 4, Article 23 (Dec. 2017), 24 pages.

[2] Branislav Bošanský, Albert Xin Jiang, Milind Tambe, and Christopher Kiekintveld. 2015. Combining Compact Representation and Incremental Generation in Large Games with Sequential Strategies. In *Proceedings of the Twenty-Ninth AAAI Conference on Artificial Intelligence.*

[3] Branislav Bošanský, Christopher Kiekintveld, Viliam Lisý, and Michal Pěchouček. 2014. An Exact Double-Oracle Algorithm for Zero-Sum Extensive-Form Games with Imperfect Information. *Journal of Artificial Intelligence Research* 51 (2014), 829–866.

[4] Branislav Bošanský and Jiří Čermák. 2015. Sequence-Form Algorithm for Computing Stackelberg Equilibria in Extensive-Form Games. In *Proceedings of the Twenty-Ninth AAAI Conference on Artificial Intelligence*. 805–811.

[5] Michael Bowling, Neil Burch, Michael Johanson, and Oskari Tammelin. 2015. Heads-up limit holdem poker is solved. *Science* 347, 6218 (2015), 145–149.

[6] Karel Durkota, Viliam Lisý, Christopher Kiekintveld, Branislav Bošanský, and Michal Pěchouček. 2016. Case Studies of Network Defense with Attack Graph Games. *IEEE Intelligent Systems* 31, 5 (2016), 24–30.

[7] Karel Durkota, Viliam Lisý, Christopher Kiekintveld, Karel Horák, Branislav Bošanský, and Tomáš Pevný. 2017. Optimal Strategies for Detecting Data Exfiltration by Internal and External Attackers. In *GameSec 2017, LNCS 10575*. 171–192.

[8] Manish Jain, Erim Kardes, Christopher Kiekintveld, Fernando Ordónez, and Milind Tambe. 2010. Security Games with Arbitrary Schedules: A Branch and Price Approach.. In *Proceedings of the Twenty-Fourth AAAI Conference on Artificial Intelligence.*

[9] Manish Jain, Milind Tambe, and Christopher Kiekintveld. 2011. Quality-bounded solutions for finite Bayesian Stackelberg games: Scaling up. In *Proceedings of the 10th International Conference on Autonomous Agents and Multiagent Systems.* 997–1004.

[10] Daphne Koller, Nimrod Megiddo, and Bernhard von Stengel. 1996. Efficient Computation of Equilibria for Extensive two-person Games. *Games and Economic Behavior* (1996), 247–259.

[11] Christian Kroer, Gabriele Farina, and Tuomas Sandholm. 2018. Robust Stackelberg Equilibria in Extensive-Form Games and Extension to Limited Lookahead. In *Proceedings of Thirty-Second AAAI Conference on Artificial Intelligence.*

[12] George Leitmann. 1978. On generalized Stackelberg strategies. *Journal of Optimization Theory and Applications* 26, 4 (1978), 637–643.

[13] Joshua Letchford and Vincent Conitzer. 2010. Computing Optimal Strategies to Commit to in Extensive-Form Games. In *Proceedings of the 11th ACM conference on Electronic commerce.* 83–92.

[14] H. Brendan McMahan, Geoffrey J. Gordon, and Avrim Blum. 2003. Planning in the Presence of Cost Functions Controlled by an Adversary. In *Proceedings of the International Conference on Machine Learning.* 536–543.

[15] Matěj Moravčík, Martin Schmid, Neil Burch, Viliam Lisý, Dustin Morrill, Nolan Bard, Trevor Davis, Kevin Waugh, Michael Johanson, and Michael Bowling. 2017. DeepStack: Expert-Level Artificial Intelligence in No-Limit Poker. *Science* (2017).

[16] Tuomas Sandholm. 2015. Steering evolution strategically: computational game theory and opponent exploitation for treatment planning, drug design, and synthetic biology. In *Proceedings of the Twenty-Ninth AAAI Conference on Artificial Intelligence.* AAAI Press, 4057–4061.

[17] Marten Van Dijk, Ari Juels, Alina Oprea, and Ronald L Rivest. 2013. FlipIt: The game of stealthy takeover. *Journal of Cryptology* 26, 4 (2013), 655–713.

[18] Ondřej Vaněk. 2013. *Computational Methods for Transportation Security.* Ph.D. Dissertation. Czech Technical University in Prague.

[19] Jiří Čermák, Branislav Bošanský, Karel Durkota, Viliam Lisý, and Christopher Kiekintveld. 2016. Using Correlated Strategies for Computing Stackelberg Equilibria in Extensive-Form Games. In *Proceedings of Thirtieth AAAI Conference on Artificial Intelligence.* 439–445.

[20] Bernhard von Stengel. 1996. Efficient Computation of Behavior Strategies. *Games and Economic Behavior* 14 (1996), 220–246.

[21] Bernhard von Stengel and Françoise Forges. 2008. Extensive-Form Correlated Equilibrium: Definition and Computational Complexity. *Mathematics of Operations Research* 33, 4 (2008), 1002–1022.

[22] Bernhard von Stengel and Shmuel Zamir. 2004. *Leadership with Commitment to Mixed Strategies.* Technical Report. CDAM Research Report LSE-CDAM-2004-01.

[23] Haifeng Xu, Rupert Freeman, Vincent Conitzer, Shaddin Dughmi, and Milind Tambe. 2016. Signaling in bayesian stackelberg games. In *Proceedings of the 2016 International Conference on Autonomous Agents & Multiagent Systems.* International Foundation for Autonomous Agents and Multiagent Systems, 150–158.

# Non-clairvoyant Dynamic Mechanism Design*

VAHAB MIRROKNI, Google Research, USA
RENATO PAES LEME, Google Research, USA
PINGZHONG TANG, Institute for Interdisciplinary Information Sciences, Tsinghua University, China
SONG ZUO, Institute for Interdisciplinary Information Sciences, Tsinghua University, China

Despite their better revenue and welfare guarantees for repeated auctions, dynamic mechanisms have not been widely adopted in practice. This is partly due to the complexity of their implementation as well as their unrealistic use of forecasting for future periods. We address these shortcomings and present a new family of dynamic mechanisms that are simple and require no distribution knowledge of future periods.

This paper introduces the concept of non-clairvoyance in dynamic mechanism design, which is a measure-theoretic restriction on the information that the seller can use. A dynamic mechanism is non-clairvoyant if the allocation and pricing rule at each period does not depend on the type distributions in future periods.

We develop a framework (bank account mechanisms) for characterizing, designing, and proving lower bounds for dynamic mechanisms (clairvoyant or non-clairvoyant). This framework is used to characterize the revenue extraction power of non-clairvoyant mechanisms with respect to mechanisms that are allowed unrestricted use of distributional knowledge.

CCS Concepts: • **Theory of computation → Algorithmic mechanism design**; **Computational pricing and auctions**; • **Applied computing** → *Economics*;

Keywords: Dynamic mechanism design; bank account mechanisms; non-clairvoyance; dynamic auctions; approximations; Internet advertising

*Thanks are due to Dirk Bergemann for his detailed comments on an early draft of this manuscript. We also thank Ilan Lobel, Santiago Balseiro and Balu Sivan, the participants of the Erice Workshop of Stochastic Methods in Game Theory and the Google Market Algorithms Workshop for their comments and suggestions.
This paper was supported in part by the National Natural Science Foundation of China Grant 61561146398, a China Youth 1000-talent program and an Alibaba Innovative Research program.
The full version of this paper is available at https://ssrn.com/abstract=2873701.

Authors' addresses: Vahab Mirrokni, Google Research, New York City, USA, mirrokni@google.com; Renato Paes Leme, Google Research, New York City, USA, renatoppl@google.com; Pingzhong Tang, Institute for Interdisciplinary Information Sciences, Tsinghua University, Beijing, China, kenshinping@gmail.com; Song Zuo, Institute for Interdisciplinary Information Sciences, Tsinghua University, Beijing, China, songzuo.z@gmail.com.


*ACM EC '18, June 18–22, 2018, Ithaca, NY, USA*

ACM ISBN 978-1-4503-5829-3/18/06.
https://doi.org/10.1145/3219166.3219224

# Robust Repeated Auctions under Heterogeneous Buyer Behavior

SHIPRA AGRAWAL, Columbia University
CONSTANTINOS DASKALAKIS, Massachusetts Institute of Technology
VAHAB S. MIRROKNI, Google Research NYC
BALASUBRAMANIAN SIVAN, Google Research NYC

We study revenue optimization in a repeated auction between a single seller and a single buyer. Traditionally, the design of repeated auctions requires strong modeling assumptions about the bidder behavior, such as it being myopic, infinite lookahead, or some specific form of learning behavior. Is it possible to design mechanisms which are simultaneously optimal against a multitude of possible buyer behaviors? We answer this question by designing a simple state-based mechanism that is simultaneously approximately optimal against a $k$-lookahead buyer for all $k$, a buyer who is a no-regret learner, and a buyer who is a policy-regret learner. Against each type of buyer our mechanism attains a constant fraction of the optimal revenue attainable against that type of buyer. We complement our positive results with almost tight impossibility results, showing that the revenue approximation tradeoffs achieved by our mechanism for different lookahead attitudes are near-optimal.

This is an extended abstract. A full version of this paper is available as [1] [1].

**ACM Reference Format:**
Shipra Agrawal, Constantinos Daskalakis, Vahab S. Mirrokni, and Balasubramanian Sivan. 2018. Robust Repeated Auctions under Heterogeneous Buyer Behavior. 1, 1 (May 2018), 1 page. https://doi.org/10.1145/3219166.3219234

## REFERENCES

[1] Shipra Agrawal, Constantinos Daskalakis, Vahab Mirrokni, and Balasubramanian Sivan. 2018. Robust Repeated Auctions under Heterogeneous Buyer Behavior. *CoRR* abs/1803.00494 (2018). http://arxiv.org/abs/1803.00494

[1]This work was done in part while Shipra Agrawal and Costis Daskalakis were visiting Google Research NYC.

Authors' addresses: Shipra Agrawal, Columbia University; Constantinos Daskalakis, Massachusetts Institute of Technology; Vahab S. Mirrokni, Google Research NYC; Balasubramanian Sivan, Google Research NYC.


*ACM EC'18, June 18–22, 2018, Ithaca, NY, USA.* ACM ISBN 978-1-4503-5829-3/18/06.
https://doi.org/10.1145/3219166.3219234

# A General Theory of Sample Complexity for Multi-Item Profit Maximization

MARIA-FLORINA BALCAN, Carnegie Mellon University, USA
TUOMAS SANDHOLM, Carnegie Mellon University, USA
ELLEN VITERCIK, Carnegie Mellon University, USA

One of the most tantalizing and long-standing open problems in mechanism design is profit maximization in multi-item, multi-buyer settings. Much of the literature surrounding this problem rests on the strong assumption that the mechanism designer knows the distribution over buyers' values. In reality, this information is rarely available. The support of the distribution alone is often doubly exponential, so obtaining and storing the distribution is impractical. We relax this assumption and instead assume that the mechanism designer only has a set of samples from the distribution. We develop learning-theoretic foundations of sample-based mechanism design. In particular, we provide *generalization guarantees* which bound the difference between the empirical profit of a mechanism over a set of samples and its expected profit on the unknown distribution.

In this paper, we present a general theory for deriving worst-case generalization bounds in multi-item settings, as well as data-dependent guarantees when the distribution over buyers' values is well-behaved. We analyze mechanism classes that have not yet been studied in the sample-based mechanism design literature and match or improve over the best-known guarantees for many of the special classes that have been studied. The classes we study include randomized mechanisms, pricing mechanisms, multi-part tariffs, and generalized VCG auctions such as affine maximizer auctions. In the following, we enumerate our main contributions.

*A general theory of worst-case generalization guarantees for profit maximization.* We uncover a key structural property shared by many mechanisms which allows us to prove strong generalization guarantees: for any fixed set of bids, profit is a piecewise linear function of the mechanism's parameters. Our main theorem provides generalization guarantees for any class exhibiting this structure. To prove this theorem, we relate the complexity of the partition splitting the parameter space into linear portions to the intrinsic complexity of the mechanism class, which we quantify via *pseudo-dimension*. In turn, pseudo-dimension bounds imply generalization bounds. We prove that many mechanisms throughout economics, artificial intelligence, and theoretical computer science share this structure, and thus our main theorem yields strong guarantees.

We prove that our main theorem applies to randomized mechanisms, making us the first to provide generalization bounds for these mechanisms. Our guarantees apply to lotteries, a general representation of randomized mechanisms. Our results imply, for example, that if the mechanism designer plans to offer a menu of $\ell$ lotteries over $m$ items to an additive or unit-demand buyer, then $\tilde{O}(U^2\ell m/\epsilon^2)$ samples are sufficient to ensure that every menu's expected profit is $\epsilon$-close to its empirical profit, where $U$ is the maximum profit achievable over the support of the buyer's valuation distribution.

We also provide guarantees for pricing mechanisms using our main theorem. These include item-pricing mechanisms, also known as *posted-price mechanisms*, where each item has a price and buyers buy their

This work was supported in part by the National Science Foundation under grants CCF-1422910, CCF-1535967, IIS-1618714, IIS-1718457, IIS-1617590, CCF-1733556, a Microsoft Research Faculty Fellowship, an Amazon Research Award, a NSF Graduate Research Fellowship, a Microsoft Research Women's Fellowship, and the ARO under award W911NF-17-1-0082.

Authors' addresses: Maria-Florina Balcan, Carnegie Mellon University, 5000 Forbes Ave, Pittsburgh, PA, 15213, USA, ninamf@cs.cmu.edu; Tuomas Sandholm, Carnegie Mellon University, 5000 Forbes Ave, Pittsburgh, PA, 15213, USA, sandholm@cs.cmu.edu; Ellen Vitercik, Carnegie Mellon University, 5000 Forbes Ave, Pittsburgh, PA, 15213, USA, vitercik@cs.cmu.edu.


*ACM EC'18, June 18–22, 2018, Ithaca, NY, USA.* ACM ISBN 978-1-4503-4529-3/18/06.
https://doi.org/10.1145/3219166.3219217

utility-maximizing bundles. Additionally, we study *multi-part tariffs*, where there is an upfront fee and a price per unit. We are the first to provide generalization bounds for these tariffs and other non-linear pricing mechanisms, which have been studied in economics for decades. For instance, our main theorem guarantees that if there are $\kappa$ units of a single good for sale, then $\tilde{O}(U^2\kappa/\epsilon^2)$ samples are sufficient to learn a nearly optimal two-part tariff.

Our main theorem implies generalization bounds for many auction classes, including second price auctions and generalized VCG auctions, such as affine maximizer auctions, virtual valuations combinatorial auctions, and mixed-bundling auctions, which have been studied in artificial intelligence and economics.

A key challenge which differentiates our generalization guarantees from those typically found in machine learning is the sensitivity of these mechanisms to small changes in their parameters. For example, changing the price of a good can cause a steep drop in profit if the buyer no longer wants to buy it. Meanwhile, for many well-understood function classes in machine learning, there is a close connection between the distance in parameter space between two parameter vectors and the distance in function space between the two corresponding functions. Understanding this connection is often the key to quantifying the class's intrinsic complexity. Intrinsic complexity typically translates to pseudo-dimension or another metric which allows us to derive learnability guarantees. Since profit functions do not exhibit this predictable behavior, we must carefully analyze the structure of the mechanisms we study in order to derive strong generalization guarantees.

*Data-dependent generalization guarantees for profit maximization.* We provide several data-dependent tools that strengthen our main theorem when the distribution over buyers' values is "well-behaved." We prove generalization guarantees that, surprisingly, are independent of the number of items for item-pricing mechanisms, second price auctions with reserves, and a subset of lottery mechanisms. Under anonymous prices, our bounds do not depend on the number of bidders either. These guarantees hold when the bidders are additive with values drawn from *item-independent distributions* (bidder $i_1$'s value for item $j$ is independent from her value for item $j'$, but her value for item $j$ may be correlated with bidder $i_2$'s value for item $j$).

We also provide data-dependent generalization guarantees that, at a high level, are robust to outliers. Worst-case generalization guarantees typically grow linearly with the maximum profit achievable over the support of the distribution. They are thus pessimistic when the highest valuations have a low probability mass. We show how to obtain stronger guarantees in this setting.

*Structural profit maximization.* Many of the mechanism classes we study exhibit a hierarchical structure. For example, when designing a pricing mechanism, the designer can segment the population into $k$ groups and charge each group a different price. This is prevalent throughout daily life: movie theaters and amusement parks have different admission prices per market segment, with groups such as Child, Student, Adult, and Senior Citizen. In the simplest case, $k = 1$ and the prices are anonymous. If $k$ equals the number of buyers, the prices are non-anonymous. In general, the designer should not choose the simplest class to optimize over simply to guarantee good generalization because more complex classes are more likely to contain nearly optimal mechanisms. We show how the mechanism designer can determine the precise level in the hierarchy assuring him the optimal tradeoff between profit maximization and generalization.

In summary, by uncovering structure shared by a myriad of pricing, auction, and lottery mechanisms, we prove strong sample complexity bounds for mechanism classes not yet studied in the sample-based mechanism design literature and match or improve over the best known guarantees for many classes. We strengthen our main results with data-dependent bounds when the distribution over buyers' values is "well-behaved." Finally, we investigate a fundamental tradeoff in sample-based mechanism design: complex mechanisms often have higher profit than simple mechanisms, but more samples are required to ensure that empirical and expected profit are close. We provide techniques for optimizing this tradeoff.

Full Paper: https://arxiv.org/pdf/1705.00243.pdf.

CCS Concepts: • **Theory of computation → Sample complexity and generalization bounds**; **Computational pricing and auctions**;

Additional Key Words and Phrases: Learning theory, machine learning, profit maximization, revenue maximization, combinatorial auctions.

# Are Two (Samples) Really Better Than One?
## On the Non-Asymptotic Performance of Empirical Revenue Maximization

MOSHE BABAIOFF, Microsoft Research
YANNAI A. GONCZAROWSKI, The Hebrew University of Jerusalem and Microsoft Research
YISHAY MANSOUR, Tel Aviv University and Google Research
SHAY MORAN, Institute for Advanced Study

The literature on "mechanism design from samples," which has flourished in recent years at the interface of economics and computer science, offers a bridge between the classic computer-science approach of worst-case analysis (corresponding to "no samples") and the classic economic approach of average-case analysis for a given Bayesian prior (conceptually corresponding to the number of samples tending to infinity). Nonetheless, the two directions studied so far are two extreme and almost diametrically opposed directions: that of asymptotic results where the number of samples grows large, and that where only a single sample is available. In this paper, we take a first step toward understanding the middle ground that bridges these two approaches: that of a fixed number of samples greater than one. In a variety of contexts, we ask what is possibly the most fundamental question in this direction: *are two samples really better than one sample?*. We present a few surprising negative results, and complement them with our main result: showing that the worst-case, over all regular distributions, expected-revenue guarantee of the *Empirical Revenue Maximization* algorithm given two samples is greater than that of this algorithm given one sample. The proof is technically challenging, and provides the first result that shows that *some* deterministic mechanism constructed using two samples can guarantee more than one half of the optimal revenue.

CCS Concepts: •**Theory of computation → Design and analysis of algorithms; Sample complexity and generalization bounds; Algorithmic game theory; Algorithmic mechanism design; Convergence and learning in games; Computational pricing and auctions;**

Additional Key Words and Phrases: Revenue maximization; empirical revenue maximiation; samples

A full version of this paper is available at https://arxiv.org/abs/1802.08037.

Authors' email addresses: Babaioff: moshe@microsoft.com; Gonczarowski: yannai@gonch.name; Mansour: mansour@tau.ac.il; Moran: shaymoran1@gmail.com.

The research was done while Mansour and Moran were co-affiliated with Microsoft Research.

Yannai Gonczarowski is supported by the Adams Fellowship Program of the Israel Academy of Sciences and Humanities; his work is supported by ISF grant 1435/14 administered by the Israeli Academy of Sciences, by Israel-USA Bi-national Science Foundation (BSF) grant number 2014389, and by the European Research Council (ERC) under the European Union's Horizon 2020 research and innovation programme (grant agreement No 740282). The research of Yishay Mansour was supported in part by a grant from the Israel Science Foundation, a grant from United States-Israel Binational Science Foundation (BSF), and the Israeli Centers of Research Excellence (I-CORE) program (Center No. 4/11). The research of Shay Moran is supported by the National Science Foundation under agreement No. CCF-1412958 and by the Simons Foundations. We thank Zhiyi Huang and Tim Roughgarden for stimulating conversations.


*ACM EC'18, June 18–22, 2018, Ithaca, NY, USA.*

ACM ISBN 978-1-4503-4529-3/18/06.
http://dx.doi.org/10.1145/3219166.3219187

# Water from Two Rocks: Maximizing the Mutual Information

YUQING KONG, University of Michigan, USA
GRANT SCHOENEBECK, University of Michigan, USA

We build a natural connection between the learning problem, co-training, and forecast elicitation without verification (related to peer-prediction) and address them simultaneously using the same information theoretic approach.[1]

In co-training/multiview learning [5] the goal is to aggregate two views of data into a prediction for a latent label. We show how to optimally combine two views of data by reducing the problem to an optimization problem. Our work gives a unified and rigorous approach to the general setting.

In forecast elicitation without verification we seek to design a mechanism that elicits high quality forecasts from agents in the setting where the mechanism does not have access to the ground truth. By assuming the agents' information is independent conditioning on the outcome, we propose mechanisms where truth-telling is a strict equilibrium for both the single-task and multi-task settings. Our multi-task mechanism additionally has the property that the truth-telling equilibrium pays better than any other strategy profile and strictly better than any other "non-permutation" strategy profile.

CCS Concepts: • **Theory of computation → Algorithmic mechanism design**; **Unsupervised learning and clustering**; • **Information systems → Incentive schemes**;

Additional Key Words and Phrases: Peer prediction, co-training, information theory

## 1 INTRODUCTION

Co-training/multiview learning is a problem that asks to aggregate two views of data into a prediction for the latent label, and was first proposed by Blum and Mitchell [5]. Although co-training is an important learning problem, it lacks a unified and rigorous approach to the general setting. The current paper will make an innovative connection between the co-training problem and a peer prediction style mechanism design problem: forecast elicitation without verification, and develop a unified theory for both of them via the same information theoretic approach.

We use "forecasting whether a startup company will succeed" as our running example. We have two possible sources of information for each startup: the features $X_A$ (e.g. products, business idea, target customer) of the startup; and the survey feedback $X_B$, collected from the crowd (e.g. a survey of amateur investors). Sometimes we have access to both the sources, and sometimes we have access to only one of the sources. We want to learn how to forecast the result $Y$ (succeed/fail) of a startup company, using both or one of the sources.

We are given a set predictor candidates $\{P_A\}$ (e.g. a set of hypotheses) such that each predictor candidate $P_A$ maps the features $X_A$ to a forecast for the result $Y$ of the startup (e.g. succeed with 73%

[1]A full version of the paper is available at https://arxiv.org/abs/1802.08887.

This work is supported by the National Science Foundation, under grant CAREER#1452915, CCF#1618187 and AitF#1535912.
Authors' addresses: Yuqing Kong, University of Michigan, Ann Arbor, USA, yuqkong@umich.edu; Grant Schoenebeck, University of Michigan, Ann Arbor, USA, schoeneb@umich.edu.


*ACM EC'18, June 18–22, 2018, Ithaca, NY, USA.* ACM ISBN 978-1-4503-5829-3/18/06...$15.00
https://doi.org/10.1145/3219166.3219194

probability, fail with 27% probability). We are also given a set predictor candidates $\{P_B\}$ (e.g. a set of aggregation algorithms like majority vote/weighted average) such that each predictor candidate $P_B$ maps the survey feedback $X_B$ to a forecast for the result $Y$. Our goal is to evaluate the performance of a specific pair $P_A, P_B$. The learning problem, learning how to forecast, can be reduced to this goal since if we know how to evaluate the two candidates $P_A, P_B$'s performance, we can select the two candidates $P_A^*, P_B^*$ which have the highest performance and use them to forecast.

Given a batch of past startup data each with the features $X_A$, the crowdsourced feedback $X_B$, and the result $Y$, we can evaluate the performance of the predictors through many existing measurements (e.g. proper scoring rules, loss functions). This evaluation method is related to the supervised learning setting. However, there may be only very few data points about the startups with results $Y$.[2] When we only use a few labeled data points to train the predictor, the predictor will likely over-fit. Thus, we can boldly ask:

(*Learning) *Can we evaluate the performance of the predictor candidates, as well as learn how to forecast the ground truth $Y$, without access to any data labeled with $Y$?* (See Figure 1)

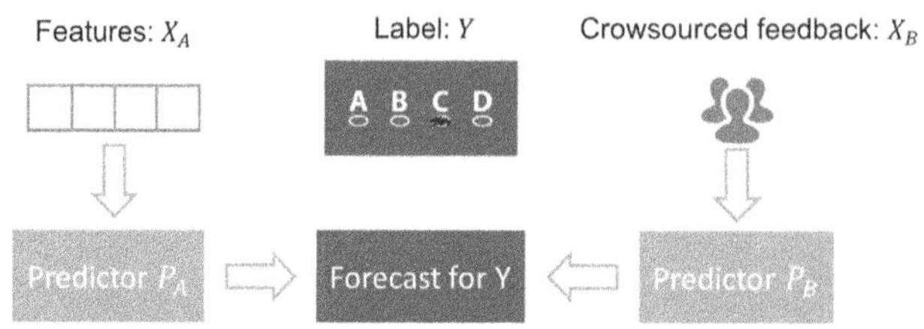


Fig. 1. Problem (*): Finding the common ground truth

It is impossible to solve this problem without making an additional assumption on the relationship between $X_A, X_B$ and $Y$. However, it turns out we can solve this problem with a natural assumption, conditioning on $Y$, $X_A$ and $X_B$ are independent. This assumption states that $Y$ contains all common information between $X_A$ and $X_B$ (see Section 3 for more discussion).

With this assumption, a naive approach is to learn the joint distribution of $X_A$ and $X_B$ using the past data, and then solve the relationship between $Y$ and $X_A, X_B$ by some calculations, using the fact that $X_A$ and $X_B$ are independent conditioning on $Y$. However, this naive approach will not work if either $X_A$ or $X_B$ has very high dimension. We will address this issue using learning methods. Before we go further on the learning problem, let's consider a corresponding mechanism design problem. In the scenario where the forecasts are provided by human beings, we want to ask a mechanism design problem:

(**Mechanism design) *Can we design proper* instant *reward schemes to incentivize high quality forecast for $Y$ without instant access to $Y$?* (See Figure 2)

People will obtain instant payments from *instant* reward schemes. If we do not require the reward schemes to be instant, proper scoring rules will work by rewarding people in the future after $Y$ is revealed. It turns out the above learning problem (*) and mechanism design problem (**) are essentially the same, since there is a natural correspondence between an evaluation of their performance and their rewards. The mechanism design applications still require the conditional independent assumption. To address the two problems, a first try would be rewarding the predictors according to their "agreement", since high quality predictors should have a lot of agreement with each other. However, if we train the predictors based on this criterion, then the output of the

[2]For example, if we focus on cryptographic or self-driving currencies, there are very few startups labeled with results.

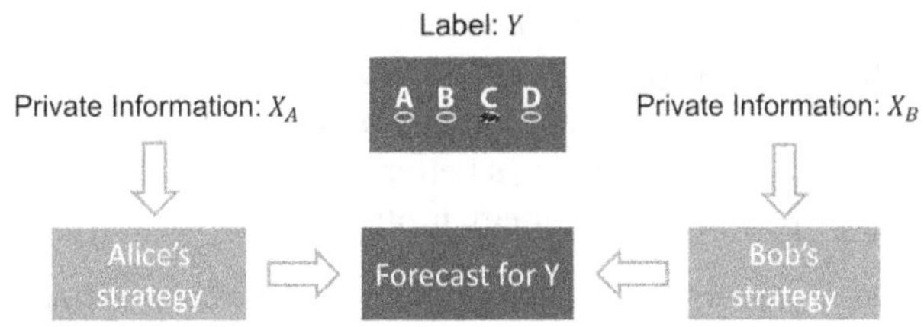


Fig. 2. Problem (**): Forecast elicitation

training process will be two meaningless constant predictors which perfectly agree with each other (e.g. always forecast 100% success). We call this problem the "naive agreement" issue.

Note that the mechanism design problem (**) is closely related to the peer prediction literature, incentivizing high quality information reports without verification. It is natural to leverage the techniques and insights from peer prediction to address problems (*) and (**). In fact, the peer prediction literature provides an information theoretic idea to address the "naive agreement" issue, that is, replacing "agreement" by mutual information. In the current paper, we will show that with a natural assumption, conditioning on $Y$, $X_A$, and $X_B$ are independent, we can address problem (*) and (**) simultaneously via rewarding the predictors the mutual information between them and using the predictors' reward as the evaluation of their performance.

*Our contribution.* We build a natural connection between mechanism design and machine learning by simultaneously addressing a learning problem and a mechanism design problem in the context where ground truth is unknown, via the same information theoretic approach.

**Learning** We focus on the co-training problem [5]: learning how to forecast $Y$ using two sources of information $X_A$ and $X_B$, without access to any data labeled with ground truth $Y$ (Section 3). By making a typical assumption in the co-training literature, conditioning on $Y$, $X_A$ and $X_B$ are independent, we reduce the learning problem to an optimization problem $\max_{P_A,P_B} MIG^f(P_A, P_B)$ such that solving the learning problem is equivalent to picking the $P_A^*, P_B^*$ that maximize $MIG^f(P_A, P_B)$, i.e., the $f$-mutual information gain between $P_A$ and $P_B$ (Section 4). Formally, we define *the Bayesian posterior predictor* as the predictor that maps any input information $X = x$ to its Bayesian posterior forecast for $Y = y$, i.e., $Pr(Y = y|X = x)$. Then when both $P_A, P_B$ are Bayesian posterior predictors, $MIG^f(P_A, P_B)$ is maximized and the maximal value is the $f$-mutual information between $X_A$ and $X_B$. With an additional mild restriction on the prior, $MIG^f(P_A, P_B)$ is maximized if and only if both $P_A, P_B$ are permuted versions of the Bayesian posterior predictor.
As is typical in related literature, we do not investigate the computation complexity or data requirement of the learning problem.
*To the best of our knowledge, this is the first optimization goal in the co-training literature that guarantees that the maximizer corresponds to the Bayesian posterior predictor, without any additional assumption.* Thus, our method optimally aggregates the two sources of information.

**Mechanism design** Consider the scenario where we elicit forecasts for ground truth $Y$ from agents and pay agents immediately. Without access to $Y$, given the prior on the distribution of $Y$, i.e., $Pr[Y]$, [3] by assuming agents' private information are independent conditioning on $Y$, in the single-task setting (there is only a single forecasting task), we design a *strictly*

[3] This is not a very strong assumption since we do not need the knowledge of the joint distribution over the event and agents' private information.

*truthful* mechanism, the *common ground mechanism*, where truth-telling is a strict equilibrium (Section 5.2); in the multi-task (there are at least two a priori similar forecasting tasks) setting, we design a family of *focal* mechanisms, the *multi-task common ground mechanism MCG($f$)s*, where the truth-telling equilibrium pays better than any other strategy profile and *strictly* higher than any non-permutation strategy profile (Section 5.1).

*Technical contribution.* Our main technical ingredient is a novel performance measurement, the *$f$-mutual information gain*, which is an unbiased estimator of the $f$-mutual information. To give a flavor of this measurement, we give an informal presentation here: both $P_A$ and $P_B$ are assigned a batch of forecasting tasks, the $f$-mutual information gain between $P_A$ and $P_B$ is

The agreements between $P_A$'s forecast and $P_B$'s forecast for the same task

$-f^{\star}$(The agreements between $P_A$'s forecast and $P_B$'s forecast for different tasks)

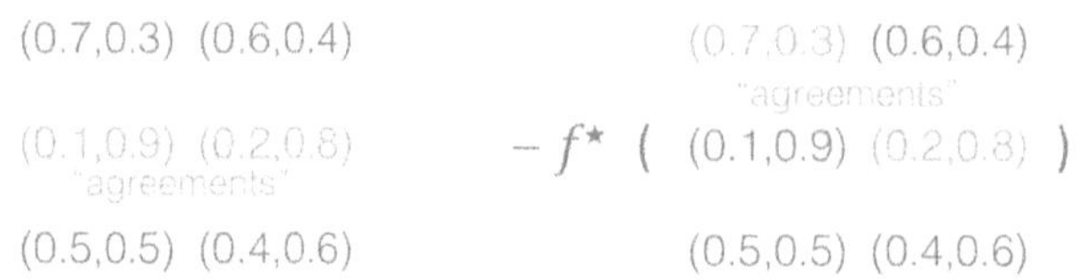


Fig. 3. An unbiased estimator of $f$-mutual information: $f$-mutual information gain. $P_A$ and $P_B$ are assigned three forecasting tasks. $P_A$'s outputs are $(0.7, 0.3), (0.1, 0.9), (0.5, 0.5)$ and $P_B$'s outputs are $(0.6, 0.4), (0.2, 0.8), (0.4, 0.6)$. To calculate the $f$-mutual information gain between them, we pick a task (e.g. Task no. 2) uniformly at random and calculate the "agreement" $a_s$ between $P_A$ and $P_B$'s forecasts for this task; we also pick a pair of distinct tasks $(i, j)$ uniformly at random (e.g. (Task no. 1, Task no. 2)) and calculate the "agreement" $a_d$ between $P_A$'s forecast for task $i$ and $P_B$'s forecast for this task $j$. The $f$-mutual information gain is then $a_s - f^{\star}(a_d)$. The formal definition (Section 4.1) actually uses the empirical expectations of $a_s$ and $f^{\star}(a_d)$.

where $f^{\star}$ is the conjugate of the convex function $f$. With this measurement, two agreeing constant predictors have small gain since their outputs have large agreements for both the same task and different tasks. The formal definition will be introduced in Section 4.1 and the agreement measure is introduced in Definition 4.2.

The $f$-mutual information gain is conceptually similar to the correlation payment scheme proposed by Dasgupta and Ghosh [10] (in the binary choice setting), and Shnayder et al. [33] (in the multiple choice setting), which pays agents "the agreement for the same task *minus* the agreement for the distinct task". In Dasgupta and Ghosh [10] and Shnayder et al. [33], the payment scheme is designed for discrete signals and the measure of agreements is a simple indicator function. Kong and Schoenebeck [17] show that this correlation payment is related to a special $f$-mutual information. Thus, the $f$-mutual information gain can be seen as an extension of the correlation payment scheme that works for forecast reports.

## 1.1 Applications

In our startup running example, we consider the situation where one source of information is the features and another source of information is the crowdsourced feedback. In fact, our results apply to all kinds of information sources. For example, we can make both sources features or crowdsourced feedback. Different setups for the information sources and predictor candidates can bring different applications of our results.

Let's consider the "learning with noisy labels" problem where the labels in the training data are a noisy version of the ground truth labels $Y$ and the noise is independent. We can map this problem into our framework by letting $X_B$ be the noisy label of features $X_A$. That is, $X_B$ is a noisy version of $Y$. Our framework guarantees that the Bayesian posterior predictor that forecasts $Y$ using $X_A$ must be part of a maximizer of the optimization problem. However, there are many other maximizers. For example, since $X_A$ and $X_B$ are independent conditioning $X_B$. The Bayesian posterior predictor that forecasts $X_B$ using $X_A$ is also part of a maximizer, since the scenario $Y = X_B$ also satisfies the conditional independence assumption. If $X_B$ has much higher dimension than $Y$, we do not have this issue. But $X_B$ has the same signal space with $Y$ in the learning with noisy label problem. Thus, it's impossible to eliminate other maximizers without any side information here. With some side information (e.g. a candidate set $\mathcal{F}$, like linear regressions, that only contains our desired maximizer.), it's possible to obtain the Bayesian posterior predictor that forecasts $Y$ using $X_A$. Note that our framework does not require a pre-estimation on the transition probability that transits the ground truth label $Y$ to the noisy ground truth label $X_B$, since our framework has this transition probability, which corresponds to the predictor $P_B$, as parameters as well and learns the correct forecaster $P_A$ and the transition probability $P_B$ simultaneously.

Ratner et al. [29] propose a method to collect massive labels by asking the crowds to write heuristics to label the instances. Each instance is associated with many noisy labels outputted by the heuristics. In their setting, the crowds use a different source of information from the learning algorithm (e.g. the learning algorithm uses the biology description of the genes and the crowds use the scientific papers about the gene). Thus, the conditional independence assumption is natural here and we can map this setting's training problem into our framework. Ratner et al. [29] preprocess the collected labels to approximate ground truth by assuming a particular information structure model on the crowds. Our framework is model-free and does not need to preprocess the collected labels since we can learn the best forecaster (predictor $P_A$) and the best processing/aggregation algorithm (predictor $P_B$) simultaneously.

Moreover, since the highest evaluation value of the predictors $P_A, P_B$ is the $f$-mutual information between $X_A$ and $X_B$, our results provide a method to calculate the $f$-mutual information between any two sources of information $X_A, X_B$ of any format. Kong and Schoenebeck [17] propose a framework for designing information elicitation mechanisms that reward truth-telling by paying each agent the $f$-mutual information between her report and her peers' report. Thus, the $f$-mutual information gain method can be combined with this framework to design information elicitation mechanisms when the information has a complicated format.

## 1.2 Related work

*Learning.* Co-training/multiview learning was first proposed by Blum and Mitchell [5] and explored by many works (e.g. Collins and Singer [7], Dasgupta et al. [11]). Li et al. [19], Xu et al. [37] give surveys on this literature. Although co-training is an important learning problem, it lacks a unified theory and a solid theoretic guarantee for the general model. Most traditional co-training methods require additional restrictions on the hypothesis space (e.g. weakly good hypotheses) to address the "naive agreement" issue and fail to deal with soft hypotheses. Soft hypotheses output a continuous signal (as opposed to hard hypothesis which output a discrete signal) and are typically required to fully aggregate the information from two sources. Becker [3] deals with a feature learning problem which is very similar to the co-training problem. Becker [3] seeks to maximize the Shannon mutual information between the output of two functions. However, their work only considers hard (not soft) hypotheses and lacks a solid theoretic analysis for the maximizer. Kakade and Foster [15] consider the multi-view regression and maximize the correlation between the two hypotheses. Their method captures the "mutual information" idea (in fact, correlation is a special $f$-mutual information [17]) but their model has a very specific set up and the analysis cannot be extended to other co-training problems.

In contrast, we propose a simple, powerful and general information theoretic framework, $f$-mutual information gain, that has a solid theoretic guarantee, works for soft hypothesis and addresses the "naive agreement" issue without any additional assumption.

Natarajan et al. [24], Sukhbaatar and Fergus [34] and many other works (e.g. [16, 32]) consider the learning with noisy labels problem. Natarajan et al. [24] consider binary labels and calibrate the original loss function such that the Bayesian posterior predictor that forecasts ground truth $Y$ is a maximizer of the calibrated loss. Sukhbaatar and Fergus [34] extend this work to the multiclass setting. These works require additional estimation steps to learn the transition probability that transits the ground truth labels to the noisy labels and fix this transition probability in their calibration step. In contrast, by mapping this problem into our framework (Section 1.1), we do not need the additional estimation steps to make the calibrated forecaster part of a maximizer of our optimization problem, and can incorporate any kind of side information to learn the calibrated forecaster and true transition probability simultaneously.

Moreover, our results can handle more complicated setting where each instance is labeled by multiple labels. Rather than preprocessing the labels by a particular algorithm (e.g. majority vote, weighted average, spectral method) and assuming some information structure model among the crowds [29], our framework is model-free and can learn the best calibrated forecaster (predictor $P_A$) and the best processing algorithm (predictor $P_B$) simultaneously.

Raykar et al. [30] also *jointly* learn the calibrated forecaster and the distribution over the crowd-sourced feedback and ground truth labels. Raykar et al. [30] uses the maximum likelihood estimator and assumes a simple generative model for the distribution over the crowdsourced feedback and the ground truth labels, which is conditioning the ground truth label, the crowdsourced feedback is drawn from a binomial distribution, while our framework is model-free.

Generative Adversarial Networks (GAN) [14] combine game theory and learning theory to make innovative progress. We also combine game theory and learning theory by proposing a peer prediction game between two predictors. The game in GAN is a zero-sum competitive game while the game in the current paper is collaborative.

Several learning problems (e.g. finding the pose of an object in an image [4], blind source separation [6]) use mutual information maximization (infomax) as their optimization goal. Some of these problems require data labeled with ground truth and some of them have a very different problem set up than our work.

We borrow the techniques about the duality of $f$-divergence from Nguyen et al. [25, 26]. Nguyen et al. [25] show a correspondence between the $f$-divergence and the surrogate loss in the *binary supervised learning* setting and Nguyen et al. [26] propose a way to estimate the $f$-divergence between two high dimensional random variables. We apply the duality of $f$-divergence to an unsupervised learning problem and not restricted to the binary setting.

We also differ from the crowdsourcing literature that infers ground truth answers from agents' reports (e.g. [38]) in the sense that their agents' reports are a simple choice (e.g. A, B, C, D) while in our setting, the report can come from a space larger than the space of ground truth answers, perhaps even a very high dimensional vector.

*Mechanism design.* Our mechanism design setting differ from the traditional peer prediction literature (e.g.[10, 17, 23, 28, 33]) since we are eliciting forecast rather than a simple signal. We can discretize the forecast report and apply the traditional peer prediction literature results. However, this will only provide approximated truthfulness and fail to design focal mechanisms which pay truth-telling *strictly* better than any other non-permutation equilibrium since the forecast is discretized, while our mechanisms are focal for $\geq 2$ tasks setting.

Witkowski et al. [36] consider the forecast elicitation situation and assume that they have an unbiased estimator of the optimal forecast while we assume an additional conditional independence assumption but do not need the unbiased estimator.

Liu and Chen [20, 21] connect mechanism design with learning by using the learning methods to design peer prediction mechanisms. In the setting where several agents are asked to label a batch of instances, Liu and Chen [20] design a peer prediction mechanism where each agent is paid according to her answer and a reference answer generated by a classification algorithm using other agents' reports. Liu and Chen [21] also use surrogate loss functions as tools to develop a multi-task mechanism that achieves truthful elicitation in dominant strategy when the mechanism designer only has access to agents' reports. Instead of using learning methods to design the peer prediction mechanisms, our work uses peer prediction mechanism design techniques to address a learning problem. Moreover, our mechanism design problem has a very different set up from Liu and Chen [20, 21]. Agarwal and Agarwal [1] connect learning theory with information elicitation by showing the equivalence between the calibrated surrogate losses in *supervised* learning and the elicitation of certain properties of the underlying conditional label distribution. Both our learning problem and mechanism design problem have a very different set up from theirs.

*Independent work.* Like the current paper, McAllester [22] also uses Shannon mutual information to propose an information theoretic training objective that can deal with soft hypotheses/classifiers. However, the optimization functions from these two works are different. We also use a more general information measure, $f$-mutual information, which has Shannon mutual information as a special case, and provide a formal analysis for this general framework. Additionally, we propose an innovative connection between co-training and peer prediction.

## 2 PRELIMINARIES

Given a finite set $[N] := \{1, 2, ..., N\}$, for any function $\phi : [N] \mapsto \mathbb{R}$, we use $(\phi(y))_{y\in[N]}$ to represent the vector $(\phi(1), \phi(2), ..., \phi(N)) \in \mathbb{R}^N$. Given a finite set $\Sigma$, $\Delta_\Sigma$ is the set of all distributions over $\Sigma$.

### 2.1 $f$-divergence and Fenchel's duality

*$f$-divergence [2, 9].* $f$-divergence $D_f : \Delta_\Sigma \times \Delta_\Sigma \mapsto \mathbb{R}$ is a non-symmetric measure of the difference between distribution $\mathbf{p} \in \Delta_\Sigma$ and distribution $\mathbf{q} \in \Delta_\Sigma$ and is defined to be

$$D_f(\mathbf{p}, \mathbf{q}) = \sum_{\sigma\in\Sigma} \mathbf{p}(\sigma) f\left(\frac{\mathbf{q}(\sigma)}{\mathbf{p}(\sigma)}\right)$$

where $f : \mathbb{R} \mapsto \mathbb{R}$ is a convex function and $f(1) = 0$.

Here we introduce two $f$-divergences in common use: KL divergence, and Total Variance Distance.

*Example 2.1 (KL divergence).* Choosing $-\log(x)$ as the convex function $f(x)$, $f$-divergence becomes KL divergence $D_{KL}(\mathbf{p}, \mathbf{q}) = \sum_\sigma \mathbf{p}(\sigma) \log \frac{\mathbf{p}(\sigma)}{\mathbf{q}(\sigma)}$

*Example 2.2 (Total Variance Distance).* Choosing $|x-1|$ as the convex function $f(x)$, $f$-divergence becomes Total Variance Distance $D_{tvd}(\mathbf{p}, \mathbf{q}) = \sum_\sigma |\mathbf{p}(\sigma) - \mathbf{q}(\sigma)|$

*Definition 2.3 (Fenchel Duality [31]).* Given any function $f : \mathbb{R} \mapsto \mathbb{R}$, we define its convex conjugate $f^\star$ as a function that also maps $\mathbb{R}$ to $\mathbb{R}$ such that

$$f^\star(x) = \sup_t tx - f(t).$$

Lemma 2.4 (Dual version of $f$-divergence [25, 26]).

$$D_f(\mathbf{p},\mathbf{q}) \geq \sup_{u\in\Sigma} \mathbb{E}_{\mathbf{p}} u - \mathbb{E}_{\mathbf{q}} f^{\star}(u) = \sup_{u\in\mathcal{G}} \sum_{\sigma} u(\sigma)\mathbf{p}(\sigma) - \sum_{\sigma} f^{\star}(u(\sigma))\mathbf{q}(\sigma)$$

*where $\mathcal{G}$ is a set of functions that maps $\Sigma$ to $\mathbb{R}$. The equality holds if and only if $u(\sigma) = u^*(\sigma) \in \partial f(\frac{\mathbf{p}(\sigma)}{\mathbf{q}(\sigma)})$, i.e., the subdifferential of $f$ on value $\frac{\mathbf{p}(\sigma)}{\mathbf{q}(\sigma)}$.*

We call $(u^*, f^{\star}(u^*))$ *a pair of best disinguishers*. This dual version of $f$-divergence is introduced by Nguyen et al. [25] and also plays a key role in the design of a type of generative adversarial networks, $f$-GANs [27].

## 2.2 $f$-mutual information

Given two random variables $X, Y$ whose realization space are $\Sigma_X$ and $\Sigma_Y$, let $\mathbf{U}_{X,Y}$ and $\mathbf{V}_{X,Y}$ be two probability measures where $\mathbf{U}_{X,Y}$ is the joint distribution of $(X, Y)$ and $\mathbf{V}_{X,Y}$ is the product of the marginal distributions of $X$ and $Y$. Formally, for every pair of $(x, y) \in \Sigma_X \times \Sigma_Y$,

$$\mathbf{U}_{X,Y}(X = x, Y = y) = \Pr[X = x, Y = y] \qquad \mathbf{V}_{X,Y}(X = x, Y = y) = \Pr[X = x]\Pr[Y = y].$$

If $\mathbf{U}_{X,Y}$ is very different from $\mathbf{V}_{X,Y}$, the mutual information between $X$ and $Y$ should be high since knowing $X$ changes the belief for $Y$ a lot. If $\mathbf{U}_{X,Y}$ equals to $\mathbf{V}_{X,Y}$, the mutual information between $X$ and $Y$ should be zero since $X$ is independent with $Y$. Intuitively, the "distance" between $\mathbf{U}_{X,Y}$ and $\mathbf{V}_{X,Y}$ represents the mutual information between them.

*Definition 2.5 ($f$-mutual information [17]).* The $f$-mutual information between $X$ and $Y$ is defined as

$$MI^f(X;Y) = D_f(\mathbf{U}_{X,Y}, \mathbf{V}_{X,Y})$$

where $D_f$ is $f$-divergence. $f$-mutual information is always non-negative [17].

$f$-mutual information is used in the peer prediction literature since if the information is measured by $f$-mutual information, any "data processing" on either of the random variables will decrease the amount of information crossing them. Thus, in peer prediction, if we pay agents according to the $f$-mutual information between her information and her peers' information, agents will be incentivized to report all information to maximize their payments[4].

Two examples of $f$-mutual information are Shannon mutual information [8] (Choosing $f$-divergence as KL divergence) and $MI^{tvd}(X;Y) := \sum_{x,y} |\Pr[X = x, Y = y] - \Pr[X = x]\Pr[Y = y]|$ (Choosing $f$-divergence as Total Variation Distance).

We define $K(X = x, Y = y)$ as the ratio between $U_{X,Y}(x, y)$ and $V_{X,Y}(x, y)$, i.e.,

$$K(X = x, Y = y) := \frac{\Pr[X = x, Y = y]}{\Pr[X = x]\Pr[Y = y]} = \frac{\Pr[Y = y|X = x]}{\Pr[Y = y]} = \frac{\Pr[X = x|Y = y]}{\Pr[X = x]}.$$

$K(X = x, Y = y)$ represents the "**pointwise mutual information**(PMI)" between $X = x$ and $Y = y$. Lemma 2.4 directly implies:

Lemma 2.6 (Dual version of $f$-mutual information).

$$MI^f(X;Y) \geq \sup_{u\in\mathcal{G}} \mathbb{E}_{U_{X,Y}} u - \mathbb{E}_{V_{X,Y}} f^{\star}(u)$$

*where $\mathcal{G}$ is a set of functions that maps $\Sigma_X \times \Sigma_Y$ to $\mathbb{R}$.*

*The equality holds if and only if $u(x, y) = u^*(x, y) \in \partial f(K(X = x, Y = y))$.*

[4]In the current paper, we do not directly use the data processing inequality of $f$-mutual information. Thus, we omit the formal introduction here. The interested reader is refer to Kong and Schoenebeck [17].

| $f$-divergence | $f(t)$ | $u^*(x,y) = \partial f(K(x,y))$ | $f^\star(u^*(x,y))$ |
|---|---|---|---|
| Total Variation Distance | $\lvert t-1 \rvert$ | $\text{sign}(\log K(x,y))$ | $\text{sign}(\log K(x,y))$ |
| KL divergence | $t\log t$ | $1+\log K(x,y)$ | $K(x,y)$ |
| Reverse KL | $-\log t$ | $-\frac{1}{K(x,y)}$ | $-1+\log K(x,y))$ |
| Pearson $\chi^2$ | $(t-1)^2$ | $2(K(x,y)-1)$ | $(K(x,y))^2-1$ |
| Squared Hellinger | $(\sqrt{t}-1)^2$ | $1-\sqrt{\frac{1}{K(x,y)}}$ | $\sqrt{K(x,y)}-1$ |

Table 1. Reference for common $f$-divergences and corresponding pairs of best distinguishers $(u^*(x,y), f^\star(u^*(x,y)))$ of $f$-mutual information. $K(x,y) = K(X=x, Y=y)$ (PMI).

### 2.3 Proper scoring rules

A scoring rule $PS : \Sigma \times \Delta_\Sigma \mapsto \mathbb{R}$ [13, 35] takes in a signal $\sigma \in \Sigma$ and a distribution over signals $\mathbf{p} \in \Delta_\Sigma$ and outputs a real number. A scoring rule is *proper* if, whenever the first input is drawn from a distribution $\mathbf{p}$, then $\mathbf{p}$ will maximize the expectation of $PS$ over all possible inputs in $\Delta_\Sigma$ to the second coordinate. A scoring rule is called *strictly proper* if this maximum is unique. We will assume throughout that the scoring rules we use are strictly proper. Slightly abusing notation, we can extend a scoring rule to be $PS : \Delta_\Sigma \times \Delta_\Sigma \mapsto \mathbb{R}$ by simply taking $PS(\mathbf{p}, \mathbf{q}) = \mathbb{E}_{\sigma \leftarrow \mathbf{p}}(\sigma, \mathbf{q})$. We note that this means that any proper scoring rule is linear in the first term.

*Example 2.7 (Log Scoring Rule [13, 35]).* Fix an outcome space $\Sigma$ for a signal $\sigma$. Let $\mathbf{q} \in \Delta_\Sigma$ be a reported distribution. The Logarithmic Scoring Rule maps a signal and reported distribution to a payoff as follows:

$$LSR(\sigma, \mathbf{q}) = \log(\mathbf{q}(\sigma)).$$

Let the signal $\sigma$ be drawn from some random process with distribution $\mathbf{p} \in \Delta_\Sigma$.
Then the expected payoff of the Logarithmic Scoring Rule

$$\mathbb{E}_{\sigma \leftarrow \mathbf{p}}[LSR(\sigma, \mathbf{q})] = \sum_\sigma \mathbf{p}(\sigma) \log \mathbf{q}(\sigma) = LSR(\mathbf{p}, \mathbf{q})$$

This value will be maximized if and only if $\mathbf{q} = \mathbf{p}$.

### 2.4 Property of the pointwise mutual information

We will introduce a simple property of the pointwise mutual information that we will use multiple times in the future. In addition to several different formats of the pointwise mutual information (e.g. joint distribution/product of the marginal distributions, posterior/prior), if there exists a latent random variable $Y$ such that random variable $X_A$ and random variable $X_B$ are independent conditioning on $Y$, we can also represent the pointwise mutual information between $X_A$ and $X_B$ by the "agreement" between the "relationship" between $X_A$ and $Y$, and the "relationship" between $X_B$ and $Y$.

Claim 2.8. *When random variables $X_A, X_B$ are independent conditioning on $Y$,*

$$\begin{aligned} K(X_A = x_A, X_B = x_B) &= \sum_y \Pr[Y=y] K(X_A = x_A, Y=y) K(X_B = x_B, Y=y) \\ &= \sum_y \Pr[Y=y \mid X_A = x_A] K(X_B = x_B, Y=y) \end{aligned}$$

$$=\sum_y \frac{\Pr[Y=y|X_A=x_A]\Pr[Y=y|X_B=x_B]}{\Pr[Y=y]}.$$

We defer the proof to the full version.

## 3 GENERAL MODEL AND ASSUMPTIONS

Let $X_A, X_B, Y$ be three random variables and we define prior $Q$ as the joint distribution over $X_A, X_B, Y$. We want to forecast the ground truth $Y$ whose realization is a signal in a finite set $\Sigma$. $X_A, X_B$ are two sources of information that are related to $Y$. $X_A$'s realization is a signal in a finite set $\Sigma_A$. $X_B$'s realization is a signal in a finite set $\Sigma_B$. We may have access to both of the realizations of $X_A$ and $X_B$ or only one of them. Thus, we need to learn the relationship between $X_A, X_B$ and $Y$ to forecast $Y$. It's impossible to learn by only accessing the samples of $X_A, X_B$ without additional assumption. We make the following conditional independence assumption:

Assumption 3.1 (Conditional independence). *We assume that conditioning on $Y$, $X_A$, and $X_B$ are independent.*

Intuitively, $Y$ can be seen as the "intersection" between $X_A$ and $X_B$. To better understand this assumption and its limitations we return to our running example where the variable $Y$ is the success of a start-up. In this case, if both $X_A$ and $X_B$ contain the sex of the CEO (which we assume is independent of $Y$), then this assumption will not hold. To make it hold, either $Y$ would need to be redefined to contain the sex of the CEO, or this information would need to be removed from either $X_A$ or $X_B$. For the mechanism design application, if the assumption is violated, for example both agents are sexists and forecast using the sex of the CEO, then it is impossible to avoid paying them for this useless/harmful information.

### 3.1 Well-defined and stable prior

We call $Z$ a *solution* if conditioning on $Z$, $X_A$, and $X_B$ are independent. $Y$ is a solution. However, there are a lot of solutions. For example, conditioning on $X_A$ or $X_B$, $X_A$ and $X_B$ are independent, which means $X_A$ and $X_B$ are both solutions. Thus, we have an additional restriction on the prior: well-defined prior and stable prior.

We will need restrictions on the prior when we analyze the strictness of our learning algorithm/mechanism. Readers can skip this section without losing the core idea of our results.

To infer the relationship between $Y$ and $X_A, X_B$ with only samples of $X_A, X_B$, we cannot do better than to just solve the system of equations (1), given the joint distribution over $X_A, X_B$: $Q$. Our goal is to obtain the Bayesian posterior predictor. Thus, we list a system that the Bayesian posterior predictor satisfies. The system below equations involve variables $\{\mathbf{a}^{x_A}, \mathbf{b}^{x_B} \in \Delta_\Sigma\}_{x_A\in\Sigma_A, x_B\in\Sigma_B}$, and $\mathbf{r} \in \Delta_\Sigma$. We insist $a_y^{x_A} = \Pr[Y=y|X_A=x_A]$, $b_y^{x_B} = \Pr[Y=y|X_B=x_B]$ and $r_y = \Pr[Y=y]$ is a solution and we call it the *desired* solution.

$$\begin{aligned}&\mathcal{S}(\{\mathbf{a}^{x_A},\mathbf{b}^{x_B}\}_{x_A\in\Sigma_A,x_B\in\Sigma_B},\mathbf{r}) \\ &:=\left\{\sum_{y\in\Sigma}\frac{a_y^{x_A}b_y^{x_B}}{r_y} - K(X_A=x_A,X_B=x_B)\right\}_{x_A\in\Sigma_A,x_B\in\Sigma_B} = 0\end{aligned} \tag{1}$$

Claim 2.8 shows the above system has the desired solution.

Note that any permutation of a solution is still a valid solution[5]. Since we cannot do better than to solve the above system, if the above system only has one "unique" solution, in the sense that any two solutions are permuted version of each other, we call the prior $Q$ a well-defined prior. Formally,

*Definition 3.2 (Well-defined).* A prior $Q$ is well-defined if for any two solutions $\{\mathbf{a}^{x_A}, \mathbf{b}^{x_B}\}_{x_A\in\Sigma_A, x_B\in\Sigma_B}$, $\mathbf{r}$ and $\{\mathbf{c}^{x_A}, \mathbf{d}^{x_B}\}_{x_A\in\Sigma_A, x_B\in\Sigma_B}$, $\mathbf{r}'$ of the system of equations (1), there exists a permutation $\pi : \Sigma \mapsto \Sigma$ such that $\mathbf{r} = \pi\mathbf{r}'$ for any $x_A, x_B$, $\mathbf{a}^{x_A} = \pi\mathbf{c}^{x_A}$, $\mathbf{b}^{x_B} = \pi\mathbf{d}^{x_B}$.

The well-defined prior exist since intuitively, if $|\Sigma_A|$ and $|\Sigma_B|$ are high and $|\Sigma|$ is low, it is likely $Y$ is the "unique intersection" since the number of constraints of the system will be much greater than the number of variables.

We say a prior is stable if fixing part of the desired solution of the system (1), in order to make it still a solution of the system, other parts of the desired solution should also be fixed.

*Definition 3.3 (Stable).* A prior $Q$ is stable if fixing $a_y^{x_A} = \Pr[Y = y|X_A = x_A]$ and $r_y = \Pr[Y = y]$, the system (1) $\mathcal{S}(\{\mathbf{a}^{x_A}, \mathbf{b}^{x_B}\}_{x_A\in\Sigma_A, x_B\in\Sigma_B}, \mathbf{r}) = 0$ has unique solution $\mathbf{b}^{x_A}$ such that $b_y^{x_B} = \Pr[Y = y|X_B = x_B]$; and fixing $b_y^{x_B} = \Pr[Y = y|X_B = x_B]$ and $r_y = \Pr[Y = y]$, the system (1) $\mathcal{S}(\{\mathbf{a}^{x_A}, \mathbf{b}^{x_B}\}_{x_A\in\Sigma_A, x_B\in\Sigma_B}, \mathbf{r}) = 0$ has unique solution $\mathbf{a}^{x_A}$ such that $a_y^{x_A} = \Pr[Y = y|X_A = x_A]$.

We require stable priors when we design *strictly* truthful mechanisms.

## 3.2 Predictors

This section gives the definition of predictors. We have two sets of samples $S_A := \{x_A^\ell\}_{\ell\in\mathcal{L}_A}$ and $S_B := \{x_B^\ell\}_{\ell\in\mathcal{L}_B}$ which are i.i.d samples of $X_A$ and $X_B$ respectively. For $\ell \in \mathcal{L}_A \cap \mathcal{L}_B$, $(x_A^\ell, x_B^\ell)$s are i.i.d samples of the joint random variable $(X_A, X_B)$.

A predictor $P_A : \Sigma_A \mapsto \Delta_\Sigma$ for $X_A$ maps $x_A \in \Sigma$ to a forecast $P_A(x_A)$ for ground truth $Y$. We similarly define the predictors for $X_B$. We define *the Bayesian posterior predictor* as the predictor that maps any input information $X = x$ to its Bayesian posterior forecast for $Y = y$, i.e., $Pr(Y = y|X = x)$.

With the conditional independence assumption, we have

$$\begin{aligned}\Pr[Y|X_A, X_B] &= \frac{\Pr[Y, X_A, X_B]}{\Pr[X_A, X_B]}\\ &= \frac{\Pr[Y]\Pr[X_A|Y]\Pr[X_B|Y]}{\Pr[X_A, X_B]} && \text{(conditional independence)}\\ &= \frac{\Pr[Y|X_A]\Pr[Y|X_B]}{K(X_A, X_B)\Pr[Y]} && (K(X_A, X_B) \text{ is the pointwise mutual information.})\end{aligned}$$

When we have access to both the sources where $X_A = x_A$ and $X_B = x_B$, given the prior of the ground truth $Y$, we can construct an aggregated forecast for $Y = y$ using $P_A, P_B$:

$$\frac{P_A(x_A)P_B(x_B)}{\Pr[Y = y]} \cdot \text{normalization}$$

In this case, if both $P_A$ and $P_B$ are the Bayesian posterior predictor, the aggregated forecast is the Bayesian posterior predictor as well. Thus, it's sufficient to only train $P_A$ and $P_B$. In the rest sections, we will show how to train $P_A$ and $P_B$ (Section 4), given the two sets of samples $S_A$ and $S_B$, as well as how to incentivize high quality predictors from the crowds (Section 5).

[5]We may be able to distinguish a solution with its permuted version if we have some side information (e.g. the prior of $Y$/a few $(x_A, x_B, y)$ samples).

## 4 CO-TRAINING: FINDING THE COMMON GROUND TRUTH

We have a set of candidates $\mathcal{H}_A$ for the predictor for $X_A$ and a set of candidates $\mathcal{H}_B$ for the predictor for $X_B$. We sometimes call each predictor candidate *a hypothesis*. Given the two sets of samples $S_A = \{x_A^\ell\}_{\ell\in\mathcal{L}_A}$ and $S_B = \{x_B^\ell\}_{\ell\in\mathcal{L}_B}$, our goal is to figure out the best hypothesis in $\mathcal{H}_A$ and the best hypothesis in $\mathcal{H}_B$ simultaneously. Thus, we need to design proper "loss function" such that the best hypotheses minimize the loss. In fact, we will show how to design a proper "reward function" such that the best hypotheses maximize the reward.

### 4.1 $f$-mutual information gain

*$f$-mutual information gain $MIG^f(R)$ (Figure 3).*

**Hypothesis** We are given $\mathcal{H}_A = \{h_A : \Sigma_A \mapsto \Delta_\Sigma\}$, $\mathcal{H}_B = \{h_B : \Sigma_B \mapsto \Delta_\Sigma\}$: the set of hypotheses/predictor candidates for $X_A$ and $X_B$, respectively.

**Gain** Given reward function $R : \Delta_\Sigma \times \Delta_\Sigma \mapsto \mathbb{R}$,
for each $\ell \in \mathcal{L}_A \cap \mathcal{L}_B$, reward "the amount of agreement" between the two predictor candidates' predictions for task $\ell$, i.e.,

$$R(h_A(x_A^\ell), h_B(x_B^\ell));$$

for each distinct pair $(\ell_A, \ell_B)$, $\ell_A \in \mathcal{L}_A, \ell_B \in \mathcal{L}_B, \ell_A \neq \ell_B$, punish both predictor candidates "the amount of agreement" between their predictions for a pair of distinct tasks $(\ell_A, \ell_B)$, i.e.,

$$f^\star(R(h_A(x_A^{\ell_A}), h_B(x_B^{\ell_B})).$$

The $f$-mutual information gain $MIG^f(R)$ that is corresponding to the reward function $R$ is

$$MIG^f(R(h_A, h_B))_{|S_A,S_B} = \frac{1}{|\mathcal{L}_A \cap \mathcal{L}_B|} \sum_{\ell\in\mathcal{L}_A\cap\mathcal{L}_B} R(h_A(x_A^\ell), h_B(x_B^\ell))$$

$$-\frac{1}{|\mathcal{L}_A||\mathcal{L}_B| - |\mathcal{L}_A \cap \mathcal{L}_B|^2} \sum_{\ell_A\in\mathcal{L}_A, \ell_B\in\mathcal{L}_B, \ell_A\neq\ell_B} f^\star(R(h_A(x_A^{\ell_A}), h_B(x_B^{\ell_B})))$$

Lemma 4.1. *The expected total $f$-mutual information gain is maximized over all possible $R$, $h_A$, and $h_B$ if and only if for any $(x_A, x_B) \in \Sigma_A \times \Sigma_B$,*

$$R(h_A(x_A), h_B(x_B)) \in \partial f(K(x_A, x_B)).$$

*The maximum is $MI^f(X_A; X_B)$.*

Proof. $(x_A^\ell, x_B^\ell)_\ell$ are i.i.d. realizations of $(X_A, X_B)$. Therefore, the expected $f$-mutual information gain is $\mathbb{E}_{U_{X_A,X_B}} R - \mathbb{E}_{V_{X_A,X_B}} f^\star(R)$. The results follow from Lemma 2.6. □

Although any reward function corresponds to an $f$-mutual information gain function, we need to properly design the reward function $R$ such that, fixing $R$, there exist hypotheses to maximize the corresponding $f$-mutual information gain $MIG^f(R)$ to the $f$-mutual information between the two sources. We will use the intuition from Lemma 4.1 to design such reward functions $R$ in the next section.

### 4.2 Maximizing the $f$-mutual information gain

In this section, we will construct a special reward function $R^f$ and then show that the maximizers of the corresponding $f$-mutual information gain $MIG^f(R^f)$ are the Bayesian posterior predictors.

*Definition 4.2 ($R^f$).* We define reward function $R^f$ as a function that maps the two hypotheses' outputs $\mathbf{p}_1, \mathbf{p}_2 \in \Delta_\Sigma$ and the vector $\mathbf{p} \in \Delta_\Sigma$ to

$$R^f(\mathbf{p}_1, \mathbf{p}_2, \mathbf{p}) := g\left(\sum_y \frac{\mathbf{p}_1(y)\mathbf{p}_2(y)}{\mathbf{p}(y)}\right)$$

where $g(t) \in \partial f(t), \forall t$. When $f$ is differentiable,

$$R^f(\mathbf{p}_1, \mathbf{p}_2, \mathbf{p}) := f'\left(\sum_y \frac{\mathbf{p}_1(y)\mathbf{p}_2(y)}{\mathbf{p}(y)}\right).$$

With this definition of the reward function, fixing $\mathbf{p} \in \Delta_\Sigma$ which can be seen as the prior over $Y$, the "amount of agreement" between two predictions $\mathbf{p}_1, \mathbf{p}_2$ are an increasing function $g$ of

$$\sum_y \frac{\mathbf{p}_1(y)\mathbf{p}_2(y)}{\mathbf{p}(y)},$$

which is intuitive and reasonable. The increasing function $g$ is the derivative of the convex function $f$. By carefully choosing convex function $f$, we can use any increasing function $g$ here.

Theorem 4.3. *With the conditional independent assumption on $X_A, X_B, Y$, given the samples $S_A, S_B$, given a convex function $f$, we define the optimization goal as the expected $f$-mutual information gain with reward function $R^f$, i.e.,*

$$MIG^f(h_A, h_B, \mathbf{p}) := \mathbb{E}_{X_A, X_B} MIG^f(R^f(h_A, h_B, \mathbf{p}))_{|S_A, S_B}$$

*and optimize over all possible hypotheses $h_A : \Sigma_A \mapsto \Delta_\Sigma$, $h_B : \Sigma_B \mapsto \Delta_\Sigma$ and distribution vectors $\mathbf{p} \in \Delta_\Sigma$. We have*

**Solution→Maximizer:** *any solution $Z$ corresponds to a maximizer of $MIG^f(h_A, h_B, \mathbf{p})$*[6]*: for any solution $Z$,*

$$h^*_A(x_A) := (\Pr[Z = y|X_A = x_A])_y \qquad h^*_B(x_B) := (\Pr[Z = y|X_B = x_B])_y$$[7]

*and the prior over $Z$, $\Pr[Z = y]_y$, is the maximizer of $MIG^f(h_A, h_B, \mathbf{p})$ and the maximum is $MI^f(X_A; X_B)$;*

**Maximizer→(Permuted) Ground truth** *when the prior is well-defined, $f$ is differentiable, and $f'$ is invertible, any maximizer of $MIG^f(h_A, h_B, \mathbf{p})$ corresponds to the (possibly permuted) ground truth $Y$: for any maximizer $(h^*_A(\cdot), h^*_B(\cdot), \mathbf{p}^*)$ of $MIG^f(h_A, h_B, \mathbf{p})$, there exists a permutation $\pi$ such that*

$$h^*_A(x_A) := (\Pr[\pi(Y) = y|X_A = x_A])_y \qquad h^*_B(x_B) := (\Pr[\pi(Y) = y|X_B = x_B])_y$$

*and $\mathbf{p}^* = \Pr[\pi(Y) = y]_y$.*

The above theorem neither investigates computation complexity (which may be affected by the choice of $f$), data requirements, nor the choice of the hypothesis class for practical implementation (see Section 6 for more discussion).

[6]Given the prior over $Y$, we can fix $\mathbf{p}$ as the prior over $Y$. Without knowing the prior over $Y$, $\mathbf{p}$ becomes a variable of the optimization goal and helps us learn the prior over $Y$.

[7]Recall that we use $(\phi(y))_{y \in [N]}$ to represent the vector $(\phi(1), \phi(2), \ldots, \phi(N)) \in \mathbb{R}^N$.

Proof for Theorem 4.3. Lemma 4.1 shows that the expected $f$-mutual information gain is maximized if and only if for any $(x_A, x_B)$,

$$R^f(h_A^*(x_A), h_B^*(x_B), \mathbf{p}^*) \in \partial f(K(x_A, x_B)).$$

(1) *Solution→Maximizer:* For any solution $Z$, we can construct

$$h_A^*(x_A) := (\Pr[Z = y | X_A = x_A])_y \qquad h_B^*(x_B) := (\Pr[Z = y | X_B = x_B])_y$$

and $\mathbf{p}^* = \Pr[Z = y]_y$. Then

$$\begin{aligned} R^f(h_A^*(x_A), h_B^*(x_B), \mathbf{p}^*) &\in \partial f\left(\sum_y \frac{\Pr[Z = y|X_A = x_A]\Pr[Z = y|X_B = x_B]}{\Pr[Z = y]}\right) \\ &= \partial f(K(x_A, x_B) && \text{(Claim 2.8)} \end{aligned}$$

Thus, based on Lemma 4.1, any solution $Z$ corresponds to a maximizer of the optimization goal.

(2)*Maximizer→(Permuted) Ground truth:* For any maximizer $(h_A^*(\cdot), h_B^*(\cdot), \mathbf{p}^*)$ of the optimization goal, when $f$ is differentiable, Lemma 4.1 shows that

$$R^f(h_A^*(x_A), h_B^*(x_B), \mathbf{p}^*) = f'(K(x_A, x_B)).$$

When $f'$ is invertible, we have

$$\sum_y \frac{h_A^*(x_A)(y) h_B^*(x_B)(y)}{\mathbf{p}^*(y)} = K(x_A, x_B)$$

for all $x_A, x_B$.

Thus, $\{(h_A^*(x_A), h_B^*(x_B), \mathbf{p}^*)\}_{x_A, x_B}$ is actually the solution of the system (1). When the prior is well-defined, there exists a permutation $\pi$ such that

$$h_A^*(x_A) := (\Pr[\pi(Y) = y | X_A = x_A])_y \qquad h_B^*(x_B) := (\Pr[\pi(Y) = y | X_B = x_B])_y$$

and $\mathbf{p}^* = \Pr[\pi(Y) = y]_y$ where $Y$ is the ground truth.

□

## 5 FORECAST ELICITATION WITHOUT VERIFICATION

This section considers the setting where the forecasts are provided by the crowds and we want to incentivize high quality forecast by providing an instant reward without instant access to the ground truth.

There is a forecasting task. Alice and Bob have private information $X_A, X_B = x_A \in \Sigma_A, x_B \in \Sigma_B$ correspondingly and are asked to forecast the ground truth $Y = y$. We denote $(\Pr[Y = y|X_A = x_A])_y$, $(\Pr[Y = y|X_B = x_B])_y$ by $\mathbf{p}_{x_A}, \mathbf{p}_{x_B}$ correspondingly. Alice and Bob are asked to report their Bayesian forecast $\mathbf{p}_{x_A}, \mathbf{p}_{x_B}$. We denote their actual reports by $\hat{\mathbf{p}}_{x_A}$ and $\hat{\mathbf{p}}_{x_B}$. Without access to the realization of $Y$, we want to incentivize both Alice and Bob play *truth-telling* strategies, i.e., honestly reporting their forecast $\mathbf{p}_{x_A}, \mathbf{p}_{x_B}$ for $Y$.

We define the *strategy* of Alice as a mapping $s_A$ from $x_A$ (private signal) to a probability distribution over the space of all possible forecast for random variable $Y$. Analogously, we define Bob's strategy $s_B$. Note that essentially each (possibly mixed) strategy $s_A$ can be seen as a (possibly random) predictor $P_A$ where $P_A(x_A)$ is a random forecast drawn from distribution $s_A(x_A)$. In particular, the truthful strategy corresponds to the Bayesian posterior predictor.

We say agents play a *permutation strategy profile* if there exists permutation $\pi : \Sigma \mapsto \Sigma$ such that each agent always reports $\pi\mathbf{p}$ given her truthful report is $\mathbf{p}$.

Note that without any side information about $Y$, we cannot distinguish the scenario where agents are honest and the scenario where agents play a permutation strategy profile. Thus, it is too much to ask truth-telling to be strictly better than any other strategy profile. The focal property defined in the following paragraph is the optimal property we can obtain.

*Mechanism Design Goals.*

**(Strictly) Truthful** Mechanism $\mathcal{M}$ is (strictly) truthful if truth-telling is a (strict) equilibrium.

**Focal** Mechanism $\mathcal{M}$ is focal if it is strictly truthful and each agent's expected payment is maximized if agents tell the truth; moreover, when agents play a non-permutation strategy profile, each agent's expected payment is *strictly* less.

We consider two settings:

**Multi-task** Each agent is assigned several independent a priori similar forecasting tasks in a random order and is asked to report her forecast for each task.

**Single-task** All agents are asked to report their forecast for the same single task.

In the single-task setting, it's impossible to design focal mechanisms since agents can collaborate to pick an arbitrary $y^* \in \Sigma$ and pretend that they know $Y = y^*$. However, we will show we can design strictly truthful mechanism in the single-task setting. In the multi-task setting, since agents may be assigned different tasks and the tasks show in random order, they cannot collaborate to pick an arbitrary $y^* \in \Sigma$ for each task. In fact, we will show if the number of tasks is greater or equal to 2, we can design a family of focal mechanisms.

Achieving the focal goal in the multi-task setting is very similar to what we did in finding the common ground truth. Note that in the forecast elicitation problem, incentivizing a truthful strategy is equivalent to incentivizing the Bayesian posterior predictor. Thus, we can directly use the $f$-mutual information gain as the reward in the multi-task setting. Achieving the strictly truthful goal in the single-task setting is more tricky and we will return to it later.

### 5.1 Multi-task: focal forecast elicitation without verification

We assume Alice is assigned tasks set $\mathcal{L}_A$ and Bob is assigned tasks set $\mathcal{L}_B$. For each task $\ell$, Alice's private information is $x_A^\ell$ and Bob's private information is $x_B^\ell$. The ground truth of this task is $y^\ell$.

*Multi-task common ground mechanism MCG($f$).* Given the prior distribution over $Y$, a convex and *differentiable* function $f$ whose convex conjugate is $f^\star$,

**Report** for each task $\ell \in \mathcal{L}_A$, Alice is asked to report $\mathbf{p}_{x_A{}^\ell} := (\Pr[Y = y|x_A^\ell])_y$; for each task $\ell \in \mathcal{L}_B$, Bob is asked to report $\mathbf{p}_{x_B{}^\ell} := (\Pr[Y = y|x_B^\ell])_y$. We denote their actual reports by $\hat{\mathbf{p}}^\ell_{x_A{}^\ell}$ and $\hat{\mathbf{p}}^\ell_{x_B{}^\ell}$.

**Payment** For each $\ell \in \mathcal{L}_A \cap \mathcal{L}_B$, reward both Alice and Bob "the amount of agreement" between their forecast in task $\ell$, i.e.,

$$R(\hat{\mathbf{p}}^\ell_{x_A{}^\ell}, \hat{\mathbf{p}}^\ell_{x_B{}^\ell});$$

for each pair of distinct tasks $(\ell_A, \ell_B), \ell_A \in \mathcal{L}_A, \ell_B \in \mathcal{L}_B, \ell_A \neq \ell_B$, punish both Alice and Bob "the amount of agreement" between their forecast in distinct tasks $(\ell_A, \ell_B)$, i.e.,

$$f^\star(R(\hat{\mathbf{p}}^{\ell_A}_{x_A{}^{\ell_A}}, \hat{\mathbf{p}}^{\ell_B}_{x_B{}^{\ell_B}}).$$

In total, both Alice and Bob are paid

$$\frac{1}{|\mathcal{L}_A \cap \mathcal{L}_B|} \sum_{\ell \in \mathcal{L}_A \cap \mathcal{L}_B} R(\hat{\mathbf{p}}^\ell_{x_A{}^\ell}, \hat{\mathbf{p}}^\ell_{x_B{}^\ell})$$

$$-\frac{1}{|\mathcal{L}_A||\mathcal{L}_B| - |\mathcal{L}_A \cap \mathcal{L}_B|^2} \sum_{\ell_A \in \mathcal{L}_A, \ell_B \in \mathcal{L}_B, \ell_A \neq \ell_B} f^{\star}(R(\hat{\mathbf{p}}^{\ell_A}_{x_A{}^{\ell_A}}, \hat{\mathbf{p}}^{\ell_B}_{x_B{}^{\ell_B}})$$

where

$$R(\mathbf{p}_1, \mathbf{p}_2) := f'(\sum_y \frac{\mathbf{p}_1(y)\mathbf{p}_2(y)}{\Pr[Y = y]}).$$

We do not want agents to collaborate with each other based on the index of the task or other information in addition to the private information. Thus, we make the following assumption to guarantee the index of the task is meaningless for all agents.

Assumption 5.1 (A priori similar and random order). *For each task $\ell$, fresh i.i.d. realizations of $(X_A, X_B, Y) = (x_A^\ell, x_B^\ell, y^\ell)$ are generated. All tasks appear in a random order, independently drawn for each agent.*

Theorem 5.2. *With the conditional independence assumption, and a priori similar and random order assumption, when the prior $Q$ is stable and well-defined, given the prior distribution over the $Y$, given a differential convex function $f$ whose derivative $f'$ is invertible, if $\max\{|\mathcal{L}_A|, |\mathcal{L}_B|\} \geq 2$, then $MCG(f)$ is focal. When both Alice and Bob are honest, each of them's expected payment in $MCG(f)$ is $MI^f(X_A; X_B)$.*

The non-negativity of $MI^f$ implies that agents are willing to participate in the mechanism. Like Theorem 4.3, in order to show Theorem 5.2, we need to first introduce a lemma which is very similar to Lemma 4.1.

Lemma 5.3. *With the conditional independence assumption, the expected total payment is maximized over Alice and Bob's strategies if and only if $\forall \ell_1 \in \mathcal{L}_A, \ell_2 \in \mathcal{L}_B$, for any $(x_A^{\ell_1}, x_B^{\ell_2}) \in \Sigma_A \times \Sigma_B$,*

$$R(\hat{\mathbf{p}}^{\ell_1}_{x_A{}^{\ell_1}}, \hat{\mathbf{p}}^{\ell_2}_{x_B{}^{\ell_2}}) = f'(K(x_A^{\ell_1}, x_B^{\ell_2})).$$

*The maximum is $MI^f(X_A; X_B)$.*

The proofs of Lemma 5.3 and Theorem 5.2 are very similar with Lemma 4.1 and Theorem 4.3. We defer the formal proofs to the full version.

## 5.2 Single-task: strictly truthful forecast elicitation without verification

This section introduces the strictly truthful mechanism in the single-task setting. If we know the realization $y$ of $Y$, we can simply apply a proper scoring rule and pay Alice and Bob $PS(y, \hat{\mathbf{p}}_{x_A})$ and $PS(y, \hat{\mathbf{p}}_{x_B})$ respectively. Then according to the property of the proper scoring rule, Alice and Bob will honestly report their truthful forecast to maximize their expected payment. However, we do not know the realization of $Y$. In the information elicitation without verification setting where Alice and Bob are required to report their information, Miller et al. [23] propose the "peer prediction" idea, that is, pays Alice the accuracy of the forecast that predicts Bob's information conditioning Alice's information, i.e., $PS(\hat{x}_B, (\Pr[X_B = x_B|\hat{x}_A])_y)$ where $\hat{x}_A$ and $\hat{x}_B$ are Alice and Bob's reported information. We note the peer prediction mechanism in Miller et al. [23] is truthful. With a similar "peer prediction" idea, we propose a strictly truthful mechanism in forecast elicitation.

*Common ground mechanism.* Given the prior distribution over $Y$,

**Report** Alice and Bob are required to report $\mathbf{p}_{x_A}, \mathbf{p}_{x_B}$. We denote their actual reports by $\hat{\mathbf{p}}_{x_A}$ and $\hat{\mathbf{p}}_{x_B}$.

**Payment** Both Alice and Bob are paid

$$\log \sum_y \frac{\hat{\mathbf{p}}_{x_A}(y)\hat{\mathbf{p}}_{x_B}(y)}{\Pr[Y = y]}.$$

THEOREM 5.4. *With the conditional independence assumption (and when the prior is stable), given the prior distribution over the $Y$, the common ground mechanism is (strictly) truthful; moreover, when both Alice and Bob are honest, each of them's expected payment in the common ground mechanism is the Shannon mutual information between their private information* $I(X_A; X_B) = MI^{KL}(X_A; X_B)$.

The (strictly) truthful property of the common ground mechanism is proved by the fact that log scoring rule *LSR* is strictly proper. We defer the proof to the full version.

## 6 CONCLUSION AND DISCUSSION

We build a natural connection between mechanism design and machine learning by addressing two related problems: (1) co-training: learning to forecast ground truth using two conditionally independent sources, without access to labeled data; (2) forecast elicitation: eliciting high quality forecasts from the crowds without verification, by the same information theoretic approach.

For the co-training problem, as usual in the related literature, we reduce the problem to an optimization problem and do not investigate the computation complexity or the data requirements. To implement our $f$-mutual information gain framework in practice, we implicitly assume that for high dimensional $X_A, X_B$, there exists a trainable set of hypotheses (e.g. neural networks) that is sufficiently rich to contain the Bayesian posterior predictor but not everything to cause over-fitting. The most apparent empirical direction will be running experiments on real data by training two neural networks to test our algorithms. Interesting theoretic directions include the analysis of the Bayesian risk and the influence of the choice of the convex function $f$ on the convergence rate.

For forecast elicitation, the most apparent direction will be performing real-world experiments. To apply our mechanisms, we do not need that every two agents' information is conditionally independent. In fact, for each agent, we only need to find a single reference agent for her such that the reference agent's information is conditionally independent of hers. Then we can run our mechanisms on the agent and her reference agent. In practice, we can pair the agents with some side information and make sure each pair of agents' information is conditionally independent.

Another interesting direction is to ensure fairness, in particular, that agents are not incentivized to coordinate on stereotypes. One solution, is suppressing information from some of the agents and using our framework. However, when this is not possible, the prior peer prediction work on cheap signals [12, 18] may be helpful in addressing this issue.

## ACKNOWLEDGEMENT

We thank Clayton Scott for useful conversations.

## REFERENCES

[1] Arpit Agarwal and Shivani Agarwal. 2015. On consistent surrogate risk minimization and property elicitation. In *Conference on Learning Theory*. 4–22.
[2] Syed Mumtaz Ali and Samuel D Silvey. 1966. A general class of coefficients of divergence of one distribution from another. *Journal of the Royal Statistical Society. Series B (Methodological)* (1966), 131–142.
[3] Suzanna Becker. 1996. Mutual information maximization: models of cortical self-organization. *Network: Computation in neural systems* 7, 1 (1996), 7–31.
[4] Anthony J Bell and Terrence J Sejnowski. 1995. An information-maximization approach to blind separation and blind deconvolution. *Neural computation* 7, 6 (1995), 1129–1159.
[5] Avrim Blum and Tom Mitchell. 1998. Combining labeled and unlabeled data with co-training. In *Proceedings of the eleventh annual conference on Computational learning theory*. ACM, 92–100.
[6] J-F Cardoso. 1997. Infomax and maximum likelihood for blind source separation. *IEEE Signal processing letters* 4, 4 (1997), 112–114.
[7] Michael Collins and Yoram Singer. 1999. Unsupervised models for named entity classification. In *1999 Joint SIGDAT Conference on Empirical Methods in Natural Language Processing and Very Large Corpora.*
[8] Thomas M Cover and Joy A Thomas. 2006. Elements of information theory 2nd edition. (2006).

[9] Imre Csiszár, Paul C Shields, et al. 2004. Information theory and statistics: A tutorial. *Foundations and Trends® in Communications and Information Theory* 1, 4 (2004), 417–528.

[10] Anirban Dasgupta and Arpita Ghosh. 2013. Crowdsourced judgement elicitation with endogenous proficiency. In *Proceedings of the 22nd international conference on World Wide Web*. 319–330.

[11] Sanjoy Dasgupta, Michael L Littman, and David A McAllester. 2002. PAC generalization bounds for co-training. In *Advances in neural information processing systems*. 375–382.

[12] A. Gao, J. R. Wright, and K. Leyton-Brown. 2016. Incentivizing Evaluation via Limited Access to Ground Truth: Peer-Prediction Makes Things Worse. *ArXiv e-prints* (June 2016). arXiv:cs.GT/1606.07042

[13] Tilmann Gneiting and Adrian E Raftery. 2007. Strictly proper scoring rules, prediction, and estimation. *J. Amer. Statist. Assoc.* 102, 477 (2007), 359–378.

[14] Ian Goodfellow, Jean Pouget-Abadie, Mehdi Mirza, Bing Xu, David Warde-Farley, Sherjil Ozair, Aaron Courville, and Yoshua Bengio. 2014. Generative adversarial nets. In *Advances in neural information processing systems*. 2672–2680.

[15] Sham M Kakade and Dean P Foster. 2007. Multi-view regression via canonical correlation analysis. In *International Conference on Computational Learning Theory*. Springer, 82–96.

[16] Roni Khardon and Gabriel Wachman. 2007. Noise tolerant variants of the perceptron algorithm. *Journal of Machine Learning Research* 8, Feb (2007), 227–248.

[17] Y. Kong and G. Schoenebeck. 2016. An Information Theoretic Framework For Designing Information Elicitation Mechanisms That Reward Truth-telling. *ArXiv e-prints* (May 2016). arXiv:cs.GT/1605.01021

[18] Y. Kong and G. Schoenebeck. 2018. Eliciting Expertise without Verification. *ArXiv e-prints* (Feb. 2018). arXiv:cs.GT/1802.08312

[19] Yingming Li, Ming Yang, and Zhongfei Zhang. 2016. Multi-view representation learning: A survey from shallow methods to deep methods. *arXiv preprint arXiv:1610.01206* (2016).

[20] Yang Liu and Yiling Chen. 2017. Machine-Learning Aided Peer Prediction. In *Proceedings of the 2017 ACM Conference on Economics and Computation (EC '17)*. ACM, New York, NY, USA, 63–80. https://doi.org/10.1145/3033274.3085126

[21] Yang Liu and Yiling Chen. 2018. Surrogate Scoring Rules and a Dominant Truth Serum for Information Elicitation. *CoRR* abs/1802.09158 (2018). arXiv:1802.09158 http://arxiv.org/abs/1802.09158

[22] D. McAllester. 2018. Information Theoretic Co-Training. *ArXiv e-prints* (Feb. 2018). arXiv:cs.LG/1802.07572

[23] N. Miller, P. Resnick, and R. Zeckhauser. 2005. Eliciting informative feedback: The peer-prediction method. *Management Science* (2005), 1359–1373.

[24] Nagarajan Natarajan, Inderjit S Dhillon, Pradeep K Ravikumar, and Ambuj Tewari. 2013. Learning with noisy labels. In *Advances in neural information processing systems*. 1196–1204.

[25] XuanLong Nguyen, Martin J Wainwright, and Michael I Jordan. 2009. On surrogate loss functions and f-divergences. *The Annals of Statistics* (2009), 876–904.

[26] XuanLong Nguyen, Martin J Wainwright, and Michael I Jordan. 2010. Estimating divergence functionals and the likelihood ratio by convex risk minimization. *IEEE Transactions on Information Theory* 56, 11 (2010), 5847–5861.

[27] Sebastian Nowozin, Botond Cseke, and Ryota Tomioka. 2016. f-gan: Training generative neural samplers using variational divergence minimization. In *Advances in Neural Information Processing Systems*. 271–279.

[28] D. Prelec. 2004. A Bayesian Truth Serum for subjective data. *Science* 306, 5695 (2004), 462–466.

[29] Alexander J Ratner, Christopher M De Sa, Sen Wu, Daniel Selsam, and Christopher Ré. 2016. Data programming: Creating large training sets, quickly. In *Advances in Neural Information Processing Systems*. 3567–3575.

[30] Vikas C Raykar, Shipeng Yu, Linda H Zhao, Gerardo Hermosillo Valadez, Charles Florin, Luca Bogoni, and Linda Moy. 2010. Learning from crowds. *Journal of Machine Learning Research* 11, Apr (2010), 1297–1322.

[31] R Tyrrell Rockafellar et al. 1966. Extension of Fenchel'duality theorem for convex functions. *Duke mathematical journal* 33, 1 (1966), 81–89.

[32] Clayton Scott, Gilles Blanchard, and Gregory Handy. 2013. Classification with asymmetric label noise: Consistency and maximal denoising. In *Conference On Learning Theory*. 489–511.

[33] Victor Shnayder, Arpit Agarwal, Rafael Frongillo, and David C Parkes. 2016. Informed truthfulness in multi-task peer prediction. In *Proceedings of the 2016 ACM Conference on Economics and Computation*. ACM, 179–196.

[34] Sainbayar Sukhbaatar and Rob Fergus. 2014. Learning from noisy labels with deep neural networks. *arXiv preprint arXiv:1406.2080* 2, 3 (2014), 4.

[35] Robert L Winkler. 1969. Scoring rules and the evaluation of probability assessors. *J. Amer. Statist. Assoc.* 64, 327 (1969), 1073–1078.

[36] Jens Witkowski, Pavel Atanasov, Lyle H Ungar, and Andreas Krause. 2017. Proper Proxy Scoring Rules.. In *AAAI*. 743–749.

[37] Chang Xu, Dacheng Tao, and Chao Xu. 2013. A survey on multi-view learning. *arXiv preprint arXiv:1304.5634* (2013).

[38] Yuchen Zhang, Xi Chen, Denny Zhou, and Michael I Jordan. 2014. Spectral methods meet EM: A provably optimal algorithm for crowdsourcing. In *Advances in neural information processing systems*. 1260–1268.

# Eliciting Expertise without Verification

YUQING KONG, University of Michigan, USA
GRANT SCHOENEBECK, University of Michigan, USA

A central question [1] of crowdsourcing is how to elicit expertise from agents. This is even more difficult when answers cannot be directly verified. A key challenge is that sophisticated agents may strategically withhold effort or information when they believe their payoff will be based upon comparison with other agents whose reports will likely omit this information due to lack of effort or expertise.

Our work defines a natural model for this setting based on the assumption that *more sophisticated agents know the beliefs of less sophisticated agents.*

We then provide a mechanism design framework for this setting. From this framework, we design several novel mechanisms, for both the single and multiple tasks settings, that (1) encourage agents to invest effort and provide their information honestly; (2) output a correct "hierarchy" of the information when agents are rational.

CCS Concepts: • **Theory of computation → Algorithmic mechanism design**; • **Information systems → Incentive schemes**;

Additional Key Words and Phrases: Peer prediction, information theory

## 1 INTRODUCTION

Crowdsourcing, outsourcing tasks to a crowd of workers (e.g. Amazon Mechanical Turk, peer grading for massive open online courses, scholarly peer review, and Yahoo answers), is a fast, cheap, and effective method for performing simple tasks even at large scales. To attract a large number of workers, crowdsourcing is usually open to the public rather than just professional experts. This makes crowdsourcing a challenge for more complicated tasks where agents with different levels of expertise may honestly report different answers. For example, in peer grading, some students may be incapable of accurate grading, missing errors other students point out.

One solution is to spot-check random tasks or equivalently to insert "gold-standard" tasks to which the mechanism already knows the answer. However, such techniques are expensive and even impossible for tasks where the agents' opinions can be very subjective (e.g. peer grading essay assignments) or individualized (e.g. experience at a restaurant).

[1] A full version of the paper is available at https://arxiv.org/abs/1802.08312.

This work is supported by the National Science Foundation, under grant CAREER#1452915, CCF#1618187 and AitF#1535912.
Authors' addresses: Yuqing Kong, University of Michigan, Ann Arbor, USA, yuqkong@umich.edu; Grant Schoenebeck, University of Michigan, Ann Arbor, USA, schoeneb@umich.edu.


*ACM EC'18, June 18–22, 2018, Ithaca, NY, USA.* ACM ISBN 978-1-4503-5829-3/18/06...$15.00
https://doi.org/10.1145/3219166.3219172

### 1.1 Our setting

This work is about the "peer-prediction" setting where such verification is unavailable or undesirable. Already, a large line of work in the peer prediction (PP) area [3, 6, 8, 12–24, 27, 28, 30–34, 36, 39–42] designed mechanisms for agents with similar expertise (without verification).

These papers study various settings. In the *single-task* setting [27, 28] agents are asked one multiple-choice question but typically share a common prior over the responses; in the *multi-tasks* setting [6, 20, 36] agents are assigned a batch of a priori similar multiple-choice questions. We consider both of these settings.

In the *detail-free* setting, the mechanism is not required to know information about the (common) prior distribution. Our mechanisms are generally in this setting, but some of them do require information about the different levels of expertise/effort agents can exhibit.

However, the aforementioned peer-prediction papers do not consider settings where

(1) **Agents have different levels of expertise** or
(2) **A lack of effort can systemically bias agents' reports**.

The following two tasks exemplify settings 1) and 2) respectively:

*Example 1.1.* Which state (from a list of all 50 states) in the United States of America is closest to Africa? (Single-task)

*Example 1.2.* Peer grading several essays by providing a grade from the set $\{1, 2, 3, 4, 5\}$. (Multi-tasks)

In the first example, an agent can guess randomly (no effort), look up the correct answer (full effort), or guess at the correct answer (partial effort). Most people will guess Florida, even though experts will know the correct answer is Maine. Thus differing levels of expertise yield different answers.

In the second example, a student can, instead of carefully grading (full effort) or assigning a random grade (zero effort), quickly check the name of the top of the paper and spot check the grammar (partial effort). Thus partial effort can systematically bias agents: consider an essay from a top student in an impeccable pose, but which contains large conceptual errors. Here partial effort can give some information about the correct answer, but also enable agents to "coordinate" on an incorrect answer.

Gao, Wright, and Leyton-Brown [9] show that the effects of the settings 1) and 2) are devastating to previous peer-prediction mechanisms, which generally fail in motivating the agents to invest effort for "expensive signals" when "cheap signals" (that ensure agreement and may even be correlated with the sought signal) exist. The main (very high-level) idea behind previous peer-prediction mechanisms can be understood as a "clever majority vote", every agent is paid according to a specific similarity between her and her peer. Thus, they point out that in the peer-grading example, coordinating on just checking the grammar can guarantee good agreement with other agents, but with substantially reduced effort.

In fact, Gao et al point out that things are likely even worse than this. If the cheap signals correlate more than the expensive signals, then the peer-prediction techniques incentivize agents to not report the true answer, but instead focus on cheap signals! For example, in the essay grading above, it is likely that assessments of grammatical correctness will agree more than assessments of overall essay quality. Because of this, peer-prediction mechanisms will pay agents more overall for lower-quality information. In Example 1.1, even if agents know the answer is Maine, they may report Florida, expecting that most others will do likewise.

Such behavior undermines the goal of applying crowdsourcing to increasingly complex tasks, and, in fact, undercuts any application of crowdsourcing to perform any task where the answers are not "common knowledge." The field must overcome this key challenge of rewarding rather than suppressing expertise in order to begin the project of expanding crowdsourcing beyond simple labeling tasks.

### 1.2 Key Insight and Assumption

Previous peer-prediction mechanisms treat all information (cheap/expensive) equally, and thus agents lack an incentive to invest the effort to obtain expensive signals. Moreover, even when an expert can easily obtain the expensive signal, the previous mechanism discourage her from providing it when she believes the non-experts will disagree.

A successful mechanism must break the symmetry between weak and expensive signals and between expert and non-expert signals. We propose the following natural assumption which will allow a mechanism to break this symmetry.

Assumption 1.3. *Agents with high effort or expertise know the beliefs of agents with less effort or less expertise.*

We can see that this assumption is very natural in Example 1.1 and Example 1.2. Agents who look up or know the answer in Example 1.1 also know most people will answer "Florida." Agents that carefully grade an essay can also approximate the score of an agent who spends very little effort. We will define a hierarchical information structure (Section 3) to naturally capture Assumption 1.3.

Our mechanisms solicit not only agents' own opinions but also their predictions for the opinions of the other agents who have less information. This differs with the previous peer prediction mechanisms which ask agents to provide their predictions for *all* other agents' opinions. For example, in the peer-grading example, we might ask agents to report their own evaluation, and to *optionally* report one or more low-effort / low expertise evaluations (e.g. scores based on grammar, thesis statement, student name, naive reading, etc).

### 1.3 Our contribution

- **Modeling:** We define a hierarchical information structure (the higher level information is more valuable and harder to obtain) model that captures the hierarchical relationship between the different expertise;
- **Mechanism design:** We employ information theory tools to provide a mechanism design framework for the aforementioned hierarchical setting—Hierarchical Mutual Information Paradigm (HMIP)—which 1) pays the higher level information more and encourages agents to invest effort for different levels of information according to their own abilities 2) incentivizes agents to report honestly; and 3) only pays agents for information they actually learn. We apply our mechanism design framework to create the following mechanisms:
  - **Multi-HMIM** which works in the multi-task setting even for a small number of tasks but requires the mechanism to know the hierarchical information structure.
  - **Learning-based Multi-HMIM** which works in the multi-task setting even when the mechanism does not know the hierarchical information structure; however requires a large number of tasks.
  - **Single-HMIM** which works in the single-task setting.
- **Algorithmic:** In the multiple task setting where the mechanism does not know the hierarchical information structure, we design an algorithm which, given agent reports as input, outputs the hierarchical structure of the information as well as the most valuable information. Note that our algorithm is robust against agents with limited (or no) information reporting biased (or totally random and useless) information. This is used as part of the *Learning-based Multi-HMIM* mechanism.

### 1.4 Road Map

The remainder of this section discusses related work; Section 2 lays out the mathematical tools we use and can be referred back to when necessary. Section 3 introduces both our model, the hierarchical information structure, and our mechanism design framework, the hierarchical mutual information paradigm (HMIP). Section 4 and section 5 apply the HMIP mechanism design framework into multi-task setting and single-task setting respectively.

In the multi-task setting (Section 4), we consider two situations: 1) the mechanism knows the information structure shared by agents but each agent is assigned a small number of tasks; 2) the mechanism does not know the information structure but each agent is assigned a large number of tasks such that the mechanism can learn the information structure. In the single-task setting (Section 5), we assume the mechanism know the information structure.

Section 6 concludes by discussing some potential applications and the robustness of our mechanisms.

### 1.5 Related Work

*Model perspective.* Prior work has modeled heterogeneous expertise where different agents receive a different number of signals [12] or expertise is embedding in several dimensions [7, 26, 37, 43]; however in these works lower expertise/effort along with a certain dimension only leads to a more noisy signal. In contrast, our model allows such signals to be systematically biased.

*Mechanism design perspective.* The most related work with the current paper is Prelec et al. [29] which uses Bayesian Truth Serum [28] to incentivize agents to report their signal and selects the most surprising signal (measured by occurring more than its average prediction) as the final answer. McCoy and Prelec [26] follow Prelec et al. [29] to propose a probabilistic model to learn the expertise of agents. Riley [35] compares the peer prediction decision rule (similar to Prelec et al. [29]) and the majority vote rule and exhibits cases where each outperforms the other. The current paper differs with Prelec et al. [29] in the model and assumptions as well as the possible applications. Prelec et al. [29] only focus on the single-task setting and assume that agents receive the signals endogenously (without effort). In contrast, this paper considers both single and multiple task settings and the model used in this paper handles both exogenous and indigenous signals.

The mechanism design framework in the current paper extends the information theoretic framework proposed in Kong and Schoenebeck [20]. Agarwal et al. [1] propose a mechanism that works for the heterogeneous participants in the multi-task setting. Mandal et al. [25] consider the setting with heterogeneous tasks. They all do not assume the hierarchy of the information and cannot be applied to identify and elicit expertise.

*Algorithmic perspective.* Several works [7, 10, 37, 43] provide clever methods to learn the expertise as well as the ground truth of the crowdsourcing tasks. The algorithm in the current paper differs in two main aspects: (1) The current paper uses a different expertise model which can successfully capture the possibly hierarchical relationship between different information/expertise as well as the most valuable information; (2) the current paper combines the algorithm with an incentive mechanism that endogenously controls the quality and structure of the input, rather than making exogenous assumptions about the quality of the input.

## 2 MECHANISM DESIGN TOOLS

We use two key information theory ingredients in designing information elicitation mechanisms. The first ingredient is $f$-mutual information $MI^f(X;Y)$ which measures the amount of information crossing two random variables $X, Y$. For example, if $X$ is independent with $Y$—no information crosses $X$ and $Y$, $MI^f(X;Y) = 0$. The second ingredient is proper scoring rule $PS(x, \mathbf{p})$ which measures the accuracy of the prediction $\mathbf{p}$ even we only have one sample $x$ of the outcome $X$.

Both two ingredients have the information monotonicity property. If the information is measured by $f$-mutual information, any "data processing" on either of the random variables will decrease the amount of information crossing them. If the accuracy of a forecast is measured by a proper scoring rule, more information implies a more accurate forecast.

## 2.1 $f$-mutual information

$f$-divergence [2, 5] $D_f : \Delta_\Sigma \times \Delta_\Sigma \to \mathbb{R}$ is a non-symmetric measure of the difference between distribution $\mathbf{p} \in \Delta_\Sigma$ and distribution $\mathbf{q} \in \Delta_\Sigma$ and is defined to be $D_f(\mathbf{p}, \mathbf{q}) := \sum_{\sigma\in\Sigma} \mathbf{p}(\sigma) f\left(\frac{\mathbf{q}(\sigma)}{\mathbf{p}(\sigma)}\right)$ where $f(\cdot)$ is a convex function and $f(1) = 0$. Two commonly used $f$-divergences are KL divergence and total variation distance. Now we start to introduce $f$-mutual information.

Given two random variables $X, Y$, let $\mathbf{U}_{X,Y}$ and $\mathbf{V}_{X,Y}$ be two probability measures where $\mathbf{U}_{X,Y}$ is the joint distribution of $(X, Y)$ and $\mathbf{V}$ is the product of the marginal distributions of $X$ and $Y$. Formally, for every pair of $(x, y)$,

$$\mathbf{U}_{X,Y}(X = x, Y = y) = \Pr[X = x, Y = y] \qquad \mathbf{V}_{X,Y}(X = x, Y = y) = \Pr[X = x] \Pr[Y = y].$$

If $\mathbf{U}_{X,Y}$ is very different with $\mathbf{V}_{X,Y}$, the mutual information between $X$ and $Y$ should be high since knowing $X$ changes the belief for $Y$ a lot. If $\mathbf{U}_{X,Y}$ equals to $\mathbf{V}_{X,Y}$, the mutual information between $X$ and $Y$ should be zero since $X$ is independent with $Y$. Intuitively, the "distance" between $\mathbf{U}_{X,Y}$ and $\mathbf{V}_{X,Y}$ represents the mutual information between them.

*Definition 2.1 ($f$-mutual information [20]).* The $f$-mutual information between $X$ and $Y$ is defined as

$$MI^f(X;Y) = D_f(\mathbf{U}_{X,Y}, \mathbf{V}_{X,Y})$$

where $D_f$ is $f$-divergence.

*Definition 2.2 (Conditional $f$-mutual information [20]).* Given three random variables $X, Y, Z$, we define $MI^f(X;Y|Z)$ as

$$\sum_z Pr[Z = z] MI^f(X;Y|Z = z)$$

where $MI^f(X;Y|Z = z) := MI^f(X';Y')$ where $Pr[X' = x, Y' = y] = Pr[X = x, Y = y|Z = z]$.

Two examples of $f$-mutual information are Shannon mutual information [4] (Choosing $f$-divergence as KL divergence) and $MI^{tvd}(X;Y) := \sum_{x,y} |\Pr[X = x, Y = y] - \Pr[X = x]\Pr[Y = y]|$ (Choosing $f$-divergence as Total Variation Distance).

Lemma 2.3 (General data processing inequality / Information monotonicity [20]). *When $f$ is convex, $f$-mutual information $MI^f$ is symmetric $MI^f(X;Y) = MI^f(Y;X)$; non-negative and satisfies data processing equality: for any transition probability $M \in \mathbb{R}^{|\Sigma_X| \times |\Sigma_X|}$, when $Y$ is independent with $M(X)$ conditioning on $X$, $MI^f(M(X);Y) \leq MI^f(X;Y)$.*

## 2.2 Proper scoring rules

Informally, a scoring rule measures the accuracy of the forecasts. Formally, a scoring rule [11, 38] $PS : \Sigma \times \Delta_\Sigma \to \mathbb{R}$ takes in a signal $x \in \Sigma$ and a distribution over signals $\delta_\Sigma \in \Delta_\Sigma$ and outputs a real number. A scoring rule is *proper* if, whenever the first input is drawn from a distribution $\delta_\Sigma$, then $\delta_\Sigma$ will maximize the expectation of $PS$ over all possible inputs in $\Delta_\Sigma$ to the second coordinate. A scoring rule is called *strictly proper* if this maximum is unique. We will assume throughout that the scoring rules we use are strictly proper. Slightly abusing notation, we can extend a scoring rule to be $PS : \Delta_\Sigma \times \Delta_\Sigma \to \mathbb{R}$ by simply taking $PS(\delta_\Sigma, \delta'_\Sigma) = \mathbb{E}_{x\leftarrow\delta_\Sigma}(x, \delta'_\Sigma)$.

## 3 MODEL AND MECHANISM DESIGN FRAMEWORK

In this section, we will define the hierarchical information structure and provide a mechanism design framework that helps design mechanisms which elicit the hierarchical information. Section 3.1 defines the information model; Section 3.2 defines our mechanism framework; and Section 3.3 analyzes the framework. We will use the peer grading process (Figure 1) as a running example to throughout this section.

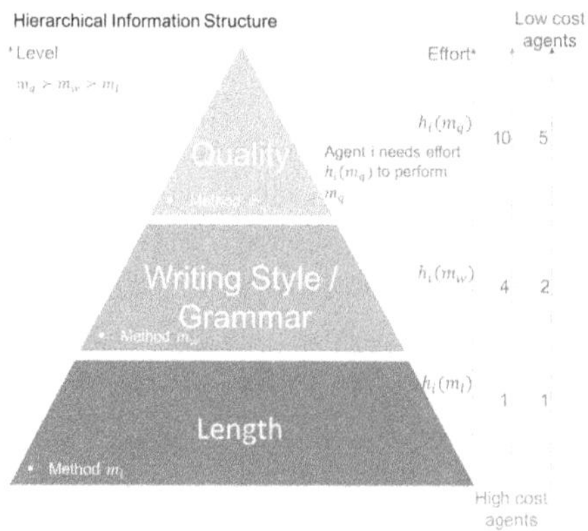


Fig. 1. An illustration of the hierarchical information structure in the peer grading process.

### 3.1 Hierarchical Information Structure

There are $n$ agents and one task. The agents have a finite set $M$ of methods to perform on the task based on the task's attributes $\mathbf{a} \in A$ where $a$ is a random (possibly high dimensional) vector drawn from a distribution $Q_A \in \Delta_A$. Each method $m : A \mapsto \Sigma_m$ maps the attributes $\mathbf{a} \in A$ to a signal $m(\mathbf{a})$ from a finite set $\Sigma_m$. We now introduce our peer grading example.

> 10 evaluators are asked to judge one essay. The essay has eight possible attributes: $\mathbf{a} = (q_i, w_j, l_k), i, j, k \in \{0, 1\}$. $(q_1, w_0, l_1)$ means the essay has (good quality, bad writing, long length); $(q_0, w_1, l_0)$ means the essay has (bad quality, good writing, short length). The distribution over the attributes space $Q_A$ is defined as:
>
> | $Q_A((q_0, w_0, *))$ | $Q_A((q_0, w_1, *))$ | $Q_A((q_1, w_0, *))$ | $Q_A((q_1, w_1, *))$ |
> |---|---|---|---|
> | 0.4 | 0.1 | 0.1 | 0.4 |
>
> With this distribution, an essay of good quality usually has good writing as well. Moreover, we assume the essay's length is independent with the essay's quality and writing and an essay has long length with probability 0.5. That is: $Q_A((q_i, w_j, l_1)) = Q_A((q_i, w_j, *)) * 0.5$, $Q_A((q_i, w_j, l_0)) = Q_A((q_i, w_j, *)) * 0.5$.
> Each evaluator can perform three methods: $m_l(\mathbf{a})$, $m_w(\mathbf{a})$, and $m_q(\mathbf{a})$ which are, respectively, (possibly noisy) signals about the essay's length; writing style and grammar; and quality. $\Sigma_l = \Sigma_w = \Sigma_q = \{☺, ☹\}$.

We define $\psi_i^m(\mathbf{a})$ as agent $i$'s received output by performing $m$ on attributes $\mathbf{a}$. Different agents may receive different signals by performing the same method on the same attributes. But we assume the distribution is symmetric/homogeneous in the sense that for any permutation $\pi : [n] \mapsto [n]$, the probability that $\psi_1^m(\mathbf{a}) = \sigma_1, \psi_2^m(\mathbf{a}) = \sigma_2, \ldots \psi_n^m(\mathbf{a}) = \sigma_n$ equals the probability that $\psi_{\pi(1)}^m(\mathbf{a}) = \sigma_1$,

$\psi^m_{\pi(2)}(\mathrm{a}) = \sigma_2, \ldots \psi^m_{\pi(n)}(\mathrm{a}) = \sigma_n$. We also assume that each agent performs methods independently (see (1)). When the attributes a is drawn from a distribution $Q_A$, we can define define $\Psi^m_i$ as agent $i$'s received output by performing $m$ on a random attributes a that is drawn from a distribution $Q_A$. Analogously, we define a random variable $\Psi^m_{-i}$ as an arbitrary agent $j \neq$'s received output by performing $m$ on a random attributes a that is drawn from a distribution $Q_A$. This definition is well-defined since we have assumed the distribution is symmetric. We define prior $Q$ as a joint distribution over all $\{\Psi^m_i\}_{i\in[n],m\in M}$.

Conditioning on the attributes of the essay $\mathrm{a} = (q_i, w_j, l_k), i, j, k \in \{0, 1\}$, for each method $m$, each agent will receive $\psi^m_i(\mathrm{a}) = ☺$ with probability $p_{m,\mathrm{a}}$ independently by performing $m$. That is, agents' received signals by performing $m$ is a Binomial distribution $B(n = 10, p_{m,\mathrm{a}})$. [a]

| | good quality essay[b] | bad quality essay |
|---|---|---|
| $\Pr[m_q(\mathrm{a}) = ☺]$ | 70% | 30% |

This means conditioning on the essay having good quality, the distribution over agents' received quality signals by performing $m_q$ is $Q_{m_q,(q_1,*,*)} = B(10, 0.7)$; while conditioning on the essay having good quality, the distribution is $Q_{m_q,(q_0,*,*)} = B(10, 0.3)$. Similarly, we have

| | good writing essay | bad writing essay |
|---|---|---|
| $\Pr[m_w(\mathrm{a}) = ☺]$ | 90% | 10% |

| | long essay | short essay |
|---|---|---|
| $\Pr[m_l(\mathrm{a}) = ☺]$ | 100% | 0% |

Note that the cheap length signal is noiseless. We also assume that fixing the attributes, every agent performs the different methods independently. That is, when $\mathrm{a} = (q_1, w_1, l_1)$

$$\Pr\left(\Psi^{m_l}_i(\mathrm{a}) = ☺, \Psi^{m_w}_i(\mathrm{a}) = ☺, \Psi^{m_q}_i(\mathrm{a}) = ☺\right) = 0.7 * 0.9 * 1. \tag{1}$$

With the above set up, the probability that agent $i$ receives a ☺ writing signal and agent $j$ receives a ☺ quality signal will be

$\Pr[\Psi^{m_w}_i = ☺, \Psi^{m_q}_j = ☺] = 0.4 * 0.1 * 0.3 + 0.1 * 0.3 * 0.9 + 0.1 * 0.7 * 0.1 + 0.4 * 0.7 * 0.9 = 0.298.$

[a] To give a concrete example, we use the Binomial distribution here. In fact, we only need the distribution to be symmetric.

[b] This means $\mathrm{a} = (q_1, *, *)$

We define a partial order on the methods. We say $m_1 \succeq m_2$—the level of $m_1$ is higher than that of $m_2$—if method $m_1$ cannot be performed without performing $m_2$. By $m_1 \succ m_2$ we mean $m_1 \succeq m_2$ but $m_2 \not\succeq m_1$. Note that the partial order $\succ$ is transitive—$m_1 \succ m_2, m_2 \succ m_3 \Rightarrow m_1 \succ m_3$. Each agent $i$ needs effort $h_i(m) > 0$ to perform method $m$ and when she spends effort $h_i(m)$ to perform $m$, the methods that have lower levels than $m$ are performed as well without additional effort. We assume, as is natural, that $h_i(m)$ is an increasing function, that is, $h_i(m_1) \geq h_i(m_2)$ when $m_1 \succeq m_2$. The higher the level of the method an agent performs, the more effort she must invest. However, it may be the case that some agents (low cost agents) can perform methods more economically than others (high cost agents). The partial order definition is essentially our key assumption (Assumption 1.3).

$m_q \succ m_w \succ m_a$. Among the 10 evaluators, there are 2 low cost evaluators who need 1, 2, 5 effort to perform $m_l, m_w, m_q$ respectively. There are 8 high cost evaluators who need 1, 4, 10 effort to perform $m_l, m_w, m_q$ respectively (Figure 1). Based on the partial order definition, when an evaluator spends sufficient effort to perform $m_q$ and obtains the quality signal, she also obtains the length and writing signals without additional effort, which is natural in real life.

We assume agents share a hierarchical information structure and allow agents to have different priors $Q$[2]. We will design mechanisms that incentivize agents to invest efforts based on their costs and report honestly.

### 3.2 Mechanism Design Framework

We start by introducing the formal definition of a mechanism.

*Definition 3.1 (Mechanism).* We define a *mechanism* $\mathcal{M}$ for $n$ agents as a tuple $\mathcal{M} := (R, S)$ where $R$ is a set of all possible reports the mechanism allows, and $S : R^n \mapsto \mathbb{R}^n$ is a mapping from all agents' reports to each agent's payment.

We will extend the Mutual Information Paradigm [20] to our Hierarchical Mutual Information Paradigm that handles the hierarchical information structure.

*Mutual Information Paradigm [20].* Kong and Schoenebeck [20] provide a Mutual Information Paradigm for Peer Prediction Mechanisms: each agent $i$ is paid the mutual information between her information and her peers' information—

$$MI(\text{her information}; \text{her peers' information}).$$

By picking $f$-mutual information $MI^f$ that satisfies data processing equality (Section 2.1), no agent can obtain strict benefit by lying since intuitively the amount of information each agent has will not increase no matter what kind of strategy she applies to her information.

We can naturally extend the Mutual Information Paradigm for Peer Prediction Mechanisms to the hierarchical model by paying agent $i$

$$MI^f(\text{her information}; \{\Psi_{-i}^m\}_{m \in M})\text{[3]}.$$

This idea has a severe drawback: sometimes low level information has very large correlation with the high level information. In this case, $MI^f(\text{her information}; \{\Psi_{-i}^m\}_{m \in M})$ will pay low level information nearly as much as high level information; and so agents will lack incentive to perform high level methods.

To solve the above problem, we pay agents method by method. For each $m$, we only value the "information gain" in the sense that we pay each agent $i$ the mutual information between her information and the method $m$'s information *conditioning on* the information output by the methods are lower than $m$.

Formally, we chose a payment scale $\alpha_m$ for each $m$ and pay each agent $i$

$$\sum_m \alpha_m MI^f(\text{her information}; \Psi_{-i}^m | \{\Psi_{-i}^{m'}\}_{m' < m}).$$

In our actual paradigm, we hope to pay each agent $i$ using the above payment when the mechanism has access to all levels of honest information provided by other agents.

In the peer grading example, the information about the writing style / grammar may already have a very high correlation with the quality of the essay. With the above concrete set up,

[2] To ease the presentation of the example, in our peer grading example, we assume agents share the same prior $Q$.

[3] Recall that $(\Psi_1^m, \Psi_2^m, ..., \Psi_n^m)$ are the random signals agents receive by performing method $m$ on the same random attributes.

we are ready to calculate the (conditional) Shannon mutual information (Euler number base) between agent $i$'s received signals and agent $j$'s received signals. For example, the $2 \times 2$ entry is the mutual information between agent $i$'s received length signal, writing signal by performing method $m_w$ and agent $j$'s writing signal, conditioning on agent $j$'s length signal, which is 0.2259. We calculate the values by first calculating the joint distribution over 6 random variables—agent $i$'s length, writing, quality signals and agent $j$'s length, writing, quality signals.
We show the values in the following table and defer the calculation to the full version. According to the information monotonicity, for each column, the values increase from bottom to top.

| $MI(\cdot;\cdot)$ agent $j$'s / agent $i$'s | length | writing\|length [a] | quality \| writing, length | length, writing, quality [b] |
|---|---|---|---|---|
| length, writing, quality | 0.6931 | 0.2259 | **0.0115** | **0.9305** |
| length, writing | 0.6931 | 0.2218 | **0.0041** | **0.9190** |
| length | 0.6931 | 0 | 0 | 0.6931 |

Even though performing the quality method provides the information that has the highest mutual information 0.9305 with other agents' information, performing writing method already outputs information that has $0.9190 \approx 0.9305 * 0.98$ mutual information with other agents' information.
In this case, what we really value is the additional quality of information after conditioning on the information of cheap signals like writing style / grammar. In other words, we value the information about an essay which has a high quality but is written carelessly (or low quality but impeccable prose).
Each agent, performing the writing method only has 0.0041 mutual information with other agents' quality signal conditioning on other agents' writing and length signals while performing the quality method has $0.0115 \approx 0.0041 * 2.80$ conditional mutual information.
Looking ahead, we seek to pay each evaluator $i$ by:

$$\begin{aligned} &\alpha_l MI^f(\text{her information; agent } j\text{'s length signal}) \quad (2)\\ &+\alpha_w MI^f(\text{her information; agent } j\text{'s writing signal}|\text{agent } j\text{'s length signal})\\ &+\alpha_q MI^f(\text{her information; agent } j\text{'s quality signal}|\text{agent } j\text{'s length and writing signal}).\end{aligned}$$

where $\alpha_q$ is set to be rather larger than $\alpha_l$ and $\alpha_w$.

[a] x|y means x conditioning on y.

[b] Since we use Shannon mutual information which satisfies chain rule, the last column is the sum of the previous columns.

*Hierarchical Mutual Information Paradigm (HMIP($MI^f$,$\{\alpha_m\}_m$)).* We now present our hierarchical Mutual Information Paradigm. We emphasize that this is not a mechanism that can be run. Instead we engage in the wishful thinking that the reports of the agents are distributions rather than draws from the distribution. Of course, this will never happen. Nonetheless, we will show that using the HMIP paradigm we can design actual mechanisms in both the multiple-task setting (Section 4) and the single-task setting (Section 5).

The paradigm requires as parameters a payment scale $\alpha_m \in \mathbb{R}_{\geq 0}$ for each method $m$.

**Report** For each agent $i$, for each $m \in M$, she is asked to optionally provide the random signal $\Psi_i^m$. We denote the set of methods whose outputs are reported by agent $i$ as $M_i$ and the actual random signal she reports for each $\ell \in M_i$ as $\hat{\Psi}_i^\ell$.

**Payment/Information Score** We define $M_{-i}$ as $\bigcup_{j\neq i} M_j$. For each $m \in M_{-i}$, we arbitrarily pick an agent $j \neq i$ who provides method $m$'s output and denote his report for method $m$'s output as $\hat{\Psi}_{-i}^m$.

Agent $i$ is paid by her information score

$$\sum_{m\in M_{-i}} \alpha_m MI^f(\{\hat{\Psi}_i^\ell\}_{\ell\in M_i}; \hat{\Psi}_{-i}^m | \{\hat{\Psi}_{-i}^{m'}\}_{m'<m, m'\in M_{-i}})$$

*Resolving "wishful thinking".* HMIP pays agents according to the information measure. The calculation of the information measure requires the knowledge of the prior, i.e., the joint distribution which is unrealistic in practice. To resolve this "wishful thinking", a key observation is that paying agents an unbiased estimator of the information measure is sufficient when we assume agents are expected utility maximizers. To construct an unbiased estimator of the information measure using agents' reports, different settings have different techniques. In the multi-task setting, either we ask a large number of questions to estimate the prior and use the prior to calculate the information measure (Learning-based multi-HMIM), or we ask a small number questions but require the knowledge of the structure and use a special $f$-mutual information, $MI^{tvd}$ (Multi-HMIM). In the single-task setting (Single-HMIM), we ask agents their posteriors (e.g. what percentage of your peers say yes?) and construct the estimator using both the first order information (e.g., Y/N) and the second order information (e.g., 80% Yes). Thus, although all proposed mechanisms are based on the HMIP, they are all detail free in the sense that they do not need any priori knowledge of the distributions (nor wishful thinking).

### 3.3 Analysis of HMIP

For each agent $i$, we define her utility as her payment minus her effort.

*Definition 3.2 (Strategy).* We define the *effort strategy* of each agent $i$ as a mapping $e_i$ from her priors to a probability distribution over the methods she will perform. We define the *report strategy* of each agent $i$ as a mapping $s_i$ from her received information to a probability distribution over $R$.

*Definition 3.3 (Amount of information in HMIP).* In HMIP, for agent $i$, the amount of information acquired with method $m_i$ is defined as

$$AOI(m_i, \text{HMIP}(MI^f, \{\alpha_m\}_m)) := \sum_{m\in M} \alpha_m MI^f(\{\Psi_i^\ell\}_{\ell\leq m_i}; \Psi_{-i}^m | \{\Psi_{-i}^{m'}\}_{m'<m}).$$

We have already give the example of the amount of information in (2). Later in the proof of Theorem 3.7, we will see the amount of information is also the optimal payment of agent $i$ who performs method $m_i$ when HMIP has access to all levels of honest signals reported by other agents.

An especially desirable strategy in HMIP is a *prudent strategy*. Informally, agents play a prudent strategy if they (a) choose the method they perform to maximize their utility—trading off the amount of information acquired with the effort it costs; (b) report all received information honestly.

*Definition 3.4 (Prudent strategy in HMIP).* For each agent $i$, we say she plays a prudent strategy in HMIP($MI^f$,$\{\alpha_m\}_m$) if she chooses to (a) perform method $m_i^*$ such that

$$m_i^* \in \arg\max_{m_i} \left(AOI(m_i, \text{HMIP}(MI^f, \{\alpha_m\}_m)) - h_i(m_i)\right); \textit{and}$$

(b) reports all received information honestly.

*Definition 3.5 (Truthful strategy in HMIP).* We say an agent plays truthful strategy if she always reports her received information honestly.

A truthful strategy is a special report strategy. An agent can play any effort strategy and truthful strategy simultaneously. If an agent invests no effort and reports nothing or meaningless information, she is still considered as playing truthful strategy.

*Mechanism design goals.* A mechanism $\mathcal{M}$ is (strictly) *potent* if for each agent, when she believes everyone else plays their prudent strategy, she can (strictly) maximize her expected utility by playing a prudent strategy as well. A mechanism $\mathcal{M}$ is *dominant truthful* if for each agent, regardless of other agents' strategies, she can maximize her expected utility by playing a pure effort strategy and truthful strategy.

The dominant truthful property is incomparable with the potent property. A flat payment scheme is dominant truthful but not potent since investing no effort and reporting nothing is also considered as a pure effort and truthful strategy. The potent property is desirable since it encourages low cost agents to invest high level effort and high cost agents to invest low level effort, and incentivizes them to report honestly as well.

In order to design potent mechanism, the coefficients $\{\alpha_m\}_m$ should be chosen appropriately. If the coefficients $\{\alpha_m\}_m$ are too low, no agent will be incentivized to invest the highest level method. In this case, the mechanism cannot access all levels of information to encourage agents to play prudent strategy. Thus, we will assume the coefficients are chosen such that it is worthwhile for at least two agents to invest the highest level method.

We say a method $m$ is *maximal* if there does not exist $m' \neq m \in M$ such that $m' > m$.

*Definition 3.6 (potent coefficients for HMIP).* Given the priors $\{Q_m\}_m$, we say the coefficients $\{\alpha_m\}_m$ are potent for HMIP($MI^f$,$\{\alpha_m\}_m$) if given the coefficients $\{\alpha_m\}_m$, for every maximal $m$, there exists at least **two** agents whose prudent strategy in HMIP($MI^f$,$\{\alpha_m\}_m$) is performing method $m$.

This is a weak requirement since we only need to set sufficiently high coefficients to incentivize **two** low cost agents such that for each agent (including one of the low cost agent), she will believe there exists a low cost agent who will be incentivized to report all levels of information. potent coefficients exist since we can always set the coefficient of the highest level information sufficiently high and the coefficients of other levels arbitrarily close to zero such that agents will be incentivized to invest the highest level effort. We use our peer grading example to show how to set potent coefficients. With our example, we will see we can always set the optimal potent coefficients that minimize the mechanism's cost by solving a linear programming.

In our example, the 2 low cost agents need efforts 1,2,5 to perform $m_l, m_w, m_q$ respectively and 8 high cost agents need efforts 1,4,10. With the above set up, we need $\alpha_q * 0.0115 + \alpha_w * 0.2259 + \alpha_l * 0.6931 - 5 > \max\{\alpha_q * 0.0041 + \alpha_w * 0.2218 + \alpha_l * 0.6931 - 2, \alpha_l * 0.6931 - 1, 0\}$ to make the coefficients potent and we also want to minimize the mechanism's cost which is

$$
\begin{aligned}
&2 * (\alpha_q * 0.0115 + \alpha_w * 0.2259 + \alpha_l * 0.6931)\\
&+ 8 * \begin{cases} v_q := \alpha_q * 0.0115 + \alpha_w * 0.2259 + \alpha_l * 0.6931 & \text{if } v_q - 10 \geq v_w - 4, v_l - 1, 0 \\ v_w := \alpha_q * 0.0041 + \alpha_w * 0.2218 + \alpha_l * 0.6931 & \text{if } v_w - 4 \geq v_q - 10, v_l - 1, 0 \\ v_l := \alpha_l * 0.6931 & \text{if } v_l - 1 \geq v_w - 4, v_q - 10, 0 \\ 0 & \text{otherwise} \end{cases}
\end{aligned}
$$

After solving this linear programming, the optimal solution is around $\alpha_l, \alpha_w, \alpha_q = \epsilon^a, 0.5562, 423.8571$ and the amount of information for performing $m_l$,$m_w$,and $m_q$ are $O(\epsilon)$, $1.86 + O(\epsilon)$, and $5 + O(\epsilon)$ respectively. The minimal cost is $2 * (5 + O(\epsilon)) = 10 + O(\epsilon)$.

[a] $\epsilon$ is an arbitrarily small positive real number, we need $\epsilon$ since we want agents will be incentivized to report the length signal as well.

Theorem 3.7. *Given a convex function $f$, HMIP($MI^f$,$\{\alpha_m\}_m$) is dominant truthful; moreover, when $\{\alpha_m\}_m$ are potent for HMIP($MI^f$,$\{\alpha_m\}_m$), HMIP($MI^f$,$\{\alpha_m\}_m$) is potent and dominant truthful.*

The proof of the theorem uses the information monotonicity of $MI^f$. The key observation in the proof is that *applying any strategy to the information is essentially data processing and thus erodes information.*

Proof for Theorem 3.7. In order to show the dominant truthful property, we will show for each agent, fixing any other agents' strategies, she can maximize her payment as well as her utility by reporting her received information honestly. The information monotonicity property of $f$-mutual information $MI^f$ (Fact 2.3) says any data processing decreases the (conditional) mutual information. For each $m \in M_{-i}$, fixing the strategies other agents use, the distribution of $\hat{\Psi}^m_{-i}$, whose randomness comes from random variable $\Psi^m_{-i}$ and the agents' strategies, is also fixed. Any strategy (data processing) agent $i$ applies to her received signals decreases

$$MI^f(\text{her received signals}; \hat{\Psi}^m_{-i}|\{\hat{\Psi}^{m'}_{-i}\}_{m'<m, m'\in M_{-i}}).$$

Thus, for agent $i$, honestly reporting her received signals maximizes her payment no matter what strategies other agents use.

We start to show HMIP is potent when the coefficients are potent . When the coefficients are potent , for every agent $i$, when she believes everyone else plays a prudent strategy, she will believe for each $m$, there exists an agent $j(m) \neq i$ who reports $\{\Psi^\ell_j\}_{\ell\leq m}$ to the mechanism. Thus, $M_{-i} = M$. In this case, agent $i$'s optimal payment for performing method $m_i$ will be

$$\sum_{m\in M} \alpha_m MI^f(\{\Psi^\ell_i\}_{\ell\leq m_i}; \Psi^m_j|\{\Psi^{m'}_j\}_{m'<m}) = \sum_{m\in M} \alpha_m MI^f(\{\Psi^\ell_i\}_{\ell\leq m_i}; \Psi^m_{-i}|\{\Psi^{m'}_{-i}\}_{m'<m})$$

which is the amount of information acquired with method $m_i$ (Definition 3.3) and can be obtained by honestly reporting all received information. The optimality of the payment is due to the information monotonicity of $MI^f$. In this case, her optimal strategy is her prudent strategy. Therefore, HMIP is potent .

□

HMIP provides a framework to design information elicitation mechanisms for our hierarchical information model. To apply the HMIP framework in different settings, it remains to design the report requirement for agents and to use agents' reports to calculate the (conditional) mutual information without underlying distributions. We apply HMIP in both the multi-task setting (Section 4) and the single-task setting (Section 5).

## 4 MULTI-TASK SETTING

In this section, we will apply the HMIP framework in the multi-task setting where each agent receives a random batch of *a priori similar* tasks: tasks are i.i.d samples for all agents. For every agent, before she invests any effort, for each $m$, for all tasks, she has the same prior belief for the signals she and other agents will receive by performing $m$.

Prior work [6, 20, 36] also makes this assumption; however, in their setting, it is much stronger than in ours. For example, it insists that the only "signal" included in a prompt is for the correct answer. In reality, some false answers are more appealing than others (see Example 1.1 where

Kansas is an unlikely answer). In our model, these appealing false answers can be modeled as "cheap" information instead of being assumed away.

Note that in the multi-task setting, we allow agents to have different priors and only require that for every agent, her prior satisfies our assumptions.

### 4.1 Known Information Structure and a Small Number of tasks

In order to avoid agents "getting something for nothing" by reporting the cheap signals instead of the expensive signals (e.g. giving a high quality grade when there are no typos in Example 1.2), we reward agents the information score of expensive signals according to not only their agreements but also the diversity of their answers *conditioning on the tasks which have the same cheap signals. (e.g. the essays which all have no typos).* We will show this idea is essentially the application of HMIP framework when $MI^f$ is chosen to be $MI^{tvd}$.

We assume agents' signals are *positively correlated.* In the peer grading example, this assumption means that for every agent, receiving ☺ for the quality signal will increase her belief for the probability other agents receive ☺ for the quality signal. We defer the formal definition to the full version.

*Multi-task Hierarchical Mutual Information Mechanism (Multi-HMIM($\{\alpha_m\}_m$)).*

**Report** Each agent $i$ is assigned a random batch of tasks (at least two). For each task $t$ which is assigned to agent $i$, she is asked to report both the method $m_i(t)$ she performed on task $t$ and method $m_i(t)$'s output $\psi_i^{m_i(t)}(t)$; for each $m \neq m_i(t)$, agent $i$ is asked to optionally report her signal $\psi_i^m(t)$. We denote her actual report for her performed method and signal for every method $m$ by $\hat{m}_i(t)$ and $\hat{\psi}_i^m(t)$ respectively.

**Information Score** For each method $m$, the mechanism collects agent $i$'s method $m$ signals and records them via a $T$ dimensional vector $\hat{\boldsymbol{\psi}}_i^m$.

$$\text{The } t^{th} \text{ coordinate of } \hat{\boldsymbol{\psi}}_i^m \text{ is } \begin{cases} \hat{\psi}_i^m(t), & \text{if agent } i \text{ provides the method } m\text{'s output } \hat{\psi}_i^m(t) \text{ for task } t; \\ \emptyset, & \text{otherwise} \end{cases}$$

We define $\hat{\boldsymbol{\psi}}_{-i}^m$ as a vector where the $t^{th}$ coordinate of $\hat{\boldsymbol{\psi}}_{-i}^m$ is

$$\begin{cases} \hat{\psi}_{-i}^m(t), & \text{we arbitrarily pick an agent (who is not agent } i\text{) whose performed method is} \geq m \text{ for task } t \\ & \text{and provides method's } m\text{'s output for task } t\text{; we denote his report by } \hat{\psi}_{-i}^m(t); \\ \emptyset, & \text{such agent does not exist} \end{cases}$$

Agent $i$ is paid by her information score

$$\sum_m 2\alpha_m Corr(\hat{\boldsymbol{\psi}}_i^m; \hat{\boldsymbol{\psi}}_{-i}^m | \{\hat{\boldsymbol{\psi}}_{-i}^{m'}\}_{m'<m})$$

and $Corr(\cdot)$[4] is a random algorithm defined in Algorithm 1.

[4] $Corr(\cdot;\cdot)$ is essentially the same concept as the payment schemes in Dasgupta and Ghosh [6], Kong and Schoenebeck [20], Shnayder et al. [36]. $Corr(\cdot;\cdot|\cdot)$ is a new concept in this paper.

**Algorithm 1** Building Block *Corr*

**procedure** $Corr(\boldsymbol{v}_1;\boldsymbol{v}_2)$ ▷ e.g. $\boldsymbol{v}_1 = (☺, \emptyset, ☺, ☺, ☺)$, $\boldsymbol{v}_2 = (☺, ☺, ☺, ☺, \emptyset)$
  **if** either $\boldsymbol{v}_1$ or $\boldsymbol{v}_2$ has fewer than two non-empty entries **then return** 0
  **else**
    $B \subset [M] \leftarrow$ the set of entries where both $\boldsymbol{v}_1$ and $\boldsymbol{v}_2$ are not empty ▷ $B \leftarrow \{1, 3, 4\}$
    **if** $B = \emptyset$ **then return** 0
    **else**
      **for** $t_B \in B$ **do** ▷ *We call* $t_B$ *a* ***reward task***
        $v_1(t_1) \leftarrow$ a random non-empty entry in $\boldsymbol{v}_1$
        ▷ $v_1(t_1) \leftarrow$ ☺
        $v_2(t_2) \leftarrow$ a random non-empty entry in $\boldsymbol{v}_2$, $t_2 \neq t_1$ ▷ $v_2(t_2) \leftarrow$ ☺
        $Corr_{t_B} \leftarrow \mathbb{1}(v_1(t_B) = v_2(t_B)) - \mathbb{1}(v_1(t_1) = v_2(t_2))$ ▷ $Corr_{t_B} \leftarrow 0$
      **return** $\sum_{t_B \in B} Corr_{t_B}$ and "success" ▷ *Return 0*

**procedure** $Corr(\boldsymbol{v}_1;\boldsymbol{v}_2|V)$ ▷ e.g. $\boldsymbol{v}_1 = (☺, ☺, ☹, ☺, ☺)$, $\boldsymbol{v}_2 = (☺, ☺, ☹, ☺, ☹)$, $V = \{v\}$, $v = (☺, ☺, ☹, ☺, ☹)$
  $C \leftarrow$ the set of entries where every $v \in V$ is not empty ▷ $C \leftarrow \{1, 2, 3, 4, 5\}$
  **if** $C = \emptyset$ **then return** $Corr(\boldsymbol{v}_1;\boldsymbol{v}_2)$
  **else**
    $t_C^* \leftarrow$ a random element in $C$ ▷ $t_C^* \leftarrow 2$
    $D \leftarrow \emptyset$
    **for** $t \in [T]$ **do**
      **if** for every $v \in V$, $v(t) = v(t_C^*)$ **then**
        put $t$ in $D$
    ▷ $D = \{1, 2, 4\}$, $\boldsymbol{v}_1(D) = \boldsymbol{v}_2(D) = (☺, ☺, ☺)$
    **return** $Corr(\boldsymbol{v}_1(D);\boldsymbol{v}_2(D))$
    ▷ Return $Corr(\boldsymbol{v}_1(D);\boldsymbol{v}_2(D)) = 0$ and "success"

We design $Corr(\hat{\boldsymbol{\psi}}_i^m;\hat{\boldsymbol{\psi}}_{-i}^m|\{\hat{\boldsymbol{\psi}}_{-i}^{m'}\}_{m'<m})$ to be an unbiased estimator of $MI^{tvd}(\hat{\Psi}_i^m;\hat{\Psi}_{-i}^m|\{\hat{\Psi}_{-i}^{m'}\}_{m'<m})$[5] if $\hat{\Psi}_i^m$ and $\hat{\Psi}_{-i}^m$ are *positively correlated*. Thus, in Multi-HMIM, agents are essentially paid based on the (conditional) mutual information by picking a special $f$-mutual information—$MI^{tvd}$, if agents are honest since we have assumed that agents' honest signals are positively correlated. This makes our Multi-HMIM a special case of HMIP framework.

With the positively correlated and other additional natural assumptions (see full version), with similar definitions for the amount of information and potent coefficients with HMIP, we can show Multi-HMIM is potent as well by mapping it into the HMIP framework. Moreover, we define truthful strategy in Multi-HMIM as the strategy where the agent honestly reports her performed method and that method's output for each task; for other methods' outputs, either she chooses to not report or she reports honestly. We can show Multi-HMIM is truthful: for each agent, when she believes other agents play a truthful strategy, she can maximize her expected utility by playing a truthful strategy as well. We defer the formal analysis of Multi-HMIM to the full version.

## 4.2 Learning Information Structure with a Large Number Tasks

Assumption 4.1 ($\delta_0$-gap). *For each m, we assume that for every $i \neq j$, each $m' \neq m$*

$$MI^f(\Psi_i^m;\Psi_j^m) > \frac{1}{\delta_0} \qquad MI^f(\Psi_i^m;\Psi_j^{m'}) < \frac{1}{\delta_0}$$

[5]In the current paper, $\hat{\boldsymbol{\psi}}_i^m$ means vector, $\hat{\Psi}_i^m$ means random variable.

The above assumption guarantees that when we can accurately learn the $f$-mutual information between two agents' answer vectors, we can accurately classify the answer vectors and then learn the maximal method's outputs correctly.

*Learning-based Multi-HMIM($\mathcal{L}$).*

**Report** Each agent $i$ is assigned $T$ tasks and asked to perform the same method for all tasks. For agent $i$ who performs method $m_i$, she is asked to report her own answer vector

$$\boldsymbol{\psi}_i^{m_i} = (\psi_i^{m_i}(1), \psi_i^{m_i}(2), ..., \psi_i^{m_i}(T))$$

and, for each method $m \neq m_i$, is asked to optionally report her answer vector $\boldsymbol{\psi}_i^m$. We denote the set of methods whose outputs are reported by agent $i$ as $M_i$ and the actual answer vector she reports for each method $\ell \in M_i$ as $\hat{\boldsymbol{\psi}}_i^\ell$. Agent $i$ can name the methods freely[6].

**Learning Information Structure** We define the distance between $\hat{\boldsymbol{\psi}}_i^m$ and $\hat{\boldsymbol{\psi}}_j^{m'}$ as $\frac{1}{MI^f(\hat{\Psi}_i^m;\hat{\Psi}_j^{m'})}$.

The mechanism starts to cluster answer vectors. A set of answer vectors are clustered into one cluster if and only if their pairwise distance is less than $\delta_0$. A cluster may have $\geq 1$ answer vector(s).

For two clusters $m_1, m_2$, $m_1 \succ m_2$ if and only if there exists an agent who's own answer vector is in cluster $m_1$ and also provides an answer vector which is classified in cluster $m_2$. The mechanism picks positive real values for the type payment scale $\alpha_m$ according to a rule $\mathcal{L}$.

**Information Score** The mechanism learns the information structure using all agents' reports excluding agent $i$. We denote the set of clusters by $M_{-i}$. For each cluster $m \in M_{-i}$, the mechanism randomly picks an answer vector, denoted $\hat{\boldsymbol{\psi}}_{-i}^m$, from it.

Agent $i$ is paid her information score:

$$\sum_{m \in M_{-i}} \alpha_m MI^f(\{\hat{\Psi}_i^\ell\}_{\ell \in M_i}; \hat{\Psi}_{-i}^m | \{\hat{\Psi}_{-i}^{m'}\}_{m' \prec m, m' \in M_{-i}})$$

which can be calculated accurately when the number of tasks is large.

We define $\boldsymbol{\alpha}(\mathcal{L}) := \{\alpha_m(\mathcal{L})\}_m$ as the coefficients determined by $\mathcal{L}$, given that the mechanism has access to all levels of honest answer vectors. Here the amount of information and prudent strategy are defined by the same way in HMIP, except that the coefficients are $\boldsymbol{\alpha}(\mathcal{L})$.

We also define potent $\mathcal{L}$ such that $\boldsymbol{\alpha}(\mathcal{L})$ is potent in the definition in HMIP. We can show with the a priori similar and random order assumption, Learning-based multi-HMIM is dominant truthful. With the gap assumption, when the rule $\mathcal{L}$ is potent , Learning-based multi-HMIM is potent , dominant truthful and will output the hierarchical information structure as well as the maximal level(s) answer vector given that agents play prudent strategy.

Learning-based multi-HMIM can be mapped to HMIP since a large number of tasks and the gap assumption allow the estimation of the prior and the learning of the information structure and correct clusters. Note that even if the mechanism clusters incorrectly, the mechanism is still dominant truthful since even each agent is paid by the mutual information between her information and "wrong" information, the information monotonicity still incentivizes the agent to report all information she has. Thus we do not need the gap assumption for the dominant truthfulness. With the gap assumption, we can cluster agents correctly and use Theorem 3.7 to show the potent property. We defer the formal statement and proof to the full version. Moreover, we want to emphasize that our mechanisms work even if every agent only has a piece of correct information for the information structure.

[6]The mechanism will ignore the name of the methods and only record the relationship that the other answer vectors reported by agent $i$ have lower level than agent $i$'s own answer vector.

## 5 SINGLE-TASK SETTING

In the single task setting without known prior, the literature usually assumes a common prior assumption and follows a signal-prediction framework [28]—asking agents not only her signal but also her prediction. To achieve truthfulness for $\geq 3$ agents, Radanovic and Faltings [31] and Kong and Schoenebeck [21] punish each agent if her predictions differ from the predictions of other agents who report the same signals with her, and reward each agent for the accuracy of her prediction. Therefore, for each agent, to maximize her accuracy reward, she will honestly report her predictions. To avoid the punishment for the "inconsistency", she will honestly report her received signals as well because of the following commonly assumed assumption—*common prior and stochastic relevance*: for every agent $i$ and $j$, they will have the same belief for the distribution of the signals received by other agents if and only if they receive the same signals.

### 5.1 Applying HMIP in the Single-task Setting

We follow the previous "signal-prediction" framework and "punishing inconsistency" idea in the hierarchical information case. We ask agents their received signals and predictions for different levels. We pay each agent the accuracy of her forecasts. The high expertise agents have accurate predictions for even high cost information reports while the low expertise agents only have accurate prediction for low cost information. Therefore, high expertise agents will be paid more.

*Single-HMIM($PS, \{\alpha_m\}_m$).*

- **Report (signals, predictions)** Each agent $i$ who performs method $m_i$ is asked to report her received signals $\{\sigma_i^m\}_{m\leq m_i}$ and her forecast $p_i^{m_i}$ for $\Psi_{-i}^{m_i}$. For each $m \neq m_i$, she is asked to optionally report her forecast $p_i^m$ for $\Psi_{-i}^m$. We denote her report for her received signals as $\{\hat{\sigma}_i^m\}_{m\leq \hat{m}_i}$ and her prediction report as $\{\hat{p}_i^m\}_{m\in M_i}$ where $M_i$ is the set of methods whose outputs are predicted by agent $i$.
- **Prediction Score** We define $M_{-i}$ as the set of methods whose outputs are reported by an agent who is not agent $i$. For each $m \in M_{-i}$, we pick an arbitrary reference agent $j \neq i$ whose performed method is higher than $m$ and denote his report for method $m$'s output by $\hat{\sigma}^m$. Agent $i$'s prediction score is $\sum_{m\in M_{-i}\cap M_i} \alpha_m PS(\sigma^m, \hat{p}_i^m)$.
- **Information Score** If there is no other agent who reports the same signals as agent $i$, then agent $i$'s information score is 0. Otherwise, arbitrarily pick a reference agent $j \neq i$ from the agents who report the same signals as agent $i$. Agent $i$'s information score is minus the inconsistency between her prediction report and agent $j$'s prediction report, that is,

$$-\left(\sum_{m\in M_i\cap M_j} \alpha_m(PS(\hat{p}_j^m, \hat{p}_j^m) - PS(\hat{p}_j^m, \hat{p}_i^m))\right).$$

In Single-HMIM, the payment of each agent is $\alpha *$ *Information Score* $+ \beta *$ *Prediction Score.*

*Definition 5.1 (Truthful strategy in Single-HMIM).* For each agent $i$ who performed method $m_i$, she plays truthful strategy if she honestly report her received signals $\{\sigma_i^m\}_{m\leq m_i}$ and forecast for $\Psi_{-i}^{m_i}$ and for each $m \neq m_i$, either she does not report or she reports her forecast for $\Psi_{-i}^m$ honestly.

With proper definition for the amount of information and potent coefficients, we will show with the common prior assumption, single-HMIM is strictly truthful; moreover, when the coefficients are potent for single-HMIM, single-HMIM is potent and strictly truthful.

The strictly truthful property follows from the common prior and stochastic relevance assumption. The potent property follows from the definition of prudent strategy and potent coefficients. We defer the formal proof to the full version.

## 6 DISCUSSION AND FUTURE WORK

Although our work is theoretical, it is not far from applications. For example, in some situations, we could simplify the information structure by roughly dividing it into two levels where the higher level requires more time. Then we can apply our Multi-HMIM or Single-HMIM to peer grading or any other situations where certain agents are only given 15 seconds to grade a work and others are expected to do a good job. We value the information *conditioning on* the reports provided by the "15 seconds" agents. We could also use machine learning to obtain the lower level information.

Race, sex, and other stereotypes can be used as "cheap" signals. One possible future application of this work is to address fairness is crowdsourcing.

There are several limitations of our mechanisms. Our Multi-HMIM requires that the hierarchy structure of the information is common knowledge. Our key assumption, that more sophisticated agents know the information of less sophisticated agents may not always hold, especially if the less sophisticated agents collude to report seemingly irrelevant information (e.g., the third letter of the third word).

Our analysis of the Learning-based HMIM requires the agents to perform an infinite number of tasks. One future direction is having the sample complexity analysis. Our Single-HMIM still requires a forecast report. A future direction is making the forecast report optional in some scenarios (we might ask agents for the most common answer if they believe it is not their reported answer). Another future direction is the information cost elicitation: tuning the coefficients of the mechanisms such that the payment matches the actual effort required by agents.

A key future direction is to test our mechanism and explore the limitations in practice by performing real-world experiments. This would require designing a suitable user interface.

## REFERENCES


[1] Arpit Agarwal, Debmalya Mandal, David C. Parkes, and Nisarg Shah. 2017. Peer Prediction with Heterogeneous Users. In *Proceedings of the 2017 ACM Conference on Economics and Computation, EC '17, Cambridge, MA, USA, June 26-30, 2017.* 81–98.

[2] Syed Mumtaz Ali and Samuel D Silvey. 1966. A general class of coefficients of divergence of one distribution from another. *Journal of the Royal Statistical Society. Series B (Methodological)* (1966), 131–142.

[3] Y. Chen, D.F. Bacon, I. Kash, D.C. Parkes, M. Rao, and M. Sridharan. 2012. Predicting Your Own Effort. In *Proceedings of the 11th International Conference on Autonomous and Multiagent Systems (AAMAS 2012).*

[4] Thomas M Cover and Joy A Thomas. 2006. Elements of information theory 2nd edition. (2006).

[5] Imre Csiszár, Paul C Shields, et al. 2004. Information theory and statistics: A tutorial. *Foundations and Trends® in Communications and Information Theory* 1, 4 (2004), 417–528.

[6] Anirban Dasgupta and Arpita Ghosh. 2013. Crowdsourced judgement elicitation with endogenous proficiency. In *Proceedings of the 22nd international conference on World Wide Web.* International World Wide Web Conferences Steering Committee, 319–330.

[7] A. P. Dawid and A. M. Skene. 1979. Maximum Likelihood Estimation of Observer Error-Rates Using the EM Algorithm. *Journal of the Royal Statistical Society. Series C (Applied Statistics)* 28, 1 (1979), 20–28.

[8] Boi Faltings, Radu Jurca, Pearl Pu, and Bao Duy Tran. 2014. Incentives to counter bias in human computation. In *Second AAAI Conference on Human Computation and Crowdsourcing.*

[9] A. Gao, J. R. Wright, and K. Leyton-Brown. 2016. Incentivizing Evaluation via Limited Access to Ground Truth: Peer-Prediction Makes Things Worse. *ArXiv e-prints* (June 2016). arXiv:cs.GT/1606.07042

[10] Arpita Ghosh, Satyen Kale, and Preston McAfee. 2011. Who moderates the moderators?: crowdsourcing abuse detection in user-generated content. In *Proceedings of the 12th ACM conference on Electronic commerce.* ACM, 167–176.

[11] Tilmann Gneiting and Adrian E Raftery. 2007. Strictly proper scoring rules, prediction, and estimation. *J. Amer. Statist. Assoc.* 102, 477 (2007), 359–378.

[12] Sharad Goel, Daniel M. Reeves, and David M. Pennock. 2009. Collective revelation: A mechanism for self-verified, weighted, and truthful predictions. In *Proceedings of the 10th ACM conference on Electronic commerce (EC 2009).*

[13] Radu Jurca and Boi Faltings. 2006. Minimum payments that reward honest reputation feedback. In *Proceedings of the 7th ACM conference on Electronic commerce (EC 2006).*

[14] Radu Jurca and Boi Faltings. 2007. Robust Incentive-Compatible Feedback Payments. In *Trust, Reputation and Security: Theories and Practice*, Vol. 4452. Springer-Verlag, 204–218.

[15] Radu Jurca and Boi Faltings. 2008. Incentives for expressing opinions in online polls. In *Proceedings of the 9th ACM conference on Electronic commerce (EC 2008)*.

[16] Radu Jurca and Boi Faltings. 2009. Mechanisms for making crowds truthful. *J. Artif. Int. Res.* 34, 1 (March 2009).

[17] R. Jurca and B. Faltings. 2011. Incentives for Answering Hypothetical Questions. In *Proceedings of the 1st Workshop on Social Computing and User Generated Content (SC 2011)*. ACM.

[18] Vijay Kamble, Nihar Shah, David Marn, Abhay Parekh, and Kannan Ramachandran. 2015. Truth Serums for Massively Crowdsourced Evaluation Tasks. *arXiv preprint arXiv:1507.07045* (2015).

[19] Yuqing Kong, Katrina Ligett, and Grant Schoenebeck. 2016. Putting peer prediction under the micro (economic) scope and making truth-telling focal. In *International Conference on Web and Internet Economics*. Springer, 251–264.

[20] Y. Kong and G. Schoenebeck. 2016. A Framework For Designing Information Elicitation Mechanisms That Reward Truth-telling. *ArXiv e-prints* (May 2016). arXiv:cs.GT/1605.01021

[21] Yuqing Kong and Grant Schoenebeck. 2018. Equilibrium selection in information elicitation without verification via information monotonicity. In *9th Innovations in Theoretical Computer Science, ITCS 2018*, Vol. 94.

[22] N. Lambert and Y. Shoham. 2008. Truthful surveys. *Proceedings of the 3rd International Workshop on Internet and Network Economics (WINE 2008)* (2008).

[23] Yang Liu and Yiling Chen. 2016. Learning to incentivize: eliciting effort via output agreement. *arXiv preprint arXiv:1604.04928* (2016).

[24] Yang Liu and Yiling Chen. 2016. Sequential Peer Prediction: Learning to Elicit Effort using Posted Prices. *arXiv preprint arXiv:1611.09219* (2016).

[25] Debmalya Mandal, Matthew Leifer, David C Parkes, Galen Pickard, and Victor Shnayder. 2016. Peer Prediction with Heterogeneous Tasks. *arXiv preprint arXiv:1612.00928* (2016).

[26] John McCoy and Drazen Prelec. 2017. A statistical model for aggregating judgments by incorporating peer predictions. *arXiv preprint arXiv:1703.04778* (2017).

[27] N. Miller, P. Resnick, and R. Zeckhauser. 2005. Eliciting informative feedback: The peer-prediction method. *Management Science* (2005), 1359–1373.

[28] D. Prelec. 2004. A Bayesian Truth Serum for subjective data. *Science* 306, 5695 (2004), 462–466.

[29] Dražen Prelec, H Sebastian Seung, and John McCoy. 2017. A solution to the single-question crowd wisdom problem. *Nature* 541, 7638 (2017), 532–535.

[30] Goran Radanovic and Boi Faltings. 2013. A robust bayesian truth serum for non-binary signals. In *Proceedings of the 27th AAAI Conference on Artificial Intelligence, AAAI 2013*. 833–839.

[31] Goran Radanovic and Boi Faltings. 2014. Incentives for truthful information elicitation of continuous signals. In *Twenty-Eighth AAAI Conference on Artificial Intelligence*.

[32] Goran Radanovic and Boi Faltings. 2015. Incentive schemes for participatory sensing. In *Proceedings of the 2015 International Conference on Autonomous Agents and Multiagent Systems*. 1081–1089.

[33] Goran Radanovic and Boi Faltings. 2015. Incentives for Subjective Evaluations with Private Beliefs. In *Twenty-Ninth AAAI Conference on Artificial Intelligence*.

[34] Blake Riley. 2014. Minimum truth serums with optional predictions. In *Proceedings of the 4th Workshop on Social Computing and User Generated Content (SC14)*.

[35] Blake Riley. 2015. Mechanisms for Making Accurate Decisions in Biased Crowds. (2015).

[36] Victor Shnayder, Arpit Agarwal, Rafael Frongillo, and David C Parkes. 2016. Informed truthfulness in multi-task peer prediction. In *Proceedings of the 2016 ACM Conference on Economics and Computation*. ACM, 179–196.

[37] Peter Welinder, Steve Branson, Serge J Belongie, and Pietro Perona. 2010. The Multidimensional Wisdom of Crowds.. In *NIPS*, Vol. 23. 2424–2432.

[38] Robert L Winkler. 1969. Scoring rules and the evaluation of probability assessors. *J. Amer. Statist. Assoc.* 64, 327 (1969), 1073–1078.

[39] Jens Witkowski, Bernhard Nebel, and David C Parkes. 2014. *Robust Peer Prediction Mechanisms*. Ph.D. Dissertation. Ph. D. Dissertation, Albert-Ludwigs-Universitat Freiburg: Institut fur Informatik.

[40] Jens Witkowski and David C Parkes. 2012. Peer prediction without a common prior. In *Proceedings of the 13th ACM Conference on Electronic Commerce*. ACM, 964–981.

[41] Jens Witkowski and David C Parkes. 2013. Learning the prior in minimal peer prediction. In *Proceedings of the 3rd Workshop on Social Computing and User Generated Content at the ACM Conference on Electronic Commerce*. Citeseer, 14.

[42] Peter Zhang and Yiling Chen. 2014. Elicitability and knowledge-free elicitation with peer prediction. In *Proceedings of the 2014 international conference on Autonomous agents and multi-agent systems*. 245–252.

[43] Denny Zhou, Sumit Basu, Yi Mao, and John C Platt. 2012. Learning from the wisdom of crowds by minimax entropy. In *Advances in Neural Information Processing Systems*. 2195–2203.

# The One-Shot Crowdfunding Game.*

ITAI ARIELI, Faculty of Industrial Engineering and Management, Technion,, Israel
MORAN KOREN, Faculty of Industrial Engineering and Management, Technion,, Israel
RANN SMORODINSKY, Faculty of Industrial Engineering and Management, Technion,, Israel

CCS Concepts: • **Theory of computation → Quality of equilibria**; **Market equilibria**; *Algorithmic game theory*; Solution concepts in game theory;

Keywords: Crowdfunding; efficiency; equilibrium; information aggregation; common value; voting

**ACM Reference Format:**
Itai Arieli, Moran Koren, and Rann Smorodinsky. 2018. The One-Shot Crowdfunding Game.. In *ACM EC '18: 2018 ACM Conference on Economics and Computation, June 18–22, 2018, Ithaca, NY, USA*. ACM, New York, NY, USA, 2 pages. https://doi.org/10.1145/3219166.3219215

In most popular crowdfunding platforms, a firm sets a revenue goal and posts a price for its product.[1] Individual contributors may choose whether or not to commit to buying the product at the posted price (an action we dub 'contribute'). Contributions are collected and the product is supplied only when the total contributions pledged exceed the revenue goal.

We model a crowdfunding campaign as a one-shot game of incomplete information, denoted $\Gamma(B, n, p, \mu, \tau)$, played among a population of $n$ potential contributors. The common value of the product, $v$, can be either one (with probability $\mu$) or zero and each player receives a private binary signal which equals the true value with probability $p > \frac{1}{2}$. Conditional on the state, signals are distributed IID across players. Each player decides whether or not to buy the product at the posted price, $\tau$, ('contribute'). If a player contributes and the total number of contributors exceeds the threshold, $B$, then her utility is $v - \tau$, otherwise it is zero. Our model extends Arieli et al. [1] who study the symmetric case, where $\mu = 0.5, \tau = 0.5$.

The campaign plays a dual role: (1) to raise funds for product development; (2) as a means to gauge the market's demand for a product. Therefore we examine two performance indices - a (market) *participation Index* which measures how well do campaigns attract contributors, and a *correctness index* which measures how well do campaigns support the high quality products while denying funds to the low quality ones.

*Extended Abstract, The full version of the paper is available at:
http://smarturl.it/oneshot-cf-game.

[1]Possibly a menu of prices for various product bundles.

Authors' addresses: Itai Arieli, Faculty of Industrial Engineering and Management, Technion, Haifa, Haifa, Israel, 3200003, iarieli@technion.ac.il; Moran Koren, Faculty of Industrial Engineering and Management, Technion, Haifa, Haifa, Israel, 3200003, ko@technion.ac.il; Rann Smorodinsky, Faculty of Industrial Engineering and Management, Technion, Haifa, Haifa, Israel, 3200003, rann@ie.technion.ac.il.


*ACM EC '18, June 18–22, 2018, Ithaca, NY, USA*

ACM ISBN 978-1-4503-5829-3/18/06
https://doi.org/10.1145/3219166.3219215

## Main findings

**Existence and uniqueness of an equilibium:** We focus our analysis on *non-trivial* equilibria, i.e, ones in which there is a positive probability that the good will be supplied. We show that in any crowdfunding game, there can be at most one non-trivial symmetric Bayes-Nash equilibrium.[2] Furthermore, for sufficiently large $n$, the existence of such an equilibrium is guaranteed.

Let $\tau_l$ denote the maximal price a player with a low signal is willing to pay and $\tau_h$ denote the corresponding price for a player with a high signal. We say that the campaign price is cheap whenever $\tau \leq \tau_l$, it is moderate whenever $\tau_l < \tau \leq \tau_h$, and it is expensive whenever $\tau > \tau_h$. We summarize our results for each of the three price levels.

**Cheap prices:** When the price is cheap, playing 'contribute' is a dominant strategy for all players. Therefore player actions are non-informative and the correctness index equals the prior $\mu$. In addition as all players contribute, the campaign surely succeeds and the participation index equals 1.

**Moderately prices:** When the price is moderate, players who receive a high signal will surely contribute. Players with low signals will contribute with a positive probability only when the threshold is above $(1-p)n$. In these cases, there is a positive probability that the sum of contributions reaches the threshold even if most players received low signals. We find that the correctness index in large markets equals, $\theta(\mu, p, \tau) = 1 - \frac{1-p}{p}\frac{1-\tau}{\tau}\mu$. Note that this expression is bounded away from one, yet, as the price is moderate, it is always greater than $\mu$. Furthermore, the correctness index increases as prices ($\tau$) and signal quality ($p$) increase but decrease in the prior ($\mu$). In addition, the asymptotic participation index equals $R(\mu, p, \tau) = \mu(1 + \frac{1-p}{p}\frac{1-\tau}{\tau})$. Note that participation decreases in both signal quality ($p$) and price ($\tau$). While it is rather intuitive that higher prices decrease participation, we also find similar effect induced by better signals.

**Expensive prices:** When the price is expensive and threshold is greater than (or equal to) $(1-p)n$, the equilibrium and the index analysis coincide with the case of moderate prices. However, when the threshold is lower than $(1-p)n$, players with high signals choose a mixed strategy while players with low signals opt-out with probability one. We find that the correctness index in large markets of expensively priced crowdfunding game is identical to that of moderately priced games. However, For some parameter values,[3] the participation index in large markets is $R(\mu, p, \tau) = \mu p + (1-\mu)\frac{1-p}{2} = \frac{(3\mu-1)p+(1-\mu)}{2}$. Note that it is increasing in $p$ as now stronger signals increase the probability of contribution of the indifferent player, which, in this case is the one with the high signal.

**Applicability of the results to small crowdfunding games:** The theoretical findings above pertain to crowdfunding campaigns with large markets. We compute equilibrium outcomes for 'realistic' market size that is derived from empirical findings using field data. The computational part demonstrates the validity of the theory to such markets.

## REFERENCES


[1] Itai Arieli, Moran Koren, and Rann Smorodinsky. 2017. The Crowdfunding Game. In *Web and Internet Economics*, Nikhil Devanur and Pinyan Lu (Eds.). Springer International Publishing, Berlin, Heidelberg, 388–389. https://arxiv.org/abs/1710.00319


[2] In what follows, when discussing equilibria we mean non-trivial symmetric Bayes-Nash equilibria.

[3] More accurately if $\mu < \frac{1}{3}$ or if $\mu > \frac{1}{3}$ and $p \leq \sqrt{3} - 1$, or if $\mu > \frac{1}{3}$, $p > \sqrt{3} - 1$ and $\tau > \frac{2\mu}{(1-\mu)p+2(1-p)\mu)}$.

# Dancing Pigs or Externalities? Measuring the Rationality of Security Decisions

ELISSA M. REDMILES, MICHELLE L. MAZUREK,
AND JOHN P. DICKERSON, University of Maryland

Accurately modeling human decision-making in security is critical to thinking about when, why, and how to recommend that users adopt certain secure behaviors. In this work, we conduct behavioral economics experiments to model the rationality of end-user security decision-making in a realistic online experimental system simulating a bank account. We ask participants to make a financially impactful security choice, in the face of transparent risks of account compromise and benefits offered by an optional security behavior (two-factor authentication). We measure the cost and utility of adopting the security behavior via measurements of time spent executing the behavior and estimates of the participant's wage. We find that more than 50% of our participants made rational (e.g., utility optimal) decisions, and we find that participants are more likely to behave rationally in the face of higher risk. Additionally, we find that users' decisions can be modeled well as a function of past behavior (anchoring effects), knowledge of costs, and to a lesser extent, users' awareness of risks and context ($R^2$=0.61). We also find evidence of endowment effects, as seen in other areas of economic and psychological decision-science literature, in our digital-security setting. Finally, using our data, we show theoretically that a "one-size-fits-all" emphasis on security can lead to market losses, but that adoption by a subset of users with higher risks or lower costs can lead to market gains.

## 1 INTRODUCTION

People's adoption, or rejection, of security behaviors can lead to system-wide consequences. While security requirements and system defaults such as automatic updates can remove many human decision-making fail-points for security-relevant systems, in many cases human decisions are still required to enable security. As such, security researchers have tried to understand and alter the decisions of the "human in the loop" [21].

Prior work has proposed two simplified theories of the human in the loop: a rational actor who chooses to ignore security behaviors because the costs always outweigh the potential losses, and an irrational actor who chooses "dancing pigs over security every time" because they neither understand nor care about security risks [39]. While these simplified models of user behavior can help to provide high-level insights, our aim is to define a more realistic medium between these two extremes: *a semi (or boundedly) rational security actor with predictable, but not always utility-optimal, behavior based on risks and costs.*

End-user decision-making in security has largely been examined hypothetically [14, 39] or qualitatively [27, 36, 42, 53, 66, 71, 78, 79]. Here, we seek to provide an empirical, economic examination of the rationality of security behavior in a particular context. We define rationality as utility-optimality: that is, a decision is rational if the utility (gain) from the decision is greater than the costs of enacting the decision. Ultimately, we seek to understand: **How do costs ($C$), risks ($R$),**

Author's address: Elissa M. Redmiles, Michelle L. Mazurek,
and John P. Dickerson, University of Maryland, [eredmiles,mmazurek,john]@cs.umd.edu.


*ACM EC'18, June 18–22, 2018, Ithaca, NY, USA.* ACM ISBN 978-1-4503-5829-3/18/06...$15.00
https://doi.org/10.1145/3219166.3219185

**and user tendencies and attributes ($U$) influence: (1) a security decision and (2) whether that decision is rational?**

By answering this question and quantifying a model of rationality in security behavior, we can guide users toward utility-maximizing behavior (or lack of behavior) in order to optimize the use of their personal, behavioral compliance budgets and maximize market gains from security [4, 10].

In this work, we construct an experimental system and conduct behavioral-economics experiments (e.g., games) to evaluate and model security decision-making. Such experiments allow for a high level of control, realism, and quantification beyond that usually achieved from traditional survey and lab-based user-studies [32]. Our experimental system operates like a bank account to which users have to regularly log in. In each game, users are assigned to a condition: in one of the endowment conditions participants are given an amount of money and are required to login once every 24 hours to retain their money, while those in one of the earn conditions begin with a small amount of money and have the opportunity to earn more every time they log on. When signing up for a game, participants are offered a security choice: whether to enable *two-factor authentication* (2FA). Prior to making this choice they are shown explicit risks (which vary by game): risk of being hacked and amount of protection offered by adopting 2FA. If they are hacked – probabilistically determined by a script regularly run on the system – participants lose all of the money in their account. At the end of a game, participants receive the real monetary value of the amount left in their account.

Participants in our experiment play the game twice, each time with a different condition (endowment/earn, hack risk, and protection offered by 2FA). We invited 150 AMT workers to play the first game. Based on the observations we record during game play, we model the factors that influence whether a participant enables 2FA and whether the decision was utility optimal (e.g., rational). We further examine the extent to which people make utility-maximizing decisions and how the optimization of choices varies based on effective risk and the endowment vs. earn condition.

We find that people's decisions to enable 2FA can be explained well (pseudo-$R^2$ = 0.612) by their prior behavior (approximately 35% of the variance), knowledge of costs (e.g., awareness of how long 2FA will take) (approx. 15% of behavior variance), and to a lesser but still significant extent, explicit risk judgements and endowment effects (9% to 15% of variance, depending on their knowledge of other factors). Further, we find that both risk and endowment effects also relate to whether the decision to enable a behavior was utility-optimal. We find that those playing in the lowest-risk conditions are far less likely to make utility-optimal decisions than those in the highest-risk conditions. Those in the medium-risk conditions make a utility-optimal decision 58% of the time the first time they play the game and 69% of the time the second. Our results suggest that, in our experiment:

- Users made rational security choices approximately 50% of the time.
- User tend to act in accordance with an anchoring effect [70]: they tend to stick with the first security decision they make. More general security tendencies (chosen password strength, security behavioral intentions) did not influence behavior.
- Users are boundedly rational: they appear to incorporate knowledge about costs and explicit risks.
- In higher-risk conditions, users enable security options more often and make rational decisions more often.
- When protecting assets they already have, especially in highest-risk games, users tend to behave more rationally and more securely (endowment effect [50]).

Using this data, we can compute estimates of utility-optimizing behaviors for a given user based on users' typical costs (e.g., login speed, account balance, and earning potential) and estimated explicit risks (risk of hacking, protection offered by a behavior). As a tangible example, we present a thought experiment using our data to theorize about market gains and losses from different approaches to user security: encouraging all users to be secure, encouraging utility-optimal behavior, and not requiring end users to engage in security behaviors. We show that a "one-size-fits-all" emphasis on security can lead to significant market *losses* from needless user costs for negligible security utility, and identify hypothetical risk thresholds at which targeted encouragement of certain security behaviors for at-risk users can lead to market gains.

Consequently, we suggest a push toward personalized security recommendations (e.g., nudges) to guide users toward utility-optimal behaviors and allow them more autonomy to make decisions based on transparently communicated risks paired with a push for more data-driven research quantifying those risks. We conclude with further discussion of the implications of our findings for predicting user behaviors and improving market, or population, security through nudging and risk communication, and suggest directions for future work.

## 2 RELATED WORK

Below, we review prior work on the decision-making in security and privacy, focusing specifically on economics-based studies when available.

**Security Decision-Making.** Herley takes the first economic approach to examining end-user security decisions [39]. In his theoretical paper, he provides a cost-benefit analysis of having end-users follow security advice. He argues that threats are so rare – and suggested behaviors so ineffective – as to make it logical for end users to never adopt security behaviors. Relatedly, Böhme and Grossklags approach user attention in security as a public good, that is, as an extremely scarce resource and examine how to facilitate optimizing rather than satisficing of user attention toward security warnings and privacy notices [14]. They theoretically explore the effect of different user interface designs on the use of attention and recommend that user interactions should be rationed, rather than just user interfaces optimized, to maximize the use of users' privacy and security compliance budgets.

The majority of security-related economics analysis of human behavior has focused on experts' (e.g., system or network administrators) responses to threat [20, 34, 43, 45], organizational responses to threat [16, 30, 54], or attackers [7, 18, 51, 52, 62, 67]. For example, Grossklags and colleagues conduct a number of different studies applying game-theoretic models to examine expert behavior in attack/defense security games [20, 33, 34, 45] finding evidence of unclear risks and bounded rationality for security professionals; and relatedly, Rounds et al. examined the impact of changes in security and reward on attacker responses, finding that as the value of an account increases, so too does the number of attacks on that account; and as the amount of security on an account increases so too does the number of attacks decrease [61]. These analyses of experts, however, provide limited insight into end-user behavior.

Christin et al. present one of the few empirical, economic-related, studies of security behavior: they incentivized users to execute arbitrary code [19]. They adjusted the incentives provided, finding that 43% of participants were willing to run untrusted executables for $1.00. Most prior work focused on end-user decision making has been more qualitative, examining people's security decisions through surveys and interview studies. These studies include explorations of why people say they update or do not update their software [53, 78, 79], why users fall for phishing attacks [42, 66], why people bypass browser warning messages [27, 36, 71], and even preliminary support for boundedly-rational decision-making in cybersecurity based on post-event surveys with university students [8]. Findings have shown evidence of the importance of fatigue from too many security demands, unclear risks, and lack of clarity on the utility of behaviors for addressing risks.

The reasonable conclusion of many of these end-user studies is a push for better education of users to get them to take security risks seriously and enable security behaviors. Indeed, especially in the corporate realm, there may often exist an implicit assumption that more security is better and our goal should be to get all users to enable all security behaviors at all times [40, 47]. Herley's work challenges this approach, arguing that security is *never* better for the end-user, and at best benefits the corporations of whom they are clients while costing the individual [39]. Underlying both approaches is also an implicit assumption that users have rational reasons for adopting or ignoring security advice, and are able to interpret and make reasonable decisions about risks if they are aware of them. In our work, we explore to what extent users are rational actors and we explore what factors, including implicit and explicit risks and costs, relate to the security decisions they make in our simulation. We also explore the impact of the "users should always be secure" and "users should never be secure" perspectives on the costs and utility of enabling 2FA for an entire population to better understand when, and whether, we should encourage end users to adopt security behaviors.

**Economics of Privacy.** Prior work on privacy has explored privacy as a good and theoretical privacy markets [6, 12, 26, 44] as well as empirical examinations of users valuations of data [9, 17, 22, 29], and especially their willingness to pay to protect private, digital information vs. willingness to disclose information for a payout [5, 63, 64]. Acquisti and colleagues have found evidence of bounded rationality – that is, semi-rational decisions in which people are only able to take into account a portion of the data (i.e., risks or evidence) in their decisions [2, 4] and have found that difficultly identifying risks and benefits can lead to significant uncertainty that muddies privacy decision-making [3]. Closely related to our work, Tsai et al. explore what happens when making privacy tradeoffs more transparent, finding that when privacy information is surfaced to users in an online shopping scenario they are more likely to make purchases from a privacy-preserving website, even at a higher cost [75]. Beyond privacy, behavioral economics experiments similar to ours have been used effectively to model bounded-ly rational decisions in business and management settings, health, and purchasing [24, 35, 68].

Our work draws on findings from these studies to explore bounded-rationality in security and examine how security-tendencies such as password strength choices influence decision-making. We combine the individual-focused analyses presented by this prior work in privacy with the market-level analyses emphasized by security economics work, presenting a perspective on how and when we should emphasize security protection for end-users.

## 3 METHODOLOGY

Below we describe our experimental system, the experiments (e.g., games), participant recruitment, our analyses, and limitations. All procedures were approved by our institution's review board.

### 3.1 System Design

We created the "bank" system to provide a similar UI flow to logging into a real bank account (Figure 1 provides a system overview). The system URL was bank.[institutiondomain], had an SSL certificate, and was thus displayed over HTTPS.

When participants began the study, they were taken to a page that had two options: log in or sign up. After choosing the signup button they were taken to a page where they could create an account. The account creation page asked the participant for their Amazon Mechanical Turk (MTurk) ID and to create a password. There were no constraints for password creation, and the provided MTurk IDs were validated against the list of workers who accepted the task on MTurk. If the participant clicked the Login button, they would be taken to a page asking for their MTurk ID and their previously created password.

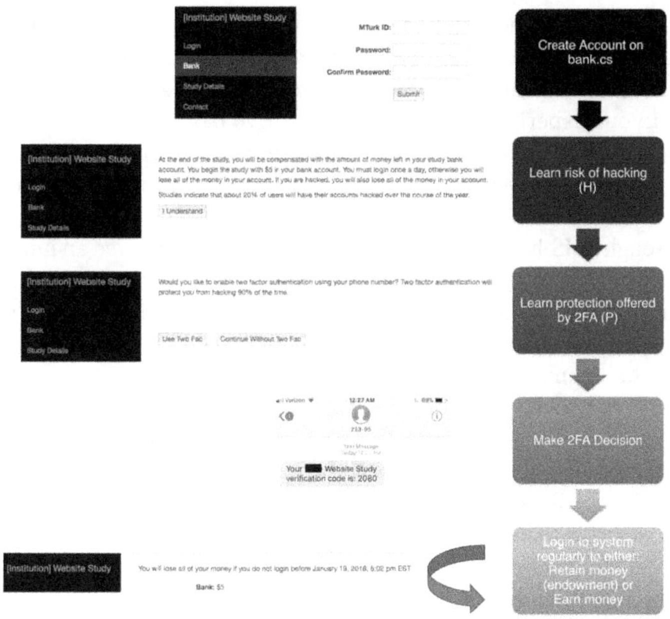


Fig. 1. Overview of the experimental system flow.

The next screen explained the study. In the study, we varied participants' game condition, which was a combination of experimental setting (Earn or Endowment), risk of hacking ($H$), and protection offered by 2FA ($P$). Those in the Earn Setting ($S : Earn$) started with \$1 in their account and could earn an extra \$1 per day up to a maximum of \$5. Those in Endowment Setting ($S : Endowment$) started with \$5 and would lose that money if they did not log in once per day. In addition to varying the conditions, we also transparently told participants their risk of getting hacked $H$. Hacking was experimentally constructed: we ran a script every evening, randomly selected a number, and "hacked" the participant (e.g., removed the money from their account) if the randomly selected number was less than their effective risk; hacking probabilities were not affected by how frequently participants chose to login. The participant's effective risk was defined as either $H$ (no 2FA selected) or $H * (1 - P)$ (2FA selected), that is, the probability of being hacked modulated by the accepted protection. In the initial consent form and study instructions it was made clear to participants that the hacking was constructed and that there were not real hackers trying to break into their study accounts.

Participants were randomly assigned one of three $H$ values: 20% (a chance of hacking popularly cited, which we use as a benchmark [55, 65, 72]), 1%, and 50%. To convey this information, participants in $S : Earn$ saw the message shown in the second screen from the top in Figure 1. Those in $S : Endowment$ saw a very similar message, which replaced the second and third sentences in the message with: "You begin the study with \$1 in your bank account. Each time you login (at most once per day) you will earn an additional \$1."

Next, participants were offered the option to enable 2FA. We chose 2FA as the exemplar behavior in our system because prior work finds that it is an "in-the-middle" behavior – understood better and adopted more often than updating, but less so than strong passwords [59]. Additionally, it was easier to create a simple, realistic system around a binary 2FA choice (enable/don't enable) than around other security behaviors such as updating or browser warnings.

We were explicit about the amount of protection offered by 2FA, just as we were explicit about the risk of being hacked. Participants were randomly assigned an arbitrarily chosen protection value, $P$, of 50% or 90%. As defined above, that value was then used in the effective risk calculation that led to a chance of "hacking" in our experiment. Thus, their effective risk was $H(1 - P)$. To communicate this, participants saw the following message: "Would you like to enable two factor authentication using your phone number? Two factor authentication will protect you from hacking $P$ of the time."

Those who selected 2FA went through SMS-based two-factor setup, where they received an initial text with a four-digit code that they needed to enter before proceeding.[1] Then, on all subsequent logins, they received an SMS with a code and had to enter this code along with their password in order to log in.

Finally, participants were shown their bank balance, and also reminded of when they must next log in, for $S : Endowment$, or when they could next earn more money, for $S : Earn$.

Upon subsequent logins, participants would see the previously described login page where they logged in using their MTurk ID, password, and, if they selected the option, 2FA. After logging in, the participant was directed to their bank balance page. At the end of the study, on their last login, they were shown a link to a Qualtrics survey which the user needed to complete in order to receive payment. The survey used two validated measures, SeBIS [25] and the Web-Use Skills Index [37], to measure the participant's general security behavior intentions and internet skill; we also collected their gender, age, and education level.

**Technical Details: Data Storage & Measurement.** Our system was built using PHP 5.6.32. The 2FA validation was handled by the AuthyAPI. All data was stored in a secure database. Only the hashed and salted password, not the cleartext password, was saved using the PHP password-hash functionwith PASSWORD_DEFAULT. Passwords were verified using the PHP password-verify function.

To measure password strength, we used the data-driven neural-network password meter [76]. To record the signup and login times, we recorded the total number of seconds for which the 2FA screen was in focus. We began recording when the page was loaded and stopped recording focus time when the pages were submitted. That is, if a user went to the login page, stayed on that page for five seconds, checked their email for two minutes, and finally came back to the website and took another ten seconds to submit their login, we would have recorded a login screen time of fifteen seconds.

### 3.2 Experimental Design

We recruited 150 workers from Amazon Mechanical Turk (MTurk) to participate in two rounds of an experiment run on our bank system. We recruited only workers from the United States and those who had a 95% approval rating or above, as prior work shows that these workers produce the highest quality results [56]. Our advertisement stated that participants would be evaluating a website for our institution and had the opportunity to earn up to $5. In the first experiment, participants completed a consent form and were then redirected to create an account on the bank site. They progressed through the steps described above, and were assigned to one of eight experimental settings: H=1%, P=50%, Endowment and Earn (Low Risk); H=1%, P=90%, Endowment; H=20%, P=50% Endowment and Earn; H=50% and P=50% Endowment; H=50% and P=90% Endowment and Earn (High Risk).

[1]While SMS-based 2FA has been shown to be insecure [57], it is still the most broadly adopted 2FA standard. Additionally, SMS-based 2FA provides a simple, quantifiable privacy and time cost for our experimental scenario: app-based 2FA would complicate cost calculations, as we would not know if certain users already had the application we chose installed on their phones. For purposes of our experiment, the actual security offered by SMS-based 2FA in practice does not matter.

We selected a non-full-factorial design due to cost constraints; we selected the following conditions that would maximize our ability to draw conclusions about the effect of various risk levels as well as the endowment condition. The experiment ran for five days. All participants who started the experiment were paid $0.50, and those who submitted their final surveys were paid the amount remaining in their bank account (ranging from $0 through $5.00).

Five days after the conclusion of Round 1 (RD1), participants received an email through MTurk inviting them to participate in the experiment again. They were told that things would work the same way as last time, but that they needed to create a new account. Participants were again randomly assigned to one of the eight experimental settings, with no relation to their RD1 settings. When participants finished Round 2 (RD2) they were not asked to take the survey again, but were again compensated as in RD1. Participants spent an average of a total of 142 seconds (Std. Dev = 34.57 (s)) logging in to RD1 and an average of a total of 158 seconds (Std. Dev = 30.40 (s)) logging into RD2, plus an average of 6 minutes completing the survey after the first game.

### 3.3 Analysis

Our analysis consists of three components: (1) modeling security behavior as a function of the variables measured and assigned in the games; (2) determining the degree to which participants' behavior was utility-optimal, that is "rational," and modeling the factors correlating with rational decision-making; and (3) presenting a thought experiment showing how we could use this information to predict utility-optimal behaviors for MTurker's and how such predictions could be used to nudge security behavior in the future. We describe our specific methodology for each analysis in more detail in Sections 5 to 7; Table 1 summarizes the regression models constructed.

| Outcome Var | Input Vars |
|---|---|
| R1 2FA Decision | S, H, P, H:S, P:S, age, gender, education, IS, pwd. strength, SeBIS |
| R2 2FA Decision | R1 2FA Decision |
| R2 2FA Decision | R1 2FA Decision, R1 Login Time, R1 Signup Time, interactions between times and 2FA decision |
| R2 2FA Decision | R1 2FA Decision, R1 Login Time, R1 Signup Time, interactions between times and 2FA decision, S, H, P, P:S |
| R1 2FA Rationality | S, H, P, H:S, P:S, age, gender, education, IS, pwd. strength, SeBIS |
| R2 2FA Rationality | S, H, P, H:S, P:S, age, gender, education, IS, pwd. strength, SeBIS |

Table 1. Regression models constructed. S stands for setting (Earn or Endowment, with Earn as baseline); H is a numeric variable for Hack percentage; P is a numeric variable for protect percentage; gender is a boolean variable with Male as the baseline; education is a three-level categorical variable with HS education or less as the baseline; decisions in prior rounds are boolean with False as the baseline; and IS (internet skill), SeBIS (security behavior intention), age, time measurements, and pwd. (password) strength are numerics. Input vars shown in table for R1 2FA Decision are those that were included prior to backward selection, only S, H, P, and P:S were retained after model selection.

### 3.4 Limitations

Behavioral economics experiments are subject to a number of limitations: participants may behave differently than in real life, our variables for the hack and protect percentages may be unrealistic, and 2FA may not be a representative security behavior. We have done our best to mitigate these limitations by setting our incentive in line with typical behavior economics incentives [46] and by choosing hack and protection percentages both higher and lower than real values suggested by popular studies for the hack percentage, and we tried to pick protection values that would provide information about whether people feel differently about a nearly "perfectly" protective security behavior and a behavior that will only work half of the time. Finally, we chose 2FA as our exemplar behavior because prior work suggests it is a reasonable "middle-of-the-road" in terms of user understanding and adoption [59].

It is also possible that the source of our sample, Amazon Mechanical Turk, and the fact that our sample is not representative of the demographics of the US may have biased our results (our participants are younger and more educated than the U.S. population, as is typicaly of AMT samples [60]); additionally it is possible that those participants who lost their money due to hacking or due to forgetting to log in would be far less likely to return their surveys or return for the second round. We chose to use Mechanical Turk because census-representative survey platforms do not allow for the deployment of experiments such as ours, and we experienced low drop out rates (17% RD1, 15% RD2) suggesting that lack of compensation for participants who were hacked or forgot to log in was not a significant source of bias.

## 4 PARTICIPANT DESCRIPTIVES

125 of the original 150 participants completed RD1. 107 of these RD1 participants finished RD2. The demographics of the two groups were nearly identical. Our samples were skewed slightly male (54% in R1, 55% in R2). Our participants were more educated than the general population, with 51% and 50% in each round, respectively, holding a college degree or above as compared to 28% of the U.S. population [77]. Finally, our samples are both skewed heavily younger than the general population, with 70% of our participants under 40 years old compared to 40% of the general population. Table 2 summarizes the demographics of our samples.

Our RD1 participants had a mean internet skill score of 4.06 on the Web-Use Skills Index [37]; our RD2 participants had a mean internet skill score of 4.016 (this difference was not significant by a Mann-Whitney U test). Our RD1 participants had a mean SeBIS score [25] of 3.17; RD2 participants had a mean SeBIS score of 3.16 (the difference in SeBIS scores across rounds was not significant by a Mann-Whitney U test).

| Metric | Round 1 | Round 2 | Census |
|---|---|---|---|
| Male | 54% | 55% | 49% |
| Female | 45% | 44% | 51% |
| HS or Less | 13% | 13% | 28% |
| Some College | 36% | 37% | 31% |
| B.S. or Above | 51% | 50% | 28% |
| 18-29 years | 31% | 32% | 23% |
| 30-39 years | 43% | 41% | 17% |
| 40-49 years | 15% | 15% | 17% |
| 50-59 years | 8% | 9% | 18% |
| 60+ years | 2% | 2% | 25% |

Table 2. Demographics of participants in our sample. Some percentages may not add to 100% due to item non-response. Census statistics from the American Community Survey [77].

## 5 WHAT FACTORS DRIVE PEOPLE'S SECURITY DECISION-MAKING?

**Analysis Approach.** To model our participants' behavior, we constructed binomial logistic regression models where enabling 2FA was the outcome variable. For modeling 2FA enablement in RD1, we included the following input variables: the participant's gender, age, educational level,

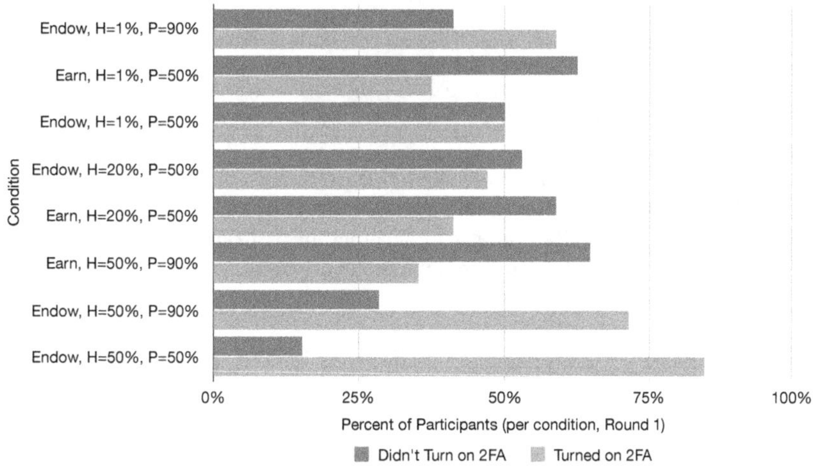


Fig. 2. Percent of participants who enabled 2FA in each of our eight experimental conditions in RD1.

internet skill, security behavior intention and password strength, as well as the protect and hack percentages presented, the setting (earn or endow), and two-way interactions between the latter three factors. We used backward selection based on the Bayesian Information Criterion to select the model of best fit [69]. We report model fit using McFadden's Pseudo-$R^2$ [15], approximating the percent of variance explained.

For modeling round two behavior, we construct three models: one with only RD1 behavior as the input variable; one with RD1 behavior, RD1 signup time (not including time spent on 2FA), and RD1 mean login time (not including time spent on 2FA); and one with RD1 behavior and times as well as RD2 equivalents of the factors found to be relevant in the RD1 2FA enablement model (a subset of: hack and protection percentages, demographics, password strength, the setting, and relevant interactions) as the input variables. We chose to construct these models in order to examine the relationship between security decision-making and anchoring effects,[2] participants' costs (e.g., tendency to login or signup slowly), and the relevant factors identified in RD1 (our "blind" experiment, in which we do not yet know participants' typical tendencies or costs). We do not include whether the participant was hacked or lost money in RD1 because fewer than 10 such participants returned to play in RD2, a quantity insufficient to provide robust regression results. We compared the fits of our three models using likelihood ratio tests [11].

We report the results of all models, including log-adjusted regression coefficients (odds ratios), 95% confidence intervals for those odds ratios, p-values (with a significance threshold of 0.05), pseudo-$R^2$, and the results of model comparison tests, when appropriate.

**Factors that Drive 2FA Decisions.** 51% of participants in RD1 and 56% in RD2 chose to enable 2FA. These decisions varied by condition, as shown in Figure 2.

We model RD1 decisions to enable 2FA as a function of attributes of the respondent (gender, age, education, internet skill), and security practices or savviness (security behavior intention, password strength), and risks and conditions assigned to the participant ($H$, $P$, $S$), as well as interactions between these risks and settings: interaction between endowment (T/F) and $H$ and interaction between endowment and $P$. We find that the model of best fit retains only the risk, protection, and setting factors, as well as the interaction between setting and protect percentage (Table 3). Those in

[2]The anchoring effect is a commonly shown psychological effect in which humans tend to stick with the first decision they make or choice they are offered [70].

| Variable | O.R. | C.I. | p-value |
|---|---|---|---|
| *Endowment* | 2.32 | [1.44, 3.76] | <0.001* |
| *H* | 2.31 | [1.22, 4.38] | 0.011* |
| *P* | 1.46 | [1.22, 1.97] | 0.043* |
| *Endowment:P* | 3.61 | [1.35, 9.67] | 0.012* |

Table 3. Logistic regression results for 2FA behavior in RD1. O.R. is the log-adjusted regression coefficient (odds ratio), CI is the 95% confidence interval of that odds ratio, and p-values marked with * are significant at the 0.05 level. Endowment is a boolean variable for whether the participant was in one of the endowment conditions, $H$ and $P$ are numeric, and ':' indicates an interaction variable.

the endowment conditions are 2.3 times more likely to enable 2FA, in line with endowment effects observed in other fields [5, 50].

Those who are shown a higher $H$, that is told that research shows a higher chance of account hacking, are more likely to enable 2FA. Those shown a higher $P$, that is, those told 2FA will be 90% rather than 50% effective, are also more likely to enable 2FA, while those in a condition that involved endowment and a higher $P$ are even more more likely to enable than just accounting for $P$ or the endowment setting separately would suggest. This model explains 14.7% of the variance in the RD1 data.[3]

As described above, we model RD2 decisions with three different sets of models. The model with just RD1 behavior as an input factor indicates that those who enabled 2FA in RD1 are 83 times more likely to do so in RD2 , in line with the expected anchoring effect. This model explains 35.3% of the variance in our RD2 data. Next, we added RD1 costs (e.g., RD1 signup and login times) to the model to understand whether RD2 behavior was explained just by repeating RD1 behavior or also by learning from the costs of RD1 behavior. The model of best fit retained all three factors, and we see that both login time in RD1 and RD1 behavior are significant in the model, with those who enabled in RD1 being more likely to enable in RD2 and those who took longer than others to login in RD1 being 6% less likely to enable 2FA in RD2.This model explains the data significantly better than the prior model ($p = 0.012$) with pseudo-$R^2$=0.522. Finally, we built a third model that included these three RD1 factors as well as the experimental settings retained in RD1. This final model shows only that enabling 2FA in RD1 is significantly related to enabling 2FA in RD2, however, we find that this final model with the experimental variables fits significantly better than the prior model ($p = 0.040$) and explains a total of 61.2% of the variance (Table 4), suggesting that the costs and experimental settings are explanatory of behavior but not as strongly as are anchoring effects.

## 6 DO PEOPLE MAKE RATIONAL SECURITY DECISIONS?

**Analysis Approach.** To examine whether participants made utility-optimal decisions and the factors related to the rationality of those decisions, we considered participants to have made a *utility-optimal* decision in the following way: it is utility-optimal to enable 2FA if the cost of doing so is less than the expected utility that would be gained from 2FA. For those who enabled 2FA in either round, we compute the cost of using 2FA for an individual user as the time it cost them to sign up (in hours) plus the sum of the time it cost them to log in each time (in hours) times their hourly wage: $C_{2fa} = (T_{signup} + \sum T_{login}) * wage_{mturk}$. To compute the value of our participants' *wage* we used the data collected in the Pew 2016 survey about MTurk workers [41] to compute a population-based estimate of \$4.97/hr. For those who did not use 2FA, and in any analysis in which

[3]We note that this is likely a *conservative* interpretation of the effect; indeed, psychologists have suggested that $R^2$ values may appear deceptively low when modeling singular events (e.g., decisions) that tend to accumulate over time, and that the true explanatory power of the significant variables in these cases may be stronger than a singular measurement indicates [1].

| Variable | O.R. | C.I. | p-value |
|---|---|---|---|
| R1 2FA Decision | 32.66 | [2.19, 486.54] | 0.011* |
| R1 Login Times | 0.81 | [0.6, 1.11] | 0.190 |
| R1 Signup Time | 0.90 | [0.69, 1.16] | 0.411 |
| *Endowment* | 1.26 | [0, 547.12] | 0.094 |
| *P* | 17.09 | [0.04, 144.74] | 0.357 |
| *H* | 72.88 | [0.57, 373.07] | 0.063 |
| *Endowment:P* | 0.99 | [0.91, 1.08] | 0.822 |
| R1 2FA:Login Times | 1.12 | [0.81, 1.56] | 0.496 |
| R1 2FA:Signup Time | 2.41 | [0.26, 22.02] | 0.435 |

Table 4. Logistic regression results for 2FA behavior in RD2 modeled as a function of RD1 2FA decision, RD1 costs (login and signup times), and RD2 experimental settings. McFadden Pseudo-$R^2$=0.612

we use the full dataset (that is the data of those who enabled and did not enable 2FA), we estimate the cost of 2FA. A sensitivity analysis reveals a linear pattern in estimations: considering 2FA cost as the mean results in an estimate of more rational choices than considering 2FA cost as 2× or 3× the mean. To generate conservative estimates of rational behavior we continue our computations by estimating 2FA cost for those who did not enable as 2× the mean.

We compute the utility of using 2FA as the potential loss (maximum amount they could earn times hack percentage) times the protection gained by using 2FA ($P$): $U_{2fa} = P[(H) * Max_{bank}]$. Where $Max_{bank}$ was \$5 for our experiment, and is the value of the money in an MTurker's account for the third analysis.

Below we examine whether 2FA users made utility-optimal decisions. We also examine the proportion of utility-optimal decisions made by our sample as a whole using the mean cost of enabling 2FA (computed from those who did choose to use it). To compare the strength of the associations between the decisions made in each round, we use a $\chi^2$ test with Cramér's V as our measure of effect size and use Holm-Bonferroni correction to account for multiple comparisons .

Finally, we model whether participants' decisions were utility-rational using regression models. We construct these models using a similar approach to that described in Section 5, with RD1 utility-optimal decision-making being modeled as a function of the participant's gender, age, educational level, internet skill, security behavior intention and password strength, as well as the protect and hack percentages presented, the setting, and two-way interactions among the latter three factors. RD2 utility-optimal decision-making (True or False) was modeled with two models: the first was a single-factor model containing only whether the RD1 decision was utility-optimal, and the second included the same factors as in RD1 as well as the RD1 decision. We performed backward selection on this second model to achieve a model of best fit for RD2.

**Were Participants' Decisions Rational?** We find that, following the approach described above, 48% of all participants made utility-optimal decisions in RD1 and 58% did so in RD2.

We also consider behavior at the extremes: that is, the lowest and highest risk conditions, as well as in the middle. We find that, in RD1, 33% of participants in the lowest-risk settings (e.g., did not enable 2FA), 48% in the medium risk, and 63% in the highest risk settings make a utility-optimal decision (e.g., enabled 2FA [4]). We observe a learning effect ($\chi^2 = 21.226$, df= 2, $p < 0.001$, V = 0.578 (medium)) with 58% of all participants in the medium-risk experiments making a rational decision in RD2, 46% in the lowest-risk settings and 75% in the highest-risk settings. Figure 3 compares the change in utility-optimal behavior by risk level for the rounds.

[4]In our particular experiment, using 2FA was always utility-optimal in the highest risk setting and never in the lowest.

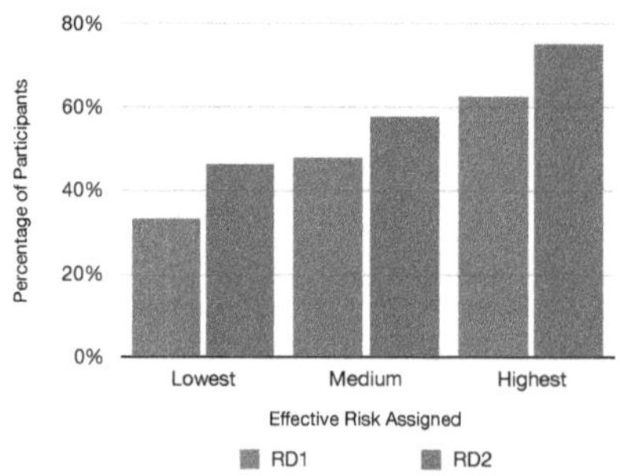


Fig. 3. Percentage of participants in each round and with a given risk setting who made a utility-optimal decision about 2FA.

**Modeling utility-optimal decision making.** We wanted to understand how these different factors, as well as participant factors, interacted to potentially explain whether participants' make utility-optimal decisions.

We first model whether participants made a utility-optimal 2FA decision in RD1 in the same way as we modeled general decision-making for RD1 in Section 5 above. The model of best fit retains only the hack percentage, setting, and internet skill factors (pseudo-$R^2$=0.141). Those in the endowment setting are 25% more likely to make a utility-optimal choice, while those with higher internet skill are 15% more likely to do so. Further, we see that those who saw a higher hack percentage are more likely to make a *utility-optimal decision* in RD1.

For RD2, we find that a single-factor consisting of only whether the RD1 decision was utility optimal is not significant. After backward selection, the multi-factor model of best fit retains SeBIS, the risk and protection factors, endowment, and interactions between risk and endowment and protection and endowment (psuedo-$R^2$=0.078). We see that those with higher SeBIS scores are nearly four times more likely to have made a utility-optimal decision in RD2, and (similar to RD1) those who saw a higher hack percentage are 21% more likely to make a utility-optimal decision.

## 7 THOUGHT EXPERIMENT: WHEN DOES SECURITY BENEFIT THE MARKET?

In order to examine the impact of different models of user behavior on market costs and utility from security, we present a simple thought experiment regarding the implementation of optional 2FA on the MTurk platform.

**Approach.** Suppose that MTurk decided to offer a 2FA option to workers. Workers who enable 2FA then must use 2FA every time they log in, exactly as in our experiment. We know from prior work [41] that 63% of MTurkers log in daily, 32% multiple times a week (for the purposes of our thought experiment, we say 3× per week), 3% log in weekly, and the rest log in less than once a week. Using costs (as defined in Section 6) from our experiment, this means 2FA would cost: $C_{2fa} = 0.065 * wage_{mturk} + 0.039 * N(logins) * wage_{mturk}$. Using this equation, we see that each week using 2FA would cost the daily login group \$0.34, the 3× a week login group \$0.18, and the weekly login group \$0.10.

Suppose also that MTurkers transfer the money they earn out of their accounts once per week, so the value of their bank (e.g., the money they stand to lose if their account is hacked) is the value of their weekly earnings. Not all MTurkers earn the same amount on MTurk; prior work shows that 17% earn all of their income on MTurk, 8% earn most (75%), 6% earn half (50%), 15% earn some (25%), and 53% earn very little (5%) of their income on the platform. We estimate, based on reports from the population that those who earn all or most of their income on MTurk make \$38,555 per

| Approach | Costs | Utility | Loss/Gain |
|---|---|---|---|
| All Secure | $275 | $148 | (-) $126 |
| Utility Optimal | $32 | $128 | (+) $96 |
| No Security | $0 | $0 | $0* |

Table 5. Estimated costs, utility, and loss or gain from each of the security approaches. Figures are per 1000 MTurk users. *We use the [39] model, in which users sustain no losses from hacking, to compute this value. If users sustained losses, the value would instead be $266.

year or $741 per week in total, with either 100% or 75% of that income coming from MTurk. Those who earn half or less of their income on MTurk earn a higher overall income of $54,300 or $1044 per week, but only 5%-50% of that income comes from MTurk.

Finally, we estimate the utility gained from 2FA for some people at an arbitrarily selected 1% risk of hacking over the course of the year and for others at an arbitrary 20% risk of hacking over the course of the year. We suppose in this thought experiment that 25% of people might choose weak passwords, thus having a hypothetically supposed 20% risk of hacking over the course of the year. The remaining 75% of the population we theorize have a 1% risk of hacking. Thus, the utility of 2FA in a given week would be calculated as follows (with a conservatively assumed 50% protection value): $U_{2fa} = P(H * Income)/52$. We again consider enabling 2FA to be utility optimal in cases where the utility is greater than the cost.

It is important to note that we choose fairly arbitrary values for this thought experiment, so the results should be considered as an example rather than taken literally. However, we believe this example (as with prior theoretical work that uses a similar approach [39]) provides a useful perspective for thinking carefully about when and how to advise users.

**Results.** We find that under the above assumptions, for all but those who earn the least on MTurk ($52 per week) those who are at a 20% risk of hacking and who log in more than once a week should always enable 2FA. Those that log in once a week could enable 2FA or not enable 2FA with no discrepancy in outcome, as the cost of enabling and the utility gain are equal. For those who earn the least on MTurk, it is never utility optimal to enable 2FA.

Based on these calculations, we compute the cost and utility, and the overall gain or loss, from the three different recommendations for user security: users should always take all security precautions, users should never take security precautions, and users should take utility-optimal security precautions. Table 5 summarizes the results per 1000 MTurkers. We see that utility-optimal behavior leads to a gain of $96 per 1000 MTurkers, while an "enable security always" solution leads to a cost of $126 per 1000 MTurkers, and a "never enable security" solution leads to a gain of $0. Estimates suggest that there are 500,000 MTurkers active at any given time [41]. Using this estimate, requiring all MTurkers to use 2FA would cost the market $63,606, while providing MTurkers with nudges for suggested behavior that is utility-optimal would lead to a gain of $47,865 if all MTurkers behaved optimally and $23,932 if 50% chose a utility optimal behavior. Of course, the current option of not presenting 2FA leads to no gain or loss.

More generally, assuming that 2FA offers protection only 50% of the time, we find that for those who have $741 in their accounts (e.g., earn $741 weekly and withdraw their income once per week) there need only be a 1.5% chance of their account being hacked over the course of the year for there to be utility gain from 2FA. For those who login weekly, a 2.7% risk for those who login three times a week, and a 4.9% risk for those who login daily. Similarly, for those who earn half their income from MTurk ($522) and login weekly there need only be a 2.2% chance of their account getting hacked over the course of the year for there to be utility gain from 2FA. (These figures include only monetary losses, not time losses or emotional consequences from cleaning up from hacking;

including these costs would cause 2FA to become utility optimal at even lower risks.) On the other hand, for those who earn very little (or keep very little money in their MTurk accounts), the risks must be very large — 68% for daily logins or 21% for weekly logins — for 2FA to be utility optimal.

## 8 DISCUSSION

**Make Risks, Costs, and Benefits Transparent.** Overall, we find that explicitly stated risks and utilities (e.g., benefits) appear to explain between 9% (Round 2) and 15% (Round 1) of the variance in our participants' behavior. While participants lean heavily on anchoring effects (e.g., their typical practices) and to a lesser extent their knowledge of their own costs (e.g., how long it takes them to perform a login) when settling on a behavior, the additional contribution of risk and utility variables to the variance explained suggests that *numeric* descriptions of risk and benefit are at least partially informing users' security decision making. This finding agrees with prior findings in privacy that showed people were able to pick between different platforms verbally described to be more or less privacy protective [75]. These findings consequently offer support for making risk and benefit information more transparent to users. Rather than telling people they "should adopt behavior X to be more secure" we may wish to give them more autonomy over their choices.

Inherently, making risks (or benefits from a given behavior) more transparent requires us to know what the risk or benefit of a particular attack or behavior is to the user. Measuring this risk effectively is a challenging open problem [40]. Recent work, such as that conducted by Bilge et al. and Thomas et al. [13, 73], pushes for more scientific and measurement oriented approaches to assessing the potential for an attack or the benefit of a security behavior. Our results provide additional motivation for this research direction, and present a parallel direction for future work exploring how best to convey risk to users (e.g., exploring how they interpret and respond to different textual and numeric estimates of risk), as well as investigating how explicit risk communication may factor into existing legal and policy frameworks around digital security and privacy disclosure.

**Recommend Utility-Optimal Behaviors.** In our experiment, being able to compute a cost for an individual's security behavior and their expected utility from that behavior allows us to predict what users should do in a particular security decision-making scenario. A similar principle could be used in a real-world system to develop personalized security recommendations to guide users toward utility-optimal behaviors, rather than always trying to encourage adoption of security behaviors. That is, by measuring users' typical time to complete certain behaviors (e.g., login), their implicit risk (e.g., password strength, security settings), and the history of attacks on a given platform for users with a similar risk profile, systems may be able to offer users personalized, suggested behaviors.

For example, a platform could display a message similar to the following on login or when the user is confronted with a security decision: "Our personalized security analysis system suggests that two-factor authentication may be a good fit for securing your account. We expect to take only an additional 30 seconds of your time." While prior work has found that encouraging users to adopt behaviors that their friends have adopted [23] can succeed, doing so may not always be of benefit to the user. A more carefully personalized system that takes into account the utility-cost ratio for the user, as well as other factors unexplored here, such as risk aversion, may offer a more trustworthy set of suggestions that are respectful of user time and reduce their security burden.

**Security-Savvy Not Necessarily Safer.** Our findings reveal that security-savvy, measured by password strength and SeBIS score, had no impact on choice to enable 2FA, and an inconsistent impact on rationality of decision. We had anticipated a relationship between 2FA use and password strength (or security behavior intention), either that stronger passwords (or more security intention) would indicate higher paranoia that would correlate with more 2FA use, or that those who picked weaker passwords would be more likely to enable 2FA, suggesting a tradeoff between the two risk-reducing behaviors. Instead, we find only a relationship between explicitly stated risks (e.g., the chance of getting hacked that we conveyed to them). This suggests that users treat different security behaviors independently without considering them as a package that influences overall risk or may be unaware of the relationship between their own choices (e.g., the strength of the password they pick) and their risks. If so, they may have difficulty making rational choices.

Thus, future work may wish to explore users' level of understanding of the risks of their security choices, how they think these risks interact, and investigate how to correct resultant misperceptions. Additionally, we may wish to understand the efficacy of translating user choices into explicit risk assessments; for example, instead of presenting a scale of password strength from weak to strong, present password strength in terms of risk of account compromise.

**Future Work.** The work presented here takes a first step toward measuring the rationality of user decision-making, assessing the contexts in which more and less rational behavior occurs, and understanding how risks, costs, and user factors influence decisions in security. Our experimental scenario presents the simplest of situations: with explicit, monetary, easily characterizable costs and risks. Future work may wish to explore rationality of decision making around data or other non-monetary assets and the impact of non-numeric risk statements, or explore other cognitive biases, e.g., present bias [31, 48, 49]. Learning and/or comparing against other models of bounded rationality is of practical interest [38, 80]. Additionally, our experiment only explores users' choice to enable 2FA, and indirectly their choice of password strength. Future work should validate, or invalidate, these results with other security behaviors.

Finally, our results show that self-report measures of security behavior intention and internet skill were not related to 2FA enablement behavior. However, we see evidence that skill and/or intent may be related to the rationality of decision-making. This suggests that self-report measures may be ineffective at predicting or assessing behaviors — a finding supported by extensive work in other fields [28, 58, 74] — but may be useful in assessing more deeply underlying constructs that are related to rationality. Future work should seek to further explore the utility of self-report measures for assessing security behavior, and whether experimental systems such as that presented here more, less, or equally as useful as self-reporting for measuring real-world behavior.

## 9 CONCLUSION

In this work we explore the rationality of decisions made by end-users when faced with security choices. We validate that, at least in our relatively realistic experimental scenario, end-users behave in accordance with bounded rationality. That is, they are able to take into account some, but not all, risk and context factors and make rational (e.g., utility optimal) decisions in more than 50% of cases. We find, further, that we are able to explain user decision making well (McFadden Pseudo-$R^2$=0.61) by accounting for participants' knowledge of costs and risks as well as accounting for the known phenomena of endowment and anchoring effects.

We find that our participants made utility-optimal decisions more often when faced with higher risks. While perhaps encouraging for corporate high-risk scenarios, this finding also suggests a challenge for day-to-day security, as many of the risks end users confront in daily digital life are less transparent, less monetarily linked, and relatively small. Thus, future work may wish to explore how rationality is affected by different methods of communicating risk, less tangible consequences than the monetary incentives provided in our experiments, and even smaller risks.

Using our data to compute utilities and costs for 2FA on the Amazon Mechanical Turk (MTurk) platform, we show that a "one-size-fits-all" approach encouraging all users to engage in all security behaviors at all times can lead to significant market and individual losses. However, we also show that there are relatively low risk thresholds at which 2FA becomes utility optimal, leading to significant market gains. This underscores the importance of quantifying the risk and utility of security behaviors through data-driven research [13, 73] in order to ensure that risks, costs, and benefits are accurately understood.

Overall, our work supports a nuanced model of the "human-in-the-loop" who is able to somewhat take into account explicit risks and personal costs, in addition to relying on typical tendencies (e.g., anchoring effects), to make frequently rational decisions but who struggles to identify less obvious risks such as those incurred from weak passwords. This argues for personalized security-behavior recommendations for users tailored based on their costs (e.g., login times), risks (e.g., password strength), and value of their account (e.g., measured through the amount of money stored), especially in cases where the optimal behavior for them goes against their typical tendencies. If accurate, such personalized recommendations could provide security benefits while helping to avoid large market and personal costs from wasted time and effort on non-utility-optimizing security behaviors.

## ACKNOWLEDGEMENTS

Elissa Redmiles acknowledges support from the National Science Foundation Graduate Research Fellowship Program under Grant No. DGE 1322106 and a Facebook Fellowship.

## REFERENCES

[1] Robert P Abelson. 1985. A variance explanation paradox: When a little is a lot. *Psychological Bulletin* 97, 1 (1985), 129.

[2] Alessandro Acquisti. 2004. Privacy in electronic commerce and the economics of immediate gratification. In *Proceedings of the ACM Conference on Electronic Commerce (EC)*. ACM, 21–29.

[3] Alessandro Acquisti, Laura Brandimarte, and George Loewenstein. 2015. Privacy and human behavior in the age of information. *Science* (2015).

[4] Alessandro Acquisti and Jens Grossklags. 2005. Privacy and rationality in individual decision making. *IEEE Security & Privacy* 3, 1 (2005).

[5] Alessandro Acquisti, Leslie K John, and George Loewenstein. 2013. What is privacy worth? *The Journal of Legal Studies* 42, 2 (2013).

[6] Alessandro Acquisti, Curtis R Taylor, and Liad Wagman. 2016. The economics of privacy. (2016).

[7] Tansu Alpcan and Tamer Basar. 2006. An intrusion detection game with limited observations. In *12th Int. Symp. on Dynamic Games and Applications, Sophia Antipolis, France*, Vol. 26.

[8] Kregg Aytes and Terry Connolly. 2004. Computer security and risky computing practices: A rational choice perspective. *JOEUC* 16, 3 (2004).

[9] Christine Bauer, Jana Korunovska, and Sarah Spiekermann. 2012. On the value of information-what Facebook users are willing to pay. *ECIS* (2012).

[10] A. Beautement, M. A. Sasse, and M. Wonham. 2008. The compliance budget: Managing security behaviour in organisations. In *workshop on new security paradigms*. DOI: http://dx.doi.org/10.1145/1595676.1595684

[11] Peter M Bentler and Douglas G Bonett. 1980. Significance tests and goodness of fit in the analysis of covariance structures. *Psychological bulletin* 88, 3 (1980).

[12] Stefan Berthold and Rainer Böhme. 2010. Valuating privacy with option pricing theory. *Economics of information security and privacy* (2010).

[13] Leyla Bilge, Yufei Han, and Matteo Dell'Amico. 2017. RiskTeller: Predicting the Risk of Cyber Incidents. In *CCS*.

[14] Rainer Böhme and Jens Grossklags. 2011. The security cost of cheap user interaction. In *NSPW*. ACM.

[15] A Colin Cameron and Frank AG Windmeijer. 1997. An R-squared measure of goodness of fit for some common nonlinear regression models. *Journal of Econometrics* 77, 2 (1997).

[16] Katherine Campbell, Lawrence A Gordon, Martin P Loeb, and Lei Zhou. 2003. The economic cost of publicly announced information security breaches: empirical evidence from the stock market. *Journal of Computer Security* 11, 3 (2003).

[17] Juan Pablo Carrascal, Christopher Riederer, Vijay Erramilli, Mauro Cherubini, and Rodrigo de Oliveira. 2013. Your browsing behavior for a big mac: Economics of personal information online. In *WWW*. ACM.

[18] Lin Chen and Jean Leneutre. 2009. A game theoretical framework on intrusion detection in heterogeneous networks. *IEEE Transactions on Information Forensics and Security* 4, 2 (2009).

[19] Nicolas Christin, Serge Egelman, Timothy Vidas, and Jens Grossklags. 2011. It's all about the Benjamins: An empirical study on incentivizing users to ignore security advice. In *FC*.

[20] Nicolas Christin, Jens Grossklags, and John Chuang. 2004. Near rationality and competitive equilibria in networked systems. In *SIGCOMM workshop on Practice and theory of incentives in networked systems*. ACM.

[21] Lorrie Faith Cranor. 2008. A framework for reasoning about the human in the loop. *UPSEC* 8, 2008 (2008).

[22] Dan Cvrcek, Marek Kumpost, Vashek Matyas, and George Danezis. 2006. A study on the value of location privacy. In *Proceedings of the 5th ACM Workshop on Privacy in Electronic Society*. ACM.

[23] S. Das, A. D.I. Kramer, L. A. Dabbish, and J. I. Hong. 2014. Increasing Security Sensitivity With Social Proof: A Large-Scale Experimental Confirmation. In *CCS*. DOI: http://dx.doi.org/10.1145/2660267.2660271

[24] Peter Diamond and Hannu Vartiainen. 2012. *Behavioral economics and its applications*. Princeton University Press.

[25] S. Egelman and E. Peer. 2015. Scaling the Security Wall: Developing a Security Behavior Intentions Scale (SeBIS). In *CHI*.

[26] Joseph Farrell. 2012. Can privacy be just another good. *Journal on Telecomm. & High Tech* 10 (2012).

[27] Adrienne Porter Felt, Robert W Reeder, Hazim Almuhimedi, and Sunny Consolvo. 2014. Experimenting at scale with google chrome's SSL warning. In *CHI*. ACM.

[28] Michael Fendrich and Connie M Vaughn. 1994. Diminished lifetime substance use over time: An inquiry into differential underreporting. *Public Opinion Quarterly* 58, 1 (1994).

[29] Allan Friedman. 2007. An Empirical Approach to Understanding Privacy Valuation. (2007).

[30] Esther Gal-Or and Anindya Ghose. 2005. The economic incentives for sharing security information. *Information Systems Research* 16, 2 (2005).

[31] Nick Gravin, Nicole Immorlica, Brendan Lucier, and Emmanouil Pountourakis. 2016. Procrastination with variable present bias. *EC* (2016).

[32] Jens Grossklags. 2007. Experimental economics and experimental computer science: A survey. In *Workshop on Experimental computer science*. ACM.

[33] Jens Grossklags, Nicolas Christin, and John Chuang. 2008. Secure or insure?: a game-theoretic analysis of information security games. In *WWW*. ACM.

[34] Jens Grossklags, Nicolas Christin, and John Chuang. 2008. Security Investment (Failures) in Five Economic Environments: A Comparison of Homogeneous and Heterogeneous User Agents.. In *WEIS*.

[35] Yaniv Hanoch, Stacey Wood, and Thomas Rice. 2007. Bounded rationality, emotions and older adult decision making: Not so fast and yet so frugal. *Human Development* 50, 6 (2007).

[36] Marian Harbach, Sascha Fahl, Polina Yakovleva, and Matthew Smith. 2013. Sorry, I don't get it: An analysis of warning message texts. In *FC*.

[37] Eszter Hargittai and Yuli Patrick Hsieh. 2012. Succinct survey measures of web-use skills. *Social Science Computer Review* 30, 1 (2012), 95–107.

[38] Jason S Hartford, James R Wright, and Kevin Leyton-Brown. 2016. Deep learning for predicting human strategic behavior. In *NIPS*. 2424–2432.

[39] C. Herley. 2009. So Long, and No Thanks for the Externalities: The Rational Rejection of Security Advice by Users. In *NPSW*. DOI: http://dx.doi.org/10.1145/1719030.1719050

[40] Cormac Herley. 2017. Justifying Security Measures: a Position Paper. In *ESoRCS*.

[41] Paul Hitlin. 2016. Research in the Crowdsourcing Age, a Case Study. (2016).

[42] Jason Hong. 2012. The state of phishing attacks. *Commun. ACM* 55, 1 (2012).

[43] Ashish R Hota and Shreyas Sundaram. 2015. Interdependent security games under behavioral probability weighting. In *International Conference on Decision and Game Theory for Security*.

[44] Kai-Lung Hui and Ivan PL Png. 2006. Economics of privacy. (2006).

[45] Benjamin Johnson, Jens Grossklags, Nicolas Christin, and John Chuang. 2010. Are Security Experts Useful? Bayesian Nash Equilibria for Network Security Games with Limited Information.. In *ESORICS*.

[46] Emir Kamenica. 2012. Behavioral economics and psychology of incentives. *Annu. Rev. Econ.* (2012).

[47] Laurie Kirsch and Scott Boss. 2007. The last line of defense: motivating employees to follow corporate security guidelines. *ICIS* (2007).

[48] Jon Kleinberg, Sigal Oren, and Manish Raghavan. 2016. Planning problems for sophisticated agents with present bias. In *EC*. ACM, 343–360.

[49] Jon Kleinberg, Sigal Oren, and Manish Raghavan. 2017. Planning with multiple biases. In *EC*. ACM, 567–584.

[50] Jack L Knetsch. 1989. The endowment effect and evidence of nonreversible indifference curves. *American Economic review* 79, 5 (1989).

[51] Yu Liu, Cristina Comaniciu, and Hong Man. 2006. A Bayesian game approach for intrusion detection in wireless ad hoc networks. In *Proceeding from the 2006 workshop on Game theory for communications and networks*. ACM.

[52] Mohammad Hossein Manshaei, Quanyan Zhu, Tansu Alpcan, Tamer Bacşar, and Jean-Pierre Hubaux. 2013. Game theory meets network security and privacy. *CSUR* 45, 3 (2013).

[53] Arunesh Mathur, Josefine Engel, Sonam Sobti, Victoria Chang, and Marshini Chetty. 2016. " They Keep Coming Back Like Zombies": Improving Software Updating Interfaces.. In *SOUPS*.

[54] R Ann Miura-Ko, Benjamin Yolken, John Mitchell, and Nicholas Bambos. 2008. Security decision-making among interdependent organizations. In *CSF*. IEEE.

[55] Norton. 2012. Norton 2012 Cybercrime Report. (2012). https://now-static.norton.com/now/en/pu/images/Promotions/2012/cybercrimeReport/2012_Norton_Cybercrime_Report_Master_FINAL_050912.pdf

[56] Eyal Peer, Joachim Vosgerau, and Alessandro Acquisti. 2014. Reputation as a sufficient condition for data quality on Amazon Mechanical Turk. *Behavior research methods* 46, 4 (2014).

[57] Bradley Reaves, Nolen Scaife, Dave Tian, Logan Blue, Patrick Traynor, and Kevin RB Butler. 2016. Sending out an SMS: Characterizing the Security of the SMS Ecosystem with Public Gateways. In *Security and Privacy (SP), 2016 IEEE Symposium on.* IEEE, 339–356.

[58] Elissa M Redmiles, Yasemin Acar, Sascha Fahl, and Michelle L Mazurek. 2017. *A Summary of Survey Methodology Best Practices for Security and Privacy Researchers.* Technical Report.

[59] Elissa M Redmiles, Sean Kross, and Michelle L Mazurek. 2016. How i learned to be secure: a census-representative survey of security advice sources and behavior. In *CCS.* ACM.

[60] Joel Ross, Lilly Irani, M Silberman, Andrew Zaldivar, and Bill Tomlinson. 2010. Who are the crowdworkers?: shifting demographics in mechanical turk. In *CHI'10 extended abstracts on Human factors in computing systems.* ACM, 2863–2872.

[61] Mark Rounds, Norman Pendegraft, and Jim Alves-Foss. 2013. An Experimental Study to Explore Attacker Response to Changes in Security and Reward. In *HICSS.* IEEE.

[62] Karin Sallhammar, Svein J Knapskog, and Bjarne E Helvik. 2005. Using stochastic game theory to compute the expected behavior of attackers. In *Applications and the Internet Workshops, 2005. Saint Workshops 2005. The 2005 Symposium on.* IEEE.

[63] Michel Schreiner and Thomas Hess. 2013. On The Willingness To Pay For Privacy As A Freemium Model: First Empirical Evidence.. In *ECIS.*

[64] Simeon Schudy and Verena Utikal. 2017. "You must not know about me" On the willingness to share personal data. *Journal of Economic Behavior & Organization* (2017).

[65] John Seymour. 2016. How Often Are Social Media Accounts Hacked? (2016). https://www.zerofox.com/blog/often-social-media-accounts-hacked/

[66] Steve Sheng, Mandy Holbrook, Ponnurangam Kumaraguru, Lorrie Faith Cranor, and Julie Downs. 2010. Who falls for phish?: a demographic analysis of phishing susceptibility and effectiveness of interventions. In *CHI.* ACM.

[67] Woohyun Shim, Luca Allodi, and Fabio Massacci. 2012. Crime pays if you are just an average hacker. In *CyberSecurity.* IEEE.

[68] Herbert A Simon. 1979. Rational decision making in business organizations. *American Economic Review* 69, 4 (1979).

[69] David J Spiegelhalter, Nicola G Best, Bradley P Carlin, and Angelika Van Der Linde. 2002. Bayesian measures of model complexity and fit. *Journal of the Royal Statistical Society: Series B (Statistical Methodology)* 64, 4 (2002).

[70] Fritz Strack and Thomas Mussweiler. 1997. Explaining the enigmatic anchoring effect: Mechanisms of selective accessibility. *Journal of personality and social psychology* 73, 3 (1997).

[71] Joshua Sunshine, Serge Egelman, Hazim Almuhimedi, Neha Atri, and Lorrie Faith Cranor. 2009. Crying Wolf: An Empirical Study of SSL Warning Effectiveness.. In *USENIX security.*

[72] Ben Taylor. 2016. Why There is a 1 in 3 Chance You'll get Hacked in 2016. (2016). https://www.bestvpn.com/privacy-news/get-hacked-one-in-three/

[73] Kurt Thomas, Frank Li, Ali Zand, Jacob Barrett, Juri Ranieri, Luca Invernizzi, Yarik Markov, Oxana Comanescu, Vijay Eranti, Angelika Moscicki, Daniel Margolis, Vern Paxson, and Elie Bursztein (Eds.). 2017. *Data breaches, phishing, or malware? Understanding the risks of stolen credentials.*

[74] Roger Tourangeau and Ting Yan. 2007. Sensitive questions in surveys. *Psychological bulletin* 133, 5 (2007).

[75] Janice Y Tsai, Serge Egelman, Lorrie Cranor, and Alessandro Acquisti. 2011. The effect of online privacy information on purchasing behavior: An experimental study. *Informs* (2011).

[76] Blase Ur, Felicia Alfieri, Maung Aung, Lujo Bauer, Nicolas Christin, Jessica Colnago, Lorrie Faith Cranor, Henry Dixon, Pardis Emami Naeini, Hana Habib, and others. 2017. Design and evaluation of a data-driven password meter. In *CHI.* ACM.

[77] U.S. Census Bureau. 2014. American Community Survey 5-Year Estimates. (2014).

[78] Kami Vaniea and Yasmeen Rashidi. 2016. Tales of software updates: The process of updating software. In *CHI.* ACM.

[79] Rick Wash and Emilee J Rader. 2015. Too Much Knowledge? Security Beliefs and Protective Behaviors Among United States Internet Users.. In *SOUPS.*

[80] James R Wright and Kevin Leyton-Brown. 2014. Level-0 meta-models for predicting human behavior in games. In *EC.* ACM, 857–874.

# Keynote Talk: High-Frequency Trading and the Design of Financial Exchanges: Will the Market Fix the Market?

ERIC BUDISH, University of Chicago, Booth School of Business

The first part of this talk will cover the argument in Budish, Cramton and Shim [1] that the predominant market design used by financial exchanges around the world, called the continuous limit order book, is flawed. The flaw – essentially, a glitch introduced in the transition from human-based financial exchanges to electronic ones – is to treat time as a continuous variable, and process requests to trade serially. This combination of continuous time and serial processing creates mechanical arbitrage opportunities based on symmetric public information --- a violation of efficient markets theory, built right into the market design! --- which in turn harms liquidity provision and induces a never-ending, socially wasteful, arms race for speed. That is, much of high-frequency trading is a *symptom* of flawed market design. We propose an alternative market design, called frequent batch auctions, in which time is discrete and orders are batch processed using auctions, and show that this directly fixes the problem with the continuous market.

The second part of this talk will ask whether the "market will fix the market?" – that is, whether market forces will lead to the adoption of discrete-time trading instead of continuous-time trading, or whether a regulatory intervention would be needed. This requires a model of how modern stock exchanges compete and earn profits, the subject of new work-in-progress with Lee and Shim [2]. The model shows that competition among stock exchanges is fierce on the dimension of traditional trading fees, but that exchanges have market power in the sale of exchange-specific speed technology – i.e., arms for the arms race. We then use the model to study the private and social returns to market design innovation. We find that even though the social returns to adopting discrete-time trading would be large and positive, the private returns can be negative, due to the loss of rents from speed technology. We discuss some modest policy interventions that could tip the balance of incentives and encourage the "market to fix the market".

Last, I will discuss some open questions about financial market design that lie at the intersection of economics and computer science.

Keywords: Market design; high-frequency trading; frequent batch auctions; sniping; efficient markets

**ACM Reference Format**
Eric Budish. 2018. Keynote Talk: High-Frequency Trading and the Design of Financial Exchanges: Will the Market Fix the Market? In ACM EC'18: Proceedings of the 2018 ACM Conference on Economics and Computation, June 18-22, Ithaca, NY. ACM, NY, NY. 2 pages. DOI: https://doi.org/10.1145/3219166.3219237

## Speaker's Bio

Eric Budish is Professor of Economics at the University of Chicago, Booth School of Business. He is also a Research Associate at the National Bureau of Economic Research and a Director of the Initiative on Global Markets at Chicago Booth.


*ACM EC'18, June 18–22, 2018, Ithaca, NY, USA.*

ACM ISBN 978-1-4503-5829-3/18/06. https://doi.org/10.1145/3219166.3219237

Budish's research is on market design: designing the "rules of the game" in a market so that self-interested behavior by market participants leads to economically attractive outcomes. Budish's research on high-frequency trading and the design of financial exchanges received the AQR Insight Award and the Leo Melamed Award, has been discussed in major policy addresses by the NY Attorney General and the SEC Chair, and has influenced exchange design proposals in the US and UK. Budish's dissertation research concerned the matching problem of assigning students to schedules of courses, or workers to schedules of shifts. Budish's proposed design, which applies price-theoretic competitive equilibrium ideas to a matching market, was successfully adopted for use in practice by the Wharton School in 2013, and is currently being used at six professional schools. Budish's research on patent design and cancer R&D received the Kauffman/iHEA Award for Health Care Entrepreneurship and Innovation Research and the Arrow Award for the best paper in Health Economics.

Budish received his PhD in Business Economics from Harvard University, his MPhil in Economics from Oxford (Nuffield College), and his BA in Economics and Philosophy from Amherst College. Prior to graduate school, Budish was an analyst at Goldman Sachs. Budish's honors include the Marshall Scholarship, the Sloan Research Fellowship, and giving the 2017 AEA-AFA joint luncheon address.

## ACKNOWLEDGMENTS

I am grateful to my dissertation advisors, Alvin Roth, Susan Athey, Ariel Pakes, and David Parkes, my collaborators, Eduardo Azevedo, Aditya Bhave, Gerard Cachon, Estelle Cantillon, Yeon-Koo Che, Peter Cramton, Judd Kessler, Fuhito Kojima, Robin Lee, Paul Milgrom, Abraham Othman, Philip Reny, Benjamin Roin, Tuomas Sandholm, John Shim, Lisa Takeyama, and Heidi Williams, and my colleagues at the University of Chicago.

## REFERENCES

[1] Budish, E, P. Cramton and J. Shim. 2015. The High-Frequency Trading Arms Race: Frequent Batch Auctions as a Market Design Response. *Quarterly Journal of Economics*, pg. 1547-1621.

[2] Budish, E, R. Lee and J. Shim. 2018. Will the Market Fix the Market? A Theory of Stock Exchange Competition and Innovation. *Manuscript in Preparation.*

# Almost Optimal Stochastic Weighted Matching with Few Queries

SOHEIL BEHNEZHAD, University of Maryland, USA
NIMA REYHANI, Upwork, USA

We consider the *stochastic matching* problem. An edge-weighted general (i.e., not necessarily bipartite) graph $G(V, E)$ is given in the input, where each edge in $E$ is *realized* independently with probability $p$; the realization is initially unknown, however, we are able to *query* the edges to determine whether they are realized. The goal is to query only a small number of edges to find a *realized matching* that is sufficiently close to the maximum matching among all realized edges.

The stochastic matching problem has received a considerable attention during the past decade after the initial paper of Chen et al. [ICALP'09] because of its numerous real-world applications in kidney-exchange, matchmaking services, online labor markets, and advertisements. Most relevant to our work are the recent papers of Blum et al. [EC'15], Assadi et al. [EC'16, EC'17] and Maehara and Yamaguchi [SODA'18] that consider the same model of stochastic matching.

Our main result is an *adaptive* algorithm that for any arbitrarily small $\epsilon > 0$, finds a $(1 - \epsilon)$-approximation in expectation, by querying only $O(1)$ edges per vertex. We further show that our approach leads to a $(1/2 - \epsilon)$-approximate *non-adaptive* algorithm that also uses $O(1)$ edges per vertex. Prior to our work, no nontrivial approximation was known for weighted graphs using a constant per-vertex budget. The state-of-the-art adaptive (resp. non-adaptive) algorithm of Maehara and Yamaguchi achieves a $(1 - \epsilon)$-approximation (resp. $(1/2 - \epsilon)$-approximation) by querying up to $O(w \log n)$ edges per vertex where $w$ denotes the maximum integer edge-weight. Our result is a substantial improvement over this bound and has an appealing message: No matter what the structure of the input graph is, one can get arbitrarily close to the optimum solution by querying only a constant number of edges per vertex.

To obtain our results, we introduce novel properties of a generalization of *augmenting paths* to weighted matchings that may be of independent interest.

Additional Key Words and Phrases: Stochastic matching, stochastic optimization, matching markets

## 1 INTRODUCTION

We consider the *stochastic weighted matching* problem where the goal is to find a maximum weighted matching under *uncertainty* assumption about the input graph. More precisely, the input contains a general (i.e., not necessarily bipartite) weighted graph $G = (V, E)$ and a constant probability $p > 0$. We are unsure about the edges of $G$ that exist in the actual *realization*, however, the assumption is that each edge of $G$ is *realized* independently with probability $p$. An algorithm is able to *query* an edge in $G$ to determine whether it exists in the actual realization. The goal is to find a sufficiently large weighted matching in the realized graph by querying only a small number of the edges. An *adaptive* algorithm in this setting can have multiple rounds of adaptivity where the queries

Portions of this work were completed while the first author was an intern at Upwork.

Authors' addresses: Soheil Behnezhad, University of Maryland, USA; Nima Reyhani, Upwork, USA.


*ACM EC'18, June 18–22, 2018, Ithaca, NY, USA.* ACM ISBN 978-1-4503-5829-3/18/06...$15.00
https://doi.org/10.1145/3219166.3219226

conducted in each round of adaptivity may depend on the results of the previous rounds. A *non-adaptive* algorithm, on the other hand, has only one round of adaptivity. That is, a non-adaptive algorithm should pick a degree bounded subgraph $H$ of $G$ whose expected matching is sufficiently close to that of $G$.

Ignoring the constraint on the number of queries, a trivial solution is to query all the edges of $G$ and report the maximum weighted matching among the realized edges. However, for many applications of the stochastic matching problem (which we elaborate on in the next section), querying an edge is *time consuming*. We are, therefore, interested in the tradeoff between the fraction of the omniscient optimum solution that we achieve and the number of edges that are queried.

Our main contribution is an adaptive algorithm, that for any arbitrarily small constant $\epsilon > 0$, finds in expectation, a $(1 - \epsilon)$-approximation of the maximum weighted matching in the realized graph, by making only a *constant* (dependant only on $\epsilon$ and $p$) number of per-vertex queries, in a constant number of rounds. We also show that it is possible to obtain a $(1/2 - \epsilon)$-approximation via a non-adaptive algorithm. This result, apart from its theoretical importance, has an appealing practical message: No matter what the structure of the input graph is, one can get arbitrarily close to the optimum solution by querying only a constant number of edges per vertex.[1]

It is worth mentioning that the dependence on both $\epsilon$ and $p$ is crucial for any algorithm that achieves a $(1 - \epsilon)$-approximation. Consider the simple example of a star graph where one vertex $v$ is connected to all other vertices by edges of weight 1. The expected weight of the omniscient maximum matching is $1 - o(1)$ since the matching size would be 1 if at least one of the edges are realized. To ensure that with probability at least $1 - \epsilon$ one of the queried edges is realized, one needs to query at least $\Omega(\log(1/\epsilon)/p)$ edges of $v$.[2]

Stochastic matching settings have been studied extensively in the past decade after the initial paper of [11]. Motivated mainly by its application in *kidney exchange*, this natural variant of stochastic matching problem was initially introduced in [9] and has received significant attention ever since [5, 6, 9, 18]. In the literature, most algorithms work only for unweighted graphs [5, 6, 9] where the goal is to approximate maximum cardinality matching. The only exception is the very recent paper of Maehara and Yamaguchi [18] that achieves a $(1 - \epsilon)$-approximation via an adaptive algorithm for general (resp. bipartite) weighted graphs with $O(w \log n/\epsilon p)$ (resp. $O(w/\epsilon p)$) queries per vertex where $w$ denotes the maximum edge weight assuming that all edge weights are positive integers. They also show that a $(1/2 - \epsilon)$-approximation is achievable via a non-adaptive algorithm using the same number of queries per vertex. Our result is a substantial improvement over this bound as it has no dependence on the structural properties of the input graph such as $n$ or $w$.

Our techniques are based on a novel set of definitions and lemmas for weighted *augmenting components* that generalize augmenting paths to weighted graphs. Despite being useful objects when the goal is to find a large cardinality matching, augmenting paths have rarely been useful for weighted graphs in different settings of the matching problem. These properties may be of independent interest for generalizing augmenting path based techniques to weighted graphs.[3]

---

[1]We note that our algorithms works even if the realization probability of the edges are different as long as they are all bounded away from 0 by a constant. In such cases, it suffices to define $p$ to be the minimum realization probability among all the edges.

[2]Note that although the matching size here is either 0 or 1, a $(1 - \epsilon)$-approximation is well defined because we are comparing the *expected* size of the realized matching to that of the original graph. Another closely related example is a complete graph for which one can show existence of a perfect matching w.h.p. and follow the same approach to prove the same lower bound for *every* vertex (e.g., see [5]).

[3]There is also a notion of "augmenting paths" for flow algorithms. Here we only refer to augmenting path based techniques that are used in matching algorithms.

## 1.1 Applications

*Kidney exchange.* One of the main applications of the stochastic matching problem is in *kidney exchange*, which includes two types of participants: an organ donor and an organ receiver. The donor is a healthy living individual willing to donate one of his/her two kidneys to the organ receiver (patient), without much of life threatening side effects. Usually, the donor is among family and friends. However, the kidney of a donor might not be a compatible match for the patient due to physiological reasons including the incompatible blood type, tissue-type, etc. The goal in kidney exchange is to provide a platform to swap kidneys between pairs of organ donors and patients in order to find a match.

Usually the donors' and the patients' medical records (e.g. blood type) are available as an early indicator of the compatibility. The basic information is not conclusive, therefore, extra medical laboratory tests such as antibody screening is required to better estimate the odds of a successful transplant. The extra medical tests are time consuming and costly; specially for the patients who have been long waiting for the transplant or are in critical life condition.

Kidney exchange can be seen as a matching problem where each incompatible donor-patient pair is a vertex and there exists an edge between two vertices when the two kidneys can be swapped between pairs. A maximum matching of the donor-patients graph finds the maximum number of the donor-patient pairs who can swap kidneys. For many reasons, such as geographic proximity, wait time, age, etc. [14], the design committee may introduce weights on the edges. This means, depending on the matching policy and the edge weights, maximizing the matching cardinality is not necessarily the best solution.

The stochastic matching problem, here, helps in reducing the number of costly and time consuming extra medical tests which should be performed to find the compatibility of the donor-patient pairs. The algorithm selects (i.e., queries) only a small set of donor-patient pairs for extra medical lab-tests so that in expectation, a sufficiently large matching exists within the selected pairs that pass the test in the realized graph.

There has been a plethora of studies on kidney exchange, particularly on stochastic settings [2–4, 7, 13, 15, 16, 19, 20]. We refer interested readers to the paper of [9] for a more detailed discussion.

*Online labour markets.* Traditional full-time employment has continuously given way to *flexible* contract work. This has resulted in a growth of demand for the services of the companies such as Upwork, Guru, Freelancer and Fiverr that facilitate working relationships between freelancers and employers. The parties in such markets have often more options than they can consider and interview with. In the stochastic matching context, job descriptions and the freelancers can be represented by vertices in a bipartite graph where an edge between a freelancer and a job posting would represent whether the freelancer is a good fit for the job. While initial job descriptions by an employer rule out some of the edges, there is no way of having a full knowledge about the actual graph beforehand. Here, querying an edge maps to the pair having an interview, and therefore, the stochastic matching procedure helps in minimizing the number of interviews while achieving a near optimal solution. Edge weights, in this context, help in maximizing, say, the social welfare or other objective functions.

By analogy, stochastic matching also contributes to other *matching services*, such as online dating services.

### 1.2 The Model

In the *stochastic setting*, for input graph $G = (V, E)$, the edges in $E$, independently from each other, are realized w.p. $p$.[4] For a subset $E'$ of $E$, we define $E'_p$ to be a random variable corresponding to different *realizations* of $E'$ where each edge in $E'$ is *realized* independently w.p. $p$.

In the *stochastic matching problem*, a graph $G = (V, E)$ with a non-negative weight $w_e$ for each edge $e \in E$ as well as the realization probability $p$ are given the input. A realization $\mathcal{E}$ of $E$ that is drawn from $E_p$ is initially fixed but is unknown to us. Our goal is to find a weighted matching of $\mathcal{E}$ that is close to $M(\mathcal{E})$, where $M(.)$ denotes the maximum weighted matching of its input edge set.[5] An algorithm is allowed to *query* the edges in $E$ to determine whether they are in $\mathcal{E}$ or not.

An *adaptive* algorithm proceeds in separate rounds. At each round $i$, based on the results of the queries thus far, the algorithm queries a new subset of the edges $Q_i$ in parallel. The goal is to maximize $\mathbb{E}[M(\cup_{i=1}^{R} Q'_i)]$, where $Q'_i$ denotes the edges in $Q_i$ that exist in $\mathcal{E}$, and guarantee that it is close to $\text{OPT} := \mathbb{E}[M(\mathcal{E})]$. These expectations are taken over the randomness of the realization $\mathcal{E}$. The total number of rounds that an adaptive algorithm takes is called its *degree of adaptivity*. A *non-adaptive* algorithm on the other hand has only one round of adaptivity.

We hope to have algorithms in which the number of per-vertex queries and the degree of adaptivity are both independent of the structure of the input graph such as the edge weights or $n$.

### 1.3 Related Work

Directly related to the model that we consider in this work are [5, 6, 9, 18], with the only difference that (except for [18]) their results only hold for unweighted graphs. More specifically, Blum *et al.* [9] give an adaptive algorithm that achieves a $(1 - \epsilon)$-approximation by querying $\frac{\log(2/\epsilon)}{p^{2/\epsilon}}$ per-vertex edges, in the same number of rounds. Assadi *et al.* [5] improve this result to get rid of the exponential dependence on $1/\epsilon$. In particular, they show that it is possible to achieve the same approximation factor by querying only $O(\log(1/\epsilon p)/\epsilon p)$ edges, with a very similar algorithm. Very recently, Maehara and Yamaguchi [18], among some other related problems, considered the stochastic weighted matching problem. They provided a $(1 - \epsilon)$-approximation via an adaptive algorithm for general (resp. bipartite) weighted graphs with $O(w \cdot \log n/\epsilon p)$ (resp. $O(w/\epsilon p)$) queries per vertex where $w$ is the maximum edge weight assuming that all edge weights are positive integers. See Section 2.1 for a comparison of our techniques to the techniques used in these papers.

For non-adaptive algorithms, all of the papers above also obtain a $(1/2 - \epsilon)$-approximation via a non-adaptive algorithm. The state-of-the-art non-adaptive algorithm for unweighted graphs is the algorithm of Assadi *et al.* [6], which achieves a slightly better than half approximation for unweighted graphs.

Stochastic matching has received a lot of attention in the last decade due to its numerous applications. A very well-studied setting is the *query-commit* model that was first introduced by Chen *et al.* [11]. In the query-commit model, a queried realized edge has to be included in the final matching [1, 8, 11, 12, 17]. Another related setting is that of [10]. In this setting, the algorithm is allowed to query at most two incident edges of each vertex and the goal is to find the optimal subset of edges to query.

## 2 OUR RESULTS AND TECHNIQUES

Our main result is the following theorem which is formally given in Section 3 as Theorem 3.

[4]Throughout the paper, we use *w.p.* to abbreviate "with probability".

[5]We may slightly abuse the notation and use $M(.)$ to both refer to a maximum weighted matching and its weight.

**Theorem 1** (Informal). *For any given $\epsilon > 0$, there exists a poly-time adaptive algorithm to achieve a $(1-\epsilon)$-approximation of the stochastic weighted matching problem by querying only $O(\frac{1}{\epsilon p^{4/\epsilon}})$ edges per vertex in $O(\frac{1}{\epsilon p^{4/\epsilon}})$ rounds of adaptivity.*

We further show that one can obtain a $(0.5-\epsilon)$-approximation via a non-adaptive algorithm with the same number of per-vertex queries.

**Theorem 2** (Informal). *For any given $\epsilon > 0$, there exists a poly-time non-adaptive algorithm to achieve a $(0.5-\epsilon)$-approximation of the stochastic weighted matching problem by querying only $O(\frac{1}{\epsilon p^{4/\epsilon}})$ edges per vertex.*

Here we focus on the adaptive algorithm and explain the main technical ingredients used in proving Theorem 1. In brief, our algorithm is as follows: take the maximum weighted matching in $G$, query its edges, and remove from $G$ the queried edges that are known to be unrealized. Repeat this for $R$ (a parameter to be determined later) rounds; then report the maximum weighted matching among the realized queried edges.

Inspired by the analysis of [9] for the unweighted variant of the problem, we first provide a proof sketch to show that this algorithm achieves a $(1-\epsilon)$-approximation for $R = O(1)$, if all the edge weights are the same (which is equivalent to the case of unweighted graphs). We then focus on challenges in generalizing this approach to the general weighted case and describe the intuitions on how we overcome them.

The idea is to maintain a *realized matching* and iteratively augment it at each round until its size becomes as large as $(1-\epsilon)$OPT. Let us denote by $O_r$ the maximum realized matching among the queried edges by round $r$. Note that if $|O_{r-1}| < (1-\epsilon)$OPT, the next matching that we pick (which is definitely of size at least OPT) augments $O_{r-1}$ by *many* vertex disjoint augmenting paths of size at most $O(1/\epsilon)$. Any of these augmenting paths increases the matching size only if all of its edges are realized. However, since the length of each of the augmenting paths is at most $O(1/\epsilon)$, the probability that all of the edges of any of the augmenting path is realized is at least $p^{O(1/\epsilon)}$. Hence roughly after $1/p^{O(1/\epsilon)}$ rounds, we achieve a $(1-\epsilon)$-approximation in expectation.

This proof contains two canonical parts: (i) there are *many* vertex disjoint augmenting paths; (ii) each of them has a relatively *small length*. Roughly speaking, these claims are correct since in unweighted graphs, each augmenting path increases the size of a matching by at most one edge. In fact, for weighted graphs, one may give an example that refutes both of these assumptions at the same time.

This difference, is perhaps, one of the main reasons that in the literature of the matching problem, augmenting paths have extensively been considered for the unweighted graphs, where in contrast, they have rarely been useful when the graph under consideration is weighted. In this work, we propose a novel direction to generalize augmenting paths to weighted graphs that may be of independent interest.

Consider two weighted matchings $M_L$ and $M_H$ of the same graph with $w(M_L) < (1-\epsilon)w(M_H)$. Further consider the graph $M_H \Delta M_L := (M_H \cup M_L) - (M_H \cap M_L)$ which is a set of connected components that are either paths or cycles since the degree of each vertex in it is at most 2. We call each of these connected components an *alternating component*. Moreover, we call each alternating component an *augmenting component* if the total weight of edges of $M_H$ in it is more than that of $M_L$.

For any alternating component $C$ in $M_H \Delta M_L$, we denote by $\Delta_C$ the amount of weight that is added to the base matching $M_L$ after we swap the edges of $M_L$ in $C$ with that of $M_H$ (we call this process *augmenting* $C$). Thus, we have $\sum_{C \in M_H \Delta M_L} \Delta_C = w(M_H) - w(M_L)$. We refer to $\Delta_C$ as the value of alternating component $C$. Hence, an augmenting component is an alternating component with a positive value. We further define the *augmenting edges* of $C$, denoted by $Q_C$, to be the set of edges in $C$ that are in $M_H$. Moreover, we define the *normalized length* of $C$, denoted by $L_C$, to be $w(Q_C)/\Delta_C$ where $w(Q_C)$ denotes the total weight of the edges in $Q_C$.

In the stochastic matching context, $M_L$ will correspond to our maintained realized matching and $M_H$ will correspond to the matching that we pick in the next iteration of the algorithm. The main theorem of this paper is obtained by coupling the following two lemmas:

(1) Querying the edges of an augmenting component $C$, increases the expected weight of the maximum realized matching by at least $\Omega(p^{O(L_C)}\Delta_C)$ in expectation. (See Lemma 7 for the formal statement.)
(2) There is always a set $S$ of *high impact* (i.e., $\sum_{C\in S}\Delta_C$ is sufficiently large) vertex-disjoint augmenting components of *small* normalized length. (See Lemma 8 for the formal statement.)

*Intuition behind (1).* Fix an augmenting component $C$. Denote the actual length (i.e., the number of edges) of $C$ by $k$. If $k \le O(L_C)$ the proof of the first lemma is trivial. Indeed, all the edges of $C$ are realized with probability $p^k$ and if they are all realized, $C$, after augmentation, adds $\Delta_C$ to the weight of the realized matching that we maintain. Hence in expectation $p^k\Delta_C$ $(\ge p^{O(L_C)}\Delta_C)$ is added to the weight of our realized matching as desired. Roughly speaking, for the case when $k$ is much larger than $L_C$, we cannot *afford* the probability by which the whole augmenting component is realized. Instead, we decompose the component into a set of vertex disjoint *sub-components* by removing some of its non-queried edges. This results in having smaller components that have a higher chance of being completely realized. We then argue that the amount of weight that these smaller components add to the matching is larger than $\Omega(p^{O(L_C)}\Delta_C)$ even considering the weight of the removed edges.

*Intuition behind (2).* The proof of this lemma is mainly based on the assumption that $w(M_L) < (1-\epsilon)w(M_H)$. If the normalized length $L_C = w(Q_C)/\Delta_C$ of an augmenting component $C$ is large, then its augmenting edges $Q_C$ should have a large total weight while its value $\Delta_C$ should be relatively small. This implies, intuitively, that a large portion of the edges in the heavier matching $M_H$ are *wasted* without augmenting the base matching $M_L$ by a large enough weight. Nonetheless, since we have $w(M_L) < (1-\epsilon)w(M_H)$, we can argue that this cannot happen for an arbitrarily large portion (based on their weights) of augmenting components.

### 2.1 Comparison of Techniques with Prior Works

The most relevant paper to our work, in terms of the techniques that are used, is that of [9] which only considers the unweighted version of the problem and the challenges in generalizing their analysis to the weighted case were discussed above. In summary, to achieve our results, we focus on properties of weighted augmenting paths. An important step is to relax the requirement that every edge in an augmenting path should be realized for it to be useful. We then show that it is possible to get $\epsilon$-close to the optimum weighted matching by constant per-vertex queries.

Assadi *et al.* [5], improve the result of [9] by achieving the same approximation factor while querying only $O(\log(1/\epsilon p)/\epsilon p)$ edges per vertex. Their ideas are mainly based on the intuition that even if parts of augmenting paths are realized, one can "patch" them together to create new augmenting paths and use Tutte-Berg to formalize this. Unfortunately, no equivalent generalization of Tutte-Berg formula is known for weighted graphs and thus our techniques are inherently different. However, our analysis is also based on the fact that parts of the edges in an augmenting path may be enough to obtain a better weighted matching.

Maehara and Yamaguchi [18] gave the only known approximation on weighted graphs prior to our work. They show that it is possible to get a $(1-\epsilon)$-approximation for general (resp. bipartite) weighted graphs with $O(w \log n)$ (resp. $O(w)$) queries per vertex where $w$ denotes the maximum edge weight assuming that all edge weights are positive integers. Their results are based on a general integer programming framework. More specifically, they formulate the stochastic matching problem by an integer program and use LP relaxations of maximum weighted matching on bipartite and general graphs to obtain their approximations. The dependence of the number of per-vertex queries on the edge weights' range ($w$) is intrinsically part of their framework, hence both of their approximations for bipartite and general graphs depend on $w$.

As an interesting side note, apart from minor differences, the descriptions of the algorithms proposed for the stochastic matching problem in the literature are all simple and similar, and the differences only appear in the analysis [5, 6, 9, 18].

## 3 $(1-\epsilon)$-APPROXIMATION VIA AN ADAPTIVE ALGORITHM

In this section we give an adaptive algorithm that returns a matching of the realized graph whose expected weight is a $(1-\epsilon)$-approximation of the optimum solution for any arbitrarily small constant $\epsilon$. The number of per-vertex queries, as well as the degree of adaptivity of our algorithm is $O(1)$ (it only depends on $\epsilon$ and $p$ — and not properties of the input graph such as $n$ or the edge weights).

The algorithm, formally given as Algorithm 1, is simple: In each round, among the edges that are either not queried yet or are queried and realized, it finds a maximum weighted matching and queries its edges. Finally after a sufficiently large (but constant) number of rounds, it reports the maximum weighted matching among the realized edges that had been queried.

**Algorithm 1** Adaptive algorithm for weighted stochastic matching: $(1-\epsilon)$-approximation.

```
Input: Input graph G = (V, E).
Parameter: R.
E* ← E
for r = 1, . . . , R do
    Find a maximum weighted matching M_r in (V, E*).
    Query the edges in M_r and remove its non-realized edges from E*.
end for
return a maximum weighted matching among realized edges in ∪_{r=1}^R M_r.
```

Note that $R$ is an upper bound on the per vertex queries and the degree of adaptivity of Algorithm 1. The main focus of this section is to show that for a constant $R$, the weight of the matching that Algorithm 1 returns is in expectation a $(1-\epsilon)$-approximation of the omniscient optimum. Theorem 3, which is the formal restatement of Theorem 1, captures this.

**Theorem 3.** *For any graph $G = (V, E)$, and any arbitrarily small constant $\epsilon > 0$, Algorithm 1 returns a matching whose expected weight is at least $(1-\epsilon)$OPT for $R = O(\frac{1}{\epsilon p^{4/\epsilon}})$.*

We start by a set of definitions for weighted matchings in Section 3.1 and then proceed to prove Theorem 3 in Section 3.2

### 3.1 Tools for Analyzing Weighted Matchings

Consider two weighted matchings $M_L$ and $M_H$ and assume that the total weight of matching $M_H$ is larger than that of $M_L$, i.e., $w(M_L) < w(M_H)$ where for any $E' \subseteq E$, we use $w(E') := \sum_{e \in E'} w_e$ to denote the total weight of edges in $E'$. Our goal in this section is to define a set of tools, among which, the most important is the notion of *augmenting components* which generalizes augmenting paths to weighted graphs.

Let us denote by $A\Delta B := (A \cup B) - (A \cap B)$ the symmetric difference of two sets $A$ and $B$. Consider the graph $D := M_L \Delta M_H$ of edges that appear in exactly one of $M_L$ and $M_H$. Since the degree of each vertex in $D$ is at most 2 (due to the fact that both $M_1$ and $M_2$ are matchings), $D$ is a collection of vertex disjoint paths and cycles. We start by defining alternating components.

**Definition 4** (Alternating components). We call any connected component of $M_L \Delta M_H$ an *alternating component*. For an alternating component $C$, we define $B_C := C \cap M_L$ to be its edges in $M_L$ and define $Q_C := C \cap M_H$ to be its edges in $M_H$. We refer to $B_C$ as the *base* edges of component $C$ and refer to $Q_C$ as the *augmenting* edges of $C$.

Note that alternating components in weighted graphs can be either cycles or paths, hence we refer to them as *components* instead of paths which is more common for cardinality matching in unweighted graphs. Next, we define a set of properties of these alternating components (see Figure 1).

**Definition 5.** For any alternating component $C$:

- We define the *value* $\Delta_C$ of $C$ to be $w(Q_C) - w(B_C)$.
- We define the *normalized length* $L_C$ of $C$ to be $w(Q_C)/\Delta_C$.

Observe that by definition, the value of an alternating component may even be negative. We use the term *augmenting components* to refer to any alternating component $C$ with $\Delta_C > 0$. Furthermore, we also use the term *augmenting* a component $C$ to denote the process of updating the matching $M_L$ to be $M_L \backslash B_C \cup Q_C$ which clearly is a valid matching since all components are vertex disjoint.

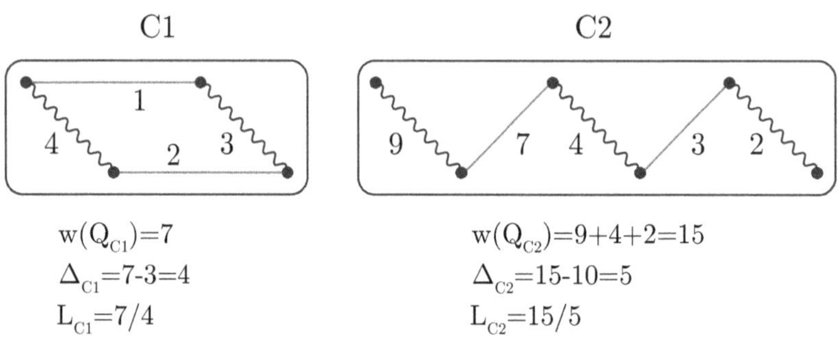


Fig. 1. Two augmenting components and their properties. The wavy (black) edges are the edges in $M_H$. The solid (red) edges are the edges in $M_L$.

## 3.2 Analysis

Let $M_r^T$ (resp. $M_r^F$) denote the edges in $M_r$ that are realized (resp., are not realized). Furthermore, denote by $O_r := M(\cup_{i=1}^r M_r^T)$ the maximum realized matching found by round $r$ (i.e., $O_R$ is what Algorithm 1 outputs). Let us denote by OPT the weight of the omniscient optimum maximum weight matching. Our goal is to show that for any round $r-1$ with $w(O_{r-1}) < (1-\epsilon)$OPT, the matching $M_r$ picked in the next round of Algorithm 1 augments $O_{r-1}$ by a constant fraction of OPT and use this to show that it takes only a constant number of rounds to obtain a $(1-\epsilon)$-approximation. We start by the following standard observation.

**Observation 6.** *For any $r \geq 1$, we have $w(M_r) \geq$ OPT.*

Proof. Matching $M_r$ is the maximum weighted matching over a set of edges that is a super set of the edges in the realization, hence $w(M_r)$ is larger than the weight of OPT which is the maximum weighted matching over the realized edges. □

Consider the two matchings $M_r$ and $O_{r-1}$ and define $U_r$ to be the set of augmenting[6] components in $M_r \Delta O_{r-1}$. We couple the following two lemmas to prove Theorem 3.

**Lemma 7.** *Querying the edges of each augmenting component $C$ in $U_r$ increases the expected matching size by at least $p^{2L_C}\Delta_C/2$.*

**Lemma 8.** *If $w(O_{r-1}) < (1-\epsilon)w(M_r)$, then $\sum_{C\in U_r : L_C < 2/\epsilon} \Delta_C \geq \frac{\epsilon}{2} w(M_r)$.*

We first show how with these two lemmas we can prove Theorem 3.

Proof of Theorem 3. By Observation 6, we know that for any round $r$, we have $w(M_r) \geq$ OPT. Suppose we have not obtained a $(1-\epsilon)$-approximation by round $r-1$, then we have

$$w(O_{r-1}) \leq (1-\epsilon)\text{OPT} \leq (1-\epsilon)w(M_r).$$

Let $S$ be the set of augmenting components in $U_r$ with normalized length at most $2/\epsilon$. The inequality above satisfies the condition of Lemma 8, thus, we have

$$\sum_{C\in S} \Delta_C \geq \frac{\epsilon}{2} w(M_r) \geq \frac{\epsilon}{2}\text{OPT}. \tag{1}$$

By Lemma 7, querying the edges of each of the augmenting components in $U_r$ increases the expected matching size by at least $p^{2L_C}\Delta_C/2$. Therefore,

$$\begin{aligned}
\mathbb{E}[w(O_r) - w(O_{r-1})] &\geq \frac{1}{2}\sum_{C\in U_r} p^{2L_C}\Delta_C \\
&\geq \frac{1}{2}\sum_{C\in S} p^{2L_C}\Delta_C && \text{Since for any } C \in U_r,\ \Delta_C > 0 \text{ and } S \subseteq U_r. \\
&\geq \frac{1}{2}\sum_{C\in S} p^{4/\epsilon}\Delta_C && \text{Since for any } C \in S,\ L_C \leq 2/\epsilon. \\
&\geq \frac{p^{4/\epsilon}}{2}\sum_{C\in S} \Delta_C \\
&\geq \frac{\epsilon p^{4/\epsilon}}{4}\text{OPT} && \text{By (1).}
\end{aligned}$$

This means that until we reach a $(1-\epsilon)$-approximation, we add, in expectation, a value of at least $\Omega(\epsilon p^{4/\epsilon}\text{OPT})$ to our maximum weighted realized matching in each round. Therefore, in expectation, it takes at most $O(\frac{1}{\epsilon p^{4/\epsilon}})$ rounds to obtain a $(1-\epsilon)$-approximation. □

[6] It is important that $U_r$ is the set of *augmenting* components in $M_r \Delta O_{r-1}$, and not all of its alternating components.

### 3.2.1 *Proof of Lemma 7.*

Proof of Lemma 7. Observe that the base edges of $C$ which are its edges that are in $O_{r-1}$ are already known to be realized by definition of $O_{r-1}$. However, the augmenting edges of $C$ which are the edges that are from matching $M_r$ might not have been queried before and thus might appear to be unrealized after being queried. The challenge, thus, is to show that in expectation the portion of augmenting edges of $C$ that will be realized augment $O_{r-1}$ by a total weight of at least $p^{2L_C}\Delta_C/2$.

Denote by $k$ the number of edges of $C$ that are from $M_r$. Since each of these edges are realized with probability at least $p$ independently from other edges, with probability at least $p^k$ all of them are realized and if they are all realized they augment the base matching $O_{r-1}$ by at least $\Delta_C$. Hence they add, in expectation, a total weight of at least $p^k\Delta_C$. If $p^k\Delta_C \geq p^{2L_C}\Delta_C/2$ we are done. However this might not be the case when $L_C$ is much smaller than $k$. To handle this, we show that even if small portions of $C$ are realized, they augment the base matching by a large enough value and argue that the expected augmentation value is at least $p^{2L_C}\Delta_C/2$.

**Definition 9.** Depending on the structure of component $C$, label its edges in the following way:

(1) If $C$ is a path starting with an edge of $M_r$, denote its edges by $(q_1, b_1, q_2, b_2, \ldots)$ that is in the order that the edges appear in the path.
(2) if $C$ is a path starting with an edge of $O_{r-1}$, denote its edges by $(b_0, q_1, b_1, q_2, b_2, \ldots)$ that is in the order that the edges appear in the path.
(3) if $C$ is a cycle, denote its edges by $(q_1, b_1, q_2, b_2, \ldots)$ that is in the order that the edges appear in the cycle, starting from an arbitrary augmenting edge of $C$.

Suppose for ease of exposition that $\alpha := 2L_C$ is an integer. For any integer $i \in [\alpha]$, define $D_i$ to be the following set of edges of $M_r$ in $C$:

$$D_i := \{q_i, q_{i+\alpha}, q_{i+2\alpha}, q_{i+3\alpha}, \ldots\}.$$

**Claim 10.** *There exists some integer $i \in [\alpha]$ for which $w(D_i) \leq w(Q_C)/\alpha$.*

Proof. It is easy to confirm by definition that for any $i, j \in [\alpha]$ with $i \neq j$, we have $D_i \cap D_j = \emptyset$ and that $\cup_{i\in[\alpha]} D_i = w(\cup_i\{q_i\}) = w(Q_C)$. That is, the edges of $Q_C$ are partitioned by $D_i$'s into $\alpha$ disjoint subsets. Thus, the average total weight of $D_i$ for $i \in [\alpha]$ is $w(Q_C)/\alpha$, meaning that there should be some $i \in [\alpha]$ with $w(D_i)$ no more than this average value. □

Now take an arbitrary $i \in [\alpha]$ for which $w(D_i) \leq w(Q_C)/\alpha$ and "delete" all the edges of $D_i$ from $C$. This procedure decomposes our augmenting component $C$ into a set $F = \{C_1, C_2, \ldots, C_t\}$ of smaller vertex disjoint connected components that we call *sub-components*. While each of these sub-components has the good property that it has a higher chance of being completely realized compared to the much longer original component $C$, we also need to take into account the loss of value resulted by deleting the edges of $D_i$ from $M_r$. Nonetheless, we argue that if we sum up the expected augmentation value of each of these vertex disjoint sub-components, the total expected value is as large as our desired value of $p^{2L_C}\Delta_C/2$.

One can confirm by the labeling procedure defined in Definition 9 that after removal of the edges in $D_i$, each sub-component $C_j \in F$ has at most $\alpha$ edges of $Q_C$. Therefore, for any sub-component $C_j$, all the edges in $C_j \cap M_r$ will be realized with probability at least $p^\alpha = p^{2L_C}$.

Denote by $\Delta_{C_j} := (C_j \cap M_r) - (C_j \cap O_{r-1})$ the *value* of sub-component $C_j$. By observation above, each sub-component $C_j$ augments its base matching by a total weight of at least $p^{2L_C}\Delta_{C_j}$ in expectation. Hence the total augmentation value of all sub-components is, in expectation, at least

$$\sum_{C_j\in F} p^{2L_C}\Delta_{C_j} = p^{2L_C}\sum_{C_j\in F}\Delta_{C_j}. \tag{2}$$

It only suffices to show that $\sum_{C_j \in F} \Delta_{C_j}$ is sufficiently large for our purpose. To see this, observe that $\sum_{C_j \in F} \Delta_{C_j}$ is essentially equal to the total value $\Delta_C$ of augmenting component $C$ minus the weight of the edges of $D_i$ since we removed them. However, since $w(D_i) \leq w(Q_C)/2L_C$ by Claim 10, we have

$$\begin{aligned}
\sum_{C_j \in F} \Delta_{C_j} &\geq \Delta_C - \frac{w(Q_C)}{2L_C} \\
&\geq \Delta_C - \frac{w(Q_C)}{2w(Q_C)/\Delta_C} && \text{By definition } L_C = w(Q_C)/\Delta_C. \\
&\geq \Delta_C - \frac{\Delta_C}{2} \\
&\geq \frac{\Delta_C}{2}. && (3)
\end{aligned}$$

Combining (2) and (3) we obtain our desired property that the total augmentation value of all sub-components is, in expectation at least $p^{2L_C}\Delta_C/2$, concluding the proof of Lemma 7. □

### 3.3 Proof of Lemma 8

Proof of Lemma 8. By Definition 5, the values of all augmenting components in $U_r$ add up to at least $w(M_r) - w(O_{r-1})$, i.e.,

$$\sum_{C \in U_r} \Delta_C \geq w(M_r) - w(O_{r-1}).$$

Separating the augmenting components based on their normalized length, we get

$$\begin{aligned}
\sum_{C \in U_r : L_C \geq 2/\epsilon} \Delta_C + \sum_{C \in U_r : L_C < 2/\epsilon} \Delta_C &\geq w(M_r) - w(O_{r-1}) \\
\sum_{C \in U_r : L_C < 2/\epsilon} \Delta_C &\geq w(M_r) - w(O_{r-1}) - \sum_{C \in U_r : L_C \geq 2/\epsilon} \Delta_C. && (4)
\end{aligned}$$

Next, we show that the total values of augmenting components with normalized length at least $2/\epsilon$ is small. Since by Definition 5, $L_C = w(Q_C)/\Delta_C$, we have

$$\sum_{C \in U_r : L_C \geq 2/\epsilon} \Delta_C = \sum_{C \in U_r : L_C \geq 2/\epsilon} \frac{w(Q_C)}{L_C}.$$

On the other hand, since the normalized length of each component in the summation above is at least $2/\epsilon$, we have

$$\sum_{C \in U_r : L_C \geq 2/\epsilon} \frac{w(Q_C)}{L_C} \leq \sum_{C \in U_r : L_C \geq 2/\epsilon} \frac{w(Q_C)}{2/\epsilon} \leq \frac{\epsilon}{2} \sum_{C \in U_r : L_C \geq 2/\epsilon} w(Q_C) \leq \frac{\epsilon}{2} w(M_r),$$

which combined with the equation above implies

$$\sum_{C \in U_r : L_C \geq 2/\epsilon} \Delta_C \leq \frac{\epsilon}{2} w(M_r). \tag{5}$$

Combining (5) and (4), we get

$$\begin{aligned}\sum_{C \in U_r : L_C < 2/\epsilon} \Delta_C &\geq w(M_r) - w(O_{r-1}) - \frac{\epsilon}{2} w(M_r) \\ &= (1 - \frac{\epsilon}{2}) w(M_r) - w(O_{r-1}) \\ &\geq (1 - \frac{\epsilon}{2}) w(M_r) - (1 - \epsilon) w(M_r) && \text{Since } w(O_{r-1}) \leq (1-\epsilon) w(M_r). \\ &= \frac{\epsilon}{2} w(M_r),\end{aligned}$$

which is the desired lower bound. □

## 4 $(0.5 - \epsilon)$-APPROXIMATION VIA A NON-ADAPTIVE ALGORITHM

In this section, we give a non-adaptive algorithm to obtain a $(1/2 - \epsilon)$-approximation of the omniscient optimum. A non-adaptive algorithm should return a degree bounded (bounded by a constant) subset $H$ of the original graph's edge set $E$ with the goal to make $\mathbb{M}[H]$ as close as possible to $\mathbb{M}[E]$ where we use $\mathbb{M}[E']$ to denote the expected weight of the maximum weighted matching of an edge set $E'$ given that each of its edges is realized independently with probability $p$.

To illustrate why it is not trivial to give a constant approximation, note that the realization probability $p$ could be any arbitrarily small constant. As such, to achieve a constant approximation, we need to pick a subset of edges that *augment* each other well. For instance, by only picking the maximum weighted matching $M$ of the input graph $G$ as our subgraph $H$, the expected matching weight would only be $p \cdot w(M)$ which might be much smaller than the omniscient optimum, especially if $p$ is small.

Our algorithm, which is formally given as Algorithm 2, is as follows: pick a maximum weighted matching, add it to the solution and remove its edges. We repeat this for $R = O(\frac{1}{\epsilon p^{4/\epsilon}})$ steps and prove it achieves a $(1/2 - \epsilon)$-approximation.

**Algorithm 2** Non-adaptive algorithm for weighted stochastic matching: $(1/2 - \epsilon)$-approximation.

**Input:** Input graph $G = (V, E)$.
**Parameter:** $R$.

```
E* ← E
for r = 1, ..., R do
    Find a maximum weighted matching M_r in (V, E*).
    E* ← E* − M_r
end for
Query the edges in ∪_{r=1}^R M_r and return the maximum realized matching in it.
```

We refer to the iterations of the for loop in Algorithm 2 as "rounds" here. However, we emphasize that this is different from the adaptivity rounds of Algorithm 1 since here we only query once at the end of algorithm in contrast to Algorithm 1 that queries the picked edges at each round.

**Theorem 11.** *For any graph $G = (V, E)$, and any arbitrarily small constant $\epsilon > 0$, Algorithm 2 returns a matching whose expected weight is at least $(1/2 - \epsilon)\mathbb{M}[E]$ for $R = O(\frac{1}{\epsilon p^{4/\epsilon}})$.*

Proof. The proof is similar to the proof of the adaptive algorithm with some minor differences that we cover here. The main difference that indeed causes the approximation factor to be $1/2 - \epsilon$ instead of $1 - \epsilon$ is that the weight of matching $M_r$ that we pick at round $r$ might be smaller than that of the omniscient optimum. However, denoting by $H_r := \cup_{i=1}^{r} M_r$ our subgraph by round $r$, we shows that until we obtain a $(1/2-\epsilon)$-approximation, the weight of the next matching that we pick is at least $1/2\mathbb{M}[E]$. We start with the following auxiliary observation.

**Observation 12.** *For any partitioning of the edge set $E$ into two subsets $E_1$ and $E_2$ with $E_1 \cup E_2 = E$, we have $w(M(E_1)) + w(M(E_2)) \geq w(M(E))$.*

Proof. Let $\mu$ be the maximum weighted matching of $E$, and define $\mu_1 = \mu \cap E_1$ and $\mu_2 = \mu \cap E_2$. Observe that $\mu_1$ and $\mu_2$ are both valid matchings of $E_1$ and $E_2$ respectively, which implies $w(M(E_1)) \geq w(\mu_1)$ and $w(M(E_2)) \geq w(\mu_2)$. Also note that $w(\mu_1) + w(\mu_2) \geq w(\mu)$ since $E_1 \cup E_2 = E$. Combining these two observations, we get

$$w(M(E_1)) + w(M(E_2)) \geq w(\mu_1) + w(\mu_2) \geq w(\mu) = w(M(E)),$$

completing the proof. □

**Lemma 13.** *For any round $r$ of Algorithm 2, if $\mathbb{M}[H_{r-1}] < \mathbb{M}[E]/2$, then $w(M_r) \geq \mathbb{M}[E]/2$.*

Proof. Let us, for any $r$, denote by $N_r$ the edges in $E \backslash H_r$. By this definition, we have $N_r \cup H_r = E$. This further implies that for any subset $E'$ of $E$, we have $(N_r \cap E') \cup (H_r \cap E') = E'$. Combining this with Observation 12, we get that for any realization $G_p = (V, E_p)$ of $G$, we have $w(M(H_r \cap E_p)) + w(M(N_r \cap E_p)) \geq w(M(E_p))$. Thus, we have

$$\begin{aligned}
\mathbb{E}_{E_p}\Big[w(M(H_r \cap E_p)) + w(M(N_r \cap E_p))\Big] &\geq \mathbb{E}_{E_p}\Big[w(M(E_p))\Big] \\
\mathbb{E}_{E_p}\Big[w(M(H_r \cap E_p))\Big] + \mathbb{E}_{E_p}\Big[w(M(N_r \cap E_p))\Big] &\geq \mathbb{E}_{E_p}\Big[w(M(E_p))\Big] \\
\mathbb{M}[H_r] + \mathbb{M}[N_r] &\geq \mathbb{M}[E].
\end{aligned}$$

Now, having $\mathbb{M}[H_{r-1}] < \mathbb{M}[E]/2$ implies that $\mathbb{M}[N_{r-1}] \geq \mathbb{M}[E]/2$ meaning that there is at least one matching of weight at least $\mathbb{M}[E]/2$ in $N_{r-1}$. Since all the edges in $N_{r-1}$ can be chosen in the matching $M_r$ picked in the next round, we have $w(M_r) \geq w(M(N_{r-1})) \geq \mathbb{M}[E]/2$ as desired. □

Our goal is to show that if $\mathbb{M}[H_{r-1}] < (1/2-\epsilon)\mathbb{M}[E]$ then $\mathbb{M}[H_r] - \mathbb{M}[H_{r-1}]$ is larger than $\Omega(p^{4/\epsilon}\epsilon\mathbb{M}[E])$ which implies that after $O(\frac{1}{\epsilon p^{4/\epsilon}})$ rounds we obtain a $(1/2-\epsilon)$-approximation. To do so, similar to the adaptive case, we maintain the maximum realized weighted matching $O_r$ obtained by round $r$ of Algorithm 2 and show that if $O_{r-1}$ is smaller than $(1/2-\epsilon)\mathbb{M}[E]$, the next matching $M_r$ augments $O_{r-1}$ by at least $\epsilon p^{4/\epsilon}\mathbb{M}[E]$ in expectation.

Recall that the argument in proving Theorem 3 was based on the fact (Observation 6) that the matching that we pick in each round has weight at least opt, and argued that querying its edges increases the weight of our maintained realized matching by a large factor in expectation. For the non-adaptive algorithm, however, the matching that we pick in each round might not be this large since we remove the previously picked edges from the graph. Instead, we know by Lemma 13, that until we obtain a $(1/2-\epsilon)$-approximation, its weight $w(M_r)$ is at least $\mathbb{M}[E]/2$. Therefore, we can adapt[7] Lemmas 7 and 8 to argue that we iteratively improve the weight of our maintained matching to obtain a $(1/2-\epsilon)$-approximation in only $O(\frac{1}{\epsilon p^{4/\epsilon}})$ iterations of Algorithm 2.

□

[7]We emphasize that it is crucial that the proofs of these two lemmas do not depend at all on the adaptivity of Algorithm 1.

## 5 OPEN PROBLEMS & FUTURE DIRECTIONS

An interesting future direction is to improve the approximation factor of our non-adaptive algorithm for weighted matchings. It was shown by Assadi et al. [6] that it is possible to obtain a slightly better than half approximation for the unweighted case, however, their analysis does not carry over to weighted graphs since it is highly tailored for cardinality matchings.

Another open question is how close we can get to the known lower bound of $\Omega(\log(1/\epsilon)/p)$ on the number of per-vertex queries to achieve a $(1-\epsilon)$-approximation adaptive algorithm. For the unweighted case, an algorithm with linear dependence on both $\epsilon$ and $p$ is known [5]. Although the techniques there were generalized to the weighted case by Maehara and Yamaguchi [18], the per-vertex queries — despite not having an exponential dependence on $\epsilon$ and $p$ — depends on structural properties of the graph such as the number of vertices or the edge-weights which we showed are not necessary.

## 6 ACKNOWLEDGEMENTS

We thank Mahsa Derakhshan for her helpful suggestions and ideas. We are also thankful to anonymous reviewers for their helpful comments.

## REFERENCES

[1] Marek Adamczyk. 2011. Improved analysis of the greedy algorithm for stochastic matching. *Inform. Process. Lett.* 111, 15 (2011), 731–737.

[2] Mohammad Akbarpour, Shengwu Li, and Shayan Oveis Gharan. 2014. Dynamic matching market design. *arXiv preprint arXiv:1402.3643* (2014).

[3] Ross Anderson, Itai Ashlagi, David Gamarnik, and Yash Kanoria. 2015. A dynamic model of barter exchange. In *Proceedings of the twenty-sixth annual ACM-SIAM symposium on Discrete algorithms*. Society for Industrial and Applied Mathematics, 1925–1933.

[4] Ross Anderson, Itai Ashlagi, David Gamarnik, and Alvin E Roth. 2015. Finding long chains in kidney exchange using the traveling salesman problem. *Proceedings of the National Academy of Sciences* 112, 3 (2015), 663–668.

[5] Sepehr Assadi, Sanjeev Khanna, and Yang Li. 2016. The Stochastic Matching Problem with (Very) Few Queries. In *Proceedings of the 2016 ACM Conference on Economics and Computation, EC '16, Maastricht, The Netherlands, July 24-28, 2016.* 43–60. https://doi.org/10.1145/2940716.2940769

[6] Sepehr Assadi, Sanjeev Khanna, and Yang Li. 2017. The Stochastic Matching Problem: Beating Half with a Non-Adaptive Algorithm. In *Proceedings of the 2017 ACM Conference on Economics and Computation, EC '17, Cambridge, MA, USA, June 26-30, 2017.* 99–116. https://doi.org/10.1145/3033274.3085146

[7] Pranjal Awasthi and Tuomas Sandholm. 2009. Online Stochastic Optimization in the Large: Application to Kidney Exchange.. In *IJCAI*, Vol. 9. 405–411.

[8] Nikhil Bansal, Anupam Gupta, Jian Li, Julián Mestre, Viswanath Nagarajan, and Atri Rudra. 2012. When LP is the cure for your matching woes: Improved bounds for stochastic matchings. *Algorithmica* 63, 4 (2012), 733–762.

[9] Avrim Blum, John P. Dickerson, Nika Haghtalab, Ariel D. Procaccia, Tuomas Sandholm, and Ankit Sharma. 2015. Ignorance is Almost Bliss: Near-Optimal Stochastic Matching With Few Queries. In *Proceedings of the Sixteenth ACM Conference on Economics and Computation, EC '15, Portland, OR, USA, June 15-19, 2015.* 325–342. https://doi.org/10.1145/2764468.2764479

[10] Avrim Blum, Anupam Gupta, Ariel Procaccia, and Ankit Sharma. 2013. Harnessing the power of two crossmatches. In *Proceedings of the fourteenth ACM conference on Electronic commerce.* ACM, 123–140.

[11] Ning Chen, Nicole Immorlica, Anna R Karlin, Mohammad Mahdian, and Atri Rudra. 2009. Approximating matches made in heaven. In *International Colloquium on Automata, Languages, and Programming.* Springer, 266–278.

[12] Kevin P Costello, Prasad Tetali, and Pushkar Tripathi. 2012. Stochastic matching with commitment. In *International Colloquium on Automata, Languages, and Programming.* Springer, 822–833.

[13] John P Dickerson, Ariel D Procaccia, and Tuomas Sandholm. 2012. Dynamic Matching via Weighted Myopia with Application to Kidney Exchange.. In *AAAI*, Vol. 2012. 98–100.

[14] John P Dickerson, Ariel D Procaccia, and Tuomas Sandholm. 2012. Optimizing kidney exchange with transplant chains: Theory and reality. In *Proceedings of the 11th International Conference on Autonomous Agents and Multiagent Systems-Volume 2.* International Foundation for Autonomous Agents and Multiagent Systems, 711–718.

[15] John P Dickerson, Ariel D Procaccia, and Tuomas Sandholm. 2013. Failure-aware kidney exchange. In *Proceedings of the fourteenth ACM conference on Electronic commerce*. ACM, 323–340.
[16] John P Dickerson and Tuomas Sandholm. 2015. FutureMatch: Combining Human Value Judgments and Machine Learning to Match in Dynamic Environments.. In *AAAI*. 622–628.
[17] Anupam Gupta and Viswanath Nagarajan. 2013. A stochastic probing problem with applications. In *International Conference on Integer Programming and Combinatorial Optimization*. Springer, 205–216.
[18] Takanori Maehara and Yutaro Yamaguchi. 2018. Stochastic Packing Integer Programs with Few Queries. In *Proceedings of the Twenty-Ninth Annual ACM-SIAM Symposium on Discrete Algorithms*. SIAM.
[19] David F Manlove and Gregg O'Malley. 2012. Paired and altruistic kidney donation in the UK: Algorithms and experimentation. In *International Symposium on Experimental Algorithms*. Springer, 271–282.
[20] M Utku Ünver. 2010. Dynamic kidney exchange. *The Review of Economic Studies* 77, 1 (2010), 372–414.

Received Mar 2018; accepted Apr 2018

# First-Choice Maximal and First-Choice Stable School Choice Mechanisms

UMUT DUR, North Carolina State University, USA
TIMO MENNLE, University of Zurich, Switzerland
SVEN SEUKEN, University of Zurich, Switzerland

We investigate the class of school choice mechanisms that are *first-choice maximal (FCM)* (i.e., they match a maximal number of students to their reported first choices) and *first-choice stable (FCS)* (i.e., no students form blocking pairs with their reported first choices). FCM is a ubiquitous desideratum in school choice, and we show that FCS is the only rank-based relaxation of stability that is compatible with FCM. The class of FCM and FCS mechanisms includes variants of the well-known Boston mechanism as well as certain Asymmetric Chinese Parallel mechanisms. Regarding incentives, we show that while no mechanism in this class is strategyproof, the Pareto efficient ones are least susceptible to manipulation. Regarding student welfare, we show that the Nash equilibrium outcomes of these mechanisms correspond precisely to the set of stable matchings. By contrast, when some students are sincere, we show that more students may be matched to their true first choices in equilibrium than under any stable matching. Finally, we show how our results can be used to obtain a new characterization of the Boston mechanism (i.e., the most widely used FCM and FCS mechanism). On a technical level, this paper provides new insights about an influential class of school choice mechanisms. For practical market design, our results yield a potential rationale for the popularity of FCM and FCS mechanisms in practice.

Full paper including appendix available at SSRN: https://ssrn.com/abstract=3180824

## 1 INTRODUCTION

School choice programs give students an opportunity to express their preferences over which public schools they would like to attend. Ideally, one would like to match all students to their respective true first choices. However, this ideal may not be achievable because schools have limited capacities and some schools may be more popular than others. Therefore, administrators need to design school choice mechanisms that reconcile students' conflicting interests with capacity constraints. Generating high student welfare is one of the key objectives in this task [4].

One way to measure student welfare is to consider the *number of students who are matched to their first choices*. This measure is particularly tangible because maximizing it is an obvious compromise between capacity constraints and the desire to ideally match all students to their top

We would like to thank (in alphabetical order) Antonio Miralles, Axel Ockenfels, Alexander Westkamp, as well as participants of the ZEW Market Design Research Seminar, the Design and Behavior Research Seminar (Uni Cologne), the 12th MiP Workshop, MATCH-UP 2017, and the EEA/ESEM 2017 for helpful comments. Part of this research was supported by the SNSF (Swiss National Science Foundation) under grant #156836.

Authors' addresses: Umut Dur, North Carolina State University, Department of Economics, 2801 Founders Drive, Raleigh, NC, 27695, USA, udur@ncsu.edu; Timo Mennle, University of Zurich, Switzerland, mennle@ifi.uzh.ch; Sven Seuken, University of Zurich, Department of Informatics, Binzmuhlestrasse 14, Zurich, CH-8050, Switzerland, seuken@ifi.uzh.ch.


*ACM EC'18, June 18--22, 2018, Ithaca, NY, USA.* ACM ISBN 978-1-4503-4529-3/18/06...$15.00
https://doi.org/10.1145/3219166.3219201

choices. It comes as no surprise that the share of students who are matched to their first choices receives attention in the media with headlines such as

> *"One in six secondary pupils in England doesn't get first school choice"*[1]

and

> *"45% of New York City 8th-graders got into top high school choice [...]."*[2]

Furthermore, administrators report the share of students who are matched to their first choices as part of their public communication. For example, Denver Public Schools prominently feature this measure on the website that informs parents about school choice.[3]

In line with the popularity of this measure, many school choice mechanisms in practice attempt to maximize it, the most prominent example being the *Boston mechanism (BM)* [4]. Arguably, BM owes much of its popularity to the intuitive way in which it attempts to maximize first choices. The common focus on first choices motivates our definition of *first-choice maximality (FCM)*, which requires that a mechanism matches a maximal number of students to their reported first choices.

A second important desideratum in school choice is stability. A matching is called *stable* if it is *non-wasteful* (i.e., no student would rather be matched to a school with unfilled seats), *individually rational* (i.e., no matched student would rather be unmatched), and if it *eliminates justified envy* (i.e., if a student prefers a different school to her match, then any student matched to that other school must have higher priority[4]) [7]. Equivalently, stability can be defined as the absence of blocking pairs.[5] A student in a blocking pair may feel as though she has been treated unfairly by the mechanism. On top of that, she may even have a basis for pursuing legal actions against the school district.[6] Administrators would naturally try to avoid both, perceived unfairness and the risk of legal actions. Stability is therefore a common criterion in school choice.

Our first insight in this paper is that FCM and stability are incompatible. This raises the question whether there exists a relaxed notion of stability that can serve as a useful second best but is not in conflict with FCM. We answer this question in the affirmative: A matching is called *first-choice stable (FCS)* if no student forms a blocking pair with her reported first choice (but students may form blocking pairs with other choices). We show that among all rank-based relaxations of stability, FCS is the only one that is compatible with FCM.[7]

This insight gives rise to a natural class of school choice mechanisms: We start with the ubiquitous desideratum to maximize the number of students who are matched to their first choices (i.e., FCM). Given this, it would be unreasonable to match these first choices in a way that violates priorities; thus, we also require FCS. On the other hand, all more demanding notions of stability are in conflict with FCM. This motivates our analysis of the class of mechanisms that satisfy both FCM and FCS. For the sake of brevity, we refer to these mechanisms as *first-choice (FC) mechanisms.*

[1] Sally Weale (June 14, 2016). *The Guardian*. Retrieved October 10, 2016: www.theguardian.com

[2] Sophia Rosenbaum and Erica Pearson (March 11, 2014). *New York Daily News*. Retrieved October 10, 2016: nydailynews.com

[3] Denver Public Schools Website. Retrieved October 10, 2016: schoolchoice.dpsk12.org/schoolchoice/

[4] Priorities are common in school choice. For example, a school may grant priority to students whose siblings attend the same school, who live nearby, or based on grades [3].

[5] A student-school-pair $(i, s)$ is *blocking* if $i$ would prefer $s$ to her current match and $s$ has unfilled seats, $s$ is $i$'s outside option, or some student who is matched to $s$ has lower priority at $s$ than $i$.

[6] A Wisconsin student's lawsuit succeeded on the grounds of *justified envy* [4]. It appears natural that students with justified envy are more likely to sue for violations of priorities at first choices than at other ranks. The admission to medical degree programs in Germany is organized via a centralized mechanism [33]. Rejected applicants sometimes obtain a seat by suing universities for leaving seats unfilled. These lawsuits succeed on the grounds of *wastefulness.*

[7] A *rank-based relaxation of stability* requires that there are no blocking pairs for which the respective school has a certain rank in the respective student's preference order.

The class of FC mechanisms includes all commonly employed variants of the Boston mechanism (e.g., with varying tie-breakers, varying limits on the length of preference lists, and where filled schools are or are not skipped in the application process). Such mechanisms are used in many school districts, including Minneapolis, Seattle, Lee County [24], San Diego, Amsterdam (until 2014) [14], Wake County (until 2015) [16], and in Nordrhein Westfalen and Freiburg (Germany) [8]. Asymmetric Chinese Parallel mechanisms with $e_0 = 1$ also belong to this class and are used for college admissions in the Chinese Beijing, Gansu, and Shandong provinces [11]. A plausible motivation for using FC mechanisms is the desire to achieve FCM and FCS. As market designers, we are of course aware of the fact that strategic misreporting by students may impede this objective. Nonetheless, administrators may find FC mechanisms appealing, for example, if they believe that students will report their preferences truthfully despite contrary incentives.[8] Moreover, even if students strategize, administrators may prefer FC mechanisms for cosmetic reasons (e.g., if they are driven by other considerations such as favorable media coverage).

For market designers, the question arises whether and to what extent *FC mechanisms actually achieve the intended desiderata* to match a maximal number of students to their *true* first choices and to avoid blocking pairs of students with their respective *true* first choices. This research question is the focus of our present paper. To answer it, we proceed in two steps:

Step 1. We identify the incentives for students under FC mechanisms (by comparing these mechanisms by their vulnerability to manipulation).

Step 2. We investigate how strategic reporting by students affects outcomes (by studying the Nash equilibria of the induced preference revelation games).

Regarding **incentives** (Step 1), our first insight is that FCM alone is already incompatible with strategyproofness, even without the additional restriction of FCS. Despite this incompatibility, some FC mechanisms may invite more strategic misreporting than others. Towards understanding these differences, we employ the concept of comparing mechanisms by their *vulnerability to manipulation*, introduced by Pathak and Sönmez [30].[9] We show that all Pareto efficient FC mechanisms are manipulable at exactly the same problems and are therefore equivalent in this sense. Moreover, we show that for any Pareto *in*efficient FC mechanism, there exists a Pareto efficient FC mechanism that Pareto dominates the original mechanism but is also at most as manipulable.

Our results have two significant consequences: First, the two most widely studied FC mechanisms are the classic *Boston mechanism (BM)* [4] and the *adaptive Boston mechanism (ABM)* [5, 15, 22, 26, 27]. One would intuitively suspect ABM to have better incentive properties than BM. However, since both mechanisms are Pareto efficient, they are manipulable at the same problems. Thus, surprisingly, the intuitive difference in their incentive properties cannot be formalized via the comparison by vulnerability to manipulation.[10] The second consequence of our results pertains to FC mechanisms used in practice that are not Pareto efficient, such as Asymmetric Chinese Parallel mechanisms [11]. Our results imply that these mechanisms are more manipulable and less efficient than necessary, even if administrators are restricted to only using FC mechanisms. Thus, the motivation for using Pareto *in*efficient FC mechanisms must rely on other considerations

[8]For example, the Teach for America (TfA) program uses a non-strategyproof mechanism to match teachers-to-be to teaching positions. However, TfA administrators feel that the use of this mechanism is justified because participants would find it hard to acquire the skills and information necessary to successfully manipulate the mechanism [19].

[9]A mechanism $\varphi$ is *at most as manipulable as* another mechanism $\psi$ if the set of problems where some student can benefit from misreporting under $\varphi$ is a subset of the respective set under $\psi$.

[10]ABM differs from BM in that students automatically skip exhausted schools in the application process under ABM, while under BM they apply to exhausted schools (thereby wasting some rounds). More nuanced assumptions are required to establish a formal understanding of the different incentive properties of BM and ABM, e.g., when school may have zero capacity or find some students unacceptable [15] or when priorities are random [26].

besides incentives. Otherwise, unambiguous improvements to these mechanisms would be possible, even within the class of FC mechanisms.

Regarding the **impact of strategic behavior on outcomes** (Step 2), we show that the set of Nash equilibrium outcomes of any FC mechanism corresponds precisely to the set of matchings that are stable with respect to the true preferences. This means that the equilibrium outcomes of any FC mechanism are first-choice stable with respect to the true preferences, but the may not match a maximal number of students to their true first choices.[11] Our result generalizes the main result of Ergin and Sönmez [18], who showed this correspondence for BM. For market designers, the most important consequence of our result is that in markets where all students are strategic (and when the primary concerns are concerns stability and matching true first choices), there is no reason for using an FC mechanism instead of the *student-proposing deferred-acceptance (DA) mechanism* [4]: DA produces the *student-optimal* stable matching, which is the unique stable matching that Pareto dominates all other stable matchings, and DA is strategyproof. In contrast, FC mechanisms merely produce *some* stable matchings, and they do this only subject to a weaker solution concept.

Our observations so far pertain to the case when *all* students strategize. In practice, however, students may exhibit varying levels of strategic sophistication. For example, it may be cognitively challenging to determine a beneficial misreport, or acquiring the necessary information may be costly. Experimental results suggest that under BM, a significant share of the participants report their preferences truthfully despite incentives to misreport [12, 13], and a lack of information further increases this share [28].[12] We therefore follow Pathak and Sönmez [29], who considered *mixed* problems with two types of students: *Sincere* students report their preferences truthfully, independent of incentives, while *sophisticated* students recognize the strategic aspect of the matching process. For these mixed problems, we identify the Nash equilibrium outcomes of FC mechanisms. Specifically, we show that, from the perspective of the sophisticated students, the set of Nash equilibrium outcomes corresponds to the set of matchings that are stable with respect to the true preferences and certain *augmented priorities*.[13] Our result partially generalizes the result of Pathak and Sönmez [29], who showed this correspondence for BM.[14] Our result also implies the existence of equilibrium outcomes that are uniformly preferred by all sophisticated students.

With these results at our disposal, we can conclusively answer our main research question: To what extent do **FC mechanisms actually achieve FCM and FCS**? Towards FCS, we show that all equilibrium outcomes of any FC mechanism are FCS with respect to the true preferences. Thus, FC mechanisms actually implement FCS, independent of which students strategize and independent of which equilibrium is chosen. Towards FCM, we isolate the effect of any individual student's decision (say $i'$) whether to strategize or to report truthfully by comparing the respective sophisticated-student-optimal equilibrium outcomes. We show that under any FC mechanism, $i'$ prefers being sophisticated to being sincere, all other sophisticated students prefer $i'$ being sincere, and for sincere students the difference is ambiguous with one notable exception: Any student who is matched to her true first choice when $i'$ is sophisticated is still matched to her true first choice when $i'$ is sincere. Thus, the number of true first choices matched in strategic-student-optimal

[11] This follows because stability implies FCS but is incompatible with FCM.

[12] In laboratory experiments conducted by Chen and Sönmez [13], this share was 13%, and it increased to 28% when priorities were random. Chen and Kesten [12] observed shares between 23% and 46% in similar experiments, and Pais and Pinter [28] found that withholding information significantly increased these shares from 47% to 87%.

[13] *Augmented priorities* arise as an adjustment of the original priorities. They account for the positions in which students rank schools and whether or not students are sophisticated (see Section 6.1).

[14] The correspondence proven by Pathak and Sönmez [29] holds for all students. Our restriction to the perspective of sophisticated students is necessary because FC mechanisms are identified by how they match students to their reported first choices but are unrestricted in how they match students to other choices (see Lemma 4.3). In equilibrium, this freedom only affects sincere students.

equilibrium outcomes is lowest if all students strategize, increases in mixed problems with more sincere students, and is maximal when all students are sincere. In this sense, FC mechanisms have the potential to match more true first choices in equilibrium than strategyproof alternatives like DA. This prediction is consistent with experimental findings that BM and ACPM both match significantly more students to their true first choices than DA (Result 4 of Chen and Kesten [12]).

Finally, we provide a new characterization of BM, the FC mechanism most widely used in practice. For this purpose, we consider an extended model where schools may have zero capacity initially. Since FCM and FCS can become void constraints in this extended model, we extend the definition of FCM to best-choice maximality by requiring that a mechanism maximizes the number of students assigned to their $k^{\text{th}}$ choice such that in any matching no students can be assigned to a better choice than $k$. We define best-choice stability analogously. We then show that best-choice maximality and best-choice stability, in combination with consistency [24], characterize BM in the extended model.

For market designers, our main results imply that the use of FC mechanisms in practice may be justified if FCM and FCS are primary desiderata and if a sufficiently large share of the students can be expected to report their preferences truthfully. Our characterization result of BM shows that, within the class of FC mechanisms, BM stands out a little more than the others, which may be a potential rationale for its popularity in practice.

## 2 PRELIMINARIES

### 2.1 Formal Model

A *school choice problem* is a tuple $(I, S, q, P, \succ)$ with a finite set of *students* $I = \{i_1, \ldots, i_n\}$ and a finite set of *schools* $S = \{s_1, \ldots, s_m\}$. $q = (q_s)_{s \in S}$ is the vector of *school capacities* (i.e., $q_s$ is the number of seats available at school $s$), $P = (P_i)_{i \in I}$ is the *preference profile* in which each $P_i$ is the strict *preference order* of student $i$ over the schools in $S$ and the *outside option*, denoted by $\emptyset$. $\succ = (\succ_s)_{s \in S}$ is the *priority profile* in which each $\succ_s$ is the *priority order* of school $s$ over students in $I$. We assume that priorities are strict, known, and fixed. In particular, this means that tie-breaking is not necessary, random or otherwise, and that schools do not strategize. $s \; P_i \; s'$ means that student $i$ strictly prefers school $s$ to school $s'$, and $i \succ_s i'$ means that student $i$ has priority over student $i'$ at school $s$. We assume that there is at least one seat at each school (i.e., $q_s \geq 1$ for all $s \in S$) and that all students can be matched to their outside option (i.e., $q_\emptyset = n$). For a preference order $P_i$, the corresponding *weak preference order* is denoted by $R_i$ (i.e., $s \; R_i \; s'$ if either $s \; P_i \; s'$ or $s = s'$). Unless stated otherwise, we fix $I$, $S$, $q$, and we use $(P, \succ)$ to denote a specific *problem* throughout the paper.

A *matching* is a function $\mu : I \longrightarrow S \cup \{\emptyset\}$. For a given matching $\mu$, $\mu(i)$ is the school to which student $i$ is matched, and $\mu^{-1}(s)$ is the set of students who are matched to schools $s$. We focus on *feasible* matchings (i.e., $|\mu^{-1}(s)| \leq q_s$ for every $s \in S \cup \{\emptyset\}$), and we simplify notation by writing $\mu_i$ and $\mu_s$ for $\mu(i)$ and $\mu^{-1}(s)$, respectively.

For a problem $(P, \succ)$ and matchings $\mu$ and $\nu$, we say that $\mu$ *weakly Pareto dominates* $\nu$ if $\mu_i \; R_i \; \nu_i$ for all students $i \in I$, and $\mu$ *Pareto dominates* $\nu$ if $\mu$ weakly Pareto dominates $\nu$ and $\mu_{i'} \; P_{i'} \; \nu_{i'}$ for at least one student $i' \in I$. The matching $\mu$ is *Pareto efficient* if it is not Pareto dominated by any other matching, $\mu$ is *individually rational* if $\mu_i \; R_i \; \emptyset$ for all students $i \in I$, $\mu$ is *wasteful* if there exists some student $i \in I$ and some school $s \in S$ such that $|\mu_s| < q_s$ but $s \; P_i \; \mu_i$, and $\mu$ is *non-wasteful* if it is not wasteful. A student $i \in I$ has *justified envy (under $\mu$)* if there exists another student $i' \in I$ and a school $s \in S$ such that $s \; P_i \; \mu_i$, $\mu_{i'} = s$, and $i \succ_s i'$, and $\mu$ is *fair* if no student has justified envy. Finally, $\mu$ is *stable* if it is individually rational, non-wasteful, and fair. Observe that for any unstable matching $\mu$, there exists at least one pair $(i, s) \in I \times (S \cup \{\emptyset\})$ such that $s \; P_i \; \mu_i$ and $|\mu_s| < q_s$ (if $\mu$ is wasteful), or $s = \emptyset$ (if $\mu$ is not individually rational), or there exists a student $i' \in I$ with $\mu_{i'} = s$ and $i \succ_s i'$ (if $i$ has justified envy). Any such student-school pair is called a *blocking pair*. Obviously,

| Mechanism | SP | PE | ST | FCM | FCS | Examples of use in practice |
|---|---|---|---|---|---|---|
| BM | | ✓ | | ✓ | ✓ | Minneapolis, Seattle, Lee County, San Diego |
| ABM | | ✓ | | ✓ | ✓ | Amsterdam (until 2014), Nordrhein Westfalen |
| DA | ✓ | | ✓ | | ✓ | New York, Boston, Mexico City |
| ACPM | | | | | ✓ | Various Chinese provinces |
| ACPM, $e_0 = 1$ | | | | ✓ | ✓ | Bejing, Gansu, and Shangdong provinces |
| TTC | ✓ | ✓ | | | | New Orleans Recovery School District (2012) |

Table 1. Mechanisms, properties, examples of use; strategyproof (*SP*), Pareto efficient (*PE*), stable (*ST*).[15]

the matching $\mu$ is stable if and only if there exist no blocking pairs. Throughout the paper, we employ this equivalent definition of stability to simplify definitions and proofs.

A *mechanism* $\varphi$ is a mapping that receives a problem $(P, \succ)$ as input and selects a matching, denoted by $\varphi(P, \succ)$. We denote by $\varphi_i(P, \succ)$ the school to which student $i$ is matched under $\varphi(P, \succ)$. A mechanism $\varphi$ is called *Pareto efficient*/*individually rational*/*non-wasteful*/*fair*/*stable* if it selects matchings with the respective property for all problems. The mechanism $\varphi$ *Pareto dominates* another mechanism $\psi$ if the matching $\varphi(P, \succ)$ weakly Pareto dominates the matching $\psi(P, \succ)$ for all problems $(P, \succ)$ and this dominance is not weak for at least one problem. Observe that these properties are formulated in terms of how the mechanisms handle reported preferences. However, students may lie about their preferences so that the input to the mechanism may differ from the true problem. Regarding incentives, a mechanism $\varphi$ is called *strategyproof* if, for all problems $(P, \succ)$, all students $i \in I$, and all preference orders $P'_i$, we have $\varphi_i(P, \succ)\ R_i\ \varphi_i((P'_i, P_{-i}), \succ)$ where $P_{-i} = (P_j)_{j \neq i}$ are the preferences of all students except $i$.

Finally, we introduce some auxiliary notation: Given a problem $(P, \succ)$, let $\text{choice}_{P_i}(k)$ be the $k^{\text{th}}$ *choice* of student $i$ according to $P_i$. For a matching $\mu$, let $I(\mu, k, P)$ be the set of students who are matched to their $k^{\text{th}}$ choice under the matching $\mu$; formally, $I(\mu, k, P) = \{i \in I : \text{choice}_{P_i}(k) = \mu_i\}$. Thus, $I(\varphi(P, \succ), k, P)$ is the set of students who are matched to their $k^{\text{th}}$ choice (according to $P$) when the mechanism $\varphi$ is applied to the problem $(P, \succ)$.

## 2.2 School Choice Mechanisms

In this section, we describe common school choice mechanisms. Table 1 provides an overview of their properties as well as examples of their use in practice.

The *Boston mechanism (BM)* [4] works in rounds. In the first round, all students apply to their respective first choices, and each school permanently accepts applications from students in order of priority until all applications are accepted or until all seats are filled. Students whose applications are not accepted enter the second round where they apply to their respective second choices. Again, schools accept applications into unfilled seats by priority and reject all remaining applications once all seats are filled. This process continues (i.e., students who were rejected in round $k - 1$ apply to their $k^{\text{th}}$ choices in round $k$) until no school receives new applications.

The *adaptive Boston mechanism (ABM)* [5, 15, 22, 26, 27] is similar to BM, except that students who are rejected in round $k - 1$ apply to their respective *most-preferred school that still has at least one unfilled seat* in round $k$. Students thus automatically skip schools in the application process when applications to these schools are bound to be rejected, independent of priority.

[15]Sources: [2, 3, 8, 10, 11, 14, 24], and Andrew Vanacore (April 16, 2012). *The Times-Picayune.* Retrieved March 22, 2017: www.nola.com

Under the *Student-Proposing Deferred Acceptance (DA) mechanism* [4, 20], students also apply to schools in rounds, and priorities determine which applications are accepted. However, acceptances are *tentative* rather than permanent. This means that students can be rejected by a school where they were tentatively accepted in a previous round if other students apply in later rounds who have higher priority. Newly rejected students apply to their most preferred school that has not yet rejected them. The application process ends when no school receives any new applications.

*Asymmetric Chinese Parallel mechanisms (ACPM)* [11] are mechanisms that combine elements of BM and DA. They are parametrized by a vector of integers $(e_0, e_1, \ldots)$ with $e_k \geq 1$. Initially, all matches are tentative as under DA. However, unlike under DA, students who are rejected by their ${e_0}^{\text{th}}$ choices pause in the application process. When all students are either matched tentatively or have been rejected by their ${e_0}^{\text{th}}$ choices, all tentative matches are finalized. In the next phase, the rejected students continue to apply but pause again when they have been rejected by their $(e_0 + e_1)^{\text{th}}$ choices. The tentative matches are again finalized if all students are either tentatively accepted at some school or pausing. This process continues until all students are matched or have been rejected by all schools on their preference list. Observe that ACPM specifies a class of mechanisms. This class subsumes BM (for $e_k = 1$ for all $k$) and DA (for $e_0 \geq |S|$).

The *Top Trade Cycles (TTC) mechanism* [4] works by forming a directed graph: Each student points to her most-preferred school with unfilled seats, each school points to the student who has highest priority at that school, and the outside option points to all students who are pointing to it. In each step, a cycle of this graph is selected and implemented (i.e., each student in the cycle is permanently matched to the school to which she is pointing, and the respective seats and students are removed from the mechanism). Students and schools then adjust where they are pointing and the process repeats. The process ends when all students have been removed.

## 3 SETTING THE STAGE: FIRST-CHOICE MAXIMALITY, FIRST-CHOICE STABILITY

As we have argued in the introduction, the number of students who are matched to their (reported) first choices receives a lot of attention. Following this observation, we define first-choice maximality.

*Definition 3.1.* Given a problem $(P, \succ)$, a matching $\mu$ is *first-choice maximal* if there exists no other matching $\nu$ such that $|I(\mu, 1, P)| < |I(\nu, 1, P)|$. A mechanism $\varphi$ is *first-choice maximal (FCM)* if, for all problems $(P, \succ)$, the matching $\varphi(P, \succ)$ is first-choice maximal.[16]

Next, we define rank-based relaxations of stability.

*Definition 3.2.* Given a problem $(P, \succ)$ and an integer $k \in \{1, \ldots, m\}$, a matching $\mu$ is *$k^{th}$-choice stable* if there exists no blocking pair $(i, s) \in I \times (S \cup \{\emptyset\})$ where $s$ is the $k^{\text{th}}$ choice of $i$, and $\mu$ is *first-choice stable* if this holds for $k = 1$. A mechanism is *$k^{th}$-choice stable (first-choice stable (FCS))* if, for all problems $(P, \succ)$, the matching $\varphi(P, \succ)$ is $k^{\text{th}}$-choice stable (first-choice stable).

We observe that FCM and FCS are compatible: It is easy to see that BM satisfies both properties. On the other hand, FCM by itself is already a severe restriction: As the next example shows, it is incompatible with strategyproofness, with stability, or even with $k^{\text{th}}$-choice stability for $k \geq 2$.

*Example 3.3.* There are three students $I = \{1, 2, 3\}$, two schools $S = \{a, b\}$ with a single seat each. The preferences and priorities are

$$\begin{aligned} P_i \text{ for } i \in I: &\quad a \; P_i \; b \; P_i \; \emptyset, \\ \succ_s \text{ for } s \in S: &\quad 1 \succ_s 2 \succ_s 3. \end{aligned}$$

[16]FCM is a strictly weaker requirement than the axiom that a mechanism *favors higher ranks* [24]: Specifically, a mechanism is FCM if and only if it favors the *first* rank.

Let $\varphi$ be an FCM mechanism. By feasibility, $\varphi$ must leave at least one student unmatched. Without loss of generality, suppose that this is student 3 (i.e., $\varphi_3(P, \succ) = \emptyset$). If student 3 reports $b\ P'_3\ a\ P'_3\ \emptyset$ instead of reporting $P_3$ truthfully, then $\varphi$ must match student 3 to school $b$. Since $\varphi_3((P'_3, P_{-3}), \succ) = b\ P_3\ \emptyset = \varphi_3(P, \succ)$, $P'_3$ is a beneficial misreport for student 3. Thus, $\varphi$ cannot be strategyproof.

Next, observe that at the problem $((P'_3, P_{-3}), \succ)$, there exists a unique stable matching $\mu$ where $\mu_1 = a$, $\mu_2 = b$, and $\mu_3 = \emptyset$. However, any FCM mechanism $\varphi$ must match student 3 to school $b$, so $\varphi$ cannot be stable. A straightforward extension illustrates that $\varphi$ also violates $k^{\text{th}}$-choice stability for any $k \geq 2$: Consider a problem with $k$ schools $S = \{s_1, \ldots, s_k\}$ with a single seat each, and $k + 1$ students $I = \{1, 1', 2, \ldots, k\}$. The preferences and priorities are

$$\begin{aligned} P_i \text{ for } i \in \{1, 1'\} : &\quad s_1\ P_i\ s_2\ P_i\ \ldots\ P_i\ s_k\ P_i\ \emptyset, \\ P_i \text{ for } i \in \{2, \ldots, k\} : &\quad s_i\ P_i\ \ldots, \\ \succ_s \text{ for } s \in S : &\quad 1 \succ_s 1' \succ_s 2 \succ_s \ldots \succ_s k. \end{aligned}$$

FCM implies that $\varphi$ matches each student $i \in \{2, \ldots, k\}$ to $s_i$. Thus, either student 1 or student 1′ is unmatched. Then that student forms a blocking pair with her $k^{\text{th}}$ choice.

It follows from Example 3.3 that among all rank-based relaxations of stability, FCS is the only one compatible with FCM. For the remainder of this paper, we therefore focus on the class of mechanisms that are both FCM and FCS.

*Definition 3.4.* A mechanism is a *first-choice (FC) mechanism* if it is FCM and FCS.

For example, BM and ABM are both FCM and FCS and known to be Pareto efficient, but they violate strategyproofness and stability. ACPMs with $e_0 = 1$ are also FCM and FCS. Their first phase is the same as the first round of BM, and the matches made in this phase are not undone in subsequent phases. These mechanisms thus satisfy FCM and FCS (by Lemma 4.3 in Section 4). Moreover, as Chen and Kesten [11] pointed out, ACPMs are not Pareto efficient unless $e_k = 1$ for all $k$, in which case they are equivalent to BM, and they are not stable unless $e_0 > m$, in which case they are equivalent to DA. DA is stable and therefore FCS. However, FCM is incompatible with stability, so DA cannot be FCM. It is straightforward to see that TTC is neither FCM nor FCS, and it is known to be strategyproof and Pareto efficient but unstable.[17]

## 4 INCENTIVES UNDER FC MECHANISMS

As Example 3.3 illustrates, no FC mechanism is strategyproof. However, some FC mechanisms may be *more manipulable* than others. Towards understanding these differences, we employ the concept of *comparing mechanisms by their vulnerability to manipulation* introduced by Pathak and Sönmez [30], which we restate formally before presenting our results.

*Definition 4.1.* A mechanism $\varphi$ is *manipulable at* $(P, \succ)$ if there exist a student $i \in I$ and a preference order $P'_i$ such that $\varphi_i((P'_i, P_{-i}), \succ)\ P_i\ \varphi_i(P, \succ)$. For two mechanisms $\varphi$ and $\psi$, we say that $\varphi$ is *at least as manipulable as* $\psi$ if, for all problems $(P, \succ)$, manipulability of $\psi$ at $(P, \succ)$ implies manipulability of $\varphi$ at $(P, \succ)$. $\varphi$ is *more manipulable than* $\psi$ if in addition there exists a problem where $\varphi$ is manipulable but $\psi$ is not.

In words, the comparison by vulnerability to manipulation classifies mechanisms by the sets of problems at which they are manipulable. If $\varphi$ is at least as manipulable as $\psi$, then the set of problems at which $\varphi$ is manipulable is a superset of the set of problems where $\psi$ is manipulable, and $\varphi$ is more manipulable if it is a strict superset.

[17] TTC violates FCM at the problem $((P'_3, P_{-3}), \succ)$ from Example 3.3, and it violates FCS at the same problem if the priorities of school $a$ are changed to $3 \succ_a 2 \succ_a 1$.

Our next results, Theorem 4.2 and Proposition 4.5, reveal how FC mechanisms compare in terms of their vulnerability to manipulation. First, we show that all Pareto efficient FC mechanisms are manipulable at *exactly the same problems.* Second, we show that any Pareto *in*efficient FC mechanism is manipulable at a (possibly strict) *superset* of these problems. In this sense, the Pareto efficient FC mechanisms form a minimally manipulable subset within the class of FC mechanisms.

THEOREM 4.2. *Let $\varphi$ and $\psi$ be two Pareto efficient FC mechanisms. Then $\varphi$ is at least as manipulable as $\psi$ and vice versa.*

PROOF. We state two lemmas, which we also use in other proofs. Recall that $\text{choice}_{P_i}(k)$ denotes the $k^{\text{th}}$ choice school according to $P_i$ and that $I(\mu, k, P)$ denotes the set of students who are matched to their $k^{\text{th}}$ choice according to $P$ under $\mu$.

LEMMA 4.3. *$\varphi$ is an FC mechanism if and only if $I(\varphi(P, \succ), 1, P) = I(BM(P, \succ), 1, P)$ for all $(P, \succ)$.*

LEMMA 4.4. *Given an FC mechanism $\varphi$, a problem $(P, \succ)$, and a subset of students $A \subsetneq I$, let $(P'_A, P_{-A})$ be a preference profile such that $\text{choice}_{P'_i}(1) = \varphi_i(P, \succ)$ for all $i \in A$. Then, $\varphi_i((P'_A, P_{-A}), \succ) = \varphi_i(P, \succ)$ for all $i \in A$.*

The proofs of these Lemmas are given in Appendices A and B of the full version of this paper. Lemma 4.3 characterizes the set of FC mechanisms as those mechanisms that match exactly the same students to their reported first choices as BM; but otherwise they are free in how they match the remaining students. Lemma 4.4 shows that when some students change their reported preferences by ranking first the school to which they are matched under an FC mechanism, then this mechanism continues to match these students to the same schools.[18]

Next, let $\varphi$ be manipulable at $(P, \succ)$. Then $\varphi_i((P'_i, P_{-i}), \succ)\ P_i\ \varphi_i(P, \succ)$ for some student $i \in I$ and some preference order $P'_i$. Without loss of generality, let $s = \varphi_i((P'_i, P_{-i}), \succ)$ be the most preferred school according to $P_i$ at which $i$ can obtain a seat by misreporting (and possibly $s = \emptyset$). By Lemma 4.4, we can choose $P'_i$ such that $s$ is ranked first. Observe that $s$ cannot be the first choice under $P_i$ (otherwise, $P'_i$ would not be a strictly beneficial deviation for $i$). There are two cases:

*Case 1: $\varphi(P, \succ) = \psi(P, \succ)$.* Then $I(\varphi((P'_i, P_{-i}), \succ), 1, P) = I(\psi((P'_i, P_{-i}), \succ), 1, P)$ by Lemma 4.3. Since $i \in I(\varphi((P'_i, P_{-i}), \succ), 1, P)$ and $s$ is $i$'s first choice under $P'_i$, we have $i \in I(\psi((P'_i, P_{-i}), \succ), 1, P)$ and $\psi_i((P'_i, P_{-i}), \succ) = s$. Hence, $\psi_i((P'_i, P_{-i}), \succ)\ P_i\ \psi_i(P, \succ)$, that is, $i$ can manipulate $\psi$ at $(P, \succ)$.

*Case 2: $\varphi(P, \succ) \neq \psi(P, \succ)$.* Since both $\varphi(P, \succ)$ and $\psi(P, \succ)$ are FCS and Pareto efficient, there exists a student $i' \in I$ such that $\varphi_{i'}(P, \succ) \neq \psi_{i'}(P, \succ)$ and $\varphi_{i'}(P, \succ)\ P_{i'}\ \psi_{i'}(P, \succ)$. Let $s' = \varphi_{i'}(P, \succ)$ and let $P'_{i'}$ be a preference order in which $s'$ is ranked first. Then $\varphi_{i'}((P'_{i'}, P_{-i'}), \succ) = s'$ by Lemma 4.3, and $I(\varphi((P'_{i'}, P_{-i'}), \succ), 1, (P'_{i'}, P_{-i'})) = I(\psi((P'_{i'}, P_{-i'}), \succ), 1, (P'_{i'}, P_{-i'}))$ by Lemma 4.4. Hence, $\psi_{i'}((P'_{i'}, P_{-i'}), \succ) = s'\ P_{i'}\ \psi_{i'}(P, \succ)$, that is, $i'$ can manipulate $\psi$ at $(P, \succ)$.

In conclusion, manipulability of $\varphi$ at $(P, \succ)$ implies manipulability of $\psi$ at $(P, \succ)$. Symmetrically, it follows that if $\psi$ is manipulable at some problem, then so is $\varphi$. □

While Theorem 4.2 pertains to Pareto efficient FC mechanisms, the next proposition closes the remaining gap for Pareto *in*efficient FC mechanisms.

[18]This corresponds to a relaxed notion of Maskin monotonicity for FC mechanisms: The preference profile $(P'_A, P_{-A})$ is a monotonic transformation of $P$ at $\varphi(P, \succ)$, and under any FC mechanism the matching of the students in $A$ may not change. Observe that this property is independent of the *rank respecting invariance* property, a different relaxation of Maskin monotonicity that Kojima and Ünver [24] used for their axiomatic characterization of BM.

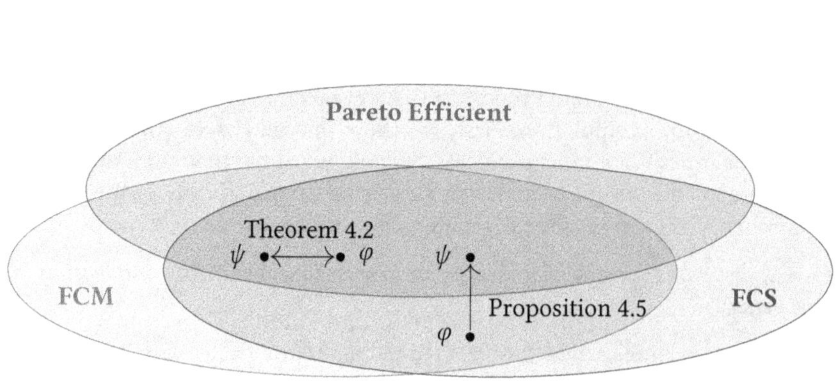


Fig. 1. Illustration of Theorem 4.2 and Proposition 4.5.

PROPOSITION 4.5. *Let $\varphi$ be an FC mechanism that violates Pareto efficiency. Then there exists a mechanism $\psi$ with the following properties:*

1. *$\psi$ is a Pareto efficient FC mechanism,*
2. *$\psi$ Pareto dominates $\varphi$,*
3. *$\varphi$ is at least as manipulable as $\psi$.*

The proof is given in Appendix C of the full version of this paper. The Venn diagram in Figure 1 illustrates the results of Theorem 4.2 and Proposition 4.5. All Pareto efficient FC mechanisms (i.e., mechanisms in the intersection of all three areas) are equivalent when comparing them by their vulnerability to manipulation. The horizontal arrow on the left symbolizes this equivalence. Moreover, any Pareto *in*efficient FC mechanism (i.e., a mechanism in the intersection of the blue and red areas at the bottom) is at least as manipulable as some (and therefore any) Pareto efficient FC mechanism. The vertical arrow on the right symbolizes this relationship.

Theorem 4.2 and Proposition 4.5 have two implications for market design: First, recall that under BM, students apply to their $k^{\text{th}}$ choices in the $k^{\text{th}}$ round, even if these schools have no more unfilled seats. Students can therefore strategize by omitting full schools in their ranking. In contrast, under ABM, students automatically skip such schools and apply to their most preferred school with one or more unfilled seats. While students may still strategize in other ways, the above-mentioned manipulation becomes unnecessary. Thus, intuitively, we would expect ABM to have better incentive properties than BM. Surprisingly, this difference does not surface because both mechanism are equivalent in this sense by Theorem 4.2.[19]

Second, ACPMs with $e_0 = 1$ are Pareto *in*efficient (unless $e_k = 1$ for all $k$, in which case they are equivalent to BM), but they are used in practice (e.g., for college admission in the Chinese Beijing, Gansu, and Shandong provinces). Proposition 4.5 shows that the choice of such mechanisms cannot be justified by the desiderata FCM, FCS, and "good" incentives alone, because administrators could choose a different FC mechanism that simultaneously yields unambiguous improvements in terms of student welfare and robustness to manipulation.

This concludes Step 1, the discussion of incentives under FC mechanisms.

[19]The indistinguishability of BM and ABM is even more severe: It cannot be recovered via the as-*strongly*-manipulable-as relation, and for random priorities, even the weak distinction by vulnerability to manipulation is inconclusive (see Appendices G and H of the full version of this paper. More nuanced approaches are needed to obtain meaningful distinctions (see, e.g., [15, 26]).

## 5 EQUILIBRIUM UNDER FC MECHANISMS

Recall that no FC mechanism is strategyproof. We must therefore be concerned about the impact of strategic reporting by students. Following prior work, we identify the equilibrium outcomes of the preference revelation game induced by the mechanisms and use *Nash equilibrium under complete information* as the main solution concept [18, 21, 23, 29].

*Definition 5.1.* Given a mechanism $\varphi$ and a problem $(P, \succ)$, a preference profile $P^*$ is a *Nash equilibrium (of $\varphi$ at $(P, \succ)$)* if, for all students $i \in I$ and all preference orders $P'_i \neq P^*_i$, we have that $\varphi_i(P^*, \succ) \; R_i \; \varphi_i((P'_i, P^*_{-i}), \succ)$.

In words, no student can be matched to a school that she strictly prefers by unilaterally deviating from the equilibrium profile.[20] For the special case of BM, Ergin and Sönmez [18] showed that the Nash equilibrium outcomes of BM correspond precisely to the matchings that are stable with respect to the true preferences and priorities.

**Fact 1** (Theorem 1 of Ergin and Sönmez [18]). *Given a problem $(P, \succ)$, a matching $\mu$ is stable if and only if there exists a Nash equilibrium $P^*$ of BM at $(P, \succ)$ with $\mu = BM(P^*, \succ)$.*

Our next theorem shows that the same result holds for all FC mechanisms.

Theorem 5.2. *Given a problem $(P, \succ)$ and an FC mechanism $\varphi$, a matching $\mu$ is stable at $(P, \succ)$ if and only if there exists a Nash equilibrium $P^*$ of $\varphi$ at $(P, \succ)$ with $\mu = \varphi(P^*, \succ)$.*

Proof. *Necessity.* Let $P^*$ be a Nash equilibrium. Assume towards contradiction that the matching $\varphi(P^*, \succ)$ is not stable wrt. $(P, \succ)$. Then there exist $i \in I$ and $s \in S \cup \{\emptyset\}$ such that $s \; P_i \; \varphi_i(P^*, \succ)$ and either $|\varphi_s(P^*, \succ)| < q_s$, or there exists $i' \in I$ such that $\varphi_{i'}(P^*, \succ) = s$ and $i \succ_s i'$. Let $P'_i$ be a preference order with $\text{choice}_{P'_i}(1) = s$. When BM is applied to the preference profile $(P'_i, P^*_{-i})$, $i$ is matched to $s$ in the first round. By Lemma 4.3 we get $\varphi_i((P'_i, P^*_{-i}), \succ) = \text{BM}_i((P'_i, P^*_{-i}), \succ) = s$. Therefore, $P^*_i$ is not a best response to $P^*_{-i}$ for $i$, a contradiction.

*Sufficiency.* Let $\mu$ be stable wrt. $(P, \succ)$. Consider a preference profile $P^*$ where each student $i$ ranks $\mu_i$ first. Since $\mu$ is feasible, $\varphi$ produces the matching $\mu$ in the first step when applied to $(P^*, \succ)$ by Lemma 4.3. Moreover, $P^*$ is a Nash equilibrium of $\varphi$: Assume towards contradiction that some student $i$ can improve her match by deviating from $P^*$ (i.e., get matched to a school $s$). By Lemma 4.4, she can do so by ranking $s$ first. Then $i$ either displaces another student with lower priority at $s$, or $s$ has unfilled seats under $\mu$. In both cases, the pair $(i, s)$ blocks $\mu$, a contradiction. □

**Remark 1.** Theorem 5.2 shows that stability (with respect to the true preferences and priorities) is the characterizing feature of the Nash equilibrium outcomes of FC mechanisms. This generalizes Fact 1 from BM to all FC mechanisms. Ergin and Sönmez [18] also showed that all monotonic rank-priority mechanisms have this property. Relatedly, within the class of rank-priority mechanisms, Jaramillo et al. [23] characterized those that Nash implement the set of stable matchings. Our Theorem 5.2 is independent of both of these results because the set of FC mechanisms is neither a subset nor a superset of the rank-priority mechanisms (see Appendix D of the full version of this paper). An interesting subject for future research would be a characterization of all direct-revelation mechanisms that Nash implement the set of stable matchings that unifies these results.

[20]The *preference revelation game induced by $\varphi$ at $(P, \succ)$* is a simultaneous move game $(N, O, \tau)$, where the students are the agents (i.e., $N = I$), the outcomes are the matchings that are possible under $\varphi$ (i.e., $O = \{\varphi(\widehat{P}, \succ) \mid \widehat{P} \text{ preference profile}\}$), and for each agent $i$, the weak preference order $\tau_i$ over outcomes is induced by the respective student's weak preference order over schools (i.e., for outcomes $x, y \in O$, $x \; \tau_i \; y$ if and only if $x_i \; R_i \; y_i$).

Observe that we simplify the formal exposition of Nash equilibrium in two ways: First, we use the term *Nash equilibrium of $\varphi$ at $(P, \succ)$* to mean a Nash equilibrium of the induced preference revelation game. Second, we consider *preference profiles* instead of strategy profiles. This is without loss of generality because we consider only direct revelation mechanisms.

DA is known to implement the *student-optimal* stable matchings in weakly-dominant strategies.[21] In contrast, by Theorem 5.2, FC mechanisms implement *all* stable matchings in Nash equilibrium, not just the student-optimal ones. Thus, DA produces (weakly) Pareto dominant matchings, and it does so subject to a more robust solution concept. This provides a partial answer to our main research question whether FC mechanisms actually achieve the desiderata FCM and FCS with respect to the true preferences: They achieve FCS because they lead to stable matchings (in equilibrium when all students strategize), but they fail to achieve FCM (which is incompatible with stability).

## 6 EQUILIBRIUM UNDER FC MECHANISMS WHEN SOME STUDENTS ARE SINCERE

In practice, students exhibit varying levels of strategic sophistication. Some students may report their preferences truthfully, e.g., because they lack the information that is necessary to determine beneficial misreports. Following Pathak and Sönmez [29], we consider *mixed problems* with two groups of students: *Sincere students* simply report their preferences truthfully, independent of incentives, while *sophisticated students* recognize the strategic nature of the preference revelation game and play best responses. In this section, we identify the Nash equilibrium outcomes of FC mechanisms (Section 6.1) and study the implications on student welfare (Section 6.2).

### 6.1 Identification of Equilibrium Outcomes

We first extend our definition of Nash equilibrium to mixed problems with both sophisticated and sincere students.

*Definition 6.1.* Given a problem $(P, \succ)$, a set of sophisticated students $A \subseteq I$, and a mechanism $\varphi$, a preference profile $P^*$ is an *A-Nash equilibrium (of $\varphi$ at $(P, \succ)$)* if $P_i^* = P_i$ for all sincere students $i \in I \backslash A$ and $\varphi_i(P^*, \succ)\ R_i\ \varphi_i((P_i', P_{-i}^*), \succ)$ for all sophisticated students $i \in A$ and all preference orders $P_i'$.

In words, in an $A$-Nash equilibrium, all sincere students report truthfully and no sophisticated student can benefit by unilaterally deviating from the equilibrium profile. Pathak and Sönmez [29] showed that the $A$-Nash equilibrium outcomes of BM correspond to the matchings that are stable with respect to the true preferences and an *augmented priority profile*. These augmented priorities capture three intuitive aspects of BM: First, students who have been accepted keep their seats, even if they have lower priority than another student who applies in a later round of BM. The fact that a student ranks a school higher thus overrules the fact that her priority at that school may be lower. Augmented priorities capture this by giving higher priority to students who rank a school higher. Second, while sincere students report their preferences truthfully, sophisticated students can misreport their preferences. In particular, they can rank any school first. Augmented priorities reflect this advantage by treating sophisticated students as if they ranked every school first. Third, BM breaks ties according to the original priority profile, and augmented priorities do the same. The next definition formalizes these aspects (where $I_k^s$ denotes the set of students who rank $s$ in $k^{\text{th}}$ position according to $P$).

*Definition 6.2.* Given a problem $(P, \succ)$ and a set of sophisticated students $A \subseteq I$, for each school $s \in S$, the *augmented priority order* $\widehat{\succ}_s$ is constructed as follows:

- $i \mathbin{\widehat{\succ}_s} j$ if $i \in A \cup I_1^s$ and $j \in I_2^s \backslash A$
- $i \mathbin{\widehat{\succ}_s} j$ if $i \in I_k^s \backslash A$ and $j \in I_{k+1}^s \backslash A$ for any $k \geq 2$
- $i \mathbin{\widehat{\succ}_s} j$ if $i \succ_s j$ and either $i, j \in A \cup I_1^s$ or $i, j \in I_k^s \backslash A$ for any $k \geq 2$
- All undefined priorities are implied by transitivity

[21] A stable matching is *student-optimal* if all students prefer it to any other stable matching. These matchings are unique for the problems we consider [31].

A matching $\mu$ is *augmented stable* if it is stable with respect to the problem $(P, \widehat{\succ})$.

With the notions of $A$-Nash equilibrium and augmented stability, we can now formally restate the main result of Pathak and Sönmez [29].

**Fact 2** (Proposition 1 of Pathak and Sönmez [29]). *Given a problem $(P, \succ)$ and a set of sophisticated students $A \subseteq I$, a matching $\mu$ is augmented stable if and only if there exists an $A$-Nash equilibrium $P^*$ of BM at $(P, \succ)$ with $\mu = BM(P^*, \succ)$.*

In words, Fact 2 means that the set of $A$-Nash equilibrium outcomes of BM corresponds precisely to the set of augmented-stable matchings. Our next result extends this characterization to the entire class of FC mechanisms, albeit with one limitation: We identify the equilibrium outcomes of FC mechanisms only up to equivalence from the perspective of the sophisticated students. Formally, we say that two matchings $\mu$ and $\nu$ are *$A$-equivalent* if $\mu_i = \nu_i$ for all students $i \in A$, denoted $\mu =_A \nu$.

Theorem 6.3. *Given a problem $(P, \succ)$, a set of sophisticated students $A \subseteq I$, and an FC mechanism $\varphi$, a matching $\mu$ is $A$-equivalent to some augmented-stable matching if and only if there exists an $A$-Nash equilibrium $P^*$ of $\varphi$ at $(P, \succ)$ with $\mu =_A \varphi(P^*, \succ)$.*

We give the proof in Appendix E of the full version of this paper. In words, Theorem 6.3 shows that augmented stability describes the equilibrium outcomes of FC mechanisms in mixed problems from the perspective of the sophisticated students. To see why the limitation to sophisticated students is needed, recall that FC mechanisms are restricted in how they handle first choices but they are free in how they to handle other choices (Lemma 4.3). In equilibrium, this freedom only affects sincere students; sophisticated students can always get their equilibrium school by ranking it first (Lemma 4.4).

If all students are sincere, then the equilibrium outcomes of FC mechanisms trivially satisfy FCM and FCS with respect to the true preferences. With sophisticated students, this may no longer be true. Example 6.4 illustrates that FCM (with respect to the true preferences) can be violated even if there is just one sophisticated student.

*Example 6.4.* There are three students $I = \{1, 2, 3\}$ and two schools $S = \{a, b\}$ with one seat each, and only student 2 is sophisticated (i.e., $A = \{2\}$). The preferences and priorities are

$$\begin{aligned} P_i \text{ for } i \in \{1,2\}: &\quad a\ P_i\ b\ P_i\ \emptyset, \\ P_3: &\quad b\ P_3\ a\ P_3\ \emptyset, \\ \succ_a: &\quad 3 \succ_a 1 \succ_a 2, \\ \succ_b: &\quad 1 \succ_b 2 \succ_b 3. \end{aligned}$$

Notice that at most two students can be matched to their true first choices. But with $A = \{2\}$, the unique augmented-stable matching is $\mu$ with $\mu_1 = a$, $\mu_2 = b$, and $\mu_3 = \emptyset$. By Thm. 6.3, student 2 is matched to school $b$ in any $\{2\}$-Nash equilibrium outcome of any FC mechanism. Thus, at most one student is matched to her first choice which violates FCM (with respect to the true preferences).

While FC mechanisms may not match a maximal number of true first choices in equilibrium, the next corollary shows that all equilibrium outcomes are FCS with respect to the true preferences.

Corollary 6.5. *Given a problem $(P, \succ)$, a set of sophisticated students $A \subseteq I$, and an FC mechanism $\varphi$, let $P^*$ be an $A$-Nash equilibrium of $\varphi$ at $(P, \succ)$. Then $\varphi(P^*, \succ)$ is FCS with respect to $(P, \succ)$.*

Proof. Assume towards contradiction that $\varphi(P^*, \succ)$ is not FCS with respect to the true problem $(P, \succ)$. Then there exists a pair $(i, s) \in I \times (S \cup \{\emptyset\})$ that blocks $\varphi(P^*, \succ)$ with $s = \text{choice}_{P_i}(1)$. If $i \in A$, then $i$ could get matched to $s$ by ranking it first, a contradiction to the assumption that $P^*$ is an $A$-Nash equilibrium. If $i \notin A$, then $i$ already ranks $s$ first. However, first choices are matched respecting priorities under any FC mechanism (by Lemma 4.3). Thus, all students matched to $s$ have priority over $i$ at $s$, again a contradiction. □

In summary, we have found that the equilibrium outcomes of FC mechanisms in mixed problems always satisfy FCS with respect to the true preferences, but they may violate FCM.

### 6.2 Student Welfare in Equilibrium

So far, we have analyzed student welfare under FC mechanisms in two extreme cases: When *all students are sophisticated*, then FC mechanisms match at most as many students to their true first choices in equilibrium as DA;[22] when *all students are sincere*, then FC mechanisms are trivially FCM. But what happens in intermediate cases, when some but not all students are sincere?

Towards this question, we consider specific equilibrium outcomes that are unanimously preferred by all sophisticated students.[23] To make this formal, fix an FC mechanism $\varphi$, a set of sophisticated students $A \subseteq I$, and a problem $(P, \succ)$. By the theory of stable matchings [32], there exists a *student-optimal augmented-stable matching*, say $\widehat{\mu}$. By Theorem 6.3, there exists an $A$-Nash equilibrium $P^*$ (of $\varphi$ at $(P, \succ)$) such that the outcome $\varphi(P^*, \succ)$ is $A$-equivalent to $\widehat{\mu}$, and all sophisticated students (weakly) prefer the matching $\varphi(P^*, \succ)$ to all other $A$-Nash equilibrium matchings. Because of this unanimous preference by the sophisticated students for $\varphi(P^*, \succ)$, we now focus on these *A-optimal Nash equilibrium matchings*.

For our analysis of student welfare in intermediate cases (i.e., with some sincere students), we identify how an individual student's behavior impacts student welfare by comparing the respective $A$-optimal Nash equilibrium matchings. First, we discuss an example to build intuition.

*Example 6.6.* There are six students $I = \{1, \ldots, 6\}$ and four schools $S = \{a, b, c, d\}$ with one seat each. The preferences and priorities are

$$\begin{aligned} P_i \text{ for } i \in \{1,2,3\}: &\quad a\ P_i\ b\ P_i\ c\ P_i\ \emptyset, \\ P_4: &\quad a\ P_4\ b\ P_4\ c\ P_4\ d\ P_4\ \emptyset, \\ P_5: &\quad a\ P_5\ b\ P_5\ d\ P_5\ \emptyset, \\ P_6: &\quad b\ P_6\ c\ P_6\ \emptyset, \\ \succ_s \text{ for } s \in S: &\quad 1 \succ_s \ldots \succ_s 6. \end{aligned}$$

Suppose that the FC mechanism ABM is used to match students to schools. For the sets of sophisticated students $A = \{6\}$ and $A' = \{3, 6\}$, the equilibrium outcomes in each case are unique and given in the following table.

| Sophisticated students | Unique equilibrium matchings under ABM |
|---|---|
| $A = \{6\}$ | $\mu_1 = a,\quad \mu_2 = c,\quad \mu_3 = \emptyset,\quad \mu_4 = \emptyset,\quad \mu_5 = d,\quad \mu_6 = b$ |
| $A' = \{3, 6\}$ | $\nu_1 = a,\quad \nu_2 = \emptyset,\quad \nu_3 = b,\quad \nu_4 = d,\quad \nu_5 = \emptyset,\quad \nu_6 = c$ |

This example illustrates four aspects of the relationship between $\mu$ and $\nu$.

(1) The sophisticated student 6 prefers the outcome when student 3 is sincere because she strictly prefers $\mu_6 = b$ to $\nu_6 = c$.
(2) Student 3, who is either sophisticated or sincere, prefers the outcome when she is sophisticated because she strictly prefers $\nu_3 = b$ to $\mu_3 = \emptyset$.

[22] Assuming truthful reporting, which is a weakly dominant strategy under DA.
[23] Note that a comparison between equilibrium outcomes may, in general, be inconclusive. We focus on the equilibrium outcomes that are unanimously preferred by all sophisticated students because they are well motivated: the strategic students would select these equilibria if they were given a choice.

(3) Whether student 3 is sophisticated or sincere has ambiguous effects for sincere students: Students 2 and 5 prefer $\mu$, student 4 prefers $\nu$, and student 1 is indifferent between $\mu$ and $\nu$.
(4) When more students are sincere, more student are matched to their true first choices: If students 3 and 6 are both sophisticated, then only student 1 is matched to her true first choice. However, if only student 6 is sophisticated, then students 1 and 6 are both matched to their true first choices.

The following theorem establishes that our observations about the relationship between $\mu$ and $\nu$ in Example 6.6 hold in general for all FC mechanisms and all mixed problems.

THEOREM 6.7. *Given a problem $(P, \succ)$, an FC mechanism $\varphi$, sophisticated students $A \subseteq I$, and a sincere student $i' \notin A$, let $\mu$ be an A-optimal Nash equilibrium matching and let $\nu$ be an $A'$-optimal Nash equilibrium matching where $A' = A \cup \{i'\}$. Then:*

1. *For all $i \in A$: $\mu_i \; R_i \; \nu_i$, i.e., all sophisticated students prefer $\mu$ to $\nu$.*
2. *For $i'$: $\nu_{i'} \; R_{i'} \; \mu_{i'}$, i.e., $i'$ prefers $\nu$ to $\mu$.*
3. *For $i \notin A \cup \{i'\}$: $\nu_i \; P_i \; \mu_i$, $\mu_i \; P_i \; \nu_i$, or $\nu_i = \mu_i$ are all possible, i.e., for all sincere students except $i'$ the impact of the behaior of $i'$ is ambiguous.*
4. *For all $i \in I$: If $\nu_i = choice_{P_i}(1)$, then $\mu_i = \nu_i$, i.e., any student who is matched to her true first choice under $\nu$ is also matched to her true first choice under $\mu$.*

A formal proof is given in Appendix F of the full version of this paper. Our result generalizes the corresponding Proposition 4 of Pathak and Sönmez [29] in two ways: First, we extend its scope from BM to all FC mechanisms. Second, beyond the impact for sophisticated students and $i'$, we also identify the impact for sincere students and for those students who are matched to their true first choices.

**Remark 2.** It is intuitive that strategizing improves the outcome for $i'$ and harms the other sophisticated students. Thus, Statements 1 and 2 in Theorem 6.7 may appear trivial. However, this intuition is deceptive: By misreporting her preferences, $i'$ changes the outcome for herself and others. But more importantly, she also changes the game for the other sophisticated students. They in turn respond by changing their own preference reports, which could deteriorate the outcome for $i'$ in general. Showing that FC mechanisms do not induce such dynamics is precisely the contribution of Theorem 6.7, and the proof critically relies on the two properties FCM and FCS.

For market designers, Theorem 6.7 answers the question whether FC mechanisms can bring us closer to achieving first-choice maximality with respect to the true preferences. In the respective optimal equilibrium outcomes, the number of students who are matched to their true first choices is lowest if all students are sophisticated, increases when more students are sincere, and peaks when all students are sincere. This provides a potential justification for the use of FC mechanisms in practice: If administrators wish to match many students to their true first choices, if they care about a minimal fairness guarantee in terms of FCS, and if they expect some share of the students to report their preferences truthfully, then FC mechanisms may be an attractive design alternative.

**Remark 3.** This insight comes with a caveat: Robust predictions of equilibrium play are not the only reason for the appeal of strategyproofness. By simplifying participation for students, strategyproofness also alleviates the cognitive cost that sophisticated students incur when they strategize [6]. On top of that, strategyproofness yields another form of fairness because it levels the playing field between students with different levels of strategic sophistication [29]. Our finding that the use of non-strategyproof FC mechanisms may be justified by the fact that they may match more students to their true first choices is agnostic to this broader role of strategyproofness as a desideratum for market design.

## 7 A CHARACTERIZATION OF THE BOSTON MECHANISM

In this section, we present a characterization of BM, the FC mechanism most commonly used in practice. Our characterization is based on extensions of the properties FCM and FCS and the well-known axiom of consistency.

Consistency requires that removing any student and her assigned seat from a problem and applying the mechanism to this reduced problem leads to the same matchings for the remaining students to the remaining seats [24]. It is easy to see that removing students with their seats may lead to problems where some school has no capacity, a case that our formal model explicitly excludes (see Section 2.1). To properly define consistency, we therefore extend the model by allowing $q_s = 0$ for some schools $s \in S$.

*Definition 7.1.* A mechanism $\varphi$ is *consistent* if, for all school choice problems $(I, S, q, P, \succ)$ and all students $i' \in I$, the following holds: Let $\mu = \varphi(I, S, q, P, \succ)$, and let $(I^-, S^-, q^-, P^-, \succ^-)$ be the reduced problem where $I^- = I \backslash \{i'\}$, $S^- = S$, $q^-_{\mu_{i'}} = q_{\mu_{i'}} - 1$, $q^-_s = q_s$ for all $s \in S \backslash \{\mu_{i'}\}$, $P^- = (P_i)_{i \in I^-}$, and $\succ^- = (\succ^-_s)_{s \in S^-}$, where $i \succ^-_s j$ whenever $i \succ_s j$ for all $i, j \in I^-$; then $\varphi_i(I, S, q, P, \succ) = \varphi_i(I^-, S^-, q^-, P^-, \succ^-)$ for all $i \in I^-$.

FCM and FCS can still be defined in the extended model. However, they become void if no student can be matched to their first choice, and void constraints are not useful in characterizing mechanisms. We therefore extend these properties in a different way: Instead of maximizing the number of matched first choices (as with FCM), we require that a mechanism maximizes the number of students matched to their $k^{\text{th}}$ choice where $k$ is the best rank for which this maximization is not trivial, and we take the same approach to extend FCS.

*Definition 7.2.* Given a problem $(P, \succ)$, let $k^{\text{best}}$ be the minimal rank for which there exist a student $i \in I$ and a school $s \in S$ such that $\text{choice}_{P_i}(k^{\text{best}}) = s$ and $q_s \geq 1$. A matching $\mu$ is *best-choice maximal* if there exists no other matching $\nu$ such that $|I(\mu, k^{\text{best}}, P)| < |I(\nu, k^{\text{best}}, P)|$; and $\mu$ is *best-choice stable* if it is $k^{best}$*-choice stable* (see Definition 3.2). A mechanism $\varphi$ is *best-choice maximal* (*best-choice stable*) if, for all problems $(P, \succ)$, the matching $\varphi(P, \succ)$ is best-choice maximal (best-choice stable).

Observe that FCM and best-choice maximality coincide for problems where all schools have at least one seat; the same is true for FCS and best-choice stability. Both properties can thus be understood as extensions of FCM and FCS, respectively. With these definitions and the extended model (where schools can have zero capacity) we can state our characterization result.

Theorem 7.3. *A mechanism $\varphi$ is best-choice maximal, best-choice stable, and consistent if and only if it is the Boston mechanism.*

Proof. Best-choice stability and best-choice maximality of BM are an immediate consequence of its definition; and Kojima and Ünver [24] showed consistency of BM. Conversely, assume towards contradiction that a mechanism $\psi$ is best-choice stable, best-choice maximal, and consistent but $\psi(I, S, P, \succ, q) \neq BM(I, S, q, P, \succ)$ for some problem $(I, S, q, P, \succ)$. First, observe that any best-choice maximal and best-choice stable mechanism assigns the same set of students to their $k^{\text{best}}$ choices for any problem. To see this, note that if $k^{\text{best}} > 1$, then we can update the preferences of all students in $I$ by truncating the first $k - 1$ choices and apply Lemma 4.3. We can remove these students with their assignments and define the reduced problem $(I^-, S^-, q^-, P^-, \succ^-)$ (as in Definition 7.1). By consistency of $\psi$, it matches the remaining students to the same schools under both $(I, S, q, P, \succ)$ and $(I^-, S^-, q^-, P^-, \succ^-)$; and the same is true for BM. Repeating this argument, we eventually arrive at a trivial problem that admits only one feasible matching (where no student is matched to any school).

The matchings from both mechanisms must coincide on this problem. Then, by construction, they must also coincide on all prior problems, a contradiction. □

Theorem 7.3 establishes the extraordinary role of BM in the set of FC mechanisms: While it is not the only FCM and FCS mechanism, it is essentially the only such mechanism that is also consistent (albeit in an extended model and with a special extension of the axioms to this model).

## 8 CONCLUSION

In school choice, FC mechanisms arise naturally, and many school choice mechanisms used in practice belong to this class. Understanding this class is therefore important for researchers and practitioners alike. The class of FC mechanisms is fairly large because FC mechanisms are only restricted in how they handle (reported) first choices. Nonetheless, we were able to analyze the incentives and equilibria of all mechanisms in this class purely based on the defining properties FCM and FCS. This suggests FCM and FCS as useful concepts analyzing school choice markets.

Our findings contribute to an ongoing debate about the respective merits and shortcomings of BM and DA. On the one hand, DA has the obvious advantage of being strategyproof [4], and its outcome weakly Pareto dominates the Nash equilibrium outcomes of BM in settings with strict priorities and when all students strategize optimally [18]. However, the comparison becomes less clear when either of the assumptions are relaxed. When priorities are weak, the equilibrium outcomes of BM can dominate those of DA from an *ex-ante* perspective [1, 17, 27]. Furthermore, if all students are sincere, BM *rank dominates* DA whenever they are comparable by rank dominance [22, 26], and BM satisfies the welfare property of *favoring higher ranks* [24]. Our present paper adds to these insights: If first choices matter and if a share of the students is expected to be sincere, then any FC mechanism (including BM) may yield more appealing matchings in equilibrium than DA. Our characterization result further shows that BM takes an elevated position among the FC mechanisms. Nevertheless, we refrain from recommending any specific mechanism in general; instead, our findings highlight the implicit trade-offs one must make when choosing between any of the mechanisms we have studied.

The prevalence of non-strategyproof mechanisms in practice has inspired new ways of thinking about incentives. For example, the concept for comparing mechanisms by their vulnerability to manipulation, put forward by [30], was instrumental in identifying a trend towards better incentive properties in the USA, UK, and Ghana. Interestingly, our results yield a criticism of this concept because it does not identify the intuitive differences between BM and ABM. To distinguish these two mechanisms by their incentive properties, more nuanced approaches are necessary (e.g., [15] for the case when schools find some students unacceptable or [26] when priorities are random).

Finally, our results give rise to promising directions for future research: Whether or not FC mechanisms can outperform DA hinges on the share of sophisticated students and their ability to coordinate on equilibrium. Some recent work has already considered field data to study student behavior and outcomes in school choice markets [9, 14, 16]. However, further research focusing specifically on sincerity and coordination would constitute an important contribution to the debate about school choice mechanisms, and we are aware of ongoing efforts in this direction.

## REFERENCES

[1] Atila Abdulkadiroğlu, Yeon-Koo Che, and Yosuke Yasuda. 2011. Resolving Conflicting Preferences in School Choice: The Boston Mechanism Reconsidered. *American Economic Review* 101, 1 (2011), 399--410.

[2] Atila Abdulkadiroğlu, Parag Pathak, and Alvin Roth. 2005. The New York City High School Match. *American Economic Review* 95, 2 (May 2005), 364--367.

[3] Atila Abdulkadiroğlu, Alvin Roth, Parag Pathak, and Tayfun Sönmez. 2006. Changing the Boston School Choice Mechanism: Strategy-proofness as Equal Access. (2006). Working Paper.

[4] Atila Abdulkadiroğlu and Tayfun Sönmez. 2003. School Choice: A Mechanism Design Approach. *American Economic Review* 93, 3 (2003), 729--747.

[5] Jose Alcalde. 1996. Implementation of Stable Solutions to Marriage Problems. *Journal of Economic Theory* 69, 1 (1996), 240--254.

[6] Eduardo Azevedo and Eric Budish. 2015. Strategy-proofness in the Large. (2015). Working Paper.

[7] Michel Balinski and Tayfun Sönmez. 1999. A Tale of Two Mechanisms: Student Placement. *Journal of Economic Theory* 84, 1 (1999), 73--94.

[8] Christian Basteck, Katharina Huesmann, and Heinrich Nax. 2015. Matching Practices for Secondary Schools - Germany. (2015). matching-in-practice.eu matching-in-practice.eu, accessed May 16, 2015.

[9] Caterina Calsamiglia and Maia Güell. 2014. The Illusion of School Choice: Empirical Evidence from Barcelona. (2014). Working Paper.

[10] Li Chen and Juan Sebastián Pereyra. 2015. Self-selection in School Choice. (2015). Working Paper.

[11] Yan Chen and Onur Kesten. 2016. Chinese College Admissions and School Choice Reforms: A Theoretical Analysis. (2016). Working Paper.

[12] Yan Chen and Onur Kesten. 2016. Chinese College Admissions and School Choice Reforms: An Experimental Study. (2016). Working Paper.

[13] Yan Chen and Tayfun Sönmez. 2006. School Choice: an Experimental Study. *Journal of Economic Theory* 127, 1 (2006), 202--231.

[14] Monique de Haan, Pieter Gautier, Hessel Oosterbeek, and Bas van der Klaauw. 2015. The Performance of School Assignment Mechanisms in Practice. (2015). Working Paper.

[15] Umut Dur. 2015. The Modified Boston Mechanism. (2015). Working Paper.

[16] Umut Dur, Robert Hammond, and Thayer Morrill. 2016. The Secure Boston Mechanism: Theory and Experiments. (2016). Working Paper.

[17] Aytek Erdil and Haluk Ergin. 2008. What's the Matter with Tie-Breaking? Improving Efficiency in School Choice. *American Economic Review* 98, 3 (2008), 669--89.

[18] Haluk Ergin and Tayfun Sönmez. 2006. Games of School Choice Under the Boston Mechanism. *Journal of Public Economics* 90, 1-2 (2006), 215--237.

[19] Clayton Featherstone. 2015. Rank Efficiency : Investigating a Widespread Ordinal Welfare Criterion. (2015). Working Paper.

[20] David Gale and Lloyd Shapley. 1962. College Admissions and the Stability of Marriage. *The American Mathematical Monthly* 69, 1 (1962), 9--15.

[21] Guillaume Haeringer and Flip Klijn. 2009. Constrained School Choice. *Journal of Economic Theory* 144, 5 (2009), 1921--1947.

[22] Patrick Harless. 2015. A School Choice Compromise: Between Immediate and Deferred Acceptance. (2015). Working Paper.

[23] Paula Jaramillo, Cağatay Kayi, and Flip Klijn. 2016. School Choice: Nash Implementation of Stable Matchings Through Rank-Priority Mechanisms. (2016). Working Paper.

[24] Fuhito Kojima and Utku Ünver. 2014. The Boston School-Choice Mechanism: an Axiomatic Approach. *Economic Theory* 55, 3 (2014), 515--544.

[25] Timo Mennle and Sven Seuken. 2017. Partial Strategyproofness: Relaxing Strategyproofness for the Random Assignment Problem. (2017). Working Paper.

[26] Timo Mennle and Sven Seuken. 2017. Trade-offs in School Choice: Comparing Deferred Acceptance, the Naïve and the Adaptive Boston Mechanism. (2017). Working Paper.

[27] Antonio Miralles. 2008. School Choice: the Case for the Boston Mechanism. (2008). Working Paper.

[28] Joana Pais and Agnes Pinter. 2008. School Choice and Information: an Experimental Study on Matching Mechanisms. *Games and Economic Behavior* 64 (2008), 303--328.

[29] Parag Pathak and Tayfun Sönmez. 2008. Leveling the Playing Field: Sincere and Sophisticated Players in the Boston Mechanism. *American Economic Review* 98, 4 (2008), 1636--52.

[30] Parag Pathak and Tayfun Sönmez. 2013. School Admissions Reform in Chicago and England: Comparing Mechanisms by Their Vulnerability to Manipulation. *American Economic Review* 103(1) (2013), 80--106.

[31] Alvin Roth. 1982. The Economics of Matching: Stability and Incentives. *Mathematical Operations Research* 7 (1982), 617--628.

[32] Alvin Roth and Marilda Sotomayor. 1990. *Two-Sided Matching: A Study in Game-Theoretic Modeling and Analysis.* Cambridge University Press.

[33] Alexander Westkamp. 2013. An Analysis of the German University Admissions System. *Economic Theory* 53, 3 (2013), 561--589.

# Stable Marriage with Multi-Modal Preferences

JIEHUA CHEN, University of Warsaw, Poland and Ben-Gurion University of the Negev, Israel
ROLF NIEDERMEIER, TU Berlin, Germany
PIOTR SKOWRON, University of Warsaw, Poland

We thoroughly study a generalized version of the famous STABLE MARRIAGE problem, now based on multi-modal preference lists. The central twist herein is to allow each agent to rank its potentially matching counterparts based on more than one "evaluation mode" (e.g., more than one criterion); thus, each agent is equipped with multiple preference lists, each ranking the counterparts in a possibly different way. We introduce and study three natural concepts of stability, investigate their mutual relations and focus on computational complexity aspects with respect to computing stable matchings in these new scenarios. Mostly encountering computational hardness (NP-hardness), we can also spot few islands of tractability and make a surprising connection to the GRAPH ISOMORPHISM problem.

Additional Key Words and Phrases: Stable matching; concepts of stability; multi-layer (graph) models; NP-hardness; parameterized complexity analysis; exact algorithms

## 1 INTRODUCTION

Information about the same "phenomenon" can come from different, possibly contradictory, sources. For instance, when evaluating applicants for an open position, data on their experience and professional achievements may give rise to a different ranking of the applicants than data on their formal qualifications and degrees. In other words, one has to deal with a multi-modal data scenario. Clearly, to make an objective and rational decision, it makes sense to take into account several information resources in order to achieve best possible results. In this work we systematically apply this point of view to the STABLE MARRIAGE problem [27]; a key observation here is that several natural and well-motivated "multi-modal variants" of STABLE MARRIAGE arise. We investigate the complexity of computing matchings that are stable according to the correspondingly varying definitions.

In the classic (conservative) STABLE MARRIAGE problem [27], we are given two disjoint sets $U$ and $W$ of $n$ agents each, where each of the agents has a *strict preference list* that ranks *every* member of the other set. The goal is to find a bijection (which we call a *matching*) between $U$ and $W$ that does not contain a *blocking pair*, *i.e.* a pair that can endanger the stability of the matching. A pair of agents is *blocking* a matching if they are not matched to each other but prefer each other to their respective partners in the matching.

Jiehua Chen was supported by the People Programme (Marie Curie Actions) of the European Union's FP7/2007-2013 (REA grant number 631163.11) and by the Israel Science Foundation (grant number 551145/14). Piotr Skowron was supported by a postdoctoral fellowship of the Alexander von Humboldt Foundation, Germany. Work started when all authors were with TU Berlin. Main work was done while Jiehua Chen was with Ben-Gurion University of the Negev and Piotr Skowron was with TU Berlin.
Authors' addresses: Jiehua Chen, University of Warsaw, Warsaw, Poland , Ben-Gurion University of the Negev, Beer-Sheva, Israel, jiehua.chen2@gmail.com; Rolf Niedermeier, TU Berlin, Berlin, Germany, rolf.niedermeier@tu-berlin.de; Piotr Skowron, University of Warsaw, Warsaw, Poland, p.skowron@mimuw.edu.pl.


*ACM EC'18, June 18–22, 2018, Ithaca, NY, USA.* ACM ISBN 978-1-4503-5829-3/18/06…$15.00
https://doi.org/10.1145/3219166.3219168

Gale and Shapley [27] introduced the Stable Marriage problem in the fields of Economics and Computer Science in the 1960s. One of their central results was that every Stable Marriage instance with $2n$ agents admits a stable matching, which can be found by their algorithm in $O(n^2)$ time. Since then Stable Marriage has been intensively studied in Economics, Computer Science, and Social and Political Science [29, 31, 32, 37, 39]. Practical applications of Stable Marriage (and its variants) include partnership issues in various real-world scenarios, matching graduating medical students (so-called residents) with hospitals [40], students with schools [1, 9], and organ donors with patients [42, 49], and the design of content delivery systems [38] and other distributed markets [50].

The original model of Stable Marriage assumes, roughly speaking, that there is a (subjective) criterion and that each agent has a single preference list depending on this criterion. In typically complex real-world scenarios, however, there are usually multiple aspects one takes into account when making a decision. For instance, if we consider the classical partnership scenario, then there could be different criteria such as working hours, family background, physical appearance, health, hobbies, etc. In other words, we face a much more complex multi-modal scenario. Accordingly, the agents may have multiple preference lists, each defined by a different criterion; we call each of these criteria a *layer* (also see Example 2.4 for another interpretation of layers). For an illustration, let us consider the following stable marriage example with two sets of two agents each, denoted as $\{u_1, u_2\}$ and $\{w_1, w_2\}$, and three layers of preferences, denoted as $P_1$, $P_2$, and $P_3$. In the diagram the preferences are depicted right above (resp. right below) the corresponding agents; preferences are represented through vertical lists where more preferred agents are put above the less preferred ones. In the first layer, all agents from the same set have the same preference list, *i.e.* both $u_1$ and $u_2$ rank $w_1$ higher than $w_2$ while both $w_1$ and $w_2$ rank $u_1$ higher than $u_2$. Similarly, in the second layer, both $u_1$ and $u_2$ rank $w_2$ higher than $w_1$ while both $w_1$ and $w_2$ rank $u_1$ higher than $u_2$. In the last layer, the preference lists of the two agents from the same set are reverse to each other. For instance, $u_1$ ranks $w_1$ higher than $w_2$, which is opposite to $u_2$. In terms of the classic Stable Marriage problem, we will have three independent instances, one for each layer. The corresponding stable matching(s) for each instance are depicted through the edges between the agents (we use different styles of lines to distinguish different stable matching). For instance, the first layer admits exactly one stable matching, which matches $u_1$ with $w_1$, and $u_2$ with $w_2$. Yet, if we want to take all these layers jointly into account, then we need to extend the traditional concept of stability.

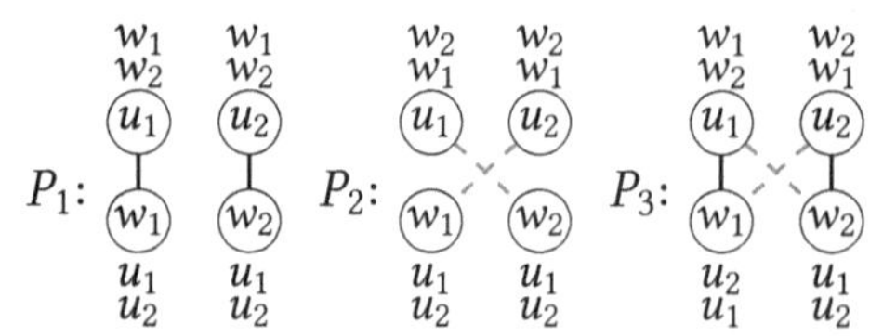


With multiple preference lists for each agent, there are three natural ways to extend the original stability notion, each leading to a new concept. In the following, we intuitively describe these concepts and defer the formal definitions and motivating examples to Section 2. Assume that each agent has $\ell$ (possibly different) preferences lists. All three new concepts are defined for a certain integer threshold $\alpha$ with $1 \leq \alpha \leq \ell$, which quantifies "the strength" of stability.

- The first concept, called *$\alpha$-layer global stability*, extends the original stability concept in a straightforward way. It assumes that the matched pairs agree on a set $S$ of $\alpha$ layers where no unmatched pair is blocking the matching in any layer from $S$. In our example, the matching $M_1 = \{\{u_1, w_1\}, \{u_2, w_2\}\}$ is stable in the first and the last layer, and thus it is 2-layer globally stable.
- The second concept, called *$\alpha$-layer pair stability*, restricts the "blocking ability" of the unmatched pairs. It *forbids* each unmatched pair to block more than $\ell - \alpha$ layers. Considering again our running example, we can verify that the 2-layer globally stable matching $M_1$ is also 2-layer pair stable as each unmatched pair is blocking at most one layer. Indeed, we will see that $\alpha$-layer pair stability is strictly weaker than $\alpha$-layer global stability (Proposition 3.1 and Example 3.2).

– The third concept, called *α-layer individual stability*, focuses on the "willingness" of an agent to stay with its partner. It requires that for each unmatched pair, at least one of the agents prefers to stay with its partner in at least $\alpha$ layers. In our example, matching $M_1$ is also 2-layer individually stable. Thus, it is tempting to assume that $\alpha$-layer individual stability also generalizes $\alpha$-layer global stability. This is, however, not true as the matching $M_2 = \{\{u_1, w_2\}, \{u_2, w_1\}\}$ is 2-layer globally stable but not 2-layer individually stable. Neither does the latter imply the former, so both concepts are incomparable. We refer to Example 3.4 for more explanations.

**Related work.** Our framework unifies and generalizes a couple of models known in the literature on stable matchings. Very recently, the Stable Marriage problem with multiple preference lists per agent has been studied by Aziz et al. [3] and Miyazaki and Okamoto [45]. Aziz et al. [3] introduced *certain stability* and *possible stability* for the case when there is a specific probability distribution over preference profiles. These two concepts are (mathematically) equivalent to our all-layer global stability and 1-layer global stability, respectively. Thus, our $\alpha$-layer global stability generalizes these two notions and defines a spectrum of solution concepts in-between. A 1-layer globally stable matching always exists. Aziz et al. showed that deciding all-layer global stability is NP-hard for $\alpha = \ell = 16$ layers; we strengthen this result by requiring only two layers (Theorem 4.6). In their work, Miyazaki and Okamoto [45] aimed to find a *jointly stable* matching that is stable in all layers, which turns out to be equivalent to our all-layer global stability as well. The authors showed that for $\alpha = \ell = 2$, checking all-layer global stability is NP-hard. We strengthen this by showing hardness for arbitrary $\alpha \leq \ell$ (Proposition 5.3). When one side of the preferences is single-layered (see Section 6.1), Miyazaki and Okamoto observed that finding an all-layer globally stable matching can be reduced to finding a super stable matching for an instance where one side of the preferences may be just a partial order; the latter is known to be polynomial-time solvable by using an extended variant of Irving's algorithm [30, 39]. The same result can be achieved as a corollary of our Propositions 3.5 and 6.1 and by using Algorithm 1. Note that Algorithm 1 decides all-layer individual stability for the general case when the input preferences may be not single-layered.

Aggregating the preference lists of multiple layers into one (by comparing each pair of agents) and then searching for a "stable" matching for the agents with aggregated preferences is an intuitive approach to stable marriage with multi-modal preferences. However, the aggregated preferences may be intransitive or even cyclic. Addressing this situation, Farczadi et al. [25] considered a generalized variant of Stable Marriage where each agent $u$ of one side, say $U$, has a strict preference list $\succ_u$ (as in the original Stable Marriage), while each agent $w$ of the other side, say $W$, may order each possible pair of partners separately, expressed by a subset $B_w \subseteq U \times U$ of ordered pairs. They called a matching $M$ *stable* if no unmatched pair $\{u, w\}$ satisfies "$w \succ_u M(u)$ and $(u, M(u)) \in B_w$". It turns out that our individual stability and their stability concept for a *more generalized* case where both sides of the agents may have intransitive preferences are related, and we can use one of their results as a subroutine. In a way, our analysis provides a more fine-grained view, since we consider a richer model and thus are able to discuss how certain assumptions on elements of this model (e.g., the number of layers, the threshold value $\alpha$, etc.) affect the computational complexity of the problem. Aziz et al. [2] considered a variant of Stable Marriage, where each agent has a probability of preferring one agent over another. Assigning a probability of 1 to either $(x, y)$ or $(y, x)$ for each $x$ and $y$, their variant is closely related to the one of Farczadi et al..

Weems [53] considered Stable Marriage where each agent has two preference lists that are the reverse of each other; this is a special case of our $\alpha$-layer global stability model for $\alpha = \ell = 2$. He provided a polynomial-time algorithm to find a matching that is stable in both layers. We refer to several expositions [8, 29, 34, 35, 37, 39] for a broader overview on Stable Marriage and related problems.

**Our contributions.** We introduce and thoroughly study three general concepts of stability for Stable Marriage with multi-modal preferences. In Section 2 we formally define these concepts, *global stability*, *pair stability*, and *individual stability*, and provide motivating and illustrating examples. In Section 3, we study the relations between the three concepts and show that pair stability is the least restrictive form while global and individual stability are in general incomparable (also see Figure 1 on the right for a more refined picture). In Section 4, we consider the special case of *all-layer* stability ($\alpha = \ell$) for our three stability concepts. On the one hand, we provide a polynomial-time algorithm for checking individual stability for an arbitrarily large number of preference lists. On the other hand, through an involved construction, we show that it is NP-hard to determine whether an all-layer globally stable (or all-layer pair stable) matching exists, whenever $\alpha \geq 2$. The hardness results demonstrate a complexity dichotomy for both global and pair stability since for $\ell = 1$, all three stability concepts are equivalent, and such stable matching(s) always exist and are polynomial-time computable. In Section 5, we investigate the case of finding stable matchings for less than all layers and only find NP-hardness. In particular, complementing the polynomial-time solvability result for checking individual stability when $\ell = \alpha$, we show that the problem becomes hard already when $\ell = 3$ and $\alpha = 2$. In Section 6, we identify two special scenarios with strong but natural restrictions on the preference lists. For the first scenario we assume that one side of the agents has *single-layered preferences*, *i.e.* the preference list of each agent remains the same in all layers. Under such restrictions, pair stability and individual stability are equivalent, and stable matchings can be computed in polynomial time; for global stability we obtain W[1]-hardness (and also NP-hardness) and XP membership for the threshold parameter $\alpha$. In the second scenario, we assume that the preferences of all agents on each side are *uniform* in each layer, *i.e.* for each fixed layer and side all agents have the same preference list. When considering individual stability we find surprisingly tight connections to the Graph Isomorphism problem. Table 1 gives a broad overview on our complexity results.

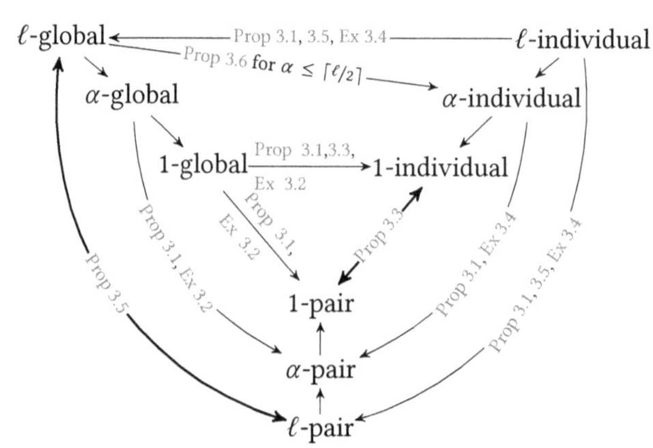


Fig. 1. Relations among the different multi-layer concepts of stability for different values of $\alpha$. Herein, an arc is to be read like an implication: one property implies the other.

Due to space constraints we deferred the whole version of the proofs marked by "proof sketch" and the proofs for results marked with the asterisk ⋆ to [16].

## 2 DEFINITIONS AND NOTATIONS

For each natural number $t$ by $[t]$ we denote the set $\{1, 2, \ldots, t\}$. Let $U = \{u_1, \ldots, u_n\}$ and $W = \{w_1, \ldots, w_n\}$ be two $n$-element disjoint sets of agents. There are $\ell$ layers of preferences, where $\ell$ is a positive integer. For each $i \in [\ell]$ and each $u \in U$, let $\succ_u^{(i)}$ be a linear order on $W$ that represents the ranking of agent $u$ over all agents from $W$ in layer $i$. Analogously, for each $i \in [\ell]$ and each $w \in W$, the symbol $\succ_w^{(i)}$ represents a linear order on $U$ that encodes preferences of $w$ in layer $i$. We

Table 1. The computational complexity of finding matchings stable according to our three introduced concepts—$\alpha$-layer global stability, $\alpha$-layer pair stability, and $\alpha$-layer individual stability—for instances with $2n$ agents and $\ell$ layers. Unless stated explicitly, all results hold for each value of $\alpha$ specified in the first column. The result marked by "◇" has also been achieved by Aziz et al. [3] and Miyazaki and Okamoto [45] for two layers and 16 layers, respectively.

| Parameters | global stability | pair stability | individual stability |
|---|---|---|---|
| Arbitrary | | | |
| $1 = \alpha$ | $O(n^2)$ [Gale and Shapley] | $O(n^2)$ [Gale and Shapley] | $O(n^2)$ [Gale and Shapley] |
| $2 \le \alpha = \ell$ | NP-h◇ [T. 4.6] | NP-h [C. 4.7] | $O(\ell \cdot n^2)$ [T. 4.5] |
| $\lfloor \ell/2 \rfloor < \alpha < \ell$ | NP-h [P. 5.3] | NP-h [P. 5.5+P. 5.6] | NP-h for $3\alpha \le 2\ell$ [T. 5.1] |
| $2 \le \alpha \le \lfloor \ell/2 \rfloor$ | NP-h [P. 5.3] | NP-h [C. 5.4] | NP-h [T. 5.2] |
| Single-layered | NP-h for unbounded $\alpha$ [T. 6.3] | NP-h for $2 \le \alpha \le \lfloor \ell/2 \rfloor$ [C. 5.4] | NP-h for $2 \le \alpha \le \lfloor \ell/2 \rfloor$ [T. 5.2] |
| | W[1]-h & in XP for $\alpha$ [T. 6.3] | | |
| | $O(\ell \cdot n^2)$ when $\alpha = \ell$ [T. 6.3] | $O(\ell \cdot n^3)$ when $\alpha > \lfloor \ell/2 \rfloor$ [P. 6.4] | $O(\ell \cdot n^3)$ when $\alpha > \lfloor \ell/2 \rfloor$ [P. 6.4] |
| Uniform | | | |
| $\alpha \ge \ell/2 + 1$ | $O(\ell \cdot n)$ [P. 6.10] | ? | $n^{O(\log(n))} + O(\ell \cdot n^2)$ [C. 6.9] |
| $\alpha = \ell/2$ | $O(\ell \cdot n)$ [P. 6.10] | ? | Graph Isom.-hard [T. 6.8] |

refer to such linear orders as preference lists. A preference profile $P_i$ of layer $i \in [\ell]$ is a collection of the preference lists of all agents in layer $i$, that is, $\{\succ_a^{(i)} \mid a \in U \cup W\}$.

A *matching* $M \subseteq \{\{u, w\} \mid u \in U \wedge w \in W\}$ is a set of pairwisely disjoint pairs, *i.e.* for each two pairs $p, p' \in M$ it holds that $p \cap p' = \emptyset$. If $\{u, w\} \in M$, then we also use $M(u)$ to refer to $w$ and $M(w)$ to refer to $u$, and we say that $u$ and $w$ are their respective partners under $M$; otherwise we say that $\{u, w\}$ is an *unmatched pair*. Example 2.1 below illustrates an example matching and recalls a graphical notation that we will use throughout the paper.

*Example 2.1.* Consider two sets of agents, $U = \{u_1, u_2, u_3\}$ and $W = \{w_1, w_2, w_3\}$, and two layers, $P_1$ and $P_2$. One can check that $P_1$ has only one stable matching $M_1 = \{\{u_1, w_3\}, \{u_2, w_1\}, \{u_3, w_2\}\}$, and $P_2$ has three stable matchings: (1) $M_1$, (2) $M_2 = \{\{u_1, w_1\}, \{u_2, w_2\}, \{u_3, w_3\}\}$, and (3) $M_3 = \{\{u_1, w_2\}, \{u_2, w_3\}, \{u_3, w_1\}\}$.

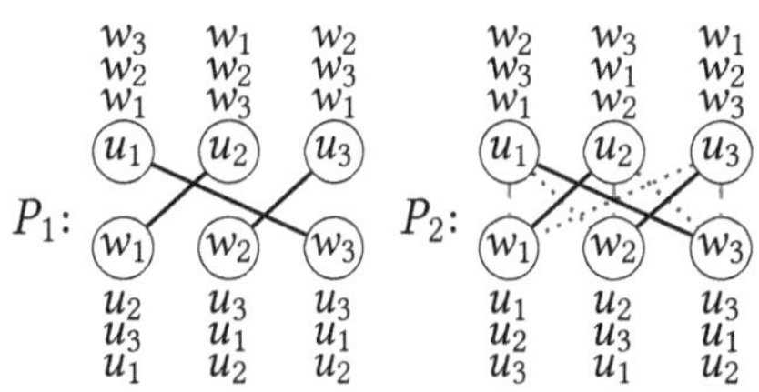

◇

Let us now introduce two notions that we will use when defining various concepts of stability.

*Definition 2.2 (Dominating and blocking).* Let $M$ be a matching over $U \cup W$. Consider an unmatched pair $\{u, w\} \notin M$ and a layer $i \in [\ell]$. We say that *$\{u, w\}$ dominates $\{u, v\}$ in layer $i$* if $w \succ_u^{(i)} v$. We say that *$\{u, w\}$ is blocking matching $M$ in layer $i$* if (1) $u$ is unmatched in $M$ or $\{u, w\}$ dominates $\{u, M(u)\}$ in layer $i$, and (2) $w$ is unmatched in $M$ or $\{u, w\}$ dominates $\{w, M(w)\}$ in layer $i$.

For an arbitrary layer, say $i$, a matching $M$ is *stable in layer $i$* if no unmatched pair is blocking $M$ in layer $i$. We illustrate the concept of dominating and blocking pairs through Example 2.1. Consider the matching $M_3 = \{\{u_1, w_2\}, \{u_2, w_3\}, \{u_3, w_1\}\}$ and profile $P_1$ of layer 1. Here, pair $\{u_1, w_3\}$ dominates both $\{u_1, w_2\}$ (since $u_1$ prefers $w_3$ to $w_2$) and $\{u_2, w_3\}$ (since $w_3$ prefers $u_1$ to $u_2$). Thus, $\{u_1, w_3\}$ is a blocking pair and so it witnesses that $M$ is not stable in profile $P_1$.

We are interested in matchings which are stable in multiple layers, *i.e.* we aim at generalizing the classic Stable Marriage problem [27, 29, 37, 39] which is defined for a single layer to the case of multiple layers.

At a high level, the ideas behind all our concepts are similar: in order to call a matching *stable* for multiple layers we require it to be stable in at least a certain, given number $\alpha$ of layers ($\alpha$ is a number indicating the "strength" of the stability). However, the three concepts require different levels of agreement with respect to which layers are required for stability. Informally speaking, on the one end of the spectrum we have a variant of stability where we require a global agreement of the agents regarding the set of $\alpha$ layers for which the matching must be stable. On the other end of the spectrum we have a variant where we assume that the agents act independently: an agent $a$ would deviate if it would find another agent, say $b$, such that $a$ prefers $b$ to its matched partner in some $\alpha$ layers, and $b$ prefers $a$ to its matched partner in another, possibly different, set of $\alpha$ layers. In the intermediate case, we require that a deviating pair must agree on the subset of layers which form the reason for deviation.

We formally define the three concepts below. Let there be $\ell$ layers of preferences.

### 2.1 $\alpha$-layer global stability

A matching $M$ is *$\alpha$-layer globally stable* if there exist $\alpha$ layers in each of which $M$ is stable.

*Definition 2.3.* A matching $M$ is *$\alpha$-layer globally stable* if there is a subset $S \subseteq [\ell]$ of $\alpha$ layers, where for each $i \in S$ and each unmatched pair $\{u, w\} \notin M$ at least one of the two conditions holds: (1) $\{u, M(u)\}$ dominates $\{u, w\}$ in layer $i$, or (2) $\{w, M(w)\}$ dominates $\{w, u\}$ in layer $i$.

The following example describes a scenario where $\alpha$-layer global stability appears to be useful.

*Example 2.4.* Assume that the preferences of the agents depend on external circumstances which are not known a priori. Assume that each layer represents a different possible state of the universe. If we want to find a matching that is stable in as many states of the universe as possible, then we need to find an $\alpha$-layer globally stable matching for the highest possible value of $\alpha$. ◇

Already for $\alpha$-layer global stability we see substantial differences compared to the original concept of stability for a single layer. It is guaranteed that such a matching always exists for $\alpha = 1$; indeed this would be a matching that is stable in an arbitrary layer. However, one can observe that as soon as $\alpha > 1$ an $\alpha$-layer globally stable matching might not exist (see Example 3.2).

### 2.2 $\alpha$-layer pair stability

While $\alpha$-layer global stability requires that the agents globally agree on a certain subset of $\alpha$ layers for which the matching should be stable, pair stability forbids each unmatched pair to block more than a certain number of layers. The formal definition, using the domination concept, is as follows:

*Definition 2.5.* A matching $M$ is *$\alpha$-layer pair stable* if for each unmatched pair $\{u, w\} \notin M$ there is a subset $S \subseteq [\ell]$ of $\alpha$ layers such that for each $i \in S$ at least one of the two conditions holds: (1) $\{u, M(u)\}$ dominates $\{u, w\}$ in layer $i$, or (2) $\{w, M(w)\}$ dominates $\{w, u\}$ in layer $i$.

Definition 2.5 can be equivalently formulated using a generalization of the concept of blocking pairs. Let $\beta \in [\ell]$. A pair $\{u, w\}$ is *$\beta$-blocking* $M$ if there is a subset $S$ of $\beta$ layers such that for each $i \in S$, pair $\{u, w\}$ is blocking $M$ in layer $i$.

PROPOSITION 2.6 (★). *A matching $M$ is $\alpha$-layer pair stable if and only if no unmatched pair is $(\ell - \alpha + 1)$-blocking $M$.*

The following example motivates $\alpha$-layer pair stability.

*Example 2.7.* Consider the case when the preferences of the agents depend on a context, yet the context is pair-specific. For instance, in matchmaking a woman may have different preferences over men depending on which country they will decide to live in. Thus, a pair of a man and a woman is blocking if they agree on certain conditions (*i.e.* layers), and if they will find each other more attractive than their current partners according to the agreed conditions. ◇

In Section 3, we show that $\alpha$-layer global stability implies $\alpha$-layer pair stability (Proposition 3.1). This, among other things, implies that for $\alpha = 1$ an $\alpha$-layer pair stable matching always exists. However, as soon as $\alpha \geq 2$ the existence is no longer guaranteed (see Example 3.2).

### 2.3 $\alpha$-layer individual stability

*Definition 2.8.* A matching $M$ is *$\alpha$-layer individually stable* if for each unmatched pair $\{u, w\} \notin M$ there is a subset $S \subseteq [\ell]$ of $\alpha$ layers such that at least one of the two conditions holds: (1) $\{u, M(u)\}$ dominates $\{u, w\}$ in each layer of $S$, or (2) $\{w, M(w)\}$ dominates $\{w, u\}$ in each layer of $S$.

The following example illustrates a potential application in the domain of partnership agencies.

*Example 2.9.* Assume that each layer describes a single criterion for preferences. The preferences of each agent may differ depending on the criterion. For instance, the two sets of agents can represent, respectively, men and women, as in the traditional Stable Marriage problem. Different criteria may correspond, for instance, to the intelligence, sense of humor, physical appearance etc. Assume that an agent $a$ will have no incentive to break his or her relationship with $b$, and to have an affair with $c$ if he or she prefers $b$ to $c$ according to at least $\alpha$ criteria. In order to match men with women so that they form stable relationships, one needs to find an $\alpha$-layer individually stable matching. ◇

Definition 2.8 can be equivalently formulated using a generalization of the concept of dominating pairs. Let $\beta \in [\ell]$. We say that a pair $\{u, w\}$ is *$\beta$-dominating* $\{u, w'\}$ if there is a subset $R$ of $\beta$ layers such that for each $i \in R$ the pair $\{u, w\}$ dominates $\{u, w'\}$ in layer $i$.

Proposition 2.10 (★). *A matching $M$ is $\alpha$-layer individually stable if and only if no unmatched pair $\{u, w\}$ exists that is both $(\ell - \alpha + 1)$-dominating $\{u, M(u)\}$ and $(\ell - \alpha + 1)$-dominating $\{w, M(w)\}$.*

For $\alpha = 1$ an $\alpha$-layer individually stable matching always exists (see Propositions 3.1 and 3.3); however, this is no longer the case when $\alpha \geq 2$ (see Proposition 3.1 and Example 3.2).

In this paper, we investigate how the three concepts relate to each other, and study the algorithmic complexity of finding matchings that are stable according to the above definitions. Now, we formally define the search problem of finding an $\alpha$-layer globally stable matching. The other two problems, Pair Stable Marriage and Individually Stable Marriage, are defined analogously.

Globally Stable Marriage
**Input:** Two disjoint sets $U$ and $W$ of $n$ agents each, $\ell$ preference profiles, and an integer $\alpha \in [\ell]$.
**Output:** Return an $\alpha$-layer globally stable matching if one exists, or report that there is no such stable matching.

## 3 RELATIONS BETWEEN THE MULTI-LAYER CONCEPTS OF STABILITY

Below we establish relations among the three concepts. We start by showing that $\alpha$-layer pair stability is a weaker notion than $\alpha$-layer global stability and $\alpha$-layer individual stability.

Proposition 3.1 (★). *An $\alpha$-layer globally stable matching is $\alpha$-layer pair stable. An $\alpha$-layer individually stable matching is $\alpha$-layer pair stable.*

Example 3.2 shows an $\alpha$-layer pair stable matching which is not $\alpha$-layer globally stable. Using Proposition 3.1, this also shows that $\alpha$-layer global stability is strictly stronger than $\alpha$-layer pair stability.

*Example 3.2.* Consider six agents with two layers of preference profiles. Observe that matching

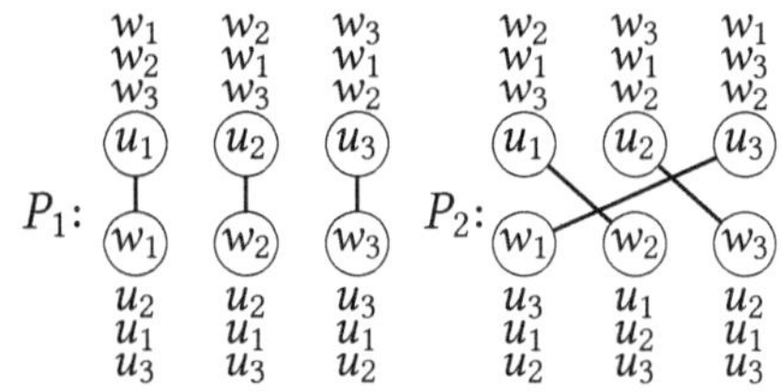


$M = \{\{u_1, w_1\}, \{u_2, w_3\}, \{u_3, w_2\}\}$ is 1-layer individually stable and, thus 1-layer pair stable. However, $M$ is blocked by $\{u_2, w_1\}$ in $P_1$ and by $\{u_1, w_2\}$ in $P_2$. Thus, $M$ is not 1-layer globally stable. Indeed the only 1-layer globally stable matchings are indicated by the solid lines, which are also 1-layer individually stable. As soon as $\alpha \geq 2$, $\alpha$-layer pair stability does not always exist, even if $\ell > \alpha$. To see this we augment the instance with one more layer whose preference lists are identical to the first layer given in Example 2.1. One can verify that for each of all six possible matchings, there is always an unmatched pair that is blocking at least two layers. ⋄

For $\alpha = 1$, we observe that 1-layer pair stability is equivalent to 1-layer individual stability.

Proposition 3.3 (★). *A matching is 1-layer pair stable iff. it is 1-layer individually stable.*

Example 3.4 shows that for $\alpha > 1$, individual stability and pair stability are not equivalent, neither is individual stability equivalent to global stability.

*Example 3.4.* Consider the example given in Section 1. Recall that both $M_1$ and $M_2$ are 2-layer globally stable (and 2-layer pair stable). However, $M_1$ is 2-layer individually stable while $M_2$ is not. To see why $M_2$ is not 2-layer individually stable, we can verify that the unmatched pair $p = \{u_1, w_1\}$ dominates $\{u_1, w_2\}$ in the first and the third layer and it dominates $\{u_2, w_1\}$ in the first two layers. By Proposition 2.10, $M_2$ is not 2-layer individually stable since $\ell - \alpha + 1 = 2$. If we restrict the example to the last two layers only, then matching $M_2$ is also evidence that an $\ell$-layer globally stable (which, by Proposition 3.5, implies $\ell$-layer pair stability) is not $\ell$-layer individually stable. ⋄

For $\alpha = \ell$ global stability and pair stability are equivalent.

Proposition 3.5 (★). *A matching is $\ell$-layer globally stable iff. it is $\ell$-layer pair stable.*

It is somehow counter-intuitive that even an $\ell$-layer globally stable matching (*i.e.* a matching that is stable in each layer) may not be $\ell$-layer individually stable (see Example 3.4). Propositions 3.1 and 3.5 imply that $\ell$-layer global stability is strictly weaker than $\ell$-layer individual stability. By Example 3.4, $\ell$-layer global stability does not imply $\ell$-layer individual stability. However, it implies $\lceil \ell/2 \rceil$-layer individual stability.

Proposition 3.6 (★). *Every $\ell$-layer globally stable matching is $\lceil \ell/2 \rceil$-layer individually stable. There exist $\ell$-layer globally stable matchings which are not $(\lceil \ell/2 \rceil + 1)$-layer individually stable.*

The relations among the different concepts of multi-layer stability are depicted in Figure 1.
A 1-layer globally stable matching always exists. By Proposition 3.1, we obtain the following.

Proposition 3.7. *An instance with $\ell$ layers always admits a matching which is 1-layer globally stable, 1-layer pair stable, and 1-layer individually stable.*

## 4 ALL-LAYERS STABILITY ($\alpha = \ell$)

In this section, we discuss the special case when $\alpha = \ell$. It turns out that deciding whether a given instance with $2n$ agents admits an $\ell$-layer individually stable matching can be solved in linear time: $O(\ell \cdot n^2)$. Moreover, we identify a close connection between our $\ell$-layer individual stability and the super stability concept for preferences with partial orders [39]. Using this connection, we could also solve our individual stability problem in a higher running time, $O(\ell \cdot n^3)$ (see [16]). For the other two concepts of stability, however, the problem is NP-hard even when $\ell = 2$.

**ALGORITHM 1:** Algorithm for finding an $\ell$-layer individually stable matching.

**Input:** A set of agents $U \cup W$ and $\ell$ layers of preferences.

1 **repeat**
2   **foreach** agent $u \in U$ **do**
3     **foreach** layer $i = 1, 2, \ldots, \ell$ **do**
4       $w \leftarrow$ the first agent in $u$'s preference list in layer $i$
5       $r \leftarrow 1$
6       **repeat**
7         **foreach** $u'$ with $w\colon u \succ_w^{(j)} u'$ for some layer $j$ **do** **mark** $\{u', w\}$
8         $r \leftarrow r + 1$
9         $w \leftarrow$ the $r^{\text{th}}$ agent in $u$'s preference list in layer $i$
10       **until** $\{u, w\}$ is *not* marked
11 **until** (some agent's preference list consists of only marked agents) **or** (no new pair was marked in the last iteration)
12 **if** some preference contains only marked agents **then** no $\ell$-layer individually stable matching exists
13 **else return** $M = \{\{u, w\} \mid u \in U$ with $w$ being the first not-yet-marked agent in $u$'s preference list$\}$ as an $\ell$-layer individually stable matching

## 4.1 Algorithm for $\ell$-layer individual stability

The algorithm for deciding $\ell$-layer individual stability is based on the following simple lemma.

Lemma 4.1 (★). *Let $u \in U$ and $w \in W$ be two agents such that $w$ is the first ranked agent of $u$ in some layer $i \in [\ell]$, and let $u' \in U \setminus \{u\}$ be another agent such that $w$ prefers $u$ over $u'$ in some layer $j \in [\ell]$. Then, no $\ell$-layer individually stable matching contains $\{u', w\}$.*

Lemma 4.1 leads to Algorithm 1 which looks quite similar to the so-called extended Gale-Shapley algorithm by Irving [30]. The crucial difference is that we loop into different layers and we cannot delete a pair $p$ of agents that does not belong to any stable matching, as it may still serve to block certain matchings. Instead of deleting such pair, we will *mark* it. Herein, *marking a pair* $\{u, w\}$ means marking the agent $u$ (resp. $w$) in the preference list of $w$ (resp. $u$) in every layer.
The correctness of Algorithm 1 follows from Lemmas 4.2 to 4.4.

Lemma 4.2 (★). *If a pair $\{u', w\}$ is marked during the execution of Algorithm 1, then no $\ell$-layer individually stable matching contains this pair.*

The following lemma ensures that in Line 13 if $w$ is matched to an agent $u$, then it is the most preferred unmarked agent of $u$ in *all* layers.

Lemma 4.3 (★). *If no agent's preference list consists of only marked agents and there is an agent $u$ and two different layers $i, j \in [\ell]$, $i \neq j$ such that the first unmarked agent in the preference list of $u$ in layer $i$ differs from the one in layer $j$, then Algorithm 1 will mark at least one more pair.*

When Algorithm 1 terminates and no agent contains a preference list that consists of only marked agents, then we can construct an $\ell$-layer individually stable matching by assigning to each agent $u$ its first unmarked agent in any preference list (note that Lemma 4.3 ensures on termination that for each agent it holds that in all layers is first unmarked agent is the same).

Lemma 4.4 (★). *If upon termination no agent's preference list consists of only marked agents, then the matching $M$ computed by Algorithm 1 is $\ell$-layer individually stable.*

Finally, we prove that Algorithm 1 computes an $\ell$-layer individually stable matching if one exists.

THEOREM 4.5. *For $\alpha = \ell$, Algorithm 1 solves* INDIVIDUALLY STABLE MARRIAGE *in $O(\ell \cdot n^2)$ time.*

PROOF SKETCH. Let $I = (U, W, P_1, P_2, \ldots, P_\ell)$ with $2n$ agents be the input of Algorithm 1. By Lemma 4.2, no $\ell$-layer individually stable matching contains a marked pair. If there is an agent whose preference list consists of only marked agents, then we can immediately conclude that the given instance is a no-instance. Otherwise, Lemma 4.4 proves that the algorithm returns an $\ell$-layer individually stable matching. □

### 4.2 NP-hardness for $\ell$-layer global stability and $\ell$-layer pair stability

In contrast to $\ell$-layer individual stability, in this section we show that deciding GLOBALLY STABLE MARRIAGE is NP-hard as soon as $\alpha = \ell = 2$. We establish this by reducing a NP-complete variant of the 3-SAT problem [28] to the decision variant of GLOBALLY STABLE MARRIAGE. The idea behind this reduction is to introduce for each variable four agents that admit exactly two possible globally stable matchings, one for each truth value. Then, we construct a satisfaction gadget for each clause by introducing six agents. These agents will have three possible globally stable matchings. We use a layer for each literal contained in the clause to enforce that setting the literal to false will exclude exactly one of the three globally stable matchings. Hence, unless one of the literals in the clause is set to true, no globally stable matching remains. Using the above idea, we can already show hardness of deciding $\alpha$-layer global stability for $\alpha = \ell = 3$. With some tweaks and using a restricted variant of 3-SAT, we can strengthen our hardness result to hold even for $\ell = 2$.

Before moving on with our result, we note that, independent from our work, Aziz et al. [3] and Miyazaki and Okamoto [45] considered all-layer global stability. While the former showed hardness for $\ell = 16$, the latter strengthened it to the case with $\ell = 2$. Using a slightly different reduction, we show the same hardness result as Miyazaki and Okamoto. Indeed, our reduction can be adapted to show hardness for many other cases. For instance, by adapting the construction we show hardness not only for the two-layer case but also for arbitrary $\alpha < \ell$ (Proposition 5.3). Moreover, we will see that our reduction can also be adapted to tackle a more general stability concept—pair stability (Proposition 5.5).

THEOREM 4.6 (★). *For each $\alpha = \ell \geq 2$,* GLOBALLY STABLE MARRIAGE *is NP-hard.*

Since $\ell$-layer global stability equals $\ell$-layer pair stability (Proposition 3.5), by Theorem 4.6 we obtain the following corollary for the pair stability.

COROLLARY 4.7. *For each $\alpha = \ell \geq 2$,* PAIR STABLE MARRIAGE *is NP-hard.*

## 5 MULTI-LAYER STABILITY WITH $\alpha < \ell$

In this section we show that for each of the three concepts that we introduced in Section 2 the problem of computing a multi-layer stable matching is computationally hard as soon as $2 \leq \alpha < \ell$.

### 5.1 NP-hardness for $\alpha$-layer individual stability

For $\alpha$-layer individual stability with $\alpha < \ell$ we no longer have the observation in Lemma 4.1 (which was crucial for solving the case with $\alpha = \ell$ in polynomial time). Indeed, we show that the problem is NP-hard even if $\ell = 3$ and $\alpha = 2$ by reducing from the NP-complete 3-SAT problem (where each clause has exactly three variables). The idea behind the reduction is a variable gadget that allows two $\alpha$-layer individually stable matchings, one for each truth value, and a clause gadget that allows exactly three $\alpha$-layer individually stable matchings, called *clause matchings*. One of the agents in the clause gadget, together with an agent from the variable gadget, will form an unmatched pair that would be $(\ell - \alpha + 1)$-dominating one clause matching if the corresponding literal in the clause is set false. Thus, unless at least one literal in the clause is set true, no $\alpha$-layer individually stable matching remains for the clause gadget. Utilizing this idea, we can show hardness for arbitrary constants $\ell$ and $\alpha$ with $\ell/2 < \alpha \leq 2\ell/3$.

Theorem 5.1. Individually Stable Marriage *is NP-hard for each* $\ell/2 < \alpha \leq 2\ell/3$.

Proof Sketch. We reduce from the NP-complete 3-SAT problem [28], where each clause has exactly three variables, to the decision version of Individually Stable Marriage for $\alpha = 2$ and $\ell = 3$. The proof for the more general case with $\ell/2 < \alpha \leq 2\ell/3$ can be found in [16].

Let $I = (X, C)$ be an instance of 3-SAT, where $X = \{x_1, x_2, \dots, x_n\}$ is the set of $n$ variables and $C = \{C_1, C_2, \dots, C_m\}$ is the set of $m$ clauses. For each variable $x_i \in X$, we create four *variable agents* $x_i, \overline{x}_i, y_i, \overline{y}_i$. We will construct three layers of preference lists for the variable agents so that each 2-layer individually stable matching contains either $M_i^{\text{true}} := \{\{x_i, y_i\}, \{\overline{x}_i, \overline{y}_i\}\}$ or $M_i^{\text{false}} := \{\{x_i, \overline{y}_i\}, \{\overline{x}_i, y_i\}\}$. Briefly put, using $M_i^{\text{true}}$ and $M_i^{\text{false}}$ will correspond to setting the variable $x_i$ to true or false, respectively. For each clause $C_j \in C$, we create six *clause agents* $a_j, b_j, c_j, d_j, e_j, f_j$. We will construct preference lists for these clause agents so that for each clause, there are exactly three different ways in which these agents are matched in a 2-layer individually stable matching. We use two layers to enforce that setting a different literal contained in the clause $C_j$ to false excludes exactly one of these ways. In total, we have $4n+6m$ agents and we divide them into two groups $U$ and $W$ with $U = \{x_i, \overline{x}_i \mid i \in [n]\}\} \cup \{a_i, b_i, c_j \mid j \in [m]\}$ and $W = \{y_i, \overline{y}_i \mid i \in [n]\} \cup \{d_j, e_j, f_j \mid j \in [m]\}$.

**Preference lists of the variable agents.** The preference lists of the variable agents restricted to the variable agents have the same pattern. We remark that here and in the description for the clause gadget, agents which were not explicitly mentioned in the preference list will be ordered behind the ones mentioned, in an arbitrary order.

$\forall i \in [n]$: Layer (1): $x_i : y_i \succ \overline{y}_i$, $\overline{x}_i : \overline{y}_i \succ y_i$, $y_i : \overline{x}_i \succ x_i$, $\overline{y}_i : x_i \succ \overline{x}_i$.
Layer (2): $x_i : y_i \succ \overline{y}_i$, $\overline{x}_i : y_i \succ \overline{y}_i$, $y_i : \overline{A}_i \succ x_i \succ A_i \succ \overline{x}_i$, $\overline{y}_i : x_i \succ \overline{x}_i$.
Layer (3): $x_i : \overline{y}_i \succ y_i$ , $\overline{x}_i : \overline{y}_i \succ y_i$, $y_i : A_i \succ \overline{x}_i \succ \overline{A}_i \succ x_i$, $\overline{y}_i : \overline{x}_i \succ x_i$.

Herein, $A_i$ denotes a list (in an arbitrary order) of all clause agents $a_j$ such that the corresponding clause $C_j$ contains the positive literal $x_i$. $\overline{A}_i$ denotes a list (in an arbitrary order) of all clause agents $a_j$ such that the corresponding clause $C_j$ contains the negative literal $\overline{x}_i$.

**Preference lists of the clause agents.** When restricted to the clause agents only, the preference lists for the clause agents are "uniform": In each layer, the preference lists of all agents corresponding to the same clause are the same (see Section 6.2). To unify the expression, for each clause $C_j = \ell_j^1 \vee \ell_j^2 \vee \ell_j^3$ and each integer $t \in \{1, 2, 3\}$ by $Y_j^{(t)}$ we denote the variable agent $y_i$ that corresponds to the literal $\ell_j^t$.

$\forall j \in [m]$:Layer (1): $a_j : d_j \succ Y_j^{(2)} \succ e_j \succ Y_j^{(3)} \succ f_j$; $b_j$ and $c_j : d_j \succ e_j \succ f_j$; $d_j$ and $e_j$ and $f_j : a_j \succ b_j \succ c_j$.
Layer (2): $a_j : e_j \succ Y_j^{(3)} \succ f_j \succ Y_j^{(1)} \succ d_j$; $b_j$ and $c_j : e_j \succ f_j \succ d_j$; $d_j$ and $e_j$ and $f_j : b_j \succ c_j \succ a_j$.
Layer (3): $a_j : f_j \succ Y_j^{(1)} \succ d_j \succ Y_j^{(2)} \succ e_j$; $b_j$ and $c_j : f_j \succ d_j \succ e_j$; $d_j$ and $e_j$ and $f_j : c_j \succ a_j \succ b_j$.

Before we show the correctness of our construction, we discuss some properties that each 2-layer individually stable matching $M$ must satisfy.

Claim 1 (★). *Let $M$ be a 2-layer individually stable matching for our three-layer preference profiles. For each variable $x_i \in X$, it holds that either $M_i^{true} \subseteq M$ or $M_i^{false} \subseteq M$.*

We obtain a similar result for the clause agents. For each clause $C_j \in C$ let $N_j^1 = \{\{a_j, d_j\}, \{b_j, e_j\}, \{c_j, f_j\}\}$, $N_j^2 = \{\{a_j, e_j\}, \{b_j, f_j\}, \{c_j, d_j\}\}$, $N_j^3 = \{\{a_j, f_j\}, \{b_j, d_j\}, \{c_j, e_j\}\}$.

Claim 2 (★). *Let $M$ be a 2-layer individually stable matching $M$. For each clause $C_j \in C$ the following holds. (1) One of $\{N_j^1, N_j^2, N_j^3\}$ belongs to $M$. (2) Let $\ell_j^{(t)}$ be the $t^{th}$ literal in $C_j$, $t \in \{1,2,3\}$ such that $N_j^t \subseteq M$. If $\ell_j^{(t)}$ is positive, then $M_i^{true} \subseteq M$. If $\ell_j^{(t)}$ is negative, then $M_i^{false} \subseteq M$.*

Using Claims 1 and 2, we can show that $(X, C)$ admits a satisfying truth assignment if and only if there exists a 2-layer individually stable matching for the thus-constructed instance. The full proof can be found in [16]. □

For each $\alpha < \ell/2$, we also obtain hardness results by reducing from the NP-hard Perfect SMTI problem, which asks to find a perfect *SMTI-stable* matching with (possibly) incomplete preference lists and ties [33, 41], defined as follows. A preference list is *incomplete* if not all agents from one side are considered acceptable to an agent from the other side. A preference list has a *tie* if there are two agents in the list which are considered to be equally good. As a result, a preference list of an agent $u$ from one side can be considered as a weak (*i.e.* transitive and complete) order $\succeq_u$ on a subset of the agents on the other side. We use $\succ_u$ and $\sim_u$ to denote the asymmetric and symmetric part of the preference list, respectively. Equivalently, two agents $x$ and $y$ are said to be tied by $u$ if $x \succeq_u y$ and $y \succeq_u x$, denoted as $x \sim_u y$. Formally, we say that a matching $M$ for a Perfect SMTI with two disjoints sets $U$ and $W$ of agents is *SMTI-stable* if there are no SMTI-blocking pairs for $M$. A pair $\{u, w\}$ is *SMTI-blocking* $M$ if all of the following three conditions are satisfied: (i) $u$ and $w$ appear in the preference lists of each other, (ii) $w \succ_u M(u)$ or $u$ is not matched to any agent from $W$, and (iii) $u \succ_w M(w)$ or $w$ is not matched to any agent from $U$.

The reduction is based on the following ideas: In a Perfect SMTI instance $I$ the preference list of an agent $z$ may have ties. To encode ties, we first "linearize" the preference list of $z$ in $I$ to obtain two linear preference lists such that the resulting lists restricted to the tied agents are reverse to each other. Then, we let half of the $\ell$ layers have one of the preference lists and let the remaining half to have the other list. Since $\alpha < \ell/2$, it is always possible to find half layers which fulfill our $\alpha$-layer individual stability constraint. In $I$, two agents, say $x$ and $y$, may not be acceptable to each other. To encode this, we add to the source instance $\ell$ pairs of dummy agents with $\ell$ layers of preferences that preclude $x$ and $y$ from being matched together. However, to make sure that an agent $x$ is not matched to any dummy agent, we have to require that $\ell \geq 4$.

Theorem 5.2 (★). *For each fixed number $\ell$ of layers with $\ell \geq 4$ and for each fixed value $\alpha$ with $2 \leq \alpha \leq \lfloor \ell/2 \rfloor$, Individually Stable Marriage is NP-hard even if on one side the preference list of each agent is the same in all layers.*

## 5.2 NP-hardness for $\alpha$-layer global stability and $\alpha$-layer pair stability

To find a matching $M$ that is $\alpha$-layer globally stable, even if $\alpha < \ell$, the main difficulty is not just to determine $\alpha$ layers where $M$ should be stable. In fact, we sometimes need to find a matching that is stable in some specific layers. This requirement allows us to adapt the construction in the proof of Theorem 4.6 to show hardness for deciding $\alpha$-layer global stability for the case when $2 \leq \alpha < \ell$.

Proposition 5.3 (★). *For each $\alpha$ with $\alpha \geq 2$, Globally Stable Marriage is NP-hard.*

We remark that our proof for Proposition 5.3 also implies hardness for $\alpha = \ell$ for arbitrary $\ell \geq 2$. Observe that in the instance constructed in the proof of Theorem 5.2 every agent from the side $W \cup R$ has the same preference list in all layers. Later on, in Proposition 6.1 we will show that in such a case the concepts of $\alpha$-layer individual stability and $\alpha$-layer pair stability are equivalent, Thus, we obtain the same hardness result for pair stability when $\alpha \leq \lfloor \ell/2 \rfloor$.

Corollary 5.4. *For each $\ell$ with $\ell \geq 4$ and each $\alpha$ with $2 \leq \alpha \leq \lfloor \ell/2 \rfloor$, Pair Stable Marriage is NP-hard even if on one side the preference lists of each agent are the same in all layers.*

For $\alpha > \lceil \ell/2 \rceil$, we use an idea similar to the one used for showing Proposition 5.3.

Proposition 5.5 (★). *For each $\alpha$ with $\lceil \ell/2 \rceil + 1 \leq \alpha \leq \ell$,* Pair Stable Marriage *is NP-hard.*

Corollary 5.4 and Proposition 5.5 cover the whole range of the potential values of $\alpha$ except for $\alpha = \lfloor \ell/2 \rfloor + 1$ when $\ell$ is odd. As we will see in the next section Theorem 5.2 cannot be strengthened to cover the value $\alpha = \lfloor \ell/2 \rfloor + 1$ (see Proposition 6.4), and so, also Corollary 5.4 cannot be directly strengthened. However, we can tweak the construction from Theorem 5.2, breaking the restriction that on one side the preference list of each agent is the same in all layers, and obtain hardness for $\alpha$-layer pair stability for $\alpha = \lfloor \ell/2 \rfloor + 1$.

Proposition 5.6 (★). *For each $\alpha \geq 3$ with $\ell = 2\alpha - 1$,* Pair Stable Marriage *is NP-hard.*

## 6 TWO SPECIAL CASES OF PREFERENCES

In this section, we consider two well-motivated special cases of our general multi-layer framework for stable matchings. We will discuss how the corresponding simplifying assumptions affect the computational complexity of finding multi-layer stable matchings. Surprisingly, even under seemingly strong assumptions some variants of our problem remain computationally hard.

### 6.1 Single-layered preferences on one side

Consider the special case where the preferences of the agents from $U$ can be expressed through a single layer. Formally, we model this by assuming that for each agent from $U$, its preference list is the same in all layers. In this case we say that the agents from $U$ have *single-layered preferences*.

Single-layered preferences on one side can arise in many real-life scenarios. For instance, consider the standard example of matching residents with hospitals and, similarly as in Example 2.9, assume that each layer corresponds to a certain criterion. It is reasonable to assume that the hospitals evaluate their potential employees with respect to the level of their qualifications only (thus, having a single layer of preferences), while the residents take into account a number of factors such as how far is a given hospital from the place they live, the level of compensation, the reputation of the hospital, etc.

First, we observe that in such a case two out of our three stability concepts are equivalent.

Proposition 6.1 (★). *If each agent from $U$ has single-layered preferences, then $\alpha$-layer pair stability and $\alpha$-layer individual stability are equivalent for each $\alpha$.*

For profiles with single-layered preferences of the agents on one side, $\alpha$-layer global stability is strictly stronger than the other two concepts:

*Example 6.2.* Consider four agents with three layers of profiles and let $M = \{\{u_1, w_2\}, \{u_2, w_1\}\}$. We show that $M$ is 2-layer pair stable but not 2-layer globally stable. Indeed, $M$ is stable only in the first layer, so it cannot be 2-layer globally stable. To see why $M$ is 2-layer pair stable, consider the unmatched pairs $\{u_1, w_1\}$ and $\{u_2, w_2\}$. The first one only blocks the third layer, and the latter one only blocks the second layer. ◇

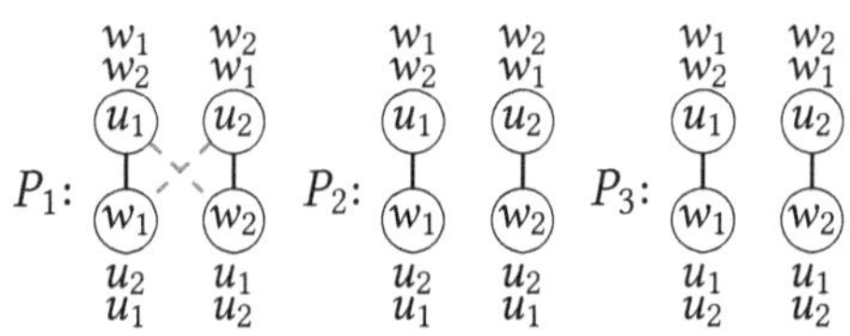


**Global stability.** By Propositions 3.5 and 6.1, we know that for the case that the input instance has single-layered preferences, all three all-layer stability concepts are the same. Thus, when $\alpha = \ell$, we can use Algorithm 1 to decide $\alpha$-layer global stability in polynomial time for the single-layered preferences case. Moreover, for $\alpha < \ell$, we can also decide $\alpha$-layer global stability in time $O(\ell^{\alpha} \cdot \alpha \cdot n^2)$

by guessing a subset of $\alpha$ layers and using Algorithm 1. However, the following result shows that fixed-parameter tractability (FPT) for the parameter $\alpha$, *i.e.*, the existence of an algorithm running in $f(\alpha) \cdot (\ell \cdot n)^{O(1)}$ time for some computable function $f$, is unlikely (for details on parameterized complexity we refer to the books of Cygan et al. [19], Downey and Fellows [21], Flum and Grohe [26], and Niedermeier [46]).

Theorem 6.3 ($\star$). *Even if the preferences of the agents from $U$ are single-layered,* Globally Stable Marriage *is NP-hard and is W[1]-hard for the threshold parameter $\alpha$. For $\alpha = \ell$, the problem is solvable in $O(\ell \cdot n^2)$ time, while for $\alpha < \ell$ it is solvable in $O(\ell^{\alpha} \cdot \alpha \cdot n^2)$ time.*

**Individual stability and pair stability.** By Theorem 5.2, checking $\alpha$-layer individual stability for preferences single-layered on one side is NP-hard if $\ell \geq 4$ and $\alpha \leq \lfloor \ell/2 \rfloor$. For the case of $\alpha \geq \lfloor \ell/2 \rfloor + 1$, we establish a relation between the individual stability for preferences single-layered on one side and the stability concept in the traditional single-layer setting, but with general incomplete and possibly intransitive preferences as studied by Farczadi et al. [25]. This relation allows us to construct a polynomial-time algorithm for checking $\alpha$-layer individual stability.

Proposition 6.4 ($\star$). *If the preferences of the agents on one side are single-layered and $\alpha \geq \lfloor \ell/2 \rfloor + 1$, then* Pair Stable Marriage *and* Individually Stable Marriage *can be solved in $O(\ell \cdot n^3)$ time.*

## 6.2 Uniform preferences in each layer

In this section we consider the case when in each layer the preferences of all agents from $U$ (resp. $W$) are the same—we call such preferences *uniform in each layer*. This special case is motivated with the following observation pertaining to Example 2.9: preferences uniform in a layer can arise if the criterion corresponding to the layer is not subjective. For instance, if a layer corresponds to the preferences regarding the wealth of potential partners, then it seems natural that everyone prefers to be matched with a wealthier partner (and so the preferences of all agents for this criterion are the same); similarly it seems reasonable that the preferences of all hospitals are the same: candidates with higher grades are ranked higher by each hospital.

First, we observe that for uniform preferences, no two of the three concepts are equivalent.

*Example 6.5.* Consider four agents with four layers of uniform preferences. Let $M_1 = \{\{u_1, w_1\}, \{u_2, w_2\}\}$ and $M_2 = \{\{u_1, w_2\}, \{u_2, w_1\}\}$. One can check that both $M_1$ and $M_2$ are *not* 3-layer globally stable and *not* 3-layer individually stable.

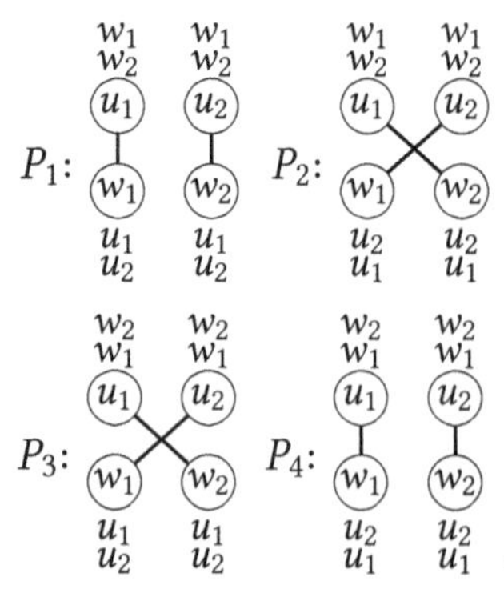


Both $M_1$ and $M_2$ are 3-layer pair stable. For instance, for $M_1$, the unmatched pairs $\{u_1, w_2\}$ and $\{u_2, w_1\}$ are only blocking layer (2) and layer (3), respectively. If we restrict the instance to only the first three layers, then we have the following results. (1) $M_1$ is not even 2-layer globally stable but it is 2-layer individually stable as for each unmatched pair $p$ with respect to $M_1$, at least one agent in $p$ obtains a partner which is its most preferred agent in at least two layers. (2) $M_2$ is 2-layer globally stable but it is not 2-layer individually stable. To see why it is not 2-layer individually stable, we consider the unmatched pair $\{u_1, w_1\}$. There are $3 - 2 + 1 = 2$ layers where $u_1$ prefers $w_1$ to its partner $M_2(u_1) = w_2$ and there are two layers where $w_1$ prefers $u_1$ to its partner $M_2(w_1) = u_2$. ◇

**Individual stability.** For preferences that are uniform in each layer, there is a close relation between Individually Stable Marriage and Graph Isomorphism, the problem of finding an isomorphism between graphs or deciding that there exists none. Herein, an instance of Graph Isomorphism consists of two undirected graphs $G$ and $H$ with the same number of vertices and the same number of edges. We want to decide whether there is an edge-preserving bijection $f: V(G) \to V(H)$ between the vertices, *i.e.* for each two vertices $u, v \in V(G)$ it holds that $\{u, v\} \in E(G)$ if and only if $\{f(u), f(v)\} \in E(H)$. We call such bijection an isomorphism between $G$ and $H$.

We explore this relation through the following construction. For an instance $I$ of INDIVIDUALLY STABLE MARRIAGE we construct two directed graphs $G_I$ and $H_I$ as follows. The agents from $U$ and $W$ will correspond to the vertices in $G_I$ and $H_I$, respectively. For each two vertices $u, u' \in U$ we add to $G_I$ an arc $(u, u')$ if the agents from $W$ prefer $u$ to $u'$ in at least $(\ell - \alpha + 1)$ layers. Analogously, for each two agents $w$ and $w'$, we add to $H_I$ an arc $(w, w')$ if the agents from $U$ prefer $w$ to $w'$ in at least $(\ell - \alpha + 1)$ layers. Let $E(G_I)$ and $E(H_I)$ denote the arc sets of $G_I$ and $H_I$, respectively.

We first explain how the so constructed graphs can be used to find an $\alpha$-layer individually stable matching in the initial instance $I$, or to claim that there is no such a matching.

PROPOSITION 6.6 (★). *A matching $M$ for instance $I$ is $\alpha$-layer individually stable if and only if for each two $u, u' \in U$ and each two $w, w' \in W$ the following two properties hold. (1) $(u, u') \in E(G_I)$ implies $(M(u'), M(u)) \notin E(H_I)$. (2) $(w, w') \in E(H_I)$ implies $(M(w'), M(w)) \notin E(G_I)$.*

Using a construction by McGarvey [43], given an arbitrary directed graph, we can indeed construct multi-layer preferences that induce this graph.

LEMMA 6.7 (★). *For each two directed graphs $G_I$ and $H_I$ with $m$ arcs each there exists an instance with $\ell = 2m$ layers of uniform preferences that induces $G_I$ and $H_I$ via McGarvey's construction, where $m$ denotes the number of arcs in $G_I$ (and thus in $H_I$).*

Using Proposition 6.6 and Lemma 6.7 as tools, we can show that for uniform preferences, INDIVIDUALLY STABLE MARRIAGE is at least as hard as GRAPH ISOMORPHISM.

THEOREM 6.8. GRAPH ISOMORPHISM *is polynomial-time reducible to* INDIVIDUALLY STABLE MARRIAGE, *where the preferences of the agents are uniform in all $\ell$ layers, $\ell$ is even, and $\alpha = \ell/2$.*

PROOF SKETCH. Let $G, H$ be two undirected graphs that form an instance of GRAPH ISOMORPHISM. Without loss of generality, assume that $n \geq 4$ (number of vertices) and $m \geq 3$ (number of edges). From $G$ and $H$ we construct an instance $I$ of the problem of deciding whether there exists an $\alpha$-layer individually stable matching for preferences being uniform in all $\ell$ layers, where $\alpha = \ell/2$. By Lemma 6.7 we can describe this instance by providing the corresponding directed graphs $G_I$ and $H_I$. We show how to construct $G_I$ from $G$. The graph $H_I$ is constructed from $H$ analogously.

Let $V$ and $E$ denote the sets of vertices and edges in $G$. We copy all vertices from $G$ to $G_I$ (we will refer to these vertices as *non-special*) and we additionally introduce five types of "special" vertices, which we call $\mathsf{prime}^G$, $\mathsf{deputy}^G$, $\binom{n}{2} + 1$ connectors, $m$ sinks, and $\binom{n}{2} - m$ sources. We specify the connectors, the sinks, and the sources formally: With each pair of vertices $p = \{v, v'\} \in \binom{V}{2}$ we associate one connector, denoted as $\mathsf{connector}_p^G$. One remaining connector is distinguished and denoted as $\mathsf{connector}_*^G$. Further, for each edge $e \in E$ we have one sink, denoted as $\mathsf{sink}_e^G$, and for each non-edge $e = \{v, v'\} \notin E$ we have a source, denoted as $\mathsf{source}_e^G$. The arcs in $G_I$ are constructed as follows. Let $\mathsf{SOURCE}^G = \{\mathsf{source}_e \mid e \in \binom{V}{2} \setminus E\}$, $\mathsf{SINK}^G = \{\mathsf{sink}_e \mid e \in E\}$, and $\mathsf{CONNECTOR}^G = \{\mathsf{connector}_e^G \mid e \in \binom{V}{2}\}$ denote the set of all sources, the set of all sinks, and the set of non-special connectors, respectively:

(1) For each pair $e = \{v, v'\} \subseteq V$ of vertices, we do the following: (i) If $\{v, v'\} \in E$, then we add to $G_I$ the following five arcs: $(v, \mathsf{sink}_e^G)$, $(v', \mathsf{sink}_e^G)$, $(v, \mathsf{connector}_e^G)$, $(v', \mathsf{connector}_e^G)$, and $(\mathsf{sink}_e^G, \mathsf{connector}_e^G)$. Otherwise, we add to $G_I$ the following five arcs: $(\mathsf{source}_e^G, v)$, $(\mathsf{source}_e^G, v')$, $(v, \mathsf{connector}_e^G)$, $(v', \mathsf{connector}_e^G)$, and $(\mathsf{source}_e^G, \mathsf{connector}_e^G)$. (ii) For each other non-special

vertex $u \in V \setminus \{v, v'\}$, we add to $G_I$ the arc $(\text{connector}_e^G, u)$. (iii) For each other source or sink $x \in \text{SOURCE}^G \cup \text{SINK}^G \setminus \{\text{sink}_e^G, \text{source}_e^G\}$, we add to $G_I$ the arc $(\text{connector}_e^G, x)$.

(2) For each source and each sink $x \in \text{SOURCE}^G \cup \text{SINK}^G$ we add to $G_I$ an arc $(x, \text{connector}_*^G)$. For each non-special vertex $v \in V$, we additionally add to $G$ the arc $(\text{connector}_*^G, v)$.

(3) For each vertex $x \in V \cup \text{SOURCE}^G \cup \text{SINK}^G \cup \text{CONNECTOR}^G \cup \{\text{connector}_*^G\}$ except for the deputy, we add to $G_I$ an arc $(\text{prime}^G, x)$.

(4) For each vertex $x \in \text{SOURCE}^G \cup \text{SINK}^G \cup \{\text{prime}^G\}$ we add to $G_I$ the arc $(\text{deputy}^G, x)$. For each connector $y \in \text{CONNECTOR}^G \cup \{\text{connector}_*^G\}$ we add to $G_I$ the arc $(y, \text{deputy}^G)$.

This completes the construction of $G_I$. The arcs in $H_I$ are constructed analogously. The correctness proof that "there is an $\alpha$-layer individually stable matching in the instance $(G_I, H_I)$ with $\alpha = \ell/2$ if and only if there is an isomorphism between $G$ and $H$" can be found in [16]. □

Theorem 6.8 implies that developing a polynomial-time algorithm for our problem is currently out of scope since the question of whether Graph Isomorphism is solvable in polynomial time is still open. Besides Theorem 6.8 there are other interesting implications of Proposition 6.6 and Lemma 6.7. For $\alpha \geq \ell/2 + 1$ our problem can be reduced to the Tournament Isomorphism problem, which, given two tournament graphs, asks whether there is an arc-preserving bijection between the vertices of the two tournaments. Tournament Isomorphism has been studied extensively in the literature (for a more detailed discussion see, e.g., [4, 51, 52]), but to the best of our knowledge it is still open whether it is solvable in polynomial time [4]. The best known algorithm solving Tournament Isomorphism runs in $n^{O(\log n)}$ time, where $n$ denotes the number of vertices.

Corollary 6.9. *If the preferences of the agents are uniform in all $\ell$ layers and $\alpha \geq \ell/2 + 1$, then* Individually Stable Marriage *can be solved in $n^{O(\log n)} + O(\ell \cdot n^2)$ time, where $n$ denotes the number of agents.*

Proof. Assume that $\alpha \geq \ell/2+1$ and construct the two directed graphs as we did for Proposition 6.6. Since $\ell - \alpha + 1 \leq \ell/2$, for each two vertices $x$ and $y$ in $G_I$ (resp. $H_I$) at least one of the arcs $(x, y)$ and $(y, x)$ exists. Note that such graphs are not necessarily tournaments. But we can deal with the case when one of the graphs is not a tournament. If both $(x, y)$ and $(y, x)$ exist in $G_I$ or in $H_I$, then by Proposition 6.6 no $\alpha$-layer individually stable matchings exists. Thus, the only non-trivial case is when the graphs $G_I$ and $H_I$ are tournaments. Moreover, in such a case, the condition from Proposition 6.6 can be reformulated as "$(x, y) \in G_I$ if and only if $(M(x), M(y)) \in H_I$" and this is the condition that $M$ is a tournament isomorphism between $G_I$ and $H_I$. Consequently, for $\alpha \geq \ell/2 + 1$ Individually Stable Marriage can be reduced to Tournament Isomorphism. Note that the number of vertices in the constructed graphs equals the number of agents in our problem. Following Babai and Luks [4], we obtain an algorithm with the desired running time. □

**Global stability.** There exists a fairly straightforward polynomial-time algorithm for checking $\alpha$-layer global stability.

Proposition 6.10 (★). *If the preferences of the agents are uniform in all $\ell$ layers, then* Globally Stable Marriage *can be solved in $O(\ell \cdot n)$ time, where $n$ denotes the number of agents.*

## 7 OPEN PROBLEMS AND CONCLUSIONS

While our work provides a rich and almost complete structure for analyzing the computational properties of deciding our proposed stability concepts for multi-layer preferences, it directly leads to the following open questions: (1) How hard is it to find an $\alpha$-layer individually stable matching for $\lceil 2\ell/3 \rceil < \alpha < \ell$? (2) When the preferences of the agents are uniform in each layer and $\alpha \geq \ell/2 + 1$, we showed that the decision variant of Individually Stable Marriage is solvable in quasi-polynomial time $n^{O(\log n)} + O(\ell \cdot n^2)$ which implies that the problem is in the complexity class LOGSNP [47]. It would be interesting to know whether it is also complete for LOGSNP.[1] However, LOGSNP-hardness for our problem would also imply LOGSNP-hardness for GRAPH ISOMORPHISM (see Theorem 6.8). (3) When the preferences of the agents are uniform in each layer, how hard is it to search for an $\alpha$-layer pair stable matching for arbitrary $\alpha > 1$ or an $\alpha$-layer individually stable matching when $\alpha < \ell/2$, or in general when the number of layers is constant.

We also believe that a number of other parameters and special cases can be motivated naturally in the context of our model, in particular parameters quantifying the degree to which the preferences of the agents differ. Analogous parameterizations have been studied in computational social choice, for instance for the NP-hard KEMENY SCORE problem [6, 7]. Continuing our research on special cases of input preferences (Section 6), it might be interesting to study STABLE MARRIAGE with multi-layer *structured* preferences, such as *single-peaked* [10], *single-crossing* [44, 48], and *1-Euclidean* [17, 18, 36] preferences. We note that it can be detected in polynomial time whether a preference profile has any of these structure [5, 14, 20, 22, 24, 36] and we refer the reader to Bredereck et al. [15] and Elkind et al. [23] for an overview of the literature on single-peakedness and single-crossingness. We also note that Bartholdi III and Trick [5] worked on stable roommates for narcissistic and single-peaked preferences, while Bredereck et al. [12] extended this line by also studying other structured preferences and including preferences with ties and incompleteness.

Finally, our multi-modal view on the bipartite variant (STABLE MARRIAGE) can be generalized to the non-bipartite variant (STABLE ROOMMATES), the case with incomplete preferences with ties, and the case where each side may have a different number of layers. It would be interesting to see whether our computational tractability results transfer to these cases.

## REFERENCES


[1] A. Abdulkadiroğlu, P.A. Pathak, and A.E. Roth. 2005. The Boston public school match. *Amer. Econ. Rev.* 95, 2 (2005), 368–âĂŞ371.

[2] H. Aziz, P. Biró, T. Fleiner, S. Gaspers, R. de Haan, N. Mattei, and B. Rastegari. 2017. Stable Matching with Uncertain Pairwise Preferences. In *Proceedings of AAMAS-17*. 344–352.

[3] H. Aziz, P. Biró, S. Gaspers, R. de Haan, N. Mattei, and B. Rastegari. 2016. Stable Matching with Uncertain Linear Preferences. In *Proceedings of SAGT-16*. 195–206.

[4] L. Babai and E. Luks. 1983. Canonical Labeling of Graphs. In *Proceedings of STOC-83*. 171–183.

[5] J.J. Bartholdi III and M. Trick. 1986. Stable Matching with Preferences Derived from a Psychological Model. *Oper. Res. Lett.* 5, 4 (1986), 165–169.

[6] N. Betzler, R. Bredereck, and R. Niedermeier. 2014. Theoretical and empirical evaluation of data reduction for exact Kemeny Rank Aggregation. *Autonomous Agents and Multi-Agent Systems* 28, 5 (2014), 721–748.

[7] N. Betzler, J. Guo, C. Komusiewicz, and R. Niedermeier. 2011. Average parameterization and partial kernelization for computing medians. *J. Comput. System Sci.* 77, 4 (2011), 774–789.

[8] P. Biró. 2017. Applications of Matching under Preferences. In *Trends in Computational Social Choice*. 345–373.

[9] P. Biró and S. Kiselgof. 2015. College admissions with stable score-limits. *Cent. Eur. J. Oper. Res.* 23, 4 (2015), 727–741.

[10] D. Black. 1958. *The Theory of Committees and Elections.* Cambridge University Press.

[11] R. Bredereck, J. Chen, P. Faliszewski, J. Guo, R. Niedermeier, and G.J. Woeginger. 2014. Parameterized Algorithmics for Computational Social Choice: Nine Research Challenges. *Tsinghua Science and Technology* 19, 4 (2014), 358–373.

[12] R. Bredereck, J. Chen, U.P. Finnendahl, and R. Niedermeier. 2017. Stable Roommate with Narcissistic, Single-Peaked, and Single-Crossing Preferences. In *Proceedings of ADT-17*. 315–330.

[13] R. Bredereck, J. Chen, S. Hartung, S. Kratsch, R. Niedermeier, O. Suchý, and G.J. Woeginger. 2014. A Multivariate Complexity Analysis of Lobbying in Multiple Referenda. *JAIR* 50 (2014), 409–446.

[14] R. Bredereck, J. Chen, and G.J. Woeginger. 2013. A Characterization of the Single-Crossing Domain. *Soc. Choice Welf.* 41, 4 (2013), 989–998.

[15] R. Bredereck, J. Chen, and G.J. Woeginger. 2016. Are There Any Nicely Structured Preference Profiles Nearby? *Math. Soc. Sci.* 79 (2016), 61–73.


[1] LOGSNP-hardness has been encountered and discussed for natural problems in Computational Social Choice [11, 13].

[16] J. Chen, R. Niedermeier, and P. Skowron. 2018. *Stable Marriage with Multi-Modal Preferences.* Technical Report. arXiv:1801.02693 [cs.MA,cs.DS].

[17] J. Chen, K. Pruhs, and G.J. Woeginger. 2017. The One-Dimensional Euclidean Domain: Finitely Many Obstructions Are Not Enough. *Soc. Choice Welf.* 48, 2 (2017), 409–432.

[18] C.H. Coombs. 1964. *A Theory of Data.* John Wiley and Sons.

[19] M. Cygan, F.V. Fomin, L. Kowalik, D. Lokshtanov, D. Marx, M. Pilipczuk, M. Pilipczuk, and S. Saurabh. 2015. *Parameterized Algorithms.* Springer.

[20] JP. Doignon and JC. Falmagne. 1994. A Polynomial Time Algorithm for Unidimensional Unfolding Representations. *J. Algorithms* 16, 2 (1994), 218–233.

[21] R.G. Downey and M.R. Fellows. 2013. *Fundamentals of Parameterized Complexity.* Springer.

[22] E. Elkind, P. Faliszewski, and A. Slinko. 2012. Clone Structures in Voters' Preferences. In *Proceedings of EC-12.* 496–513.

[23] E. Elkind, M. Lackner, and D. Peters. 2017. Structured Preferences. In *Trends in Computational Social Choice.* 187–207.

[24] B. Escoffier, J. Lang, and M. Öztürk. 2008. Single-Peaked Consistency and its Complexity. In *Proceedings of ECAI-08.* 366–370.

[25] L. Farczadi, K. Georgiou, and J. Könemann. 2016. Stable Marriage with General Preferences. *Theory Comput. Syst.* 59, 4 (2016), 683–699.

[26] J. Flum and M. Grohe. 2006. *Parameterized Complexity Theory.* Springer.

[27] D. Gale and L. S. Shapley. 1962. College Admissions and the Stability of Marriage. *The American Mathematical Monthly* 120, 5 (1962), 386–391.

[28] M.R. Garey and D.S. Johnson. 1979. *Computers and Intractability—A Guide to the Theory of NP-Completeness.* W. H. Freeman and Company.

[29] D. Gusfield and R.W. Irving. 1989. *The Stable Marriage Problem–Structure and Algorithms.* MIT Press.

[30] R.W. Irving. 1994. Stable marriage and indifference. *Discrete Applied Mathematics* 48, 3 (1994), 261–272.

[31] R.W. Irving. 2016. Optimal Stable Marriage. In *Encyclopedia of Algorithms,* Ming-Yang Kao (Ed.). 1470–1473.

[32] R.W. Irving. 2016. Stable Marriage. In *Encyclopedia of Algorithms,* Ming-Yang Kao (Ed.). 2060–2064.

[33] K. Iwama, D. Manlove, S. Miyazaki, and Y. Morita. 1999. Stable Marriage with Incomplete Lists and Ties. In *Proceedings of ICALP-99.* 443–452.

[34] K. Iwama and S. Miyazaki. 2008. A Survey of the Stable Marriage Problem and Its Variants. In *International Conference on Informatics Education and Research for Knowledge-Circulating Society.* 131–136.

[35] B. Klaus, D.F. Manlove, and F. Rossi. 2016. Matching under Preferences. In *Handbook of Computational Social Choice.*

[36] V. Knoblauch. 2010. Recognizing one-dimensional Euclidean preference profiles. *J. Math. Econ.* 46, 1 (2010), 1–5.

[37] D. Knuth. 1976. *Mariages Stables.* Les Presses de L'Université de Montréal.

[38] B.M. Maggs and R.K. Sitaraman. 2015. Algorithmic Nuggets in Content Delivery. *SIGCOMM Computer Communication Review* 45, 3 (2015), 52–66.

[39] D.F. Manlove. 2013. *Algorithmics of Matching Under Preferences.* Vol. 2. WorldScientific.

[40] D. Manlove. 2016. Hospitals/Residents Problem. In *Encyclopedia of Algorithms,* Ming-Yang Kao (Ed.).

[41] D. Manlove, R.W. Irving, K. Iwama, S. Miyazaki, and Y. Morita. 2002. Hard variants of stable marriage. *Theor. Comput. Sci.* 276, 1-2 (2002), 261–279.

[42] D.F. Manlove and G. O'Malley. 2014. Paired and Altruistic Kidney Donation in the UK: Algorithms and Experimentation. *ACM Journal of Experimental Algorithmics* 19, 1 (2014), 2.6:1–2.6:21.

[43] D.C. McGarvey. 1953. A Theorem on the Construction of Voting Paradoxes. *Econometrica* 21, 4 (1953), 608–610.

[44] J.A. Mirrlees. 1971. An Exploration in the Theory of Optimal Income Taxation. *Rev. Econ. Studies* 38 (1971), 175–208.

[45] S. Miyazaki and K. Okamoto. 2017. Jointly Stable Matchings. In *Proc. ISAAC-17.* 56:1–56:12.

[46] R. Niedermeier. 2006. *Invitation to Fixed-Parameter Algorithms.* Oxford University Press.

[47] C.H. Papadimitriou and M. Yannakakis. 1996. On Limited Nondeterminism and the Complexity of the V-C Dimension. *J. Comput. System Sci.* 53, 2 (1996), 161–170.

[48] K.W.S. Roberts. 1977. Voting over income tax schedules. *J. Public Econ.* 8, 3 (1977), 329–340.

[49] A.E. Roth, T. Sönmez, and M. Utku Ünver. 2007. Efficient Kidney Exchange: Coincidence of Wants in Markets with Compatibility-Based Preferences. *Amer. Econ. Rev.* 97, 3 (2007), 828–851.

[50] A.E. Roth and M.A.O. Sotomayor. 1992. *Two-Sided Matching: A Study in Game-Theoretic Modeling and Analysis.* Part of Econometric Society Monographs.

[51] P. Schweitzer. 2017. A Polynomial-Time Randomized Reduction from Tournament Isomorphism to Tournament Asymmetry. In *Proceedings of ICALP-17.* 66:1–66:14.

[52] F. Wagner. 2007. Hardness Results for Tournament Isomorphism and Automorphism. In *Proceedings of MFCS-07.* 572–583.

[53] B.P. Weems. 1999. Bistable Versions of the Marriages and Roommates Problems. *J. Comput. System Sci.* 59, 3 (1999), 504–520.

# Delegated Search Approximates Efficient Search

JON KLEINBERG, Cornell University, USA
ROBERT KLEINBERG, Cornell University, USA

There are many settings in which a principal performs a task by *delegating* it to an agent, who searches over possible solutions and proposes one to the principal. This describes many aspects of the workflow within organizations, as well as many of the activities undertaken by regulatory bodies, who often obtain relevant information from the parties being regulated through a process of delegation. A fundamental tension underlying delegation is the fact that the agent's interests will typically differ – potentially significantly – from the interests of the principal, and as a result the agent may propose solutions based on their own incentives that are inefficient for the principal. A basic problem, therefore, is to design mechanisms by which the principal can constrain the set of proposals they are willing to accept from the agent, to ensure a certain level of quality for the principal from the proposed solution.

In this work, we investigate how much the principal loses – quantitatively, in terms of the objective they are trying to optimize – when they delegate to an agent. We develop a methodology for bounding this loss of efficiency, and show that in a very general model of delegation, there is a family of mechanisms achieving a universal bound on the ratio between the quality of the solution obtained through delegation and the quality the principal could obtain in an idealized benchmark where they searched for a solution themself. Moreover, it is possible to achieve such bounds through mechanisms with a natural threshold structure, which are thus structurally simpler than the optimal mechanisms typically considered in the literature on delegation. At the heart of our framework is an unexpected connection between delegation and the analysis of *prophet inequalities*, which we leverage to provide bounds on the behavior of our delegation mechanisms.

CCS Concepts: • **Theory of computation → Design and analysis of algorithms**; • **Applied computing → Economics**;

Additional Key Words and Phrases: Delegated search, prophet inequalities.

## 1 INTRODUCTION

There are many settings in which a decision-maker is faced with a difficult problem that they cannot solve on their own, and so they instead approach it in two steps: they first *delegate* the search for possible solutions to an *agent* who is able to invest more time in the process, and then they evaluate the solution(s) that the agent proposes. One concrete example arises in organizations or firms, where the management may delegate the search for solutions to a division that reports to them, ultimately making a decision on the solution that is proposed by the division [2, 6, 18]. A second example arises in regulation, where a governmental agency needs to decide whether there is a way to structure a proposed corporate merger in a way that is compatible with regulatory guidelines; the companies seeking to merge study possible ways of structuring the merger, propose one or more to the regulator, and seek the regulator's approval. In this way, the search over structures for the merger has implicitly been delegated from the regulator to the companies, with the regulator

Authors' addresses: Jon Kleinberg, Cornell University, Ithaca, NY, 14853, USA; Robert Kleinberg, Cornell University, Ithaca, NY, 14853, USA.


*ACM EC'18, June 18–22, 2018, Ithaca, NY, USA.* ACM ISBN 978-1-4503-5829-3/18/06...$15.00
https://doi.org/10.1145/3219166.3219205

retaining decision-making control over the the proposed solution [11, 20]. A similar scenario could be described for regulation in other settings, where a company may be searching over possible solutions that comply with environmental law, employment law, or other guidelines.

The interesting tension in all these situations is that the decision-maker who delegates the task (henceforth referred to as the "principal") has a particular objective function that they are seeking to optimize; but the agent who actually performs the task might have interests that are not directly aligned with the principal's. For example, in the regulatory context, the regulator (acting as principal) may reasonably suspect that a merger proposed by a set of companies (acting as the agent) will be structured in a way that strongly benefits the companies, even if other feasible structures would have been better for the market or for society as a whole. Similarly, a group within an organization tasked with solving a problem may well preferentially search for a solution that benefits them in particular. Given this natural set of incentives, how should the principal structure the delegation to the agent so as to ensure that the solution the agent proposes performs well under the principal's own objective function?

A rich literature has developed in economics around the formalization and analysis of delegation, focusing on this tension between the conflicting objectives of the principal and the agent; see Holmstrom [13, 14] for influential early research, and [3–6] for recent work. A dominant theme in this line of work is that the principal does not offer monetary compensation to the agent as a way of favoring certain proposed solutions over others (though see Krishna and Morgan [17]); this is consistent with the motivating applications, in which for example regulators in many contexts can accept or reject proposals from companies, but cannot selectively offer varying amounts of compensation to these companies based on the content of the proposal. This lack of monetary transfers between the parties imparts a fundamental structure to the problem, in which the principal can simply define a mechanism implicitly specifying the subset of all "eligible" proposals that they are willing to accept, and the agent is then incentivized to search for solutions that are good for them but that also lie in this eligible set. A long line of work has gone into determining the structure of eligible sets that produce optimal mechanisms for the principal, yielding constructions that are often quite intricate [3, 6, 19].

**The Present Work.** Given how broadly delegation is used across a range of contexts, it is interesting to consider how precarious a process it is — the principal is ceding control of their search problem to an agent whose interests might be completely misaligned with their own, and the only leverage the principal has is to accept or reject the solution that is eventually proposed. How much does the principal give up — quantitatively, measured in terms of the objective they are trying to optimize — when they delegate to an agent? Is there some robust, intrinsic reason why things don't turn out as badly as we might fear? And how do the answers to these questions depend on what the principal is actually able to observe about the agent's solution — including how much effort the agent put into finding the solution, and how good it is not just for the principal but also for the agent?

In their most natural formulation, these are inherently comparative questions, since they seek to relate the solution quality obtained through delegation to the solution quality in an alternate, ideal setting where delegation was not necessary. As such, they address an issue fundamentally distinct from the primary focus of the existing literature on delegation, which as noted above has centered on characterizing mechanisms that produce optimal delegation for the principal, without this type of comparative evaluation.

There is a natural benchmark to use for our comparison: we could measure the quality of the outcome under delegation versus the quality of the solution that the principal could obtain were they to perform the search task themself, investing the same level of effort in the search that the agent does. Now, there are many settings where it may be too costly or otherwise infeasible for the principal to actually conduct this search, but this benchmark nonetheless provides a conceptual reference point to make clear how much payoff to the principal is lost through delegation. In this sense, it plays the role of an optimal point of comparison, much like the role of the intractable optimum in an approximation algorithm or the societal optimum in a price-of-anarchy analysis.

In this paper we develop a methodology to bound the performance of delegated search, relative to the benchmark in which the principal searches for a solution on their own. Our methodology builds on a set of links that we identify between bounds on delegated search and the analysis of some fundamental models of decision-making under uncertainty — in particular, a surprisingly strong connection between delegated search and bounds on *prophet inequalities*. The connections between these formalisms turn out be quite natural and useful, but to our knowledge they have not been previously identified in either of the literatures on delegated search or on prophet inequalities. This connection not only provides bounds on the quality of delegated solutions relative to an ideal benchmark; it also shows that strong bounds can be obtained using eligible sets that are structurally very simple — in a number of cases defined simply by a carefully chosen threshold rule — and hence in contrast with the complex constructions associated with optimal mechanisms.

### Overview of Models

**A Distributional Model.** We begin by describing the models in which we perform our analysis. Our main model, which is essentially the one considered in Armstrong and Vickers [6], has the principal and the agent agree that the agent will consider $n$ candidate solutions and propose one to the principal; $n$ thus represents the level of effort that the agent commits to the problem. The principal will only see the solution that is proposed, not the other $n-1$ that the agent also considers.

What does it means for the agent to consider a candidate solution? We assume that the solutions belong to an abstract space $\Omega$ with a probability measure on it, and the agent's search for a solution consists of performing $n$ independent and identically distributed draws from $\Omega$, resulting in a set of candidate solutions $\omega_1, \omega_2, \ldots, \omega_n \in \Omega$.[1] Each solution $\omega_i$ drawn by the agent has a quality for the principal, denoted $x(\omega_i)$, and a possibly different quality for the agent, denoted $y(\omega_i)$. The agent selects one of its candidate solutions, say $\omega_i$, to present to the principal. (Below, we will discuss the contrast between the model in which the principal is able to determine both $x(\omega_i)$ and $y(\omega_i)$ — the value to both the agent and themself — for the proposed solution, and the model in which the principal is only able to determine $x(\omega_i)$.)

Now, if the principal imposed no constraint on the agent's behavior, then the agent would simply choose the solution $\omega_i$ that maximizes $y(\omega_i)$, and the principal would receive whatever corresponding $x(\omega_i)$ value resulted from this choice. To improve on this, the principal could specify at the outset that they will only accept $\omega$ values that satisfy some predicate on $x(\omega_i)$ and (in the case that they can determine it) $y(\omega_i)$; we will refer to the set of all $\omega$ satisfying the principal's predicate as the *eligible set* of solutions. It is thus in the agent's interest to propose a solution belonging to the eligible set; we ask whether one can design eligible sets that provide provable bounds on the expected quality of the solution to the principal, relative to the scenario in which the principal simply were to draw $n$ times from $\Omega$ and select the sampled solution $\omega$ with maximum $x(\omega)$.

**A Binary Model.** In our first, distributional model, the agent draws a set of candidate solutions $\omega_1, \ldots, \omega_n$ that the principal cannot observe, and then must choose one to present to the principal. This models a setting in which the agent explores a design space and cannot fully anticipate which

[1]Later we will also consider the case in which different draws by the agent can come from different probability measures on $\Omega$; for example, this can model the case in which the agent is a group of $n$ employees in an organization, and the $i^{\text{th}}$ solution is drawn by the $i^{\text{th}}$ agent, who may have a different distribution over solutions from the $j^{\text{th}}$ agent.

$\omega_i$ it will encounter until it begins this exploration. But we can also imagine settings where the principal and agent both know that the set of potential options comes from a large discrete set $\omega_1, \omega_2, \ldots, \omega_m$, and the only question is which of these options is actually feasible to implement. For example, there may be $m$ standard ways of structuring a merger in a given industry, and the only question is which are possible for the companies in question.

We model this version with publicly known binary options as follows. There is a set of options $\omega_1, \omega_2, \ldots, \omega_m$, and for each $i$, there is a known probability $p_i > 0$ such that option $\omega_i$ is *feasible* with probability $p_i$, and *infeasible* otherwise. If option $\omega_i$ turns out to be feasible, then it produces a known payoff of $x(\omega_i)$ for the principal and a known payoff $y(\omega_i)$ for the agent; if it turns out to be infeasible, then it produces a payoff of 0 for both. The only way to evaluate the feasibility of option $\omega_i$ is to pay a cost of $c_i$ to investigate it.

The principal delegates to the agent the task of proposing a feasible option, which the principal can either accept or reject. The principal will not be able to see which options the agent decides to pay to evaluate as part of this task, but again the principal can specify a predicate defining the eligible subset of $\omega_i$ that they will accept. Subject to this constraint, the agent then must decide how to evaluate options in a way that maximizes its own benefit $y(\omega_i)$ from the option $\omega_i$ it proposes, minus the evaluation cost. Here too we evaluate the principal's payoff relative to the scenario in which they performed the evaluation of options themself. We also consider an extension of this model in which there is a budget of $n < m$ on the number of options that the agent can evaluate — a constraint analogous to the bound on the number of samples the agent can evaluate in our first distributional model.

## Overview of Results

We begin by showing that for an arbitrary instance of the distributional model, there is a mechanism the principal can specify to the agent so that the principal's expected payoff from delegation is within a factor of 2 of the expected payoff they'd receive were they able to search for the solution by themself. (If the principal were to search by themself, they would examine $n$ candidate solutions and choose the one that was best for them.) This mechanism only requires knowledge of the principal's $x(\omega_i)$ values, not the agent's $y(\omega_i)$ values, and it has a very simple structure: depending on the distribution of values, it can be written as a threshold rule with either a weak threshold, in which the principal only accepts proposals $\omega$ for which $x(\omega) \geq \theta$ for some $\theta$, or a strict threshold, in which the principal only accepts proposals $\omega$ for which $x(\omega) > \theta$ for some $\theta$. In the case when $x(\omega)$ and $y(\omega)$ are distributed independently with no point masses, the factor of 2 in this bound can be improved to $e/(e-1)$.

There are several things worth remarking on about this result. First, the fact that arbitrary instances of the problem have mechanisms providing provable guarantees of this form suggests a qualitative argument for the robustness of delegation: no matter how misaligned the agent's interests are, the principal can ensure an absolute bound on how much is lost in the quality of the solution. Second, the mechanism that achieves this bound is very simple and detail-free, consisting of just a (weak or strict) threshold on the quality of the solution for the principal. And third, the mechanism requires knowledge of $n$ (the number of samples drawn by the agents) but not the values $y(\omega)$. In this sense, it suggests that it is more important for the principal to know how much effort the agent has spent on the search (via $n$) than to know how good the proposed solution is for the agent (via $y(\omega)$).

**A connection to prophet inequalities.** These results on threshold mechanisms and their guarantees follow from a general result at the heart of our analysis — a close connection between bounds for delegated search and *prophet inequalities*. Prophet inequalities are guarantees for the following type of decision under uncertainty: we see a sequence of values $s_1, s_2, \ldots, s_n$ in order, with $s_i$ drawn from a distribution $S_i$, and when we see the value $s_i$ we must irrevocably decide whether to stop and accept $s_i$, or continue (in the hope of finding a better value in the future). Research on prophet inequalities has established the non-trivial fact that it is possible to design rules whose expected payoff comes within a constant fraction of the maximum achievable by a decision-maker who could see all the realized values $s_1, s_2, \ldots, s_n$ in advance.

Prophet inequalities tend to be established by designing carefully constructed *threshold rules*, in which the decision-maker accepts $s_i$ if and only if $s_i$ (weakly or strictly) exceeds a specified threshold $\theta_i$ that can depend on the position $i$. The key component of our analysis is to establish a close, though subtle, technical connection between delegated search and prophet inequalities: roughly speaking, the sequence of values $x(\omega_1), x(\omega_2), \ldots, x(\omega_n)$ sampled by the agent from the set of possible solutions $\Omega$ plays the role of the process generating $s_1, s_2, \ldots, s_n$; and the principal and the agent jointly — through the principal's specification of the threshold and the agent's incentive to obey it — play the role of the decision-maker who uses a threshold rule for deciding when to stop. Again, the notion of "stopping" here is a bit oblique, since the principal never sees the full sequence $x(\omega_1), x(\omega_2), \ldots, x(\omega_n)$ that the agent generates; this is the sense in which the stopping rule is jointly constructed by the behavior of the principal and the agent together.

**Stronger bounds for independent values.** Using this connection to threshold rules for prophet inequalities, we can design a much more powerful policy for the principal in the case when the values of $x(\omega)$ and $y(\omega)$ on a draw $\omega$ from $\Omega$ are distributed independently, and when the principal can see both $x(\omega_i)$ and $y(\omega_i)$ (rather than only $x(\omega_i)$) in the solution $\omega_i$ proposed by the agent.

To do this, we begin with a stopping rule from the prophet inequality literature achieving an expected payoff that is at least 0.745 times the optimum when the distributions of the $s_i$ values are independent and identically distributed [1, 9, 12, 15]. This stopping rule uses a sequence of thresholds $\theta_i$ that decrease with $i$, making the decision-maker naturally more prone to stop and accept a value as the end of the sequence nears — effectively following the idea that one should only accept a value early if it's very good.

In the context of delegated search when the principal can observe both $x(\omega_i)$ and $y(\omega_i)$ for a proposed solution $\omega_i$, a related concept is useful for designing mechanisms: the principal should only accept a solution $\omega_i$ with $y(\omega_i)$ very large if $x(\omega_i)$ is very large as well. The analogy between requiring strong incentive to accept a value with large $y(\omega_i)$ in delegated search and requiring strong incentive to accept a value early in the sequence in the prophet inequality context can be made precise, and it reveals that the $y(\omega_i)$ values (over the set of candidate solutions considered by the agent) can be used as a kind of "continuous time" parameter for deriving a threshold: if we think of the candidate solution $\omega_i$ as arriving at continuous time $y(\omega_i)$, then we can derive a threshold function $\theta(\cdot)$ in which the principal only accepts $\omega_i$ if $x(\omega_i)$ (weakly or strictly) exceeds $\theta(y(\omega_i))$.[2] In this sense, the principal and agent again jointly construct the stopping rule, with the agent's payoff providing a type of synthetic temporal ordering that is useful in formulating a threshold policy.

**Bounds for the binary model.** We also use the connection to prophet inequalities to derive bounds for the binary model, where the agent pays to evaluate the feasibility of pairs from a known list of options $\omega_1, \omega_2, \ldots, \omega_m$. Here too the principal can designate a predefined eligible set of proposals so that the mechanism that accepts any eligible proposed $\omega_i$ yields an expected payoff that is within a factor of two of the benchmark in which the principal performs the search on their

[2]We observe that this continuous time defined by the $y(\omega_i)$ runs "in reverse," in the sense that large values of $y(\omega_i)$, like small values of time, place stricter demands on the $x(\omega_i)$ values that can be accepted.

own. However, the eligibility criterion in this case is subtler: it depends not only on the principal's assessment of the proposal's quality, $x(\omega_i)$, but also on the cost $c_i$ and the *a priori* probability of feasibility, $p_i$.

To establish this bound, we draw on both prophet inequality bounds and on work of Kleinberg et al for the *box problem* [16, 22]; by considering an ordering of the options by the notion of *reservation price* (or, equivalently, *strike price*) defined in those works, we can establish a provable guarantee that correctly handles not only the payoff arising from the $x(\omega_i)$ and $y(\omega_i)$ values but also the cost incurred by the agent in evaluating the feasibility of options.

Finally, we derive similar bounds in the more general case where the agent also has a budget of $n < m$ on the number of options they can evaluate. The approach using reservation prices does not directly extend to this case, but we show that by combining the approach of Kleinberg et al. [16] with bounds for stochastic optimization due to Asadpour and Nazerzadeh [7], we can obtain more general bounds for a budgeted variant of the box problem that contains the case we need for our delegated search guarantee.

We note that it would be a natural open question to consider a variant of the problem combining characteristics of the two main versions we consider here: as in the distributional model, the agent performs independent draws from a space $\Omega$; but as in the binary model, the agent does not have a fixed bound $n$ on the number of allowed draws, instead incurring a cost to perform each draw that must be traded off against the eventual payoff from the sample selected.

### Further Discussion of Related Work on Delegation

The theory of delegation in the economics literature is often viewed as beginning with Bengt Holmstrom's Ph.D. thesis [13, 14]; this work articulates the basic tension that we see in these models, between allowing an agent to optimize in a large space and restricting the agent's freedom of action to prevent them from pursuing their own objectives too aggressively. Holmstrom's model considered delegating an optimization problem over an interval, and a sequence of subsequent papers analyzed the case in which the agent optimizes over a continuum [3, 19]. Armstrong and Vickers [6] propose a model that is very close to what we consider here, where the optimization takes place over a discrete set that the agent samples from an underlying distribution. By way of comparison between our work and that of Armstrong and Vickers [6], we noted the key contrast earlier in this section: their paper is largely devoted to identifying cases of the delegated search problem for which the structure of the optimal mechanism can be identified, whereas we focus on bounding the inefficiency of delegated search relative to a benchmark in which the principal performs the task themself. It is through our emphasis on these types of bounds that we develop the connection to the analysis of prophet inequalities.

A distinct line of work in delegation relaxes the constraint that the principal may only allow or forbid each proposed solution, and instead allows the principal to add arbitrary amounts of cost to certain subsets of proposed solutions [4, 5, 8]. One of the key motivations for such a condition is to model the strategic role of bureaucracy within an organization: if management wants to dissuade units within the organization from proposing certain types of solutions, they can use bureaucratic measures (requiring more extensive justifications and processes) that make these solutions selectively more costly without explicitly forbidding them, and without engaging in explicit monetary transfers. Ambrus and Egorov [5] propose a model in which such selective cost increases are in fact part of the optimal delegation scheme.

## 2 MODEL AND PRELIMINARIES

We begin by making the precise the way in which the principal and the agent interact, resulting in the principal's selection of (at most) one element from a set $\Omega$ of potential solutions. There are functions $x : \Omega \to \mathbb{R}$ and $y : \Omega \to \mathbb{R}$ such that if $\omega \in \Omega$ is selected, then the principal's utility is $x(\omega)$ and the agent's utility is $y(\omega)$. To formalize the possibility that the principal selects no solution (i.e., perpetuating the status quo) we identify this possiblity with a special "null outcome", denoted $\perp$, and we extend the utility functions from $\Omega$ to $\Omega_+ \triangleq \Omega \cup \{\perp\}$ by setting $x(\perp) = y(\perp) = 0$.

The set $\Omega$ is a probability space, with probability measure $\mu$, and the agent has the power to draw independent samples from $\Omega$ according to $\mu$. The principal, on the other hand, can neither draw samples from $\Omega$ nor directly observe the outcome of the agent's sampling; she must rely on her interaction with the agent to arrive at a selected element of $\Omega$.[3]

Before formalizing our model of interaction, it is useful to first note some of the ways in which our basic model can be generalized or specialized.

- We will initially consider the case of a single probability measure $\mu$ on $\Omega$, but it is also useful to consider cases in which there are multiple probability measures $\mu_1, \mu_2, \ldots, \mu_m$ on $\Omega$, and the agent has the power to draw independent samples from any of these distributions.
- We will generally assume there is a *sampling budget* of $n$ on the number of samples that the agent can draw. In some of our models, we will also introduce a *sampling cost* $c \geq 0$ for each draw by the agent — or in the case of multiple probability measures, a cost $c_i \geq 0$ for sampling from $\mu_i$.
- We consider both the *full-information case* — in which the principal knows both the functions $x : \Omega \to \mathbb{R}$ and $y : \Omega \to \mathbb{R}$, and hence can evaluate the utility of a solution $\omega$ to both herself and to the agent — and the *limited-information case*, in which the principal only knows her own utility function $x$.
- The functions $x : \Omega \to \mathbb{R}$ and $y : \Omega \to \mathbb{R}$ define random variables on $\Omega$, and we consider both the case in which they can be arbitrary non-negative functions, and the case of *independent utilities*, when they are independent random variables.

In a later section, we will specialize the formalism to the *binary model* discussed in Section 1, in which each distribution $\mu_i$ is supported on a two-element set $\{\omega_{0i}, \omega_{1i}\}$ such that $(x(\omega_{0i}), y(\omega_{0i})) = (0, 0)$. In this case we will let $(x_i, y_i)$ denote the pair $(x(\omega_{1i}), y(\omega_{1i}))$. The binary model captures a setting in which the feasibility of the $i^{\text{th}}$ solution is unknown until the agent investigates it, but the value of the solution to both parties (if feasible) is known *a priori*.

## 2.1 A General Definition of Mechanisms for the Principal and Agent

Let us now formalize how the principal and the agent interact, resulting in the principal's selection of a solution. Thus far, our discussion in Section 1 has focused on interactions of a very structured form: the agent draws a set of samples from $\Omega$; the agent selects one of these samples to present to the principal; and the principal accepts or rejects it. But it would be useful to be able to consider more general formulations for their allowed interactions, within which the transmission of a single proposal from the agent to the principal is a particular special case.

To do this, we begin by defining a *mechanism* as follows. A mechanism $M = (\Sigma, g)$ defines a set of signals, $\Sigma$, that the agent may send, and an allocation function $g : \Sigma \to \Omega_+$ that specifies which solution the principal will choose given the agent's signal. In such a mechanism, a *strategy* for the agent is specified by a mapping $\sigma : \Omega^* \to \Sigma$, where $\Omega^*$ denotes the set of finite sequences over $\Omega$, such that $\sigma(\omega_1, \ldots, \omega_n)$ represents the signal the agent sends if he sampled $n$ solutions and observed the sequence $\omega_1, \ldots, \omega_n$.

Suppose the agent observes sequence $\omega_1, \ldots, \omega_n$ and sends signal $\sigma$, resulting in outcome $\omega = g(\sigma)$. In this case, the principal's and agent's utilities are $x(\omega)$ and $y(\omega)$, respectively, if

[3]Throughout this paper we use feminine pronouns for the principal and masculine pronouns for the agents.

$\omega \in \{\omega_1, \ldots, \omega_n\} \cup \{\perp\}$. Otherwise the principal's utility is 0 and the agent's is $-1$. In other words, we assume that if the mechanism results in the principal selecting a solution that was never sampled by the agent, that solution cannot be adopted. Instead the status quo is preserved and the agent suffers a penalty. This assumption is consistent with our assumption that the principal lacks the power to directly search for solutions herself; she can only adopt solutions that the agent has discovered.

In models with costly sampling, the specification of an agent's strategy must also include a sequential policy $\pi$ for deciding which sample (if any) to observe next, given the set of samples already observed. The principal's and agent's utilities are both diminished by the sum of costs $c_i$ for the samples $i$ that the agent observed when running policy $\pi$. (We deduct this sum from the principal's utility because we think of the cost incurred by the agent in searching for a solution as a kind of "waste" that the principal views as detracting from the overall utility.)

Under our definition of mechanisms, the sequence of solutions sampled by the agent leads to a signal (via the agent's strategy $\sigma$), and this signal leads to a solution in $\Omega_+$ (via the principal's allocation function $g$). Composing these two functions, we get a mapping from the agent's sampled solutions to a single solution:

*Definition 2.1 (interim allocation function).* If $M$ is a mechanism and $\sigma$ is an agent's strategy, the interim allocation function of the pair $(M, \sigma)$ is the mapping $f_{M,\sigma} : \Omega^* \to \Omega_+$ obtained by composing the strategy $\sigma$ with the allocation function $g$. In other words, $f_{M,\sigma}(\omega_1, \ldots, \omega_n)$ is the outcome resulting from mechanism $M$, when the agent draws sample sequence $(\omega_1, \ldots, \omega_n)$ and plays according to $\sigma$.

## 2.2 Single Proposal Mechanisms

We now show that there is a sense in which it is without loss of generality to focus on interactions in which the agent proposes a single solution from among the ones they sampled, and the principal either accepts or rejects it. To do this, we define a simple type of mechanism called a *single proposal mechanism*, and we show in Lemma 1 below that any other mechanism can be simulated by a single proposal mechanism.

**Definition 1.** A *single-proposal mechanism* with eligible set $R \subseteq \Omega$ is a mechanism in which the agent proposes one outcome, and the mechanism accepts this proposal if and only if it belongs to $R$. More formally, $M = (\Sigma, g)$ is a single-proposal mechanism with eligible set $R$ if $\Sigma = \Omega_+$ and $g$ restricts to the identity function on $R$ and the constant function $\omega \mapsto \perp$ on $\Omega_+ \setminus R$.

Lemma 1. *If $M$ is any mechanism and $\sigma$ is any strategy constituting a best response to $M$, then there exists a single proposal mechanism $M'$ and a best response $\sigma'$ to $M'$, such that the interim allocation functions $f_{M,\sigma}$ and $f_{M',\sigma'}$ are identical.*

Proof. Let $R$ be the range of the interim allocation function $f_{M,\sigma}$, i.e. the set of all possible outcomes of $M$, other than $\perp$, when the agent acts according to $\sigma$. Define $M'$ to be the single-proposal mechanism with eligible set $R$. Let $\sigma'$ be the strategy in which the agent observes his tuple of samples, $\boldsymbol{\omega} = (\omega_1, \ldots, \omega_n)$, and chooses strategy $\sigma'(\boldsymbol{\omega}) = g(\sigma(\boldsymbol{\omega}))$. By construction the interim allocation functions $f_{M,\sigma}$ and $f_{M',\sigma'}$ are identical. To prove that $\sigma'$ is a best response to $M'$, consider any $\boldsymbol{\omega} \in \Omega^n$ and any $v \neq \sigma'(\boldsymbol{\omega})$. Let $y_0 = y(g'(\sigma'(\boldsymbol{\omega})))$ denote the agent's utility when playing according to $\sigma'$; note that $y_0 \geq 0$. We wish to show that the agent cannot benefit by playing $v$ instead, i.e.

$$y(g'(v)) \leq y_0. \tag{1}$$

If $v \notin R$ then $g'(v) = \perp$ which implies (1) since $y_0 \geq 0$. If $v \in R$ then $v = g(\tilde{\sigma})$ for some $\tilde{\sigma} \in \Sigma$. Now (1) follows because strategy $\sigma$ is a best response for mechanism $M$, and $y(g'(v))$ denotes the agent's utility when playing strategy $\tilde{\sigma}$ in $M$ whereas $y_0$ denotes his utility when playing $\sigma$. □

## 3 ANALYZING DELEGATED SEARCH VIA PROPHET INEQUALITIES

In this section we develop a formal link between delegated search mechanisms and prophet inequalities. It turns out that the relevant prophet inequalities involve random variables arriving at discrete points in continuous time, rather than the usual assumption that they arrive at time points $1, 2, \ldots, n$. Accordingly, we will begin by explaining the formal model of continuous-time prophet inequalities in Section 3.1 below. Then in Section 3.2 we explain the reduction from delegated search (in the distributional model) to continuous-time prophet inequalities.

### 3.1 Continuous-time prophet inequalities

In this section we will be concerned with problems which involve designing a selection rule to choose (at most) one element from a random finite set of pairs $(x_i, t_i) \in \mathbb{R}_+ \times [0, 1]$, with the goal of maximizing the expected $x$-coordinate of the chosen element. The $t$-coordinate is thought of as a time coordinate, and we will generally (but not exclusively) be concerned with selection rules that make their choice without looking into the future, as is ordinarily the case in the analysis of prophet inequalities.

**Definition 2** (selection rules). A *selection rule* is a function $\rho$ from finite subsets of $\mathbb{R}_+ \times [0, 1]$ to the set $(\mathbb{R}_+ \times [0, 1]) \cup \{\perp\}$, with the property that $\rho(S) \in S \cup \{\perp\}$ for every $S$.

A *stopping rule* is a selection rule that chooses element $(x, t)$ from set $S$ without looking at the set of elements whose time coordinate is greater than $t$. Formally, $\rho$ is a stopping rule if it satisfies the following property: for any $(x, t) \in \mathbb{R}_+ \times [0, 1]$ and any two sets $S, S'$ such that $S \cap (\mathbb{R}_+ \times [0, t]) = S' \cap (\mathbb{R}_+ \times [0, t])$, we have

$$\rho(S) = (x, t) \iff \rho(S') = (x, t).$$

An *oblivious stopping rule* with eligible set $Q \subseteq \mathbb{R}_+ \times [0, 1]$ is a stopping rule $\rho_Q$ such that for every $S$, $\rho_Q(S)$ is an earliest element of $S \cap Q$ (i.e., an element of that set with minimum $t$ coordinate) or $\rho_Q(S) = \perp$ if $S \cap Q$ is empty.

A *threshold stopping rule* with threshold $\theta$ is an oblivious stopping rule whose eligible set is of the form $(\theta, \infty) \times [0, 1]$ or $[\theta, \infty) \times [0, 1]$.

**Definition 3** (CTSPs and prophet inequalities). A *continuous-time selection problem* (CTSP) is an ordered pair $(\mathscr{D}, R)$ where $\mathscr{D}$ is a set of probability distributions over finite subsets of $\mathbb{R}_+ \times [0, 1]$, and $\mathscr{R}$ is a set of selection rules.

A CTSP $(\mathscr{D}, R)$ satisfies a *prophet inequality with factor* $\alpha$ if it is the case that for every $\mathrm{D} \in \mathscr{D}$ there exists some $\rho \in \mathscr{R}$ such that

$$\mathbb{E}_{S \sim \mathrm{D}}[X_{\rho(S)}] \geq \alpha \cdot \mathbb{E}_{S \sim \mathrm{D}}[X_{*(S)}].$$

Here the random variable $X_{\rho(S)}$ is defined by specifying that if $\rho(S) = (x, t)$ then $X_{\rho(S)} = x$, and if $\rho(S) = \perp$ then $X_{\rho(S)} = 0$. The random variable $X_{*(S)}$ is defined to be $\max\{x \mid (x, t) \in S\}$.

We now present the prophet inequalities we will use in this work. To state them, we define the following families of stopping rules and distributions on subsets of $\mathbb{R}_+ \times [0, 1]$.

- $\mathscr{R}_{\text{obliv}}$ is the family of oblivious stopping rules.
- $\mathscr{R}_{\text{thresh}}$ is the family of threshold stopping rules.

- $\mathscr{D}_{\text{ind}}$ is the family of random sets whose elements are obtained by sampling independently from $n$ joint distributions. In other words, a distribution $\mathbf{D} \in \mathscr{D}_{\text{ind}}$ is specified by giving a positive number $n$, a tuple of joint distributions $\mathbf{D}_1, \ldots, \mathbf{D}_n$ on $\mathbb{R}_+ \times [0,1]$, and defining $\mathbf{D}$ to be the distribution on $n$-element sets obtained by drawing one sample independently from each of $\mathbf{D}_1, \ldots, \mathbf{D}_n$.
- $\mathscr{D}_{\text{iid},n}$ is the family of random sets whose $n$ elements are i.i.d. samples from an atomless distribution with $x$ and $t$ independent, i.e. a distribution on $\mathbb{R}_+ \times [0,1]$ which is a product of atomless distributions.
- $\mathscr{D}_{\text{iid}}$ is the union of $\mathscr{D}_{\text{iid},n}$ over all $n \geq 1$.

Our first prophet inequality is Samuel-Cahn's famous prophet inequality for threshold stopping rules [21].

Theorem 1. *(Samuel-Cahn [21]) There is a prophet inequality with factor $\frac{1}{2}$ for $(\mathscr{D}_{ind}, \mathscr{R}_{thresh})$.*

The second is an improved prophet inequality for threshold stopping rules when samples are drawn i.i.d. from atomless product distributions; it can be derived as a corollary of either [10, Theorem 19] or [9, Corollary 2.2].

Theorem 2. *(Correa et al. [9], Ehsani et al. [10]) There is a prophet inequality with factor $1 - \frac{1}{e}$ for $(\mathscr{D}_{iid}, \mathscr{R}_{thresh})$.*

Our third prophet inequality again pertains to the case when samples are drawn i.i.d. from atomless product distributions, but it allows for oblivious stopping rules rather than threshold stopping rules. The discrete-time counterpart to this prophet inequality can be found in [9, 12, 15].

Theorem 3. *Let $\alpha = 0.745\ldots$ be the solution to $\int_0^1 \left(y - y\ln y + 1 - \frac{1}{\alpha}\right)^{-1} dy = 1$. There is a prophet inequality with factor $\alpha - O\left(\frac{\log n}{n}\right)$ for $(\mathscr{D}_{iid,n}, \mathscr{R}_{obliv})$.*

Since the distincton between discrete time and continuous time is immaterial from the standpoint of analyzing threshold stopping rules, the first two of these theorems are equivalent to the existing results for discrete-time prophet inequalities that we have cited before the theorem statements. On the other hand, because oblivious stopping rules are less powerful than general stopping rules, the third theorem is not an immediate consequence of the corresponding discrete-time prophet inequality.

To complete this section, we will describe the stopping rules which achieve the bounds stated in the three prophet inequalities above.

When the points $\{(x_i, t_i)\}_{i=1}^n$ are independent but not necessarily identically distributed, choose threshold $\theta_{1/2}$ to be the median of the distribution of $\max\{x_i\}$. In other words, $\theta_{1/2}$ is defined such that the events $\max\{x_1, \ldots, x_n\} > \theta_{1/2}$ and $\max\{x_1, \ldots, x_n\} < \theta_{1/2}$ both have probability at most $\frac{1}{2}$. Consider the threshold stopping rule that selects the first pair $(x_i, t_i)$ with $x_i > \theta_{1/2}$, and consider the one whose selection criterion is $x_i \geq \theta_{1/2}$. The proof of Theorem 1 shows that at least one of these two stopping rules fulfills a prophet inequality with factor 1/2.

When the points $\{(x_i, t_i)\}_{i=1}^n$ are i.i.d. and the distributions of $x_i$ and $t_i$ are atomless and independent, with cumulative distribution functions $F$ and $G$, respectively, choose threshold $\theta_{1-1/e}$ such that $\Pr(\max\{x_1, \ldots, x_n\} > \theta_{1-1/e}) = 1 - \frac{1}{e}$. The proof of Theorem 2 shows that the threshold stopping rule that selects the first pair $(x_i, t_i)$ such that $x_i > \theta_{1-1/e}$ fulfills a prophet inequality with factor $1 - \frac{1}{e}$. Now let $\beta_n$ be the solution to

$$\int_0^n (1 + z + \beta_n e^z)^{-1} \, dz = 1,$$

and let $z_n(s)$ be the solution of the differential equation

$$\frac{dz}{ds} = 1 + z + \beta_n e^z$$

with initial condition $z(0) = 0$. The oblivious stopping rule that accepts the first $(x_i, t_i)$ such that

$$1 - F(x_i) < z(G(t_i))/n$$

fulfills a prophet inequality with factor $\alpha - \frac{\log n}{n}$.

### 3.2 Reducing delegated search to prophet inequalities

Although delegated search problems and prophet inequalities appear unrelated at first glance, the tight technical connection between them is explained by an observation which is extremely natural in hindsight. Consider a change of variables that maps the agent's utility $y$ to a point $t(y) \in [0, 1]$, where the function $t$ is monotonically decreasing. In a single proposal mechanism with eligible set $R$, the agent submits the eligible proposal $(x, y)$ with the highest $y$ value. Similarly, an oblivious stopping rule with eligible set $Q$ selects the earliest eligible point $(x, t)$. Since the change of variables $t(y)$ is monotonically decreasing, the two selection criteria are equivalent! Thus, designing single proposal mechanisms that yield high utility for the principal is equivalent to designing oblivious stopping rules that yield a high expected value.

In more detail, let $t$ be any continuous, monotonically decreasing bijection from $[0, \infty)$ to $(0, 1]$, for example $t(y) = e^{-y}$. Under the mapping $H : \Omega \to (\mathbb{R}_+ \times [0, 1])$ defined by $H(\omega) = (x(\omega), t(y(\omega)))$, any distribution on sets of solutions $\{\omega_1, \dots, \omega_n\}$ induces a distribution $\mathbf{D}$ on sets of pairs $\{(x_1, t_1), \dots, (x_n, t_n)\}$. In particular, our distributional model in which the agent draws $n$ i.i.d. samples from $\Omega$ is mapped, under this correspondence, to a member of the family of distributions $\mathscr{D}_{\text{iid}, n}$.

There is also a reverse correspondence from oblivious stopping rules to single proposal mechanisms and their interim allocation functions. The oblivious stopping rule $\rho_Q$ with eligible set $Q$ corresponds to the single proposal mechanism with eligible set $H^{-1}(Q)$. More precisely, if $R = H^{-1}(Q)$ and $\sigma$ is a best response to the single proposal mechanism $M$ with eligible set $R$, then for any sequence of samples $\boldsymbol{\omega} = (\omega_1, \dots, \omega_n)$, we have

$$\rho_Q(H(\boldsymbol{\omega})) = H(f_{M,\sigma}(\boldsymbol{\omega})).$$

In other words, suppose we run the mechanism $M$; the agent draws a sequence of samples; and we let the agent choose the best one (for the agent) that belongs to $R$. This procedure is equivalent to running the oblivious stopping rule $\rho_Q$ on the sequence obtained by transforming all of the agents' samples to points $(x_i, t_i) = (x_i, t(y_i))$, and selecting the earliest such point (ordered by $t_i$) that belongs to $Q$. Under this correspondence, threshold stopping rules correspond to single proposal mechanisms in which a solution is deemed eligible if the principal's utility exceeds a specified threshold. Note that this subset of single proposal mechanisms can be implemented even when the agent's utility is unobservable.

Combining these observations with Theorems 1 to 3, we obtain the following theorem.

THEOREM 4. *In the distributional model, suppose the agent draws n i.i.d. samples, and let $x^*$ denote the utility the principal would attain if she could directly choose her favorite among these n samples.*

(1) *There is always a set $X$ of the form $(\theta, \infty)$ or $[\theta, \infty)$ such that a single proposal mechanism with eligible set $\{\omega \mid x(\omega) \in X\}$ ensures that the principal's expected utility is at least $\frac{1}{2}\mathbb{E}[x_*]$.*
(2) *If the principal and agent have independent utilities, each drawn from an atomless distribution, then a single proposal mechanism that accepts any proposal satisfying $x(\omega) > \theta$, for a suitable choice of $\theta$, ensures that the principal's expected utility is at least $\left(1 - \frac{1}{e}\right)\mathbb{E}[x_*]$.*

(3) *If the principal and agent have independent utilities, each drawn from an atomless distribution, and the principal can observe the agent's utility, then a single proposal mechanism that accepts any proposal satisfying $x(\omega) > \theta(y(\omega))$, for a suitable choice of the function $\theta(\cdot)$, ensures that the principal's expected utility is at least $\left(\alpha - O\left(\frac{\log n}{n}\right)\right)\mathbb{E}[x_*]$, where $\alpha$ is the constant defined in* Theorem 3.

It is possible to show that the bounds in all three parts of the theorem are tight with respect to the assumptions made in their respective statements.

## 4 BINARY OUTCOMES

Recall the binary model from Section 1: The potential solutions come from a large discrete set $\Omega = \{\omega_1, \omega_2, \ldots, \omega_m\}$ and the agent's role is to explore which of these options are feasible to implement. If $\omega_i$ is feasible, it yields utility $x_i$ for the principal and $y_i$ for the agent — where the pair $(x_i, y_i)$ is commonly known to both parties — and if $\omega_i$ is infeasible it yields zero utility for both parties. To explore the feasibility of solution $\omega_i$ the agent must incur a cost of $c_i \geq 0$, and the probability of success is $p_i > 0$, independently of the success of other solutions. These quantities $c_i, p_i$ are again commonly known to both parties. We will assume that $c_i \leq p_i y_i$ for each solution $y_i$, since otherwise it is against the agent's self-interest to explore $\omega_i$, even if it were assured that the solution would be adopted if feasible.

### 4.1 Optimal search policies: Weitzman's box problem

If the principal were conducting the search by herself (without delegation to an agent), this model would correspond to a special case of the *box problem* introduced by Weitzman [22]. The optimal search policy is simple but surprisingly subtle: it assigns to each option a priority $z_i$ satisfying $\mathbb{E}[(x_i - z_i)^+] = c_i$ — which in our case entails setting $z_i = x_i - c_i/p_i$ — and then explores options in decreasing order of priority, selecting the first feasible one in this ordering or stopping when all remaining unexplored options have $z_i < 0$.

Now suppose that the principal instead delegates the search to an agent who bears the cost of exploration, by running a single-proposal mechanism with eligible set $R$. Then the agent faces a different instance of the box problem, in which the set of options is limited to $R$, and the costs and success probabilities of the options is the same as before, but the value of option $i$ (if feasible) is $y_i$ rather than $x_i$. This means the agent prioritizes boxes in decreasing order of $w_i = y_i - c_i/p_i$ rather than $z_i = x_i - c_i/p_i$, and recommends the first box in this ordering that is discovered to be feasible.

To summarize, the delegated search problem in the binary model is analogous to Weitzman's box problem, but with the important distinction that the searcher (the principal) is not allowed to choose the order in which to open the boxes. Instead the problem specifies an exogenous ordering of the boxes — corresponding to the agent's ranking of options by decreasing $w_i$ — and the searcher is only free to decide which boxes in this sequence should be opened and which ones should be skipped, corresponding to the principal's problem of choosing the set $R$. Since this problem may be of independent interest, we devote Theorem 5 below to presenting a solution that always achieves at least half of the expected value of running the optimal search procedure that is allowed to inspect the boxes in any order it desires. Interestingly, the analysis is based on prophet inequalities, specifically Theorem 1 and its proof. It implies there is an approximately optimal mechanism with the following structure. For any half-infinite interval $X$ of the form $X = (\theta, \infty)$ or $X = [\theta, \infty)$, let $R(X) = \{\omega_i \mid z_i \in X\}$ and define $M(X)$ to be the single-proposal mechanism in which a proposal $\omega_i$ is eligible if it is feasible and belongs to $R(X)$.

### 4.2 The Box Problem with an Exogenous Ordering

In this section we recapitulate some background material about Weitzman's 1979 box problem. In this problem[4] there are $m$ boxes, each containing an independent random prize. The prize in box $i$ is denoted $v_i$, and the cost of opening the box is $c_i$. A searcher may open any number of boxes sequentially, or may cease the search at any time and claim a prize from at most one of the open boxes. The problem is to design an optimal sequential search policy. Weitzman proves that if each box is assigned a *priority* $z_i$ defined by the equation $\mathbb{E}[(v_i - z_i)^+] = c_i$, then the optimal sequential search policy opens boxes in decreasing order of priority, stopping at the first time when the highest prize inside an open box exceeds the highest priority of a closed box, or at the first time when the priority of every remaining closed box is negative, whichever comes sooner.

Kleinberg et al. [16] provided a proof of optimality of Weitzman's procedure in which the priority $z_i$ is interpreted as the "strike price" of a real option with fair value $c_i$. An important quantity in their analysis is the "covered call value", which is simply the random variable $\kappa_i = \min\{v_i, z_i\}$. We restate the following lemma[5] from their work.

LEMMA 2. *(Kleinberg et al. [16]) For any sequential search procedure and any box i, let $A_i, B_i$ be the indicator random variables of the event that the procedure selects box i and the event that it opens box i, respectively. The inequality*

$$\mathbb{E}[A_i v_i - B_i c_i] \leq \mathbb{E}[A_i \kappa_i] \tag{2}$$

*is satisfied by every search procedure, and equality holds if and only if the search procedure is* non-exposed, *meaning that $A_i = B_i$ at every sample point where $v_i > z_i$.*

COROLLARY 1. *For any sequential search procedure, the expected net value of running the procedure (i.e., the value of the selected box minus the combined cost of opening boxes) is bounded above by the expectation of the maximum covered call value, i.e.*

$$\mathbb{E}\left[\sum_{i=1}^{m} A_i v_i - \sum_{i=1}^{m} B_i c_i\right] \leq \mathbb{E}\left[\sum_{i=1}^{m} A_i \kappa_i\right]. \tag{3}$$

The corollary is immediate, by summing inequality (2) over boxes $i = 1, \ldots, m$.

Now consider the box problem with an exogenous ordering of boxes, where the searcher is limited to considering the boxes one by one in the specified order, and once she decides to leave a box closed or to leave the prize within unclaimed, she cannot later return to the box and open it or claim its prize. We define a type of policy that we call a *$\kappa$-thresholding policy*; the reason for the name will become apparent in the subsequent Lemma 3, which shows that these policies correspond to a threshold rule applied to the sequence of covered call values $\kappa_i$.

**Definition 4.** A *$\kappa$-thresholding policy* for the box problem with exogenous ordering is a policy that operates as follows. There is a half-infinite interval $X = (\theta, \infty)$ or $X = [\theta, \infty)$ called the *target interval.* The policy declines to open any box $i$ with $z_i \notin X$. Otherwise, if $z_i \in X$, the policy opens the box and claims the prize inside if and only if $v_i \in X$.

LEMMA 3. *Every $\kappa$-thresholding policy is non-exposed. The expected net value of running a $\kappa$-thresholding policy with target interval X is exactly the same as the expected value selected by the threshold stopping rule that observes the random sequence $\kappa_1, \kappa_2, \ldots, \kappa_n$ and selects the first element of this sequence that belongs to X.*

[4] The following description constitutes a special case of Weitzman's problem. The general case incorporates geometric time discounting and time delays.

[5] Lemma 1 of the full version of their paper, http://dx.doi.org/10.2139/ssrn.2753858.

Proof. The policy is non-exposed because $z_i \notin X$ implies $A_i = B_i = 0$, while $z_i \in X$ and $v_i > z_i$ imply $A_i = B_i = 1$. Hence the left and right sides of (2) are equal for every box, and the net value of running the policy is $\mathbb{E}\left[\sum_{i=1}^{m} A_i \kappa_i\right]$, i.e. the expected covered call value of the box the policy selects. By design, the policy perfectly simulates the threshold stopping rule that chooses the first element of the sequence $\kappa_1, \ldots, \kappa_n$ that belongs to $X$; this is because it selects the first box such that $z_i$ and $v_i$ both belong to $X$, which is also the first box such that $\kappa_i$ belongs to $X$. □

Theorem 5. *For every instance of the box problem with exogenous ordering, there is a $\kappa$-thresholding policy whose expected net value is at least half that of Weitzman's optimal search procedure (which endogenously selects the ordering of the boxes).*

Proof. Lemma 3 reduces the analysis of $\kappa$-thresholding policies to a question about prophet inequalities. In particular, the expected net value of running a $\kappa$-thresholding policy is equal to the expected covered call value of the random element selected from the sequence $\kappa_1, \ldots, \kappa_n$ by a particular threshold stopping rule. Since Samuel-Cahn's 1984 prophet inequality (Theorem 1 above) implies that threshold stopping rules can always attain at least half the expectation of the maximum random variable in the sequence, it follows that there is a $\kappa$-thresholding policy whose expected net value is at least half the expectation of the maximum covered call value. Corollary 1 ensures that the latter is an upper bound on the expected net value of Weitzman's optimal search procedure. □

### 4.3 An approximately optimal mechanism

Recall that for a half-infinite interval $X = (\theta, \infty)$ or $X = [\theta, \infty)$, the mechanism $M(X)$ is defined to be the single proposal mechanism whose eligible set consists of solutions $\omega_i$ that are feasible and satisfy $z_i \in X$.

Theorem 6. *There exists a choice of $X$ such that the expected net value of mechanism $M(X)$ — i.e., the principal's value for adopting the agent's proposal, if adopted, minus combined cost of all the alternatives explored — is at least half of the expected net value the principal could achieve by performing the optimal search herself (without delegation).*

Proof. Convert the delegated search problem into a box problem with exogenous order, where the order is defined by sorting the solutions $\omega_1, \ldots, \omega_m$ in non-increasing order of the agent's priority value $w_i = y_i - c_i/p_i$, and the value $v_i$ inside box $i$ is defined to be $x_i$ if $\omega_i$ turns out to be feasible, 0 otherwise.

According to Theorem 5 there exists a choice of $X$ such that the $\kappa$-thresholding policy with target set $X$ attains at least half the expected net value of the optimal search procedure. This thresholding policy goes through boxes in the given order, i.e. descending $w_i$, and opens only those with $z_i \in X$, selecting the first one such that $v_i \in X$. Note that among the boxes which the policy opens, the first one with $v_i \in X$ is also the first one corresponding to a feasible $\omega_i$. This is because an infeasible $\omega_i$ has $v_i = 0$ hence $v_i \notin X$, whereas a feasible $\omega_i$ has $v_i = x_i \geq z_i$, hence $v_i \in X$.

Recall from Section 4.1 that the agent's best response to mechanism $M(X)$ is to go through the elements of $R(X)$ in decreasing order of $w_i$, stopping and proposing the first one that is discovered to be feasible. This is exactly the behavior of the $\kappa$-thresholding policy with target set $X$, as derived in the preceding paragraph. Hence the mechanism $M(X)$ coupled with the agent's best response behavior emulates the $\kappa$-thresholding policy which attains at least half the expected net value of the optimal search procedure. □

### 4.4 Limiting the number of samples

In some cases the number of distinct potential solutions, $m$, may be prohibitively large, and the agent may only have the power to explore the feasibility of a limited number of them, $n < m$. In this case, if the principal were to conduct the search autonomously without delegation — subject to the same costs $c_i$ and the same upper bound, $n$, on the total number of solutions that can be tested for feasibility — it may require a very complex procedure. Nevertheless, we will provide in this section a simple delegated search mechanism such that it is easy for the agent to compute a search procedure that is a best response to the mechanism, and the outcome of running the mechanism with this best response attains at least $\frac{1}{2}\left(1 - \frac{1}{e}\right) \approx 0.316$ of the net expected value of the (potentially complex) optimal procedure.

The key observation is the following lemma, which provides a useful upper bound on the value of running the optimal search procedure.

Lemma 4. *In the box problem with $m > n$ boxes, if the searcher is limited to open at most $n$ boxes before claiming a prize, then the expected net value of any search procedure is bounded above by $\mathbb{E}[\max_{i \in S} \kappa_i]$ where $S$ is the random set of boxes that the procedure opens.*

Proof. Sum up the inequality (2) over all boxes and note that $A_i = 0$ for $i \notin S$, to derive

$$\mathbb{E}\left[\sum_{i=1}^{m} A_i v_i - \sum_{i=1}^{m} B_i c_i\right] \leq \mathbb{E}\left[\sum_{i \in S} A_i \kappa_i\right].$$

The lemma follows by noting that $\sum_{i \in S} A_i \kappa_i \leq \max_{i \in S} \kappa_i$ because $\sum_{i \in S} A_i \leq 1$. □

Lemma 5. *There exists a (non-random) set $T$ of cardinality $n$, such that $\mathbb{E}[\max_{i \in T} \kappa_i] \geq (1 - \frac{1}{e})\mathbb{E}[\max_{i \in S} \kappa_i]$, where $S$ is the random set of solutions explored by the optimal search procedure subject to a contraint of exploring at most $n$ solutions.*

Proof. The problem of adaptively exploring a random set $S$ of at most $n$ solutions to maximize $\mathbb{E}[\max_{i \in S} \kappa_i]$ is a special case of the stochastic monotone submodular function maximization problem studied by Asadpour and Nazerzadeh [7], in which the role of the monotone submodular function $f : \mathbb{R}_+^n \to \mathbb{R}_+$ is played by the function $f(\lambda_1, \ldots, \lambda_n) = \max\{\lambda_i\}$, and role of the matroid constraint is played by the cardinality constraint that at most $n$ elements may be probed. Theorem 1 of [7], which asserts that the adaptivity gap of stochastic monotone submodular maximization is $\frac{e}{e-1}$, specializes in the present case to the assertion stated in the lemma. □

Theorem 7. *Consider delegated search in the binary model with a constraint that no more than $n$ solutions can be examined for feasibility. There exists a mechanism that attains at least $\frac{1}{2}\left(1 - \frac{1}{e}\right)$ fraction of the expected net value of the optimal search procedure subject to the same limitation of examining at most $n$ solutions.*

Proof. According to Lemmas 4 and 5, there is an $n$-element set $T \subseteq \Omega$ such that the optimal search procedure that is limited to explore only solutions in $T$ is able to attain at least $1 - \frac{1}{e}$ fraction of the expected net value of the optimal search procedure that is limited to examine at most $n$ solutions but can (adaptively) choose any $n$ elements of $\Omega$ during its search. When the set of solutions is restricted to $T$, the constraint that at most $n$ solutions can be examined becomes irrelevant since $T$ only has $n$ elements. Thus, Theorem 6 guarantees the existence of a delegated search mechanism that is at least half as good as the optimal search procedure limited to $T$, and is consequently at least $\frac{1}{2}\left(1 - \frac{1}{e}\right)$ times as good as the optimal search procedure limited to examine at most $n$ solutions. Moreover, by applying the algorithm in Asadpour and Nazerzadeh [7] used to prove Lemma 5, we can implement this policy in polynomial time with a loss of a further additive $\varepsilon$ in the approximation ratio, thus obtaining a bound of $\frac{1}{2}\left(1-\frac{1}{e}-\varepsilon\right)$ efficiently. □

**Acknowledgements.** This work was supported in part by NSF grants CCF-1512964, CCF-1740822, and SES-1741441, a grant from the MacArthur Foundation, and a Simons Investigator Award. The authors would like to thank Brendan Lucier, Jens Ludwig, Sendhil Mullainathan, Rad Niazadeh, and Glen Weyl for helpful discussions, and The Nines in Ithaca, NY, for the many deep-dish pizzas that were consumed during the course of this research.

## REFERENCES

[1] Melika Abolhassani, Soheil Ehsani, Hossein Esfandiari, MohammadTaghi Hajiaghayi, Robert D. Kleinberg, and Brendan Lucier. 2017. Beating 1-1/e for ordered prophets. In *Proceedings of the 49th Annual ACM SIGACT Symposium on Theory of Computing, STOC 2017, Montreal, QC, Canada, June 19-23, 2017.* 61–71. DOI: http://dx.doi.org/10.1145/3055399.3055479

[2] Philippe Aghion and Jean Tirole. 1997. Formal and Real Authority in Organizations. *Journal of Political Economy* 105, 1 (Feb. 1997), 1–29.

[3] Ricardo Alonso and Niko Matouschek. 2008. Optimal Delegation. *Review of Economic Studies* 75, 1 (Jan. 2008), 259–293.

[4] Manuel Amador and Kyle Bagwell. 2013. The Theory of Optimal Delegation With an Application to Tariff Caps. *Econometrica* 81, 4 (July 2013), 1541–1599.

[5] Attila Ambrus and Georgy Egorov. 2017. Delegation and nonmonetary incentives. *Journal of Economic Theory* 171 (2017), 101–135.

[6] Mark Armstrong and John Vickers. 2010. A model of delegated project choice. *Econometrica* 78, 1 (Jan. 2010), 213–244.

[7] Arash Asadpour and Hamid Nazerzadeh. 2016. Maximizing Stochastic Monotone Submodular Functions. *Management Science* 62, 8 (2016), 2374–2391. DOI: http://dx.doi.org/10.1287/mnsc.2015.2254

[8] Susan Athey, Kyle Bagwell, and Chris Sanchirico. 2004. Collusion and Price Rigidity. *Review of Economic Studies* 71, 2 (April 2004), 317–349.

[9] José R. Correa, Patricio Foncea, Ruben Hoeksma, Tim Oosterwijk, and Tjark Vredeveld. 2017. Posted Price Mechanisms for a Random Stream of Customers. In *Proceedings of the 2017 ACM Conference on Economics and Computation, EC '17, Cambridge, MA, USA, June 26-30, 2017.* 169–186. DOI: http://dx.doi.org/10.1145/3033274.3085137

[10] Soheil Ehsani, MohammadTaghi Hajiaghayi, Thomas Kesselheim, and Sahil Singla. 2018. Prophet Secretary for Combinatorial Auctions and Matroids. In *Proc. 29th Annual ACM-SIAM Symposium on Discrete Algorithms (SODA 2018).* 700–714.

[11] Joseph Farrell and Michael L. Katz. 2006. The economics of welfare standards in antitrust. *Competition Policy International* 2 (2006), 3–28.

[12] Theodore P Hill and Robert P Kertz. 1982. Comparisons of stop rule and supremum expectations of iid random variables. *The Annals of Probability* 10, 2 (1982), 336–345.

[13] Bengt Holmstrom. 1977. *On Incentives and Control in Organizations.* Ph.D. Dissertation. Stanford University.

[14] Bengt Holmstrom. 1984. On the Theory of Delegation. In *Bayesian Models in Economic Theory*, M. Boyer and R. Kihlstrom (Eds.). Elsevier, 115–141.

[15] Robert P Kertz. 1986. Stop rule and supremum expectations of iid random variables: a complete comparison by conjugate duality. *Journal of Multivariate Analysis* 19, 1 (1986), 88–112.

[16] Robert D. Kleinberg, Bo Waggoner, and E. Glen Weyl. 2016. Descending Price Optimally Coordinates Search. In *Proceedings of the 2016 ACM Conference on Economics and Computation, EC '16, Maastricht, The Netherlands, July 24-28, 2016.* 23–24. DOI: http://dx.doi.org/10.1145/2940716.2940760

[17] Vijay Krishna and John Morgan. 2008. Contracting for information under imperfect commitment. *RAND Journal of Economics* 39, 4 (2008), 905–925.

[18] Jin Li, Niko Matouschek, and Michael Powell. 2017. Power Dynamics in Organizations. *American Economic Journal: Microeconomics* 9, 1 (2017), 217–241.

[19] Nahum D. Melumad and Toshiyuki Shibano. 1991. Communication in Settings with No Transfers. *RAND Journal of Economics* 22, 2 (1991), 173–198.

[20] Volker Nocke and Michael D. Whinston. 2010. Dynamic Merger Review. *Journal of Political Economy* 118, 6 (2010), 1200–1251.

[21] Ester Samuel-Cahn. 1984. Comparison of threshold stop rules and maximum for independent nonnegative random variables. *Annals of Probability* 12, 4 (1984), 1213–1216.

[22] Martin L. Weitzman. 1979. Optimal Search for the Best Alternative. *Econometrica* 47 (1979), 641–654.

# Prophet Secretary: Surpassing the $1 - 1/e$ Barrier

YOSSI AZAR, Tel Aviv University, Israel
ASHISH CHIPLUNKAR*, École Polytechnique Fédérale de Lausanne, Switzerland
HAIM KAPLAN, Tel Aviv University, Israel

In the Prophet Secretary problem, samples from a known set of probability distributions arrive one by one in a uniformly random order, and an algorithm must irrevocably pick one of the samples as soon as it arrives. The goal is to maximize the expected value of the sample picked relative to the expected maximum of the distributions. This is one of the most simple and fundamental problems in online decision making that models the process selling one item to a sequence of costumers. For a closely related problem called the Prophet Inequality where the order of the random variables is adversarial, it is known that one can achieve in expectation $1/2$ of the expected maximum, and no better ratio is possible. For the Prophet Secretary problem, that is, when the variables arrive in a random order, Esfandiari et al. (2015) showed that one can actually get $1 - 1/e$ of the maximum. The $1 - 1/e$ bound was recently extended to more general settings by Ehsani et al. (2018). Given these results, one might be tempted to believe that $1 - 1/e$ is the correct bound. We show that this is not the case by providing an algorithm for the Prophet Secretary problem that beats the $1 - 1/e$ bound and achieves $1 - 1/e + 1/400$ times the expected maximum. We also prove a hardness result on the performance of algorithms under a natural restriction which we call deterministic distribution-insensitivity.

Additional Key Words and Phrases: Optimal stopping, posted price mechanisms, competitive analysis

## 1 INTRODUCTION

The Prophet Inequality problem of Krengel and Sucheston [13, 14] is one of the cornerstones in optimal stopping theory. In this problem, probability distributions $\mathcal{D}_1, \ldots, \mathcal{D}_n$ of a sequence of independent non-negative random variables is given to an algorithm. Thereafter, samples $X_1 \sim \mathcal{D}_1, \ldots, X_n \sim \mathcal{D}_n$ are revealed to the algorithm one by one, and the algorithm is required to pick (at most) one of the $X_i$'s irrevocably as soon as it is revealed. The goal of the algorithm is to maximize its profit, that is, the value of the sample that it picks. It is easy to see that we may only look for *threshold algorithms*, that is, algorithms which come up with a threshold $\alpha_i$ in each round $i$, and accept $X_i$ if and only if $X_i \geq \alpha_i$.

The primary motivation behind studying the Prophet Inequality and its related problems comes from mechanism design. Consider the sale of a single item where customers arrive online, and the

*This work was done when the author was a post-doc at Tel Aviv University.

The authors thank Amos Fiat for his insightful involvement in the discussions. The second author thanks Matt Weinberg for introducing him to optimal stopping theory. The first author is supported in part by the Israel Science Foundation (grant No. 1506/16) and by the ICRC Blavatnik Fund. The third author is partially supported by the Israel Science Foundation grant no. 1841-14, the Blavatnik Fund, and the German-Israeli Foundation for Scientific Research and Development (GIF) grant no. 1367/2017.

Authors' addresses: email; Yossi Azar, Tel Aviv University, Ramat Aviv, Tel Aviv, 6997801, Israel, azar@tau.ac.il; Ashish Chiplunkar, École Polytechnique Fédérale de Lausanne, 1015, Lausanne, Switzerland, ashish.chiplunkar@gmail.com; Haim Kaplan, Tel Aviv University, Ramat Aviv, Tel Aviv, 6997801, Israel, haimk@post.tau.ac.il.


*ACM EC'18, June 18–22, 2018, Ithaca, NY, USA.* ACM ISBN 978-1-4503-4529-3/18/06...$15.00
https://doi.org/10.1145/3219166.3219182

item is to be sold irrevocably to one of the customers. Suppose that the probability distribution of the valuation of each customer is known in advance. A threshold algorithm naturally translates to a *posted price mechanism*, which is inherently *truthful*, and the goal of maximizing the sample picked translates to maximizing the *social welfare*.

Indeed, if the algorithm knew all the samples $X_1, \ldots, X_n$ in advance, it would pick $\max_i X_i$, resulting in an expected profit of $\mathbb{E}[\max_i X_i]$. The algorithm's performance is, therefore, compared against the benchmark of $\mathbb{E}[\max_i X_i]$. An algorithm is said to have a *competitive ratio* of $c$ if its expected profit is at least $c \cdot \mathbb{E}[\max_i X_i]$, on any sequence $\mathcal{D}_1, \ldots, \mathcal{D}_n$ of distributions, where $X_i \sim \mathcal{D}_i$. The classical results of Krengel and Sucheston [13, 14] and Samuel-Cahn [17] state that $(1/2)$-competitive algorithms exist, and no algorithm can have a better competitive ratio. One such $(1/2)$-competitive algorithm is the following simple algorithm by Kleinberg and Weinberg [12]: compute $T = \mathbb{E}[\max_i X_i]/2$, and pick the first $X_i$ which exceeds $T$, if one exists.

Another well known problem in the domain of optimal stopping is the Secretary problem [6, 9], where a set of values $\{x_1, \ldots x_n\}$ is chosen adversarially, and revealed to an algorithm in a random order. As before, an algorithm has to pick one of the $x_i$'s as soon as it is revealed. Inspired from this problem, Esfandiari, Hajiaghayi, Liaghat, and Monemizadeh [8] defined a natural variant of the Prophet Inequality problem called the Prophet Secretary problem. In the Prophet Secretary problem, the set $\{\mathcal{D}_1, \ldots, \mathcal{D}_n\}$ of probability distributions is adversarial and known to the algorithm in advance, while the samples $\{X_i \sim \mathcal{D}_i\}$ are revealed in a uniformly random order. Naturally, the Prophet Secretary problem models selling a single item to a randomly permuted set of customers, the distributions of whose valuations are known in advance.

Since the arrival order is no longer adversarial in the Prophet Secretary problem, it is natural to expect that algorithms with competitive ratio larger than 1/2 will exist. Esfandiari et al. gave an algorithm which does the following. The algorithm chooses a sequence $1 > \alpha_1 > \cdots > \alpha_n > 0$ of thresholds determined completely by $n$ and independent of the set of distributions. Suppose $\sigma \in \mathcal{S}_n$ is the random order in which the samples are revealed, that is, the $k^{\text{th}}$ sample to be revealed is $X_{\sigma(k)}$. Then the algorithm picks $X_{\sigma(k)}$ for the smallest $k$ such that $X_{\sigma(k)} \geq \alpha_k \cdot \mathbb{E}[\max_i X_i]$, if such an index $k$ exists, otherwise it picks nothing. Esfandiari et al. proved that, for a suitable choice of thresholds $\alpha_1, \ldots, \alpha_n$, the algorithm is $(1 - 1/e)$-competitive. This was believed to be the optimal competitive ratio, and Ehsani et al. [7] mention improving this bound as a challenging problem.

As an impossibility result, Esfandiari et al. [8] also proved that no algorithm for the prophet secretary problem can have a competitive ratio better than 3/4. However, observe that the competitive ratio in the particular case where $X_1, \ldots, X_n$ are identically distributed and independent is trivially an upper bound on the competitive ratio of the Prophet Secretary problem. Moreover, if $X_1, \ldots, X_n$ are identically distributed, then the Prophet Inequality and the Prophet Secretary problems are equivalent. Hill and Kertz [11] had already proved that the competitive ratio for IID Prophet Inequality, which we call $c_{\text{iid}}$, is at most $(1.341)^{-1} \approx 0.746$. No upper bound better than $c_{\text{iid}}$ is known for the Prophet Secretary problem.

## 1.1 Our results

Our main result is that the (algorithmic) lower bound of $1 - 1/e$ on the competitive ratio of Prophet Secretary by Esfandiari et al. [8] is not tight. By introducing new techniques in addition to those of Esfandiari et al., we give an algorithm for the Prophet Secretary problem that has a competitive ratio better than $1 - 1/e$. (It is noteworthy that, in contrast to Abolhassani et al. [1] who beat the $1 - 1/e$ bound provided there are enough copies of each distinct random variable, we beat the bound unconditionally.)

Theorem 1.1. *There is an algorithm for the Prophet Secretary problem with competitive ratio larger than* $1 - 1/e + 1/400$.

Observe that the algorithm for the Prophet Inequality problem by [12] as well as the algorithm for the Prophet Secretary problem by [8], which we stated previously, are both simple in the following sense. Both algorithms are actually oblivious to the probability distributions $\mathcal{D}_1, \ldots, \mathcal{D}_n$ of $X_1, \ldots, X_n$; they only need to know $\mathbb{E}[\max_i X_i]$, which they compete against. Moreover, both algorithms choose their threshold(s) deterministically. We call such algorithms *deterministic distribution-insensitive algorithms*. Our second result is a hardness result for deterministic distribution-insensitive algorithms.

Theorem 1.2. *Deterministic distribution-insensitive algorithms for the Prophet Secretary problem cannot have a competitive ratio larger than* $11/15 \approx 0.733$.

This improves the upper bound of $3/4$ by [8], as well as the better upper bound of $c_{\text{iid}} \approx 0.746$ due to [11], for deterministic distribution-insensitive algorithms.

## 1.2 Our techniques

We give here the high-level ideas behind the design of our algorithm for the Prophet Secretary problem. Assume without loss of generality that $\mathbb{E}[\max_i X_i] = 1$. Observe that for any $a$, $\mathbb{E}[\max_i X_i] = \mathbb{E}[\min(a, \max_i X_i)] + \mathbb{E}[\max(0, \max_i X_i - a)]$. We divide the Prophet Secretary instances into three categories as follows. Loosely speaking, the first category contains instances in which $\mathbb{E}[\min(a, \max_i X_i)]$ is small, for a suitable $a \approx 1 - 1/e$. The second category contains instances in which, in expectation, more than one $X_i$ exceed a certain threshold $T$. For each of these categories, we strengthen Esfandiari et al.'s algorithm to achieve a better performance.

The third category is most interesting and includes all the remaining instances. For these instances we prove that one of the $X_i$'s (say $X_1$) is larger than all the rest with high probability, and also has a sufficiently large expectation. For these instances, our algorithm sets the same threshold for all samples. We prove that with high probability, the algorithm does not pick a sample before it encounters $X_1$. As a consequence, it extracts most of the expected value of $X_1$ as its profit. Moreover, the algorithm encounters, on an average, half of the other $X_i$'s before it sees $X_1$, because the samples arrive in a uniformly random order. Thus, even in the unlikely event that one of the $X_i$'s ($i > 1$) exceeds the threshold, the algorithm extracts its value with probability close to $1/2$. (This is necessary because $\mathbb{E}[X_1]$, although large, is not guaranteed to be sufficient by itself for the algorithm to achieve its targeted competitive ratio.)

## 1.3 Related Work

**Prophet Inequalities (worst case arrival order):** Ever since the seminal work of Krengel and Sucheston [13, 14], the Prophet Inequality problem has been studied in a variety of settings. One of the most natural variants is perhaps the multiple choice Prophet Inequality, where the algorithm is required to pick at most $k$ of the $x_i$'s ($k > 1$), and has to compete against the expectation of the sum of the $k$ largest random variables. Alaei [2] gave an algorithm for this problem with competitive ratio $1 - O(k^{-1/2})$, which is known to be asymptotically optimal. Kleinberg and Weinberg [12] considered the Matroid Prophet Inequality problem, where the feasible subsets of random variables are independent sets of a given matroid. They gave a $(1/2)$-competitive algorithm even for this more general problem than the classical Prophet Inequality problem. Going beyond this, Prophet Inequalities where the feasibility constraint is an intersection of matroids [12], or even an arbitrary downward-closed set system [15, 16], have been studied.

**IID Prophet Inequalities:** The case of identical distributions is particularly interesting because in this setting, the Prophet Inequality and the Prophet Secretary problems coincide. Already more than two decades ago, Hill and Kertz [11] gave an implicit characterization of $c_{\text{iid}}$, the competitive ratio for identical distributions, by analyzing the natural dynamic programming algorithm which performs optimally on every instance. However, they could only find the numerical value of $c_{\text{iid}}(n)$, the competitive ratio when we have $n$ independent identical random variables, for all $n \leq 10000$. They conjectured that $c_{\text{iid}}(n)$ decreases as $n$ increases, and proved that for $n = 10000$, the competitive ratio is approximately $(1.341)^{-1} \approx 0.746$. For $n > 10000$, they could only prove a lower bound of $1 - 1/e$ on $c_{\text{iid}}(n)$. Only recently, Abolhassani et al. [1] improved the lower bound for large $n$ to $0.738$ by giving a new algorithm. Shortly thereafter, Correa, Foncea, Hoeksma, Oosterwijk, and Vredeveld [5] took an entirely new approach to the problem and came up with yet another algorithm. They proved that its competitive ratio is at least $c_{\text{cfhov}} > 0.745$, a constant which they defined implicitly. Surprisingly, Hill and Kertz's implicit characterization of $c_{\text{iid}}$ and Correa et al's implicit definition of $c_{\text{cfhov}}$, although quite different from their appearance, are actually the same. This means that $c_{\text{iid}} = c_{\text{cfhov}} \in [0.745, 0.746]$, and that the algorithm of Correa et al. [5], in fact, achieves the optimal competitive ratio.

**Best case arrival order:** A natural variant of the Prophet Inequality and the Prophet Secretary problems is the one where the order in which the samples are revealed is chosen by the algorithm (the best order case). Yan [18] proved that the $(1-1/e)$-approximate revenue maximization algorithm of Chawla et al. [4] can be adapted to get a $(1 - 1/e)$-competitive algorithm for the best case arrival order variant of Prophet Inequality. Esfandiari et al. [8] proved that this bound holds even if the arrival order is random, as stated earlier, which suggests that the best case competitive ratio might be substantially better. Pursuing this line of research, Abolhassani et al. [1] proved that as long as there are sufficiently many (independent) copies of each random variable, an algorithm can come up with an appropriate order for which the competitive ratio is arbitrarily close to $c_{\text{iid}}$.[1] In the absence of the multiplicity assumption, it is not known whether we can attain a competitive ratio for the best order case which is better than the random order case.

**Matroid Prophet Secretary:** Very recently, Ehsani et al. [7] have considered the generalization of Prophet Secretary to matroids, analogous to Kleinberg and Weinberg's generalization of Prophet Inequality to matroids. Ehsani et al. give an algorithm that achieves the $1 - 1/e$ bound even with matroid feasibility constraint and random arrival order, and hence, can be seen as a generalization of the results of Yan [18] (matroid constraint, best case order) and Esfandiari et al. [8] (single choice constraint, random order).

**Posted price mechanism design:** As remarked earlier, algorithms for problems like the Prophet Inequality and Prophet Secretary correspond to posted price mechanisms for approximately maximizing social welfare. A parallel line of work has been to design posted price mechanisms under similar settings for approximate revenue maximization, taking as benchmark the revenue obtained by Myerson's mechanism. For more information on posted price mechanisms for online arrival of buyers, see [2, 4, 5, 10, 18], and the references therein.

### 1.4 Organization of the paper

Towards proving Theorem 1.1, we introduce some notation in Section 2. Since we reuse some part of Esfandiari et al.'s proof, we give an overview of that proof in Section 3. We present our algorithm in Section 4, and its analysis in the subsequent subsections, thereby proving Theorem 1.1. We devote Section 5 to prove Theorem 1.2, where we give an adversarial strategy to defeat every distribution-insensitive algorithm.

[1] In fact, this claim holds even in the random order case, where $O(\log n)$ multiplicity is sufficient. If the algorithm is allowed to choose the order, even $O(1)$ multiplicity is sufficient.

## 2 PRELIMINARIES

Let $\mathcal{D}_1, \ldots, \mathcal{D}_n$ be probability distributions on $\mathbb{R}^+$ and let $X_1, \ldots, X_n$ be independent non-negative random variables, where $X_i \sim \mathcal{D}_i$. Let $X = \max_i X_i$. By scaling the random variables appropriately, we assume $\mathbb{E}[X] = 1$ without loss of generality throughout this paper.

In the *Prophet Secretary* problem, the following interaction takes place between an adversary ADV, an algorithm ALG, and a third player, say RAND, responsible for all the randomness. (We abuse notation and also denote the expected profit of the algorithm by ALG.)

(1) ADV declares a set $\{\mathcal{D}_1, \ldots, \mathcal{D}_n\}$ of probability distributions of independent random variables $X_1, \ldots, X_n$ such that $\mathbb{E}[\max_i X_i] = 1$.
(2) RAND samples a permutation $\sigma \in \mathcal{S}_n$ over the indices $\{1, \ldots, n\}$ uniformly at random and keeps it private.
(3) For $k = 1$ to $n$,
   (a) ALG declares a threshold $\alpha_k$.
   (b) RAND samples $X_{\sigma(k)} \sim \mathcal{D}_{\sigma(k)}$. If $X_{\sigma(k)} \geq \alpha_k$, then the ALG is given the profit $X_{\sigma(k)}$ and the loop breaks.

Note that in the above setting, we assume that the algorithm does not know $\sigma$, and it does not know $X_{\sigma(k)}$ even after it rejects $X_{\sigma(k)}$.

In the more restricted setting of the *Distribution-Insensitive Prophet Secretary* problem, ADV, instead of making the distributions $\mathcal{D}_1, \ldots, \mathcal{D}_n$ public, sends them to RAND only. Thus, the algorithm only knows that $\mathbb{E}[\max_i X_i]$ is one. The thresholds $\alpha_1, \ldots, \alpha_n$ chosen by the algorithm are thus determined solely by $n$, and are oblivious to the distributions $\mathcal{D}_1, \ldots, \mathcal{D}_n$. Moreover, if an algorithm chooses $\alpha_1, \ldots, \alpha_n$ deterministically, we call it a *deterministic distribution-insensitive* algorithm. The $(1 - 1/e)$-competitive algorithm of Esfandiari at al. [8] is a deterministic distribution-insensitive algorithm. In contrast, the algorithm that we design is sensitive to the distributions $\mathcal{D}_1, \ldots, \mathcal{D}_n$.

## 3 OVERVIEW OF THE OLD ANALYSIS

We briefly restate those parts of the analysis by Esfandiari et al. [8] which we require in our proof. Let $\alpha_1, \ldots, \alpha_n$ be the thresholds chosen by an algorithm. Let the random variable $z_k$ denote the profit obtained by the algorithm from the $k^{\text{th}}$ round. That is, $z_k$ is equal to $X_{\sigma(k)}$ if the algorithm picked $X_{\sigma(k)}$, the $k^{\text{th}}$ sample; otherwise $z_k$ is zero. Then

$$\text{ALG} = \sum_{k=1}^{n} \mathbb{E}[z_k] = \sum_{k=1}^{n} \int_0^\infty \Pr[z_k \geq x]dx = \sum_{k=1}^{n} \int_0^{\alpha_k} \Pr[z_k \geq x]dx + \sum_{k=1}^{n} \int_{\alpha_k}^{\infty} \Pr[z_k \geq x]dx. \quad (1)$$

Observe that if we treat ALG as a posted price mechanism, then the first term in the last expression above is the expected revenue for the seller, whereas the second term is the expected utility of the buyer. The revenue and the utility components above are bounded from below as follows. Let $\theta(k)$ denote the probability that the algorithm does not choose a value from the first $k$ samples. Let $\alpha_{n+1} = 0$. Then we have,

Proposition 3.1 (Lemma 10 of [8]). *The expected revenue of ALG is given by*

$$\sum_{k=1}^{n} \int_0^{\alpha_k} \Pr[z_k \geq x]dx = \sum_{k=1}^{n} (1 - \theta(k))(\alpha_k - \alpha_{k+1}) = \alpha_1 - \sum_{k=1}^{n} \theta(k)(\alpha_k - \alpha_{k+1})$$

Proposition 3.2 (Lemma 11 of [8]). $\Pr[z_k \geq x] \geq \frac{\theta(k)}{n}\Pr[X \geq x]$ *for* $x \geq \alpha_k$, *and the expected utility of ALG is bounded as*

$$\int_{\alpha_k}^{\infty} \Pr[z_k \geq x]dx \geq \frac{\theta(k)}{n}\left(1 - \int_0^{\alpha_k} \Pr[X \geq x]dx\right) \geq \frac{\theta(k)}{n} \cdot (1 - \alpha_k).$$

Substitution of these bounds into (1) results in a lower bound on ALG which depends on the $\theta(k)$'s. Esfandiari et al. carefully choose the thresholds $\alpha_1, \dots, \alpha_n$ in such a way that this dependence is eliminated, and $\alpha_1 \approx 1 - 1/e$ is a lower bound on ALG, and hence, on the competitive ratio.

## 4 THE IMPROVED ALGORITHM

The main intuition behind our Prophet Secretary algorithm is the following. Suppose that the set $\{\mathcal{D}_1, \dots, \mathcal{D}_n\}$ of probability distributions is such that for some $a$ and $c < 1$, $\mathbb{E}[\min(a, X)] \leq c \cdot a$. Then we can use this to strengthen Proposition 3.2. Next, suppose that for some $T$, $b$, and $d$, the expected number of $X_i$'s exceeding $T$ is at least $b$, and $\int_T^{\infty} \Pr[X \geq x]dx = d$. Then we also exploit this to strengthen Proposition 3.2. In either case, we improve the competitive ratio. However, there exist instances in which none of these improvements is possible. We prove that such instances must have one of the $X_i$'s that is bounded away from zero with high probability, while the rest are close to zero with high probability. In this case, we prove that using a uniform threshold for all samples suffices.

Our improved algorithm for the Prophet Secretary problem has the following four parameters: $a \in [0, 1 - 1/e]$, $b > 1$, $c \in [0, 1]$, and $d \in [0, 1]$, chosen such that

$$ac + d > 1. \tag{2}$$

These are absolute constants independent of $n$ and the distributions of the random variables, and their values will be fixed later. Let $T$ be such that $\mathbb{E}[\max(0, X - T)] = \int_T^{\infty} \Pr[X \geq x]dx = d$. Since we assumed that $\mathbb{E}[X] = \int_0^{\infty} \Pr[X \geq x]dx = 1$, we get $\mathbb{E}[\min(T, X)] = \int_0^T \Pr[X \geq x]dx = 1 - d$, which trivially implies the following lower bound on $T$.

$$T \geq 1 - d. \tag{3}$$

The thresholds $\alpha_1, \dots, \alpha_n$ of the algorithm are determined as follows.

- **Case 1:** If $\mathbb{E}[\min(a, X)] \leq c \cdot a$, then

$$\alpha_k = \begin{cases} 1 - e^{(k-1)/n-1} & \text{if } \frac{k-1}{n} > 1 + \ln(1-a), \\ \frac{1}{c} - \left(\frac{1}{c} - a\right)\left(\frac{e^{(k-1)/n-1}}{(1-a)}\right)^c & \text{otherwise.} \end{cases}$$

- **Case 2:** else if $\mathbb{E}[|\{i : X_i \geq T\}|] \geq b$, then

$$\alpha_k = \begin{cases} \left(1 - e^{b((k-1)/n-1)}\right) \cdot \frac{b+d-bd}{b} & \text{if } \frac{k-1}{n} > 1 - \frac{1}{b}\ln\frac{b+d-bd}{d}, \\ 1 - d \cdot \left(\frac{b+d-bd}{d}\right)^{1/b} \cdot e^{(k-1)/n-1} & \text{otherwise.} \end{cases}$$

- **Case 3:** else $\alpha_1 = \dots = \alpha_n = T$.

Our analyses of Case 1 and Case 2 reuse some parts of the analysis by Esfandiari et al. [8], whereas the analysis of Case 3 uses a novel approach. We present the analyses of the three cases in the upcoming subsections, and then choose our parameters to get the final bound on the competitive ratio.

### 4.1 Analysis of Case 1

Suppose that the input set of distributions falls into Case 1, that is,

$$\mathbb{E}[\min(a, X)] = \int_0^a \Pr[X \geq x]dx \leq c \cdot a.$$

Using this upper bound on $\int_0^a \Pr[X \geq x]dx$, we get the following strengthened version of Proposition 3.2.

Lemma 4.1. *If* $\frac{k-1}{n} \leq 1 + \ln(1-a)$ *then* $\int_{\alpha_k}^{\infty} \Pr[z_k \geq x]dx \geq \frac{\theta(k)}{n} \cdot (1 - c\alpha_k)$.

Proof. From the later part of Proposition 3.2, we have,

$$\int_{\alpha_k}^{\infty} \Pr[z_k \geq x]dx \geq \frac{\theta(k)}{n}\left(1 - \int_0^{\alpha_k} \Pr[X \geq x]dx\right). \tag{4}$$

Suppose $(k-1)/n \leq 1 + \ln(1-a)$. Then from the definition of $\alpha_k$ in Case 1 of the algorithm, it is easy to verify that $\alpha_k \geq a$. Thus, for any $x \geq 0$, $ax/\alpha_k \leq x$, and hence, $\Pr[X \geq x] \leq \Pr[X \geq ax/\alpha_k]$. Therefore,

$$\int_0^{\alpha_k} \Pr[X \geq x]dx \leq \int_0^{\alpha_k} \Pr\left[X \geq \frac{ax}{\alpha_k}\right]dx = \frac{\alpha_k}{a}\int_0^a \Pr[X \geq y]dy \leq \frac{\alpha_k}{a} \cdot ca = c\alpha_k$$

where we get the first equality with the substitution $y = ax/\alpha_k$ and the second last inequality follows from the assumption that we apply Case 1. Substituting this upper bound on $\int_0^{\alpha_k} \Pr[X \geq x]dx$ in (4), the claim follows. □

Using Lemma 4.1 to bound $\int_{\alpha_k}^{\infty} \Pr[z_k \geq x]dx$ for positions $k$ such that $(k-1)/n \leq 1 + \ln(1-a)$, and Proposition 3.2 for positions $k$ such that $(k-1)/n > 1 + \ln(1-a)$, we get a stronger lower bound on $\sum_{k=1}^n \int_{\alpha_k}^{\infty} \Pr[z_k \geq x]dx$ than what is obtained by using Proposition 3.2 alone. Adding to this the bound on $\sum_{k=1}^n \int_0^{\alpha_k} \Pr[z_k \geq x]dx$ given by Proposition 3.1, we get a lower bound on ALG that depends on the $\theta(k)$'s. Our next lemma is helpful in proving that our choice of the values of $\alpha_k$'s reduces this dependence to an $O(n^{-1})$ error term, and as a result we get a lower bound on the algorithm's expected profit.

Lemma 4.2. *Let* $\tau = \lfloor n(1 + \ln(1-a)) + 1 \rfloor$. *Suppose* $\alpha_1 \ldots, \alpha_n$ *are defined as in Case 1 of the algorithm. Then there exist absolute positive constants,* $\gamma_1^>, \gamma_1^=, \gamma_1^<$, *such that*

(1) *For* $k > \tau$, $\frac{1-\alpha_k}{n} - \alpha_k + \alpha_{k+1} \geq -\frac{\gamma_1^>}{n^2}$.
(2) *For* $k = \tau$, $\frac{1-c\alpha_k}{n} - \alpha_k + \alpha_{k+1} \geq -\frac{\gamma_1^=}{n}$.
(3) *For* $k < \tau$, $\frac{1-c\alpha_k}{n} - \alpha_k + \alpha_{k+1} \geq -\frac{\gamma_1^<}{n^2}$.

The proof of this lemma is deferred to the full version of this paper [3] (Lemma 14 in the Appendix).

Theorem 4.3. *Suppose that the input set of distributions falls into Case 1 of the algorithm. Then the algorithm's expected profit is at least* $\frac{1}{c} - \left(\frac{1}{c} - a\right)(e(1-a))^{-c} - \frac{\gamma_1}{n}$, *for an absolute constant* $\gamma_1$.

Proof. Let $\tau$ be as defined in the statement of Lemma 4.2. We have

$$\begin{aligned}\sum_{k=1}^n \int_{\alpha_k}^{\infty} \Pr[z_k \geq x]dx &= \sum_{k=1}^{\tau} \int_{\alpha_k}^{\infty} \Pr[z_k \geq x]dx + \sum_{k=\tau+1}^{n} \int_{\alpha_k}^{\infty} \Pr[z_k \geq x]dx \\ &\geq \sum_{k=1}^{\tau} \theta(k) \cdot \frac{1 - c\alpha_k}{n} + \sum_{k=\tau+1}^{n} \theta(k) \cdot \frac{1 - \alpha_k}{n}.\end{aligned}$$

Here we used Lemma 4.1 for the first term and Proposition 3.2 for the second term. Substituting this and the bound of Proposition 3.1 in Equation (1), we get

$$\text{ALG} \geq \alpha_1 + \sum_{k=1}^{\tau} \theta(k) \cdot \left( \frac{1 - c\alpha_k}{n} - \alpha_k + \alpha_{k+1} \right) + \sum_{k=\tau+1}^{n} \theta(k) \cdot \left( \frac{1 - \alpha_k}{n} - \alpha_k + \alpha_{k+1} \right).$$

Using Lemma 4.2 and the fact that $\theta(k) \leq 1$, we have,

$$\text{ALG} \geq \alpha_1 - \sum_{k=1}^{\tau-1} \theta(k) \cdot \frac{\gamma_1^<}{n^2} - \theta(\tau) \cdot \frac{\gamma_1^=}{n} - \sum_{k=\tau+1}^{n} \theta(k) \cdot \frac{\gamma_1^>}{n^2} \geq \alpha_1 - \frac{\gamma_1^< + \gamma_1^= + \gamma_1^>}{n}.$$

Substituting the value of $\alpha_1$ and using $\gamma_1 = \gamma_1^< + \gamma_1^= + \gamma_1^>$, we have,

$$\text{ALG} \geq \frac{1}{c} - \left( \frac{1}{c} - a \right) (e(1-a))^{-c} - \frac{\gamma_1}{n}.$$

□

### 4.2 Analysis of Case 2

Suppose that the input set of distributions falls into Case 2, that is,

$$\mathbb{E}[|\{i : X_i \geq T\}|] = \sum_{i=1}^{n} \Pr[X_i \geq T] \geq b.$$

Then $\sum_{i=1}^{n} \Pr[X_i \geq x] \geq b$ for all $x \leq T$, because each $\Pr[X_i \geq x]$ can only increase as $x$ decreases. This gives us the following strengthened version of Proposition 3.2.

Lemma 4.4. *If* $\frac{k-1}{n} \geq 1 - \frac{1}{b} \ln \frac{b+d-bd}{d}$ *then* $\int_{\alpha_k}^{\infty} \Pr[z_k \geq x]dx \geq \frac{\theta(k)}{n} \cdot (b + d - bd - b\alpha_k)$.

Proof. Suppose $\frac{k-1}{n} \geq 1 - \frac{1}{b} \ln \frac{b+d-bd}{d}$. From the definition of $\alpha_k$ in Case 2 of the algorithm, it is clear that $\alpha_k \leq 1 - d$. Thus, from (3), we have $\alpha_k \leq 1 - d \leq T$. For $x \in [\alpha_k, T]$, we have

$$\Pr[z_k \geq x] \geq \frac{\theta(k)}{n} \sum_{i=1}^{n} \Pr[X_i \geq x] \geq \frac{\theta(k)}{n} \sum_{i=1}^{n} \Pr[X_i \geq T] \geq b \cdot \frac{\theta(k)}{n}. \tag{5}$$

Thus,

$$\begin{aligned}
\int_{\alpha_k}^{\infty} \Pr[z_k \geq x]dx &= \int_{\alpha_k}^{T} \Pr[z_k \geq x]dx + \int_{T}^{\infty} \Pr[z_k \geq x]dx \\
&\geq \int_{\alpha_k}^{T} b \cdot \frac{\theta(k)}{n} dx + \int_{T}^{\infty} \frac{\theta(k)}{n} \Pr[X \geq x]dx \\
&\geq \frac{\theta(k)}{n} \cdot b \cdot (1 - d - \alpha_k) + \frac{\theta(k)}{n} \cdot d \\
&= \frac{\theta(k)}{n} \cdot (b + d - bd - b\alpha_k).
\end{aligned}$$

Here, in the first inequality, we used Equation (5) for the first term and the earlier part of Proposition 3.2 for the second term. In the second inequality, we used the lower bound (3) on $T$ for the first term and the definition of $T$ for the second term. □

Analogous to Case 1, using Lemma 4.4 to bound $\int_{\alpha_k}^{\infty} \Pr[z_k \geq x]dx$ for positions $k$ such that $(k-1)/n \geq 1 - \frac{1}{b} \ln \frac{b+d-bd}{d}$, and Proposition 3.2 for positions $k$ such that $(k-1)/n < 1 - \frac{1}{b} \ln \frac{b+d-bd}{d}$, we get better bound on $\sum_{k=1}^{n} \int_{\alpha_k}^{\infty} \Pr[z_k \geq x]dx$. Using this bound and Proposition 3.1, we again get a bound ALG which depends on the $\theta(k)$'s. As before, our next lemma helps us prove that our choice of the values of $\alpha_k$'s reduces this dependence to an $O(n^{-1})$ error term, and as a result we get a lower bound on the algorithm's expected profit.

Lemma 4.5. *Suppose $\alpha_1 \ldots, \alpha_n$ are defined as in Case 2 of the algorithm. Then there exist absolute positive constants, $\gamma_2^>, \gamma_2^=, \gamma_2^<$, such that*

(1) *For $k < \tau$, $\frac{1-\alpha_k}{n} - \alpha_k + \alpha_{k+1} \geq -\frac{\gamma_2^<}{n^2}$.*
(2) *For $k = \tau$, $\frac{1-\alpha_k}{n} - \alpha_k + \alpha_{k+1} \geq -\frac{\gamma_2^=}{n}$.*
(3) *For $k > \tau$, $\frac{b+d-bd-b\alpha_k}{n} - \alpha_k + \alpha_{k+1} \geq -\frac{\gamma_2^>}{n^2}$.*

The proof of this lemma is deferred to the full version of this paper [3] (Lemma 15 in the Appendix).

Theorem 4.6. *Suppose that the input set of distributions falls into Case 2 of the algorithm. Then the algorithm's expected profit is at least $1 - \frac{d}{e} \cdot \left(\frac{b+d-bd}{d}\right)^{1/b} - \frac{\gamma_2}{n}$, for an absolute constant $\gamma_2$.*

Proof. Let $\tau$ be as defined in the statement of Lemma 4.5. We have

$$\begin{aligned}\sum_{k=1}^{n} \int_{\alpha_k}^{\infty} \Pr[z_k \geq x]dx &= \sum_{k=1}^{\tau} \int_{\alpha_k}^{\infty} \Pr[z_k \geq x]dx + \sum_{k=\tau+1}^{n} \int_{\alpha_k}^{\infty} \Pr[z_k \geq x]dx \\ &\geq \sum_{k=1}^{\tau} \theta(k) \cdot \frac{1-\alpha_k}{n} + \sum_{k=\tau+1}^{n} \theta(k) \cdot \frac{b+d-bd-b\alpha_k}{n}.\end{aligned}$$

Here we used Proposition 3.2 for the first term and Lemma 4.4 for the second term. Substituting this and the bound of Proposition 3.1 in Equation (1), we get

$$\text{ALG} \geq \alpha_1 + \sum_{k=1}^{\tau} \theta(k) \cdot \left(\frac{1-\alpha_k}{n} - \alpha_k + \alpha_{k+1}\right) + \sum_{k=\tau+1}^{n} \theta(k) \cdot \left(\frac{b+d-bd-b\alpha_k}{n} - \alpha_k + \alpha_{k+1}\right).$$

Using Lemma 4.5 and the fact that $\theta(k) \leq 1$, we have,

$$\text{ALG} \geq \alpha_1 - \sum_{k=1}^{\tau-1} \theta(k) \cdot \frac{\gamma_2^<}{n^2} - \theta(\tau) \cdot \frac{\gamma_2^=}{n} - \sum_{k=\tau+1}^{n} \theta(k) \cdot \frac{\gamma_2^>}{n^2} \geq \alpha_1 - \frac{\gamma_2^< + \gamma_2^= + \gamma_2^>}{n}.$$

Substituting the value of $\alpha_1$ and using $\gamma_2 = \gamma_2^< + \gamma_2^= + \gamma_2^>$, we have,

$$\text{ALG} \geq 1 - \frac{d}{e}\left(\frac{b+d-bd}{d}\right)^{1/b} - \frac{\gamma_2}{n}.$$

□

### 4.3 Analysis of Case 3

Suppose the set $\{X_1, \ldots, X_n\}$ of random variables falls into Case 3 of the algorithm. Then the algorithm chooses $\alpha_1 = \cdots = \alpha_n = T$, where $\int_T^{\infty} \Pr[X \geq x]dx = d$ and $\int_0^T \Pr[X \geq x]dx = 1 - d$. Consider the event that the algorithm does not pick any of the samples, and recall that its probability is $\theta(n)$, by definition. This event happens if and only if all the samples are less than $T$, or equivalently, the maximum of the samples is less than $T$. Our first lemma states that this event is not too likely.

Lemma 4.7. *Define $h = \frac{ca-1+d}{a-1+d}$. Then the algorithm chooses some sample with probability at least $h$, that is,*

$$1 - \theta(n) = \Pr[\exists i\, X_i \geq T] = \Pr[X \geq T] > h.$$

Proof. Since we are in Case 3, we have $\int_0^a \Pr[X \geq x]dx > ca$. Recall Equation (2), which stated that we choose $a$, $c$, and $d$ such that $ac + d > 1$. Thus,

$$\int_0^T \Pr[X \geq x]dx = 1 - d < ac < \int_0^a \Pr[X \geq x]dx.$$

This implies $T < a$. For any $x \in [T, a]$, $\Pr[X \geq x] \leq \Pr[X \geq T]$. Thus,

$$1 - d + (a - T)\Pr[X \geq T] \geq \int_0^T \Pr[X \geq x]dx + \int_T^a \Pr[X \geq x]dx = \int_0^a \Pr[X \geq x]dx > ca.$$

Therefore,

$$1 - \theta(n) = \Pr[X \geq T] > \frac{ca - 1 + d}{a - T} \geq \frac{ca - 1 + d}{a - 1 + d} = h$$

where we used the lower bound on $T$ given by (3) for the second inequality. □

Next, we bound $\sum_{k=1}^n \int_0^{\alpha_k} \Pr[z_k \geq x]dx$ and $\sum_{k=1}^n \int_{\alpha_k}^{\infty} \Pr[z_k \geq x]dx$ from below. Substituting these lower bounds in Equation (1), we get a lower bound on the algorithm's profit. From Proposition 3.1 and recalling that $\alpha_{n+1} = 0$, we have,

$$\sum_{k=1}^n \int_0^{\alpha_k} \Pr[z_k \geq x]dx = \alpha_1 - \sum_{k=1}^n \theta(k)(\alpha_k - \alpha_{k+1}) = T - \theta(n) \cdot T = (1 - \theta(n))T \geq h(1 - d) \quad (6)$$

where we used Lemma 4.7 and Equation (3) for the last inequality.

Reusing some notation and arguments from Esfandiari et al. [8], let $q_{-i}(k)$ denote the probability that the algorithm rejects the first $k$ samples, given that none of them came from $X_i$. Then

$$\Pr[z_k \geq x] = \sum_{i=1}^n \Pr[\sigma(k) = i] \cdot \Pr[z_k \geq x \mid \sigma(k) = i] = \frac{1}{n} \sum_{i=1}^n \Pr[z_k \geq x \mid \sigma(k) = i].$$

Suppose $x \geq \alpha_k = T$. Conditioned on $\sigma(k) = i$, the event $z_k \geq x$ happens if and only if the following two independent events happen: the algorithm rejects the first $k - 1$ samples, and $X_i \geq x$. Thus, $\Pr[z_k \geq x \mid \sigma(k) = i] = q_{-i}(k - 1) \cdot \Pr[X_i \geq x]$, and consequently, $\Pr[z_k \geq x] = \frac{1}{n} \sum_{i=1}^n q_{-i}(k - 1) \cdot \Pr[X_i \geq x]$. Therefore,

$$\sum_{k=1}^n \int_{x=\alpha_k}^{\infty} \Pr[z_k \geq x]dx = \sum_{k=1}^n \int_{x=T}^{\infty} \frac{1}{n} \sum_{i=1}^n q_{-i}(k - 1) \cdot \Pr[X_i \geq x]dx.$$

Interchanging the order of summations and integration, we get,

$$\sum_{k=1}^n \int_{x=\alpha_k}^{\infty} \Pr[z_k \geq x]dx = \sum_{i=1}^n \left(\frac{1}{n} \sum_{k=1}^n q_{-i}(k - 1)\right) \cdot \left(\int_{x=T}^{\infty} \Pr[X_i \geq x]dx\right).$$

Define $\mu_i = \int_{x=T}^{\infty} \Pr[X_i \geq x]dx$, the quantity in the second pair of parentheses above. Thus,

$$\sum_{k=1}^n \int_{x=\alpha_k}^{\infty} \Pr[z_k \geq x]dx = \sum_{i=1}^n \left(\frac{1}{n} \sum_{k=1}^n q_{-i}(k - 1)\right) \cdot \mu_i.$$

Define $E_i$ to be the event that the algorithm encounters $X_i$, that is, it does not choose a sample before it sees $X_i$. Then observe that $\Pr[E_i | \sigma(k) = i] = q_{-i}(k-1)$, and thus, $\Pr[E_i] = \sum_{k=1}^n \Pr[\sigma(k) = i] \cdot \Pr[E_i | \sigma(k) = i] = \frac{1}{n} \sum_{k=1}^n q_{-i}(k - 1)$, the expression in the parentheses above. Therefore,

$$\sum_{k=1}^n \int_{x=\alpha_k}^{\infty} \Pr[z_k \geq x]dx = \sum_{i=1}^n \Pr[E_i] \cdot \mu_i. \quad (7)$$

In order to lower bound the above, we need a crucial lemma, which states that there is one *prominent* random variable among $\{X_1, \ldots, X_n\}$ which is larger than $T$ with a large probability, whereas the others are unlikely to exceed $T$. For the rest of this section, we assume, without loss of generality, that $\Pr[X_1 \geq T] = \max_i \Pr[X_i \geq T]$ (that is, the *prominent* random variable is $X_1$).

Lemma 4.8. *Define $g \in (0, 1]$ to be the unique*[2] *number such that $(1-g)^{1/g} = (1-h)^{1/b}$. Then $\Pr[X_1 \geq T] \geq g$ and $\sum_{i=2}^n \Pr[X_i \geq T] \leq b - g$.*

The proof of Lemma 4.8 relies on the following technical result.

Lemma 4.9. *Suppose $y_1, \ldots, y_n$ are such that $0 \leq y_i \leq p$ for all $i$, and $\sum_{i=1}^n y_i \leq b$, where $p \in [0, 1]$. Then we have $\prod_{i=1}^n (1-y_i) \geq (1-p)^{b/p}$.*

Proof. Let $(y_1, \ldots, y_n)$ minimize $\prod_{i=1}^n (1-y_i)$ subject to the constraints $0 \leq y_i \leq p$ for all $i$, and $\sum_{i=1}^n y_i \leq b$. If $np \leq b$, then it is easy to see that $y_1 = \ldots = y_n = p$ is the optimum. Then $\prod_{i=1}^n (1-y_i) = (1-p)^n \geq (1-p)^{b/p}$, because $1-p \in [0, 1]$ and $n \leq b/p$. This implies the claim.

Now suppose $np > b$. Then some $y_i$ must be less than $p$. Further, $\sum_{i=1}^n y_i$ must be equal to $b$, otherwise we can increase one of the $y_i$s, resulting in a decrease in the objective value while maintaining feasibility. If we have $0 < y_i \leq y_j < p$ for some $i \neq j$, then we may choose an appropriate $\varepsilon > 0$ and replace $(y_i, y_j)$ by $(y_i - \varepsilon, y_j + \varepsilon)$, thereby decreasing $\prod_{i=1}^n (1-y_i)$ while still maintaining feasibility, and contradicting the optimality of $(y_1, \ldots, y_n)$. Thus, we must have at most one $y_i$ which is in $(0, p)$. This forces that $\lfloor b/p \rfloor$ many $y_i$s are $p$, one $y_i$ is $b - p\lfloor b/p \rfloor = p(b/p - \lfloor b/p \rfloor)$, and the rest are zero. Thus,

$$\prod_{i=1}^n (1-y_i) = (1-p)^{\lfloor b/p \rfloor}(1 - p(b/p - \lfloor b/p \rfloor)) \geq (1-p)^{\lfloor b/p \rfloor}(1-p)^{(b/p - \lfloor b/p \rfloor)} = (1-p)^{b/p}$$

where we used the identity $1 - xz \geq (1-x)^z$ for $x, z \in [0, 1]$ as long as $1-x$ and $z$ are not both zero. □

As a consequence, Lemma 4.8 is proved as follows.

Proof of Lemma 4.8. Suppose, for contradiction, that $\Pr[X_1 \geq T] = \max_i \Pr[X_i \geq T] < g$. We have $\sum_{i=1}^n \Pr[X_i \geq T] < b$, otherwise the algorithm would execute Case 2 and not Case 3. Applying Lemma 4.9 (with $y_i = \Pr[X_i \geq T]$), we have

$$\Pr[\exists i\, X_i \geq T] = 1 - \prod_{i=1}^n (1 - \Pr[X_i \geq T]) \leq 1 - (1-g)^{b/g} = 1 - (1-h) = h.$$

This contradicts Lemma 4.7. Thus, $\Pr[X_1 \geq T] \geq g$, which also implies $\sum_{i=2}^n \Pr[X_i \geq T] \leq b - g$, because $\sum_{i=1}^n \Pr[X_i \geq T] < b$. □

Lemma 4.8 enables us to prove Lemma 4.10, which gives a lower bound on $\Pr[E_i]$. Lemma 4.10 states that the *prominent* random variable $X_1$ is encountered with probability close to 1, whereas each of the others is encountered with probability almost 1/2. An intuitive explanation for this is the following. Lemma 4.8 states that $X_2, \ldots, X_n$ are together unlikely to cause the algorithm to stop. Therefore, the algorithm must see $X_1$ with probability close to one. Moreover, each $X_i$ ($i > 1$) appears before $X_1$ with probability 1/2. Given that this happens, the algorithm is unlikely to stop before it sees $X_i$. Thus, $X_i$ is seen with probability close to 1/2.

Lemma 4.10. $\Pr[E_1] \geq 1 - \frac{b-g}{2}$, *and for $i > 1$, we have* $\Pr[E_i] \geq \frac{1}{2}\left(1 - \frac{b-g}{3}\right)$.

[2] Observe that $\zeta : (0, 1] \longrightarrow [0, 1/e)$ defined as $\zeta(z) = (1-z)^{1/z}$ is a monotonically decreasing function with $\zeta(1) = 0$ and $\lim_{z \to 0} \zeta(z) = 1/e$. We will ensure that $0 \leq (1-h)^{1/b} < 1/e$, so that $g$ exists.

Proof. Let $S_i = \{j \in [n] \mid \sigma^{-1}(j) < \sigma^{-1}(i)\} \subseteq [n] \setminus i$ be the random subset of indices $j$ whose position is before $i$ in the random permutation $\sigma$. Then

$$\Pr[E_i \mid S_i] = \Pr[X_j < T\ \forall j \in S_i] \geq 1 - \sum_{j \in S_i} \Pr[X_j \geq T] = 1 - \sum_{j \neq i} \Pr[X_j \geq T] \cdot \mathbb{I}[j \in S_i] \quad (8)$$

where the inequality follows by the union bound.

First, consider the case of $i = 1$. By (8), we have,

$$\Pr[E_1] \geq \mathbb{E}_{S_1}\left[1 - \sum_{j=2}^{n} \Pr[X_j \geq T] \cdot \mathbb{I}[j \in S_1]\right] = 1 - \sum_{j=2}^{n} \Pr[X_j \geq T] \cdot \Pr[j \in S_1].$$

Every $j \neq 1$ is equally likely to be before 1 and after 1 in the random permutation. Thus, $\Pr[j \in S_1] = 1/2$. Therefore,

$$\Pr[E_1] \geq 1 - \frac{1}{2}\sum_{j=2}^{n} \Pr[X_j \geq T] \geq 1 - \frac{b-g}{2}$$

where we used Lemma 4.8 for the second inequality.

Next, let $i > 1$. Again, by (8), we have,

$$\begin{aligned}\Pr[E_i \mid 1 \notin S_i] &\geq \mathbb{E}_{S_i}\left[1 - \sum_{j \neq i} \Pr[X_j \geq T] \cdot \mathbb{I}[j \in S_i] \mid 1 \notin S_i\right] \\ &= 1 - \sum_{j \notin \{1,i\}} \Pr[X_j \geq T] \cdot \Pr[j \in S_i \mid 1 \notin S_i].\end{aligned}$$

Given $1 \notin S_i$, that is, 1 is after $i$, it is equally likely that $j \notin \{1, i\}$ is before $i$, between $i$ and 1, and after 1, in the random permutation. Thus, $\Pr[j \in S_i \mid 1 \notin S_i] = 1/3$. Therefore,

$$\Pr[E_i \mid 1 \notin S_i] \geq 1 - \frac{1}{3}\sum_{j \notin \{1,i\}} \Pr[X_j \geq T] \geq 1 - \frac{1}{3}\sum_{j \neq 1} \Pr[X_j \geq T] \geq 1 - \frac{b-g}{3}$$

where we used Lemma 4.8 for the last inequality. Therefore,

$$\Pr[E_i] \geq \Pr[1 \notin S_i] \cdot \Pr[E_i \mid 1 \notin S_i] \geq \frac{1}{2}\left(1 - \frac{b-g}{3}\right)$$

as required. □

Substituting the bounds given by Lemma 4.10 in Equation (7), we get,

$$\begin{aligned}\sum_{k=1}^{n} \int_{\alpha_k}^{\infty} \Pr[z_k \geq x]dx &\geq \left(1 - \frac{b-g}{2}\right) \cdot \mu_1 + \frac{1}{2}\left(1 - \frac{b-g}{3}\right) \cdot \sum_{i=2}^{n} \mu_i \\ &= \left(\frac{1}{2} - \frac{b-g}{3}\right) \cdot \mu_1 + \frac{1}{2}\left(1 - \frac{b-g}{3}\right) \cdot \sum_{i=1}^{n} \mu_i. \quad (9)\end{aligned}$$

We are thus left to bound $\mu_1$ and $\sum_{i=1}^{n} \mu_i$ from below.

Lemma 4.11. *$\mu_1 \geq ca - (1-d) - (a-1+d)(b-g)$.*

Proof. By the union bound, we have,

$$\int_T^a \sum_{i=1}^{n} \Pr[X_i \geq x]dx \geq \int_T^a \Pr[X \geq x]dx = \int_0^a \Pr[X \geq x]dx - \int_0^T \Pr[X \geq x]dx.$$

Using the facts that $\int_0^a \Pr[X \geq x]dx > ca$ (else we would be in Case 1) and $\int_0^T \Pr[X \geq x]dx = 1-d$ (definition of $T$), we have,

$$\int_T^a \sum_{i=1}^{n} \Pr[X_i \geq x]dx \geq ca - (1-d). \tag{10}$$

On the other hand, using Lemma 4.8 and Equation (3), we also have,

$$\int_T^a \sum_{i=2}^{n} \Pr[X_i \geq x]dx \leq (a-T)(b-g) \leq (a-1+d)(b-g). \tag{11}$$

Subtracting Equation 11 from Equation 10, we get,

$$\int_T^a \Pr[X_1 \geq x]dx \geq ca - (1-d) - (a-1+d)(b-g).$$

The claim follows by observing that $\mu_1 = \int_T^\infty \Pr[X_1 \geq x]dx \geq \int_T^a \Pr[X_1 \geq x]dx$. □

Finally, $\sum_{i=1}^n \mu_i$ is easily bounded as

$$\sum_{i=1}^n \mu_i = \sum_{i=1}^n \int_T^\infty \Pr[X_i \geq x]dx = \int_T^\infty \sum_{i=1}^n \Pr[X_i \geq x]dx \geq \int_T^\infty \Pr[X \geq x]dx = d \tag{12}$$

where the inequality is due to union bound.

As a result of the above analysis, we get the following bound on the competitive ratio.

Theorem 4.12. *Suppose that the input set of distributions falls into Case 3 of the algorithm. Then the algorithm's expected profit is at least*

$$h(1-d) + \left(\frac{1}{2} - \frac{b-g}{3}\right) \cdot (ca - (1-d) - (a-1+d)(b-g)) + \frac{1}{2}\left(1 - \frac{b-g}{3}\right) \cdot d.$$

Proof. Substituting Equation (6) and Equation (9) into Equation (1), and then using the bounds given by Equation (12) and Lemma 4.11, the claim follows. □

## 4.4 The Overall Competitive Ratio

We take $a$, $c$, $d$, and $g$ as independent parameters, so that $h = \frac{ca-1+d}{a-1+d}$, and because $(1-g)^{1/g} = (1-h)^{1/b}$, we get that $b = g\ln(1-h)/\ln(1-g)$. We numerically verified that for $a = 1 - 1.31/e$, $c = 0.98$, $d = 0.62$, and $g = 0.88$, we get the desired competitive ratio. It is easy to check $ac + d > 1$, which we promised earlier. We get $h \approx 0.925$, $b \approx 1.075$, and the competitive ratio lower bounds given by Theorems 4.3, 4.6, and 4.12 are all at least $c^* - O(n^{-1})$, for some $c^* > 1 - 1/e + 1/400$. It remains to show how the $O(n^{-1})$ term can be eliminated.

Lemma 4.13. *If there exists a $c$-competitive algorithm for the Prophet Secretary problem with $N$ random variables, then there exists a $c$-competitive algorithm for the Prophet Secretary problem with $n$ random variables for every $n < N$.*

Proof. Let ALG($N$) denote the algorithm. The required algorithm ALG($n$) behaves as follows. Given $n$ random variables $X_1, \ldots, X_n$, it adds $N - n$ ghost random variables $X_{n+1}, \ldots, X_N$ which take value zero deterministically. This does not change the expectation of the maximum. We now argue that ALG($n$) can essentially simulate the behavior of ALG($N$). Given a permutation $\sigma$ of $[n]$, we can generate a permutation $\sigma'$ of $[N]$ as follows. Arrange $n+1, \ldots, N$ uniformly at random in $N - n$ out of $N$ locations, then place $1, \ldots, n$ in the $n$ vacant locations in the order specified by $\sigma$. If $\sigma$ is a uniformly random permutation of $[n]$, then $\sigma'$ is a uniformly random permutation of $[N]$. ALG($n$) uses this trick as follows. First it places the ghost random variables into $N - n$ out of $N$

locations, and starts running ALG($N$). As soon as it encounters a vacant location, it asks for the next real input, and passes it on to ALG($N$). Clearly, since ALG($N$) is $c$-competitive, so is ALG($n$).

It is instructive to simplify the working of ALG($n$). Given the sequence of thresholds $\alpha_1, \ldots, \alpha_N$ chosen by ALG($N$), ALG($n$) essentially chooses a random subsequence of $n$ thresholds and uses them. Clearly, since the algorithm is $c$-competitive on an average, there exists a subsequence of $\alpha_1, \ldots, \alpha_N$ with $n$ thresholds which achieves $c$-competitiveness. □

Corollary 4.14. *If there exists an algorithm with competitive ratio $c - O(n^{-1})$ for the Prophet Secretary problem on n random variables, then for any $\varepsilon > 0$ there exists a $(c-\varepsilon)$-competitive algorithm for the Prophet Secretary problem.*

Proof. Given an instance of the Prophet Secretary problem on $n$ random variables, choose $N$ large enough so that the $O(N^{-1})$ term in the competitive ratio is less than $\varepsilon$, and apply Lemma 4.13. □

As a consequence of the above corollary, we have an algorithm for the Prophet Secretary problem with competitive ratio $c^* - \varepsilon$ for every $\varepsilon > 0$. Since $c^* > 1 - 1/e + 1/400$, Theorem 1.1 follows.

## 5 A HARDNESS RESULT FOR DISTRIBUTION-INSENSITIVE ALGORITHMS

Recall the definition of a deterministic distribution-insensitive algorithm from Section 2: such an algorithm chooses its thresholds $\alpha_1, \ldots, \alpha_n$ deterministically merely with the knowledge of the expected value of the maximum of the random variables, which we assumed to be one. Therefore, the adversary may adapt the input set of random variables to the algorithm subject to keeping the expectation of their maximum to be one. We now give an adversarial strategy which forces an upper bound of $11/15$ on the competitive ratio of any deterministic distribution-insensitive algorithm ALG. This proves Theorem 1.2.

Let $n = 3$, and let $\alpha_1, \alpha_2, \alpha_3$ be the thresholds chosen by a deterministic distribution-insensitive algorithm ALG. Without loss of generality, we assume $\alpha_3 = 0$, because if the algorithm does not pick any of the first two samples, then it can only benefit by picking the last one, no matter how small it is. Depending on the values of $\alpha_1$ and $\alpha_2$, the adversary chooses one of the following instances as input to the algorithm, where $\varepsilon > 0$ is an arbitrarily small constant.

(1) $X_1$ is 1 deterministically; $X_2$ and $X_3$ are both 0 deterministically.
(2) $X_1$ is 1 deterministically; $X_2$ and $X_3$ are both $\alpha_1$ deterministically.
(3) $X_1$ is $(1-(1-\varepsilon)(\alpha_1-\varepsilon))/\varepsilon$ with probability $\varepsilon$ and $\alpha_1 - \varepsilon$ with probability $1-\varepsilon$; $X_2$ and $X_3$ are both $\alpha_2$ deterministically. (This instance is used only if $\alpha_1 > \alpha_2$.)
(4) $X_1$ is $(1-(1-\varepsilon)(\min(\alpha_1,\alpha_2)-\varepsilon))/\varepsilon$ with probability $\varepsilon$ and $\min(\alpha_1,\alpha_2) - \varepsilon$ with probability $1-\varepsilon$; $X_2$ and $X_3$ are both 0 deterministically. (This instance is used only if $\min(\alpha_1,\alpha_2) > 0$.)

Observe that for each of the instances above, $\mathbb{E}[\max_i X_i] = \mathbb{E}[X_1] = 1$. In order to prove an upper bound on the competitive ratio of ALG, we first consider the case where one of $\alpha_1$ and $\alpha_2$ is larger than 1, and analyze the algorithm's performance on Instance 1.

Lemma 5.1. *If $\alpha_1 > 1$ or $\alpha_2 > 1$, then the competitive ratio of ALG is no larger than $2/3$.*

Proof. Consider the first instance, where $X_1$ is 1 deterministically, and $X_2$ and $X_3$ are both 0 deterministically. Suppose $\alpha_1 > 1$. Then ALG misses $X_1$ with probability at least $1/3$, so the expectation of its profit is at most $2/3$. The same argument holds if $\alpha_2 > 1$. □

We therefore assume for the rest of this section that both $\alpha_1$ and $\alpha_2$ are at most 1. In the next three lemmas, we analyze the algorithm's performance on Instances 2-4, each resulting in an upper bound on the algorithm's competitive ratio as a function of $\alpha_1$ and $\alpha_2$. Then we argue that the minimum of the three bounds is at most $11/15$ for any choice of $\alpha_1$ and $\alpha_2$.

LEMMA 5.2. *The competitive ratio of ALG is no larger than* $(1 + 2\alpha_1)/3$.

PROOF. Consider the second instance, where $X_1$ is 1 deterministically, and $X_2$ and $X_3$ are both $\alpha_1$ deterministically. ALG necessarily accepts the first sample, because all the random variables are at least $\alpha_1$ with probability one. With probability 1/3, $X_1$ appears first and ALG's profit is 1, whereas with probability 2/3, one of $X_2$ and $X_3$ comes first, resulting in the ALG's profit being $\alpha_1$. Thus, the expectation of ALG's profit is $(1 + 2\alpha_1)/3$. □

LEMMA 5.3. *If* $\alpha_1 > \alpha_2$*, then the competitive ratio of ALG is no larger than* $(2 - \alpha_1 + 2\alpha_2)/3$.

PROOF. Consider the third instance, where $X_1$ is $(1 - (1 - \varepsilon)(\alpha_1 - \varepsilon))/\varepsilon$ with probability $\varepsilon$ and $\alpha_1 - \varepsilon$ with probability $1 - \varepsilon$, whereas both $X_2$ and $X_3$ are $\alpha_2$ deterministically. Suppose $X_1$ appears first. If its value is realized to be $(1 - (1 - \varepsilon)(\alpha_1 - \varepsilon))/\varepsilon$, then the algorithm picks it; otherwise the algorithm picks $\alpha_2$ in the next round. Suppose $X_1$ appears second. Then the first sample, which is necessarily $\alpha_2$, is rejected, and since $X_1 \geq \alpha_2$ with probability one, the algorithm picks whatever value is realized for $X_1$. If $X_1$ appears last, then the algorithm rejects the first sample, which is $\alpha_2$, and accepts the second one, which is also $\alpha_2$. Thus, the expected profit of the algorithm is

$$\frac{1}{3} \cdot \left(\varepsilon \cdot \frac{1 - (1 - \varepsilon)(\alpha_1 - \varepsilon)}{\varepsilon} + (1 - \varepsilon) \cdot \alpha_2\right) + \frac{1}{3} \cdot \mathbb{E}[X_1] + \frac{1}{3} \cdot \alpha_2 = \frac{1}{3} \cdot (1 - (1 - \varepsilon)(\alpha_1 - \varepsilon - \alpha_2) + 1 + \alpha_2).$$

As $\varepsilon \to 0$, this approaches $(2 - \alpha_1 + 2\alpha_2)/3$. □

LEMMA 5.4. *If* $\min(\alpha_1, \alpha_2) = \alpha > 0$*, then the competitive ratio of ALG is no larger than* $(3 - 2\alpha)/3$.

PROOF. Consider the fourth instance, where $X_1$ is $(1 - (1 - \varepsilon)(\alpha - \varepsilon))/\varepsilon$ with probability $\varepsilon$ and $\alpha - \varepsilon$ with probability $1 - \varepsilon$, whereas both $X_2$ and $X_3$ are 0 deterministically. If $X_1$ appears first or second, then the algorithm picks it if and only if its realized value is $(1 - (1 - \varepsilon)(\alpha - \varepsilon))/\varepsilon$. If $X_1$ appears last, then the algorithm picks it irrespective of its realized value. Thus, the expected profit of the algorithm is

$$\frac{2}{3} \cdot \left(\varepsilon \cdot \frac{1 - (1 - \varepsilon)(\alpha - \varepsilon)}{\varepsilon}\right) + \frac{1}{3} \cdot \mathbb{E}[X_1] = \frac{1}{3} \cdot (2 - 2(1 - \varepsilon)(\alpha - \varepsilon) + 1).$$

As $\varepsilon \to 0$, this approaches $(3 - 2\alpha)/3$. □

The above lemmas allow us to prove Theorem 1.2 as follows.

PROOF OF THEOREM 1.2. First, suppose $\alpha_1 > \alpha_2 > 0$. Then by Lemmas 5.2, 5.3, and 5.4, the competitive ratio of the algorithm is at most

$$\frac{\min(1 + 2\alpha_1, 2 - \alpha_1 + 2\alpha_2, 3 - 2\alpha_2)}{3} \leq \frac{1 \cdot (1 + 2\alpha_1) + 2 \cdot (2 - \alpha_1 + 2\alpha_2) + 2 \cdot (3 - 2\alpha_2)}{(1 + 2 + 2) \cdot 3} = \frac{11}{15}.$$

Next, suppose $\alpha_1 > \alpha_2 = 0$. Then by Lemmas 5.2 and 5.3, the competitive ratio of the algorithm is at most

$$\frac{\min(1 + 2\alpha_1, 2 - \alpha_1)}{3} \leq \frac{1 \cdot (1 + 2\alpha_1) + 2 \cdot (2 - \alpha_1)}{(1 + 2) \cdot 3} = \frac{5}{9} < \frac{11}{15}.$$

On the other hand, if $0 < \alpha_1 \leq \alpha_2$, then by Lemmas 5.2 and 5.4, the competitive ratio of the algorithm is at most

$$\frac{\min(1 + 2\alpha_1, 3 - 2\alpha_1)}{3} \leq \frac{1 + 2\alpha_1 + 3 - 2\alpha_1}{6} = \frac{2}{3} < \frac{11}{15}.$$

Finally, if $0 = \alpha_1 \leq \alpha_2$, then by Lemma 5.2, the competitive ratio of the algorithm is at most $1/3 < 11/15$. □

## 6 CONCLUDING REMARKS

Our understanding of the Prophet Secretary problem is still limited, and there is a lot of scope for diving deeper. We showed that $1 - 1/e$ is not the correct competitive ratio for the Prophet Secretary problem. Under the natural restriction of deterministic distribution-insensitivity, we showed that no algorithm can have competitive ratio larger than $11/15$. We conjecture that none of the bounds known bounds for the Prophet Secretary problem is tight. As this is a fundamental problem, finding the right competitive ratio is an important question which is still wide open.

## REFERENCES

[1] Melika Abolhassani, Soheil Ehsani, Hossein Esfandiari, MohammadTaghi Hajiaghayi, Robert D. Kleinberg, and Brendan Lucier. 2017. Beating 1-1/e for ordered prophets. In *STOC*. 61–71. https://doi.org/10.1145/3055399.3055479

[2] Saeed Alaei. 2011. Bayesian Combinatorial Auctions: Expanding Single Buyer Mechanisms to Many Buyers. In *FOCS*. 512–521. https://doi.org/10.1109/FOCS.2011.90

[3] Yossi Azar, Ashish Chiplunkar, and Haim Kaplan. 2017. Prophet Secretary: Surpassing the 1-1/e Barrier. *CoRR* abs/1711.01834 (2017). arXiv:1711.01834 http://arxiv.org/abs/1711.01834

[4] Shuchi Chawla, Jason D. Hartline, David L. Malec, and Balasubramanian Sivan. 2010. Multi-parameter mechanism design and sequential posted pricing. In *STOC*. 311–320. https://doi.org/10.1145/1806689.1806733

[5] José R. Correa, Patricio Foncea, Ruben Hoeksma, Tim Oosterwijk, and Tjark Vredeveld. 2017. Posted Price Mechanisms for a Random Stream of Customers. In *EC*. 169–186. https://doi.org/10.1145/3033274.3085137

[6] E.B. Dynkin. 1963. The optimum choice of the instant for stopping a markov process. *Soviet Math. Dokl.* (1963).

[7] Soheil Ehsani, MohammadTaghi Hajiaghayi, Thomas Kesselheim, and Sahil Singla. 2018. Prophet Secretary for Combinatorial Auctions and Matroids. In *SODA*. 700–714. https://doi.org/10.1137/1.9781611975031.46

[8] Hossein Esfandiari, MohammadTaghi Hajiaghayi, Vahid Liaghat, and Morteza Monemizadeh. 2015. Prophet Secretary. In *ESA*. 496–508. https://doi.org/10.1007/978-3-662-48350-3_42

[9] Thomas S. Ferguson. 1989. Who Solved the Secretary Problem? *Statist. Sci.* 4, 3 (1989), 282–289. http://www.jstor.org/stable/2245639

[10] Mohammad Taghi Hajiaghayi, Robert D. Kleinberg, and Tuomas Sandholm. 2007. Automated Online Mechanism Design and Prophet Inequalities. In *AAAI*. 58–65. http://www.aaai.org/Library/AAAI/2007/aaai07-009.php

[11] T.P. Hill and Robert P. Kertz. 1982. Comparisons of stop rule and supremum expectations of I. I. D. random variables. *The Annals of Probability* 10 (1982), 336–345.

[12] Robert Kleinberg and S. Matthew Weinberg. 2012. Matroid prophet inequalities. In *STOC*. 123–136. https://doi.org/10.1145/2213977.2213991

[13] Ulrich Krengel and Louis Sucheston. 1977. Semiamarts and finite values. *Bull. Amer. Math. Soc.* 83 (1977), 745–747.

[14] Ulrich Krengel and Louis Sucheston. 1978. On semiamarts, amarts, and processes with finite value. *Adv. in Prob. Related Topics* 4 (1978), 197–266.

[15] Aviad Rubinstein. 2016. Beyond matroids: secretary problem and prophet inequality with general constraints. In *STOC*. 324–332. https://doi.org/10.1145/2897518.2897540

[16] Aviad Rubinstein and Sahil Singla. 2017. Combinatorial Prophet Inequalities. In *SODA*. 1671–1687. https://doi.org/10.1137/1.9781611974782.110

[17] Ester Samuel-Cahn. 1984. Comparison of threshold stop rules and maximum for independent nonnegative random variables. *The Annals of Probability* 12, 4 (1984), 1213–1216.

[18] Qiqi Yan. 2011. Mechanism Design via Correlation Gap. In *SODA*. 710–719. https://doi.org/10.1137/1.9781611973082.56

# Prophets and Secretaries with Overbooking

TOMER EZRA, Tel Aviv University, Israel
MICHAL FELDMAN, Tel Aviv University, Israel
ILAN NEHAMA, Kyushu University, Japan

The prophet and secretary problems demonstrate online scenarios involving the optimal stopping theory. In a typical prophet or secretary problem, selection decisions are assumed to be immediate and irrevocable. However, many online settings accommodate some degree of revocability. To study such scenarios, we introduce the *$\ell$-out-of-k* setting, where the decision maker can select up to $k$ elements immediately and irrevocably, but her performance is measured by the top $\ell$ elements in the selected set. Equivalently, the decision makes can hold up to $\ell$ elements at any given point in time, but can make up to $k - \ell$ returns as new elements arrive. We give upper and lower bounds on the competitive ratio of *$\ell$-out-of-k* prophet and secretary scenarios.

For *$\ell$-out-of-k* prophet scenarios we provide a single-sample algorithm with competitive ratio $1-\ell \cdot e^{-\Theta\left(\frac{(k-\ell)^2}{k}\right)}$. The algorithm is a single-threshold algorithm, which sets a threshold that equals the $(\frac{\ell+k}{2})^{th}$ highest sample, and accepts all values exceeding this threshold, up to reaching capacity $k$. On the other hand, we show that this result is tight if the number of possible returns is linear in $\ell$ (i.e., $k - \ell = \Theta(\ell)$). In particular, we show that no single-sample algorithm obtains a competitive ratio better than $1 - \frac{2^{-(2k+1)}}{k+1}$.

We also present a deterministic single-threshold algorithm for the 1*-out-of-k prophet* setting which obtains a competitive ratio of $1 - \frac{3}{2} \cdot e^{-k/6}$, knowing only the distribution of the maximum value. This result improves the result of [Assaf & Samuel-Cahn, J. of App. Prob., 2000].

Furthermore, we show that no *$\ell$-out-of-k prophet* algorithm, even one that has full information on the distributions of values from the outset, can achieve a better competitive ratio than $1 - \frac{1}{(2k+2)!}$.

For *$\ell$-out-of-k secretary* scenarios, we provide an algorithm with a competitive ratio $1 - \ell e^{-\frac{k-4\ell}{2+2\ln \ell}} - e^{-k/6}$. The algorithm divides the values into $\ell + 1$ segments, numbered from 0 to $\ell$. In the $j$-th segment the algorithm accepts the $i^{th}$ element if it belongs to the $j$ highest values seen so far, and the capacity $k$ is not exhausted. On the negative side, we show that no *$\ell$-out-of-k secretary* algorithm achieves a better competitive ratio than $1 - \frac{1}{e^k} + \frac{2}{3n}$.

Beyond the contribution to online algorithms and optimal stopping theory, our results have implications to mechanism design. In particular, we use our prophet algorithms to derive *overbooking* mechanisms with good welfare and revenue guarantees; these are mechanisms that sell more items than the seller's capacity, then allocate to the agents with the highest values among the selected agents.

Our results are summarized in Tables 1 and 2 below.

Full Paper: http://arxiv.org/abs/1805.05094

CCS Concepts: • **Theory of computation → Online algorithms**; **Algorithmic mechanism design**;

This work was partially supported by the European Research Council under the European Union's Seventh Framework Programme (FP7/2007-2013) / ERC grant agreement number 337122, by the Israel Science Foundation (grant number 317/17), and by JSPS KAKENHI Grant Numbers JP17H00761 and JP17H04695.

Authors' addresses: Tomer Ezra, Tel Aviv University, Israel, tomer.ezra@gmail.com; Michal Feldman, Tel Aviv University, Israel, mfeldman@tau.ac.il; Ilan Nehama, Kyushu University, Japan, ilan.nehama@mail.huji.ac.il.


*ACM EC'18, June 18–22, 2018, Ithaca, NY, USA.* ACM ISBN 978-1-4503-4529-3/18/06.
https://doi.org/10.1145/3219166.3219211

| | Lower bound | Upper bound |
|---|---|---|
| Single-sample algorithm | $1 - \ell \cdot e^{-\Theta\left(\frac{(k-\ell)^2}{k}\right)}$ | $1 - \frac{2^{-(2k+1)}}{k+1}$ |
| $D_{max}$ algorithm | $1 - \frac{3}{2} \cdot e^{-k/6}$ | $1 - \frac{1}{(2k+2)!}$ |

Table 1. *ℓ-out-of-k prophet*

| | Lower bound | Upper bound |
|---|---|---|
| Secretary | $1 - \ell e^{-\frac{k-4\ell}{2+2\ln \ell}} - e^{-k/6}$ | $1 - \frac{1}{e^k} + \frac{2}{3n}$ |

Table 2. *ℓ-out-of-k secretary*

Additional Key Words and Phrases: prophet inequality, secretary problem, online algorithms, mechanism design, welfare approximation

# Multiplicative Weights Update in Zero-Sum Games

JAMES P. BAILEY, Singapore University of Technology and Design
GEORGIOS PILIOURAS, Singapore University of Technology and Design

We study the classic setting where two agents compete against each other in a zero-sum game by applying the Multiplicative Weights Update (MWU) algorithm. In a twist of the standard approach of [11], we focus on the K-L divergence from the equilibrium but instead of providing an upper bound about the rate of increase we provide a nonnegative lower bound for games with interior equilibria. This implies movement away from equilibria and towards the boundary. In the case of zero-sum games without interior equilibria convergence to the boundary (and in fact to the minimal product of subsimplexes that contains all Nash equilibria) follows via an orthogonal argument. In that subspace divergence from the set of NE applies for all nonequilibrium initial conditions via the first argument. We argue the robustness of this non-equilibrating behavior by considering the following generalizations:

- **Step size:** Agents may be using different and even decreasing step sizes.
- **Dynamics:** Agents may be using Follow-the-Regularized-Leader algorithms and possibly apply different regularizers (e.g. MWU versus Gradient Descent). We also consider a linearized version of MWU.
- **More than two agents:** Multiple agents can interact via arbitrary networks of zero-sum polymatrix games and their affine variants.

Our results come in stark contrast with the standard interpretation of the behavior of MWU (and more generally regret minimizing dynamics) in zero-sum games, which is typically referred to as "converging to equilibrium". If equilibria are indeed predictive *even for the benchmark class of zero-sum games*, agents in practice must deviate robustly from the axiomatic perspective of optimization driven dynamics as captured by MWU and variants and apply carefully tailored equilibrium-seeking behavioral dynamics.

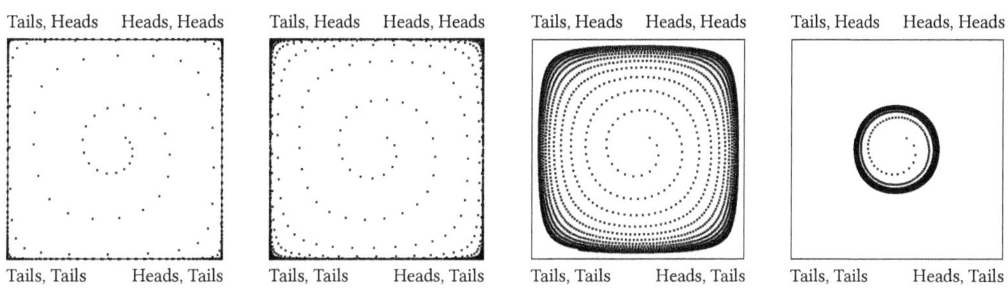


(a) $\epsilon_t = .5$ (b) $\epsilon_t = 1/\sqrt[3]{t}$ (c) $\epsilon_t = 1/\sqrt{t}$ (d) $\epsilon_t = 1/\sqrt[3]{t^2}$

Fig. 1. Player Strategies Spiraling Outwards in Matching Pennies when Updated with 2500 Iterations of Multiplicative Weights. All Experiments Start with the Same Initial Condition.

Authors' addresses: James P. Bailey, Singapore University of Technology and Design, james_bailey@sutd.edu.sg; Georgios Piliouras, Singapore University of Technology and Design, georgios@sutd.edu.sg.


*ACM EC'18, June 18–22, 2018, Ithaca, NY, USA.* ACM ISBN 978-1-4503-4529-3/18/06...$15.00
https://doi.org/10.1145/3219166.3219235

## 1 INTRODUCTION

We study arguably the most well known online learning dynamic, Multiplicative Weights Update (MWU) [12, 16] in the most well studied class of games (zero-sum games). Naturally, the prominence of each of these objects in their respective fields, i.e., the centrality of MWU for online learning, optimization and classification and similarly of zero-sum games for game theory is indisputable. In fact, both of these objects as well as the question about how does MWU behave in zero-sum games is a subject matter that is typically studied in undergrad and graduate courses on these subjects.

Our current understanding and interpretation of this setting revolves around a classic work by Freund and Schapire [11]. Their analysis focuses on establishing strong regret guarantees. In the case of a zero-sum game this produces a simple proof of von Neumann's min-max theorem and a provable method of approximately solving a game. Specifically, given that both agents apply (MWU), both the time average of the mixed strategy profiles as well as the utility of both agents converge approximately to their Nash equilibrium values, where the approximation error can become arbitrarily close to zero by choosing a sufficiently small step size. This result extends straightforwardly to general no-regret dynamics, and, in fact, the other desirable properties of the Nash equilibria such as polynomial-time tractability and convexity can be shown to readily follow from this close connection between no-regret learning and equilibration.

In the game theoretic literature, this major result is typically celebrated by the shorthand statement "MWU (no-regret dynamics) converges to equilibria in zero-sum games". Naturally, this statement is not formally accurate as it indicates a much stronger result, i.e., that the actual day-to-day behavior of MWU converges to equilibria. In spite of the classic nature of the problem, we are not aware of any formal analysis of the asymptotic behavior of MWU even for a specific instance of a zero-sum game (e.g., Matching Pennies).

To some extent, this lack of formal theoretical arguments is not surprising, as even a single dimensional discrete time dynamical system can exhibit totally unpredictable, chaotic behavior that is hard to characterize theoretically [15]. To make matters worse, recent results strongly suggest that the behavior of MWU in 2x2 coordination/potential games[1] is impossibly hard to completely characterize and predict. Specifically, [21] has shown that there exist specific instances of 2x2 potential games where the behavior of MWU exhibits bifurcations at critical values of its step size. For small values the system always converges to equilibria whereas if we keep increasing the step size eventually limit cycles emerge. For a different 2x2 potential game it is proven that MWU can exhibit chaotic behavior. Simulations of this system suggest that as we increase the step size of MWU, the system undergoes an infinite number of period doubling phase transitions. This behavior is not universal in 2x2 potential games as there seem to exist instances where it is impossible to induce chaotic behavior no matter how large we choose the step size to be. If the behavior MWU is so complex in 2x2 potential games, why should we expect it to be any simpler in 2x2 zero-sum games, let alone general constant-sum games?

Well, at least in the case of Matching Pennies, the simulations of MWU in Figure 1 seem to suggest an intuitively clear story. Given any fixed step size, e.g., $\epsilon = .5$ the dynamic converges to the boundary with the rate of convergence being an increasing function of $\epsilon$. For decreasing step sizes, e.g., $\epsilon_t = 1/\sqrt[3]{t}$ or $1/\sqrt{t}$, the system moves away from the equilibrium along a spiral. Interestingly enough, we get qualitatively different limit behavior depending on the rate of decrease of the step size with the $1/\sqrt{t}$ rate encoding the boundary between the two. For slower decreasing step sizes we still quickly converge to the boundary, whereas for faster rates the system converges to a closed curve in the interior. With hindsight, this curve is the boundary of a K-L divergence ball.

[1]These are games that lie on the antipode of zero-sum games. In coordination/potential games, the agents' incentives are strongly aligned and all agents act as if they wish to maximize a common potential function.

That is, this set contains all points at a fixed K-L divergence from the equilibrium. For the special case of $1/\sqrt{t}$ we still diverge to the boundary. We will show that this intuitive picture largely carries over to general zero-sum games, and furthermore present several extensions for different games and dynamics.

### 1.1 Results

We begin by showing that the K-L divergence from any fully mixed Nash equilibrium (NE) to the player strategies is increasing when players update their strategies using the MWU. This implies that the set of Nash equilibria repel player strategies explaining the outward spirals we observe in Figure 1. Building on this result, we establish that player strategies converge to the boundary for any constant $\epsilon$. Importantly, this analysis is robust. Our results extend to constant-sum polymatrix games and even if individual players opt to use different values for $\epsilon$. Moreover, our results apply even to the setting where agents use shrinking step sizes. Formally, player strategies converge to the boundary iff $\sum_{t=1}^{\infty} \epsilon_t^2 = \infty$ perfectly describing the contrast between the different phase portraits in Figure 1.

Otherwise, in the event where the only Nash equilibrium of the game is on the boundary, the K-L divergence may actually decrease in an iteration of MWU. Using different proof techniques we establish that player strategies converge to the smallest face containing the set of Nash equilibria. In that subspace divergence away from the set of NE applies for all nonequilibrium initial conditions via the first argument, completing our picture for the behavior of the MWU dynamics.

Finally we consider other standard regret minimizing dynamics. We show how our results carry over to the more general class of Follow-the-Regularized-Leader algorithms. In addition, our results hold for the linear version of MWU[2] in skew-symmetric games.

### 1.2 Related Work

The study of learning dynamics in game theory has a long history dating back to the work of Brown and Robinson [2, 26] on fictitious play in zero-sum games, which followed shortly after von Neumann's seminal work on zero-sum games [30, 31]. A good reference book cataloguing these developments is [13]. The classic results about time-average convergence of no-regret dynamics have been successfully generalized to include multiplayer extensions of network constant-sum games [3, 4, 9].

*Non-equilibrating dynamics in game theory.* Although traditionally research in the area aims at proving results about convergence of dynamics to equilibria, within the algorithmic game theory (AGT) community, there has been a steady stream of results cataloguing interesting non-equilibrium effects. Proving such non-equilibrium effects is typically rather hard, and results in this area typically revolve around specific examples of games with a handful of agents and strategies. [7] showed that MWU does not converge even in a time-average sense in the case of a specific 3x3 game. [14] established non-convergence for a continuous-time variant of MWU, known as the replicator dynamic, for a 2x2x2 game and show that as a result the system social welfare converges to states that dominate all Nash equilibria. Balcan et al. [1] studied MWU in rank-1 games (i.e., games where the summation of the payoff matrices of the two agents results in a rank-1 matrix). This games are in some sense almost constant-sum, and the paper shows that there exist such games where not even the time-average of MWU converges to equilibria. [21] proved the existence of Li-Yorke chaos in MWU dynamics of 2x2 potential games.

[2]This is a well known variant of MWU, where the weights are updated as $w \leftarrow w(1+\epsilon)^u$ they are updated as $w \leftarrow w(1+\epsilon u)$. This variant enjoys strong connections to biological and evolutionary dynamics [5, 18, 19].

*Continuous time dynamics in game theory.* From the perspective of evolutionary game theory, which typically studies continuous time dynamics, numerous nonconvergence results are known but again typically for small games [27]. In [23, 24], the authors show that replicator dynamics, the continuous time version of MWU exhibit a specific type of near periodic behavior, which is known as Poincaré recurrence. Recently, [20] showed how to generalize this cyclic behavior for replicator to more general continuous time variants of follow the regularized leader (FTRL) dynamics. Finally, [17] showed that this arguments can also be adapted in the case of dynamically evolving games. The papers in this category combine delicate arguments such as volume preservation and the existence of constants of motions for the dynamics to establish cyclic behavior. In the case of discrete time dynamics, such as the MWU, the system trajectories are more "rough" and these arguments which are suited for smooth dynamics are no longer valid. Finally, [22] has put forward a program for a general connection between game theoretic dynamics and concepts in topology that holds the promise of becoming a universal tool for analyzing non-equilibrium dynamics in games.

*Fast convergence to low regret states.* It is widely known that the time-average of no-regret algorithms converge to the set of coarse correlated equilibria. The "black-box" rate of convergence is $O(1/\sqrt{t})$ and it is achieved by MWU with suitably shrinking step size without making any assumptions about its environment. Recently, several authors have focused instead on obtaining stronger regret guarantees for systems of learning algorithms in games. [6] and [25] developed dynamics with a $O(\log t/t)$ regret minimization rate in two-player zero-sum games. [28] further analyzed a recency biased variant of follow the regularized leader (FTRL) in more general games and showed a $O(t^{-3/4})$ regret minimization rate. The social welfare converges at a rate of $O(1/t)$, a result which was extended to standard versions of FRTL dynamics in [10]. Finally, [8] studies the convergence properties of a specifically tailored dynamic in bilinear saddle problems and show convergence of the daily behavior to equilibrium. Based on this, they develop novel training algorithms for generative adversarial neural networks (GANs).

## 2 DEFINITIONS

### 2.1 Normal Form Games

We begin with basic definitions from game theory. A finite normal-form game $\Gamma \equiv \Gamma(\mathcal{N}, \mathcal{S}, u)$ consists of a set of players $\mathcal{N} = \{1, ..., N\}$ where player $i$ may select from a finite set of actions or pure strategies $\mathcal{S}_i$. Each player has a payoff function $u_i : \mathcal{S} \equiv \prod_i \mathcal{S}_i \to \mathbb{R}$ assigning reward $u_i(s)$ to player $i$. It is common to describe $u_i$ with a payoff tensor $A^{(i)}$ where $u_i(s) = A^{(i)}_s$.

Players are also allowed to use mixed strategies $x_i = (x_{is_i})_{s_i \in \mathcal{S}_i} \in \Delta(\mathcal{S}_i) \equiv \mathcal{X}_i$. The set of mixed strategies is $\mathcal{X} = \prod_i \mathcal{X}_i$. A strategy is fully mixed if $x_{is_i} > 0$ for all $s_i \in \mathcal{S}_i$ and $i \in \mathcal{N}$. Individuals the payoff of a mixed strategy linearly using expectation. Formally,

$$u_i(x) = \sum_{s \in \mathcal{S}} u_i(s) \prod_{i \in \mathcal{N}} x_{is_i}. \tag{1}$$

We also introduce additional notation to express player payouts for brevity in our analysis later. Let $v_{is_i}(x) = u_i(s_i; x_{-i})$[3] denote the reward $i$ receives if $i$ opts to play pure strategy $s_i$ when everyone else commits to their strategies described by $x$. This results in $u_i(x) = \langle v_i(x), x_i \rangle$. Let $P_i(x) = v_{is_i}(x)$ with probability $x_{is_i}$ be a random variable corresponding to the payout for player $i$ given the mixed profile $x$. Using this definition, only player $i$ introduces randomness to $i$'s reward and $x_{-i}$ is treated as a deterministic strategy. We can then write $u_i(x) = E[P_i(x)]$.

[3] $(s_i; x_{-i})$ denotes the strategy $x$ after replacing $x_i$ with $s_i$.

The most commonly used solution concept for games is the *Nash equilibrium*. A Nash equilibrium (NE) is a strategy $x^* \in \mathcal{X}$ where no player can do better by deviating from $x_i^*$. Formally,

$$u_i(x_i^*; x_{-i}^*) \geq u_i(x_i; x_{-i}^*) \text{ for all } x_i \in \mathcal{X}_i \text{ and } i \in \mathcal{N}. \tag{NE}$$

### 2.2 2-Player and Polymatrix Constant-Sum Games

The most commonly studied class of games are 2-player zero-sum games. A two-player zero-sum game $\Gamma$ is such that $\mathcal{N} = \{1, 2\}$ and $u_1 + u_2 = 0$. Letting $u \equiv u_1 = -u_2$, the value of a 2-player zero-sum game is

$$u_\Gamma = \max_{x_1 \in \mathcal{X}_1} \min_{x_2 \in \mathcal{X}_2} u(x_1; x_2) = \min_{x_2 \in \mathcal{X}_2} \max_{x_1 \in \mathcal{X}_1} u(x_1; x_2) \tag{2}$$

where equality comes from von Neuman's min-max theorem [30]. The solutions to (2) are the set of Nash equilibria of the game.

Constant-sum games are closely related to zero-sum games. A constant-sum game with parameter $c$ is such that $u_1 + u_2 = c$. By shifting either players utility function, a two-player constant-sum game can be transformed into a zero-sum game without changing the set of Nash equilibria.

Also of interest in this paper are games featuring a network of competitors. An $N$-player pairwise constant-sum polymatrix game $\Gamma$ consists of an interaction graph $\mathcal{G} = \mathcal{G}(\mathcal{N}, \mathcal{E})$ where the set of nodes $\mathcal{N}$ represent of players and where $\{i, j\}$ is an edge in $\mathcal{E}$ only if $i$ and $j$ compete in a constant-sum game with parameter $c_{ij}$.

Player $i$'s utility, $u_i$ is now expressed as a sum of the utilities gained in the games $i$ plays in the graph $\mathcal{G}$. Formally, let $u_{ij} = c_{ij} - u_{ji}$ be utility gained in $i$'s game against $j$ and

$$u_i(x) = \sum_{j:\{i,j\} \in \mathcal{E}} u_{ij}(x). \tag{3}$$

Without loss of generality we can assume $\mathcal{G}$ is a complete graph by letting $u_{ij}(x) = 0$ for all $x$ if $i$ and $j$ do not compete. Under this assumption, we can write the simpler $u_i(x) = \sum_{j \in \mathcal{N} \setminus \{i\}} u_{ij}(x)$.

### 2.3 Bregman Divergence from a Nash Equilibrium

Let $x^* \in \mathcal{X}$ be a Nash equilibrium and let $x \in \mathcal{X}$ be an arbitrary strategy profile. Then the Bregman divergence from $x^*$ to $x$ with respect to convex function $h$ is

$$D_h(x^* || x) = h(x^*) - h(x) - \langle \nabla h(x), x^* - x \rangle. \tag{Bregman Divergence}$$

A convex function we will be particularly interested in the course of this paper is the negative entropy function, $h(x) = \sum_{s_i \in S_i} x_{is_i} \ln(x_{is_i})$. The Bregman divergence for this function is referred to as the Kullback-Leibler (K-L) divergence and is given by

$$D_{KL}(x^* || x) = \sum_{i \in N} \sum_{s_i \in S_i} x_{is_i}^* \left( \ln x_{is_i}^* - \ln x_{is_i} \right) \tag{K-L Divergence}$$

### 2.4 Follow-the-Regularized-Leader

$$x_i^t = \operatorname*{argmax}_{x_i \in \mathcal{X}_i} \eta \sum_{s=0}^{t-1} u_i(x_i; x_{-i}^s) - h(x_i) \tag{FTRL}$$

If the negative entropy function is used as the regularizer, then FTRL results in the exponential weighted update algorithm given by

$$x_{is_i}^t = \frac{x_{is_i}^{t-1}(1+\epsilon)^{v_{is_i}(x^{t-1})}}{\sum_{s_i' \in S_i} x_{is_i'}^{t-1}(1+\epsilon)^{v_{is_i'}(x^{t-1})}} = \frac{x_{is_i}^t (1+\epsilon)^{v_{is_i}(x^{t-1})}}{E\left[(1+\epsilon)^{P_i(x^{t-1})}\right]} \tag{$MWU_e$}$$

where $\epsilon = e^{\eta} - 1$.

We will also consider the Linear Multiplicative Weight Update algorithm. While Linear MWU is not a FTRL algorithm, it is a regret minimizing algorithm for decaying values of $\epsilon$. It is given by

$$x^t_{is_i} = \frac{x^{t-1}_{is_i}(1 + \epsilon v_{is_i}(x^{t-1}))}{\sum_{s'_i \in S_i} x^{t-1}_{is'_i}(1 + \epsilon v_{is'_i}(x^{t-1}))} = \frac{x^{t-1}_{is_i}(1 + \epsilon v_{is_i}(x^{t-1}))}{1 + \epsilon u_i(x^{t-1})} \tag{$MWU_\ell$}$$

## 3 CONVERGENCE TO BOUNDARY IN MULTIPLICATIVE WEIGHTED UPDATE

We start our analysis by proving the repelling property of Nash equilibria.

THEOREM 3.1. *The K-L divergence between player strategies and any fully mixed Nash equilibrium is non-decreasing when strategies are updated with ($MWU_e$) for any 2-player constant-sum game.*

PROOF. Plugging ($MWU_e$) into (K-L Divergence), we obtain

$$D_{KL}(x^*||x^t) = \sum_{i\in N}\sum_{s_i\in S_i} x^*_{is_i}\left(\ln x^*_{is_i} - \ln x^t_{is_i}\right) \tag{4}$$

$$= \sum_{i\in N}\sum_{s_i\in S_i} x^*_{is_i}\left(\ln x^*_{is_i} - \ln x^{t-1}_{is_i} - v_{is_i}(x^{t-1})\ln(1+\epsilon) + \ln E\left[(1+\epsilon)^{P_i(x^{t-1})}\right]\right) \tag{5}$$

$$= D_{KL}(x^*||x^{t-1}) + \sum_{i\in N}\sum_{s_i\in S_i} x^*_{is_i}\left(\ln E\left[(1+\epsilon)^{P_i(x^{t-1})}\right] - v_{is_i}(x^{t-1})\ln(1+\epsilon)\right) \tag{6}$$

$$= D_{KL}(x^*||x^{t-1}) + \sum_{i\in N}\left(\ln E\left[(1+\epsilon)^{P_i(x^{t-1})}\right] - u_i(x^*_i; x^{t-1}_{-i})\ln(1+\epsilon)\right) \tag{7}$$

$$= D_{KL}(x^*||x^{t-1}) + \sum_{i\in N}\left(\ln E\left[(1+\epsilon)^{P_i(x^{t-1})}\right] - u_i(x^{t-1})\ln(1+\epsilon)\right) \tag{8}$$

The equlibrium $x^*$ is fully mixed implying $u_i(x^*_i, x^{t-1}_{-i}) = u_i(x^*)$ and $\sum_{i\in N} u_i(x^*_i; x^{t-1}_{-i}) = \sum_{i\in N} u_i(x^*) = \sum_{i\in N} u_i(x^{t-1})$ since the game is constant-sum. Therefore in the $t^{th}$ iteration of ($MWU_e$) the K-L divergence changes by

$$D_{KL}(x^*||x^t) - D_{KL}(x^*||x^{t-1}) = \sum_{i\in N} \ln E\left[(1+\epsilon)^{P_i(x^{t-1}) - u_i(x^{t-1})}\right] \tag{9}$$

$$\geq \sum_{i\in N} E\left[P_i(x^{t-1}) - u_i(x^{t-1})\right]\ln(1+\epsilon) = 0 \tag{10}$$

where the last inequality follows from Jensen's Inequality. □

*Definition 3.2.* Strategy $s_i \in S_i$ is *essential* iff there is a Nash equilibrium $x^*$ where $x^*_{is_i} > 0$.

It is straightforward to check that there is no fully mixed Nash equilibrium iff there is a non-essential strategy. The backward direction follows by definition, whereas the forward follows from the convexity of the equilibrium set.

We are now ready to prove our main result.

THEOREM 3.3. *For almost every 2-player constant-sum game, there exists $\epsilon_0 > 0$, such that as long as all agents use ($MWU_e$) with $\epsilon < \epsilon_0$, all non-equilibrium initial conditions converge to the boundary.*

*Specifically, in any game that has at least one interior NE, for all $\epsilon$, all non-equilibrium initial conditions converge to the boundary. In any game with no interior NE, as long as it has a unique NE (a genericity assumption), all non-equilibrium initial conditions converge to the minimal subspace that contains all essential strategies.*

We present the proof of convergence in two parts. First we show that if there is a fully mixed Nash equilibrium then the K-L divergence between the Nash equilibrium and the player strategies goes to infinity implying convergence to the boundary. This portion of the proof works for any $\epsilon$. In the second part of the proof, for the case of games with non-interior Nash equilibria, we show that under the generic assumption that the zero-sum game in question has a unique equilibrium[4] the probability of playing any non-essential strategy goes to 0 completing the proof of the theorem.

Proof of Theorem 3.3. First suppose there is a fully mixed Nash equilibrium $x^*$. By Lemma 3.1, $D_{KL}(x^*||x^t)$ is non-decreasing and there is a compact set $B$ such that $x^t \in B$ for all $t$ and $x^* \notin B$.

For contradiction, suppose $x^t$ does not converge to the boundary. This implies there exists $w > 0$ such $D_{KL}(x^*||x^t) \leq w$ for all $t$ since $D_{KL}(x^*||x^t)$ is non-decreasing. Thus we may assume that $B$ also excludes the boundary. (10) is saturated only if $x^t = x^*$ or $x^t$ is on the boundary. Therefore $D_{KL}(x^*||x^t) - D_{KL}(x^*||x^{t-1}) > 0$ for all $x^t$ since $x^t \in B$. $D_{KL}(x^*||x^t) - D_{KL}(x^*||x^{t-1})$ is continuous with respect to $x^t$ and each $x^t$ is in the compact $B$. Thus, there is a constant $d > 0$ such that $D_{KL}(x^*||x^t) - D_{KL}(x^*||x^{t-1}) \geq d$. This implies

$$\lim_{t\to\infty} D_{KL}(x^*||x^t) = D_{KL}(x^*||x^0) + \sum_{t=1}^{\infty} \left(D_{KL}(x^*||x^t) - D_{KL}(x^*||x^{t-1})\right) \quad (11)$$

$$\geq D_{KL}(x^*||x^0) + \sum_{t=0}^{\infty} d = \infty \quad (12)$$

and thus we reach a contradiction.

Now suppose there is no fully mixed Nash equilibrium and that player $i$ has a non-essential strategy $s_i$. Iteratively, the update ($MWU_e$) can be written as

$$x^t_{is_i} = \frac{x^0_{is_i}(1+\epsilon)^{t\cdot v_{is_i}(\bar{x}^{t-1})}}{E\left[(1+\epsilon)^{t\cdot P_i(\bar{x}^{t-1})}\right]} \quad (13)$$

where $\bar{x}^t = \sum_{s=0}^{t} \frac{x^s}{t+1}$ is the time average of player strategies and where the expectation is taken with respect to $x_i^{t-1}$. Since ($MWU_e$) has an $O(\epsilon)$ time-average regret, $\bar{x}^t$ converges to a $O(\epsilon)$-approximate Nash equilibrium.[5] Since for $\epsilon \to 0$ the set of $O(\epsilon)$-approximate Nash equilibria converges to the set of Nash equilibria, given any open neighborhood around the set of Nash equilibria we can choose an appropriate $\epsilon$ so that all the $O(\epsilon)$-approximate Nash equilibria are contained in that neighborhood.

For this portion of the proof we assume without loss of generality that $u_i(x^*) = 0$. Almost every constant-sum game has a unique Nash equilibrium $x^*$ [29]. Moreover, by [20] we have that that for every non-essential strategy $i$, $v_{is_i}(x^*) < u_i(x^*) = 0$. Let $\delta = v_{is_i}(x^*) < 0$. By the continuity of payoffs we have that for any mixed strategy profile $y$ in a small enough neighborhood around the equilibrium set, $v_{is_i}(y) < 2\delta/3$ whereas for any strategy $s_i'$ in the equilibrium support $v_{is_i'}(y) > \delta/3$. Let $\epsilon_0$ in the statement of the theorem be such that all $O(\epsilon_0)$-approximate Nash equilibria as strictly

[4]The set of zero-sum games with a unique equilibrium is open and dense in the space of all zero-sum games. Moreover, this slightly stronger result is also true. Within the set of all zero-sum games, the complement of the set of zero-sum games with unique equilibrium is closed and has Lebesgue measure zero [29].

[5]This is a well known fact. By the $O(\epsilon)$-regret property of the second agent, the time average utility of the first agent cannot be larger than $u_\Gamma + O(\epsilon)$. By the $O(\epsilon)$-regret property of the first agent, his utility for deviating to any strategy is at most $O(\epsilon)$ greater that his current time average utility which is at most $u_\Gamma + O(\epsilon)$. Specifically, his expected utility at $\bar{x}^t$ when both agents play their time average strategies is at most $u_\Gamma + O(\epsilon)$. A similar argument from the perspective of the second agent produces the analogous lower bound. This strategy profile is thus an $O(\epsilon)$ equilibrium of the game.

contained in the above neighborhood. We have that $t \cdot \left(v_{is_i}(\bar{x}^t) - v_{is_i'}(\bar{x}^t)\right) \to -\infty$ as $t \to \infty$. As a result, $x^t_{is_i}/x^t_{is_i'} \to 0$ as $t \to \infty$ and since $x^t_{is_i'}$ is upper bounded by 1, $x^t_{is_i} \to 0$ as $t \to \infty$. This completes the proof of the theorem. □

### 3.1 Exponential MWU Convergence in Polymatrix Games

THEOREM 3.4. *For every polymatrix constant-sum game with a fully mixed Nash equilibrium, every (non-equilibrium) initial strategy converges to the boundary when updated with ($MWU_e$) for any $\epsilon > 0$.*

Let $x$ denote an arbitrary strategy profile. Observe that

$$\sum_{i\in N} u_i(x_i^*; x_{-i}) = \sum_{i\in N}\sum_{j\in N\setminus\{i\}} u_{ij}(x_i^*; x_j) \tag{14}$$

$$= \sum_{j\in N}\sum_{i\in N\setminus\{j\}} u_{ij}(x_i^*; x_j) \tag{15}$$

$$= \sum_{j\in N}\sum_{i\in N\setminus\{j\}} u_{ij}(x^*) \tag{16}$$

$$= \sum_{i\in N} u_i(x^*) \tag{17}$$

$$= \sum_{i\in N} u_i(x) \tag{18}$$

The proof of Theorem 3.4 then follows analogously to Theorems 3.1 and 3.3.

### 3.2 Exponential MWU with Different Step Sizes

Players may opt to use a different value of $\epsilon$ in each iteration of ($MWU_e$). For instance, a common selection is $\epsilon_t = \frac{1}{\sqrt{t}}$ which guarantees vanishing regret. We extend our results to this setting.

$$x^t_{is_i} = \frac{x^{t-1}_{is_i}(1+\epsilon_t)^{v_{is_i}(x^{t-1})}}{E\left[(1+\epsilon_t)^{P_i(x^{t-1})}\right]} \tag{$MWU_e^{\epsilon_t}$}$$

THEOREM 3.5. *For every polymatrix constant-sum game with a fully mixed Nash equilibrium, every (non-equilibrium) initial strategy converges to the boundary when updated with ($MWU_e^{\epsilon_t}$) iff $\sum_{t=1}^{\infty}\epsilon_t^2 = \infty$.*

The proof of Theorem 3.5 requires showing that the $K-L$ divergence increases by approximately $\sum_{i\in N}\frac{Var[P_i(x^t)]}{2}\epsilon_t^2$. The remainder of the proof then follows analogously to Theorem 3.3. The details of this proof appear in Appendix A.

In practice, there is no reason all players update their weights using the same $\epsilon_t$, i.e., players $i$ may instead use weight $\epsilon_{it}$. As we show next, the result holds even if players all use different values for $\epsilon_t$ under certain conditions.

THEOREM 3.6. *The statement of Theorem 3.5 holds even if players are allowed to select different values for $\epsilon_{it}$, as long as $\frac{\prod_{k\in N\setminus\{i\}}\ln(1+\epsilon_{kt})}{\sum_{j\in N}\ln(1+\epsilon_{jt})}$ is time invariant for all $i \in N$.*

The proof of Theorem 3.6 requires examining $\sum_{i\in N}\frac{\prod_{k\in N\setminus\{i\}}\ln(1+\epsilon_{kt})}{\sum_{j\in N}\ln(1+\epsilon_{jt})}D_{KL}(x_i^*||x_i^t) \le c\cdot D_{KL}(x^*||x^t)$ for some constant $c > 0$ and then follows analogously to Theorems 3.1 and 3.5. As a corollary, for arbitrary, fixed but possibly different step-sizes $\epsilon_i$ ($MWU_e$) converges to the boundary.

While Theorem 3.6 guarantees there are many possible selections of $\epsilon_{it}$ that guarantee convergence of the boundary, we also show that $\epsilon_{it}$ may be selected so that the K-L divergence between player strategies and any fully mixed Nash equilibrium may actually decrease.

Proposition 3.7. *The K-L divergence between player strategies and any fully mixed Nash equilibrium may decrease when strategies are updated with (MWU$_e$) if players are allowed to select values for $\epsilon_{it}$ arbitrarily.*

The proof of Proposition 3.7 appears in Appendix B.

## 4 EXTENSIONS

In this section we examine other regret-minimizing dynamics. Specifically, we consider (i) Follow-the-Regularized-Leader algorithms (FTRL) and (ii) the linear version of MWU (MWU$_\ell$) in strictly adversarial settings and establish divergence away from Nash equilibria.

### 4.1 FTRL

Theorem 4.1. *For every constant-sum game with a fully mixed Nash equilibrium and every (non-equilibrium) initial strategy, the Bregman divergence from the NE will strictly increase in every iteration when player strategies are updated with (FTRL) and a strictly convex regularizer, as long as the updated strategies are fully mixed.*

Proof. The $KKT$ optimality conditions for (FTRL) are

$$\begin{aligned}
\nabla h_i(x_i^t) &= \eta \sum_{s=0}^{t-1} v_i(x_{-i}^s) - \lambda^t \mathbf{1} + \delta^t \\
\sum_{s_i \in \mathcal{S}_i} x_{is_i}^t &= 1 \\
x_{is_i} &\geq 0 \\
\delta^t &\geq 0 \\
\langle \delta^t, x_i^t \rangle &= 0
\end{aligned} \tag{FTRL KKT Conditions}$$

where $\lambda^t \in \mathbb{R}$ is the variable associated with the constraint $\sum_{s_i \in \mathcal{S}_i} x_{is_i}^t = 1$ and $\delta^t \in \mathbb{R}_{\geq 0}^{|\mathcal{S}_i|}$ is the vector associated with the constraints $x_{is_i} \geq 0$ for all $s_i \in \mathcal{S}_i$. Therefore,

$$D_h(x_i^* || x_i^t) = h(x_i^*) - h(x_i^t) - \langle \nabla h(x_i^t), x_i^* - x_i^t \rangle \tag{19}$$

$$= h(x_i^*) - h(x_i^t) - \langle \eta \sum_{s=0}^{t-1} v_i(x_{-i}^s) - \lambda^t \mathbf{1} + \delta^t, x_i^* - x_i^t \rangle \tag{20}$$

$$= h(x_i^*) - h(x_i^t) + \eta \sum_{s=0}^{t-1} \left( u_i(x_i^t, x_{-i}^s) - u_i(x_i^*, x_{-i}^s) \right) - \langle \delta^t, x_i^* \rangle \tag{21}$$

$$\leq h(x_i^*) - h(x_i^t) + \eta \sum_{s=0}^{t-1} \left( u_i(x_i^t, x_{-i}^s) - u_i(x^*) \right) . \tag{22}$$

Now suppose $x_i^t$ is fully mixed implying $\delta^t = \mathbf{0}$ and (22) holds with equality. Through similar reasoning and by strict convexity of $h$,

$$h(x_i^{t-1}) > h_i(x_i^t) + \langle \nabla h_i(x_i^t), x_i^{t-1} - x_i^t \rangle \tag{23}$$

$$= h_i(x_i^t) + \eta \sum_{s=0}^{t-1} \left( u_i(x_i^{t-1}, x_{-i}^s) - u_i(x_i^t; x_{-i}^s) \right) \tag{24}$$

Combining (22) and (24), we have

$$D_h(x^*||x^t) - D_h(x^*||x^{t-1}) = \sum_{i \in \mathcal{N}} \left( D_h(x_i^*||x_i^t) - D_h(x_i^*||x_i^{t-1}) \right) \tag{25}$$

$$> \sum_{i \in \mathcal{N}} \eta \left( u_i(x^{t-1}) - u_i(x^*) \right) = 0 \tag{26}$$

completing the proof of the theorem. □

Theorem 4.1 guarantees that when the strategy and its update are fully mixed the update will move further from the Nash equilibrium explaining the outward spirals in Figure 1. Moreover, it guarantees that the Bregman divergence continues to increase when the current strategy isn't fully mixed as long as its update is. Let $r > 0$ be the maximum value such that $D_h(x^*||x) \geq r$ for all $x$ on the boundary. If $x^{t-1}$ is on the boundary, then either (1) $x^t$ is on the boundary and $D_h(x^*||x^t) \geq r$ by definition or (2) $x^t$ is fully mixed and $D_h(x^*||x^t) > D_h(x^*||x^{t-1}) \geq r$ by Theorem 4.1. Thus, once the updated strategies hit the boundary, the strategies will never again enter the smallest ball centered at the Nash equilibrium that intersects with the boundary.

Theorem 4.2. *For every 2-player constant-sum game with a fully mixed equilibrium, if all agents use (FTRL) with fixed $\eta$ and a strongly convex regularizer, any (non-equilibrium) initial strategies come arbitrarily close to the boundary infinitely often.*

Proof. For contradiction, suppose there exists a $T$ such that that $x^t$ never comes close to boundary and there is a $w$ such that $D_h(x^*||x^t) \leq w$ for all $t \geq T$. This implies $x_{is_i}^t > 0$ and that we can disregard the constraint $x_{is_i} \geq 0$ in (FTRL) for all $t \geq T$. By Theorem 4.1 there exists an $r > 0$ such that $D_h(x^*||x^t) \geq r$ for all $t$ and therefore there is a compact $B$ excluding $x^*$ and the boundary such that $x^t \in B$ for all $t \geq T$.

Let $\hat{h}$, $\hat{u}$, and $\hat{v}$ be the functions obtained by plugging $x_{is_i} = 1 - \sum_{s_i' \in \mathcal{S}_i \setminus \{s_i\}} x_{is_i}$ into $h$, $u$, and $v$ respectively for an arbitrarily selected $s_i$. Once this substitution is made, $x^t$ is determined by

$$x_i^t = \operatorname{argmax} \eta \sum_{s=0}^{t-1} \hat{u}_i(x_i; x_{-i}^s) - \hat{h}(x_i) \tag{Unconstrained FTRL}$$

where $x_{is_i}^t$ is assigned $1 - \sum_{s_i' \in \mathcal{S}_i \setminus \{s_i\}} x_{is_i}$. This function has KKT optimality conditions

$$\nabla \hat{h}(x_i^{t+1}) = \eta \sum_{s=0}^{t} \hat{v}_i(x_{-i}^s) = \eta \nabla \hat{h}(x_i^t) + \eta \hat{v}_i(x_{-i}^t). \tag{27}$$

Thus $x^{t+1}$ is uniquely determined from $x^t$ and therefore $f(x^t) = ||x^{t+1} - x^t||_2^2$ is well-defined. Since $x^t$ is fully mixed, $x^t = x^{t+1}$ if and only if $x^t = x^s$ for all $s \geq t$. This only occurs if $x^t = x^*$ which cannot occur since $x^t \in B$ and therefore $f(x^t) > 0$ for all $t \geq T$. By compactness of $B$, there exists a $d > 0$ such that $f(x^t) \geq d$ for all $t \geq T$.

If $h$ is strongly convex with parameter $m > 0$, then the proof of Theorem 4.1 can readily be modified to show that the divergence increases by at least $m||x^{t+1} - x^t||_2^2$ in iteration $t$ of (FTRL) since $x^t$ is always fully mixed for $t \geq T$. Thus,

$$\lim_{t\to\infty} D_h(x^*||x^t) = D_h(x^*||x^T) + \sum_{t=T}^{\infty}\left(D_h(x^*||x^{t+1}) - D_h(x^*||x^t)\right) \tag{28}$$

$$\geq D_h(x^*||x^T) + \sum_{t=T}^{\infty} m||x^{t+1} - x^t||_2^2 \tag{29}$$

$$\geq D_h(x^*||x^T) + \sum_{t=T}^{\infty} md = \infty \tag{30}$$

a contradiction. □

Theorems 4.1 and 4.2 imply that if the regularizer used in (FTRL) guarantees $x^t$ will be fully mixed for each $t$ then $x^t$ converges to the boundary. An example of such a regularizer is the negative entropy function yielding the update rule ($MWU_e$). However, not all regularizers come with this guarantee. For instance in Figure 2, we see that for the regularizer $h(x) = ||x||_2^2$ (yielding the Gradient Descent algorithm) that player strategies move outward until they collide with the boundary. After this initial collision however, we see that the strategies may once again become fully mixed until they eventually again hit the boundary. Interestingly, we see that player strategies still appear to converge to the boundary in the absolute sense. However, the proof techniques we established for ($MWU_e$) cannot capture this simply because the Bregman divergence may decrease when player strategies are on the boundary.

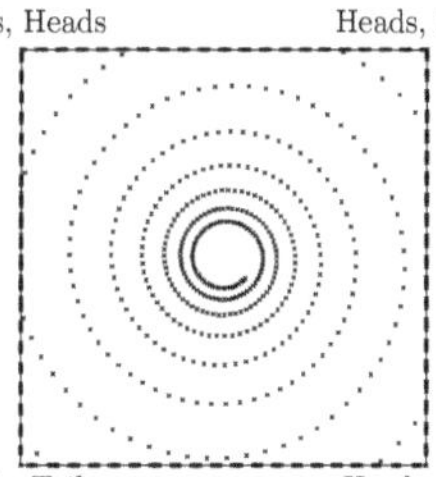


Fig. 2. Matching Pennies updated 1000 times with (FTRL), Regularizer $h(x) = ||x||_2^2$ and $\eta = .08$.

Similar to our results for ($MWU_e$) Theorem 4.2 holds in polymatrix games even when individuals select different values of $\eta$ so long as $\frac{\prod_{k\in N\setminus\{i\}} \eta_{kt}}{\sum_{j\in N} \eta_{jt}}$ is time invariant and the selection of $\eta$ can guarantee arbitrarily low regret. The proof of the results follow analogously to Theorems 3.4, 3.6, and 4.2. In addition, Theorem 4.2 holds even if players use different regularizers. The proof of Theorems 4.1 only makes use of the convexity of the regularizer.

Theorem 4.3. *For almost every 2-player constant-sum game with no fully mixed equilibria, there exists $\eta_0 > 0$, such that as long as all agents use (FTRL) with $\eta < \eta_0$ any (non-equilibrium) initial strategies converge to the boundary.*

This proof follows similarly to the second part of Theorem 3.3 and is deferred to Appendix C.

## 4.2 Linear MWU

The linear variant of MWU ($MWU_\ell$) is similar to the ($MWU_e$) in that they have the same first order approximation for the update in player strategies and thus we may expect that the two algorithms should behave similarly. However, as shown in Figure 3, the algorithms can result in player strategies evolving in very different ways. Figure 3 suggests that ($MWU_\ell$) still implies convergence to the boundary.

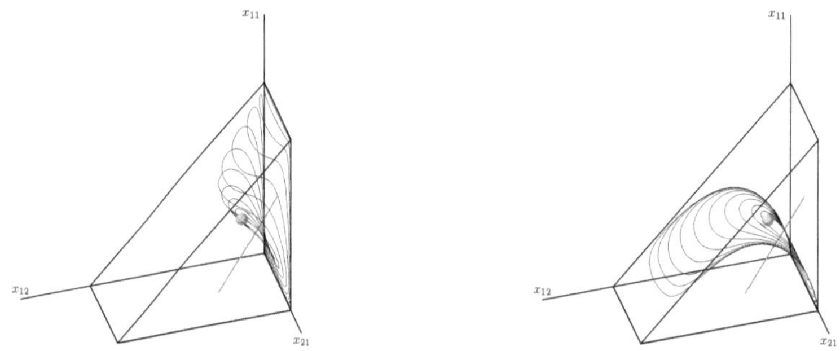


(a) Linear Update (b) Exponential Update

Fig. 3. Player Strategies Spiraling Outwards for the Zero-Sum Game with Player 1 Payoff Matrix $\begin{pmatrix} 1 & -1 \\ 2 & -2 \\ -1 & 1 \end{pmatrix}$ with $\epsilon = .5$.

We explore convergence of ($MWU_\ell$) in this section. We establish that the proof techniques used in Theorem 3.3 combined with the K-L divergence are insufficient for showing convergence to the boundary in ($MWU_\ell$) – The K-L divergence may actually decrease when players update their strategies with ($MWU_\ell$). The proof techniques are however sufficient to guarantee convergence to the boundary in the large class of zero-sum games, skew-symmetric games. A two-player game is *skew-symmetric* if both players have the same payoff matrix. Rock, Paper, Scissors is a classical example of a skew-symmetric game.

Theorem 4.4. *Let $\Gamma$ be a 2-player constant-sum game that admits an interior Nash equilibrium. If both players update their strategies according to ($MWU_\ell$) in iteration t, then the K-L divergence increases by* $\sum_{i\in N}\left(\ln\left(1+\epsilon u_i(x^{t-1})\right) - \sum_{s_i\in S_i} x_i^* \ln\left(1+\epsilon v_{is_i}(x^{t-1})\right)\right)$.

The proof of Theorem 4.4 follows analogously to Theorem 3.1.

Proposition 4.5. *There exists a 2-player zero-sum game $\Gamma$ with an interior point equilibrium and a fully mixed strategy $x^0$ so that the K-L divergences decreases whenever players update strategies with ($MWU_\ell$) with a sufficiently small $\epsilon$.*

Proof. Consider the zero-sum game with payoff matrix $A_1 = \begin{pmatrix} 3 & -2 \\ -1 & 4 \end{pmatrix}$. The unique Nash equilibrium of this game is $x_1^* = (1/2, 1/2)$ and $x_2^* = (3/5, 2/5)$. By Theorem 4.4, the change in KL divergence after one iteration given the initial strategies $x_1^0 = (1/4, 3/4)$ and $x_2^0 = (1/3, 2/3)$ is

$$\ln\left(1+\frac{5}{3}\epsilon\right) + \ln\left(1-\frac{5}{3}\epsilon\right) - \frac{1}{2}\ln\left(1-\frac{1}{3}\epsilon\right) - \frac{1}{2}\ln\left(1+\frac{7}{3}\epsilon\right) - \frac{2}{5}\ln\left(1-\frac{5}{2}\epsilon\right) < 0 \quad (31)$$

for $\epsilon \lessapprox 0.1736$. □

Theorem 4.6. *Let $\Gamma$ be a 2-player skew-symmetric game that admits an interior Nash equilibrium. Further suppose that $x_1^0 = x_2^0$ is a fully mixed non-equilibrium initial strategy and both players update* *their strategies according to ($MWU_\ell$) then $x^t$ converges to the boundary. In the case of time evolving $\epsilon_t$, its ($MWU_\ell^{\epsilon_t}$) variant converges to the boundary iff $\sum_{t=1}^{\infty} \epsilon^2 = \infty$.*

Since the game is skew-symmetric and since players are playing the same strategies, $u_1(x) = u_2(x) = 0$ for any strategy $x$. Therefore in an iteration of ($MWU_\ell$) the K-L divergence increases by $-2\sum_{s_1 \in S_1} x_1^* \ln\left(1 + \epsilon v_{1s_1}(x^{t-1})\right)$. The proof then follows analogously to Theorem 3.5 and obtains a similar rate of convergence to the boundary.

## 5 CONCLUSIONS

Our results suggest that the behavior of MWU (as well as of most classic no-regret dynamics) is more intricate than what is suggested by regret-minimizing algorithms' guarantee of "convergence to equilibrium". Even though the time-average of strategies converge, actual player strategies are repelled away from the equilibrium. If equilibria are predictive and we expect individual strategies to approach equilibria over time then the standard no-regret approach to updating strategies via MWU is inadequate and we must consider other equilibrium-seeking algorithms. Our work opens up the possibility of a much tighter understanding of the true, realized behavior of such dynamics in many contexts and raises interesting questions from a behavioral game theory standpoint. For example, what type of learning dynamics do people apply in practice? Can we exploit our understanding of the shape of these trajectories (e.g. the geometry of the limit cycles) to perform behavioral model fitting?

## ACKNOWLEDGEMENTS

We acknowledge SUTD grant SRG ESD 2015 097, MOE AcRF Tier 2 Grant 2016-T2-1-170 and NRF 2018 Fellowship NRF-NRFF2018-07.

## REFERENCES

[1] Maria-Florina Balcan, Florin Constantin, and Ruta Mehta. 2012. The Weighted Majority Algorithm does not Converge in Nearly Zero-sum Games. In *ICML Workshop on Markets, Mechanisms and Multi-Agent Models.*

[2] G.W. Brown. 1951. Iterative Solutions of Games by Fictitious Play. *In Activity Analysis of Production and Allocation, T.C. Koopmans (Ed.), New York: Wiley.* (1951).

[3] Yang Cai, Ozan Candogan, Constantinos Daskalakis, and Christos Papadimitriou. 2016. Zero-Sum Polymatrix Games: A Generalization of Minmax. *Mathematics of Operations Research* 41, 2 (2016), 648–655.

[4] Yang Cai and Costantinos Daskalakis. 2011. On Minmax Theorems for Multiplayer Games. In *ACM-SIAM Symposium on Discrete Algorithms (SODA).* 217–234.

[5] Erick Chastain, Adi Livnat, Christos Papadimitriou, and Umesh Vazirani. 2014. Algorithms, games, and evolution. *Proceedings of the National Academy of Sciences (PNAS)* 111, 29 (2014), 10620–10623.

[6] Constantinos Daskalakis, Alan Deckelbaum, and Anthony Kim. 2011. Near-optimal No-regret Algorithms for Zero-sum Games. In *Proceedings of the Twenty-second Annual ACM-SIAM Symposium on Discrete Algorithms (SODA '11).* Society for Industrial and Applied Mathematics, Philadelphia, PA, USA, 235–254. http://dl.acm.org/citation.cfm?id=2133036.2133057

[7] C. Daskalakis, R. Frongillo, C. Papadimitriou, G. Pierrakos, and G. Valiant. 2010. On learning algorithms for Nash equilibria. *Symposium on Algorithmic Game Theory (SAGT)* (2010), 114–125.

[8] Constantinos Daskalakis, Andrew Ilyas, Vasilis Syrgkanis, and Haoyang Zeng. 2018. Training GANs with Optimism.

[9] Constantinos Daskalakis and Christos Papadimitriou. 2009. On a Network Generalization of the Minmax Theorem. In *ICALP.* 423–434.

[10] Dylan J Foster, Thodoris Lykouris, Karthik Sridharan, and Eva Tardos. 2016. Learning in games: Robustness of fast convergence. In *Advances in Neural Information Processing Systems.* 4727–4735.

[11] Yoav Freund and Robert E Schapire. 1999. Adaptive game playing using multiplicative weights. *Games and Economic Behavior* 29, 1-2 (1999), 79–103.

[12] Drew Fudenberg and David K Levine. 1995. Consistency and cautious fictitious play. *Journal of Economic Dynamics and Control* 19, 5-7 (1995), 1065–1089.

[13] Drew Fudenberg and David K. Levine. 1998. *The Theory of Learning in Games.* The MIT Press.

[14] R. Kleinberg, K. Ligett, G. Piliouras, and É. Tardos. 2011. Beyond the Nash equilibrium barrier. In *Symposium on Innovations in Computer Science (ICS)*.

[15] Tien-Yien Li and James A. Yorke. 1975. Period Three Implies Chaos. *The American Mathematical Monthly* 82, 10 (1975), 985–992.

[16] Nick Littlestone and Manfred K Warmuth. 1994. The weighted majority algorithm. *Information and computation* 108, 2 (1994), 212–261.

[17] T. Mai, I. Panageas, W. Ratcliff, V. V. Vazirani, and P. Yunker. 2017. Rock-Paper-Scissors, Differential Games and Biological Diversity. *ArXiv e-prints* (Oct. 2017). arXiv:math.DS/1710.11249

[18] Ruta Mehta, Ioannis Panageas, and Georgios Piliouras. 2015. Natural Selection as an Inhibitor of Genetic Diversity: Multiplicative Weights Updates Algorithm and a Conjecture of Haploid Genetics. In *Innovations in Theoretical Computer Science*.

[19] R. Mehta, I. Panageas, G. Piliouras, and S. Yazdanbod. 2016. The Computational Complexity of Genetic Diversity. *European Symposium on Algorithms (ESA)* (2016).

[20] Panayotis Mertikopoulos, Christos Papadimitriou, and Georgios Piliouras. 2018. Cycles in adversarial regularized learning. In *SODA*.

[21] Gerasimos Palaiopanos, Ioannis Panageas, and Georgios Piliouras. 2017. Multiplicative Weights Update with Constant Step-Size in Congestion Games: Convergence, Limit Cycles and Chaos. In *Proceedings of the 30th International Conference on Neural Information Processing Systems (NIPS'17)*.

[22] Christos Papadimitriou and Georgios Piliouras. 2016. From Nash equilibria to chain recurrent sets: Solution concepts and topology. In *ITCS*.

[23] Georgios Piliouras, Carlos Nieto-Granda, Henrik I. Christensen, and Jeff S. Shamma. 2014. Persistent Patterns: Multi-agent Learning Beyond Equilibrium and Utility. In *AAMAS*. 181–188.

[24] Georgios Piliouras and Jeff S Shamma. 2014. Optimization despite chaos: Convex relaxations to complex limit sets via Poincaré recurrence. In *Proceedings of the twenty-fifth annual ACM-SIAM symposium on Discrete algorithms*. SIAM, 861–873.

[25] Sasha Rakhlin and Karthik Sridharan. 2013. Optimization, learning, and games with predictable sequences. In *Advances in Neural Information Processing Systems*. 3066–3074.

[26] J. Robinson. 1951. An Iterative Method of Solving a Game. *Annals of Mathematics* 54 (1951), 296–301.

[27] William H. Sandholm. 2010. *Population Games and Evolutionary Dynamics*. MIT Press.

[28] Vasilis Syrgkanis, Alekh Agarwal, Haipeng Luo, and Robert E. Schapire. 2015. Fast Convergence of Regularized Learning in Games. In *Proceedings of the 28th International Conference on Neural Information Processing Systems (NIPS'15)*. MIT Press, Cambridge, MA, USA, 2989–2997. http://dl.acm.org/citation.cfm?id=2969442.2969573

[29] Eric Van Damme. 1991. *Stability and perfection of Nash equilibria*. Vol. 339. Springer.

[30] John von Neumann. 1928. Zur Theorie der Gesellschaftsspiele. *Math. Ann.* 100 (1928), 295–300.

[31] John von Neumann and Oskar Morgenstern. 1944. *Theory of Games and Economic Behavior*. Princeton University Press.

## A PROOF OF THEOREM 3.5

The first proof we present is a bound on the generalized binomial coefficient which will allow us to bound the change in K-L divergence in each iteration of ($MWU_e^{\epsilon_t}$).

Lemma A.1. *The generalized binomial coefficient* $\binom{x}{k} = x(x-1)\cdots(x-k+1)$ *is such that* $\binom{x}{k} = \sum_{j=1}^{k} a_{jk}x^j$ *where* $\sum_{j=1}^{k} |a_{jk}| = k!$.

Proof. Recursively, it follows that $a_{kk} = 1$, $a_{1k} = (1-k)a_{1,k-1}$ and $a_{jk} = (1-k)a_{j,k-1} + a_{j-1,k-1}$. We now proceed by induction. The statement of the lemma trivially holds for $k = 1$. Assume the result hold for $k-1$. Then by the the inductive hypothesis,

$$\sum_{j=1}^{k} |a_{jk}| = |a_{kk}| + |a_{1k}| + \sum_{j=2}^{k-1} |a_{jk}| \tag{32}$$

$$= 1 + (k-1)|a_{1,k-1}| + \sum_{j=2}^{k-1} \Big((k-1)|a_{j,k-1}| + |a_{j-1,k-1}|\Big) \tag{33}$$

$$= 1 + (k-1)\sum_{j=1}^{k-1} |a_{j,k-1}| + \sum_{j=1}^{k-1} |a_{j,k-1}| - |a_{k-1,k-1}| \tag{34}$$

$$= 1 + (k-1)(k-1)! + (k-1)! - 1 = k! \tag{35}$$

completing the proof of the lemma. □

Lemma A.2. *Let* $\Gamma$ *be a game with a fully mixed Nash equilibrium. Let* $b = \max\left\{1, \max_{s,s'\in\mathcal{S}}\{u_1(s) - u_1(s')\}\right\}$ *and suppose* $\epsilon_t \leq \frac{1}{2b}$. *If player's update their strategies according to* ($MWU_e^{\epsilon_t}$) *then* $D_{KL}(x^*||x^t) - D_{KL}(x^*||x^{t-1}) \leq \sum_{i\in\mathcal{N}} \frac{Var[P_i(x^t)]}{2}\epsilon_t^2 + 4b^3\epsilon_t^3$.

Proof. Let $a_{jk}$ be as described in Lemma A.1. By Theorem 3.1,

$$D_{KL}(x^*||x^t) - D_{KL}(x^*||x^{t-1}) = \sum_{i\in\mathcal{N}} \ln E\left[(1+\epsilon_t)^{P_i(x^t)-u_i(x^t)}\right] \tag{36}$$

$$= \sum_{i\in\mathcal{N}} \ln E\left[\sum_{k=0}^{\infty} \binom{P_i(x^t)-u_i(x^t)}{k}\epsilon_t^k\right] \tag{37}$$

$$= \sum_{i\in\mathcal{N}} \ln\left(1 + \frac{Var[P_i(x^t)]}{2}\epsilon_t^2 + \sum_{k=3}^{\infty} \frac{\sum_{j=1}^{k} a_{jk}E\left[(P_i(x^t)-u_i(x^t))^j\right]}{k!}\epsilon_t^k\right). \tag{38}$$

Next observe that $E\left[(P_i(x^t)-u_i(x^t))^j\right] \leq b^j \leq b^k$ for $k \geq j$. Therefore,

$$D_{KL}(x^*||x^t) - D_{KL}(x^*||x^{t-1}) \le \sum_{i\in\mathcal{N}} \ln\left(1 + \frac{Var[P_i(x^t)]}{2}\epsilon_t^2 + \sum_{k=3}^{\infty} \frac{\sum_{j=1}^{k} |a_{jk}| b^k}{k!}\epsilon_t^k\right) \tag{39}$$

$$= \sum_{i\in\mathcal{N}} \ln\left(1 + \frac{Var[P_i(x^t)]}{2}\epsilon_t^2 + \sum_{k=3}^{\infty} b^k \epsilon_t^k\right) \tag{40}$$

$$= \sum_{i\in\mathcal{N}} \ln\left(1 + \frac{Var[P_i(x^t)]}{2}\epsilon_t^2 + \frac{b^3\epsilon_t^3}{1-b\epsilon_t}\right) \tag{41}$$

$$\le \sum_{i\in\mathcal{N}} \ln\left(1 + \frac{Var[P_i(x^t)]}{2}\epsilon_t^2 + 2b^3\epsilon_t^3\right) \tag{42}$$

following from the Taylor series expansion of $\frac{y^3}{1-y}$ and since $\epsilon_t \le \frac{1}{2b}$. Furthermore $\ln(1+y) \le y$ and

$$D_{KL}(x^*||x^t) - D_{KL}(x^*||x^{t-1}) \le \sum_{i\in\mathcal{N}} \left(\frac{Var[P_i(x^t)]}{2}\epsilon_t^2 + 2b^3\epsilon_t^3\right) \tag{43}$$

$$= \sum_{i\in\mathcal{N}} \frac{Var[P_i(x^t)]}{2}\epsilon_t^2 + 4b^3\epsilon_t^3 \tag{44}$$

completing the proof of the lemma. □

Lemma A.2 is sufficient to give the "only if" portion of Theorem 3.5. To obtain the "if" portion, we need a similar lower bound.

Lemma A.3. *Let $\Gamma$ be a game with a fully mixed Nash equilibrium. Let* $b = \max\left\{1, \max_{s,s'\in\mathcal{S}}\{u_1(s) - u_1(s')\}\right\}$ *and suppose $\epsilon_t \le \frac{1}{2b}$. If player's update their strategies according to ($MWU_e^{\epsilon_t}$) then* $D_{KL}(x^*||x^t) - D_{KL}(x^*||x^{t-1}) \ge \sum_{i\in\mathcal{N}} \frac{Var[P_i(x^t)]}{4}\epsilon_t^2 - 2b^3\epsilon_t^3$.

Proof. Following symmetrically with the proof of Lemma A.2 for $\epsilon_t \le \frac{1}{2b}$,

$$D_{KL}(x^*||x^t) - D_{KL}(x^*||x^{t-1}) \ge \sum_{i\in\mathcal{N}} \ln\left(1 + \frac{Var[P_i(x^t)]}{2}\epsilon_t^2 - 2b^3\epsilon_t^3\right) \tag{45}$$

$$\ge \sum_{i\in\mathcal{N}} \frac{Var[P_i(x^t)]}{4}\epsilon_t^2 - 2b^3\epsilon_t^3 \tag{46}$$

since $\ln(1+y) \ge \frac{y}{2}$ completing the proof of the lemma. □

The statement of Lemma A.3 can be tightened to $\frac{Var[P_i(x^t)]}{2c}\epsilon_t^2$ for any $c > 1$ by taking $\epsilon_t$ sufficiently small. However, Lemma A.3 as written is sufficient for the proof of Theorem 3.5.

Proof of Theorem 3.5. We show the result only for 2-player games. The extension to polymatrix games follows in the same fashion as Theorem 3.4. We begin by showing player strategies do not converge to the boundary if $\sum_{t=1}^{\infty} \epsilon_t^2 < \infty$. Let $b$ be as defined in Lemma A.2. Since the sum is finite, there must be a $T$ such that $\epsilon_t \le \frac{1}{2b}$ for all $t \ge T$. Any fully mixed strategy updated by ($MWU_e^{\epsilon_t}$) remains fully mixed and therefore $D_{KL}(x^*||x^{T-1}) < \infty$. Thus,

$$\lim_{t\to\infty} D_{KL}(x^*||x^t) = D_{KL}(x^*||x^{T-1}) + \sum_{t=T}^{\infty}\left(D_{KL}(x^*||x^t) - D_{KL}(x^*||x^{t-1})\right) \tag{47}$$

$$\leq D_{KL}(x^*||x^{T-1}) + \sum_{t=T}^{\infty}\left(\sum_{i\in N}\frac{Var[P_i(x^t)]}{2}\epsilon_t^2 + 4b^3\epsilon_t^3\right) \tag{48}$$

$$\leq D_{KL}(x^*||x^{T-1}) + \sum_{t=T}^{\infty}\left(\sum_{i\in N}\frac{b^2}{2}\epsilon_t^2 + 4b^3\epsilon_t^2\right) < \infty \tag{49}$$

by Lemma A.2, since $Var[P_i(x^t)] \leq b^2$, and $\sum_{t=1}^{\infty}\epsilon_t^2 < \infty$. Thus player strategies move outward but do not converge to the boundary completing the first part of the proof.

We now show that player strategies converge to the boundary if $\sum_{t=1}^{\infty}\epsilon_t^2 = \infty$. Let $x^*$ be a fully mixed Nash equilibrium. For contradiction, suppose player strategies do not converge to the boundary and there is a $w > 0$ such that $D_{KL}(x^*||x^t) < w$ for all $t$. Thus, as in the proof of Theorem 3.3, there exists a compact $B$ such that $x^t \in B$ for all $t$ but $B$ excludes the boundary and $x^*$. $\sum_{i\in N} Var[P_i(x)] > 0$ for all $x \in B$ and since $B$ is compact and $Var[P_i(x)]$ is continuous in $x$, there exists a $d > 0$ such that $\sum_{i\in N} Var[P_i(x^t)] \geq d$ for all $t$.

If there are infinitely many $t$ such that $\epsilon_t > \min\{\frac{1}{2b}, \frac{d}{16b^3}\}$ then the proof follows identically to Theorem 3.3 and we may assume there exists a $T$ such that $\epsilon_t \leq \min\{\frac{1}{2b}, \frac{d}{16b^3}\}$ for all $t \geq T$. Finally,

$$\lim_{t\to\infty} D_{KL}(x^*||x^t) = D_{KL}(x^*||x^{T-1}) + \sum_{t=T}^{\infty}\left(D_{KL}(x^*||x^t) - D_{KL}(x^*||x^{t-1})\right) \tag{50}$$

$$\geq D_{KL}(x^*||x^{T-1}) + \sum_{t=T}^{\infty}\left(\sum_{i\in N}\frac{Var[P_i(x^t)]}{4}\epsilon_t^2 - 2b^3\epsilon_t^3\right) \tag{51}$$

$$\geq D_{KL}(x^*||x^{T-1}) + \sum_{t=T}^{\infty}\left(\frac{d}{4}\epsilon_t^2 - \frac{d}{8}\epsilon_t^2\right) = \infty \tag{52}$$

by Lemma A.3 and since $\epsilon_t \leq \frac{d}{16b^3}$ and $\sum_{t=1}^{\infty}\epsilon_t^2 = \infty$. This is a contradiction, completing the proof of the theorem. □

## B PROOF OF PROPOSITION 3.7

To show this proposition, we actually show that for almost every 2x2 constant-sum game with a fully mixed Nash equilibria $x^*$ that there exists $\{\{\epsilon_{it}\}_{i\in N}\}_{t=1}^{\infty}$ so that $\lim_{t\to\infty} x^t \to x^*$

The process for achieving this is quite simple; it requires at most 4 unique selections for $\epsilon_{it}$ to come arbitrarily close to $x^*$. Moreover if we allow $\epsilon_{it}$ to be arbitrarily large we can come arbitrarily close to the Nash equilibrium in 3 steps with 3 unique selections for $\epsilon_{it}$. Rather than give the full proof, we describe selection process used to achieve convergence to $x^*$.

If $u_1(x^1) > u_1(x^*)$ then player 1 is profiting (relative to the Nash strategy) and selects $\epsilon_{1t} = 0$ so that strategy does not change. The game is constant-sum and $u_2(x^1) < u_2(x^*)$ implying player 2 is losing utility. He assigns $\epsilon_{it} = c$ for some $c > 0$. MWU is myopic and after some number of iterations $u_2(x^T) - u_2(x^*)$ becomes positive. In a 2x2 game $u_i(x^T) = u_i(x^*)$ if and only if at least one player is playing a Nash strategy. Therefore by re-selecting $\epsilon_{2T}$ so that $u_2(x^T)$ is arbitrarily close to $u_2(x^*)$, he also ensures that $x_2^T$ is arbitrarily close to $x_2^*$. Moreover, he can do this so that $u_2(x^T) > u_2(x^*)$. Since $u_2(x^T) > u_2(x^*)$, $u_1(x^T) < u_1(x^*)$ and the players can repeat a symmetric process so that for $T' > T$, $x_1^{T'}$ is arbitrarily close to $x_1^*$. Moreover, since $\epsilon_{2t} = 0$ for all $t \in \{T+1, ..., T'\}$, $x_2^T = x_2^{T'}$ and both players are submitting a strategy arbitrarily close to the Nash equilibrium.

Since this process requires for $u_i(x^t) \neq u_i(x^*)$, it may require one additional step at the beginning if $x_i^0 = x_i^*$ for either player. However, this process is trivial since almost every selection of $\epsilon_{i1}$ will result in $x_i^* \neq x_i^1$ for both $i$. Moreover, if we allow $\epsilon_{it}$ to be arbitrarily large then we can select $\epsilon_{it}$ so that $T = 2$ and $T' = 3$.

## C PROOF OF THEOREM 4.3

Similar to Theorem 3.3, we show the probability of playing a non-essential strategy goes to 0 as $t \to \infty$. Suppose player $i$ has a non-essential strategy $s_i$. Without loss of generality we assume $u_i(x^*) = 0$. For almost every zero-sum game there is a unique Nash equilibrium $x^*$. Suppose $x^t$ is updated according to (FTRL). Let $f_i^t(x_i)$ be the function optimized in (FTRL) to find $x_i^t$.

$$f_i^t(x_i) = t \cdot \eta \cdot u_i(x_i; \bar{x}_{-i}^{t-1}) - h(x_i) \tag{53}$$

where $\bar{x}^t = \sum_{s=0}^t x^s/t$ is the time-average of the player strategies.

As in the proof of Theorem 3.3, let $\delta = v_{is_i}(x^*) < 0$. For any $y$ sufficiently close to $x^*$, $v_{is_i}(y) < 2\delta/3$ by continuity of payoffs. Let $\eta_0$ in the statement of the theorem be such that the time average of FTRL converges to the interior of the above neighborhood. For any $c > 0$ and any $x_i$ where $x_{is_i} > c$, $f_i^t(x_1) \to -\infty$ as $t \to \infty$. However, $u_i(x_i^*; y_-i) \geq 0$ implying that for sufficiently large $t$, $f_i^t(x_i^*) > f_i^t(x_i)$. Thus, for arbitrary $c > 0$, $\limsup x_{is_i}^t < c$ implying $x_{is_i}^t \to 0$ for every non-essential $s_i$.

# Cycles in Zero-Sum Differential Games and Biological Diversity

TUNG MAI, Georgia Institute of Technology
MILENA MIHAIL, Georgia Institute of Technology
IOANNIS PANAGEAS, MIT
WILL RATCLIFF, Georgia Institute of Technology
VIJAY VAZIRANI, UC Irvine
PETER YUNKER, Georgia Institute of Technology

Negative frequency-dependent selection (i.e., declining fitness with increased frequency in the population) is thought to be one of the factors that maintains biological diversity. In this paper, we give a concrete mathematical argument supporting this. Our model is as follows: A collection of species derive their fitnesses via a rock-paper-scissors-type game whose precise payoffs are a function of the environment. The new aspect of our model lies in adding a feedback loop: the environment changes according to the relative fitnesses of the species (hence, payoffs change as a function of fitness, which in turn changes as a function of payoffs). The changes in the payoffs are in keeping with the principle of negative frequency-dependent selection, which is widespread in nature. In order to model our game as a continuous time dynamical system, we cast it in the setting of a differential game. We show that for certain parameters, this dynamics cycles, i.e., no species goes extinct and diversity is maintained.

We believe that our techniques can be applied to optimization and machine learning to show that first order methods (e.g., gradient descent/ascent) do cycle even in online settings in which the loss function changes with time.

CCS Concepts: • **Theory of computation → Convergence and learning in games**; **Convergence and learning in games**;

## 1 INTRODUCTION

Game theory has yielded deep insights into biological phenomena for almost a century. For example, the work of Fisher, Haldane, and Wright gave the central model of replicator dynamics which has been used extensively to study evolutionary processes. In this paper, we use game theory to give a concrete mathematical argument supporting the belief that negative frequency-dependent selection maintains biological diversity.

Negative frequency-dependent selection (*i.e.*, declining fitness with increased frequency in the population) is widespread in biology, and is thought to be one of the main factors maintaining biological diversity within a community [24, 30]. There are many different mechanisms that reduce the fitness of common genotypes or species, but two interactions are nearly ubiquitous, operating

Vijay Vazirani was supported by NSF Grant 1815901.
Authors' addresses: Tung Mai, Georgia Institute of Technology, tmai9@gatech.edu; Milena Mihail, Georgia Institute of Technology, milena.mihail@gmail.com; Ioannis Panageas, MIT, ioannis@csail.mit.edu; Will Ratcliff, Georgia Institute of Technology, will.ratcliff@biology.gatech.edu; Vijay Vazirani, UC Irvine, vazirani@ics.uci.edu; Peter Yunker, Georgia Institute of Technology, peter.yunker@gatech.edu.


*ACM EC'18, June 18–22, 2018, Ithaca, NY, USA.* ACM ISBN 978-1-4503-5829-3/18/06...$15.00
https://doi.org/10.1145/3219166.3219227

at all levels of biological complexity, from microbes to metazoans. First, common organisms tend to be more susceptible to natural enemies, like predators [24], parasites [19] and pathogens [32, 36]. Pathogens themselves also face negative frequency-dependent selection [12] as they co-evolve with a rapidly-changing host population. Natural selection often favors traits that increase diversity, allowing common organisms to produce uncommon offspring. Perhaps the best example of this is the evolution of eukaryotic sex, which may have evolved and persisted by allowing common genotypes to generate rare, pathogen-resistant offspring genotypes [23]. Second, the intensity of competition for limiting resources (*e.g.*, food [10], reproductive opportunities [11], *etc.*) often scales with frequency. In fact, a classic pattern observed within community ecology is âĂŸniche partitioningâĂŹ [7], in which organisms that compete for different limiting resources stably coexist. When organisms compete for the same limiting resource, the most competitive organism for the shared limiting resource usually ends up dominating the population [37].

When fitness is frequency dependent, game theoretic approaches that use fixed payoff matrices do not accurately represent the behavior of the system. One approach is to make the games dynamic, allowing the payoff matrix to change with time and organismal frequency. Two main categories of such games are stochastic games [34] which are discrete, with the payoff matrix being governed by a Markov chain, and differential games [14], the state space of which is described via a differential equation (continuous time dynamical system). An example of the first is [21], which studies evolution via the so-called 'multiplicative weights update' algorithm, and an example of the second is the recent elegant model of Weitz et al. [38], studying a dynamical version of the tragedy of the commons.

The work presented here is inspired by the last paper, [38]. A tragedy of the commons occurs when a large number of agents simultaneously play a Prisoner's Dilemma-type game. Selfish behavior on the part of agents, i.e., defection, leads to a highly sub-optimal outcome as compared to the globally best outcome in which all agents cooperate. An early, and motivating example, of this phenomena was cattle grazing in a common pasture. Each shepherd's selfish strategy of letting his cattle overgraze leads to a depleted pasture land. The novel idea in [38] was to model a situation in which the actions of the agents slowly change the environment, and hence the payoff matrix, so that the selfish strategy of agents itself changes. They give differential equations modeling this situation and show regimes of parameters under which the game cycles between the two extremes of replete and depleted environments, with selfish behavior cycling between cooperation and defection.

The underlying game analyzed by Weitz et al. is particularly simple in that each agent has only two strategies. In this paper, we consider a more complex class of games which are non-transitive, namely rock-paper-scissors, which has three strategies, and its generalization to $n$ strategies. The rock-paper-scissors (RPS) game belongs to a general class of negative feedbacks in biology caused by non-transitivity. In such scenarios, there is no global optimum, as each strategy beats one of the other two, and is beaten by a third. Non-transitive dynamics appear to be widespread in biology, and rock-paper-scissors games have been reported in diverse organisms, including plants [4, 20], animals [35], and microorganisms [16–18]. In general, rock paper scissors dynamics maintain biological diversity (i.e., individuals, genes, or species), as no single strategy is capable of outright dominance [17, 20, 31]. Most prior models of RPS dynamics used in biology assumed fixed payoff matrices. This is an incongruity with biology, where the fitness of most strategies will be frequency-dependent. On the other hand, analyzing complex games, such as RPS, in the setting of differential games is not straightforward and there is a need to develop techniques for doing this.

**Differential games:** In a differential game, payoffs change continuously with time and are defined over a continuous state space. The state variables of such a game evolve over time according to a differential equation. These games were first introduced by Isaacs [15] to study pursuer–evader games, with military applications in mind. Over the years, such games have had numerous applications in control theory, especially as applied to aerospace, e.g., see [39], and later in economics, e.g., see [6]. To the best of our knowledge, [38] is the first application of such games to biology.

**Our model:** Our model is as follows: We assume that the fitness of a collection of species is given by a rock-paper-scissors-type game. Additionally, the precise payoff matrix is a function of the environment. The new aspect of our model lies in adding a feedback loop: the environment changes according to the relative fitnesses of the species; in particular, it gives a boost to the species having smaller populations. We cast our model in the setting of a differential game and we show that for a certain setting of parameters, this dynamics cycles.

More precisely, assume a population of $n$ species and let $\boldsymbol{x}$ give the relative population of each species at any point in time, i.e., $x_i$ gives the fraction of population of species $i$. We define $\boldsymbol{P}_1, \ldots, \boldsymbol{P}_n$ to be $n$ RPS-type payoff matrices, where $\boldsymbol{P}_i$ favors species $i$ over other species. At any point in time, the payoff matrix $\boldsymbol{P}$ is a convex combination of these $n$ matrices given by weights $\boldsymbol{w}$. We now define two replicator dynamics:

(1) The population $\boldsymbol{x}$ follows a replicator dynamics based on payoff matrix $\boldsymbol{P}$.
(2) The weights $\boldsymbol{w}$ change according to a second replicator dynamics, based on $\boldsymbol{x}$, in such a way that for smaller population species $i$, the weight of $\boldsymbol{P}_i$ tends to increase, hence giving species $i$ a boost.

## 1.1 Our techniques

For the model defined above, we show that the dynamics as defined in (1) "cycle" in the following sense: For all but a measure zero of initial population vectors $\boldsymbol{x}_0 > 0$ and weight vectors $\boldsymbol{w}_0 > 0$ (strictly positive coordinates) and for any $\epsilon > 0$, the trajectory of (1) will return to a distance at most $\epsilon$ from $(\boldsymbol{x}_0, \boldsymbol{w}_0)$ infinitely often (for an illustration of the theorem, see Figures 1,2). In order to prove this recurrence we follow a proof outline that was developed first by in [28] and [22]. The proof relies on the Poincaré recurrence theorem 2.3, a well known theorem established a century ago. In words, the theorem says that systems that satisfy the two conditions of conservation of volume and that no orbit goes to the boundary will, after finite time, return to a state very close to the initial state and this will happen an infinite number of times. We proved that under a certain homeomorphic transformation $\Pi$ (see Definition 3.2), our dynamics satisfies both conditions of Poincaré's theorem.

We established the second condition (Lemma 3.3) by coming up with a log-barrier function (a similar idea is used in constrained optimization) which is finite in the interior of the state space and infinite at the boundary and by proving that this function is constant with respect to time. This suffices to prove that the orbits do not reach the boundary of $\Delta_n \times \Delta_n$ (and hence the orbits for the transformed system under $\Pi$ are bounded). The former condition can be proved via Liouville's theorem 2.2 (see also [33]). Finally, it can be shown that $\Pi^{-1}$ exists and is continuous, hence the result for the transformed dynamics carries over to the original dynamics (1). Our results hold for any dimensions in contrast to [38]; their results hold for 2 dimensions ($2 \times 2$ payoff matrices) only.

## 1.2 Model

*1.2.1 Classic RPS.* RPS is a game between two players, each of whom has three strategies. The payoff matrix can be written as

$$\boldsymbol{P} = \begin{bmatrix} 0 & -1 & 1 \\ 1 & 0 & -1 \\ -1 & 1 & 0 \end{bmatrix}.$$

The RPS game can be generalized to more than three strategies, with the $n \times n$ payoff matrix being:

$$\boldsymbol{P} = \begin{bmatrix} 0 & -\alpha & 0 & 0 & \dots & 0 & 0 & \alpha \\ \alpha & 0 & -\alpha & 0 & \dots & 0 & 0 & 0 \\ \vdots & \vdots & \vdots & \vdots & \vdots & \vdots & \vdots & \vdots \\ 0 & 0 & 0 & 0 & \dots & \alpha & 0 & -\alpha \\ -\alpha & 0 & 0 & 0 & 0 & \dots & \alpha & 0 \end{bmatrix}, \text{ where } \alpha > 0.$$

In the context of biology, we will have $n$ competing species corresponding to the $n$ strategies, Let $\boldsymbol{x}$ be the population vector where $x_i$ is the fraction of the population that is species $i$ and $\boldsymbol{r}$ be the fitness vector. Note that $\boldsymbol{r}$ can be computed given $\boldsymbol{x}$, i.e., $\boldsymbol{r} = \boldsymbol{P}\boldsymbol{x}$. The replicator dynamics under $\boldsymbol{P}$ is

$$x_i' = x_i(r_i - \overline{r}) \quad \forall i,$$

where $\overline{r} = \boldsymbol{x}^\top \boldsymbol{P}\boldsymbol{x}$ is the average fitness (if $\boldsymbol{P}$ is antisymmetric, $\overline{r}$ is zero).

We will call the above the *static* setting, since $\boldsymbol{P}$ is fixed. Replicator dynamics in zero sum games have already been analyzed, proving that it has limit cycles or is recurrent (e.g., see [1, 26–28, 33]).

*1.2.2 Dynamic payoff matrix.* We next define a *dynamic* setting, where at all times the payoff matrix is a convex combination of $n$ matrices:

$$\boldsymbol{P}^{\boldsymbol{w}} = w_1\boldsymbol{P}_1 + w_2\boldsymbol{P}_2 + \dots + w_n\boldsymbol{P}_n,$$

where

$$\boldsymbol{P}_1 = \boldsymbol{P} + \begin{bmatrix} 0 & \mu & \dots & \mu & \mu \\ -\mu & 0 & \dots & 0 & 0 \\ \vdots & \vdots & \vdots & \vdots & \vdots \\ -\mu & 0 & \dots & 0 & 0 \end{bmatrix}, \boldsymbol{P}_2 = \boldsymbol{P} + \begin{bmatrix} 0 & -\mu & 0 & \dots & 0 \\ \mu & 0 & \mu & \dots & \mu \\ 0 & -\mu & 0 & \dots & 0 \\ \vdots & \vdots & \vdots & \vdots & \vdots \\ 0 & -\mu & 0 & \dots & 0 \end{bmatrix}, \dots,$$

$$\boldsymbol{P}_n = \boldsymbol{P} + \begin{bmatrix} 0 & 0 & \dots & 0 & -\mu \\ 0 & 0 & \dots & 0 & -\mu \\ \vdots & \vdots & \vdots & \vdots & \vdots \\ 0 & 0 & \dots & 0 & -\mu \\ \mu & \mu & \dots & \mu & 0 \end{bmatrix}.$$

Formally, $\boldsymbol{P}_i - \boldsymbol{P}$ is a matrix with entries $\mu$ at the $i$-th row and $-\mu$ at the $i$-th column (rest of the entries and diagonal entry $(i, i)$ are zero). It can be seen that for $\mu > 0$ (for the rest of the paper $\mu \geq 0$), $\boldsymbol{P}_i$ favors type $i$ by increasing the payoff of $i$ when competing with other types. The weight vector $\boldsymbol{w} = (w_1, \dots, w_n)$ changes according to the replicator dynamics under the following matrix

$$= \begin{bmatrix} 0 & x_2 - x_1 & x_3 - x_1 & \dots & x_{n-1} - x_1 & x_n - x_1 \\ x_1 - x_2 & 0 & x_3 - x_2 & \dots & x_{n-1} - x_2 & x_n - x_2 \\ \vdots & \vdots & \vdots & \vdots & \vdots & \vdots \\ x_1 - x_n & x_2 - x_n & x_3 - x_n & \dots & x_{n-1} - x_n & 0 \end{bmatrix}.$$

In words, $\boldsymbol{P}^{\boldsymbol{w}}$ changes with time. The idea behind the way $\boldsymbol{w}$ changes, is that species with small population should be favored. Since is also anti-symmetric and has 0 entries in the diagonal, the replicator dynamics update rule of $\boldsymbol{w}$ is

$$w_i' = w_i \sum_j w_j(x_j - x_i) \quad \forall i.$$

By model's definition,

$$P^w = \begin{bmatrix} 0 & -\alpha + \mu(w_1 - w_2) & \mu(w_1 - w_3) & \dots & \alpha + \mu(w_1 - w_n) \\ \alpha + \mu(w_2 - w_1) & 0 & -\alpha + \mu(w_2 - w_3) & \dots & \mu(w_2 - w_n) \\ \vdots & \vdots & \vdots & \vdots & \vdots \\ \mu(w_{n-1} - w_1) & \mu(w_{n-1} - w_2) & \mu(w_{n-1} - w_3) & \dots & -\alpha + \mu(w_{n-1} - w_n) \\ -\alpha + \mu(w_n - w_1) & \mu(w_n - w_2) & \mu(w_n - w_3) & \dots & 0 \end{bmatrix}.$$

Note that $P$ is anti-symmetric and has 0 entries in the diagonal. The replicator dynamics of $x$ becomes

$$x_i' = x_i \cdot s_i \quad \forall i,$$

where $s = P^w x$ is the fitness vector of population $x$ under $P^w$. Summing up, the system of ordinary differential equations that we would like to analyze is captured by ($w_i$ depends on $x_i$)

$$x_i' = x_i \sum_j P_{ij}^w x_j, \; w_i' = w_i \sum_j w_j (x_j - x_i) \quad \forall i. \tag{1}$$

**Connections to training GANs and min-max optimization in online settings:**

Generative Adversarial Networks (GANs) Goodfellow et al. [9] have been really successful over the last 3 years in Machine/Deep Learning, especially in generating images that look "superficially authentic". The framework is as follows: There are two deep neural networks, the Generator (G) and the Discriminator (D). The generator gets noise as input and produces a sample in the same space of the sampled data set (e.g, an image), with the aim to approximate a sample from the underlying distribution. In the meantime, the discriminator is trying to discriminate a sample produced from generator and a true sample. This framework is modeled as a zero sum game between the two neural nets.

The aforementioned framework and also the framework of WGANs [2] has increased the interest of researchers in the areas of optimization and machine learning to work on min-max optimization (generator chooses $x$ and discriminator $y$):

$$\min_x \max_y f(x, y). \tag{2}$$

In [5] the authors showed that using gradient descent on $x$ and gradient ascent on $y$ might yield cycles for the problem (2). Moreover, in [22] it was essentially proved that any continuous time learning dynamics that consists an instance of FTRL (Followed the regularized leader), cycles when $f$ is essentially a bilinear function.

Our setting applies in the online framework of (2) where function $f$ changes with the time (iterations if the time is discrete, continuously otherwise). Our model is a specific case of such an online setting, where $f_t(x, y) = x^T A_t y, A_t$ is antisymmetric for all $t$ and in which we showed that cycles persist. It would be interesting to analyze more general online settings and design learning algorithms in which the last iterate converges (under assumptions on the sequence $\{A_t\}_{t \in \mathbb{N}}$).

**Notation:** We denote the probability simplex on a set of size $n$ as $\Delta_n$. Vectors in $\mathbb{R}^n$ are denoted in bold-face letters $x$ and are considered as column vectors. The $i$-th coordinate is denoted by $x_i$. To denote a row vector we use $x^\top$. The time derivative of a function $y = y(t)$ is denoted by $y'$.

# 2 PRELIMINARIES

## 2.1 Dynamical Systems

Let $f : \mathcal{S} \to \mathcal{S}$ be continuously differentiable with $\mathcal{S} \subset \mathbb{R}^n$, $\mathcal{S}$ an open set. A *continuous (time) dynamical system* is of the form

$$y' \equiv \frac{dy}{dt} = f(y). \tag{3}$$

Since $f$ is continuously differentiable, the system of ordinary differential equations (ode (3)) along with the initial condition $y(0) = y_0 \in \mathcal{S}$ has a unique solution for $t \in \mathcal{I}(y_0)$ (some time interval) and we can present it by $\phi(t, y_0)$, called the *flow* of the system. $\phi_t(y_0) \equiv \phi(t, y_0)$ corresponds to a function of time which captures the *trajectory/orbit* of the system with $y_0$ the given starting point. It is continuously differentiable, its inverse exists (denoted by $\phi_{-t}(y_0)$) and is also continuously differentiable (called *diffeomorphism*) in the so called maximal interval of existence $\mathcal{I}$. It is also true that $\phi_t \circ \phi_s = \phi_{t+s}$ for $t, s, t+s \in \mathcal{I}$. $y_0 \in \mathcal{S}$ is called an *equilibrium* if $f(y_0) = \mathbf{0}$. In that case holds $\phi_t(y_0) = y_0$ for all $t \in \mathcal{I}$, i.e., $y_0$ is a *fixed point* of the function $\phi_t(y)$ for all $t \in \mathcal{I}$.

If $f$ is globally Lipschitz then the flow is defined for all $t \in \mathbb{R}$, i.e., $\mathcal{I} = \mathbb{R}$. One way to enforce the dynamical system to have a well-defined flow for all $t \in \mathbb{R}$ is to renormalize the vector field by $\|f(y)\| + 1$, i.e., the resulting dynamical system will be $\frac{dy}{dt} = \frac{f(y)}{\|f(y)\|+1}$, because the function becomes globally 1-Lipschitz. The two dynamical systems (before and after renormalization) are topologically equivalent ([25], p. 184). Formally this means that there exists a homeomorphism $H$ which maps trajectories of (3) onto trajectories of the renormalized flow and preserves the direction of time. In words it means that the two systems have the same behavior/geometry (same fixed points, convergence properties, phase portrait). For the rest of the paper, we may assume that the flow of dynamics (1) is well-defined for all $t \in \mathbb{R}$.

*Definition 2.1 (**Volume preserving**).* The differential equation (3) is said to be volume preserving on $\mathcal{S}$ if for any measurable set $B \subseteq \mathcal{S}$, we have $v(\phi_t(B)) = v(B)$ for all $t \in \mathbb{R}$, where $v$ is the Lebesgue measure and $\phi_t$ the flow of the ode.

The most common way to prove that the flow is volume preserving is via the Liouville's theorem.

Theorem 2.2 (**Liouville theorem** [33]). *Let $y' = f(y)$ be an ode with flow $\phi_t$. It holds that*

$$\frac{dv(\phi_t(B))}{dt} = \int_{\phi_t(B)} (\nabla \cdot f) dv, \text{ for each Lebesgue measurable set } B.$$

*Therefore, as long as $\nabla \cdot f = 0$, the flow preserves volume.*

In 1890, Poincaré [29] showed that whenever a dynamical system preserves volume, almost all trajectories return arbitrarily close to their initial position an infinite number of times.

Theorem 2.3 (**Poincaré Recurrence** [3, 29]). *If a flow preserves volume and has only bounded orbits then for each open set there exist orbits that intersect the set infinitely often.*

For more information on dynamical systems see [25] and for readers familiar with game theory see [13, 33].

## 2.2 Replicator Dynamics and Evolution

Replicator equations, first were introduced by Fisher [8] in 30's for genotype evolution. The simplest form of replicator equations is the following:

$$x_i'(t) = x_i(t)((Ax(t))_i - x(t)^\top Ax(t)).$$

where $A$ is a payoff matrix (generally non-negative), $\boldsymbol{x}$ a vector that lies in simplex and $(A\boldsymbol{x})_i$ denotes $\sum_j A_{ij}x_j$. Observe that in the nonlinear dynamics above, simplex is invariant (if we start from a probability distribution, the vector remains a probability distribution). This dynamics is called replicator dynamics and has been used numerous times in biology, evolution, game theory and genetic algorithms. The dynamics we analyze in this paper is a version of replicator dynamics (on generalized RPS with dynamics payoff matrix).

## 3 OUR RESULTS

In this section we state and prove our main result. Our main theorem can be stated formally as follows (see also Figures 1,2):

THEOREM 3.1. *For all but measure zero of initial positions, the trajectories of the dynamics (1) return arbitrarily close to their initial position an infinite number of times.*

*Definition 3.2 (**Natural transformation** [13]).* We define the natural transformation $\Pi : \text{int}(\Delta_n) \to \mathbb{R}^{n-1}$ to be $\Pi(y) = \left(\log\left(\frac{y_1}{y_n}\right), ..., \log\left(\frac{y_{n-1}}{y_n}\right)\right)$. In words, we map every point $\boldsymbol{y}$ of the interior of simplex to a point in $\mathbb{R}^{n-1}$. It is not hard to see that the map is injective and surjective. The reason is that $\Pi^{-1}$ exists and is equal to $\Pi^{-1}(z) = \left(\frac{e^{z_1}}{1+\sum_{j=1}^{n-1} e^{z_j}}, \ldots, \frac{e^{z_{n-1}}}{1+\sum_{j=1}^{n-1} e^{z_j}}, \frac{1}{1+\sum_{j=1}^{n-1} e^{z_j}}\right)$. The points on the boundary of simplex correspond to vectors with infinity Euclidean norm in $\mathbb{R}^{n-1}$.

LEMMA 3.3. *Let $(\boldsymbol{x}^0, \boldsymbol{w}^0)$ be an initial point in the interior of $\Delta_n \times \Delta_n$. The dynamics mapped to $\mathbb{R}^{n-1} \times \mathbb{R}^{n-1}$ (under natural mapping $(\Pi, \Pi)$) has bounded orbits $(\Pi(\boldsymbol{x}^t), \Pi(\boldsymbol{w}^t))$.*

PROOF. We define the log-barrier function

$$D(\boldsymbol{x}) = \sum_{i=1}^{n} \log\left(\frac{1}{x_i}\right).$$

Computing the derivative we get,

$$\begin{aligned} D'(\boldsymbol{x}) &= -\sum_i \frac{x_i'}{x_i} = -\sum_i s_i = -\sum_i \sum_j P_{ij}^{\boldsymbol{w}} x_j \\ &= -\left(\sum_j x_j \left(\mu \sum_i (w_i - w_j) + \alpha - \alpha\right)\right) \\ &= -\mu\left(\sum_j x_j(1 - n w_j)\right) \\ &= -\mu\left(1 - n\sum_j w_j x_j\right). \end{aligned}$$

We also define the log-barrier function

$$D(\boldsymbol{w}) = \sum_{i=1}^{n} \log\left(\frac{1}{w_i}\right),$$

and we have

$$
\begin{aligned}
D'(\mathbf{w}) &= -\sum_i \frac{w_i'}{w_i} = -\sum_i \sum_j w_j(x_j - x_i) \\
&= -\sum_j \sum_i w_j(x_j - x_i) \\
&= -\sum_j w_j(nx_j - 1) \\
&= -\left(n \sum_j w_j x_j - 1\right).
\end{aligned}
$$

Therefore,

$$
\begin{aligned}
D'(\mathbf{x}) + \mu D'(\mathbf{w}) &= -\mu\left(1 - n\sum_j w_j x_j\right) - \mu\left(n\sum_j w_j x_j - 1\right) \\
&= \left(n \sum_j w_j x_j - 1\right)(\mu - \mu) = 0.
\end{aligned}
$$

Hence,

$$D(\mathbf{x}) + \mu D(\mathbf{w})$$

is a constant motion of time (independent of time). It is also clear that $D(\mathbf{x}), D(\mathbf{w}) \geq 0$ and become infinity only on the boundary of $\Delta_n \times \Delta_n$. Since $D(\mathbf{x}^0) + \mu D(\mathbf{w}^0)$ is bounded (i.e., $(\mathbf{x}^0, \mathbf{w}^0)$ is an interior point), we get that $D(\mathbf{x}^t) + \mu D(\mathbf{w}^t)$ is bounded for all times $t$, hence there is no subsequence of times $t_k$ so that $(\mathbf{x}^{t_k}, \mathbf{w}^{t_k})$ converges to the boundary of $\Delta_n \times \Delta_n$. Therefore there is no subsequence of times $t_k$ so that $\|(\Pi(\mathbf{x}^{t_k}), \Pi(\mathbf{w}^{t_k}))\|_2$ goes to infinity, i.e., the dynamics on $\mathbb{R}^{n-1} \times \mathbb{R}^{n-1}$ (under natural mapping $(\Pi, \Pi)$) has bounded orbits. □

Proof of Theorem 3.1. Under the mapping $\Pi$ for $\mathbf{x}, \mathbf{w}$, set $\mathbf{y} \equiv \Pi(\mathbf{x})$ and $\mathbf{z} \equiv \Pi(\mathbf{w})$. We shall show that the dynamics $(\mathbf{y}', \mathbf{z}') = g(\mathbf{y}, \mathbf{z})$ satisfies the conditions of the Poincaré recurrence theorem (Theorem 2.3), where $g$ is the vector field of the resulting dynamics, after the transformation $(\Pi, \Pi)$.

The vector field becomes $y_i' = \frac{x_n}{x_i}\frac{x_i' x_n - x_i x_n'}{x_n^2} = \frac{x_i'}{x_i} - \frac{x_n'}{x_n} = \sum_j (P_{ij}^{w} - P_{nj}^{w}) x_j = \alpha(x_1 + x_{i-1} - x_{n-1} - x_{i+1}) + \mu(w_i - w_n)$ (with the convention that $x_0 = x_n$). Similarly $z_i' = \frac{w_n}{w_i}\frac{w_i' w_n - w_i w_n'}{w_n^2} = \frac{w_i'}{w_i} - \frac{w_n'}{w_n} = \sum_j w_j(x_n - x_i) = x_n - x_i$.

After substitution (using $\Pi^{-1}$) we get

$$y_i' = \alpha \cdot \frac{e^{y_1} + e^{y_{i-1}} - e^{y_{n-1}} - e^{y_{i+1}}}{1 + \sum_{j=1}^{n-1} e^{y_j}} + \mu \frac{e^{z_i} - 1}{1 + \sum_{j=1}^{n-1} e^{z_j}}, \quad z_i' = \frac{1 - e^{y_i}}{1 + \sum_{j=1}^{n-1} e^{y_j}}. \tag{4}$$

We shall prove that the flow of the dynamics (4) preserves the volume, by showing that $\nabla \cdot g = 0$ (then it follows from Liouville's theorem 2.2).

Set $S = \sum_{j=1}^{n-1} e^{y_j}$. We compute the partial derivatives and we get that

$$\begin{aligned}\frac{\partial g}{\partial y_1} &= \alpha \cdot \frac{e^{y_1}(1+S) - e^{y_1}(1+e^{y_1}-e^{y_2}-e^{y_{n-1}})}{(1+S)^2},\\ \frac{\partial g}{\partial y_j} &= -\alpha \cdot \frac{e^{y_j}(e^{y_1}+e^{y_{j-1}}-e^{y_{j+1}}-e^{y_{n-1}})}{(1+S)^2}, \text{ for } 2 \le j \le n-2,\\ \frac{\partial g}{\partial y_{n-1}} &= \alpha \cdot \frac{-e^{y_{n-1}}(1+S) - e^{y_{n-1}}(e^{y_1}+e^{y_{n-2}}-1-e^{y_{n-1}})}{(1+S)^2},\\ \frac{\partial g}{\partial z_j} &= 0 \text{ for } 1 \le j \le n-1.\end{aligned} \tag{5}$$

Therefore we get that

$$\begin{aligned}\nabla \cdot g &= \sum_{j=1}^{n-1} \frac{\partial g}{\partial y_j} + \sum_{j=1}^{n-1} \frac{\partial g}{\partial z_j}\\ &= \frac{-\alpha \cdot \sum_{j=1}^{n-1} e^{y_j}(e^{y_1} + e^{y_{j-1}} - e^{y_{j+1}} - e^{y_{n-1}}) + \alpha \cdot (e^{y_1} - e^{y_{n-1}})(1 + \sum_{j=1}^{n-1} e^{y_j})}{(1+S)^2},\end{aligned}$$

with the convention that $y_0 = y_n = 0$. We get that all the terms of the form $e^{y_j}e^{y_{j+1}}$ cancel out (telescopically) and also terms $e^{y_1}e^{y_j}, e^{y_{n-1}}e^{y_j}$ also cancel out for all $j$, i.e., it turns out that $\nabla \cdot g = 0$. Hence we conclude from Liouville theorem that the dynamical system (4) preserves volume.

Using the fact that the flow preserves the volume and that the orbits are bounded (Lemma 3.3), we apply Poincaré recurrence theorem on $(\tilde{y}, \tilde{z}) = g(y, z)$ for a small open ball around any initial point $(\tilde{y}_0, \tilde{z}_0)$ and the claim follows for the transformed dynamics. Since $\Pi^{-1}$ is continuous, if the distance between two points goes to zero in $\mathbb{R}^{n-1} \times \mathbb{R}^{n-1}$, so it does in $\Delta_n \times \Delta_n$ and the claim follows for the dynamics (1). □

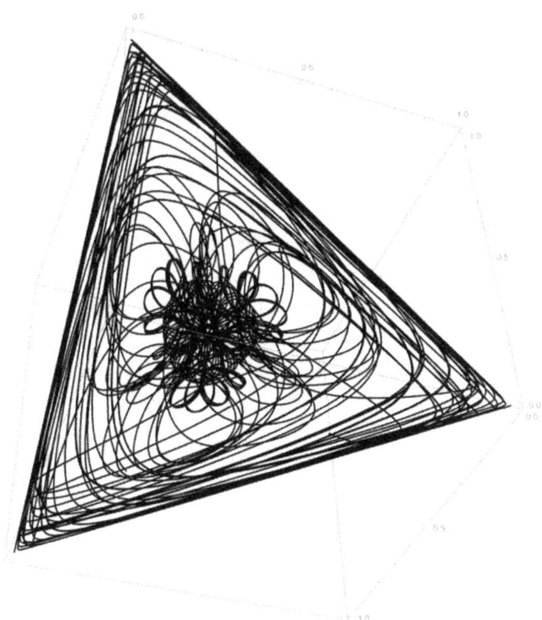

Fig. 1. Trajectories of the vector $x$ for different initial positions with $\mu = 0.1$. Trajectories intersect due to the fact 6 dimensions are projected to a 3D figure. The "cycling" behavior is observed.

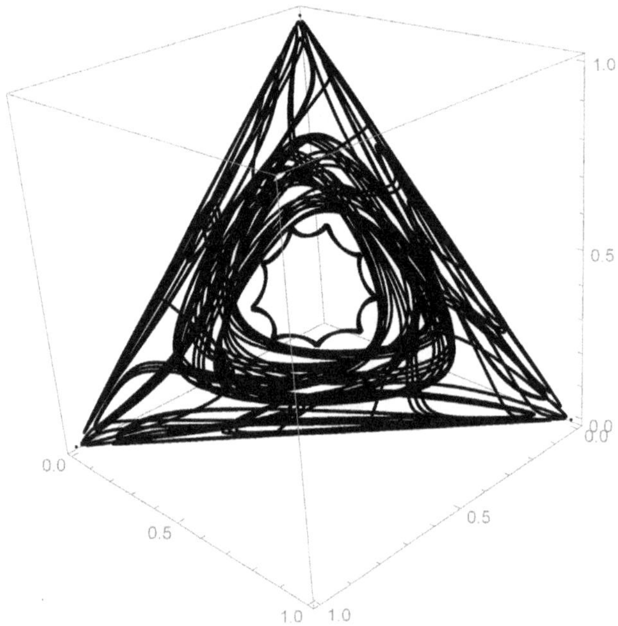


Fig. 2. Trajectories of the vector $\boldsymbol{w}$ for different initial positions with $\mu = 0.1$. Trajectories intersect due to the fact 6 dimensions are projected to a 3D figure. The "cycling" behavior is observed.

## 4 DISCUSSION

We believe that our work and that of [38] are opening up the possibility of modeling more complex biological phenomena using the setting of differential games, thereby potentially leading to new insights into biological phenomena. Additionally, we believe that the kinds of techniques used in this paper, and highlighted in Section 1.1, will be useful for studying other models of non-transitive dynamics.

We are not aware of other uses of the Poincaré theorem in differential games. It will be nice to see other applications of this powerful theorem to learning dynamics, other than replicator dynamics (such as FTRL), where the state space (payoff matrix) changes as per a differential equation.

There are several generalizations of our model which are worth studying. For example, what happens if each matrix $\boldsymbol{P}_i$ has its own parameter $\mu_i$? So far we have not been able to prove cycling for this general case but simulations indicate that the system does cycle. Understanding the range of parameters which lead to cycling and those that do not will be interesting.

## REFERENCES


[1] E. Akin and V. Losert. 1984. Evolutionary dynamics of zero-sum games. *J. of Math. Biology* (1984).

[2] Martín Arjovsky, Soumith Chintala, and Léon Bottou. 2017. Wasserstein Generative Adversarial Networks. In *Proceedings of the 34th International Conference on Machine Learning, ICML 2017, Sydney, NSW, Australia, 6-11 August 2017.* 214–223.

[3] L. Barreira. 2006. Poincaré recurrence: old and new. *XIVth International Congress on Mathematical Physics. World Scientific.* (2006), 415–422.

[4] D. D. Cameron, A. White, and J. Antonovics. 2009. ParasiteâĂŞgrassâĂŞforb interactions and rockâĂŞpaperâĂŞscissor dynamics: predicting the effects of the parasitic plant Rhinanthus minor on host plant communities. *Journal of Ecology* (2009), 1311–1319.

[5] Constantinos Daskalakis, Andrew Ilyas, Vasilis Syrgkanis, and Haoyang Zeng. 2018. Training GANs with Optimism. *To appear in ICLR* (2018). arXiv:1711.00141

[6] Engelbert Dockner. 2000. *Differential games in economics and management science.* Cambridge University Press.

[7] Deborah L. Finke and William E. Snyder. 2008. Niche Partitioning Increases Resource Exploitation by Diverse Communities. *Science* 321, 5895 (2008), 1488–1490.

[8] R.A. Fisher. 1999. *The Genetical Theory of Natural Selection. A complete variorum edition.* Clarendon Press, Oxford.

[9] Ian J. Goodfellow, Jean Pouget-Abadie, Mehdi Mirza, Bing Xu, David Warde-Farley, Sherjil Ozair, Aaron C. Courville, and Yoshua Bengio. 2014. Generative Adversarial Nets. In *Advances in Neural Information Processing Systems 27: Annual Conference on Neural Information Processing Systems 2014, December 8-13 2014, Montreal, Quebec, Canada.* 2672–2680.

[10] Jeremy JD Greenwood. 1984. The functional basis of frequency-dependent food selection. *Biological Journal of the Linnean Society* 23, 2-3 (1984), 177–199.

[11] Mart R Gross. 1982. Sneakers, satellites and parentals: polymorphic mating strategies in North American sunfishes. *Ethology* 60, 1 (1982), 1–26.

[12] James Haven, Levy C Vargas, Emmanuel F Mongodin, Vincent Xue, Yozen Hernandez, Pedro Pagan, Claire M Fraser-Liggett, Steven E Schutzer, Benjamin J Luft, Sherwood R Casjens, and others. 2011. Pervasive recombination and sympatric genome diversification driven by frequency-dependent selection in Borrelia burgdorferi, the Lyme disease bacterium. *Genetics* 189, 3 (2011), 951–966.

[13] J. Hofbauer and K. Sigmund. 1998. *Evolutionary Games and Population Dynamics.* Cambridge University Press, Cambridge.

[14] R. Isaacs. 1999. *Differential Games.* Dover.

[15] Rufus Isaacs. 1999. *Differential games: a mathematical theory with applications to warfare and pursuit, control and optimization.* Courier Corporation.

[16] B. Kerr, C. Neuhauser, B. J. M. Bohannan, and A. M. Dean. 2006. Local migration promotes competitive restraint in a host-pathogen'tragedy of the commons'. *Nature* (2006).

[17] B. Kerr, M. A. Riley, M. W. Feldman, and B. J. M. Bohannan. 2002. Local dispersal promotes biodiversity in a real-life game of rock-paper-scissors. *Nature* (2002).

[18] B. C. Kirkup and M. A. Riley. 2004. Antibiotic-mediated antagonism leads to a bacterial game of rock-paper-scissor in vivo. *Nature* (2004).

[19] Britt Koskella and Curtis M Lively. 2009. Evidence for negative frequency-dependent selection during experimental coevolution of a freshwater snail and a sterilizing trematode. *Evolution* 63, 9 (2009), 2213–2221.

[20] R. A. Lankau and S. Y. Strauss. 2007. Mutual feedbacks maintain both genetic and species diversity in a plant community. *Science* (2007), 1561–1563.

[21] R. Mehta, I. Panageas, G. Piliouras, P. Tetali, and V. V. Vazirani. 2017. Mutation, Sexual Reproduction and Survival in Dynamic Environments. *Innovations in Theoretical Computer Science (ITCS)* (2017).

[22] Panayotis Mertikopoulos, Christos Papadimitriou, and Georgios Piliouras. 2018. Cycles in Adversarial Regularized Learning. In *Proceedings of the Twenty-Ninth Annual ACM-SIAM Symposium on Discrete Algorithms, SODA 2018, New Orleans, LA, USA, January 7-10, 2018.* 2703–2717.

[23] Levi T Morran, Olivia G Schmidt, Ian A Gelarden, Raymond C Parrish, and Curtis M Lively. 2011. Running with the Red Queen: host-parasite coevolution selects for biparental sex. *Science* 333, 6039 (2011), 216–218.

[24] Robert Olendorf, F Helen Rodd, David Punzalan, Anne E Houde, Carla Hurt, David N Reznick, and Kimberly A Hughes. 2006. Frequency-dependent survival in natural guppy populations. *Nature* 441, 7093 (2006), 633–636.

[25] L. Perko. 1991. *Differential Equations and Dynamical Systems* (3nd. ed.). Springer.

[26] G. Piliouras, C. Nieto-Granda, H. I. Christensen, and J. S. Shamma. 2014. Persistent patterns: multi-agent learning beyond equilibrium and utility. In *International conference on Autonomous Agents and Multi-Agent Systems, AAMAS.* 181–188.

[27] Georgios Piliouras and Leonard J. Schulman. 2018. Learning Dynamics and the Co-Evolution of Competing Sexual Species. In *9th Innovations in Theoretical Computer Science Conference, ITCS 2018, January 11-14, 2018, Cambridge, MA,*

*USA*. 59:1–59:3.

[28] G. Piliouras and J. S. Shamma. 2014. Optimization Despite Chaos: Convex Relaxations to Complex Limit Sets via Poincaré Recurrence. *ACM-SIAM symposium on Discrete algorithms (SODA)* (2014).

[29] H. Poincaré. 1890. Sur le probléme des trois corps et les équations de la dynamique. *Acta Math* 13 (1890), 1–270.

[30] Paul B Rainey, Angus Buckling, Rees Kassen, and Michael Travisano. 2000. The emergence and maintenance of diversity: insights from experimental bacterial populations. *Trends in ecology & evolution* 15, 6 (2000), 243–247.

[31] T. Reichenbach, M. Mobilia, and E. Frey. 2007. Local migration promotes competitive restraint in a host-pathogen' tragedy of the commons'. *Nature* (2007), 1046–1049.

[32] Volker HW Rudolf and Janis Antonovics. 2005. Species coexistence and pathogens with frequency-dependent transmission. *The American Naturalist* 166, 1 (2005), 112–118.

[33] W. H. Sandholm. 2010. *Population Games and Evolutionary Dynamics.* MIT Press.

[34] L. S. Shapley. 1953. Stochastic games. *Proceedings of the National Academy of Sciences (PNAS)* (1953), 1095–1100.

[35] B. Sinervo and C. M. Lively. 1996. The rock-paper-scissors game and the evolution of alternative male strategies. *Nature* (1996).

[36] Peter H Thrall, Arjen Biere, and Marcy K Uyenoyama. 1995. Frequency-dependent disease transmission and the dynamics of the Silene-Ustilago host-pathogen system. *The American Naturalist* 145, 1 (1995), 43–62.

[37] David Tilman. 1982. *Resource competition and community structure.* Princeton university press.

[38] J. S. Weitz, C. Eksin, K. Paarporn, S. P. Brown, and W. C. Ratcliff. 2016. An oscillating tragedy of the commons in replicator dynamics with game-environment feedback. *Proceedings of the National Academy of Sciences.* 113 (2016), 7518–7525.

[39] RE Wong. 1967. Some aerospace differential games. *Journal of Spacecraft and Rockets* 4, 11 (1967).

# Dynamics of Distributed Updating in Fisher Markets

YUN KUEN CHEUNG, Max Planck Institute for Informatics, Saarland Informatics Campus, Germany

RICHARD COLE and YIXIN TAO, Courant Institute, NYU, USA

A major goal in Algorithmic Game Theory is to justify equilibrium concepts from an algorithmic and complexity perspective. One appealing approach is to identify natural distributed algorithms that converge quickly to an equilibrium. This paper established new convergence results for two generalizations of proportional response in Fisher markets with buyers having CES utility functions. The starting points are respectively a new convex and a new convex-concave formulation of such markets. The two generalizations correspond to suitable mirror descent algorithms applied to these formulations. Several of our new results are a consequence of new notions of strong Bregman convexity and of strong Bregman convex-concave functions, and associated linear rates of convergence, which may be of independent interest.

Among other results, we analyze a damped generalized proportional response and show a linear rate of convergence in a Fisher market with buyers whose utility functions cover the full spectrum of CES utilities aside the extremes of linear and Leontief utilities; when these utilities are included, we obtain an empirical $O(1/T)$ rate of convergence.

CCS Concepts: • **Theory of computation → Algorithmic game theory and mechanism design**; *Market equilibria*;

Additional Key Words and Phrases: Proportional response, mirror descent, Bregman divergence, Fisher market.

## 1 INTRODUCTION

One of the most important results in Algorithmic Game Theory is the PPAD-hardness of finding a Nash Equilibrium in finite games [8, 17], which serves as a strong evidence that there is no efficient algorithm to compute Nash Equilibria. Similar hardness results have been established for markets [7, 9, 10, 14, 47]. By viewing the players and the environment collectively as implicitly performing a computation, these hardness results indicate that, in general, a market cannot reach an equilibrium quickly. In Kamal Jain's words: "If your laptop cannot find it, neither can the market" [40, Chapter 2.1].

As a result, a lot of attention has been given to the design of polynomial-time algorithms to find equilibria, either exactly or approximately, for specific families of games and markets. Most of these algorithms can be categorized as either simplex-like (e.g., Lemke-Howson), numerical

The work of Richard Cole and Yixin Tao was supported in part by NSF grant CCF-1527568.

Authors' addresses: Yun Kuen Cheung, Max Planck Institute for Informatics, Saarland Informatics Campus, Germany, ycheung@mpi-inf.mpg.de; Richard Cole; Yixin Tao, Courant Institute, NYU, USA, cole@cs.nyu.edu,yt851@nyu.edu.


*ACM EC'18, June 18–22, 2018, Ithaca, NY, USA.* ACM ISBN 978-1-4503-5829-3/18/06...$15.00
https://doi.org/10.1145/3219166.3219189

methods (e.g., the interior-point method or the ellipsoid method), or some carefully-crafted combinatorial algorithm (e.g., flow-based algorithms for computing a market equilibrium for linear utility functions).

However, it seems implausible that these algorithms describe the implicit computations in games or markets. For many markets would appear to have a highly distributed environment, or need to make rapid decisions on an ongoing basis. These features would appear to preclude computations which require centralized coordination, which is essential for the three categories of algorithms above. Consequently, in order to justify equilibrium concepts, we want natural algorithms which could plausibly be running (in an implicit form) in the associated distributed environments.

This paper will focus on Fisher markets (or economies[1]). In a Fisher market there are buyers who start with money which they have no desire to keep, and sellers who have goods to sell, which they wish to sell in their entirety for money. This is a modest generalization of the notion of Competitive Equilibrium from Equal Incomes (CEEI) [27, 46]. In prior work on computing equilibria for these markets, there has been a particular focus on Eisenberg-Gale markets, a term coined by Jain and Vazirani, and their generalizations [28]; Eisenberg-Gale markets are Fisher markets in which demands are determined by homothetic utility functions. The latter markets have been seen to capture the notion of proportional fairness, as defined in the networking community [30], which is also equivalent to the optimum Nash Social Welfare [29, 35].

Two natural dynamics have been studied in the context of Fisher markets. The first, which is perhaps the most intuitive candidate for a natural algorithm, is tatonnement, in which the price of a good is raised if the demand exceeds the supply of the good, and decreased if the demand is too small. Implicitly, buyers' demands are assumed to be a best-response to the current prices. This highly intuitive algorithm was proposed by Walras well over a century ago [48].

Proportional Response, in contrast, is a buyer-oriented update, originally analyzed in an effort to explain the behavior of peer-to-peer networks [31, 49]. Here, buyers update their spending in proportion to the contribution each good makes to its current utility. While its meaning is clear for linear and other separable utilities, for other classes of utilities this needs more interpretation, which we provide in Section 2. Here prices are assumed to equal the current spending. An $O(1/T)$ rate of convergence was shown in [2] for Fisher markets with buyers having linear utilities, and for the substitutes domain excluding linear utilities, a faster linear rate (i.e., $\exp(-\Omega(T))$ rate) of convergence was shown in [50].

This paper continues the exploration of the connection between distributed dynamic processes and convex optimization, and more specifically the relation of proportional response to mirror descent.

Our first set of results starts by rederiving Zhang's bounds for CES substitutes utilities, by showing that for this setting proportional response amounts to mirror descent on a suitable convex function. To achieve the linear rate of convergence he obtained, we need to go beyond the standard $O(1/T)$ rate of convergence for mirror descent with a Bregman divergence. We proceed by analogy with gradient descent. Gradient descent with a Lipschitz constraint on the gradients guarantees only an $O(1/T)$ rate of convergence, but a faster linear rate of convergence is obtained when the objective function $f$ is strongly convex. For mirror descent with Bregman Divergences we introduce the notion of *strong Bregman convexity* and show that it also leads to a linear convergence rate. It turns out that the convex function associated with the CES substitutes utilities satisfies strong Bregman convexity, thereby obtaining Zhang's bound anew. In addition, for complementary CES

[1]In the CS literature the term market has been widely used to refer to economies; we follow this practice.

utilities, the same now concave function satisfies an analogous strong Bregman concavity property, which also yields a linear rate of convergence for these utilities. In addition, if we include linear utilities in the substitutes utilities, we obtain an $O(1/T)$ rate of convergence; likewise, including Leontief utilities in the complementary utilities also yields an $O(1/T)$ rate.

Next, we seek to handle substitute and complementary CES utilities simultaneously. The challenge we face is that the objective function used for the first set of results becomes a mixed concave-convex function in this setting, and the equilibrium corresponds to a saddle point of this function. We introduce the further notion of strongly-Bregman convex-concave functions, and for these functions we obtain a linear rate of convergence to the saddle point. Again, our objective function of the mixed CES utilities satisfies this property, thereby yielding linear convergence, albeit now for a *damped* proportional response, rather than the undamped proportional response analyzed in the first set of results. Here, including linear utilities and Leontief utilities yields an *empirical* $O(1/T)$ rate of convergence.

We note that our results are not a straightforward application of the existing mirror descent toolbox. The Bregman notions and the related convergence results in this paper are new. While the results for strong Bregman convex (resp. concave) functions are natural generalizations of gradient descent (resp. ascent) on standard strong convex (resp. concave) functions, the technique for demonstrating convergence for strong Bregman convex-concave functions appears to be new. It is not evident that suitable damping (i.e., reducing the step-size) permits a clean convergence analysis. Indeed, results showing linear point-wise convergence on convex-concave functions are rare ; in fact, the only such work we are aware of is [26]. We believe the new notions and convergence results for optimization problems may be of wider interest.

*Roadmap.* In Section 2 we give necessary definitions and notation, and in Section 3 we state our results precisely. Then, in Section 4, we describe related work. In Section 5 we carry out the analysis of mirror descent when Strong Bregman convexity holds, and then derive the convergence behavior of Proportional Response in each of the substitutes and complements domains. In Section 7, we perform an analogous analysis for strong Bregman convex-concave functions, and deduce the convergence behavior of a damped Proportional Response in combined substitutes and complements domains. Finally, in Section 9 we discuss the rates of convergence under some alternate measures.

## 2 NOTATION AND DEFINITIONS

We use bold symbols, e.g., $\mathbf{p}, \mathbf{x}, \mathbf{e}$, to denote vectors.

*Fisher Market.* In a Fisher market, there are $n$ perfectly divisible goods and $m$ buyers. Without loss of generality, the supply of each good $j$ is normalized to be one unit. Each buyer $i$ has a utility function $u_i : \mathbb{R}^n_+ \rightarrow \mathbb{R}$, and a budget of size $e_i$. At any given price vector $\mathbf{p} \in \mathbb{R}^n_+$, each buyer purchases a maximum utility affordable collection of goods. More precisely, $\mathbf{x}_i \in \mathbb{R}^n_+$ is said to be a demand of buyer $i$ if $\mathbf{x}_i \in \arg\max_{\mathbf{x}':\, \mathbf{x}'\cdot\mathbf{p}\leq e_i} u_i(\mathbf{x}')$.

A price vector $\mathbf{p}^* \in \mathbb{R}^n_+$ is called a *market equilibrium* if at $\mathbf{p}^*$, there exists a demand $\mathbf{x}_i$ of each buyer $i$ such that

$$p_j^* > 0 \Rightarrow \sum_{i=1}^{m} x_{ij} = 1 \quad \text{and} \quad p_j^* = 0 \Rightarrow \sum_{i=1}^{m} x_{ij} \leq 1.$$

The collection of $\mathbf{x}_i$ is said to be an *equilibrium allocation* to the buyers.

*CES utilities.* In this paper, each buyer $i$'s utility function is of the form

$$u_i(\mathbf{x}_i) = \left( \sum_{j=1}^{n} a_{ij} \cdot (x_{ij})^{\rho_i} \right)^{1/\rho_i},$$

for some $-\infty \leq \rho_i \leq 1$. $u_i(\mathbf{x}_i)$ is called a Constant Elasticity of Substitution (CES) utility function. They are a class of utility functions often used in economic analysis. The limit as $\rho_i \to -\infty$ is called a Leontief utility, usually written as $u_i(\mathbf{x}_i) = \min_j \frac{x_{ij}}{c_{ij}}$ [2]; and the limit as $\rho_i \to 0$ is called a Cobb-Douglas utility, usually written as $\prod_j x_{ij}{}^{a_{ij}}$, with $\sum_j a_{ij} = 1$. The utilities with $\rho_i \geq 0$ capture goods that are substitutes, and those with $\rho_i \leq 0$ goods that are complements.

*Notation.* Buyer $i$'s spending on good $j$, denoted by $b_{ij}$, is given by $b_{ij} = x_{ij} \cdot p_j$. Also, $z_j = \sum_i x_{ij} - 1$ denotes the excess demand for good $j$. We sometimes index prices, spending, and demands by $t$ to indicate the relevant value at time $t$. Finally, we use a superscript of $^*$ to indicate an equilibrium value.

*Bregman Divergence and Mirror Descent.* Let $C$ be a compact and convex set. Given a differentiable convex function $h(\mathbf{x})$ with domain $C$, the *Bregman divergence* generated by kernel $h$ is denoted by $d_h$, and is defined as:

$$d_h(\mathbf{x}, \mathbf{y}) = h(\mathbf{x}) - [\, h(\mathbf{y}) + \langle \nabla h(\mathbf{y}) \,,\, \mathbf{x} - \mathbf{y} \rangle \,], \ \forall \mathbf{x} \in C \text{ and } \mathbf{y} \in \mathrm{rint}(C),$$

where $\mathrm{rint}(C)$ is the relative interior of $C$. We note that, in general, $d_h$ is asymmetric, i.e., $d_h(\mathbf{x}, \mathbf{y}) \neq d_h(\mathbf{y}, \mathbf{x})$. In this paper, we use the Kullback-Leibler or KL divergence extensively; it is the Bregman divergence generated by $h(\mathbf{x}) = \sum_j (x_j \cdot \ln x_j - x_j)$. When $\sum_j x_j = \sum_j y_j$, the explicit formula is:

$$\mathrm{KL}(\mathbf{x}||\mathbf{y}) := \sum_j x_j \cdot \ln \frac{x_j}{y_j}.$$

For the problem of minimizing a convex function $f(\mathbf{x})$ subject to $\mathbf{x} \in C$, the mirror descent method w.r.t. Bregman divergence $d_h$ is given by the following update rule:

$$\mathbf{x}^{t+1} = \arg\min_{\mathbf{x} \in C} \left\{ f(\mathbf{x}^t) + \left\langle \nabla f(\mathbf{x}^t) \,,\, \mathbf{x} - \mathbf{x}^t \right\rangle + \frac{1}{\Gamma_t} \cdot d_h(\mathbf{x}, \mathbf{x}^t) \right\}, \tag{1}$$

where $\Gamma_t > 0$, and may be dependent on $t$.

*Proportional Response.* For linear utility functions, Proportional Response is the dynamic given by the spending update rule:

$$b_{ij}^{t+1} = e_i \cdot \frac{a_{ij} x_{ij}^t}{\sum_k a_{ik} x_{ik}^t} = e_i \cdot \frac{a_{ij} \frac{b_{ij}^t}{p_j^t}}{\sum_k a_{ik} \frac{b_{ik}^t}{p_k^t}} \quad \text{with } p_k^t = \sum_i b_{ik}^t.$$

For substitutes CES utilities, [50] generalized this rule to:

$$b_{ij}^{t+1} = e_i \cdot \frac{a_{ij} (x_{ij}^t)^{\rho_i}}{\sum_k a_{ik} (x_{ik}^t)^{\rho_i}} = e_i \cdot \frac{a_{ij} \left( \frac{b_{ij}^t}{p_j^t} \right)^{\rho_i}}{\sum_k a_{ik} \left( \frac{b_{ik}^t}{p_k^t} \right)^{\rho_i}} \tag{2}$$

[2]Here, the utility function $u_i(\mathbf{x}) = \min_j \frac{x_{ij}}{c_{ij}}$ can be seen as the limit of $u_i(\mathbf{x}) = \left( \sum_j \left( \frac{x_{ij}}{c_{ij}} \right)^{\rho_i} \right)^{\frac{1}{\rho_i}}$ as $\rho_i$ tends to $-\infty$.

obtaining a linear convergence rate for the resulting dynamic, assuming $0 < \rho_i < 1$. The above rule has a natural distributed interpretation in the Fisher market setting: in each round, each buyer splits her spending on different goods in proportion to the values of $a_{ik}(x^t_{ik})^{\rho_i}$. The seller of good $j$ then allocates the good to buyers in proportion to the spending received from each buyer.

## 3 RESULTS

### 3.1 Proportional Response

It is natural to seek to extend the Proportional Response rule (2) to the complementary domain, but this rule does not lead to convergent behavior in general. Set $\rho = -1$. Suppose there are two buyers and two items. Both buyers have the same preference for each item and the same budgets; i.e. $a_{11} = a_{12} = a_{21} = a_{22} = \frac{1}{2}$, and $e_1 = e_2 = 1$. Initially, at time $t = 0$, suppose that $b^{(0)}_{11} = \frac{1}{4}$, $b^{(0)}_{12} = \frac{3}{4}$, $b^{(0)}_{21} = \frac{3}{4}$, and $b^{(0)}_{22} = \frac{1}{4}$. A simple calculation shows that applying update rule (2) gives $b^{(1)}_{11} = \frac{3}{4}$, $b^{(1)}_{12} = \frac{1}{4}$, $b^{(1)}_{21} = \frac{1}{4}$, and $b^{(1)}_{22} = \frac{3}{4}$. So this simple example shows that in this setting, the spending will not converge to the market equilibrium; rather, it will cycle among 2 states.

Instead, we observe that in the substitutes domain, excluding Cobb-Douglas utilities, this rule is the mirror descent updating rule using the KL divergence for the following optimization problem.

$$\min_{\mathbf{b}} \quad \Phi(\mathbf{b}) = -\sum_{ij} \frac{b_{ij}}{\rho_i} \log \frac{a_{ij}(b_{ij})^{\rho_i - 1}}{(\sum_h b_{hj})^{\rho_i}}$$
$$\text{subject to } \ \textstyle\sum_j b_{ij} = e_i \ \text{ for all } i, \quad \text{and } b_{ij} \geq 0 \text{ for all } i, j.$$

We exclude Cobb-Douglas utilities, because as $\rho_i \to 0$ the corresponding term in $\Phi$ tends to $\infty$. When restricted to linear utilities, i.e. $\rho_i = 1$ for all $i$, this is simply Shmyrev's convex program [44] for these markets.

In the complementary domain, the mirror descent updating rule for this function is:

$$b^{t+1}_{ij} = e_i \cdot \frac{\left(\frac{a_{ij}}{(p^t_j)^{\rho_i}}\right)^{\frac{1}{1-\rho_i}}}{\sum_k \left(\frac{a_{ik}}{(p^t_k)^{\rho_i}}\right)^{\frac{1}{1-\rho_i}}} \quad \text{for } -\infty < \rho_i < 0, \qquad \text{and } b^{t+1}_{ij} = e_i \cdot \frac{c_{ij} p^t_j}{\sum_k c_{ik} p^t_k} \quad \text{for } \rho_i = -\infty,$$
$$\text{where } p^t_k = \textstyle\sum_i b^t_{ik}. \tag{3}$$

Accordingly, we adopt this as the generalization of Proportional Response to the complementary domain. This rule can be easily implemented in the distributed environment of Fisher markets. In each round, each buyer only needs the prices computed in the previous round to compute its update. Thus, to implement the update rule, it suffices to have the sellers broadcast their prices by the end of each round.

Interestingly, this update rule is also the best response action to the current prices for each buyer. We note that this rule can be viewed as a tatonnement update if we define $x^{t+1}_{ij} = b^{t+1}_{ij}/p^t_j$, for then $p^{t+1}_j = \sum_i b^{t+1}_{ij} = \sum_i x^{t+1}_{ij} p^t_j = p^t_j(1 + z^{t+1}_j)$. However, this is not the same rule as was used for the tatonnement analyzed in recent works regarding Fisher markets [11, 16].

For linear utilities, update rule (2) was analyzed in [2]. For the substitutes domain excluding linear utilities, a faster linear rate of convergence was shown in [50], but not based on considering the above optimization problem. To obtain a linear rate of convergence for an analysis based on optimizing $\Phi$ via a mirror descent with a KL Divergence, we introduce the notion of *strong Bregman convexity*. We also coin the term Bregman convexity for an analogous notion introduced in [2]).

Definition 1. *The function $f$ is $L$-Bregman convex w.r.t. Bregman divergence $d_h$ if, for any* $\mathbf{y} \in \mathrm{rint}(C)$ *and* $\mathbf{x} \in C$,

$$f(\mathbf{y}) + \langle \nabla f(\mathbf{y}), \mathbf{x} - \mathbf{y} \rangle \leq f(\mathbf{x}) \leq f(\mathbf{y}) + \langle \nabla f(\mathbf{y}), \mathbf{x} - \mathbf{y} \rangle + L \cdot d_h(\mathbf{x}, \mathbf{y}).$$

*The function $f$ is $(\sigma, L)$-strongly Bregman convex w.r.t. Bregman divergence $d_h$ if, $0 < \sigma \leq L$, and, for any* $\mathbf{y} \in \mathrm{rint}(C)$, $\mathbf{x} \in C$,

$$f(\mathbf{y}) + \langle \nabla f(\mathbf{y}), \mathbf{x} - \mathbf{y} \rangle + \sigma \cdot d_h(\mathbf{x}, \mathbf{y}) \leq f(\mathbf{x}) \leq f(\mathbf{y}) + \langle \nabla f(\mathbf{y}), \mathbf{x} - \mathbf{y} \rangle + L \cdot d_h(\mathbf{x}, \mathbf{y}).$$

*If the direction of the inequalities and the signs on the $d_h(\mathbf{x}, \mathbf{y})$ terms are reversed, the function is said to be Bregman concave (or strongly Bregman concave respectively).* ($\mathrm{rint}(C)$ *denotes the relative interior of* $C$.)

Consider the update rule:

$$\mathbf{x}^{t+1} \leftarrow \arg\min_{\mathbf{y}} \left\{ \left\langle \nabla f(\mathbf{x}^t), \mathbf{y} - \mathbf{x}^t \right\rangle + L \cdot d_h(\mathbf{y}, \mathbf{x}^t) \right\}. \tag{4}$$

Theorem 3.1. *Suppose that $f$ is $(\sigma, L)$-strongly Bregman convex w.r.t. $d_h$. If update rule (4) is applied, then, for all $t \geq 1$,*

$$f(\mathbf{x}^t) - f(\mathbf{x}^*) \leq \frac{\sigma}{\left(\frac{L}{L-\sigma}\right)^t - 1} \cdot d_h(\mathbf{x}^*, \mathbf{x}^0).$$

An analogous Theorem for $L$-Bregman convex functions was given in [2]:

Theorem 3.2. *[2] Suppose $f$ is an $L$-Bregman convex function w.r.t. $d$, and $\mathbf{x}^T$ is the point reached after $T$ applications of the mirror descent update rule (4). Then,*

$$f(\mathbf{x}^T) - f(\mathbf{x}^*) \leq \frac{L \cdot d(\mathbf{x}^*, \mathbf{x}^0)}{T}.$$

We show that in the CES substitutes domain, excluding linear utilities, $\Phi$ is a strongly Bregman convex function w.r.t. the KL-divergence on spending, thereby providing an alternative derivation of Zhang's result. In addition, in the CES complements domain, excluding Leontief utilities, $\Phi$ is a strongly Bregman concave function w.r.t. the KL divergence on spending, which yields a proof of linear convergence in this domain. These analyses are readily modified to give a $1/T$ rate of convergence if we include respectively the linear and Leontief utilities. These results are made precise in the following theorem.

Theorem 3.3. *Suppose buyers with substitutes utilities repeatedly update their spending using Proportional Response rule (2), and those with complementary utilities use rule (3). Then the potential function $\Phi$ converges to the market equilibrium as follows.*

- *If all buyers have substitutes CES utilities, then*

$$\Phi(\mathbf{b}^T) - \Phi(\mathbf{b}^*) \leq \frac{1}{T} \sum_i \frac{1}{\rho_i} \mathrm{KL}(b_i^* || b_i^0).$$

- *Suppose that in addition no buyer has a linear utility. Let $\sigma = \min_i\{1 - \rho_i\}$. Then,*

$$\Phi(\mathbf{b}^T) - \Phi(\mathbf{b}^*) \leq \frac{\sigma(1-\sigma)^T}{1 - (1-\sigma)^T} \sum_i \frac{1}{\rho_i} \mathrm{KL}(b_i^* || b_i^0).$$

- *If all buyers have complementary CES utilities, then*[3]

$$\Phi(\mathbf{b}^*) - \Phi(\mathbf{b}^T) \leq \frac{1}{T}\sum_i \frac{\rho_i - 1}{\rho_i}\mathrm{KL}(b_i^*||b_i^0).$$

- *Suppose that in addition no buyer has a Leontief utility. Let* $\sigma = \min_i \left\{\frac{1}{1-\rho_i}\right\}$. *Then,*

$$\Phi(\mathbf{b}^*) - \Phi(\mathbf{b}^T) \leq \frac{\sigma(1-\sigma)^T}{1-(1-\sigma)^T}\sum_i \frac{\rho_i - 1}{\rho_i}\mathrm{KL}(b_i^*||b_i^0).$$

The first two results are shown in Corollaries 6.4, 6.5, respectively, and the remaining results can be found in the full version of the paper. We also note that as shown in Lemma 13 in [2], if $b_{ij} = e_i/m$ for all $i$ and $j$, then $\mathrm{KL}(\mathbf{b}^*||\mathbf{b}) \leq \log mn$, which provides a possibly more intuitive version of the above bounds.

Theorem 3.3 does not cover buyers with Cobb-Douglas utilities, because, as already noted, the terms in $\Phi$ for such buyers are equal to $\infty$. Note that these buyers always wish to allocate their spending in fixed proportions regardless of the prices. Thus, arguably, it would be natural for these buyers to always have the equilibrium spending. But even if this were not true initially, after one update this property would hold, and remain true henceforth. Thus the presence of these buyers would seem to have little effect on the convergence. Indeed, the above bounds hold with $\mathrm{KL}(\mathbf{b}_i^*||\mathbf{b}_i^0)$ replaced by $\mathrm{KL}(\mathbf{b}_i^*||\mathbf{b}_i^1)$ and $T$ replaced by $T-1$ on the RHS. But to obtain bounds in terms of $\mathrm{KL}(\mathbf{b}_i^*||\mathbf{b}_i^0)$ appears to require substantially more effort; this analysis is given in the full paper. The rates of convergence are similar to those given in Theorem 3.3.

## 3.2 Damped Proportional Response

But what if we want to allow a mix of substitutes and complementary utilities? The difficulty we face is that the objective function $\Phi$ is no longer either convex or concave. Rather, if we fix the spending of the buyers with complementary utilities, the resulting restricted $\Phi$ is convex, while if we fix the spending of the buyers with substitutes utilities, the resulting restricted $\Phi$ is concave. As it happens, the equilibrium corresponds to a saddle point of the function $\Phi$. Also, a suitable dynamic will converge to this saddle point. To show this, we introduce a saddle-point convergence analysis. To this end, we define the following notion.

Definition 2. *Function $f$ is $(L_X, L_Y)$-convex-concave w.r.t. the pair of Bregman divergences $(d_g, d_h)$, if it satisfies the following constraints.*

(1) *For fixed* $\mathrm{y}$, $f(\cdot, \mathrm{y})$ *is a convex function;*

(2) *For fixed* $\mathrm{x}$, $f(\mathrm{x}, \cdot)$ *is a concave function;*

(3) *There exist parameters* $L_X, L_Y > 0$ *such that for any* $\mathrm{x} \in X$, $\mathrm{x}' \in X$, $\mathrm{y} \in Y$ *and* $\mathrm{y}' \in Y$,

$$-L_Y \cdot d_h(\mathrm{y},\mathrm{y}') \overset{(a)}{\leq} f(\mathrm{x},\mathrm{y}) - f(\mathrm{x}',\mathrm{y}') - \langle \nabla f(\mathrm{x}',\mathrm{y}'), (\mathrm{x},\mathrm{y}) - (\mathrm{x}',\mathrm{y}')\rangle \overset{(b)}{\leq} L_X \cdot d_g(\mathrm{x},\mathrm{x}'). \quad (5)$$

The saddle point is the "optimal" point of the convex-concave function, which is the minimum point in the $x$-direction and the maximum point in the $y$-direction, defined formally as follows.

Definition 3. *$(x^*, y^*)$ is a saddle point of $f$ if and only if*

$$f(x, y^*) \geq f(x^*, y^*) \geq f(x^*, y) \text{ for any } x \in X \text{ and } y \in Y.$$

[3]For $\rho_i = -\infty$, we define $\frac{\rho_i - 1}{\rho_i}$ to equal 1.

Now consider the following update rule:

$$\mathbf{x}^{t+1} = \arg\min_{\mathbf{x}}\{\langle \nabla_x f(\mathbf{x}^t, \mathbf{y}^t), \mathbf{x} - \mathbf{x}^t \rangle + 2L_X \cdot d_g(\mathbf{x}, \mathbf{x}^t)\};$$
$$\mathbf{y}^{t+1} = \arg\min_{\mathbf{y}}\{\langle -\nabla_y f(\mathbf{x}^t, \mathbf{y}^t), \mathbf{y} - \mathbf{y}^t \rangle + 2L_Y \cdot d_h(\mathbf{y}, \mathbf{y}^t)\}. \tag{6}$$

We can then show an $O(1/T)$ empirical rate of convergence, as stated in the next theorem.

Theorem 3.4. *Suppose that $f$ is $(L_X, L_Y)$-convex-concave, and there exists a saddle point $(\mathbf{x}^*, \mathbf{y}^*)$. In addition, suppose that $(\mathbf{x}, \mathbf{y})$ are updated according to (6). Then:*

*(i)* $\displaystyle\sum_{t=1}^{T}\Big(f(\mathbf{x}^t, \mathbf{y}^*) - f(\mathbf{x}^*, \mathbf{y}^t)\Big) \le 2L_X \cdot d_g(\mathbf{x}^*, \mathbf{x}^0) + 2L_Y \cdot d_h(\mathbf{y}^*, \mathbf{y}^0).$

*Note that $f(\mathbf{x}^t, \mathbf{y}^*) - f(\mathbf{x}^*, \mathbf{y}^t) \ge 0$ since $f(\mathbf{x}^t, \mathbf{y}^*) \ge f(\mathbf{x}^*, \mathbf{y}^*) \ge f(\mathbf{x}^*, \mathbf{y}^t)$.*

*(ii) Also, if $\bar{\mathbf{x}} = \frac{1}{T}\sum_{t=1}^{T}\mathbf{x}^t$ and $\bar{\mathbf{y}} = \frac{1}{T}\sum_{t=1}^{T}\mathbf{y}^t$, then:*

$$f(\bar{\mathbf{x}}, \mathbf{y}^*) - f(\mathbf{x}^*, \bar{\mathbf{y}}) \le \frac{1}{T}[2L_X \cdot d_g(\mathbf{x}^*, \mathbf{x}^0) + 2L_Y \cdot d_h(\mathbf{y}^*, \mathbf{y}^0)].$$

Note that the second part of the theorem follows immediately from the first part because $f(\cdot, \mathbf{y}^*)$ is a convex function and $f(\mathbf{x}^*, \cdot)$ is a concave function.

The objective function $\Phi$ is $(1,1)$-convex-concave w.r.t. $d_g = \sum_{i:\rho_i>0}\frac{1}{\rho_i}\mathrm{KL}(b_i||b_i')$ and $d_h = \sum_{i:\infty<\rho_i<0}\frac{\rho_i-1}{\rho_i}\mathrm{KL}(b_i||b_i') + \sum_{i:\rho_i=-\infty}\mathrm{KL}(b_i||b_i')$. Consequently, we obtain an empirical $O(1/T)$ rate of convergence for the following *Damped* Proportional Response update.

$$b_{ij}^{t+1} = e_i \cdot \frac{\left[b_{ij}^t \cdot a_{ij}\left(\frac{b_{ij}^t}{p_j^t}\right)^{\rho_i}\right]^{\frac{1}{2}}}{\sum_k\left[b_{ik}^t \cdot a_{ik}\left(\frac{b_{ik}^t}{p_k^t}\right)^{\rho_i}\right]^{\frac{1}{2}}}, \text{ for } \rho_i > 0; \quad b_{ij}^{t+1} = e_i \cdot \frac{\left[b_{ij}^t \cdot \left(\frac{a_{ij}}{(p_j^t)^{\rho_i}}\right)^{\frac{1}{1-\rho_i}}\right]^{\frac{1}{2}}}{\sum_k\left[b_{ik}^t \cdot \left(\frac{a_{ik}}{(p_k^t)^{\rho_i}}\right)^{\frac{1}{1-\rho_i}}\right]^{\frac{1}{2}}}, \text{ for } -\infty < \rho_i < 0;$$
$$b_{ij}^{t+1} = e_i \cdot \frac{\left[b_{ij}^t \cdot \left(\frac{c_{ij}}{p_j^t}\right)^{-1}\right]^{\frac{1}{2}}}{\sum_k\left[b_{ik}^t \cdot \left(\frac{c_{ik}}{p_k^t}\right)^{-1}\right]^{\frac{1}{2}}}, \text{ for } \rho_i = -\infty; \tag{7}$$

We say it is damped because the update rule uses the geometric mean of the current value and the standard Proportional Response update.

A natural question is whether a linear convergence rate is possible if the linear and Leontief utilities are excluded. The answer is yes, and to obtain this we need a stronger condition on the convex-concave objective function, as given in the following definition.

Definition 4. *$f$ is a $(\sigma_X, \sigma_Y, L_X, L_Y)$-strongly Bregman convex-concave function, w.r.t. Bregman divergences $d_g, d_h$, if, for all $\mathbf{x} \in X$, $\mathbf{x}' \in X$, $\mathbf{y} \in Y$, and $\mathbf{y}' \in Y$, function $f$ satisfies:*

$$-L_Y \cdot d_h(\mathbf{y}, \mathbf{y}') + \sigma_X \cdot d_g(\mathbf{x}, \mathbf{x}') \le f(\mathbf{x}, \mathbf{y}) - f(\mathbf{x}', \mathbf{y}') - \langle \nabla f(\mathbf{x}', \mathbf{y}'), (\mathbf{x}, \mathbf{y}) - (\mathbf{x}', \mathbf{y}') \rangle$$
$$\le L_X \cdot d_g(\mathbf{x}, \mathbf{x}') - \sigma_Y \cdot d_h(\mathbf{y}, \mathbf{y}'). \tag{8}$$

Theorem 3.5. *If $f$ is a $(\sigma_X, \sigma_Y, L_X, L_Y)$-strongly Bregman convex-concave function w.r.t $d_g$ and $d_h$, and there exists a saddle point, then update rule (6) converges to the saddle point with a linear convergence rate:*

$$\Big(f(\mathbf{x}^T, \mathbf{y}^*) - f(\mathbf{x}^*, \mathbf{y}^T)\Big) \le \left(1 - \frac{\min\left\{\frac{\sigma_X}{L_X}, \frac{\sigma_Y}{L_Y}\right\}}{2}\right)^{T-1}\Big((2L_X - \sigma_X)d_g(\mathbf{x}^*, \mathbf{x}^0) + (2L_Y - \sigma_Y)d_h(\mathbf{y}^*, \mathbf{y}^0)\Big).$$

$\Phi$ is $(\min_{i:\rho_i>0}\{1-\rho_i\}, \min_{i:\rho_i<0}\left\{\frac{1}{1-\rho_i}\right\}, 1, 1)$-strongly Bregman convex-concave, and thus we can deduce that the damped Proportional Response achieves a linear convergence rate if linear and Leontief utilities are excluded.

As before, the above results exclude Cobb-Douglas utilities.

Arguably, the buyers with Cobb-Douglas utilities should always have the equilibrium spending, or failing that, should immediately update to this spending. But for mathematical consistency, we suppose they are performing the same type of damped update as the other buyers. In this case, our previous potential function can't be used when we include Cobb-Douglas utility functions. We now need to include a term in the potential function for each buyer with a Cobb-Douglas utility as their spending keeps changing.

We will need the following notation. Let $\mathbf{b}_{>0}$, $\mathbf{b}_{=0}$, and $\mathbf{b}_{<0}$ denote the spending of those buyers with $\rho_i > 0$, $\rho_i = 0$, and $\rho_i < 0$, respectively. Accordingly, we will write $\Phi(\mathbf{b}) = \Phi(\mathbf{b}_{>0}, \mathbf{b}_{=0}, \mathbf{b}_{<0})$. The resulting function is still convex in $\mathbf{b}_{>0}$ and concave in $\mathbf{b}_{<0}$. The construction is given in the full paper. We note that the update rule for the buyers with $\rho_i = 0$ is given by:

$$b_{ij}^{t+1} = e_i \cdot \frac{\left[b_{ij}^t \cdot a_{ij}^t\right]^{\frac{1}{2}}}{\sum_k \left[b_{ik}^t \cdot a_{ik}^t\right]^{\frac{1}{2}}}, \qquad \text{for } \rho_i = 0.$$

THEOREM 3.6. *Suppose buyers repeatedly update their spending using the Damped Proportional Response rule (7). Then*

$$\mathrm{KL}(\mathbf{b}_{=0}^T||\mathbf{b}_{=0}^*) \le \frac{1}{2^T}\mathrm{KL}(\mathbf{b}_{=0}^0||\mathbf{b}_{=0}^*),$$

*and the potential function $\Phi$ converges to the market equilibrium as follows:*

*i.*
$$\sum_{t=1}^{T}\left[\Phi(\mathbf{b}_{>0}^t, \mathbf{b}_{=0}^*, \mathbf{b}_{<0}^*) - \Phi(\mathbf{b}_{>0}^*, \mathbf{b}_{=0}^*, \mathbf{b}_{<0}^t)\right]$$
$$\le 4\sum_{i:\rho_i=0}\mathrm{KL}(\mathbf{b}_i^*||\mathbf{b}_i^0) + \sum_{i:-\infty<\rho_i<0}\frac{2(\rho_i-1)}{\rho_i}\mathrm{KL}(\mathbf{b}_i^*||\mathbf{b}_i^0) + \sum_{i:\rho_i>0}\frac{2}{\rho_i}\mathrm{KL}(\mathbf{b}_i^*||\mathbf{b}_i^0) + \sum_{i:\rho_i=-\infty}\mathrm{KL}(\mathbf{b}_i^*||\mathbf{b}_i^0).$$

*ii. If in addition no buyer has a linear or Leontief utility,*

$$\text{Let } \sigma = \min\left\{\min_{i:\rho_i>0}\left\{\frac{2}{1+\rho_i}\right\}, \min_{i:\rho_i<0}\left\{\frac{2(\rho_i-1)}{2\rho_i-1}\right\}\right\} \qquad \text{(so } 1<\sigma<2\text{). Then,}$$

$$\Phi(\mathbf{b}_{>0}^T, \mathbf{b}_{=0}^*, \mathbf{b}_{<0}^*) - \Phi(\mathbf{b}_{>0}^*, \mathbf{b}_{=0}^*, \mathbf{b}_{<0}^T) \le \frac{1}{\sigma^{T-1}}\left[\frac{4}{2-\sigma}\sum_{i:\rho_i=0}\mathrm{KL}(\mathbf{b}_i^*||\mathbf{b}_i^0) + \sum_{i:\rho_i<0}\frac{2\rho_i-1}{\rho_i}\mathrm{KL}(\mathbf{b}_i^*||\mathbf{b}_i^0) + \sum_{i:\rho_i>0}\frac{1+\rho_i}{\rho_i}\mathrm{KL}(\mathbf{b}_i^*||\mathbf{b}_i^0)\right].$$

Weaker bounds are shown in Corollaries 8.2 and 8.3, respectively. The complete proof is given in the full paper.

## 4 RELATED WORK

The concept of a market equilibrium was first proposed by Walras [48] along with a description of the tatonnement process. Since then, studies of market equilibria and tatonnement have received much attention in economics, operations research, and most recently in computer science. A fairly recent account of the classic perspective in economics is given in [34].

Computer scientists, beginning with the work by Deng et al. [19], showed that computing equilibria was a hard problem in general; see also [18, 41]. This led to much work on polynomial time algorithms for restricted classes of markets, e.g. [13, 20, 21, 25].

The Eisenberg-Gale program for the case of linear utilities was formulated in [24] and then generalized to homothetic functions in [23]; further generalizations were given in [28]. The maxima of these convex programs correspond to the equilibria of the corresponding markets. In particular, when buyer or agent utilities are homothetic, the optimum of the Eisenberg-Gale program corresponds to the optimum Nash Social Welfare; interestingly, this optimum also appears to provide good outcomes when apportioning indivisible goods [4, 5]. Recently, Cole et al. [15] identified another variant of the Eisenberg-Gale program that captured the best currently-known polynomial-time approximate solution for the indivisible setting.

The analysis most similar to ours is the one in [2] which considers convex functions that obey a constraint which we name $L$-Bregman convexity w.r.t. a Bregman divergence (see Definition 1). Our work generalizes this notion substantially.

The earliest analyses of tatonnement showed convergence in exchange economies with gross substitutes utilities, first for continuous updating [1] and then for discrete updates [45], but it was shown to diverge in general [43]. Recent works have analyzed its convergence properties in specific markets, primarily Fisher markets [11, 12, 16]. Cheung et al. [11] showed that tatonnement is equivalent to coordinate descent on a convex function for several classes of Fisher markets, and consequently that a suitable tatonnement converges toward the market equilibrium in two classes of markets: complementary-CES Fisher markets and Leontief Fisher markets.

Other dynamics have been considered. In particular, Dvijotham et al. [22] study sellers best responding in a setting in which they form beliefs about other sellers' strategies. They obtain linear convergence in Fisher markets where buyers have weak gross substitutes utilities. In the context of network flow control, Low and Lapsley [32] adopted an optimization approach to derive a dynamic protocol where both prices (of links) and flow demands of agents are updated, and showed that the protocol converges to a social-welfare maximizing state. The update rules (2), (3) look quite similar to a game-learning dynamic called *log-linear learning* [3, 33] (by suitably viewing spendings as probability densities), but due to different contexts (games vs. markets), the actual behaviors and the analyses have significant qualitative differences.

Convex-concave saddle-point problems can be reduced to non-smooth convex minimization problems, for which algorithms yielding $O(1/\sqrt{T})$ convergence rate exist. Its wide applications (e.g., to two-person zero-sum game equilibrium) have motivated exploration of properties of the underlying function which support faster converging algorithms [36–39, 42]. In this paper, we present a new property and a simple algorithm which yields an $O(1/T)$ empirical convergence rate. In our opinion, its analysis is quite simple, which may well open the door to further exploration. Indeed, we have taken such a step by presenting a variant of our new property for which the same algorithm yields a linear *point-wise* convergence rate.

## 5 LINEAR CONVERGENCE WITH STRONG BREGMAN CONVEXITY

Our proof will use the following lemmas.

LEMMA 5.1. *[6] If $\mathbf{x}^+$ is the optimal point for the optimization problem:*

$$\begin{aligned} \textit{minimize} \quad & g(\mathbf{x}) + d(\mathbf{x}, \mathbf{y}) \\ \textit{subject to} \quad & \mathbf{x} \in C, \end{aligned}$$

*where $C$ is a compact convex set, then, for any $\mathbf{x} \in C$,*

$$g(\mathbf{x}^+) + d(\mathbf{x}^+, \mathbf{y}) + d(\mathbf{x}, \mathbf{x}^+) \le g(\mathbf{x}) + d(\mathbf{x}, \mathbf{y}).$$

LEMMA 5.2. *[2] Suppose that $f$ is a L-Bregman convex function w.r.t. $d(\mathbf{x}, \mathbf{x}')$, and $\mathbf{x}^t$ and $\mathbf{x}^{t+1}$ are the points reached after $t$ and $t+1$ applications of the mirror descent update rule (4). Then*

$$f(\mathbf{x}^{t+1}) \le f(\mathbf{x}^t).$$

PROOF OF THEOREM 3.1. By Lemma 5.1 with $\mathbf{y} = \mathbf{x}^t$, $\mathbf{x}^+ = \mathbf{x}^{t+1}$, and $\mathbf{x} = \mathbf{x}^*$,

$$\left\langle \nabla f(\mathbf{x}^t)\,,\; \mathbf{x}^{t+1} - \mathbf{x}^t \right\rangle + L \cdot d_h(\mathbf{x}^{t+1}, \mathbf{x}^t) \le \left\langle \nabla f(\mathbf{x}^t)\,,\; \mathbf{x}^* - \mathbf{x}^t \right\rangle + L \cdot \left[ d_h(\mathbf{x}^*, \mathbf{x}^t) - d_h(\mathbf{x}^*, \mathbf{x}^{t+1}) \right]. \tag{9}$$

By strong Bregman-convexity, with $\mathbf{y} = \mathbf{x}^t$, and $\mathbf{x} = \mathbf{x}^{t+1}$,

$$\left\langle \nabla f(\mathbf{x}^t)\,,\; \mathbf{x}^{t+1} - \mathbf{x}^t \right\rangle + L \cdot d_h(\mathbf{x}^{t+1}, \mathbf{x}^t) \ge f(\mathbf{x}^{t+1}) - f(\mathbf{x}^t); \tag{10}$$

and with $\mathbf{y} = \mathbf{x}^t$ and $\mathbf{x} = \mathbf{x}^*$,

$$\nabla f(\mathbf{x}^t) \cdot (\mathbf{x}^* - \mathbf{x}^t) \le f(\mathbf{x}^*) - f(\mathbf{x}^t) - \sigma \cdot d_h(\mathbf{x}^*, \mathbf{x}^t). \tag{11}$$

Combining (9), (10), and (11), gives, for $t \ge 0$,

$$f(\mathbf{x}^{t+1}) - f(\mathbf{x}^*) \le (L - \sigma) \cdot d_h(\mathbf{x}^*, \mathbf{x}^t) - L \cdot d_h(\mathbf{x}^*, \mathbf{x}^{t+1}). \tag{12}$$

On multiplying both sides of the above inequality by $\left(\frac{L}{L-\sigma}\right)^t$, and then summing over $0 \le t < T$, the RHS becomes a telescoping sum, and hence

$$\sum_{t=0}^{T-1} \left(\frac{L}{L-\sigma}\right)^t \cdot \left[ f(\mathbf{x}^{t+1}) - f(\mathbf{x}^*) \right] \le (L - \sigma) \cdot d_h(\mathbf{x}^*, \mathbf{x}^0).$$

By Lemma 5.2, $f(\mathbf{x}^{t+1}) \le f(\mathbf{x}^t)$; thus:

$$\frac{L-\sigma}{\sigma} \cdot \left[ \left(\frac{L}{L-\sigma}\right)^T - 1 \right] \cdot \left[ f(\mathbf{x}^T) - f(\mathbf{x}^*) \right] = \left( \sum_{t=0}^{T-1} \left(\frac{L}{L-\sigma}\right)^t \right) \cdot \left[ f(\mathbf{x}^T) - f(\mathbf{x}^*) \right] \le (L-\sigma) \cdot d_h(\mathbf{x}^*, \mathbf{x}^0),$$

and the result follows. □

## 6 CONVERGENCE OF PROPORTIONAL RESPONSE

We consider the following potential function:

$$p_j(\mathbf{b}) = \textstyle\sum_i b_{ij},$$

$$\Phi(\mathbf{b}) = -\sum_{i:\rho_i \ne \{0, -\infty\}} \frac{1}{\rho_i} \sum_j b_{ij} \log \frac{a_{ij} b_{ij}^{\rho_i - 1}}{[p_j(\mathbf{b})]^{\rho_i}} - \sum_{i:\rho_i = -\infty} \sum_j b_{ij} \log \frac{b_{ij}}{c_{ij} p_j(\mathbf{b})}.$$

For those $i$ for which $\rho_i \neq -\infty$,

$$\nabla_{b_{ij}}\Phi(\mathbf{b}) = -\frac{1}{\rho_i}\log a_{ij} - \frac{\rho_i - 1}{\rho_i}(\log b_{ij} + 1) + \log p_j(\mathbf{b}) + \sum_h b_{hj}\frac{1}{p_j(\mathbf{b})}$$
$$= \frac{1}{\rho_i}\left(1 - \log\frac{a_{ij}b_{ij}^{\rho_i - 1}}{p_j^{\rho_i}(\mathbf{b})}\right);$$

and for those $i$ for which $\rho_i = -\infty$, $\quad \nabla_{b_{ij}}\Phi(\mathbf{b}) = -\log\dfrac{b_{ij}}{c_{ij}p_j}$.

We deduce:

Lemma 6.1.

$$\sum_{i:\rho_i \neq -\infty}\frac{1-\rho_i}{\rho_i}\mathrm{KL}(\mathbf{b}_i||\mathbf{b}'_i) - \sum_{i:\rho_i = -\infty}\mathrm{KL}(\mathbf{b}_i||\mathbf{b}'_i) \leq \Phi(\mathbf{b}) - \Phi(\mathbf{b}') - \langle\nabla\Phi(\mathbf{b}'), \mathbf{b} - \mathbf{b}'\rangle \leq \sum_{i:\rho_i \neq -\infty}\frac{1}{\rho_i}\mathrm{KL}(\mathbf{b}_i||\mathbf{b}'_i).$$

Proof.

$$\Phi(\mathbf{b}) - \Phi(\mathbf{b}') - \langle\nabla\Phi(\mathbf{b}'), \mathbf{b} - \mathbf{b}'\rangle = -\sum_{i:\rho_i \neq \{0,-\infty\}}\frac{\rho_i - 1}{\rho_i}\mathrm{KL}(\mathbf{b}_i||\mathbf{b}'_i) - \sum_{i:\rho_i = -\infty}\mathrm{KL}(\mathbf{b}_i||\mathbf{b}'_i) + \mathrm{KL}(\mathbf{p}||\mathbf{p}')$$
$$= \sum_{i:\rho_i \neq -\infty}\frac{1}{\rho_i}\mathrm{KL}(\mathbf{b}_i||\mathbf{b}'_i) - \left(\sum_i \mathrm{KL}(\mathbf{b}_i||\mathbf{b}'_i) - \mathrm{KL}(\mathbf{p}||\mathbf{p}')\right).$$

Since $\sum_i \mathrm{KL}(\mathbf{b}_i||\mathbf{b}'_i) \geq \mathrm{KL}(\mathbf{p}||\mathbf{p}')$, the result follows. □

*The Substitutes Domain.* The following lemma states the equivalence between mirror descent and proportional response in the substitutes domain; it follow readily from the definition of $\mathbf{b}^{t+1}$ for Proportional Response (given by (2)).

Lemma 6.2. *For buyers with CES substitutes utilities, the Proportional Response update is the same as the mirror descent update, given by:*

$$\mathbf{b}_i^{t+1} = \arg\min_{\mathbf{b}_i:\sum_j b_{ij} = e_i}\left\{\langle\nabla_{\mathbf{b}_i}\Phi(\mathbf{b}^t), \mathbf{b}_i - \mathbf{b}_i^t\rangle + \frac{1}{\rho_i}\mathrm{KL}(\mathbf{b}_i||\mathbf{b}_i^t)\right\}.$$

The next lemma states several properties of the potential function in the substitutes domain.

Lemma 6.3. *[i.]*

(1) *If $\rho_i > 0$ for all $i$, then $\Phi$ is a 1-Bregman convex function w.r.t. $\sum_i \frac{1}{\rho_i}\mathrm{KL}(\mathbf{b}_i||\mathbf{b}'_i)$;*

(2) *if $0 < \rho_i < 1$ for all $i$, then $\Phi$ is a $(\min_i\{1 - \rho_i\}, 1)$-strong Bregman convex function w.r.t. $\sum_i \frac{1}{\rho_i}\mathrm{KL}(\mathbf{b}_i||\mathbf{b}'_i)$;*

(3) *$\mathbf{b}$ is the spending at the market equilibrium if and only if $\mathbf{b}$ is the minimum point of $\Phi$.*

Proof. The first two claims follow from Lemma 6.1 with a little calculation. We show the third claim for CES utilities, leaving the cases of linear utilities to the full paper.

First, we note that the update rule will leave $\mathbf{b}$ unchanged exactly if $\mathbf{b} = \mathbf{b}^*$. This implies that for every $i$, the values $a_{ij}(b_{ij})^{\rho_i - 1}/p_j^{\rho_i}$ are the same at a minimum of $\Phi$, for if $\mathbf{b}^t$ is optimal then $\mathbf{b}^{t+1} = \mathbf{b}^t$, and so for all $j$ the multipliers on $b_{ij}^t$ are the same, and these multipliers are $a_{ij}(b_{ij})^{\rho_i - 1}/p_j^{\rho_i}$. But this is exactly the condition that holds when buyer $i$ is maximizing her utility at prices $\mathbf{p}$: $a_{ij}(x_{ij})^{\rho_i-1}/p_j$ are the same for all $j$, and since $x_{ij} = b_{ij}/p_j$, this means $a_{ij}(b_{ij})^{\rho_i-1}/p_j^{\rho_i}$ are the same for all $j$. □

Let $\mathbf{b}^*$ be the spending at some market equilibrium. Applying Theorem 3.2 yields:

Corollary 6.4.

$$\Phi(\mathbf{b}^T) - \Phi(\mathbf{b}^*) \leq \frac{1}{T}\sum_i \frac{1}{\rho_i}\mathrm{KL}(\mathbf{b}_i^*||\mathbf{b}_i^0).$$

Furthermore, if there is no buyer with a linear utility function, then, applying Theorem 3.1 yields:

Corollary 6.5. *Let* $\sigma = \min_i\{1-\rho_i\}$. *Then,*

$$\Phi(\mathbf{b}^T) - \Phi(\mathbf{b}^*) \leq \frac{\sigma(1-\sigma)^T}{1-(1-\sigma)^T}\sum_i \frac{1}{\rho_i}\mathrm{KL}(\mathbf{b}_i^*||\mathbf{b}_i^0).$$

We now explain how to recover Zhang's bound [50]. From (12),

$$\sum_i \frac{1}{\rho_i}\mathrm{KL}(\mathbf{b}_i^*||\mathbf{b}_i^t) \leq \frac{L-\sigma}{L}\sum_i \frac{1}{\rho_i}\mathrm{KL}(\mathbf{b}_i^*||\mathbf{b}_i^{t-1}) \leq \left(\frac{L-\sigma}{L}\right)^t \sum_i \frac{1}{\rho_i}\mathrm{KL}(\mathbf{b}_i^*||\mathbf{b}_i^0) = \left(\max_i \rho_i\right)^t \sum_i \frac{1}{\rho_i}\mathrm{KL}(\mathbf{b}_i^*||\mathbf{b}_i^0).$$

In [50], $\phi(t)$ is used to denote $\sum_i \frac{1}{\rho_i}\mathrm{KL}(\mathbf{b}_i^*||\mathbf{b}_i^t)$. We have obtained the exact same bound on $\sum_i \frac{1}{\rho_i}\mathrm{KL}(\mathbf{b}_i^*||\mathbf{b}_i^t)$ as in [50], and thus can deduce the identical convergence rate.

*The Complementary Domain.* The analysis here is similar to that for the substitutes domain and is given in the full version of the paper.

## 7 SADDLE POINT ANALYSIS

Proof of Theorem 3.4. Recall that $\mathbf{x}^{t+1} = \arg\min_{\mathbf{x}\in X}\{\langle\nabla_{\mathbf{x}} f(\mathbf{x}^t,\mathbf{y}^t),\mathbf{x}-\mathbf{x}^t\rangle + 2L_X d_g(\mathbf{x},\mathbf{x}^t)\}$. Applying Lemma 5.1 with $\mathbf{x}=\mathbf{x}^*$, $d(\cdot,\cdot) = 2L_X d_g(\cdot,\cdot)$, $\mathbf{y}=\mathbf{x}^t$, $\mathbf{x}^+ = \mathbf{x}^{t+1}$, and $g(\mathbf{x}) = \langle\nabla_x f(\mathbf{x}^t,\mathbf{y}^t)\rangle, \mathbf{x}-\mathbf{x}^t\rangle$ gives

$$\langle\nabla_X f(\mathbf{x}^t,\mathbf{y}^t),\mathbf{x}^{t+1}-\mathbf{x}^t\rangle + 2L_X d_g(\mathbf{x}^{t+1},\mathbf{x}^t) \leq \langle\nabla_X f(\mathbf{x}^t,\mathbf{y}^t),\mathbf{x}^*-\mathbf{x}^t\rangle + 2L_X d_g(\mathbf{x}^*,\mathbf{x}^t) - 2L_X d_g(\mathbf{x}^*,\mathbf{x}^{t+1}).$$

This is equivalent to

$$\underbrace{f(\mathbf{x}^t,\mathbf{y}^t) + \langle\nabla f(\mathbf{x}^t,\mathbf{y}^t),(\mathbf{x}^{t+1},\mathbf{y}^{t+1})-(\mathbf{x}^t,\mathbf{y}^t)\rangle + 2L_X d_g(\mathbf{x}^{t+1},\mathbf{x}^t)}_{\mathsf{LHS}}$$
$$\leq \underbrace{f(\mathbf{x}^t,\mathbf{y}^t) + \langle\nabla f(\mathbf{x}^t,\mathbf{y}^t),(\mathbf{x}^*,\mathbf{y}^{t+1})-(\mathbf{x}^t,\mathbf{y}^t)\rangle + 2L_X d_g(\mathbf{x}^*,\mathbf{x}^t) - 2L_X d_g(\mathbf{x}^*,\mathbf{x}^{t+1})}_{\mathsf{RHS}}. \quad (13)$$

Since $f$ is $(L_X, L_y)$-convex-concave, the third property — see (5) — gives:

$$f(\mathbf{x}^{t+1},\mathbf{y}^{t+1}) + L_X d_g(\mathbf{x}^{t+1},\mathbf{x}^t) \overset{(1)}{\leq} \mathsf{LHS} \leq \mathsf{RHS}$$
$$\overset{(2)}{\leq} f(\mathbf{x}^*,\mathbf{y}^{t+1}) + L_Y d_h(\mathbf{y}^{t+1},\mathbf{y}^t) + 2L_X d_g(\mathbf{x}^*,\mathbf{x}^t) - 2L_X d_g(\mathbf{x}^*,\mathbf{x}^{t+1}), \quad (14)$$

where (1) is deduced from $(b)$ in Definition 2 with $(x',y') = (\mathbf{x}^t,\mathbf{y}^t)$ and (2) is deduced from $(a)$ in Definition 2 with $(x',y') = (\mathbf{x}^t,\mathbf{y}^t)$ and $(x,y) = (\mathbf{x}^*,\mathbf{y}^{t+1})$.

Now, let's consider $-f(x, y)$ and $\mathbf{y}^{t+1} = \arg\min_{\mathbf{y}\in Y}\{\langle -\nabla_{\mathbf{y}} f(\mathbf{x}^t, \mathbf{y}^t), \mathbf{y} - \mathbf{y}^t\rangle + 2L_Y d_h(\mathbf{y}, \mathbf{y}^t)\}$. Using a similar argument, we obtain:

$$-f(\mathbf{x}^{t+1}, \mathbf{y}^{t+1}) + L_Y d_h(\mathbf{y}^{t+1}, \mathbf{y}^t) \le -f(\mathbf{x}^{t+1}, \mathbf{y}^*) + L_X d_g(\mathbf{x}^{t+1}, \mathbf{x}^t) + 2L_Y d_h(\mathbf{y}^*, \mathbf{y}^t) - 2L_Y d_h(\mathbf{y}^*, \mathbf{y}^{t+1}). \tag{15}$$

Adding these two inequalities gives:

$$f(\mathbf{x}^{t+1}, \mathbf{y}^*) - f(\mathbf{x}^*, \mathbf{y}^{t+1}) \le 2L_X d_g(\mathbf{x}^*, \mathbf{x}^t) + 2L_Y d_h(\mathbf{y}^*, \mathbf{y}^t) - 2L_X d_g(\mathbf{x}^*, \mathbf{x}^{t+1}) - 2L_Y d_h(\mathbf{y}^*, \mathbf{y}^{t+1}).$$

Summing over $t$ yields: $\sum_{t=1}^{T}\left(f(\mathbf{x}^t, \mathbf{y}^*) - f(\mathbf{x}^*, \mathbf{y}^t)\right) \le 2L_X d_g(\mathbf{x}^*, \mathbf{x}^0) + 2L_Y d_h(\mathbf{y}^*, \mathbf{y}^0)$. □

Proof of Theorem 3.5. Using (8) instead of (5), we deduce the following from (13) instead of (14):

$$f(\mathbf{x}^{t+1}, \mathbf{y}^{t+1}) + L_X d_g(\mathbf{x}^{t+1}, \mathbf{x}^t) \le f(\mathbf{x}^*, \mathbf{y}^{t+1}) + L_Y d_h(\mathbf{y}^{t+1}, \mathbf{y}^t) + (2L_X - \sigma_X) d_g(\mathbf{x}^*, \mathbf{x}^t) - 2L_X d_g(\mathbf{x}^*, \mathbf{x}^{t+1}).$$

Also, (15) is replaced by:

$$-f(\mathbf{x}^{t+1}, \mathbf{y}^{t+1}) + L_Y d_h(\mathbf{y}^{t+1}, \mathbf{y}^t) \le -f(\mathbf{x}^{t+1}, \mathbf{y}^*) + L_X d_g(\mathbf{x}^{t+1}, \mathbf{x}^t) + (2L_Y - \sigma_Y) d_h(\mathbf{y}^*, \mathbf{y}^t) - 2L_Y d_h(\mathbf{y}^*, \mathbf{y}^{t+1}).$$

Summing up these two inequalities gives:

$$\begin{aligned} &f(\mathbf{x}^{t+1}, \mathbf{y}^*) - f(\mathbf{x}^*, \mathbf{y}^{t+1}) \\ &\quad \le (2L_X - \sigma_X) d_g(\mathbf{x}^*, \mathbf{x}^t) + (2L_Y - \sigma_Y) d_h(\mathbf{y}^*, \mathbf{y}^t) - 2L_X d_g(\mathbf{x}^*, \mathbf{x}^{t+1}) - 2L_Y d_h(\mathbf{y}^*, \mathbf{y}^{t+1}). \end{aligned}$$

Let $\sigma = \min\left\{\frac{\sigma_X}{L_X}, \frac{\sigma_Y}{L_Y}\right\}$. Then:

$$\sum_{t=0}^{T-1}\left(\frac{2}{2-\sigma}\right)^t \left(f(\mathbf{x}^{t+1}, \mathbf{y}^*) - f(\mathbf{x}^*, \mathbf{y}^{t+1})\right) \le (2L_X - \sigma_X) d_g(\mathbf{x}^*, \mathbf{x}^0) + (2L_Y - \sigma_Y) d_h(\mathbf{y}^*, \mathbf{y}^0).$$

Note that $f(\mathbf{x}^t, \mathbf{y}^*) - f(\mathbf{x}^*, \mathbf{y}^t)$ is positive for each $t$, so the result follows. □

## 8 ANALYSIS OF DAMPED PROPORTIONAL RESPONSE

*Excluding Cobb-Douglas Utility Functions.* First, we consider a simplified situation where there is no buyer with a Cobb-Douglas utility function. We want to use the technique developed in the saddle point analysis to obtain a convergence result. The potential function is the same as before.

We make the following observations.

Lemma 8.1. *If $\rho_i > 0$ for buyer i, then the Damped Proportional Response (given by (7)) is equivalent to mirror descent with a halved step size, defined as follows:*

$$\mathbf{b}_i^{t+1} = \arg\min_{\mathbf{b}_i : \sum_j b_{ij} = e_i}\left\{\langle \nabla_{\mathbf{b}_i}\Phi(\mathbf{b}^t), \mathbf{b}_i - \mathbf{b}_i^t\rangle + \frac{2}{\rho_i}\mathrm{KL}(\mathbf{b}_i || \mathbf{b}_i^t)\right\};$$

*if $-\infty < \rho_i < 0$ for buyer i, then the Damped Proportional Response (given by (7)) is equivalent to mirror descent (really ascent as this is a concave function) with a halved step size defined as follows:*

$$\mathbf{b}_i^{t+1} = \arg\min_{\mathbf{b}_i : \sum_j b_{ij} = e_i}\left\{-\langle \nabla_{\mathbf{b}_i}\Phi(\mathbf{b}^t), \mathbf{b}_i - \mathbf{b}_i^t\rangle + \frac{2(\rho_i - 1)}{\rho_i}\mathrm{KL}(\mathbf{b}_i || \mathbf{b}_i^t)\right\};$$

*and if $\rho_i = -\infty$ for buyer i, then the Damped Proportional Response (given by (7)) is equivalent to mirror descent (really ascent as this is a concave function) with a halved step sizem defined as follows:*

$$\mathbf{b}_i^{t+1} = \arg\min_{\mathbf{b}_i:\sum_j b_{ij}=e_i}\{-\langle \nabla_{\mathbf{b}_i}\Phi(\mathbf{b}^t), \mathbf{b}_i - \mathbf{b}_i^t\rangle + 2\mathrm{KL}(\mathbf{b}_i||\mathbf{b}_i^t)\}.$$

Proof. By calculation. □

By Lemma 6.1 and with a simple calculation one can show that, in Definition 2, if we set $\mathbf{x} = \mathbf{b}_{>0}$, $\mathbf{y} = \mathbf{b}_{<0}$, $d_g(\mathbf{x}) = \sum_{i:\rho_i>0}\frac{1}{\rho_i}\mathrm{KL}(\mathbf{b}_i||\mathbf{b}_i')$, and $d_h(\mathbf{y}) = \sum_{i:\infty<\rho_i<0}\frac{\rho_i-1}{\rho_i}\mathrm{KL}(\mathbf{b}_i||\mathbf{b}_i')+\sum_{i:\rho_i=-\infty}\mathrm{KL}(\mathbf{b}_i||\mathbf{b}_i')$ , then $\Phi$ is $(1,1)$-convex-concave function.

Furthermore, let $\mathbf{b}_{>0}^*$ and $\mathbf{b}_{<0}^*$ be the market equilibrium of the Fisher market. Then,

$$\mathbf{b}_{>0}^* \text{ minimizes } \Phi(\cdot, \mathbf{b}_{<0}^*), \text{ and } \mathbf{b}_{<0}^* \text{ maximizes } \Phi(\mathbf{b}_{>0}^*, \cdot),$$

which implies $(\mathbf{b}_{>0}^*, \mathbf{b}_{<0}^*)$ is a saddle point of the potential function $\Phi$. Theorem 3.4 yields the following corollary.

Corollary 8.2. *The Damped Proportional Response (given by (7)) converges to the equilibrium with a convergence rate of:*

$$\sum_{t=1}^{T}\left[\Phi(\mathbf{b}_{>0}^t, \mathbf{b}_{<0}^*) - \Phi(\mathbf{b}_{>0}^*, \mathbf{b}_{<0}^t)\right]$$
$$\leq \sum_{i:-\infty<\rho_i<0}\frac{2(\rho_i-1)}{\rho_i}\mathrm{KL}(\mathbf{b}_i^*||\mathbf{b}_i^0) + \sum_{i:\rho_i>0}\frac{2}{\rho_i}\mathrm{KL}(\mathbf{b}_i^*||\mathbf{b}_i^0) + \sum_{i:\rho_i=-\infty}2\mathrm{KL}(\mathbf{b}_i^*||\mathbf{b}_i^0).$$

Moreover, if we assume there is no buyer with either a linear utility of a Leontief utility function, then, by Lemma 6.1, $\Psi(\cdot,\cdot)$ is a $(\min_{i:\rho_i>0}\{1-\rho_i\}, \min_{i:\rho_i<0}\{\frac{1}{1-\rho_i}\}, 1, 1)$-strong Bregman convex-concave function with $\mathbf{x} = \mathbf{b}_{>0}$, $\mathbf{y} = \mathbf{b}_{<0}$, $d_g(\mathbf{x}) = \sum_{i:\rho_i>0}\frac{1}{\rho_i}\mathrm{KL}(\mathbf{b}_i||\mathbf{b}_i')$ and $d_h(\mathbf{y}) = \sum_{i:\infty<\rho_i<0}\frac{\rho_i-1}{\rho_i}\mathrm{KL}(\mathbf{b}_i||\mathbf{b}_i')$ (see Definition 4). Theorem 3.5 yields the following corollary.

Corollary 8.3. *Suppose there is no buyer with either a linear utility or a Leontief utility. Let*

$$\sigma_{>0} = \min_{i:\rho_i>0}\{1-\rho_i\} \quad \textit{and} \quad \sigma_{<0} = \min_{i:\rho_i<0}\left\{\frac{1}{1-\rho_i}\right\}.$$

*Then the Damped Proportional Response (given by (7)) converges to the equilibrium with a convergence rate of*

$$\Phi(\mathbf{b}_{>0}^T, \mathbf{b}_{<0}^*) - \Phi(\mathbf{b}_{>0}^*, \mathbf{b}_{<0}^T)$$
$$\leq \left(1 - \frac{\min\{\sigma_{>0}, \sigma_{<0}\}}{2}\right)^{T-1}\left[\sum_{i:\rho_i<0}(2-\sigma_{<0})\frac{\rho_i-1}{\rho_i}\mathrm{KL}(\mathbf{b}_i^*||\mathbf{b}_i^0) + \sum_{i:\rho_i>0}(2-\sigma_{>0})\frac{1}{\rho_i}\mathrm{KL}(\mathbf{b}_i^*||\mathbf{b}_i^0)\right].$$

*The Entire CES Range* Now we consider the Damped Proportional Response with a damping factor of 2 over the entire CES range, i.e. including Cobb-Douglas utilities. Recall that we modify our potential function to include terms for the buyers with $\rho_i = 0$. However, for this new modified function, the buyers with Cobb-Douglas utility functions don't actually perform mirror descent. Fortunately, we can make two observations.

First, the buyers with Cobb-Douglas utility functions converge quickly to the equilibrium independently of everyone else's spending. Second, the buyers whose utility functions are not Cobb-Douglas will still perform the mirror descent (ascent) procedure.

So, intuitively, in our analysis, we regard the spending of the buyers with Cobb-Douglas utility functions as a parameter, $\theta$, of $f_\theta(\mathbf{x}, \mathbf{y})$, where $\mathbf{x}$ represents the spending of the strictly substitutes buyers and $\mathbf{y}$ represents the spending of the strictly complementary buyers. Remember, in the case with no Cobb-Douglas utilities, the market equilibrium corresponded to a saddle point. Here, similarly, a market equilibrium corresponds to a saddle point of $f_{\theta^*}(\cdot,\cdot)$, where $\theta^*$ is the spending at the market equilibrium of those buyers with Cobb-Douglas utility functions. We prove the following two claims.

(1) $\theta$ converges to $\theta^*$ quickly;
(2) when $\theta$ tends to $\theta^*$, though $\mathbf{x}$ and $\mathbf{y}$ perform the mirror descent based on the gradient of $f_\theta(\mathbf{x}, \mathbf{y})$ and not of $f_{\theta^*}(\mathbf{x}, \mathbf{y})$, $(\mathbf{x}, \mathbf{y})$ will still converge quickly to $(\mathbf{x}^*, \mathbf{y}^*)$, the saddle point of $f_{\theta^*}(\cdot,\cdot)$.

We thereby show that Damped Proportional Response converges to the market equilibrium even when faced with the entire range of CES utilities.

## 9 OTHER MEASURES OF CONVERGENCE

The potential function $\phi$ appears to be closely related to the Eisenberg-Gale program. In particular, we can show that in the substitutes domain, when applying update rule (2), the Proportional Response update, the objective function $\Psi$ for the Eisenberg-Gale program converges at least as fast as $\Phi$, i.e. that $\Psi(\mathbf{x}(\mathbf{b}^*_{>0}, \mathbf{b}^*_{=0})) - \Psi(\mathbf{x}(\mathbf{b}_{>0}, \mathbf{b}^*_{=0})) \le \Phi(\mathbf{b}_{>0}, \mathbf{b}^*_{=0}) - \Phi(\mathbf{b}^*_{>0}, \mathbf{b}^*_{=0})$, and that in the complementary domain, when applying update rule (3), the objective function for the dual of the Eisenberg-Gale program converges at least as fast as $\Phi$. These claims are shown in the full paper.

Lemma 6.1 allows us to make some observations about the rate of convergence of the spending. For update rule (2), in the substitutes domain excluding linear utilities, we can deduce that $\sum_i \mathrm{KL}(\mathbf{b}_i || \mathbf{b}^*_i) \le \max_i \frac{\rho_i}{1-\rho_i}[\Phi(\mathbf{b}) - \Phi(\mathbf{b}^*)]$, and for update rule (3) in the complementary domain excluding Leontief utilities, that $\sum_i \mathrm{KL}(\mathbf{b}_i || \mathbf{b}^*_i) \le \max_i -\rho_i[\Phi(\mathbf{b}) - \Phi(\mathbf{b}^*)]$. As the equilibrium need not be unique in terms of spending for either linear or Leontief utilities, this lemma is not going to yield a bound on the convergence rate of the spending in these cases, as it can be applied to any equilibrium. Similarly in the combined domain, still excluding linear and Leontief utilities, we can observe that

$$\sum_{i:\rho_i>0} \frac{1-\rho_i}{\rho_i} \mathrm{KL}(\mathbf{b}_i || \mathbf{b}^*_i) + \sum_{i:\rho_i<0} \frac{-1}{\rho_i} \mathrm{KL}(\mathbf{b}_i || \mathbf{b}^*_i) \le [\Phi(\mathbf{b}_{>0}, \mathbf{b}^*_{<0}) - \Phi(\mathbf{b}^*)] + [\Phi(\mathbf{b}^*) - \Phi(\mathbf{b}^*_{>0}, \mathbf{b}_{<0})].$$

In addition, since $\mathrm{KL}(\mathbf{p}||\mathbf{p}^*) \le \mathrm{KL}(\mathbf{b}||\mathbf{b}^*)$ we can immediately obtain analogous bounds on the KL divergence of the prices. Furthermore, for the substitutes domain, including linear utilities, Lemma 6.1 also implies that $\mathrm{KL}(\mathbf{p}||\mathbf{p}^*) \le [\Phi(\mathbf{b}) - \Phi(\mathbf{b}^*)]$.

## ACKNOWLEDGMENTS

We are grateful to the anonymous referees for their insightful comments which helped improve the presentation.

## REFERENCES

[1] Kenneth J. Arrow, H. D. Block, and Leonid Hurwicz. 1959. On the Stability of Competitive Equilibrium, II. *Econometrica* 27, 1 (1959), 82–109.

[2] Benjamin Birnbaum, Nikhil R. Devanur, and Lin Xiao. 2011. Distributed Algorithms via Gradient Descent for Fisher Markets. In *Proceedings of the 12th ACM Conference on Electronic Commerce (EC '11)*. ACM, 127–136. DOI: http://dx.doi.org/10.1145/1993574.1993594

[3] Lawrence E. Blume. 1993. The Statistical Mechanics of Strategic Interaction. *Games and Economic Behavior* 5, 3 (1993), 387–424.

[4] Eric Budish. 2011. The Combinatorial Assignment Problem: Approximate Competitive Equilibrium from Equal Incomes. *Journal of Political Economy* 119, 6 (2011), 1061–1103.

[5] Ioannis Caragiannis, David Kurokawa, Hervé Moulin, Ariel D. Procaccia, Nisarg Shah, and Junxing Wang. 2016. The Unreasonable Fairness of Maximum Nash Welfare. In *Proceedings of the 2016 ACM Conference on Economics and Computation (EC '16)*. ACM, 305–322. DOI: http://dx.doi.org/10.1145/2940716.2940726

[6] Gong Chen and Marc Teboulle. 1993. Convergence Analysis of a Proximal-Like Minimization Algorithm Using Bregman Functions. *SIAM Journal on Optimization* 3, 3 (1993), 538–543.

[7] X. Chen, D. Dai, Y. Du, and S. H. Teng. 2009. Settling the Complexity of Arrow-Debreu Equilibria in Markets with Additively Separable Utilities. In *2009 50th Annual IEEE Symposium on Foundations of Computer Science*. 273–282. DOI: http://dx.doi.org/10.1109/FOCS.2009.29

[8] Xi Chen, Xiaotie Deng, and Shang-Hua Teng. 2009. Settling the Complexity of Computing Two-player Nash Equilibria. *J. ACM* 56, 3, Article 14 (May 2009), 57 pages.

[9] Xi Chen, Dimitris Paparas, and Mihalis Yannakakis. 2017. The Complexity of Non-Monotone Markets. *J. ACM* 64, 3 (2017), 20:1–20:56. DOI: http://dx.doi.org/10.1145/3064810

[10] Xi Chen and Shang-Hua Teng. 2009. Spending Is Not Easier Than Trading: On the Computational Equivalence of Fisher and Arrow-Debreu Equilibria. In *Algorithms and Computation, 20th International Symposium, ISAAC 2009, Honolulu, Hawaii, USA, December 16-18, 2009. Proceedings*. 647–656. DOI: http://dx.doi.org/10.1007/978-3-642-10631-6_66

[11] Yun Kuen Cheung, Richard Cole, and Nikhil Devanur. 2013. Tatonnement Beyond Gross Substitutes?: Gradient Descent to the Rescue. In *Proceedings of the Forty-fifth Annual ACM Symposium on Theory of Computing (STOC '13)*. ACM, 191–200. DOI: http://dx.doi.org/10.1145/2488608.2488633

[12] Yun Kuen Cheung, Richard Cole, and Ashish Rastogi. 2012. Tatonnement in Ongoing Markets of Complementary Goods. In *Proceedings of the 13th ACM Conference on Electronic Commerce (EC '12)*. ACM, 337–354. DOI: http://dx.doi.org/10.1145/2229012.2229039

[13] Bruno Codenotti, Benton McCune, and Kasturi Varadarajan. 2005. Market Equilibrium via the Excess Demand Function. In *Proceedings of the Thirty-seventh Annual ACM Symposium on Theory of Computing (STOC '05)*. ACM, 74–83. http://doi.acm.org/10.1145/1060590.1060601

[14] Bruno Codenotti, Amin Saberi, Kasturi Varadarajan, and Yinyu Ye. 2006. Leontief Economies Encode Nonzero Sum Two-player Games. In *Proceedings of the Seventeenth Annual ACM-SIAM Symposium on Discrete Algorithm (SODA '06)*. Society for Industrial and Applied Mathematics, 659–667.

[15] Richard Cole, Nikhil Devanur, Vasilis Gkatzelis, Kamal Jain, Tung Mai, Vijay V. Vazirani, and Sadra Yazdanbod. 2017. Convex Program Duality, Fisher Markets, and Nash Social Welfare. In *Proceedings of the 2017 ACM Conference on Economics and Computation (EC '17)*. ACM, 459–460. DOI: http://dx.doi.org/10.1145/3033274.3085109

[16] Richard Cole and Lisa Fleischer. 2008. Fast-converging Tatonnement Algorithms for One-time and Ongoing Market Problems. In *Proceedings of the Fortieth Annual ACM Symposium on Theory of Computing (STOC '08)*. ACM, 315–324. DOI: http://dx.doi.org/10.1145/1374376.1374422

[17] Constantinos Daskalakis, Paul W. Goldberg, and Christos H. Papadimitriou. 2009. The Complexity of Computing a Nash Equilibrium. *SIAM J. Comput.* 39, 1 (2009), 195–259.

[18] Xiaotie Deng and Ye Du. 2008. The Computation of Approximate Competitive Equilibrium is PPAD-hard. *Inf. Process. Lett.* 108, 6 (Nov. 2008), 369–373.

[19] Xiaotie Deng, Christos Papadimitriou, and Shmuel Safra. 2003. On the complexity of price equilibria. *Journal of Computer System Sciences (JCSS)* 67 (2003), 311–324.

[20] Nikhil R. Devanur. 2004. The Spending Constraint Model for Market Equilibrium: Algorithmic, Existence and Uniqueness Results. In *Proceedings of the Thirty-sixth Annual ACM Symposium on Theory of Computing (STOC '04)*. ACM, 519–528. DOI: http://dx.doi.org/10.1145/1007352.1007431

[21] Nikhil R. Devanur, Christos H. Papadimitriou, Amin Saberi, and Vijay V. Vazirani. 2008. Market equilibrium via a primal-dual algorithm for a convex program. *J. ACM* 55, 5 (2008), 22:1–22:18.

[22] Krishnamurthy Dvijotham, Yuval Rabani, and Leonard J. Schulman. 2017. Convergence of Incentive-driven Dynamics in Fisher Markets. In *Proceedings of the Twenty-Eighth Annual ACM-SIAM Symposium on Discrete Algorithms (SODA '17)*. Society for Industrial and Applied Mathematics, 554–567.

[23] E. Eisenberg. 1961. Aggregation of Utility Functions. *Management Sciences* 7 (1961), 337–350.

[24] E. Eisenberg and D. Gale. 1959. Consensus of subjective probabilities: the Pari-Mutuel method. *The Annals of Mathematical Statistics* 30 (1959), 165–168.

[25] Rahul Garg and Sanjiv Kapoor. 2006. Auction Algorithms for Market Equilibrium. *Math. Oper. Res.* 31, 4 (Nov. 2006), 714–729.
[26] Gauthier Gidel, Tony Jebara, and Simon Lacoste-Julien. 2017. Frank-Wolfe Algorithms for Saddle Point Problems. In *The 20th International Conference on Artificial Intelligence and Statistics.*
[27] Aanund Hylland and Richard Zeckhauser. 1979. The Efficient Allocation of Individuals to Positions. *Journal of Political Economy* 87, 2 (April 1979), 293–314.
[28] Kamal Jain and Vijay V. Vazirani. 2007. Eisenberg-Gale Markets: Algorithms and Structural Properties. In *Proceedings of the Thirty-ninth Annual ACM Symposium on Theory of Computing (STOC '07).* ACM, 364–373. DOI: http://dx.doi.org/10.1145/1250790.1250845
[29] Mamoru Kaneko and Kenjiro Nakamura. 1979. The Nash social welfare function. *Econometrica* (1979), 423–435.
[30] Frank Kelly. 1997. Charging and rate control for elastic traffic. *European Transactions on Telecommunications* 8, 1 (1997), 33–37.
[31] Dave Levin, Katrina LaCurts, Neil Spring, and Bobby Bhattacharjee. 2008. Bittorrent is an Auction: Analyzing and Improving Bittorrent's Incentives. *SIGCOMM Comput. Commun. Rev.* 38, 4 (Aug. 2008), 243–254. DOI: http://dx.doi.org/10.1145/1402946.1402987
[32] Steven H Low and David E Lapsley. 1999. Optimization flow control. I. Basic algorithm and convergence. *IEEE/ACM Transactions on networking* 7, 6 (1999), 861–874.
[33] Jason R. Marden and Jeff S. Shamma. 2012. Revisiting log-linear learning: Asynchrony, completeness and payoff-based implementation. *Games and Economic Behavior* 75, 2 (2012), 788–808.
[34] L. W. McKenzie. 2002. *Classical General Equilibrium Theory.* The MIT press.
[35] J. F. Nash. 1950. The Bargaining Problem. *Econometrica* 18 (1950), 155–162.
[36] Arkadi Nemirovski. 2004. Prox-Method with Rate of Convergence O(1/t) for Variational Inequalities with Lipschitz Continuous Monotone Operators and Smooth Convex-Concave Saddle Point Problems. *SIAM Journal on Optimization* 15, 1 (2004), 229–251.
[37] Yurii Nesterov. 2005. Excessive Gap Technique in Nonsmooth Convex Minimization. *SIAM Journal on Optimization* 16, 1 (2005), 235–249.
[38] Yurii Nesterov. 2005. Smooth minimization of non-smooth functions. *Math. Program.* 103, 1 (2005), 127–152.
[39] Yurii Nesterov. 2007. Dual extrapolation and its applications to solving variational inequalities and related problems. *Mathematical Programming* 109, 2-3 (2007), 319–344.
[40] Noam Nisan, Tim Roughgarden, Eva Tardos, and Vijay V. Vazirani. 2007. *Algorithmic Game Theory.* Cambridge University Press, New York, NY, USA.
[41] Christos H. Papadimitriou and Mihalis Yannakakis. 2010. An Impossibility Theorem for Price-adjustment Mechanisms. *PNAS* 5, 107 (2010), 1854–1859.
[42] Alexander Rakhlin and Karthik Sridharan. 2013. Optimization, Learning, and Games with Predictable Sequences. In *Advances in Neural Information Processing Systems 26: Twenty-seventh Annual Conference on Neural Information Processing Systems 2013.* 3066–3074.
[43] H. Scarf. 1960. Some examples of global instatibility of the competitive equilibrium. *International Economic Review* 3, 13 (1960), 157–172.
[44] Vadim I Shmyrev. 2009. An algorithm for finding equilibrium in the linear exchange model with fixed budgets. *Journal of Applied and Industrial Mathematics* 3, 4 (2009), 505.
[45] Hirofumi Uzawa. 1960. Walras' Tatonnement in the Theory of Exchange. *Review of Economic Studies* 27, 3 (1960), 182–194.
[46] H.R. Varian. 1974. Equity, envy, and efficiency. *Journal of Economic Theory* 9, 1 (1974), 63–91.
[47] Vijay V. Vazirani and Mihalis Yannakakis. 2011. Market equilibrium under separable, piecewise-linear, concave utilities. *J. ACM* 58, 3 (2011), 10:1–10:25.
[48] Léon Walras. 1874. *Eléments d'Economie Politique Pure.* Corbaz. (Translated as: *Elements of Pure Economics.* Homewood, IL: Irwin, 1954.).
[49] Fang Wu and Li Zhang. 2007. Proportional Response Dynamics Leads to Market Equilibrium. In *Proceedings of the Thirty-ninth Annual ACM Symposium on Theory of Computing (STOC '07).* ACM, 354–363. DOI: http://dx.doi.org/10.1145/1250790.1250844
[50] Li Zhang. 2011. Proportional response dynamics in the Fisher market. *Theor. Comput. Sci.* 412, 24 (2011), 2691–2698.

# Interdependent Values without Single-Crossing [Abstract]

ALON EDEN, Tel-Aviv University
MICHAL FELDMAN, Tel-Aviv University and Microsoft Research
AMOS FIAT, Tel-Aviv University
KIRA GOLDNER, University of Washington

We consider a setting where an auctioneer sells a single item to $n$ potential agents with *interdependent values*. That is, each agent has her own private signal, and the valuation of each agent is a known function of all $n$ private signals. This captures settings such as valuations for oil drilling rights, broadcast rights, pieces of art, and many more.

In the interdependent value setting, all previous work has assumed a so-called *single-crossing condition*. Single-crossing means that the impact of a private signal, $s_i$, on the valuation of agent $i$, is greater than the impact of $s_i$ on the valuation of any other agent. It is known that without the single-crossing condition, an efficient outcome cannot be obtained. We ask what approximation to the optimal social welfare can be obtained when valuations do not exhibit single-crossing.

We show that, in general, without the single-crossing condition, one cannot hope to approximate the optimal social welfare any better than assigning the item to a random bidder. Consequently, we consider a relaxed version of single-crossing, *c-single-crossing*, with some parameter $c \geq 1$, which means that the impact of $s_i$ on the valuation of agent $i$ is at least $1/c$ times the impact of $s_i$ on the valuation of any other agent ($c = 1$ is single-crossing). Using this relaxed notion, we obtain a host of positive results. These include a prior-free universally truthful $2\sqrt{n}c^{3/2}$-approximation to welfare, and a prior-free deterministic $(n-1)c$-approximation to welfare. Under appropriate concavity conditions, we improve this to a prior-free universally truthful $2c$ approximation to welfare as well as a universally truthful $O(c^2)$-approximation to the optimal revenue.

CCS Concepts: •**Theory of computation → Algorithmic game theory and mechanism design;**

Additional Key Words and Phrases: Interdependent values; single-crossing; welfare maximization; prior-free

A full version of this paper is available at https://www.cs.tau.ac.il/~alonarde/interdependent.pdf.

Author's email addresses: alonarden@gmail.com; michal.feldman@cs.tau.ac.il; fiat@tau.ac.il; kgoldner@cs.washington.edu.

The work of A. Eden, M. Feldman, and K. Goldner was partially supported by the European Research Council under the European Union's Seventh Framework Programme (FP7/2007-2013) / ERC grant agreement number 337122, and by the Israel Science Foundation (grant number 317/17). The work of A. Eden and A. Fiat was partially supported by ISF 1841/14. The work of K. Goldner was supported in part by NSF award CCF-1420381 and by a Microsoft Research PhD Fellowship.



*ACM EC'18, June 18–22, 2018, Ithaca, NY, USA.*



ACM ISBN 978-1-4503-4529-3/18/06.
https://doi.org/10.1145/3219166.3219173

# Credible Mechanisms

MOHAMMAD AKBARPOUR, Stanford University, USA
SHENGWU LI, Harvard University, USA

Consider an extensive-form mechanism, run by an auctioneer who communicates sequentially and privately with agents. Suppose the auctioneer can make any deviation that no single agent can detect. We study the mechanisms such that it is incentive-compatible for the auctioneer not to deviate – the *credible* mechanisms. Consider the optimal auctions in which only winners make transfers. The first-price auction is the unique credible static mechanism. The ascending auction is the unique credible strategy-proof mechanism.

Full Paper: https://ssrn.com/abstract=3033208

CCS Concepts: • **Applied computing → Economics; Electronic commerce**;

Additional Key Words and Phrases: Mechanism design, auction, credible, strategy-proof

We thank Ben Brooks, Jeremy Bulow, Alex Frankel, Ben Golub, Matthew Jackson, Scott Kominers, David Kreps, Elliot Lipnowski, Erik Madsen, Eric Maskin, Paul Milgrom, Roger Myerson, Michael Ostrovsky, Doron Ravid, Ilya Segal, Andy Skrzypacz, Cameron Taylor, Alex Teytelboym, Bob Wilson, Alex Wolitzky, and several seminar participants for valuable comments and advice.

Authors' addresses: Mohammad Akbarpour, Stanford University, 655 Knight way, E251, Stanford, CA, 94305, USA, mohamwad@stanford.edu; Shengwu Li, Harvard University, 1805 Cambridge Street, Cambridge, MA, 02138, USA, shengwu_li@fas.harvard.edu.



*ACM EC'18, June 18–22, 2018, Ithaca, NY, USA.* ACM ISBN 978-1-4503-5829-3/18/06.
https://doi.org/10.1145/3219166.3219213

# The Best of Both Worlds: Asymptotically Efficient Mechanisms with a Guarantee on the Expected Gains-From-Trade

MOSHE BABAIOFF, Microsoft Research
YANG CAI, McGill University
YANNAI A. GONCZAROWSKI, The Hebrew University of Jerusalem and Microsoft Research
MINGFEI ZHAO, McGill University

The seminal impossibility result of Myerson and Satterthwaite [1983] states that for bilateral trade, there is no mechanism that is individually rational (IR), incentive compatible (IC), weakly budget balanced, and efficient. This has led follow-up work on two-sided trade settings to weaken the efficiency requirement and consider approximately efficient simple mechanisms, while still demanding the other properties. The current state-of-the-art of such mechanisms for two-sided markets can be categorized as giving one (but not both) of the following two types of approximation guarantees on the *gains from trade*: a constant *ex-ante* guarantee, measured with respect to the *second-best* efficiency benchmark, or an asymptotically optimal *ex-post* guarantee, measured with respect to the *first-best* efficiency benchmark. Here the second-best efficiency benchmark refers to the highest gains from trade attainable by any IR, IC and weakly budget balanced mechanism, while the first-best efficiency benchmark refers to the maximum gains from trade (attainable by the VCG mechanism, which is not weakly budget balanced).

In this paper, we construct simple mechanisms for double-auction and matching markets that *simultaneously* achieve both types of guarantees: these are ex-post IR, Bayesian IC, and ex-post weakly budget balanced mechanisms that 1) ex-ante guarantee a constant fraction of the gains from trade of the second-best, and 2) ex-post guarantee a realization-dependent fraction of the gains from trade of the first-best, such that this realization-dependent fraction converges to 1 (full efficiency) as the market grows large.

We believe that mechanisms that not only provide a worst-case guarantee, but also provide a guarantee of performing very well on "easy instances" are appealing and more likely to be used. In our setting, we implement this agenda by postulating that "nice instances" are large-market instances, and we are able to achieve the best of both worlds: a guaranteed constant approximation on one hand, and asymptotic optimality when the markets are large on the other hand. We believe that presenting similar results in other settings is an interesting research direction.

CCS Concepts: •**Theory of computation → Design and analysis of algorithms; Graph algorithms analysis; Algorithmic game theory; Algorithmic mechanism design; Computational pricing and auctions;**

Additional Key Words and Phrases: Two-sided market; double auction; matching markets; trade reduction

A full version of this paper is available at https://arxiv.org/abs/1802.08023.

Authors' email addresses: Babaioff: moshe@microsoft.com; Cai: cai@cs.mcgill.ca; Gonczarowski: yannai@gonch.name; Zhao: mingfei.zhao@mail.mcgill.ca.

Yang Cai is supported by NSERC Discovery RGPIN-2015-06127 and FRQNT 2017-NC-198956. Yannai Gonczarowski is supported by the Adams Fellowship Program of the Israel Academy of Sciences and Humanities; his work is supported by ISF grant 1435/14 administered by the Israeli Academy of Sciences, by Israel-USA Bi-national Science Foundation (BSF) grant number 2014389, and by the European Research Council (ERC) under the European Union's Horizon 2020 research and innovation programme (grant agreement No 740282). Mingfei Zhao is supported by NSERC Discovery RGPIN-2015-06127 and Richard H. Tomlinson Doctoral Fellowship.



*ACM EC'18, June 18–22, 2018, Ithaca, NY, USA.*



ACM ISBN 978-1-4503-4529-3/18/06.
http://dx.doi.org/10.1145/3219166.3219203

# Network Pricing: How to Induce Optimal Flows Under Strategic Link Operators

JOSÉ CORREA, Universidad de Chile
CRISTÓBAL GUZMÁN, Pontificia Universidad Católica de Chile
THANASIS LIANEAS, National Technical University of Athens
EVDOKIA NIKOLOVA, University of Texas at Austin
MARC SCHRÖDER, RWTH Aachen University.

Network pricing games provide a framework for modeling real-world settings with two types of strategic agents: owners (operators) of the network and users of the network. Owners of the network post a price for usage of the link they own so as to attract users and maximize profit; users of the network select routes based on price and level of use by other users. We point out that an equilibrium in these games may not exist, may not be unique and may induce an arbitrarily inefficient network performance.

Our main result is to observe that a simple regulation on the network owners market solves all three issues above. Specifically, if an authority could set appropriate caps (upper bounds) on the tolls (prices) operators can charge, then: the game among the link operators has a unique and strong Nash equilibrium and the users' game results in a Wardrop equilibrium that achieves the optimal total delay. We call any price vector with these properties a great set of tolls. As a secondary objective, we want to compute great tolls that minimize total users' payments and we provide a linear program that does this. We obtain multiplicative approximation results compared to the optimal total users' payments for arbitrary networks with polynomial latencies of bounded degree, while in the single-commodity case we obtain a bound that only depends on the topology of the network. Lastly, we show how the same mechanism of setting appropriate caps on the allowable prices extends to the model of elastic demands.

CCS Concepts: •**Theory of computation → Algorithmic game theory and mechanism design; Quality of equilibria; Network games; Exact and approximate computation of equilibria;**

## 1 INTRODUCTION

Network pricing games provide a framework for modeling real-world settings with two types of strategic agents: users of the network and owners (operators) of the network. Owners of the network post a price for usage of the links they own, while users of the network select routes based on price and level of use by other users. A landmark example of this type of interaction, that sets the ground in which we describe our work, occurs in transportation networks. Here, link owners

This work was partially supported by CONICYT through grants ISCI FB0816, PCI PII 20150140, FONDECYT 11160939, and FONDECYT 1160079; by NSF through grants CCF-1216103, CCF-1331863, CCF-1350823 and CCF-1733832; and by ICM through the Millennium Nucleus Information and Coordination in Networks RC130003, and the Millennium Institute for Research in Market Imperfections and Public Policy IS130002. Part of the work was done while a subset of the authors was visiting the Simons Institute for the Theory of Computing, Berkeley, CA.


*ACM EC'18, June 18–22, 2018, Ithaca, NY, USA.*
 ACM ISBN 978-1-4503-4529-3/18/06..$15.00.
https://doi.org/10.1145/3219166.3219190

are road operators and may toll the usage of their road. Users are travelers that seek to minimize their travel time plus tolls.

The challenge in these games is that there are two levels of competition: one, among the owners to attract users to their link so as to maximize profit; and second, among users of the network to select routes that are cheap yet not too congested. In the absence of self-interested link owners, these games reduce to the well-studied network congestion games—a widely accepted and practically useful model for selfish resource allocation in transportation and communication networks (see, e.g., [4, 13, 33] and references therein). In congestion games, self-interested users travel in a network from their origin to their destination with the goal of minimizing their own travel cost. The natural solution concept of the game is the so-called Wardrop equilibrium flow, under which all users route along shortest paths, given the strategic choices of other users.

Since selfish behavior usually drives systems to socially inefficient situations, a central authority is typically interested in optimizing the social welfare for the network users—a task that, in the absence of self-interested link owners, can be implemented by appropriate *marginal tolls* [4], which simply charge each user the negative externality she imposes on the system. However, the presence of link owners, who set tolls so as to maximize their profits, is at odds with user welfare. For instance, under marginal tolls, some operators may want to increase their toll in order to make a higher profit. In this regard, an equilibrium for the link owners is a toll vector, such that, a change in a single toll does not increase the profit of the corresponding toll operator (under the implied user Wardrop equilibrium flow).

In this more complex game-theoretic environment, (i) an equilibrium may fail to exist; (ii) it might not be unique and; (iii) the network performance at equilibrium can be arbitrarily inefficient. Specifically, the only case where an equilibrium is proved to exist is in parallel link networks with affine latency functions [1, 20, 21]. Additionally, equilibria might not be unique [2, 20], implying that we might not be able to predict the outcome of the game. Further, the network's performance at the Wardrop equilibrium flow under a Nash equilibrium toll vector can be arbitrarily degraded, which implies that the network can behave arbitrarily worse than the case where tolls (prices) are completely absent.

In the face of these challenges, we set out to find ways to mitigate the effect of selfish toll operator behavior. We introduce competition regulation by allowing a regulator to set specific price caps on the toll values that each toll operator can set on her link. Different price caps for different operators is consistent with the practice in some privately operated networks of highways. For example, in Santiago de Chile there are currently 12 different operators who set tolls on different urban highways, as shown in Fig. 1. The current regulation sets a price cap that is unique to each highway and the toll operators are allowed to set tolls below the caps [19]. As it turns out, introducing such regulation can resolve all of the above issues, as there are caps for which the game has a unique Nash equilibrium, under which the Wardrop equilibrium is optimal.

## Contribution

We first study the network pricing game in its original form, i.e. without regulation, providing examples regarding the nonexistence of Nash equilibria and the inefficiency of the resulting Wardrop equilibrium flow. The first example, Example 3.1, shows that Nash equilibria may not exist in the case of extension-parallel networks[1] with affine latencies. Interestingly, the source of the problem is twofold. On the one hand, the best-response mapping cannot be bounded a priori: there are instances of the game in which the best response of operators is to increase their toll and thus,

[1]Extension-parallel networks are recursively defined as a single link or two extension-parallel networks connected in parallel or a single link connected in series with an extension-parallel network [16].

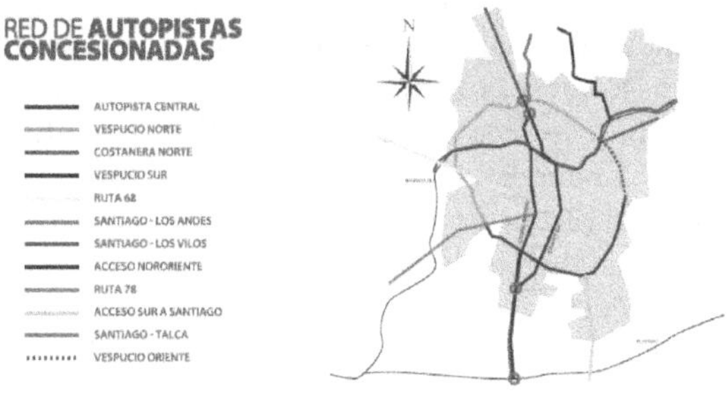


Fig. 1. Privately operated highways in Santiago de Chile. Each highway has its own toll cap.

iterated best responses lead to unbounded tolls. On the other hand, and quite surprisingly, the best-response mapping may turn out to be discontinuous so that iterated best responses actually cycle. From the latter it turns out that even if we impose a priori caps on the tolls, equilibria may fail to exist. The second example (Example 3.2) provides an instance where a Nash equilibrium exists yet the network performance, quantified by total users' delay of the Wardrop flow, is arbitrarily worse than optimal.

Since the unregulated network pricing game behaves so poorly, in Section 4 we set out to study mechanisms to improve it. In particular, we investigate the simple regulatory policy of setting upper bounds (caps) on the toll values that each operator is allowed to set. Note that there is a tension between the toll charged by the operator and the amount of flow she will get. It is plausible for a toll operator to gain from decreasing her toll since her link will attract more flow, which may result in an overall higher profit. For large enough caps it indeed happens that it is optimal for the operator to set a toll below the cap. Our main result, Theorem 4.4, shows that using such a vector as toll caps leads to every operator charging precisely the cap. Moreover, we show this equilibrium is robust to coalitions, a concept known as *strong Nash equilibrium.* A direct corollary of this result is that if the caps are set to be the marginal tolls, then the unique Nash equilibrium is the set of marginal tolls itself, which is known to induce the optimal flow as a Wardrop equilibrium. A surprising fact is that even though the flow on a given link is a decreasing function of the toll on that link (as we show in Lemmas 4.1 and 4.2), the profit of the toll operator as a function of the toll she charges is an increasing function up to a certain point (Lemma 4.3), which is a key tool to prove Theorem 4.4. Also, we give an example to show that our results do not extend to the setting in which a regulator owns multiple links of the network.

Inspired by Theorem 4.4 we study *great tolls* in more detail. These are toll vectors that induce the optimal flow as a Wardrop equilibrium and when set as caps are themselves the unique Nash equilibrium. As great tolls are guaranteed to exist and need not be unique, a basic question is that of finding the great tolls minimizing the users' payments. Note that the users' total delay under great tolls is fixed, since all great tolls induce the optimal flow; thus, our question is equivalent to that of finding great tolls that minimize the total (delays plus payments) users' cost. By the results in Section 4, any vector that induces the optimal flow and is upper bounded by the marginal toll vector, is a great set of tolls, yet simple examples show that these are not the only ones. While a characterization of great tolls seems to be out of reach, by restricting to those which are upper bounded by marginal tolls we formulate a linear program for optimizing the total users' cost over this restricted set of great tolls. Section 5 is devoted to finding bounds on the performance of such great tolls in terms of the induced total users' cost. To this end, we use as a benchmark the *minimum payment tolls*, defined as those that while inducing optimal flows, minimize the total users' cost. Minimum payment tolls can also be computed by a linear program.

We prove that the ratio of these linear programs can be bounded in two fundamentally different ways, and these bounds are tight. First, we prove a functional bound (Theorem 5.2) for instances where latency functions satisfy a bounded relative growth condition, which for example gives a $(d + 1)$-approximation on the total cost incurred by users, when latencies are polynomial functions of degree at most $d$. Notice that all the results so far hold for multicommodity instances. Second, we prove a structural bound (Theorem 5.5) for single-commodity instances that only depends on the structure of the network but not on the underlying latency functions. As a corollary, we get that for series-parallel networks the previous ratio is actually one and thus our linear programming approach is optimal.

To test the robustness of our results, we finally consider the setting with elastic traffic demands. Here users have a valuation for traveling through the network and may opt out from traveling if the travel cost exceeds their valuation. We show that, similar to the fixed demand model, any toll vector that induces the optimal flow and is at most equal to the marginal toll vector is a great set of tolls (Theorem 6.1). Moreover, even though the consumer surplus under great tolls can be arbitrary worse than the optimal surplus, we prove that it is at least as high as the optimal surplus if each user had half the original valuation (Theorem 6.5).

### Related Work

Acemoglu and Ozdaglar [1] introduced a model of price competition between link operators where each user has some fixed reservation value for travel. They show that increasing competition among operators from a monopoly to an oligopoly may cause a reduction in efficiency, measured as the difference between users' willingness to pay and delay costs, and provide a (tight) bound on efficiency in pure strategy equilibria. In a follow up work, Acemoglu and Ozdaglar [2] generalized the above study to slightly more general topologies in which parallel paths with multiple links may replace the parallel links. They showed that even this slight generalization can make the game arbitrarily inefficient, where the efficiency is measured as mentioned above.

Hayrapetyan et al. [21] considered instances on parallel links where the demand to be routed is elastic and decreases in a concave way as the cost for using the network increases. The social cost in that work is the sum of the players' profits plus a term that represents the utility gathered by the traffic that gets routed. For that game they showed that in a network with parallel links and linear latencies, there is always a pure Nash equilibrium with the price of anarchy, i.e. the measure for inefficiency, being bounded by a constant factor even when the latency functions are relaxed to be convex. For the case where latencies have zero value under zero flow, they improve the constant in the above bound. Following that work, Ozdaglar [29] studied the same model and managed to prove tight bounds on the efficiency of that game. Musacchio [26] and Musacchio and Wu [27] rederived and generalized those (upper) bounds for the case of series-parallel networks via a connection to electrical circuits; see the survey by Ozdaglar and Srikant [30] for further discussion.

With respect to the congestion model itself, the most closely related work to ours is that of Harks et al. [20]. There, a regulator is able to set a unique price cap for all toll operators. As it turns out this restricts the regulator enough so that the induced network performance is not always optimal. For two-link parallel networks this reduction in performance is characterized for different classes of latency function.

Our price competition model corresponds to Bertrand competition in a network setting [15, Chapter 6]. Under this setting Chawla et al. [11] addressed questions regarding the price of anarchy and price of stability with respect to two objectives: the social welfare of all the players (users and sellers), and the total profit obtained by all the sellers. The main differences with our work are that only capacity-based congestion is considered,[2] and no regulation is imposed on the game. Their results show a dependence of the price of anarchy/stability on the number of monopolistic links, namely the links whose removal disconnects an origin-destination pair. In contrast, our model does not suffer from monopolies: setting caps on prices prevents monopolistic links from charging arbitrarily large prices. Following the same model and focusing on the social welfare of the consumers as the objective, Chawla and Niu [10] extended the results of Chawla et al. [11].

An interesting and related model is raised by Anshelevich and Sekar [3]. In that work, the edges of a network correspond to goods, and each edge is owned by a different profit maximizing seller. In the first stage of the game, sellers set prices for the use of their edges and have production costs depending on the level of use. In the second stage, the users of the network, i.e., the buyers, choose origin to destination paths so as each of them maximizes her utility minus the payments to the sellers. The main difference with the model presented here (in particular, the extension to the elastic demand case in Section 6) is that users impose an externality on the sellers, via the production costs, and not on the other users, as is the case in our model. This crucially affects the equilibrium pricing and the social welfare (e.g., for single commodity networks, if no monopolies are present, there is always an optimal equilibrium, which is not the case in our model).

In other related work, Papadimitriou and Valiant [31] consider the case where the routing is no longer selfish, but is controlled by the edges of the network, and each edge either minimizes its average latency, or announces a suitable price to its neighbors in order to maximize its profit. Caragiannis et al. [8] consider a model of buyers and sellers of a similar product, that under some reformulation can be seen as a variant of the parallel links model of Acemoglu and Ozdaglar [1] with heterogeneous buyers but constant latencies. Instead of minimizing traffic costs, maximizing the profit from tolls, has been considered in the past [7, 9, 24]. There, a central authority/unique owner has control of all the toll-able edges, yet, more importantly, the edge costs are constants rather than flow dependent.

The study of network congestion games where a central operator is allowed to charge tolls in order to improve efficiency has a long history, starting with Beckmann et al. [4]. Cole et al. [12] and Fleischer [17] provided upper bounds on tolls that induce the optimal flow as an equilibrium, and Dial [14] considered the objective of minimizing users' payments among optimal flow-inducing tolls. The study of network users games where for each link a (potentially adversarially chosen) upper bound on the toll is present was first considered by Bonifaci et al. [6] and later by Jelinek et al. [22] and Fotakis et al. [18]. Results in these papers show that when upper bounds are present, optimality cannot in general be achieved, yet, on the positive side, algorithms are proposed under rather restrictive settings with provable guarantees regarding the efficiency of the network.

## 2 PRELIMINARIES

We study a network pricing game, where nonatomic players, which we call *users*, selfishly minimize their cost (delays plus tolls) across a network; on top of this, each network link is operated by a different selfish agent which maximizes profit by charging tolls on users traversing her link.

### The Network Users' Game: Selfish Routing

Let $G = (V, E)$ be a network, with $V$ the set of nodes, and $E$ the set of directed edges/links of the network. We consider a multi-commodity flow instance, described by origin-destination node pairs $\{(o^k, d^k)\}_{k\in K}$, for a finite set of commodities $K$. For each commodity $k$, $r^k > 0$ units of demand

[2]Capacity-based congestion corresponds to latency functions which are identically zero until capacity is reached, and then jump to infinity.

need to be routed from $o^k$ to $d^k$. For each link $e \in E$, there is a latency function $\ell_e : \mathbb{R}_+ \to \mathbb{R}_+$, that represents the delay experienced by users traversing this link, as a function of the total flow on the link; we will assume this function to be strictly increasing, convex and smooth.[3]

**Paths and Flows.** For each commodity $k \in K$, let $\mathcal{P}^k$ denote the set of $o^k - d^k$ paths and let $\mathcal{P} = \cup_k \mathcal{P}^k$ be the union of all these paths. A *flow* for commodity $k$ is a nonnegative vector $\boldsymbol{x}^k = (x_P^k)_{P \in \mathcal{P}^k}$ such that $\sum_{P \in \mathcal{P}^k} x_P^k = r^k$. A *flow* $\boldsymbol{x}$ is a vector $(\boldsymbol{x}^k)_{k \in K}$, where each $\boldsymbol{x}^k$ is a flow for commodity $k$. For a flow $\boldsymbol{x}$ and $e \in E$, let $x_e^k = \sum_{P \in \mathcal{P}^k : e \in P} x_P^k$ be the amount of flow that $\boldsymbol{x}^k$ routes on each link $e$ and let $x_e = \sum_{k \in K} x_e^k$ be the amount of flow that $\boldsymbol{x}$ routes on $e$. With a slight abuse of notation, we will also denote $\boldsymbol{x} = (x_e)_{e \in E}$, the link-wise description of a flow.

**Wardrop Equilibria and Optimal Flows.** Given flow $\boldsymbol{x}$, the delay experienced on $e$ is $\ell_e(x_e)$. In the case a toll $t_e \geq 0$ is charged for link usage, the combined cost of traversing $e$ is $[\ell_e(x_e) + \alpha \cdot t_e]$, where $\alpha$ represents the trade-off factor between delay and tolls and is assumed to be identical for all users. Without loss of generality, we can assume $\alpha$ to be equal to 1 because we can always divide all tolls by $\alpha$. A flow is a *Wardrop equilibrium* if it is supported on paths of minimum cost. Formally, $\boldsymbol{x}$ is a Wardrop equilibrium if, for every $k$, for every path $P \in \mathcal{P}^k$ with $x_P^k > 0$, and every path $P' \in \mathcal{P}^k$, $\sum_{e \in P}[\ell_e(x_e) + t_e] \leq \sum_{e \in P'}[\ell_e(x_e) + t_e]$. Given such a flow, any $o^k - d^k$ path achieving the minimum end-to-end cost will be called an *active path*, and any link that belongs to an active path will be called an *active link*.

For any toll vector $\boldsymbol{t} \geq 0$, a Wardrop equilibrium exists, moreover it minimizes the convex Wardrop potential $\Phi_t(\boldsymbol{x})$ [4], and thus is given by:

$$\boldsymbol{x}(\boldsymbol{t}) \triangleq \arg \min_{\boldsymbol{x} \geq 0 \text{ flow}} \left\{ \Phi_t(\boldsymbol{x}) \triangleq \sum_{e \in E} \int_0^{x_e} (\ell_e(x) + t_e)\, dx \right\}. \tag{1}$$

Notice that by our choice of latency functions, $\Phi_t$ is strictly convex, implying that the link-wise description of the Wardrop equilibrium is unique, and therefore $(x_e(\boldsymbol{t}))_{e \in E}$ is a well-defined function, which is moreover continuous by Berge's theorem [5].

Given flow $\boldsymbol{x}$, the total delay experienced by users is $\sum_{e \in E} x_e \ell_e(x_e)$, and it is the standard measure of network performance. Notice this function is strictly convex in $\boldsymbol{x}$. The optimal flow $\boldsymbol{x}^*$ is the flow that minimizes the total delay. In general, it is known [32] that the untolled Wardrop flow $\boldsymbol{x}(\boldsymbol{0})$ is not necessarily optimal. However, a classical result [4] shows that the vector of marginal tolls $\hat{\boldsymbol{t}}$, defined as $\hat{t}_e = x_e^* \ell_e'(x_e^*)$, *induces* the optimal flow, that is $\boldsymbol{x}(\hat{\boldsymbol{t}}) = \boldsymbol{x}^*$. Any toll vector with this property will be called *optimal*.

### The Network Operators' Game: Price Competition on Tolls

In our model, additionally, every link $e \in E$ is operated by a different operator: these are the players of the price competition game. Each player $e$ is allowed to charge a nonnegative toll $t_e$ for its usage. Under the resulting toll vector $\boldsymbol{t}$, each link gets flow $x_e(\boldsymbol{t})$ according to the induced Wardrop equilibrium, and thus the profit of player $e$ is given by $\pi_e(\boldsymbol{t}) \triangleq t_e x_e(\boldsymbol{t})$. We are interested in the equilibrium outcomes of this game.

**Profit functions.** For each player $e \in E$, her strategy is given by toll $t_e$, and her profit is given by $\pi_e(t_e, \boldsymbol{t}_{-e}) = t_e x_e(t_e, \boldsymbol{t}_{-e})$, where we have used the standard game-theoretic notation $\boldsymbol{t} = (t_e, \boldsymbol{t}_{-e})$. Whenever $\boldsymbol{t}_{-e}$ is clear from context, we will simply write $x_e(t_e)$ and $\pi_e(t_e)$.

**Regulated Network Pricing Game and Nash Equilibria.** The regulated network pricing game we consider is the following. A central planner may choose a cap vector $\bar{\boldsymbol{t}} \geq 0$ for tolls, and each

[3]More general assumptions have been studied in the literature, but we will restrict to this setting in order to avoid some minor technicalities.

player wants to maximize her own profit under this constraint. We study two solution concepts, (pure) Nash equilibrium and strong (pure) Nash equilibrium. Tolls $\boldsymbol{t}$ are a Nash equilibrium for the network pricing game if for every $e$, $t_e$ is the best response of player $e$ to $\boldsymbol{t}_{-e}$, i.e. we have $t_e \in \mathcal{BR}_e(\boldsymbol{t}_{-e})$, where the best response mapping $\mathcal{BR}_e(\boldsymbol{t}_{-e})$ is defined as

$$\mathcal{BR}_e(\boldsymbol{t}_{-e}) \triangleq \arg\max\{\pi_e(s_e, \boldsymbol{t}_{-e}) : 0 \le s_e \le \bar{t}_e\}.$$

Tolls $\boldsymbol{t}$ are a strong Nash equilibrium if there is no possible coalition that jointly deviates, resulting in an improvement of their individual profits. Formally, tolls $\boldsymbol{t}$ are a strong Nash equilibrium if for any set $E^\Delta \subset E$ (the coalition) and $\boldsymbol{t}'$ (the deviation) such that $E^\Delta = \{e \in E : t'_e \neq t_e\}$, if there is a player $e \in E^\Delta$ who gains by deviating with $\pi_e(\boldsymbol{t}') > \pi_e(\boldsymbol{t})$ then there exists another player $f \in E^\Delta$ who is worse off with $\pi_f(\boldsymbol{t}') < \pi_f(\boldsymbol{t})$. Notice that any strong Nash equilibrium is a Nash equilibrium.

*Definition 2.1 (Cap equilibrium and great tolls).* Given an instance of the profit maximization game, we say that a (nonnegative) vector $\bar{\boldsymbol{t}} = (\bar{t}_e)_{e\in E}$ is

(a) a cap equilibrium if when restricting the strategy space for every player $e$ to tolls $s_e \in [0, \bar{t}_e]$, then $(s_e)_{e\in E} = (\bar{t}_e)_{e\in E}$ is a strong Nash equilibrium;
(b) a great set of tolls if it is optimal (i.e., induces the optimal flow) and a cap equilibrium.

The case where $\bar{t}_e = \infty$ for every $e \in E$ corresponds to the unregulated game, which will be the main focus of the next section. Observe that there are situations where the unregulated game may not have equilibrium at all, for instance in the presence of a monopoly, i.e. a link that cuts a commodity. In order to avoid such cases, we will assume that each commodity has at least two disjoint $o^k - d^k$ paths. Notice this will only be necessary for the unregulated game, as when imposing caps we immediately prevent monopolies from setting arbitrarily large prices.

## 3 UNREGULATED NETWORK PRICING GAME

We address the question of existence of equilibria in the network pricing game without caps. In this setting, the only case where equilibria are known to exist is for parallel link networks and affine latencies, and, additionally, if one drops the affine latencies requirement while keeping the parallel links topology, then equilibria may fail to exist (see e.g. [1, 20]). To highlight and add on the brittleness of existence of equilibria for the unregulated game, we show that if one drops the network topology requirement, in the simplest nontrivial way, while keeping the affine latencies requirement, then equilibria may again fail to exist. We conclude the section by showing that even when equilibria exist, the resulting performance may be arbitrarily bad with respect to the social optimum.

**Nonexistence of Equilibria.** To begin with, we show that even for affine latencies and rather simple topologies, an equilibrium is not guaranteed to exist.

*Example 3.1.* Consider the extension-parallel network on the left side of Figure 2, with vertex set $\{o, u, d\}$, link set $E = \{e_1 = (o, u), e_2 = (u, d), e_3 = (u, d), e_4 = (o, d)\}$, latencies $\ell_{e_1}(x) = \ell_{e_3}(x) = \ell_{e_4}(x) = x$ and $\ell_{e_2}(x) = 2$, and a single $o, d$ commodity with demand $r = 2$. This instance does not have a Nash equilibrium.[4]

[4] In this example, as well as in other examples, constant latencies are present. This violates the assumption that latencies are strictly increasing, yet this assumption was adopted for technical simplicity in order to have uniqueness of Wardrop flow, so that profits are well defined. All examples present in our work indeed satisfy such uniqueness, and moreover they can be modified to satisfy the strictly increasing assumption, e.g. by adding an $\varepsilon x$ factor to each of the constant latencies for $\varepsilon > 0$ sufficiently small.

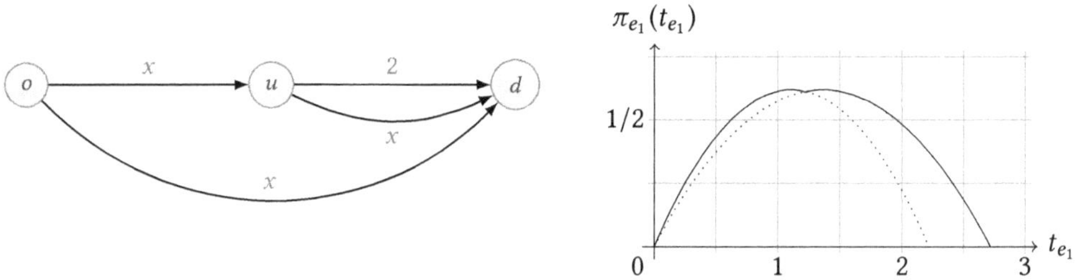


Fig. 2. On the left, the network of Example 3.1. On the right, the profit function of player 1 when $t_{e_2} = 0$, $t_{e_3} = 3/2$ and $t_{e_4} = (2 + \sqrt{6})/2$.

To get an intuition why no Nash equilibrium exists, suppose that $t_{e_2} = 0$, $t_{e_3} = 3/2$ and $t_{e_4} = (2 + \sqrt{6})/2$. Figure 2 on the right, shows the profit function of player 1. Notice that the profit function is not concave and has two maxima, one at $(2 + \sqrt{6})/4$ and one at $(3 + \sqrt{6})/4$. This implies that the best-response correspondence of player 1 is not convex. Yet, convexity of the best-response correspondences seems to be a crucial property as, on the one hand, it is necessary for the existence proof for the parallel links with affine latencies case (which is using Kakutani's fixed-point theorem), and, on the other hand, it is also absent from other nonexistence examples with parallel links [1, 20]. □

**Unboundedness of Total Delay.** Next, we show that even when Nash equilibria exist, the resulting Wardrop flows may be arbitrarily inefficient, in terms of total delay. Our example is a parallel link network with two links and affine latencies.

*Example 3.2.* Consider a single-commodity instance where $r = 1$ units of flow is routed through a two-link parallel network with $\ell_{e_1}(x) = Ax$ and $\ell_{e_2}(x) = a$ for $0 < a < A$. By direct computation, we get the optimal flow $\boldsymbol{x}^* = (\frac{a}{2A}, \frac{2A-a}{2A})$, achieving total delay $[4aA - a^2]/[4A]$.

On the other hand, for any toll vector $\boldsymbol{t}$, the Wardrop flow is $\boldsymbol{x}(\boldsymbol{t}) = ([a + t_{e_2} - t_{e_1}]/A, [A - a - t_{e_2} + t_{e_1}]/A)$ (provided these values lie in $[0, 1]$). By the first-order conditions on the profit maximization problem for players 1 and 2, we get a Nash equilibrium $(t_{e_1}, t_{e_2}) = ([a + A]/3, [2A - a]/3)$, and the respective Wardrop flow $\boldsymbol{x}(\boldsymbol{t}) = ([A + a]/[3A], [2A - a]/[3A])$, resulting in total delay $[A^2 + 8Aa - 2a^2]/[9A]$.

As a consequence, the ratio of the total delay at the Nash equilibrium over the optimal delay is $\frac{4[A^2+8Aa-2a^2]}{9[4aA-a^2]}$. Keeping $A > 0$ fixed and taking $a \to 0$, we have that the ratio diverges. □

## 4 REGULATED NETWORK PRICING GAME

In this section, we study the profit maximization game and some of its structural properties. We prove that the marginal tolls, when used as caps, are always a Nash equilibrium for the profit maximization game, thus resolving the issues of equilibrium existence, uniqueness and inefficiency raised in the previous section. Our main result, presented in Theorem 4.4, strengthens the above by showing that a potentially larger set of optimal tolls, when used as caps, leads to a unique Nash equilibrium, which is furthermore robust to coalitions.

We start by studying the behavior of the Wardrop equilibrium flow as a function of tolls. The following result states some monotonicity properties that are standard. Its proof is omitted since we prove a more general result right after.

Lemma 4.1 (Monotonicity). *Let $e \in E$ and $\boldsymbol{t}_{-e}$ be a fixed toll vector for the rest of the players. If $t'_e > t_e$ then*

(i) $x_e(t'_e) \leq x_e(t_e)$, *and*
(ii) $\ell_e(x_e(t'_e)) + t'_e \geq \ell_e(x_e(t_e)) + t_e$.

In this work we need a generalization of the previous result, establishing how flows may change as several tolls decrease. This generalization is stated and proved below.

Lemma 4.2. *Let $\boldsymbol{t}, \boldsymbol{t}' \geq 0$ be two toll vectors such that $\boldsymbol{t} \leq \boldsymbol{t}'$ and $E^< = \{e \in E : t_e < t'_e\}$ is nonempty. Then, there exist $e_1, e_2 \in E^<$ such that:*

(i) $x_{e_1}(\boldsymbol{t}') \leq x_{e_1}(\boldsymbol{t})$,
(ii) $[x_{e_2}(\boldsymbol{t}') - x_{e_2}(\boldsymbol{t})][\ell_{e_2}(x_{e_2}(\boldsymbol{t}')) + t'_{e_2} - \ell_{e_2}(x_{e_2}(\boldsymbol{t})) - t_{e_2}] \leq 0$.

Proof. To prove (i) we compare flows $\boldsymbol{x}(\boldsymbol{t})$ and $\boldsymbol{x}(\boldsymbol{t}')$ with respect to the Wardrop potentials, $\Phi_t(\boldsymbol{x})$ and $\Phi_{t'}(\boldsymbol{x}) = \Phi_t(\boldsymbol{x}) + \sum_{e \in E^<}[t'_e - t_e]x_e$. By the optimality of the Wardrop flow on its respective potential, we get the following inequalities

$$\begin{aligned} \Phi_t(\boldsymbol{x}(\boldsymbol{t})) &\leq \Phi_t(\boldsymbol{x}(\boldsymbol{t}')) \\ \Phi_t(\boldsymbol{x}(\boldsymbol{t}')) + \sum_{e \in E^<}[t'_e - t_e]x_e(\boldsymbol{t}') &\leq \Phi_t(\boldsymbol{x}(\boldsymbol{t})) + \sum_{e \in E^<}[t'_e - t_e]x_e(\boldsymbol{t}). \end{aligned}$$

Combining these inequalities we get

$$\sum_{e \in E^<}[t'_e - t_e][x_e(\boldsymbol{t}') - x_e(\boldsymbol{t})] \leq 0,$$

and thus there must exist $e_1 \in E^<$ such that $x_{e_1}(\boldsymbol{t}') \leq x_{e_1}(\boldsymbol{t})$, proving $(i)$.

Let us now prove $(ii)$. Notice that since $\boldsymbol{x}(\boldsymbol{t}) + (\boldsymbol{x}(\boldsymbol{t}') - \boldsymbol{x}(\boldsymbol{t})) = \boldsymbol{x}(\boldsymbol{t}')$ is a feasible flow, then $\boldsymbol{x}(\boldsymbol{t}') - \boldsymbol{x}(\boldsymbol{t})$ is a feasible direction for $\boldsymbol{x}(\boldsymbol{t})$. By the first-order optimality conditions,

$$\sum_e [\ell_e(x_e(\boldsymbol{t})) + t_e][x_e(\boldsymbol{t}) - x_e(\boldsymbol{t}')] \leq 0.$$

Analogously, $x(\boldsymbol{t}) - x(\boldsymbol{t}')$ is a feasible direction for $x(\boldsymbol{t}')$, and thus

$$\sum_e [\ell_e(x_e(\boldsymbol{t}')) + t'_e][x_e(\boldsymbol{t}') - x_e(\boldsymbol{t})] \leq 0.$$

Adding up these inequalities, we obtain

$$\sum_{e \in E^=}[x_e(\boldsymbol{t}') - x_e(\boldsymbol{t})][\ell_e(x_e(\boldsymbol{t}')) - \ell_e(x_e(\boldsymbol{t}))] + \sum_{e \in E^<}[x_e(\boldsymbol{t}') - x_e(\boldsymbol{t})][\ell_e(x_e(\boldsymbol{t}')) + t'_e - \ell_e(x_e(\boldsymbol{t})) - t_e] \leq 0,$$

where $E^= = \{e \in E : t_e = t'_e\}$. Observe now that the first summation term is nonnegative, as $\ell_e$ is increasing for all $e$. Thus, $\sum_{e \in E^<}[x_e(\boldsymbol{t}') - x_e(\boldsymbol{t})][\ell_e(x_e(\boldsymbol{t}')) + t'_e - \ell_e(x_e(\boldsymbol{t})) - t_e] \leq 0$, implying that there exists $e_2 \in E^<$ such that $[x_{e_2}(\boldsymbol{t}') - x_{e_2}(\boldsymbol{t})][\ell_{e_2}(x_{e_2}(\boldsymbol{t}')) + t'_{e_2} - \ell_{e_2}(x_{e_2}(\boldsymbol{t})) - t_{e_2}] \leq 0$, proving $(ii)$. □

The following result gives an intriguing inequality satisfied by any profit maximizing toll. This property is a consequence of the first-order optimality conditions, in combination with the monotonicity properties stated above. We will later see this lemma is crucial for our main result.

Lemma 4.3. *Let $\boldsymbol{t} \geq 0$ be a toll vector and $e \in E$ with $t_e > 0$. If $t_e$ is a local optimum for the profit maximization problem (that is, for objective $\pi_e(\cdot, \boldsymbol{t}_{-e})$) then $x_e(t_e) \cdot \ell'_e(x_e(t_e)) \leq t_e$.*

Proof. Notice first that in the case $x_e(t_e) = 0$ the result obviously holds, thus we may restrict ourselves to the case $x_e(t_e) > 0$. In order to use the first-order optimality conditions, we need to ensure that the flow on $e$ neither suddenly drops to zero nor it remains constant. By continuity, there exists an interval $[t_e, t_e + \delta']$ where $x_e(\cdot) > 0$, with $\delta' > 0$; furthermore, by local optimality, we may choose $0 < \delta < \delta'$ so that $t_e$ is a profit maximizing toll on the interval. This in particular implies that $0 < x_e(s_e) < x_e(t_e)$ for any $s_e \in [t_e, t_e + \delta]$.

Now, since $t_e$ is a local maximizer, we can use the first-order optimality conditions, $D^+[\pi_e(t_e)] \leq 0$, where $D^+[\cdot]$ is the upper-right Dini derivative.[5] Using the linearity of Dini derivatives, we get

$$x_e(t_e) + t_e D^+[x_e(t_e)] = D^+[\pi_e(t_e)] \leq 0; \tag{2}$$

notice in particular $D^+[x_e(t_e)] < 0$.

On the other hand, since $x_e(s_e) < x_e(t_e)$ for any $s_e \in [t_e, t_e + \delta]$, by Lemma 4.1 (ii), we have that $[\ell_e(x_e(s_e)) + s_e - \ell_e(x_e(t_e)) - t_e]/[x_e(s_e) - x_e(t_e)] \leq 0$. After re-arranging terms, we get

$$\frac{\ell_e(x_e(s_e)) - \ell_e(x_e(t_e))}{x_e(s_e) - x_e(t_e)} \leq -\frac{s_e - t_e}{x_e(s_e) - x_e(t_e)}.$$

Taking $\limsup_{s_e \to t_e^+}$ in the expression above, we get that the left hand side converges to $\ell_e'(x_e(t_e))$, whereas the right hand side converges to $-(D^+[x_e(t_e)])^{-1}$ (recall the Dini derivative is nonzero); we conclude that $\ell_e'(x_e(t_e)) \leq -\frac{1}{D^+[x_e(t_e)]}$. This, in combination with (2), gives

$$x_e(t_e)\ell_e'(x_e(t_e)) \leq -\frac{x_e(t_e)}{D^+[x_e(t_e)]} \leq t_e,$$

which proves the result. □

Our main result below shows a strong consequence of the lemma above. Consider tolls that induce the optimal flow, and are at most the marginal tolls (in particular, marginal tolls satisfy these two conditions). Then these tolls, when used as caps, lead to a unique and strong Nash equilibrium.

Theorem 4.4. *Let $\bar{t} \leq \hat{t}$ be an optimal toll vector. For the profit maximization problem with caps $\bar{t}$, there exists a unique Nash equilibrium, given by $\bar{t}$, which, moreover, is a strong Nash equilibrium.*

Proof. First we prove that $\bar{t}$ is a strong Nash equilibrium for the game. By way of contradiction, let $E^<$ be a set of links for which the corresponding players, without losing profit, deviate to some smaller toll value and let $t \leq \bar{t}$ be the toll vector after these deviations. In particular, for all $e \in E^<$ we have $t_e x_e(t) \geq \bar{t}_e x_e(\bar{t}) > t_e x_e(\bar{t})$, which implies $t_e > 0$ along with $x_e(t) > x_e(\bar{t})$ and

$$t_e \geq \frac{\bar{t}_e x_e(\bar{t})}{x_e(t)}. \tag{3}$$

By Lemma 4.2 *(ii)*, there exists $e \in E^<$ such that $[x_e(\bar{t}) - x_e(t)][\ell_e(x_e(\bar{t})) + \bar{t}_e - \ell_e(x_e(t)) - t_e] \leq 0$, which in combination with $x_e(t) > x_e(\bar{t})$ gives

$$\ell_e(x_e(\bar{t})) + \bar{t}_e \geq \ell_e(x_e(t)) + t_e. \tag{4}$$

Let $e \in E^<$ be a link satisfying (4). We have the following inequalities

$$\ell_e'(x_e(\bar{t}))(x_e(t) - x_e(\bar{t})) \leq \ell_e(x_e(t)) - \ell_e(x_e(\bar{t})) \leq \bar{t}_e - t_e \leq \bar{t}_e\left(1 - \frac{x_e(\bar{t})}{x_e(t)}\right), \tag{5}$$

where the first inequality follows from convexity of $\ell_e$, the second from (4), and the third from (3). Since $\bar{t}_e \leq \hat{t}_e = \ell_e'(x_e(\bar{t}))x_e(\bar{t})$, we obtain from (5) that

$$\ell_e'(x_e(\bar{t}))(x_e(t) - x_e(\bar{t})) \leq \ell_e'(x_e(\bar{t}))x_e(\bar{t})\left(\frac{x_e(t) - x_e(\bar{t})}{x_e(t)}\right).$$

Since $\ell_e'(x_e(\bar{t})) > 0$ and $x_e(t) > x_e(\bar{t})$, we conclude that $x_e(t) \leq x_e(\bar{t})$, a contradiction.

[5] Recall the definition of the upper-right Dini derivative, $D^+[f(x)] \triangleq \limsup_{h \to 0^+} \frac{f(x+h) - f(x)}{h}$.

Now that we have proved existence, we show there is a unique Nash equilibrium. By way of contradiction, suppose there exists another Nash equilibrium $\boldsymbol{t} \neq \bar{\boldsymbol{t}}$ for the profit maximization game with caps $\bar{\boldsymbol{t}}$. Since all players are playing their best response, we may assume $t_e > 0$ for all players $e$ such that $\bar{t}_e > 0$, and thus we can use Lemma 4.3, concluding that $x_e(\boldsymbol{t})\ell'_e(x_e(\boldsymbol{t})) \leq t_e$ for all $e \in E^< = \{e \in E : t_e < \bar{t}_e\}$ (nonempty by assumption) which in turn gives

$$x_e(\boldsymbol{t})\ell'_e(x_e(\boldsymbol{t})) \leq t_e < \bar{t}_e \leq \hat{t}_e = x^*_e\ell'_e(x^*_e),$$

concluding that $x_e(\boldsymbol{t}) < x^*_e = x_e(\bar{\boldsymbol{t}})$ for all $e \in E^<$. But from Lemma 4.2 (*i*) there exists $e_1 \in E^<$ such that $x_{e_1}(\boldsymbol{t}) \geq x_{e_1}(\bar{\boldsymbol{t}})$, a contradiction. □

REMARK 4.5. *Theorem 4.4 cannot be extended to the setting where an operator owns more than one link. For an example, consider the network of Figure 3 with unit demand and suppose that all links are owned by a single operator. The marginal tolls, and thus the caps, are given by* $(\hat{t}_{ou}, \hat{t}_{uv}, \hat{t}_{vd}) = (2/3, 1/3, 2/3)$*, yielding a total profit of 1 for the operator (links* $(o,v)$ *and* $(u,d)$ *have zero caps). If, however, the operator charges a toll vector of* $(t_{ou}, t_{uv}, t_{vd}) = (2/3, 0, 2/3)$*, then it induces a flow of* $2/9$ *on each of the upper and lower paths, and a flow of* $5/9$ *on the zig-zag path, gaining a profit of* $28/27$*. Hence, the marginal tolls are not a cap equilibrium.*

## 5 MINIMIZING USERS' COSTS

Theorem 4.4 implies that any opt-inducing toll vector that is not above the marginals is itself a cap equilibrium, and thus is a great set of tolls. The fact that great tolls need not be unique, motivates the question of whether it is possible to compute the great tolls vector that minimizes the total users' costs. If all great tolls were not above the marginals, then computing the great tolls vector that minimizes the total users' costs would reduce to solving a linear program (see program (BMT) below). Yet, this is not the case, since, as the following example suggests, there are great tolls that are above the marginals for some edges and additionally incur smaller costs for the users.

*Example 5.1.* Consider the Braess network of Figure 3 with unit demand. The optimal flow is obtained by sending one third of the flow on each of the upper and lower paths, and one third of the flow on the zig-zag path; leading to a total delay of $21/9$. The marginal tolls are given by $(\hat{t}_{ou}, \hat{t}_{uv}, \hat{t}_{vd}) = (2/3, 1/3, 2/3)$, yielding a total profit of 1. Hence the users' costs under the marginal tolls are $21/9 + 1$. Notice that the only great tolls that are not above the marginal tolls are the marginal tolls themselves.

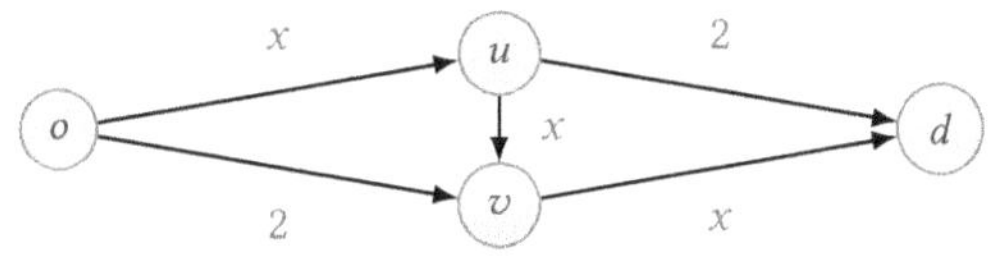


Fig. 3. The network of Remark 4.5 and Example 5.1. Under unit demand, the optimal flow routes one third of the flow to each of the upper, zig-zag and lower paths.

Taking $S = \{o, v\}$ as a cut, we can decrease the tolls by some $\varepsilon > 0$ for outgoing links (namely, $(o,u)$ and $(v,d)$) and increase them by $\varepsilon$ on incoming links (i.e., $(u,v)$). This procedure maintains optimality of tolls, however it is unclear whether the cap equilibrium property is maintained. Solving the profit maximization problem explicitly for link $(u,v)$ we have that these modified tolls are a cap equilibrium if and only if $\varepsilon \leq 1/6$, and therefore the minimum users' cost among great tolls is $21/9 + 5/6$. □

The mathematical program for obtaining great tolls that minimize users' costs while keeping $\boldsymbol{x}^*$ as a Wardrop equilibrium flow is (BGT stands for *Best Great Tolls*):

$$\text{(BGT)} \begin{cases} \min & \sum_{e\in E}[\ell_e(x_e^*) + t_e]x_e^* \\ v_u^k - v_v^k + t_e & = & -\ell_e(x_e^*) & \forall k,\ e=(u,v): x_e^{*k} > 0 \\ v_u^k - v_v^k + t_e & \geq & -\ell_e(x_e^*) & \forall k,\ e=(u,v): x_e^{*k} = 0 \\ \boldsymbol{t} & & \text{is a cap equilibrium} \\ \boldsymbol{t} & \geq & 0, \end{cases}$$

The program, in variables $(\boldsymbol{t}, \boldsymbol{v})$, defines a potential $v^k$ for each commodity $k$, in such a way that any flow-carrying path is indeed a shortest path. A careful reader may also notice that we included in the objective the constant term $\sum_e \ell_e(x_e^*)x_e^*$, corresponding to the total delay experienced by users. This is of course part of the cost experienced by users, but it also turns out to be important in order to obtain some of the approximation bounds we are aiming to prove.

In the formulation above, the problem (BGT) does not have any amenable structure for efficient methods, particularly due to the cap equilibrium constraint. However, by Theorem 4.4, optimal tolls upper bounded by the marginal tolls are always a cap equilibrium, thus within this restricted set of tolls we can write the following LP, that encodes all possible great set of tolls upper bounded by marginals (BMT stands for *Below Marginal Tolls*):

$$\text{(BMT)} \begin{cases} \min & \sum_{e\in E}[\ell_e(x_e^*) + t_e]x_e^* \\ v_u^k - v_v^k + t_e & = & -\ell_e(x_e^*) & \forall k,\ e=(u,v): x_e^{*k} > 0 \\ v_u^k - v_v^k + t_e & \geq & -\ell_e(x_e^*) & \forall k,\ e=(u,v): x_e^{*k} = 0 \\ t_e & \leq & \hat{t}_e & \forall e \in E \\ t_e & \geq & 0 & \forall e \in E. \end{cases}$$

Since by Example 5.1 the value of (BMT) does not necessarily coincide with the value of (BGT), the next natural question to ask is how efficient program (BMT) can be. In order to answer this question, we can use as benchmark the value of *Minimum Payment Tolls*: These are the optimal tolls that minimize the total payments. These tolls can be computed by a similar linear program, where we only drop the cap equilibrium constraints (MPT stands for *Minimum Payment Tolls*):

$$\text{(MPT)} \begin{cases} \min & \sum_{e\in E}[\ell_e(x_e^*) + t_e]x_e^* \\ v_u^k - v_v^k + t_e & = & -\ell_e(x_e^*) & \forall k, e=(u,v): x_e^{*k} > 0 \\ v_u^k - v_v^k + t_e & \geq & -\ell_e(x_e^*) & \forall k, e=(u,v): x_e^{*k} = 0 \\ t_e & \geq & 0 & \forall e \in E. \end{cases}$$

In what follows, $\bar{\boldsymbol{t}}$ and $\boldsymbol{t}^*$ are optimal solutions of (BMT) and (MPT), respectively.

### 5.1 Functional Approximation Bound on Cost

We consider an approximation bound based on properties of the latency functions.

THEOREM 5.2. *Suppose all latency functions $\ell$ in the profit maximization game satisfy* $\sup_{x\geq 0} \frac{x\ell'(x)}{\ell(x)} \leq \gamma$, *then* val(BMT) $\leq (\gamma+1)$ val(MPT).

PROOF. By the assumption on latency functions,

$$\begin{aligned} \text{val(BMT)} &= \sum_e [\ell_e(x_e^*) + \bar{t}_e]x_e^* \leq \sum_e [\ell_e(x_e^*) + x_e^*\ell_e'(x_e^*)]x_e^* \\ &\leq \sum_e (1+\gamma)\ell_e(x_e^*)x_e^* \leq (\gamma+1)\,\text{val(MPT)}, \end{aligned}$$

proving the result. □

For polynomial functions with nonnegative coefficients and degree at most $d$ it is known that one can choose $\gamma = d$ above, which gives the following corollary:

Corollary 5.3. *For polynomial latency functions of degree at most d and nonnegative coefficients,* val(BMT)$\leq (d+1)$ val(MPT).

The proposed approximation bound looks rather weak. However, this bound is tight even for single-commodity networks.

### 5.2 Topological Approximation Bound on Cost

As shown above, having a Braess type subnetwork can lead to a gap between the linear programs (BMT) and (MPT), and moreover a *generalized Braess subnetwork* will further worsen this gap. Notice however that these examples in order to achieve large gaps need both a complex network structure and large degree latencies. Is it possible that, e.g., simple networks with high-degree latencies still achieve a small gap? Fortunately, the answer is yes.

In this subsection we will restrict ourselves to single-commodity instances and will assume that, without loss of generality, they have unit demand. With this, the (BMT) linear program simplifies substantially,

$$\text{(BMT)}\quad \begin{cases} \min & \sum_{e\in E}[\ell_e(x_e^*)+t_e]x_e^* \\ v_u - v_v + t_e & = & -\ell_e(x_e^*) & \forall e=(u,v): x_e^*>0 \\ v_u - v_v + t_e & \geq & -\ell_e(x_e^*) & \forall e=(u,v): x_e^*=0 \\ t_e & \leq & \hat{t}_e & \forall e \in E \\ t_e & \geq & 0 & \forall e\in E. \end{cases}$$

We start with a structural lemma, which allows us to upper bound the value of (BMT). This is naturally important in order to derive an approximation bound. We will first need some definitions. Consider a directed network $G$ and the undirected network $G^u$ that comes from $G$ if we drop the directions of its links. Any path in $G^u$ is called an undirected path in $G$. For an undirected path $P$, the links that are traversed in their actual direction are called *forward* links, denoted by $P^+$, and the ones traversed in their reversed direction are called *backward* links, denoted by $P^-$. Finally, an undirected path has $J$ alternations if, when traversing it, there are exactly $J$ times where a forward link is followed by a backward link.[6]

Lemma 5.4. *There exists an undirected $o-d$ path $P$ such that the first and the last link of $P$ belong in $P^+$, all $e \in P^+$ are flow carrying, and the value of* (BMT) *is equal to*

$$\sum_{e\in P^+}\ell_e(x_e^*) - \sum_{e\in P^-}[\ell_e(x_e^*)+\hat{t}_e].$$

We make the following assumption on the instance: there exists a $J\geq 0$ such that any simple $o-d$ undirected path has at most $J$ alternations. The smallest constant $J$ satisfying this condition will be called the *alternation number*, and our approximation bound will only depend on this number.

Theorem 5.5. *Consider a single-commodity and unit demand instance of the network pricing game whose underlying network has alternation number $J$. We have,* val(BMT) $\leq (J+1)\cdot$ val(MPT).

Proof. By Lemma 5.4, we have val(BMT)$= \sum_{e\in P_+}\ell_e(x_e^*) - \sum_{e\in P_-}[\ell_e(x_e^*)+\hat{t}_e]$. Since the alternation number of $G$ is $J$, we can decompose $P$ in at most $J$ segments of consecutive forward and backward links, $P = A_1 - B_1 - A_2 - B_2 - \ldots - B_J - A_{J+1}$, from which val(BMT)$\leq \sum_{j=1}^{J+1}\left[\sum_{e\in A_j}\ell_e(x_e^*)\right]$. Let now $(\boldsymbol{t}^*, \boldsymbol{v}^*)$ be an optimal solution for (MPT); since all links $e\in A_j, j=1,\ldots,J+1$ are flow

[6]For such alternating paths, see also, e.g., [23, 25, 28]

carrying, for each $j = 1, \ldots, J+1$, we have $\sum_{e \in A_j} \ell_e(x_e^*) \leq v_d^* - v_o^*$. Combining the inequalities, we obtain val(BMT)$\leq \sum_{j=1}^{J+1} \left[\sum_{e \in A_j} \ell_e(x_e^*)\right] \leq (J+1)[v_d^* - v_o^*] = (J+1)\cdot$ val(MPT). □

Since $J = 0$ for series-parallel networks, we get the following corollary, which implies that our approach is optimal in this case.

Corollary 5.6. *For instances on series-parallel networks, $\bar{t}$ minimizes the users' cost and payments.*

The bound obtained in Theorem 5.5 is tight for single-commodity instances and it does not extend to multi-commodity instances, or even single-source multi-commodity instances.

## 6 ELASTIC DEMAND

In this section, we assume that the total amount of traffic for each $o^k - d^k$ pair is dependent on the costs the traffic experiences; the higher the costs, the lower the traffic. We analyze the elastic traffic demand model as introduced by Beckmann et al. [4] and later used for network pricing games by Hayrapetyan et al. [21] and Ozdaglar [29]. We model elastic demand with a *utility function* $u^k : [0, r^k] \to \mathbb{R}_+$ for each $k \in K$, where $u^k(x)$ captures the reservation value for travel of the particle of the demand (i.e., the infinitesimally small user) at level $x$. We assume that $u^k(\cdot)$ is nonincreasing and continuous for each $k \in K$, so that, in a sense, the users are ordered decreasingly according to their utility for traveling. Let $u = (u^k)_{k \in K}$ be the vector of all utility functions. Define the aggregate utility function $U^k : [0, r^k] \to \mathbb{R}_+$ by $U^k(x) = \int_0^x u^k(y)\, dy$. By definition, this function is nondecreasing, concave and continuously differentiable.

A *flow* for commodity $k$ is a nonnegative vector $\boldsymbol{x}^k = (x_P^k)_{P \in \mathcal{P}^k}$ such that $\sum_{P \in \mathcal{P}^k} x_P^k \leq r^k$. For each commodity $k \in K$, let $r_x^k = \sum_{P \in \mathcal{P}^k} x_P^k$ be the amount of flow that is routed on the network by $\boldsymbol{x}^k$. A *flow* $\boldsymbol{x}$ is a vector $(\boldsymbol{x}^k)_{k \in K}$, where each $\boldsymbol{x}^k$ is a flow for commodity $k$.

A flow $\boldsymbol{x}$ is a *Wardrop equilibrium* if all the routed traffic goes through shortest paths for the respective commodity, the utility for each traveling user is at least equal to the common shortest path cost of her commodity, and the utility of each user not traveling is at most equal to the common shortest path cost of her commodity. Mathematically, for every $k$, for every path $P \in \mathcal{P}^k$ with $x_P^k > 0$, and every path $P' \in \mathcal{P}^k$, $\sum_{e \in P}[\ell_e(x_e) + t_e] \leq \sum_{e \in P'}[\ell_e(x_e) + t_e]$ and $\sum_{e \in P}[\ell_e(x_e) + t_e] \leq u^k(r_x^k)$ with $r_x^k = r^k$ if $\sum_{e \in P}[\ell_e(x_e) + t_e] < u^k(r_x^k)$.

For any toll vector $\boldsymbol{t} \geq 0$, a Wardrop equilibrium exists, and moreover can be found by solving the following maximization problem [4]:

$$\boldsymbol{x}(\boldsymbol{t}) \triangleq \arg \max_{\boldsymbol{x} \geq 0 \text{ flow}} \left\{ \sum_{k \in K} U^k(r_x^k) - \sum_{e \in E} \int_0^{x_e} (\ell_e(x) + t_e)\, dx \right\}. \tag{6}$$

Assuming that each $\ell_e(x_e)$ is strictly increasing for each $e \in E$, the link-wise description of the Wardrop equilibrium is unique, and therefore $(x_e(\boldsymbol{t}))_{e \in E}$ is a well-defined function, which is moreover continuous by Berge's theorem [5].

Given flow $\boldsymbol{x}$ and toll vector $\boldsymbol{t}$, define the *total users' cost* by $C(\boldsymbol{x}, \boldsymbol{t}) = \sum_{e \in E}[\ell_e(x_e) + t_e]x_e$ and the *consumer surplus* by

$$CS(\boldsymbol{x}, \boldsymbol{t}, u) = \sum_{k \in K} U^k(r_x^k) - C(\boldsymbol{x}, \boldsymbol{t}).$$

We define the *social welfare* by

$$SW(\boldsymbol{x}, u) = \sum_{k \in K} U^k(r_x^k) - \sum_{e \in E} \ell_e(x_e) \cdot x_e.$$

Notice that tolls do not appear in the social welfare, as they are transfers from users to toll operators.

An *optimal flow* $\boldsymbol{x}^*(u)$ is a flow that maximizes the social welfare w.r.t. to $u$. Similarly to the fixed demand model, we have the classical result by Beckmann et al. [4] showing that a flow $\boldsymbol{x}^*(u)$ is an optimal flow if and only if $\boldsymbol{x}^*(u) = \boldsymbol{x}(\hat{\boldsymbol{t}}(u))$, where $\hat{t}_e(u) = x_e^*(u)\ell_e'(x_e^*(u))$. Also, for every network and demand vector there exist utility functions such that all users travel under the optimal solution, i.e. $r^k_{x^*(u)} = r^k$ for each $k \in K$. Observe that, in this case, this optimal flow is the same optimal flow as defined in Section 2. For a given instance, we denote this particular optimal flow by $\boldsymbol{x}^*$.

### 6.1 Regulated Network Pricing Game

The elastic traffic demand model generalizes the fixed demand one. Fortunately, the main result of Section 4, i.e., Theorem 4.4, can be generalized as well.

THEOREM 6.1. *Let $\bar{\boldsymbol{t}} \leq \hat{\boldsymbol{t}}(u)$ be an optimal toll vector. For the profit maximization problem with caps $\bar{\boldsymbol{t}}$, there exists a unique Nash equilibrium, given by $\bar{\boldsymbol{t}}$, which, moreover, is a strong Nash equilibrium.*

For a proof, one has first to prove an analogue of Lemma 4.2. That provided, an analogue of Lemma 4.3 follows directly and the same proof as the one for Theorem 4.4 can be applied.

### 6.2 Maximizing Consumer Surplus

We now consider the question of which great tolls vector maximizes the consumer surplus. The main result in this subsection, Theorem 6.5, only applies to single-source, single-sink networks, and thus we will restrict ourselves to these instances.

By Theorem 6.1, optimal tolls upper bounded by the marginal tolls are always a cap equilibrium, thus within this restricted set of tolls we can write the following LP, that encodes all possible great set of tolls upper bounded by marginals:

$$(\text{BMT2}) \begin{cases} \max \quad CS(\boldsymbol{x}^*(u), \boldsymbol{t}, u) & & & \\ \quad v_v - v_w + t_e & = & -\ell_e(x_e^*(u)) & \forall e = (v,w) : x_e^*(u) > 0 \\ \quad v_v - v_w + t_e & \geq & -\ell_e(x_e^*(u)) & \forall e = (v,w) : x_e^*(u) = 0 \\ \quad v_t - v_s & \leq & u(r_{x^*(u)}) & \text{where the inequality is tight if } r_{x^*(u)} < r \\ \quad t_e & \leq & \hat{t}_e(u) & \forall e \in E \\ \quad t_e & \geq & 0 & \forall e \in E. \end{cases}$$

A natural question to ask is how efficient our program (BMT2) can be. In order to answer this question, we can use as benchmark the value of Minimum Payment Tolls: these are the optimal tolls that minimize the total payments. These tolls can be computed by a similar linear program, where we only drop the cap equilibrium constraints:

$$(\text{MPT2}) \begin{cases} \max \quad CS(\boldsymbol{x}^*(u), \boldsymbol{t}, u) & & & \\ \quad v_v - v_w + t_e & = & -\ell_e(x_e^*(u)) & \forall e = (v,w) : x_e^*(u) > 0 \\ \quad v_v - v_w + t_e & \geq & -\ell_e(x_e^*(u)) & \forall e = (v,w) : x_e^*(u) = 0 \\ \quad v_t - v_s & \leq & u(r_{x^*(u)}) & \text{where the inequality is tight if } r_{x^*(u)} < r \\ \quad t_e & \geq & 0 & \forall e \in E. \end{cases}$$

In what follows, $\boldsymbol{t}^B$ and $\boldsymbol{t}^M$ are toll vectors that belong to some optimal solutions of (BMT2) and (MPT2), respectively. The following example shows that when all users travel, the objective of the maximization problem (BMT2) can be arbitrary higher than the objective of (MPT2).

*Example 6.2.* Consider the Braess network of Figure 4 with unit demand and $u(x) = 2$ for $x \in [0, 1]$.

An optimal flow in this case is to split the demand of one by half among the upper and lower paths; in particular, no flow traverses the middle $uv$ link. This way, marginal tolls are given by

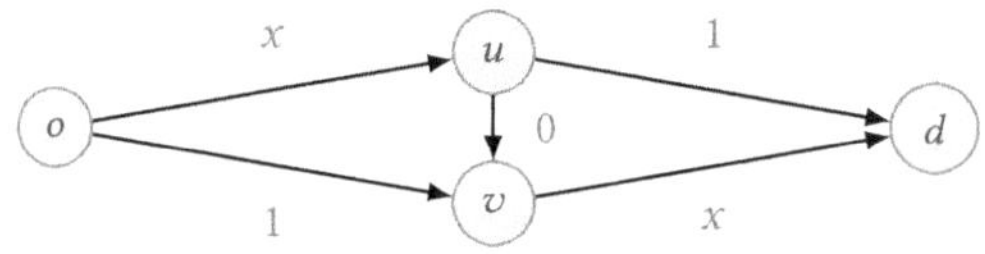


Fig. 4. The network of Example 6.2.

$(\hat{t}_{ou}, \hat{t}_{uv}, \hat{t}_{vd}) = (1/2, 0, 1/2)$, and notice this is the only feasible solution for (BMT2), achieving a value of $2 - 2 = 0$. On the other hand, it is easy to see that the LP solution for (MPT2) just needs to assign a sufficiently large value for $t_{uv}$ (more precisely, $t_{uv} \geq 1/2$) and the rest of the tolls can be zero, therefore the value of (MPT2) is $2 - 3/2 = 1/2$. □

The main result of this subsection is a comparison in the spirit of the bicriteria bound of Roughgarden and Tardos [34]: by how much should we decrease the utility function in order to induce the same level of consumer surplus when comparing (BMT2) to (MPT2). A corollary of the result is that multiplying the utility function by 1/2 is sufficient. In other words, the consumers' surplus under $\boldsymbol{t}^B$ is at least as much as the optimal surplus if each of them had half the valuation.

First we need two lemmas:

Lemma 6.3. *If $r_{x^*(u)} < r$, then $CS(\boldsymbol{x}^*(u), \boldsymbol{t}, u) = U(r_{x^*(u)}) - r_{x^*(u)} \cdot u(r_{x^*(u)})$ for all optimal $\boldsymbol{t}$.*

Lemma 6.4. *Let $\tilde{u}$ and $u$ be utility functions so that $\tilde{u}(x) = \alpha \cdot u(x)$, where $0 < \alpha \leq 1$. Then*

(i) $r_{x^*(u)} \geq r_{x^*(\tilde{u})}$,
(ii) $CS(\boldsymbol{x}^*(u), \boldsymbol{t}^B, u) \geq CS(\boldsymbol{x}^*(\tilde{u}), \boldsymbol{t}^B, \tilde{u})$,
(iii) $CS(\boldsymbol{x}^*(u), \boldsymbol{t}^M, u) \geq CS(\boldsymbol{x}^*(\tilde{u}), \boldsymbol{t}^M, \tilde{u})$.

We are now ready for our main result.

Theorem 6.5. *Let $C(\boldsymbol{x}^*, \boldsymbol{t}^B) \leq \beta \cdot C(\boldsymbol{x}^*, \boldsymbol{t}^M)$ for some $\beta \in [1, \infty)$.*[7] *Then*

$$CS(\boldsymbol{x}^*(u), \boldsymbol{t}^B, u) \geq CS(\boldsymbol{x}^*(\tilde{u}), \boldsymbol{t}^M, \tilde{u}),$$

*where $\tilde{u}(x) = \frac{\beta}{2\beta-1} \cdot u(x)$.*

Proof. Recall, $x^*$ is the optimal flow when all $r$ units are being routed. By the optimal flow characterization of Beckmann et al. [4], we have that $r_{x^*(u)} < r$ for all $u$ with $C(\boldsymbol{x}^*, \hat{\boldsymbol{t}}) > r \cdot u(r)$, and $r_{x^*(u)} = r$ for all $u$ with $C(\boldsymbol{x}^*, \hat{\boldsymbol{t}}) \leq r \cdot u(r)$.

We consider the following three cases: (1) $u(r) < C(\boldsymbol{x}^*, \hat{\boldsymbol{t}})/r$, (2) $C(\boldsymbol{x}^*, \hat{\boldsymbol{t}})/r \leq u(r) < \frac{2\beta-1}{\beta} \cdot C(\boldsymbol{x}^*, \hat{\boldsymbol{t}})/r$ and (3) $u(r) \geq \frac{2\beta-1}{\beta} \cdot C(\boldsymbol{x}^*, \hat{\boldsymbol{t}})/r$.

Case (1). Assume that $u(r) < C(\boldsymbol{x}^*, \hat{\boldsymbol{t}})/r$. Then $r_{x^*(u)} < r$ and thus

$$CS(\boldsymbol{x}^*(u), \boldsymbol{t}^B, u) = CS(\boldsymbol{x}^*(u), \boldsymbol{t}^M, u) \geq CS(\boldsymbol{x}^*(\tilde{u}), \boldsymbol{t}^M, \tilde{u}),$$

where the equality follows by Lemma 6.3 and the inequality by Lemma 6.4.

Case (2). Assume that $C(\boldsymbol{x}^*, \hat{\boldsymbol{t}})/r \leq u(r) < \frac{2\beta-1}{\beta} \cdot C(\boldsymbol{x}^*, \hat{\boldsymbol{t}})/r$. Then $r_{x^*(u)} = r$ and since $\tilde{u}(r) = \frac{\beta}{2\beta-1} \cdot u(r) < C(\boldsymbol{x}^*, \hat{\boldsymbol{t}})/r$, we have $r_{x^*(\tilde{u})} < r$. Thus

$$CS(\boldsymbol{x}^*(u), \boldsymbol{t}^B, u) \geq CS(\boldsymbol{x}^*(\tilde{u}), \boldsymbol{t}^B, \tilde{u}) = CS(\boldsymbol{x}^*(\tilde{u}), \boldsymbol{t}^M, \tilde{u}),$$

[7] Notice that, first, there is always such a $\beta$, since if all the demand is routed, the feasible space of MPT2 is at least as big as that of BMT2, while if the demand is partially routed we assume $\boldsymbol{t}^B = \boldsymbol{t}^M$, and, second, if $r_{x^*(u)} = r$, then $\boldsymbol{t}^B = \boldsymbol{t}^{BMT}$ and $\boldsymbol{t}^M = \boldsymbol{t}^{MPT}$, and so, for particular values of $\beta$, one can use Theorem 5.2 and Theorem 5.5.

where the inequality follows by Lemma 6.4 and the equality by Lemma 6.3.

Case (3). Assume that $u(r) \geq \frac{2\beta-1}{\beta} \cdot C(\boldsymbol{x}^*, \hat{\boldsymbol{t}})/r$. Then $r_{x^*(u)} = r$ and since $\tilde{u}(r) = \frac{\beta}{2\beta-1} \cdot u(r) \geq C(\boldsymbol{x}^*, \hat{\boldsymbol{t}})/r$, we have $r_{x^*(\tilde{u})} = r$. Thus,

$$\begin{aligned} C(\boldsymbol{x}^*, \boldsymbol{t}^B) - C(\boldsymbol{x}^*, \boldsymbol{t}^M) &\leq \left(1 - \frac{1}{\beta}\right) \cdot C(\boldsymbol{x}^*, \boldsymbol{t}^B) \\ &\leq \left(1 - \frac{1}{\beta}\right) \cdot C(\boldsymbol{x}^*, \hat{\boldsymbol{t}}) \\ &\leq r \cdot \frac{\beta - 1}{2\beta - 1} \cdot u(r) - \int_0^r u(x)dx + \int_0^r u(x)dx \\ &\leq - \int_0^r \tilde{u}(x)dx + \int_0^r u(x)dx = U(r) - \tilde{U}(r), \end{aligned}$$

where the first inequality follows from $C(\boldsymbol{x}^*, \boldsymbol{t}^B) \leq \beta \cdot C(\boldsymbol{x}^*, \boldsymbol{t}^M)$, which is true by assumption, the second from $C(\boldsymbol{x}^*, \boldsymbol{t}^B) \leq C(\boldsymbol{x}^*, \hat{\boldsymbol{t}})$, the third from $\frac{\beta}{2\beta-1} \cdot u(r) \geq C(\boldsymbol{x}^*, \hat{\boldsymbol{t}})/r$, and the fourth from $r \cdot u(r) \leq \int_0^r u(x)dx$ and the definition of $\tilde{u}(x)$. Rearranging terms yields

$$CS(\boldsymbol{x}^*(u), \boldsymbol{t}^B, u) = U(r) - C(\boldsymbol{x}^*, \boldsymbol{t}^B) \geq \tilde{U}(r) - C(\boldsymbol{x}^*, \boldsymbol{t}^M) = CS(\boldsymbol{x}^*(\tilde{u}), \boldsymbol{t}^M, \tilde{u}),$$

as needed. □

Remark 6.6. *Theorem 6.5 cannot be extended to multicommodity networks. For an example, consider the network of Figure 5. Commodities $o - d_1$, $o - d_2$ have a maximum demand of 1. If $u^1(x) = 8$ for $x \in [0, 1]$ and $u^2(x) = 4$ for $x \in [0, 1]$, then the optimal flow is $3/4$ for commodity 1 and 1 for commodity 2. The unique optimal toll vector is $(3/4, 7/4)$; inducing a consumer surplus of $1/2$.*

*If $u^1(x) = 4$ for $x \in [0, 1]$ and $u^2(x) = 2$ for $x \in [0, 1]$, then the optimal flow is 0 for commodity 1 and 1 for commodity 2. The unique optimal toll vector is $(0, 0)$; inducing a consumer surplus of 1.*

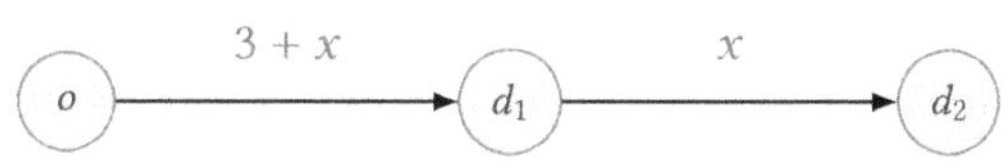


Fig. 5. The network of Remark 6.6.

## REFERENCES


[1] D. Acemoglu and A. Ozdaglar. 2007. Competition and Efficiency in Congested Markets. *Mathematics of Operations Research* 32, 1 (2007), 1–31.

[2] D. Acemoglu and A. Ozdaglar. 2007. Competition in parallel-serial networks. *IEEE Journal on selected areas in communications* 25, 6 (2007), 1180–1192.

[3] E. Anshelevich and S. Sekar. 2015. Price Competition in Networked Markets: How Do Monopolies Impact Social Welfare. In *WINE 2015, Amsterdam, The Netherlands, December 9-12, 2015, Proceedings.* 16–30.

[4] M. Beckmann, C. McGuire, and C. Winsten. 1956. *Studies in the economics of transportation.* Yale Univ. Press.

[5] C. Berge. 1963. *Topological Spaces: Including a Treatment of Multi-valued Functions, Vector Spaces, and Convexity.* Dover Publications.

[6] V. Bonifaci, M. Salek, and G. Schäfer. 2011. Efficiency of Restricted Tolls in Non-atomic Network Routing Games. In *SAGT 2011, Amalfi, Italy, October 17-19, 2011, Proceedings.* 302–313.

[7] P. Briest, M. Hoefer, and P. Krysta. 2012. Stackelberg Network Pricing Games. *Algorithmica* 62, 3-4 (2012).

[8] I. Caragiannis, X. Chatzigeorgiou, P. Kanellopoulos, G.A. Krimpas, N. Protopapas, and A. Voudouris. 2017. Efficiency and Complexity of Price Competition Among Single-Product Vendors. *Artificial Intelligence* 248 (2017), 9–25.

[9] L. Castelli, M. Labb, and A. Violin. 2017. Network pricing problem with unit toll. *Networks* 69, 1 (2017), 83–93.

[10] S. Chawla and F. Niu. 2009. The Price of Anarchy in Bertrand Games. In *EC '09, Stanford, CA, USA, July 6-10, 2009, Proceedings.* ACM, New York, NY, USA, 305–314.

[11] S. Chawla, F. Niu, and T. Roughgarden. 2008. Bertrand competition in networks. In *SAGT 2008, Paderborn, Germany, April/May, 2008, Proceedings.* 70–82.

[12] R. Cole, Y. Dodis, and T. Roughgarden. 2003. Pricing network edges for heterogeneous selfish users. In *STOC '03, San Diego, CA, USA, June 9-11, 2003, Proceedings*, Vol. 3. 444–467.

[13] J.R. Correa and N.E. Stier-Moses. 2011. Wardrop equilibria. *Wiley encyclopedia of op. research and man. science* (2011).

[14] R. Dial. 1999. Minimal-revenue congestion pricing part I: A fast algorithm for the single-origin case. *Transportation Research Part B: Methodological* 33, 3 (1999), 189 – 202.

[15] H. Dixon. 2001. *Surfing Economics : Essays for the Inquiring Economist.* Palgrave Macmillan.

[16] A. Epstein, M. Feldman, and Y. Mansour. 2009. Efficient graph topologies in network routing games. *Games and Economic Behavior* 66, 1 (2009), 115 – 125.

[17] L. Fleischer. 2005. Linear Tolls Suffice: New Bounds and Algorithms for Tolls in Single Source Networks. *Theoretical Computer Science* 348 (2005), 217–225.

[18] D. Fotakis, D. Kalimeris, and T. Lianeas. 2015. Improving Selfish Routing for Risk-Averse Players. In *WINE 2015, Amsterdam, The Netherlands, December 9-12, 2015, Proceedings.* 328–342.

[19] A. Gonzalez. 2016. Controversias por reducciones en la demanda en las concesiones de carreteras en Chile. *Revista de Derecho Económico* 76 (2016).

[20] T. Harks, M. Schröder, and D. Vermeulen. 2018. Toll Caps in Privatized Road Networks. (2018). arXiv preprint arXiv:1802.10514.

[21] A. Hayrapetyan, E. Tardos, and T. Wexler. 2007. A network pricing game for selfish traffic. *Distributed Computing* 19, 4 (2007), 255–266.

[22] T. Jelinek, M. Klaas, and G. Schäfer. 2014. Computing Optimal Tolls with Arc Restrictions and Heterogeneous Players. In *STACS 2014, Lyon, France, March 5-8, 2014, Proceedings.*

[23] P. Kleer and G. Schäfer. 2016. The Impact of Worst-Case Deviations in Non-Atomic Network Routing Games. In *SAGT 2016, Liverpool, UK, September 19-21, 2016, Proceedings.* 129–140.

[24] A. Kuiteing, P. Marcotte, and G. Savard. 2016. Network Pricing of Congestion-Free Networks: The Elastic and Linear Demand Case. *Transportation Science* 51, 3 (2016), 791–806.

[25] H. Lin, T. Roughgarden, E. Tardos, and A. Walkover. 2011. Stronger Bounds on Braess's Paradox and the Maximum Latency of Selfish Routing. *SIAM Journal on Discrete Mathematics* 25, 4 (2011), 1667–1686.

[26] J. Musacchio. 2009. The Price of Anarchy in Parallel-Serial Competition with Elastic Demand. (2009). Technical Report No. UCSC-SOE-09-20.

[27] J. Musacchio and S. Wu. 2007. The Price of Anarchy in a Network Pricing Game. In *Allerton Conference, Monticello, IL, USA, September 26-28, 2007, Proceedings.*

[28] E. Nikolova and N. Stier-Moses. 2015. The Burden of Risk Aversion in Mean-Risk Selfish Routing. In *EC '15, Portland, OR, USA, June 15-19, 2015, Proceedings.* 489–506.

[29] A. Ozdaglar. 2008. Price Competition with Elastic Traffic. *Networks* 52, 3 (2008), 141–155.

[30] A. Ozdaglar and R. Srikant. 2007. Incentives and pricing in communication networks. In *Algorithmic Game Theory.* Cambridge Press, 571–591.

[31] C. Papadimitriou and G. Valiant. 2010. A New Look at Selfish Routing. In *ICS 2010, Beijing, China, January 5-7, 2010, Proceedings.* 178–187.

[32] A. Pigou. 1920. *The economics of welfare.* Macmillan.

[33] T. Roughgarden. 2005. *Selfish Routing and the Price of Anarchy.* MIT press.

[34] T. Roughgarden and E. Tardos. 2002. How bad is selfish routing? *J. ACM* 49, 2 (2002), 236–259.

# Polynomial Time Equilibria in Bottleneck Congestion Games

COSTAS BUSCH, Louisiana State University, USA
RAJGOPAL KANNAN, US Army Research Lab-West, USA

We consider bottleneck congestion games in an arbitrary graph $G$ where player strategies are flows in $G$. The player's objective is to select a flow that minimizes the maximum load on any edge, that is, minimize the bottleneck congestion. We consider splittable and unsplittable games with pure strategies. It has been an open problem for many years to determine whether it is possible to compute in polynomial time Nash equilibriums for bottleneck congestion games in arbitrary graphs. For splittable games we provide a polynomial time algorithm to compute a Nash equilibrium which is also a global optimum. The unsplittable game problem is known to be PLS-complete, and so we focus on approximate Nash equilibria where players are approximately stable. For uniform player demands we give an algorithm to compute a $O(\log m)$-approximate unsplittable equilibrium in polynomial time, where $m$ is the number of edges. For non-uniform player demands we give an algorithm to compute a $O(\zeta \log(\zeta m))$-approximate unsplittable equilibrium in polynomial time, where $\zeta = O(1 + \log(d_{\max}/d_{\min}))$ and $d_{\max}$, $d_{\min}$ are the respective maximum and minimum player demands. To our knowledge, these are the first general results for efficiently computing equilibria of pure bottleneck congestion games in arbitrary graphs, both for the splittable and unsplittable cases.

CCS Concepts: • **Theory of computation → Algorithmic game theory**; **Exact and approximate computation of equilibria**; **Network games**;

Additional Key Words and Phrases: Nash equilibrium; bottleneck congestion; equilibrium computation; polynomial time; arbitrary graphs

## 1 INTRODUCTION

We consider non-cooperative congestion games for $n$ players on a graph $G$ with $m$ edges. Each player $i$ has a positive demand $d_i$ to be sent from a source to a destination node in $G$. We consider both the splittable case, where a player sends its demand as a splittable flow on available paths in $G$, and the unsplittable case, where a player assigns all its demand along a single path in $G$. Congestion occurs when multiple players use the same edge in their flow assignments. The congestion of an edge corresponds to the total flow that goes through it.

We consider *bottleneck congestion games* where the utility cost of a player is the maximum congestion (*bottleneck congestion*) experienced in any of the edges in its chosen flow assignment. Players aim to minimize their utility cost, that is, obtain smaller bottleneck congestion. In the splittable game, the strategy set of a player consists of all possible flow assignments (splittable or unsplittable) in $G$. In the unsplittable game, the strategy set of a player consists of all possible unsplittable flow assignments (i.e. all possible paths from source to destination). Here, we consider only pure strategies, where only one strategy is picked by the player. A game state consists of the flow assignments of all players. The *social cost* of a state is the maximum bottleneck congestion

Authors' addresses: Costas Busch, Louisiana State University, Division of Computer Science & Engineering, 3272E Patrick F. Taylor Hall, Baton Rouge, LA, 70803, USA, busch@csc.lsu.edu; Rajgopal Kannan, US Army Research Lab-West, Los Angeles, CA, 90094, USA, rajgopal.kannan.civ@mail.mil.


*ACM EC'18, June 18–22, 2018, Ithaca, NY, USA.* ACM ISBN 978-1-4503-5829-3/18/06...$15.00
https://doi.org/10.1145/3219166.3219221

in any edge. A state is a Nash equilibrium if each player is *stable*, that is, there is no alternative strategy for the player with smaller utility cost.

Bottleneck congestion games are important in networks, since bottleneck edges are network hot-spots with the possibility to partition the network and expose it to malicious attacks [1]. Bottleneck congestion games are also important in packet and machine scheduling problems, since the bottleneck congestion is a dominant factor in the schedule time performance [7, 12, 13, 16, 17, 23].

## 1.1 Contributions

We give polynomial time algorithms to compute equilibria for bottleneck games. We first consider the case of splittable games where we provide an algorithm that computes a Nash equilibrium in polynomial time. The algorithm is based on repeatedly applying a LP formulation to compute a global optimum. It identifies a set of edges as a *cut* for a set of players, where these players are found to be stable on the cut. Then the cut edges are removed and the respective players are replaced with a set of "constant-players" that send their demand directly along a single edge of the cut. The process repeats for the remaining players and edges of the graph until either all edges or players are depleted. The resulting state is stable for all players, and it is also globally optimal.

We then turn to unsplittable games (atomic games). Harks *et al.* [9] observe that computing pure equilibriums in unsplittable bottleneck congestion games is a PLS-complete problem. Hence, we consider approximate Nash equilibria. We say that a player is $\alpha$-stable if it cannot improve its utility cost by more than a factor of $\alpha$. In an $\alpha$-approximate Nash equilibrium all players are $\alpha$-stable.

For unsplittable games, we first present an algorithm that computes an equilibrium for uniform demands where all players have unit demands. The idea of the algorithm is to first compute the Nash equilibrium of the respective splittable game and convert it to an approximate unsplittable equilibrium using randomized rounding. This gives an $O(\log m)$-approximate Nash equilibrium for the unsplittable game in polynomial time, where $m$ is the number of edges in $G$.

We observe that the algorithm for uniform demands may not be as efficient when applied for arbitrary (non-uniform) demands, since for some game instances that have big variation on the players' demands the resulting equilibrium may have a large approximation ratio. Therefore, for non-uniform demands we provide an alternative polynomial time algorithm with a better approximation ratio. The algorithm works in several phases where at each phase it computes an equilibrium for a residual splittable game which is converted to an unsplittable assignment. At each phase, a set of edges is identified as a cut, and the respective players on the cut convert their splittable assignments to unsplittable with randomized rounding. At the end of this process, the algorithm returns a $O(\zeta \log(\zeta m))$-approximate Nash equilibrium, where $\zeta = O(1 + \log(d_{\max}/d_{\min}))$ and $d_{\max}$, $d_{\min}$ are the respective maximum and minimum player demands.

## 1.2 Related Work

Banner and Orda [1] consider bottleneck congestion games, and provide a comprehensive analysis of the *Price of Anarchy* (*PoA*), the worst ratio of the social cost in an equilibrium to the optimal social cost. They study both splittable and unsplittable games. They show that *PoA* of splittable bottleneck games is unbounded. They also evaluate the computational complexity of achieving equilibrium flows in bottleneck games under sequential best-response strategies. They demonstrate the weakness of best-response strategies in splittable bottleneck games by showing examples in which players playing their best-responses in a given sequence take unbounded time to converge to an equilibrium flow.

With respect to computing efficiently bottleneck game equilibriums, Caragiannis *et al.* [5] give a polynomial time algorithm for computing Nash Equilibria for the special case where the network (graph) has the same single sink or source for all players (on the other hand, the algorithms we present here are not restricted to a single source or sink). Harks *et al.* [9] also provide efficient algorithms for special bottleneck games such as matroid games and single source games.

In the literature, congestion games have been extensively studied considering the typical aggregate congestion cost model, where the utility cost of a player relates to the sum of the congestions (instead of maximum) along all edges in its strategy [6, 15, 18, 20–22, 24]. Rosenthal [18] proves that congestion games have always pure Nash equilibria. Computing pure Nash equilibria in this congestion model is a PLS-complete problem as well. For such aggregate utility costs it is already known how to obtain $O(1)$-approximate Nash equilibriums in polynomial time [4]. However, prior to the work that we present here the same question was open for general bottleneck congestion games.

Most of the literature in algorithmic game theory is focused on bounding the price of anarchy for the aggregate cost model. The notion of price of anarchy (or coordination ratio) was introduced by Koutsoupias and Papadimitriou [11] in the context of the *parallel link networks* model for which they provide the bound on price of anarchy $PoA = 3/2$. Roughgarden and Tardos [21] provide the first price of anarchy result for splittable flows in general networks in which they showed that $PoA \leq 4/3$. There exist more works on pure equilibria with atomic flow (unsplittable games) [3, 6, 14, 24], and with splittable flow [19–22], mostly focused on bounding the price of anarchy.

Price of anarchy has also been the main research subject in the literature for bottleneck games. Harks *et al.* [10] give a proof for the existence of strong Nash equilibria (which concern coalitions of players) for games with the lexicographic improvement property; such games include the model for bottleneck congestion games that we consider here. Keijzer *et al.* [8] study the price of anarchy in linear resource allocation games. Busch and Magdon-Ismail [3] consider atomic bottleneck congestion games in graphs where they prove that $\ell \leq PoA \leq c(\ell^2 + log^2|V|)$, where $\ell$ is the size of the largest edge-simple cycle in the network graph and $c$ is a constant. Bottleneck games with the $C + D$ (congestion + dilation) metric have also been studied with respect to price of anarchy [2].

### Roadmap

In Section 2 we give the model of the bottleneck congestion game. In Section 3 we prove the existence of equilibria for unsplittable games using improvement move dynamics (we do this for completeness). In Section 4 we give an algorithm to compute in polynomial time an equilibrium for a splittable game. In Section 5 we give an algorithm to compute in polynomial time an equilibrium for unsplittable games with uniform demands, while in Section 6 we give an algorithm for arbitrary demands. We finish with a conclusion and open problems in Section 7.

## 2 GAME MODEL

Consider a set of players $\mathcal{N} = \{1, \ldots, n\}$ and an undirected graph $G = (V, E)$. Without loss of generality, assume that $G$ is connected. Each player $i \in \mathcal{N}$ has a non-negative demand $d_i$ that needs to be routed from a source node $s_i \in V$ to a destination node $t_i \in V$. Suppose that we replace each undirected edge $e = (u, v) \in E$ with two directed edges $e' = (u, v)$ and $e'' = (v, u)$ on opposite directions on the adjacent nodes of $e$. For convenience, when we consider flows we will consider the converted graph and we will assume that $E$ corresponds to the directed set of edges in the converted graph and that $m = |E|$.

For a player $i$, flow $f_i$ is a distribution in the classic sense of the demand $d_i$ along $G$ from $s_i$ to $t_i$. If $f_i$ consists of a single path from $s_i$ to $t_i$ then we say that the flow is *unsplittable*; otherwise, it is *splittable*. For any edge $e \in E$ we denote by $f_{i,e}$ the assigned flow of player $i$ through $e$.

A flow $f$ on $G$ is a collection of players flows $f = (f_1, \ldots, f_n)$. We say that $F$ is unsplittable if $f_i$ is unsplittable for all players; otherwise, $F$ is splittable. For any edge $e \in G$, the *congestion* on $e$ is $f(e) = \sum_{i \in \mathcal{N}} f_{i,e}$.

*Bottleneck Games.* A *bottleneck congestion game* is a strategic game $(G, \mathcal{N}, \mathcal{D}, \mathcal{S})$ with graph $G = (V, E)$, players $N = \{1, \ldots, n\}$, demands $\mathcal{D} = \{d_1, \ldots, d_n\}$, while the strategy space of the game is $\mathcal{S} = \mathcal{S}_1 \times \cdots \times \mathcal{S}_n$, where $\mathcal{S}_i$ denotes the (pure) strategy set of player $i$.

In a *splittable game*, the strategy set $\mathcal{S}_i$ of each player $i \in \mathcal{N}$ consists of all possible flows on $G$ (unsplittable and splittable) for demand $d_i$, which includes all possible ways of splitting the demand along the paths from source $s_i$ to destination $t_i$. In an *unsplittable game*, the strategy set $\mathcal{S}_i$ of each player $i \in \mathcal{N}$ consists of all possible unsplittable flows for demand $d_i$, which is all possible paths from $s_i$ to $t_i$.

A *game state* $S \in \mathcal{S}$, corresponds to a flow $f_S = (f_1, \ldots, f_n) \in \mathcal{S}$ (oftentimes we will denote the state $S$ with the respective $f_S$). Let $E(f_i) = \{e : f_{i,e} > 0\}$ denote the set of edges used by player $i$ in $f_i$. In any game state $S \in \mathcal{S}$, each player $i \in \mathcal{N}$ has a *utility cost* $c_i(S) = \max_{e \in E(f_i)} f(e)$, which is equal to the maximum congestion on any edge in its flow. We also say that $c_i(S)$ is the *bottleneck congestion* of player $i$.

Player $i$ is *stable* (*locally optimal*) in state $S$ if $c_i(S) \leq c_i(S')$ for any state $S' \in \mathcal{S}$. An *improvement move* by a player $i$ is any change of its strategy leading from a state $S \in \mathcal{S}$ to a state $S' \in \mathcal{S}$, which improves the player cost, that is, $c_i(S') < c_i(S)$. A state $S$ is a *Nash Equilibrium* if every player is locally optimal; in other words, no improvement move is available to any player.

Given a game instance $I = (G, \mathcal{N}, \mathcal{D}, \mathcal{S})$, and any state $S \in \mathcal{S}$, we will consider a *social cost* (or *global cost*) function, denoted $C(S)$, which measures the state's impact to the global welfare. In bottleneck congestion games, $C(S) = \max_{i \in \mathcal{N}} c_i(S)$, that is, the social cost is the maximum cost of any player. Note that $C(S)$ also corresponds to the maximum edge congestion in state $S$. We also refer to $C(S)$ as the bottleneck congestion of state $S$. A state $S^* \in \mathcal{S}$ is called *optimal* (or *global optimum*) if it has minimum attainable social cost: for any other state $S \in \mathcal{S}$, $C(S^*) \leq C(S)$.

We can also define the notion of approximate Nash equilibria. We say that a player is $\alpha$-stable if it cannot improve its cost by a factor of more than $\alpha$. That is, player $i$ is *$\alpha$-stable* in state $S$ if $c_i(S) \leq \alpha \cdot c_i(S')$ for any state $S' \in \mathcal{S}$. We say that a state $S$ is an *$\alpha$-approximate Nash Equilibrium* if every player is $\alpha$-stable; namely, no player can improve its utility cost by a factor of more than $\alpha$. If $\alpha = 1$, then the equilibrium is exact and the definitions coincide with the earlier (precise) definitions of stability and equilibrium.

## 3 EXISTENCE OF UNSPLITTABLE EQUILIBRIA

Consider an unsplittable game instance $(G, \mathcal{N}, \mathcal{D}, \mathcal{S})$. We define a potential function for the unsplittable game which can help to obtain a Nash equilibrium in finite time. Let $\delta = \sum_{i \in \mathcal{N}} d_i$. For state $S \in \mathcal{S}$, consider the *congestion vector* of variables $Z_S = (z_0, \ldots, z_\delta)$, such that $z_i$ denotes the number of edges in $G$ which have congestion $i$. The list of numbers $0, \ldots, \delta$ includes all possible distinct values of congestions that we can obtain by combining demands of the players from the powerset $2^{\mathcal{N}}$. Vectors can be compared according to lexicographical order such that $(z'_0, \ldots, z'_\delta) < (z_0, \ldots, z_\delta)$ if there is a $j$, $0 \leq j \leq \delta$, such that $z'_i = z_i$ for all $i > j$, and $z'_j < z_j$. The potential function maps a state $S$ to its respective congestion vector. The following result is an adaptation from [3].

Lemma 3.1. *An improvement move by a player $i$ changes the game state $S$ to a game state $S'$ such that $Z_{S'} < Z_S$.*

Proof. Let $c_1 = c_i(S)$ and $c_2 = c_i(S')$. Clearly, $c_1 > c_2$, since $i$ performs an improvement move. Let $Z_S = (z_0, \ldots, z_\delta)$ and $Z_{S'} = (z'_0, \ldots, z'_\delta)$ denote the respective congestion vectors in $S$ and $S'$. Since player $i$ abandons edges with congestion $c_1$ in the improvement move, the number of edges with congestion $c_1$ decreases by at least one from $S$ to $S'$, hence, $z_{c_1} > z'_{c_1}$. Edges with congestion higher than $c_1$ are not affected because they are not used in the path of player $i$. Therefore, $Z_{S'} < Z_S$. □

**ALGORITHM 1:** Splittable Game Equlibrium

**Input:** A splittable bottleneck congestion game $(G, \mathcal{N}, \mathcal{D}, \mathcal{S})$
**Output:** A Nash equilibrium $S \in \mathcal{S}$ with $f_s = (f_1, \ldots, f_n)$
$A \leftarrow E$; `// remaining edges`
$\Pi \leftarrow \mathcal{N}$; `// remaining players`
$K \leftarrow \emptyset$; `// constant-players`
**while** $A \neq \emptyset$ *and* $\Pi \neq \emptyset$ **do**
    Use LP to compute a flow $f^*$ for players $\Pi \cup K$ on the induced subgraph $G_A$ by $A$;
    Let $C^*$ be the bottleneck congestion in $f^*$;
    Let $B \subseteq A$ be the set of edges that have congestion $C^*$;
    Let $\Pi_B \subseteq \Pi \cup K$ be the set of all players that use the edges $B$ in $f^*$;
    Let $B' \subseteq B$ be a minimal cut in $G_A$ for some non-empty set of players $Y \subseteq \Pi_B$;
    **foreach** *player* $i \in Y \cap \mathcal{N}$ **do**
        $f_i \leftarrow f_i^*$; `// flow assignment for player i`
        **foreach** *edge* $e = (u, v) \in A \cap E(f_i)$ *used by player* $i$ *in* $f_i$ **do**
            create a new "constant-player" $i_e$ with source $s_{i_e} = u$, destination $t_{i_e} = v$ and demand $d_{i_e} = f^*_{i,e}$;
            $K \leftarrow K \cup \{i_r\}$;
        **end**
    **end**
    $A \leftarrow A \setminus B'$;
    $\Pi \leftarrow \Pi \setminus Y$;
**end**

The following result follows directly from Lemma 3.1 by starting from an arbitrary initial state in $\mathcal{S}$ (arbitrary path for each player from its source to destination) and repeatedly applying improvement moves for players, since there are only a finite number of vectors $Z_S$.

Theorem 3.2 (Existence of Unsplittable Equilibrium). *Any unsplittable game has a Nash equilibrium.*

There could possibly be multiple different Nash equilibrium states which might be reached by starting from different initial states. If the initial state is optimal then the resulting equilibrium state will also be optimal, since improvement moves never increase edge congestion. Note however that improvement moves may take too long to converge to an equilibrium since there could be an exponential number of intermediate states. For this reason, we examine alternative approaches to compute equilibria faster.

## 4 EQUILIBRIA FOR SPLITTABLE GAMES

Consider a splittable bottleneck congestion game instance $(G, \mathcal{N}, \mathcal{D}, \mathcal{S})$. We give an algorithm which computes a Nash Equilibrium in polynomial time with respect to the number of edges $m$ and number of players $n$.

In the algorithm we use the notion of a *minimal cut* for a set of players. For a singe player $i$ a *cut* is a set of edges such that any flow $f_i$ from $s_i$ to $t_i$ must use at least one edge in the cut. A *cut* for a set a players $\Pi \subseteq \mathcal{N}$ is a set of edges $E' \subseteq E$ such that for each $i \in \Pi$, any possible flow $f_i$ must use at least one edge in $E'$. A cut $E'$ is *minimal* for $\Pi$ if no strict subset of $E$ is a cut for $\Pi$.

### 4.1 Algorithm

The Nash equilibrium is computed by Algorithm 1. The algorithm repeatedly computes a flow $f^*$ and identifies stable players on appropriately defined cuts with maximum congestion edges. Those players and edges on the cut are removed in subsequent steps of the algorithm until no more players and edges remain.

In Algorithm 1, sets $A$ and $\Pi$ represent the remaining edges and players, which are initially set to $E$ and $\mathcal{N}$, respectively. There is also a set of "constant-players" $K$ which are artificially created throughout the execution of the algorithm. A constant-player $j \in K$ has adjacent source and destination, that is, $(s_j, t_j) \in E$. The algorithm forces the demand of constant-player $j$ to be sent directly on the edge $(s_j, t_j)$. For convenience, we define the cut of $j$ to be simply its edge $(s_j, t_j)$. Initially, $K$ is empty.

The algorithm works in multiple iterations (while-loop). In each iteration it uses a LP to find a flow $f^*$ with bottleneck congestion $C^*$ for the remaining players $\Pi$ on the induced subgraph $G_A$ defined by the remaining edges $A$. Then, it identifies a minimal cut $B'$ for a set of players $Y \subseteq \Pi \cup K$ that have bottleneck congestion $C^*$. The players in $Y \cap \mathcal{N}$ are stable, since the cut does not allow these players to have better alternate flows. Thus, we can assign to each player $i \in Y \cap \mathcal{N}$ the currently computed flow $f_i^*$. The players in $Y$ and edges $B'$ are removed and the algorithm proceeds to find new stable players in the residual graph. The algorithm repeats until no original players in $\mathcal{N}$ or edges of $E$ remain.

In the algorithm, when we proceed with the next iteration we need to be sure that the flows of players computed in earlier iterations are preserved. To achieve this, in any given iteration all the players in $Y$ are replaced with new artificial "constant-players" on the edges that their flows use. The constant-players maintain the computed flow of the removed players in subsequent iterations. More specifically, for each player $i \in Y$ and for each edge $e = (u, v) \in E(f_i^*)$, we introduce a new artificial player $i_e$ with source $u$ and destination $v$ with demand $d_{i_e} = f_i^*(e)$ and we insert $i_e$ in the set of constant-players $K$. The players $Y$ are removed from subsequent iterations but their constant-player replacements will remain. The LP guarantees that the demand of each constant-player flows directly through the edge connecting its source and destination, which preserves the flows of the players in $Y$.

Below is the LP formulation that we use in Algorithm 1. The LP computes a flow $f^* = (f_{i_1}^*, \ldots, f_{i_{n'}}^*)$ for players $\Pi \cup K$ in the induced subgraph of $G_A$ by the edges $A$. The LP may return a splittable flow $f^*$, which is the reason why the algorithm computes a splittable equilibrium. Note that the LP forces the constant-players $K$ to send all their demand directly on the edge connecting the source and destination.

*Minimize C such that:*

$$\sum_i f_{i,e}^* \le C, \ \forall i \in \Pi \cup K \wedge \forall e \in A \text{ (maximum congestion bound)},$$

$$\sum_{u:(u,v)\in A} f_{i,(u,v)}^* = \sum_{u':(v,u')\in A} f_{i,(v,u')}^*, \ \forall i \in \Pi \wedge \forall v \in V \setminus \{s_i, t_i\} \text{ (flow preservation on nodes)},$$

$$\sum_{v:(s_i,v)\in A} f_{i,(s_i,v)}^* = d_i, \ \forall i \in \Pi \text{ (source flow preservation)},$$

$$\sum_{u:(u,t_i)\in A} f_{i,(u,t_i)}^* = d_i, \ \forall i \in \Pi \text{ (destination flow preservation)},$$

$$f_{i,(s_i,t_i)}^* = d_i, \ \forall i \in K \wedge (s_i, t_i) \in A \text{ (constant-player flow)}.$$

## 4.2 Analysis

Here we prove that Algorithm 1 returns a Nash equilibrium. We first prove some useful properties for a while-loop iteration of Algorithm 1, where either $A \neq \emptyset$ or $\Pi \neq \emptyset$.

LEMMA 4.1. *Sets $B'$ and $Y$ are non-empty and can be computed in polynomial time.*

PROOF. Set $B'$ can be computed as follows. Start with $B' = B$. Let $\Pi' \subseteq \Pi$ be all players which use edges in $B'$ but $B'$ is not a cut in $G_A$. Thus each player $i \in \Pi'$ has a path $p$ in $G_A$ from $s_i$ to $t_i$ such that $p \cap B' = \emptyset$. Clearly, each edge in $p$ has congestion less that $C^*$. Thus, each such player $i$ can achieve lower congestion than $C^*$ by redistributing $\epsilon > 0$ portion of the demand $d_i$ outside $B'$ through $p$. Therefore, suppose that the players $\Pi'$ indeed redistribute their demands accordingly outside $B'$. Then, update $B' = B' \setminus X$. Repeat until $B'$ can be no further reduced.

The resulting $B'$ has to be non-empty, since otherwise, in the specific while-loop iteration of Algorithm 1 the LP would have returned a $f^*$ with lower bottleneck congestion than $C^*$. Clearly, the set of players $Y = \Pi \cap K$ which use edges on $B'$ is non-empty as well. Moreover, $B'$ is minimal for $Y$, since otherwise we can continue with the process above and reduce $B'$ even further. Set $B'$ can be easily computed in polynomial time with respect to $m$ and $n$, since each time the excluded players $\Pi'$ can be easily detected by checking for alternate paths outside $B'$. □

LEMMA 4.2. *The bottleneck congestion resulting by the LP solution in any given while-loop iteration does not increase in any subsequent while-loop iteration.*

PROOF. After we apply the LP solution $f^*$, all the edges in $A$ have congestion at most $C^*$. The players in $\Pi \setminus Y$ have flows with bottleneck congestion at most $C^*$ and do not use any of the $B'$ edges that are about to be removed. When we replace the players in $Y$ with constant-players (in the inner for-loop) and send the flows along the respective single edges, the current flows of the players in $\Pi \setminus Y$ are not affected since the bottleneck congestion remains at most $C^*$. Therefore, in the next iteration for the new set of players $\Pi \leftarrow \Pi \setminus Y$ in the remaining edges $A \leftarrow A \setminus B'$, there is a flow $f$ with congestion at most $C^*$. □

Let $Y_l$ denote the set of players $Y$ in while-loop iteration $l$. Let $Y'_l = Y_l \cap \mathcal{N}$, which are the players whose flow $f_i$ is assigned in iteration $l$. Let $\Pi'_l = Y'_1 \cup \cdots \cup Y'_l$.

LEMMA 4.3. *At while-loop iteration $l$, the players in $\Pi'_l$ are stable with respect to their flow assignments in $G$.*

PROOF. We prove the claim by induction on $l$. For $l = 1$, consider the first while-loop iteration where we have that $\Pi'_1 = Y'_1$. According to Algorithm 1, the flow $f_i \leftarrow f^*_i$ of each player $i \in Y'_1$, which is assigned in the first iteration, has bottleneck congestion equal to the current bottleneck congestion $C^*$ of $f^*$. Since $A$ is initially empty, $G_A = G$. Moreover, since $B'$ is a cut for $Y'_1$ and all edges in $B'$ have congestion $C^*$, no player in $Y'$ has a better alternative flow choice with lower bottleneck congestion. Hence, the players $Y'_1$ are stable in $G$ in flow $f^*$,

Assume now that the players in $\Pi'_l$ are stable for all $1 \leq l < k$. Consider now the $k$th while-loop iteration. We have that $\Pi'_{k-1} \cup Y'_k = \Pi'_k$. Similar to the reasoning in the induction basis, the players in $Y'_k$ are stable with respect to the current induced subgraph $G_A$. For each player $i \in Y'_k$ any alternative flow $f'_i$ in the original graph $G$ may use edges in the removed cuts of players in $\Pi'_{k-1}$ (those edges were removed at earlier while-loop iterations). From Lemma 4.2, the congestion in the cuts of the players in $\Pi'_{k-1}$ was at least $C^*$ when their flow was assigned. Therefore, given the flow assignment of $\Pi'_{k-1}$, any alternative flow for the players in $Y'_k$ has congestion at least $C^*$. Thus, players $Y'_k$ are stable in iteration $k$ with respect to $G$ and the current flow assignments in $\Pi'_k$.

From induction hypothesis, the players in $\Pi'_{k-1}$ were stable in $G$ at iteration $k-1$. They will remain stable in $G$ in iteration $k$, since the congestion on their cut edges was at least $C^*$ at iteration $k-1$ and is not affected in iteration $k$ (those edges were removed earlier), and also any edge in their flows in $G_A$ in iteration $k$ has congestion at most $C^*$ (Lemma 4.2).

Therefore, the players $\Pi'_{k-1} \cup Y'_k = \Pi'_k$ are stable in $G$ with respect to their current flow assignments in $G$. □

We finally give the main result for this section which proves that we can compute a splittable Nash equilibrium in polynomial time. This equilibrium is also a global optimum.

Theorem 4.4 (Equilibrium for Splittable Game). *For a splittable bottleneck congestion game, Algorithm 1 computes a Nash Equilibrium in polynomial time. The equilibrium is a global optimum.*

Proof. The algorithm terminates when either $A = \emptyset$ or $\Pi = \emptyset$. From Lemma 4.1, in each iteration of the while-loop, $B'$ is not empty, and therefore set $A$ is reduced each time. This implies that the number of while-loop iterations is bounded by $m = |E|$. The size of the LP in each while-loop iteration is polynomial with respect to $m$ and $n$. Moreover, from Lemma 4.1, the total computation involved in each iteration is polynomial as well. Since the number of iterations is bounded by $\max(m, n)$, the total time is polynomial with respect to $m$ and $n$.

Next, we show that every player in $\mathcal{N}$ will be included in the final flow assignment $f$. In the beginning, each player in $\mathcal{N}$ uses some edge in the assignment $f^*$ of the first while-loop iteration. If a player was using an edge in $B'$, then the player will be included in the output assignment $f$ and will be removed from $\Pi$. Otherwise, the player was using some other edge outside $B'$ which will be in $A$ in the next iteration. Eventually, since in the last iteration either $A = \emptyset$ or $\Pi = \emptyset$, each player will be included in some iteration in the final flow $f$.

Lemma 4.3 implies that the flow assignment $f$ corresponds to a stable state for all players in $\mathcal{N}$. The resulting flow $f$ is also a global optimum, since in the first while-loop iteration $f^*$ is a global optimum, and from Lemma 4.2, the bottleneck congestion does not increase in subsequent while-loop iterations. □

## 5 UNSPLITTABLE GAMES WITH UNIFORM DEMANDS

Consider an unsplittable bottleneck congestion game instance $I = (G, \mathcal{N}, \mathcal{D}, \mathcal{S})$ where each player has unit demand, that is, $d_i = 1$, for each $i \in \mathcal{N}$ (uniform demands), and players are only allowed to use a single path in their respective flows. We present Algorithm 2 that computes an approximate unsplittable Nash equilibrium for $I$ in polynomial time (with respect to $m$ and $n$). The basic idea behind the algorithm is that it first computes an equilibrium $S$ (possibly splittable) for the respective splittable game based on Algorithm 1, and then converts $S$ to an unsplittable equilibrium $\overline{S}$ with randomized rounding.

### 5.1 Algorithm

Algorithm 2 performs the following steps. Let $I' = (G, \mathcal{N}, \mathcal{D}, \mathcal{S}')$ be the respective splittable game instance where players are allowed to use all possible flows (splittable and unsplittable). Execute Algorithm 1 with input $I'$ and let $S$ be the resulting Nash equilibrium with flow assignment $f = (f_1, \ldots, f_n)$. Flow $f$ (possibly splittable) can be converted to an unsplittable flow assignment $\overline{f} = (\overline{f}_1, \ldots, \overline{f}_n)$ with randomized rounding. First, using path decomposition, flow $f$ is converted to a flow $f'$ such that for each player $i$ its flow $f_i$ is sent along a set of paths $P_i = \{p_{i,1}, \ldots, p_{i,k_i}\}$ (each path has source $s_i$ and destination $t_i$). Each path $p_{i,j}$ has flow allocation $f'_{i,p_{i,j}}$ with $\sum_{j=1}^{k_i} f'_{i,p_{i,j}} = d_i = 1$. Player's $i$ flow allocation on the paths in $P_i$ represents a probability distribution. Player

**ALGORITHM 2:** Unsplittable Game Equilibrium for Uniform Demands

**Input:** An unsplittable bottleneck game $(G, \mathcal{N}, \mathcal{D}, \mathcal{S})$ with demand $d_i = 1$ for each $i \in \mathcal{N}$
**Output:** An approximate Nash equilibrium $\overline{S} \in \mathcal{S}$ with unsplittable flow $\overline{f} = (\overline{f}_1, \ldots, \overline{f}_n)$
Let $I' = (G, \mathcal{N}, \mathcal{D}, \mathcal{S}')$ be the respective splittable game;
Use Algorithm 1 to compute a Nash equilibrium $S$ for $I'$;
Let $f = (f_1, \ldots, f_n)$ be the respective assignment in $S$;
Use path decomposition to convert $f$ to a flow $f'$ such that for each player $i$ the flow $f_i$ is sent over a path set $P_i = \{p_{i,1}, \ldots, p_{i,k_i}\}$ with respective flow allocations on the paths $f'_{i,p_{i,1}}, \ldots, f'_{i,p_{i,k_i}}$ such that $\sum_{j=1}^{k_i} f'_{i,p_{i,j}} = d_i = 1$;
Each player $i \in \mathcal{N}$ chooses a path $p_{i,j} \in P_i$ with probability $f'_{i,p_{i,j}}$;
Each player $i \in \mathcal{N}$, sends in $\overline{f}_i$ all its unit demand to the respective chosen path $p_{i,j}$;

$i$ picks to send all its unit demand along one of the paths $p_{i,j} \in P_i$ with probability $f'_{i,p_{i,j}}$. The resulting flow on the chosen path is the assigned unsplittable flow $\overline{f}_i$ for player $i$.

### 5.2 Analysis

From Theorem 4.4, assignment $f$ is a Nash equilibrium computed in polynomial time. We will show that $\overline{f}$ is an approximate unsplittable equilibrium. We use the following Chernoff bounds.

Lemma 5.1 (Chernoff bounds). *Let $X_1, X_2, \cdots, X_m$ be independent Poisson trials such that, for $1 \le i \le m$, $X_i \in \{0,1\}$. Then, for $X = \sum_{i=1}^m X_i$, and $\mu = E[X]$:*

$$\mathbf{Pr}[X \ge (1+\delta)\mu] \le e^{-\frac{\delta\mu}{3}}, \qquad 1 < \delta, \tag{1}$$

$$\mathbf{Pr}[X \le (1-\delta)\mu] \le e^{-\frac{\delta^2\mu}{2}}, \qquad 0 < \delta < 1. \tag{2}$$

Lemma 5.2. *With probability at least $1 - 3/m$, the following hold for all edges in $E$:*

(a) *For any $e \in E$ with $f(e) \le 8 \ln m$, $\overline{f}(e) \le 32 \ln m$.*
(b) *For any $e \in E$ with $f(e) \ge 8 \ln m$, $f(e)/4 \le \overline{f}(e) \le 4f(e)$.*

Proof. Consider a edge $e \in E$. For any player $i$, we have that $f_{i,e} = f'_{i,e}$, and hence $f(e) = f'(e)$. In flow $\overline{f}$ the probability that a player $i$ picks any of its path in $P_i$ that uses edge $e$ to send its unit demand is equal to $f'_{i,e} = f_{i,e}$. Therefore, in flow assignment $\overline{f}$ the expected congestion on edge $e$ is $\mu = E[\overline{f}(e)] = f'(e) = f(e)$.

We first prove that if $f(e) \le 2 \ln m$, then $\mathbf{Pr}[\overline{f}(e) \ge 8 \ln m] \le 1/m^2$. Let $\delta = 8 \ln m / f(e) - 1$. From Equation 1 we obtain:

$$\mathbf{Pr}[\overline{f}(e) \ge 8 \ln m] = \mathbf{Pr}[\overline{f}(e) \ge (1+\delta)f(e)] \le e^{-\frac{\delta f(e)}{3}} = e^{-\frac{8 \ln m - f(e)}{3}} \le e^{-2 \ln m} = \frac{1}{m^2}. \tag{3}$$

Next, we prove that if $f(e) \ge 2 \ln m$, then $\mathbf{Pr}[\overline{f}(e) \ge 4f(e)] \le 1/m^2$. Let $\delta = 3$. From Equation 1 we obtain:

$$\mathbf{Pr}[\overline{f}(e) \ge 4f(e)] = \mathbf{Pr}[\overline{f}(e) \ge (1+\delta)f(e)] \le e^{-\frac{\delta f(e)}{3}} = e^{-f(e)} \le e^{-2 \ln m} = \frac{1}{m^2}. \tag{4}$$

Last, we prove that if $f(e) \ge 8 \ln m$, then $\mathbf{Pr}[\overline{f}(e) \le f(e)/4] \le 1/m^2$. Let $\delta = 3/4$. From Equation 2 we obtain:

$$\mathbf{Pr}[\overline{f}(e) \le f(e)/4] = \mathbf{Pr}[\overline{f}(e) \le (1-\delta)f(e)] \le e^{-\frac{\delta^2 f(e)}{2}} = e^{-\frac{72 \ln m}{32}} \le e^{-2 \ln m} = \frac{1}{m^2}. \tag{5}$$

Consider now the case where $f(e) \leq 8 \ln m$. From Equation 3, if $f(e) \leq 2 \ln m$ then $\overline{f}(e) \leq 8 \ln m < 32 \ln m$ with probability at least $1 - 1/m^2$. From Equation 4, if $2 \ln m \leq f(e) \leq 8 \ln m$, then $\overline{f}(e) \leq 4f(e) \leq 32 \ln m$ with probability at least $1 - 1/m^2$. Therefore, $\overline{f}(e) \leq 32 \ln m$ with probability at least $1 - 1/m^2$.

Consider now the case where $f(e) \geq 8 \ln m$. From Equation 4, we have that $\overline{f}(e) \leq 4f(e)$ with probability at least $1 - 1/m^2$. From Equation 5, we also have that $\overline{f}(e) \geq f(e)/4$ with probability at least $1 - 1/m^2$. Therefore, $f(e)/4 \leq \overline{f}(e) \leq 4f(e)$ with probability at least $1 - 2/m^2$.

Consequently, for any specific edge $e$ parts (a) and (b) of the claim hold with probability at least $1 - 3/m^2$. Therefore, considering the union bound for all the $m$ edges in $E$, parts (a) and (b) hold together with probability at least $1 - 3/m$. □

Theorem 5.3 (Equilibrium for unsplittable game with uniform demands). *For an unsplittable game instance $I$ with uniform demands, Algorithm 2 computes in polynomial time an unsplittable flow assignment $\overline{f}$ which with high probability (at least $1 - 3/m$) is an $O(\log m)$-approximate Nash equilibrium.*

Proof. From Theorem 4.4, the flow $f$ is a splittable Nash equilibrium. Let $c_i$ and $\overline{c}_i$ denote the bottleneck congestion of player $i$ in $f$ and $\overline{f}$, respectively. Let also $p_{i,j} \in P_i$ be the chosen path for player $i$ to allocate all the unit flow in $\overline{f}_i$. It has to be that in $f$ for each edge $e \in p_{i,j}$, $f(e) \leq c_i$.

Consider the case where $c_i \leq 8 \ln m$. From part (a) of Lemma 5.2, we have that for each edge $e \in p_{i,j}$, $\overline{f}(e) \leq 32 \ln m$ (with high probability). Consequently, $\overline{c}_i \leq 32 \ln m$. Therefore, player $i$ is $32 \ln m$-stable in the unsplittable game $I$ since any alternative unsplittable strategy has bottleneck congestion at least 1.

Consider now the case where $c_i > 8 \ln m$. From part (b) of Lemma 5.2, we have that for each edge $e \in p_{i,j}$, $\overline{f}(e) \leq 4f(e) \leq 4c_i$ (with high probability). Since player $i$ is stable in $f$, for each $p_{i,j'} \in P_i$, $j' \neq j$, there is an edge $e'$ with $f(e') = c_i$. Moreover, each path from $s_i$ to $t_i$ must use one of the edges in $P_i$ with congestion $c_i$, since otherwise, there would be an alternative path $p'$ that could be used to redirect some of the flow in $f_i$ in order to lower the congestion $c_i$, which would imply that $i$ is not stable in $f_i$. From part (b) of Lemma 5.2 we have that $\overline{f}(e') \geq f(e')/4 = c_i/4$ (with high probability). Hence, player $i$ is 16-stable in the unsplittable game $I$.

Combining the two cases above, it follows that each player $i$ is $O(\log m)$-stable. From Lemma 5.2, $\overline{f}$ is an unsplittable Nash equilibrium with probability at least $1 - 3/m$. For each player $i$ the path decomposition $P_i$ can be computed in polynomial time with respect to $m$ (giving polynomial number of paths of length at most $m$). Moreover, from Theorem 4.4, the flow $f$ is computed in polynomial time with respect to $m$ and $n$. Therefore, the time complexity of Algorithm 2 is polynomial with respect to $m$ and $n$. □

## 6 UNSPLITTABLE GAMES WITH ARBITRARY DEMANDS

Consider an unsplittable game $I = (G, \mathcal{N}, \mathcal{D}, \mathcal{S})$ with arbitrary demands. Let $d_{\max}$ and $d_{\min}$ denote the maximum and minimum demands, respectively, in $\mathcal{D}$. Without loss of generality, we may assume that $d_{\min} = 1$, since otherwise, we can scale the demands of all players by a factor $1/d_{\min}$. We present Algorithm 3 which computes a poly-log approximate Nash equilibrium for $I$.

We do not use Algorithm 2 directly because the randomized rounding for all players is conditioned only upon the one-time output of the splittable game and the approximation factor (due to the way the Chernoff bounds are applied) is a direct function of the equilibrium congestion at any edge. However, a direct application of this technique will not work directly when the players have arbitrary demands since the splittable equilibrium congestion $C$ at any edge with players to be rounded might be significantly lower than the maximum demand of hitherto unrounded players with high demands.

For example, consider a game instance with two classes of players, the first class with small demands, i.e. 1, and the second class with very high demands. The respective splittable game may have low overall bottleneck congestion, since the flows of the second class players may possibly split in multiple disjoint paths (depending of $G$). After rounding, some edges may contain players of both classes, which could be rounded in the higher demands that will cause the low demand players to be unstable. This may result to a large approximation factor for an approximate equilibrium, possibly as large as the ratio of the demands which can be arbitrary.

In order to overcome this difficulty, we develop in Algorithm 3 an *iterative rounding* technique based on multiple iterations of computing stable splittable equilbria. Our key observation is that highly congested edges at any phase can occur due to two different (but not mutually exclusive) scenarios: (1) high congestion at an edge is due to a large number of players with small demands, and (2) high congestion is mainly due to a few players with very high demands. We therefore propose a novel iterative rounding technique conditioned on *both* of these factors.

## 6.1 Algorithm

Algorithm 3 works in phases, where each phase corresponds to a while-loop iteration. At each phase, there is a set of remaining edges $A$ and players $\Pi$ (initialized to $E$ and $\mathcal{N}$, respectively). At the beginning of a phase, the algorithm computes a stable Nash equilibrium $f$ through Algorithm 1 for the respective splittable game $I'$. Then it identifies all edges $X$ whose congestion is at least a certain threshold $64 \cdot \widehat{d}\zeta \ln(\zeta m)$, where $\widehat{d}$ is the maximum demand of any player in that phase, and $\zeta = \lceil \log d_{\max} \rceil + 1$ (log is base 2). The players $\Phi \subseteq \Pi$ have a flow $f_i$ that uses edges in $X$. The players in $\Psi$ are players whose demands are at least $\widehat{d}/2$.

Each player $i \in (\Phi \cup \Psi) \cap \mathcal{N}$ is "rounded" to some path from $s_i$ to $t_i$ using randomized rounding. As before, using path decomposition, the flow $f_i$ is first converted to a flow $f_i'$ over a path set $P_i = \{p_{i,1}, \ldots, p_{i,k_i}\}$ with flow allocations on the paths $f'_{i,p_{i,1}}, \ldots, f'_{i,p_{i,k_i}}$, where $\sum_{j=1}^{k_i} f'_{i,p_{i,j}} = d_i$ (each path has source $s_i$ and destination $t_i$). Player $i$ then picks at random one of the paths in $p_{i,j} \in P_i$ to assign the whole demand $d_i$ with probability $f'_{i,p_{i,1}}/d_i$, which gives its resulting unsplittable flow assignment $\overline{f}_i$.

As we show in the analysis, since flow $f$ is an equilibrium in $I'$, the set $X$ is a cut for the players in $\Phi$, which is crucial for providing their approximately stability after rounding, by giving upper and lower bounds for the congestion of each edge in $X$. Further, the rounding of the players in $\Psi$ guarantees that the maximum demand is halved each time, which helps to provide approximate equilibria for players in subsequent rounds whose congestion was not as high in the current round. The rounded players are "dissolved" into several constant-players of small demand in the range $[1, 2)$, so that they are not rounded again in the following phases. Note that inside Algorithm 1, the set $K$ is initialized to the current set of constant players $K$ in the particular phase (instead of the empty set assumed in the initialization of Algorithm 1).

At the end of a phase we remove the edges $X$ and the rounded players from $A$ and $\Pi$ respectively, and the whole process repeats in the next iteration of the while-loop. The algorithm terminates when either $A$ or $\Pi$ are empty, at which point every player in $\mathcal{N}$ is rounded, and hence, a corresponding final unsplittable flow assignment $\overline{f}$ is returned.

## 6.2 Analysis

According to Algorithm 3, each player will be included eventually in one of the sets $\Phi$ or $\Psi$. The algorithm requires $\sigma \leq \zeta$ phases since at each phase $k$, $1 \leq k \leq \sigma$, any remaining player $i$ with

**ALGORITHM 3:** Unsplittable Game Equilibrium

```
Input: An unsplittable bottleneck game (G, N, D, S) with arbitrary demands d_i ≥ 1 for each i ∈ N
Output: An approximate Nash equilibrium S̄ ∈ S with unsplittable flow f̄ = (f̄_1, ..., f̄_n)
d_max ← max_{i∈N} d_i; ζ ← ⌈log d_max⌉ + 1;
A ← E; // remaining edges
Π ← N; // remaining players
K ← ∅; // constant-players
while A ≠ ∅ and Π ≠ ∅ do
    f ← Nash equilibrium of Algorithm 1 for respective splittable game I' = (G_A, Π ∪ K, D, S') on the
      induced subgraph G_A by the edges A on G;
    d̂ ← max_{i∈Π} d_i;
    X ← all edges e ∈ A with f(e) ≥ 64 · d̂ζ ln(ζm);
    Φ ← all players in Π that in f use edges in X;
    Ψ ← all players i ∈ Π with d_i ≥ d̂/2;
    foreach player i ∈ (Φ ∪ Ψ) ∩ N do
        // randomized rounding
        Use path decomposition to convert f_i to a flow f'_i over a path set P_i = {p_{i,1}, ..., p_{i,k_i}} with flow
          allocations on the paths f'_{i,p_{i,1}}, ..., f'_{i,p_{i,k_i}}, where Σ_{j=1}^{k_i} f'_{i,p_{i,j}} = d_i;
        Player i chooses a path p_{i,j} ∈ P_i with probability f'_{i,p_{i,j}}/d_i;
        f̄_i ← an unsplittable flow assignment where demand d_i is sent on p_{i,j};
        // dissolve rounded player into constant-players
        foreach edge e = (u, v) ∈ p_{i,j} do
            Replace i in e with a set of ⌊d_i⌋ constant-players Z, such that each player i' ∈ Z has source
              s_{i'} = u destination t_{i'} = v and demand d_{i'} = d_i/⌊d_i⌋;
            K ← K ∪ Z;
        end
    end
    A ← A \ X;
    Π ← Π \ (Φ ∪ Ψ);
end
```

demand $d_i \geq d_{\max}/2^k$ is included in $\Psi$, and then dissolved into multiple constant-players of demand $d_i/\lfloor d_i \rfloor \in [1, 2)$. Therefore, each player $i \in \mathcal{N}$ is eventually rounded at some of the algorithm's phases, and hence finally by the $\zeta$th phase the algorithm returns an unsplittable flow assignment $\overline{f}$ for all players in $\mathcal{N}$.

The total computation time is polynomial with respect to parameters $m$ and $n$ and $\zeta$, since Algorithm 1 is polynomial with $m$ and $n$ (Theorem 4.4), and path decomposition returns paths in polynomial time with respect to $m$ for each player. It remains to show that $\overline{f}$ is an approximate Nash equilibrium. Below, when we say "high probability" we assume a probability $1 - 1/g(m, \zeta)$, where $g$ is a polynomial function on $m$ and $\zeta$.

Let $I^k = (G_A, \Pi \cup K, \mathcal{D}, \mathcal{S}')$ denote the splittable game at the beginning of the $k$th phase, $1 \leq k \leq \sigma$, where $\mathcal{S}'$ is the splittable strategy space on the induced subgraph $G_A$ by $A$ (assume that $\mathcal{D}$ has been adjusted to include only demands of players $\Pi \cup K$). Let $\widehat{d_k}$ denote the maximum demand in the beginning of phase $k$ of any player in $A$. Note that $\widehat{d_k}$ is strictly decreasing as $k$ increases.

Lemma 6.1. *At any phase $k \geq 1$, $X$ is a cut for the players in $\Phi$ with respect to edges $A$ in game $I^k$.*

Proof. Suppose there is a player $i \in \Phi$ for which $X$ is not a cut. Player $i$ is stable in flow assignment $f_i$, since flow $f$ is a Nash equilibrium for $I^k$ (Theorem 4.4). Therefore, there is a path $p'$ in $G_A$ from $s_i$ to $t_i$, such that $p'$ does not use any edge in $X$. From the definition of $X$, for each $e' \in p'$, since $e' \notin X$, $f(e') < 64 \cdot \widehat{d_k}\zeta \ln(\zeta m)$. From the definition of $\Phi$, flow $f_i$ uses an edge of $X$, and hence the bottleneck congestion cost of player $i$ in $f$ is $c_i \geq 64 \cdot \widehat{d_k}\zeta \ln(\zeta m)$. However, due to the existence of $p'$ player $i$ can lower is cost by redirecting some of the flow in path $p'$, which can result in a flow with bottleneck congestion $c_i' < c_i$. Thus, player $i$ is unstable in $f$, a contradiction. □

Consider the flow $f$ for splittable game $I^k$ in the $k$th phase, as computed by Algorithm 1. Flow $f$ is a Nash equilibrium in $G_A$ (Theorem 4.4). Consider also an edge $e \in A$ which in equilibrium $f$ has flow $f(e)$. After the players in $(\Phi \cup \Psi) \cap \mathcal{N}$ (rounding players) pick their random unsplittable assignment, the bottleneck congestion in $f(e)$ is possibly modified. For simplicity, let $\overline{f}(e)$ denote the respective total flow in $e$ after all the rounding steps in the $k$th phase. In the lemma below, we give upper and lower bounds for $\overline{f}(e)$. In the proof of the lemma, it is not necessary to distinguish the players which are rounding than those that are not, since it does not make any difference in the provided bounds of $\overline{f}(e)$ (non-rounding players can be treated as constant-players in $e$ which with probability 1 pick their single edge path choice). Let $d_e$ denote the maximum demand of all players that have $e$ in their flow, namely, $d_e = \max_{i:e \in E(f_i)} d_i$, and let $\zeta_e = \lceil \log d_e \rceil + 1$.

Lemma 6.2. *With probability at least* $1 - 2/m$*, in any phase:*

(a) *For any edge* $e \in A$, $\overline{f}(e) \leq 8f(e) + 64 \cdot d_e \ln(\zeta m)$.

(b) *For any edge* $r \in A$, *if* $f(e) \geq 64 \cdot d_e \zeta_e \ln(\zeta m)$ *then* $\overline{f}(e) \geq f(e)/16$.

Proof. Consider for now a specific phase $k$ and game $I^k$. Let $Q \subseteq \Pi$ denote the set of players which in flow $f$ use edge $e$ (for each $i \in Q$, $f_i(e) > 0$). For any player $i \in Q$, we have that $f_{i,e} = f'_{i,e}$. and hence $f(e) = f'(e)$ (assume there no other players than $Q$ using $e$, as noted above). With probability $f'_{i,e}/d_i = f_{i,e}/d_i$, each player $i \in Q$ assigns all its flow to some path in $P_i$ that uses $e$ so that $\overline{f}_i(e) = d_i$.

We partition $Q$ into subsets $Q_j$, $0 \leq j < \zeta_e$, according to the players' demands, such that for each $i \in Q_j$, $d_i \in [2^j, 2^{j+1})$. Let $M_j = \sum_{i \in Q_j} f_{i,e}$. Therefore, $f(e) = \sum_j M_j$.

Let $Y_j$ be a random variable that denotes the number of players in $Q_j$ whose selected rounded path uses $e$. Denote $\mu_j = E[Y_j] = \sum_{i \in Q_j} f_{i,e}/d_i$. Therefore, $M_j/2^{j+1} < \mu_j \leq M_j/2^j$. Using the Chernoff bounds (Lemma 5.1) as in Lemma 5.2, we can prove:

i. If $\mu_j \leq 2\ln(\zeta m)$, then $\mathbf{Pr}[Y_j \geq 8 \ln m] \leq 1/(\zeta m)^2$.

ii. If $\mu_j \geq 2\ln(\zeta m)$, then $\mathbf{Pr}[Y_j \geq 4\mu_j] \leq 1/(\zeta m)^2$.

iii. If $\mu_j \geq 8\ln(\zeta m)$, then $\mathbf{Pr}[Y_j \leq \mu_j/4] \leq 1/(\zeta m)^2$.

Combining parts i and ii, we obtain $Y_j \leq 4\mu_j + 8\ln(\zeta m) \leq 4M_j/2^j + 8\ln(\zeta m)$, with probability at least $1 - 1/(\zeta m)^2$. Therefore,

$$
\begin{aligned}
\overline{f}(e) &< \sum_{0 \leq j < \zeta_e} |Y_j| 2^{j+1} \\
&\leq \sum_{0 \leq j < \zeta_e} (4M_j/2^j + 8\ln(\zeta m))2^{j+1} \\
&= \sum_{0 \leq j < \zeta_e} (8M_j + 2^{j+4}\ln(\zeta m)) \\
&< 8f(e) + 2^{\zeta_e + 4}\ln(\zeta m) \\
&\leq 8f(e) + 64 \cdot d_e \ln(\zeta m). \qquad (6)
\end{aligned}
$$

Equation 6 holds with probability at least $1 - \zeta_e/(\zeta m)^2 \geq 1 - 1/(\zeta m^2)$, since $\zeta_e \leq \zeta$ and parts i and ii have been applied $\zeta_e$ times in the involved summation.

Suppose now that $f(e) \geq 64 \cdot d_r \zeta_e \ln(\zeta m)$. Let $\xi_1$ and $\xi_2$ denote the number of subsets $Q_j$ with $M_j < 32 \cdot d_e \ln(\zeta m)$ and $M_j \geq 32 \cdot d_e \ln(\zeta m)$, respectively. Let $L_1$ and $L_2$ denote the sum of $M_j$ for the $\xi_1$ and $\xi_2$ subsets, respectively. Since $L_1 + L_2 = f(e)$, and $L_1 < 32 \cdot d_e \zeta_e \ln(\zeta m) \leq f(e)/2$, we get that $L_2 \geq f(e)/2$. For each of the $\xi_2$ sets it holds that $M_j \geq 32 \cdot d_e \ln(\zeta m)$, and since $d_e \geq 2^{\zeta_e - 2}$ and $j < \zeta_e$, we get $\mu_j > M_j/2^{j+1} \geq 8 \ln(\zeta m)$. Therefore, from part iii, for all the $\xi_2$ sets we obtain $Y_j \geq \mu_j/4 > M_j/2^{j+3}$, with probability at least $1 - 1/(\zeta m)^2$. Let $\Xi_2$ denote the set that contains all the $\xi_2$ sets $Q_j$. We have:

$$\overline{f}(e) \geq \sum_{j:Q_j \in \Xi_2} |Y_j| 2^j > \sum_{j:Q_j \in \Xi_2} (M_j/2^{j+3}) 2^j = \sum_{j:Q_j \in \Xi_2} (M_j/8) = L_2/2 \geq f(e)/16. \tag{7}$$

Equation 7 holds with probability at least $1 - \zeta_e/(\zeta m)^2 \geq 1 - 1/(\zeta m^2)$, since $\zeta_e \leq \zeta$ and part iii has been applied at most $\zeta_e$ times in the involved summation with $\Xi_2$.

When we consider the two Equations 6 and 7 over all edges $e \in A$, which are bounded by $m$, by taking the union of the respective probability bounds, we obtain probability $1 - 2/(\zeta m)$. The result follows by taking the union bound when considering all $\zeta$ phases. □

Lemma 6.2 can be used to give an upper bound on the bottleneck congestion of any edge in any phase $k > 1$.

Lemma 6.3. *In phase $k > 1$, in flow $f$ each edge $e \in A$ has $f(e) < 9 \cdot 64 \cdot \widehat{d}_{k-1} \zeta \ln(\zeta m)$, with high probability.*

Proof. Consider first the previous phase $k - 1 \geq k$. Let $\widehat{f}$ be the flow assignment for splittable game $I^{k-1}$ with respective edges $A'$. All edges $e \in A'$ with $\widehat{f}(e) \geq 64 \cdot \widehat{d}_{k-1} \zeta \ln(\zeta m)$, are included in the respective $X'$. For each $e \in A' \setminus X'$, it has to be that $\widehat{f}(e) < 64 \cdot \widehat{d}_{k-1} \zeta \ln(\zeta m)$. Let $f''$ be the respective flow assignment after rounding all players in the $k - 1$ phase. From Lemma 6.2, after the rounding phase, the total flow in $f''$ on each edge $e \in A' \setminus X'$ becomes $\overline{f}(e) \leq 8\widehat{f}(r) + 64 \cdot d_r \ln(\zeta m) < 8(64 \cdot \widehat{d}_{k-1} \zeta \ln(\zeta m)) + 64 \cdot \widehat{d}_{k-1} \ln(\zeta m) \leq 9 \cdot 64 \cdot \widehat{d}_{k-1} \zeta \ln(\zeta m)$.

The players which are not rounded in the $k - 1$ phase continue as players $\Pi$ to the next phase $k$, including the so far created constant-players. Thus, $f''$ corresponds to a valid possible splittable flow assignment for phase $k$ and players $\Pi$ in $I^k$, if we exclude all removed edges and players from the previous phase. However, $f''$ may not be an equilibrium and neither optimal. The flow $f$ returned by Algorithm 1 for $I^k$ is a Nash equilibrium and at the same time a global optimum (Theorem 4.4). Hence, the bottleneck congestion in $f$ cannot exceed the bottleneck congestion in $f''$. Therefore, in phase $k$ for any edge $e \in A$, $f(e) < 9 \cdot 64 \cdot \widehat{d}_{k-1} \zeta \ln(\zeta m)$. □

We continue to show that in the $k$th phase each player in $(\Phi \cup \Psi) \cap \mathcal{N}$ will be approximately stable after rounding with respect to the game $I^k$.

Lemma 6.4. *At the $k$th phase after rounding, each player $i \in (\Phi \cup \Psi) \cap \mathcal{N}$ is $O(\zeta \ln(\zeta m))$-stable in flow assignment $\overline{f}_i$ with respect to game $I^k$, with high probability.*

Proof. For each player in $i \in (\Phi \cup \Psi) \cap \mathcal{N}$, let $c_i$ and $\overline{c}_i$ denote the bottleneck congestion cost of $i$ in $f_i$ and $\overline{f}_i$, respectively.

Each player $i \in \Phi \cap \mathcal{N}$ is stable in $f$. Let $Y = X \cap E(f_i)$. For any $e \in Y$ it holds that $c_i \geq f(e) \geq 64 \cdot \widehat{d}_k \zeta \ln(\zeta m)$, since from Lemma 6.1, $X$ is a cut for $i$ and in addition $i$ is also stable in $f$ (otherwise, player $i$ would redistribute its demand on alternative paths to obtain lower bottleneck congestion). For any edge $e \in E(f_i)$ it holds that $f(e) \leq c_i$. and from part a of Lemma 6.2 we get,

$\overline{f}(e) \leq 8f(e) + 64 \cdot d_e \ln(\zeta m) \leq 8c_i + 64 \cdot \widehat{d}_k \ln(\zeta m) \leq 9c_i$. Further, for any $e \in X$, from part b of Lemma 6.2, since $f(e) \geq 64 \cdot \widehat{d}_k \zeta \ln(\zeta m) \geq 64 \cdot d_e \zeta_e \ln(\zeta m)$, we get that $\overline{f}(e) \geq f(e)/16 = c_i/16$. Consequently, since $\overline{c}_i = \overline{f}(e')$ for some $e' \in E(f_i)$, and $X$ is a cut, we obtain that the players in $\Phi \cap \mathcal{N}$ are $9 \cdot 16 = 144$-stable.

Consider now a player $i \in (\Psi \setminus \Phi) \cap \mathcal{N}$. Player $i$ demand is $d_i \geq \widehat{d}_k/2$, and the player $i$ in $f_i$ must be using edges $E(f_i) \subseteq A \setminus X$, each with $f(e) < 64 \cdot \widehat{d}_k \zeta \ln(\zeta m)$. Therefore, $c_i < 64 \cdot \widehat{d}_k \zeta \ln(\zeta m)$. After rounding, from part a of Lemma 6.2 we get that for $e \in E(f_i)$, $\overline{f}(e) \leq 8f(e) + 64 \cdot d_e \ln(\zeta m) < 9 \cdot 64 \cdot \widehat{d}_k \zeta \ln(\zeta m) \leq 18 \cdot 64 \cdot d_i \zeta \ln(\zeta m)$. Since in $\overline{f}_i$ player $i$ must assign all the demand $d_i$ to one path $p_{i,j} \in P_i$, we get $\overline{c}_i \geq d_i$. Consequently, player $i$ is $18 \cdot 64 \cdot \zeta \ln(\zeta m) = O(\zeta \ln(\zeta m))$-stable.

The claim follows by combining the two cases above. □

Lemma 6.4 shows that in any phase $k$ the rounded players are approximately stable in the respective game $I^k$. However, this result alone does not guarantee that the players will remain stable until the last phase, since rounding of new players may destabilize the previously stable players. In the following theorem we show that the players that have been rounded at previous phases, will remain stable in subsequent phases. This is then used to show that in the final flow assignment $\overline{f}$ in the last phase, each player is approximately stable with respect to the original unsplittable game $I$.

Theorem 6.5 (Equilibrium for unsplittable game). *For unsplittable game $I$, Algorithm 3 returns in polynomial time an unsplittable flow $\overline{f}$ which with high probability is a $O(\zeta \log(\zeta m))$-approximate Nash equilibrium.*

Proof. The time complexity has been discussed earlier. Hence, we focus on proving that $\overline{f}$ is an approximate Nash equilibrium for the original unsplittable game $I$. In order to do this, we will show that the rounded players of each phase remain approximately stable in the next phases. In phase $k$ let $\Phi_k$ be the players $\Phi \cap \mathcal{N}$, and let $\Psi_k$ be the players $(\Psi \setminus \Phi) \cap \mathcal{N}$. That is, $\Phi_k$ and $\Psi_k$ are the players that are rounded in phase $k$. Let $X_k$ be the set $X$ at phase $k$. Denote $Y_k = \bigcup_{1 \leq i \leq k} X_i$. Let $\ell_k = \widehat{d}_{k-1} \zeta \ln(\zeta m)$, for $k > 1$.

Each edge $e' \in X_{k'}$, $1 \leq k' < k$, has $f(e') \geq 64 \cdot \widehat{d}_{k'} \zeta \ln(\zeta m) \geq 64 \cdot \widehat{d}_{k-1} \zeta \ln(\zeta m) = 64 \cdot \ell_k$, since $\widehat{d}_{k'} \geq \widehat{d}_{k-1}$. From part b of Lemma 6.2, $\overline{f}(e') \geq f(e')/16$, and hence, $\overline{f}(e') \geq 4 \cdot \ell_k$.

From Lemma 6.3, each edge $e'' \in E \setminus Y_k$, in any phase $k'' > k$, has $f(e'') < 9 \cdot 64 \cdot \widehat{d}_{k''-1} \zeta \ln(\zeta m) \leq 9 \cdot 64 \cdot \widehat{d}_{k-1} \zeta \ln(\zeta m) = 9 \cdot 64 \cdot \ell_k$, and therefore, from part a of Lemma 6.2, $\overline{f}(e'') \leq 8f(e'') + 64 \cdot d_{e''} \ln(\zeta m) < 73 \cdot 64 \cdot \ell_k$.

From Lemma 6.1, for any $k \geq 1$, $X_k$ is a cut for the players in $\Phi_k$ with respect to game $I^k$. Therefore, $Y_k$ is a cut for the players in $\Phi_k$ with respect to the original game $I$, since $Y_k$ includes all removed edges from previous phases.

From Lemma 6.3, for each phase $k > 1$, for each edge $e \in X_k$ it holds that $f(e) < \ell'_k$ where $\ell'_k = 9 \cdot 64 \cdot \ell_k$. From the proof of Lemma 6.4, we have that each player $i \in \Phi_k$ is 144-stable in $I^k$ and in $\overline{f}_i$ it has cost $\overline{c}_i \leq 9c_i < 9\ell'_k = 81 \cdot 64 \cdot \ell_k$. This cost may increase in later phases for player $i$ due to the possibility of utilizing an edge $e'' \in E \setminus Y_k$ in assignment $\overline{f}_i$. However, as proven above this does not exceed $73 \cdot 64 \cdot \ell_k$. Thus, in $I$, it holds that $\overline{c}_i < 81 \cdot 64 \cdot \ell_k$. Further, as we proved above each edge $e' \in X'_k$, $1 \leq k' < k$, has bottleneck congestion at least $4 \cdot \ell_k$.

Therefore, the players in $\Phi_k$, $k > 1$, are $\max(144, (81 \cdot 64)/4) = O(1)$-stable in $I$. For $k = 1$, using part b of Lemma 6.2, we obtain for each player $i \in \Phi_1$ that $\overline{c}_i \geq 4 \cdot d_{max} \zeta \ln(\zeta m)$. From above, we have that each edge $r'' \in E \setminus Y_1$ has bottleneck congestion at most $73 \cdot 64 \cdot \ell_k < 73 \cdot 64 \cdot d_{\max} \zeta \ln(\zeta m)$. Hence, the players in $\Phi_1$ are $73 \cdot 64/4 = O(1)$-stable in $I$.

As shown in the proof of Lemma 6.4, the players $\Psi_k$ are $O(\zeta \log(\zeta m))$-stable in $I^k$. The players may destabilize in later rounds if the congestion increases in any edge they appear as dissolved constant-players in later rounds. In phase $k$ each player $i \in \Psi_k$ assigns all its demand to a path $p_{i,j} \in P_i$ that uses only edges in $E \setminus Y_{k-1}$. As described above, for each edge $e'' \in E \setminus Y_{k-1}$ its bottleneck congestion in phase $k'' > k$ will not exceed $73 \cdot 64 \cdot \widehat{d}_{k''-1}\zeta \ln(\zeta m) \leq 73 \cdot 64 \cdot \widehat{d}_k \zeta \ln(\zeta m) \leq 73 \cdot 64 \cdot 2d_i \zeta \ln(\zeta m)$, since $\widehat{d}_k \leq 2d_i$ (due to the definition of $\Psi_k$). Any unsplittable flow for player $i$ must have bottleneck congestion at least $d_i$. Therefore, player $i$ remains $O(\zeta \log(\zeta m))$-stable in $I$.

Thus, the result of stability follows by combining all the different player cases above. □

Note that Theorem 6.5 can still be applied even if we consider arbitrary $d_{\min} > 0$ (instead of assuming that $d_{\min} = 1$). For this, first we scale all demands by a factor $1/d_{\min}$ which normalizes all players to have demands at least 1 (as required by Algorithm 3), and the maximum demand becomes $d_{\max}/d_{\min}$. Then, we can apply Algorithm 3 which according to Theorem 6.5 gives a state $S$ which is an unsplittable $O(\zeta \log(\zeta m))$-approximate Nash equilibrium, such that $\zeta = \lceil \log(d_{\max}/d_{\min}) \rceil + 1$. Then, we recover the original demands by multiplying each player's demand with $d_{\min}$. Since each edge has scaled the bottleneck congestion by the same factor, the resulting state remains an unsplittable $O(\zeta \log(\zeta m))$-approximate Nash equilibrium.

## 7 CONCLUSION

We provided algorithms that compute Nash equilibria for bottleneck congestion games in polynomial time. We presented an algorithm to compute an equilibrium for splittable games, and we also gave algorithms to compute approximate equilibria for unsplittable games for uniform and non-uniform demands. Based on the proofs of the respective main theorems for the unsplittable games, it can be shown that the resulting equilibria are also poly-logarithmic approximations for the global unsplittable optimums.

Several future problems remain to be explored. We have considered in this work the identity player cost function on the bottleneck congestion. It would be interesting to examine other player cost functions as well, for example, linear cost functions on the congestion. Moreover, another possibility is to consider non-uniform cost functions for the players or the edges. Another problem is to improve the poly-logarithmic approximation factor, and remove the dependence on the demand values. Furthermore, it would be interesting to de-randomize the algorithms.

## REFERENCES


[1] Ron Banner and Ariel Orda. 2007. Bottleneck Routing Games in Communication Networks. *IEEE Journal on Selected Areas in Communications* 25, 6 (2007), 1173–1179.

[2] Costas Busch, Rajgopal Kannan, and Athanasios V. Vasilakos. 2012. Approximating Congestion + Dilation in Networks via 'Quality of Routing' Games. *IEEE Trans. Comput.* 61, 9 (September 2012), 1270–1283.

[3] Costas Busch and Malik Magdon-Ismail. 2009. Atomic Routing Games on Maximum Congestion. *Theoretical Computer Science* 410, 36 (August 2009), 3337–3347.

[4] Ioannis Caragiannis, Angelo Fanelli, Nick Gravin, and Alexander Skopalik. 2011. Efficient Computation of Approximate Pure Nash Equilibria in Congestion Games. In *Proceedings of the 2011 IEEE 52nd Annual Symposium on Foundations of Computer Science (FOCS '11)*. IEEE Computer Society, Washington, DC, USA, 532–541. DOI: http://dx.doi.org/10.1109/FOCS.2011.50

[5] Ioannis Caragiannis, Clemente Galdi, and Christos Kaklamanis. 2005. Network Load Games. In *ISAAC'05*. 809–818.

[6] George Christodoulou and Elias Koutsoupias. 2005. The price of anarchy of finite congestion games. In *Proceedings of the 37th Annual ACM Symposium on Theory of Computing (STOC)*. ACM, Baltimore, MD, USA, 67–73.

[7] Robert Cypher, Friedhelm Meyer auf der Heide, Christian Scheideler, and Berthold Vöcking. 1996. Universal Algorithms for Store-and-Forward and Wormhole Routing. In *In Proc. of the 28th ACM Symp. on Theory of Computing*. 356–365.

[8] Bart de Keijzer, Guido Schäfer, and Orestis A. Telelis. 2010. On the inefficiency of equilibria in linear bottleneck congestion games. In *Proceedings of the Third international conference on Algorithmic game theory (SAGT'10)*. Athens, Greece, 335–346.

[9] Tobias Harks, Martin Hoefer, Max Klimm, and Alexander Skopalik. 2013. Computing pure Nash and strong equilibria in bottleneck congestion games. *Mathematical Programming* 141, 1 (2013), 193–215. DOI: http://dx.doi.org/10.1007/s10107-012-0521-3

[10] Tobias Harks, Max Klimm, and Rolf H. Möhring. 2009. Strong Nash Equilibria in Games with the Lexicographical Improvement Property. In *WINE '09: Proceedings of the 5th International Workshop on Internet and Network Economics*. Rome, Italy, 463–470.

[11] Elias Koutsoupias and Christos Papadimitriou. 1999. Worst-case equilibria. In *Proceedings of the 16th Annual Symposium on Theoretical Aspects of Computer Science (STACS) (LNCS)*, Vol. 1563. Springer-Verlag, Trier, Germany, 404–413.

[12] F. T. Leighton, B. M. Maggs, and S. B. Rao. 1994. Packet routing and job-scheduling in $O(congestion + dilation)$ steps. *Combinatorica* 14 (1994), 167–186.

[13] Tom Leighton, Bruce Maggs, and Andrea W. Richa. 1999. Fast Algorithms for Finding O(Congestion + Dilation) Packet Routing Schedules. *Combinatorica* 19 (1999), 375–401.

[14] Lavy Libman and Ariel Orda. 2001. Atomic Resource Sharing in Noncooperative Networks. *Telecomunication Systems* 17, 4 (2001), 385–409.

[15] D. Monderer and L. S. Shapely. 1996. Potential Games. *Games and Economic Behavior* 14 (1996), 124–143.

[16] Rafail Ostrovsky and Yuval Rabani. 1997. Universal $O(\text{congestion+dilation+}\log^{1+\varepsilon} N)$ Local Control Packet Switching Algorithms. In *Proceedings of the 29th Annual ACM Symposium on the Theory of Computing*. New York, 644–653.

[17] Yuval Rabani and Éva Tardos. 1996. Distributed Packet Switching in Arbitrary Networks. In *Proceedings of the Twenty-Eighth Annual ACM Symposium on the Theory of Computing*. Philadelphia, Pennsylvania, 366–375.

[18] R. W. Rosenthal. 1973. A Class of Games Possesing Pure-Strategy Nash Equilibria. *International Journal of Game Theory* 2 (1973), 65–67.

[19] Tim Roughgarden. 2004. The maximum latency of selfish routing. In *Proceedings of the Fifteenth Annual ACM-SIAM Symposium on Discrete Algorithms (SODA)*. New Orleans, Louisiana, (USA), 980–981.

[20] Tim Roughgarden. 2005. Selfish routing with atomic players. In *Proc. 16th Symp. on Discrete Algorithms (SODA)*. ACM/SIAM, 1184–1185.

[21] Tim Roughgarden and Éva Tardos. 2002. How bad is Selfish Routing. *J. ACM* 49, 2 (March 2002), 236–259.

[22] Tim Roughgarden and Éva Tardos. 2004. Bounding the Inefficiency of Equilibria in Nonatomic Congestion Games. *Games and Economic Behavior* 47, 2 (2004), 389–403.

[23] Aravind Srinivasan and Chung-Piaw Teo. 1997. A Constant-factor Approximation Algorithm for Packet Routing, and Balancing Local vs. Global Criteria. In *Proceedings of the Twenty-ninth Annual ACM Symposium on Theory of Computing (STOC '97)*. ACM, New York, NY, USA, 636–643. DOI: http://dx.doi.org/10.1145/258533.258658

[24] Subhash Suri, Csaba D. Toth, and Yunhong Zhou. 2007. Selfish Load Balancing and Atomic Congestion Games. *Algorithmica* 47, 1 (Jan. 2007), 79–96.

# Spatio-Temporal Games Beyond One Dimension

SOHEIL BEHNEZHAD, University of Maryland
MAHSA DERAKHSHAN, University of Maryland
MOHAMMADTAGHI HAJIAGHAYI, University of Maryland
SAEED SEDDIGHIN, University of Maryland

Protecting valuable *targets* from an adversary is an ever-important international concern with far-reaching applications in wildlife protection, border protection, counter-terrorism, protection of ships from piracy, etc. As a successful recent approach, *security games* cast these issues as two-player games between a *defender* and an *attacker*. The defender decides on how to allocate the available *resources* to protect targets against the attacker who strives to inflict damage on them. The main question of interest here is equilibrium computation.

Our focus in this paper is on *spatio-temporal* security games. However, inspired by the paper of Xu [EC'16], we start with a general model of security games and show that any approximation (of any factor) for the defender's best response (DBR) problem leads to an approximation of the same factor for the actual game.

In most applications of security games, the targets are mobile. This leads to a well-studied class of succinct games, namely *spatio-temporal* security games, that is played in space and time. In such games, the defender has to specify a time-dependent patrolling strategy over a spatial domain to protect a set of moving targets. We give a generalized model of prior spatio-temporal security games that is played on a base graph $G$. That is, the patrols can be placed on the vertices of $G$ and move along its edges over time. This unifies and generalizes prior spatio-temporal models that only consider specific spatial domains such as lines or grids. Graphs can further model many other domains of practical interest such as roads, internal maps of buildings, etc.

Finding an optimal defender strategy becomes NP-hard on general graphs. To overcome this, we give an LP relaxation of the DBR problem and devise a rounding technique to obtain an almost optimal integral solution. More precisely, we show that one can achieve a $(1 - \epsilon)$-approximation in polynomial time if we allow the defender to use $\lceil \ln(1/\epsilon) \rceil$ times more patrols. We later show that this result is in some sense the best possible polynomial time algorithm (unless P=NP). Furthermore, we show that by using a novel *dependent rounding* technique, the same LP relaxation gives an optimal solution for specific domains of interest, such as one-dimensional spaces. This result simplifies and improves upon the prior algorithm of Behnezhad *et al.* [EC'17] on several aspects and can be generalized to other graphs of interest such as cycles.

Lastly, we note that most prior algorithms for security games assume that the attacker attacks only once and become intractable for a super-constant number of attacks. Our algorithms are fully polynomial in the input size and work for any given number of attacks.

CCS Concepts: • **Theory of computation** → **Algorithmic game theory and mechanism design**;

Additional Key Words and Phrases: security games, Nash equilibrium, ellipsoid method, approximation

Supported in part by NSF CAREER award CCF-1053605, NSF BIGDATA grant IIS-1546108, NSF AF:Medium grant CCF-1161365, DARPA GRAPHS/AFOSR grant FA9550-12-1-0423, and another DARPA SIMPLEX grant

Authors' addresses: Soheil Behnezhad, University of Maryland, soheil@cs.umd.edu; Mahsa Derakhshan, University of Maryland, mahsa@cs.umd.edu; MohammadTaghi Hajiaghayi, University of Maryland, hajiagha@cs.umd.edu; Saeed Seddighin, University of Maryland, saeedreza.seddighin@gmail.com.


*ACM EC'18, June 18–22, 2018, Ithaca, NY, USA.* ACM ISBN 978-1-4503-5829-3/18/06...$15.00
https://doi.org/10.1145/3219166.3219226

## 1 INTRODUCTION

Protecting a set of valuable *targets* from an adversary is a critical international concern with far-reaching applications in wildlife protection, border protection, counter-terrorism, protection of ships from piracy, etc. As a successful recent approach, security games cast these issues as two-player games between a *defender* and an *attacker*. The defender has to decide on how to allocate her *resources* to provide the *best* protection against the attacker who strives to inflict damage on the targets.

The most common solution concept that is adopted for security games in the literature is a *strong Stackelberg equilibrium*. The defender commits to a particular randomized allocation (e.g., a randomized patrolling schedule) whereas the attacker attacks at will. The defender's strategy is assumed to be revealed to the attacker due to the ability of the attacker in using surveillance to learn about the defender's strategy. The attacker then best-responds to this strategy by attacking a target that maximizes the expected damage. Therefore, the defender's goal is to play her optimal maximin strategy.

This approach has inspired a plethora of studies and research activities, including several awards and nominations (see Section 1.2 for an overview of related work). Remarkably, it has also been adopted in real-world scenarios such as airport checkpoints, US air marshals, urban transit systems and wildlife protection; many of these were recognized with commendations and awards. Security games also have other potential applications in protecting ships from piracy or protecting aid convoys in unstable regions.

In most applications of security games, the targets are mobile. This leads to a well-studied class of security games that is played in space and time [3, 8, 19]. In *spatio-temporal security games*, the defender has to specify a time-dependent patrolling strategy over a spatial domain to protect a set of moving targets. Figure 1 illustrates a spatio-temporal security game that is played on a discretized one-dimensional space. Time and space are respectively illustrated on x- and y-axis. The paths denote the trajectory of two patrols and the stars denote targets. The hatched area around the patrol paths denote their protection area.

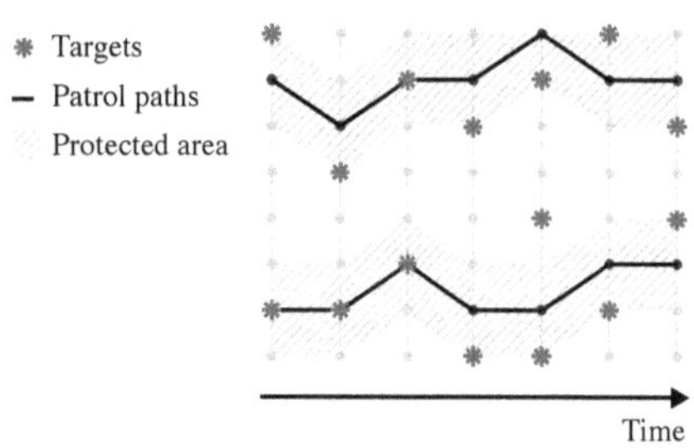


Fig. 1. A game instance on a path.

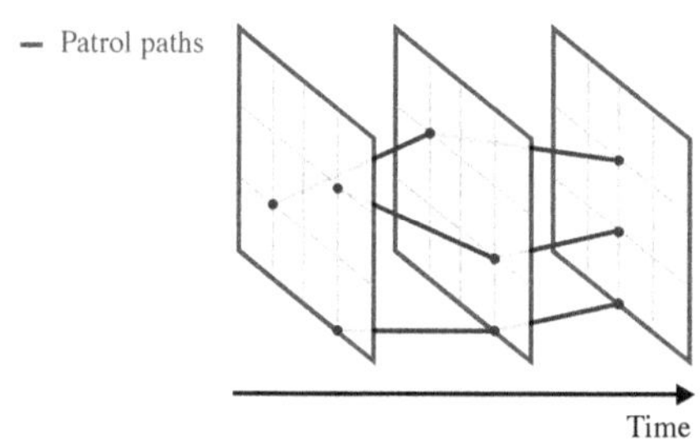


Fig. 2. Patrols moving on a grid.

The number of pure strategies of the defender in spatio-temporal security games is often exponentially large. This, combined with the overlapping *protection ranges* of the patrols, makes it notoriously difficult to find an optimal strategy in polynomial time. Even the seemingly easy case of discretized one-dimensional domains is quite a challenge and existence of a polynomial time algorithm remained open until the recent algorithm of [3] that solves it in polynomial time.

For some real-world applications of spatio-temporal security games such as border protection, the spatial domain is indeed one-dimensional. However, for many cases, the space is much more complicated. In wildlife protection, for instance, the targets (animals) can move in a rather complicated two-dimensional area. Ignoring complex natural objects such as hills or rivers, such environments can be modeled by grids [9]. However, there are many different instances that require even more complicated spatial domains.

In this paper, we consider spatio-temporal security games on graphs. That is, we assume that the underlying spatial domain is represented by an undirected graph $G$ where the patrols can be placed on the vertices of $G$ and move along its edges. This unifies and generalizes the aforementioned prior models. For instance, the graph for one-dimensional domains is simply a path[1] and discretized two-dimensional spaces can be modeled by grids (Figure 2). Graphs allow us to model even more complicated spatial domains such as roads, internal map of buildings, etc.

### 1.1 Our Results & Techniques

Most variants of security games can be shown to be *bilinear games* (see Section 3). That is, for any *fixed* strategy of the attacker, the defender's utility can be computed by a linear function (and vice versa). This allows us to compute the optimal minimax strategy of the defender via a linear program with roughly the same number of variables as the number of strategies of the defender and the same number of constraints as the number of strategies of the attacker (see LP 1).

The main challenge, however, lies in the fact that the number of strategies of both the defender and the attacker is exponentially large. That is, the defender can put her $K$ patrols in any subset of the vertices at the first time point and move them over time. On the other hand, the attacker can attack any subset of size up to $Q$ of the targets.

The huge number of strategies of the players leads to having an LP with exponentially many variables and exponentially many constraints which cannot be solved in polynomial time. The overall approach is to reduce the number of variables to a polynomial and then use the ellipsoid method to handle the exponential number of constraints. For this, we first take dual of LP 1 — given as LP 2 — which corresponds to the attacker's maximin strategy. LP 2 also has exponentially many variables and constraints, however, the difference is that the variables of LP 2 correspond to the attacker's pure strategies, whereas, the variables of LP 1 correspond to the defender's. We show that, fortunately, the inherent symmetry in attacker's strategies can be used to obtain an equivalent LP - given as LP 3 - with only polynomially many variables.

LP 3 can be solved using the ellipsoid method if we have access to a polynomial time *separating oracle*. The separating oracle is, in fact, equivalent to the defender's best response (DBR) problem which is the following combinatorial problem: Given a set of weighted targets over time, what is the pure strategy of the defender that *covers* the maximum weight? (See Definition 3 for the formal statement.) Therefore the complexity of solving spatio-temporal security games is linked directly to the complexity of this combinatorial problem. Indeed the main body of work in this work is devoted to solving (or approximating) the defender's best response problem for different variants of the game.

Using the oracle-based approach is nothing new and it has been used in the literature to find optimal strategies of certain types of succinct games, including security games [1, 10, 11, 13, 18, 19]. However, the DBR problem is not necessarily easier to solve than the actual game. In fact, the recent paper of Xu [18] shows that any exact solution for the actual game leads to an exact solution for the DBR problem. Therefore, unsurprisingly, there had been many instances where the actual game is solved directly without any attempts to solve the DBR problem (e.g. see [3]).

[1] In paths the *speed limit* of patrols is 1, i.e., they can only move to an adjacent location after each time point. To generalize this to an arbitrary speed limit $\Delta$ that is considered in prior work, the graph would be a *pseudo-path*, where each vertex is connected to $\Delta$ nearby vertices.

The DBR problem turns out to be NP-hard for many natural variants of spatio-temporal security games. Therefore, unless P = NP, we can only solve it *approximately* in polynomial time. An approximate solution might relax the number of patrols that are used or the fraction of the optimal solution that it achieves. Define a solution to be an $(\alpha, \beta)$-approximation if it achieves an $\alpha$ fraction of the optimal solution by using up to at most $\beta$ times more patrols (i.e., $\alpha \leq 1$ and $\beta \geq 1$). A natural question is whether an approximate DBR solution leads to an approximation of the actual game. Our first result answers this affirmatively.

**Result 1.** (Formally as Theorem 6). Any $(\alpha, \beta)$-approximation of the DBR problem leads to an $(\alpha, \beta)$-approximation of the actual game.

Using the known low-regret learning techniques, one can obtain an $\epsilon$-minimax equilibrium by having access to an additive FPTAS of DBR (see e.g., [10]). However, Result 1 is essentially different in that it preserves the multiplicative approx factors $\alpha$ and $\beta$. This generalization is essential for our contributions since the DBR does not admit any additive FPTAS in the general case (see Section 7). Having Result 1, we then focus on solving the DBR problem for different variants of spatio-temporal security games.

For spatio-temporal security games, the DBR problem is as follows: given $N$ targets that move over time, find a deterministic (i.e., pure) scheduling for $K$ homogeneous patrols that together maximize the total weight of protected targets. What complicates computation of the optimal scheduling is the existence of *protection range* around the patrols and the fact that *double coverage* has no benefit. To illustrate the computational hardness of the DBR problem, consider a game instance that is played only in one time unit (i.e., the targets and patrols do not move) and when there is a target of weight 1 on each vertex. Also assume that the protection range of each patrol is 1 (i.e., all targets at distance at most 1 are protected). If one can cover all the targets by $K$ patrols, then the dominating set of the base graph is at most $K$. A problem that is not only NP-hard, but also Log-APX-complete [7]. Also recall that the original DBR problem is much more complicated than this example; patrols and targets may move over time and the targets are not homogeneous.

Generally, to solve the DBR problem, we focus on an LP relaxation (formally given as LP 4) of the problem where we allow the patrols to move *fractionally*. That is, instead of integral paths, we assume that any flow of size one is a valid scheduling for a patrol. Note that the LP that computes the optimal fractional solution has to incorporate other constraints to prevent double coverage. Therefore, the standard integrality of network flow is not necessarily the case for our problem. After all, the problem is NP-hard in the general case, therefore, the integrality gap of this relaxation cannot be one. As such, the main technicality of our work is centered around different rounding techniques for the LP solution.

We first show that for general graphs, there exists a rounding scheme that achieves an almost optimal solution by using at most $\lceil \ln(1/\epsilon) \rceil$ times more patrols. To obtain this, we first decompose the fractional solution into $K$ flows of size 1, then pick $\lceil \ln(1/\epsilon) \rceil$ paths independently (but not uniformly) at random from each of these flows. We later show that, at least for specific values of $\epsilon$, this bound is essentially tight (see Theorem 18).

**Result 2.** (Formally as Theorem 15). For any $\epsilon > 0$, one can, in expectation, find in polynomial time, a $(1 - \epsilon, \lceil \ln \frac{1}{\epsilon} \rceil)$-approximation of the DBR problem, and therefore a $(1 - \epsilon, \lceil \ln \frac{1}{\epsilon} \rceil)$-approximation of the actual game, on general graphs.

The inapproximability results use, in an essential way, the generality of the underlying graph. However, in practice, we may be dealing with very specific graphs. For example, an important class of spatio-temporal security games are played in discretized one-dimensional (Figure 1) domains [3, 8, 9, 19] where the base graph would be a line. Therefore the question is: *can we obtain any better rounding scheme when we have certain assumptions about the input graph?* We show that, perhaps surprisingly, the integrality gap of LP 4 is indeed one for the one-dimensional case. Obtaining the following result.

**Result 3.** (Formally as Theorem 12). One can find in polynomial time, the optimal solution to the DBR problem, and therefore the actual game, for discretized one-dimensional spaces (i.e., lines or *pseudo-lines*).

To prove Result 3, we first pick a *mass variable* $\sigma \in [0, 1]$ uniformly at random; then construct each of the patrol paths according to $\sigma$. Roughly speaking, the main role of $\sigma$ is that, unlike the rounding for general graphs where the patrol paths are constructed independently from each other, it correlates how different patrols are rounded in a way that, we argue, will minimize double-coverage. We then show that this procedure, in expectation, achieves the same coverage as the fractional solution. Recall that any integral solution is also a valid fractional solution, thus, no rounded solution can achieve a better coverage. This implies that in order to achieve the same expected coverage, for every choice of $\sigma$, we indeed achieve the same coverage as the fractional solution.

Result 3 improves the recent polynomial time algorithm of [3] on several aspects. First, [3] assume that the attacker attacks only once and their algorithm becomes intractable for even two attacks, whereas, our solution works for any given number of attacks. Second, we show that our solution can be generalized to many related graphs of interest, such as cycles, where it is arguably impossible to generalize the approach of [3] to obtain exact solutions. Third, our solution is significantly simpler than that of [3]. We also note that a problem similar to the DBR problem was considered in [19] for which the authors give a $(1 - 1/e, 1)$-approximation. Combining this approximation with Result 1, one can achieve a $(1 - 1/e, 1)$-approximation of the actual game. Result 3 improves this by obtaining the exact solution.

### 1.2 Related Work

Security games have attracted a plethora of studies in the past decade, see the book [17] as well as more recent work, e.g. [3, 4, 8, 14, 18, 19]. Remarkably, this research has concerned both theory and practice; real-world deployments include: Canine-patrol and vehicle-checkpoints scheduling in Los Angeles airport (LAX) [15], US Coast Guard patrol boats [8], airport passenger screening by US Transportation Security Administration [5], scheduling flights for air marshals by US Federal Air Marshal Service [12], fare inspection in Los Angeles transit system [20], and wildlife protection in Malaysia [9].

Security game papers that are most relevant to this work address moving targets and patrols [3, 4, 8, 19] (as previously discussed). Other work concerned solving security games that are not (necessarily) spatio-temporal, e.g. [6, 13, 18].

Our work, in a broader context, is also related to Stackelberg games and equilibrium computation in succinct games. While it is known to be PPAD-hard in general, polynomial time algorithms exist for many natural variants. For background, see a survey [16]; or more recent papers in this context [1, 2, 10].

### 1.3 Paper Organization

In Section 2 we describe the model. In Section 3 we cover required game theory basics and describe, in Section 4, the overall oracle-based approach. In Section 5 we show how to solve (or approximate) the defender's best response problem for general graphs and specific domains (specifically one-dimensional domains) and in Section 6 show why this leads to an approximation of the actual game. Finally, in Section 7 we cover the hardness results.

## 2 THE MODEL

Security games are two-player games which are played between a *defender* and an *attacker*. In this paper, we focus on *spatio-temporal* security games where the goal of the defender is to protect a set of *moving targets* (e.g., ferries carrying passengers) from an attacker by choosing a time-dependent patrolling strategy (Figure 2 and Figure 1).

**Environment.** The game is played on a given graph $G = (V, E)$ where the defender's *patrols* and the targets can be positioned on the vertices of $G$. Furthermore, the temporal domain is assumed to be discretized into $T$ time points. We consider the full-information case where both the defender and the attacker have complete knowledge about the targets' movements a priori.[2] The defender has $K$ *homogeneous* patrols that can move, in each time step, to any adjacent vertex. However, we assume that the state of targets in one time point does not give us any information about them at other time points (e.g., the targets are not restricted, in contrast to the patrols, to move only to adjacent vertices in one time step).[3] In fact, from now on, we treat targets of different time points as $N$ totally different objects (i.e., $N = K \cdot N'$ where $N'$ denotes the number of targets in each time point). For any $i \in [N]$ we respectively denote by $t_i \in [T]$ and $\ell_i \in V$ the time and location of the $i$th target.

**Strategies.** As it was already mentioned, the defender has $K$ homogenous patrols that after each time step can either move to an adjacent vertex or remain at their current location. Moreover, the patrols have a *protection range* $R$ within which any target is *protected*. More precisely, a patrol that is located at vertex $v$ protects any target in location $u$ as long as $\text{dist}_G(v, u) \leq R$. A *patrol path*, which denotes the trajectory of a patrol, is a list $(v_1, v_2, \ldots, v_T)$ of size $T$ of vertices in $G$ where for any $t \in [T-1]$, either $v_{t+1} = v_t$ or $v_{t+1}$ is a neighbor of $v_t$ in $G$. A pure strategy of the defender is a set of $K$ patrol paths. A pure strategy of the attacker, on the other hand, is a subset $S_A \subseteq [N]$ of size at most $Q$ of the targets to attack.

**Utilities.** Associated to each target $i \in [N]$ is a weight $w_i \in \mathbb{R}_+$ and a cost $c_i \in \mathbb{R}_+$. For any $i \in [N]$, we denote the *partial utility* of the defender (resp. attacker) on target $i$ by $\text{U}_i^{\text{D}}$ (resp. $\text{U}_i^{\text{A}}$) and define it as follows.

$$\text{U}_i^{\text{D}} = \begin{cases} w_i & \text{if } i \text{ is not attacked,} \\ w_i - c_i & \text{if } i \text{ is attacked but protected,} \\ 0 & \text{if } i \text{ is attacked and unprotected.} \end{cases} \qquad \text{U}_i^{\text{A}} = \begin{cases} 0 & \text{if } i \text{ is not attacked,} \\ c_i & \text{if } i \text{ is attacked but protected,} \\ w_i & \text{if } i \text{ is attacked and unprotected.} \end{cases}$$

The overall utility of the defender (resp. attacker), which we denote by $\text{U}^{\text{D}}$ (resp. $\text{U}^{\text{A}}$) is simply sum of utilities on all targets, i.e.,

$$\text{U}^{\text{D}} = \textstyle\sum_{i \in [N]} \text{U}_i^{\text{D}}, \qquad \text{U}^{\text{A}} = \textstyle\sum_{i \in [N]} \text{U}_i^{\text{A}}. \tag{1}$$

Note that the game is constant sum with $\Gamma := \sum_{i=1}^{N} w_i$ being the sum of utilities. We assume that $c_i < w_i$ for any target $i$; meaning that protecting a target is strictly beneficial to the defender than not protecting it. Intuitively, for patrolling ferries, one can think of $w_i$ as the number of passengers

[2] We remark that the stochastic case, where the players are only given the distribution of target locations can be reduced to the full-information case.

[3] The independence of targets of different time points is a standard assumption in the literature [3, 8, 19]. We also note that all of our hardness results in Section 7 work for the unit time case when $T = 1$; meaning that it is essentially impossible to have any form of a time-dependent assumption on targets that makes the game solvable in polynomial time.

in ferry $i$. All of the passengers get hurt if the attacker attacks it and the defender does not protect it; however, only $c_i$ passengers get hurt if the attacker attacks the ferry but the defender protects it. The defender's overall utility is the number of unhurt passengers and the attacker's overall utility is the number of passengers that get hurt. Therefore, sum of utilities is always the total number of passengers in the ferries.

**The input.** Any instance of the game can be uniquely represented by $G = (V, E), T, K, R, Q$, and the weights and costs of targets. The total input size, therefore, is of $\Omega(|V| + |E| + N + \log(K \cdot R \cdot Q))$ bits. All the algorithms that we give are polynomial time in the input size.

## 3 GAME THEORY BACKGROUND

**Bilinear games.** Consider a two-player constant-sum game $\mathcal{G}$ with $\Gamma$ denoting the sum of utilities and polytopes $\mathcal{S}_1$ and $\mathcal{S}_2$ denoting the players' strategy spaces. As in the literature, we call $\mathcal{G}$ a *bilinear* game if there exists a *utility matrix* $M$ such that for any strategy profile $(\mathbf{x}, \mathbf{y}) \in \mathcal{S}_1 \times \mathcal{S}_2$, the first player gets utility $\mathbf{x}^T M\mathbf{y}$ (implying that the second player gets utility $\Gamma - \mathbf{x}^T M\mathbf{y}$).

Our model is not bilinear. However, the strategy spaces can be reformulated in a compact way that transforms the game into a payoff-equivalent bilinear game. To do so, let us represent each pure strategy of the defender by a vector $(x_1, \dots, x_N)^T$ where $x_i = 1$ if target $i$ is protected in the strategy and $x_i = 0$ otherwise. Note that any valid strategy maps to a point in $\{0, 1\}^N$ but the reverse is not always true, i.e., a point in $\{0, 1\}^N$ does not necessarily represent a valid strategy. We denote by $\mathcal{S}^D$ the set of pure strategies of the defender in the new space. Furthermore, we represent each pure strategy of the attacker by a vector $(y_1, \dots, y_N)^T$ in $\{0, 1\}^N$ where $y_i = 1$ if the attacker attacks target $i$ and $y_i = 0$ otherwise. Similarly, we denote by $\mathcal{S}^A$ the set of all valid strategies of the attacker in the new space.

Mixed strategies are basically linear combinations of pure strategies. Therefore, in the new space, each mixed strategy of the defender and the attacker can be represented by a vector of size $N$, where each entry is a (possibly fractional) number in $[0, 1]$. The $i$th entry of any strategy of the defender denotes the *marginal coverage probability* of target $i$. Similarly, the $i$th entry of any strategy of the attacker denotes the *marginal attacking probability* of target $i$.

By representing strategies in the marginal probability spaces, spatio-temporal security games become bilinear. If the defender and the attacker respectively play pure strategies $\mathbf{x} \in \mathcal{S}^D$ and $\mathbf{y} \in \mathcal{S}^A$, the utilities of the defender and the attacker respectively become

$$\mathrm{U}^D(\mathbf{x}, \mathbf{y}) := \sum_{i \in [N]} (w_i - c_i)x_i y_i - w_i y_i + w_i, \qquad \mathrm{U}^A(\mathbf{x}, \mathbf{y}) := \sum_{i \in [N]} (c_i - w_i)x_i y_i + w_i y_i. \quad (2)$$

Note that this is indeed a bilinear function of a slightly different form of $\mathbf{x}^T A\mathbf{y} + B\mathbf{y} + c$. The following lemma shows that utilities can essentially be computed via the same function for mixed strategies too.

**Lemma 1.** *Given a mixed strategy $\mathbf{x}'$ of the defender and a mixed strategy $\mathbf{y}'$ of the attacker, the expected utility of the defender can be computed via the following function where $x_i'$ and $y_i'$ respectively denote the marginal coverage and marginal attacking probabilities for target $i$.*

$$U^D(\mathbf{x}', \mathbf{y}') := \sum_{i \in [N]} (w_i - c_i)x_i' y_i' - w_i y_i' + w_i, \qquad U^A(\mathbf{x}', \mathbf{y}') := \sum_{i \in [N]} (c_i - w_i)x_i' y_i' + w_i y_i'. \quad (3)$$

The proof of Lemma 1 is included in the full-version of the paper.

**Solution concepts.** Many different solution concepts are of interest for security games. For example, a *strong Stackelberg Equilibrium* captures an equilibrium scenario where the *leader* (the defender) commits to a mixed strategy and the *follower* (the attacker) best-responds to this mixed-strategy. Other well-known solution concepts, such as the *Nash equilibrium* or *minimax* solutions have also been considered. The celebrated minimax theorem of von Neumann, states that all these solution concepts are equivalent to one another for constant-sum games. Hence, throughout the paper, we seek to compute only a maximin solution. That is, our goal is to find a strategy profile $(\mathbf{x}, \mathbf{y})$ where,

$$\mathbf{x} = \arg\max_{\mathbf{x}'} \left[ \min_{\mathbf{y}'}(\mathrm{U}^D(\mathbf{x}', \mathbf{y}')) \right], \qquad \text{and} \qquad \mathbf{y} = \arg\max_{\mathbf{y}'} \left[ \min_{\mathbf{x}'}(\mathrm{U}^A(\mathbf{x}', \mathbf{y}')) \right].$$

Since it becomes computationally difficult to find the exact maximin strategies in some cases, we are also interested in finding *approximate maximin strategies.* A strategy $\mathbf{x}$ is an $\alpha$-approximate minimax strategy for the defender if it guarantees receiving an $\alpha$ fraction of the maximin value, or more precisely,

$$\min_{\mathbf{y}'}[\mathrm{U}^D(\mathbf{x}, \mathbf{y}')] \geq \alpha \cdot \max_{\mathbf{x}'} \left( \min_{\mathbf{y}'}[\mathrm{U}^D(\mathbf{x}', \mathbf{y}')] \right).$$ [4]

## 4 A GENERAL APPROACH FOR SOLVING SECURITY GAMES

Maximin strategies can be efficiently computed for bilinear games using a simple linear program if the players have polynomially many pure strategies. Unfortunately, the number of pure strategies of the defender in our game is exponentially large. Nevertheless, since our solutions essentially build upon this linear program, we start by stating defender's minimax linear program as LP 1.[5]

$$\begin{array}{lll} \min & u, & \\ \text{s.t.} & 0 \leq p_d & \forall \mathbf{d} \in \mathcal{S}^D, \\ & \sum_{\mathbf{d} \in \mathcal{S}^D} p_d = 1, & \\ & \sum_{\mathbf{d} \in \mathcal{S}^D} p_d \cdot \mathbf{d} = \mathbf{x}, & \\ & \sum_{i \in [N]} (c_i - w_i) x_i a_i + w_i a_i \leq u & \forall \mathbf{a} \in \mathcal{S}^A. \end{array}$$

LP 1. Defender's minimax strategy. Variables are $x_i$ (probability of protecting target $i$), $p_d$ (probability of playing pure strategy $d$ of the defender), and $u$ (the attacker's utility).

LP 1 has exponentially many variables and constraints, thus, we cannot directly solve it in polynomial time. Our goal is to convert it to another LP with polynomially many variables (but still with exponentially many constraints) and use ellipsoid method to solve it. To do this, consider the dual form of LP 1 which is formally stated as LP 2.

$$\begin{array}{lll} \max & \mathbf{y} \cdot \mathbf{w} - c, & \\ \text{s.t.} & 0 \leq p_a & \forall \mathbf{a} \in \mathcal{S}^A, \\ & \sum_{\mathbf{a} \in \mathcal{S}^A} p_a = 1, & \\ & \sum_{\mathbf{a} \in \mathcal{S}^A} p_a \cdot \mathbf{a} = \mathbf{y} & \\ & h_i = (w_i - c_i) y_i & \forall i \in [N], \\ & \mathbf{h} \cdot \mathbf{d} \leq c & \forall \mathbf{d} \in \mathcal{S}^D. \end{array}$$

LP 2. Dual form of LP 1, which corresponds to attacker's maximin strategy. Variables are $y_i$ (marginal probability of attacking target $i$), $p_a$ (probability of playing strategy $a$ of the attacker), $h_i$, and $c$ (the defender's *coverage*).

[4] An additive form of approximation, called $\epsilon$-minimax or $\epsilon$-equilibrium is also common in the literature; however, we emphasize that all of our approximation factors are multiplicative.

[5] We remark that our results in this section have no assumption on the structure of the defender's strategy set $\mathcal{S}^D$ and can be adopted to other models of security games (i.e., not necessarily spatio-temporal) with similar payoff structures.

Note that LP 2 also has exponentially many variables. However, the simplicity of valid pure strategies of the attacker helps us in obtaining an equivalent LP with only polynomially many variables. To elaborate more on this, first note that the first 3 constraints of LP 2 ensure only that $\mathbf{y}$ is a valid mixed strategy of the attacker. That is, $\mathbf{y}$ must be a linear combination of the strategies in $\mathcal{S}^A$. To do this, LP 2 includes a variable $p_a$ for every strategy $\mathbf{a} \in \mathcal{S}^A$, indicating the probability of playing strategy $\mathbf{a}$. Since the attacker has $\binom{N}{Q}$ different pure strategies, this leads to an exponential (in $Q$) number of variables. However, observe that these variables are only used to ensure validity of vector $\mathbf{y}$ (i.e., they do not appear in the other constraints). To simplify LP 2 and get rid of the exponential number of variables, we show an alternative way that ensures validity of $\mathbf{y}$ via only polynomially many variables. Note that any valid mixed strategy $\mathbf{y}$ of the attacker should satisfy the following two conditions:

(1) For any $i \in [N]$, $0 \le y_i \le 1$,
(2) $\sum_{i\in[N]} y_i = Q$.

In Lemma 2 we show that these conditions are also sufficient to ensure $\mathbf{y}$ is a valid strategy.

**Lemma 2.** *Let* $\mathbf{y} = (y_1, \ldots, y_N)$ *be a vector satisfying* $\sum_{i\in[N]} y_i = Q$ *and* $0 \le y_i \le 1$ *for any* $i \in [N]$. *There exists a mixed strategy for the attacker that provides marginal attacking probability* $\mathbf{y}$.

In the interest of space, we defer the proof of Lemma 2 to the full-version of the paper. Roughly speaking, given a vector $\mathbf{y}$ that satisfies the aforementioned constraints, we iteratively extract a pure strategy $\mathbf{s} \in \mathcal{S}^A$ with an assigned probability $p$ and update $\mathbf{y}$ to be $\mathbf{y} - p\mathbf{s}$. The challenge is to make sure that there are at least $Q$ non-zero entries in $\mathbf{y}$ at every step and that the probabilities that we assign to the strategies does not exceed 1 when $\mathbf{y}$ becomes zero.

As a result of Lemma 2, we can simplify LP 2 to obtain an equivalent LP — formally given as LP 3 — with only polynomially many variables.

$$
\begin{array}{lll}
\max & \mathbf{y}\cdot\mathbf{w} - c, & \\
\text{s.t.} & 0 \le y_i \le 1 & \forall i \in [N], \\
& \sum_{i\in[N]} y_i = Q, & \\
& h_i = (w_i - c_i)y_i & \forall i \in [N], \\
& \mathbf{h}\cdot\mathbf{d} \le c & \forall \mathbf{d} \in \mathcal{S}^D.
\end{array}
$$

LP 3. A simplified version of LP 2 with polynomially many variables. Variables are $y_i$ (probability of attacking target $i$), $h_i$, and $c$ (the defender's *coverage*).

Despite having a polynomial number of variables, the number of constraints in LP 3 is still exponentially large. Nevertheless, we can use the ellipsoid method to solve LP 3 in polynomial time if we have access to a polynomial time *separation oracle* that for any assignment to the variables of LP 3 either asserts that the assignment does not violate any of the constraints or otherwise returns a violated constraint. Verifying that the first three constraint sets in LP 3 are not violated can easily be done in polynomial time since there are only $2N + 1$ such constraints. The main challenge is to confirm that no constraint of the fourth type is violated. This can be achieved by solving the *defender's best response* problem, which we formally define as follows.

**Definition 3** (Defender's best response problem). For a given *weight vector* $\mathbf{h} \in \mathbb{R}_+^N$, the defender's best response problem,

$$\mathrm{DBR}(\mathbf{h}) := \arg\max_{\mathbf{s}\in\mathcal{S}^D} [\mathbf{h}\cdot\mathbf{s}],$$

is to find a pure strategy that *covers* the maximum possible weight. Moreover, we denote by $\mathrm{C}(\mathbf{h}) := \max_{\mathbf{s}\in\mathcal{S}^D}[\mathbf{h}\cdot\mathbf{s}]$ the best possible *coverage* for the defender, i.e., $\mathrm{C}(\mathbf{h}) = \mathbf{h}\cdot\mathrm{DBR}(\mathbf{h})$.

**Observation 4.** *The separation oracle of LP 3 can be solved in polynomial time if DBR can be solved in polynomial time.*

It does not immediately follow that a solution for the dual LP implies a solution for the primal LP since the primal LP has exponentially many variables and even constructing a solution may require exponential time. However, it has been proven that in such cases, there always exists a primal solution with polynomially many non-zero variables and that a separation oracle for the dual LP along with the ellipsoid method obtains such a solution (see e.g. [1]). So far, it was shown that if the DBR problem can be solved in polynomial time, the actual game can also be solved in polynomial time. The DBR problem, however, is generally NP-hard even for restricted cases where $T = 1$. However, we show that, roughly, any approximation of the DBR problem leads to an approximation of the actual game with the same approx factor. We start by defining approximate DBR.

**Definition 5** (Approximate DBR). For any $\alpha \leq 1$ and $\beta \geq 1$, and any given weight vector $\mathbf{h} \in \mathbb{R}_+^N$, a pure strategy $\mathbf{s}$ of the defender is an $(\alpha, \beta)$-approximation of the DBR problem, if it uses up to $\beta K$ patrols and

$$\mathbf{h} \cdot \mathbf{s} \geq \alpha[\mathbf{h} \cdot \mathrm{DBR}(\mathbf{h})].$$

Theorem 6 implies that both approximation factors ($\alpha$ and $\beta$) can be preserved in polynomial time for the actual game. The proof is technical and we defer it to Section 6.

**Theorem 6.** *Having access to an oracle that provides a $(\alpha, \beta)$-approximation of the defender's best response problem, one can achieve in polynomial time, an $\alpha$-approximate maximin strategy of the defender that uses up to $\beta K$ patrols.*

## 5 APPROXIMATING DEFENDER'S BEST RESPONSE

We showed that even an approximate solution for the defender's best response (DBR) problem leads to an approximation of the actual game. As such, in this section, we focus on the DBR problem and give a general approach for solving or approximating it.

Recall that in the DBR problem, given a weight vector $\mathbf{h} \in \mathbb{R}_+^N$, the solution is a defender's pure strategy $\mathbf{s} \in \mathcal{S}$ that maximizes $\mathbf{h} \cdot \mathbf{s}$. In other words, the solution is a pure strategy of the defender that maximizes the total weight of protected targets.

The general approach is to relax the integrality assumption of patrol paths. Roughly speaking, we allow the patrols to be partitioned into fractions with each fraction moving independently. For example, 0.6 fraction of a patrol might pass through a patrol path and the remaining 0.4 fraction through another one. This relaxation allows us to solve the problem optimally via an LP. We then analyse the integrality gap of this LP using different rounding techniques.

We first define a directed graph $\mathcal{T}(V_\mathcal{T}, E_\mathcal{T})$, which we refer to as the *temporal graph*, in such a way that any patrol path maps to a path in $\mathcal{T}$. Also any *fractional patrol path* can be represented as a flow of size 1 in this graph. We use this representation to write the Linear Program 4 which finds a fractional solution to the defender's best response problem. Recall that the game is played on graph $G = (V, E)$ where the defender's patrols and the targets can be positioned on the vertices of $G$. Also, recall that the temporal domain has $T$ discretized time points.

**Definition 7** (Temporal graph). Given the base graph $G = (V, E)$ on which the game is played, the *temporal graph* $\mathcal{T} = (V_\mathcal{T}, E_\mathcal{T})$ is defined as follows.

- The vertex set of $\mathcal{T}$ is composed of $T$ copies $V_1, \ldots, V_T$ of $V$. For any $v \in V$, we denote by $v^{(t)}$ its equivalent vertex in $V_t$.
- For any edge $\{u, v\} \in E$ and for any time point $t \in [T-1]$, the edge set $E_\mathcal{T}$ of $\mathcal{T}$ contains two directed edges: one from $u^{(t)}$ to $v^{(t+1)}$ and one from $v^{(t)}$ to $u^{(t+1)}$.

Before proceeding, we need a few definitions over the temporal graph. For any target $a \in [N]$ in time $t_a$ and at vertex $\ell_a$, we denote by $\text{cover}(a) := \{v^{(t_a)} : v^{(t_a)} \in V_{t_a}, \text{dist}_G(v, \ell_a) \le R\}$ the set of all vertices in $V_{t_a}$ from which $a$ is protected in the base graph. Moreover, for any $v \in V_{\mathcal{T}}$, sets $A^+(v)$ and $A^-(v)$ respectively denote incoming and outgoing edges of $v$.

It is not hard to imagine a one-to-one mapping between the set of all possible patrol paths and paths of length $T$ in $\mathcal{T}$. Note that a path $P$ of length $T$ in $\mathcal{T}$ must start from a vertex in $V_1$ and end at a vertex in $V_T$ since there are no *backward* edges. The equivalent patrol path in the base graph is a path of length $T$ that traverses the vertices equivalent to that of $P$ in $G$ in the same order. Throughout the paper, we may slightly abuse the notation and refer to such paths in $\mathcal{T}$ as patrol paths.

Any pure strategy of the defender can be represented by $K$ patrol paths in graph $\mathcal{T}$. To be able to solve the DBR problem in polynomial time, we relax the *integrality assumption* on the patrol paths. More precisely, we assume that any network flow of size $K$ that starts from the vertices in $V_1$ and ends at the vertices in $V_T$ is a valid pure strategy. We then write a linear program — which is formally given as LP 4 — to find a relaxed pure strategy that maximizes the total coverage.

$$
\begin{array}{lll}
\max & \mathbf{p} \cdot \mathbf{h} & \\
\text{s.t.} & 0 \le f_v & \forall v, t : t \in [T], v \in V_t \\
& \sum_{v \in V_t} f_v = K & \forall t : t \in [T] \\
& \sum_{e \in A^-(v)} f_e = f_v & \forall t, v : t \in [T-1], v \in V_t \\
& \sum_{e \in A^+(v)} f_e = f_v & \forall t, v : t \in [2, T], v \in V_t \\
& p_i \le \sum_{v \in \text{cover}(i)} f_v & \forall i \in [N] \\
& p_i \le 1 & \forall i \in [N]
\end{array}
$$

LP 4. LP relaxation of the DBR problem. Variables are $p_i$ (protection of target $i$) and $f_a$ (amount of flow passing through vertex or edge $a$). Find the informal description of the LP in the text.

**Description of LP 4.** Variable $f_a$ denotes the amount of flow passing through $a$ where $a$ may be either an edge or a vertex in graph $\mathcal{T}$. The first four constraints are standard network flow constraints to ensure we get a valid flow of size $K$. To maximize the coverage, for any target $i \in [N]$ we use a variable $p_i$ that indicates the total coverage of target $i$ in the solution. More precisely, 1 indicates that the target is fully covered and 0 indicates that the target is not covered by any patrol. Note that generally, the amount of flow around a target might be more than 1, to prevent double coverage in such scenarios, we add a constraint to ensure $p_i$ never exceeds 1. The objective function, clearly, is to maximize the total coverage which is basically $\mathbf{p} \cdot \mathbf{h}$.

The rest of this section is mainly focused on different rounding methods that help us achieve approximation algorithms for the integral DBR problem.

### 5.1 One Dimensional Domains

An important class of security games is played on one-dimensional domains, that is the patrols could move over a discretized line (see Figure 1). This model has been considered several times in the literature because of its numerous real-world applications. A polynomial time algorithm (though, under the assumption that the attacker attacks only once) was previously given by [3]. In this section, we show how by a dependent rounding technique, one can solve LP 4 to obtain an exact solution for the DBR problem in one-dimensional domains and solve the actual game. We note that a similar DBR problem has been considered in [19] where the authors give a $1 - 1/e$ approximation for it, using submodular maximization algorithms. Combining this approximation with Theorem 6 one can achieve a $1 - 1/e$ approximation of the actual game. Our focus in this section is to show how the DBR problem could be optimally solved by rounding LP 4.

We can model the one-dimensional space via a path of length $M$. However, this limits the patrols to only move to an adjacent vertex in after each time point. The original model is more general than this, given a speed limit $\Delta$, each patrol is able to move to any other location with distance at most $\Delta$. To consider this, we construct the base graph $G_1 = (V_1, E_1)$ as follows: The vertex set $V_1$ contains $M$ vertices $\{v_1, v_2, \ldots, v_M\}$, and two vertices $v_i$ and $v_j$ are connected to each other iff $|i - j| \leq \Delta$. Intuitively, we add edges between any two locations (i.e., vertices) that are accessible from each other in one time step. Throughout the section, we say a vertex $v_i$ is above $v_j$ or vertex $v_j$ is below vertex $v_i$, if $i > j$.

Consider the solution $(\mathbf{f}, \mathbf{p})$ of LP 4 for graph $G_1$. Recall that $\mathcal{T} = (V_\mathcal{T}, E_\mathcal{T})$ denotes the temporal graph of $G_1$ and that $f_v$ denotes the amount of flow passing through a vertex $v \in V_\mathcal{T}$. The intuition behind our rounding algorithm, as illustrated in Figure 3, is as follows: (1) Choose a fractional number $\sigma$ uniformly at random from $[0, 1]$. (2) For any time point $t$, and for any $k \in [K]$, put the $k$th patrol at the top-most vertex in time $t$ where the amount of flow passing through the vertices below it is less than $k + \sigma$. To prove that this rounding technique works we need to prove two things: That the patrol paths are valid (i.e., the speed limits are not violated), and that it provides the same coverage. Roughly speaking, the validity of patrol paths is proved by the structure of the flows. The amount of coverage is also preserved since, we show, this rounding method minimizes double coverage.

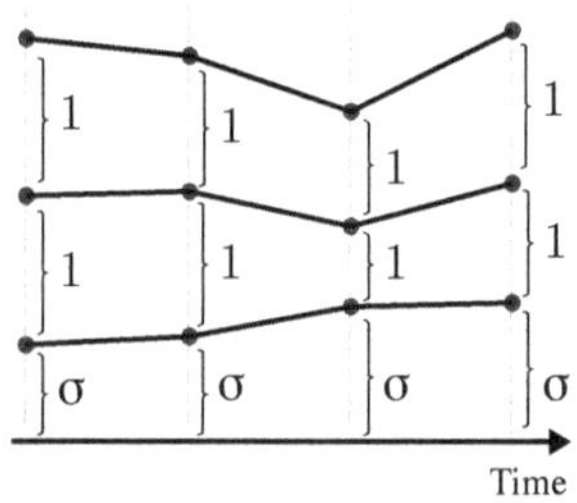


Fig. 3. Intuition of Algorithm 1.

---

**Algorithm 1** Rounding technique for the fractional solution of LP 4 in the one-dimensional case.

1: Choose a fractional number $\sigma$ in range $[0, 1]$ u.a.r. ▷ Remark: any choice of $\sigma$ works.

2: For any $k \in [K]$ and any $t \in [T]$, let $\mathrm{P}(k, t) := \max\{i : \sum_{j=1}^{i-1} f_{v_j^{(t)}} < k + \sigma\}$ be the top-most vertex at time $t$ that the amount of flow passing through the vertices below it is less than $k + \sigma$.

3: Return $\left\{(v_{\mathrm{P}(k,1)}, \ldots, v_{\mathrm{P}(k,T)})\right\}_{k \in [K]}$. ▷ Lemma 8 shows this is a valid set of patrol paths.

---

**Lemma 8.** *The solution of Algorithm 1 is a valid set of patrol paths. That is, for any $k \in [K]$ and any $t \in [T - 1]$, we have $|\mathrm{P}(k, t) - \mathrm{P}(k, t + 1)| \leq \Delta$.*

**Proof.** We first assume that the path assigned to patrol $k \in [K]$ violates the condition at time $t \in [T - 1]$, then we obtain a contradiction. Let $a := \mathrm{P}(k, t)$ and $b := \mathrm{P}(k, t + 1)$. This violation means that due to the patrols' limited speed, it is not possible for them to move from vertex $v_a$ to $v_b$ at one unit of time. More formally, $|a - b| > \Delta$. Therefore, either $b > a + \Delta$ or $a > b + \Delta$.

We first consider the case where $a > b + \Delta$. By Line 2 of Algorithm 1,

$$\textstyle\sum_{j=1}^{a-1} f_{v_j^{(t)}} < k + \sigma, \qquad \text{and} \qquad \sum_{j=1}^{b} f_{v_j^{(t+1)}} \geq k + \sigma;$$

therefore,

$$\textstyle\sum_{j=1}^{a-1} f_{v_j^{(t)}} < \sum_{j=1}^{b} f_{v_j^{(t+1)}}. \tag{4}$$

Let $A$ and $B$ respectively denote the set of vertices $\{v_1^{(t)}, \ldots, v_{a-1}^{(t)}\}$ and $\{v_1^{(t+1)}, \ldots, v_b^{(t+1)}\}$. Inequality 4 implies that the overall amount of flow passing through vertices in set $A$ is less than that of set $B$. However, by the structure of graph $\mathcal{T}$ and the assumption $a > b + \Delta$, all the incoming edges to vertices in set $B$ are from vertices in set $A$. Hence, any flow passing though $B$ comes from the vertices in $A$. This implies that the amount of flow passing through vertices in $A$ cannot be less than the amount of flow passing through $B$ which contradicts Inequality 4.

The case of $b > a + \Delta$ also follows from a similar argument. By Line 2 of Algorithm 1,

$$\sum_{j=1}^{a} f_{v_j^{(t)}} \geq k + \sigma, \qquad \text{and} \qquad \sum_{j=1}^{b-1} f_{v_j^{(t+1)}} < k + \sigma;$$

therefore,

$$\sum_{j=1}^{b-1} f_{v_j^{(t+1)}} < \sum_{j=1}^{a} f_{v_j^{(t)}}. \tag{5}$$

Let $A' = \{v_1^{(t)}, \ldots, v_a^{(t)}\}$ and let $B' = \{v_1^{(t+1)}, \ldots, v_{b-1}^{(t+1)}\}$. Inequality 5 implies that the overall amount of flow passing through vertices in set $B'$ is less than that of set $A'$. However, by the structure of graph $\mathcal{T}$ and the assumption $b > a + \Delta$, all the outgoing edges of the vertices in $A'$ are to a vertex in $B'$. Hence, any flow passing though $A'$ also passes through $B'$; which contradicts Inequality 4. □

In Lemma 9 we prove that the expected coverage of the integral solution given by Algorithm 1 is equal to that of the fractional one. Let $\text{OPT}_4$ denote the coverage of the fractional solution given by LP 4. Also let vector $\mathbf{x}$ be the marginal coverage probability of the pure strategy that is obtained by Algorithm 1. Note that $\mathbf{x}$ is a random variable due to the randomness in the rounding algorithm.

**Lemma 9.** *Algorithm 1 provides the same coverage as LP 4 in expectation, that is* $\mathbb{E}[\mathbf{h} \cdot \mathbf{x}] = OPT_4$.

**Proof.** Since $\text{OPT}_4 = \mathbf{p} \cdot \mathbf{h}$, by linearity of expectation it suffices to prove that for any $a \in [N]$, we have $\mathbb{E}[x_a] \geq p_a$ holds. For an arbitrary target $a$, let $i$ and $j$ respectively denote the smallest and the greatest number in $[M]$ where $v_i^{(t_a)}, v_j^{(t_a)} \in \text{cover}(a)$. Note that for any $k \in [i, j]$, vertex $v_k^{(t_a)}$ is also in cover$(a)$. We prove our claim using the fact that $x_a = 1$ iff there exists a $k \in [M]$, where $\text{P}(k, t_a) \in [i, j]$. Let $l_a := \sum_{k \in [i-1]} f_{v_k^{(t)}}$ and $r_a := \sum_{k \in [j]} f_{v_k^{(t)}}$. Note that $p_a \leq r_a - l_a$. We consider 3 different cases based on values of $l_a$ and $r_a$.

- $\lceil l_a \rceil = \lceil r_a \rceil$: let $k := \lceil l_a \rceil$. In this case, $p(k, t_a) \in [i, j]$ iff $l_a - \lfloor l_a \rfloor < \sigma \leq r_a - \lfloor r_a \rfloor$. Therefore, $\mathbb{E}[x_a] = r_a - l_a$, and $\mathbb{E}[x_a] \geq p_a$.
- $\lceil r_a \rceil - \lceil l_a \rceil = 1$: let $k_1 := \lceil l_a \rceil$ and $k_2 := \lceil r_a \rceil$. In this case, $l_a - \lfloor l_a \rfloor < \sigma \leq 1$ iff $p(k_1, t_a) \in [i, j]$. Also, $0 \leq \sigma \leq r_a - \lfloor r_a \rfloor$ iff $p(k_2, t_a) \in [i, j]$. Therefore, $\mathbb{E}[x_a] = \min(1, r_a - l_a)$ and $\mathbb{E}[x_a] \geq p_a$.
- $\lceil r_a \rceil - \lceil l_a \rceil > 1$: in this case, $p(\lceil r_a \rceil + 1, t_a) \in [i, j]$ always holds, therefore $1 = p_i = \mathbb{E}[x_a]$.

Three mentioned cases covers all the possiblities for the relation between $l_a$ and $r_a$, and $p_a \leq \mathbb{E}[x_a]$ holds in three of them. Thus for any $a \in [N]$, $p_a \leq \mathbb{E}[x_a]$ and as a result, $\text{OPT}_4 = \mathbb{E}[h \cdot x]$. □

Note that, any integral solution is also a valid fractional solution for LP 4. Since LP 4 finds the solution with maximum coverage, no integral solution can provide a higher coverage than the solution of LP 4. Implying that in order for the expected value of $\mathbb{E}[\mathbf{h} \cdot \mathbf{x}]$ to be the same as $\text{OPT}_4$, for every choice of $\sigma$, the integral solution should provide the same coverage as LP 4.

**Corollary 10** (of Lemma 9). *For any choice of* $\sigma$, *Algorithm 1 provides the same coverage as LP 4.*

To summarize, recall that the input to the DBR problem is a weight vector $\mathbf{h} \in \mathbb{R}_+^N$. We first find a an optimal fractional solution using LP 4; then round it using Algorithm 1 to obtain an integral solution. The output of this algorithm is $k$ patrol paths, each assigned to a patrol. In Lemma 8, we prove that these paths do not violate the speed limit and show in Corollary 10 that for any choice of $\sigma$, this algorithm provides the same coverage as LP 4. Meaning that the integrality gap of LP 4, is 1 for the one dimensional case (i.e., over graph $G_1$) and that we can solve the DBR problem optimally in polynomial time.

**Theorem 11.** *There exists an algorithm that solves the defender's best response (DBR) problem optimally for the one-dimensional case (i.e., over graph $G_1$) in polynomial time.*

Combined with Theorem 6 (for $\alpha = \beta = 1$), this implies that the optimal minimax strategy of the defender for the one-dimensional case can be obtained in polynomial time.

**Corollary 12** (of Theorem 12)**.** *There exists a polynomial time algorithm to find the defender's optimal minimax strategy for the one-dimensional case (i.e., over graph $G_1$) in polynomial time.*

**Generalization to cycles.** Assume that the base graph is a cycle, or even a *pseudo-cycle* where each node of the cycle also has edges to its $\Delta$ nearby vertices. We argue here that essentially the same rounding procedure can be slightly modified to obtain an exact solution. For space limits, we do not provide a detailed proof and only describe the high level ideas behind the solution. Roughly speaking, the challenge compared to path graph, is that the patrols may need to *rotate* around the cycle over time. That is, the same approach of starting from the bottom-most vertex and putting a patrol at the first vertex that contains a flow of size $\sigma + k$ below it does not work for cycles. Instead, for each time point $t$, we fix a different vertex $v_t$ and start the same procedure from this vertex. To fix these vertices, we first decompose the flow of LP 4 into $K$ flows of size 1 in such a way that the $i$th flow is *sandwiched* between the $i-1$th and the $i+1$th flows.[6] Next, it suffices to pick two flows, say the first and the second, and for each time point $t$, fix a vertex $v_t$ that is sandwiched between the first and the second flow.

## 5.2 General Graphs

The goal of this section is to show that one can achieve, in polynomial time, a near-optimal solution of defender's best response problem by allowing the defender to have a slightly greater number of patrols. Theorem 15 formalizes the main result of this section. To prove this theorem we first give a rounding technique in Algorithm 2 for converting the fractional solution given by LP 4 to an integral one. Note that the integral solution is an integral pure strategy of the defender. We, then prove that solving the LP combined with this rounding technique gives us the approximation mentioned in Theorem 15.

Given a solution of LP 4 and an $\epsilon > 0$, Algorithm 2 outputs an integral pure strategy of the defender that uses up to $\lceil \ln(1/\epsilon) \rceil \cdot K$ patrols. Graph $\mathcal{T} = (V_{\mathcal{T}}, E_{\mathcal{T}})$ is the temporal graph of graph $G$. Recall that any solution of LP 4 is a flow of size $K$ from $V_1$ to $V_T$ in graph $\mathcal{T}$. Let $F$ denote this flow. Algorithm 2, first decomposes $F$ into a set of paths denoted by $P$. (The definition of flow decomposition is given in Definition 13.) There exists a simple greedy algorithm that decomposes $F$ into polynomially many paths. It is possible to iteratively choose a flow path and remove it from $F$ such that the remaining flow of at least one edge decreases to 0 after each iteration. Therefore, the greedy algorithm returns a set $P$ where $|P|$ is polynomial in the size of $E_{\mathcal{T}}$. In the next step, Algorithm 2, partitions $P$ into $K$ subsets denoted by $P_1 \dots P_K$ where for any $i \in K$, $\sum_{p \in P_i} f_p = 1$. Note that, paths in $P$ can be decomposed to some fractions, thus it is possible to find such a partitioning in $O(|P|)$ time. For any $i \in K$, Algorithm 2 independently at random chooses $\lceil \ln(1/\epsilon) \rceil$ patrol paths from each $P_i$. The randomness is in a way that the probability of choosing any path is equal to the flow assigned to that. In Lemma 14, we prove that in expectation this algorithm gives a $(1-\epsilon, \lceil \ln(1/\epsilon) \rceil)$-approximation of for defender's best response problem.

**Definition 13** (Flow decomposition)**.** Flow $F$ denotes a flow on graph $\mathcal{T}$ from $V_1$ to $V_T$. Let $f_e$ be the amount of flow that passes through any edge $e \in E_{\mathcal{T}}$ in $F$. Decomposition of $F$ is a set $P$ of paths from $V_1$ to $V_T$ with a nonzero amount of flow assigned to any one. For any path $p \in P$,

[6]This requires a postprocessing step on the solution of LP 4 to remove its crossing edges.

denote by $f_p$ the amount of flow that is assigned to $p$. Let $P_e = \{p : p \in P, e \in p\}$. For any valid flow decomposition of $F$, $\sum_{p \in P_e} f_p = f_e$ and $|P|$ is polynomial in the size of $E_{\mathcal{T}}$.

**Algorithm 2** Rounding technique for the fractional solution of LP 4 in general graphs

Let flow $F$ on graph $\mathcal{T}$ (from $V_1$ to $V_T$) denote the solution of LP 4.
Denote by $P$ the decomposition of flow $F$ which is defined in Definition 13.
Partition $P$ to $K$ subsets $P_1, \dots, P_K$ such that $\sum_{p \in P_i} f_p = 1$ holds for any $i \in K$. (One might need to decompose some of the paths in $P$ to make it possible.)
**for** any $i \in [K]$ and $j \in [\lceil \ln(1/\epsilon) \rceil]$ **do**
    Choose a path in $P_i$ randomly where each path $p \in P_i$ is chosen with probability $f_p$.
**end for**
Assign a patrol to any chosen path.

The following lemma shows that Algorithm 2 indeed provides a $(1-\epsilon)$-approximation. Due to space limit, the proof of this lemma is left to the full-version of the paper.

**Lemma 14.** *For any given weight vector* $\mathbf{h} \in \mathbb{R}_+^N$ *and any constant* $\epsilon > 0$, *there exists an* approximate defender best response *(ADBR) algorithm that using* $K' = \lceil \ln(1/\epsilon) \rceil \cdot K$ *patrols, finds a random strategy* $\mathbf{s} \in \mathcal{S}_{K'}$ *in polynomial time, where*

$$\mathbb{E}[\mathbf{h} \cdot \mathbf{s}] \geq (1-\epsilon) \cdot C_K(\mathbf{h}).$$

By combining this with Theorem 6 we get the following results.

**Theorem 15.** *For any* $\epsilon > 0$, *there exists an algorithm, that in time* $\text{poly}(\eta, \log(1/\epsilon))$ *finds in expectation a* $(1-\epsilon)$*-approximate minimax strategy of the defender, using up to* $\lceil \ln(1/\epsilon) \rceil \cdot K$ *patrols.*

We remark there is also another way to obtain the result above using a greedy algorithm that provides the same approximation factor exactly (i.e., not in expectation).

## 6 PRESERVING THE APPROXIMATION FACTOR

The goal of this section is to show that any approximation (of a certain type) for the defender's best response problem, even when we relax the assumption that the defender has to use at most $K$ patrols, leads to an approximate minimax strategy.

Since in this section we allow the defender to use more than $K$ patrols, we need to slightly modify some notations to clearly state the number of patrols that are used in different parts of the algorithm. Recall that we denote by $\mathcal{S}^D$ the set of all pure strategies of the defender. Here, we use $\mathcal{S}_j^D$ to denote the set of all pure strategies of the defender that use up to $j$ patrols; meaning that $\mathcal{S}_K^D = \mathcal{S}^D$. Moreover, we generalize Definition 3 and denote by $\text{DBR}_j(\mathbf{h}) := \arg\max_{\mathbf{s} \in \mathcal{S}_j^D}[\mathbf{h} \cdot \mathbf{s}]$ the defender's best response to weight vector $\mathbf{h}$ when she is able to use $j$ patrols. Similarly, we use $\text{C}_j(\mathbf{h}) := \max_{\mathbf{s} \in \mathcal{S}_j^D}[\mathbf{h} \cdot \mathbf{s}]$ to denote the coverage of defender's best response that uses up to $j$ patrols.

We are now ready to formally define approximate DBR and state the main theorem of this section.

**Definition 16** (Approximate DBR). For any $\alpha \leq 1$ and $\beta \geq 1$, we call an oracle $O : \mathbb{R}_+^N \to \mathcal{S}_{\beta K}^D$, an $(\alpha, \beta)$-approximation of the defender's best response problem, if for any $\mathbf{h} \in \mathbb{R}_+^N$, we have

$$\mathbf{h} \cdot O(\mathbf{h}) \geq \alpha \cdot \text{C}_K(\mathbf{h}).$$

To simplify notations, when $\beta = 1$, we simply use $\alpha$-approximation instead of $(\alpha, 1)$-approximation.

Theorem 6 *Having access to an $(\alpha, \beta)$-approximation oracle for the defender's best response problem, one can achieve in polynomial time, an $\alpha$-approximate maximin strategy of the defender that uses up to $\beta K$ patrols.*

We cannot directly use an approximate best response as the separating oracle of LP 3 since the found strategies can use more than $K$ patrols by definition, whereas, LP 3 constraints the defender to use at most $K$ patrols. More precisely, the violating constraint that is implied by the oracle might not exist in LP 3. To overcome this, we write a modified version of LP 3, which first allows the defender to use up to $K' := \beta K$ patrols, and second, converts the maximization problem to a feasibility problem. Here we restate LP 3 and state its modified version as LP 5.

$$\begin{array}{lll} \max & \mathbf{y} \cdot \mathbf{w} - c, & \\ \text{s.t.} & 0 \leq y_i & \forall i \in [N], \\ & \sum_{i \in [N]} y_i = Q, & \\ & h_i = (w_i - c_i) y_i & \forall i \in [N], \\ & \mathbf{h} \cdot \mathbf{s} \leq c & \forall \mathbf{s} \in \mathcal{S}_K^D. \end{array}$$

LP 3 (restated): Variables are $y_i$, $h_i$, and $c$.

$$\begin{array}{lll} \max & 0, & \\ \text{s.t.} & \mathbf{y} \cdot \mathbf{w} - c \geq b, & \\ & 0 \leq y_i & \forall i \in [N], \\ & \sum_{i \in [N]} y_i = Q, & \\ & h_i = (w_i - c_i) y_i & \forall i \in [N], \\ & \mathbf{h} \cdot \mathbf{s} \leq c & \forall \mathbf{s} \in \mathcal{S}_{K'}^D. \end{array}$$

LP 5. Variables are $y_i$, $h_i$, and $c$.

We need a few notations before proceeding. Let us denote by $\text{OPT}_3$ the optimum value of LP 3. We also denote by $\text{FEAS}_5(b') \in \{0, 1\}$ whether LP 5 has any feasible solution by setting the constant value $b$ to be $b'$ or not (1 indicates feasibility and 0 indicates infeasibility). LP 5 does not have a direct objective function, but we denote by $\text{OPT}_5 := \max\{b' : \text{FEAS}_5(b') = 1\}$ the maximum possible value of $b$ for which a feasible solution exists. Notice that $\text{OPT}_3$ and $\text{OPT}_5$ respectively denote the optimal utility of the attacker when the defender can use up to $K$ and $K'$ patrols. Therefore, since $K' \geq K$, the value of $\text{OPT}_5$ cannot be more than $\text{OPT}_3$.

**Observation 17.** *$OPT_5 \leq OPT_3$.*

We cannot compute either of $\text{OPT}_3$ or $\text{OPT}_5$ in polynomial time. What we show, however, is that we can *approximate* $\text{OPT}_5$ in polynomial time to obtain a solution that we later argue is sufficiently close to $\text{OPT}_3$.

For a fixed $b$, we approximately check the feasibility of LP 5 by using the approximate best response as the separating oracle of ellipsoid method. Let us denote the obtained solution by AFEAS($b$), where AFEAS($b$) = 1 if the ellipsoid method finds a feasible solution, and AFEAS($b$) = 0 otherwise. Obviously, since the ellipsoid method uses an approximate separating oracle, it does not always return the correct solution, i.e., AFEAS($b$) is not necessarily equal to FEAS($b$). However, it is still possible to have the following deduction about the value of AFEAS($b$).

**Claim 6.1.** *If AFEAS($b$) = 0, then FEAS($b$) = 0.*

We do not argue here whether if AFEAS($b$) = 1 implies AFEAS($b'$) = 1 for any $b' < b$ or not (which might or might not be the case). Regardless, we can binary search in range $[0, W]$ to find at least a *locally maximum* value $b^\star$ where AFEAS($b^\star$) = 1 and for some $\epsilon' > 0$ and any $\delta$ with $0 < \delta < \epsilon'$, AFEAS($b^\star + \delta$) = 0. Claim 6.2 formalizes our claim and emphasizes that it takes only polynomial time to find $b^\star$. The following figure illustrates the values of FEAS($b$) and AFEAS($b$) based on $b$.

**Claim 6.2.** *There exists a polynomial time algorithm that returns $b^\star$ where AFEAS($b^\star$) = 1 and for some $\epsilon' > 0$ and any $\delta$ with $0 < \delta < \epsilon'$, AFEAS($b^\star + \delta$) = 0.*

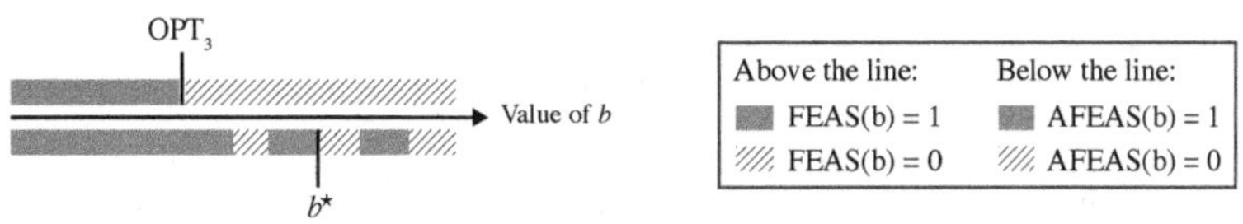


We now prove that $b^\star$ is indeed close to $\mathrm{OPT}_5$, and therefore, $\mathrm{OPT}_3$.

**Claim 6.3.** $b^\star \leq OPT_3 + (1-\alpha)(\mathbf{y}^\star \cdot \mathbf{w})$.

Recall, again, that $b^\star$ and $\mathrm{OPT}_3$ specify the attacker's payoff. To analyze the approximation ratio for the defender, we need to give a lower bound for $(\Gamma - b^\star)/(\Gamma - \mathrm{OPT}_3)$.

**Claim 6.4.** $(\Gamma - b^\star)/(\Gamma - OPT_3) \geq \alpha$.

In the interest of space, proof of Claim 6.4 is deferred to the full-version of the paper.

We are now ready to prove Theorem 6.

**Proof of Theorem 6:** Let $O$ be the $(\alpha, \beta)$-aproximate oracle. We first find a locally optimal solution $b^\star$ for LP 5 in polynomial time by Claim 6.2 and by using $O$ as the oracle. We know by Claim 6.4 that

$$\frac{\Gamma - b^\star}{\Gamma - \mathrm{OPT}_3} \geq \alpha. \tag{6}$$

Note that $\Gamma - b^\star$ and $\Gamma - \mathrm{OPT}_3$ respective indicate the defender's utility in the approximate solution and the optimal solution, hence, the approximation factor is precisely $\frac{\Gamma - b^\star}{\Gamma - \mathrm{OPT}_3}$ which is shown to be at least $\alpha$. □

## 7 HARDNESS RESULTS

**Hardness of defender's best response.** We show in this section that the DBR problem is NP-hard to even approximate within a $(1 - 1/e + o(1), 1)$ factor. A matching upper bound of $(1 - 1/e, 1)$ can be obtained in polynomial time by setting $\epsilon$ to be $1/e$ in Theorem 15.

**Theorem 18.** *There is no $(1 - 1/e + o(1))$-approximation of the defender's best response problem unless* P = NP.

**Reducing the game to defender's best response.** We showed in Section 4 that by solving the DBR problem in polynomial time, one can solve the actual game in polynomial time. However, in some cases, the DBR problem turns out to be hard to solve in polynomial time, as it was shown in the previous section. Does this imply that the game is also hard to solve? In this section, we partially answer this in the affirmative. The proof adopts the recent results of [18] to our settings. We defer the proof to the full-version of the paper.

**Theorem 19.** *When $Q = 1$, an instance of spatio-temporal security games can be solved in polynomial time if and only if the DBR problem can be solved in polynomial time.*

## 8 ACKNOWLEDGMENTS

We thank Alex Slivkins for many useful discussions and his previous collaboration in [3] that started this work.

## REFERENCES

[1] AmirMahdi Ahmadinejad, Sina Dehghani, MohammadTaghi Hajiaghayi, Brendan Lucier, Hamid Mahini, and Saeed Seddighin. 2016. From Duels to Battlefields: Computing Equilibria of Blotto and Other Games.. In *AAAI*. 376–382.

[2] Soheil Behnezhad, Sina Dehghani, Mahsa Derakhshan, MohammadTaghi HajiAghayi, and Saeed Seddighin. 2017. Faster and Simpler Algorithm for Optimal Strategies of Blotto Game. In *Proceedings of the Thirty-First AAAI Conference on Artificial Intelligence.*

[3] Soheil Behnezhad, Mahsa Derakhshan, MohammadTaghi Hajiaghayi, and Aleksandrs Slivkins. 2017. A Polynomial Time Algorithm for Spatio-Temporal Security Games. In *Proceedings of the 2017 ACM Conference on Economics and Computation.* ACM, 697–714.

[4] Branislav Bošanský, Viliam Lisý, Michal Jakob, and Michal Pěchouček. 2011. Computing time-dependent policies for patrolling games with mobile targets. In *The 10th International Conference on Autonomous Agents and Multiagent Systems-Volume 3.* International Foundation for Autonomous Agents and Multiagent Systems, 989–996.

[5] Matthew Brown, Arunesh Sinha, Aaron Schlenker, and Milind Tambe. 2016. One Size Does Not Fit All: A Game-Theoretic Approach for Dynamically and Effectively Screening for Threats. In *Proceedings of the Thirtieth AAAI Conference on Artificial Intelligence.* 425–431.

[6] Vincent Conitzer and Tuomas Sandholm. 2006. Computing the optimal strategy to commit to. In *Proceedings 7th ACM Conference on Electronic Commerce (EC-2006).* 82–90.

[7] Bruno Escoffier and Vangelis Th Paschos. 2006. Completeness in approximation classes beyond apx. *Theoretical computer science* 359, 1-3 (2006), 369–377.

[8] Fei Fang, Albert Xin Jiang, and Milind Tambe. 2013. Optimal patrol strategy for protecting moving targets with multiple mobile resources. In *Proceedings of the 2013 international conference on Autonomous agents and multi-agent systems.* International Foundation for Autonomous Agents and Multiagent Systems, 957–964.

[9] Fei Fang, Thanh Hong Nguyen, Rob Pickles, Wai Y Lam, Gopalasamy R Clements, Bo An, Amandeep Singh, Milind Tambe, and Andrew Lemieux. 2016. Deploying PAWS: Field Optimization of the Protection Assistant for Wildlife Security.. In *AAAI.* 3966–3973.

[10] Nicole Immorlica, Adam Tauman Kalai, Brendan Lucier, Ankur Moitra, Andrew Postlewaite, and Moshe Tennenholtz. 2011. Dueling algorithms. In *Proceedings of the forty-third annual ACM symposium on Theory of computing.* ACM, 215–224.

[11] Manish Jain, Erim Kardes, Christopher Kiekintveld, Fernando Ordónez, and Milind Tambe. 2010. Security Games with Arbitrary Schedules: A Branch and Price Approach.. In *AAAI.*

[12] Christopher Kiekintveld, Manish Jain, Jason Tsai, James Pita, Fernando Ordóñez, and Milind Tambe. 2009. Computing optimal randomized resource allocations for massive security games. In *Proceedings of The 8th International Conference on Autonomous Agents and Multiagent Systems-Volume 1.* International Foundation for Autonomous Agents and Multiagent Systems, 689–696.

[13] Dmytro Korzhyk, Vincent Conitzer, and Ronald Parr. 2010. Complexity of Computing Optimal Stackelberg Strategies in Security Resource Allocation Games.. In *AAAI.*

[14] Joshua Letchford and Vincent Conitzer. 2013. Solving Security Games on Graphs via Marginal Probabilities. In *Proceedings of the Twenty-Seventh AAAI Conference on Artificial Intelligence.*

[15] James Pita, Manish Jain, Janusz Marecki, Fernando Ordóñez, Christopher Portway, Milind Tambe, Craig Western, Praveen Paruchuri, and Sarit Kraus. 2008. Deployed ARMOR protection: the application of a game theoretic model for security at the Los Angeles International Airport. In *Proceedings of the 7th international joint conference on Autonomous agents and multiagent systems: industrial track.* International Foundation for Autonomous Agents and Multiagent Systems, 125–132.

[16] Tim Roughgarden. 2010. Computing Equilibria: A Computational Complexity Perspective. *Economic Theory* 42, 1 (2010), 193–236.

[17] Milind Tambe. 2011. *Security and game theory: algorithms, deployed systems, lessons learned.* Cambridge University Press.

[18] Haifeng Xu. 2016. The mysteries of security games: Equilibrium computation becomes combinatorial algorithm design. In *Proceedings of the 2016 ACM Conference on Economics and Computation.* ACM, 497–514.

[19] Haifeng Xu, Fei Fang, Albert Xin Jiang, Vincent Conitzer, Shaddin Dughmi, and Milind Tambe. 2014. Solving Zero-Sum Security Games in Discretized Spatio-Temporal Domains.. In *AAAI.* Citeseer, 1500–1506.

[20] Zhengyu Yin, Albert Xin Jiang, Milind Tambe, Christopher Kiekintveld, Kevin Leyton-Brown, Tuomas Sandholm, and John P Sullivan. 2012. TRUSTS: Scheduling randomized patrols for fare inspection in transit systems using game theory. *AI Magazine* 33, 4 (2012), 59.

# Optimal Deterministic Mechanisms for an Additive Buyer

MOSHE BABAIOFF, Microsoft Research
NOAM NISAN, Hebrew University and Microsoft Research
AVIAD RUBINSTEIN, Harvard University

We study revenue maximization by *deterministic* mechanisms for the simplest case for which Myerson's characterization does not hold: a single seller selling two items, with independently distributed values, to a single additive buyer. We prove that optimal mechanisms are submodular and hence monotone. Furthermore, we show that in the IID case, optimal mechanisms are symmetric. Our characterizations are surprisingly non-trivial, and we show that they fail to extend in several natural ways, e.g. for correlated distributions or more than two items. In particular, this shows that the optimality of symmetric mechanisms does *not* follow from the symmetry of the IID distribution.

CCS Concepts: •**Theory of computation → Design and analysis of algorithms; Algorithmic game theory; Algorithmic mechanism design; Computational pricing and auctions;**

Additional Key Words and Phrases: revenue maximization; multi-parameter domains; additive buyer; deterministic mechanism; revenue monotonicity

A full version of this paper is available at https://arxiv.org/abs/1804.06867.

Authors' email addresses: Babaioff: moshe@microsoft.com; Nisan: noam@cs.huji.ac.il; Rubinstein: aviad@cs.stanford.edu.

Nisan is supported by funding from the European Research Council (ERC) under the European Unionfis Horizon 2020 research and innovation programme (grant agreement No 740282).
Rubinstein's work was mostly done while he was an intern at Microsoft Research, and a visitor at Hebrew University (supported by the above ERC grant). Parts of this work were also done while at Harvard University (supported by the Rabin Postdoctoral Fellowship).


*ACM EC'18, June 18–22, 2018, Ithaca, NY, USA.*

ACM ISBN 978-1-4503-4529-3/18/06.
http://dx.doi.org/10.1145/3219166.3219188

# Revenue Loss in Shrinking Markets

SHAHAR DOBZINSKI, Weizmann Institute of Science, Israel
NITZAN UZIELY, Weizmann Institute of Science, Israel

We analyze the revenue loss due to market shrinkage. Specifically, consider a simple market with one item for sale and $n$ bidders whose values are drawn from some joint distribution. Suppose that the market shrinks as a single bidder retires from the market. Suppose furthermore that the value of this retiring bidder is fixed and always strictly smaller than the values of the other bidders. We show that even this slight decrease in competition might cause a significant fall of a multiplicative factor of $\frac{1}{e+1} \approx 0.268$ in the revenue that can be obtained by a dominant strategy ex-post individually rational mechanism.

In particular, our results imply a solution to an open question that was posed by Dobzinski, Fu, and Kleinberg [STOC'11].

*"Take heed of the children of the poor, for from them will Torah come forth."*
*— Babylonian Talmud, Nedarim 81a.*

## 1 INTRODUCTION

How much revenue might a firm lose due to market shrinkage? We study this question in a simple market with $n$ bidders and one item. The private values of the bidders $(v_1, \ldots, v_n)$ are drawn from some known distribution. Now suppose that one bidder retires from the market. Our goal is to compare the maximum revenue that can be extracted in the original market by a dominant-strategy mechanism that is also ex-post individually rational to the maximum revenue that can be obtained by a similar mechanism in the smaller market.

Obviously, if the value of the retiring bidder is always much larger than the values of the rest of the bidders then almost all revenue will be lost. Thus, we consider an extreme situation where the retiring bidder is the weakest competitor in the market: in every realization $(v_1, \ldots, v_n)$ the value of the retiring bidder $v_i$ is always strictly smaller than the value of any other bidder $v_j$. Furthermore, we will assume that $v_i$ is identical in all realizations, so the value of the retiring bidder $v_i$ conveys no information at all about the values of other bidders.

One might speculate that as the number of bidders increases the relative contribution to the revenue of payments by this retiring bidder diminishes. However, we show that – perhaps counter-intuitively – even this slight decrease in competition, i.e., the same large market but with the absence of its least valuable consumer, might cause the revenue to fall by a constant multiplicative factor, independently of the size of the market:

The second author was partially supported by BSF grant no. 2016192.

Authors' addresses: Shahar Dobzinski, Weizmann Institute of Science, Israel, shahar.dobzinski@weizmann.ac.il; Nitzan Uziely, Weizmann Institute of Science, Israel, nitzan.uziely@gmail.com.


*ACM EC'18, June 18–22, 2018, Ithaca, NY, USA.* ACM ISBN 978-1-4503-5829-3/18/06...$15.00
https://doi.org/10.1145/3219166.3219196

**Theorem (informal):** For any $n$, there exists a joint distribution $\mathcal{H}_n$ over the values of $n$ bidders with the following properties:

- Bidder $n$ is a "weak" bidder (as discussed above).
- The maximum expected revenue that can be extracted by a dominant strategy ex-post individually rational mechanism in a market with $n$ bidders whose values are distributed according to $\mathcal{H}_n$ is at least 1.
- Let $\mathcal{H}_{n-1}$ be the joint distribution over $n-1$ values that is obtained from $\mathcal{H}_n$ by removing the value of bidder $n$. The maximum expected revenue that can be extracted by a dominant strategy ex-post individually rational mechanism in a market with $n-1$ bidders whose values are distributed according to $\mathcal{H}_{n-1}$ is at most $\frac{e}{e+1} \approx 0.731$.

A dual interpretation of our result is that in some markets firms should consider investing effort in market expansion, as even recruiting a single low value consumer might lead to a revenue surge. Obviously there are markets in which recruiting low value consumers does not lead to a significant increase in the revenue – understanding whether there are practical distributions in which recruiting low value consumers leads to a significant increase in the revenue is an interesting open question.

As we will discuss later, the $\frac{e}{e+1}$ ratio is essentially tight, by a result of [3]. Interestingly, we cannot hope to obtain a similar result with independent valuations: when the values are distributed independently and identically, it is easy to see (directly or by applying market-expansion theorems like Bulow-Klemperer [1]) that a removal of any single bidder decreases the revenue by a factor of at most $\frac{1}{n}$, where $n$ is the number of bidders in the market. A more careful argument gives that this factor continues to hold when removing the weakest bidder from a market in which the values are distributed independently but not necessarily identically [9].

We note that our theorem holds regardless of whether we compare the best randomized truthful in expectation mechanisms in both markets or the best deterministic mechanisms.

### Connection to Previous Work

Our result is directly connected to the literature on approximating revenue maximizing auctions when the values of the bidders are correlated. This line of research was initiated by Ronen [9]. In particular, Ronen introduces the Lookahead auction: this is the dominant strategy, ex-post individually rational revenue maximizing auction among all auctions that are only allowed to sell to the bidder with the highest value. Ronen shows that the Lookahead auction extracts in expectation at least half of the expected revenue of the *unconstrained* dominant-strategy individually rational revenue maximizing mechanism[1].

The $k$-lookahead auction is a natural generalization: this is the dominant strategy, ex-post individually rational revenue maximizing auction among all auctions that are only allowed to sell the item to one of the $k$ bidders with the highest values. Dobzinski, Fu, and Kleinberg [5] show that the $k$-lookahead extracts a fraction of at least $\frac{2k-1}{3k-1}$ of the revenue of the unconstrained revenue maximizing mechanism. The analysis was improved by [3] where it was shown that the fraction is at least $\frac{e^{1-\frac{1}{k}}}{e^{1-\frac{1}{k}}+1}$ and that this is tight for $k = 2$.

However, a question that was left open in [3, 5] is to determine whether the expected revenue of the $k$-lookahead auction approaches 1 as $k < n$ increases[2]. Our result answers this question and

[1]Cremer and Mclean [4] show that under certain assumptions on the distribution there is a dominant-strategy mechanism that extracts *all* the surplus of the bidders. However, their mechanism is only ex-interim individually rational, whereas our interest here is in ex-post individually rational mechanisms.

[2]Previously, for $k > 2$ the best result was that for every $k$ there is a distribution for which the $k$-lookahead auction does not extract more than $\frac{k}{k+2}$ of the revenue [3], improving over the $\frac{k}{k+1}$ factor obtained by [5].

shows that it does not since in the presence of a weak bidder the revenue of the $k$-lookahead auction on the original market is actually identical to the revenue of the revenue-maximizing mechanism on the smaller market. Furthermore, our result is asymptotically tight since the revenue of the $k$-lookahead auction is at least $\frac{e^{1-\frac{1}{k}}}{e^{1-\frac{1}{k}}+1}$ of the revenue of the optimal auction [3], and this expression approaches $\frac{e}{e+1}$ as $k$ grows. Note that there is a gap between the bounds for any constant $k \geq 3$, closing it remains an interesting open question.

Our result also has some implications on the computational complexity of approximating revenue maximizing auctions [2, 3, 5, 8]. Specifically, we show that the analysis of the best currently known polynomial time truthful in expectation mechanism cannot be improved.

We now elaborate on this point. It is known that determining the revenue of the revenue-maximizing *deterministic* auction for three bidders or more is NP hard within some constant factor [2, 8]. In contrast, a revenue maximizing *truthful in expectation* mechanism can be computed in polynomial time for any fixed number of bidders [5]. Thus, for every constant $k$ the $k$-lookahead auction can be implemented in polynomial time. Combining with the bound of [3], we get that there is a polynomial time truthful in expectation mechanism that extracts in expectation an $\frac{e}{e+1}$ fraction of the revenue of the optimal truthful in expectation mechanism. This is the best bound known for truthful in expectation mechanisms. As we discussed, it was not known whether the analysis of the approximation ratio of the $k$-lookahead auction is tight or not. Our result implies that we cannot hope to improve the bound by improving the analysis of the $k$-lookahead auction.

## 2 PRELIMINARIES

We consider a single item auction setting with $n$ bidders. Each bidder $i$ has a (privately known) value $v_i$ for the item. The values are drawn from some joint distribution $\mathcal{D}$. A (direct) mechanism $M$ takes a profile $v = (v_1, \ldots, v_n)$ and returns an allocation probability and a non-negative expected price for each bidder. We use $M(v) = \left(\left(x_1^{M(v)}, p_1^{M(v)}\right), \ldots, \left(x_n^{M(v)}, p_n^{M(v)}\right)\right)$ to denote the outcome. Thus, given $v$, $M$ allocates to bidder $i$ with probability $x_i^{M(v)}$ and bidder $i$ pays $\frac{p_i^{M(v)}}{x_i^{M(v)}}$ if allocated. A mechanism $M$ is *ex-post individually rational* (IR) if for all $v$ and $i$: $x_i^{M(v)} \cdot v_i \geq p_i^{M(v)}$.

A mechanism $M$ is *truthful in expectation* if for every $v_i, v_i'$ and $v_{-i}$: $x_i^{M(v_i,v_{-i})} \cdot v_i - p_i^{M(v_i,v_{-i})} \geq x_i^{M(v_i',v_{-i})} \cdot v_i - p_i^{M(v_i',v_{-i})}$. Notice that truthfulness should hold also for profiles that are not in the support of $\mathcal{D}$. The expected revenue of $M$ over $\mathcal{D}$ is $\sum_{v\in\mathcal{D}} \Pr_{\mathcal{D}}[v] \left(\sum_{i=1}^{n} p_i^{M(v)}\right)$. A truthful in expectation mechanism $M$ is *optimal* if the revenue of $M$ is at least that of any other mechanism $M'$. We let $rev(\mathcal{D})$ denote the supremum of the revenue[3] that can be extracted by a truthful mechanism when the values are distributed according to $\mathcal{D}$ and $rev_{\mathcal{D}}(M)$ the revenue of a specific mechanism $M$. We will sometimes omit the subscript $\mathcal{D}$ when $\mathcal{D}$ is known from the context.

A mechanism $M$ is *monotone* if for every $i$, $v_i, v_i', v_{-i}$ s.t. $v_i < v_i'$ we have that $x_i^{M(v_i,v_{-i})} \leq x_i^{M(v_i',v_{-i})}$. It is well known that a mechanism can be implemented truthfully if and only if it is monotone. The following proposition gives the payments:

Proposition 2.1 ([7]). *A mechanism $M$ is truthful in expectation if and only if*

$$p_i^{M(v)} = \int_0^{v_i} z \cdot \frac{d}{dz} x_i^{M(z,v_{-i})} dz$$

[3]The support of the distribution that we consider are infinite, so possibly no mechanism attains this supremum.

## 3 A MARKET WITH A REVENUE LOSS OF $\frac{1}{e+1}$

Let $\mathcal{H}_n$ be a distribution over the values of $n$ bidders. We say that bidder $i$ is a weak bidder in $\mathcal{H}_n$ if $v_i$ is the same in every profile $(v_1, \ldots, v_n)$ in the support of $\mathcal{H}_n$ and furthermore we have that $v_i < v_{i'}$ for all $i \neq i'$. $\mathcal{H}_n$ *contains a weak bidder* if there is some bidder that is weak in $\mathcal{H}_n$. Without loss of generality, we will assume that the weak bidder is bidder $n$. Given a distribution $\mathcal{H}_n$ which contains a weak bidder, let $\mathcal{H}_{n-1}$ be the *distribution of* $\mathcal{H}_n$ *after shrinkage*: a distribution over the values of bidders $1, ..., n-1$ which is obtained by sampling from $\mathcal{H}_n$ and ignoring the value of the weak bidder $n$. Our main result analyzes the revenue loss due to the shrinkage:

THEOREM 3.1. *For every $n \geq 3$ and $\delta > 0$, there exist a distribution $\mathcal{H}_n$ that contains a weak bidder and a distribution $\mathcal{H}_{n-1}$ of $\mathcal{H}_n$ after shrinkage such that $\frac{rev(\mathcal{H}_{n-1})}{rev(\mathcal{H}_n)} < \frac{e}{e+1} + \delta$.*

As noted in the introduction, this ratio ($\approx 0.731$) is asymptotically tight [3]. For $n = 2$ the right ratio is $\frac{1}{2}$ [9] and for $n = 3$ the right ratio is $\frac{\sqrt{e}}{1+\sqrt{e}}$ [3].

The rest of this section is devoted to proving Theorem 3.1 and we start by giving some intuition on the proof. We will construct $\mathcal{H}_n$, a distribution over the values of $n$ bidders with the following properties:

- The value of bidder 1 will be selected from a family of equal revenue distributions, each with an expected revenue of $\frac{e}{e-1}$.
- We will always have $v_2, \ldots, v_{n-1} \approx 1$ in the support of $\mathcal{H}_{n-1}$. The precise values of $v_2, \ldots, v_{n-1}$ will jointly encode a parameter $h$ that will determine the specific distribution of $v_1$.
- The value of bidder $n$ is always fixed to 1.

We will see that to maximize revenue one has to determine the parameter $h$ by observing $v_2, \ldots, v_{n-1}$, and offer bidder 1 to purchase the item at a price that is a function of $h$. If bidder 1 declines to purchase the item at the requested price, we obviously want to sell the item to one of the bidders $2, \ldots, n$ at the highest price possible, which is approximately 1 (since the values of bidders $2, \ldots, n$ is approximately 1). However, we will not be able to sell the item to bidders $2, \ldots, n-1$. The intuitive reason is that we've used their values in order to determine $h$. However, we may sell to bidder $n$ since we have not used $v_n$ to determine the price for bidder 1. Thus, the revenue is maximized in a mechanism that determines the take-it-or-leave-it offer to bidder 1 by querying the values of $v_2, \ldots, v_{n-1}$, and if bidder 1 rejects the offer the item is sold to bidder $n$ for price 1.

The point is that bidder $n$ is a weak bidder in $\mathcal{H}_n$. In particular, to maximize revenue in the distribution $\mathcal{H}_{n-1}$ (that is obtained from $\mathcal{H}_n$ by removing bidder $n$), one still has to determine $h$ by querying $v_2, \ldots, v_{n-1}$ and set accordingly a take-it-or-leave-it offer to bidder 1. However, if bidder 1 rejects the offer we cannot sell the item at all. The gap in the revenue between the optimal mechanisms before and after the shrinkage is therefore exactly the probability that optimal mechanisms for $\mathcal{H}_n$ sell the item to bidder $n$. Equivalently, this is the probability that the item is not sold at all in an optimal mechanism for the distribution $\mathcal{H}_{n-1}$.

### 3.1 The Distribution over $n$ Bidders

We start with defining the distribution over the values of $n$ bidders $\mathcal{H}_n$. The next definition will be used to determine the specific values of $v_2, \ldots, v_{n-1}$ which in turn will be used to determine the value of the parameter $h$.

*Definition 3.2.* Let $X_\epsilon^d$ be a random variable with support over the positive integers. Let $1 > \epsilon > 0$. $X_\epsilon^d$ is $(\epsilon, d)$ *– balanced* if for every integer $i \geq 1$ s.t. $i \mod d = 1$:

(1) $\Pr\left[X_\epsilon^d = i\right] = \Pr\left[X_\epsilon^d = i+1\right] = \cdots = \Pr\left[X_\epsilon^d = i + (d-1)\right]$.

(2) $(1-\epsilon)\Pr\left[X_\epsilon^d = i\right] = \Pr\left[X_\epsilon^d = i + d\right]$.

Note that if $X_\epsilon^d$ is $(\epsilon, d)$-balanced then for all $\ell \geq 1$ and $j \in \{1, \ldots, d\}$, $\Pr\left[X_\epsilon^d = \ell\right] \geq \Pr\left[X_\epsilon^d = \ell + j\right] \geq (1-\epsilon)\Pr\left[X_\epsilon^d = \ell\right]$. When $\epsilon$ is known from the context we sometimes refer to $(\epsilon, d)$-balanced random variables as $d$-balanced. Appendix A.1 shows the existence of $(\epsilon, d)$-balanced distributions.

Define $\mathcal{H}_n$, a distribution (with parameters $d$,$\epsilon$) over the values of $n$ bidders: let $z = \frac{e}{e-1}$, $m = \left\lfloor \frac{d}{z} - 1 \right\rfloor$. Let $\mathcal{D}_0, \ldots, \mathcal{D}_{m-1}$ be $m$ distributions over $\mathbb{R}$ that will be defined in Subsection 3.1.1:

- $v_n$ is always fixed to $1 - 2\epsilon$.
- For every $2 \leq i < n$, let $v_i = 1 - 2\epsilon + \epsilon \cdot \Sigma_{j=1}^{X_i} \frac{1}{2^j}$ where $X_i$ is an independent $(\epsilon, d)$-balanced variable.
- Let $h(v_{-1}) = \min\left(\sum_{j=2}^{n-1} X_i \mod d, m-1\right)$. $v_1$ is distributed $\mathcal{D}_{h(v_{-1})}$.

*3.1.1 The Distributions $\mathcal{D}_0, \ldots, \mathcal{D}_{m-1}$.* We now describe the distributions $\mathcal{D}_0, \ldots, \mathcal{D}_{m-1}$. All are equal revenue distributions. The description is technical and might require some time to digest. However, we do note that for the analysis we will mostly refer to the simple properties that are stated in Lemma 3.3.

Define the probabilities $q_0, \ldots, q_{m-2} \in \mathbb{R}$ and $\overline{q_0}, \ldots \overline{q_{m-1}} \in \mathbb{R}$:

- For every $y \in \{0, \ldots, m-2\}$: $q_y = \frac{(z-1)d}{(d-y)(d-y-1)}$.
- For every $y \in \{0, \ldots, m-1\}$: $\overline{q_y} = 1 - \sum_{j=0}^{y-1} q_j$.

Define the values $t_0, t_1, \ldots, t_{m-1} \in \mathbb{R}$: $t_y = \frac{z}{\left(1-\Sigma_{j=0}^{y-1} q_j\right)} = \frac{z}{\overline{q_y}}$. Note that $z = t_0 < t_1 < \cdots < t_{m-1}$. We now define $\mathcal{D}_0, \ldots, \mathcal{D}_{m-1}$. First, $D_0(x) = t_0 = z$ with probability 1. For every $1 \leq y \leq m-1$:

$$\mathcal{D}_y(x) = \begin{cases} t_0 & \text{w.p. } q_0 \\ t_1 & \text{w.p. } q_1 \\ \vdots & \vdots \\ t_{y-1} & \text{w.p. } q_{y-1} \\ t_y & \text{w.p. } \overline{q_y} \end{cases}$$

Notice that the support of each distribution $\mathcal{D}_{i+1}$ contains the support of $\mathcal{D}_i$ and one additional value. Moreover, all distributions are equal revenue distributions (see Lemma 3.3). We note that:

- For every $y \in \{0, \ldots, m-1\}$ and every $j \in \{y, \ldots, m-1\}$: $\overline{q_y} = \Pr\left[v_1 = t_y | h(v_{-1}) = y\right] = \Pr\left[v_1 \geq t_y | h(v_{-1}) = j\right]$.
- For every $y \in \{0, \ldots, m-2\}$: $q_y = \Pr\left[v_1 = t_y | y < h(v_{-1}) \leq m-1\right]$.

Proof. We prove only the first claim, the second part is immediate from the definitions. For the first bullet point, let $y \in \{1, \ldots, m-1\}$ and let $m-1 \geq j \geq l$. Consider $\mathcal{D}_y$ and $\mathcal{D}_j$. The probability that bidder 1's value is lower than $t_y$ if his value is distributed $\mathcal{D}_y$ or $\mathcal{D}_j$ is $\sum_{k=0}^{j-1} q_k$, as his probability for every value $t_k$ is $q_k$ for every $k \in \{0, \ldots, y-1\}$. Thus the probability of his valuation being higher is $1 - \sum_{k=0}^{j-1} q_k$. For $\mathcal{D}_y$, the only higher value possible is $t_y$. □

Next we prove some simple and useful facts related to $\mathcal{D}_0, \ldots, \mathcal{D}_{m-1}$.

Lemma 3.3. *For $d \geq 4$ the following holds:*

(1) *For all $y \in \{0, \ldots, m-1\}$, $\overline{q_y} \cdot t_y = z$ (i.e., $\mathcal{D}_0, \ldots, \mathcal{D}_{m-1}$ are equal revenue distributions).*
(2) *For all $y \in \{0, \ldots, m-2\}$, $\overline{q_{y+1}} + q_y = \overline{q_y}$.*
(3) *For all $y \in \{1, \ldots, m-1\}$, $\sum_{j=0}^{y-1} q_j = \frac{(z-1)}{(d-y)} y$.*
(4) *For all $y \in \{0, \ldots, m-1\}$, $\overline{q_y} = \frac{d-z \cdot y}{d-y}$.*

(5) *For all* $y \in \{0, \dots, m-2\}$, $\overline{q_y} + (d-y-1)\, q_y = z = \overline{q_y} \cdot t_y$.

Proof.

(1) $\overline{q_y} \cdot t_y = \overline{q_y} \cdot \frac{z}{\overline{q_y}} = z$.

(2) $\overline{q_{y+1}} + q_y = \left(1 - \sum_{j=0}^{y} q_y + q_y\right) = \left(1 - \sum_{j=0}^{y-1} q_y\right) = \overline{q_y}$.

(3) $\sum_{j=0}^{y-1} q_j = \sum_{j=0}^{y-1} \frac{(z-1)d}{(d-j)(d-j-1)} = (z-1)\,d \cdot \sum_{j=0}^{y-1} \frac{1}{(d-j)(d-j-1)} = (z-1)\,d \cdot \sum_{r=d-(y-1)}^{d} \frac{1}{r(r-1)} = (z-1)\,d \cdot \sum_{r=d-(y-1)}^{d} \left(\frac{1}{r-1} - \frac{1}{r}\right) = (z-1) \cdot d \cdot \left(\frac{1}{d-y} - \frac{1}{d}\right) = (z-1) \cdot d \cdot \frac{y}{d(d-y)} = \frac{(z-1)}{(d-y)} \cdot y$.

(4) If $y = 0$ then $\overline{q_y} = 1 = \frac{d-z\cdot 0}{d-0}$. If $y > 0$ then, using property 3, $\overline{q_y} = \left(1 - \sum_{j=0}^{y-1} q_j\right) = 1 - \frac{(z-1)}{d-y} \cdot y = \frac{d-z\cdot y}{d-y}$.

(5) $\overline{q_y} + (d-y-1)\, q_y = \frac{d-z\cdot y}{(d-y)} + (d-y-1)\frac{(z-1)d}{(d-y)(d-y-1)} = \frac{d-z\cdot y+z\cdot d-d}{(d-y)} = \frac{z\cdot(d-y)}{(d-y)} = z$.

□

Claim 3.4. *$\mathcal{D}_0, \dots, \mathcal{D}_{m-1}$ are valid distributions.*

Proof. $\mathcal{D}_0$ is valid, as it is a probability distribution over one value with probability 1. For $\mathcal{D}_j$ where $1 \le j \le m-1$, we need to show that $1 > q_j > 0$, $1 > \overline{q_j} > 0$, $\sum_{i=0}^{j-1} q_i < 1$ and that $\sum_{i=0}^{j-1} q_i + \overline{q_j} = 1$. By definition $\sum_{i=0}^{j-1} q_i + \overline{q_j} = \sum_{i=0}^{j-1} q_i + \left(1 - \sum_{i=0}^{j-1} q_i\right) = 1$. We will show that $\sum_{i=0}^{j-1} q_i < 1$ and the rest follows, as $\overline{q_i} = 1 - \sum_{j=0}^{i-1} q_j$ and $q_i$ are positive. Using property 3:

$$\sum_{i=0}^{j-1} q_i \le \frac{(z-1)}{(d-(m-1))}(m-1) \overset{m=\left\lfloor \frac{d}{z} \right\rfloor -1}{=} (z-1)\frac{\left\lfloor \frac{d}{z} - 1 \right\rfloor}{d - \left\lfloor \frac{d}{z} \right\rfloor + 2} < (z-1)\frac{\frac{d}{z}}{d - \left\lfloor \frac{d}{z} \right\rfloor} = \frac{d - \frac{d}{z}}{d - \left\lfloor \frac{d}{z} \right\rfloor} \le 1$$

□

### 3.2 Outline of the Proof of Theorem 3.1

We will now derive the main result by applying a few lemmas. The proof of Lemma 3.6 is in Subsection 3.3 and the proof of Lemma 3.7 can be found in Subsection 3.4.

We first want to claim that to maximize revenue we should not sell the item to bidders $2, \dots, n-1$. We will do so in two steps. In Lemma 3.6 we claim that we can focus on high priced mechanisms (a technical notion that we will shortly define). Claim 3.7 shows that high priced mechanisms maximize the revenue by not selling to bidders $2, \dots, n-1$.

*Definition 3.5.* A mechanism for $n-1$ bidders is *high priced* if in every profile $v \in \mathcal{H}_{n-1}$ where bidder 1 is allocated with positive probability it holds that $v_1 \ge t_{h(v_{-1})}$.

The next lemma shows that we can alter any mechanism to be high priced without changing the revenue (with respect to $\mathcal{H}_{n-1}$). The heart of this transformation is based on the observation that by the construction of $\mathcal{H}_{n-1}$ given the values of bidders $2, \dots, n-1$, bidder 1's value is drawn from an equal revenue distribution. We use this observation as follows (for simplicity we assume in this paragraph that the mechanism is deterministic): if, given $v_2, \dots, v_{n-1}$, bidder 1 is offered to buy the item at price $p < t_{h(v_{-1})}$, set the price in these instances to $p = t_{h(v_{-1})}$. Note that the expected revenue remains the same because of the equal revenue distribution and since the allocation function to bidders $2, \dots, n-1$ is unchanged. Feasibility is not violated by the transformation, since in every instance in which bidder 1 purchases the item after the transformation he also purchases the item in the original mechanism, before the transformation. Finally, notice that given $v_{-1}$ the possible values of bidder 1 in the support of $\mathcal{H}_{n-1}$ are at most $t_{h(v_{-1})}$, so the item will never be sold if $p > t_{h(v_{-1})}$.

Lemma 3.6. *Let $M_{n-1}$ be a mechanism for $n-1$ bidders. Then, there exists a high priced mechanism $M'_{n-1}$ such that $rev_{\mathcal{H}_{n-1}}(M'_{n-1}) \ge rev_{\mathcal{H}_{n-1}}(M_{n-1})$.*

Lemma 3.7. *Let $M_{n-1}$ be a high priced mechanism for $n-1$ bidders. Then, there exists a high priced mechanism $M'_{n-1}$ such that for every $i = 2, \ldots, n-1$ and $v \in \mathcal{H}_{n-1}$ we have that $x_i^{M_{n-1}(v)} = 0$ (i.e., bidders $2, \ldots, n-1$ are never allocated) and with $rev_{\mathcal{H}_{n-1}}(M'_{n-1}) \geq rev_{\mathcal{H}_{n-1}}(M_{n-1})$.*

The two lemmas give us that the revenue of every mechanism for $\mathcal{H}_{n-1}$ is dominated by a mechanism that only allocates to bidder 1. This allows us to bound the revenue that can be obtained by any mechanism:

Corollary 3.8. *Let $M_{n-1}$ be a mechanism for $n-1$ bidders. Then, $rev_{\mathcal{H}_{n-1}}(M_{n-1}) \leq \frac{e}{e-1}$.*

Proof. By Lemmas 3.6 and 3.7, there exists a mechanism $M'_{n-1}$ such that the revenue of $M_{n-1}$ is at most the revenue of $M'_{n-1}$, and $M'_{n-1}$ only allocates to bidder 1. Now, for every realization of $v_{-1}$, bidder 1's value is distributed according to an equal revenue distribution with revenue $\frac{e}{e-1}$. Thus, $rev_{\mathcal{H}_{n-1}}(M_{n-1}) \leq rev_{\mathcal{H}_{n-1}}\left(M'_{n-1}\right) \leq \frac{e}{e-1}$. □

The next lemma shows a simple connection between the revenue of mechanisms for $\mathcal{H}_{n-1}$ and mechanisms for $\mathcal{H}_n$:

Lemma 3.9. *Let $M_{n-1}$ be a mechanism for $n-1$ bidders. There exists a mechanism $M_n$ for $n$ bidders such that: $rev_{\mathcal{H}_n}(M_n) \geq rev_{\mathcal{H}_{n-1}}(M_{n-1}) + \Pr_{v\sim\mathcal{H}_n}\left[v_1 \neq t_{h(v_{-1})}\right] \cdot (1-2\epsilon)$.*

Proof. Given $M_{n-1}$, let $M'_{n-1}$ be the high priced mechanism that allocates the item only to bidder 1 and has at least the same revenue of $M_{n-1}$, as guaranteed by Lemmas 3.6 and 3.7.

Consider the following mechanism $M_n$: if $v_1 \geq t_{h(v_{-1})}$ then allocate to bidder 1 with probability $x_1^{M'_{n-1}}(v)$ and charge $x_1^{M'_{n-1}}(v)\cdot t_{h(v_{-1})}$. Otherwise, allocate to bidder $n$ and charge $1-2\epsilon$ (if $v_n \geq 1-2\epsilon$, else do not allocate the item at all). The mechanism is clearly truthful and ex-post IR. The revenue is $rev_{\mathcal{H}_{n-1}}\left(M'_{n-1}\right) + \Pr_{v\sim\mathcal{H}_n}\left[v_1 \neq t_{h(v_{-1})}\right] \cdot (1-2\epsilon) \geq rev_{\mathcal{H}_{n-1}}(M_{n-1}) + \Pr_{v\sim\mathcal{H}_n}\left[v_1 \neq t_{h(v_{-1})}\right] \cdot (1-2\epsilon)$. □

Corollary 3.10. $\frac{rev(\mathcal{H}_{n-1})}{rev(\mathcal{H}_n)} \leq \frac{\frac{e}{e-1}}{\frac{e}{e-1}+\frac{1}{e-1}\left(\sum_{j=d-\lfloor\frac{d}{z}\rfloor+1}^{d}\frac{1}{j}\right)(1-2\epsilon)}$.

Proof. By Corollary 3.8, Lemma 3.9 and a simple calculation of $\Pr_{v\sim\mathcal{H}_n}\left[v_1 \neq t_{h(v_{-1})}\right]$:

$$\begin{aligned}
\Pr_{v\sim\mathcal{H}_n}\left[v_1 \neq t_{h(v_{-1})}\right] &= \sum_{j=0}^{m-2} \Pr\left[v_1 = t_j \wedge h(v_{-1}) \neq j\right] = \sum_{j=0}^{m-2} \Pr\left[v_1 = t_j | h(v_{-1}) > j\right] \cdot \Pr\left[h(v_{-1}) > j\right] \\
&= \sum_{j=0}^{m-2} \Pr\left[v_1 = t_j | h(v_{-1}) > j\right] \cdot \left(1 - \Pr\left[h(v_{-1}) \leq j\right]\right) \\
&= \sum_{j=0}^{m-2} \overbrace{\Pr\left[v_1 = t_j | h(v_{-1}) > j\right]}^{=q_j=\frac{d\cdot(z-1)}{(d-j-1)(d-j)}} \cdot \overbrace{\left(1 - \frac{j+1}{d}\right)}^{\frac{d-j-1}{d}} \\
&= (z-1)\sum_{j=0}^{m-2} \frac{1}{(d-j)} \overset{m=\lfloor\frac{d}{z}-1\rfloor}{=} (z-1) \sum_{j=d-\lfloor\frac{d}{z}\rfloor+1}^{d} \frac{1}{j}
\end{aligned}$$

□

We can now finish the proof of Theorem 3.1. Applying Lemma A.2 (in the appendix), we have that $\lim_{d\to\infty,\epsilon\to 0} \frac{rev(\mathcal{H}_{n-1})}{rev(\mathcal{H}_n)} \le \frac{\frac{e}{e-1}}{\frac{e}{e-1}+\left(\frac{e}{e-1}-1\right)} = \frac{e}{2e-(e-1)} = \frac{e}{e+1}$. Thus, by Corollary 3.10, for every $\delta > 0$ there exist $d \ge 4$ and $\epsilon > 0$ such that $\frac{rev(\mathcal{H}_{n-1})}{rev(\mathcal{H}_n)} < \frac{e}{e+1} + \delta$.

### 3.3 Proof of Lemma 3.6

Consider a mechanism $M_{n-1}$, and let $M'_{n-1}$ be the following high priced mechanism for $n-1$ bidders. The allocation and payments of bidders $2, \ldots, n-1$ remain the same as in $M_{n-1}$. The allocation and payment of bidder 1 are defined as follows:

$$\begin{cases} \left(x_1^{M_{n-1}\left(t_{h(v_{-1})}, v_{-1}\right)}, t_{h(v_{-1})} \cdot x_1^{M_{n-1}\left(t_{h(v_{-1})}, v_{-1}\right)}\right) & v_1 \ge t_{h(v_{-1})}; \\ (0, 0) & \text{otherwise.} \end{cases}$$

Claim 3.11. *$M'_{n-1}$ always outputs a feasible allocation and is truthful in expectation.*

Proof. Notice that for every $v$ the allocation is valid since bidders $2, \ldots, n-1$ are allocated identically and the allocation probability of bidder 1 does not increase: when $v_1 < t_{h(v_{-1})}$ then bidder 1 is not allocated at all in $M'_{n-1}$. When $v_1 = t_{h(v_{-1})}$ then the allocation is identical. When $v_1 > t_{h(v_{-1})}$ the allocation probability of bidder 1 in $M_{n-1}$ is by monotonicity at least $x_1^{M_{n-1}}\left(t_{h(v_{-1})}, v_{-1}\right)$. This last expression is the allocation probability of bidder 1 in $M'_{n-1}$.

As for truthfulness, clearly, for bidders $2, \ldots, n-1$ the mechanism is truthful in expectation, as we have not changed their allocation probabilities or payments. As for bidder 1, his allocation function is clearly monotone and the payments are according to Proposition 2.1. Hence $M'_{n-1}$ is truthful in expectation. □

It is left is to show that $rev\left(M'_{n-1}\right) \ge rev\left(M_{n-1}\right)$. The payments of bidders $2, \ldots, n-1$ are identical in both mechanisms, thus it remains to show that the expected payment of bidder 1 has not decreased. We show that for every fixed $v_{-1}$. Let $h(v_{-1}) = y$ and $x_1 = x_1^{M_{n-1}(t_y, v_{-1})}$. When the values of all other bidders are $v_{-1}$, bidder 1's expected payment is $\Pr[v_1 = t_y | v_{-1}] \cdot t_y \cdot x_1 = \overline{q_y} \cdot t_y \cdot x_1 = z \cdot x_1$.

Since the allocation function of $M_{n-1}$ is monotone, for every $v'_1 \le v_1$, $M_{n-1}$ allocates to bidder 1 with probability at most $x_1$. We now bound from above the revenue of the optimal revenue of a mechanism $M''$ for a single bidder that is distributed $\mathcal{D}_y$ and never allocates with probability larger than $x_1$. We will show that the revenue of $M''$ is at most $z \cdot x_1$, which will imply that $rev(M'_{n-1}) \ge rev(M_{n-1})$. To see this, recall that by [5, 6], any truthful in expectation mechanism for a single bidder can be implemented as a universally truthful mechanism: a distribution over deterministic mechanisms. Now, for a single bidder a deterministic mechanism is simply a take-it-or-leave-it price. Since $\mathcal{D}_y$ is an equal revenue distribution with revenue $z$, and since the maximum allocation is $x_1$, the revenue of $M_{n-1}$ is at most $z \cdot x_1$, as needed.

### 3.4 Proof of Lemma 3.7

The proof plan is to take the high priced mechanism $M_{n-1}$ and look for profiles in the support of $\mathcal{H}_{n-1}$ in which some bidder $i > 1$ is allocated with positive probability. We will obtain $M'_{n-1}$ by "fixing" those profiles, essentially by shifting the allocation probability of bidder $i$ to bidder 1 and then showing that the shifting has not decreased the revenue.

We will transform $M_{n-1}$ to $M'_{n-1}$ in steps: we will find a "minimal" profile $v'$ (in a sense that will be formally defined) in which the allocation probability of some bidder $i > 1$ is positive. We will "fix" this profile as well as some "neighboring" profiles and continue. Notice that in principle there might be an infinite number of profiles that require a fix. Fortunately, the support of $\mathcal{H}_{n-1}$ is countable so the process is guaranteed to eventually reach every specific profile.

Now for the formal description. We first apply a "pre processing step": consider some profile $v$ which is not in the support of $\mathcal{H}_{n-1}$. Suppose that there is some bidder $i$ with a non-zero allocation probability. We set the allocation probability of this bidder $i$ to 0 if for each $v_i' < v_i$ it holds that $v' = (v_i', v_{-i})$ is not in $\mathcal{H}_{n-1}$ or the allocation probability of bidder $i$ is 0. Note that this preprocessing does not affect monotonicity and that the revenue does not decrease.

We say that a profile $v$ in the support of $\mathcal{H}_{n-1}$ is *problematic* if for some $i > 1$, $x_i^{M_{n-1}(v)} > 0$ and $v_1 = t_{h(v_{-1})}$.

We first claim that if there is some $v$ in the support of $\mathcal{H}_{n-1}$ and some bidder $i > 1$ with $x_i^{M_{n-1}(v)} > 0$, then there exists a problematic profile. To see this, let $v^1$ be the minimal profile $(v_1, \dots, v_{i-1}, s, v_{i+1}, \dots, v_n)$ which is in the support of $\mathcal{H}_{n-1}$ that is strictly bigger coordinate-wise than $v$, let $v^2$ be the minimal profile $(v_1, \dots, v_{i-1}, s', v_{i+1}, \dots, v_n) \in \mathcal{H}_{n-1}$ which is strictly bigger than $v^1$ and so on (notice that the instances $v, v^1, v^2, \dots$ differ only in bidder $i$'s value). Since bidder $i$'s allocation probability is positive in $v'$, by monotonicity the allocation probability of bidder $i$ is also positive in $v^k$, for every $k \geq 1$. Now observe that for some profile $j$, $1 \leq j \leq d$ it holds that $v_1^j = t_{h(v_{-1}^j)}$ thus $v^j$ is problematic.

If there are no problematic profiles we are already done. If there are several such profiles, let $v'$ be a problematic profile such that there is no problematic profile $v'' \neq v'$ with $v_{i'}'' \leq v_{i'}'$ for every $i' > 1$. Note that the existence of one problematic profile $v'$ implies the existence of a "minimal" problematic profile since the number of profiles in the support of $\mathcal{H}_{n-1}$ that are dominated by $v'$ coordinate-wise is finite. Let $I$ be the set of bidders (excluding bidder 1) with a positive allocation probability in $v'$ and let $y = h(v_{-1}')$.

We now "fix" the mechanism $M_{n-1}$ by defining a high priced mechanism $M'$ with higher revenue. The behavior of $M'$ and $M_{n-1}$ will differ only in the profile $v'$ and "neighboring" profiles. We then continue fixing the other problematic profiles: we take $M'$ and fix the next problematic profile by obtaining $M''$, then fix the next problematic profile in $M''$, and so on.

Let $M'$ be the mechanism with the following allocation function: the allocations of all bidders that are not in $I \cup \{1\}$ remain the same. We set the allocation probability of every bidder $i \in I$ in $v'$ to 0. By monotonicity, we have to set the allocation probability of bidder $i \in I$ in each of the profiles in the set $G_i = \{v | v_{-i} = v_{-i}' \text{ and } v_i \leq v_i'\}$ to 0.

In addition, we shift the allocation probability mass in $v'$ from each bidder $i \in I$ to bidder 1: $x_1^{M'(v')} = x_1^{M_{n-1}(v')} + \Sigma_{i \in I} x_i^{M_{n-1}(v')}$. To guarantee monotonicity, we set the allocation probability of bidder 1 to $x_1^{M'(v')}$, and the probability of bidders $2, \dots, n-1$ to 0 in every profile in $G_1 = \{v | v_{-1} = v_{-1}' \text{ and } v_1 > v_1'\}$. Notice that profiles in $G_1$ are not in the support of $\mathcal{H}_{n-1}$ since $v_1' = t_{h(v_{-1}')}$. The payment of bidder 1 in the profiles $\{v'\} \cup G_1$ is $t_y \cdot \left(x_1^{M_{n-1}(v')} + \Sigma_{i \in I} x_i^{M_{n-1}(v')}\right)$. The allocation in profiles that are not in $G_1 \cup (\cup_{i \in I} G_i)$ is identical to the allocation of the mechanism $M_{n-1}$.

Claim 3.12. *For every bidder i, the allocation of $M'$ is feasible and monotone. In addition, M' is high priced.*

Proof. We will first show that in every profile the total allocation probability of $M'$ is at most that of $M_{n-1}$. The allocation in every valuation profile that is not in $G_1 \cup (\cup_{i \in I} G_i)$ is identical to that of $M_{n-1}$, hence feasible. In $v'$ and in profiles in $G_1$, the total allocation probability in $M'$ is the total allocation probability of $M_{n-1}$ in the profile $v'$, which by feasibility of $M_{n-1}$ is at most 1.

As for monotonicity, given a minimal problematic vector $v'$ as above, $M'$ is monotone for all bidders except bidder 1 and bidders in $I$, as their allocations remain the same. Bidder 1's allocation function is monotone since we have just changed the profile $v'$ and profiles in $G_1$: monotonicity requires that the allocation probability of bidder 1 in each profile $v \in G_1$ will be at least his allocation probability in $v'$, and in $M'$ these two probabilities are equal. Similarly, the allocation of bidder

$i \in I$ has changed only for $v'$ and profiles in $G_i$: bidder $i$'s allocation probability in $v'$ is 0 and this probability remains 0 when $v_i$ decreases in any other profile $v \in G_i$.

To finish the monotonicity proof, suppose that for some bidder $i$ and $v \in G_1$ which was altered due to a minimal problematic vector $v'$ the mechanism is not monotone (observe that $v_{-1} = v'_{-1}$). That is, there exists a profile $v''$ where $v_{-i} = v'_{-i}$ but $v_i > v''_i$, and bidder $i$'s allocation in $v''_i$ is greater than bidder $i$'s allocation in $v'_i$. If $v''$ is in the support of $\mathcal{H}_{n-1}$ then we reach a contradiction since $v'$ is not a minimal vector ($v''$ is "smaller" – notice that minimality is only defined with respect to bidders $2, \ldots, n-1$). If $v''$ is not in the support, then by our "preprocessing" there must be some $u = (u_i, v''_{-i}) \in \mathcal{H}_{n-1}$ with $u_i < v''_i$ in which the allocation probability of bidder $i$ is not 0. But similarly to before this $u$ is in contradiction to the minimality of $v'$.

Finally, in every allocation $v \in G_i$ $(i > 1)$ the allocation is identical to that of $M_{n-1}$, except that the allocation probability of bidder $i$ is 0. It is also not hard to see that if $M_{n-1}$ is high priced then $M'$ is high priced as well. □

The claim guarantees that the allocation function is monotone, hence there are payments that make it truthful in expectation. The next claim analyzes these payments:

Claim 3.13. *For every profile $v \neq v', v \in \mathcal{H}_{n-1}$: $p_1^{M_{n-1}(v)} = p_1^{M'(v)}$. For the profile $v'$, $p_1^{M'(v)} = p_1^{M_{n-1}(v')} + t_y \cdot \Sigma_{i \in I} x_i^{M_{n-1}(v')}$. For every bidder $i > 1$ and profile $v \notin \{v'\} \cup G_i$, $p_i^{M_{n-1}(v)} \leq p_i^{M'(v)}$.*

Proof. The claim regarding the payments of bidder 1 is a direct consequence of Proposition 2.1. As for the payments of bidder $i > 1$, recall that by Proposition 2.1, for any mechanism $M$ it holds that $p_i^{M(v)} = \int_0^{v_i} z \cdot \frac{d}{dz} x_i^{M(z, v_{-i})} dz$. That is, when drawing the allocation probability as a function of the value, the payment is the area between the allocation curve and the $y$-axis. Reducing the allocation probability at some points clearly increases the payments. □

We show that $rev\ (M') > rev\ (M_{n-1})$ by proving that even though $M'$ extracts less revenue from bidders in $I$ in $v'$ and profiles in $\cup_{i \in I} G_i$ it compensates by extracting more revenue from bidder 1 in $v'$.

Towards this end, consider some bidder $i \in I$ and denote $s^0 = v'_i$. Fixing $v'_{-i}$, let $s^{-1}$ denote the highest value that bidder $i$ gets in $v \in \mathcal{H}_{n-1}$ subject to the constraints that $v_{-i} = v'_{-i}$ and $v_i < v'_i$. Define $s^{-j}$ similarly but with respect to the $j$'th highest value that bidder $i$ gets. Note that $h(v_2, \ldots, v_{i-1}, s^{-d}, v_{i+1}, \ldots, v_{n-1}) = y$ and that in the valuation profile $(s^{-d}, v'_{-i})$ bidder $i$'s allocation probability is 0, otherwise we get a contradiction to the minimality of $v'$.

$M'$ extracts more revenue than $M_{n-1}$ from bidder 1 in the valuation profile $(s^0, v'_{-i})$ due to the shifted mass from bidder $i$ to bidder 1. By our discussion above, $M'$ potentially extracts less revenue than $M_{n-1}$ precisely in the valuation profiles $(s^{-j}, v'_{-i})$, for $j = 1, \ldots, d-1$ where the allocation probability of bidder $i$ has possibly decreased. We conservatively assume the in profiles that are not in $\{v'\} \cup G_i$ the payments of bidder $i$ in $M'$ and $M_{n-1}$ are the same (by Claim 3.13 they might be higher in $M'$). In fact, it is enough to focus on instances $(s^{-j}, v'_{-i})$ for $j \geq d - y + 1$ since otherwise the probability (given the values of the other bidders) that $v_1 = t_y$ is 0.

We will show that $x_i^{M_{n-1}(v')} \cdot \left(\Pr[v'] \left(t_y - v'_i\right)\right) > x_i^{M_{n-1}(v')} \cdot \sum_{j=d-y+1}^{d-1} \Pr\left[\left(s^{-j}, v'_{-i}\right)\right] \cdot v'_i$ (i.e., the additional revenue due to the mass shifted from bidder $i$ to bidder 1 is higher than the revenue loss due to not allocating to bidder $i$ in $\{v'\} \cup G_i$). Notice that by individual rationality we use the value of bidder $i$ as an upper bound to his payment, and by monotonicity we have that $x_i^{M_{n-1}(v')}$ is an upper bound to the allocation probability of $M_{n-1}$ to bidder $i$ in every profile in $G_i$.

Recall that by the definition of $\mathcal{H}_{n-1}$:

$$\Pr\left[\left(s^0, v'_{-i}\right)\right] = \overbrace{\Pr\left[v_1 = t_y | h\left((v'_2, \ldots)\right) = y\right]}^{\overline{q_y}} \cdot \Pr\left[\left(v'_2, \ldots, v'_{i-1}, s^0, v'_{i+1}, \ldots, v'_{n-1}\right)\right]$$
$$= \overline{q_y} \cdot \Pr\left[s^0\right] \cdot \Pi_{t\in\{2,\ldots,n-1\}\setminus\{i\}} \Pr\left[v'_t\right]$$

Where the last equality is by the fact that the values of bidders $2, \ldots, n-1$ are $(n-2)$-wise independent. Additionally, for every $j \in \{d-y+1, \ldots, d-1\}$:

$$\Pr\left[\left(v'_1, \ldots, s^{-j}, \ldots, v'_{n-1}\right)\right] = \Pr\left[v_1 = t_y | h\left(\left(v'_2, \ldots, s^{-j}, \ldots, v'_{n-1}\right)\right) > y\right] \cdot \Pr\left[\left(v'_2, \ldots, s^{-j}, \ldots, v'_{n-1}\right)\right]$$
$$= q_y \cdot \Pr\left[s^{-j}\right] \cdot \Pi_{t\in\{2,\ldots,n-1\}\setminus\{i\}} \Pr\left[v'_t\right]$$

Thus:

$$\Pr\left[v'\right]\left(t_y - v'_i\right) - \sum_{j=d-y+1}^{d-1} \Pr\left[\left(s^{-j}, v'_{-i}\right)\right] \cdot v'_i$$

$$= \Pi_{t\in\{2,\ldots,n-1\}\setminus\{i\}} \Pr\left[v'_t\right] \cdot \left(\overline{q_y} \cdot \overbrace{\Pr\left[s^0\right]}^{\geq(1-\epsilon)\Pr\left[s^{-d}\right]} \cdot \left(t_y - \overbrace{v'_i}^{<1}\right) - \sum_{j=d-y+1}^{d-1} \overbrace{v'_i}^{<1-\epsilon} \cdot q_y \cdot \overbrace{\Pr\left[s^{-j}\right]}^{\leq\Pr\left[s^{-d}\right]}\right) \quad (1)$$

$$> \Pi_{t\in\{2,\ldots,n-1\}\setminus\{i\}} \Pr\left[v'_t\right] \cdot (1-\epsilon) \cdot \Pr\left[s^{-d}\right]\left(\overline{q_y} \cdot \left(t_y - 1\right) - \sum_{j=1}^{d-y-1} q_y\right) \quad (2)$$

$$= \Pi_{t\in\{2,\ldots,n-1\}\setminus\{i\}} \Pr\left[v'_t\right] \cdot (1-\epsilon)\left[s^{-d}\right]\left(\overbrace{\overline{q_y} \cdot t_y}^{z} - \left(\overbrace{\overline{q_y} + (d-y-1)\, q_y}^{z}\right)\right)$$

$$= 0 \quad (3)$$

(1) is by Definition 3.2, as $\Pr\left[s^0\right] \geq (1-\epsilon)\Pr\left[s^{-d}\right]$ and $\Pr\left[s^{-j}\right] \leq \Pr\left[s^{-d}\right]$ because the value of bidder $i$ is distributed $1 - 2\epsilon + \epsilon \cdot \Sigma_{j=1}^{X_i} \frac{1}{2^j}$ and $X_i$ is $d$-balanced. (2) is by the fact that $1 > (1-\epsilon) > v_i$. (3) is by Lemma 3.3, specifically $\overline{q_y} + (d-y-1)\, q_y = z$. This shows that the revenue of $M'$ is higher than that of $M_{n-1}$.

## REFERENCES


[1] Jeremy Bulow and Paul Klemperer. 1996. Auctions versus Negotiations. *American Economic Review* 86, 1 (1996), 180–94.

[2] Ioannis Caragiannis, Christos Kaklamanis, and Maria Kyropoulou. 2016. Limitations of deterministic auction design for correlated bidders. *ACM Transactions on Computation Theory (TOCT)* 8, 4 (2016), 13.

[3] Xue Chen, Guangda Hu, Pinyan Lu, and Lei Wang. 2011. On the approximation ratio of k-lookahead auction. In *Internet and Network Economics*. Springer, 61–71.

[4] Jacques Cremer and Richard P McLean. 1988. Full extraction of the surplus in Bayesian and dominant strategy auctions. *Econometrica: Journal of the Econometric Society* (1988), 1247–1257.

[5] Shahar Dobzinski, Hu Fu, and Robert D Kleinberg. 2011. Optimal auctions with correlated bidders are easy. In *Proceedings of the forty-third annual ACM symposium on Theory of computing*. ACM, 129–138.

[6] Aranyak Mehta and Vijay V Vazirani. 2004. Randomized truthful auctions of digital goods are randomizations over truthful auctions. In *Proceedings of the 5th ACM conference on Electronic commerce*. ACM, 120–124.

[7] Roger B Myerson. 1981. Optimal auction design. *Mathematics of operations research* 6, 1 (1981), 58–73.

[8] Christos H Papadimitriou and George Pierrakos. 2011. On optimal single-item auctions. In *Proceedings of the forty-third annual ACM symposium on Theory of computing*. ACM, 119–128.

[9] Amir Ronen. 2001. On approximating optimal auctions. In *Proceedings of the 3rd ACM conference on Electronic Commerce.* ACM, 11–17.

# A MISSING PROOFS

## A.1 Existence of Balanced Distributions

PROPOSITION A.1. *For every $d \geq 1, 0 < \epsilon < 1$ there exists an $(\epsilon, d)$-balanced distribution.*

Let $X_\epsilon^d$ be the following random variable (for $0 < \epsilon < 1$ and $k \geq 1$): $\Pr\left[X_\epsilon^d = k\right] = \frac{\epsilon(1-\epsilon)^{\left\lceil \frac{k}{d} \right\rceil - 1}}{d}$. Notice that for $d = 1$ this is a regular Geometric distribution with $p = \epsilon$. We show that $X_\epsilon^d$ is an $(\epsilon, d)$ balanced distribution (as defined in Definition 3.2):

(1) Clearly, the positive integers are the support.

(2) $X_\epsilon^d$ is well defined. For every positive integer $k$, $0 < \Pr[k] < 1$, and $\sum_{j=1}^{\infty} \frac{\epsilon(1-\epsilon)^{\left\lceil \frac{j}{d} \right\rceil - 1}}{d} = 1$.

(3) For $i = c \cdot d + 1$ (where $c \in (\mathbb{N} \cup \{0\})$, i.e. $i \mod d = 1$):

(a) For $j \in \{0, \ldots, d-1\}$ $\Pr\left[X_\epsilon^d = i + j\right] = \frac{\epsilon(1-\epsilon)^{\left\lceil \frac{c \cdot d + 1 + j}{d} \right\rceil - 1}}{d} = \frac{\epsilon(1-\epsilon)^{c - 1 + \left\lceil \frac{1+j}{d} \right\rceil}}{d} \overset{1+j \leq d}{=} \frac{\epsilon(1-\epsilon)^c}{d}$.

(b) $\Pr\left[X_\epsilon^d = i\right] = \frac{\epsilon(1-\epsilon)^c}{d}$ and $\Pr\left[X_\epsilon^d = i + d\right] = \frac{\epsilon(1-\epsilon)^{c+1}}{d} = \frac{\epsilon(1-\epsilon)^c}{d}(1-\epsilon) = \Pr\left[X_\epsilon^d = i\right](1-\epsilon)$.

## A.2 The Limit of $\sum_{j=d-\left\lfloor \frac{d}{z} \right\rfloor + 1}^{d} \frac{1}{j}$

LEMMA A.2. $\lim_{d \to \infty} z + (z-1)(1-2\epsilon) \sum_{j=d-\left\lfloor \frac{d}{z} \right\rfloor + 1}^{d} \frac{1}{j} = z + (z-1)(1-2\epsilon)$

Recall that for general $a$ and $b$:

$$\ln\left(\frac{a+1}{b}\right) = \int_b^{a+1} \frac{1}{j} dj \leq \sum_b^a \frac{1}{j} \leq \int_{j=b+1}^{a} = \ln\left(\frac{a}{b+1}\right)$$

In our case: $a = d$ and $b = d - \left\lfloor \frac{d}{z} \right\rfloor + 1$. On one hand, as $\left(\frac{a+1}{b}\right) = \frac{d+1}{d - \left\lfloor \frac{d}{z} \right\rfloor + 1}$:

$$\lim \frac{d+1}{d - \left\lfloor \frac{d}{z} \right\rfloor} = \lim \frac{d+1}{d - \frac{d}{z} + 1} = \lim \frac{zd + z}{(z-1)d + z} = \frac{z}{z-1}$$

On the other hand, as $\frac{a}{b+1} = \frac{d+1}{d - \left\lfloor \frac{d}{z} \right\rfloor + 2}$:

$$\lim \frac{d+1}{d - \left\lfloor \frac{d}{z} \right\rfloor + 2} = \lim \frac{zd + z}{d(z-1) + 2z} = \frac{z}{z-1}$$

Therefore, by the Squeeze Theorem:

$$\lim_{d \to \infty} z + (z-1)(1-2\epsilon) \sum_{j=d-\left\lfloor \frac{d}{z} \right\rfloor + 1}^{d} \frac{1}{j} = z + (z-1)(1-2\epsilon) \log\left(\frac{z}{z-1}\right) = z + (z-1)(1-2\epsilon)$$

where the last equality follows as $\log\left(\frac{z}{z-1}\right) = \log\left(\frac{\frac{e}{e-1}}{\frac{e}{e-1} - 1}\right) = 1$.

# 99% Revenue via Enhanced Competition

MICHAL FELDMAN, Computer Science, Tel-Aviv University, and Microsoft Research., Israel
OPHIR FRIEDLER, Computer Science, Tel-Aviv University., Israel
AVIAD RUBINSTEIN, Harvard University., USA

A sequence of recent studies show that even in the simple setting of a single seller and a single buyer with additive, independent valuations over $m$ items, the revenue-maximizing mechanism is prohibitively complex. This problem has been addressed using two main approaches:

- *Approximation:* the best of two simple mechanisms (sell each item separately, or sell all the items as one bundle) gives 1/6 of the optimal revenue [1].
- *Enhanced competition:* running the simple VCG mechanism with additional $m$ buyers extracts at least the optimal revenue in the original market [17].

Both approaches, however, suffer from severe drawbacks: On the one hand, losing 83% of the revenue is hardly acceptable in any application. On the other hand, attracting a linear number of new buyers may be prohibitive. We show that by combining the two approaches one can achieve the best of both worlds. Specifically, for any constant $\epsilon$ one can obtain a $(1 - \epsilon)$ fraction of the optimal revenue by running simple mechanisms — either selling each item separately or selling all items as a single bundle — with substantially fewer additional buyers: logarithmic, constant, or even none in some cases.

CCS Concepts: • **Theory of computation → Algorithmic game theory and mechanism design**; **Computational pricing and auctions**;

Additional Key Words and Phrases: Mechanism Design, Revenue, Simple Mechanisms, Pricing

## 1 INTRODUCTION

The scenario of a buyer with an additive, independent valuation over $m$ items has become the paradigmatic setting for studying optimal (revenue-maximizing) mechanisms. In this setting, the buyer's valuation is drawn from a distribution $D$ that is known to the seller, and the seller wishes to design a selling mechanism that extracts as much revenue as possible.

By now it is well known that the optimal mechanism requires randomization [22], infinite, uncountable menus [16], is non-monotone [23], and computationally intractable [15][1]. Thus it is mostly interesting as a theoretic benchmark to which one can compare more plausible mechanisms (much like the way an offline optimum serves as a benchmark in online settings). In recent years,

This work was partially supported by the European Research Council under the European Union's Seventh Framework Programme (FP7/2007-2013) / ERC grant agreement number 337122, Israel Science Foundation (grant number 317/17), and a Rabin Postdoctoral Fellowship.

[1]Similar undesired properties have been observed with respect to the optimal mechanism in additional related (multi-dimensional) models, e.g., unit-demand buyers [3, 13, 14, 31]

Authors' addresses: Michal Feldman, Computer Science, Tel-Aviv University, and Microsoft Research. Tel-Aviv, Israel, michal.feldman@cs.tau.ac.il; Ophir Friedler, Computer Science, Tel-Aviv University. Tel-Aviv, Israel, ophirfriedler@gmail.com; Aviad Rubinstein, Harvard University. Cambridge, MA, USA, aviad@seas.harvard.edu.



*ACM EC'18, June 18–22, 2018, Ithaca, NY, USA.* ACM ISBN 978-1-4503-5829-3/18/06...$15.00
https://doi.org/10.1145/3219166.3219202

two main approaches have been taken with respect to this challenge, both of which proposed simple mechanisms and measured their performance against the theoretic optimum:

The first line of work approaches this problem through the lens of *approximation* [1, 2, 6, 8–12, 18, 21, 26, 27, 29, 34–36]. In particular, the breakthrough result of [1] shows that the better of two simple mechanisms – selling each item separately or selling all items together in a grand bundle – obtains at least 1/6 (but at most 1/2 [33]) of the optimal revenue.

The second approach is to enhance the competition for the merchandise by increasing the population of potential buyers [4, 17, 28, 32]. This approach is often termed resource augmentatation in computer science. The state of the art for additive buyers is by Eden *et al.* [17], who showed that adding $m$ additional buyers is sufficient to recover the original optimal revenue with a simple mechanism. It is also known that at least $\Omega(\log m)$ additional buyers are required to achieve this benchmark. This result from [17] generalizes the seminal work of Bulow and Klemperer [4] who showed that for a market with a single item, under a regularity assumption, running the second price auction with one additional buyer extracts at least as much revenue as the original optimal revenue. However, when $m$ is large, adding $m$ additional buyers may be prohibitive. We therefore believe that the most interesting question here is whether the linear dependence on $m$ is necessary.

To summarize, the "optimal" benchmark is intractable. The approximation approach is stuck at a 1/6-approximation (forfeiting 83% of potential revenue). And if we wish to follow the enhanced competition approach, the best known bound on the number of additional buyers is linear in the number of items.

### 1.1 Our Contribution

We show that one can combine the two approaches (of approximation and enhanced competition) in a way that achieves the best of both worlds. We establish a host of results for various settings, but they all convey one theme: in order to obtain revenue that is very close to optimum, there is no need to recruit a linear number (in $m$) of additional buyers; that is:

**Main take away (informal):** *A seller can obtain 99% of the optimal revenue in a simple mechanism (selling each item separately or selling all items together in a singe bundle) with substantially fewer additional buyers — logarithmic (in m), constant, or even none in some cases.*

The constant 99% above is arbitrary of course. More generally, we show what we think of as the **mechanism-design analog of computational PTAS**: an efficient mechanism that obtains a $(1-\varepsilon)$-approximation, for any constant $\varepsilon > 0$ (where in our case *efficient* means "few additional buyers" instead of "polynomial time").

All of our results apply to the paradigmatic scenario of a seller who sells $m$ items to a single buyer with additive, independent valuations over the items, with a known prior. Some of our results extend to the more general scenario of $n$ i.i.d. buyers, namely where buyers' values are drawn independently according to the same distribution. The induced product distribution is then denoted by $\mathcal{D}$. Our first set of results consider the simple mechanism that sells each item separately.

Theorem 1.1. *For every constant $\varepsilon > 0$, selling each item separately to $O(\log m)$ i.i.d. buyers extracts at least $(1-\varepsilon)$-fraction of the optimal revenue achievable by a single buyer.*

This result improves upon the $O(m)$ bound shown in [17], at the loss of $\varepsilon$ fraction in revenue. In fact, this result can be extended even to a setting with $n$ i.i.d. buyers and $m$ items. The following theorem fully characterizes, up to constant factors, the number of additional buyers necessary as a function of the number of items.

Theorem 1.2. *(implies Theorem 1.1) For a setting with n i.i.d. buyers and m items, for every constant $\varepsilon > 0$, selling each item separately achieves at least $(1-\varepsilon)$-fraction of the optimal revenue if we* *increase the number of buyers by a factor of $O(\log(2 + m/n))$, and this is tight up to constant factors. Moreover, if $m = o(n)$, then selling each item separately achieves $(1-\varepsilon)$-fraction of the optimal revenue even with no additional buyers.*

Theorem 1.2 essentially fully characterizes (up to constant factors) the number of additional buyers necessary for achieving $(1 - \varepsilon)$ of the optimal revenue. In particular, we consider three different regimes of $m$ and $n$: For $m = \omega(n)$ we prove that increasing the number of buyers by a factor of $O(\log(m/n))$ is both necessary (Theorem 4.12) and sufficient (Theorem 4.1). For $m = \Theta(n)$, our new lower bound implies that the previous results of [17] (who showed that a linear number of additional buyer suffice) are essentially tight. Finally, for $m = o(n)$, we show that *no* additional buyers are necessary (Theorem 5.1). We note that our lower bound generalizes the special case of $\Omega(\log m)$-factor for the case of a single buyer in [17] [2].

Let us return to the single buyer setting. Theorem 1.2 implies that we can recover $(1-\varepsilon)$-fraction of the optimal revenue by adding $O(\log m)$ buyers. However, one may argue that for a large value of $m$, $O(\log m)$ is still too large. We address this issue by showing that the better of selling items separately and selling the grand bundle requires only a constant number of additional buyers[3].

THEOREM 1.3. *For every constant $\varepsilon > 0$, the better of selling each item separately and selling the grand bundle, to a constant number of i.i.d. buyers, extracts at least $(1 - \varepsilon)$-fraction of the optimal revenue achievable from one buyer.*

Up until now, we concentrated on *prior-dependent* mechanisms; namely, mechanisms that use the knowledge of the distribution of values. Our work, however, contributes also to the literature on *prior-independent* mechanisms. As in previous literature on prior-independent mechanisms, to achieve any meaningful result, we assume that the underlying single-dimensional distributions are regular (note that this does not generally imply regularity of the grand bundle's distribution). Since bidders are additive, the prior-independent VCG mechanism simply runs the second price auction for each item simultaneously. Thus, Theorem 1.2 combined with the original result of Bulow and Klemperer [4] immediately implies the following corollary:

COROLLARY 1.4. *If $\mathcal{D}$ is a product of regular distributions, then for every constant $\varepsilon > 0$, running the VCG mechanism with a factor $O(\log(2 + m/n))$ increase in the number of buyers (and with no additional buyers in the case of $m = o(n)$) extracts at least $(1 - \varepsilon)$-fraction of the original optimal revenue.*

It would be highly desirable to obtain such an analog to Theorem 1.3. An immediate barrier, however, is that the seller must know in advance whether to sell the items separately or sell the grand bundle. How can the seller determine which one of these mechanisms to run in the absence of a prior? This barrier is overcome by the surprising result that when $\mathcal{D}$ is a product of regular distributions, the seller *never* needs to sell items separately; selling the grand bundle is always the "correct" strategy:

THEOREM 1.5. *If $\mathcal{D}$ is a product of regular distributions, then for every constant $\varepsilon > 0$, selling the grand bundle in a second price auction to a constant number of i.i.d. additive buyers extracts at least $(1 - \varepsilon)$-fraction of the optimal revenue achievable from one buyer.*

[2]The lower bound in [17] was proven for mechanisms that target 100% of the optimal revenue, but it can be easily extended to mechanisms that target 99% or any constant fraction.

[3]There is no contradiction to the $\Omega(\log m)$ lower bound, which applies only for selling items separately.

### 1.2 The Case for 99% AGT

Constant factor approximations, and the heavy use of asymptotics in general, are one of the distinctive characteristics of Algorithmic Game Theory (in contrast to "standard" Economics), and we are by no means innocent. Note that in all our theorem statements hidden constants are lurking, and we do not even attempt to explicitly state them (obtaining reasonable constants remains an interesting open problem). We hope, as we always do when we make such asymptotic analysis, that our mathematically precise models tell an insightful story about how our guarantees degrade when we extend our single item / neighborhood grocery store intuition to auctioneers selling a huge number of items[4], especially online. (And this goes without mentioning our "standard" but absurd assumptions: rational bidders, independent valuation distributions, etc.)

That being said, we argue that some constants are more important than others, and constant factor approximation of the revenue are particularly problematic. Consider the $1/6$-approximation by [1]. This is an extremely interesting result, but ultimately, losing 83% (or even the most optimistic 50%) of the revenue doesn't actually *solve* the auctioneer's mechanism problem[5]. On the other hand, a seller might be willing to compromise on optimality if guaranteed 99% of the optimal revenue. (For example, merchants around the world pay small fees to credit card companies in return for simple selling mechanisms). We therefore argue that in general the most interesting agenda, in 99% of mechanism design problems, should be obtaining 99% of the optimal revenue.

### 1.3 Relation to work on approximate revenue maximization

As already mentioned, our work is related to and inspired by a long line of research that aims at understanding what fraction of the optimal revenue can be guaranteed with simple mechanisms (without adding buyers), including [1, 20, 27] and references therein. It is interesting to note that obtaining a 0.99-approximation to the optimal revenue with $k$ additional buyers has implications on approximation results without additional buyers. In particular, if one can obtain a 0.99-approximation to the optimal revenue using mechanism $\mathcal{M}$ with $k$ additional buyers, then, by revenue submodularity, this immediately implies a $0.99/(k+1)$-approximation of the optimal revenue with a single buyer. Hence, our Theorem 1.1 implies the result of [27] that selling each item separately is an $\Omega(1/\log m)$-approximation of the optimal revenue. Similarly, our Theorem 1.3 implies the main result of [1] that the better of selling separately and selling the grand bundle yields a constant fraction of the optimal revenue. Of course, the reverse implication is not true, since the seller only has a single copy of each item to allocate to all buyers. Therefore, while our analysis builds on the techniques of [1, 27], it is significantly more challenging.

Recently, Goldner and Karlin [20] built on the result of Babaioff *et al.* [1], and showed that for regular distributions, the prior-independent mechanism which sells either each item separately or the grand bundle, and sets the price according to a single sample from the valuations distribution, obtains a constant fraction of the optimal revenue. As a corollary of our Theorem 1.5, we can obtain the following qualitative strengthening of [20, Corollary 2] for the case of a single buyer:

Corollary 1.6. *If $\mathcal{D}$ is a product of regular distributions, taking a single sample of the value of the grand bundle and selling the grand bundle for that price (to a single buyer) extracts at least a constant fraction of the optimal revenue.*

[4]For example, in 2012 Google was estimated to serve an average of 29,741,270,774 ($\approx$ 30 billion) impressions per day[25].

[5]There are still many great reasons to study constant-factor approximations in mechanism design; see, e.g., [24] for an excellent discussion.

For the special case where the single-dimensional distributions satisfy the monotone hazard rate (MHR) condition[6], Cai and Huang [7] gave a PTAS for the revenue maximizing auction. En route to obtaining their computational result, they prove the following structural lemma, which holds even for heterogeneous buyers. 99% of the optimal revenue can be obtained by one of the following simple mechanisms: (i) selling every item separately; or (ii) selling all but a constant number of items via a VCG-like mechanism. In other words, they show that when the single-dimensional distributions satisfy the MHR condition, no additional buyers are necessary to obtain 99% of the optimal revenue with mechanisms that are simple (in the above sense). Moreover, inspired by [5], they show that for MHR distributions, when the number of buyers is larger than some constant, selling items separately obtains 99% of the *social welfare*. (In contrast, note that for regular distributions the ratio of social welfare to revenue may be unbounded, even when adding any number of buyers.)

### 1.4 Organization

In Section 2 we provide a succinct overview of the techniques for all our results. Model definitions and other preliminaries appear in Section 3. An abridged version of the proof of Theorem 1.2 appears in the following two sections: Section 4 deals with the regime where the number of items is greater than the number of buyers, whereas the regime of more buyers than items is considered in Section 5. The full version of this paper with detailed proofs of all theorems is available at https://arxiv.org/abs/1801.02908.

## 2 OVERVIEW OF PROOFS

Our techniques build upon the now-standard approach for approximately optimal revenue analysis: Separately reason about revenue contribution from rare events of extremely high value ("tail" events), and revenue contribution from lower values ("core" events). This approach is made formal via the core-tail decomposition framework of Li and Yao [27]. Separation between core and tail events is done by setting a cutoff for each item, and then proving a "core-tail decomposition" lemma that upper bounds the optimal revenue by the sum of total value from core events in which items are below their cutoffs (a.k.a. contribution from the core), and the total revenue from tail events in which items are above their cutoffs (a.k.a. contribution from the tail).

For approximation results, the next step would typically be to show that simple mechanisms approximate both the contribution from the core and the tail, hence the best simple mechanism approximates the optimal revenue. However, when targeting 99% of the optimal revenue, even if one shows that simple mechanisms fully recover the contribution from the core and the tail, it does not yet imply that simple mechanisms recover the *sum* of the contributions. Hence this approach alone cannot yield better than a 1/2-approximation. Instead, we carefully set the cutoffs so that the contribution from the core is almost fully recovered using simple mechanisms with either $O(1)$ buyers (Theorems 1.3 and 1.5) or $O(\log m)$ buyers (Theorem 1.2), and the contribution from the tail is only a tiny fraction of the revenue from simple mechanisms with $O(1)$ buyers[7].

Before delving into the specificities of each result, we provide a few general notes about the tail and the core.

*Tail.* Since tail events are rare, they are approximately "separable" across items and across buyers. First, since the probability of two or more items in the tail of any buyer is low, the revenue contribution from tail items is roughly "separable" across items, i.e., approximating revenue contribution of tail events by the revenue contribution from selling items separately loses only a moderate factor.

[6]Roughly speaking, MHR distribution (a special case of regular distributions) has a tail that is thinner than that of an exponential distribution.

[7]In other words, for heavy-tailed distributions, adding a few buyers *increases* the revenue by a lot.

Furthermore, each buyer is likely to have tail valuations for disjoint subsets of items ("separability across buyers"). Thus in an enhanced competition setting with more buyers we can simultaneously serve all of them, quickly increasing the revenue.

*Core.* Since the value of core items is bounded, a concentration bound typically suggests a near-optimal grand bundle price whenever the sum of item values is significantly larger than the revenue from selling items separately.

In what follows we elaborate on cases where interesting artifacts arise in the analysis. We use Rev, SRev, and BRev to denote the optimal revenue from any mechanism, the optimal revenue from selling each item separately, and the optimal revenue from selling the grand bundle, respectively. [8]

*Theorem 1.3 (*$\max\{$*SRev, BRev*$\}$*).* An optimistic approach for proving Theorem 1.3 would use the same cutoff for all items, and apply a concentration bound (Chebyshev's inequality) to suggest a bundle price that almost fully recovers the contribution from the core with constant probability, then improve this probability to almost 1 by considering additional buyers. Unfortunately, such strong concentration does not hold in general: a small number of items may still exhibit a large variance, even inside the core. To overcome this challenge, we separate the set of items to items that exceed their cutoffs with constant probability, which we call "high items", and the remaining we call "low items". We then use a concentration bound only for the sum of low items to get a good bundle price for the low items. We set the cutoff so that the number of high items is a constant, hence with probability close to 1, one of our additional $O(1)$ buyers simultaneously exceeds the cutoff of all the "high items". We conclude that BRev with $O(1)$ buyers recovers almost all of the contribution from the core with probability almost 1.

*Theorem 1.5 (BRev, regular distributions).* Single dimensional regular distributions are appealing since they have a "small tail" property. While the grand bundle distribution need not be regular even when the individual item distributions are, we show that the underlying regularity of the individual items still maintains some well behaved properties that we can exploit. Specifically, we can set cutoffs so that in the resulting core-tail decomposition, the contribution from the tail is significantly smaller than the contribution from the core. This is important since we are only allowed to sell the grand bundle, while the tail is typically covered by selling items separately.

It is now left to guarantee that the core is almost fully recovered. The challenge is that a small number of outlier items may have very large variance, ruining the naive concentration bound argument. (In Theorem 1.3 we sometimes sold the outliers separately, but here we are only allowed to sell the grand bundle.) We show that given a large (but still constant) number of additional buyers, two of them are likely to have high values simultaneously for all of the outlier items. We can then use a concentration bound to suggest a good price for the remaining items, so that VCG on the grand bundle gives high revenue.

*Theorem 1.2 (SRev), $m = \omega(n)$ regime.* Instead of a concentration bound for the grand bundle (which is irrelevant when considering SRev) we further separate the contribution from the core to the contributions from lower and higher values. We then show that the contributions of lower values to the core can be almost fully recovered with probability almost 1 by SRev with $O(n \cdot \log(m/n))$ buyers, while the contributions of higher values to the core form only a tiny fraction of the revenue that can be extracted by SRev with $O(n \cdot \log(m/n))$ buyers. The proof appears in Section 4.

[8] SRev and BRev essentially perform Myerson's mechanism either on each item separately or on the grand bundle respectively.

*Theorem 1.2 (SRev), $m = o(n)$ regime.* We show that selling each item separately achieves 99% of the optimal auction without adding *any buyers at all.* Proving this result requires yet new ideas. The intuition is simple: with so many buyers, we can afford to set the cutoff much higher - so high that *most buyers* have at most one item in the tail - while the contribution from the core can be almost fully recovered by selling each item to a tiny fraction of the buyers. Therefore, we can set aside a small subset of special buyers, and offer the items at high (tail) prices to all other buyers; we can then recover the rest of the revenue by auctioning the items not previously sold to the special buyers. (Note that this mechanism is for analysis purposes only — once we establish guarantees for any mechanism for selling items separately, we can use Myerson's optimal mechanism for selling items separately.) This part of the analysis also takes into account the probability that an item was sold in tail events.

Formalizing the above intuition is quite subtle. With high probability, there are still *some* buyers with multiple items in the tail - and each of those items has many other buyers whose valuations are in the tail, etc. Thus even after the core-tail decomposition, we have to reason about a multiple buyer, multiple item setting. To cope with this difficulty, we consider a bipartite graph of buyers and items, where we draw an edge $\{i, j\}$ whenever buyer $i$'s value of item $j$ is in the tail. We then argue that we can analyze the revenue from each connected component separately. In particular, while there are, w.h.p., large components in the graph (with $\omega(1)$ buyers and items), we use simple ideas from percolation theory to bound the expected size of each connected component. The proof appears in Section 5.

## 3 MODEL AND PRELIMINARIES

We consider a setting in which a monopolist seller sells a set $[m] = \{1, 2, \dots, m\}$ of heterogeneous items to $n$ additive buyers. Buyer $i$'s value is additive if there exist values $v_1^i, \dots, v_m^i$ such that buyer $i$'s value for a set of items $A$ is $\sum_{j \in A} v_j^i$. The seller does not know the buyers' values, but knows the distribution from which they are sampled. For every item $j$, the value of each agent $i$ for item $j$ is independently sampled from a single-dimensional distribution $D_j$.

A mechanism is given by a pair of an allocation function $\pi$, and a payment function $\mathbf{p}$. The mechanism receives a valuation profile $\mathbf{v} = \{v_j^i\}_{i,j}$ as input. Based on $\mathbf{v}$, the allocation function determines the (possibly random) allocation of items to buyers, and the payment function determines the payment $\mathbf{p}^i$ of every buyer $i$. Buyers are quasi-linear; namely, buyer $i$'s utility from a mechanism that allocates her each item $j$ with probability $\pi_j^i$ and charges her a payment $\mathbf{p}_i$ is $\sum_j \pi_j^i \cdot v_j^i - \mathbf{p}^i$.

A mechanism is Bayesian Individually Rational (BIR) if every buyer's expected utility (over the randomness of the mechanism and other buyers' values, assuming they are drawn from $\times_j D_j$) is non-negative. A mechanism is Bayesian Incentive Compatible (BIC) if every buyer's expected utility is maximized when the buyer reports her valuation truthfully. Throughout the paper, a BIR-BIC mechanism is termed a *truthful* mechanism. The expected revenue of a truthful mechanism is $\mathbb{E}\left[\sum_i \mathbf{p}^i(\mathbf{v})\right]$, where for every buyer $i$ and item $j$ buyer $i$'s value for item $j$ is drawn independently from $D_j$. The *optimal revenue* is the optimal[9] expected revenue among all truthful mechanisms.

For any single dimensional distribution $D$ and any $q \in [0, 1]$, we assume w.l.o.g. that there exists $v(q) \in \mathbb{R}$ such that $\Pr_{x \sim D}[x \geq v(q)] = q$. When the distribution is continuous this is true by the intermediate value theorem. When the distribution has point masses, we can smooth it with an infinitesimal perturbation; see e.g., [34] for a formal discussion. We note that when $D$ is regular, the perturbed distribution may not be regular. However, it will not be hard to see that our proof in

[9]In general for distributions of infinite support, the optimum revenue may not be achieved by any mechanism (i.e. it is the supremum of all revenues achievable by truthful mechanisms). This is not so important for our purposes since we are only trying to approximate the optimum.

Section ?? will also work with distributions that are infinitesimally-close to regular distributions. For a set of items $A \subseteq [m]$, let $\bar{A} = [m] \setminus A$. We use $\mathbf{v}^i_A = \{\mathbf{v}^i_j\}_{j\in A}$, therefore $\mathbf{v}^i = (\mathbf{v}^i_A, \mathbf{v}^i_{\bar{A}})$. Also, we use $\mathbf{v}_j = \{\mathbf{v}^i_j\}_{i\in[n]}$, and more generally, for a set $S \subseteq [n] \times [m]$, we use $\mathbf{v}_S = \{\mathbf{v}^i_j\}_{(i,j)\in S}$ and $\mathbf{v}_{-S} = \{\mathbf{v}^i_j\}_{(i,j)\notin S}$. Let $\mathcal{D} = \times_{j\in[m]} D_j$. Therefore, in a setting with $n$ i.i.d. buyers, each drawn from $\mathcal{D}$, the prior distribution is $\mathcal{D}^n$ [10].

Let $\mathcal{M}$ be a truthful mechanism with an allocation function $\pi$ and a payment function $\mathbf{p}$, i.e., given the submitted bids $\mathbf{v}$, each buyer $i$ is allocated item $j$ with probability $\pi^i_j(\mathbf{v})$ and pays $\mathbf{p}^i(\mathbf{v})$. Let $\textsc{Rev}_{\mathcal{M}}(\cdot)$ be mechanism $\mathcal{M}$'s expected revenue, e.g., $\textsc{Rev}_{\mathcal{M}}(\mathcal{D}^h)$ is mechanism $\mathcal{M}$'s expected revenue from $h$ buyers, where each buyer's valuation $\mathbf{v}^i$ is drawn i.i.d. from $\mathcal{D}$, i.e., $\textsc{Rev}_{\mathcal{M}}(\mathcal{D}^h) = \mathbb{E}_{\mathbf{v}\leftarrow\mathcal{D}^h}\left[\sum_{i\in[h]} \mathbf{p}^i(\mathbf{v})\right]$. Let $\textsc{Rev}(\cdot)$ be the optimal expected revenue by any truthful mechanism, e.g., $\textsc{Rev}(\mathcal{D}^h)$ is the optimal expected revenue by any truthful mechanism for $h$ i.i.d. buyers drawn from $\mathcal{D}$. Similarly, $\textsc{SRev}(\cdot)$ is the optimal expected revenue when selling the items separately, and $\textsc{BRev}(\cdot)$ is the optimal expected revenue when selling all items in a bundle. Let $\textsc{Val}(\cdot)$ be the expected value of the optimal allocation. Since we consider additive, independently drawn buyers, $\textsc{Val}(\mathcal{D}^h) = \sum_j \mathbb{E}\left[\max_{i\in[h]} \mathbf{v}^i_j\right]$.

For a single dimensional distribution $D$, and a number $p \in [0,1]$, let $\textsc{Rev}_p(\cdot)$ denote the revenue of an optimal mechanism, among all truthful mechanisms that *sell with ex-ante probability of at most* $p$, i.e., mechanisms with allocation function $\pi$ that satisfies $\mathbb{E}_{\mathbf{v}}\left[\sum_i \pi^i(\mathbf{v})\right] \leq p$.

Throughout the analysis, for $h$ that is not an integer, we slightly abuse notation and use, e.g., $D^h$ instead of $D^{\lceil h\rceil}$ to denote the product distribution $\times_{i\in\lceil h\rceil} D$. For a random variable $X$ drawn from distribution $D$, we use $\textsc{Rev}(X)$ and $\textsc{Rev}(D)$ interchangeably (and similarly for $\textsc{SRev}$, $\textsc{BRev}$, etc.). Also, let $\mathbb{I}[\mathcal{E}]$ be the indicator random variable that equals 1 when event $\mathcal{E}$ occurs, and 0 otherwise.

Finally, we will use the following previously shown lemma.

Lemma 3.1. *[1] For any nm dimensional distribution $\mathcal{D}$, $\textsc{Rev}(\mathcal{D}) \leq n \cdot m \cdot \textsc{SRev}(\mathcal{D})$.*

### 3.1 Lemmas for single dimensional distributions.

We recall and develop tools for our analysis in the remaining sections. Let $v$ be drawn from a single dimensional distribution $D$ (i.e., $v \leftarrow D$), and consider some cutoff $\mathcal{T} \in \mathbb{R}$.

Lemma 3.2. *[21] $\textsc{Rev}(v|v > \mathcal{T}) = \frac{\textsc{Rev}(v\cdot\mathbb{I}[v>\mathcal{T}])}{\Pr[v>\mathcal{T}]}$.*

Lemma 3.3. *[27] Let $\gamma > 0$. Then $\Pr[v > \gamma \cdot \textsc{Rev}(D)] \leq \frac{1}{\gamma}$.*

Let $\mathrm{Var}(D)$ denote the variance of $D$.

Lemma 3.4. *[27] Let $\gamma > 0$, and supposed that both $\textsc{Rev}(D) \leq \gamma$ and that the support of $D$ is in $[0, t\gamma]$. Then $\mathrm{Var}(D) \leq (2t-1)\gamma^2$.*

The following lemma shows that for $\delta > 0$ that is not too small, the optimal revenue from $\lceil 1/\delta \rceil$ i.i.d. buyers drawn from $D$ is at least a $1/(2\delta)$ factor larger than the optimal revenue that can be extracted from a buyer with value distributed according to $v \cdot \mathbb{I}[v > \mathcal{T}]$. This lemma will be used to bound the contribution (both to the core and tail) of higher values.

Lemma 3.5. *Suppose that $\delta \geq 2 \cdot \Pr[v > \mathcal{T}]$. Then $\textsc{Rev}(v \cdot \mathbb{I}[v > \mathcal{T}]) \leq 2\delta \cdot \textsc{Rev}(D^{1/\delta})$.*

The following lemma will be used to cover the contribution of values from the core.

Lemma 3.6. *Let $\mathcal{T}_\alpha$ satisfy $\Pr_{v\leftarrow D}[v > \mathcal{T}_\alpha] \geq \alpha$. For any $h \geq 1$: $\textsc{Rev}(D^h) \geq (1 - e^{-\alpha\cdot h}) \cdot \mathcal{T}_\alpha$.*

[10] By $\mathcal{D}^n$ we mean the product distribution $\times_{i\in[n]} \mathcal{D}$.

The following lemma is a specified analog to Lemma 3.6 that bounds the contribution from values in the core using the second price auction, and its proof is similar to the proof of Lemma 3.6. Let $\textsc{Rev}_{\text{VCG}}$ denote the revenue from the second price auction.

Lemma 3.7. *Let $\mathcal{T}_\alpha$ satisfy $\Pr_{v \leftarrow D}[v > \mathcal{T}_\alpha] \geq \alpha$. For any $h \geq 1$: $\textsc{Rev}_{VCG}\left(D^{2h}\right) \geq (1 - e^{-\alpha \cdot h})^2 \cdot \mathcal{T}_\alpha$*

*3.1.1 Regular distributions.* For ease of exposition, we assume $D$ has a density $f$ and is strictly increasing. Nevertheless, our results extend to arbitrary regular distributions. A distribution $D$ with density $f$ is *regular* if $v - (1 - D(v))/f(v)$ is non-decreasing in $v$. Our analysis is done in quantile space, which is defined below.

*Definition 3.8.* (Quantiles, demand curve, and revenue curve.)

- Let $q(v) = \Pr_{x \leftarrow D}[x \leq v] = D(v)$ be the *quantile* of $v$.
- Let $V(q) = v$ for which $D(v) = q$, i.e., $V(q) = D^{-1}(q)$ is the *demand curve* of $D$.
- Let $\text{rev}(q) = (1 - q) \cdot V(q)$, i.e., the revenue from the posted price $V(q)$ that sells w.p. $1 - q$.

Observe that $V$ is increasing in $q$. By change of variables, the expected value $v$ can be computed as follows: [11] $\mathbb{E}[v] = \int_0^\infty v f(v) dv = \int_0^1 V(q) dq = \mathbb{E}_{q \leftarrow U[0,1]}[V(q)]$. The following lemma is a well known characterization of regular distributions.

Lemma 3.9. *[30] A distribution $D$ is regular if and only if rev$(q)$ is concave, i.e., for every $\alpha, \beta, \gamma \in [0, 1]$, it holds that rev$(\gamma \cdot \alpha + (1 - \gamma)\beta) \geq \gamma \cdot$ rev$(\alpha) + (1 - \gamma) \cdot$ rev$(\beta)$.*

The following corollary is the only way we use regularity (and is only used to prove Lemma 3.11).

Corollary 3.10. *If $D$ is regular and $0 \leq \beta \leq \alpha \leq 1$, then rev$(\beta) \geq \alpha \cdot$ rev$(\beta) \geq \beta \cdot$ rev$(\alpha)$.*

The following lemma shows that if the probability of exceeding the cutoff $\mathcal{T}$ is $\varepsilon$, then $\mathcal{T}$ is a price that provides a $1 - \varepsilon$ approximation to the optimal revenue from the random variable $v \cdot \mathbb{I}[v > \mathcal{T}]$.

Lemma 3.11. *For a cutoff $\mathcal{T} = V(1 - \varepsilon)$, it holds that rev$(1 - \varepsilon) \geq (1 - \varepsilon) \cdot \textsc{Rev}(v \cdot \mathbb{I}[v > \mathcal{T}])$.*

The following lemma relates the contribution from the core to the contribution from the tail.

Lemma 3.12. *For a cutoff $\mathcal{T} = V(1 - \varepsilon_1)$, for every $0 < \varepsilon_2 < 1$ and $k \in \mathbb{N}$ such that $\varepsilon_1 \cdot \varepsilon_2^{-k} < 1$ it holds that: $\mathbb{E}_{v \leftarrow D}[v \cdot \mathbb{I}[v \leq \mathcal{T}]] \geq k \cdot (1 - \varepsilon_2) \cdot (1 - \varepsilon_1 \cdot \varepsilon_2^{-k}) \textsc{Rev}(v \cdot \mathbb{I}[v > \mathcal{T}])$*

*3.1.2 Mechanisms with restricted probability of sale.* We describe optimal single item mechanisms with restricted probability of sale. The lemmas established in this section are used in Section 5. In particular, we formally show that a naive generalization of Myerson's optimal auction for the unrestricted case is also optimal for the restricted case.

Fix a number $p \in [0, 1]$ and $x$ i.i.d. buyers, each buyer $i$ with value $\mathbf{v}^i$ drawn from a single dimensional distribution $D$. A mechanism with allocation function $\pi$ that satisfies $\mathbb{E}_{\mathbf{v}}\left[\sum_{i \in [x]} \pi^i(\mathbf{v})\right] \leq p$, is said to *sell with ex-ante probability of at most $p$*.

Recall that by Myerson's theory, a mechanism with allocation rule $\pi$ and payment $\mathbf{p}$ is truthful if and only if each buyer $i$'s allocation rule $\pi^i$ is monotone, and buyer $i$'s payment function is fully determined by $\pi^i$ via the equality $\mathbf{p}^i(\mathbf{v}) = \mathbf{v}^i \cdot \pi^i(\mathbf{v}) - \int_{z=0}^{\mathbf{v}^i} \pi^i(z, \mathbf{v}^{-i}) dz$. Furthermore, Myerson defines *virtual value* functions[12] $\varphi^D : \text{supp}(D) \to \mathbb{R}$ for single dimensional distributions $D$ (we henceforth drop the superscript $D$). The virtual value function is particularly useful because one can re-amortize the expected payment to a term that uses the virtual value functions, and this term can be optimized point wise. This becomes apparent in Myerson's payment identity:

[11] By $v = V(q)$, we get $dv = V'(q)dq = [D^{-1}]'(q) = \frac{1}{f(D^{-1}(q))} = \frac{1}{f(V(q))}$, so $vf(v)dv = V(q)\frac{f(V(q))}{f(V(q))}dq$

[12] When $D$ has a density $f$, its virtual value function is defined by $\varphi(v) = v - \frac{1-D(v)}{f(v)}$. See e.g., [6, 19] for the general case.

Lemma 3.13. *[30] (Payment identity) In every truthful mechanism with allocation function $\pi$ and payment function* $\mathbf{p}$*, for every buyer $i$ it holds that* $\mathbb{E}\left[\varphi(\mathbf{v}^i)\cdot\pi^i(\mathbf{v})\right]=\mathbb{E}\left[\mathbf{p}^i(\mathbf{v})\right]$

A regular distribution is a distribution whose corresponding virtual value function $\varphi$ is monotone. For irregular distributions, Myerson defines yet another transformation that transforms the virtual value function to an *ironed* virtual value function $\bar{\varphi}$ (the details are not so important for our application; for more details see e.g., [24, 30]). The key point is that ironed virtual value functions are always monotone, and furthermore, maintain the following property:

Theorem 3.14. *([24, Theorem 3.12]) For every truthful mechanism with allocation function $\pi$, for every buyer $i$,* $\mathbb{E}\left[\varphi(\mathbf{v}^i)\cdot\pi^i(\mathbf{v})\right]\leq\mathbb{E}\left[\bar{\varphi}(\mathbf{v}^i)\cdot\pi^i(\mathbf{v})\right]$*, with equality if $\pi^i(\cdot,\mathbf{v}^{-i})$ is constant on ironed intervals.*

In order to construct the optimal mechanism with restricted probability of sale, we will need the following definitions. Let $\mathbf{v}^*=\max_{i\in[x]}\mathbf{v}^i$, and let $S=\{y\geq 0:\Pr[\bar{\varphi}(\mathbf{v}^*)\geq y]\leq p\}$ and $\phi=\inf S$.

Note that if $\phi\in S$, then it must be that $\phi=0$ or that $\Pr[\bar{\varphi}(\mathbf{v}^*)\geq\phi]=p$. [13] Otherwise, it must be that $\Pr[\bar{\varphi}(\mathbf{v}^*)>\phi]\leq p$, [14] but $\Pr[\bar{\varphi}(\mathbf{v}^*)\geq\phi]>p$, i.e, $\Pr[\bar{\varphi}(\mathbf{v}^*)=\phi]=\Pr[\bar{\varphi}(\mathbf{v}^*)\geq\phi]-\Pr[\bar{\varphi}(\mathbf{v}^*)>\phi]>0$.

Consider the mechanism $\mathcal{M}$ that sells a single item to $x$ buyers as follows. If $\phi\in S$, the mechanism allocates the item to a random buyer $i$ among those with $\bar{\varphi}(\mathbf{v}^i)=\bar{\varphi}(\mathbf{v}^*)$ whenever $\bar{\varphi}(\mathbf{v}^*)\geq\phi$, and otherwise does not allocate.

If $\phi\notin S$, then the mechanism allocates the item to a random buyer $i$ among those with $\bar{\varphi}(\mathbf{v}^i)=\bar{\varphi}(\mathbf{v}^*)$ whenever $\bar{\varphi}(\mathbf{v}^*)>\phi$, and whenever $\bar{\varphi}(\mathbf{v}^*)=\phi$ the mechanism draws a Bernoulli random variable that equals 1 w.p. $\frac{p-\Pr[\bar{\varphi}(\mathbf{v}^*)>\phi]}{\Pr[\bar{\varphi}(\mathbf{v}^*)=\phi]}$, and if the variable equals 1 the mechanism allocates to a random buyer $i$ among those with $\bar{\varphi}(\mathbf{v}^i)=\phi$.

Lemma 3.15. *For $x$ i.i.d. buyers drawn from a single dimensional distribution $D$, and $p,\phi,\mathbf{v}^*$ as above, the mechanism $\mathcal{M}$ described above sells with ex-ante probability of at most $p$, and extracts expected revenue of:* $\mathbb{E}\left[\bar{\varphi}(\mathbf{v}^*)\cdot\mathbb{I}[\bar{\varphi}(\mathbf{v}^*)>\phi]\right]+\phi\cdot(p-\Pr[\bar{\varphi}(\mathbf{v}^*)>\phi])$.
*Moreover, every buyer contributes the same amount of expected revenue.*

We will now prove the optimality of $\mathcal{M}$ among mechanisms with restricted probability of sale.

Lemma 3.16. *For $D,x,p$ as above, the mechanism $\mathcal{M}$ above is a revenue maximizing mechanism among all truthful mechanisms that sell to $x$ i.i.d. buyers drawn from $D$ with ex-ante probability of at most $p$, i.e.,* $\textsc{Rev}_p(D^x)=\textsc{Rev}_{\mathcal{M}}(D^x)$.

Corollary 3.17. *Let $0\leq\delta<1$. Then* $\textsc{Rev}_p(D^x)\leq\frac{1}{1-\delta}\textsc{Rev}_p(D^{(1-\delta)\cdot x})$

Lemma 3.18. $\textsc{Rev}_p(D^k)$ *is non-decreasing in $k$.*

Lemma 3.19. *Fix a cutoff $\mathcal{T}$. Let $\mathbf{v}\leftarrow D^n$. Let $\hat{D}$ denote the distribution of $\mathbf{v}^i|(\mathbf{v}^i>\mathcal{T})$ for every buyer $i$. Then for every $k\leq n$ and $p\in[0,1]$:* $\textsc{Rev}_p\left(\hat{D}^k\right)\leq\frac{\textsc{Rev}_p(D^n)}{\Pr[|\{i:\mathbf{v}^i>\mathcal{T}\}|\geq k]}$

### 3.2 Partition of the support.

Recall that for every buyer $i$ and item $j$, $\mathbf{v}^i_j\leftarrow D_j$, and that $\mathcal{D}=\times_{j\in[m]}D_j$. Every item $j$ is assigned a cutoff $\mathcal{T}_j$. If the value of an item is greater than its cutoff (i.e., $\mathbf{v}^i_j>\mathcal{T}_j$) then it is said to be in the tail w.r.t. $\mathbf{v}^i$, and otherwise it is in the core w.r.t $\mathbf{v}^i$.

[13] Otherwise $\Pr[\bar{\varphi}(\mathbf{v}^*)\geq\phi]=p-\epsilon$ but for every $0<a<\phi$ we have $\Pr[\phi>\bar{\varphi}(\mathbf{v}^*)\geq a]>\epsilon$.

[14] Otherwise $\Pr[\bar{\varphi}(\mathbf{v}^*)>\phi]=p+\epsilon$ but for every $a>\phi$ we have $\Pr[a>\bar{\varphi}(\mathbf{v}^*)>\phi]\geq\epsilon$.

For a set of items $A$, let $\mathcal{D}^A$ be the distribution $\mathcal{D}$ conditioned on $A$ being exactly the set of items in the tail. Let $p_A$ be the probability of $A$ being exactly the set of items in the tail, i.e., $p_A = \prod_{j\in A}\Pr[\mathbf{v}^i_j > \mathcal{T}_j]\cdot\prod_{j\notin A}\Pr[\mathbf{v}^i_j \le \mathcal{T}_j]$. Let $\mathcal{D}^A_C$ (resp., $\mathcal{D}^A_T$) be the distribution $\mathcal{D}^A$ restricted to just items in the core (resp., tail).

For every buyer $i$ consider some $\mathcal{A}^i \subseteq [m]$, and let $\mathcal{A} = \{\mathcal{A}^i\}_{i\in[n]}$. Let $\mathcal{A}$ represent the event that for every $i$ it holds that $\mathcal{A}^i$ is exactly the set of items that are in the tail with respect to buyer $i$'s valuation, i.e., for every item $j \in \mathcal{A}^i$ it holds that $\mathbf{v}^i_j > \mathcal{T}_j$, and for every $j \notin \mathcal{A}^i$ it holds that $\mathbf{v}^i_j \le \mathcal{T}_j$. Denote by $p_{\mathcal{A}}$ the probability of event $\mathcal{A}$, i.e., $p_{\mathcal{A}} = \prod_i p_{\mathcal{A}^i}$, and let $\mathcal{D}^{\mathcal{A}}$ be the distribution $\mathcal{D}^n$ conditioned on the event $\mathcal{A}$, i.e., $\mathcal{D}^{\mathcal{A}} = \times_{i\in[n]}\mathcal{D}^{\mathcal{A}^i}$.

The following lemma appeared previously and is included for completeness.

Lemma 3.20. *[21] (Sub-domain stitching) Let $\mathcal{L} = \{\mathcal{A} : \forall i, \mathcal{A}^i \subseteq [m]\}$ be all possible $\mathcal{A}$. Then $\textsc{Rev}(\mathcal{D}^n) \le \sum_{\mathcal{A}\in\mathcal{L}} p_{\mathcal{A}}\cdot \textsc{Rev}(\mathcal{D}^{\mathcal{A}})$*

## 4 MANY ITEMS: SRev WITH $O(n\cdot\log\frac{m}{n})$ BUYERS

In this section we prove that for $m \gg n$, increasing the number of buyers by a factor of $O(\log(m/n))$ suffices to recover 99% of the optimal revenue by selling the items separately.

Theorem 4.1 (Theorem 1.2, case $m \gg n$). *For any constant $\varepsilon > 0$ there exists a constant $\delta = \delta(\varepsilon) > 0$ such that whenever $m \ge 2n/\delta$,*

$$(1-\varepsilon)\textsc{Rev}(\mathcal{D}^n) \le \textsc{SRev}(\mathcal{D}^{\frac{n\cdot\log\frac{m}{n}}{\delta}})$$

This implies the following corollary for the special case of a single buyer:

Corollary 4.2 (Theorem 1.1). *For any constant $\varepsilon > 0$ there exists a constant $\delta(\varepsilon) > 0$ such that whenever $m \ge 2/\delta$, $(1-\varepsilon)\textsc{Rev}(\mathcal{D}) \le \textsc{SRev}(\mathcal{D}^{\frac{\log m}{\delta}})$*

### 4.1 Proof outline

We first partition the domain of the valuations distribution into sub-domains (using the Subdomain Stiching Lemma (Lemma 3.20)). We henceforth condition on the event (or sub-domain) $\mathcal{A}$ that describes which items are in the tail or core for which buyer (we still don't know their values within the tail/core).

We now describe a "marginal mechanism lemma" (Lemma 4.3) that shows that the optimal revenue from $\mathcal{D}^{\mathcal{A}}$, is bounded by the sum of expected item values in the core in event $\mathcal{A}$, plus the revenue from selling to each buyer the items that are in her tail in event $\mathcal{A}$ (conditioned on them being in the tail). This implies a core-tail decomposition lemma (Lemma 4.4) that bounds the optimal revenue using two terms: the core and tail.

We bound the tail in Section 4.3. In Lemma 4.5 we show that the tail is bounded by the revenue from selling items separately and using only prices that are higher than the cutoffs. Since the probability that two buyers are interested in the same item at a high price is extremely low, the supply constraint is hardly restricting. Therefore when we increase the number of buyers, the revenue increases almost linearly. This is used in Lemma 4.6 that shows that the tail is a tiny fraction of the revenue after multiplying the number of buyers by a (large) constant.

We bound the core in Section 4.4. We separate the core into regions of lower values and higher values. Lower values are upper bounded by a maximum of two cutoffs, and are handled in two lemmata (4.7 and 4.8).

In Lemma 4.10 we bound the contribution from "higher" values (still in the core). First, we observe that they lie in a bounded region: bounded from above since they are in the core, and bounded from below since we handle low values separately. We use this property to show that their expected value is at most $O(\log(m/n))$-factor larger than the revenue from selling each item separately at "higher" prices. Now, similarly to the tail, since at high prices buyers are likely to want disjoint sets of items, the above revenue scales almost linearly when increasing the number of buyers. Therefore, multiplying the number of buyers by $O(\log(m/n))$ suffices to extract revenue much larger than the contribution from high values.

Finally, we complete the proof by combining the core-tail decomposition with the above arguments.

### 4.2 Core-tail decomposition.

The following lemma may be seen as a generalization of Lemma 24 in [21] for $n > 1$ buyers. In [21], the authors note that the proof of their Lemma 24 implies a generalization for $n > 1$, by considering for each item the maximal value among all buyers' values. This method still allows to partition the support of $\mathcal{D}^n$ to only $2^m$ subsets (according to the set of items that have a maximal value above the cutoff). We show a more fine-grained generalization that partitions the support of $\mathcal{D}^n$ to $2^{m \cdot n}$ subsets, thereby leading to a tighter analysis.

Recall that for some $\mathcal{A}^i$, $\mathcal{D}_T^{\mathcal{A}^i}$ is the distribution $\mathcal{D}$ conditioned on $\mathcal{A}^i$ being exactly the set of items in the tail, restricted only to the items in the tail ($\mathcal{A}^i$).

Lemma 4.3. *(Marginal Mechanism on Sub-Domain) For $\mathcal{A}$ as above,*

$$\textsc{Rev}\left(\mathcal{D}^{\mathcal{A}}\right) \leq \sum_{j\in[m]} \mathop{\mathbb{E}}_{\mathbf{v}\leftarrow\mathcal{D}^n}\left[\max_{i:j\notin\mathcal{A}^i} \mathbf{v}_j^i \middle| \mathcal{A}\right] + \sum_{i\in[n]} \textsc{Rev}\left(\mathcal{D}_T^{\mathcal{A}^i}\right)$$

The following core-tail decomposition upper bounds the optimal revenue from $n$ buyers. In contrast to the decomposition in [1], our decomposition provides a tail that relates to single buyer settings.

To simplify notation, once cutoffs $\mathcal{T}_j$ are fixed for every $j$, we use $\mathcal{D}_{\textsc{Tail}}$ to denote the product distribution of the random variables $\{v_j \cdot \mathbb{I}[v_j > \mathcal{T}_j]\}_{j\in[m]}$, and $\mathcal{D}_{\textsc{Core}}$ to denote the product distribution of the random variables $\{v_j \cdot \mathbb{I}[v_j \leq \mathcal{T}_j]\}_{j\in[m]}$, where $v_j \leftarrow D_j$ for every $j$.

Lemma 4.4. *(Core-tail decomposition) $\textsc{Rev}(\mathcal{D}^n) \leq \textsc{Val}(\mathcal{D}^n_{\textsc{Core}}) + n \cdot \sum_{A\subseteq[m]} p_A \cdot \textsc{Rev}(\mathcal{D}_T^A)$*

*Cutoff setting.* For every item $j$ fix $\mathcal{T}_j$ to be so that $\Pr_{\mathbf{v}_j\leftarrow D_j}[\mathbf{v}_j > \mathcal{T}_j] = m^{-1}$.

### 4.3 Tail

The main lemma of this section is Lemma 4.6 which states that the contribution from the tail is a tiny fraction of the revenue from SRev with $n \cdot C$ buyers where $C$ is some constant. Lemma 4.5 shows (in the spirit of Proposition 1 in [1]) that we can approximately recover the tail of one buyer ($\sum_{A\subseteq[m]} p_A \cdot \textsc{Rev}(\mathcal{D}_T^A)$) by selling items separately, only using prices that are higher than the cutoffs. Recall that $\mathcal{D}_{\textsc{Tail}}$ is the product distribution of the random variables $\{\mathbf{v}_j \cdot \mathbb{I}[\mathbf{v}_j > \mathcal{T}_j]\}_{j\in[m]}$, and therefore $\textsc{SRev}(\mathcal{D}_{\textsc{Tail}}) = \sum_{j\in[m]} \textsc{Rev}(\mathbf{v}_j \cdot \mathbb{I}[\mathbf{v}_j > \mathcal{T}_j])$.

Lemma 4.5. *$\sum_{A\subseteq[m]} p_A \cdot \textsc{Rev}(\mathcal{D}_T^A) \leq 2 \cdot \textsc{SRev}(\mathcal{D}_{\textsc{Tail}})$*

Combining the above lemma with Lemma 3.5 shows that SRev with $n \cdot C$ buyers (where $C$ is a constant) extracts *much more* revenue than the contribution from the tail.

Lemma 4.6. *Let $\delta \geq 2n/m$. Then $n \cdot \sum_{A\subseteq[m]} p_A \textsc{Rev}(\mathcal{D}_T^A) \leq 4 \cdot \delta \cdot \textsc{SRev}(\mathcal{D}^{n/\delta})$*

### 4.4 Core

For ease of exposition, let $\mathbf{v}_j^*$ denote the random variable $\mathbf{v}_j^* = \max_{i\in[n]}\{\mathbf{v}_j^i \cdot \mathbb{I}[\mathbf{v}_j^i \le \mathcal{T}_j]\}$ where $\mathbf{v}_j^i \leftarrow D_j$ for each $i \in [n]$. In this section we upper bound the core $\text{VAL}(\mathcal{D}^n_{\text{CORE}}) = \sum_{j\in[m]} \mathbb{E}[\mathbf{v}_j^*]$.

*Cutoff setting in the core.* Fix some constant $\varepsilon_1 \le 1$. For each item $j$, set $\mathcal{T}_j{}'$ so that $\Pr_{v\leftarrow D_j}[v > \mathcal{T}_j{}'] = \frac{\varepsilon_1}{n\cdot\log\frac{m}{n}}$, and set $\mathcal{T}_j{}'' = \max\{\frac{n}{m}\cdot\mathcal{T}_j, \mathcal{T}_j{}'\}$. In order to bound the contribution from the core, for each item we separate to "tiny values" (at most $\frac{n}{m}\mathcal{T}_j$), "low values" (at most $\mathcal{T}_j{}'$), and "higher values" (above $\max\{\frac{n}{m}\cdot\mathcal{T}_j, \mathcal{T}_j{}'\}$).

In the following we bound the contribution from values that are at most $\mathcal{T}_j{}''$. In Lemma 4.7 we show that "tiny values" contribute a tiny fraction of the revenue that is achievable by increasing the number of buyers by a constant factor, and in Lemma 4.8 we show that the contribution of "lower values" to the core can be almost completely covered by the revenue that is achievable by increasing the number of buyers by a factor of $O(\log\frac{m}{n})$.

Lemma 4.7. *(Tiny values) Let $\delta \ge 2n/m$. Then for each item $j$ $\frac{n}{m}\mathcal{T}_j \le 2\delta\cdot \text{REV}(D_j^{n/\delta})$*

Lemma 4.8. *(Lower values) Let $\delta < \varepsilon_1$. Then for each item $j$, $\mathcal{T}_j{}' \le (1-e^{-\frac{\varepsilon_1}{\delta}})^{-1}\cdot \text{REV}(D_j^{n\cdot\log(\frac{m}{n})/\delta})$*

Putting Lemmas 4.7 and 4.8 gives the following corollary

Corollary 4.9. *Let $\frac{2n}{m} \le \delta \le \min\{\frac{1}{2}, \varepsilon_1\}$. Then for each item $j$, $\mathcal{T}_j{}'' \le (1-e^{-\frac{\varepsilon_1}{\delta}})^{-1}\cdot \text{REV}(D_j^{n\cdot\log(\frac{m}{n})/\delta})$*

Lemma 4.10 shows that "higher values" in the core contribute a tiny fraction of the revenue that is achievable by increasing the number of buyers by a factor of $O(\log\frac{m}{n})$.

Lemma 4.10. *Let $\delta < 2\varepsilon_1$. Then for each $j$, $\mathbb{E}[\mathbf{v}_j^*\cdot\mathbb{I}[\mathbf{v}_j^* > \mathcal{T}_j{}'']] \le 8\cdot\varepsilon_1\cdot \text{REV}(D_j^{\frac{n\cdot\log\frac{m}{n}}{\delta}})$.*

We are now ready to bound the contribution from the core. Let $\varepsilon_2$ be so that $1+\varepsilon_2 = (1-e^{-\frac{\varepsilon_1}{\delta}})^{-1}$.

Lemma 4.11. *Let $2n/m \le \delta \le \min\{1/2, \varepsilon_1\}$. Then, $\text{VAL}(\mathcal{D}^n_{\text{CORE}}) \le (1+\varepsilon_2+8\cdot\varepsilon_1)\cdot \text{SREV}(\mathcal{D}^{\frac{n\cdot\log\frac{m}{n}}{\delta}})$.*

### 4.5 Matching Lower Bound for Many Items

Theorem 4.12. *Let $m = \Omega(n)$. There exists a distribution $\mathcal{D}$ so that for every $\varepsilon > 0$ there exists some $\delta > 0$ so that*

$$\text{SREV}(\mathcal{D}^{\delta\cdot n\cdot\ln\frac{m}{n}}) \le \varepsilon\cdot \text{REV}(\mathcal{D}^n).$$

*Proof sketch:* Each item is drawn from the equal revenue (ER) distribution on the support $[1, m]$. Let $\mathcal{ER} = \times_{j\in[m]}\text{ER}$. One can easily show that $\text{SREV}(\mathcal{ER}^{\delta\cdot n\cdot\ln(\frac{m}{n})}) \le \delta\cdot m\cdot n\cdot\ln\left(\frac{m}{n}\right)$. Therefore, it suffices to show a mechanism that achieves revenue of $\Omega(m\cdot n\cdot\ln\left(\frac{m}{n}\right))$. Consider the mechanism that orders the buyers (arbitrarily), and offers each buyer in her turn to purchase her favorite bundle of size $\frac{m}{4\cdot n}$ at price $\frac{m}{8}\cdot\ln\frac{m}{n}$. As $\frac{m}{n}$ grows to a large enough constant, one can show that for every buyer w.h.p. there are at least $\frac{m}{4n}$ items valued above $n$. Conditioned on that event, the expected value of the sum of these items is at least $\frac{m}{4}\cdot\ln\frac{m}{n}$. Also, w.h.p. every buyer will purchase a bundle (observe that there are always enough items), thus extracting revenue of $\frac{n\cdot m}{8}\cdot\ln\frac{m}{n}$, w.h.p., as required.

## 5 MANY BUYERS: SREV WITH NO ADDITIONAL BUYERS

In this section we show that adding more buyers is not required for a number of buyers $n$ that is sufficiently larger than the number of items $m$. Specifically, we prove the following theorem:

Theorem 5.1 (Theorem 1.2, case $n \gg m$). *For any constant $\varepsilon > 0$ there exists a constant $\delta(\varepsilon) > 0$ such that whenever $n \geq \frac{m}{\delta}$:*

$$(1 - \varepsilon)\textsc{Rev}(\mathcal{D}^n) \leq \textsc{SRev}(\mathcal{D}^n)$$

### 5.1 Proof outline (a tale of three tails)

We first partition the domain of the valuation distributions into sub-domains, using the Subdomain Stiching Lemma (Lemma 3.20). In our analysis, we condition on the event (or sub-domain) $\mathcal{A}$ that describes which items are in the tail or core for which buyer (we still don't know their values within the tail/core). For each event we define a bipartite graph with buyer-nodes $[n]$ and item-nodes $[m]$, where an edge $\{i, j\}$ between buyer $i$ and item $j$ exists if and only if item $j$ is in buyer $i$'s tail. Crucially, the revenue is separable across connected components (because in different connected components, disjoint sets of buyers are interested in disjoint sets of items).

We now establish a "marginal mechanism lemma" (Lemma 5.2) that shows that the optimal revenue from $\mathcal{D}^{\mathcal{A}}$ is bounded from above by the sum of expected item values in the core in event $\mathcal{A}$, plus the revenue from selling items in each connected component to the buyers in that connected component (conditioned on them being in the tail).

For a connected component that contains only one item (i.e., the buyers in this connected component have only this item in their tails), the lemma provides an even tighter bound. Namely, we can restrict attention to mechanisms that sell the item to buyers in the connected component with probability at most $p$, where $p$ is the upper bound on the ex-ante probability that the optimal mechanism (for event $\mathcal{A}$) sells this item. Then, with probability $1 - p$ we can resell the item to other buyers. Essentially, this means that we can use most buyers and some items to (almost) recover the contribution from the tail, and then use the rest of the buyers and items to (almost) recover the contribution from the core. Note that while we partition the buyers in advance, the partitioning of the items is only done after seeing which items are bought by the first subset of buyers. Note also that the mechanism of partitioning the buyers is for analysis purpose only: once we establish that it achieves a good revenue by selling each item separately, we can only improve the revenue by running Myerson's optimal mechanism.

Since we consider a setting with many buyers, the expected number of buyers that have a specific item in their tail (henceforth termed *interested buyers*) is concentrated. This implies a core-tail decomposition lemma (Lemma 5.3) that bounds the optimal revenue using four terms: one core, and three tails. The three tails are (1) the contribution from selling item $j$ whenever the number of interested buyers does not exceed the expected number of interested buyers by much, (2) the contribution from selling item $j$ whenever the number of interested buyers *does* exceed the expected number of interested buyers by a significant constant, and (3) the contribution from selling items in connected components with at least two items.

We bound the three tails in Section 5.4. In Lemma 5.5 we show that the first tail is almost completely recovered by the revenue from selling items separately to all but a small fraction of the buyers, and restricting the ex-ante probability of sale as described above. Note that the tail is not fully recovered, but this is a sufficient guarantee due to the probability of sale restriction (see above). In particular, the items can be resold to other buyers with sufficiently high probability.

In Lemma 5.6 we show that the second tail is a tiny fraction of the revenue from selling items separately. This is done by arguing that the event where the number of interested buyers significantly exceeds the expectation is extremely rare.

In Lemma 5.9 we show that the third tail is also a tiny fraction of the revenue from selling items separately. This part is more involved, since we need to bound the expected size of a connected component, as well as some of the higher moments. Here we use some simple ideas from percolation theory. See Section 5.4.1 for details.

Finally, we conclude the proof in Section 5.5 by integrating the above arguments into the core-tail decomposition.

### 5.2 The item-buyer bipartite graph

We adopt all the notation from Section 3.2, and introduce some more notation. For a single dimensional distribution $v \leftarrow D$ and cutoff $\mathcal{T}$, let $\hat{D}$ denote the distribution of $v|v > \mathcal{T}$. Fix an event $\mathcal{A}$ as described in Section 3.2. Consider the bipartite graph $H_{\mathcal{A}} = ([n], [m], E[\mathcal{A}])$ over buyers and items. The set of edges is defined to be $E[\mathcal{A}] = \{\{i, j\} : j \in \mathcal{A}^i\}$, i.e., for each item $j$ in the tail of $i$, ($\mathbf{v}^i_j > \mathcal{T}_j$) there exists an edge $\{i, j\}$. For each node $k$, let $\mathcal{A}[k]$ denote $k$'s neighbors in $H_{\mathcal{A}}$, i.e., for an item $j \in [m]$, $\mathcal{A}[j] = \{i : j \in \mathcal{A}^i\}$, and for a buyer $i \in [n]$, $\mathcal{A}[i] = \mathcal{A}^i$. Note that $H_{\mathcal{A}}$ is a random graph where each edge $\{i, j\}$ exists independently w.p. $\Pr[\mathbf{v}^i_j > \mathcal{T}_j]$. Let $P^{\mathcal{A}}$ be the partition of the graph $H_{\mathcal{A}}$ to connected components. For a connected component $X \in P^{\mathcal{A}}$, let $X_n = X \cap [n]$ be the nodes in $X$ associated with buyers, and similarly $X_m = X \cap [m]$ are the nodes in $X$ associated with items. For a connected component $X \in P^{\mathcal{A}}$, let $\mathcal{D}^X_T$ be the product distribution over the buyers $X_n$, where each buyer $i$ has only values $\mathbf{v}^i_j$ for items $j$ in $\mathcal{A}[i]$, and each such $\mathbf{v}^i_j$ is drawn from the conditional distribution $\hat{D}_j$, i.e., $D^X_T = \times_{i \in X_n} \mathcal{D}^{\mathcal{A}[i]}_T$.

### 5.3 Core-tail decomposition.

We introduce a new "marginal mechanism" lemma (Lemma 5.2) that is suitable for the case $n \gg m$. Fix some $\mathcal{A}$ as in Section 3.2, and let $\mathcal{M}$ be an optimal mechanism w.r.t. $\mathcal{D}^{\mathcal{A}}$, i.e., $\textsc{Rev}_{\mathcal{M}}(\mathcal{D}^{\mathcal{A}}) = \textsc{Rev}(\mathcal{D}^{\mathcal{A}})$. Let $\pi$ be the mechanism's allocation function, and let $\bar{\pi}_j = \sum_{i \in \mathcal{A}[j]} \mathbb{E}_{\mathbf{v} \leftarrow \mathcal{D}^{\mathcal{A}}}[\pi^i_j(\mathbf{v})]$. Recall that for a connected component $X \in P^{\mathcal{A}}$, $X_n = X \cap [n]$ and similarly $X_m = X \cap [m]$. Also, recall that given $v \leftarrow D_j$, we use $\hat{D}_j$ to denote the distribution of $v|v > \mathcal{T}_j$.

Lemma 5.2. *(Marginal Mechanism on Sub-Domain) Fix $\mathcal{A}$, and let $\bar{\pi}$ be as above. Let $P^{\mathcal{A}}_2$ be all the connected components $X$ in $P^{\mathcal{A}}$ so that $|X_m| \geq 2$. Then*

$$\textsc{Rev}(\mathcal{D}^{\mathcal{A}}) \leq \sum_{j \in [m]} \left( \textsc{Rev}_{\bar{\pi}_j} \left( \hat{D}_j^{|\mathcal{A}[j]|} \right) + \mathcal{T}_j \cdot (1 - \bar{\pi}_j) \right) + \sum_{X \in P^{\mathcal{A}}_2} \textsc{Rev}(\mathcal{D}^X_T)$$

*I.e., the revenue from $\mathcal{D}^{\mathcal{A}}$ is bounded by the revenue from selling items separately, each item $j$ to $|\mathcal{A}[j]|$ buyers in the tail at $\bar{\pi}_j$ ex-ante probability of sale, plus the contribution to the core ($\mathcal{T}_j \cdot (1 - \bar{\pi}_j)$), plus the revenue from connected components with more than one item.*

One can show that for fixed item $j$, cutoff $\mathcal{T}_j$, and $\delta = 2 \cdot \Pr_{v \leftarrow D_j}[v > \mathcal{T}_j]$, for any $k \leq 1/\delta$: $\textsc{Rev}(\hat{D}^k_j) \leq 4 \cdot k \cdot \textsc{Rev}(D_j^{1/\delta})$, (see full version for details). This in turns allows to show the following core-tail decomposition,

Lemma 5.3. *(Core-tail decomposition) For cutoffs $\mathcal{T}_j$ so that $\Pr_{v \leftarrow D_j}\left[v > \mathcal{T}_j\right] \geq \frac{1}{2n}$, and a cutoff $\mathcal{T}^*$*

$$\begin{aligned}
\textsc{Rev}(\mathcal{D}^n) \leq & \sum_{j \in [m]} \mathcal{T}_j \cdot \mathbb{E}\left[1 - \bar{\pi}_j\right] && \textit{Core} \\
& + \sum_{j \in [m]} \mathbb{E}\left[\textsc{Rev}_{\bar{\pi}_j}\left(\hat{D}_j^{|\mathcal{A}[j]|}\right) \cdot \mathbb{I}\left[|\mathcal{A}[j]| \leq \mathcal{T}^*\right]\right] && \textit{Tail 1} \\
& + 4 \cdot \sum_{j \in [m]} \textsc{Rev}\left(\mathcal{D}^n_j\right) \cdot \mathbb{E}\left[|\mathcal{A}[j]| \cdot \mathbb{I}\left[|\mathcal{A}[j]| > \mathcal{T}^*\right]\right] && \textit{Tail 2} \\
& + 4 \cdot \sum_{j \in [m]} \textsc{Rev}\left(\mathcal{D}^n_j\right) \cdot \mathbb{E}\left[\left|X^j_m\right| \cdot \left|X^j_n\right|^2 \cdot \mathbb{I}[\left|X^j_m\right| \geq 2]\right] && \textit{Tail 3}
\end{aligned}$$

*Cutoff setting.* Fix some $0 < \varepsilon_1, \varepsilon_2, \varepsilon_3, \varepsilon_4 < 1$. Throughout this section, for every item $j$ fix $\mathcal{T}_j$ to be the value for which $\Pr_{v \leftarrow D_j}\left[v > \mathcal{T}_j\right] = \frac{1}{n \cdot \varepsilon_1}$. Clearly the expected number of buyers that have item $j$ in their tail is $\frac{1}{\varepsilon_1}$. We set $\mathcal{T}^* = \frac{(1+\varepsilon_2)}{\varepsilon_1}$, i.e., we use $\varepsilon_2$ as a deviation from this expected size.

We will first sell items separately at high prices to a $1 - \varepsilon_4$ fraction of the buyers. In this case the expected number of buyers that have item $j$ in their tail is $\frac{1-\varepsilon_4}{\varepsilon_1}$. We will use $\varepsilon_3$ as a deviation from this expected size.

Whenever an item $j$ is not sold to one of the $1 - \varepsilon_4$ fraction of the buyers, we will sell the item to one of the remaining $\varepsilon_4$ buyers at price $\mathcal{T}_j$. This will suffice to to almost fully recover the contribution from the core.

Lemma 5.4. *(Core.) For every item $j$, $\mathcal{T}_j \cdot \mathbb{E}\left[(1 - \bar{\pi}_j)\right] \leq \mathbb{E}\left[(1 - \bar{\pi}_j)\right](1 - e^{-\varepsilon_4/\varepsilon_1})^{-1}\textsc{Rev}(D_j^{\varepsilon_4 \cdot n})$*

## 5.4 Tail.

The following lemma essentially combines Lemma 3.19 with a concentration bound, to show that Tail 1 can be almost fully recovered by selling items separately to a $1 - \varepsilon_4$ fraction of the buyers. Let $\varepsilon_5 = \varepsilon_5(\varepsilon_1, \varepsilon_2, \varepsilon_4, \varepsilon_3)$ be so that $1 + \varepsilon_5 = \frac{1+\varepsilon_2}{(1-\varepsilon_4)\cdot(1-\varepsilon_3)} \cdot \left(1 - \exp\left(-\frac{(1-\varepsilon_4)\cdot \varepsilon_3^2}{2 \cdot \varepsilon_1}\right)\right)^{-1}$. It is only important to note that $\varepsilon_5 \to 0$ as $\varepsilon_1 \to 0$.

Lemma 5.5. *(Tail 1). Fix an item $j$. For $k \leq \frac{(1+\varepsilon_2)}{\varepsilon_1}$, $\textsc{Rev}_p\left(\hat{D}_j^k\right) \leq (1 + \varepsilon_5) \cdot \textsc{Rev}_p(D_j^{(1-\varepsilon_4)\cdot n})$*

Lemma 5.6 shows that the coefficient of SRev in Tail 2 tends to 0 with $\varepsilon_1$. Let $\varepsilon_6 = \frac{4}{\varepsilon_1} \cdot \exp\left(-\frac{\varepsilon_2^2}{8 \cdot \varepsilon_1}\right)$.

Lemma 5.6. *(Tail 2) Fix item $j$. $\mathbb{E}\left[|\mathcal{A}[j]| \cdot \mathbb{I}\left[|\mathcal{A}[j]| > \mathcal{T}^*\right]\right] \leq \varepsilon_6$*

### 5.4.1 The 3rd tail (a non-trivial connected component).

The following lemmas ultimately show that the coefficient of $\textsc{SRev}(\mathcal{D}^n)$ in Tail 3 tends to 0 as as $\varepsilon_1$ tends to 0. This will be proved in Lemma 5.9. We will develop the proof in steps. Recall that for a connected component $X \in P^{\mathcal{A}}$, $X_n = X \cap [n]$ and $X_m = X \cap [m]$. Lemma 5.7 upper bounds the term we wish to bound into two terms. Note that in both terms, at a loss of a constant factor, we free ourself from the dependence on the number of buyers that have at most one item in their tail (and are in $j$'s connected component).

Lemma 5.7. *For every $\mathcal{A}$, let $S \subseteq [n]$ denote the buyers $i$ with at least two items in their tail, i.e., $\mathcal{A}[i] \geq 2$. For every item $j$, let $\hat{\mathbb{I}} = \mathbb{I}[|X_m^j| \geq 2]$, then*

$$\mathbb{E}[|X_m^j| \cdot |X_n^j|^2 \cdot \hat{\mathbb{I}}] \leq 3 \cdot \varepsilon_1^{-1} \cdot \mathbb{E}[(|X_m^j| + |X_n^j \cap S|)^3 \cdot \hat{\mathbb{I}}] + \varepsilon_1^{-2} \cdot \mathbb{E}[|X_m^j| \cdot \hat{\mathbb{I}}]$$

Clearly, showing that $\mathbb{E}\left[\left(\left|X_m^j\right| + \left|X_n^j \cap S\right|\right)^3\right]$ is small implies that $\mathbb{E}\left[\left|X_m^j\right|\right]$ is small. For every $j$ it holds that $\mathbb{E}\left[\left|X_m^j\right|\right] \leq \frac{1}{1 - \frac{m}{n \cdot \varepsilon_1^2}}$ (this follows from simple ideas from percolation theory, see full version for details). Similar techniques can be used to prove Lemma 5.8.

Lemma 5.8. *For every $\mathcal{A}$, let $S \subseteq [n]$ denote the buyers $i$ with at least two items in their tail. There exists a (universal) constant $c$ so that for every item $j$, $\mathbb{E}\left[\left(\left|X_m^j\right| + \left|X_n^j \cap S\right|\right)^3\right] \leq \frac{1 + c \cdot \frac{m}{n \cdot \varepsilon_1^2}}{1 - c \cdot \frac{m}{n \cdot \varepsilon_1^2}}$*

Lemma 5.8 is then used to prove that Tail 3 contributes only a tiny fraction. Let $\varepsilon_7 = \varepsilon_7(m, n, \varepsilon_1)$ be so that for the universal constant $c$ from Lemma 5.8, $\varepsilon_7 = \frac{4}{n \cdot \varepsilon_1^4} + \frac{m}{n} \cdot \frac{6 \cdot c}{\varepsilon_1^3 \cdot \left(1 - c \cdot \frac{m}{n \cdot \varepsilon_1^2}\right)} + \frac{m}{n} \cdot \frac{1}{\varepsilon_1^4 \cdot \left(1 - \frac{m}{n \cdot \varepsilon_1^2}\right)}$.

Lemma 5.9. *(Tail 3) For every $j$: $\mathbb{E}\left[\left|X_m^j\right| \cdot \left|X_n^j\right|^2 \cdot \mathbb{I}\left[\left|X_m^j\right| \geq 2\right]\right] \leq \varepsilon_7$*

### 5.5 Proof of Theorem 5.1

Combine the core-tail decomposition (Lemma 5.3) with Lemma 5.4, Lemma 5.5 with $p = \bar{\pi}_j$, Lemma 5.6, and Lemma 5.9 to get:

$$\textsc{Rev}(\mathcal{D}^n) \leq \left(1 - e^{-\varepsilon_4/\varepsilon_1}\right)^{-1} \cdot \sum_{j\in[m]} \mathbb{E}\left[(1-\bar{\pi}_j)\right] \cdot \textsc{Rev}(D_j^{\varepsilon_4 \cdot n}) + (1+\varepsilon_5) \cdot \sum_{j\in[m]} \mathbb{E}\left[\textsc{Rev}_{\bar{\pi}_j}(D_j^{(1-\varepsilon_4)\cdot n})\right]$$
$$+ 4 \cdot \varepsilon_6 \cdot \sum_{j\in[m]} \textsc{Rev}\left(\mathcal{D}_j^n\right) + 4 \cdot \varepsilon_7 \cdot \sum_{j\in[m]} \textsc{Rev}\left(\mathcal{D}_j^n\right)$$

Consider a seller that sells the items separately. Each item $j$ is first auctioned to $(1-\varepsilon_4) \cdot n$ buyers using an optimal mechanism with restricted ex-ante probability of sale of $\bar{\pi}_j$. Whenever the mechanism does not allocate the item, the seller proceeds and sells the item to the remaining $\varepsilon_4 \cdot n$ buyers optimally. Clearly, the revenue of the suggested mechanism is at least[15] $\textsc{Rev}_{\bar{\pi}_j}(D_j^{(1-\varepsilon_4)\cdot n}) + \textsc{Rev}(D_j^{\varepsilon_4 \cdot n}) \cdot (1-\bar{\pi}_j)$. The above mechanism, by definition, does not make more than $\textsc{Rev}(D_j^n)$ revenue, hence, $\textsc{Rev}(\mathcal{D}^n) \leq (\max\{(1-e^{-\varepsilon_4/\varepsilon_1})^{-1}, (1+\varepsilon_5)\} + 4 \cdot (\varepsilon_6 + \varepsilon_7)) \cdot \sum_{j\in[m]} \textsc{Rev}(D_j^n)$ As required.

## REFERENCES


[1] Moshe Babaioff, Nicole Immorlica, Brendan Lucier, and S Matthew Weinberg. 2014. A Simple and Approximately Optimal Mechanism for an Additive Buyer. In *Proceedings of the 2014 IEEE 55th Annual Symposium on Foundations of Computer Science*. IEEE Computer Society, 21–30.

[2] MohammadHossein Bateni, Sina Dehghani, MohammadTaghi Hajiaghayi, and Saeed Seddighin. 2015. Revenue Maximization for Selling Multiple Correlated Items. In *Algorithms - ESA 2015 - 23rd Annual European Symposium, Patras, Greece, September 14-16, 2015, Proceedings*. 95–105. DOI: http://dx.doi.org/10.1007/978-3-662-48350-3_9

[3] Patrick Briest, Shuchi Chawla, Robert Kleinberg, and S Matthew Weinberg. 2010. Pricing randomized allocations. In *Proceedings of the twenty-first annual ACM-SIAM symposium on Discrete Algorithms*. Society for Industrial and Applied Mathematics, 585–597.

[4] Jeremy Bulow and Paul Klemperer. 1996. Auctions Versus Negotiations. *The American Economic Review* (1996), 180–194.

[5] Yang Cai and Constantinos Daskalakis. 2011. On Minmax Theorems for Multiplayer Games. In *Proceedings of the Twenty-Second Annual ACM-SIAM Symposium on Discrete Algorithms, SODA 2011, San Francisco, California, USA, January 23-25, 2011*. 217–234. DOI: http://dx.doi.org/10.1137/1.9781611973082.20

[6] Yang Cai, Nikhil R Devanur, and S Matthew Weinberg. 2016. A duality based unified approach to Bayesian mechanism design. In *Proceedings of the 48th Annual ACM SIGACT Symposium on Theory of Computing*. ACM, 926–939.

[7] Yang Cai and Zhiyi Huang. 2013. Simple and Nearly Optimal Multi-Item Auctions. In *the 24th Annual ACM-SIAM Symposium on Discrete Algorithms (SODA)*.

[8] Yang Cai and Mingfei Zhao. 2017. Simple Mechanisms for Subadditive Buyers via Duality. In *Proceedings of the 49th Annual ACM SIGACT Symposium on Theory of Computing*. ACM, 170–183.

[9] Shuchi Chawla, Jason D Hartline, and Robert Kleinberg. 2007. Algorithmic pricing via virtual valuations. In *Proceedings of the 8th ACM conference on Electronic commerce*. ACM, 243–251.

[10] Shuchi Chawla, Jason D Hartline, David L Malec, and Balasubramanian Sivan. 2010. Multi-parameter mechanism design and sequential posted pricing. In *Proceedings of the forty-second ACM symposium on Theory of computing*. ACM, 311–320.

[11] Shuchi Chawla, David L. Malec, and Balasubramanian Sivan. 2015. The power of randomness in bayesian optimal mechanism design. *Games and Economic Behavior* 91 (2015), 297–317.

[12] Shuchi Chawla and J. Benjamin Miller. 2016. Mechanism Design for Subadditive Agents via an Ex Ante Relaxation. In *Proceedings of the 2016 ACM Conference on Economics and Computation (EC '16)*. ACM, New York, NY, USA, 579–596. DOI: http://dx.doi.org/10.1145/2940716.2940756

[13] Xi Chen, Ilias Diakonikolas, Anthi Orfanou, Dimitris Paparas, Xiaorui Sun, and Mihalis Yannakakis. 2015. On the Complexity of Optimal Lottery Pricing and Randomized Mechanisms. In *IEEE 56th Annual Symposium on Foundations*


[15] The mechanism does not extract exactly this quantity, because it might sell to the $(1-\varepsilon_4) \cdot n$ buyers with ex-ante probability that is *lower* than $\bar{\pi}_j$, in which case it will make even more than the above.

*of Computer Science, FOCS 2015, Berkeley, CA, USA, 17-20 October, 2015.* 1464–1479. DOI: http://dx.doi.org/10.1109/FOCS.2015.93

[14] Xi Chen, Ilias Diakonikolas, Dimitris Paparas, Xiaorui Sun, and Mihalis Yannakakis. 2014. The Complexity of Optimal Multidimensional Pricing. In *Proceedings of the Twenty-Fifth Annual ACM-SIAM Symposium on Discrete Algorithms, SODA 2014, Portland, Oregon, USA, January 5-7, 2014.* 1319–1328. DOI: http://dx.doi.org/10.1137/1.9781611973402.97

[15] Constantinos Daskalakis, Alan Deckelbaum, and Christos Tzamos. 2014. The complexity of optimal mechanism design. In *Proceedings of the Twenty-Fifth Annual ACM-SIAM Symposium on Discrete Algorithms*. Society for Industrial and Applied Mathematics, 1302–1318.

[16] Constantinos Daskalakis, Alan Deckelbaum, and Christos Tzamos. 2016. Strong Duality for a Multiple-Good Monopolist. *Econometrica* (2016).

[17] Alon Eden, Michal Feldman, Ophir Friedler, Inbal Talgam-Cohen, and S. Matthew Weinberg. 2017. The Competition Complexity of Auctions: A Bulow-Klemperer Result for Multi-Dimensional Bidders. In *Proceedings of the 2017 ACM Conference on Economics and Computation, EC '17, Cambridge, MA, USA, June 26-30, 2017.* 343. DOI: http://dx.doi.org/10.1145/3033274.3085115

[18] Alon Eden, Michal Feldman, Ophir Friedler, Inbal Talgam-Cohen, and S. Matthew Weinberg. 2017. A Simple and Approximately Optimal Mechanism for a Buyer with Complements: Abstract. In *Proceedings of the 2017 ACM Conference on Economics and Computation, EC '17, Cambridge, MA, USA, June 26-30, 2017.* 323. DOI: http://dx.doi.org/10.1145/3033274.3085116

[19] Edith Elkind. 2007. Designing and learning optimal finite support auctions. In *Proceedings of the eighteenth annual ACM-SIAM symposium on Discrete algorithms*. Society for Industrial and Applied Mathematics, 736–745.

[20] Kira Goldner and Anna Karlin. 2016. A Prior-Independent Revenue-Maximizing Auction for Multiple Additive Bidders. In *The 12th Conference on Web and Internet Economics (WINE).*

[21] Sergiu Hart and Noam Nisan. 2012. Approximate revenue maximization with multiple items. In *Proceedings of the 13th ACM Conference on Electronic Commerce*. ACM, 656–656.

[22] Sergiu Hart and Noam Nisan. 2013. The menu-size complexity of auctions. In *Proceedings of the 14th ACM Conference on Economics and Computation*. 565–566.

[23] Sergiu Hart and Philip J. Reny. 2012. Maximal Revenue with Multiple Goods: Nonmonotonicity and Other Observations. *Discussion Paper Series dp630, The Center for the Study of Rationality, Hebrew University, Jerusalem* (2012).

[24] Jason D Hartline. 2013. Mechanism design and approximation. (2013).

[25] Larry Kim. 2012. How Many Ads Does Google Serve In A Day? Read more at https://www.business2community.com/online-marketing/how-many-ads-does-google-serve-in-a-day-0322253. *Bussines2Community* (Nov 2012). https://www.business2community.com/online-marketing/how-many-ads-does-google-serve-in-a-day-0322253

[26] Robert Kleinberg and Seth Matthew Weinberg. 2012. Matroid prophet inequalities. In *Proceedings of the forty-fourth annual ACM symposium on Theory of computing*. ACM, 123–136.

[27] Xinye Li and Andrew Chi-Chih Yao. 2013. On Revenue Maximization for Selling Multiple Independently Distributed Items. *Proceedings of the National Academy of Sciences* 110, 28 (2013), 11232–11237.

[28] Siqi Liu and Christos-Alexandros Psomas. 2018. On the Competition Complexity of Dynamic Mechanism Design. In *SODA*. To appear.

[29] Will Ma and David Simchi-Levi. 2015. Reaping the Benefits of Bundling under High Production Costs. *CoRR* abs/1512.02300 (2015). http://arxiv.org/abs/1512.02300

[30] Roger B. Myerson. 1981. Optimal Auction Design. *Mathematics of Operations Research* 6, 1 (1981), 58–73.

[31] Jean-Charles Rochet and Philippe Chone. 1998. Ironing, Sweeping, and Multidimensional Screening. *Econometrica* 66, 4 (July 1998), 783–826.

[32] Tim Roughgarden, Inbal Talgam-Cohen, and Qiqi Yan. 2015. Robust Auctions for Revenue via Enhanced Competition. (2015). Working paper; a preliminary version appeared in EC'12.

[33] Aviad Rubinstein. 2016. On the computational complexity of optimal simple mechanisms. In *Proceedings of the 2016 ACM Conference on Innovations in Theoretical Computer Science*. ACM, 21–28.

[34] Aviad Rubinstein and S Matthew Weinberg. 2015. Simple mechanisms for a subadditive buyer and applications to revenue monotonicity. In *Proceedings of the Sixteenth ACM Conference on Economics and Computation*. ACM, 377–394.

[35] Andrew Chi-Chih Yao. 2017. On Revenue Monotonicity in Combinatorial Auctions. *CoRR* abs/1709.03223 (2017). arXiv:1709.03223 http://arxiv.org/abs/1709.03223

[36] Andrew Chi-Chih Yao. 2015. An n-to-1 bidder reduction for multi-item auctions and its applications. In *Proceedings of the Twenty-Sixth Annual ACM-SIAM Symposium on Discrete Algorithms*. SIAM, 92–109.

# The A/B Testing Problem

EDUARDO M. AZEVEDO, Wharton
ALEX DENG, Microsoft Corporation
JOSÉ LUIS MONTIEL OLEA, Columbia University
JUSTIN RAO, HomeAway
E. GLEN WEYL, Microsoft Research

Randomized experiments are increasingly central to innovation in many fields.[2] In the tech sector, major platforms run thousands of experiments (called A/B tests) each year on tens of millions of users at any given time and use the results to screen most product innovations. In the policy and academic circles, governments, nonprofit organizations, and academics use randomized control trials to evaluate social programs and shape public policy.

Experiments are not only prevalent, but also highly heterogeneous in design. Policy makers and tech giants typically focus on a "go big" approach, obtaining large sample sizes for a small number of experiments to ensure they that can detect even small benefits of a policy intervention. In contrast, many start-ups and entrepreneurs take a different "go lean" approach, running many small tests and discarding any innovation without outstanding success. The idea is to quickly and cheaply experiment with many ideas, abandon or pivot from ideas that do not work, and scale up ideas that do work. In this paper, we study when each of these approaches is appropriate. To do so, we propose a new framework for optimal experimentation that we call the A/B testing problem. The frameworks also yields an optimal strategy of what innovations to implement and methods to calculate the value of data and experimentation. The key insight is that the optimal experimentation strategy depends crucially on the tails of the distribution of innovation quality, and whether these tails have "black swan" outliers, of innovations with a very large positive or negative impact.

The A/B testing problem is as follows. A firm has a set of potential innovations $i = 1, \dots, I$ to implement. The quality $\Delta_i$ of innovation $i$ is unknown and comes from a distribution $G$. Quality is independently distributed across innovations. The firm selects a number of users $n_i$ to allocate to an A/B test evaluating innovation $i$. This yields a signal with mean equal to the true quality of idea $i$ and variance $\sigma^2/n_i$. The firm is subject to the constraint that the total number of users assigned to experiments is no greater than the number $N$ of users available for experimentation. After seeing the realization of the signals, the firm selects a subset $S$ of ideas to implement. The firm's objective is to maximize the expected sum of the true quality of the ideas that are implemented.

Authors' addresses: Eduardo M. Azevedo, Wharton, 3620 Locust Walk, Philadelphia, PA 19104, eazevedo@wharton.upenn.edu, http://www.eduardomazevedo.com; Alex Dang, Microsoft Corporation, 555 110th Ave NE, Bellevue, WA 98004, shaojie.deng@microsoft.com, http://alexdeng.github.io/; José Luis Montiel Olea, Department of Economics, Columbia University, 1022 International Affairs Building, New York, NY 10027, montiel.olea@gmail.com, http://www.joseluismontielolea.com/; Justin Rao, HomeAway, 11800 Domain Blvd., Austin, TX 78758, justinmrao@outlook.com, http://www.justinmrao.com; E. Glen Weyl, Microsoft Research, One Memorial Drive, Cambridge, MA 02142 and Department of Economics, Yale University, glenweyl@microsoft.com, http://www.glenweyl.com.

[1] A full version of this paper is available at https://eduardomazevedo.github.io/papers/azevedo-et-al-ab.pdf.

 978-1-4503-5829-3/18/06
https://doi.org/10.1145/3219166.3219204

The A/B testing problem is related to standard models of optimal experimentation, such as Wald's sequential decision problem [3] and the bandits literature [1, 2]. The A/B testing problem is simpler than the standard bandit frameworks in three ways. First, there is no exploration versus exploitation tradeoff, because the firm simply wants to acquire the best possible information for making a decision. Thus, the A/B testing problem is relevant in cases where the payoff from an innovation once it is scaled up is much greater than the payoffs in the relatively short experimentation phase. Second, the innovations are not rival, because the firm is free to implement all innovations with positive expected value. This is in contrast to the bandit problem where pulling one arm precludes pulling another. Third, the dynamics in the A/B testing problem are trivial, because the firm makes its experimentation decisions simultaneously, and then uses the results of the experiments to make the implementation decisions. This is relevant when there are restrictions to how flexible experimentation has to be. This is a reasonable approximation in online A/B testing settings due to practical constraints. At the same time, a crucial ingredient of the A/B testing problem is that we allow for a fat-tailed distribution of idea quality. Fat tails are typically assumed away in the optimal experimentation literature but are crucial to our results.

In broad terms, our main results are the following. If the tail of the distribution of quality are sufficiently thin, the go big approach is optimal. Intuitively, a small test has little value as it is unlikely to move the experimenter away from her prior beliefs. The value of information is thus convex and experiments have a minimum efficient scale. This is roughly the intuition behind the usual practice of performing power calculations. In contrast, with sufficiently fat tails, this conventional wisdom reverses and the go lean approach of trying many small experiments is preferred. Intuitively, with sufficiently fat tails, even small experiments are sufficient to detect the largest effects that in this case account for most total value. Larger experiments detect subtler effects, but these constitute less of the total value; making the value of information concave. This case also has different implications for the marginal value of information. The dividing line between these cases turns out to be, under our main assumptions, whether the third moment of the innovation value distribution exists.

To test this distinction, we studied Microsoft Bing's EXP platform, which conducts hundreds of A/B tests of the search engine every year. We find both reduced form and structural, model-based evidence of extremely fat tails. This suggests that it is possible to considerably increase innovation productivity in that setting by moving towards a lean experimentation strategy, such as by eliminating triage of ideas prior to online A/B tests.

## KEYWORDS

A/B testing; innovation screening; optimal experimentation strategy

## REFERENCES

[1] Robbins, Herbert, "Some aspects of the sequential design of experiments", in Herbert Robbins Selected Papers (Springer, 1985), pp. 169--177.

[2] Thompson, William R., "On the likelihood that one unknown probability exceeds another in view of the evidence of two samples", Biometrika 25, 3/4 (1933), pp. 285--294.

[3] Wald, Abraham, "Foundations of a general theory of sequential decision functions", Econometrica, Journal of the Econometric Society (1947), pp. 279--313.

# A Personalized BDM Mechanism for Efficient Market Intervention Experiments

IMANOL ARRIETA-IBARRA, Stanford University, USA
JOHAN UGANDER, Stanford University, USA

The BDM mechanism, introduced by Becker, DeGroot, and Marschack in the 1960's, employs a second-price auction against a random bidder to elicit the willingness to pay of a consumer. The BDM mechanism has been recently used as a treatment assignment mechanism in order to estimate the treatment effects of policy interventions while simultaneously measuring the demand for the intervention. In this work, we develop a personalized extension of the classic BDM mechanism, using modern machine learning algorithms to predict an individual's willingness to pay and personalize the "random bidder" based on covariates associated with each individual. We show through a mock experiment on Amazon Mechanical Turk that our personalized BDM mechanism results in a lower cost for the experimenter, provides better balance over covariates that are correlated with both the outcome and willingness to pay, and eliminates biases induced by ad-hoc boundaries in the classic BDM algorithm. We expect our mechanism to be of use for policy evaluation and market intervention experiments, in particular in development economics. Personalization can provide more efficient resource allocation when running experiments while maintaining statistical correctness.

CCS Concepts: • **Computing methodologies** → **Machine learning**; • **Applied computing** → **Economics**; Psychology;

Additional Key Words and Phrases: personalization; BDM; second price auctions; causal inference

## 1 INTRODUCTION

Measuring the success of a market intervention, where a new product or service is introduced to an existing market, requires evaluating the convolved causal effects of both the product itself and the effects of the price at which the product is introduced, while also estimating the market demand for the product at different prices. The BDM mechanism [9] provides an elegant method for evaluating market interventions, and it has been recently employed in field experiments by development economists to simultaneously evaluate causal treatment effects as well as market demand [10].

Imagine that we want to estimate the average treatment effect of a water filter on a household's health. A simple way to estimate the effect is to run a randomized controlled trial—randomly give away water filters to some households and not to others—and measure the treatment effect by comparing the health of the households. However, this experiment would produce no information about the demand for the product, since we'd be giving the product away. It would also prevent us from studying the interaction effect of the price on the water filter's effectiveness, where previous

The authors would like to thank Anup Malani for discussions that inspired this work. This work supported in part by NSF grant IIS-1657104 and a Facebook Faculty Research Grant.

Authors' addresses: Imanol Arrieta-Ibarra, Stanford University, Management Science and Engineering, Stanford, CA, 94305, USA; Johan Ugander, Stanford University, Management Science and Engineering, Stanford, CA, 94305, USA.


*ACM EC'18, June 18–22, 2018, Ithaca, NY, USA.* ACM ISBN 978-1-4503-5829-3/18/06...$15.00
https://doi.org/10.1145/3219166.3219220

field experiments have shown that price paid for a product can have a significant effect on its adoption [6]. As another approach, we could propose a (random) price to the treatment households where we randomly offer the product, applying the so-called "take it or leave it" mechanism. But this approach would tell us relatively little about the willingness of the household to pay for the product at other prices, and the households that purchase the product would skew towards wealthier homes, creating a difference between the treatment and control population that would be hard to discern.

The BDM mechanism, meanwhile, gathers the willingness to pay of the households in an incentive compatible way, allowing us to derive demand curves for the product while also making it possible to exactly compute the household's probability of treatment when bidding against the BDM mechanism's random bidder. The mechanism can therefore be viewed as performing a randomized controlled trial with heterogeneous but known probabilities of assignment to treatment or control (known once the willingness to pay has been elicited). In addition to the average treatment effect (ATE), we can use BDM to estimate the conditional average treatment effect (CATE) conditional on willingness to pay which is key to making policy decisions about an intervention.

In this work we observe that the BDM mechanism can be improved upon using personalization to provide less volatile causal effect estimates at a lower expected cost for researchers, all while maintaining the incentive compatibility of traditional BDM. In particular, we can use personalization to reduce (1) the variance of effect estimators, (2) the budget regret of running the experiment, all while (3) maintaining incentive compatibility. The variance is reduced by balancing the treatment probabilities so individuals are more equally likely to land it both treatment and control based on what we know about them a priori. The budget regret is reduced by essentially avoiding situations where we would be giving away the product for much less than what the person is willing to pay for it, again based on what we know about them a priori. In order to perform our personalization we employ standard tools from machine learning, taking care to maintain incentive compatibility.

We evaluate our personalized BDM (PBDM) mechanism under different simulation specifications and run a small field experiment on Amazon Mechanical Turk as a demonstration. The experiment consists of a data-labelling task where we simultaneously evaluate both the *causal effect of* and *demand against* time constraints during the task. How much better or worse are subjects at labelling when there are tight time constraints? How much would they be willing to pay to remove time constraints? The results of this field experiment suggest that a personalized BDM mechanism can provide large efficiency gains during market intervention experiments, where the personalization can also enable statistically efficient estimation of heterogeneous effects that would otherwise be infeasible to estimate reliably.

## 2 BACKGROUND

The BDM mechanism has been previously utilized as an assignment instrument in [10], which compared it against a "take it or leave it" mechanism for the provision of water filters in Ghana. The BDM mechanism is particularly convenient in such settings because of its double randomization, both of treatment and of prices paid, whereby it is possible to estimate both price effects as well as treatment effects conditioned on willingness to pay. Using BDM as an assignment tool thus improved over [27], which used a two-step intervention in order to achieve this double randomization. Furthermore, eliciting user's willingness to pay allows for the estimation of demand curves for the offered product or service. This capability can be of great use in circumstances where a clean randomized control trial can't be performed, or where there is both the need to estimate the demand for a product as well as its potential benefits.

The effectiveness of the BDM mechanism as an elicitation mechanism has been thoroughly tested in auction theory: for lotteries [19, 26, 40], applied to environmental commodities [12], and in comparison to "take it or leave it" mechanisms and Vickrey auctions and against other individuals

[10, 34]. However, many of these studies report some practical problems with BDM. One problem that we focus on is that, in practice, setting and announcing the bounds for the bidding distribution of the BDM mechanism has been found to introduce bias in individual bids in empirical settings [11], meaning that the mechanism is not "behaviorally incentive compatible." One consequence of our personalized mechanism is that it solves this issue by not requiring the specification of these bounds, which makes the BDM mechanism distribution independent [31]. For our personalized mechanism, the proposal distribution is learned as users make bids.

This work is aligned with a larger effort to design adaptive experiments that optimize resources. Similar endeavors include adaptive designs to elicit time preference from subjects [23] and the adaptation of experiments to subpopulations to increase the precision of estimators [4]. Most broadly this research question sits between machine learning and economics, where other recent work [1, 7, 8, 21, 28, 39] has started to bridge the gap between the two fields. Our proposed methodology exemplifies a clear case where the statistical methods for policy evaluations can be improved by the powerful predictive capacities of modern artificial intelligence and machine learning techniques.

## 3 ESTIMATING CAUSAL EFFECTS

The idea of estimating causal effects was first formalized into the *potential outcomes* framework by Neyman [33], but it was Fisher [16], some years later, who commented on the importance of randomization in order to be able to make causal claims. The field has since then been expanded to include controlled as well as observational studies through work by Rubin [36], who was the first to formalize how causal statements could still be made even when researchers were not in total control of the assignment mechanism. See also the recent textbook by Imbens and Rubin [24]. We'll begin this section with a brief review of causal inference in the potential outcomes framework, presenting four different estimators commonly used for estimating average treatment effects [5].

The potential outcomes framework assumes that users present different outcomes depending on whether they are assigned to a treatment condition or a control condition. Let $T_i$ represent whether the observation unit $i$ is assigned to treatment ($T_i = 1$) or control ($T_i = 0$), for example if a water filter was given to a household (with possibly impacting health) or if an individual received paid legal counsel (possibly impacting court trial outcomes). Let $Y_i(T_i)$ be the outcome of interest for unit $i$, e.g. the number of times members of the household became sick during a year or the outcome of a trial. We use $Y_i(1)$ and $Y_i(0)$ to denote the potential outcomes when the unit is assigned to treatment or control, respectively. We make the standard Stable Unit Treatment Value Assumption (SUTVA) that the potential outcomes for one unit is not affected by the treatments of other units, and the potential outcomes are fixed in that there are no different forms or versions of each treatment level. Under these conditions we denote the Average Treatment Effect (ATE) as $\tau = N^{-1}\sum_{i=1}^{N} Y_i(1) - Y_i(0)$, taken over the whole population of $N$ units. We are interested in this average, but for each individual we can only observe one of $Y_i(0)$ or $Y_i(1)$.

One way to estimate the ATE $\tau$ is to simply take an average of the given quantity from a sample of observed values. The most commonly used estimator of the ATE is the difference in means (DM) estimator, where we let $N_C$ be the number of units assigned to the control group while $N_T$ are assigned to the treatment group:

$$\hat{\tau}_{DM} = \frac{1}{N_T}\sum_{i=1}^{N} Y_i(1)T_i - \frac{1}{N_C}\sum_{i=0}^{N} Y_i(0)(1 - T_i). \tag{1}$$

In order for this estimator to be unbiased we need to make three more assumptions: that each unit has positive probability of being treated or controlled, that the treatment of each unit is independent from the treatment of the rest, and that conditional on observables, the assignment to treatment or control is random [24].

If the probability of assignment to treatment depends on observables, the difference in means estimator would be biased, but this bias can be corrected by inverse probability weighting. Let $e(X_i)$ be the *propensity score* or the probability of unit $i$ being treated given a vector of covariates $X_i$, i.e. $e(X_i) = P(Ti = 1|X_i)$. Generally a great deal of attention is given to conditions under which these propensities can be estimated. However, in this work we are in control of the assignment mechanism and we'll be dealing with known true probabilities of assignment. We still call them propensities by convention.

Given these propensity scores, the Horvitz-Thompson estimator (HT) [22] is an unbiased estimator that employs inverse probability weighting:

$$\hat{\tau}_{HT} = \frac{1}{N}\left[\sum_{i=1}^{N} \frac{1}{e(X_i)} Y_i(1)T_i - \sum_{i=1}^{N} \frac{1}{1-e(X_i)} Y_i(0)(1-T_i)\right]. \quad (2)$$

Although the HT estimator is unbiased, it tends to be very volatile in practice. The reason is that the probability of being treated for some units may be very close to zero or one, making for very high variance. The Hajek estimator [20] is a refinement of the HT estimator where instead of dividing by $N$, one divides by the sum of the propensity weights (the expected value of which is $N$). This causes the normalizing denominator to move with the same magnitude as the weights; for this reason the Hajek estimator is sometimes called the self-normalizing estimator [38]. The Hajek estimator is defined as:

$$\hat{\tau}_{\text{Hajek}} = \frac{\sum_{i=1}^{N} \frac{1}{e(X_i)} Y_i(1)T_i}{\sum_{i=1}^{N} \frac{1}{e(X_i)} T_i} - \frac{\sum_{i=1}^{N} \frac{1}{1-e(X_i)} Y_i(0)(1-T_i)}{\sum_{i=1}^{N} \frac{1}{(1-e(X_i))}(1-T_i)}. \quad (3)$$

A final family of estimators we consider is that of *blocking estimators* that employ stratification. These estimators recognize that, for populations with close propensity scores, we have an almost random assignment to treatment or control. We can then estimate the ATE using post-stratification techniques assuming some smoothness in the effects as follows:

(1) Choose $M$ points $q_1, ..., q_M$ from the domain of $e(X_i)$.
(2) Given an $\epsilon > 0$, for each point $q_j$ select all units $i$ whose propensity score is close to this point, $\{X_i : |e(X_i) - q_j| < \epsilon\}$.
(3) For each $j = 1, \ldots, M$, compute the Horvitz-Thompson estimator for those units, $\hat{\tau}^j_{HT}$.
(4) Compute $\hat{\tau}_{\text{block}} = \sum_{j=1}^{M} \frac{N_j}{N} \hat{\tau}^j_{HT}$ as the post-stratified weighted average of the HT estimators, where $N_j = |\{X_i : |e(X_i) - q_j| < \epsilon\}|$ is the number of units near $q_j$.

For this estimator it is often recommended to do some trimming beforehand to improve its variance; for indications about how to perform this trimming without falling into involuntary $p$-hacking, see [24].

Beyond average treatment effects, there has been a growing interest in the estimation of so-called heterogeneous treatment effects in contexts where treatment effects are thought to differ widely for different subpopulations [7]. In these contexts, one aims to estimate the conditional average treatment effect (CATE), $\tau(x) = \frac{1}{|\{i:x_i=x\}|} \sum_{i \in \{i:x_i=x\}} Y_i(1) - Y_i(0)$. We estimate the CATE conditional on willingness to pay, making it possible to investigate how the treatment effect varies with revealed wealth.

## 4 A PERSONALIZED BDM MECHANISM

In this section we propose a way of personalizing the BDM mechanism that we call simply personalized BDM (or PBDM for short). We first show how BDM achieves incentive compatibility, but can produce high variance estimators with high budget regret. By contrast a simple "randomized controlled trial mechanism" (randomization without any willingness to pay component) would minimize the variance of the treatment effect estimators, but at the same time it would only be weakly incentive compatible and it would also achieve the upper bound of budget regret. Personalized BDM can be incentive compatible, produce estimators with lower expected variance, and achieves lower budget regret than both the BDM and RCT mechanisms. As a concrete summary, we will discuss how personalization can deliver a mechanism that is superior to BDM in three specific aspects:

(1) PBDM results in lower variance than BDM for the HT and Hajek estimators.
(2) PBDM has a smaller budget regret than BDM (the ex-post cost from treated units is smaller).
(3) Under PBDM, elicited valuations are distribution independent.

It is important to note that the types of interventions that have been analyzed in this context, and the ones we experiment with, involve giving out subsidies, e.g. water filters to households or legal representation to accused defendants, that would normally cost $C$ on the open market. Then, because of the nature of the problem, we are interested only in units with a willingness to pay $W < C$. However, not all market interventions have an easily knowable upper bound for the population of interest, and indeed that is a difficulty highlighted by the work by Bohm et al. [11]. And even knowing $C$, a researcher could run an inefficient implementation of the BDM mechanism. Imagine, for example, that a vaccine costs $C$ dollars to produce, but the maximum people are willing to pay for it is $\frac{C}{10}$. Every treated user would be very expensive to subsidize, but we won't know if the medical benefits of the vaccine outweigh the cost of the subsidy without a controlled experiment.

Let $\Phi$ be the randomized price offered by BDM's phantom bidder. At the heart of our personalized mechanism is a choice of conditional price distribution $\Phi|X_i$, where $X_i$ are observable characteristics of $i$ that can not be manipulated. Given a choice of $\Phi|X_i$, the mechanism is carried out in the following manner:

(1) Offer a product with cost $C$ to a subject with $X_i$ observable characteristics,
(2) Draw a price $\phi$ from $\Phi|X_i$ without showing it to the subject,
(3) Ask the subject to report her willingness to pay $w_i$, which we assume is drawn from $W|X_i$,
(4) If $\phi < w$ the user gets the product and pays $\phi$. Otherwise there is no exchange.

How should we design $\Phi|X_i$? It is clear that we want to make our choice using estimated properties of $W|X_i$, the willingness to pay of previous subjects conditional on their covariates. The problem is made easier by assuming that $W|X_i$ has support in $[0, C]$ for all $X_i$ for a fixed outside cost $C$, as discussed above. We will now describe our choice of $\Phi|X_i$ before elaborating on why this choice embodies favorable tradeoffs between the three objectives at the start of this section.

The conditional price distribution $\Phi|X_i$ we propose consists of two point masses of probability $\epsilon/2$ at the lower and upper bounds of the price range (0 and $C$) combined with a uniform distribution over a range $[a, b]$, where $a$ and $b$ are quantiles of $W|X_i$ given by $b = F^{-1}_{W|X_i}(1-\frac{\delta}{2})$ and $a = F^{-1}_{W|X_i}(\frac{\delta}{2})$. The cumulative distribution function $F_{\Phi|X_i}(w; a, b, \epsilon)$ is then:

$$F_{\Phi|X_i}(w) = \frac{\epsilon}{2} + (1-\epsilon)\frac{w\mathbf{I}\{a \le x \le b\}}{b-a} + \frac{\epsilon}{2}\mathbf{I}\{w \ge C\}. \tag{4}$$

In practice $a$ and $b$ must be estimated from observed willingness to pay data, furnishing estimates $\hat{a}$ and $\hat{b}$. We leave the estimation of $\epsilon$ for future work, and choose to set it before the experiment begins based on simulations. For different specifications of the data generating process, we find that $\epsilon = 0.05$ is a conservative value that balances cost and variance while maintaining incentive compatibility[1].

We propose the above family of distributions for two reasons. First, we want a mechanism that in the absence of any signal from the covariates reverts to BDM, which the mechanism clearly does (when $\epsilon = 0$). Second, if $\epsilon = 0$ there may be cases where the probability of assignment will either be zero or one (if someone bids outside the range of $[a, b]$), so the point masses of $\epsilon/2$ serve to bound the variance of our estimates (which is unbounded if any of the treatment probabilities reach 0 or 1).

Given that we estimate $\hat{F}_{W|X_i}$ for user $i$ from the dataset $\{(x_1, w_1), ..., (x_{i-1}, w_{i-1})\}$, the probability of being treated depends heavily on the history of users that have come before user $i$. This means that, contrary to BDM (where conditional on $W$ the assignment to treatment is random), for PBDM one needs to condition on all the previous history. However all the previous history is summarized by the choice of $F_{\Phi|X_i}$ so that

$$P(T_i = 1|\{(x_1, w_1), ..., (x_{i-1}, w_{i-1})\}) = F_{\Phi|X_i}(w_i)$$

for the realized $w_i$. In order to compute the HT or Hajek estimators of the average treatment effect, it suffices to save $F_{\Phi|X_i}(w_i)$ at the point when it was computed.

There are three immediate benefits from this setup. First as [31] conclude, not making the exact distribution explicit to users prevents distribution-dependence bids. Second, in the case where there is little predictive power of $X_i$ on $W$, the mechanism reverts to a well-centered BDM. Third, the point masses at the boundaries of this distribution help bound the variance of the ATE estimators. The following sub-sections show how the objectives specified in the introduction (low variance, low budget regret, and incentive compatibility) help inform the choice of this distribution for our mechanism. We detail how PBDM is superior to BDM in terms of lower variance, lower budget regret, and superior to a pure RCT in terms of stronger incentive-compatibility and lower budget regret. An RCT that gives away water filters can be thought of as randomizing people to either get a price of 0 (treatment) or $C$ (control) since they could possibly still buy it on the open market.

### 4.1 HT estimator variance

One can use the BDM mechanism to compute the Average Treatment Effect (ATE) of a particular intervention [10] as explained in the previous section, utilizing the probabilities of treatment and control as "propensities" (conditional on the willingness to pay they are true probabilities, not estimates). Post-stratification can be used for populations that are unbalanced in terms of their willingness to pay. However, since the probability of treatment depends fully on $W$, these estimates may be highly volatile. Equation (5) makes evident how the variance of the HT estimator can grow to infinity if the probability of treatment is close to 0 or 1. The variance of the Horviz-Thompson estimator is [5]:

$$Var(\hat{\tau}_{HT}) = \frac{1}{N^2}\left(\sum_{i=1}^{N} \frac{1 - e(X_i)}{e(X_i)} Y_i(1)^2 + \frac{e(X_i)}{1 - e(X_i)} Y_i(0)^2\right). \tag{5}$$

In the event of unavoidable extreme propensity scores close to 0 or 1, one could restrict the population of interest (change the estimand) to a subset of the propensity scores through trimming [24], though this can quickly turn into an invitation for "$p$-hacking" if not preconceived as part of the experimental design. Therefore we would like to have better balance of treated and control individuals for every willingness to pay $w$. This achieves two goals. First, both the ATE and CATE estimates would have lower variance. Second, by reducing the "profit" of the treated consumers (the

[1]This is consistent with notions of trimming specified in [24].

difference between their willingness to pay and the price they paid), researchers would have less regret about their subsidy of the product as will be explained in more detail in the next subsection.

The Hajek estimator's variance can be related to the HT variance. The standard approach here is to linearize the Hajek estimator around the HT estimator and then take the variance and truncate higher order terms. We thus concentrate on the HT estimator for comparing variance across mechanisms; the results presented in this section apply for the Hajek estimator asymptotically[2].

How should we design the conditional price distribution, $\Phi|X$, to balance the treatment and control? The variance in equation (5) can be modified by replacing the propensities with $F_{\Phi|X}$, the (true) probability of being treated by our personalized mechanism:

$$Var(\hat{\tau}_{HT}) = \frac{1}{N^2}\left(\sum_{i=1}^{N} \frac{1 - F_{\Phi|X_i}(W_i)}{F_{\Phi|X_i}(W_i)} Y_i(1)^2 + \frac{F_{\Phi|X_i}(W_i)}{1 - F_{\Phi|X_i}(W_i)} Y_i(0)^2\right). \tag{6}$$

Under a (rather strong) null hypothesis of no individual treatment effect (Fisher's null, see [15]) where $Y_i(1) - Y_i(0) = 0\ \forall i$, meaning $Y_i(1) = Y_i(0) = \alpha_i$, we can write the variance as:

$$Var(\hat{\tau}_{HT}) = \frac{1}{N^2}\sum_{i=1}^{N} \alpha_i \left(\frac{1 - F_{\Phi|X_i}(W_i)}{F_{\Phi|X_i}(W_i)} + \frac{F_{\Phi|X_i}(W_i)}{1 - F_{\Phi|X_i}(W_i)}\right). \tag{7}$$

This expression is minimized when $F_{\Phi|X_i}(W_i) = \frac{1}{2}$ for all $W_i$ , for any realization of $w_1, ..., w_N$. If we are only interested in minimizing $Var(\hat{\tau}_{HT})$ under the null, there is a simple solution: we can just place half of the probability mass of $\Phi$ on 0 and the other half on the upper bound for $W_i$. This provides an intuition for why randomized control trials are the gold standard for estimating causal effects. Yet, our objective is not only the estimation of an ATE: we are also interested in estimating the demand for the product and reducing the regret over our spent budget. Deploying an RCT actually achieves the upper bound for the budget regret (for any subject treated, they would pay 0 and we would lose the full value of the product, $C$). With respect to estimating the demand, RCTs provide no incentive to users for revealing their true willingness to pay, making the mechanism only weakly incentive compatible.

Guaranteeing minimum variance for any realization of $W$ is a very strong condition. We instead focus on the expected variance, conditional on the observed characteristics $X_i$, with the expectation being taken over realizations of $W_1, ..., W_N$. Using a Taylor expansion of Equation (6) around the mean and taking a first degree approximation, we then are interested in minimizing:

$$E[Var(\hat{\tau}_{HT})|X_1, ...X_N] \approx \frac{1}{N^2}\sum_{i=1}^{N}\left(\frac{1 - F_{\Phi|X_i}(E[W_i|X_i])}{F_{\Phi|X_i}(E[W_i|X_i])} Y_i(1)^2 + \frac{F_{\Phi|X_i}(E[W_i|X_i])}{1 - F_{\Phi|X_i}(E[W_i|X_i])} Y_i(0)^2\right). \tag{8}$$

Again assuming the Fisher null of no individual effect, this expected variance is minimized whenever $F_{\Phi|X_i}(E[W_i|X_i]) = \frac{1}{2}$, meaning that the median from the price distribution thus needs to be equal to the conditional expectation of the willingness to pay distribution.

One of the biggest advantages of PBDM over BDM is that it "smooths" the probability of a unit to be treated or controlled, depending on the distribution of $W|X_i$. This is, if the distribution of $W|X_i$ is skewed to the right, where users would be rarely treated, PBDM would "focus" in this part of the distribution and would increase the probability of treatment. On the other hand if $W|X_i$ is skewed to the left then PBDM could diminish the probability of "high spenders" to be treated. Our objective however is clearly underspecified in that there is an infinite number of distributions that achieve this goal. We can therefore target additional goals within this space of distributions.

[2]See [37], pages 172–176.

In particular, we would like for the variance of our estimator to be bounded. In order to achieve this, it is enough to require for

$$P(F_{\Phi|X_i}(W_i) > 1 - \frac{\epsilon}{2}) = 0, \tag{9}$$

$$P(F_{\Phi|X_i}(W_i) < \frac{\epsilon}{2}) = 0. \tag{10}$$

These conditions can be achieved by placing a probability mass of $\frac{\epsilon}{2}$ at both 0 and $C$ as PBDM does.

If we assume that $W|X_i$ is symmetric, this price distribution achieves the minimum expected conditional variance while at the same time bounding the probability of it escalating to infinity. It is important to note that BDM also achieves these two principles, but only in the case where the lower and upper bounds are chosen appropriately and $W$ is independent from $X_i$. For any other case BDM would provide a higher variance in expectation than PBDM.

## 4.2 Budget Regret

If we knew in advance a user's willingness to pay, the optimal pricing mechanism would be to randomize the price uniformly between $w_i - \epsilon$ and $w_i + \epsilon$ for some small value of $\epsilon$. This would mean that every user effectively pays their willingness to pay for the product or service and would result in the estimator with minimal variance. However, due to the uncertainty in $W$ we incur some level of regret every time we assign someone to treatment.

We define *budget regret* as:

$$BR(X, W) = E_\Phi\left[(W - \Phi)|\Phi < W, X, W\right], \tag{11}$$

and *expected budget regret* as:

$$br(F_\Phi) = E_{X,W}[BR(X, W)]. \tag{12}$$

Expected budget regret is the expected subsidy paid when assigning a unit to treatment. For any realization of $W$, an RCT price mechanism achieves the upper bound for $br(\Phi)$ among all possible price distributions: when $\mathrm{I}\{W_i > \Phi_i\} = 1$ it must be that $\Phi_i = 0$.

Meanwhile, for BDM we have that the budget regret is equal to:

$$br_{BDM}(F_\Phi) = E\left[\frac{W}{2}\right]. \tag{13}$$

For PBDM, if $\hat{b} = F^{-1}_{W|X_i}(1 - \frac{\delta}{2})$ and $\hat{a} = F^{-1}_{W|X_i}(\frac{\delta}{2})$ and $\epsilon = 0$ (assume an asymptotic setting where $\hat{a}$, $\hat{b}$ have converged on $a$, $b$):

$$br_{PBDM}(F_\Phi) = E\left[\frac{W - \hat{a}}{2}\right]. \tag{14}$$

These budget regret expressions mean that less variance in $W|X$ translates to less regret on average.

## 4.3 Balancing Cost and Variance

The choice of $\epsilon$ and $\delta$ for the PBDM mechanism is equivalent to choosing a trade-off between experiment cost and estimator variance, where larger values of $\epsilon$ or smaller values of $\delta$ correspond to lower variance and higher costs. On the other hand, a good reason to want to decrease the cost of treating an individual is to be able to treat more people and thereby have lower variance for the experiment at a given budget (or for the same variance, have lower costs). We propose a way to summarize this trade-off under a single minimization problem. We'll assume that sending people to control is costless and that there is no information in $X$ about $W$. Let the expected number of treated units under no budget constraints be $N_u$ and the expected number of treated units under budget constraint be $N_b$, taking the expectation over both willingness to pay and the random draws. It is evident that $N_u \geq N_b$. Let $N$ be the maximum number of units that can be treated.

We can write $N_u$ as:

$$N_u = \sum_{i=1}^{N} \mathbb{I}\{W_i > \Phi_i\} \approx Np(\epsilon, \delta), \tag{15}$$

where we define $p(\epsilon, \delta) = P(W > \Phi)$. Meanwhile in the setting with a budget $B$ we want to approximately spend the full budget:

$$B \approx \sum_{i=1}^{N} (C_i - P_i)\mathbb{I}\{W_i > P_i\} \approx N_b c(\epsilon, \delta) \tag{16}$$

where $c(\epsilon, \delta) = E\left[(C - P)|W > P\right]$.

We then have that

$$N_u \geq N_b \Rightarrow Np(\epsilon, \delta) \gtrapprox \frac{B}{c(\epsilon, \delta)} \Rightarrow N \gtrapprox \frac{B}{p(\epsilon, \delta)c(\epsilon, \delta)}. \tag{17}$$

From Equation (7) we get that the variance for this simplified case is

$$Var(\hat{\tau}_{HT}|W) \propto \frac{1}{N^2}\left(\sum_{i=1}^{N} \frac{p(\epsilon, \delta, W_i)}{1 - p(\epsilon, \delta, W_i)} + \frac{1 - p(\epsilon, \delta, W_i)}{p(\epsilon, \delta, W_i)}\right) \tag{18}$$

$$\lessapprox \left(\frac{p(\epsilon, \delta)c(\epsilon, \delta)}{B}\right)^2 \left(\sum_{i=1}^{N} \frac{p(\epsilon, \delta, W)}{1 - p(\epsilon, \delta, W)} + \frac{1 - p(\epsilon, \delta, W)}{p(\epsilon, \delta, W)}\right). \tag{19}$$

For a given budget $B$ we would like to minimize $E[Var(\hat{\tau}_{HT}|W)]$. For the purposes of this work, we chose to fix $\epsilon$ to preserve incentive compatibility (otherwise, the variance would be minimized with $\epsilon = 1$, corresponding to an RCT). We ran simulations to select $\delta$ by minimizing the expectation of Equation (19) over our prior belief of the distribution of $W_i$. We chose $\delta$ after some robustness checks prior to running the experiment. In practice, $\delta$ could be personalized by being calculated at every point in time after having better estimates of the distribution of $W$. We believe there is ample room to fine tune these parameters but leave this as future work.

### 4.4 Incentive Compatibility

Finally, for BDM and PBDM if a user is an expected-utility maximizer she gains nothing by providing a wrong valuation of the product offered. Let's say that the user has a valuation of $v_i$ for the product. If she were to report $v_i - \epsilon$ as her valuation for all those prices between $v_i - \epsilon$ and $v_i$ she would lose the product, which is still more valuable than the price she would have to pay. If she were to offer $v_i + \epsilon$ she would have to pay more than her valuation with $\epsilon$ probability.

For an RCT mechanism the user is indifferent between reporting her true valuation or not. This is because she would always be offered 0 or $C$ as the price. This could happen in PBDM if the user's willingness to pay is between 0 and $F^{-1}_{W|X_i}(\frac{\epsilon}{2})$, but this would only happen with small probability. Even if users know PBDM is being used, they don't know their order of arrival. As a result they would be uncertain about the distribution from which prices are being sampled. And as Mazar et al. [31] show, as long as users don't know the underlying distribution, their offers will be distribution-independent.

### 4.5 Why not use the predicted median as the price?

We have thus far described a personalized mechanism that outperforms BDM in all of the described dimensions. One may ask however why not just predict the median $W_i|X_i$ and use this as the offered price. This was actually the original mechanism we envisioned for this problem, running a simple median regression on $W_i|X_i$. If the covariates are highly predictive of $W_i$ we would achieve a 50-50 split and achieve close to minimum budget regret. However, we would not be able to assume that $W_i$ is fixed (but previously unknown) for every user, since doing so would make the probability of being assigned to treatment *conditional on* $W_i$ either 0 or 1, losing randomness in the conditional assignment and breaking the assumption that treatment needs to be assigned at random in order to make causal interpretations. Even if we assumed that the randomness comes from some probabilistic process in how people elicit their willingness to pay, one could have an unobserved variable correlated with both the willingness to pay and the outcome which would complicate causal interpretations.

## 5 EMAIL CLASSIFICATION MOCK EXPERIMENT

In order to test our method we designed a Mechanical Turk task where users performed email spam classification [17]. After performing several rounds of classification, the users were offered the opportunity to spend part of their wages in order to forgo a time restriction on their work. The time restriction made the task significantly more difficult, and they experienced the task both with and without the time restriction before being offered the opportunity to remove it. The offer to pay to remove the restriction was formulated as a willingness to pay experiment. Users were randomly assigned to either the standard BDM mechanism or our PBDM mechanism. The objective in this mock experiment was thus to estimate both the demand for time freedom (the willingness to pay for it) and the causal effect of being time-restricted on performance (better or worse spam classification).

We conducted our experiment on Amazon Mechanical Turk for its convenience and simplicity for running experiments. Mechanical Turk compares favorably to traditional ways of conducting behavioral experiments [13]; see [30, 35] for discussions of best practices for behavioral research using Mechanical Turk.

We collected a range of covariates as the basis for our personalization under the PBDM mechanism. First, our task was hosted on a server that allowed us to gather browser-level features of the web users. Second, we included two surveys at the onset of the task: a demographic survey in order to compare our population with that of Mechanical Turk [25] and a risk survey, adapted from [18]. For computing the risk profile of users from this survey we used the index for general risk aversion as in [29]. Lastly, we also collected additional covariates from the behavior of users during the early tutorial phase of our task.

The users were not made aware that their browser configuration or survey responses impacted the phantom bidder of the PBDM mechanism. We had no true way of verifying the validity of the demographic survey responses or the risk survey responses, and it is important to be clear that these responses ultimately impacted the price at which these users were offered the time freedom. As a result, in settings where the subject may realize the connection between their responses to early questions and the price offered in a later stage of an experiment, it may be appropriate to only use survey questions for which answers can be validated. Examples of questions from development economics field experiments used in similar contexts include "How many members are there in your household?" or "How many rooms do you have in your home?" [2]. Note, however, that even if the users are able to impact their offer distribution in their favor, it is still in their interest to bid their true willingness to pay, regardless of how much they've been able to manipulate the

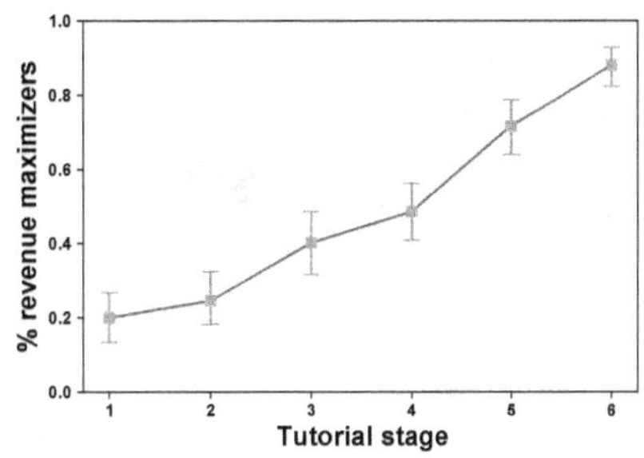


Fig. 1. As the tutorial progresses, more participants bid the revenue-maximizing number of credits.

mechanisms offer distribution (or not). It may, however, impact the price they pay. Thus if the main effect of interest is the effect of the price, it is critical to only use covariates that participants cannot strategically manipulate.

Following the initial demographic surveys, users were subject to three phases of labelling tasks designed to demonstrate and evaluate our task and mechanism. First, users were shown a selection of six emails to classify into spam or non-spam, with no time restriction. The proportion of spam/non-spam was always kept balanced (three spam, three non-spam), and the emails were showed in random order. Users were instructed that for each email classified correctly, they would earn 10 credits, otherwise they would lose 10 credits. Credits were converted to dollars at a rate of 0.5 cents per credit. These first six emails were then followed by another six emails, again balanced (three spam, three non-spam), but for these emails there was a time restriction of $t$ seconds per email (we varied $t$ between tasks), meaning that if the user did not answer within $t$ seconds their answer was marked as wrong. If the user accumulated a net loss during these phases it did not carry on to later phases.

In the second phase, users were introduced to the idea of the BDM mechanism. For 6 rounds we offered users a chance to earn $k$ credits without any work, where $k$ was a random integer from 0 to 20. Users were instructed to make a bid stating the most they were willing to pay for the $k$ credits and they were told that they would be in direct competition against an artificial intelligence. If the AI's offer was smaller than their bid, we gave them $k$ credits and charged them the AI's price. The optimal bid under the assumption of expected utility maximization should have been $k$ if the user fully understood the mechanism. We thus used this phase in order to evaluate users' understanding of the mechanism.

## 5.1 Understanding the mechanism

Figure 1 shows to what extent users were understanding the mechanism and behaving as rational agents. For the tutorial stages we measure the difference between the credits offered and a worker's willingness to pay. If users understand the mechanism, this number should be either 0 or 1, given that we are working with a discrete space. If offered $k$ credits the user should be indifferent between bidding $k$ or $k-1$; in both cases if the random draw is $k$ they get nothing and any other draw gives them back the same amount of credits. In order to evaluate the last phase, we asked participants if they regretted their decision once our random offer was shown to them. Regret here does not necessarily mean that participants didn't understand the mechanism. It is not clear to what extent people are conscious of their willingness to pay, so when a price is shown it may work as an anchor on valuation. In total 88% of participants seemed to understand the mechanism (by bidding rationally) by the end of the tutorial. Meanwhile in a post-experiment survey 33% said they regretted their bid in the final (non-tutorial) round.

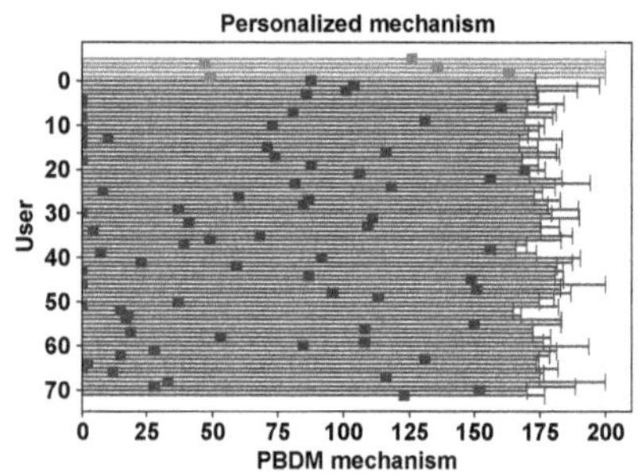


Fig. 2. For each user treated with the PBDM mechanism, intervals corresponding to the range of $\Phi|X_i$ with points correspond to the offer made by the mechanism. The first 5 users encounter the non-personalized BDM mechanism (and are counted towards that treatment arm). User 0 and onward encountered the PBDM mechanism, trained on the previous users. Probability mass below 0 and above 200 is placed at the respective boundaries (no user could have more than 200 credits). It is hard to visualize, but many of these intervals have significant probability mass at zero, which is their main difference compared to the BDM bidder distribution. Since ridge regression assumes normality and our intervals are very wide, we get that 10% of the normal intervals have lower bounds below zero.

The final phase begins with a final encounter with the willingness to pay mechanism where users were instructed to make a bid to remove the timer from a long round of spam labeling. If the AI's offer was below their bid, they will pay the AI's offer and not be subject to a timer for the final tasks. Otherwise they would be time-restricted for these tasks (though not have to pay anything). They were not told if they were in the BDM condition or the PBDM condition.

As mentioned before, we used the information from a brief demographic survey and risk profile survey executed before the first phase, the browser information, and behavioral measurements from the tutorials to inform the personalized mechanism for the final bidding. Since the mechanism is incentive compatible no matter the distribution from which we sample [9], we can easily evaluate how other offer distributions would have fared. Thus, we only needed to run one mock experiment and can then test different ways of predicting willingness to pay.

Our experiment assigned 142 users to either BDM or PBDM at random. For the personalization, we used Bayesian ridge regression (i.e. $L_2$-regularized linear regression) as our model for predicting willingness to pay, discussed in further detail below. In tests on synthetic data we saw little difference between this model and other models such as Random Forests, Lasso, or Gradient Boosting Decision Trees. PBDM can also be implemented without any user covariates with the goal of just estimating the mean and variance of the distribution for $W$. Even in this case a researcher would find improvements since the intervals over which samples are taken would be positioned optimally (but "personalized" only to the population, not individually personalized).

## 5.2 PBDM for this mock experiment

In order to specify the PBDM mechanism for our mock experiment we only need to determine how to compute $F_{\Phi|X_i}(w)$ as in Equation 4, which means estimating $a = F^{-1}_{W|X_i}(\frac{\epsilon}{2})$ and $b = F^{-1}_{W|X_i}(1 - \frac{\epsilon}{2})$. Because of the small size of the participant pool for our mock experiment, we decided to restrict ourselves to linear predictors. In particular we chose a simple ridge regression with a prior on the size of the parameters. The Bayesian interpretation of ridge regression is key, allowing us to interpret a posterior on $W|X_i$ from the model. We used STAN [14] for all computations.

Under the reasonable assumption that willingness to pay responses were not influenced by the choice of the prediction algorithm, we can use their covariates and responses to test other

| | BDM | PBDM |
|---|---|---|
| Number of participants | 71 | 71 |
| Percentage treated | 31% | 52% |
| Total cost (credits) | 5469 | 6146 |
| Cost per person treated (credits) | 237 | 161 |
| Average budget regret | 65 | 45 |
| HT ATE | -0.63 (-38,36) | 12.09 (2.09,22.09) |
| Hajek ATE | 2.23 (-4.55,9.03) | 4.26 (2.78,5.73) |
| Block ATE | 5.19 (3.56,6.81) | 3.8 (1.91,5.70) |

Table 1. PBDM improves on BDM in terms of cost per person, budget regret, and variance of the average treatment effect estimators.

prediction algorithms such as Gradient Boosting Decision Trees, Adaboost, and Lasso post-fact[3]. We observe that none of these algorithms did a good job of predicting the personalized willingness to pay from the covariates we gathered for our mock application, with all the models reverting to the population mean to predict $W$. This highlights an important basic benefit of PBDM: for all BDM experiments there is a basic population-level personalization problem of what the population of responses will look like. A PBDM mechanism that simply learns the population of bids with reasonable fidelity therefore delivers significant improvements over BDM, as our results show. Figure 2 shows the estimated intervals as well as the PBDM phantom bid for every user.

## 6 RESULTS

We use the email classification task in the previous section to evaluate our PBDM mechanism in contrast with an ordinary BDM mechanism. Our evaluation is five fold: we examine the cost of running our experiment, the cost per person treated, the variance of the average treatment effect (ATE) estimators, the CATE conditional on $W$, and the expected budget regret. Table 1 summarizes these differences. For costs, the credits we pay to user $i$ is 10 times the difference between the number of correct answers, $Y_i$, and the number of incorrect answers (out of 20), $20 - Y_i$, minus the amount paid in case of treatment: $10(Y_i - (20 - Y_i)) - \Phi_i \mathbb{I}\{W_i > \Phi_i\}$.

For the variance of the average treatment effect estimators, we focus on the variance of the Horvitz-Thompson estimator and the consistent estimator of this variance [4]:

$$\widehat{Var}(\hat{\tau}_{HT}) = \frac{1}{N^2}\left(\sum_{i=1}^{N} T_i(1 - e(X_i))\left[\frac{Y_i(1)}{e(X_i)}\right]^2 + (1 - T_i)(e(X_i))\left[\frac{Y_i(0)}{1 - e(X_i)}\right]^2\right). \tag{20}$$

Here $e(X_i)$ is the probability of assignment to treatment, which we can compute exactly given the known distribution of $\Phi_i|X_i$ at every stage of the experiment. As detailed in Section 4.1, we can obtain Hajek variances estimates from HT variance estimates by linearization and Taylor expansion to obtain $\widehat{Var}(\hat{\tau}_{\text{Hajek}})$. We use this estimate $\widehat{Var}(\hat{\tau}_{\text{Hajek}})$ to construct conservative Wald-type confidence intervals for the ATE, $\hat{\tau}_{\text{Hajek}} \pm z_{1-\alpha}\sqrt{\widehat{Var}(\hat{\tau}_{\text{Hajek}})}$. Furthermore, we build bootstrap confidence intervals for $\widehat{Var}(\hat{\tau}_{\text{Hajek}})$ under Fisher's null (no individual treatment effect [15]). We

[3]In practice, researchers can run a variety of prediction algorithms at runtime (rather than post-fact) and make predictions with the one with the best performance under a pre-specified metric.

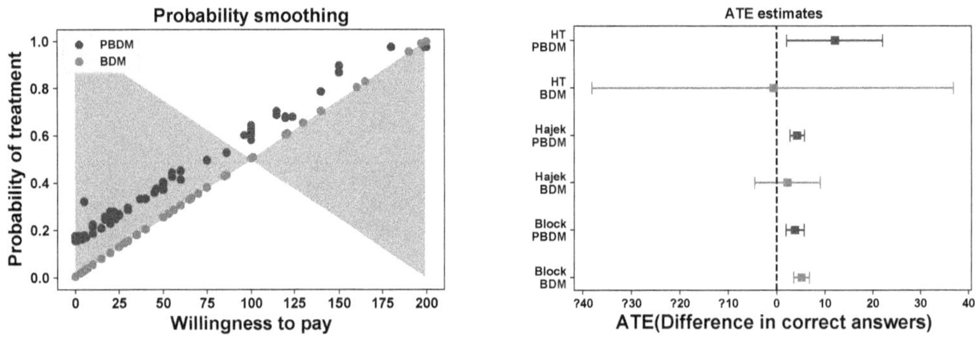


Fig. 3. (a) The probability of treatment as a function of willingness to pay for the BDM and PBDM mechanisms in our email labelling experiment. The green areas correspond to reduced contributions to the estimator variance. PBDM smoothes probabilities for most users. (b) The ATE estimates computed for both BDM and PBDM experiments for the HT, Hajek, and block estimators, with bootstrapped [5%, 95%] confidence intervals shown. For each of the three estimators, PBDM provides tighter confidence intervals than BDM.

require this null assumption because otherwise the probability of treatment is dependent on the order of arrival, and we only observe one of the two potential outcomes.

For the CATE we proceeded as in [10], computing a non-parametric kernel regression with the willingness to pay as the dependent variable of interest. We compute confidence intervals based on bootstrapping the residuals as in [32].

Finally, we estimate expected budget regret as:

$$\widehat{br} = \frac{\sum_{i=1}^{N} (W_i - \Phi_i)\mathbb{I}\{\Phi_i < W_i\}}{\sum_{i=1}^{N} \mathbb{I}\{\Phi_i < W_i\}}. \tag{21}$$

Table 1 shows a summary comparing PBDM to BDM under these varied metrics. The percentage of people treated is more balanced in PBDM compared to BDM, as can be seen in more detail in Figure 3a, helping reduce the variance of the estimators under Fisher's null.

In terms of costs, from a first glance at Table 1, it may seem that BDM is cheaper than PBDM. However, the cost per person treated is much lower for PBDM. In Figure 3b we how, for the same number of units in the experiment, PBDM achieves tighter confidence intervals than BDM.

As Figure 4 shows, at every budget level, the variance of the Hajek estimator is lower for PBDM than for BDM (we achieve the same results for the other two estimators). Finally Figure 5 shows that there is no difference between the two methods in terms of computing a demand curve (as there shouldn't be).

For our mock experiment of email labeling, these improvements were an example of a worst case scenario for the mechanism, in the sense that there was little individual personalization to learn. We were not able to predict the willingness to pay based on any of the covariates, and using the population mean and variance was the resulting strategy. As such, the main improvement of PBDM against BDM in this case was the correct centering of the distribution allowing us to increase the number of individuals treated at every level of willingness to pay. As Figure 6a shows, none of the covariates had a significant effect on $W$.

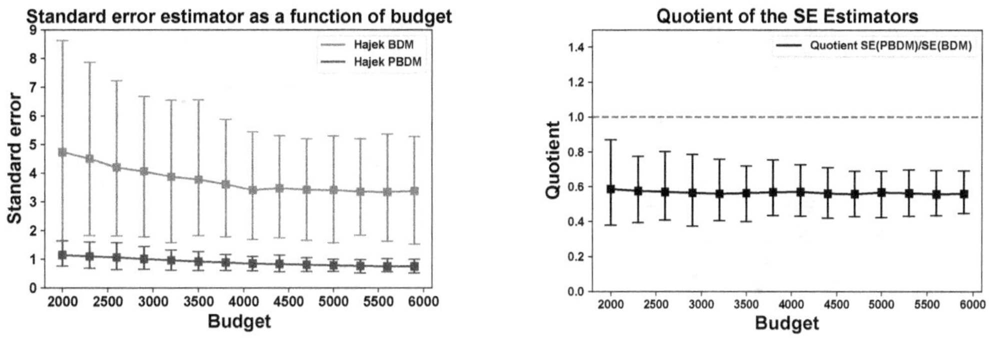


Fig. 4. (Left) Bootstrapped confidence intervals for the standard error of the Hajek ATE estimators under BDM and PBDM. The plot shows how, at each budget level, the standard errors computed for PBDM are lower than those for BDM. (Right) Bootstrapped confidence intervals for the quotient between the standard error of the Hajek ATE estimator for PBDM and BDM. The standard error under PBDM is estimated to be around 25% of the estimator under BDM.

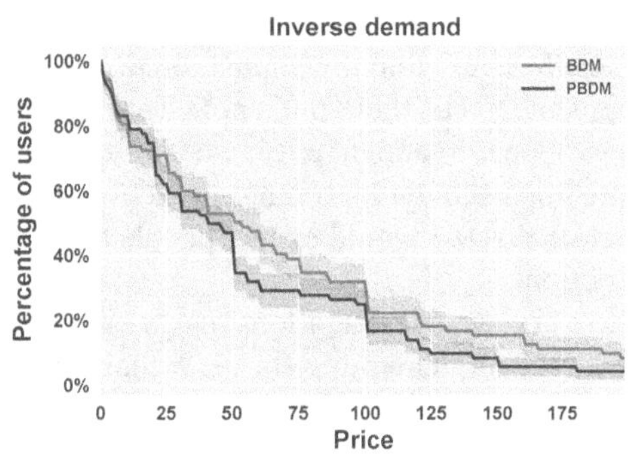


Fig. 5. The demand for not having a time limit in the email classification mock experiment, computed using the elicited willingness to pay of users under the two mechanisms, priced in units of credit.

Figure Figure 6b shows the CATE, the ATE conditional on willingness to pay. The wide confidence bands here show that the ATE did not vary significantly among people with different willingness to pay. Based on these estimates we believe that removing time restrictions on classification tasks such as ours would not have a heterogeneous effect across users of different willingness to pay levels. Our results here are all in terms of a mock experiment, but the real importance of this analysis would come by e.g. analyzing the CATE of water filters on health conditional on willingness to pay.

## 7 DISCUSSION AND EXTENSIONS

Overall our experiment shows how personalized BDM (PBDM) can improve on classic BDM in terms of budget regret, average cost, and estimator variance all at once. PBDM makes it possible to forego any assumptions about the bounds of the bid interval (except for the natural bounds that constrain the population of interest), which eliminates potential biases observed when telling users that interval. Under PBDM, the interval is quickly learned from data. While we found little to no signal in the covariates about a user's willingness to pay in our specific experiment, the

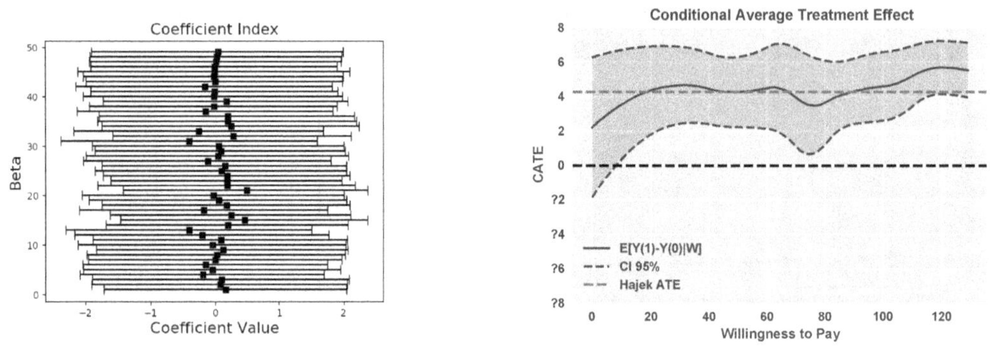


Fig. 6. (a) The coefficients corresponding to the predictors of $W$, with confidence intervals. We found no effect on any of these predictors in our mock experiment (and post-hoc found no effects with several other prediction models as well). (b) The Hajek estimator finds a significant average treatment effect (see Table 1), but no significant heterogeneous treatment effects as a function of $W$. The non-uniform confidence bands reveal that most bids were on the lower end of the interval.

personalization still served to effectively find the population distribution. We did not observe any evidence of conditional treatment effects, though it's not clear that we should have expected any: in our mock experiment a conditional treatment effect would imply that individuals with a greater willingness to pay were more impacted by the timing restriction than individuals with a smaller willingness to pay. It's not clear that we would expect people to be good judges of the value, to them, of the lifted time restriction.

In a more general note there are two considerations that we did not utilize in our current work but that we believe may be key to implementing these mechanisms in contexts where we can't assume unconfoundedness. There are different reasons why unconfoundedness may be violated. First, it may be that there are omitted variables correlated with outcomes and/or with the treatment. For example, wealthy people may have a higher willingness to pay for some health service but receive smaller benefits from it. It may also be that some users don't comply in certain settings once they have been assigned to treatment. Compliance is a fairly common problem when dealing with this type of mechanisms since it is often difficult to force people to pay after they win a bid. To address these confoundedness issues, one can use the instrumental variable framework as in [3]. The original BDM mechanism offers an external source of randomness that can be used as an instrument in these settings, as noted by [10]. For our mock experiment we didn't concern ourselves with this problem since we had perfect compliance and no dropouts. However in practice, and in particular in development settings, one could see how this would be an important issue to address.

## 8 CONCLUSIONS

In market intervention experiments the classic BDM mechanism has recently been shown to facilitate the simultaneous estimation of treatment effects (of an intervention) and demand (for the intervention). We show that both the statistical efficiency and cost of running such an experiment using BDM can be significantly improved by personalizing the mechanism. As a basic matter, we find that our personalized BDM (PBDM) mechanism can learn the overall distribution of the population of willingnesses to pay, $W$, which reduces both the cost of the experiment and variance of the estimate. As a more advanced matter, we designed our PBDM mechanism to be able to tailor the mechanism to the known covariates of each individual, learning $W|X_i$. That said, in our practical demonstration using a spam labelling task, we found that no covariates that we collected were able to meaningfully predict individual willingnesses to pay.

In terms of personalization, we believe there are further improvements to be made. Recent work in the estimation of confidence intervals for machine learning techniques (see [7] would allow more sophisticated algorithms to be used as predictors of $W$'s distribution. Furthermore, a more sophisticated characterization of the phantom bidder distribution could yield better results in contexts where the distributional properties of the demand may be known a priori, as in well established markets.

Even with the simple representation of the phantom bidder used in this work we have high confidence that a personalized BDM mechanism can result in substantial savings in experimentation costs as well as improvements in statistical efficiency for a broad class of willingness to pay experiments.

## REFERENCES


[1] Alekh Agarwal, Sarah Bird, Markus Cozowicz, Luong Hoang, John Langford, Stephen Lee, Jiaji Li, Dan Melamed, Gal Oshri, Oswaldo Ribas, Siddhartha Sen, and Alex Slivkins. 2016. Making Contextual Decisions with Low Technical Debt. *arXiv preprint arXiv:1606.03966* (2016).

[2] Vivi Alatas, Ririn Purnamasari, Matthew Wai-Poi, Abhijit Banerjee, Benjamin A Olken, and Rema Hanna. 2016. Self-targeting: Evidence from a field experiment in Indonesia. *Journal of Political Economy* 124, 2 (2016), 371–427.

[3] Joshua D Angrist and Jörn-Steffen Pischke. 2008. *Mostly harmless econometrics: An empiricist's companion.* Princeton University Press.

[4] Peter M Aronow. 2016. Data-Adaptive Causal Effects and Superefficiency. *Journal of Causal Inference* 4, 2 (2016).

[5] Peter M Aronow and Cyrus Samii. 2017. Estimating average causal effects under general interference, with application to a social network experiment. *The Annals of Applied Statistics* 11, 4 (2017), 1912–1947.

[6] Nava Ashraf, James Berry, and Jesse M Shapiro. 2010. Can higher prices stimulate product use? Evidence from a field experiment in Zambia. *American Economic Review* 100, 5 (2010), 2383–2413.

[7] Susan Athey and Guido Imbens. 2016. Recursive partitioning for heterogeneous causal effects. *Proceedings of the National Academy of Sciences* 113, 27 (2016), 7353–7360.

[8] Hamsa Bastani, Mohsen Bayati, and Khashayar Khosravi. 2017. Exploiting the Natural Exploration In Contextual Bandits. *arXiv preprint arXiv:1704.09011* (2017).

[9] Gordon M Becker, Morris H DeGroot, and Jacob Marschak. 1964. Measuring utility by a single-response sequential method. *Behavioral science* 9, 3 (1964), 226–232.

[10] James Berry, Greg Fischer, and Raymond P Guiteras. 2015. Eliciting and utilizing willingness to pay: evidence from field trials in Northern Ghana. (2015).

[11] Peter Bohm, Johan Lindén, and Joakim Sonnegård. 1997. Eliciting reservation prices: Becker–DeGroot–Marschak mechanisms vs. markets. *The Economic Journal* 107, 443 (1997), 1079–1089.

[12] Rebecca R Boyce, Thomas C Brown, Gary H McClelland, George L Peterson, and William D Schulze. 1992. An experimental examination of intrinsic values as a source of the WTA-WTP disparity. *The American Economic Review* 82, 5 (1992), 1366–1373.

[13] Michael Buhrmester, Tracy Kwang, and Samuel D Gosling. 2011. Amazon's Mechanical Turk a new source of inexpensive, yet high-quality, data? *Perspectives on psychological science* 6, 1 (2011), 3–5.

[14] Bob Carpenter, Andrew Gelman, Matt Hoffman, Daniel Lee, Ben Goodrich, Michael Betancourt, Michael A Brubaker, Jiqiang Guo, Peter Li, and Allen Riddell. 2016. Stan: A probabilistic programming language. *Journal of Statistical Software* 20, 2 (2016), 1–37.

[15] Peng Ding. 2017. A paradox from randomization-based causal inference. *Statistical science* 32, 3 (2017), 331–345.

[16] Ronald A Fisher. 1937. *The design of experiments.* Oliver And Boyd; Edinburgh; London.

[17] Daniel G Goldstein, Siddharth Suri, R Preston McAfee, Matthew Ekstrand-Abueg, and Fernando Diaz. 2014. The economic and cognitive costs of annoying display advertisements. *Journal of Marketing Research* 51, 6 (2014), 742–752.

[18] Ramu Govindasamy and John Italia. 1999. Predicting willingness-to-pay a premium for organically grown fresh produce. *Journal of Food Distribution Research* 30 (1999), 44–53.

[19] David M Grether and Charles R Plott. 1979. Economic theory of choice and the preference reversal phenomenon. *The American Economic Review* 69, 4 (1979), 623–638.

[20] Jaroslav Hájek. 1971. Comment on "An essay on the logical foundations of survey sampling, part one". *The foundations of survey sampling* 236 (1971).

[21] Jason Hartford, Greg Lewis, Kevin Leyton-Brown, and Matt Taddy. 2016. Counterfactual Prediction with Deep Instrumental Variables Networks. *arXiv preprint arXiv:1612.09596* (2016).

[22] Daniel G Horvitz and Donovan J Thompson. 1952. A generalization of sampling without replacement from a finite universe. *Journal of the American statistical Association* 47, 260 (1952), 663–685.

[23] Taisuke Imai and Colin F Camerer. 2016. Estimating Time Preferences from Budget Set Choices Using Optimal Adaptive Design. *Working Paper* (2016).

[24] Guido W Imbens and Donald B Rubin. 2015. *Causal inference in statistics, social, and biomedical sciences.* Cambridge University Press.

[25] Panagiotis G Ipeirotis. 2010. Demographics of mechanical turk. (2010).

[26] Steven J Kachelmeier and Mohamed Shehata. 1992. Examining risk preferences under high monetary incentives: Experimental evidence from the People's Republic of China. *The American Economic Review* (1992), 1120–1141.

[27] Dean Karlan and Jonathan Zinman. 2009. Observing unobservables: Identifying information asymmetries with a consumer credit field experiment. *Econometrica* 77, 6 (2009), 1993–2008.

[28] Lihong Li, Wei Chu, John Langford, and Robert E Schapire. 2010. A contextual-bandit approach to personalized news article recommendation. In *Proceedings of the 19th international conference on World wide web.* ACM, 661–670.

[29] Carter A Mandrik and Yeqing Bao. 2005. Exploring the concept and measurement of general risk aversion. *NA-Advances in Consumer Research Volume 32* (2005).

[30] Winter Mason and Siddharth Suri. 2012. Conducting behavioral research on Amazon's Mechanical Turk. *Behavior research methods* 44, 1 (2012), 1–23.

[31] Nina Mazar, Botond Koszegi, and Dan Ariely. 2014. True context-dependent preferences? The causes of market-dependent valuations. *Journal of Behavioral Decision Making* 27, 3 (2014), 200–208.

[32] Timothy L McMurry and Dimitris N Politis. 2008. Bootstrap confidence intervals in nonparametric regression with built-in bias correction. *Statistics & Probability Letters* 78, 15 (2008), 2463–2469.

[33] Jerzey Neyman. 1923. On the application of probability theory to agricultural experiments. Essay on principles. Section 9. Edited and translated by DM Dabrowska and TP Speed. *Statist. Sci.* 5 (1923), 465–72.

[34] Charles Noussair, Stephane Robin, and Bernard Ruffieux. 2004. Revealing consumers' willingness-to-pay: A comparison of the BDM mechanism and the Vickrey auction. *Journal of economic psychology* 25, 6 (2004), 725–741.

[35] Gabriele Paolacci, Jesse Chandler, and Panagiotis G Ipeirotis. 2010. Running experiments on amazon mechanical turk. (2010).

[36] Donald B Rubin. 1974. Estimating causal effects of treatments in randomized and nonrandomized studies. *Journal of educational Psychology* 66, 5 (1974), 688.

[37] Carl-Erik Särndal, Bengt Swensson, and Jan Wretman. 1992. *Model assisted survey sampling.* Springer Science & Business Media.

[38] Adith Swaminathan and Thorsten Joachims. 2015. The self-normalized estimator for counterfactual learning. In *Advances in Neural Information Processing Systems.* 3231–3239.

[39] Stefan Wager and Susan Athey. 2017. Estimation and inference of heterogeneous treatment effects using random forests. *J. Amer. Statist. Assoc.* just-accepted (2017).

[40] Nathaniel T Wilcox. 1993. On a lottery pricing anomaly: time tells the tale. *Journal of Risk and Uncertainty* 7, 3 (1993), 311–324.

# The Costs of Entering through Tying: Experimental Evidence[1]

HYUNJIN KIM, Harvard Business School
MICHAEL LUCA, Harvard Business School

In recent years, Google has entered into a growing set of markets that are adjacent to its general search engine, launching new products such as Google Flights, Google Shopping, and Google Local. To leverage its dominance in general search, Google has often tied these products to its general search page, excluding competitor content. In this paper, we explore the strategic tradeoffs platforms face when pursuing a tying strategy to enter complementary markets, empirically investigating Google's decision to tie Google Local (its reviews product) to its search engine. We experimentally vary the content displayed on top of organic search results (called the "Onebox"), to show either exclusively Google reviews (the status quo), or reviews from multiple platforms that are determined to be the best-performing by Google's own organic search algorithm. We find that users prefer the OneBox and are more likely to engage with it when it includes competitor content. This suggests that Google's strategy of excluding competitor content leaves customers with a lower quality product. However, the number of reviews contained in Google Local has increased rapidly in recent years, suggesting that there may be a benefit of excluding competitors as well. Overall, these results shed light on a strategic tradeoff for companies that enter a complementary market using a tying strategy: while companies have successfully used this strategy, it can also come at a cost to consumers in the form of a lower-quality product.

## 1 INTRODUCTION

When Google was founded, it consisted of an innovative general search algorithm and a simple interface to match users with content-creating platforms. In 2010, Google developed an interface for online reviews, later called Google Local, and began allowing searchers to write reviews. At the time, businesses like Yelp and TripAdvisor had amassed millions of reviews, but Google could in principle take advantage of its dominant position in search to increase traction for this new product by tying it to the search engine. They faced the following strategic decision: should they exclude competitor content and show only Google reviews, or should they draw on content from other platforms as well?

In practice, different platforms have made different decisions. For example, Google developed the "Onebox" that sits on top of any organic content and excludes content from other downstream platforms. In contrast, Bing has a partnership with downstream platforms like Yelp and TripAdvisor. Another easily implementable alternative would be to show the best subset of content as assessed by the platform's organic search algorithm.

In this paper, we empirically investigate Google's decision to tie its local reviews product to the search engine as it entered the reviews market. To explore, we conducted an experiment on UsabilityHub, a user testing platform that provides tools for companies to test website designs, and recruited 15,166 users from Mechanical Turk, an online labor market where companies can hire freelancers for short online tasks. Users were prompted with instructions that asked how they would search for a local pizza restaurant if they were in a new city, where we selected the 100 largest US cities by population. We then showed users a corresponding screenshot of a Google search result.

[1]Byron Perpetua and Patrick Rooney provided excellent research assistance. We thank Travis Brooks, Sebastien Couvidat, Dan Frank, and Will Seltzer for valuable support and feedback on the design and implementation of the experiment. We thank Susan Athey, Benjamin Edelman, Joshua Gans, and Timothy Wu for constructive comments on this paper. This project received financial support from Yelp. Kim and Luca have done consulting for tech companies including Yelp, but have no compensation tied to the results of this paper. All remaining errors are our own.
Full Paper appears at: **https://ssrn.com/abstract=3180721**


ACM ISBN 978-1-4503-5829-3/18/06. https://doi.org/10.1145/3219166.3219232

We randomly assigned users to one of three conditions, varying the content of the Onebox within the Google search results screenshot. In the "Google + Text" condition, reviews from Google were shown in the Onebox while competitor content was excluded. The Onebox also contained information on hours, location, and prices, and snippets of text. This is exactly what Google was showing as of 2016. In the *Google Only* condition, the same Google reviews were shown, but without the information snippets – this allowed us to create a "tying" condition that was comparable to our counterfactual strategy. In the *Google + Competitor* condition, the content in the Onebox was modified by using a Chrome Browser Extension called "Focus on the User" that pulled review content from multiple platforms determined to be the highest ranking by Google's organic search algorithm. The plugin detected the presence of a OneBox in the Google search results and conducted a separate search in the background to extract the most highly ranked local review results. All three experimental conditions shared the display structure of Google's search results, only modifying the review content shown in the OneBox -- with *Google* and *Google + Text* conditions representing Google's tying strategy, and *Google + Competitor* representing a feasible counterfactual.

We find that Google's exclusionary strategy degrades search quality: users are less likely to click on the OneBox when competitor content is excluded. Moreover, users prefer the Onebox that includes competitor content, when shown the different options side by side. These results suggest that by excluding downstream competitors, Google faces a tradeoff. On the one hand, tying has led to a worse primary product at least in the short run, by providing less useful search results. On the other hand, tying may lead to other long-term benefits, such as entry deterrence, customer acquisition, and economies of scale and scope. While a full analysis of the benefits of tying is outside the scope of this paper, Google Local reviews has grown significantly—at almost double the rate of its competitors—since its launch, amassing 3 million reviews within its first few months (one-fifth of Yelp's content at the time).[2]

Our paper relates to the broader literature on tying, which has explored the motivations and implications of using a tying strategy to enter complementary markets (Whinston 1990, Nalebuff 2004, Carlton, Gans, and Waldman 2010). Our results contribute by providing empirical evidence of the implications of tying, looking at a market with considerable quality variation. Our results highlight a quality reduction in short-term quality, and the ability of firms to use the market share resulting from tying to develop a better product.

Our paper also contributes to the debate on dominant online platforms, which have been drawing increasing scrutiny from policymakers concerned about rising industry concentration. While there has been increasing evidence that industry concentration is on the rise, there has been less insight on whether or to what extent incumbent firms are providing better quality products or preventing rivals who can offer better quality products from entering and growing (Autor et al 2017, Rognlie 2015, Barkai 2016, de Loecker and Eeckhout 2017). Our results suggest that dominant platforms may at times be degrading products for strategic purposes, such as excluding competitors in adjacent markets that they are looking to enter or grow in.

## REFERENCES

[1] Michael M. Whinston. 1990. Tying, foreclosure and exclusion. *American Economic Review* 80: 837–859.

[2] Barry Nalebuff. 2004. Bundling as an entry deterrent. *Quarterly Journal of Economics* 119: 159–187.

[3] Dennis W. Carlton, Joshua S. Gans, and Michael Waldman. 2010. Why tie a product consumers don't use? *American Economic Journal: Microeconomics* 2: 85-105 (August 2010).

[4] David Autor, David Dorn, Lawrence F. Katz, Christina Patterson, and John Van Reenen (2017). The Fall of the Labor Share and the Rise of Superstar Firms. *No. 23396. National Bureau of Economic Research, Inc.*

[5] Matthew Rognlie. 2015 Deciphering the fall and rise in the net capital share: accumulation or scarcity? *Brookings papers on economic activity.1: 1-69* (2015).

[6] Simcha Barkai. 2016. Declining labor and capital shares. S*tigler Center for the Study of the Economy & the State New Working Paper Series 2.*

[7] Jan De Loecker and Jan Eeckhout. 2017. The Rise of Market Power and the Macroeconomic Implications. *National Bureau of Economic Research No. w23687.*

[2] http://blog.kelseygroup.com/index.php/2011/03/12/googles-marissa-mayer-at-sxsw-hotpot-heating-up/

# Reputation Inflation

APOSTOLOS FILIPPAS, New York University, USA
JOHN JOSEPH HORTON, New York University, USA
JOSEPH GOLDEN, Collage.com, USA

A solution to marketplace information asymmetries is to have trading partners publicly rate each other post-transaction. Many have shown these ratings are effective; we show that their effectiveness deteriorates over time. The problem is that ratings are prone to inflation, with raters feeling pressure to leave "above average" ratings, which in turn pushes the average higher. This pressure stems from raters' desire to not harm the rated seller. As the potential to harm is what makes ratings effective, reputation systems, as currently designed, sow the seeds of their own irrelevance. Full Paper: https://papers.ssrn.com/sol3/papers.cfm?abstract_id=3136473

CCS Concepts: • **Applied computing → Electronic commerce**; **Economics**; • **Computing methodologies →** *Machine learning*;

Additional Key Words and Phrases: Marketplaces; Reputation systems; Experimentation

Scores of various kinds have long been important sources of information for market participants. In online marketplaces, "reputations" are typically calculated from the numerical feedback scores left by past trading partners. As many have noted, the distribution of feedback scores in various online marketplaces seems implausibly rosy. We examine the reputation system of a large online labor market, and find that the distribution of recent employer feedback for workers is highly top-censored, with an overwhelming majority receiving perfect feedback. However, the distribution has not always been this skewed—the fraction of workers receiving the highest possible rating of 5 stars went from 33% to 85% in just 6 years. Feedback scores in four other online marketplaces for which we could obtain longitudinal data exhibit a similar increase over time (see Figure 1).

To disentangle whether the increase is caused by raters becoming more satisfied or by raters lowering standards, we use longitudinal data that include both the feedback scores and an alternative measure of rater satisfaction. The idea is that if rater satisfaction is also captured by an alternative channel that does not inflate—or inflates at a lower rate—then we can exploit this difference to produce an estimate of inflation in the measure of interest. We find that although alternative satisfaction measures have increased over time, presumably due to improvements in fundamentals—reasons such as higher work quality, associated with higher rater satisfaction—they have not increased nearly as much as the actual, numerical feedback scores. Our estimates vary across different specifications and measures, but show that at least 50% of the increase is inflationary.

We argue that the key to understanding reputation inflation is appreciating the role of costs, and how these costs affect raters. The cost of giving "bad" feedback could provide an explanation for why feedback scores are higher than they would be if more employers reported truthfully. However, it cannot by itself explain the dynamics of ever-higher scores we observe. Inflation requires the cost

Authors' addresses: Apostolos Filippas, New York University, New York, NY, USA, apostolosfilippas@gmail.com; John Joseph Horton, New York University, New York, NY, USA, john.joseph.horton@gmail.com; Joseph Golden, Collage.com, San Francisco, CA, USA, jgolden9@gmail.com.


*ACM EC'18, June 18–22, 2018, Ithaca, NY, USA.* ACM ISBN 978-1-4503-5829-3/18/06.
https://doi.org/10.1145/3219166.3219222

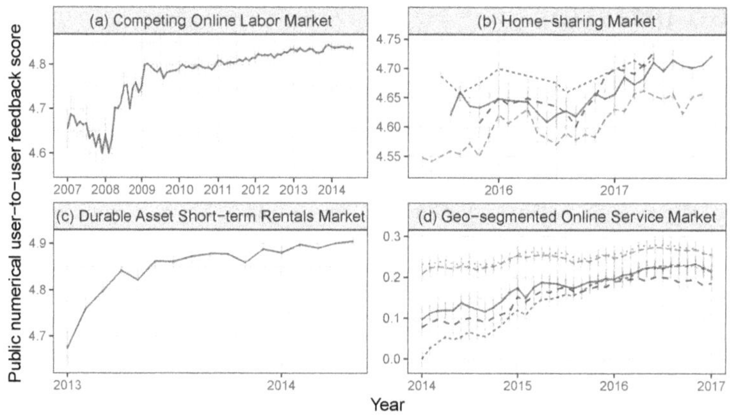


Fig. 1. Longitudinal buyer-on-seller feedback scores for a collection of online marketplaces.

of leaving a given "bad" score to increase over time. We hypothesize this is precisely what happens, with the same nominal feedback score (e.g., 2 "stars") becoming costlier to the rated worker over time, and hence costlier for the rater to give. In other words, the cause of inflation is that what constitutes "bad" feedback—feedback that causes worse market outcome for raters receiving that score—is endogenous, depending on the current distribution of feedback scores, which in turn determines what inferences future buyers make from a score. To formally illustrate how reputations can inflate, we develop a simple model of a marketplace with a reputation system. We show that there exists a unique, stable equilibrium in which sellers only report "good" feedback, regardless of actual performance, and reputations are universally inflated, even when raters derive some benefit from telling the truth.

While our observed data is consistent with our model, we also report evidence from a platform intervention that allows us to test the predictions of our model directly. After collecting private feedback for 10 months, the platform began releasing batched *aggregates* of this private feedback score to would-be employers. With this aggregation, private feedback remained quasi-anonymous, but the private scores became consequential to workers. To the extent that employers care about the fate of workers and do not want to harm their future prospects—or believe that it could get "back" to them—giving "bad" feedback suddenly had a cost, whereas before it had none. Consistent with the predictions of our model, private feedback scores began increasing immediately but there was limited change in the sentiment of written feedback—the no-longer-private feedback became inflated, mirroring what we observed with public feedback.

The complete list of citations and results this study are reported in the full version of this paper [1].

## REFERENCES

[1] Apostolos Filippas, John J Horton, and Joseph Golden. 2018. Reputation inflation. (2018).

# The Price of Prior Dependence in Auctions

PINGZHONG TANG, Tsinghua University, China
YULONG ZENG, Tsinghua University, China

In the standard form of mechanism design, a key assumption is that the designer has reliable information and technology to determine a prior distribution over types of the agents. In the meanwhile, as pointed out by the *Wilson's Principle*, a mechanism should rely as little as possible on the prior type distribution. In this paper, we put forward a simple model to formalize this statement.

In our model, each agent has a true type distribution, according to which his type is drawn. In addition, the agent is able to commit to a fake type distribution and bids rationally as if his type were from the fake distribution (e.g., plays a Bayes equilibrium under the fake distributions).

We investigate the equilibria of the induced distribution-reporting games among bidders, under the context of single-item auctions. We obtain several interesting findings: (1) the game induced by Myerson auction under our model is strategically equivalent to the first-price auction under the standard model. Consequently, the two games are revenue-equivalent. (2) the second-price auction, a well known prior independent auction, yields (weakly) more revenue than several reserve-based and virtual-value-based truthful, prior-dependent auctions, under our model. Our results complement the current literature which aims to show the superiority of prior-independent mechanisms.

CCS Concepts: • **Theory of computation → Algorithmic game theory**; **Computational pricing and auctions**;

Additional Key Words and Phrases: fake distribution, true distribution, Myerson auction, prior-dependent auction

## 1 INTRODUCTION

When designing and analyzing auction mechanisms with incomplete information, it has been assumed that buyers' prior type distributions are common knowledge among all buyers and the seller. For example, *Myerson auction* [20] uses distribution knowledge to calculate the so-called *virtual values*, which are used to determine both allocations and payments of the auction. As another example, in the first-price auction with incomplete information, one must also use distribution knowledge to calculate or verify a Bayes equilibrium (if one can).

This assumption, however, does not always hold in practice for at least two reasons: first, the seller may not have enough data of each bidder, due to lack of sufficient previous interactions; second, it is difficult for the seller to infer the buyers' valuations even if she has sufficient bidding data to do so [21]. Vulnerability of the common knowledge assumption compromises practicality of prior-dependent mechanisms. The central problem of this paper, is to *evaluate a prior-dependent mechanism, under these limitations.*

The problem raised above is both academically important and industrially meaningful. On the one hand, proving superiority of prior-dependent mechanisms, especially those concerning repeated

Authors' addresses: Pingzhong Tang, Tsinghua University, Beijing, 100084, China, kenshinping@gmail.com; Yulong Zeng, Tsinghua University, Beijing, 100084, China, freeof123@qq.com.


*ACM EC'18, June 18–22, 2018, Ithaca, NY, USA.* ACM ISBN 978-1-4503-5829-3/18/06...$15.00
https://doi.org/10.1145/3219166.3219183

interactions between seller and buyers, has been a central research agenda in the mechanism design literature [2, 3, 9, 13, 14]; on the other hand, the problem is important on its own right – a notoriously difficult problem currently faced by major search engines when designing their keywords auctions. In fact, a core project of Baidu advertising is on the design choices between GSP auction with prior-(in)dependent reserves and variants of Myerson auction. For a related choice problem faced by Yahoo! a few years ago between prior dependent and independent reserve prices, see [22].

## 1.1 Description of the model

In this paper, we put forward a model that addresses a type of strategic behaviors in prior-dependent mechanisms and show the consequences (performances of the mechanisms) caused by such strategic behaviors. In our model, each strategic buyer has a true type distribution, the same as in the standard mechanism design formulation. In addition, each buyer can pretend his type is from another distribution, which we call *the fake distribution* in this paper. The way that he convinces others, including the seller, that his type is indeed drawn from the fake distribution, is by consistently playing a Bayes Nash equilibrium in the mechanism *under the fake distribution.* Such strategies are feasible as long as the buyers can indeed commit to such a distribution and doing so increases their expected payoffs. We now demonstrate via Myerson auction that doing so can indeed lead to a higher playoff for the buyer.

*Example 1.1.* Consider the Myerson auction and a setting where there are two bidders, each with valuation drawn independently identically from the uniform distribution on $[0, 1]$. Assume that the first bidder always bids his true valuation. In other words, the bidder's bid distribution is also a uniform distribution on $[0, 1]$. We are interested in how the second bidder reacts. Suppose that the second bidder always bids $\epsilon$ (a sufficient small positive number). By observing the bids distributions for a sufficiently long period, the seller, who believes in truthfulness of Myerson auction, would infer that the first bidder's valuation from the uniform $[0, 1]$, while the second bidder's valuation is exactly $\epsilon$.

Running the Myerson auction with these prior beliefs, the first bidder's virtual value is $2v_1 - 1$ when his true type is $v_1$, while the second bidder's virtual value is always $\epsilon$. The item is allocated to the second buyer if and only if $2v_1 - 1 < \epsilon$, of which the probability is $(\epsilon + 1)/2$. As a result, the second bidder obtains an expected utility of $\int_0^1 \frac{(\epsilon+1)}{2}(v - \epsilon)dv = 1/4 + \epsilon/4 - \epsilon^2/2$.

Compared to the case where the second bidder bids according to the true distribution (i.e., uniform $[0, 1]$) and obtains an expected utility of $1/12$, his utility strictly increases. We will later prove that each bidder reporting a uniform distribution on $[1/4, 1/2]$ is an equilibrium in the induced (distribution-reporting) game.

The model captures a number of important ingredients in applied mechanism design that are not addressed in theory. First of all, it captures the fact that prior information is not endogenous to the mechanism, but has to be inferred from the players' past data. For example, in sponsored search auctions [12], prior distributions are frequently estimated and updated from the past bidding data [7, 22]. This makes prior distributions a part of agents' strategy in the repeated game, rather than constant inputs to the mechanism.

Secondly, it captures a certain dynamic aspect of mechanism design. Our model can be regarded as a sequence of iterations between 1) the seller adjusts their prior estimates of the buyers' valuations based on the bids observed so far; and 2) the buyers strategically best respond, given the current prior estimate and the fact that their current bids will be used against them in the future. Analysis of such dynamics can be complicated. Alternatively, our model focus on the analysis of the steady state resulted from a long, converged sequence of iterations where the seller no longer needs to update the prior and the buyers indeed bid according to this prior. In our model, this steady state corresponds to an equilibrium distribution profile of the induced distribution-reporting game.

Thirdly, it helps explain certain underbidding behaviors of prior-dependent auctions in practice, at least observed and commonly understood within certain major search engines. Many truthful auctions in standard setting are no longer "truthful" in the fake distribution setting.

Last but not least, the model allows one to quantify the damage caused by relying on prior information and to prescribe more less optimistically the outcomes one should expect in these auctions.

## 1.2 Assumptions

The model described above can be reduced to a clean form of distribution-reporting game (Definition 2.4) under the following two assumptions.

(1) The seller's commitment to run an auction of a particular form.
(2) The buyers' commitment to play based on their "fake distributions" in order to optimize long term utility.

The first assumption is directly motivated by the current approach adopted by Baidu (the largest search engine in China). It has been public knowledge (explicitly written in the manual to advertisers) that the search engine has committed to a particular form of prior-dependent mechanism (e.g., GSP with some prior-dependent reserve, which Baidu has been using for the past five years). It is also public knowledge that the search engine regularly updates priors based recent past bids.

The second assumption has been adopted by a recent literature on strategic agents [1, 8, 19]. All these works consider only one bidder, whose valuation is drawn independently from the same type distribution in each round (e.g., a random impression arrives in each round in a sponsored search auction). These work studies the case where the bidder may place suboptimal bidding in each round to optimize their long-term utility. Similar to their work, our bidders also have independent valuation draws each round and play strategically in order to optimize long-term expected utility.

This assumption has also been adopted by [5] who interprets each bidder (or advertiser) as a principal-agent pair. The principal (e.g., the manager of a company) knows how characteristics map into true values, e.g., knows that keyword X is worth 50 cents per click. The agent (e.g., the employee who bids in the auctions) is given instructions by the principal, that keyword X is worth 50 cents. The employee might be myopic and just wants to maximize profit within the current auction, whereas the principal foresees that the instructions she gives will shape the design of future auctions. More specifically, in Burkett's model, the principal proposes to the agent a "contract" that maps the agent's type $t$ to a "new type" $\theta(t)$, as the input to the mechanism. One can regard the fake distribution in our model as a "contract" of the principal – a mapping between each value of buyers' true distribution to a value in the fake distribution – and the agent's behavior follows the contract.

## 1.3 Our contributions

We now report our main findings when applying this model to the single-item auction domain. Our first result, perhaps the least surprising one, states that

**Theorem 1.1** For any prior-independent, truthful mechanism family, it is a weakly dominant strategy for each buyer to report his true distribution.

This suggests that it might be more interesting to look at prior-dependent auctions. We then apply this model to the revenue-optimal auction, aka. the Myerson auction, where we prove one of our main theorems that says the Myerson auction under the fake distribution model is strategically equivalent to the first-price auction in the standard model.

**Theorem 1.2.** The induced distribution-reporting game of Myerson auction is strategically equivalent to first-price auction in the standard setting.

As a result, the two games are revenue equivalent. In other words, Myerson revenue in the fake distribution model is reduced to the revenue of the first-price auction game in the standard setting.

We extend our analysis to a similar prior-dependent auction, called the second-price auction with monopoly (i.e., Myerson's) reserve [15]. This auction is also related to the current Baidu keywords auction mechanism.

**Theorem 1.3** Given that the buyers' true distributions are i.i.d. regular, the revenue of second-price auction with monopoly reserve under the equilibrium of fake distribution is the same as the revenue of second-price auction under the true distribution.

It is important to distinguish Myerson auction and second-price auction with monopoly reserve, even in the i.i.d. case. The allocation rules of the two auctions are the same under the true distribution, but different when computing the equilibrium of fake distributions: to consider a possible deviation, a buyer can report any fake distribution, creating an instance of non-i.i.d. distributions, where the allocation rules for the two auctions differ.

We further generalize the idea of prior-dependent reserve pricing by analyzing second price auction with a random reserve [11, 16].

**Theorem 1.4** Given that the buyers' true distributions are i.i.d., the revenue of second-price auction with any random reserve under the equilibrium of fake distribution is no more than the revenue of second-price auction under the true distribution.

We finally apply this model to a general class of truthful auctions called virtual efficient auctions, where the allocation rule is efficient with respect to an extended definition of virtual value function.

**Theorem 1.5** Given that the buyers' true distributions are i.i.d., the revenue of any virtual efficient mechanism family under the equilibrium of fake distribution is no more than the revenue of second-price auction under the true distribution.

To sum up, for all symmetric cases, second-price auction is (weakly) superior compared to other auctions considered in this paper.

### 1.4 Related work

Recently, driven by online applications at the interface of economics and computer science, there has been a large body of literature on the problem of prior-independent mechanism design [2, 3, 9, 13, 14]. One of the major motivations of these papers is the so-called Wilson's principle [25] , which states that a mechanism should rely as little as possible on the prior distributions. Over the years, the principle has guided many practical auction designs and has been consistent with experiences: auctions that heavily rely on prior distributions are in general not robust and rarely used. Our model can be regarded as a quantitative model for the Wilson's principle.

Independent of our work, a few recent papers [1, 8, 10, 17–19] also consider the general problem where a *single* strategic buyer repeatedly interacts with the seller. The focus of all these papers is on the dynamic and learning aspect of the problem where the buyer learns to play equilibrium. Amin et al. [1], Mohri and Munoz [19] consider a model where the seller posts a price in each time period to a buyer whose valuation is independent random draw in each period. Amin et al. [1] define the strategic regret over $T$ rounds to be the revenue difference between the chosen algorithm and the optimal pricing given each buyer bids truthfully over all rounds. They design an algorithm that yields desirable regret bound. It is interesting that Amin et al. [1] show that for any posted price auction, the optimal fake distribution for a *savvy* buyer would trivially be a small constant function so that the seller wants to set a small price. Mohri and Munoz [19] introduce a notation called $\epsilon - strategic$ buyer where the buyer does not necessarily best respond in each round. They design a sequential posted prices that achieves additive bounds to optimal revenue in two different settings. Chen and Wang [8] study the same setting and make the assumption that the action of the buyer in each round is so chosen as to maximize his overall discounted utility. They show that the seller can design a posted price mechanism that can almost surely learn the buyer's true type and achieve constant additive bound to optimal revenue. Devanur et al. [10], Immorlica et al. [17] analyze the perfect Bayesian equilibria in a repeated game where the buyers act strategically and the seller updates his belief of the prior distributions. Kanoria and Nazerzadeh [18] study a repeated game where each round is a single item second-price auction with reserve price. They give a method for setting the reserve prices dynamically, in order to maximize the seller's total revenue in $T$ rounds. They prove that their method can guarantee $\epsilon$-incentive-compatibility for the buyers and less than $T\epsilon$ revenue difference to the benchmark, when $T$ is large. We remark that our model, even though admits a dynamic and learning interpretation, is essentially a single-shot distribution-reporting game.

Works by Shen et al. [23, 24] analyze similar setting where buyers select distributions. In [23] it is supposed that the distributions chosen by buyers are indeed their true distributions. In [24] the buyer chooses a set of posterior distributions of which the linear combination equals to the prior distribution.

## 2 THE FAKE DISTRIBUTION MODEL

In a single item auction, an auctioneer sells one unit of item to $n$ buyers. Each buyer $i$ has a private valuation $v_i$ towards the item, where each $v_i$ is drawn from a distribution $F_i$. Buyer $i$ reports a bid $b_i(v_i)$ for each $v_i$. We use $B_i$ to denote the distribution of $b_i(v_i), v_i \sim F_i$.

We use a convenient representation of a distribution called *quantile* to establish the mapping between $F_i$ and $B_i$ [4].

*Definition 2.1.* (Quantile). Given a random variable $v$ with cumulative distribution $F(v)$, let $q = 1 - F(v) \in [0, 1]$ denote the quantile of $v$. The function $v(q) = F^{-1}(1 - q) : [0, 1] \to \mathbb{R}_+$ is a mapping from the quantile space to valuation space, and is uniquely determined by distribution $F$.

We use $v_i(\cdot)$ and $b_i(\cdot)$ to denote $F_i$ and $B_i$ in the quantile space respectively, with the independent variable $q$. Note that $q$ is always uniformly distributed on [0,1] and $v_i(\cdot), b_i(\cdot)$ is weakly decreasing. We write $\mathbf{q} = (q_1, q_2, ..., q_n)$ for the profile of quantiles for all buyers.

Let $\mathcal{V}$ denote the set of all weakly decreasing functions that maps $[0, 1]$ to $\mathbb{R}_+$. Let $\Phi$ denote the set of all arrangements[1] $\phi : [0, 1] \to [0, 1]$.

So buyer $i$'s action is to choose a bid distribution $b_i(\cdot) \in \mathcal{V}$ and an arrangement $\phi_i \in \Phi$ such that when buyer $i$'s value is $v_i(q)$, i.e., with quantile $q$, he bids $b_i(\phi_i(q))$. We call $b_i(\cdot)$ the fake distribution, which may be different from $v_i(\cdot)$. We use $\mathbf{b}(\cdot) = (b_1(\cdot), ..., b_n(\cdot))$ to denote the profile of fake distributions.

Standard auction setting takes $F_i$'s as buyers' prior distributions, while in our setting, mathematically speaking, the auctioneer takes $B_i$'s as the priors.

*Definition 2.2.* (Bayesian incentive compatible (BIC) mechanism (Standard))

Given prior $\mathbf{b}(\cdot)$, a (direct) BIC mechanism consists of an allocation rule $x_i : \mathbb{R}_+^n \to [0, 1]$ and a payment rule $t_i : \mathbb{R}_+^n \to \mathbb{R}$, for $i = 1, 2, ..., n$, such that

$$b_i(q_i) \in \arg\max_b \int_{q_{-i}} (b_i(q_i)x_i(b, b_{-i}(q_{-i})) - t_i(b, b_{-i}(q_{-i})))dq_{-i}, \ \forall i = 1, ..., n \ \forall q_i \in [0, 1]$$

We are interested in the outcomes at the truthful Bayes-Nash equilibrium. At such an equilibrium, for each buyer $i$ and his quantile $q_i$, define the *interim allocation* as follows:

[1]An arrangement here is the continuous analogue of permutation, which maps one quantile space (a uniform distribution on [0,1]) to another (also a uniform distribution on [0,1])

$$x_i^*(q_i) = \int_{\mathbf{q}_{-i}} x_i(b_i(q_i), \mathbf{b}_{-i}(\mathbf{q}_{-i}))d\mathbf{q}_{-i},$$

and *interim payment* as follows:

$$t_i^*(q_i) = \int_{q_{-i}} t_i(b_i(q_i), \mathbf{b}_{-i}(\mathbf{q}_{-i}))d\mathbf{q}_{-i}.$$

Note that both $x_i$ and $t_i$ are implicitly dependent on the prior. This motivates the following definition of mechanism family, which makes this fact explicit.

*Definition 2.3.* (Mechanism Family)
A mechanism family $\{M^{\mathbf{w}(\cdot)}|\mathbf{w}(\cdot) \in \mathcal{V}^n\}$ is a collection of mechanisms, one for each prior, so that each mechanism $M^{\mathbf{w}(\cdot)}$ in it takes $\mathbf{w}(\cdot)$ as the prior.

A mechanism family is truthful if every mechanisms in it is BIC.
With the notations ready, the timing of our model can be conveniently described as follows:

(1) The seller commits to a mechanism family $\{M^{\mathbf{w}(\cdot)}|\mathbf{w}(\cdot) \in \mathcal{V}^n\}$.
(2) Buyers report fake distributions $\mathbf{b}(\cdot) \in \mathcal{V}$ and $\phi_i \in \Phi$.
(3) Run the mechanism $M^{\mathbf{b}(\cdot)}$ to give the outcomes (interim allocation and payment).

We are interested in the equilibrium of the induced game:

*Definition 2.4.* (Induced game) Given a mechanism family $\{M^{\mathbf{w}(\cdot)}|\mathbf{w}(\cdot) \in \mathcal{V}^n\}$), the induced game is a normal-form game $(N, A, U)$ where

- $N = \{1, ..., n\}$ is the set of buyers,
- $A = A_1 \times ... \times A_n$. where $A_i = \mathcal{V} \times \Phi$ is the set of actions of buyer $i$.
- $U = \{U_1, ..., U_n\}$: the utility function for each buyer.

In the definition above, $U_i : A \to \mathbb{R}$ denotes the utility function of buyer $i$, such that

$$U_i((b_1(\cdot), \phi_1), ..., (b_n(\cdot), \phi_n) = \int_0^1 (x_i^*(q_i)v_i(\phi_i(q_i)) - t_i^*(q_i))dq_i$$

Where $x_i^*(q_i)$ and $t_i^*(q_i)$ are the interim allocation and payment in mechanism $M^{\mathbf{b}(\cdot)}$.

We will prove immediately in the next section that each buyer $i$ will always want to choose $\phi_i(q_i) = q_i, \forall q_i \in [0, 1]$. As a result, we can omit $\phi$ from the definition of the induced game and equivalently write $A_i = \mathcal{V}$ for brevity:

$$U_i(\mathbf{b}(\cdot)) = \int_0^1 (x_i^*(q_i)v_i(q_i) - t_i^*(q_i))dq_i$$

Denote by $u^*(q_i) = x_i^*(q_i)v_i(q_i) - t_i^*(q_i)$ the *interim utility* for any $q_i$, so that

$$U_i(\mathbf{b}(\cdot)) = \int_0^1 u^*(q_i)dq_i.$$

Game theoretical notions, such as Nash Equilibrium and best response are standard in the induced game. We sometimes refer to Nash equilibrium simply as equilibrium in the induced game.

*Definition 2.5.* Given $\mathbf{b}(\cdot)$, the seller's expected revenue is

$$REV = \sum_{i=1}^n \int_0^1 t_i^*(q_i)dq_i = \sum_{i=1}^n \int_{\mathbf{q}} t_i(\mathbf{b}(\mathbf{q}))d\mathbf{q}$$

## 3 PRELIMINARIES

In this section, we present several technical lemmas useful for the analyses of equilibrium in the induced game of various mechanism families.

In the following, we adopt the interim notations and analyze from buyer $i$'s point of view, as if he is the only buyer. We can therefore omit the subscript $i$ when it is clear from the context.

LEMMA 3.1. *For any truthful mechanism family and fixed* $\mathbf{b}(\cdot)$*, the arrangement* $\phi(q) = q, \forall q \in [0, 1]$ *maximizes the buyer's utility among all possible arrangements.*

In other words, in the induced game, the buyer will always want to map a value that is in quantile $q$ in the true distribution to a value that is also in quantile $q$ in the fake distribution, no matter what the fake distribution is.

Following the approach in Myerson's characterization of BNE [20], we can derive the *payment identity* formula using the quantile representation.

LEMMA 3.2. *(Payment identity) In a BIC mechanism* $M^{\mathbf{b}(\cdot)}$*, suppose* $b(\cdot)$ *is continuous, then the interim allocation* $x^*(q)$ *is weakly decreasing in* $q$*. Moreover, given the buyer's quantile* $q$*, the interim payment satisfies*

$$t^*(q) = b(q)x^*(q) + \int_{r=q}^{1} x^*(r)b'(r)dr - b(1)x^*(1) + t^*(1) \tag{1}$$

Given allocation rule $\mathbf{x} : \mathbb{R}_+^n \to [0, 1]^n$ such that $x^*(q)$ is weakly decreasing, the auctioneer can implement (1) by choosing payment rule

$$t(\mathbf{b}(\mathbf{q})) = b(q)x(\mathbf{b}(\mathbf{q})) - \int_{z=b(1)}^{b(q)} x(z, \mathbf{b}_{-i}(\mathbf{q}_{-i}))dz, \ \forall \mathbf{q} \in [0, 1]^n \tag{2}$$

Payment rule (2) satisfies $-b(1)x^*(1) + t^*(1) = 0$

Lemma 3.2 requires the continuity and boundedness of $b(\cdot)$, In fact, it can be proved that it is sufficient to only consider continuous, bounded fake distributions. So WLOG, we can make this assumption throughout the paper.

LEMMA 3.3. *Given fake distribution profile* $\mathbf{b}(\cdot)$*, the expected utility of the buyer is*

$$U = \int_0^1 x^*(q)(v(q) - r(q))dq + b(1)x^*(1) - t^*(1) \tag{3}$$

*where* $r(q) = b(q) + qb'(q)$*, is known as the virtual value (in [20]).*

The lemma shows that the expected utility equals expectation over true valuation minus virtual value, then times the interim allocation rule. It is similar to the utility formula given in [20] ($\int x^*(q)(b(q) - r(q))dq$) by replacing the fake value into true value but remaining virtual part the same.

LEMMA 3.4. *Given the fake distribution profile* $\mathbf{b}(\cdot)$*, the expected revenue is*

$$REV = \sum_{i=1}^{n}(\int_0^1 x_i^*(q)r(q)dq - b_i(1)x_i^*(1) + t_i^*(1)) \tag{4}$$

Lemme 3.4 follows directly from Lemma 3.3 and Definition 2.5.

For discontinuous or unbounded cases, we have the following:

LEMMA 3.5. *For any auctions considered in this payer, all results for any discontinuous or unbounded distribution are limitations of series of continuous and bounded distribution.*

## 4 PRIOR-INDEPENDENT MECHANISM FAMILIES

We first analyze the easy case where the mechanism family under consideration is independent of priors. We show that in any such mechanism family, it is a weak dominant strategy for each buyer to report the true distribution.

*Definition 4.1.* (Prior-independent mechanism family)
A mechanism family $\{M^{\mathbf{w}(\cdot)} | \mathbf{w}(\cdot) \in \mathcal{V}^n\}$ is prior independent if it is truthful, and when taking any bid profile $\mathbf{b} = (b_1, b_2, ..., b_n)$ as input, $M^{\mathbf{w}(\cdot)}$ returns the same outcome for any $\mathbf{w}(\cdot)$.

By definition, second-price auction (SPA) is a prior-independent mechanism family, while the Myerson auction, second-price auction with monopoly reserve price, are not.

Theorem 4.2. *For any prior-independent mechanism family, it is a weakly dominant strategy for each buyer to report the true distribution in the induced game. Moreover, the buyer's utility increases as $b(q)$ approaches $v(q)$ for any $q$ in a monotone way.*

This theorem is obvious according to the definition of prior-independent family: Since the fake distributions do not affect the choice of the mechanism, the agent should simply bid truthfully according to the true value. Here we still give a formal proof by the payment identity, for the convenience of proofs in section 6.

Proof of Lemma 4.2. Fix other buyers' reports $b_{-i}(\cdot)$, given the quantile $q$ of buyer $i$, by definition of prior-independent mechanism family, the interim allocation $x^*(q)$ only depends on the value of $b(\cdot)$ at quantile $q$, regardless the whole fake distribution $b(\cdot)$. We write $x(b(q)) = x^*(q)$ to reflect this observation. By Lemma 3.2, the buyer's interim utility

$$u^*(q) = v(q)x(b(q)) - b(q)x(b(q)) + \int_0^{b(q)} x(z)dz$$

Note that the term is independent to any other the value $b(q')$ such that $q' \neq q$, so we can maximize $\int_0^1 u^*(r)dr$ case by case for each $r \in [0, 1]$

Define $x'(v) = \frac{dx}{dv}$. We have

$$\frac{du^*(q)}{db(q)} = x'(b(q))(v(q) - b(q))$$

Since $x'(b(q)) \geq 0$, $u_i^*(q)$ is maximized at $b(q) = v(q)$. So the buyer will always want to report $b(q) = v(q)$ at quantile $q$. In addition, for any $q$, the buyer's utility increases as the value of $b(q)$ approaches $v(q)$.

□

## 5 THE MYERSON AUCTION

In this section, we prove our main result that the Myerson auction in the fake distribution model is strategically equivalent to the first-price auction in the standard model.

We first consider the case where we restrict the set of possible fake distributions to regular distributions, i.e., when the virtual value $r(q) = b(q) + qb'(q)$ is weakly decreasing.

Given a buyer's prior distribution $w(\cdot)$ and a bid $b$, define the virtual bid $\phi(b) = b - \frac{1-G(b)}{g(b)}$, where $G$ is the cumulative distribution function on $w(\cdot)$ and $g$ is the probability density function.

*Definition 5.1.* A mechanism $M^{\mathbf{w}(\cdot)}$ in the Myerson mechanism family allocates the item to the buyer with the largest positive virtual bid $\phi(b)$ (with respect to $w(\cdot)$). (If no buyer has positive virtual bid, the seller keeps the item). The payment rule is according to (2).

Under any regular fake distribution profile, it is a truthful mechanism family.

Fix other buyers' fake distributions $b_{-i}(\cdot)$, given the quantile $q$, the interim allocation only depends on the value of $r(\cdot)$ at quantile $q$, but not the whole distribution. As a result, we use $x(r(q))$ to denote $x^*(q)$.

Theorem 5.2. *In Myerson mechanism family, for fixed $b_{-i}(\cdot)$, buyer i's best response of the induced game is*

$$b(q) = \frac{\int_0^q r(s)ds}{q}, q \in [0,1], \quad r(q) = \arg\max_{r(q)\geq 0} x(r(q))(v(q) - r(q)), q \in [0,1] \tag{5}$$

*Furthermore, $b(q)$ is weakly monotone decreasing and regular.*

Proof. For fixed $b_{-i}(\cdot)$, by Lemma 3.3, the buyer's best response $b(q)$ maximizes

$$\int_0^1 x(r(q))(v(q) - r(q))dq. \tag{6}$$

Define $F(q) = x(r(q))(v(q) - r(q))$. The problem becomes to find a $r(\cdot)$ that maximizes $\int_0^1 F(q)dq$. We maximize $\int_0^1 F(q)$ case by case for each $q \in [0,1]$. For any $q$, the solution is

$$r(q) = \arg\max_{r(q)\geq 0} x(r(q))(v(q) - r(q)), q \in [0,1]$$

.

In particular,

$$b(q) = \frac{x(r(q))}{x'(r(q))} + r(q),$$

if $\frac{x(r(q))}{x'(r(q))} + r(q) \geq 0$, where $x'(r) = \frac{dx}{dr}$.

Given such $r(q)$, we solve the differential equation $r(q) = b(q) + qb'(q)$,$q \in [0,1]$ to get $b(q)$. One of the solutions is

$$b(q) = \frac{\int_0^q r(s)ds}{q}.$$

In order to ensure that such $b(q)$ is a distribution and is regular, we need to show the monotonicity of $b(q)$ and $r(q)$. Actually this naturally follows from monotonicity of the BNE in a first-price auction, which is later shown Theorem 5.5.

□

*Example 5.3.* For the case of $n = 2$ and both buyers' true distributions are i.i.d. from uniform [0,1], i.e., $v_1(q) = v_2(q) = 1 - q$. Suppose that buyer two reports the true distribution, i.e. $b_2(q) = 1 - q$, so $r_2(q) = 1 - 2q$. The best response of buyer one in the induced game is $b_1(q) = 0^+$.

It shows that the buyer who executes the manipulate way gets more utility while the others do not.

Proof of Example 5.3. For buyer one's quantile $q$, $F_1(q)$ in (6) is $\frac{r_1(q)+1}{2}(v_1(q) - r_1(q))$,

The optimal non-negative $r_1(q)$ to maximize $F_1(q)$ is $r_1(q) = 0$, for all $q \in [0,1]$.

So the buyer 1's best response in the is $b_1(q) = \epsilon$ (meanwhile, $r(q) = \epsilon$ ). Note that $r_2(q) < 0$ when $q \in (\frac{1}{2}, 1]$. Let $\epsilon \to 0$, buyer 1 guarantees a constant allocation probability $x_1^*(q) = \frac{1}{2}$ for any $q$, with the payment tends to 0.

□

In this example, buyer one's utility is $\frac{1}{4}$, greater than $\frac{1}{12}$, the utility buyer one gets when reporting the true distribution.

*Example 5.4.* For the case of $n = 2$ and both buyers' true distributions are i.i.d. from uniform [0,1], i.e., $v_1(q) = v_2(q) = 1 - q$. Each buyer reports fake distribution $b(q) = \frac{1}{2} - \frac{1}{4}q$ is an equilibrium of induced game in Myerson's mechanism family.

Proof of Example 5.4. Given the other buyer's fake distribution $b_{-i}(q) = \frac{1}{2} - \frac{1}{4}q$, so the corresponding virtual value function $r_{-i}(q) = \frac{1-q}{2}$. So $x(r(q)) = Pr_{q\in[0,1]}[\frac{1-q}{2} \le r(q)] = 2r(q)$. By (6), buyer $i$'s utility is

$$\int_0^1 2r(q)(v(q) - r(q))$$

Fix $q$, $2r(q)(v(q) - r(q))$ get its maximum if $r(q) = \frac{v(q)}{2} = \frac{1-q}{2}$
Solving the differential equation $b(q) + qb'(q) = \frac{1-q}{2}$ we get the solution $b(q) = \frac{1}{2} - \frac{1}{4}q$

□

For the equilibrium in Example 5.4, $U_1 = U_2 = \frac{1}{6}$, expected social welfare $SW = E[\max\{v_1(q), v_2(q)\}] = \frac{2}{3}$, and expected revenue $REV = \frac{1}{3}$.

Compared to the Myerson auction in the standard setting: $U_1 = U_2 = \frac{1}{12}$, $REV = \frac{5}{12}$, $SW = \frac{7}{12}$, the equilibrium in the induced game yields higher buyer utility and social welfare, but less revenue. As a result, it is desirable for the buyers to commit to such fake distributions.

We now prove our main theorem of the section, the equivalence between Myerson auction in the fake distribution model and first-price auction in the standard model.

Theorem 5.5. **(Main Theorem)** *Given* $\mathbf{v}(\cdot)$*, the induced game of Myerson mechanism family is strategically equivalent to the first-price auction in standard setting.*

Note that the utility of Myerson mechanism family only depends on the virtual value function $r(\cdot)$, i.e., for a set of fake distributions that corresponding to a same virtual value function, (the differential function $b(q) + qb'(q) = r(q)$ has multiple solutions of $b(q)$), the buyer has the same utility. So we can simplify the buyer's action to reporting the virtual value function $r(q)$, instead of reporting the fake distribution $b(q)$.

To describe the main theorem of this section, we first rewrite the induced game of Myerson mechanism family in an equivalent way as follows:

*Definition 5.6.* The induced game of Myerson mechanism family given true distribution profile $\mathbf{v}(\cdot)$ is a normal-form game $(N, A, U)$ where

- $N = \{1, ..., n\}$ buyers, indexed by $i$.
- $A = A_1 \times A_2 ... \times A_n$, where $A_1 = A_2 = ... = A_n = \mathcal{V}$. We use $r_i(\cdot) \in \mathcal{V}$ to denote an action of buyer $i$, in other words, the action of buyer $i$ is to choose a virtual value distribution.
- $U = \{U_1, ..., U_n\}$, where $U_i : A \to \mathbb{R}$ denote the utility function of buyer $i$ such that (from 6)

$$U_i(r_1(\cdot), r_2(\cdot), ..., r_n(\cdot)) = \int_0^1 (\int_{q_{-i}} x_i^M(\mathbf{r}(\mathbf{q}))dq_{-i})(v_i(q_i) - r_i(q_i))dq_i$$

where $\mathbf{x}^M$ is the allocation vector in Myerson mechanism, taking $n$ buyers' virtual values as inputs.

Consider a standard first-price auction (FPA) with type distribution profile $\mathbf{v}(\cdot)$, which is a Bayesian game. The buyer's bidding strategy is a function $c(q) : [0, 1] \to \mathbb{R}$ that maps each quantile (equivalently, value) to bid.

Lemma 5.7. *In first-price auction, given buyers' bidding strategy profile* $\mathbf{c}(\cdot)$, *buyer i's expected utility is*

$$\int_0^1 \left(\int_{q_{-i}} x_i^F(\mathbf{c}(\mathbf{q}))dq_{-i}\right)(v_i(q_i) - c_i(q_i))dq_i$$

*where* $\mathbf{x}^F$ *is the allocation vector in first-price auction, given n bids as inputs.*

Proof. In FPA, for a fixed quantile profile $\mathbf{q}$, the buyer pays his/her bid if he/she get the item, and pay 0 otherwise, so the utility is $x_i^F(\mathbf{c}(\mathbf{q}))(v_i(q_i) - b = c_i(q_i))$. As an result, the expected utility is

$$\int_{\mathbf{q}} x_i^F(\mathbf{c}(\mathbf{q}))(v_i(q_i) - c_i(q_i))d\mathbf{q} = \int_0^1 \left(\int_{q_{-i}} x_i^F(\mathbf{c}(\mathbf{q}))dq_{-i}\right)(v_i(q_i) - c_i(q_i))dq_i$$

□

In the same spirit as we defined for induced game of Myerson mechanism family, we can regard the first-price auction as a normal-form game, where each player's action is simply choosing a bidding strategy, and the utility is the expected utility defined above. Formally,

*Definition 5.8.* The induced game of first-price auction given type distribution profile $\mathbf{v}(\cdot)$ is normal-form game $(N, A, U)$ where

- $N = \{1, ..., n\}$ buyers, indexed by $i$
- $A = A_1 \times A_2 ... \times A_n$, where $A_1 = A_2 = ... = A_n = \mathcal{V}$. We use $c_i(\cdot) \in \mathcal{V}$ to denote an action of buyer $i$, in other words, the action of buyer $i$ is to choose a bidding strategy.
- $U = \{U_1, ..., U_n\}$, where $U_i : A \to \mathbb{R}$ denotes the utility function of buyer $i$ such that

$$U_i(c_1(\cdot), c_2(\cdot), ..., c_n(\cdot)) = \int_0^1 \left(\int_{q_{-i}} x_i^F(\mathbf{c}(\mathbf{q}))dq_{-i}\right)(v_i(q_i) - c_i(q_i))dq_i$$

It is natural to only consider decreasing bidding strategy in FPA, since it is not hard to show that any non-decreasing bidding strategy is weakly dominated by a decreasing bidding strategy.

Theorem 5.9. *Given* $\mathbf{v}(\cdot)$, *the induced game of Myerson mechanism family* $(N, \mathcal{V}^n, U^1)$ *is identical to the induced game of FPA* $(N, \mathcal{V}^n, U^2)$.

Proof of Theorem 5.9. To verify that $U^1$ and $U^2$ are the same function, we need to prove that given the same input, i.e, $\mathbf{c}(\cdot) = \mathbf{r}(\cdot)$, we have $U^1(\mathbf{c}(\cdot)) = U^2(\mathbf{r}(\cdot))$.

In fact, $x_F^*$ and $x_M^*$ are exactly the same function: Given a quantile profile $\mathbf{q}$, FPA allocates the item to the buyer with the largest bid $c(q)$, and the Myerson mechanism allocates the item to the buyer with the largest virtual value $r(q)$. As $\mathbf{c}(\cdot) = \mathbf{r}(\cdot)$, the two utilities are indeed the same. This proves the theorem. □

As a result, the two games are revenue equivalent. In other words, Myerson's revenue in the fake distribution setting is reduced to that of the first-price auction in the standard setting.

See again Example 5.4, it is well known that the BNE for first-price auction is $c(v) = \frac{v}{2}$ for valuation distribution uniform in [0,1]. So the virtual value of fake distribution $r(q) = \frac{v(q)}{2} = \frac{1-q}{2}$, the same as the proof of Example 5.4.

Given this result, it is easy to prove the monotonicity of $r(q)$. Since $r(q)$ is the optimal bidding strategy in the corresponding FPA, it must be monotone.

All results so far extend to the case where we allow the buyers to report any, possibly irregular fake distribution. The Myerson auction also extends the general distributions via ironing, a procedure that maps the irregular distribution to a regular distribution, then run Myerson mechanism for the ironed distributions. All our results in this section remain the same, because whenever a buyer reports an irregular distribution, it is equivalent to report the ironed distribution instead.

## 6 SECOND-PRICE AUCTION WITH MONOPOLY RESERVES

Second-price auction with monopoly reserve [15] is an auction that first rejects all the bids below the respective monopoly reserves and run second-price auction on the remaining bids. Since we allow buyers to report any distributions, we need to extend the definition of monopoly reserve to the irregular case. We begin by introducing the revenue curve.

Given a distribution $w(\cdot) \in \mathcal{V}$, let $R(q) = qw(q)$ denote the *revenue curve* of distribution $w(\cdot) \in \mathcal{V}$. The quantile $q^*$ such that $q^* = \arg\max_q R(q)$ is called the reserve quantile for distribution $w(\cdot)$. If there are multiple reserve quantiles, set the reserve quantile to be the largest one. The value $w(q^*)$ is called the monopoly reserve price for distribution $w(\cdot)$.

*Definition 6.1.* (Second-price auction with monopoly reserve (SPAMR) mechanism family)
For any mechainism $M^{\mathbf{w}(\cdot)}$ in a SPAMR mechanism family, it first computes the monopoly reserve price for each buyer $i$ and then allocates the item to the buyer with the largest bid $b$ which is not less than the monopoly reserve price. (If no buyer satisfies this, the seller keeps the items). The payment rule is according to (2).

Clearly, this is a truthful mechanism family.

In this section we fix $b_{-i}(q)$, take distribution $b(q)$ as a variable to be determined.

When reserve price of $b(q)$ is fixed, for a given quantile $q$, and the value of $b(q)$, the interim allocation is all the same in each mechanism from a Second-Price Auction With Monopoly Reserve mechanism family. We write $x^*(q) = x(v(q))$ if it is the case.

Unlike Lemma 4.2, reporting truthfully now leads to a potentially bad reserve price and thus may no longer be a dominant strategy.

In this section, we assume that the true distributions $\mathbf{v}(\cdot)$ are regular. We further consider two cases: in this first case, the mechanism family allows buyers to report any fake distributions, while in the second case, the mechanism family only allows buyers to report regular fake distributions.

### 6.1 Case one: buyers can report any fake distribution

In this case, we have the following two results, which essentially state that there are cases where there does not exist a symmetric equilibrium in the induced game.

THEOREM 6.2. *In the induced game of SPAMR mechanism family, fix $b_{-i}(\cdot)$, there exists R such that, it is WLOG to consider $b(\cdot)$ with the following form:*

- *for $q_3 \le q \le 1$, $b(q) = R$*
- *for $q_2 \le q < q_3$ or $0 \le q < q_1$, $b(q) = v(q)$*
- *for $q_1 \le q < q_2$, $b(q) = \frac{R}{q}$*

*Where $q_1 v(q_1) = R$, $q_2 v(q_2) = R$, $q_1 < q_2$, $v(q_3) = R$.*

THEOREM 6.3. *For any buyers' true distributions that are i.i.d. regular with minimum support at 0 and do not have a point mass, there does not exist a symmetric equilibrium in the induced game.*

First let $q^*$ denote the reserve quantile of $v(\cdot)$ (where the revenue curve $qv(q)$ get its maximum), and define $R^* = q^* v(q^*)$. $q^*$ and $R^*$ are constants given the true distribution. Let $\hat{q}^*$ denote the reserve quantile of $b(\cdot)$, and define $R = \hat{q}^* b(\hat{q}^*)$. $\hat{q}^*$ and $R$ are to be determined.

To prove Theorem 6.2 and 6.3, we introduce following lemmas:

LEMMA 6.4. *Subject to $\hat{q}^*$, $R$ unchanging, for any $q$, the buyer's utility weakly increases when the value of $b(q)$ approaches $v(q)$.*

PROOF. Note that by the definition, the reserve price $b(q^*) = \frac{R}{\hat{q}^*}$ is also fixed. Directly from the proof of Lemma 4.2, $u^*(q)$ increases for all $q < q^*$, as $b(q)$ approaches $v(q)$. So the buyer's utility also increases.

□

LEMMA 6.5. *It is without loss of generality to only consider $b(\cdot)$ subject to $R \leq R^*$.*

PROOF. Suppose $R > R^* = v(q^*)q^*$. We change the distribution $b(\cdot)$ as follows: for all $q < \hat{q}^*$ such that $qb(q) > R^*$, set $b(q) = \frac{R^*}{q}$. After the change, every $b(q)$ get closer to $v(q)$ and the reserve price decreases. (Note that after the change the reserve quantile $\hat{q}^*$ remains the same.) By Lemma 4.2, each interim utility $u^*(q)$ increases for all $q < q^*$. Since for $q > q^*$, the utility is always 0, we can conclude that the overall utility increases. □

So we only need to consider the case where $R \leq R^*$. Since $v(\cdot)$ is a regular distribution, $qv(q)$ is concave with $q$, let $q_1, q_2$ denote the two intersection points between revenue curve $qv(q)$ and straight line $y = R$. (If $R = R^*$, set $q_1 = q_2$. If $v(1) > R$, set $q_2 = 1$). It's easy to see that it is not optimal when $\hat{q}^* < q_2$. Let $q_3$ denote the quantile of the intersection between revenue curve $y = qv(q)$ and straight line $((0, 0), (\hat{q}^*, R))$. If $v(1) > R$, set $q_3 = 1$, otherwise $q_3$ always exists and $q_2 < q_3 < 1$.

LEMMA 6.6. *For fixed R subject to $R \leq R^*$ and fixed reserve quantile $\hat{q}^*$, it is without loss of generality to consider only $b(\cdot)$ with the following form.*

- *For q s.t. $\hat{q}^* < q < 1$, $b(q)$ can be any value less than $\frac{R}{q^*}$,*
- *For q s.t. $q_3 < q < q^*$, $b(q) = \frac{R}{\hat{q}^*}$ (constant),*
- *For q s.t. $q_2 < q < q_3$ or $0 < q < q_1$, $b(q) = v(q)$ (truthful)*
- *For q s.t. $q_1 < q < q_2$, $b(q) = \frac{R}{v}(q)$ (equal revenue curve)*

*(the revenue curve of $b(q)$ is the red line (line $Oq_1q_2q_3\hat{q}^*$) in Figure 1.*

PROOF. Given $R$ and $\hat{q}^*$ fixed, the feasible domain of $b(q)$ is $[\frac{R}{\hat{q}^*}, \frac{R}{q}]$, i.e. the revenue curve $qb(q)$ in figure 1 should below the line $y = R$ and above the line $((0, 0), (\hat{q}^*, R))$. Then by Lemma 6.4 we should choose the value in the feasible region that is the closest to $v(q)$, so the revenue curve of the best response distribution is the red line (line $Oq_1q_2q_3\hat{q}^*$). □

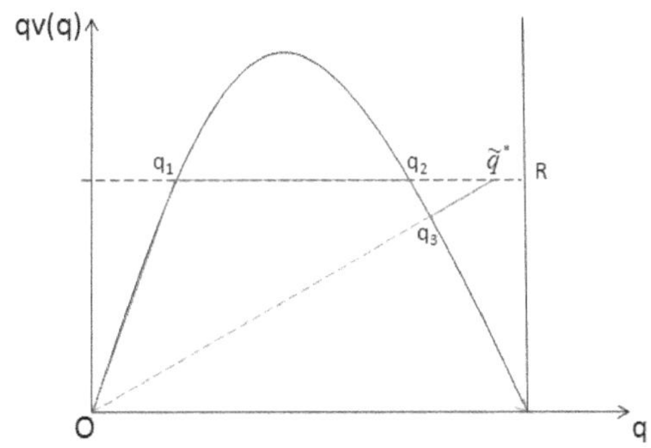


Fig. 1. Best response to SPA with Myerson reserve

LEMMA 6.7. *For fixed R, and suppose $b(\cdot)$ has the form in Lemma 6.6, it is without loss of generality to set $\hat{q}^* = 1$.*

So Theorem 6.2 is proved.

Lemma 6.8. *For fixed R, the buyer's utility by reporting the best response distribution described in Lemmas 6.6 and 6.7 is given by,*

$$U = \int_0^{q_1} x(v(q))(-qv'(q))dq + \int_{q_1}^{q_2} x(\frac{R}{q})v(q)dq + \int_{q_2}^{q_3} x(v(q))(-qv'(q)) + \int_{q_3}^{1} x(R)(v(q) - R)dq$$

*where* $q_1 v(q_1) = R, q_2(q_2) = R, v(q_3) = R$.

To prove 6.3, we first show that $b(\cdot)$ with the form given in Theorem 6.2 can not be in a symmetric equilibrium.

Lemma 6.9. *For any buyers' true distributions that are i.i.d. regular, if* $v(1) = 0$ *and the best response given by Lemma 6.6 and 6.7 is unique, then there does not exist a symmetric equilibrium of fake distribution.*

It remains to show that the best response of fake distribution is unique. We have following lemmas.

Lemma 6.10. *For any buyers' true distributions that are i.i.d. regular and do not have a point mass, the symmetric equilibrium of fake distribution can not have a point mass.*

Lemma 6.11. *For any buyers' true distributions that are i.i.d. regular and do not have a point mass, if there exists a symmetric equilibrium of fake distribution with fixed R and reserve quantile* $\hat{q}^*$, *then the best response of fake distribution given by Lemma 6.6 is unique.*

Theorem 6.3 then follows from Lemmas 6.10 and 6.11.

Combining Lemma 6.6, Lemma 6.10 and Lemma 6.11, we conclude that in symmetric environment there is no equilibrium of fake distribution. Nevertheless, Theorem 6.2 can be used to solve equilibriums in asymmetric cases.

### 6.2 Case two: buyer can only report a regular fake distribution

In this subsection, we focus on the case where buyers can only report regular fake distributions. Any mechanism family can achieve this by leaving buyers who reporting irregular fake distribution 0 utility. We show that, if buyers distribution are i.i.d, then SPAMR in the induced game yields the same revenue as second price auction with the same true type distributions.

Theorem 6.12. *There exists a quantile* $q_0$ *such that it is without generality to only consider* $b(\cdot)$ *with the following form*

- *For all* $q < q_0$, $b(q) = v(q)$
- *For all* $q \geq q_0$, $b(q) = \frac{q_0 v(q_0)}{q}$

We call the corresponding $q_0$ the incident quantile of the buyer.

*Example 6.13.* In SPAMR mechanism family, for the case where $n = 2$ and the buyers' true distribution are i.i.d. from uniform [0,1], i.e. $v_1(q) = v_2(q) = 1 - q$, then the following fake distribution is an equilibrium of the induced game.

- for $0 \leq q < \frac{1}{4}$ ,$b_i(q) = 1 - q$,
- for $\frac{1}{4} \leq q \leq 1$, $b_i(q) = \frac{3}{16q}$

Theorem 6.14. *In SPAMR family, for the case where the buyers' true distributions are i.i.d. regular, the revenue yielded by the symmetric Nash equilibrium of the induced game is equal to the revenue of the SPA under the true distribution.*

In this setting, the revenue curve of fake distribution is a concave function. Let $\hat{q}^*$ denote the reserve quantile (where the $qb(q)$ is maximized), then from 0 to $\hat{q}^*$, $qb(q)$ is weakly increasing. Define $R = \hat{q}^* b(\hat{q}^*)$. $R$ and $q^*$ are to be determined.

Lemma 6.15. *It is without loss of generality to only consider $b(\cdot)$ subject to $\hat{q}^* = 1$.*

Proof. If $\hat{q}^* < 1$, set $b(q) = \frac{R}{q}$ for all $q \in [\hat{q}^*, 1]$. The utility increases by $\int_{\hat{q}^*}^1 x(\frac{R}{q})v(q)dq > 0$. So $\hat{q}^* = 1$ □

Proof of Theorem 6.12. First of all, by a similar argument as in Lemma 6.5, we have $R \le R^*$.

By Lemma 6.15, we can assume WLOG that $\hat{q}^* = 1$. So the revenue curve $qb(q)$ is weakly increasing in [0,1]. Let $q_2$ denote the quantile of the intersection between $qb(q)$ and the right part of revenue curve $qv(q)$ ($q \in [q^*, 1]$). If $q_2$ does not exist (i.e. $v(1) > b(1)$), set $q_2 = 1$.

For all $q \in [0, q_2]$, since $qb(q)$ is increasing, $b(q) \le \frac{q_2 b(q_2)}{q}$. By Lemma 4.2, $b(q)$ should be the value in this region that is the closest to $v(q)$, i.e. $\hat{q} = \min\{\frac{q_2 b(q_2)}{q}, v(q)\}$. Let $q_1$ denote the quantile of the intersection between straight line $y = q_2 b(q_2)$ and the left part of revenue curve $qv(q)$ ($q \in [0, q^*]$). So $b(q) = v(q)$ for $q \in [0, q_1]$ and $b(q) = \frac{q_2 b(q_2)}{q}$ for $q \in [q_1, q_2]$.

For $q \in [q_2, 1]$, set $b(q) = \frac{q_2 b(q_2)}{q}$, which is the minimum possible value of revenue curve (since $qb(q)$ is increasing). After this change, the reserve price $b(1)$ weakly decreases, and all $b(q)$ gets closer to $v(q)$ (since $qv(q)$ is decreasing for $q > q_2$). By Lemma 4.2 the total utility increases.

To sum up, the fake distribution $b(\cdot)$ has the form in the Theorem 6.12 (the incident quantile is $q_1$), and satisfies concavity and monotonicity. □

For each buyer $i$, let $q_i$ denote the incident quantile.

Lemma 6.16. *Buyer $i$'s utility of reporting the best response in Lemma Theorem 6.12 is*

$$U_i = \int_0^{q_i} x(v(q))(-qv'(q))dq + \int_{q_i}^1 x(v(\frac{q_i v(q_i)}{q}))v(q)dq$$

*In an equilibrium of the induced game, $\frac{dU_1}{q_1} = \frac{dU_2}{q_2} = \ldots = \frac{dU_n}{q_n} = 0$*

For the i.i.d case, the following lemma shows the property of the incident quantile. We first proof the case where $n = 2$ for a better understanding.

Lemma 6.17. *Suppose $n = 2$ and true distributions are i.i.d. regular, for symmetric equilibrium of the induced game, the incident quantile $q_0$ (identical to both buyers) satisfies*

$$q_0 - 1 + \frac{1}{q_0 v(q_0)} \int_{q_0}^1 qv(q)dq = 0$$

Proof of Example 6.13. By Lemma 6.17, we have $q_0 - 1 + \frac{1}{q_0(1-q_0)}(\frac{1}{6} - \frac{1}{2}q_0^2 + \frac{1}{3}q_0^3) = 0$
Solving this equation we get $q_0 = \frac{1}{4}$. □

The revenue in the example is $REV = 2\int_0^{\frac{1}{4}}(1-q)(1-2q)dq = \frac{1}{3}$

Compared to SPA in the standard setting, buyer's utility and social welfare increase, while the revenue remains the same. This is not a coincidence. In the following, we prove Theorem 6.14 that says for i.i.d., regular true distributions, the revenue of the equilibrium in SPAMR equals to the revenue of SPA in standard setting.

Proof of Theorem 6.14. We prove the case when $n = 2$. For $n > 2$ a similar proof applies. By Theorem 6.12 and Lemma 3.4

$$\begin{aligned} REV &= 2\int_0^{q_0}(1-q)(v(q)+qv'(q))dq = 2\int_0^{q_0}(1-q)d(qv(q)) \\ &= 2q_0(1-q_0)v(q_0)+2\int_0^{q_0}qv(q)dq \end{aligned}$$

By Lemma 6.18, we have $(1-q_0)q_0v(q_0) = \int_{q_0}^1 qv(q)dq$

Combine the two equations above together we get $REV = 2\int_0^1 qv(q)dq$

Note that the revenue of second-price auction is

$$REV_2 = 2\int_0^1(1-q)(v(q)+qv'(q))dq = 2\int_0^1 qv(q)dq,$$

So $REV = REV_2$ □

## 7 SECOND-PRICE AUCTION WITH RESERVES IN QUANTILE

In this section, we study further an type of auction family in which the reserves are described in quantile. Our conclusion of this section is, when buyers are i.i.d, this auction family yields less revenue than second price auction in the fake distribution model.

*Definition 7.1.* Second-price auction with random quantile reserve (SPARQR)

Each mechanism $M^{w(\cdot)}$ in the mechanism family first draws a random quantile $q_r$ from uniform $[0, 1]$, and allocates the item to the buyer with the largest bid $b$ subject to $b \geq w(q_r)$ (If none of the buyers satisfies the constraint, the seller keeps the items). The payment rule is derived by (2).

If the distribution $w(\cdot)$ does not have a point mass, the mechanism is known as the *single sample mechanism* [16].

Theorem 7.2. *In SPARQR mechanism family, for the case where $n = 2$ and buyers' true distributions are i.i.d., fake distribution $b(\cdot)$ subject to $v(q) = b(q) - qb'(q)$, $\forall q \in [0, 1]$ and $v(1) = b(1)$ is weakly decreasing and is an equilibrium distribution of the induced game.*

*Example 7.3.* In SPARQR mechanism family, for the case where $n = 2$ and buyers' true distributions are i.i.d. from uniform [0,1], then $b(q) = 1 - q + q\ln q$ is an equilibrium of the induced game.

Note that $\ln q > \frac{q-1}{q}$ so $b(q) \geq 0$, $b'(q) = \ln q \leq 0$, which is a feasible distribution.

Theorem 7.4. *In the SPARQR mechanism family, if n buyers' true distributions are i.i.d., the revenue under the equilibrium of the induced game is no more than the revenue of second price auction under the true distribution.*

## 8 VIRTUAL EFFICIENT MECHANISM FAMILY

Most auction families in the single-item case can be regarded as a comparison of specific "virtual value" [6], in which each mechanism allocates the item to the buyers with the largest "virtual value" and the payments are set according to (2). Here, the "virtual value" is defined with respect to a buyer's fake distribution. In this section, we consider a class of truthful mechanism family in which the "virtual value" $R$ can be written as a functional of the fake distribution $b(\cdot)$, i.e., $R = R(q, b(q), b'(q))$.

For the buyer with fake distribution $b(\cdot)$, in the value space, we define $R$ equivalently, i.e., $R(v) = R(v, G, g)$, where $G$ is the cumulative distribution function on $b(\cdot)$ and $g$ is the probability density function. Given a bid $b$, let $R(b)$ denote the "virtual bid" .

*Definition 8.1.* In a virtual efficient mechanism family (VE), each mechanism allocate the item to the buyers with the largest "virtual bid" $R(b)$. The payment rule is set according to (2).

Note the Myerson mechanism and second-price with monopoly reserve are not included in this definition, since both auctions use the ironed virtual value $\bar{r}(q)$, which can not be written as a simple functional for irregular fake distributions.

LEMMA 8.2. *For a truthful VE mechanism family,* $\frac{\partial R}{\partial b'(q)} = 0$, $\frac{\partial R}{\partial q} \leq 0$, $\frac{\partial R}{\partial b(q)} \geq 0$.

PROOF OF LEMMA 8.2. Since the mechanism family is truthful, for any fake distribution $b(\cdot)$, the allocation rule is monotone. Then $\frac{dR}{dq} \leq 0$ for any decreasing function $b(\cdot)$, so for any $q \in [0, 1]$

$$\frac{dR(q, b(q), b'(q))}{dq} = \frac{\partial R}{\partial q} + \frac{\partial R}{\partial b}b'(q) + \frac{\partial R}{\partial b'}b''(q) \leq 0 \tag{7}$$

For any given $q, b(q), b'(q)$, if $\frac{\partial R}{\partial b'} \neq 0$, set $b''(q)$ to be a sufficiently large value (for positive $\frac{\partial R}{\partial b'}$) or sufficiently small (for negative $\frac{\partial R}{\partial b'}$), then the left side of (7) is positive, contradiction.

So $\frac{\partial R}{\partial b'} = 0$. Given this, for any given $q, b(q)$, set $b'(q) = 0$, from (7) we get $\frac{\partial R}{\partial q} \leq 0$. Set $b'(q)$ sufficiently small, we get $\frac{\partial R}{\partial b(q)} \geq 0$. □

Fix the other buyer's fake distribution, given quantile $q$, the interim allocation can be written as a function of $R$, and by Lemma 8.2, we write $x^*(q) = x(R(q, b(q)))$

LEMMA 8.3. *For a truthful, VE mechanism family, in the i.i.d. case, if there exists a symmetric equilibrium, then the fake distribution $b(\cdot)$ in equilibrium satisfies $b(q) \leq v(q)$ for any $q$.*

THEOREM 8.4. *If the buyers' true distributions are i.i.d., the revenue of any VE family under the equilibrium of induced game is no more than the revenue of second-price auction under the true distributions.*

PROOF OF THEOREM 8.4. The revenue on equilibrium of fake distribution is

$$REV = n\int_0^1 (1-q)^{n-1}(b(q) + qb(q))dq = n\int_0^1 (1-q)^{n-1}d(qb(q)) = \int_0^1 (n-1)(1-q)^{n-2}b(q)dq$$

Substitute $b$ for $v$ we get the revenue of second-price auction $\int_0^1 (n-1)(1-q)^{n-2}v(q)dq$
By Lemma 8.3, we get $REV \leq REV_2$.

□

## ACKNOWLEDGMENTS

This paper is supported in part by the National Natural Science Foundation of China Grant 61561146398, a China Youth 1000-talent Program and an Alibaba Innovative Research Program.

A previous version of the paper has been presented at AGT and Data Science workshop of EC-16. The authors are grateful for comments provided by the participants of the workshop.

## REFERENCES


[1] Kareem Amin, Afshin Rostamizadeh, and Umar Syed. 2013. Learning prices for repeated auctions with strategic buyers. In *Advances in Neural Information Processing Systems*. 1169–1177.

[2] Dirk Bergemann and K Schlag. 2011. Should I stay or should I go? Search without priors. mimeo, available at: http://www. gtcenter. org/Archive/2011/Conf/Schlag1314. pdf (last accessed 18 April 2014).

[3] Dirk Bergemann and Karl H Schlag. 2008. Pricing without priors. *Journal of the European Economic Association* 6, 2-3 (2008), 560–569.

[4] Jeremy Bulow and John Roberts. 1989. The simple economics of optimal auctions. *The Journal of Political Economy* (1989), 1060–1090.

[5] Justin Burkett. 2016. Optimally constraining a bidder using a simple budget. *Theoretical Economics* 11, 1 (2016), 133–155.

[6] Yang Cai, Constantinos Daskalakis, and S Matthew Weinberg. 2012. An algorithmic characterization of multi-dimensional mechanisms. In *Proceedings of the forty-fourth annual ACM symposium on Theory of computing*. ACM, 459–478.

[7] Shuchi Chawla, Jason Hartline, and Denis Nekipelov. 2014. Mechanism design for data science. In *Proceedings of the fifteenth ACM conference on Economics and computation*. ACM, 711–712.

[8] Xi Chen and Zizhuo Wang. 2016. Bayesian Dynamic Learning and Pricing with Strategic Customers. *Available at SSRN 2715730* (2016).

[9] Nikhil Devanur, Jason Hartline, Anna Karlin, and Thach Nguyen. 2011. Prior-independent multi-parameter mechanism design. In *Internet and Network Economics*. Springer, 122–133.

[10] Nikhil R Devanur, Yuval Peres, and Balasubramanian Sivan. 2015. Perfect bayesian equilibria in repeated sales. In *Proceedings of the Twenty-Sixth Annual ACM-SIAM Symposium on Discrete Algorithms*. SIAM, 983–1002.

[11] Peerapong Dhangwatnotai, Tim Roughgarden, and Qiqi Yan. 2015. Revenue maximization with a single sample. *Games and Economic Behavior* 91 (2015), 318–333.

[12] Benjamin Edelman, Michael Ostrovsky, and Michael Schwarz. 2005. *Internet advertising and the generalized second price auction: Selling billions of dollars worth of keywords*. Technical Report. National Bureau of Economic Research.

[13] Hu Fu, Jason Hartline, and Darrell Hoy. 2013. Prior-independent auctions for risk-averse agents. In *Proceedings of the fourteenth ACM conference on Electronic commerce*. ACM, 471–488.

[14] Hu Fu, Nicole Immorlica, Brendan Lucier, and Philipp Strack. 2015. Randomization beats second price as a prior-independent auction. In *Proceedings of the Sixteenth ACM Conference on Economics and Computation*. ACM, 323–323.

[15] Jason D Hartline and Tim Roughgarden. 2009. Simple versus optimal mechanisms. In *Proceedings of the 10th ACM conference on Electronic commerce*. ACM, 225–234.

[16] Zhiyi Huang, Yishay Mansour, and Tim Roughgarden. 2015. Making the most of your samples. In *Proceedings of the Sixteenth ACM Conference on Economics and Computation*. ACM, 45–60.

[17] Nicole Immorlica, Brendan Lucier, Emmanouil Pountourakis, and Samuel Taggart. 2017. Repeated sales with multiple strategic buyers. In *Proceedings of the 2017 ACM Conference on Economics and Computation*. ACM, 167–168.

[18] Yash Kanoria and Hamid Nazerzadeh. 2014. Dynamic reserve prices for repeated auctions: Learning from bids. *Available at SSRN 2444495* (2014).

[19] Mehryar Mohri and Andres Munoz. 2015. Revenue optimization against strategic buyers. In *Advances in Neural Information Processing Systems*. 2530–2538.

[20] Roger B Myerson. 1981. Optimal auction design. *Mathematics of operations research* 6, 1 (1981), 58–73.

[21] Denis Nekipelov, Vasilis Syrgkanis, and Eva Tardos. 2015. Econometrics for learning agents. In *Proceedings of the Sixteenth ACM Conference on Economics and Computation*. ACM, 1–18.

[22] Michael Ostrovsky and Michael Schwarz. 2011. Reserve prices in internet advertising auctions: A field experiment. In *Proceedings of the 12th ACM conference on Electronic commerce*. ACM, 59–60.

[23] Weiran Shen, Pingzhong Tang, and Yulong Zeng. 2018. Buyer-Optimal Distribution. In *Proceedings of the 17th Conference on Autonomous Agents and MultiAgent Systems*. International Foundation for Autonomous Agents and Multiagent Systems.

[24] Weiran Shen, Pingzhong Tang, and Yulong Zeng. 2018. A Closed-Form Characterization of Buyer Signaling Schemes in Monopoly Pricing. In *Proceedings of the 17th Conference on Autonomous Agents and MultiAgent Systems*. International Foundation for Autonomous Agents and Multiagent Systems.

[25] Robert Wilson. 1985. *Game-Theoretic Analysis of Trading Processes*. Technical Report. DTIC Document.

# Prior-Independent Optimal Auctions

AMINE ALLOUAH, Columbia University, USA
OMAR BESBES, Columbia University, USA

Auctions are widely used in practice. While also extensively studied in the literature, most of the developments rely on significant assumptions about common knowledge on the seller and buyers' sides. In this work, we study the design of optimal prior-independent selling mechanisms. In particular, the seller faces buyers whose values are drawn from an unknown distribution, and only knows that the distribution belongs to a particular class. We analyze a competitive ratio objective, in which the seller attempts to optimize the worst-case fraction of revenues garnered compared to those of an oracle with knowledge of the distribution. Our results are along two dimensions. We first characterize the structure of optimal mechanisms. Leveraging such structure, we then establish tight lower and upper bounds on performance, leading to a crisp characterization of optimal performance for a spectrum of families of distributions. In particular, our results imply that a second price auction is an optimal mechanism when the seller only knows that the distribution of buyers has a monotone increasing hazard rate, and guarantees at least 71.53% of the optimal revenue against any distribution within this class. Furthermore, a second price auction is near-optimal when the class of admissible distributions is that of those with increasing virtual values (aka regular). Under this class, it guarantees a fraction of 50% of optimal revenues and no mechanism can guarantee more than 55.6%.

Full Paper: https://ssrn.com/abstract=3124738

CCS Concepts: • **Theory of computation → Algorithmic mechanism design**;

Additional Key Words and Phrases: optimal auctions; limited information; prior-independent; maximin ratio.

We thank the reviewers for their valuable feedback.

Authors' addresses: Amine Allouah, Columbia University, 3022 Broadway , New York, NY, 10027, USA, mallouah19@gsb.columbia.edu; Omar Besbes, Columbia University, 3022 Broadway , New York, NY, 10027, USA, ob2105@gsb.columbia.edu.


*ACM EC'18, June 18–22, 2018, Ithaca, NY, USA.* ACM ISBN 978-1-4503-5829-3/18/06.
https://doi.org/10.1145/3219166.3219212

# Learning to Bid Without Knowing your Value

ZHE FENG, Harvard University, USA
CHARA PODIMATA, Harvard University, USA
VASILIS SYRGKANIS, Microsoft Research, New England, USA

We address online learning in complex auction settings, such as sponsored search auctions, where the value of the bidder is unknown to her, evolving in an arbitrary manner and observed only if the bidder wins an allocation. We leverage the structure of the utility of the bidder and the partial feedback that bidders typically receive in auctions, in order to provide algorithms with regret rates against the best fixed bid in hindsight, that are *exponentially faster* in convergence in terms of dependence on the action space, than what would have been derived by applying a generic bandit algorithm and almost equivalent to what would have been achieved in the full information setting. Our results are enabled by analyzing a new online learning setting with outcome-based feedback, which generalizes learning with feedback graphs. We provide an online learning algorithm for this setting, of independent interest, with regret that grows only logarithmically with the number of actions and linearly only in the number of potential outcomes (the latter being very small in most auction settings). Last but not least, we show that our algorithm outperforms the bandit approach experimentally and that this performance is robust to dropping some of our theoretical assumptions or introducing noise in the feedback that the bidder receives.

CCS Concepts: • **Information systems → Sponsored search advertising**; • **Theory of computation → Online learning algorithms**; **Algorithmic game theory and mechanism design**;

## 1 INTRODUCTION

A standard assumption in the majority of the literature on auction theory and mechanism design is that participants that arrive in the market have a clear assessment of their valuation for the goods at sale. This assumption might seem acceptable in small markets with infrequent auction occurrences and amplitude of time for participants to do market research on the goods. However, it is an assumption that is severely violated in the context of the digital economy.

In settings like online advertisement auctions or eBay auctions, bidders participate very frequently in auctions that they have very little knowledge about the good at sale, e.g. the value produced by a user clicking on an ad. It is unreasonable, therefore, to believe that the participant has a clear picture of this value. However, the inability to pre-assess the value of the good before arriving to the market is alleviated by the fact that due to the large volume of auctions in the digital economy, participants can employ *learning-by-doing* approaches.

In this paper we address exactly the question of *how would you learn to bid approximately optimally in a repeated auction setting where you do not know your value for the good at sale and where that value could potentially be changing over time.* The setting of learning in auctions with an unknown value poses an interesting interplay between exploration and exploitation that is not

Authors' addresses: Zhe Feng, Harvard University, 33 Oxford Street, Cambridge, MA, 02138, USA, zhe_feng@g.harvard.edu; Chara Podimata, Harvard University, 33 Oxford Street, Cambridge, MA, 02138, USA, podimata@g.harvard.edu; Vasilis Syrgkanis, Microsoft Research, New England, 1 Memorial Drive, Cambridge, MA, 02142, USA, vasy@microsoft.com.


*ACM EC'18, June 18–22, 2018, Ithaca, NY, USA.* ACM ISBN 978-1-4503-4529-3/18/06...$15.00
https://doi.org/10.1145/3219166.3219208

standard in the online learning literature: in order for the bidder to get feedback on her value she has to bid high enough to win the good with higher probability and hence, receive some information about that underlying value. However, the latter requires paying a higher price. Thus, there is an inherent trade-off between value-learning and cost. The main point of this paper is to address the problem of learning how to bid in such unknown valuation settings with partial *win-only feedback*, so as to minimize the regret with respect to the best fixed bid in hindsight.

On one extreme, one can treat the problem as a Multi-Armed Bandit (MAB) problem, where each possible bid that the bidder could submit (e.g. any multiple of a cent between 0 and some upper bound on her value) is treated as an arm. Then, standard MAB algorithms (see e.g. [14]) can achieve regret rates that scale *linearly* with the number of such discrete bids. The latter can be very slow and does not leverage the structure of utilities and the form of partial feedback that arises in online auction markets. Recently, the authors in [42] addressed learning with such type of partial feedback in the context of repeated single-item second-price auctions. However, their approach does not address more complex auctions and is tailored to the second-price auction.

**Our Contributions.** Our first main contribution is to introduce a novel online learning setting with partial feedback, which we denote *learning with outcome-based feedback* and which could be of independent interest. We show that our setting captures online learning in many repeated auction scenarios including all types of single-item auctions, value-per-click sponsored search auctions, value-per-impression sponsored search auctions and multi-item auctions.

Our setting generalizes the setting of learning with feedback graphs [4, 35], in a way that is crucial for applying it to the auction settings of interest. At a high level, the setting is defined as follows: The learner chooses an action $b \in B$ (e.g. a bid in an auction). The adversary chooses an *allocation function* $x_t$, that maps an action to a distribution over a set of potential outcomes $O$ (e.g. the probability of getting a click) and a *reward function* $r_t$ that maps an action-outcome pair to a reward (utility conditional on getting a click with a bid of $b$). Then, an outcome $o_t$ is chosen based on distribution $x_t(b)$ and a reward $r_t(b, o_t)$ is observed. The learner also gets to observe the function $x_t$ and the reward function $r_t(\cdot, o_t)$ for the realized outcome $o_t$ (i.e. in our auction setting: she learns the probability of a click, the expected payment as a function of her bid and, *if she gets clicked*, her value).

Our second main contribution is an algorithm which we call WIN-EXP, which achieves regret $O\left(\sqrt{T|O|\log(|B|)}\right)$. The latter is inherently better than the generic multi-armed bandit regret of $O\left(\sqrt{T|B|}\right)$, since in most of our applications $|O|$ will be a small constant (e.g. $|O| = 2$ in sponsored search) and takes advantage of the particular feedback structure. Our algorithm is a variant of the EXP3 algorithm [8], with a carefully crafted unbiased estimate of the utility of each action, which has lower variance than the unbiased estimate used in the standard EXP3 algorithm. This result could also be of independent interest and applicable beyond learning in auction settings. Our approach is similar to the importance weighted sampling approach used in EXP3 so as to construct unbiased estimates of the utility of each possible action. Our main technical insight is how to incorporate the allocation function feedback that the bidder receives to construct unbiased estimates with small variance, leading to dependence only in the number of outcomes and not the number of actions. As we discuss in the related work, despite the several similarities, our setting has differences with existing partial feedback online learning settings, such as learning with experts [8], learning with feedback graphs [4, 35] and contextual bandits [2].

This setting engulfs learning in many auctions of interest where bidders learn their value for a good only when they win the good and where the good which is allocated to the bidder is determined by some randomized allocation function. For instance, when applied to the case of single-item first-price, second-price or all-pay auctions, our setting corresponds to the case where the bidders observe their value for the item auctioned at each iteration only when they win the item. Moreover, after every iteration, they observe the critical bid they would have needed to submit to win (for instance, by observing the bids of others or the clearing price). The latter is typically the case in most government auctions or in auction settings similar to eBay.

Our flagship application is that of *value-per-click sponsored search auctions.* These are auctions were bidders repeatedly bid in an auction for a slot in a keyword impression on a search engine. The complexity of the sponsored search ecosystem and the large volume of repeated auctions has given rise to a plethora of automated bidding tools (see e.g. [43]) and has made sponsored search an interesting arena for automated learning agents. Our framework captures the fact that in this setting the bidders observe their value for a click only when they get clicked. Moreover, it assumes that the bidders also observe the average probability of click and the average cost per click for any bid they could have submitted. The latter is exactly the type of feedback that the automated bidding tools can receive via the use of *bid simulators* offered by both major search engines [24–26, 38]. In Figure 1 we portray example interfaces from these tools, where we see that the bidders can observe exactly these allocation and payment curves assumed by our outcome-based-feedback formulation. Not using this information seems unreasonable and a waste of available information. Our work shows how one can utilize this partial feedback given by the auction systems to provide improved learning guarantees over what would have been achieved if one took a fully bandit approach. In the experimental section, we also show that our approach outperforms that of the bandit one even if the allocation and payment curves provided by the system have some error that could stem from errors in the machine learning models used in the calculation of these curves by the search engines. Hence, even when these curves are not fully reliable, our approach can offer improvements in the learning rate.

Fig. 1. Example interfaces of bid simulators of two major search engines, Google Adwords (left) and BingAds (right), that enables learning the allocation and the payment function. (sources [33, 41])

We also extend our results to cases where the space of actions is a continuum (e.g. all bids in an interval $[0, 1]$). We show that in many auction settings, under appropriate assumptions on the utility functions, a regret of $O\left(\sqrt{T\log(T)}\right)$ can be achieved by simply discretizing the action space to a sufficiently small uniform grid and running our WIN-EXP algorithm. This result encompasses the results of [42] for second price auctions, learning in first-price and all-pay auctions, as well as learning in sponsored search with smoothness assumptions on the utility function. We also show how smoothness of the utility can easily arise due to the inherent randomness that exists in the mechanism run in sponsored search.

Finally, we provide two further extensions: *switching regret* and *feedback-graphs over outcomes.* The former adapts our algorithm to achieve good regret against a sequence of bids rather than a fixed bid, which has implications on the faster convergence to approximate efficiency of the outcome (price of anarchy). Feedback graphs address the idea that in many cases the learner could be receiving information about other items other than the item he won (through correlations in the values for these items). This essentially corresponds to adding a feedback graph over outcomes and when outcome $o_t$ is chosen, then the learner learns the reward function $r_t(\cdot, o)$ for all neighboring outcomes $o$ in the feedback graph. We provide improved results that mainly depend on the dependence number of the graph rather than the number of possible outcomes.

**Related Work.** Our work lies on the intersection of two main areas: No regret learning in Game Theory and Mechanism Design and Contextual Bandits.

*No regret learning in Game Theory and Mechanism Design.* No regret learning has received a lot of attention in the Game Theory and Mechanism Design literature [18]. Most of the existing literature, however, focuses on the problem from the side of the auctioneer, who tries to maximize revenue through repeated rounds without knowing a priori the valuations of the bidders [5, 6, 12, 13, 16, 20, 21, 23, 29, 32, 36, 37, 39]. These works are centered around different auction formats like the sponsored search ad auctions, the pricing of inventory and the single-item auctions. Our work is mostly related to Weed et al. [42], who adopt the point of view of the bidders in repeated second-price auctions and who also analyze the case where the true valuation of the item is revealed to the bidders only when they win the item. Their setting falls into the family of settings for which our novel and generic WIN-EXP algorithm produces good regret bounds and as a result, we are able to fully retrieve the regret that their algorithms yield, up to a tiny increase in the constants. Hence, we give an easier way to recover their results. Closely related to our work are the works of [22] and [9]. Dikkala and Tardos [22] analyzes a setting where bidders have to experiment in order to learn their valuations, and show that the seller can increase revenue by offering an initial credit to them, in order to give them incentives to experiment. Balseiro and Gur [9] introduce a family of dynamic bidding strategies in repeated second-price auctions, where advertisers adjust their bids throughout the campaign. They analyze both regret minimization and market stability. There are two key differences to our setting; first, Balseiro and Gur consider the case where the goal of the bidders is the expediture rate in a way that guarantees that the available campaign budget will be spent in an optimal *pacing* way and second, because of their target being the expenditure rate at every timestep $t$, they assume that the bidders get information about the value of the slot being auctioned and based on this information they decide how to adjust their bid. Moreover, several works analyze the properties of auctions when bidders adopt a no-regret learning strategy [11, 15, 40]. None of these works, however, addresses the question of learning more efficiently in the unknown valuation model and either invokes generic MAB algorithms or develops tailored full information algorithms when the bidder knows his value. Another line of research takes a Bayesian approach to learning in repeated auctions and makes large market assumptions, analyzing learning to bid with an unknown value under a Mean Field Equilibrium condition [1, 10, 28][1].

*Learning with partial feedback.* Our work is also related to the literature in *learning with partial feedback* [2, 14]. To establish this connection we observe that the *policies* and the *actions* in contextual bandit terminology translate into *discrete bids* and *groups of bids for which we learn the rewards* in our work. The difference between these two is the fact that for each *action* in contextual bandits we get a single reward, whereas for our setting we observe a *group* of rewards; one for each action in the group. Moreover, the fact that we allow for randomized outcomes adds extra complication, non existent in contextual bandits. In addition, our work is closely related to the literature in *online learning with feedback graphs* [3, 4, 19, 35]. In fact, we propose a new setting in online learning, namely, *learning with outcome-based feedback*, which is a generalization of learning with feedback graphs and is essential when applied to a variety of auctions which include sponsored search, single-item second-price, single-item first-price and single-item all-pay auctions. Moreover, the fact

[1]No-regret learning is complementary and orthogonal to the mean field approach, as it does not impose any stationarity assumption on the evolution of valuations of the bidder or the behavior of his opponents.

that the learner only learns the probability of each outcome and not the actual realization of the randomness, is similar in nature to a feedback graph setting, but where the bidder does not observe the whole graph. Rather, she observes a distribution over feedback graphs and for each bid she learns with what probability each feedback graph would arise. For concreteness, consider the case of sponsored search and suppose for now that the bidder gets even more information than what we assume and also observes the bids of her opponents. She still does not observe whether she would get a click if she falls on the slot below but only the probability with which she would get a click in the slot below. If she could observe whether she would still get a click in the slot below, then we could in principle construct a feedback graph that would say that for all bids were the bidder gets a slot her reward is revealed, and for every bid that she does not get a click, her reward is not revealed. However, this is not the structure that we have and essentially this corresponds to the case where the feedback graph is not revealed, as analyzed in [19] and for which no improvement over the full bandit feedback is possible. However, we show that this impossibility is amended by the fact that the learner observes the probability of a click and hence for each possible bid, she observes the probability with which each feedback graph would have happened. This is enough for a low variance unbiased estimate.

## 2 LEARNING IN AUCTIONS WITHOUT KNOWING YOUR VALUE

For simplicity of exposition, we start with a simple single-dimensional mechanism design setting, but our results extend to multi-dimensional (multi-item) mechanisms, as we will see in Section 4. Let $n$ be the number of bidders. Each bidder has a value $v_i \in [0, 1]$ *per-unit of a good* and submits a bid $b_i \in B$, where $B$ is a discrete set of bids (e.g. a uniform $\epsilon$-grid of $[0, 1]$). Given the bid profile of all bidders, the auction allocates a unit of the good to the bidders. The allocation rule for bidder $i$ is given by $X_i(b_i, b_{-i})$. Moreover, the mechanism defines a per-unit payment function $P_i(b_i, b_{-i}) \in [0, 1]$. The overall utility of the bidder is quasi-linear, i.e. $u_i(b_i, b_{-i}) = (v_i - P_i(b_i, b_{-i})) \cdot X_i(b_i, b_{-i})$.

*Online Learning with Partial Feedback.* The bidders participate in this mechanism repeatedly. At each iteration, each bidder has some value $v_{it}$ and submits a bid $b_{it}$. The mechanism has some time-varying allocation function $X_{it}(\cdot, \cdot)$ and payment function $P_{it}(\cdot, \cdot)$. We assume that the bidder does *not* know her value $v_{it}$, nor the bids of her opponents $b_{-i,t}$, nor the allocation and payment functions, *before* submitting a bid.

At the end of each iteration, she gets an item with probability $X_{it}(b_{it}, b_{-i,t})$ and observes her value $v_{it}$ for the item only when she gets one [2]. Moreover, we assume that she gets to observe her allocation and payment functions for that iteration, i.e. she gets to observe two functions $x_{it}(\cdot) = X_{it}(\cdot, b_{-i,t})$ and $p_{it}(\cdot) = P_{it}(\cdot, b_{-i,t})$. Finally, she receives utility $(v_{it} - p_{it}(b_{it})) \cdot \mathbb{1}\{\text{item is allocated to her}\}$ or in other words expected utility $u_{it}(b_{it}) = (v_{it} - p_{it}(b_{it})) \cdot x_{it}(b_{it})$. Given that we focus on learning from the perspective of a single bidder we will drop the index $i$ from all notation and instead write, $x_t(\cdot)$, $p_t(\cdot)$, $u_t(\cdot)$, $v_t$, etc. The goal of the bidder is to achieve small expected regret with respect to any fixed bid in hindsight: $R(T) = \sup_{b^* \in B} \mathbb{E}\left[\sum_{t=1}^{T} (u_t(b^*) - u_t(b_t))\right] \leq o(T)$.

## 3 ABSTRACTION: LEARNING WITH WIN-ONLY FEEDBACK

Let us abstract the learner's problem to a setting that could be of interest beyond auction settings.

*Learning with Win-Only Feedback.* Every day a learner picks an action $b_t$ from a finite set $B$. The adversary chooses a reward function $r_t : B \to [-1, 1]$ and an allocation function $x_t : B \to [0, 1]$. The learner wins a reward $r_t(b)$ with probability $x_t(b)$. Let $u_t(b) = r_t(b)x_t(b)$ be the learner's

[2] E.g. in sponsored search, the good allocated is the probability of getting clicked, and you only observe your value if you get clicked.

expected utility from action $b$. After each iteration, if she won the reward then she learns the whole reward function $r_t(\cdot)$, while she *always* learns the allocation function $x_t(\cdot)$.

*Can the learner achieve regret $O(\sqrt{T}\log(|B|))$ rather than bandit-feedback regret $O(\sqrt{T|B|})$?*

In the case of the auction learning problem, the reward function $r_t(b)$ takes the parametric form $r_t(b) = v_t - p_t(b)$ and the learner needs to learn $v_t$ and $p_t(\cdot)$ at the end of each iteration, when she wins the item. This is in line with the feedback structure we described in the previous section.

We consider the following adaptation of the EXP3 algorithm with unbiased estimates based on the information received. It is notationally useful throughout the section to denote with $A_t$ the event of *winning a reward at time t*. Then, we can write: $\Pr[A_t|b_t = b] = x_t(b)$ and $\Pr[A_t] = \sum_{b\in B} \pi_t(b)x_t(b)$, where with $\pi_t(\cdot)$ we denote the multinomial distribution from which bid $b$ is drawn. With this notation we define our WIN-EXP algorithm in Algorithm 1. We note here that our generic family of the WIN-EXP algorithms can be parametrized by the step-size $\eta$, the estimate of the utility $\tilde{u}_t$ that the learner gets at each round and the feedback structure that she receives.

**Algorithm 1** WIN-EXP algorithm for learning with win-only feedback

Let $\pi_1(b) = \frac{1}{|B|}$ for all $b \in B$ (i.e. the uniform distribution over bids), $\eta = \sqrt{\frac{2\log(|B|)}{5T}}$
**for** each iteration t **do**
  Draw a bid $b_t$ from the multinomial distribution based on $\pi_t(\cdot)$
  Observe $x_t(\cdot)$ and if reward is won also observe $r_t(\cdot)$
  Compute estimate of utility:
    If reward is won $\tilde{u}_t(b) = \frac{(r_t(b)-1)\Pr[A_t|b_t=b]}{\Pr[A_t]}$; otherwise, $\tilde{u}_t(b) = -\frac{\Pr[\neg A_t|b_t=b]}{\Pr[\neg A_t]}$.
  Update $\pi_t(\cdot)$ as in Exponential Weights Update: $\forall b \in B : \pi_{t+1}(b) \propto \pi_t(b) \cdot \exp\{\eta \cdot \tilde{u}_t(b)\}$

*Bounding the Regret.* We first bound the first and second moment of the unbiased estimates built at each iteration in the WIN-EXP algorithm.

Lemma 3.1. *At each iteration t, for any action $b \in B$, the random variable $\tilde{u}_t(b)$ is an unbiased estimate of the true expected utility $u_t(b)$, i.e.: $\forall b \in B : \mathbb{E}[\tilde{u}_t(b)] = u_t(b) - 1$ and has expected second moment bounded by: $\forall b \in B : \mathbb{E}\left[(\tilde{u}_t(b))^2\right] \le \frac{4\Pr[A_t|b_t=b]}{\Pr[A_t]} + \frac{\Pr[\neg A_t|b_t=b]}{\Pr[\neg A_t]}$.*

Proof. Let $A_t$ denote the event that the reward was won. We have:

$$\begin{aligned}\mathbb{E}[\tilde{u}_t(b)] &= \mathbb{E}\left[\frac{(r_t(b)-1)\cdot\Pr[A_t|b_t=b]}{\Pr[A_t]}\mathbb{1}\{A_t\} - \frac{\Pr[\neg A_t|b_t=b]}{\Pr[\neg A_t]}\mathbb{1}\{\neg A_t\}\right]\\ &= (r_t(b)-1)\Pr[A_t|b_t=b] - \Pr[\neg A_t|b_t=b]\\ &= r_t(b)\Pr[A_t|b_t=b] - 1 = u_t(b) - 1\end{aligned}$$

Similarly for the second moment:

$$\begin{aligned}\mathbb{E}\left[\tilde{u}_t(b)^2\right] &= \mathbb{E}\left[\frac{(r_t(b)-1)^2\cdot\Pr[A_t|b_t=b]^2}{\Pr[A_t]^2}\mathbb{1}\{A_t\} + \frac{\Pr[\neg A_t|b_t=b]^2}{\Pr[\neg A_t]^2}\mathbb{1}\{\neg A_t\}\right]\\ &= \frac{(r_t(b)-1)^2\cdot\Pr[A_t|b_t=b]^2}{\Pr[A_t]} + \frac{\Pr[\neg A_t|b_t=b]^2}{\Pr[\neg A_t]} \le \frac{4\Pr[A_t|b_t=b]}{\Pr[A_t]} + \frac{\Pr[\neg A_t|b_t=b]}{\Pr[\neg A_t]}\end{aligned}$$

where the last inequality holds since $r_t(\cdot) \in [-1, 1]$ and $x_t(\cdot) \in [0, 1]$. □

We are now ready to prove our main theorem:

Theorem 3.2 (Regret of WIN-EXP). *The regret of the WIN-EXP algorithm with the aforementioned unbiased estimates and step size* $\sqrt{\frac{2\log(|B|)}{5T}}$ *is:* $4\sqrt{T\log(|B|)}$.

Proof. Observe that regret with respect to utilities $u_t(\cdot)$ is equal to regret with respect to the translated utilities $u_t(\cdot) - 1$. We use the fact that the exponential weights update with an unbiased estimate $\tilde{u}_t(\cdot) \leq 0$ of the true utilities, achieves expected regret of the form[3]:

$$R(T) \leq \frac{\eta}{2}\sum_{t=1}^{T}\sum_{b\in B}\pi_t(b)\cdot\mathbb{E}\left[(\tilde{u}_t(b))^2\right] + \frac{1}{\eta}\log(|B|)$$

Invoking the bound on the second moment by Lemma 3.1, we get:

$$R(T) \leq \frac{\eta}{2}\sum_{t=1}^{T}\sum_{b\in B}\pi_t(b)\cdot\left(\frac{4\Pr[A_t|b_t=b]}{\Pr[A_t]} + \frac{\Pr[\neg A_t|b_t=b]}{\Pr[\neg A_t]}\right) + \frac{1}{\eta}\log(|B|) \leq \frac{5}{2}\eta T + \frac{1}{\eta}\log(|B|)$$

Picking $\eta = \sqrt{\frac{2\log(|B|)}{5T}}$, we get the theorem. □

## 4 BEYOND BINARY OUTCOMES: OUTCOME-BASED FEEDBACK

In the win-only feedback framework there were two possible outcomes that could happen: either you win the reward or not. We now consider a more general problem, where there are more than two outcomes and you learn your reward function for the outcome you won. Moreover, the outcome that you won is also a probabilistic function of your action. The proofs for the results presented in this section can be found in Appendix B in the full version[4].

*Learning with Outcome-Based Feedback.* Every day a learner picks an action $b_t$ from a finite set $B$. There is a set of payoff-relevant outcomes $O$. The adversary chooses a reward function $r_t : B \times O \to [-1, 1]$, which maps an action and an outcome to a reward and he also chooses an allocation function $x_t : B \to \Delta(O)$, which maps an action to a distribution over the outcomes. Let $x_t(b, o)$ be the probability of outcome $o$ under action $b$. An outcome $o_t \in O$ is chosen based on distribution $x_t(b_t)$. The learner wins reward $r_t(b_t, o_t)$ and observes the whole outcome-specific reward function $r_t(\cdot, o_t)$. She *always* learns the allocation function $x_t(\cdot)$ after the iteration. Let $u_t(b) = \sum_{o\in O} r_t(b, o)\cdot x_t(b, o)$ be the expected utility from action $b$.

We consider the following adaptation of the EXP3 algorithm with unbiased estimates based on the information received. It is notationally useful throughout the section to consider $o_t$ as the random variable of the outcome chosen at time $t$. Then, we can write: $\Pr_t[o_t|b] = x_t(b, o_t)$ and $\Pr_t[o_t] = \sum_{b\in B}\pi_t(b)\Pr_t[o_t|b] = \sum_{b\in B}\pi_t(b)\cdot x_t(b, o_t)$. With this notation and based on the feedback structure, we define our WIN-EXP algorithm for learning with outcome-based feedback in Algorithm 2.

Theorem 4.1 (Regret of WIN-EXP with outcome-based feedback). *The regret of Algorithm 2 with* $\tilde{u}_t(b) = \frac{(r_t(b,o_t)-1)\Pr_t[o_t|b]}{\Pr_t[o_t]}$ *and step size* $\sqrt{\frac{\log(|B|)}{2T|O|}}$ *is:* $2\sqrt{2T|O|\log(|B|)}$.

[3] A detailed proof of this claim can be found in Appendix G.
[4] https://arxiv.org/pdf/1711.01333.pdf

**Algorithm 2** WIN-EXP algorithm for learning with outcome-based feedback

Let $\pi_1(b) = \frac{1}{|B|}$ for all $b \in B$ (i.e. the uniform distribution over bids), $\eta = \sqrt{\frac{\log(|B|)}{2T|O|}}$
**for** each iteration t **do**
  Draw an action $b_t$ from the multinomial distribution based on $\pi_t(\cdot)$
  Observe $x_t(\cdot)$, observe chosen outcome $o_t$ and associated reward function $r_t(\cdot, o_t)$
  Compute estimate of utility:

$$\tilde{u}_t(b) = \frac{(r_t(b, o_t) - 1)\Pr_t[o_t|b]}{\Pr_t[o_t]} \tag{1}$$

  Update $\pi_t(\cdot)$ based on the Exponential Weights Update:

$$\forall b \in B : \pi_{t+1}(b) \propto \pi_t(b) \cdot \exp\{\eta \cdot \tilde{u}_t(b)\} \tag{2}$$

*Applications to Learning in Auctions.* We now present a series of applications of the main result of this section to several learning in auction settings, even beyond single-item or single-dimensional ones.

*Example 4.2 (Second-price auction).* Suppose that the mechanism ran at each iteration is just the second price auction. Then, we know that the allocation function $X_i(b_i, b_{-i})$ is simply of the form: $\mathbb{1}\{b_i \geq \max_{j \neq i} b_j\}$ and the payment function is simply the second highest bid. In this case, observing the allocation and payment functions at the end of the auction boils down to observing the highest other bid. In fact, in this case we have a trivial setting where the bidder gets an allocation of either 0 or 1 and if we let $B_t = \max_{j \neq i} b_{jt}$, then the unbiased estimate of the utility takes the simpler form (assuming the bidder always loses in case of ties) of: if $b_t > B_t : \tilde{u}_t(b) = \frac{(v_{it} - B_t - 1)\mathbb{1}\{b > B_t\}}{\sum_{b' > B_t} \pi_t(b')}$ and $\tilde{u}_t(b) = \frac{\mathbb{1}\{b \leq B_t\}}{\sum_{b' \leq B_t} \pi_t(b')}$ in any other case. Our main theorem gives regret $4\sqrt{T\log(|B|)}$. We note that this theorem recovers exactly the results of Weed et al. [42], by using as $B$ a uniform $1/\Delta^o$ discretization of the bidding space, for an appropriately defined constant $\Delta^o$ (see Appendix B.1 for an exact comparison of the results).

*Example 4.3 (Value-per-click auctions).* This is a variant of the binary outcome case analyzed in Section 3, where $O = \{A, \neg A\}$, i.e. get clicked or not. Hence, $|O| = 2$, and $r_t(b, A) = v_t - p_t(b)$, while $r_t(b, \neg A) = 0$. Our main theorem gives regret $4\sqrt{T\log(|B|)}$.

*Example 4.4 (Unit-demand multi-item auctions).* Consider the case of $K$ items at an auction where the bidder has value $v_k$ for only one item $k$. Given a bid $b$, the mechanism defines a probability distribution over the items that the bidder will be allocated and also defines a payment function, which depends on the bid of the bidder and the item allocated. When a bidder gets allocated an item $k$ she gets to observe her value $v_{kt}$ for that item. Thus, the set of outcomes is equal to $O = \{1, \ldots, K+1\}$, with outcome $K+1$ associated with not getting any item. The rewards are also of the form: $r_t(b, k) = v_{kt} - p_t(b, k)$ for some payment function $p_t(b, k)$ dependent on the auction format. Our main theorem then gives regret $2\sqrt{2(K+1)T\log(|B|)}$.

### 4.1 Batch Rewards Per-Iteration and Sponsored Search Auctions

We now consider the case of sponsored search auctions, where the learner participates in multiple auctions per-iteration. At each of these auctions she has a chance to win and get feedback on her value. To this end, we abstract the *learning with win-only feedback* setting to a setting where multiple rewards are awarded per-iteration. The allocation function remains the same throughout the iteration but the reward functions can change.

*Outcome-Based Feedback with Batch Rewards.* Every iteration $t$ is associated with a set of *reward contests* $I_t$. The learner picks an action $b_t$, which is used at *all* reward contests. For each $\tau \in I_t$ the adversary picks an outcome specific reward function $r_\tau : B \times O \to [-1, 1]$. Moreover, the adversary chooses an allocation function $x_t : B \to \Delta(O)$, which is not $\tau$-dependent. At each $\tau$, an outcome $o_\tau$ is chosen based on distribution $x_t(b_t)$ and independently. The learner receives reward $r_\tau(b_t, o_\tau)$ from that contest. The overall realized utility from that iteration is the average reward: $\frac{1}{|I_t|}\sum_{\tau \in I_t} r_\tau(b_t, o_\tau)$, while the expected utility from any bid $b$ is: $u_t(b) = \frac{1}{|I_t|}\sum_{\tau \in I_t}\sum_{o \in O} r_\tau(b, o) \cdot x_t(b, o)$. We assume that at the end of each iteration the learner receives as feedback the average reward function conditional on each realized outcome, i.e. if we let $I_{to} = \{\tau \in I_t : o_\tau = o\}$, then the learner learns the function: $Q_t(b, o) = \frac{1}{|I_{to}|}\sum_{\tau \in I_{to}} r_\tau(b, o)$ (with the convention that $Q_t(b, o) = 0$ if $|I_{to}| = 0$) as well as the realized frequencies $f_t(o) = \frac{|I_{to}|}{|I_t|}$ for all outcomes $o$.

With this at hand we can define the *batch-analogue* of our unbiased estimates of the previous section. To avoid any confusion we define: $\Pr_t[o|b] = x_t(b, o)$ and $\Pr_t[o] = \sum_{b \in B} \pi_t(b)\Pr_t[o|b]$, to denote that these probabilities only depend on $t$ and not on $\tau$. The estimate of the utility will be:

$$\tilde{u}_t(b) = \sum_{o \in O} \frac{\Pr_t[o|b]}{\Pr_t[o]} f_t(o)\left(Q_t(b, o) - 1\right) \tag{3}$$

We show the full algorithm with outcome-based batch-reward feedback in Algorithm 3.

---

**Algorithm 3** WIN-EXP algorithm for learning with outcome-based batch-reward feedback

---

Let $\pi_1(b) = \frac{1}{|B|}$ for all $b \in B$ (i.e. the uniform distribution over bids), $\eta = \sqrt{\frac{\log(|B|)}{2T|O|}}$

**for** each iteration t **do**

Draw an action $b_t$ from the multinomial distribution based on $\pi_t(\cdot)$

Observe $x_t(\cdot)$, chosen outcomes $o_\tau, \forall \tau \in I_t$, average reward function conditional on each realized outcome $Q_t(b, o)$ and the realized frequencies for each outcome $f_t(o) = \frac{|I_{to}|}{|I_t|}$.

Compute estimate of utility:

$$\tilde{u}_t(b) = \sum_{o \in O} \frac{\Pr_t[o|b]}{\Pr_t[o]} f_t(o)\left(Q_t(b, o) - 1\right) \tag{4}$$

Update $\pi_t(\cdot)$ based on the Exponential Weights Update:

$$\forall b \in B : \pi_{t+1}(b) \propto \pi_t(b) \cdot \exp\left\{\eta \cdot \tilde{u}_t(b)\right\} \tag{5}$$

---

Corollary 4.5. *The WIN-EXP algorithm with the latter unbiased utility estimates and step size* $\sqrt{\frac{\log(|B|)}{2T|O|}}$*, achieves regret in the outcome-based feedback with batch rewards setting at most:* $2\sqrt{2T|O|\log(|B|)}$.

It is also interesting to note that the same result holds if instead of using $f_t(o)$ in the expected utility (Equation (10)), we used its *mean value*, which is $x_t(o, b_t) = \Pr_t[o|b_t]$. This would not change any of the derivations above. The nice property of this alternative is that the learner does not need to learn the realized fraction of each outcome, but only the expected fraction of each outcome. This is already contained in the function $x_t(\cdot, \cdot)$, which we assumed was given to the learner at the end of each iteration. Thus, with these new estimates, the learner does not need to observe $f_t(o)$. In Appendix C we also discuss the case where different periods can have different number of rewards and how to extend our estimate to that case. The batch rewards setting finds an interesting application in the case of learning in sponsored search, as we describe below.

*Example 4.6 (Sponsored Search).* In the case of sponsored search auctions, the latter boils down to learning the average value $\hat{v} = \frac{1}{\#clicks} \sum_{clicks} v_{click}$ for the clicks that were generated, as well as the cost-per-click function $p_t(b)$, which is assumed to be constant throughout the period $t$. Given these quantities, the learner can compute: $Q(b, A) = \hat{v} - p_t(b)$ and $Q(b, \neg A) = 0$. An advertiser can keep track of the traffic generated by a search engine ad and hence, can keep track of the number of clicks from the search engine and the value generated by each of these clicks (conversion). Thus, she can estimate $\hat{v}$. Moreover, she can elicit the probability of click (aka click-through-rate or CTR) curves $x_t(\cdot)$ and the cost-per-click (CPC) curves $p_t(\cdot)$ over relatively small periods of time of about a few days. See for instance the Adwords bid simulator tools offered by Google [24–26, 38][5]. Thus, with these at hand we can apply our batch reward outcome based feedback algorithm and get regret that does not grow linearly with $|B|$, but only as $4\sqrt{T \log(|B|)}$. Our main assumption is that the expected CTR and CPC curves during this relatively small period of a few days remains approximately constant. The latter holds if the distribution of click-through-rates does not change within these days and if the bids of opponent bidders also do not significantly change. This is a reasonable assumption when feedback can be elicited relatively frequently, which is the case in practice.

## 5 CONTINUOUS ACTIONS WITH PIECEWISE-LIPSCHITZ REWARDS

Until now we only considered discrete action spaces. In this section, we extend our discussion to continuous ones; that is, we allow the action of each bidder to lie in a continuous action space $\mathcal{B}$ (e.g. a uniform interval in $[0, 1]$). To assist us in our analysis, we are going to use the discretization result in [31] [6]. For what follows in this section, let $R(T, \mathcal{B}) = \sup_{b^* \in \mathcal{B}} \mathbb{E}\left[\sum_{t=1}^{T} (u_t(b^*) - u_t(b_t))\right]$ be the regret of the bidder, after $T$ rounds with respect to an action space $\mathcal{B}$. Moreover, for any pairs of action spaces $B$ and $\mathcal{B}$ we let: $DE(B, \mathcal{B}) = \sup_{b \in \mathcal{B}} \sum_{t=1}^{T} u_t(b) - \sup_{b' \in B} \sum_{t=1}^{T} u_t(b')$, denote the discretization error incurred by optimizing over $B$ instead of $\mathcal{B}$. The proofs of this section can be found in Appendix E.

Lemma 5.1. *([30, 31]) Let $\mathcal{B}$ be a continuous action space and $B$ a discretization of $\mathcal{B}$. Then:*

$$R(T, \mathcal{B}) \leq R(T, B) + DE(B, \mathcal{B})$$

Observe now that in the setting of Weed et al. [42] the discretization error was: $DE(B, \mathcal{B}) = 0$ if $\epsilon < \Delta^o$, as we discussed in Section 4 and that was *the key* that allowed us to recover this result, without adding an extra $\epsilon T$ in the regret of the bidder. To achieve that, we construct the following general class of utility functions:

*Definition 5.2 ($\Delta^o$-Piecewise Lipschitz Average Utilities).* A learning setting with action space $\mathcal{B} = [0, 1]^d$, is said to have $\Delta^o$-Piecewise Lipschitz Cumulative Utilities if the average utility function $\frac{1}{T} \sum_{t=1}^{T} u_t(b)$ satisfies the following conditions: the bidding space $[0, 1]^d$ is divided into $d$-dimensional cubes with edge length at least $\Delta^o$ and within each cube the utility is $L$-Lipschitz with respect to the $\ell_\infty$ norm. Moreover, for any boundary point there exists a sequence of non-boundary points whose limit cumulative utility is at least as large as the cumulative utility of the boundary point.

Lemma 5.3 (Discretization Error for Piecewise Lipschitz). *Let $\mathcal{B} = [0, 1]^d$ be a continuous action space and $B$ a uniform $\epsilon$-grid of $[0, 1]^d$, such that $\epsilon < \Delta^o$ (i.e. $B$ consists of all the points*

[5]One could argue that the CTRs that the bidder gets in this case are not accurate enough. Nevertheless, even if they have random perturbations, we show in our experimental results that for reasonable noise assumptions, WIN-EXP is preferrable compared to EXP3.

[6]Kleinberg [31] discuss the uniform discretization of continuum-armed bandits and Kleinberg et al. [30] extend the results for the case of Lipschitz-armed bandits.

*whose coordinates are multiples of a given $\epsilon$). Assume that the average utility function is $\Delta^o$-Piecewise L-Lipschitz. Then, the discretization error of B is bounded as: $DE(B, \mathcal{B}) \leq \epsilon LT$.*

If we know the Lipschitzness constant $L$ mentioned above, the time horizon $T$ and $\Delta^o$, then our WIN-EXP algorithm for Outcome-Based Feedback with Batch Rewards yields regret as defined by the following theorem. In Appendix E, we also show how to deal with unknown parameters $L$, $T$ and $\Delta^o$ by applying a standard doubling trick.

THEOREM 5.4. *Let $\mathcal{B} = [0, 1]^d$ be the action space as defined in our model and let B be a uniform $\epsilon$-grid of $\mathcal{B}$. The WIN-EXP algorithm with unbiased estimates given by $\tilde{u}_t(b) = \sum_{o \in O} \frac{\Pr_t[o|b]}{\Pr_t[o]} f_t(o) (Q_t(b, o) - 1)$ (6) on B with $\eta = \sqrt{\frac{\log(|B|)}{2T|O|}}$, $\epsilon = \min\left\{\frac{1}{LT}, \Delta^o\right\}$ achieves expected regret at most $2\sqrt{2T|O|d \log\left(\max\left\{\frac{1}{\Delta^o}, LT\right\}\right)} + 1$ in the outcome-based feedback with batch rewards and $\Delta^o$-Piecewise L–Lipschitz average utilities* [7].

*Example 5.5 (First Price and All-Pay Auctions).* Consider the case of learning in first price or all-pay auctions. In the former, the highest bidder wins and pays her bid, while in the latter the highest bidder wins and every bidder pays her bid whether she wins or loses. Let $B_t$ be the highest other bid at time $t$. Then the average hindsight utility of the bidder in each auction is [8]:

$$\frac{1}{T} \sum_{t=1}^{T} u_t(b) = \frac{1}{T} \sum_{t=1}^{T} v_t \cdot \mathbb{1}\{b > B_t\} - b \cdot \frac{1}{T} \sum_{t=1}^{T} \mathbb{1}\{b > B_t\} \quad \text{(first price)}$$

$$\frac{1}{T} \sum_{t=1}^{T} u_t(b) = \frac{1}{T} \sum_{t=1}^{T} v_t \cdot \mathbb{1}\{b > B_t\} - b \quad \text{(all-pay)}$$

Let $\Delta^o$ be the *smallest* difference between the highest other bid at any two iterations $t$ and $t'$ [9]. Then observe that the average utilities in this setting are $\Delta^o$-Piecewise 1-Lipschitz: Between any two highest other bids, the average allocation, $\frac{1}{T} \sum_{t=1}^{T} v_t \cdot \mathbb{1}\{b > B_t\}$, of the bidder remains constant and the only thing that changes is his payment which grows linearly. Hence, the derivative at any bid between any two such highest other bids is upper bounded by 1. Hence, by applying Theorem 5.4, our WIN-EXP algorithm with a uniform discretization on a $\epsilon$-grid, for $\epsilon = \min\left\{\Delta^o, \frac{1}{T}\right\}$, achieves regret $4\sqrt{T \log\left(\max\left\{\frac{1}{\Delta^o}, T\right\}\right)} + 1$, where we used that $|O| = 2$ and $d = 1$ for any of these auctions.

## 5.1 Sponsored Search with Lipschitz Utilities

In this subsection, we extend our analysis of learning in the sponsored search auction model (Example 4.6) to the continuous bid space case, i.e., each bidder can submit a bid $b \in [0, 1]$. As a reminder, the utility function is: $u_t(b) = x_t(b)(\hat{v}_t - p_t(b))$, where $b \in [0, 1]$, $\hat{v}_t \in [0, 1]$ is the average value for the clicks at iteration $t$, $x_t(\cdot)$ is the CTR curve and $p_t(\cdot)$ is the CPC curve. These curves are implicitly formed by running some form of a Generalized Second Price auction (GSP) at each iteration to determine the allocation and payment rules. As we show in this subsection, the form of the GSP ran in reality gives rise to Lipschitz utilities, under some minimal assumptions. Therefore, we can apply the results in Section 5 to get regret bounds even with respect to the continuous bid space $\mathcal{B} = [0, 1]$ [10]. We begin by providing a brief description of the type of Generalized Second Price auction ran in practice.

[7]Interestingly, the above regret bound can help to retrieve two familiar expressions for the regret. First, when $L = 0$ (i.e. when the function is constant within each cube), in is the case for the second price auction analyzed in [42], $R(T) = 2\sqrt{2dT|O|\log\left(\frac{1}{\Delta^o}\right)} + 1$. Hence, we recover the bounds from the prior sections up to a tiny increase. Second, when $\Delta^o \to \infty$, then we have functions that are $L$-Lipschitz in the whole space $\mathcal{B}$ and the regret bound that we retrieve is: $R(T) = 2\sqrt{2dT|O|\log(LT)} + 1$, which is of the type achieved in continuous lipschitz bandit settings.

[8]For simplicity, we assume the bidder loses in case of ties, though we can handle arbitrary random tie-breaking rules.

[9]This is an analogue of the $\Delta^o$ used by [42] in second price auctions.

[10]The aforementioned Lipschitzness is also reinforced by real world data sets from Microsoft's sponsored search auction system.

*Definition 5.6 (Weighted-GSP).* Each bidder $i$ is assigned a *quality score* $s_i \in [0, 1]$. Bidders are ranked according to their score-weighted bid $s_i \cdot b_i$, typically called the *rank-score*. Every bidder whose rank-score does not pass a reserve $r$ is discarded. Bidders are allocated slots in decreasing order of *rank-score*. Each bidder is charged per-click the lowest bid she could have submitted and maintained the same slot. Hence, if a bidder $i$ is allocated a slot $k$ and $\rho_{k+1}$ is the rank-score of the bidder in slot $k+1$, then she is charged $\rho_{k+1}/s_i$ per-click. We denote with $U_i(\mathbf{b}, \mathbf{s}, r)$, the utility of bidder $i$ under a bid profile $\mathbf{b}$ and score profile $\mathbf{s}$.

The quality scores are typically highly random, dependent on the features of the ad and the user that is currently viewing the page. Hence, a reasonable modeling assumption is that the scores $s_i$ at each auction are drawn i.i.d. from some distribution with CDF $F_i$. We now show that if the CDF $F_i$ is Lipschitz (i.e. admits a bounded density), then the utilities of the bidders are also Lipschitz.

THEOREM 5.7 (LIPSCHITZNESS OF THE UTILITY OF WEIGHTED GSP). *Suppose that the score $s_i$ of each bidder $i$ in a weighted GSP is drawn independently from a distribution with an $L$−Lipschitz CDF $F_i$. Then, the expected utility $u_i(b_i, \mathbf{b}_{-i}, r) = \mathbb{E}_{\mathbf{s}}[U_i(b_i, \mathbf{b}_{-i}, \mathbf{s}, r)]$ is $\frac{2nL}{r}$−Lipschitz wrt $b_i$.*

Thus, we see that when the quality scores in sponsored search are drawn from $L$-Lipschitz CDFs $F_i, \forall i \in n$ and the reserve is lower bounded by $\delta > 0$, then the utilities are $\frac{2nL}{\delta}$-Lipschitz and we can achieve good regret bounds by using the WIN-EXP algorithm with batch rewards, with action space $B$ being a uniform $\epsilon$-grid, $\epsilon = \frac{\delta}{2nLT}$ and unbiased estimates given by Equation (6) or Equation (3). In the case of sponsored search the second unbiased estimate takes the following simple form:

$$\tilde{u}_t(b) = \frac{x_t(b) \cdot x_t(b_t)}{\sum_{b' \in B} \pi_t(b') x_t(b')} (\hat{v}_t - p_t(b) - 1) - \frac{(1 - x_t(b)) \cdot (1 - x_t(b_t))}{\sum_{b' \in B} \pi_t(b')(1 - x_t(b'))} \tag{7}$$

where $\hat{v}_t$ is the average value from the clicks that happened during iteration $t$, $x_t(\cdot)$ is the CTR curve, $b_t$ is the realized bid that the bidder submitted and $\pi_t(\cdot)$ is the distribution over discretized bids of the algorithm at that iteration. We can then apply Theorem 5.4 to get the following guarantee:

COROLLARY 5.8. *The WIN-EXP algorithm run on a uniform $\epsilon$-grid with $\epsilon = \frac{\delta}{2nLT}$, step size $\sqrt{\frac{\log(1/\epsilon)}{4T}}$ and unbiased estimates given by Equation (6) or Equation (3), when applied to the sponsored search auction setting with quality scores drawn independently from distributions with L-Lipschitz CDFs, achieves regret at most:* $4\sqrt{T \log\left(\frac{2nLT}{\delta}\right)} + 1$.

## 6 FURTHER EXTENSIONS

In this section, we discuss an extension to switching regret and the implications on Price of Anarchy and one to the feedback graphs setting.

### 6.1 Switching Regret and Implications for Price of Anarchy

We show below that our results can be extended to capture the case where, instead of having just one optimal bid $b^*$, there is a sequence of $C \geq 1$ *switches* in the optimal bids. Using the results presented in [27] and adapting them for our setting we get the following corollary (with proof in Appendix F).

COROLLARY 6.1. *Let $C \geq 0$ be the number of times that the optimal bid $b^* \in \mathcal{B}$ switches in a horizon of $T$ rounds. Then, using Algorithm 2 in [27] with $\mathcal{A} \equiv$ WIN-EXP and any $\alpha \in (0, 1)$ we can achieve expected* switching regret *at most:* $O\left(\sqrt{(C+1)^2 \left(2 + \frac{1}{\alpha}\right) 2d|O| T \log\left(\max\left\{LT, \frac{1}{\Delta^o}\right\}\right)}\right)$

This result has implications on the price of anarchy (PoA) of auctions. In the case of sponsored search where bidders' valuations are changing over time adversarially but non-adaptively, our result shows that if the valuation does not change more than $C$ times, we can compete with any bid that is a function of the value of the bidder at each iteration, with regret rate given by the latter theorem. Therefore, by standard PoA arguments [34], this would imply convergence to an approximately efficient outcome at a faster rate than bandit regret rates.

### 6.2 Feedback Graphs over Outcomes

We now extend Section 5, by assuming that there is a directed feedback graph $G = (O, E)$ over the outcomes. When outcome $o_t$ is chosen, the bidder observes not only the outcome specific reward function $r_t(\cdot, o_t)$, for that outcome, but also for any outcome $o$ in the out-neighborhood of $o_t$ in the feedback graph, which we denote with $N^{out}(o_t)$. Correspondingly, we denote with $N^{in}(o)$ the incoming neighborhood of $o$ in $G$. Both neighborhoods include self-loops. Let $G_\epsilon = (O_\epsilon, E_\epsilon)$ be the sub-graph of $G$ that contains only outcomes for which $\Pr_t[o_t] \geq \epsilon$ and subsequently, let $N_\epsilon^{in}$ and $N_\epsilon^{out}$ be the in and out neighborhoods of this sub-graph.

Based on this feedback graph we construct a WIN-EXP algorithm with step-size $\eta = \sqrt{\frac{\log(|B|)}{8T\alpha\ln\left(\frac{16|O|^2T}{\alpha}\right)}}$, utility estimate $\tilde{u}_t(b) = \mathbb{1}\{o_t \in O_\epsilon\}\sum_{o\in N_\epsilon^{out}(o_t)}\frac{(r_t(b,o)-1)\Pr_t[o|b]}{\sum_{o'\in N_\epsilon^{in}(o)}\Pr_t[o']}$ and feedback structure as described in the previous paragraph. With these changes we can show that the regret grows as a function of the *independence number of the feedback graph*, denoted with $\alpha$, rather than the *number of outcomes*. The full Algorithm can be found in Appendix A.

Theorem 6.2 (Regret of WIN-EXP-G). *The regret of the WIN-EXP-G algorithm with step size* $\eta = \sqrt{\frac{\log(|B|)}{8T\alpha\ln\left(\frac{16|O|^2T}{\alpha}\right)}}$ *is bounded by:* $R(T) \leq 2\sqrt{8\alpha T\log(|B|)\ln\left(\frac{16|O|^2T}{\alpha}\right)} + 1$.

In the case of learning in auctions, the feedback graph over outcomes can encode the possibility that winning an item can help you uncover your value for other items. For instance, in a combinatorial auction for $m$ items, the reader should think of each node in the feedback graph as a bundle of items. Then the graph encodes the fact that winning bundle $o$ can teach you the value for all bundles $o' \in N^{out}(o)$. If the feedback graph has small dependence number then a much better regret is achieved than the dependence on $\sqrt{2^m}$, that would have been derived by our outcome-based feedback results of prior sections, if we treated each bundle of items separately as an outcome.

## 7 EXPERIMENTAL RESULTS

In this section, we present our results from our comparative analysis between EXP3 and WIN-EXP on a simulated sponsored search system that we built and which is a close proxy of the actual sponsored search algorithms deployed in the industry. We implemented the weighted GSP auction as described in definition 5.6. The auctioneer draws i.i.d rank scores that are bidder and timestep specific; as is the case throughout our paper, here we have assumed a stochastic auctioneer with respect to the rank scores. After bidding, the bidder will always be able to observe the allocation function. Now, if the bidder gets allocated to a slot and she gets clicked, then, she is able observe the *value* and the payment curve. Values are assumed to lie in $[0, 1]$ and they are obliviously adversarial. Finally, the bidders choose bids from some $\epsilon$-discretized grid of $[0, 1]$ (in all experiments, apart from the ones comparing the regrets for different discretizations, we use $\epsilon = 0.01$) and update the probabilities of choosing each discrete bid according to EXP3 or WIN-EXP. Regret is measured with respect to the best fixed discretized bid in hindsight.

We distinguish three cases of the bidding behavior of the rest of the bidders (apart from our learner): i) all of them are *stochastic* adversaries drawing bids at random from some distribution, ii) there is a subset of them that are bidding *adaptively*, by using an EXP3 online learning algorithm and iii) there is a subset of them that are bidding *adaptively* but using a WINEXP online learning algorithm (self play). Validating our theoretical claims, in all three cases, WIN-EXP outperforms EXP3 in terms of regret. We generate the event of whether a bidder gets clicked or not as follows: we draw a timestep specific threshold value in $[0, 1]$ and the learner gets a click in case the CTR of the slot she got allocated (if any) is greater than this threshold value. Note here that the choice of a timestep specific threshold imposes *monotonicity*, i.e. if the learner did not get a click when allocated to a slot with CTR $x_t(b)$, she should not be able to get a click from slots with lower CTRs. We ran simulations with 3 different distributions of generating CTRs, so as to understand what is the effect of different levels of click-through-rates on the variance of our regret: i) $x_t(b) \sim U[0.1, 1]$, ii) $x_t(b) \sim U[0.3, 1]$ and iii) $x_t(b) \sim U[0.5, 1]$. Finally, we address robustness of our results to errors in CTR estimation. For this, we add random noise to the CTRs of each slot and we report to the learners the allocation and payment functions that correspond to the erroneous CTRs. The noise was generated according to a normal distribution $\mathcal{N}(0, \frac{1}{m})$, where $m$ could be viewed as the number of training samples on which a machine learning algorithm was ran in order to output the CTR estimate ($m = 100, 1000, 10000$).

For each of the following simulations, there are $N = 20$ bidders, $k = 3$ slots and we ran the experiment for each round for a total of 30 times. For the simulations that correspond to adaptive adversaries we used $a = 4$ adversaries. Our results for the *cumulative regret* are presented below. We measured ex-post regret with respect to the realized thresholds that determine whether a bidder gets clicked or not. Note that the solid plots correspond to the emprical mean of the regret, whereas the opaque bands correspond to the 10-th and 90-th percentile.

*Different discretizations.* In Figure 2 we present the comparative analysis of the estimated average regret of WIN-EXP vs EXP3 for different discretizations, $\epsilon$, of the bidding space when the learner faces adversaries that are stochastic, adaptive using EXP3 and adaptive using WINEXP. As it was expected from the theoretical analysis, the regret of WIN-EXP, as the disretized space ($|B|$) increases exponentially, remains almost unchanged compared to the regret of EXP3. In summary, *finer discretization of the bid space helps our WIN-EXP algorithm's performance, but hurts the performance of EXP3.*

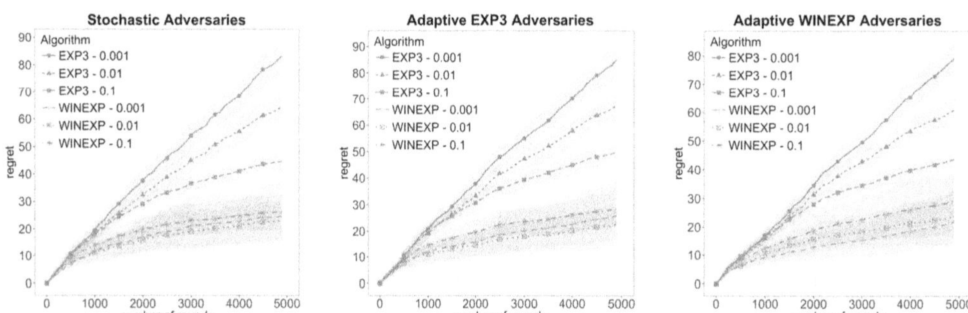


Fig. 2. Regret of WIN-EXP vs EXP3 for different discretizations $\epsilon$ (CTR $\sim U[0.5, 1]$).

*Different CTR Distributions.* In Figures 3, 4 and 5 we present the results of the regret performance of WIN-EXP compared to EXP3, when the learner discretizes the bidding space with $\epsilon = 0.01$ and when she faces stochastic, adaptive adversaries using EXP3 and adaptive adversaries using WINEXP, respectively. For all three cases, the estimated average regret of WIN-EXP is less than the estimated average regret that EXP3 yields.

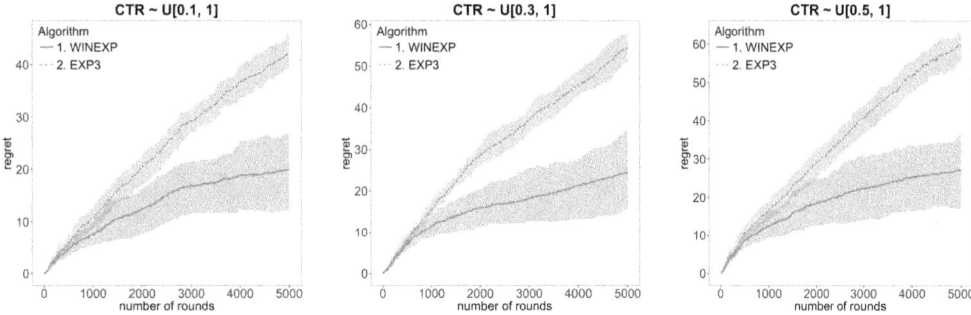


Fig. 3. Regret of WIN-EXP vs EXP3 for different CTR distributions and stochastic adversaries, $\epsilon = 0.01$.

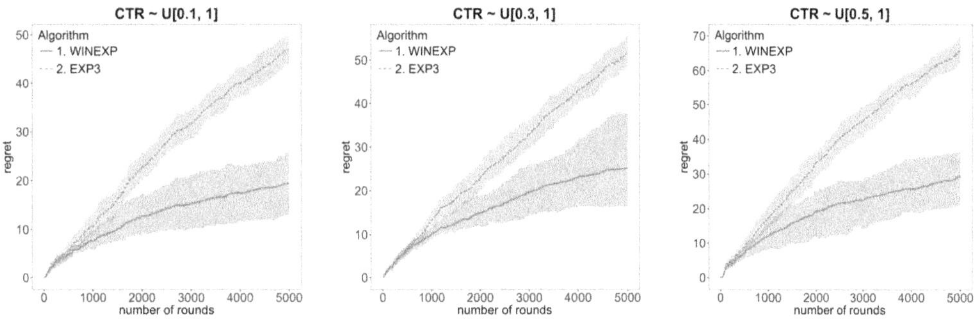


Fig. 4. Regret of WIN-EXP vs EXP3 for different CTR distributions and adaptive EXP3 adversaries, $\epsilon = 0.01$.

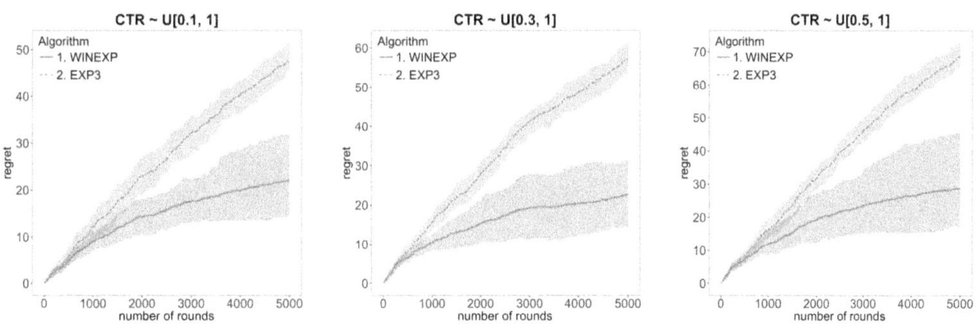


Fig. 5. Regret of WIN-EXP vs EXP3 for different CTR distributions and adaptive WINEXP adversaries, $\epsilon = 0.01$.

*Robustness to Noisy CTR Estimates.* In Figures 6, 7, 8 we empirically tested the robustness of our algorithm to random perturbations of the allocation function that the auctioneer presents to the learner, for perturbations of the form $\mathcal{N}\left(0, \frac{1}{m}\right)$, where $m$ could be viewed as the number of training examples used from the auctioneer in order to derive an approximation of the allocation curve. When the number of training samples is relatively small ($m = 100$) the empirical mean of WINEXP outperforms EXP3 in terms of regret, i.e., it is more robust to such perturbations. As the number of training samples increases, WINEXP clearly outperforms EXP3. The latter validates one of our claims throughout the paper; namely, that even though the learner might not see the exact allocation curve, but a randomly perturbed proxy, WIN-EXP still performs better than the EXP3.

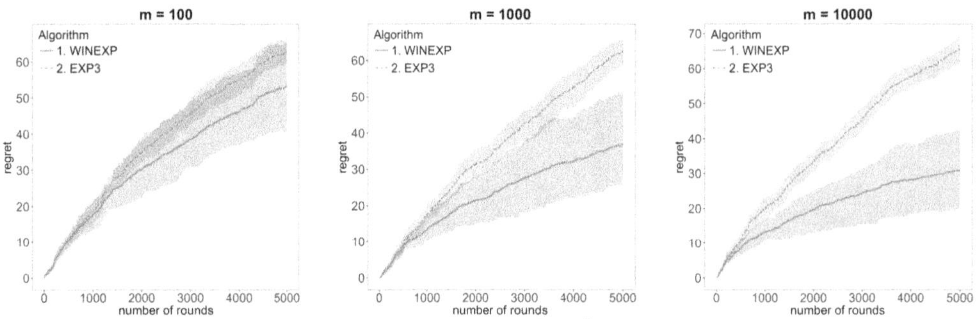


Fig. 6. Regret of WIN-EXP vs EXP3 with noise $\sim \mathcal{N}\left(0, \frac{1}{m}\right)$ for stochastic adversaries, $\epsilon = 0.01$.

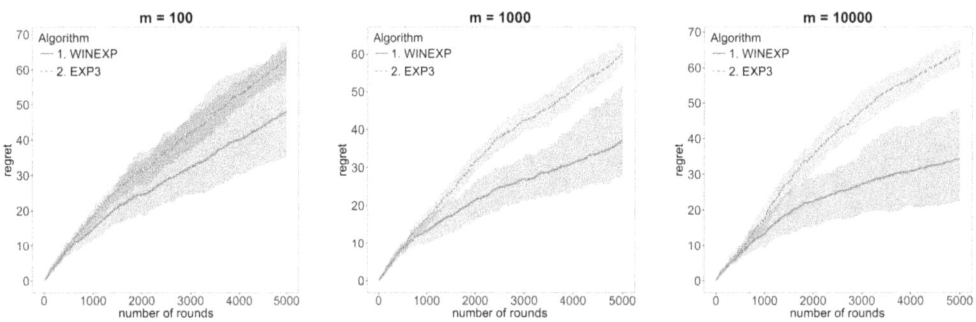


Fig. 7. Regret of WIN-EXP vs EXP3 with noise $\sim \mathcal{N}\left(0, \frac{1}{m}\right)$ for adaptive EXP3 adversaries, $\epsilon = 0.01$.

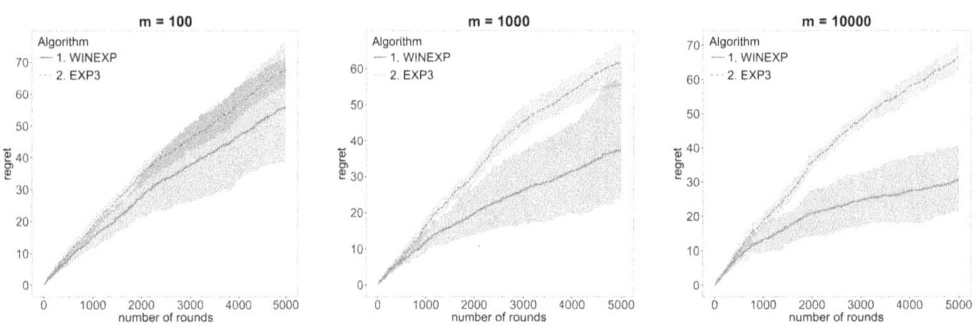


Fig. 8. Regret of WIN-EXP vs EXP3 with noise $\sim \mathcal{N}\left(0, \frac{1}{m}\right)$ for adaptive WINEXP adversaries, $\epsilon = 0.01$.

## 8 CONCLUSION

We addressed learning in repeated auction scenarios were bidders do not know their valuation for the items at sale. We formulated an online learning framework with partial feedback which captures the information available to bidders in typical auction settings like sponsored search and provided an algorithm which achieves almost full information regret rates. Hence, we portrayed that not knowing your valuation is a benign form of incomplete information for learning in auctions. Our experimental evaluation also showed that the improved learning rates are robust to violations of our assumptions and are valid even when the information assumed is corrupted. We believe that exploring further avenues of relaxing the informational assumptions (e.g., what if the value is only later revealed to a bidder or is contigent upon the competitiveness of the auction) or being more robust to erroneous information given by the auction system is an interesting future research direction. We believe that our outcome-based learning framework can facilitate such future work.

## REFERENCES


[1] Sachin Adlakha and Ramesh Johari. 2013. Mean field equilibrium in dynamic games with strategic complementarities. *Operations Research* 61, 4 (2013), 971–989.

[2] Alekh Agarwal, Daniel Hsu, Satyen Kale, John Langford, Lihong Li, and Robert Schapire. 2014. Taming the Monster: A Fast and Simple Algorithm for Contextual Bandits. In *Proceedings of the 31st International Conference on Machine Learning (Proceedings of Machine Learning Research)*, Eric P. Xing and Tony Jebara (Eds.), Vol. 32. PMLR, Bejing, China, 1638–1646.

[3] Noga Alon, Nicolo Cesa-Bianchi, Ofer Dekel, and Tomer Koren. 2015. Online learning with feedback graphs: Beyond bandits. In *Conference on Learning Theory*. 23–35.

[4] Noga Alon, Nicolo Cesa-bianchi, Claudio Gentile, and Yishay Mansour. 2013. From Bandits to Experts: A Tale of Domination and Independence. In *Advances in Neural Information Processing Systems 26*, C.j.c. Burges, L. Bottou, M. Welling, Z. Ghahramani, and K.q. Weinberger (Eds.). 1610–1618.

[5] Kareem Amin, Rachel Cummings, Lili Dworkin, Michael Kearns, and Aaron Roth. 2015. Online Learning and Profit Maximization from Revealed Preferences.. In *AAAI*. 770–776.

[6] Kareem Amin, Afshin Rostamizadeh, and Umar Syed. 2014. Repeated contextual auctions with strategic buyers. In *Advances in Neural Information Processing Systems*. 622–630.

[7] Sanjeev Arora, Elad Hazan, and Satyen Kale. 2012. The Multiplicative Weights Update Method: a Meta-Algorithm and Applications. *Theory of Computing* 8, 1 (2012), 121–164.

[8] Peter Auer, Nicolo Cesa-Bianchi, Yoav Freund, and Robert E Schapire. 2002. The nonstochastic multiarmed bandit problem. *SIAM journal on computing* 32, 1 (2002), 48–77.

[9] Santiago Balseiro and Yonatan Gur. 2017. Learning in Repeated Auctions with Budgets: Regret Minimization and Equilibrium. (2017).

[10] Santiago R Balseiro, Omar Besbes, and Gabriel Y Weintraub. 2015. Repeated auctions with budgets in ad exchanges: Approximations and design. *Management Science* 61, 4 (2015), 864–884.

[11] Avrim Blum, MohammadTaghi Hajiaghayi, Katrina Ligett, and Aaron Roth. 2008. Regret minimization and the price of total anarchy. In *Proceedings of the fortieth annual ACM symposium on Theory of computing*. ACM, 373–382.

[12] Avrim Blum, Vijay Kumar, Atri Rudra, and Felix Wu. 2004. Online learning in online auctions. *Theoretical Computer Science* 324, 2-3 (2004), 137–146.

[13] Avrim Blum, Yishay Mansour, and Jamie Morgenstern. 2015. Learning Valuation Distributions from Partial Observation.. In *AAAI*. 798–804.

[14] Sébastien Bubeck, Nicolo Cesa-Bianchi, and others. 2012. Regret analysis of stochastic and nonstochastic multi-armed bandit problems. *Foundations and Trends® in Machine Learning* 5, 1 (2012), 1–122.

[15] Ioannis Caragiannis, Christos Kaklamanis, Panagiotis Kanellopoulos, Maria Kyropoulou, Brendan Lucier, Renato Paes Leme, and Éva Tardos. 2015. Bounding the inefficiency of outcomes in generalized second price auctions. *Journal of Economic Theory* 156 (2015), 343–388.

[16] Nicolo Cesa-Bianchi, Claudio Gentile, and Yishay Mansour. 2015. Regret minimization for reserve prices in second-price auctions. *IEEE Transactions on Information Theory* 61, 1 (2015), 549–564.

[17] Nicolò Cesa-Bianchi and Gábor Lugosi. 2006. *Prediction, learning, and games*. Cambridge University Press.

[18] Shuchi Chawla, Jason D. Hartline, and Denis Nekipelov. 2014. Mechanism design for data science. In *ACM Conference on Economics and Computation, EC '14, Stanford , CA, USA, June 8-12, 2014*. 711–712.

[19] Alon Cohen, Tamir Hazan, and Tomer Koren. 2016. Online learning with feedback graphs without the graphs. In *International Conference on Machine Learning*. 811–819.

[20] Richard Cole and Tim Roughgarden. 2014. The sample complexity of revenue maximization. In *Proceedings of the forty-sixth annual ACM symposium on Theory of computing*. ACM, 243–252.

[21] Peerapong Dhangwatnotai, Tim Roughgarden, and Qiqi Yan. 2015. Revenue maximization with a single sample. *Games and Economic Behavior* 91 (2015), 318–333.

[22] Nishanth Dikkala and Éva Tardos. 2013. Can Credit Increase Revenue?. In *Web and Internet Economics - 9th International Conference, WINE 2013, Cambridge, MA, USA, December 11-14, 2013, Proceedings*. 121–133.

[23] Michal Feldman, Tomer Koren, Roi Livni, Yishay Mansour, and Aviv Zohar. 2016. Online Pricing with Strategic and Patient Buyers. In *Advances in Neural Information Processing Systems 29*, D. D. Lee, M. Sugiyama, U. V. Luxburg, I. Guyon, and R. Garnett (Eds.). Curran Associates, Inc., 3864–3872.

[24] Google. 2018. AdWords Bid Simulator. https://support.google.com/adwords/answer/2470105?hl=en&ref_topic=3122864. (2018). [Online; accessed 15-February-2018].

[25] Google. 2018. Bid Landscapes. https://developers.google.com/adwords/api/docs/guides/bid-landscapes. (2018). [Online; accessed 15-February-2018].

[26] Google. 2018. Bid Lanscapes. https://developers.google.com/adwords/api/docs/reference/v201710/DataService.BidLandscape. (2018). [Online; accessed 15-February-2018].

[27] András Gyorgy, Tamás Linder, and Gábor Lugosi. 2012. Efficient tracking of large classes of experts. *IEEE Transactions on Information Theory* 58, 11 (2012), 6709–6725.

[28] Krishnamurthy Iyer, Ramesh Johari, and Mukund Sundararajan. 2011. Mean field equilibria of dynamic auctions with learning. *ACM SIGecom Exchanges* 10, 3 (2011), 10–14.

[29] Yash Kanoria and Hamid Nazerzadeh. 2014. Dynamic Reserve Prices for Repeated Auctions: Learning from Bids - Working Paper. In *Web and Internet Economics - 10th International Conference, WINE 2014, Beijing, China, December 14-17, 2014. Proceedings.* 232.

[30] Robert Kleinberg, Aleksandrs Slivkins, and Eli Upfal. 2008. Multi-armed bandits in metric spaces. In *Proceedings of the fortieth annual ACM symposium on Theory of computing.* ACM, 681–690.

[31] Robert D Kleinberg. 2005. Nearly tight bounds for the continuum-armed bandit problem. In *Advances in Neural Information Processing Systems.* 697–704.

[32] Tomer Koren, Roi Livni, and Yishay Mansour. 2017. Bandits with Movement Costs and Adaptive Pricing. In *Proceedings of the 2017 Conference on Learning Theory (Proceedings of Machine Learning Research)*, Satyen Kale and Ohad Shamir (Eds.), Vol. 65. PMLR, Amsterdam, Netherlands, 1242–1268.

[33] Search Engine Land. 2014. Bing Ads Launches âĂIJBid LandscapeâĂİ, A Keyword Level Bid Simulator Tool. https://searchengineland.com/bing-ads-launches-bid-landscape-keyword-level-bid-simulator-tool-187219. (2014). [Online; accessed 15-February-2018].

[34] Thodoris Lykouris, Vasilis Syrgkanis, and Éva Tardos. 2016. Learning and efficiency in games with dynamic population. In *Proceedings of the Twenty-Seventh Annual ACM-SIAM Symposium on Discrete Algorithms.* Society for Industrial and Applied Mathematics, 120–129.

[35] Shie Mannor and Ohad Shamir. 2011. From Bandits to Experts: On the Value of Side-Observations.. In *NIPS*, John Shawe-Taylor, Richard S. Zemel, Peter L. Bartlett, Fernando C. N. Pereira, and Kilian Q. Weinberger (Eds.). 684–692.

[36] Andres M Medina and Mehryar Mohri. 2014. Learning theory and algorithms for revenue optimization in second price auctions with reserve. In *Proceedings of the 31st International Conference on Machine Learning (ICML-14).* 262–270.

[37] Andrés Muñoz Medina and Sergei Vassilvitskii. 2017. Revenue Optimization with Approximate Bid Predictions. *CoRR* abs/1706.04732 (2017). arXiv:1706.04732 http://arxiv.org/abs/1706.04732

[38] Microsoft. 2018. BingAds, Bid Landscapes. https://advertise.bingads.microsoft.com/en-us/resources/training/bidding-and-traffic-estimation. (2018). [Online; accessed 15-February-2018].

[39] Michael Ostrovsky and Michael Schwarz. 2011. Reserve prices in internet advertising auctions: A field experiment. In *Proceedings of the 12th ACM conference on Electronic commerce.* ACM, 59–60.

[40] Tim Roughgarden. 2009. Intrinsic robustness of the price of anarchy. In *Proceedings of the forty-first annual ACM symposium on Theory of computing.* ACM, 513–522.

[41] Search Marketing Standard. 2014. Google AdWords Improves The Bid Simulator Tool Feature. http://www.searchmarketingstandard.com/google-adwords-improves-the-bid-simulator-tool-feature. (2014). [Online; accessed 15-February-2018].

[42] Jonathan Weed, Vianney Perchet, and Philippe Rigollet. 2016. Online learning in repeated auctions. In *Conference on Learning Theory.* 1562–1583.

[43] Wordstream. 2018. Bid Management Tools. https://www.wordstream.com/bid-management-tools. (2018). [Online; accessed 15-February-2018].


## APPENDIX

The Appendix is available in our full version on arXiv.

# Selling to a No-Regret Buyer

MARK BRAVERMAN, Princeton University, USA
JIEMING MAO, Princeton University, USA
JON SCHNEIDER, Princeton University, USA
MATT WEINBERG, Princeton University, USA

We consider the problem of a single seller repeatedly selling a single item to a single buyer (specifically, the buyer has a value drawn fresh from known distribution $\mathcal{D}$ in every round). Prior work assumes that the buyer is fully rational and will perfectly reason about how their bids today affect the seller's decisions tomorrow. In this work we initiate a different direction: the buyer simply runs a no-regret learning algorithm over possible bids. We provide a fairly complete characterization of optimal auctions for the seller in this domain. Specifically:

- If the buyer bids according to EXP3 (or any "mean-based" learning algorithm), then the seller can extract expected revenue arbitrarily close to the expected welfare. This auction is independent of the buyer's valuation $\mathcal{D}$, but somewhat unnatural as it is sometimes in the buyer's interest to overbid.
- There exists a learning algorithm $\mathcal{A}$ such that if the buyer bids according to $\mathcal{A}$ then the optimal strategy for the seller is simply to post the Myerson reserve for $\mathcal{D}$ every round.
- If the buyer bids according to EXP3 (or any "mean-based" learning algorithm), but the seller is restricted to "natural" auction formats where overbidding is dominated (e.g. Generalized First-Price or Generalized Second-Price), then the optimal strategy for the seller is a pay-your-bid format with decreasing reserves over time. Moreover, the seller's optimal achievable revenue is characterized by a linear program, and can be unboundedly better than the best truthful auction yet simultaneously unboundedly worse than the expected welfare.

CCS Concepts: • **Theory of computation → Online learning algorithms**; **Algorithmic game theory**; **Convergence and learning in games**;

Additional Key Words and Phrases: mechanism design, auctions, multi-armed bandits, no-regret learning

## 1 INTRODUCTION

Consider a bidder trying to decide how much to bid in an auction (for example, a sponsored search auction). If the auction happens to be the truthful Vickrey-Clarke-Groves auction [7, 15, 31], then the bidder's decision is easy: simply bid your value. If instead, the bidder is participating in a Generalized First-Price (GFP) or Generalized Second-Price (GSP) auction, the optimal strategy is less clear. Bidders can certainly attempt to compute a Bayes-Nash equilibrium of the associated

This work is supported by NSF CAREER award (CCF-1149888), NSF CCF-1215990, NSF CCF-1525342, NSF CCF-1412958, a Packard Fellowship in Science and Engineering, the Simons Collaboration on Algorithms and Geometry and NSF CCF-1717899.

Authors' addresses: Mark Braverman, Princeton University, 35 Olden St, Princeton, NJ, 08540, USA, mbraverm@cs.princeton.edu; Jieming Mao, Princeton University, 35 Olden St, Princeton, NJ, 08540, USA, jiemingm@cs.princeton.edu; Jon Schneider, Princeton University, 35 Olden St, Princeton, NJ, 08540, USA, js44@cs.princeton.edu; Matt Weinberg, Princeton University, 35 Olden St, Princeton, NJ, 08540, USA, smweinberg@princeton.edu.


*ACM EC'18, June 18–22, 2018, Ithaca, NY, USA.* ACM ISBN 978-1-4503-5829-3/18/06...$15.00
https://doi.org/10.1145/3219166.3219233

game and play accordingly, but this is unrealistic due to the need for accurate priors and extensive computation.

Alternatively, the bidders may try to learn a best-response over time (possibly offloading the learning to commercial bid optimizers). We specifically consider bidders who *no-regret learn*, as empirical work of [27] shows that bidder behavior on Bing is largely consistent with no-regret learning (i.e. for most bidders, there exists a per-click value such that their behavior guarantees no-regret for this value). From the perspective of a revenue-maximizing auction designer, this motivates the following question: **If a seller knows that buyers are no-regret learning over time, how should they maximize revenue?**

This question is already quite interesting even when there is just a single item for sale to a single buyer. We consider a model where in every round $t$, the seller solicits a bid $b_t \in [0, 1]$ from the buyer, then allocates the item according to some allocation rule $x_t(\cdot)$ and charges the bidder according to some pricing rule $p_t(\cdot)$ (satisfying $p_t(b) \leq b \cdot x_t(b)$ for all $t, b$).[1] Note that the allocation and pricing rules (henceforth, auction) can differ from round to round, and that the auction need not be truthful. Each round, the bidder has a value $v_t$ drawn independently from $\mathcal{D}$, and uses some no-regret learning algorithm to decide which bid to place in round $t$, based on the outcomes in rounds $1, \ldots, t-1$ (we will make clear exactly what it means for a buyer with changing valuation to play no-regret in Section 2, but one can think of $v_t$ as providing a "context" for the bidder during round $t$). The same mathematical model can also represent a population $\mathcal{D}$ of many indistinguishable buyers with fixed values who each separately no-regret learn - see Section 2.3 for further details.

One default strategy for the seller is to simply to set Myerson's revenue-optimal reserve price for $\mathcal{D}$, $r(\mathcal{D})$, in every round (that is, $x_t(b_t) = I(b_t \geq r(\mathcal{D}))$, $p_t(b_t) = r(\mathcal{D}) \cdot I(b_t \geq r(\mathcal{D}))$ for all $t$, where $I(\cdot)$ is the indicator function). It's not hard to see that *any* no-regret learning algorithm will eventually learn to submit a winning bid during all rounds where $v_t > r(\mathcal{D})$, and a losing bid whenever $v_t < r(\mathcal{D})$. Note that this observation appeals only to the fact that the buyer guarantees no-regret, and makes no reference to any specific algorithm the buyer might use. So if $\mathsf{Rev}(\mathcal{D})$ denotes the expected revenue of the optimal reserve price when a single buyer is drawn from $\mathcal{D}$, the default strategy guarantees the seller revenue $T \cdot \mathsf{Rev}(\mathcal{D}) - o(T)$ over $T$ rounds. The question then becomes whether or not the seller can beat this benchmark, and if so by how much.

The answer to this question isn't a clear-cut yes or no, so let's start with the following instantiation: how much revenue can the seller extract if the buyer runs EXP3 [3]? In Theorem 3.1, we show that the seller can actually do *much* better than the default strategy: it's possible to extract revenue per round equal to (almost) the full expected welfare! That is, if $\mathsf{Val}(\mathcal{D}) = \mathbb{E}_{v \leftarrow \mathcal{D}}[v]$, there exists an auction that extracts revenue $T \cdot \mathsf{Val}(\mathcal{D}) - o(T)$ for all $\mathcal{D}$.[2] It turns out this result holds not only for EXP3, but for any learning algorithm with the following (roughly stated) property: if at time $t$, the mean reward of action $a$ is significantly larger than the mean reward of action $b$, the learning algorithm will choose action $b$ with negligible probability. We call a learning algorithm with this property a "mean-based" learning algorithm and note that many commonly used learning algorithms - EXP3, Multiplicative Weights Update [1], and Follow-the-Perturbed-Leader [16, 18, 19] - are 'mean-based' (see Section 2 for a formal definition).

We postpone all intuition until Section 3.1 with a worked-through example, but just note here that the auction format is quite unnatural: it "lures" the bidder into submitting high bids early on by giving away the item for free, and then charging very high prices (but still bounded in [0, 1])

[1] Of course, the pricing rule can be implemented by charging $p_t(b)/x_t(b)$ whenever the item is awarded if ex-post individual rationality is desired.

[2] The order of quantifiers in this sentence is correct: it is actually the same auction format that works for all $\mathcal{D}$.

near the end. The transition from "free" to "high-price" is carefully coordinated across different bids to achieve the revenue guarantee.

This result motivates two further directions. First, do there exist other no-regret algorithms for which full surplus extraction is impossible for the seller? In Theorem 3.2, we show that the answer is yes. In fact, there is a simple no-regret algorithm $\mathcal{A}$, such that when the bidder uses algorithm $\mathcal{A}$ to bid, the default strategy (set the Myerson reserve every round) is optimal for the seller. We again postpone a formal statement and intuition to Section 3.2, but just note here that the algorithm is a natural adaptation of EXP3 (or in fact, any existing no-regret algorithm) to our setting.

Finally, it is reasonable to expect that bidders might use off-the-shelf no-regret learning algorithms like EXP3, so it is still important to understand what the seller can hope to achieve if the buyer is specifically using such a "mean-based" algorithm (formal definition in Section 2). Theorem 3.1 is perhaps unsatisfying in this regard because the proposed auction is so unnatural. It turns out that the key property separating natural untruthful auctions (e.g. GSP/GFP) from the unnatural auction above is whether overbidding is a dominated strategy. That is, in our unnatural auction, if the bidder truly hopes to guarantee low regret they must seriously consider overbidding (and this is how the auction lures them into bidding way above their value). In both GSP and GFP, overbidding is dominated, so the bidder can guarantee no regret while overbidding with probability 0 in every round.

The final question we ask is the following: if the buyer is using EXP3 (or any "mean-based" algorithm), never overbids (we call such a bidder *conservative*), how much revenue can the seller extract using an auction where overbidding is dominated in every round? It turns out that the auctioneer can still outperform the default strategy, but not extract full welfare. Instead, we identify a linear program (as a function of $\mathcal{D}$) that tightly characterizes the optimal revenue the seller can achieve in this setting when the buyer's values are drawn from $\mathcal{D}$. Moreover, we show that the auction that achieves this guarantee is natural, and can be thought of as a pay-your-bid auction with decreasing reserves over time. Finally, we show that this "mean-based revenue" benchmark, $\mathsf{MBRev}(\mathcal{D})$ lies truly in between the Myerson revenue and the expected welfare: for all $c$, there exists a distribution $\mathcal{D}$ over values such that $c \cdot T \cdot \mathsf{Rev}(\mathcal{D}) < \mathsf{MBRev}(\mathcal{D}) < \frac{1}{c} \cdot T \cdot \mathsf{Val}(\mathcal{D})$. In other words, the seller's mean-based revenue may be unboundedly better than the default strategy, yet simultaneously unboundedly far from the expected welfare. We provide formal statements and a detailed proof overview of these results in Section 3.3. To briefly recap, our main results are the following:

(1) If the buyer uses a "mean-based" learning algorithm like EXP3, the seller can extract revenue $(1-\varepsilon)T \cdot \mathsf{Val}(\mathcal{D}) - o(T)$ for any constant $\varepsilon > 0$ (Theorem 3.1).
(2) There exists a natural no-regret algorithm $\mathcal{A}$ such that when the buyer bids according to $\mathcal{A}$, the seller's default strategy (charging the Myerson reserve every round) is optimal (Theorem 3.2).
(3) If the buyer uses a "mean-based" algorithm only over undominated strategies, the seller can extract revenue $\mathsf{MBRev}(\mathcal{D})$ using an auction where overbidding is dominated in every round. Moreover, we characterize $\mathsf{MBRev}(\mathcal{D})$ as the value of a linear program, and show it can be simultaneously unboundedly better than $T \cdot \mathsf{Rev}(\mathcal{D})$ and unboundedly worse than $T \cdot \mathsf{Val}(\mathcal{D})$ (Theorems 3.6, 3.4 and 3.8).

Our plan for the remaining sections is as follows. Below, we overview our connection to related work. Section 2 formally defines our model. Section 3 works through a concrete example, providing intuition for all three results. Section 4 discusses conclusions and open problems.

### 1.1 Related Work

There are two lines of work that are most related to ours. The first is that of *dynamic auctions*, such as [2, 21–23, 28]. Like our model, there are $T$ rounds where the seller has a single item for sale to a single buyer, whose value is drawn from some distribution every round. However, the buyer is fully strategic and processes fully how their choices today affect the seller's decisions tomorrow (e.g. they engage with deals of the form "pay today to get the item tomorrow"). Additional closely related work is that of Devanur et al. studying the Fishmonger problem [12, 17]. Here, there is again a single buyer and seller, and $T$ rounds of sale. Unlike our model, the buyer draws a value from $\mathcal{D}$ once during round 0 and that value is fixed through all $T$ rounds (so the seller could try to learn the buyer's value over time). Also unlike our model, they study perfect Bayesian equilibria (where again the buyer is fully strategic, and reasons about how their actions today affect the seller's behavior tomorrow).

In contrast to these works, while buyers in our model do care about the future (e.g. they value learning), they don't reason about how their actions today might affect the seller's decisions tomorrow. Our model better captures settings where full information about the auction is not public (and fully strategic reasoning is simply impossible without the necessary information).

Other related work considers the *Price of Anarchy* of simple combinatorial auctions when bidders no-regret learn [9, 27, 29, 30]. One key difference between this line of work and ours is that these all study welfare maximization for combinatorial auctions with rich valuation functions. In contrast, our work studies revenue maximization while selling a single item. Additionally, in these works the seller commits to a publicly known auction format, and the only reason for learning is due to the strategic behavior of other buyers. In contrast, buyers in our model have to learn *even when they are the only buyer*, due to the strategic nature of the seller.

Recent work has also considered learning from the perspective of the seller. In these works, the buyer's (or buyers') valuations are drawn from an unknown distribution, and the seller's goal is to learn an approximately optimal auction with as few samples as possible [6, 8, 11, 13, 14, 24, 25]. These works consider numerous different models and achieve a wide range of guarantees, but all study the learning problem from the perspective of the *seller*, whereas the buyer is simply myopic and participates in only one round. In contrast, it is the buyer in our model who does the learning (and there is no information for the seller to learn: the buyer's values are drawn fresh in every round).

Finally, no-regret learning in online decision problems is an extremely well-studied problem. When feedback is revealed for every possible action, one well-known solution is the multiplicative weight update rule which has been rediscovered and applied in many fields (see survey [1] for more details). Another algorithmic scheme for the online decision problem is known as Follow the Perturbed Leader [16, 18, 19]. When only feedback for the selected action is revealed, the problem is referred to as the multi-armed bandit problem. Here, similar ideas to the MWU rule are used in developing the EXP3 algorithm [3] for adversarial bandit model, and also for the contextual bandit problem [20]. Our algorithm in Theorem 3.2 bears some similarities to the low swap regret algorithm introduced in [4]. See the survey [5] for more details about the multi-armed bandit problem. Our results hold in both models (i.e. whether the buyer receives feedback for every bid they could have made, or only the bid they actually make), so we will make use of both classes of algorithms.

In summary, while there is already extensive work related to repeated sales in auctions, and even no-regret learning with respect to auctions (from both the buyer and seller perspective), our work is the first to address how a seller might adapt their selling strategy when faced with a no-regret buyer.

## 2 MODEL AND PRELIMINARIES

We consider a setting with 1 buyer and 1 seller. There are $T$ rounds, and in each round the seller has one item for sale. At the start of each round $t$, the buyer's value $v(t)$ (known only to the buyer) for the item is drawn independently from some distribution $\mathcal{D}$ (known to both the seller and the buyer). For simplicity, we assume $\mathcal{D}$ has a finite support[3] of size $m$, supported on values $0 \leq v_1 < v_2 < \cdots < v_m \leq 1$. For each $i \in [m]$, $v_i$ has probability $q_i$ of being drawn under $\mathcal{D}$.

The seller then presents $K$ options for the buyer, which can be thought of as "possible bids" (we will interchangeably refer to these as *options*, *bids*, or *arms* throughout the paper, depending on context). Each arm $i$ is labelled with a bid value $b_i \in [0, 1]$, with $b_1 < \ldots, < b_K$. Upon pulling this arm at round $t$, the buyer receives the item with some allocation probability $a_{i,t}$, and must pay a price $p_{i,t} \in [0, a_{i,t} \cdot b_i]$. These values $a_{i,t}$ and $p_{i,t}$ are chosen by the seller during time $t$, but remain unknown to the buyer until he plays an arm, upon which he learns the values for that arm. All of our positive results (i.e. strategies for the seller) are *non-adaptive* (in some places called *oblivious*), in the sense that that $a_{i,t}, p_{i,t}$ are set before the first round starts. All of our negative results (i.e. upper bounds on how much a seller can possibly attain) hold even against *fully adaptive* sellers, where $a_{i,t}$ and $p_{i,t}$ can be set *even after learning the distribution of arms the buyer intends to pull in round t*.

In order for the selling strategies to possibly represent natural auctions, we require the allocation/price rules to be monotone. That is, if $i > j$, then for all $t$, $a_{i,t} \geq a_{j,t}$ and $p_{i,t} \geq p_{j,t}$. In other words, bidding higher should result in a (weakly) higher probability of receiving the item and (weakly) higher expected payment. We'll also insist on the existence of an arm 0 with bid $b_0 = 0$ and $a_{0,t} = 0$ for all $t$; i.e., an arm which charges nothing but does not give the item. Playing this arm can be thought of as not participating in the auction.

### 2.1 Bandits and experts

Our goal is to understand the behavior of such mechanisms when the buyer plays according to some no-regret strategy for the multi-armed bandit problem. In the classic multi-armed bandit problem a learner (in our case, the buyer) chooses one of $K$ arms per round, over $T$ rounds. On round $t$, the learner receives a reward $r_{i,t} \in [0, 1]$ for pulling arm $i$ (where the values $r_{i,t}$ are possibly chosen adversarially). The learner's goal is to maximize his total reward.

Let $I_t$ denote the arm pulled by the principal at round $t$. The *regret* of an algorithm $\mathcal{A}$ for the learner is the random variable $\text{Reg}(\mathcal{A}) = \max_i \sum_{t=1}^{T} r_{i,t} - \sum_{t=1}^{T} r_{I_t,t}$. We say an algorithm $\mathcal{A}$ for the multi-armed bandit problem is *$\delta$-no-regret* if $\mathbb{E}[\text{Reg}(\mathcal{A})] \leq \delta$ (where the expectation is taken over the randomness of $\mathcal{A}$). We say an algorithm $\mathcal{A}$ is *no-regret* if it is $\delta$-no-regret for some $\delta = o(T)$.

In the multi-armed bandits setting, the learner only learns the value $r_{i,t}$ for the arm $i$ which he pulls on round $t$. In our setting, the learner will learn $a_{i,t}$ and $p_{i,t}$ explicitly (from which they can compute $r_{i,t}$). Our results (both positive and negative) also hold when the learner learns the value $r_{i,t}$ for *all* arms $i$ (we refer this full-information setting as the *experts setting*, in contrast to the partial-information *bandits setting*). Simple no-regret algorithms exist in both the experts setting and the bandits setting. Of special interest in this paper will be a class of learning algorithms for the bandits problem and experts problem which we term 'mean-based'.

*Definition 2.1 (Mean-Based Learning Algorithm).* Let $\sigma_{i,t} = \sum_{s=1}^{t} r_{i,s}$. An algorithm for the experts problem or multi-armed bandits problem is *$\gamma$-mean-based* if it is the case that whenever $\sigma_{i,t} < \sigma_{j,t} - \gamma T$, then the probability that the algorithm pulls arm $i$ on round $t$ is at most $\gamma$. We say an algorithm is *mean-based* if it is *$\gamma$-mean-based* for some $\gamma = o(1)$.

[3]If $\mathcal{D}$ instead has infinite support, all our results hold approximately after discretization to multiples of $\varepsilon$. If $\mathcal{D}$ is bounded in $[0, H]$, then all our results hold after normalizing $\mathcal{D}$ by dividing by $H$.

Intuitively, 'mean-based' algorithms will rarely pick an arm whose current mean is significantly worse than the current best mean. Many no-regret algorithms, including commonly used variants of EXP3 (for the bandits setting), the Multiplicative Weights algorithm (for the experts setting) and the Follow-the-Perturbed-Leader algorithm (experts setting), are mean-based (see full version of this paper).

*Contextual bandits.* In our setting, the buyer has the additional information of their current value for the item, and hence is actually facing a *contextual bandits* problem. In (our variant of) the contextual bandits problem, each round $t$ the learner is additionally provided with a *context* $c_t$ drawn from some distribution $\mathcal{D}$ supported on a finite set $C$ (in our setting, $c_t = v(t)$, the buyer's valuation for the item at time $t$). The adversary now specifies rewards $r_{i,t}(c)$, the reward the learner receives if he pulls arm $i$ on round $t$ while having context $c$. If we are in the full-information (experts) setting, the learner learns the values of $r_{i,t}(c_t)$ for all arms $i$ after round $t$, where as if we are in the partial-information (bandits) setting, the learner only learns the value of $r_{i,t}(c_t)$ for the arm $i$ that he pulled.

In the contextual bandits setting, we now define the regret of an algorithm $\mathcal{A}$ in terms of regret against the best "context-specific" policy $\pi$; that is, $\text{Reg}(\mathcal{A}) = \max_{\pi:C\to[K]} \sum_{t=1}^{T} r_{\pi(c_t),t}(c_t) - \sum_{t=1}^{T} r_{I_t,t}(c_t)$, where again $I_t$ is the arm pulled by $M$ on round $t$. As before, we say an algorithm is $\delta$-low regret if $\mathbb{E}[\text{Reg}(M)] \le \delta$, and say an algorithm is no-regret if it is $\delta$-no-regret for some $\delta = o(T)$.

If the size of the context set $C$ is constant with respect to $T$, then there is a simple way to construct a no-regret algorithm $M'$ for the contextual bandits problem from a no-regret algorithm $M$ for the classic bandits problem: simply maintain a separate instance of $M$ for every different context $v \in C$ (in the contextual bandits literature, this is sometimes referred to as the $S$-EXP3 algorithm [5]). We call the algorithm we obtain this way its *contextualization*, and denote it as $\text{cont}(M)$.

If we start with a mean-based learning algorithm, then we can show that its contextualization satisfies an analogue of the mean-based property for the contextual-bandits problem (proof in the full version of this paper).

*Definition 2.2 (Mean-Based Contextual Learning Algorithm).* Let $\sigma_{i,t}(c) = \sum_{s=1}^{t} r_{i,s}(c)$. An algorithm for the contextual bandits problem is *$\gamma$-mean-based* if it is the case that whenever $\sigma_{i,t}(c) < \sigma_{j,t}(c) - \gamma T$, then the probability $p_{i,t}(c)$ that the algorithm pulls arm $i$ on round $t$ if it has context $c$ satisfying $p_{i,t}(c) < \gamma$. We say an algorithm is *mean-based* if it is *$\gamma$-mean-based* for some $\gamma = o(1)$.

THEOREM 2.3. *If an algorithm for the experts problem or multi-armed bandits problem is mean-based, then its contextualization is also a mean-based algorithm for the contextual bandits problem.*

Finally, we will refer to learning algorithms that never overbid as *conservative*. We will sometimes abuse notation and instead refer to a buyer employing a conservative algorithm as conservative.

## 2.2 Welfare and monopoly revenue

In order to evaluate the performance of our mechanisms for the seller, we will compare the revenue the seller obtains to two benchmarks from the single-round setting of a seller selling a single item to a buyer with value drawn from distribution $\mathcal{D}$.

The first benchmark we consider is the *welfare* of the buyer, the expected value the buyer assigns to the item. This quantity clearly upper bounds the expected revenue that the seller can hope to extract per round.

*Definition 2.4.* The *welfare*, $\text{Val}(\mathcal{D})$ is equal to $\mathbb{E}_{v\sim\mathcal{D}}[v]$.

The second benchmark we consider is the *monopoly revenue*, the maximum possible revenue attainable by the seller in one round against a rational buyer. Seminal work of Myerson [26] shows that this revenue is attainable by setting a fixed price ("monopoly/Myerson reserve") for the item, and hence can be characterized as follows.

*Definition 2.5.* The *monopoly revenue* (alternatively, *Myerson revenue*) $\mathsf{Mye}(\mathcal{D})$ is equal to $\max_p p \cdot \Pr_{v \sim \mathcal{D}}[v \geq p]$.

### 2.3 A final note on the model

For concreteness, we chose to phrase our problem as one where a single bidder whose value is repeatedly drawn independently from $\mathcal{D}$ each round engages in no-regret learning with their value as context. Alternatively, we could imagine a population of $m$ different buyers, each with a *fixed* value $v_i$. Each round, exactly one buyer arrives at the auction, and it is buyer $i$ with probability $q_i$. The buyers are indistinguishable to the seller, and each buyer no-regret learns (without context, because their value is always $v_i$). This model is mathematically equivalent to ours, so all of our results hold in this model as well if the reader prefers this interpretation instead.

## 3 AN ILLUSTRATIVE EXAMPLE

In this section, we overview an illustrative example to show the difference between mean-based and non-mean-based learning algorithms, and between conservative and non-conservative learners. We will not prove all claims in this section (nor carry out all calculations) as it is only meant to illustrate and provide intuition. Throughout this section, the running example will be when $\mathcal{D}$ samples $1/4$ with probability $1/2$, $1/2$ with probability $1/4$, and 1 with probability $1/4$. Note that $\mathsf{Val}(\mathcal{D}) = 1/2$ and $\mathsf{Rev}(\mathcal{D}) = 1/4$.

### 3.1 Mean-Based Learning

Let's first consider what the seller can do with an auction when the buyer is running a mean-based (non-conservative) learning algorithm like EXP3. The seller will let the buyer bid 0 or 1. If the buyer bids 0, they pay nothing but do not receive the item (recall that an arm of this form is required). If the buyer bids 1 in round $t$, they receive the item and pay some price $p_t$ as follows: for the first half of the game ($1 \leq t \leq T/2$), the seller sets $p_t = 0$. For the second half of the game ($T/2 < t \leq T$), the seller sets $p_t = 1$.

Let's examine the behaviour of the buyer, recalling that they run a mean-based learning algorithm, and therefore (almost) always pull the arm with highest cumulative utility. The buyer with value 1 will happily bid 1 all the way through, since he is always offered the item for less than or equal to his value for the item. The buyer with value $1/2$ will bid 1 for the first $T/2$ rounds, accumulating a surplus (i.e., negative regret) of $1/2$ per round. For the next $T/2$ rounds, this surplus slowly disappears at the rate of $1/2$ per round until it disappears at time $T$, so the bidder with value $1/2$ will bid 1 all the way through. Finally, the bidder with value $1/4$ will bid 1 for the first $T/2$ rounds, accumulating surplus at a rate of $1/4$ per round. After round $T/2$, this surplus decreases at a rate of $3/4$ per round, until at round $2T/3$ his cumulative utility from bidding 1 reaches 0 and he switches to bidding 0.

Now let's compute the revenue. From round $T/2$ through $2T/3$, the buyer always buys the item at a price of 1, so the seller obtains $T/6$ revenue. Finally, from round $2T/3$ through $T$, the buyer purchases the item with probability $1/2$ and pays 1. The total revenue is $0 + T/6 + T/6 = T/3$. Note that if the seller used the default strategy, they would extract revenue only $T/4$.

Where did our extra revenue come from? First, note that the welfare of the buyer in this example is quite high: the bidder gets the item the whole way through when $v \geq 1/2$, and two-thirds of the way through when $v = 1/4$. One reason why the welfare is so high is because we give the item away for free in the early rounds. But notice also that the utility of the buyer is quite low: the buyer actually has zero utility when $v \leq 1/2$, and utility $1/2$ when $v = 1$. The reason we're able to keep the utility low, despite giving the item away for free in the early rounds is because we overcharge the bidders in later rounds (and they choose to overpay, exactly because their learning is mean-based).

In fact, by offering additional options to the buyer, we show that *it is possible for the seller to extract up to the full welfare from the buyer* (e.g. a net revenue of $T/2 - o(T)$ for this example). As in the above example, our mechanism makes use of arms which are initially very good for the buyer (giving the item away for free, accumulating negative regret), followed by a period where they are very bad for the buyer (where they pay more than their value). The trick in the construction is making sure that the good/bad intervals line up so that: a) the buyer purchases the item in every round, no matter their value (this is necessary in order to possibly extract full welfare) and b) by round $T$, the buyer has zero (arbitrarily small) utility, no matter their value.

Getting the intervals to line up properly so that any mean-based learner will pick the desired arms still requires some work. But interestingly, our constructed mechanism is non-adaptive and prior-independent (i.e. the same mechanism extracts full welfare *for all* $\mathcal{D}$). Theorem 3.1 below formally states the guarantees. The construction itself and the proof appear in the full version of this paper.

THEOREM 3.1. *If the buyer is running a mean-based algorithm, for any constant* $\varepsilon > 0$, *there exists a strategy for the seller which obtains revenue at least* $(1 - \varepsilon)\mathsf{Val}(\mathcal{D})T - o(T)$.

Two properties should jump out as key in enabling the result above. The first is that the buyer *only* has no regret towards fixed arms and *not* towards the policy they would have used with a lower value (this is what leads the buyer to continue bidding 1 with value $1/2$ even though they have already learned to bid 0 with value $1/4$). This suggests an avenue towards an improved learning algorithm: have the bidder attempt to have no regret not only towards each fixed arm, but also towards the policy of play produced when having different values. This turns out to be exactly the right idea, and is discussed in the following subsection below.

The second key property is that we were able to "lure" the bidders into playing an arm with a free item, then overcharge them later to make up for lost revenue. This requires that the bidder consider pulling an arm with maximum bid exceeding their value, which will never happen for a conservative bidder. It turns out it is still possible to do better than the default strategy against conservative bidders, but not as well as against non-conservative mean-based bidders. Section 3.3 explores conservative mean-based bidders for this example.

### 3.2 Better Learning

In our bad example above, the buyer with value $1/2$ for the item slowly spends the second half of the game losing utility. While his behaviour is still no-regret (he ends up with zero net utility, which indeed is at least as good as only bidding 0), he would have been much happier to follow the actions of the buyer with value $1/4$, who started bidding 0 at $2T/3$.

Using this idea, we show how to construct a no-regret algorithm for the buyer (Algorithm 1) such that the seller receives at most the Myerson revenue every round. We accomplish this by extending an arbitrary no-regret algorithm (e.g. EXP3) by introducing "virtual arms" for each value, so that each buyer with value $v$ has low regret not just with respect to every fixed bid, but also no-regret with respect to the policy of play as if they had a different value $v'$ for the item (for all $v' < v$). In some ways, our construction is very similar to the construction of low internal-regret (or swap-regret) algorithms from low external-regret algorithms. The main difference is that instead of having low regret with respect to swapping actions, we have low regret with respect to swapping *contexts* (i.e. values). Theorem 3.2 below states that the seller cannot outperform the default strategy against buyers who use such algorithms to learn.

THEOREM 3.2. *There exists a no-regret algorithm (Algorithm 1) for the buyer against which every seller strategy extracts no more than* $\mathsf{Mye}(\mathcal{D})T + O(m\sqrt{\delta T})$ *revenue.*

**Algorithm 1** No-regret algorithm for buyer where the seller achieves no more than $\mathsf{Mye}(\mathcal{D})T + o(T)$ revenue.

Let $M$ be a $\delta$-no-regret algorithm for the classic multi-armed bandit problem, with $\delta = o(T)$. Initialize $m$ copies of $M$, $M_1$ through $M_m$.
Instance $M_i$ of $M$ will learn over $K + i - 1$ arms.
The first $K$ arms of $M_i$ ("bid arms") correspond to the $K$ possible menu options $b_1, b_2, \ldots, b_K$.
The last $i - 1$ arms of $M_i$ ("value arms") correspond to the $i - 1$ possible values (contexts) $v_1, \ldots, v_{i-1}$.
**for** $t = 1$ to $T$ **do**
    **if** buyer has value $v_i$ **then**
        Use $M_i$ to pick one arm from the $K + i - 1$ arms.
        **if** the arm is a bid arm $b_j$ **then**
            Pick the menu option $j$ (i.e. bid $b_j$).
        **else if** the arm is a value arm $v_j$ **then**
            Sample an arm from $M_j$ (but don't update its state). If it is a bid arm, pick the corresponding menu option. If it is a value arm, recurse.
        **end if**
        Update the state of algorithm $M_i$ with the utility of this round.
    **end if**
**end for**

A more further discussion of the algorithm along with a proof of Theorem 3.2 appear in the full version of this paper. The key observation in the proof is that "not regretting playing as if my value were $v'$" sounds a lot like "not preferring to report value $v'$ instead of $v$." This suggests that the aggregate allocation probabilities and prices paid by any buyer using our algorithm should satisfy the same constraints as a truthful auction, proving that the resulting revenue cannot exceed the default strategy (and indeed the proof follows this approach).

Finally, observe that the following corollary immediately follows. Because the seller cannot hope to get more than $\mathsf{Mye}(\mathcal{D})T + o(T)$ per round when the buyer is using Algorithm 1, and the buyer cannot hope to do better than telling the truth against a truthful auction, it is in fact a Nash for the buyer to use Algorithm 1 and the seller to set price equal to the Myerson reserve every round.

COROLLARY 3.3. *It is an $o(T)$-Nash equilibrium for the seller to set the Myerson reserve $p(\mathcal{D})$ in every round (any bid $\geq p(\mathcal{D})$ reserve wins the item and pays $p(\mathcal{D})$), and the buyer to use Algorithm 1.*

### 3.3 Mean-Based Learning and Conservative Bidders

Recall in our example that to extract revenue $T/3$, bidders with values $1/4$ and $1/2$ had to consider bidding 1. If bidders are conservative, they will simply never do this.

Although the auction in Section 3.1 is no longer viable, consider the following auction instead: in addition to the zero arm, the bidder can bid $1/4$ or $1/2$. If they bid $1/2$ in any round, they will get the item with probability 1 and pay $1/2$. If they bid $1/4$ in round $t \leq T/3$, they get nothing. If they bid $1/4$ in round $t \in (T/3, T]$, they get the item and pay $1/4$. Let's again see what the bidder will choose to do, remembering that they will always pull the arm that has provided highest cumulative utility (due to being mean-based).

Clearly, the bidder with value $1/4$ will bid $1/4$ every round (since they are conservative, they won't even consider bidding $1/2$), making a total payment of $2T/3 \cdot 1/4 \cdot 1/2 = T/12$. The bidder with value $1/2$ will bid $1/2$ for the first $T/3$ rounds, and then immediately switch to bidding $1/4$, making a total payment of $T/3 \cdot 1/2 \cdot 1/4 + 2T/3 \cdot 1/4 \cdot 1/4 = T/12$.

The bidder with value 1 will actually bid $1/2$ for the entire $T$ rounds. To see this, observe that their cumulative surplus through round $t$ from bidding $1/2$ is $t \cdot 1/2 \cdot 1/4 = t/8$ ($t$ rounds by utility $1/2$ per round by probability $1/4$ of having value 1). Their cumulative surplus through round $t$ from bidding $1/4$ is instead $(t - T/3) \cdot 3/4 \cdot 1/4 = 3t/16 - T/16 \leq t/8$ (for $t \leq T$). Because they are mean-based, they will indeed bid $1/2$ for the entire duration due to its strictly higher utility. So their total payment will be $T \cdot 1/2 \cdot 1/4 = T/8$. The total revenue is then $7T/24 > T/4$, again surpassing the default strategy (but not reaching the $T/3$ achieved against non-conservative buyers).

Let's again see where our extra revenue comes from in comparison to a truthful auction. Notice that the bidder receives the item with probability 1 conditioned on having value $1/2$, and also conditioned on having value 1. Yet somehow the bidder pays an average of $1/3$ conditioned on having value $1/2$, but an average of $1/2$ conditioned on having value 1. *This could never happen in a truthful auction*, as the bidder would strictly prefer to pretend their value was $1/2$ rather than 1. But it is entirely possible when the buyer does mean-based learning, as evidenced by this example.

In the full version of this paper, we define $\mathsf{MBRev}(\mathcal{D})$ as the value of the LP in Figure 1. In Theorems 3.6 and 3.4, we show that $\mathsf{MBRev}(\mathcal{D})T$ tightly characterizes (up to $\pm o(T)$) the optimal revenue a seller can extract against a conservative buyer. The proofs can be found in the full version of this paper.

$$\begin{aligned} \textbf{maximize} \quad & \sum_{i=1}^{m} q_i(v_i x_i - u_i) \\ \textbf{subject to} \quad & u_i \geq (v_i - v_j) \cdot x_j, \quad \forall\, i, j \in [m] : i > j \\ & u_i \geq 0, 1 \geq x_i \geq 0, \quad \forall\, i \in [m] \end{aligned}$$

Fig. 1. The mean-based revenue LP.

Before stating our theorems, let us parse this LP. $q_i$ is a constant representing the probability that the buyer has value $v_i$ (also a constant). $x_i$ is a variable representing the average probability that the bidder gets the item with value $v_i$, and $u_i$ is a variable representing the average utility of the bidder when having value $v_i$. Therefore, this bidder's average value is $v_i x_i$, the average price they pay is $v_i x_i - u_i$, and the objective function is simply the average revenue. The second constraints are just normalization, ensuring that everything lies in $[0, 1]$. The first line of constraints are the interesting ones. These look a lot like IC constraints that a truthful auction must satisfy, but something's missing: the LHS is clearly the utility of the buyer with value $v_i$ for "telling the truth," but the utility of the buyer for "reporting $v_j$ instead" is $(v_i - v_j) \cdot x_j + u_j$ (so the $u_j$ term is missing on the RHS).

Here is a brief proof outline for why no seller can extract more revenue than $\mathsf{MBRev}(\mathcal{D})$:

(1) Since the buyer has no regret conditioned on having value $v_i$, their utility is at least as high as playing arm $j$ every round, for all $j \leq i$.

(2) Since the auction never charges arm $j$ more than $v_j$ (conditioned on awarding the item), the buyer's utility for playing arm $j$ every round is at least $y_j \cdot (v_i - v_j)$, where $y_j$ is the average probability that arm $j$ awards the item.
(3) Since the auction is monotone, and the buyer never considers overbidding, if the buyer gets the item with probability $x_j$ conditioned on having value $v_j$, we must have $y_j \geq x_j$.

These three facts together show that no seller can extract more than $\mathsf{MBRev}(\mathcal{D})$ against a no-regret buyer who doesn't overbid. Observe also that step 3 is *exactly* the step that doesn't hold for buyers who consider overbidding (and is exactly what's violated in our example in Section 3.1): if the buyer ever overbids, then they might receive the item with higher probability than had they just played their own arm every round.

THEOREM 3.4. *Any strategy for the seller achieves revenue at most* $\mathsf{MBRev}(\mathcal{D})T + o(T)$ *against a conservative buyer.*

The full proof of Theorem 3.4 appears in the the full version of this paper - all of the key ideas have been overviewed above.

It turns out that the previous theorem is tight; there exists an auction (taking the form of a first-price auction with descending reserve) which achieves revenue $\mathsf{MBRev}(\mathcal{D})T$ against a conservative mean-based buyer. More specifically, this auction is defined by a threshold $r_t$ that decreases over time. If at time $t$ you bid $b_t \geq r_t$, then you receive the item and must pay $b_t$; otherwise, you receive nothing and pay nothing. Moreover, the threshold function $r_t$ which achieves optimal revenue is determined from the optimal solution to the mean-based LP: the threshold $r_t$ drops from $v_i$ to $v_{i+1}$ at round $x_i$ (where the $x_i$ belong to some optimal solution).

To show that this is a valid strategy for the seller, we need to show that the values $x_i$ are monotone increasing. Luckily, this follows simply from the structure of the mean-based revenue LP.

LEMMA 3.5. *Let* $x_1, x_2, \ldots, x_m, u_1, u_2, \ldots, u_m$ *be an optimal solution to the mean-based revenue LP. Then for all* $i < j$, $x_i < x_j$.

PROOF. We proceed by contradiction. Suppose that the sequence of $x_i$ are not monotone; then there exists an $1 \leq i \leq m-1$ such that $x_i > x_{i+1}$. Now consider another solution of the LP, where we increase $x_{i+1}$ to $x_i$, keeping the value of all other variables the same. This new solution does not violate any constraints in the LP since for all $j > i+1$, $u_j \geq (v_j - v_i) \cdot x_i \geq (v_j - v_{i+1}) \cdot x_i$. However this change increases the value of the objective by $v_{i+1}q_{i+1}(x_i - x_{i+1}) > 0$, thus contradicting the fact that $x_1, \ldots, x_m, u_1, \ldots, u_m$ was an optimal solution of the mean-based revenue LP. □

We now show that this strategy indeed achieves $\mathsf{MBRev}(\mathcal{D})T$ against a conservative buyer.

THEOREM 3.6. *For any constant* $\varepsilon > 0$, *there exists a strategy for the seller gets revenue at least* $(\mathsf{MBRev}(\mathcal{D}) - \varepsilon)T - o(T)$ *against a buyer running a mean-based algorithm who overbids with probability* 0. *The strategy sets a decreasing cutoff* $r_t$ *and for all* $t$ *awards the item with probability* 1 *to any bid* $b_t \geq r_t$ *for price* $b_t$, *and with probability* 0 *to any bid* $b_t < r_t$.

PROOF. We will show that: i) the buyer with value $v_i$ receives the item for at least $x_i T - o(T)$ turns (receiving $v_i x_i T - o(T)$ total utility from the items), and ii) this buyer's net utility is at most $(u_i + \varepsilon)T + o(T)$. This implies that this buyer pays the seller at least $x_i v_i T - (u_i + \varepsilon)T - o(T)$ over the course of the $T$ rounds; taking expectation over all $v_i$ completes the proof.

Assume the buyer is running a $\gamma$-mean-based learning algorithm. Consider the buyer when they have value $v_i$. Note that

$$\sigma_{j,t}(v_i) = (v_i - v_j + \varepsilon) \cdot \max(0, t - (1 - x_j)T).$$

We first claim that after round $(1-x_i)T+\gamma T/\varepsilon$, the buyer will buy the item (i.e., choose an option that results in him getting the item) each round with probability at least $1-m\gamma$. To see this, first note that $\sigma_{i,t}(v_i) \geq \gamma T$ when $t \geq (1-x_i)T + \gamma T/\varepsilon$. Then, since the cumulative utility of any arm is 0 until it starts offering the item, it follows from the mean-based condition that the buyer will pick a specific arm that is not offering the item with probability at most $\gamma$, and therefore choose some good arm with probability at least $1-m\gamma$. It follows that, in expectation, the buyer with value $v_i$ receives the item for at least $(1-m\gamma)(x_iT - \gamma T/\varepsilon) = x_iT - o(T)$ turns.

We now proceed to upper bound the overall expected utility of the buyer. For each index $j \leq i$, let $S_j$ be the set of $t$ where $\sigma_{j,t}(v_i) > \sigma_{j',t}(v_i)$ for all other $j'$. Note that since each $\sigma_{j,t}(v_i)$ is a linear function in $t$ (when positive), each $S_j$ is either the empty set or an interval $(y_jT, z_jT)$. Since all the $v_i$ are distinct, note that these intervals partition the interval $((1-x_i)T, T)$ (with the exception of up to $m$ endpoints of these intervals); in particular, $\sum_{j\geq i}(z_j - y_j) = x_i$.

Let $\varepsilon' = \min_j(v_{j+1} - v_j)$. Note that, if $t \in (y_jT + \gamma T/\varepsilon', z_jT - \gamma T/\varepsilon')$, then for all $j' \neq j$, $\sigma_{j,t}(v_i) > \sigma_{j',t}(v_i) + \gamma T$. This follows since $\sigma_{j,t}(v_i) - \sigma_{j',t}(v_i)$ is linear in $t$ with slope $v_j - v_{j'}$, and $|v_j - v_{j'}| > \varepsilon'$. It follows that if $t$ is in this interval, then the buyer will choose option $j$ with probability at least $1-m\gamma$ (by a similar argument as before).

Define $j(t) = \arg\max_j \sigma_{j,t}(v_i)$ to be the index of the arm with the current largest cumulative reward, and let $\sigma_{max,t}(v_i) = \sum_{s=1}^{t} r_{j(s),s}(v_i)$ be the cumulative utility of always playing the arm with the current highest cumulative reward for the first $t$ rounds. The following lemma shows that $\sigma_{max,T}(v_i)$ is close to $\max_j \sigma_{j,T}(v_i)$. (In other words, playing the best arm every round and playing the best-at-the-end arm every round have similar payoffs if the historically best arm does not change often).

Lemma 3.7. *$|\sigma_{max,T}(v_i) - \max_j \sigma_{j,T}(v_i)| \leq m$.*

Proof. Let $W = |\{t | j(t) \neq j(t+1)\}|$ equal the number of times the best arm switches values; note that since each $\sigma_{j,t}(v_i)$ is linear, $W$ is at most $m$. Let $t_1 < t_2 < \cdots < t_W$ be the values of $t$ such that $j(t) \neq j(t+1)$. Additionally define $t_0 = 1$ and $t_{W+1} = T$. Then, dividing the cumulative reward $\sigma_{max,t}$ into intervals by these $t_i$, we get that

$$\begin{aligned}
\sigma_{max,t}(v_i) &= \sum_{s=1}^{t} r_{j(s),s}(v_i)\\
&= \sum_{i=1}^{W+1} (\sigma_{j(t_i),t_i}(v_i) - \sigma_{j(t_i),t_{i-1}}(v_i))\\
&= \sigma_{j(T),T}(v_i) + \sum_{i=1}^{W+1} (\sigma_{j(t_{i-1}),t_{i-1}}(v_i) - \sigma_{j(t_i),t_{i-1}}(v_i))\\
&= \max_j \sigma_{j,t}(v_i) + \sum_{i=1}^{W+1} (\sigma_{j(t_{i-1}),t_{i-1}}(v_i) - \sigma_{j(t_i),t_{i-1}}(v_i))
\end{aligned}$$

It therefore suffices to show that $|\sigma_{j(t_{i-1}),t_{i-1}}(v_i) - \sigma_{j(t_i),t_{i-1}}(v_i)| \leq 1$ for all $i$. To see this, note that (by the definition of $j(t)$), $\sigma_{j(t_{i-1}),t_{i-1}}(v_i) - \sigma_{j(t_i),t_{i-1}}(v_i) > 0$, and that $\sigma_{j(t_{i-1}),t_{i-1}+1}(v_i) - \sigma_{j(t_i),t_{i-1}+1}(v_i) < 0$. However,

$$(\sigma_{j(t_{i-1}),t_{i-1}+1}(v_i) - \sigma_{j(t_i),t_{i-1}+1}(v_i)) = (\sigma_{j(t_{i-1}),t_{i-1}}(v_i) - \sigma_{j(t_i),t_{i-1}}(v_i)) + (r_{j(t_{i-1}),t_{i-1}+1}(v_i) - r_{j(t_i),t_{i-1}+1}(v_i))$$

Since $0 \leq r_{j,t}(u) \leq 1$, it follows that $|\sigma_{j(t_{i-1}),t_{i-1}}(v_i) - \sigma_{j(t_i),t_{i-1}}(v_i)| \leq 1$. This completes the proof. □

Let $\sigma_T(v_i) = \sum_{t=1}^{T} \mathbb{E}[r_{I_t,t}(v_i)]$ denote the expected cumulative utility of this buyer at time $T$. We claim that $\sigma_T \leq \max_j \sigma_{j,T}(v_i) + o(T)$. To see this, recall that, for $t \in (y_jT + \gamma T/\varepsilon', z_jT - \gamma T/\varepsilon')$, $\Pr[I_t \neq j] \leq m\gamma$, and therefore $\mathbb{E}[r_{I_t,t}] \leq r_{j,t} + m\gamma$. Furthermore, note that for $t \in S_j$, $j(t) = j$, so $r_{j,t} = r_{j(t),t}$ and $\mathbb{E}[r_{I_t,t}] \leq r_{j(t),t} + m\gamma$. It follows that

$$
\begin{aligned}
\sigma_T(v_i) &= \sum_{t=1}^{T} \mathbb{E}[r_{I_t,t}(v_i)] \\
&\leq \sum_{t=(1-x_i)T}^{T} \mathbb{E}[r_{I_t,t}(v_i)] \\
&= \sum_{j=1}^{i} \sum_{t=y_jT}^{z_jT} \mathbb{E}[r_{I_t,t}(v_i)] \\
&\leq \sum_{j=1}^{i} \left( \frac{2\gamma T}{\varepsilon'} + \sum_{t=y_jT+\gamma T/\varepsilon'}^{z_jT-\gamma T/\varepsilon'} \mathbb{E}[r_{I_t,t}(v_i)] \right) \\
&\leq \sum_{j=1}^{i} \left( \frac{2\gamma T}{\varepsilon'} + \sum_{t=y_jT+\gamma T/\varepsilon'}^{z_jT-\gamma T/\varepsilon'} (r_{j(t),t}(v_i) + m\gamma) \right) \\
&\leq \frac{2m\gamma T}{\varepsilon'} + m\gamma T + \sum_{t=1}^{T} r_{j(t),t}(v_i) \\
&= \frac{2m\gamma T}{\varepsilon'} + m\gamma T + \sigma_{max,T}(v_i) \\
&\leq \frac{2m\gamma T}{\varepsilon'} + m\gamma T + m + \max_j \sigma_{j,T}(v_i) \\
&= \max_j \sigma_{j,T}(v_i) + o(T).
\end{aligned}
$$

Finally, note that

$$
\begin{aligned}
\max_j \sigma_{j,T}(v_i) &= \max_{j<i} (v_i - v_j + \varepsilon) x_j T \\
&\leq (\max_{j<i} (v_i - v_j) x_j + \varepsilon) T \\
&= (u_i + \varepsilon) T
\end{aligned}
$$

It follows that $\sigma_T(v_i) \leq (u_i + \varepsilon)T + o(T)$, as desired.

□

Finally, we show that this quantity MBRev($\mathcal{D}$) is in fact significantly different from both Val($\mathcal{D}$) and Rev($\mathcal{D}$); in particular, it is a constant-factor approximation to neither. In particular, the multiplicative gap between MBRev($\mathcal{D}$) and Rev($\mathcal{D}$) can grow as large as $\log\log H$ for distributions $\mathcal{D}$ supported on $[1, H]$. In comparison, the gap between Val($\mathcal{D}$) and Rev($\mathcal{D}$) can grow as large as $\log H$ on this same interval, and in fact both gaps are maximized for the same distribution: the equal-revenue curve $\mathcal{D}_{ERC}$ truncated at $H$.

Theorem 3.8. *For distributions $\mathcal{D}$ supported on $[1, H]$,* MBRev($\mathcal{D}$) $= O(\log\log H)$*, and there exist $\mathcal{D}$ supported on $[1, H]$ such that* MBRev($\mathcal{D}$) $= \Theta(\log\log H)$*. For this same $\mathcal{D}$,* Val($\mathcal{D}$) $= \Theta(\log H)$.

The proof of Theorem 3.8 is included in the full version of this paper. The proof is divided into two parts (after extending the definition of $\mathrm{MBRev}(\mathcal{D})$ to hold for continuous distributions $\mathcal{D}$): 1. showing that $\mathrm{MBRev}(\mathcal{D}_{ERC}) \leq O(\log\log H)$, and 2. showing that $\mathrm{MBRev}(\mathcal{D}_{ERC}) \geq O(\log\log H)$.

To show the first part, it suffices to simply demonstrate a solution to the mean-based LP with value at least $O(\log\log H)$. It suffices to choose $x(v) = \frac{\log v}{\log H}$ (equivalently, the reserve for the associated second-price auction should exponentially decay over time).

To show the second part, we examine the dual of the LP. Effectively, this involves rewriting $\mathrm{MBRev}(\mathcal{D})$ in the form

$$\mathrm{MBRev}(\mathcal{D}) = \max_x \mathbb{E}_{v_i \sim \mathcal{D}} \left[ v_i x_i - \max_j (v_i - v_j) x_j \right]$$

(in particular, note that for a fixed choice of $x$, $u_j = \max_j (v_i - v_j)x_j$), and finding an appropriate function $j(i)$ (which corresponds to an assignment to the dual).

### 3.4 A Final Note on the Example

While reading through our examples, the reader may think that the mean-based learner's behavior is clearly irrational: why would you continue paying above your value? Why would you continue paying more than necessary, when you can safely get the item for less?

But this is exactly the point: a more thoughtful learner can indeed do better (for instance, by using the algorithm of Section 3.2). It is also perhaps misleading to believe that the bidder should "obviously" stop overpaying: we only know this because we know the structure of the example. But in principle, how is the bidder supposed to know that the overcharged rounds are the new norm and not an anomaly? Given that most standard no-regret algorithms are mean-based, it's important to nail down the seller's options for exploiting this behavior.

## 4 CONCLUSION AND FUTURE DIRECTIONS

We consider a revenue-maximizing seller with a single item (each round) to sell to a single buyer. We show that when the buyer uses mean-based algorithms like EXP3, the seller can extract revenue equal to the expected welfare with an unnatural auction. We then provide a modified no-regret algorithm $\mathcal{A}$ such that the seller cannot extract revenue exceeding the monopoly revenue when the buyer bids according to $\mathcal{A}$. Finally, we consider a mean-based buyer who never overbids. We tightly characterize the seller's optimal revenue with a linear program, and show that a pay-your-bid auction with decreasing reserves over time achieves this guarantee. Moreover, we show that the mean-based revenue can be unboundedly better than the monopoly revenue while simultaneously worse than the expected welfare. In particular, for the equal revenue curve truncated at $H$, the monopoly revenue is 1, the expected welfare is $\ln(H)$, and the mean-based revenue is $\Theta(\ln(\ln(H)))$.

While our work has already shown the single-buyer problem is quite interesting, the most natural direction for future work is understanding revenue maximization with multiple learning buyers. Of our three main results, only Theorem 3.2 extends easily (that if every buyer uses our modified learning, the default strategy, which now runs Myerson's optimal auction every round, is optimal). Our work certainly provides good insight into the multi-bidder problem, but there are still clear barriers. For example, in order to obtain revenue equal to the expected welfare, the auction must necessarily also maximize welfare. In our single-bidder model, this means that we can give away the item for free for $\Omega(T)$ rounds, but with multiple bidders, such careless behaviour would immediately make it impossible to achieve the optimal welfare. Regarding the mean-based revenue, while there is a natural generalization of our LP to multiple bidders, it's no longer clear how to achieve this revenue against conservative bidders, as all the relevant variables now implicitly depend on the actions of the other bidders. These are just examples of concrete barriers, and there are likely interesting conceptual barriers for this extension as well.

Another interesting direction is understanding the consequences of our work from the perspective of the buyer. Aside from certain corner configurations (e.g. the seller extracting the buyer's full welfare), it's not obvious how the buyer's utility changes. For instance, is it possible that the buyer's utility actually *increases* as the seller switches from the default strategy to the optimal mean-based revenue? Does the buyer ever benefit from using an "exploitable" learning strategy, so that the seller can exploit it and make them both happier?

## REFERENCES


[1] Sanjeev Arora, Elad Hazan, and Satyen Kale. 2012. The Multiplicative Weights Update Method: a Meta-Algorithm and Applications. *Theory of Computing* 8, 6 (2012), 121–164. DOI: http://dx.doi.org/10.4086/toc.2012.v008a006

[2] Itai Ashlagi, Constantinos Daskalakis, and Nima Haghpanah. 2016. Sequential Mechanisms with Ex-post Participation Guarantees. In *Proceedings of the 2016 ACM Conference on Economics and Computation, EC '16, Maastricht, The Netherlands, July 24-28, 2016.* 213–214. DOI: http://dx.doi.org/10.1145/2940716.2940775

[3] Peter Auer, Nicolò Cesa-Bianchi, Yoav Freund, and Robert E. Schapire. 2003. The Nonstochastic Multiarmed Bandit Problem. *SIAM J. Comput.* 32, 1 (Jan. 2003), 48–77. DOI: http://dx.doi.org/10.1137/S0097539701398375

[4] Avrim Blum and Yishay Mansour. 2007. From External to Internal Regret. *Journal of Machine Learning Research* 8 (2007), 1307–1324. http://dl.acm.org/citation.cfm?id=1314543

[5] Sébastien Bubeck and Nicolò Cesa-Bianchi. 2012. Regret Analysis of Stochastic and Nonstochastic Multi-armed Bandit Problems. *Foundations and Trends in Machine Learning* 5, 1 (2012), 1–122. DOI: http://dx.doi.org/10.1561/2200000024

[6] Yang Cai and Constantinos Daskalakis. 2017. Learning Multi-item Auctions with (or without) Samples. In *FOCS.*

[7] Edward H. Clarke. 1971. Multipart Pricing of Public Goods. *Public Choice* 11, 1 (1971), 17–33.

[8] Richard Cole and Tim Roughgarden. 2014. The Sample Complexity of Revenue Maximization. In *Proceedings of the Forty-sixth Annual ACM Symposium on Theory of Computing (STOC '14).* ACM, New York, NY, USA, 243–252. DOI: http://dx.doi.org/10.1145/2591796.2591867

[9] Constantinos Daskalakis and Vasilis Syrgkanis. 2016. Learning in Auctions: Regret is Hard, Envy is Easy. In *IEEE 57th Annual Symposium on Foundations of Computer Science, FOCS 2016, 9-11 October 2016, Hyatt Regency, New Brunswick, New Jersey, USA.* 219–228. DOI: http://dx.doi.org/10.1109/FOCS.2016.31

[10] Constantinos Daskalakis and S. Matthew Weinberg. 2012. Symmetries and Optimal Multi-Dimensional Mechanism Design. In *the 13th ACM Conference on Electronic Commerce (EC).*

[11] Nikhil R. Devanur, Zhiyi Huang, and Christos-Alexandros Psomas. 2016. The Sample Complexity of Auctions with Side Information. In *Proceedings of the Forty-eighth Annual ACM Symposium on Theory of Computing (STOC '16).* ACM, New York, NY, USA, 426–439. DOI: http://dx.doi.org/10.1145/2897518.2897553

[12] Nikhil R. Devanur, Yuval Peres, and Balasubramanian Sivan. 2015. Perfect Bayesian Equilibria in Repeated Sales. In *Proceedings of the Twenty-sixth Annual ACM-SIAM Symposium on Discrete Algorithms (SODA '15).* Society for Industrial and Applied Mathematics, Philadelphia, PA, USA, 983–1002. http://dl.acm.org/citation.cfm?id=2722129.2722196

[13] Miroslav Dudík, Nika Haghtalab, Haipeng Luo, Robert E. Schapire, Vasilis Syrgkanis, and Jennifer Wortman Vaughan. 2017. Oracle-Efficient Learning and Auction Design. In *FOCS.*

[14] Yannai A. Gonczarowski and Noam Nisan. 2017. Efficient Empirical Revenue Maximization in Single-parameter Auction Environments. In *Proceedings of the 49th Annual ACM SIGACT Symposium on Theory of Computing (STOC 2017).* ACM, New York, NY, USA, 856–868. DOI: http://dx.doi.org/10.1145/3055399.3055427

[15] Theodore Groves. 1973. Incentives in Teams. *Econometrica* 41, 4 (1973), 617–631.

[16] James Hannan. 1957. Approximation to bayes risk in repeated play. In *Contributions to the Theory of Games.* 3:97–139.

[17] Nicole Immorlica, Brendan Lucier, Emmanouil Pountourakis, and Samuel Taggart. 2017. Repeated Sales with Multiple Strategic Buyers. In *Proceedings of the 2017 ACM Conference on Economics and Computation.* ACM, 167–168.

[18] Adam Kalai and Santosh Vempala. 2002. Geometric Algorithms for Online Optimization. In *Journal of Computer and System Sciences.* 26–40.

[19] Adam Kalai and Santosh Vempala. 2005. Efficient Algorithms for Online Decision Problems. *J. Comput. Syst. Sci.* 71, 3 (Oct. 2005), 291–307. DOI: http://dx.doi.org/10.1016/j.jcss.2004.10.016

[20] John Langford and Tong Zhang. 2008. The Epoch-Greedy Algorithm for Multi-armed Bandits with Side Information. In *Advances in Neural Information Processing Systems 20,* J. C. Platt, D. Koller, Y. Singer, and S. T. Roweis (Eds.). Curran Associates, Inc., 817–824. http://papers.nips.cc/paper/3178-the-epoch-greedy-algorithm-for-multi-armed-bandits-with-side-information.pdf

[21] Siqi Liu and Christos-Alexandros Psomas. 2017. On the Competition Complexity of Dynamic Mechanism Design. *CoRR* abs/1709.07955 (2017). arXiv:1709.07955 http://arxiv.org/abs/1709.07955

[22] Vahab S. Mirrokni, Renato Paes Leme, Pingzhong Tang, and Song Zuo. 2016. Dynamic Auctions with Bank Accounts. In *Proceedings of the Twenty-Fifth International Joint Conference on Artificial Intelligence, IJCAI 2016, New York, NY, USA, 9-15 July 2016*. 387–393. http://www.ijcai.org/Abstract/16/062

[23] Vahab S. Mirrokni, Renato Paes Leme, Pingzhong Tang, and Song Zuo. 2016. Optimal dynamic mechanisms with ex-post IR via bank accounts. *CoRR* abs/1605.08840 (2016). arXiv:1605.08840 http://arxiv.org/abs/1605.08840

[24] Jamie Morgenstern and Tim Roughgarden. 2015. The Pseudo-dimension of Near-optimal Auctions. In *Proceedings of the 28th International Conference on Neural Information Processing Systems - Volume 1 (NIPS'15)*. MIT Press, Cambridge, MA, USA, 136–144. http://dl.acm.org/citation.cfm?id=2969239.2969255

[25] Jamie Morgenstern and Tim Roughgarden. 2016. Learning Simple Auctions. In *29th Annual Conference on Learning Theory (Proceedings of Machine Learning Research)*, Vitaly Feldman, Alexander Rakhlin, and Ohad Shamir (Eds.), Vol. 49. PMLR, Columbia University, New York, New York, USA, 1298–1318. http://proceedings.mlr.press/v49/morgenstern16.html

[26] Roger B. Myerson. 1981. Optimal Auction Design. *Mathematics of Operations Research* 6, 1 (1981), 58–73.

[27] Denis Nekipelov, Vasilis Syrgkanis, and Eva Tardos. 2015. Econometrics for Learning Agents. In *Proceedings of the Sixteenth ACM Conference on Economics and Computation (EC '15)*. ACM, New York, NY, USA, 1–18. DOI: http://dx.doi.org/10.1145/2764468.2764522

[28] Christos Papadimitriou, George Pierrakos, Christos-Alexandros Psomas, and Aviad Rubinstein. 2016. On the Complexity of Dynamic Mechanism Design. In *Proceedings of the Twenty-seventh Annual ACM-SIAM Symposium on Discrete Algorithms (SODA '16)*. Society for Industrial and Applied Mathematics, Philadelphia, PA, USA, 1458–1475. http://dl.acm.org/citation.cfm?id=2884435.2884535

[29] Tim Roughgarden. 2012. The Price of Anarchy in Games of Incomplete Information. In *Proceedings of the 13th ACM Conference on Electronic Commerce (EC '12)*. ACM, New York, NY, USA, 862–879. DOI: http://dx.doi.org/10.1145/2229012.2229078

[30] Vasilis Syrgkanis and Eva Tardos. 2013. Composable and Efficient Mechanisms. In *Proceedings of the Forty-fifth Annual ACM Symposium on Theory of Computing (STOC '13)*. ACM, New York, NY, USA, 211–220. DOI: http://dx.doi.org/10.1145/2488608.2488635

[31] William Vickrey. 1961. Counterspeculations, Auctions, and Competitive Sealed Tenders. *Journal of Finance* 16, 1 (1961), 8–37.

# Fair Allocation of Indivisible Goods: Improvements and Generalizations

MOHAMMAD GHODSI, Sharif University of Technology and Institute for Research in Fundamental Sciences (IPM) School of Computer Science
MOHAMMADTAGHI HAJIAGHAYI, University of Maryland
MASOUD SEDDIGHIN, Sharif University of Technology
SAEED SEDDIGHIN, University of Maryland
HADI YAMI, University of Maryland

We study the problem of fair allocation for indivisible goods. We use *the maxmin share* paradigm introduced by Budish [16] as a measure for fairness. Kurokawa, Procaccia, and Wang [36] were the first to investigate this fundamental problem in the additive setting. They show that a maxmin guarantee (1-MMS allocation) is not always possible even when the number of agents is limited to 3. While the existence of an approximation solution (e.g. a 1/2-MMS allocation) is quite straightforward, improving the guarantee becomes subtler for larger constants. Kurokawa *et al.* [36] provide a proof for the existence of a 2/3-MMS allocation and leave the question open for better guarantees.

Our main contribution is an answer to the above question. We improve the result of Kurokawa *et al.* to a 3/4 factor in the additive setting. The main idea for our 3/4-MMS allocation method is clustering the agents. To this end, we introduce three notions and techniques, namely *reducibility*, *matching allocation*, and *cycle-envy-freeness*, and prove the approximation guarantee of our algorithm via non-trivial applications of these techniques. Our analysis involves coloring and double counting arguments that might be of independent interest.

One major shortcoming of the current studies on fair allocation is the additivity assumption on the valuations. We alleviate this by extending our results to the case of submodular, fractionally subadditive, and subadditive settings. More precisely, we give constant approximation guarantees for submodular and XOS agents, and a logarithmic approximation for the case of subadditive agents. Furthermore, we complement our results by providing close upper bounds for each class of valuation functions. Finally, we present algorithms to find such allocations for additive, submodular, and XOS settings in polynomial time. The reader can find a summary of our results in Table 1. [1]

CCS Concepts: • **Theory of computation → Algorithmic game theory and mechanism design**;

---

Supported in part by NSF CAREER award CCF-1053605, NSF BIGDATA grant IIS-1546108, NSF AF:Medium grant CCF-1161365, DARPA GRAPHS/AFOSR grant FA9550-12-1-0423, and another DARPA SIMPLEX grant

[1] In the interest of space, proofs and some of the results have been omitted in this version. For full technical details please see [30].

Authors' addresses: Mohammad Ghodsi, Sharif University of Technology , Institute for Research in Fundamental Sciences (IPM) School of Computer Science, ghodsi@sharif.edu; MohammadTaghi Hajiaghayi, University of Maryland, hajiagha@cs.umd.edu; Masoud Seddighin, Sharif University of Technology, mseddighin@ce.sharif.edu; Saeed Seddighin, University of Maryland, saeedreza.seddighin@gmail.com; Hadi Yami, University of Maryland, hadi.yami93@gmail.com.


*ACM EC'18, June 18–22, 2018, Ithaca, NY, USA.* ACM ISBN 978-1-4503-5829-3/18/06...$15.00
https://doi.org/10.1145/3219166.3219238

Additional Key Words and Phrases: Fairness, maximin-share, approximation, additive, submodular, XOS, subadditive

## 1 INTRODUCTION

Suppose we have a set of $m$ indivisible items, and wish to distribute them among $n$ agents. Agents have valuations for each set of items that are not necessarily identical. How hard is it to divide the items between the agents to make sure everyone receives a fair share?

Fair division problems have been vastly studied in the past 60 years, (see, e.g. [3, 5, 13, 16, 21, 36, 42]). This line of research was initiated by the work of Steinhaus [42] in which the author introduced the *cake cutting* problem as follows: given a heterogeneous cake and a set of agents with different valuation functions, the goal is to find a fair allocation of the cake to the agents.

In order to study this problem, several notions of fairness have been proposed, the most famous of which are *proportionality* and *envy-freeness*, introduced by Steinhaus [42] and Foley [28]. A division is called proportional, if the total value of the allocated pieces to each agent is at least $1/n$ fraction of his total value for the entire cake, where $n$ is the number of agents. In an envy-free division, no agent wishes to exchange his share with another agent, i.e., every agent's valuation for his share is at least as much as his valuation for the other agents' shares. Clearly, proportionality is implied by envy-freeness.

Dubins and Spanier [21] propose a simple *moving knife* procedure that can guarantee a proportional division of the cake. For envy-freeness, Selfridge and Conway design an algorithm that guarantees envy-freeness when the number of agents is limited to 3. Later, Brams and Taylor extend this guarantee to an arbitrary number of agents in the additive setting [14]. However, their method for allocating the cake makes an un-bounded number of cuts. Recently, bounded protocols are proposed for envy-free allocation of cake and chore [6, 19].

The problem becomes even more subtle when we assume the items are indivisible. It is not hard to show that for indivisible items, neither proportionality nor envy-freeness can be guaranteed; for instance, when the number of items is smaller than the number of agents, at least one agent receives no items.

From a theoretical standpoint, proportionality and envy-freeness are too strong to be delivered in the case of indivisible goods. Therefore, Budish [16] proposed a newer notion of fairness for indivisible goods, namely *the maxmin share*, which has attracted a lot of attention in recent years [1–3, 7–9, 13, 23, 36]. Imagine that we ask an agent $a_i$ to partition a set $\mathcal{M}$ of $m$ items into $n$ bundles and collect the bundle with the smallest value. To maximize his profits, agent $a_i$ tries to divide $\mathcal{M}$ in a way that maximizes the value of the bundle with the lowest value to him. Based on this, the maxmin share of an agent $a_i$, denoted by $\mathsf{MMS}_i$, is the value of the least valuable bundle in agent $a_i$'s allocation; that is, the maximum profit $a_i$ can obtain in this procedure. Clearly, $\mathsf{MMS}_i$ is the most that can be guaranteed to an agent, since if all valuations are the same, at least one agent obtains a valuation of at most $\mathsf{MMS}_i$ from his allocated set. The question is then, whether there exists an allocation which guarantees $\mathsf{MMS}_i$ for every agent $a_i$? Therefore, we call an allocation MMS, if every agent $a_i$ receives a collection of items that are together worth at least $\mathsf{MMS}_i$ to him. Bouveret and Lemaitre [13] showed that for the restricted cases, when the valuations of the items for each agent are either 0 or 1, or when $m \leq n + 3$, an MMS allocation is guaranteed to exist. In other words, each $a_i$ can be guaranteed to receive a profit of at least $\mathsf{MMS}_i$ from his allocated items.

While the experiments support the existence of an MMS allocation in general [13], this conjecture was refuted by the pioneering work of Kurokawa, Procaccia, and Wang [36]. Kurokawa *et al.* [36] provided a surprising counter-example that admits no MMS allocation. They also show that a 2/3-MMS allocation always exists, i.e. there exists an algorithm that allocates the items to the agents in such a way that every agent $a_i$ receives a share that is worth at least $2/3\mathsf{MMS}_i$ to him.

In particular, they show for $n \leq 4$, their algorithm finds a $3/4$-MMS allocation. However, their algorithm does not run in polynomial time unless we assume the number of agents is bounded by a constant number. Following this work, Amanatidis, Markakis, Nikzad, and Saberi [3], improve this result by presenting a polynomial time algorithm for finding a $(2/3 - \epsilon)$-MMS allocation to any number of agents for constant $\epsilon$. However, the heart of their algorithm is the same as [36]. In addition to this, Amanatidis *et al.* prove that for $n = 3$, a $7/8$-MMS allocation is always possible. Note that, the counter example provided by Kurokawa *et al.* [36] requires a number of goods that is exponential to the number of agents. Kurokawa *et al.*in [35] provided a better construction for the counter-example with a linear number of goods.

In this work, we improve the result of Kurokawa *et al.* [36] by proving that a $3/4$-MMS allocation always exists. We also give a polynomial time algorithm to find such an allocation. Of course, this only holds if the valuation of the agents for the items are additive. We further go beyond the additive setting and extend this result to the case of submodular, XOS, and subadditive settings. More precisely, we give constant approximation algorithms for submodular and XOS settings that run in polynomial time. For the subadditive case, we prove that a $1/10\lceil\log m\rceil$-MMS allocation is guaranteed to exist. We emphasize that finding the exact value of $\mathsf{MMS}_i$ for an agent is NP-hard. Furthermore, to the best of our knowledge, no PTAS is known for computing the MMS values in non-additive settings. Thus, any $\alpha$-MMS allocation algorithm in non-additive settings must overcome the difficulty that the value of $\mathsf{MMS}_i$ is not known in advance. Therefore, our algorithms don't immediately follow from our existential proofs.

In order to present the results and techniques, we briefly state the fair allocation problem. Note that you can find a formal definition of the problem with more details in Section 2. The input to a maxmin fair allocation problem is a set $\mathcal{M}$ of $m$ items and a set $\mathcal{N}$ of $n$ agents. Fix an agent $a_i \in \mathcal{N}$ and let $V_i : 2^{\mathcal{M}} \rightarrow \mathbb{R}^+$ be the valuation function of $a_i$. Consider the set $\Pi_r$ of all partitions of the items in $\mathcal{M}$ into $r$ non-empty sets. We define $\mathsf{MMS}^r_{V_i}(\mathcal{M})$ as follows:

$$\mathsf{MMS}^r_{V_i}(\mathcal{M}) = \max_{P^*=\langle P^*_1, P^*_2, \ldots, P^*_r\rangle \in \Pi_r} \min_{1\leq j\leq r} V_i(P^*_j).$$

In the context of fair allocation, we denote the maxmin value of an agent $a_i$ by $\mathsf{MMS}_i = \mathsf{MMS}^n_{V_i}(\mathcal{M})$. The fair allocation problem is defined as follows: *for a given parameter $\alpha$, can we distribute the items among the agents in such a way that every agent $a_i$ receives a set of items with a value of at least $\alpha\mathsf{MMS}_i$ to him?* Such an allocation is called an $\alpha$-MMS allocation. We consider the fair allocation problem in both additive and non-additive settings (including submodular, XOS, and subadditive valuations). For non-additive settings, we use oracle queries to access the valuations. Note that, for non-additive settings, eliciting the entire valuation function of each agent needs an exponential number of queries. However, our methods for allocating the items in non-additive settings only use a polynomial number of queries.

There are many applications for finding fair allocations in the additive and non-additive settings. For example, *spliddit*, a popular fair division website[2] suggests indisputable and provably fair solutions for many real-world problems such as sharing rents, distributing tasks, dividing goods, etc. For dividing goods, *spliddit* uses the maximum Nash welfare allocation (the allocation that maximizes the product of utilities). In [17], Caragiannis et.al., proved with a tight analysis that a maximum Nash welfare allocation is a $2/(1 + \sqrt{4n-3})$-MMS allocation. However, the current best approximation guarantee and the state-of-the-art method for allocating indivisible goods is based on the result of [36] that guarantees a $2/3$-MMS allocation. We believe our results can improve

[2] http://www.spliddit.org

Table 1. Summary of the results

| Previous work | Additive | Submodular | XOS | Subadditive |
|---|---|---|---|---|
| Existential proof | 2/3-MMS [36] | 1/10-MMS [9] | - | - |
| Polytime algorithm | $2/3-\epsilon$-MMS [3] | 1/31-MMS [9] | - | - |
| Upper bound | $1-\epsilon$-MMS [36] | - | - | - |
| **Our results** | **Additive** | **Submodular** | **XOS** | **Subadditive** |
| Existential proof | 3/4-MMS Theorem 1.1 | 1/3-MMS Theorem 4.7 | 1/5-MMS Theorem 1.2 | $1/10\lceil\log m\rceil$-MMS Theorem 1.5 |
| Polytime algorithm | $3/4-\epsilon$-MMS Theorem 1.1 | 1/3-MMS Theorem 4.8 | 1/8-MMS Theorem 1.3 | - |
| Upper bound | - | 3/4-MMS Theorem 4.2 | 1/2-MMS Theorem 4.1 | 1/2-MMS Theorem 4.1 |

their performance. We would like to mention that despite the complexity of analysis, the idea behind our algorithm is simple and it can be easily implemented [3].

It is worth mentioning that other than maximin share, there are other fairness criteria that attracted considerable attention, especially in recent years: envy-free up to one good (EF1) and envy-free up to any good (EFX). In these settings, we seek to find allocations with limited (but not necessarily zero) envy between the agents [10, 17, 41]. Also, recent studies have established a connection between *Nash Social Welfare* (NSW) and these fairness criteria [10, 17]. NSW is defined as the geometric mean of the agents' utilities. Maximizing NSW has been subject to many recent studies [4, 10, 11, 18].

## 1.1 Our Results and Techniques

Throughout this paper, we study the fair allocation problem for additive and non-additive agents. Kurokawa *et al.* [36] study the fair allocation problem and show a 2/3-MMS allocation is guaranteed to exist for any number of additive agents. We improve this result in two different dimensions: (i) we improve the factor 2/3 to a factor 3/4 for additive agents. (ii) we provide similar guarantees for submodular, fractionally subadditive, and subadditive agents. Moreover, we provide algorithms that find such allocations in polynomial time. A brief summary of our results is illustrated in Table 1.

*1.1.1 Additive Setting.* As mentioned before, the pioneering work of Kurokawa *et al.* [36] present the first proof to the existence of a 2/3-MMS allocation in the additive setting. On the negative side, they show that their analysis is tight, i.e. their method cannot be used to obtain a better approximation guarantee. However, whether or not a better bound could be achieved via a more efficient algorithm remains open as Kurokawa *et al.* [36] pose it as an open problem.

We answer the above question in the affirmative. Our main contribution is a proof to the existence of a 3/4-MMS allocation for additive agents. Furthermore, we show that such an allocation can be found in polynomial time.

THEOREM 1.1. *Any fair allocation problem with additive agents admits a* 3/4-MMS *allocation. Moreover, a* $(3/4-\epsilon)$-MMS *allocation can be found in time* $\text{poly}(n, m)$ *for any* $\epsilon > 0$.

[3]The reader can find a set of materials including the implementation of our method and an animated explanation of our algorithm in https://www.cs.umd.edu/~saeedrez/fair.html.

The result of Theorem 1.1 is surprising, since most of the previous methods provided for proving the existence of a 2/3-MMS allocation were tight. This convinced many in the community that 2/3 is the best that can be guaranteed. This shows that the current techniques and known structural properties of maxmin share are not powerful enough to prove the bounds better than 2/3. In this paper, we provide a better understanding of this notion by demonstrating several new properties of maxmin share. For example, we introduce a generalized form of reducibility and develop double counting techniques that are closely related to the concept of maxmin-share.

For a better understanding of our algorithm, we start with the case where valuations of the agents for all items are small enough. More precisely, let $0 < \alpha < 1$ be a constant number and assume for every agent $a_i$ and every item $b_j$, the value of agent $a_i$ for item $b_j$ is bounded by $\alpha\mathsf{MMS}_i$. In this case, we propose the following simple procedure to allocate the items to the agents.

- Arrange the items in an arbitrary order.
- Start with an empty bag and add the items to the bag one by one with respect to their order.
- Every time the valuation of an agent $a_i$ for the set of items in the bag reaches $(1-\alpha)\mathsf{MMS}_i$, give all items of the bag to that agent, and continue with an empty bag. In case many agents are qualified to receive the items, we choose one of them arbitrarily. From this point on, we exclude the agent who received the items from the process.

We call this procedure the bag filling algorithm. One can see this algorithm as an extension of the famous moving knife algorithm for indivisible items. It is not hard to show that the bag filling algorithm guarantees a $(1-\alpha)$-MMS allocation to all of the agents. The crux of the argument is to show that every agent receives at least one bag of items. To this end, one could argue that every time a set of items is allocated to an agent $a_i$, no other agent $a_j$ loses a value more than $\mathsf{MMS}_j$. This, together with the fact that $V_i(\mathcal{M}) \geq n\mathsf{MMS}_i$, shows that at the end of the algorithm, every agent receives a fair share ($(1-\alpha)$-MMS) of the items.

This observation sheds light on the fact that low-value items can be distributed in a more efficient way. Therefore, the main hardness is to allocate the items with higher values to the agents. To overcome this hardness, we devise a clustering method. Roughly speaking, we divide the agents into three clusters according to their valuation functions. We prove desirable properties for the agents of each cluster. Finally, via a procedure that is similar in spirit to the bag filling algorithm but more complicated, we allocate the items to the agents.

Our clustering method is based on three important principles: *reducibility*, *matching allocation*, and *cycle-envy-freeness*. We give a brief description of each principle in the following.

**Reducibility:** The reducibility principle is very simple and elegant but plays an important role in the allocation process. Roughly speaking, consider a situation where for an agent $a_i$ and a set $S$ of items we have the following properties: $V_i(S) \geq \alpha\mathsf{MMS}_i$, and for all $a_j \neq a_i$, $\mathsf{MMS}_j^{n-1}(\mathcal{M} \setminus S) \geq \mathsf{MMS}_j$, where $V_i(S)$ is the valuation of agent $a_i$ for subset $S$ of items. Intuitively, since the maxmin shares of all agents except $a_i$ for all the items other than set $S$ are at least as much as their current maxmin shares, allocating set $S$ to $a_i$ cannot hurt the guarantee. In other words, given that an $\alpha$-MMS allocation is possible for all agents except $a_i$ with items not in $S$, we can allocate set $S$ to agent $a_i$ and recursively solve the problem for the rest of the agents. Although the definition of reducibility is more general than what mentioned above, the key idea is that reducible instances of the problem can be transformed into irreducible instances (see Observation 2.1). This makes the problem substantially simpler, since $\alpha$-irreducible instances of the problem have many desirable properties. For example, in such instances, the value of every agent $a_i$ for each item is less than $\alpha\mathsf{MMS}_i$ (see Lemma 2.2). By setting $\alpha = 1/2$, this observation along with the analysis of the bag filling algorithm, proves the existence of a $1/2$-MMS allocation. It is worth to mention that a special form of reducibility, where $|S| = 1$ is used in the previous works [3, 36].

**Matching allocation:** At the core of the clustering part, we use a well-structured type of matching to allocate the items to the agents. Intuitively, we cluster the agents to deal with high-value or in other words *heavy* items. In order to cluster a group of agents, we find a subset $T$ of agents and a subset $S$ of items, together with a matching $M$ from $S$ to $T$. We choose $T$, $S$, and $M$ in a way that (i) every item assigned to an agent has a value of at least $\beta$ to him, (ii) agents who do not receive any items have a value less than $\beta$ for each of the assigned items. Such an allocation requires careful application of several properties of maximal matchings in bipartite graphs (see [30] for details). A matching with similar structural properties is previously used by Kurokawa *et al.* [36] to allocate the bundles to the agents. We reveal more details and precisely characterize the structure of such matchings.

**Cycle-envy-freeness:** Envy-freeness is itself a well-known notion for fairness in the resource allocation problems. However, this notion is perhaps more applicable to the allocation of divisible goods. In our algorithm, we use a much weaker notion of envy-freeness, namely *cycle-envy-freeness.* A cycle-envy-free allocation contains no cyclic permutation of agents, such that each agent envies the next agent in the cycle. In the clustering phase, we choose a matching $M$ in a way that preserves cycle-envy-freeness for the clustered agents. More details about this can be found in the full version [30].

Cycle-envy-freeness plays a key role in the second phase of the algorithm. As aforementioned, our method in the assignment phase is closely related to the bag filling procedure described above. The difference is that the efficiency of our method depends on the order of the agents who receive the items. Based on the notion of cycle-envy-freeness, we prioritize the agents and, as such, we show the allocation is fair. An analogous concept is previously used in [39], albeit with a different application than ours.

In section 3, we present the ideas behind each step of the algorithm and show how the entire algorithm leads to a proper allocation.

*1.1.2 Submodular, XOS, and Subadditive Agents.* Although the problem was initially proposed for additive agents, it is very well-motivated to extend the definition to other classes of set functions. For instance, it is quite natural to expect that an agent prefers to receive two items of value 400, rather than receiving 1000 items of value 1. Such a constraint cannot be imposed in the additive setting. However, submodular functions which encompass $k$-demand valuations are strong tools for modeling these constraints. Such generalizations have been made to many similar problems, including the *Santa Claus max-min fair allocation, welfare maximization*, and *secretary* problems [12, 24, 25, 31]. The most common classes of set functions that have been studied before are submodular, XOS, and subadditive functions. We consider the fair allocation problem when the agents' valuations are in each of these classes. In contrast to the additive setting in which finding a constant MMS allocation is trivial, the problem becomes much more subtle even when the agents' valuations are *monotone submodular.* For instance, the bag filling algorithm does not promise any constant approximation factor for submodular agents, while it is straight-forward to show it guarantees a $(1 - \alpha)$-MMS allocation for additive agents.

We begin with submodular set functions. In Section 4, we show that the fair allocation problem with submodular agents admits a $1/3$-MMS allocation. In addition, we show, given access to *query oracles*, one can find such an allocation in polynomial time. We further complement our result by showing that a $3/4$-MMS is the best guarantee that one can hope to achieve in this setting. This is in contrast to the additive setting for which the only upper bound is that 1-MMS allocation is not always possible. We begin by stating an existential proof.

THEOREM 4.7. *The fair allocation problem with submodular agents admits a* 1/3-MMS *allocation.*

Our proof for submodular agents is fundamentally different from that of the additive setting. First, without loss of generality, we assume $\mathsf{MMS}_i = 1$ for every agent $a_i \in \mathcal{N}$. Moreover, we assume the problem is 1/3-irreducible since otherwise we can reduce the problem. Next, given a function $f(.)$, we define the *ceiling function* $f^x(.)$ as follows:

$$f^x(S) = \min\{x, f(S)\} \qquad \forall S \subseteq \mathsf{ground}(f).$$

An important property of the ceiling functions is that they preserve submodularity, fractionally subadditivity, and subadditivity (see Lemma 4.4). We define the bounded welfare of an allocation $\mathcal{A}$ as $\sum V_i^{2/3}(A_i)$. Given that, we show an allocation that maximizes the bounded welfare is 1/3-MMS. To this end, let $\mathcal{A}$ be an allocation with the maximum bounded welfare and suppose for the sake of contradiction that in such an allocation, an agent $a_i$ receives a bundle of worth less than 1/3 to him. Since $\mathsf{MMS}_i = 1$, agent $a_i$ can divide the items into $n$ sets, where each set is of worth at least 1 to him. For a valuation function $V$, define the contribution of an item $b_j$ in set $S$ ($b_j \in S$) as $V(S) - V(S \setminus \{b_j\})$. Now, we randomly select an element $b_j$ which is *not* allocated to $a_i$. By the properties of submodular functions, we show that if we allocate $b_j$ to $a_i$, the expected contribution of $b_j$ to the bounded valuation function of $a_i$ would be more than the current expected contribution of $b_j$ to the bounded welfare of the allocation. Therefore, there exists an item $b_j$ such that if we allocate that item to agent $a_i$, the total bounded welfare of the allocation will be increased. This contradicts the maximality of the allocation.

Notice that Theorem 4.7 is only an existential proof. A natural approach to find such a solution is to start with an arbitrary allocation and iteratively increase its bounded welfare until it becomes 1/3-MMS. The main challenge though is that we do not even know what the MMS values are. Furthermore, unlike the additive setting, we do not have any PTAS algorithm that provides us a close estimate to these values. To overcome this challenge, we propose a combinatorial trick to guess these values without incurring any additional factor to our guarantee. The high level idea is to start with large numbers as estimates to the MMS values. Every time we run the algorithm on the estimated values, it either finds a desired allocation, or reports that the maxmin value of an agent is misrepresented by at least a multiplicative factor. Given this, we divide the maxmin value of that agent by that factor and continue on with the new estimates. Therefore, at every step of the algorithm, we are guaranteed that our estimates are not less than the actual MMS values. Based on this, we show that the running time of the algorithm is polynomial, and that the resulting allocation has the desired properties. The reader can find a detailed discussion in Section 4.

THEOREM 4.8. *Given access to query oracles, one can find a* 1/3-MMS *allocation to submodular agents in polynomial time.*

Finally, we show that in some instances with submodular agents, no allocation is better than 3/4-MMS.

THEOREM 4.1. *For any $n \geq 2$, there exists an instance of the fair allocation problem with $n$ submodular agents where no allocation is better than* 3/4-MMS.

We show Theorem 4.1 by a counter-example. In this counter-example we have $n$ agents and $2n$ items. Moreover, the valuation functions of the first $n-1$ agents are the same, but the last agent has a slightly different valuation function that makes it impossible to find an allocation which is better than 3/4-MMS. The number of agents in this example can be arbitrarily large.

We also study the problem with fractionally subadditive (XOS) agents. Similar to the submodular setting, we provide an upper bound on the quality of any allocation in the XOS setting. We show Theorem 4.2 by a counter-example.

THEOREM 4.2. *For any integer number c, there is an instance of the fair allocation problem with XOS agents where $n \geq c$ and no allocation is better than* $1/2$-MMS.

Next, we state the main theorem for XOS valuations.

THEOREM 1.2. *The fair allocation problem with XOS agents admits a* $1/5$-MMS *allocation.*

Our approach for proving Theorem 1.2 is similar to the proof of Theorem 4.7. Again, we scale the valuations to make sure $\mathsf{MMS}_i = 1$ all agents and define the notion of bounded welfare, but this time as $\sum V_i^{2/5}(A_i)$. However, as XOS functions do not adhere to the nice structure of submodular functions, we use a different analysis to prove this theorem. Let $\mathcal{A}$ be an allocation with the maximum bounded welfare. In case all agents receive a value of at least $1/5$, the proof is complete. Otherwise, let $a_i$ be an agent that receives a set of items whose value to him is less than $1/5$. In contrast to the submodular setting, giving no item alone to $a_i$ can guarantee an increase in the bounded welfare of the allocation. However, this time, we show there exists a set $S$ of items such that if we take them back from their recipients and instead allocate them to agent $a_i$, the bounded welfare of the allocation increases. The reason this holds is the following: since $\mathsf{MMS}_i = 1$, agent $a_i$ can split the items into $2n$ sets where every set is worth at least $2/5$ to $a_i$, otherwise the problem is $1/5$-reducible. Moreover, since the valuation functions are XOS, we show that giving one of these $2n$ sets to $a_i$ will increase the bounded welfare of the allocation. Therefore, if $\mathcal{A}$ is maximal, then $\mathcal{A}$ is also $1/5$-MMS.

Finally, we show that a $1/8$-MMS allocation in the XOS setting can be found in polynomial time. Our algorithm only requires access to demand and XOS oracles. Note that this bound is slightly worse than our existential proof due to some computational hardnesses. However, the blueprint of the algorithm is based on the proof of Theorem 1.2.

THEOREM 1.3. *Given access to demand and XOS oracles, we can find a* $1/8$-MMS *allocation for the problem with XOS agents in polynomial time.*

We start with an arbitrary allocation and increase the bounded welfare until the allocation becomes $1/8$-MMS. The catch is that if the allocation is not $1/8$-MMS, then there exists an agent $a_i$ and a set $S$ of items such that if we take back these items from their current recipients and allocate them to agent $a_i$, the bounded welfare of the allocation increases. In order to increase the bounded welfare, there are two computational barriers that need to be lifted. First, similar to the submodular setting, we do not have any estimates to the MMS values. Analogously, we resolve the first issue by iteratively guessing the MMS values. The second issue is that in every step of the algorithm, we have to find a set $S$ of items to allocate to an agent $a_i$ that results in an increase in the bounded welfare. Such a set $S$ cannot be trivially found in polynomial time. That is where the demand and XOS oracles take part. The high-level idea is the following: first, by accessing the XOS oracles, we determine the contribution of every item to the bounded welfare of the allocation. Next, we set the price of every element equal to three times the contribution of that element to the bounded welfare and run the demand oracle to find which subset has the highest profit for agent $a_i$. We show this subset has a value of at least $1/4$ to $a_i$. Next, we sort the elements of this set based on the ratio of contribution to the overall value of the set over the price of the item, and select a prefix for them that has a value of at least $1/4$ to $a_i$. Finally, we argue that allocating this set to $a_i$ increases the bounded welfare of the allocation by at least some known lower bound. This, married with the combinatorial trick to guess the MMS values, gives us a polynomial time algorithm to find a 1/8-MMS allocation.

An immediate corollary of Theorems 1.3 and 4.8 is a polynomial time algorithm for approximating the maxmin value of a submodular and an XOS function within factors 1/3 and 1/8, respectively.

Corollary 1.4. *Let $f$ be a submodular/XOS function on a set of ground elements $S$, and let $n$ be an integer number. Given access to query oracle/demand and XOS oracles of $f$, we can partition the elements of $S$ into $n$ disjoint subsets $S_1, S_2, \ldots, S_n$ such that*

$$\min_{i=1}^{n} f(S_i) \geq c \cdot \mathsf{MMS}_f^n$$

*where $\mathsf{MMS}_f^n$ denotes the maxmin value for function $f$ on $n$ subsets. Constant $c$ equals $1/3$ if $f$ is submodular and is equal to $1/8$ for the XOS case.*

Finally, we investigate the problem when the agents are subadditive and present an existential proof based on a well-known reduction to the XOS setting.

Theorem 1.5. *The fair allocation problem with subadditive agents admits a $1/10\lceil \log m \rceil$-MMS allocation.*

### 1.2 Organization of the Paper

The organization of the rest of the paper is as follows: Section 2 contains the notations and definitions, including different set functions and the tools to be needed for the main results. Next, in Section 3 we briefly review the general ideas behind our 3/4-MMS allocation algorithm. In interest of space, the detailed description of the algorithm and the approximation proof are removed from this version. You can find the details and the approximation proof and a flowchart of the algorithm in the full version [30].

In Section 4, we present our results for the submodular setting. The proofs for the XOS and the subadditive settings follow from the same ideas and can be found in the full version [30].

## 2 PRELIMINARIES

Throughout this paper we assume the set of agents is denoted by $\mathcal{N}$ and the set of items is referred to by $\mathcal{M}$. Let $|\mathcal{N}| = n$ and $|\mathcal{M}| = m$, we refer to the agents by $a_i$ and to the items by $b_i$, i.e., $\mathcal{N} = \{a_1, a_2, \ldots, a_n\}$ and $\mathcal{M} = \{b_1, b_2, \ldots, b_m\}$. We denote the valuation of agent $a_i$ for a set $S$ of items by $V_i(S)$. Our interest is in valuation functions that are monotone and non-negative. More precisely, we assume $V_i(S) \geq 0$ for every agent $a_i$ and $S \subseteq \mathcal{M}$, and for every two sets $S_1$ and $S_2$ we have $V_i(S_1 \cup S_2) \geq \max\{V_i(S_1), V_i(S_2)\}$. Due to obvious impossibility results for the general valuation functions , we restrict our attention to four classes of set functions:

- **Additive**: A set function $V(.)$ is additive if $V(S_1) + V(S_2) = V(S_1 \cup S_2) + V(S_1 \cap S_2)$ for every two sets $S_1, S_2 \in \mathsf{ground}(V)$.
- **Submodular**: A set function $V(.)$ is submodular if $V(S_1) + V(S_2) \geq V(S_1 \cup S_2) + V(S_1 \cap S_2)$ for every two sets $S_1, S_2 \in \mathsf{ground}(V)$.
- **Fractionally Subadditive (XOS)**: An XOS set function $V(.)$ can be shown via a finite set of additive functions $\{V_1, V_2, \ldots, V_\alpha\}$ where $V(S) = \max_{i=1}^{\alpha} V_i(S)$ for any set $S \subseteq \mathsf{ground}(V)$.
- **Subadditive**: A set function $V(.)$ is subadditive if $V(S_1) + V(S_2) \geq V(S_1 \cup S_2)$ for every two sets $S_1, S_2 \subseteq \mathsf{ground}(V)$.

For additive functions, we assume the value of the function for every element is given in the input. However, representing other classes of set functions requires access to oracles. For submodular functions, we assume we have access to *query oracle* defined below. Query oracles are great identifier for submodular functions, however, they are too weak when it comes to XOS and subadditive settings. For such functions, we use a stronger oracle which is called *demand oracle*. It is shown that for some functions, such as gross substitutes, a demand oracle can be implemented via a query oracle in polynomial time [38]. In addition to this, we consider a special oracle for XOS functions which is called *XOS oracle*. Access to query oracles for submodular functions, XOS oracle for XOS functions, and demand oracles for XOS and subadditive functions are quite common and have been very fruitful in the literature [20, 24–27, 38, 43]. In what follows, we formally define the oracles:

- **Query oracle:** Given a function $f$, a query oracle $O$ is an algorithm that receives a set $S$ as input and computes $f(S)$ in time $O(1)$.
- **Demand oracle:** Given a function $f$, a demand oracle $O$ is an algorithm that receives a sequence of prices $p_1, p_2, \ldots, p_n$ as input and finds a set $S$ such that $f(S) - \sum_{e \in S} p_e$ is maximized. We assume the running time of the algorithm is $O(1)$.
- **XOS oracle:** (defined only for an XOS functions $f$) Given a set $S$ of items, it returns the additive representation of the function that is maximized for $S$. In other words, it reveals the contribution of each item in $S$ to the value of $f(S)$.

Let $\Pi_r$ be the set of all partitions of $\mathcal{M}$ into $r$ disjoint subsets. For every $r$-partitioning $P^* \in \Pi_r$, we denote the partitions by $P_1^*, P_2^*, \ldots, P_r^*$. For a set function $f(.)$, we define $\mathsf{MMS}_f^r(\mathcal{M})$ as follows:

$$\mathsf{MMS}_f^r(\mathcal{M}) = \max_{P^* \in \Pi_r} \min_{1 \le j \le r} f(P_j^*).$$

For brevity we refer to $\mathsf{MMS}_{f_i}^n(\mathcal{M})$ by $\mathsf{MMS}_i$.

An allocation of items to the agents is a vector $\mathcal{A} = \langle A_1, A_2, \ldots, A_n \rangle$ where $\bigcup A_i = \mathcal{M}$ and $A_i \cap A_j = \emptyset$ for every two agents $a_i, a_j \in \mathcal{N}$. An allocation $\mathcal{A}$ is $\alpha$-MMS, if every agent $a_i$ receives a subset of the items whose value to that agent is at least $\alpha$ times $\mathsf{MMS}_i$. More precisely, $\mathcal{A}$ is $\alpha$-MMS if and only if $V_i(A_i) \ge \alpha \mathsf{MMS}_i$ for every agent $a_i \in \mathcal{N}$.

We define the notion of *reducibility* for an instance of the problem as follows.

*Definition 2.1.* We say an instance of the problem is $\alpha$-reducible, if there exist a set $T \subset \mathcal{N}$ of agents, a set $S$ of items, and an allocation $\mathcal{A} = \langle A_1, A_2, \ldots, A_{|T|} \rangle$ of $S$ to agents of $T$ such that

$$\forall a_i \in T \qquad V_i(A_i) \ge \alpha \mathsf{MMS}_i$$

and

$$\forall a_i \notin T \qquad \mathsf{MMS}_{V_i}^{n-|T|}(\mathcal{M} \setminus S) \ge \mathsf{MMS}_i.$$

Similarly, we call an instance *$\alpha$-irreducible* if it is not $\alpha$-reducible. The intuition behind Definition 2.1 is the following: In order to prove the existence of an $\alpha$-MMS allocation for every instance of the problem, it only suffices to prove this for the $\alpha$-irreducible instances.

Observation 2.1. *Every instance of the fair allocation problem admits an $\alpha$-MMS allocation if this holds for all $\alpha$-irreducible instances.*

The reducibility argument plays an important role in both the existential proofs and algorithms that we present in the paper. As we see, irreducible instances of the problem exhibit several desirable properties for additive and non-additive agents. We take advantage of these properties to improve the approximation guarantee for different classes of set functions. As an example, Lemma 2.2 shows a simple consequence of irreducibility.

Lemma 2.2. *For every $\alpha$-irreducible instance of the problem we have*

$$\forall a_i \in \mathcal{N}, b_j \in \mathcal{M} \qquad V_i(b_j) < \alpha.$$

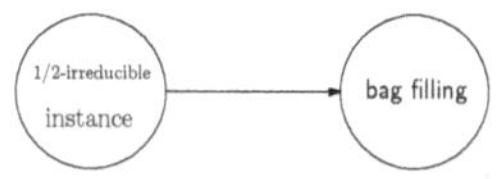


Fig. 1. 1/2-MMS Algorithm

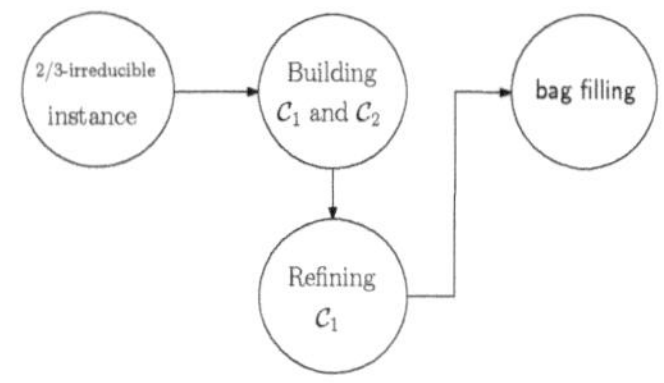


Fig. 2. 2/3-MMS Algorithm

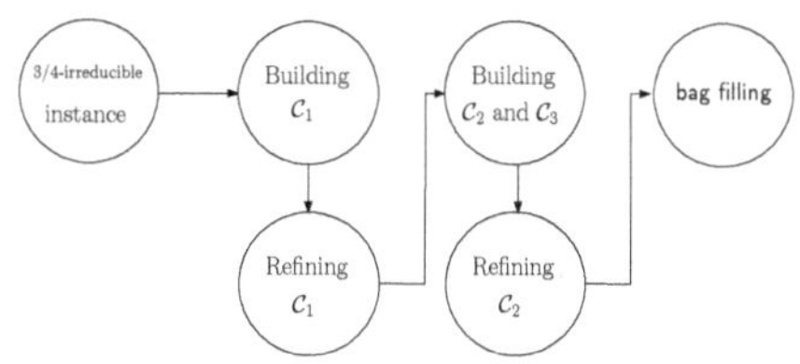


Fig. 3. 3/4-MMS Algorithm

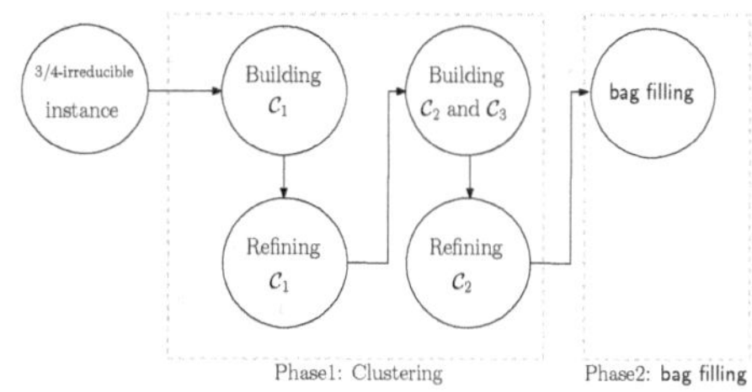


Fig. 4. Algorithm Phases

## 3 A BRIEF OVERVIEW OF THE 3/4-MMS ALGORITHM

The purpose of this section is to present an abstract overview over the ideas behind our algorithm for finding a 3/4-MMS allocation in the additive setting. For simplicity, we start with a simple 1/2-MMS algorithm mentioned in Section 1.1. Recall that the bag filling procedure guarantees a $1 - \alpha$ approximation solution when the valuations of the agents for each item is smaller than $\alpha$. Furthermore, we know that in every $\alpha$-irreducible instance, all the agents have a value less than $\alpha$ for every item. Thus, the following simple procedure yields a 1/2-MMS allocation:

(1) Reduce the problem until no agent has a value more than 1/2 for any item.
(2) Allocate the items to the agents via a bag filling procedure.

Figure 1 shows a schematic representation of this algorithm. We can extend the idea in 1/2-MMS algorithm to obtain a more efficient algorithm. Here is the sketch of the 2/3-MMS algorithm: consider a 2/3-irreducible instance of the problem. In this instance, we have no item with a value more than or equal to 2/3 to any agent. Nevertheless, the items are not yet small enough to run a bag filling procedure. The idea here is to divide the agents into two clusters $C_1$ and $C_2$. Along this clustering, the items with a value in range $[1/3, 2/3)$ are given to the agents. In particular, one item is allocated to every agent in $C_1$ that is worth at least 1/3 to him and less than 1/3 to any agent not in $C_1$. Next, we refine Cluster $C_1$. In the refining procedure, if any remaining item could singly satisfy an agent in $C_1$, we do so. After building $C_1$ and $C_2$ and refining $C_1$, the remaining items preserve the following two invariants:

(1) The value of every remaining item is less than 1/3 to every remaining agent.
(2) No remaining item can singly satisfy an agent in $C_1$ (regarding the item that is already allocated to them)

These two invariants enable us to run a bag filling procedure over the remaining items. For this case, the bag filling procedure must be more intelligent: in the case that multiple agents are qualified to receive the items of the bag, we prioritize the agents. Roughly speaking, the priorities are determined by two factors: the cluster they belong to, and the cycle-envy-freeness property of the agents in $C_1$. In Figure 2 you can see a flowchart for this algorithm.

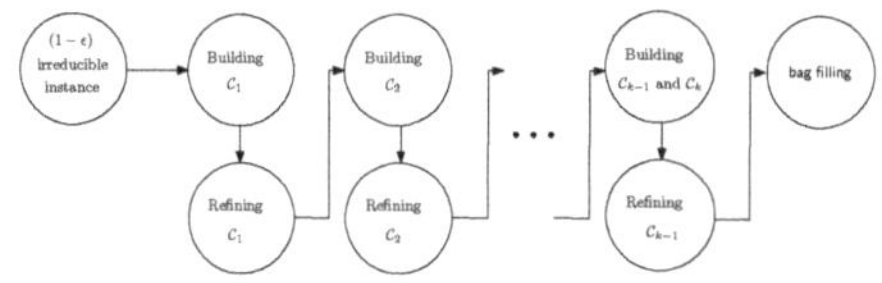


Fig. 5. Generalizing the algorithm into $k$ clusters

Our method for a 3/4-MMS allocation takes one step further from the previous 2/3-MMS algorithm. Again, we assume that the input is 3/4-irreducible since otherwise it can be further simplified. Via similar ideas, we build Cluster $C_1$ and refine it. Next, we build Clusters $C_2$ and $C_3$ and refine $C_2$. After refining Cluster $C_2$, the following invariants are preserved for the remaining items:

(1) Almost every remaining item has a value less than 1/4 to every remaining agent. More precisely, for every remaining agent $a_i$, there is at most one remaining item $b_j$ with $V_i(\{b_j\}) \geq 1/4$.
(2) No remaining item can singly satisfy an agent in $C_1$ and $C_2$ (regarding the item that is already allocated to them).

Finally, we run a bag filling procedure. Again, in the bag filling procedure, the priorities of the agents are determined by the cluster they belong to, and the cycle-envy-freeness of the clusters. In Figure 3, a flowchart for this algorithm is shown. Our assumption is that the input is 3/4-irreducible. Hence, we describe our algorithm in two phases: a clustering phase and the bag filling phase, as shown in Figure 4.

We show that all the steps of the algorithm can be implemented in polynomial time. Furthermore, we show that the assumption that the input is 3/4-irreducible is without loss of generality. In fact, we show that it suffices to check some invariants of irreducibility to be held in certain points of the algorithm.

As a future work, one can consider a more generalized form of this algorithm, where the agents are divided into more than 3 clusters (see Figure 5). We believe that this generalization might yield a $(1 - \epsilon)$-MMS allocation, where $\epsilon$ is a small value that depends on the number of agents. However, such a generalization is faced with two main barriers. First, In order to extend the idea to more than 3 clusters, we need a generalized form of reducibility for more than two items. Furthermore, a challenging part of our approximation proof is to show that the second cluster is empty at the end of the algorithm. For this, we define a graph on the items in the second cluster and prove some bounds on the number of edges in this graph. To extend the idea for more clusters, we need to define hypergraphs on the items in the clusters and show similar bounds, which requires deeper and more complicated techniques.

## 4 SUBMODULAR AGENTS

Previous work on the fair allocation problem was limited to the additive agents [3, 36]. In real-world, however, valuation functions are usually more complex than additive ones. As an example, imagine an agent is interested in at most $k$ items. More precisely, he is indifferent between receiving $k$ items or more than $k$ items. Such a valuation function is called $k$-demand and cannot be modeled by additive functions. $k$-demand functions are a subclass of submodular set functions which have been extensively studied the literature of different contexts, e.g., optimization, mechanism design, and game theory [15, 29, 32–34, 37, 40, 43].

In this section, we study the fair allocation problem where the valuations of agents are submodular. We begin by presenting an impossibility result; We show in Section 4.1 that the best guarantee that we can achieve for submodular agents is upper bounded by 3/4. Next, we give a proof to the existence of a 1/3-MMS allocation in this setting. This is followed by an algorithm that finds such an allocation in polynomial time. This is surprising since even finding the MMS of a submodular function is NP-hard and cannot be implemented in polynomial time unless P=NP [22]. In our algorithm, we assume we have access to query oracle for the valuation of agents; That is, for any set $S$ and any agent $a_i$, $V_i(S)$ can be computed via a given query oracle in time $O(1)$.

### 4.1 Upper Bound

We begin by providing an upper bound. In this section, we show for some instances of the problem with submodular agents, no allocation can be better than 3/4-MMS. Our counter-example is generic; We show this result for any number of agents.

Theorem 4.1. *For any $n \geq 2$, there exists an instance of the fair allocation problem with $n$ submodular agents where no allocation is better than* 3/4-MMS.

**Proof.** We construct an instance of the problem that does not admit any $3/4 + \epsilon$-MMS allocation. To this end, let $n$ be the number of agents and $\mathcal{M} = \{b_1, b_2, \ldots, b_m\}$ where $m = 2n$. Furthermore, let $f : 2^{\mathcal{M}} \to \mathbb{R}$ be as follows:

$$f(S) = \begin{cases} 0, & \text{if } |S| = \emptyset \\ 1, & \text{if } |S| = 1 \\ 2, & \text{if } |S| > 2 \\ 2, & \text{if } S = \{b_{2i}, b_{2i+1}\} \text{ for some } i \\ 3/2, & \text{if } |S| = 2 \text{ and } S \neq \{b_{2i}, b_{2i+1}\} \text{ for any } i. \end{cases}$$

Notice that $\text{MMS}_f^n = 2$. Moreover, in what follows we show that $f$ is submodular. To this end, suppose for the sake of contradiction that there exist sets $S$ and $S'$ such that $S \subsetneq S'$ and for some element $b_i$ we have:

$$f(S' \cup \{b_i\}) - f(S') > f(S \cup \{b_i\}) - f(S). \quad (1)$$

Since $f$ is monotone and $S' \neq S$, $f(S' \cup \{b_i\}) - f(S') > 0$ holds and thus $S'$ cannot have more than two items. Therefore, $S'$ contains at most two items and thus $S$ is either empty or contains a single element. If $S$ is empty, then adding every element to $S$ has the highest increase in the value of $S$ and thus Inequality (1) doesn't hold. Therefore, $S$ contains a single element and $S'$ contains exactly two elements. Thus, $f(S) = 1$ and $f(S') \geq 3/2$. Therefore, f(S $\cup\{b_i\}) - f(S) \geq 1/2$ and $f(S' \cup \{b_i\}) - f(S') \leq 1/2$ which contradicts Inequality (1).

Now, for agents $a_1, a_2, \ldots, a_{n-1}$ we set $V_i = f$ and for agent $a_n$ we set $V_n = f(\text{inc}(S))$ where $b_i$ is in $\text{inc}(S)$ if and only if either $i > 1$ and $b_{i-1} \in S$ or $i = 1$ and $b_m \in S$.

The crux of the argument is that for any allocation of the items to the agents, someone receives a value of at most 3/2. In case an agent receives fewer than two items, his valuation for his items would be at most 1. Similarly, if an agent receives more than two items, someone has to receive fewer than 2 items and the proof is complete. Therefore, the only case to investigate is where everybody receives exactly two items. We show in such cases, $\min V_i(A_i) = 3/2$ for all possible allocations. If all agents $a_1, a_2, \ldots, a_{n-1}$ receive two items whose value for them is exactly equal to 2, then by the construction of $f$, the value of the remaining items is also equal to 2 to them. Thus, $a_n$'s valuation for the items he receives is equal to 3/2. □

Remark that one could replace function $f$ with an XOS function

$$g(S) = \begin{cases} 0, & \text{if } |S| = \emptyset \\ 1, & \text{if } |S| = 1 \\ 2, & \text{if } |S| > 2 \\ 2, & \text{if } S = \{b_{2i}, b_{2i+1}\} \text{ for some } i \\ 1, & \text{if } |S| = 2 \text{ and } S \neq \{b_{2i}, b_{2i+1}\} \text{ for any } i. \end{cases}$$

and make the same argument to achieve a 1/2-MMS upper bound for XOS and subadditive agents.

THEOREM 4.2. *For any $n > 1$, there exists an instance of the fair allocation problem with $n$ XOS agents where no allocation is better than* 1/2-MMS.

### 4.2 Existential Proof

In this section we provide an existential proof to a 1/3-MMS allocation. Due to the algorithmic nature of the proof, we show in Section 4.3 that such an allocation can be computed in time poly$(n, m)$. For simplicity, we scale the valuation functions to ensure $\mathsf{MMS}_i = 1$ for every agent $a_i$.
We begin by introducing the ceiling functions.

*Definition 4.3.* Given a set function $f(.)$, we define $f^x(.)$ as follows:

$$f^x(S) = \begin{cases} f(S), & \text{if } f(S) \leq x \\ x, & \text{if } f(S) > x. \end{cases}$$

A nice property of the ceiling functions is that they preserve submodularity, fractionally subadditivity, and sub-additivity.

LEMMA 4.4. *For any real number $x \geq 0$, we have:*
*(1) Given a submodular set function $f(.)$, $f^x(.)$ is submodular.*
*(2) Given an XOS set function $f(.)$, $f^x(.)$ is XOS.*
*(3) Given an subadditive set function $f(.)$, $f^x(.)$ is also subadditive.*

The idea behind the existence of a 1/3-MMS allocation is simple: Suppose the problem is 1/3-irreducible and let $\mathcal{A} = \langle A_1, A_2, \ldots, A_n \rangle$ be an allocation of items to the agents that maximizes the following expression:

$$\sum_{a_i \in \mathcal{N}} V_i^{2/3}(A_i) \tag{2}$$

We refer to Expression (2) by $\mathsf{ex}^{(2/3)}(\mathcal{A})$. We prove $V_i(A_i) \geq 1/3$ for every agent $a_i \in \mathcal{N}$. By the reducibility principal, it only suffices to show every 1/3-irreducible instance of the problem admits a 1/3-MMS allocation. The main ingredients of the proof are Lemmas 2.2, 4.5 and 4.6.

LEMMA 4.5. *Let $S_1, S_2, \ldots, S_k$ be $k$ disjoint sets and $f_1, f_2, \ldots, f_k$ be $k$ submodular functions. We remove an element $e$ from $\bigcup S_i$ uniformly at random to obtain sets $S_1^* = S_1 \setminus \{e\}, S_2^* = S_2 \setminus \{e\}, \ldots, S_k^* = S_k \setminus \{e\}$. In this case we have*

$$\mathbb{E}[\sum f_i(S_i^*)] \geq \sum f_i(S_i) \frac{|\bigcup S_i| - 1}{|\bigcup S_i|}.$$

The high-level intuition behind the proof of Lemma 4.5 is as follows: For submodular functions, the smaller the size of a set is, the higher the marginal values for adding items to that set will be. Based on that, we show the summation of marginal decreases for removing each element is bounded by the total value of the set and that completes the proof.

Lemma 4.6. *Let $f$ be a submodular function and $S_1, S_2, \ldots, S_k$ be $k$ disjoint sets such that $f(S_i) \geq 1$ for every set $S_i$. Moreover, let $S \subseteq \bigcup S_i$ be a set such that $f(S) < 1/3$. If we pick an element $\{e\}$ of $\bigcup S_i \setminus S$ uniformly at random, we have:*

$$\mathbb{E}[f(S \cup \{e\}) - f(S)] \geq \frac{2k/3}{|\bigcup S_i \setminus S|}.$$

The proof of Lemma 4.6 is very similar to that of Lemma 4.5. The main point is that in submodular functions, the marginal increase decreases as the sizes of sets grow.

Next, we show the fair allocation problem with submodular agents admits a 1/3-MMS allocation.

Theorem 4.7. *The fair allocation problem with submodular agents admits a 1/3-MMS allocation.*

**Proof.** By Lemma 2.1, the problem boils down to the case of 1/3-irreducible instances. Let the problem be 1/3-irreducible and $\mathcal{A}$ be an allocation that maximizes $\text{ex}^{(2/3)}$. Suppose for the sake of contradiction that $V_i(A_i) < 1/3$ for some agent $a_i$. In this case we select an item $b_r$ from $\mathcal{M} \setminus A_i$ uniformly at random to create a new allocation $\mathcal{A}^r$ as follows:

$$A_j^r = \begin{cases} A_j \setminus \{b_r\}, & \text{if } i \neq j \\ A_j \cup \{b_r\} & \text{if } i = j. \end{cases}$$

In the rest we show $\mathbb{E}[\text{ex}^{(2/3)}(\mathcal{A}^r)] > \text{ex}^{(2/3)}(\mathcal{A})$ which contradicts the maximality of $\mathcal{A}$. Note that by Lemma 4.5 the following inequality holds:

$$\mathbb{E}[\sum_{j \neq i} V_j^{2/3}(A_j^r)] \geq \sum_{j \neq i} V_j^{2/3}(A_j) \frac{|\mathcal{M} \setminus A_i| - 1}{|\mathcal{M} \setminus A_i|}. \tag{3}$$

Moreover, by Lemma 4.6 we have

$$\mathbb{E}[V_i(A_i^r) - V_i(A_i)] \geq \frac{2n/3}{|\mathcal{M} \setminus A_i|}. \tag{4}$$

Inequality (3) along with Inequality (4) shows

$$\begin{aligned}
\mathbb{E}[\text{ex}^{(2/3)}(\mathcal{A}^r)] &= \mathbb{E}[\sum_{j \neq i} V_j^{2/3}(A_j^r)] + \mathbb{E}[V_i(A_i^r)] \\
&\geq \sum_{j \neq i} V_j^{2/3}(A_j) \frac{|\mathcal{M} \setminus A_i| - 1}{|\mathcal{M} \setminus A_i|} + \mathbb{E}[V_i(A_i^r)] \\
&\geq \sum_{j \neq i} V_j^{2/3}(A_j) \frac{|\mathcal{M} \setminus A_i| - 1}{|\mathcal{M} \setminus A_i|} + \frac{2n/3}{|\mathcal{M} \setminus A_i|} + V_i(A_i) \\
&\geq \sum_{j \neq i} V_j^{2/3}(A_j) \frac{|\mathcal{M} \setminus A_i| - 1}{|\mathcal{M} \setminus A_i|} + \frac{2n/3}{|\mathcal{M} \setminus A_i|} + V_i^{(2/3)}(A_i) \\
&\geq \sum_{j \neq i} V_j^{2/3}(A_j) \frac{|\mathcal{M} \setminus A_i| - 1}{|\mathcal{M} \setminus A_i|} + \frac{2n/3}{|\mathcal{M} \setminus A_i|} + V_i^{(2/3)}(A_i) \frac{|\mathcal{M} \setminus A_i| - 1}{|\mathcal{M} \setminus A_i|} \\
&= \text{ex}^{(2/3)}(\mathcal{A}) \frac{|\mathcal{M} \setminus A_i| - 1}{|\mathcal{M} \setminus A_i|} + \frac{2n/3}{|\mathcal{M} \setminus A_i|}.
\end{aligned} \tag{5}$$

Recall that by Lemma 2.2, the value of agent $a_i$ for any item alone is bounded by 1/3 and thus $\mathbb{E}[V_i(A_i^r) - V_i(A_i)] = \mathbb{E}[V_i^{2/3}(A_i^r) - V_i^{2/3}(A_i)]$. Notice that by the definition, $V_j^{(2/3)}$ is always bounded by 2/3 and also $V_i(A_i) < 1/3$, therefore, $\mathsf{ex}^{(2/3)}(\mathcal{A}) \leq 2n/3 - 1/3$ and thus

$$\begin{aligned}\mathbb{E}[\mathsf{ex}^{(2/3)}(\mathcal{A}^r)] &\geq \mathsf{ex}^{(2/3)}(\mathcal{A})\frac{|\mathcal{M} \setminus A_i| - 1}{|\mathcal{M} \setminus A_i|} + \frac{2n/3}{|\mathcal{M} \setminus A_i|} \\ &\geq \mathsf{ex}^{(2/3)}(\mathcal{A}) + \frac{1/3}{|\mathcal{M} \setminus A_i|} \\ &\geq \mathsf{ex}^{(2/3)}(\mathcal{A}) + 1/3m.\end{aligned} \tag{6}$$

□

### 4.3 Algorithm

In this section we give an algorithm to find a 1/3-MMS allocation for submodular agents. We show our algorithm runs in time $\text{poly}(n, m)$.

For simplicity, we assume for every agent $a_i$, $\mathsf{MMS}_i$ is given as input to the algorithm. However, computing $\mathsf{MMS}_i$ alone is an NP-hard problem. Nonetheless, we show that such a computational barrier can be lifted by a combinatorial trick. We refer the reader to the full version for a more detailed discussion. The procedure is illustrated in Algorithm 1: Based on Theorem 4.7, one can show

**ALGORITHM 1:** Finding a 1/3-MMS allocation for submodular agents

**Data:** $\mathcal{N}, \mathcal{M}, \langle V_1, V_2, \ldots, V_n \rangle, \langle \mathsf{MMS}_1, \mathsf{MMS}_2, \ldots, \mathsf{MMS}_n \rangle$

For every $a_j$, scale $V_j$ to ensure $\mathsf{MMS}_j = 1$;
**while** *there exist an agent* $a_i$ *and an item* $b_j$ *such that* $V_i(\{b_j\}) \geq 1/3$ **do**
  Allocate $\{b_j\}$ to $a_i$;
  $\mathcal{M} = \mathcal{M} \setminus b_j$;
  $\mathcal{N} = \mathcal{N} \setminus a_i$;
$\mathcal{A}$ = an arbitrary allocation of the items to the agents;
**while** $\min V_j^{2/3}(A_j) < 1/3$ **do**
  $i$ = the agent who receives the lowest value in allocation $\mathcal{A}$;
  Find an item $b_e$ such that:
   $\mathsf{ex}(\langle A_1 \setminus \{b_e\}, A_2 \setminus \{b_e\}, \ldots, A_{i-1} \setminus \{b_e\}, A_i \cup \{b_e\}, A_{i+1} \setminus \{b_e\}, \ldots, A_n \setminus \{b_e\} \rangle) \geq \mathsf{ex}(\mathcal{A}) + 1/3m$;
  $\mathcal{A} = \langle A_1 \setminus \{b_e\}, A_2 \setminus \{b_e\}, \ldots, A_{i-1} \setminus \{b_e\}, A_i \cup \{b_e\}, A_{i+1} \setminus \{b_e\}, \ldots, A_n \setminus \{b_e\} \rangle$;
For every $a_i \in \mathcal{N}$ allocate $A_i$ to $a_i$;

that in every iteration of the algorithm value of $\mathsf{ex}^{2/3}(\mathcal{A})$ is increased by at least $1/3m$. Moreover, such an element $b_e$ can be easily found by iterating over all items in time $O(m)$. Furthermore, the number of iterations of the algorithm is bounded by $2nm$, since $\mathsf{ex}^{2/3}(\mathcal{A})$ is bounded by $2n/3$. Therefore, Algorithm 1 finds a 1/3-MMS allocation in time $\text{poly}(n, m)$.

Theorem 4.8. *Given access to query oracles, one can find a* 1/3-MMS *allocation for submodular agents in polynomial time.*

As a corollary of Theorem 4.8, one can show that the problem of finding the maxmin value of a submodular function admits a 3 approximation algorithm.

Corollary 4.9. *For a given submodular function $f$, we can in polynomial time split the elements of ground set into $n$ dijsoint sets $S_1, S_2, \ldots, S_n$ such that for every $1 \leq i \leq n$,*

$$f(S_i) \geq \mathsf{MMS}_f^n/3.$$

## REFERENCES


[1] Georgios Amanatidis, Georgios Birmpas, George Christodoulou, and Evangelos Markakis. 2017. Truthful allocation mechanisms without payments: Characterization and implications on fairness. In *Proceedings of the 2017 ACM Conference on Economics and Computation*. ACM, 545–562.

[2] Georgios Amanatidis, Georgios Birmpas, and Evangelos Markakis. 2016. On truthful mechanisms for maximin share allocations. In *Proceedings of the Twenty-Fifth International Joint Conference on Artificial Intelligence*. AAAI Press, 31–37.

[3] Georgios Amanatidis, Evangelos Markakis, Afshin Nikzad, and Amin Saberi. 2017. Approximation algorithms for computing maximin share allocations. *ACM Transactions on Algorithms (TALG)* 13, 4 (2017), 52.

[4] Nima Anari, Tung Mai, Shayan Oveis Gharan, and Vijay V Vazirani. 2018. Nash social welfare for indivisible items under separable, piecewise-linear concave utilities. In *Proceedings of the Twenty-Ninth Annual ACM-SIAM Symposium on Discrete Algorithms*. SIAM, 2274–2290.

[5] Arash Asadpour and Amin Saberi. 2007. An approximation algorithm for max-min fair allocation of indivisible goods. In *Proceedings of the thirty-ninth annual ACM symposium on Theory of computing*. ACM, 114–121.

[6] Haris Aziz and Simon Mackenzie. 2016. A discrete and bounded envy-free cake cutting protocol for any number of agents. In *Foundations of Computer Science (FOCS), 2016 IEEE 57th Annual Symposium on*. IEEE, 416–427.

[7] Haris Aziz, Gerhard Rauchecker, Guido Schryen, and Toby Walsh. 2016. Approximation algorithms for max-min share allocations of indivisible chores and goods. *arXiv preprint arXiv:1604.01435* (2016).

[8] Haris Aziz, Gerhard Rauchecker, Guido Schryen, and Toby Walsh. 2017. Algorithms for Max-Min Share Fair Allocation of Indivisible Chores.. In *AAAI*, Vol. 17. 335–341.

[9] Siddharth Barman and Sanath Kumar Krishna Murthy. 2017. Approximation algorithms for maximin fair division. In *Proceedings of the 2017 ACM Conference on Economics and Computation*. ACM, 647–664.

[10] Siddharth Barman, Sanath Kumar Krishnamurthy, and Rohit Vaish. 2017. Finding Fair and Efficient Allocations. *arXiv preprint arXiv:1707.04731* (2017).

[11] Siddharth Barman, Sanath Kumar Krishnamurthy, and Rohit Vaish. 2018. Greedy Algorithms for Maximizing Nash Social Welfare. *arXiv preprint arXiv:1801.09046* (2018).

[12] MohammadHossein Bateni, Mohammadtaghi Hajiaghayi, and Morteza Zadimoghaddam. 2013. Submodular secretary problem and extensions. *ACM Transactions on Algorithms (TALG)* 9, 4 (2013), 32.

[13] Sylvain Bouveret and Michel Lemaître. 2016. Characterizing conflicts in fair division of indivisible goods using a scale of criteria. *Autonomous Agents and Multi-Agent Systems* 30, 2 (2016), 259–290.

[14] Steven J Brams and Alan D Taylor. 1995. An envy-free cake division protocol. *Amer. Math. Monthly* (1995), 9–18.

[15] Niv Buchbinder, Moran Feldman, Joseph Naor, and Roy Schwartz. 2012. A Tight Linear Time (1/2)-Approximation for Unconstrained Submodular Maximization. In *Foundations of Computer Science (FOCS), 2012 IEEE 53rd Annual Symposium on*. IEEE, 649–658.

[16] Eric Budish. 2011. The combinatorial assignment problem: Approximate competitive equilibrium from equal incomes. *Journal of Political Economy* 119, 6 (2011), 1061–1103.

[17] Ioannis Caragiannis, David Kurokawa, Hervé Moulin, Ariel D Procaccia, Nisarg Shah, and Junxing Wang. 2016. The unreasonable fairness of maximum Nash welfare. In *Proceedings of the 2016 ACM Conference on Economics and Computation*. ACM, 305–322.

[18] Richard Cole, Nikhil Devanur, Vasilis Gkatzelis, Kamal Jain, Tung Mai, Vijay V Vazirani, and Sadra Yazdanbod. 2017. Convex program duality, fisher markets, and nash social welfare. In *Proceedings of the 2017 ACM Conference on Economics and Computation*. ACM, 459–460.

[19] Sina Dehghani, Alireza Farhadi, MohammadTaghi HajiAghayi, and Hadi Yami. 2018. Envy-free Chore Division for An Arbitrary Number of Agents. In *Proceedings of the Twenty-Ninth Annual ACM-SIAM Symposium on Discrete Algorithms*. SIAM, 2564–2583.

[20] Shahar Dobzinski, Noam Nisan, and Michael Schapira. 2005. Approximation algorithms for combinatorial auctions with complement-free bidders. In *Proceedings of the thirty-seventh annual ACM symposium on Theory of computing*. ACM, 610–618.

[21] Lester E Dubins and Edwin H Spanier. 1961. How to cut a cake fairly. *American mathematical monthly* (1961), 1–17.

[22] Leah Epstein and Asaf Levin. 2014. An efficient polynomial time approximation scheme for load balancing on uniformly related machines. *Mathematical Programming* 147, 1-2 (2014), 1–23.

[23] Alireza Farhadi, MohammadTaghi Hajiaghayi, Mohammad Ghodsi, Sebastien Lahaie, David Pennock, Masoud Seddighin, Saeed Seddighin, and Hadi Yami. 2017. Fair Allocation of Indivisible Goods to Asymmetric Agents. In *Proceedings of the 16th Conference on Autonomous Agents and MultiAgent Systems*. International Foundation for Autonomous Agents and Multiagent Systems, 1535–1537.

[24] Uriel Feige. 2009. On maximizing welfare when utility functions are subadditive. *SIAM J. Comput.* 39, 1 (2009), 122–142.

[25] Uriel Feige, Vahab S Mirrokni, and Jan Vondrak. 2007. Maximizing Non-Monotone Submodular Functions. In *Foundations of Computer Science, 2007. FOCS'07. 48th Annual IEEE Symposium on.* IEEE, 461–471.

[26] Uriel Feige and Jan Vondrak. 2006. Approximation algorithms for allocation problems: Improving the factor of 1-1/e. In *Foundations of Computer Science, 2006. FOCS'06. 47th Annual IEEE Symposium on.* IEEE, 667–676.

[27] Michal Feldman, Nick Gravin, and Brendan Lucier. 2015. Combinatorial auctions via posted prices. In *Proceedings of the twenty-sixth annual ACM-SIAM symposium on Discrete algorithms.* Society for Industrial and Applied Mathematics, 123–135.

[28] Duncan K Foley. 1967. Resource allocation and the public sector. *YALE ECON ESSAYS, VOL 7, NO 1, PP 45-98, SPRING 1967. 7 FIG, 13 REF.* (1967).

[29] Satoru Fujishige. 2005. *Submodular functions and optimization.* Vol. 58. Elsevier.

[30] Mohammad Ghodsi, Mohammad Taghi Hajiaghayi, Masoud Seddighin, Saeed Seddighin, and Hadi Yami. 2017. Fair Allocation of Indivisible Goods: Improvement and Generalization. *CoRR* abs/1704.00222 (2017). arXiv:1704.00222 http://arxiv.org/abs/1704.00222

[31] Daniel Golovin. 2005. Max-min fair allocation of indivisible goods. (2005).

[32] Anupam Gupta, Aaron Roth, Grant Schoenebeck, and Kunal Talwar. 2010. Constrained non-monotone submodular maximization: Offline and secretary algorithms. In *International Workshop on Internet and Network Economics.* Springer, 246–257.

[33] Gunhee Kim, Eric P Xing, Li Fei-Fei, and Takeo Kanade. 2011. Distributed cosegmentation via submodular optimization on anisotropic diffusion. In *Computer Vision (ICCV), 2011 IEEE International Conference on.* IEEE, 169–176.

[34] Andreas Krause. 2010. Sfo: A toolbox for submodular function optimization. *The Journal of Machine Learning Research* 11 (2010), 1141–1144.

[35] David Kurokawa, Ariel D Procaccia, and Junxing Wang. 2016. When Can the Maximin Share Guarantee Be Guaranteed?. In *AAAI*, Vol. 16. 523–529.

[36] David Kurokawa, Ariel D Procaccia, and Junxing Wang. 2018. Fair Enough: Guaranteeing Approximate Maximin Shares. *Journal of the ACM (JACM)* 65, 2 (2018), 8.

[37] Jon Lee, Vahab S Mirrokni, Viswanath Nagarajan, and Maxim Sviridenko. 2009. Non-monotone submodular maximization under matroid and knapsack constraints. In *Proceedings of the forty-first annual ACM symposium on Theory of computing.* ACM, 323–332.

[38] R Paes Leme. 2014. Gross substitutability: An algorithmic survey. *preprint* (2014).

[39] Richard J Lipton, Evangelos Markakis, Elchanan Mossel, and Amin Saberi. 2004. On approximately fair allocations of indivisible goods. In *Proceedings of the 5th ACM conference on Electronic commerce.* ACM, 125–131.

[40] Michel Minoux. 1978. Accelerated greedy algorithms for maximizing submodular set functions. In *Optimization Techniques.* Springer, 234–243.

[41] Benjamin Plaut and Tim Roughgarde. 2018. Almost envy-freeness with general valuations. In *Proceedings of the Twenty-Ninth Annual ACM-SIAM Symposium on Discrete Algorithms.* SIAM, 2584–2603.

[42] Hugo Steinhaus. 1948. The problem of fair division. *Econometrica* 16, 1 (1948).

[43] Jan Vondrák. 2008. Optimal approximation for the submodular welfare problem in the value oracle model. In *Proceedings of the fortieth annual ACM symposium on Theory of computing.* ACM, 67–74.

# Finding Fair and Efficient Allocations

SIDDHARTH BARMAN, Indian Institute of Science, India
SANATH KUMAR KRISHNAMURTHY, Chennai Mathematical Institute, India
ROHIT VAISH, Indian Institute of Science, India

We study the problem of allocating a set of *indivisible* goods among a set of agents in a *fair* and *efficient* manner. An allocation is said to be *fair* if it is envy-free up to one good (EF1), which means that each agent prefers its own bundle over the bundle of any other agent up to the removal of one good. In addition, an allocation is deemed *efficient* if it satisfies Pareto efficiency. While each of these well-studied properties is easy to achieve separately, achieving them together is far from obvious. Recently, Caragiannis et al. [11] established the surprising result that when agents have additive valuations for the goods, there always exists an allocation that simultaneously satisfies these two seemingly incompatible properties. Specifically, they showed that an allocation that maximizes the Nash social welfare objective is both EF1 and Pareto efficient. However, the problem of maximizing Nash social welfare is NP-hard. As a result, this approach does not provide an efficient algorithm for finding a fair and efficient allocation.

In this paper, we bypass this barrier, and develop a pseudopolynomial time algorithm for finding allocations that are EF1 and Pareto efficient; in particular, when the valuations are bounded, our algorithm finds such an allocation in polynomial time. Furthermore, we establish a stronger existence result compared to Caragiannis et al. [11]: For additive valuations, there always exists an allocation that is EF1 and *fractionally* Pareto efficient.

Another key contribution of our work is to show that our algorithm provides a polynomial-time 1.45-approximation to the Nash social welfare objective. This improves upon the best known approximation ratio for this problem (namely, the 2-approximation algorithm of Cole et al. [12]), and also matches the lower bound on the integrality gap of the convex program of Cole et al. [12]. Unlike many of the existing approaches, our algorithm is completely combinatorial, and relies on constructing *integral* Fisher markets wherein specific equilibria are not only efficient, but also fair.

CCS Concepts: • **Theory of computation** → **Approximation algorithms analysis**; **Market equilibria**; *Algorithmic game theory*; • **Mathematics of computing** → *Combinatorial algorithms*;

Additional Key Words and Phrases: Fair division, Nash Social Welfare, Approximation Algorithms

## 1 INTRODUCTION

The theory of fair division addresses the fundamental problem of allocating goods or resources among agents in a fair and efficient manner. Such problems arise in many real-world settings such as government auctions, divorce settlements, and border disputes. Starting with the work of Steinhaus [30], there is now a vast literature in economics and mathematics to formally address fair division [7, 8, 26]. Many interesting connections have also been found between fair division and fields such as topology, measure theory, combinatorics, and algorithms [25].

Authors' addresses: Siddharth Barman, Indian Institute of Science, Bangalore, India, 560012, barman@iisc.ac.in; Sanath Kumar Krishnamurthy, Chennai Mathematical Institute, Kelambakkam, India, 603103, sanathkumar9@cmi.ac.in; Rohit Vaish, Indian Institute of Science, Bangalore, India, 560012, rohitv@iisc.ac.in.


*ACM EC'18, June 18–22, 2018, Ithaca, NY, USA.* ACM ISBN 978-1-4503-5829-3/18/06....$15.00.
https://doi.org/10.1145/3219166.3219176

Much of the prior work in fair division, though, has focused on *divisible* goods, which model resources that can be fractionally allocated (such as land). A standard fairness concept in this setting is *envy-freeness* [17], which requires that each agent prefers its own allocation over that of any other agent. A well-known result of Varian [31] shows that for the divisible setting, there always exists an allocation that is both envy-free (i.e., fair) and *Pareto efficient*. Furthermore, such an allocation can be computed in polynomial time [15, 16]. These results, however, do not extend to the setting of *indivisible* goods, which model discrete resources such as courses at universities [29] or inherited artwork. In fact, many of the classical solution concepts and algorithms that have been developed for divisible goods are not directly applicable to the indivisible setting. For example, an envy-free allocation fails to exist even in the simple setting of a single indivisible good and two agents.

These considerations have motivated recent work in the theoretical computer science and economics communities on developing relevant notions of fairness, along with existence results and algorithms for the problem of fairly allocating indivisible goods [5, 9, 21, 23]. We contribute to this line of work by showing that guarantees analogous to the fundamental result of Varian [31] hold even for indivisible goods in terms of a natural and necessary relaxation of envy-freeness. Specifically, we show that for additive valuations,[1] a fair and efficient allocation always exists, and such an allocation can be computed in (pseudo)-polynomial time.

We consider an allocation of indivisible goods to be fair if it is *envy-free up to one good* (EF1). This notion was defined by Budish [9], and provides a compelling relaxation of the envy-freeness property.[2] An allocation is said to be EF1 if each agent prefers its own bundle over the bundle of any other agent up to the removal of the most valuable good from the other agent's bundle. Although the existence of envy-free allocations is not guaranteed in the context of indivisible goods, an EF1 allocation always exists—even under general, combinatorial valuations—and can be found in polynomial time [23].

With this notion of fairness in hand, it is relevant to ask whether we can achieve *efficiency along with fairness* while allocating indivisible goods.[3] This question was recently studied by Caragiannis et al. [11], who showed a striking result that there is no need to trade efficiency for fairness: For additive valuations, an allocation that maximizes the *Nash social welfare* [20, 27]—defined to be the geometric mean of the agents' valuations—is both fair (EF1) and Pareto efficient. However, maximizing the Nash social welfare (NSW) over integral allocations is an NP-hard problem [28]. (In fact, the problem is known to be APX-hard [22]). Therefore, this existence result does not automatically provide an efficient algorithm for finding a fair and efficient allocation of indivisible goods. Our work bypasses this limitation by providing *a pseudopolynomial time algorithm for finding an EF1 and Pareto efficient allocation* of indivisible goods under additive valuations. In particular, when the valuations are *bounded*, our algorithm finds such an allocation in *polynomial time*. It is worth pointing out that the problem of maximizing NSW remains APX-hard even for bounded valuations [22].

A related problem is that of developing approximation algorithms for NSW maximization. This problem has received considerable attention in recent years [1, 2, 4, 12, 13, 18]. The first constant-factor (specifically, 2.89) approximation for this problem was provided by Cole and Gkatzelis [13]. This approximation factor was subsequently improved to $e$ [2], and most recently to 2 [12]. Similar

[1] *Additivity* means that an agent's valuation for a set of goods is the sum of its valuations for the individual goods in that set.
[2] The notion of EF1 has found practical appeal on the popular fair division website "Spliddit" [19] and in course allocation at Wharton School of Business [10].
[3] Note that fairness, by itself, does not guarantee efficiency; in fact, an EF1 allocation can be highly inefficient (refer to the full version [3] for an example).

approximation guarantees have also been developed for more general market models such as piecewise-linear concave utilities [1], budget additive valuations [18], and multi-unit markets [4].

While the problem of approximating NSW is interesting in its own right, it is relevant to note that an allocation that approximates this objective is, in and of itself, not guaranteed to be EF1 or Pareto efficient (refer to the full version [3] for an example).[4] A second key contribution of our work is to show that our algorithm provides *a polynomial-time* 1.45*-approximation to the* NSW *maximization problem*. Thus, not only does our algorithm improve upon the best-known approximation ratio for this problem (namely, the 2-approximation algorithm of Cole et al. [12]), it is also guaranteed to return a fair and efficient outcome. The following list summarizes our contributions.

**Our contributions**

- We develop an *algorithm* for computing an EF1 and Pareto efficient allocation for additive valuations. The running time of our algorithm is pseudopolynomial for general integral valuations (Theorem 3.1) and polynomial when the valuations are bounded (Remark 1). In addition, our algorithm can find an approximate EF1 and approximate Pareto efficient allocation in polynomial time even without the bounded valuations assumption (Remark 2).
- We establish a *stronger existence result* compared to Caragiannis et al. [11]: For additive valuations, there always exists an allocation that is EF1 and *fractionally* Pareto efficient (Theorem 3.2). In other words, the problem of finding an EF1 and fractionally Pareto efficient allocation is *total*. An interesting complexity-theoretic implication of this result is that there exists a nondeterministic polynomial time algorithm for finding an EF1 and Pareto efficient allocation (Remark 3). This implication does not directly follow from the existence result of Caragiannis et al. [11], as the problem of verifying whether an arbitrary allocation is Pareto efficient is known to be co-NP-complete [14].
- We show that our algorithm provides a *polynomial-time* 1.45*-approximation* for the Nash social welfare (NSW) maximization problem (Theorem 3.3). This improves upon the best known approximation factor for this problem (namely, the 2-approximation algorithm of Cole et al. [12]), and also matches the lower bound of $e^{1/e} \approx 1.44$ on the integrality gap of the convex program of Cole et al. [12]. An interesting byproduct of our analysis is a novel connection between envy-freeness and NSW: Under identical valuations, an EF1 allocation provides a 1.45-approximation to the maximum NSW (Lemma 3.4).

**Our techniques** It is known from the fundamental theorems of welfare economics that markets tend toward efficiency. Intuitively, our results are based on establishing a complementary result that markets can be *fair* as well. In particular, we construct a Fisher market along with an underlying equilibrium which is integral (i.e., corresponding to an allocation of the indivisible goods) and EF1. The fact that this allocation is a market equilibrium ensures, via the first welfare theorem, that it is Pareto efficient as well.

More concretely, we start with a Pareto efficient allocation, and iteratively modify the allocation by exchanging goods between the agents. The goal of the exchange step is to locally move toward a fair allocation. Additionally, throughout these exchanges, we maintain a set of prices that ensure that the current allocation corresponds to an equilibrium outcome for the existing market. We stop when the equilibrium of the market (i.e., the allocation at hand) satisfies *price envy-freeness up to one good* (refer to Section 4.1 for a formal definition). Essentially, this property ensures that under the given market prices, the spending of an agent is at least that of any other agent up to the removal of the highest priced good from the other agent's bundle. Requiring the spendings to

[4]We also provide an example in the full version [3] in which *every* rounding of the "spending restricted outcome"—a market equilibrium notion used in the design of approximation algorithms for NSW [1, 12, 13]—violates EF1.

be balanced in this manner implies the desired EF1 property for the corresponding fair division instance; see Section 4 for a detailed description of this construction.

At a conceptual level, our approach differs from the existing approaches in two important ways: First, our algorithm works with an *integral* Fisher market at every step, thereby breaking away from the standard *relax-and-round* paradigm where a fractional market equilibrium is first computed (typically as a solution of some convex program) followed by a rounding step [1, 2, 12, 13, 18]. Second, unlike all existing approaches, our algorithm uses the notion of *price envy-freeness up to one good* as a measure of balanced spending in the Fisher market. To the best of our knowledge, this notion is novel to this work, and might find future use in the design of fair and efficient algorithms for other settings.

## 2 PRELIMINARIES

### 2.1 The Fair Division Model

**Problem instance** An *instance* of the fair division problem is a tuple $\langle [n], [m], \mathcal{V} \rangle$, where $[n] = \{1, 2, \ldots, n\}$ denotes the set of $n \in \mathbb{N}$ *agents*, $[m] = \{1, 2, \ldots, m\}$ denotes the set of $m \in \mathbb{N}$ *goods*, and the *valuation profile* $\mathcal{V} = \{v_1, v_2, \ldots, v_n\}$ specifies the preferences of each agent $i \in [n]$ over the set of goods $[m]$ via a *valuation function* $v_i : 2^{[m]} \rightarrow \mathbb{Z}_+ \cup \{0\}$. We will assume throughout that the valuation functions are *additive*, i.e., for each agent $i \in [n]$ and any set of goods $G \subseteq [m]$, $v_i(G) := \sum_{j \in G} v_i(\{j\})$.[5] For simplicity, we will write $v_{i,j}$ instead of $v_i(\{j\})$ for a singleton good $j \in [m]$. Thus, $v_{i,j}$ is non-negative and integral for each agent $i \in [n]$ and each good $j \in [m]$. We will also assume, without loss of generality, that for each good $j \in [m]$, there exists some agent $i \in [n]$ with a nonzero valuation for it, i.e., $v_{i,j} > 0$. Finally, we let $v_{\max} := \max_{i,j} v_{i,j}$.

**Allocation** An *allocation* $\mathbf{x} \in \{0, 1\}^{n \times m}$ refers to an $n$-partition $(\mathbf{x}_1, \ldots, \mathbf{x}_n)$ of $[m]$, where $\mathbf{x}_i \subseteq [m]$ is the *bundle* allocated to agent $i$. We let $\mathcal{X}$ denote the set of all $n$ partitions of $[m]$. Given an allocation $\mathbf{x}$, the valuation of an agent $i \in [n]$ for the bundle $\mathbf{x}_i$ is $v_i(\mathbf{x}_i) = \sum_{j \in \mathbf{x}_i} v_{i,j}$.

Another useful notion is that of a fractional allocation. A *fractional allocation* $\mathbf{x} \in [0, 1]^{n \times m}$ refers to a (possibly) fractional assignment of the goods to the agents such that no more than one unit of each good is allocated, i.e., for all $j \in [m]$, we have $\sum_{i \in [n]} x_{i,j} \leq 1$. We will use the term *allocation* to refer to an integral allocation, and explicitly write *fractional allocation* otherwise.

### 2.2 Fairness Notions

**Envy-freeness and its variants** Given an instance $\langle [n], [m], \mathcal{V} \rangle$ and an allocation $\mathbf{x}$, we say that an agent $i \in [n]$ *envies* another agent $k \in [n]$ if $i$ strictly prefers the bundle of $k$ over its own bundle, i.e., $v_i(\mathbf{x}_k) > v_i(\mathbf{x}_i)$. An allocation $\mathbf{x}$ is said to be *envy-free* (EF) if each agent prefers its own bundle over that of any other agent, i.e., for every pair of agents $i, k \in [n]$, we have $v_i(\mathbf{x}_i) \geq v_i(\mathbf{x}_k)$.

An allocation $\mathbf{x}$ is said to be *envy-free up to one good* (EF1) if for every pair of agents $i, k \in [n]$, there exists a good $j \in \mathbf{x}_k$ such that $v_i(\mathbf{x}_i) \geq v_i(\mathbf{x}_k \setminus \{j\})$. Given any $\varepsilon > 0$, an allocation $\mathbf{x}$ is said to be *$\varepsilon$-approximately envy-free up to one good* ($\varepsilon$-EF1) if for every pair of agents $i, k \in [n]$, there exists a good $j \in \mathbf{x}_k$ such that $(1 + \varepsilon) v_i(\mathbf{x}_i) \geq v_i(\mathbf{x}_k \setminus \{j\})$.

**Nash social welfare** Given an allocation $\mathbf{x}$, write $\mathrm{NSW}(\mathbf{x}) := \left(\prod_{i \in [n]} v_i(\mathbf{x}_i)\right)^{\frac{1}{n}}$ to denote the *Nash social welfare* of $\mathbf{x}$. An allocation $\mathbf{x}^*$ said to be *Nash optimal* if $\mathbf{x}^* \in \arg\max_{\mathbf{x} \in \mathcal{X}} \mathrm{NSW}(\mathbf{x})$.

### 2.3 Efficiency Notions

**Pareto efficiency** Given an instance $\langle [n], [m], \mathcal{V} \rangle$ and an allocation $\mathbf{x}$, we say that $\mathbf{x}$ is Pareto dominated by another allocation $\mathbf{y}$ if $v_k(\mathbf{y}_k) \geq v_k(\mathbf{x}_k)$ for every agent $k \in [n]$, and $v_i(\mathbf{y}_i) > v_i(\mathbf{x}_i)$

[5]We will assume that $v_i(\{\emptyset\}) = 0$ for all $i \in [n]$.

for some agent $i \in [n]$. An allocation is said to be *Pareto efficient* or *Pareto optimal* (PO) if it is not Pareto dominated by any other allocation. Similarly, $\mathbf{x}$ is $\varepsilon$*-Pareto efficient* ($\varepsilon$-PO) if it is not $\varepsilon$-Pareto dominated by any other allocation $\mathbf{y}$, i.e., there does not exist an allocation $\mathbf{y}$ such that $v_k(\mathbf{y}_k) \geq (1+\varepsilon)v_k(\mathbf{x}_k)$ for every agent $k \in [n]$ and $v_i(\mathbf{y}_i) > (1+\varepsilon)v_i(\mathbf{x}_i)$ for some agent $i \in [n]$.

Some of our results use a generalization of Pareto efficiency, which we call *fractional Pareto efficiency*. An allocation is said to be fractionally Pareto efficient (fPO) if it not Pareto dominated by any fractional allocation. Thus, a fractionally Pareto efficient allocation is also Pareto efficient, but the converse is not necessarily true (refer to the full version [3] for an example).

## 3 MAIN RESULTS

This section provides the statements of our three main results: an algorithm for finding an EF1 and PO allocation (Theorem 3.1), an existence result for EF1 and fPO allocation (Theorem 3.2), and an approximation algorithm for Nash social welfare (Theorem 3.3).

**Algorithmic Result:**

THEOREM 3.1. *Given any fair division instance* $\mathcal{I} = \langle [n], [m], \mathcal{V} \rangle$ *with additive valuations, an allocation that is envy-free up to one good (EF1) and Pareto efficient (PO) can be found in* $O\left(\text{poly}(m, n, v_{\max})\right)$ *time, where* $v_{\max} = \max_{i,j} v_{i,j}$.

REMARK 1. *Note that when all valuations are* polynomially bounded *(i.e., there exists a polynomial* $f(m,n)$ *such that for all* $i \in [n]$ *and* $j \in [m]$, $v_{i,j} \leq f(m,n)$*), an EF1 and PO allocation can be computed in* polynomial *time. In particular, this is true when all valuations are bounded by a constant. As mentioned earlier in Section 1, the problem of maximizing* NSW *remains APX-hard even for constant valuations [22], and therefore our result circumvents the intractability associated with computing a Nash optimal allocation in order to achieve these two properties.*

REMARK 2. *If we relax the fairness and efficiency requirements in Theorem 3.1 to their approximate analogues, then our algorithm is guaranteed to run in polynomial time. Specifically, our algorithm can find an* $\varepsilon$*-EF1 and* $\varepsilon$*-PO allocation in* $O\left(\text{poly}(m, n, \frac{1}{\varepsilon}, \ln v_{\max})\right)$ *time, where* $v_{\max} = \max_{i,j} v_{i,j}$*. (Refer to Lemma 5.5 in Section 5.2).*

The proof of Theorem 3.1 is provided in Section 5.

**Existence Result:**

THEOREM 3.2. *Given any fair division instance with additive valuations, there always exists an allocation that is envy-free up to one good (EF1) and fractionally Pareto efficient (fPO).*

REMARK 3. *Consider the canonical binary relation* $\mathcal{R}^{EF1+PO}$ *associated with the problem of finding an EF1 and PO allocation, defined as follows: For a fair division instance* $\mathcal{I}$ *and an allocation* $\mathbf{x}$*, the relation* $\mathcal{R}^{EF1+PO}(\mathcal{I}, \mathbf{x})$ *holds if and only if* $\mathbf{x}$ *is an EF1 and PO allocation of* $\mathcal{I}$*. It is relevant to note that under standard complexity theoretic assumptions,* $\mathcal{R}^{EF1+PO}$ *is not in* TFNP.[6] *By contrast, the binary relation* $\mathcal{R}^{EF1+fPO}(\mathcal{I}, \mathbf{x})$*, which holds if and only if* $\mathbf{x}$ *is an EF1 and fPO allocation for the instance* $\mathcal{I}$*, admits efficient verification.*[7] *Since Theorem 3.2 shows that* $\mathcal{R}^{EF1+fPO}$ *is total, we get that the binary relation* $\mathcal{R}^{EF1+fPO}$ *is in* TFNP*. Thus, there exists a nondeterministic polynomial time algorithm for finding an EF1 and fPO (and hence EF1 and PO) allocation.*

The proof of Theorem 3.2 is deferred to the full version of the paper.

[6] It is known that determining whether an arbitrary allocation is PO is co-NP-complete [14]. This fact can be used to show that verifying whether a given allocation is EF1 and PO is also co-NP-complete. Hence, the binary relation $\mathcal{R}^{\text{EF1+PO}}$ cannot be efficiently verified (i.e., it is not in FNP), unless P = NP.

[7] EF1 requires checking $O(n^2)$ inequalities, and fPO can be verified by a linear program (refer to the full version).

**Approximating Nash Social Welfare:**

THEOREM 3.3. *For additive valuations, there exists a polynomial-time* 1.45*-approximation algorithm for the Nash social welfare maximization problem.*

Our proof of Theorem 3.3 draws on the following interesting connection between approximate envy-freeness and Nash social welfare:

LEMMA 3.4. *Given a fair division instance with identical and additive valuations, any $\varepsilon$-EF1 allocation provides a $e^{(1+\varepsilon)/e}$-approximation to Nash social welfare.*

The proof of Theorem 3.3 is provided in Section 6.

## 4 OUR ALGORITHM

This section presents our algorithm. We start with the relevant preliminaries in Section 4.1 that provide the necessary definitions required for describing the algorithm. The pseudocode of the algorithm appears in Section 4.2 along with a brief description.

### 4.1 Market Terminology

**Fisher market** The Fisher market is a fundamental model in the economics of resource allocation [6]. It captures the setting where a set of buyers enter the market with prespecified budgets, and use it to buy goods that provide maximum utility per unit of money spent. Specifically, a Fisher market consists of a set $[n] = \{1, 2, \dots, n\}$ of $n$ *buyers*, a set $[m] = \{1, 2, \dots, m\}$ of $m$ divisible *goods* (exactly one unit of each good is available), and a *valuation profile* $\mathcal{V} = \{v_1, v_2, \dots, v_n\}$. Each buyer $i \in [n]$ has an initial *endowment* (or budget) $e_i > 0$. The endowment holds no intrinsic value for a buyer and is only used for buying the goods. We call $\mathbf{e} = (e_1, \dots, e_n)$ the *endowment vector*, and denote a *market instance* by $\langle [n], [m], \mathcal{V}, \mathbf{e} \rangle$.

A *market outcome* is given by the pair $\langle \mathbf{x}, \mathbf{p} \rangle$, where the *allocation vector* $\mathbf{x} = (\mathbf{x}_1, \dots, \mathbf{x}_n)$ is a fractional allocation of the $m$ goods, and the *price vector* $\mathbf{p} = (p_1, \dots, p_m)$ associates a price $p_j \geq 0$ with each good $j \in [m]$. The *spending* of buyer $i$ under the market outcome $\langle \mathbf{x}, \mathbf{p} \rangle$ is given by $\mathbf{p}(\mathbf{x}_i) = \sum_{j=1}^{m} x_{i,j} p_j$. The *valuation* derived by the buyer $i$ under the market outcome $\langle \mathbf{x}, \mathbf{p} \rangle$ is given by $v_i(\mathbf{x}_i) = \sum_{j=1}^{m} x_{i,j} v_{i,j}$.

Given a price vector $\mathbf{p} = (p_1, \dots, p_m)$, define the *bang per buck* ratio of buyer $i$ for good $j$ as $\alpha_{i,j} := v_{i,j}/p_j$, and its *maximum bang per buck* ratio as $\alpha_i := \max_j \alpha_{i,j}$.[8] Let $\text{MBB}_i := \{j \in [m] : v_{i,j}/p_j = \alpha_i\}$ denote the set of all goods that maximize the bang per buck ratio for buyer $i$ at the price vector $\mathbf{p}$. We call $\text{MBB}_i$ the *maximum bang per buck set* (or MBB set) of buyer $i$ at the price vector $\mathbf{p}$.

An outcome $\langle \mathbf{x}, \mathbf{p} \rangle$ is said to be a *Fisher market equilibrium* if it satisfies the following conditions:

- *Market clearing*: Each good is either priced at zero or is completely allocated. That is, for each good $j \in [m]$, either $p_j = 0$ or $\sum_{i=1}^{n} x_{i,j} = 1$.
- *Budget exhaustion*: Buyers spend their endowments completely, i.e., $\mathbf{p}(\mathbf{x}_i) = e_i$ for all $i \in [n]$.
- *Maximum bang per buck allocation*: Each buyer's allocation is a subset of its MBB set. That is, for any buyer $i \in [n]$ and any good $j \in [m]$, $x_{i,j} > 0 \implies j \in \text{MBB}_i$. Stated differently, each buyer only spends on its maximum bang per buck goods. Notice that a consequence of spending only on MBB goods is that each buyer maximizes its utility at the given prices $\mathbf{p}$ under the budget constraints.

We refer the reader to the full version for additional market preliminaries.

[8] If $v_{i,j} = 0$ and $p_j = 0$, then we define $\alpha_{i,j} = 0$.

Proposition 1 (First Welfare Theorem; [24, Chapter 16]). *For a Fisher market with additive valuations, any equilibrium outcome is fractionally Pareto efficient (fPO).*

**Price envy-freeness and its variants** Several of our results rely on constructing market outcomes with a property called *price envy-freeness*—a notion we consider to be of independent interest. Specifically, let $\mathbf{x}$ be an allocation and let $\mathbf{p}$ be a price vector for a given Fisher market. We say that $\mathbf{x}$ is *price envy-free* (pEF) with respect to $\mathbf{p}$ if for every pair of buyers $i, k \in [n]$, we have $\mathbf{p}(\mathbf{x}_i) \geq \mathbf{p}(\mathbf{x}_k)$.[9] Similarly, $\mathbf{x}$ is said to be *price envy-free up to one good* (pEF1) with respect to $\mathbf{p}$ if for every pair of buyers $i, k \in [n]$, there exists a good $j \in \mathbf{x}_k$ such that $\mathbf{p}(\mathbf{x}_i) \geq \mathbf{p}(\mathbf{x}_k \setminus \{j\})$. Finally, given any $\varepsilon > 0$, we say that an allocation $\mathbf{x}$ is *$\varepsilon$-approximately price envy-free up to one good* ($\varepsilon$-pEF1) with respect to $\mathbf{p}$ if for every pair of buyers $i, k \in [n]$, there exists a good $j \in \mathbf{x}_k$ such that $(1 + \varepsilon)\mathbf{p}(\mathbf{x}_i) \geq \mathbf{p}(\mathbf{x}_k \setminus \{j\})$.

MBB **graph and alternating paths** The MBB *graph* of a Fisher market instance with a price vector $\mathbf{p}$ is defined as a bipartite graph $G$ whose vertex set consists of the set of agents $[n]$ and the set of goods $[m]$, and there is an edge between an agent $i \in [n]$ and a good $j \in [m]$ if $j \in \text{MBB}_i$ (called an MBB *edge*). Given an allocation $\mathbf{x}$, we can augment the MBB graph by adding *allocation edges*, i.e., an edge between an agent $i \in [n]$ and a good $j \in [m]$ such that $j \in \mathbf{x}_i$. For an augmented MBB graph, we define an *alternating path* $P = (i, j_1, i_1, j_2, i_2, \ldots, i_{\ell-1}, j_\ell, k)$ from agent $i$ to agent $k$ (and involving the agents $i_1, i_2, \ldots, i_{\ell-1}$ and the goods $j_1, j_2, \ldots, j_\ell$) as a series of alternating MBB and allocation edges such that $j_1 \in \text{MBB}_i \cap \mathbf{x}_{i_1}, j_2 \in \text{MBB}_{i_1} \cap \mathbf{x}_{i_2}, \ldots, j_\ell \in \text{MBB}_{i_{\ell-1}} \cap \mathbf{x}_k$. If such a path exists, we say that the agent $k$ is *reachable* from agent $i$ via an alternating path. Notice that no agent or good is allowed to repeat in an alternating path. We say that the path $P$ is of *length* $2\ell$ since it consists of $\ell$ MBB edges and $\ell$ allocation edges.

**Hierarchy structure** Let $G$ denote the augmented MBB graph for a Fisher market instance with the market outcome $(\mathbf{x}, \mathbf{p})$. Fix a *source* agent $i \in [n]$ in $G$. Define the *level* of an agent $k \in [n]$ as half the length of the shortest alternating path from $i$ to $k$ (if one exists). The level of the source agent $i$ is defined to be zero. If there is no alternating path from $i$ to some agent $k$ in $G$ (i.e., if $k$ is not reachable from $i$), then the level of $k$ is set to be $n$. The *hierarchy* structure $\mathcal{H}_i$ of agent $i$ is defined as a level-wise collection of all agents that are reachable from $i$, i.e., $\mathcal{H}_i = \{\mathcal{H}_i^0, \mathcal{H}_i^1, \mathcal{H}_i^2, \ldots, \}$, where $\mathcal{H}_i^\ell$ denotes the set of agents that are at level $\ell$ with respect to the agent $i$. The full version provides a polynomial time subroutine called BuildHierarchy for constructing the hierarchy.

Given a hierarchy $\mathcal{H}_i$, we will overload the term *alternating path* to refer to a series of alternating MBB and allocation edges *connecting agents at a lower level to those at a higher level.* That is, a path $P = (i, j_1, i_1, j_2, i_2, \ldots, i_{\ell-1}, j_\ell, k)$ involving agents from the hierarchy $\mathcal{H}_i$ is said to be an alternating path if (1) $j_1 \in \text{MBB}_i \cap \mathbf{x}_{i_1}, j_2 \in \text{MBB}_{i_1} \cap \mathbf{x}_{i_2}, \ldots, j_\ell \in \text{MBB}_{i_{\ell-1}} \cap \mathbf{x}_k$, and (2) $\text{level}(i) < \text{level}(i_1) < \text{level}(i_2) < \cdots < \text{level}(i_{\ell-1}) < \text{level}(k)$. In particular, an alternating path in a hierarchy cannot have edges between agents at the same level.

**Violators and path-violators** Given a Fisher market instance and a market outcome $(\mathbf{x}, \mathbf{p})$, an agent $i \in [n]$ with the smallest spending among all the agents is called the *least spender*, i.e., $i \in \arg\min_{k \in [n]} \mathbf{p}(\mathbf{x}_k)$ (ties are broken according to a prespecified ordering over the agents). An agent $k \in [n]$ is said to be a *violator* if for every good $j \in \mathbf{x}_k$, we have that $\mathbf{p}(\mathbf{x}_k \setminus \{j\}) > \mathbf{p}(\mathbf{x}_i)$, where $i$ is the least spender. Similarly, agent $k \in [n]$ is said to be an *$\varepsilon$-violator* if for every good $j \in \mathbf{x}_k$, we have that $\mathbf{p}(\mathbf{x}_k \setminus \{j\}) > (1 + \varepsilon)\mathbf{p}(\mathbf{x}_i)$. Notice that an agent can be a violator without being an *$\varepsilon$-violator.* Also notice that if no agent is a violator ($\varepsilon$-violator), then the allocation $\mathbf{x}$ is pEF1 ($\varepsilon$-pEF1) with respect to $\mathbf{p}$.

[9] Equivalently, for every pair of buyers $i, k \in [n]$, we require $\mathbf{p}(\mathbf{x}_i) = \mathbf{p}(\mathbf{x}_k)$.

A closely related notion is that of a *path-violator*. Let $i$ denote the least spender, and let $\mathcal{H}_i$ denote the hierarchy of agent $i$. An agent $k \in \mathcal{H}_i$ is said to be a *path-violator* with respect to the alternating path $P = (i, j_1, i_1, j_2, i_2, \ldots, i_{\ell-1}, j_\ell, k)$ if $\mathbf{p}(\mathbf{x}_k \setminus \{j_\ell\}) > \mathbf{p}(\mathbf{x}_i)$. Observe that a path-violator (along a path $P$) need not be a violator, since there can be a good $j \in \mathbf{x}_k$ not on the path $P$ such that $\mathbf{p}(\mathbf{x}_k \setminus \{j\}) \leq \mathbf{p}(\mathbf{x}_i)$. Similarly, an agent $k \in \mathcal{H}_i$ is said to be an *$\varepsilon$-path-violator* with respect to the alternating path $P = (i, j_1, i_1, j_2, i_2, \ldots, i_{\ell-1}, j_\ell, k)$ if $\mathbf{p}(\mathbf{x}_k \setminus \{j_\ell\}) > (1+\varepsilon)\mathbf{p}(\mathbf{x}_i)$.

### 4.2 Description of the Algorithm

Given any fair division instance $\mathcal{I} = \langle [n], [m], \mathcal{V} \rangle$ as input and a parameter $\varepsilon > 0$, our algorithm (Algorithm 1), referred to as Alg from here onwards, constructs a market equilibrium $(\mathbf{x}, \mathbf{p})$ with respect to a Fisher market instance $\langle [n], [m], \mathcal{V}, \mathbf{e} \rangle$ (for a suitable endowment vector $\mathbf{e}$). The pair $(\mathbf{x}, \mathbf{p})$ has the following two properties: (1) $\mathbf{x}$ is an integral allocation, and (2) $\mathbf{x}$ is $3\varepsilon$-pEF1 with respect to $\mathbf{p}$. The second property allows us to show that the allocation $\mathbf{x}$ is $3\varepsilon$-EF1 for the corresponding fair division instance $\mathcal{I}$ (see Lemma 4.1 below). Furthermore, by the first welfare theorem (Proposition 1), the allocation $\mathbf{x}$ is also guaranteed to be fractionally Pareto efficient (fPO) for the Fisher market instance, and consequently for the fair division instance $\mathcal{I}$.

Lemma 4.1. *Let $\varepsilon \geq 0$, and let $\mathbf{x}$ and $\mathbf{p}$ be an allocation and a price vector respectively for a market instance $\langle [n], [m], \mathcal{V}, \mathbf{e} \rangle$ such that (1) $\mathbf{x}$ is $\varepsilon$-approximately price-envy-free up to one good ($\varepsilon$-pEF1), and (2) $\mathbf{x}_i \subseteq \mathrm{MBB}_i$ for each buyer $i \in [n]$. Then, $\mathbf{x}$ is $\varepsilon$-approximately envy-free up to one good ($\varepsilon$-EF1) for the associated fair division instance $\langle [n], [m], \mathcal{V} \rangle$.*

Proof. Since $\mathbf{x}$ is $\varepsilon$-pEF1 with respect to the price vector $\mathbf{p}$, for any pair of buyers $i, k \in [n]$, there exists a good $j \in \mathbf{x}_k$ such that $(1+\varepsilon)\mathbf{p}(\mathbf{x}_i) \geq \mathbf{p}(\mathbf{x}_k \setminus \{j\})$. Multiplying both sides by the maximum bang per buck ratio $\alpha_i$ of agent $i$, we get

$$\begin{aligned} & \alpha_i \cdot (1+\varepsilon)\mathbf{p}(\mathbf{x}_i) \geq \alpha_i \cdot \mathbf{p}(\mathbf{x}_k \setminus \{j\}) \\ \implies \quad & (1+\varepsilon) v_i(\mathbf{x}_i) \geq \alpha_i \cdot \mathbf{p}(\mathbf{x}_k \setminus \{j\}) \quad (\text{since } \mathbf{x}_i \subseteq \mathrm{MBB}_i) \\ \implies \quad & (1+\varepsilon) v_i(\mathbf{x}_i) \geq v_i(\mathbf{x}_k \setminus \{j\}), \end{aligned}$$

which is the $\varepsilon$-EF1 guarantee for the allocation $\mathbf{x}$. □

In order to construct the desired Fisher market equilibrium, our algorithm starts with a welfare-maximizing allocation $\mathbf{x}$ and a price vector $\mathbf{p}$ such that $\mathbf{x}$ is fPO and each agent gets a subset of its MBB goods (this is Phase 1 of Alg). If the allocation $\mathbf{x}$ is $3\varepsilon$-pEF1 with respect to $\mathbf{p}$, then the algorithm terminates with the output $(\mathbf{x}, \mathbf{p})$. Otherwise, the algorithm proceeds to the next phase.

In Phase 2, the algorithm works with the hierarchy of the least spending agent, and performs a series of exchanges (or swaps) of goods between the agents in the hierarchy (without changing the prices). The swaps are aimed at ensuring that at the end of Phase 2, no agent in the hierarchy is $\varepsilon$-pEF1 envied by the least spender. Furthermore, all exchanges in Phase 2 happen only along the MBB edges, thus maintaining at each stage the condition that $\mathbf{x}$ is an equilibrium allocation, and hence, fPO.

If, at the end of Phase 2, the current allocation $\mathbf{x}$ is still not $3\varepsilon$-pEF1 with respect to the price vector $\mathbf{p}$, the algorithm moves to Phase 3. This phase consists of uniformly raising the prices of the goods owned by the members of the hierarchy. The prices are raised until either the allocation $\mathbf{x}$ becomes $3\varepsilon$-pEF1 with respect to the new price vector $\mathbf{p}$, or a new agent gets added to the hierarchy. In the latter case, the algorithm goes back to the start of Phase 2.

It is relevant to note that establishing the time complexity of this algorithm is an intricate task; a priori, it is not even clear whether the algorithm terminates. The stated running time bound is in fact obtained via a number of involved arguments which, in particular, rely on analyzing the spending of the agents in different phases.

## 5 PROOF OF THEOREM 3.1

This section presents the analysis of our algorithm and a proof of Theorem 3.1. Section 5.1 presents the analysis of our algorithm for valuations that satisfy the power-of-$(1+\varepsilon)$ property. Section 5.2 extends this analysis to general valuations, culminating in the proof of Theorem 3.1.

### 5.1 Analysis of ALG when the Valuations are power-of-$(1+\varepsilon)$

In this section, we will analyze ALG under the assumption that all valuations are *power-of-*$(1+\varepsilon)$, i.e., there exists $\varepsilon > 0$ such that for each agent $i \in [n]$ and each good $j \in [m]$, we have $v_{i,j} \in \{0, (1+\varepsilon)^a\}$ for some natural number $a$ (possibly depending on $i$ and $j$). We will start by defining the notion of a *time step* that will be useful in the subsequent analysis.

**Time steps and events** The execution of ALG can be described in terms of the following four *events*: (1) *Swap* operation in Phase 2, (2) *Change* in the identity of least spender in Phase 2, (3) *Price-rise* by a factor of $\alpha$ in Phase 3, and (4) *Termination step.* We use the term *time step* (or simply a *step*) to denote the indexing of any execution of ALG, e.g., ALG might perform a swap operation on the first and second time steps, followed by a price-rise in the third time step, and so on. We will use the phrase "at time step $t$" to denote the state of the algorithm *before* the event at time step $t$ takes place. Notice that each event stated above runs in polynomial time, and therefore it suffices to analyze the running time of ALG in terms of the total number of events (or time steps).

We will now proceed to analyzing the correctness (Lemma 5.1) and the running time (Lemma 5.2) of ALG for power-of-$(1+\varepsilon)$ valuations.

LEMMA 5.1 (**CORRECTNESS OF ALG FOR POWER-OF–$(1+\varepsilon)$ INSTANCE**). *Given any power-of-$(1+\varepsilon)$ instance as input, the allocation returned by* ALG *is $3\varepsilon$-approximately envy-free up to one good ($3\varepsilon$-EF1) and fractionally Pareto efficient (fPO).*

PROOF. Let the output of ALG be $(\mathbf{x}, \mathbf{p})$. The fact that $\mathbf{x}$ is fPO follows from the observation that at each step of the algorithm, the allocation of any agent is a subset of its MBB goods, i.e., at each time step, we have $\mathbf{x}_i \subseteq \text{MBB}_i$ for each agent $i \in [n]$. This is certainly true at the end of Phase 1 by way of setting the prices. In Phase 2, each swap operation only happens along an alternating MBB-allocation edge, which maintains the MBB condition. Phase 3 involves raising the prices of the goods owned by the members of the hierarchy $\mathcal{H}_i$ without changing the allocation. We will argue that for each agent $k \in [n]$, if $\mathbf{x}_k \subseteq \text{MBB}_k$ before the price-rise, then the same continues to hold after the price-rise. Indeed, for any agent $k \notin \mathcal{H}_i$, we have $\mathbf{x}_k \cap \mathbf{x}_{\mathcal{H}_i} = \emptyset$. As a result, raising the prices of the goods in $\mathbf{x}_{\mathcal{H}_i}$ does not affect the bang per buck ratio of agent $k$ for the goods in $\mathbf{x}_k$ (and can only reduce its bang per buck ratio for the goods in $\mathbf{x}_{\mathcal{H}_i}$), thus maintaining the above condition. For any agent $k \in \mathcal{H}_i$, we have $\text{MBB}_k \subseteq \mathbf{x}_{\mathcal{H}_i}$ by construction of the hierarchy. Raising the prices of the goods in $\mathbf{x}_{\mathcal{H}_i}$ therefore corresponds to lowering the MBB ratios for the agents in $\mathcal{H}_i$. By choice of $\alpha_1$, the price-rise stops as soon as a new MBB-edge appears between an agent $k \in \mathcal{H}_i$ and a good $j \notin \mathbf{x}_{\mathcal{H}_i}$. This ensures that the *new* maximum bang per buck ratio for any agent $k \in \mathcal{H}_i$ does not fall below its second highest bang per buck ratio prior to the price-rise, thus guaranteeing $\mathbf{x}_k \subseteq \text{MBB}_k$.

We can now define a Fisher market where each agent's endowment equals its spending under $\mathbf{x}$. Since $(\mathbf{x}, \mathbf{p})$ is an equilibrium for this market, we have that $\mathbf{x}$ is fPO (Proposition 1).

Next, we will argue that $\mathbf{x}$ is $3\varepsilon$-EF1. Notice that ALG terminates only if either the current outcome $(\mathbf{x}, \mathbf{p})$ is $3\varepsilon$-pEF1, or when $\alpha = \alpha_2$ (Line 23). In the first case, we get that $\mathbf{x}$ is $3\varepsilon$-EF1 for the underlying fair division instance (Lemma 4.1). Therefore, we only need to analyze the second case.

**ALGORITHM 1:** Alg

**Input:** An instance $\mathcal{I} = \langle [n], [m], \mathcal{V} \rangle$ such that valuations are power-of-$(1+\varepsilon)$.
**Output:** An integral allocation $\mathbf{x}$ and a price vector $\mathbf{p}$.

// ------------------------------Phase 1: Initialization------------------------------

1 $\mathbf{x} \leftarrow$ Welfare-maximizing allocation (allocate each good $j$ to the agent $i \in \arg\max_{k \in [n]} v_{k,j}$)
2 $\mathbf{p} \leftarrow$ For each good $j \in [m]$, set $p_j = v_{i,j}$ if $j \in \mathbf{x}_i$.
3 **if** $(\mathbf{x}, \mathbf{p})$ *is* $3\varepsilon$-pEF1 **then return** $(\mathbf{x}, \mathbf{p})$

// ------------------Phase 2: Removing price-envy within hierarchy------------------

4 $i \leftarrow$ least spender under $(\mathbf{x}, \mathbf{p})$ /* break ties lexicographically */
5 $\mathcal{H}_i \leftarrow$ BuildHierarchy$(i, \mathbf{x}, \mathbf{p})$
6 $\ell \leftarrow 1$
7 **while** $\mathcal{H}_i^\ell$ *is non-empty and* $(\mathbf{x}, \mathbf{p})$ *is not* $3\varepsilon$-pEF1 **do**
8   **if** $h \in \mathcal{H}_i^\ell$ *is an* $\varepsilon$*-path-violator along the alternating path* $P = \{i, j_1, h_1, \ldots, j_{\ell-1}, h_{\ell-1}, j, h\}$ **then**
9     $\mathbf{x}_h \leftarrow \mathbf{x}_h \setminus \{j\}$ and $\mathbf{x}_{h_{\ell-1}} \leftarrow \mathbf{x}_{h_{\ell-1}} \cup \{j\}$ /* Swap operation */
10     Repeat Phase 2 starting from Line 4
11   **else**
12     $\ell \leftarrow \ell + 1$
13 **if** $(\mathbf{x}, \mathbf{p})$ *is* $3\varepsilon$-pEF1 **then**
14   **return** $(\mathbf{x}, \mathbf{p})$
15 **else**
16   Move to Phase 3 starting from Line 17

// ------------------------------Phase 3: Price-rise------------------------------

17 $\alpha_1 \leftarrow \min_{h \in \mathcal{H}_i,\, j \in [m] \setminus \mathbf{x}_{\mathcal{H}_i}} \frac{\alpha_h}{v_{h,j}/p_j}$, where $\alpha_h$ is the maximum bang per buck ratio for agent $h$, and $\mathbf{x}_{\mathcal{H}_i}$ is the set of goods currently owned by members of the hierarchy $\mathcal{H}_i$
/* $\alpha_1$ corresponds to raising prices until a new agent gets added to the hierarchy */
18 $\alpha_2 \leftarrow \frac{1}{\mathbf{p}(\mathbf{x}_i)} \max_{k \in [n] \setminus \mathcal{H}_i} \min_{j \in \mathbf{x}_k} \mathbf{p}(\mathbf{x}_k \setminus \{j\})$
/* $\alpha_2$ corresponds to raising prices until the pEF1 condition is satisfied */
19 $\alpha_3 \leftarrow (1+\varepsilon)^s$, where $s$ is the smallest integral power of $(1+\varepsilon)$ such that $(1+\varepsilon)^s > \frac{\mathbf{p}(\mathbf{x}_h)}{\mathbf{p}(\mathbf{x}_i)}$; here $i$ is the least spender and $h \in \arg\min_{k \in [n] \setminus \mathcal{H}_i} \mathbf{p}(\mathbf{x}_k)$.
/* $\alpha_3$ corresponds to raising prices in multiples of $(1+\varepsilon)$ until the identity of the least spender changes */
20 $\alpha \leftarrow \min(\alpha_1, \alpha_2, \alpha_3)$
21 **foreach** *good* $j \in \mathbf{x}_{\mathcal{H}_i}$ **do**
22   $p_j \leftarrow \alpha \cdot p_j$
23 **if** $\alpha = \alpha_2$ **then**
24   **return** $(\mathbf{x}, \mathbf{p})$
25 **else**
26   Repeat Phase 2 starting from Line 4

Let us suppose that the termination happens at time step $t$, and let $\mathbf{q}$ be the price vector maintained by ALG just *before* the price-rise step that lead to termination. After the time step $t$, ALG terminates with the allocation $\mathbf{x}$ and price vector $\mathbf{p}$. Since Phase 3 does not change the ownership of the goods, the allocation maintained by ALG just before termination is also $\mathbf{x}$.

Let $i$ be the least spender at time step $t$, and let $\mathcal{H}_i$ be the hierarchy of agent $i$. Since Phase 3 only affects the prices of the goods in $\mathbf{x}_{\mathcal{H}_i}$, we have that $\mathbf{p}(\mathbf{x}_k) = \mathbf{q}(\mathbf{x}_k)$ for all $k \in [n] \setminus \mathcal{H}_i$, and $\mathbf{p}(\mathbf{x}_k) = \alpha_2 \mathbf{q}(\mathbf{x}_k)$ for all $k \in \mathcal{H}_i$. Additionally, at the end of (any execution of) Phase 2, no agent in the least spender's hierarchy is an $\varepsilon$-path-violator (and hence is also not an $\varepsilon$-violator). Thus,

$$\begin{aligned}(1+\varepsilon)\mathbf{q}(\mathbf{x}_i) &\geq \max_{k \in \mathcal{H}_i} \min_{j \in \mathbf{x}_k} \mathbf{q}(\mathbf{x}_k \setminus \{j\}) \\ \implies (1+\varepsilon)\mathbf{p}(\mathbf{x}_i) &\geq \max_{k \in \mathcal{H}_i} \min_{j \in \mathbf{x}_k} \mathbf{p}(\mathbf{x}_k \setminus \{j\}). \qquad (1)\end{aligned}$$

By definition of $\alpha_2$, we have the following condition for the agents outside the hierarchy:

$$\mathbf{p}(\mathbf{x}_i) = \alpha_2 \mathbf{q}(\mathbf{x}_i) \geq \max_{k \in [n] \setminus \mathcal{H}_i} \min_{j \in \mathbf{x}_k} \mathbf{q}(\mathbf{x}_k \setminus \{j\}) = \max_{k \in [n] \setminus \mathcal{H}_i} \min_{j \in \mathbf{x}_k} \mathbf{p}(\mathbf{x}_k \setminus \{j\}). \qquad (2)$$

Equations (1) and (2) together imply that

$$(1+\varepsilon)\mathbf{p}(\mathbf{x}_i) \geq \max_{k \in [n]} \min_{j \in \mathbf{x}_k} \mathbf{p}(\mathbf{x}_k \setminus \{j\}), \qquad (3)$$

which means that the outcome $(\mathbf{x}, \mathbf{p})$ is $\varepsilon$-pEF1 for agent $i$. If agent $i$ is a least spender under $(\mathbf{x}, \mathbf{p})$ (i.e., $i$ continues to a least spender after the price rise), then $\mathbf{x}$ is $\varepsilon$-pEF1 with respect to $\mathbf{p}$, and the lemma follows. Otherwise, an agent $h \in \arg\min_{k \in [n] \setminus \mathcal{H}_i} \mathbf{q}(\mathbf{x}_k)$ must become the least spender after the final price-rise step. In this case, we have that

$$\begin{aligned} & (1+\varepsilon)\mathbf{q}(\mathbf{x}_h) \geq \alpha_3 \mathbf{q}(\mathbf{x}_i) && \text{(by definition of } \alpha_3) \\ \implies & (1+\varepsilon)\mathbf{q}(\mathbf{x}_h) \geq \alpha_2 \mathbf{q}(\mathbf{x}_i) && (\alpha = \alpha_2 \implies \alpha_2 \leq \alpha_3) \\ \implies & (1+\varepsilon)\mathbf{p}(\mathbf{x}_h) \geq \mathbf{p}(\mathbf{x}_i) && \text{(since } \mathbf{p}(\mathbf{x}_i) = \alpha_2 \mathbf{q}(\mathbf{x}_i) \text{ and } \mathbf{p}(\mathbf{x}_h) = \mathbf{q}(\mathbf{x}_h)) \\ \implies & (1+\varepsilon)^2 \mathbf{p}(\mathbf{x}_h) \geq \min_{j \in \mathbf{x}_k} \mathbf{p}(\mathbf{x}_k \setminus \{j\}) && \text{for all } k \in [n], \end{aligned}$$

where the last inequality follows from Equation (3). Since $0 < \varepsilon < 1$, we have that $(1+\varepsilon)^2 < 1 + 3\varepsilon$. Thus, the new least spender (agent $h$) satisfies $(1+3\varepsilon)\mathbf{p}(\mathbf{x}_h) \geq \min_{j \in \mathbf{x}_k} \mathbf{p}(\mathbf{x}_k \setminus \{j\})$ for all $k \in [n]$. This implies that $(\mathbf{x}, \mathbf{p})$ is $3\varepsilon$-pEF1. The stated claim now follows from Lemma 4.1. □

LEMMA 5.2 (**RUNNING TIME BOUND FOR POWER-OF-$(1+\varepsilon)$ INSTANCE**). *Given any power-of-$(1+\varepsilon)$ instance as input, ALG terminates in time $O\left(\text{poly}(m, n, \frac{1}{\varepsilon}, \ln v_{\max})\right)$, where $v_{\max} = \max_{i,j} v_{i,j}$.*

The proof of Lemma 5.2 appears in the full version of the paper.

## 5.2 Analysis of ALG for General Valuations: Proof of Theorem 3.1

In this section, we will show that for any given fair division instance $\mathcal{I} = \langle [n], [m], \mathcal{V} \rangle$ with integral valuations, an allocation that is envy-free up to one good (EF1) and Pareto efficient (PO) can be found in pseudopolynomial time (Theorem 3.1). In particular, for bounded valuations, this result provides a polynomial time algorithm for computing an EF1 and PO allocation (Remark 1).

We will prove Theorem 3.1 by running ALG on a *$\varepsilon$-rounded version* $\mathcal{I}' = \langle [n], [m], \mathcal{V}' \rangle$ of the given instance $\mathcal{I}$ for some parameter $\varepsilon > 0$. The instance $\mathcal{I}'$ is a power-of-$(1+\varepsilon)$ instance[10] constructed by *rounding up* the valuations in $\mathcal{I}$ to the nearest integer power of $(1+\varepsilon)$. From Lemma 5.1, we know that the allocation returned by ALG is $3\varepsilon$-EF1 and fPO with respect to $\mathcal{I}'$ (for any given

[10]Recall that in a *power-of-*$(1+\varepsilon)$ instance, we have $v_{i,j} \in \{0, (1+\varepsilon)^a\}$ for some $a \in \mathbb{N}$ (possibly depending on $i$ and $j$).

$\varepsilon > 0$). We will show that for an appropriate choice of $\varepsilon$, the same allocation turns out to be EF1 and PO with respect to the original instance $\mathcal{I}$. In addition, the running time bound in Lemma 5.2 instantiated for this choice of $\varepsilon$ will show that ALG runs in pseudopolynomial time.

More formally, the *$\varepsilon$-rounded version $\mathcal{I}' = \langle [n], [m], \mathcal{V}' \rangle$* of the given instance $\mathcal{I}$ is constructed as follows: For each agent $i \in [n]$ and each good $j \in [m]$, the valuation $v'_{i,j}$ is given by

$$v'_{i,j} := \begin{cases} (1+\varepsilon)^{\lceil \log_{1+\varepsilon} v_{i,j} \rceil} & \text{if } v_{i,j} > 0, \\ 0 & \text{if } v_{i,j} = 0. \end{cases}$$

Notice that $v_{i,j} \le v'_{i,j} \le (1+\varepsilon)v_{i,j}$ for each agent $i$ and each good $j$.

Lemma 5.3 below establishes that for an appropriate choice of $\varepsilon$, an allocation that is fPO for the $\varepsilon$-rounded instance $\mathcal{I}'$ is PO with respect to the original instance $\mathcal{I}$. The proof of Lemma 5.3 appears in the full version of the paper.

Lemma 5.3. *Let $\mathcal{I} = \langle [n], [m], \mathcal{V} \rangle$ be a fair division instance, and let $\varepsilon \le \frac{1}{6m^3 v_{\max}^4}$. Then, an allocation $\mathbf{x}$ that is fPO for $\mathcal{I}'$ (the $\varepsilon$-rounded version of $\mathcal{I}$) is PO for the original instance $\mathcal{I}$.*

Lemma 5.4 establishes that for a small enough $\delta$, a $\delta$-EF1 allocation is in fact EF1.

Lemma 5.4. *Let $\mathcal{I} = \langle [n], [m], \mathcal{V} \rangle$ be a fair division instance, and let $0 < \delta \le \frac{1}{2mv_{\max}}$. Then, an allocation $\mathbf{x}$ is $\delta$-EF1 for $\mathcal{I}$ if and only if it is EF1 for $\mathcal{I}$.*

Proof. If $\mathbf{x}$ is $\delta$-EF1, we have that for every pair of agents $i, k \in [n]$, there exists a good $j \in \mathbf{x}_k$ such that $(1+\delta)v_i(\mathbf{x}_i) \ge v_i(\mathbf{x}_k \setminus \{j\})$. The bound on $\delta$ implies that $v_i(\mathbf{x}_k \setminus \{j\}) - v_i(\mathbf{x}_i) \le \frac{1}{2}$. Integrality of valuations gives $v_i(\mathbf{x}_k \setminus \{j\}) - v_i(\mathbf{x}_i) \le 0$, as desired. □

Theorem 3.1. *Given any fair division instance $\mathcal{I} = \langle [n], [m], \mathcal{V} \rangle$ with additive valuations, an allocation that is envy-free up to one good (EF1) and Pareto efficient (PO) can be found in $O(\text{poly}(m, n, v_{\max}))$ time, where $v_{\max} = \max_{i,j} v_{i,j}$.*

Proof. Let $\mathcal{I}' = \langle [n], [m], \mathcal{V}' \rangle$ be the $\varepsilon$-rounded version of $\mathcal{I}$ with $\varepsilon = \frac{1}{14m^3 v_{\max}^4}$. From Lemmas 5.1 and 5.2, we know that an allocation $\mathbf{x}$ that is $3\varepsilon$-EF1 and fPO for $\mathcal{I}'$ can be found in $O\left(\text{poly}(m, n, \frac{1}{\varepsilon}, \ln v_{\max})\right)$ time. Under the stated choice of $\varepsilon$, Lemma 5.3 implies that $\mathbf{x}$ must be Pareto efficient (PO) for $\mathcal{I}$. Therefore, we only need to show that $\mathbf{x}$ is EF1 for the instance $\mathcal{I}$.

Since $\mathbf{x}$ is $3\varepsilon$-EF1 for $\mathcal{I}'$, we have that for every pair of agents $i, k \in [n]$, there exists a good $j \in \mathbf{x}_k$ such that $(1+3\varepsilon)v'_i(\mathbf{x}_i) \ge v'_i(\mathbf{x}_k \setminus \{j\})$. Furthermore, since $\mathcal{I}'$ is a $\varepsilon$-rounded version of $\mathcal{I}$, we have that $v'_{i,j} \le (1+\varepsilon)v_{i,j}$ for each good $j \in [m]$. Hence, $(1+\varepsilon)(1+3\varepsilon)v_i(\mathbf{x}_i) \ge v'_i(\mathbf{x}_k \setminus \{j\})$. Finally, since the valuations in $\mathcal{I}'$ are a rounded-up version of those in $\mathcal{I}$, we have that $v_{i,j} \le v'_{i,j}$ for each good $j \in [m]$, and thus $(1+\varepsilon)(1+3\varepsilon)v_i(\mathbf{x}_i) \ge v_i(\mathbf{x}_k \setminus \{j\})$. For $\varepsilon \le 1$, this expression simplifies to $(1+7\varepsilon)v_i(\mathbf{x}_i) \ge v_i(\mathbf{x}_k \setminus \{j\})$, which means that $\mathbf{x}$ is $7\varepsilon$-EF1 for the instance $\mathcal{I}$. Instantiating Lemma 5.4 for $\delta = 7\varepsilon$ gives that $\mathbf{x}$ is EF1 for $\mathcal{I}$. □

Lemma 5.5. *Given the $\varepsilon$-rounded version $\mathcal{I}'$ (of the instance $\mathcal{I}$) as input, ALG finds a $7\varepsilon$-EF1 and $\varepsilon$-PO allocation for $\mathcal{I}$ in $O(\text{poly}(m, n, \frac{1}{\varepsilon}, \ln v_{\max}))$ time.*

Proof. Let $\mathbf{x}$ be the allocation returned by ALG. From Lemma 5.1, we know that $\mathbf{x}$ is $3\varepsilon$-EF1 and fPO for the $\varepsilon$-rounded instance $\mathcal{I}'$. By an argument similar to the one in the proof of Theorem 3.1, this implies that $\mathbf{x}$ is $7\varepsilon$-EF1 for the original instance $\mathcal{I}$. The running time guarantee follows from Lemma 5.2. Hence, we only need to show that $\mathbf{x}$ is $\varepsilon$-PO.

Suppose, for contradiction, that $\mathbf{x}$ is $\varepsilon$-Pareto dominated by an allocation $\mathbf{y}$. Thus, $v_k(\mathbf{y}_k) \ge (1+\varepsilon)v_k(\mathbf{x}_k)$ for every agent $k \in [n]$ and $v_i(\mathbf{y}_i) > (1+\varepsilon)v_i(\mathbf{x}_i)$ for some agent $i \in [n]$. By construction of the $\varepsilon$-rounded instance $\mathcal{I}'$, we know that $v_{k,j} \leq v'_{k,j} \leq (1+\varepsilon)v_{k,j}$ for each agent $k$ and each good $j$. Using the inequality $v'_{k,j} \leq (1+\varepsilon)v_{k,j}$ in a good-by-good manner for the bundle $\mathbf{x}_k$, along with the additivity assumption of valuations in the instance $\mathcal{I}$, we get that $(1+\varepsilon)v_k(\mathbf{x}_k) \geq v'_k(\mathbf{x}_k)$. By a similar application of the inequality $v_{k,j} \leq v'_{k,j}$ for the bundle $\mathbf{y}_k$, we get $v'_k(\mathbf{y}_k) \geq v_k(\mathbf{y}_k)$. Combining these relations gives $v'_k(\mathbf{y}_k) \geq v'_k(\mathbf{x}_k)$ for every agent $k \in [n]$ and $v'_i(\mathbf{y}_i) > v'_i(\mathbf{x}_i)$ for some agent $i \in [n]$. However, this means that the allocation $\mathbf{y}$ Pareto dominates the allocation $\mathbf{x}$ in the instance $\mathcal{I}'$, which is a contradiction since $\mathbf{x}$ is fPO for $\mathcal{I}'$. □

## 6 NASH SOCIAL WELFARE APPROXIMATION: PROOF OF THEOREM 3.3

This section proves that Alg provides a 1.45 ($\approx e^{1/e}$)-approximation for the Nash social welfare maximization problem in polynomial time. We begin by showing (in Lemma 3.4) that if the valuations of all the agents are identical, then any $\varepsilon$-EF1 allocation provides a $e^{(1+\varepsilon)/e}$-approximation to Nash social welfare. We will then use this result, along with an appropriate choice of $\varepsilon$, to prove the desired approximation bound in Theorem 3.3.

Lemma 3.4. *Given a fair division instance with identical and additive valuations, any $\varepsilon$-EF1 allocation provides a $e^{(1+\varepsilon)/e}$-approximation to Nash social welfare.*

The proof of Lemma 3.4 makes use a structural result stated as Lemma 6.1. A relevant notion used in these results is that of *partially-fractional allocations*, defined as follows: Given a subset $B \subset [m]$ of the set of goods, a partially-fractional allocation (with respect to $B$) is one where the goods in $B$ have to be integrally allocated and the remaining goods in $[m] \setminus B$ can be fractionally allocated. Formally, a partially-fractional allocation $\mathbf{y} \in [0,1]^{n \times m}$ is such that for each agent $i \in [n]$, we have $\mathbf{y}_{i,j} \in \{0,1\}$ for each $j \in B$, and $\mathbf{y}_{i,j} \in [0,1]$ for each $j \in [m] \setminus B$. We write $\mathcal{F}_B$ to denote the set of all partially-fractional allocations with respect to $B$.

Lemma 6.1. *Let $\mathcal{I} = \langle [n], [m], \mathcal{V} \rangle$ be an instance with additive and identical valuation functions (denoted by $v$ for each agent) such that $m \geq n$. Let $B \subset [m]$ be a subset of goods such that $|B| < n$. Then, there is a partially-fractional allocation $\omega = (\omega_1, \ldots, \omega_n) \in \mathcal{F}_B$ that maximizes Nash social welfare (among allocations in $\mathcal{F}_B$) such that*

1. *Each agent gets at most one good from $B$ under $\omega$. That is, for each agent $i \in [n]$, we have that $|\{j \in [m] : \omega_{i,j} > 0\} \cap B| \leq 1$.*
2. *Any agent with strictly-better-than-the-worst allocation under $\omega$ gets exactly one integral good (and no fractional good). That is, for any agent $i \in [n]$ such that $v(\omega_i) > \min_k v(\omega_k)$, we have $\omega_{i,j} = 1$ for some $j \in B$, and $\omega_{i,j'} = 0$ for all $j' \neq j$.*

Proof. (of Lemma 6.1) We will consider a partially-fractional allocation $\omega = (\omega_1, \omega_2, \ldots, \omega_n) \in \mathcal{F}_B$ that maximizes the Nash social welfare over $\mathcal{F}_B$, and show that it can be transformed (without decreasing NSW) into an allocation in $\mathcal{F}_B$ that satisfies the stated properties.

Observe that if an agent $i \in [n]$ receives a fractional good under $\omega$ (i.e., $\omega_{i,j'} > 0$ for some $j' \notin B$), then its value $v(\omega_i)$ is equal to $\mu := \min_k v(\omega_k)$. This is because if $v(\omega_i) > \mu$, then we can "redistribute" $j'$ between agent $i$ and the least valued agent $\arg\min_k v(\omega_k)$ to obtain another fractional allocation in $\mathcal{F}_B$ with Nash social welfare strictly greater than that of $\omega$. This contradicts the optimality of $\omega$.

Therefore, any agent with value strictly greater than $\mu$ can only receive integral goods. We will show that any such agent necessarily receives exactly one integral good, and hence establish property (2). Suppose, for contradiction, that some agent $i \in [n]$ receives distinct goods $a, b \in B$ (i.e., $\omega_{i,a} = \omega_{i,b} = 1$), and $v(\omega_i) > \mu$. Since $|B| < n$, there exists some agent $k \in [n]$ that does not receive any integral good from $B$. Since agent $k$ only receives fractional goods under $\omega$, it follows from the above argument that $v(\omega_k) = \mu$. We can now assign one of the integral goods (say $a$) to agent $k$, and redistribute the fractional goods in $\omega_k$ between the agents $i$ and $k$ to obtain a new partially-fractional allocation with strictly greater Nash social welfare than $\omega$. This contradicts the optimality of $\omega$. Therefore, any agent with value strictly greater than $\mu$ must receive exactly one integral good under $\omega$.

Next we address property (1). Note that this property already holds for agents with value strictly greater than $\mu$. Hence, we only need to consider agents whose value is exactly equal to $\mu$. Let $i \in [n]$ be an agent that receives two distinct goods $a, b \in B$ such that $v(\omega_i) = \mu$. Since $|B| < n$, there must exist an agent $k \in [n]$ that only receives fractional goods under $\omega$. We can now perform a "swap" by assigning one of the integral goods (say $a$) to agent $k$, and fractional goods of total value $v(a)$ in $\omega_k$ to agent $i$ to obtain a new partially-fractional allocation in $\mathcal{F}_B$ with the same Nash social welfare as $\omega$. Such a swap is always possible, since $v(a) \leq v(\omega_i) = \mu = v(\omega_k)$. By repeating this process at most $n$ times, we can obtain an NSW maximizer satisfying property (1). □

We will now prove Lemma 3.4.

Proof. (of Lemma 3.4) Let $\mathcal{I} = \langle [n], [m], \mathcal{V} \rangle$ denote the given instance with identical and additive valuations, and let $v$ denote the valuation function of all the agents. Write $\mathbf{x} = (\mathbf{x}_1, \mathbf{x}_2, \ldots, \mathbf{x}_n)$ to denote an $\varepsilon$-EF1 allocation of $\mathcal{I}$. Let $\ell$ denote the value of the least valued bundle in $\mathbf{x}$, i.e., $\ell := \min_{i \in [n]} v(\mathbf{x}_i)$. By reindexing, we have that $v(\mathbf{x}_1) \geq v(\mathbf{x}_2) \geq \ldots \geq v(\mathbf{x}_n) = \ell$.

We will use $g_i$ to denote a largest valued good in the bundle $\mathbf{x}_i$ of agent $i$, i.e., $g_i \in \arg\max_{g \in \mathbf{x}_i} v(g)$. The fact that $\mathbf{x}$ is an $\varepsilon$-EF1 allocation implies that

$$v(\mathbf{x}_i \setminus \{g_i\}) \leq (1+\varepsilon)\ell \qquad \text{for all } i \in [n]. \tag{4}$$

Define $B := \{g_1, g_2, \ldots, g_{n-1}\}$. Let $\omega = (\omega_1, \ldots, \omega_n) \in \mathcal{F}_B$ be a partially-fractional allocation (with respect to $B$) that maximizes Nash social welfare among all allocations in $\mathcal{F}_B$. Since $\mathcal{F}_B$ contains all the integral allocations, we have $\mathrm{NSW}(\omega) \geq \mathrm{NSW}(\mathbf{x}^*)$, where $\mathbf{x}^*$ is a Nash optimal (integral) allocation. Hence, to prove the lemma, it suffices to show that $\mathrm{NSW}(\mathbf{x}) \geq \frac{1}{e^{(1+\varepsilon)/e}} \mathrm{NSW}(\omega)$.

Define $\alpha := \min_{k \in [n]} v(\omega_k)/\ell$, and let $H := \{k \in [n] : v(\mathbf{x}_k) > \alpha\ell\}$. We will now consider partially-fractional allocations wherein only (and all) the goods in $\mathbf{x}_H$ have to be allocated integrally, and the remaining goods can be fractionally allocated. Write $\mathcal{F}_{\mathbf{x}_H}$ to denote the set of all such partially-fractional allocations.

The rest of the proof consists of four parts: First, we will construct an allocation $\mathbf{x}' \in \mathcal{F}_{\mathbf{x}_H}$ such that $\mathrm{NSW}(\mathbf{x}') \leq \mathrm{NSW}(\mathbf{x})$. (Doing this will allow us to work with the ratio $\frac{\mathrm{NSW}(\mathbf{x}')}{\mathrm{NSW}(\omega)}$, which is convenient to bound from below.) Second, we will derive a lower bound on $\mathrm{NSW}(\mathbf{x}')$ in terms of the relevant parameters $\alpha$, $\ell$, and $n$ (and two other parameters $h$ and $t$ that we will define shortly). Third, we will derive an upper bound on $\mathrm{NSW}(\omega)$ in terms of the same parameters. Finally, we will derive relationships between these parameters in order to achieve the stated approximation ratio.

- *Constructing the allocation* $\mathbf{x}'$: We start by initializing $\mathbf{x}' \leftarrow \mathbf{x}$. While there exist two agents $i, k \in [n]$ such that $\ell < v(\mathbf{x}'_i) < v(\mathbf{x}'_k) < \alpha\ell$, we transfer goods of value $\Delta := \min\{v(\mathbf{x}'_i) - \ell, \alpha\ell - v(\mathbf{x}'_k)\}$ from $\mathbf{x}'_i$ (the lesser valued bundle) to $\mathbf{x}'_k$ (the larger valued bundle). In particular, this transfer of goods ensures that the Nash social welfare does not increase. Also, this process must terminate because after every iteration of the while-loop, either $v(\mathbf{x}'_i) = \ell$ or $v(\mathbf{x}'_k) = \alpha\ell$, and therefore at least one of these agents does not participate in future iterations of the while-loop. Moreover, we have $\mathbf{x}'_k = \mathbf{x}_k$ for all $k \in H$, as the agents in $H$ do not participate in the transfer. This proves that $\mathbf{x}' \in \mathcal{F}_{\mathbf{x}_H}$.

- *Lower bound for* NSW($\mathbf{x}'$): Notice that there can be at most one agent $s$ in the allocation $\mathbf{x}'$ such that $v(\mathbf{x}'_s) \in (\ell, \alpha\ell)$. This is because the while-loop continues to execute if there are two or more such agents. For every other agent $k \in [n] \setminus H$, $v(\mathbf{x}'_k)$ is either $\ell$ or $\alpha\ell$.
  Let $h := |\{k \in [n] : v(\mathbf{x}_k) > \alpha\ell\}|$ denote the cardinality of the set $H$ (i.e., $h = |H|$). Let $t := |\{k \in [n] : v(\mathbf{x}'_k) \geq \alpha\ell\}|$ denote the number of agents with a valuation at least $\alpha\ell$ in the allocation $\mathbf{x}'$. Thus, there are $(n-t)$ agents with valuation strictly below $\alpha\ell$ in $\mathbf{x}'$. We lower bound the valuations of these agents by $\ell$ in order to obtain the following relation:
$$\text{NSW}(\mathbf{x}') \geq \left( \prod_{i=1}^{h} v(\mathbf{x}_i) \times (\alpha\ell)^{(t-h)} \times \ell^{(n-t)} \right)^{1/n}. \tag{5}$$
- *Upper bound for* NSW($\omega$): Recall that $\omega = (\omega_1, \ldots, \omega_n) \in \mathcal{F}_B$ is a partially-fractional allocation (with respect to $B$) that maximizes Nash social welfare, and $|B| < n$. Using Lemma 6.1, we can assume, without loss of generality, that $\omega$ has the following two properties: (1) each agent $i \in [n-1]$ gets the good $g_i$ under $\omega$ (this can be ensured via reindexing since the valuations are identical), and (2) if $v(\omega_i) > \min_{k\in[n]} v(\omega_k)$ for any $i \in [n]$, then agent $i$ gets exactly one integral good under $\omega$ (and no fractional good).
  We will now argue that $v(\omega_k) \leq v(\mathbf{x}_k)$ for all $k \in H$. Suppose, for contradiction, that there exists an agent $k \in H$ such that $v(\omega_k) > v(\mathbf{x}_k)$. By definition of $H$, $v(\mathbf{x}_k) > \alpha\ell$ for all $k \in H$, and therefore $v(\omega_k) > \alpha\ell$. We also know that $\min_{k\in[n]} v(\omega_k) = \alpha\ell$, and therefore, by property (2), agent $k$ must get exactly one integral good $g_k$ under $\omega$ (and no fractional good). However, since $g_k \subseteq \mathbf{x}_k$, this contradicts the condition $v(\omega_k) > v(\mathbf{x}_k)$.
  By a similar reasoning, we can show that $v(\omega_k) = \alpha\ell$ for all $k \in [n]\setminus H$. Indeed, if $v(\omega_k) > \alpha\ell = \min_a v(\omega_a)$ for some $k \in [n] \setminus H$, then by property (2), agent $k$ must get exactly one integral good $g_k$ under $\omega$ (and no fractional good). This would imply that $v(\mathbf{x}_k) \geq v(g_k) = v(\omega_k) > \alpha\ell$, which contradicts the fact that $k \in [n] \setminus H$.
  These observations imply the following upper bound on the Nash social welfare of $\omega$:
$$\text{NSW}(\omega) \leq \left( \prod_{i=1}^{h} v(\mathbf{x}_i) \times (\alpha\ell)^{(n-h)} \right)^{1/n}. \tag{6}$$
- *Deriving relationship between the parameters*: From Equation (4) and from the fact that $\mathbf{x}'_k = \mathbf{x}_k$ for all $k \in H$, we have $v(\mathbf{x}'_k \setminus \{g_k\}) = v(\mathbf{x}_k \setminus \{g_k\}) \leq (1+\varepsilon)\ell$ for all $k \in H$. Hence, we can upper bound the value of all goods in $[m]$ excluding the $h$ goods in the set $\bigcup_{k\in H}\{g_k\}$, as follows:
$$\sum_{i\in H} v(\mathbf{x}'_i \setminus \{g_i\}) + \sum_{i\in[n]\setminus H} v(\mathbf{x}'_i) \leq (1+\varepsilon)h\ell + \alpha\ell(t-h+1) + \ell(n-t-1). \tag{7}$$
  Next, we will derive a lower bound for this total value by considering $\omega$. Note that all the goods in the set $\bigcup_{k\in H}\{g_k\}$ are integrally allocated under $\omega$. Hence, at least $(n-h)$ agents do not receive any good from the set $\bigcup_{k\in H}\{g_k\}$. The cumulative value derived by these agents under $\omega$ is at least $\alpha\ell(n-h)$, since $\min_k v(\omega_k) = \alpha\ell$. Using Equation (7) and the fact that $h \leq t$, we get
$$\alpha\ell(n-h) \leq (1+\varepsilon)t\ell + \alpha\ell(t-h+1) + \ell(n-t-1).$$
  Simplification gives that $t \geq \frac{(\alpha-1)(n-1)}{\alpha+\varepsilon}$, which can be further simplified to obtain
$$(n-t) \leq \frac{n(1+\varepsilon)+\alpha-1}{\alpha+\varepsilon} \leq \frac{n(1+\varepsilon)}{\alpha} + \frac{\alpha-1}{\alpha} \leq \frac{n(1+\varepsilon)}{\alpha} + 1.$$

Recall that $\text{NSW}(\mathbf{x}) \geq \text{NSW}(\mathbf{x}')$. Using the above relation with Equations (5) and (6) gives

$$\frac{\text{NSW}(\mathbf{x})}{\text{NSW}(\omega)} \geq \frac{\text{NSW}(\mathbf{x}')}{\text{NSW}(\omega)} \geq \frac{\left(\prod_{i=1}^{h} v(\mathbf{x}_i) \times (\alpha\ell)^{(t-h)} \times \ell^{n-t}\right)^{1/n}}{\left(\prod_{i=1}^{h} v(\mathbf{x}_i) \times (\alpha\ell)^{(n-h)}\right)^{1/n}} = \alpha^{-\frac{n-t}{n}} \geq \alpha^{-\frac{1+\varepsilon}{\alpha} - \frac{1}{n}}. \tag{8}$$

The $-1/n$ term in the exponent of $\alpha$ can be neglected via a scaling argument, as follows: Construct (for analysis only) a *scaled-up* instance $\mathcal{I}'$ consisting of $c \geq 1$ copies of the instance $\mathcal{I}$. For any allocation $\mathbf{y}$ that is $\varepsilon$-EF1 for $\mathcal{I}$, the allocation $\mathbf{y}' = (\mathbf{y}, \mathbf{y}, \ldots, \mathbf{y})$ is $\varepsilon$-EF1 for $\mathcal{I}'$. Write $n', \alpha', \ell', \omega'$ to denote the analogues of $n, \alpha, \ell, \omega$ in $\mathcal{I}'$. Also, let $\tilde{\omega}$ denote the fractional allocation $(\omega, \omega, \ldots, \omega)$ in $\mathcal{I}'$. It is easy to see that $n' = cn$, $\alpha' = \alpha$, and $\ell' = \ell$. Moreover,

$$\frac{\text{NSW}(\mathbf{y})}{\text{NSW}(\omega)} = \frac{\text{NSW}(\mathbf{y}')}{\text{NSW}(\tilde{\omega})} \geq \frac{\text{NSW}(\mathbf{y}')}{\text{NSW}(\omega')} \geq \alpha^{-\frac{1+\varepsilon}{\alpha} - \frac{1}{cn}},$$

where the first term is for the instance $\mathcal{I}$, and the remaining terms are for the instance $\mathcal{I}'$. In addition, the relation $\text{NSW}(\omega') \geq \text{NSW}(\tilde{\omega})$ follows from the optimality of $\omega'$ for $\mathcal{I}'$. By choosing a sufficiently large value of $c$, the term $-1/cn$ in the exponent can be made arbitrarily small. Therefore, the lower bound in Equation (8) is (arbitrarily close to) $\alpha^{-\frac{1+\varepsilon}{\alpha}}$. Finally, notice that the function $z^{-\frac{1+\varepsilon}{z}}$ with $z \geq 0$ is minimized at $z = e$. This gives a lower bound of $e^{-(1+\varepsilon)/e}$, as desired. □

We will now proceed to the proof of Theorem 3.3. The proof relies on transforming a general fair division instance into one with identical valuations, and showing that the Nash social welfare of the allocation returned by Alg is preserved in this transformation.

Theorem 3.3. *For additive valuations, there exists a polynomial-time* 1.45*-approximation algorithm for the Nash social welfare maximization problem.*

Proof. For a given instance $\mathcal{I} = \langle [n], [m], \mathcal{V} \rangle$, let $\mathbf{z}$ and $\mathbf{q}$ denote the allocation and the price vector respectively that are returned by Alg when provided as input the $\varepsilon$-rounded version of $\mathcal{I}$ (the parameter $\varepsilon$ is set to a small constant). Let $\alpha_i \neq 0$ denote the maximum bang per buck ratio of agent $i$ with respect to $\mathbf{q}$. Construct a scaled instance $\mathcal{I}^{\text{sc}} = \langle [n], [m], \mathcal{V}^{\text{sc}} \rangle$ such that $v^{\text{sc}}_{i,j} = \frac{1}{\alpha_i} v_{i,j}$ for all $i$ and $j$.[11] Then, for any allocation $\mathbf{y}$, $\text{NSW}(\mathbf{y})$ in $\mathcal{I}^{\text{sc}}$ is $\frac{1}{(\prod_{i=1}^{n} \alpha_i)^{1/n}}$ times $\text{NSW}(\mathbf{y})$ in the original instance $\mathcal{I}$. Therefore, in order to obtain the desired approximation guarantee, it suffices to show that $\mathbf{z}$ achieves an approximation factor of 1.45 in the scaled instance $\mathcal{I}^{\text{sc}}$.

Let $\omega$ denote a Nash optimal (integral) allocation in the original instance $\mathcal{I}$. By the above argument, $\omega$ is Nash optimal in the scaled instance $\mathcal{I}^{\text{sc}}$ as well. Additionally, for each agent $i$ in $\mathcal{I}^{\text{sc}}$, we have that $v^{\text{sc}}_{i,j} = q_j$ for all $j \in \text{MBB}_i$, and $v^{\text{sc}}_{i,j} < q_j$ for all $j \notin \text{MBB}_i$. Therefore, for any agent $i$, we have $v^{\text{sc}}(\mathbf{z}_i) = \mathbf{q}(\mathbf{z}_i)$ (since, from Lemma 5.1, we have that $\mathbf{z}_i \subseteq \text{MBB}_i$), and $v^{\text{sc}}_i(\omega_i) \leq \mathbf{q}(\omega_i)$. Consequently, the Nash social welfare of the computed allocation $\mathbf{z}$ and the optimal allocation $\omega$ satisfy the following relations in the scaled instance $\mathcal{I}^{\text{sc}}$:

$$\left(\prod_{i=1}^{n} v^{\text{sc}}_i(\mathbf{z}_i)\right)^{1/n} = \left(\prod_{i=1}^{n} \mathbf{q}(\mathbf{z}_i)\right)^{1/n} \tag{9}$$

and

$$\left(\prod_{i=1}^{n} v^{\text{sc}}_i(\omega_i)\right)^{1/n} \leq \left(\prod_{i=1}^{n} \mathbf{q}(\omega_i)\right)^{1/n}. \tag{10}$$

[11] A similar scaling was used by Cole and Gkatzelis [13] in their analysis of NSW approximation.

We will further transform the valuations in $\mathcal{I}^{\text{sc}}$ to obtain an instance $\mathcal{I}^{\text{id}} = \langle [n], [m], \mathcal{V}^{\text{id}} \rangle$ with *identical* valuations. Specifically, we set $v^{\text{id}}_{i,j} = q_j$ for all $i$ and $j$. We know from Lemma 5.1 that $\mathbf{z}$ is $3\varepsilon$-pEF1 with respect to $\mathbf{q}$ in the original instance $\mathcal{I}$, and that $\mathbf{z}_i \subseteq \text{MBB}_i$ for each agent $i \in [n]$. It then follows that $z$ is $3\varepsilon$-EF1 in the identical valuations instance $\mathcal{I}^{\text{id}}$. Furthermore, when $\varepsilon = \frac{1}{300}$, the allocation $z$ is $\frac{1}{100}$-EF1 in $\mathcal{I}^{\text{id}}$, and therefore from Lemma 3.4, we have that

$$\begin{aligned}
\left(\prod_{i=1}^{n} \mathbf{q}(\mathbf{z}_i)\right)^{1/n} &\geq e^{-(1+0.01)/e} \max_{\mathbf{y}\in\mathcal{X}} \left(\prod_{i=1}^{n} \mathbf{q}(\mathbf{y}_i)\right)^{1/n} \\
&\geq \frac{1}{1.45} \max_{\mathbf{y}\in\mathcal{X}} \left(\prod_{i=1}^{n} \mathbf{q}(\mathbf{y}_i)\right)^{1/n} \\
&\geq \frac{1}{1.45} \left(\prod_{i=1}^{n} \mathbf{q}(\omega_i)\right)^{1/n} \\
&\geq \frac{1}{1.45} \left(\prod_{i=1}^{n} v_i^{\text{sc}}(\omega_i)\right)^{1/n} \qquad \text{(using Equation (10)).}
\end{aligned}$$

The previous inequality and Equation (9) together give us an approximation factor of 1.45 under the valuation profile $\mathcal{V}^{\text{sc}}$:

$$\left(\prod_{i=1}^{n} v_i^{\text{sc}}(\mathbf{z}_i)\right)^{1/n} \geq \frac{1}{1.45} \left(\prod_{i=1}^{n} v_i^{\text{sc}}(\omega_i)\right)^{1/n},$$

which provides a similar approximation guarantee for the original instance $\mathcal{I}$. Finally, observe that the allocation $z$ can be computed in polynomial time for the above choice of $\varepsilon$ (Lemma 5.5). This completes the proof of Theorem 3.3. □

## 7 CONCLUDING REMARKS

We studied the problem of finding a fair and efficient allocation of indivisible goods. Our work provided a framework based on integral Fisher markets and an (approximate) price envy-freeness condition resulting in a pseudopolynomial algorithm for finding an EF1 and PO allocation, and a polynomial time 1.45-approximation algorithm for Nash social welfare. Determining whether there exists a (strongly) polynomial time algorithm for the problem of finding an EF1 and PO allocation remains an interesting direction for future work. Extensions of our results to more general classes of valuations (e.g., submodular) will also be interesting.

## ACKNOWLEDGMENTS

SB was supported in part by a Ramanujan Fellowship (SERB - SB/S2/RJN-128/2015). The second author gratefully acknowledges the support of a Google travel grant.

## REFERENCES

[1] Nima Anari, Shayan Oveis Gharan, Tung Mai, and Vijay V Vazirani. 2018. Nash Social Welfare for Indivisible Items under Separable, Piecewise-Linear Concave Utilities. In *Proceedings of the 29th Annual ACM-SIAM Symposium on Discrete Algorithms (SODA)*. 2274–2290.

[2] Nima Anari, Shayan Oveis Gharan, Amin Saberi, and Mohit Singh. 2017. Nash Social Welfare, Matrix Permanent, and Stable Polynomials. In *Proceedings of the 8th Conference on Innovations in Theoretical Computer Science (ITCS)*.

[3] Siddharth Barman, Sanath Kumar Krishnamurthy, and Rohit Vaish. 2017. Finding Fair and Efficient Allocations. *arXiv preprint arXiv:1707.04731* (2017). https://arxiv.org/abs/1707.04731

[4] Xiaohui Bei, Jugal Garg, Martin Hoefer, and Kurt Mehlhorn. 2017. Earning Limits in Fisher Markets with Spending-Constraint Utilities. In *Proceedings of the International Symposium on Algorithmic Game Theory (SAGT)*. 67–79.

[5] Sylvain Bouveret and Michel Lemaître. 2016. Characterizing Conflicts in Fair Division of Indivisible Goods Using a Scale of Criteria. *Autonomous Agents and Multi-Agent Systems* 30, 2 (2016), 259–290.

[6] William C Brainard and Herbert Scarf. 2000. *How to Compute Equilibrium Prices in 1891.* Technical Report. Cowles Foundation for Research in Economics, Yale University.

[7] Steven J Brams and Alan D Taylor. 1996. *Fair Division: From Cake-cutting to Dispute Resolution.* Cambridge University Press.

[8] Felix Brandt, Vincent Conitzer, Ulle Endriss, Ariel D Procaccia, and Jérôme Lang. 2016. *Handbook of Computational Social Choice.* Cambridge University Press.

[9] Eric Budish. 2011. The Combinatorial Assignment Problem: Approximate Competitive Equilibrium from Equal Incomes. *Journal of Political Economy* 119, 6 (2011), 1061–1103.

[10] Eric Budish, Gérard P Cachon, Judd B Kessler, and Abraham Othman. 2016. Course Match: A Large-scale Implementation of Approximate Competitive Equilibrium from Equal Incomes for Combinatorial Allocation. *Operations Research* 65, 2 (2016), 314–336.

[11] Ioannis Caragiannis, David Kurokawa, Hervé Moulin, Ariel D Procaccia, Nisarg Shah, and Junxing Wang. 2016. The Unreasonable Fairness of Maximum Nash Welfare. In *Proceedings of the 2016 ACM Conference on Economics and Computation (EC)*. 305–322.

[12] Richard Cole, Nikhil Devanur, Vasilis Gkatzelis, Kamal Jain, Tung Mai, Vijay V Vazirani, and Sadra Yazdanbod. 2017. Convex Program Duality, Fisher Markets, and Nash Social Welfare. In *Proceedings of the 2017 ACM Conference on Economics and Computation (EC)*. 459–460.

[13] Richard Cole and Vasilis Gkatzelis. 2015. Approximating the Nash Social Welfare with Indivisible Items. In *Proceedings of the Forty-Seventh Annual ACM on Symposium on Theory of Computing (STOC)*. 371–380.

[14] Bart de Keijzer, Sylvain Bouveret, Tomas Klos, and Yingqian Zhang. 2009. On the Complexity of Efficiency and Envy-freeness in Fair Division of Indivisible Goods with Additive Preferences. In *International Conference on Algorithmic Decision Theory (ADT)*. 98–110.

[15] Nikhil R Devanur, Christos H Papadimitriou, Amin Saberi, and Vijay V Vazirani. 2008. Market Equilibrium via a Primal–Dual Algorithm for a Convex Program. *Journal of the ACM (JACM)* 55, 5 (2008), 22.

[16] Edmund Eisenberg and David Gale. 1959. Consensus of Subjective Probabilities: The Pari-mutuel Method. *The Annals of Mathematical Statistics* 30, 1 (1959), 165–168.

[17] Duncan Foley. 1967. Resource Allocation and the Public Sector. *Yale Economic Essays* (1967), 45–98.

[18] Jugal Garg, Martin Hoefer, and Kurt Mehlhorn. 2018. Approximating the Nash Social Welfare with Budget-Additive Valuations. In *Proceedings of the 29th Annual ACM-SIAM Symposium on Discrete Algorithms (SODA)*. 2326–2340.

[19] Jonathan Goldman and Ariel D Procaccia. 2015. Spliddit: Unleashing Fair Division Algorithms. *ACM SIGecom Exchanges* 13, 2 (2015), 41–46.

[20] Mamoru Kaneko and Kenjiro Nakamura. 1979. The Nash Social Welfare Function. *Econometrica: Journal of the Econometric Society* (1979), 423–435.

[21] David Kurokawa, Ariel D Procaccia, and Junxing Wang. 2018. Fair Enough: Guaranteeing Approximate Maximin Shares. *Journal of the ACM (JACM)* 65, 2 (2018), 8.

[22] Euiwoong Lee. 2017. APX-hardness of Maximizing Nash Social Welfare with Indivisible Items. *Inform. Process. Lett.* 122 (2017), 17–20.

[23] Richard J Lipton, Evangelos Markakis, Elchanan Mossel, and Amin Saberi. 2004. On Approximately Fair Allocations of Indivisible Goods. In *Proceedings of the 5th ACM Conference on Electronic Commerce (EC)*. 125–131.

[24] Andreu Mas-Colell, Michael Dennis Whinston, and Jerry R Green. 1995. *Microeconomic Theory.* Vol. 1. Oxford university press New York.

[25] Jiri Matousek. 2008. *Using the Borsuk-Ulam theorem: Lectures on Topological Methods in Combinatorics and Geometry.* Springer Science & Business Media.

[26] Hervé Moulin. 2004. *Fair Division and Collective Welfare.* MIT Press.

[27] John F Nash Jr. 1950. The Bargaining Problem. *Econometrica: Journal of the Econometric Society* (1950), 155–162.

[28] Nhan-Tam Nguyen, Trung Thanh Nguyen, Magnus Roos, and Jörg Rothe. 2014. Computational Complexity and Approximability of Social Welfare Optimization in Multiagent Resource Allocation. *Autonomous Agents and Multi-agent Systems* 28, 2 (2014), 256–289.

[29] Abraham Othman, Tuomas Sandholm, and Eric Budish. 2010. Finding Approximate Competitive Equilibria: Efficient and Fair Course Allocation. In *Proceedings of the 9th International Conference on Autonomous Agents and Multiagent Systems (AAMAS)*. 873–880.

[30] Hugo Steinhaus. 1948. The Problem of Fair Division. *Econometrica* 16 (1948), 101–104.

[31] Hal R Varian. 1974. Equity, Envy, and Efficiency. *Journal of Economic Theory* 9, 1 (1974), 63–91.

# Fair Allocation of Indivisible Public Goods

BRANDON FAIN, Duke University, USA
KAMESH MUNAGALA, Duke University, USA
NISARG SHAH, University of Toronto, Canada

We consider the problem of fairly allocating indivisible public goods. We model the public goods as elements with feasibility constraints on what subsets of elements can be chosen, and assume that agents have additive utilities across elements. Our model generalizes existing frameworks such as fair public decision making and participatory budgeting. We study a groupwise fairness notion called the *core*, which generalizes well-studied notions of proportionality and Pareto efficiency, and requires that each subset of agents must receive an outcome that is fair relative to its size.

In contrast to the case of divisible public goods (where fractional allocations are permitted), the core is not guaranteed to exist when allocating indivisible public goods. Our primary contributions are the notion of an *additive* approximation to the core (with a tiny multiplicative loss), and polynomial time algorithms that achieve a small additive approximation, where the additive factor is relative to the largest utility of an agent for an element. If the feasibility constraints define a matroid, we show an additive approximation of 2. A similar approach yields a constant additive bound when the feasibility constraints define a matching. For feasibility constraints defining an arbitrary packing polytope with mild restrictions, we show an additive guarantee that is logarithmic in the *width* of the polytope. Our algorithms are based on the convex program for maximizing the Nash social welfare, but differ significantly from previous work in how it is used. As far as we are aware, our work is the first to approximate the core in indivisible settings.

Additional Key Words and Phrases: Fairness, public goods, indivisible goods, core, proportionality

## 1 INTRODUCTION

In fair resource allocation, most work considers *private goods*; each good must be assigned to a particular agent (and no other). However, not all goods are private. *Public goods* are those which can be enjoyed by multiple agents simultaneously, like a public road. Allocation of public goods generalizes the problem of allocation of private goods, and, as we will see, can provide new difficulties from both a normative and an algorithmic perspective.

Consider an example to highlight what a public resource allocation problem might look like, and why fairness might be a concern. Suppose that the next time you vote, you see that there are four referendums for your consideration on the ballot, all of which concern the allocation of various public goods in your city: A = a new school, B = enlarging the public library, C = renovating the community college, and D = improving a museum. In 2016, residents of Durham, North Carolina faced precisely these options [24]. Suppose the government has resources to fund only two of the four projects, and the (hypothetical) results were as follows: a little more than half of the population voted for $(A, B)$, a little less than half voted for $(C, D)$, and every other combination received a small number of votes. Which projects should be funded?

If we naïvely tally the votes, we would fund A and B, and ignore the preferences of a very large minority. In contrast, funding A and C seems like a reasonable compromise. Of course, it

The full version of this paper is available at https://arxiv.org/abs/1805.03164.


*EC'18, June 18-22, 2018, Ithaca, NY, USA.* ACM ISBN 978-1-4503-5829-3/18/06... $15.00

https://doi.org/10.1145/3219166.3219174

is impossible to satisfy *all* voters, but given a wide enough range of possible outcomes, perhaps we can find one that fairly reflects the preferences of large subsets of the population. This idea is not captured by fairness axioms like proportionality or their approximations [9], which view fairness from the perspectives of *individual* agents. Indeed, in the aforementioned example, *every* allocation gives zero utility to *some* agent, and would be deemed equally good according to such fairness criteria.

### 1.1 Public Goods Model

We consider a fairly broad model for public goods allocation that generalizes much of previous work [3, 8–10, 12, 23, 29]. There is a set of voters (or agents) $N = [n]$. Public goods are modeled as elements of a ground set $W$. We denote $m = |W|$. An *outcome* $\mathbf{c}$ is a subset of $W$. Let $\mathcal{F} \subseteq 2^W$ denote the set of feasible outcomes.

The utility of agent $i$ for element $j \in W$ is denoted $u_{ij} \in \mathbb{R}_{\geq 0}$. We assume that agents have additive utilities, i.e., the utility of agent $i$ under outcome $\mathbf{c} \in \mathcal{F}$ is $u_i(\mathbf{c}) = \sum_{j \in \mathbf{c}} u_{ij}$. Since we are interested in scale-invariant guarantees, we assume without loss of generality that $\max_{j \in W} u_{ij} = 1$ for each agent $i$, so that $u_{ij} \in [0, 1]$ for all $i, j$. Crucially, this does not restrict the utility of an agent for an outcome to be 1: $u_i(\mathbf{c})$ can be as large as $m$. Specifically, let $V_i = \max_{\mathbf{c} \in \mathcal{F}} u_i(\mathbf{c})$, and $V_{\max} = \max_{i \in N} V_i$. Our results differ by the feasibility constraints imposed on the outcome. We consider three types of constraints, special cases of which have been studied previously in literature.

*Matroid Constraints.* In this setting, we are given a matroid $\mathcal{M}$ over the ground set $W$, and the feasibility constraint is that the chosen elements must form a basis of $\mathcal{M}$ (see Kung [21] for a formal introduction to matroids).

This generalizes the *public decision making* setting introduced by Conitzer et al. [9]. In this setting, there is a set of issues $T$, and each issue $t \in T$ has an associated set of alternatives $A^t = \{a_1^t, \ldots, a_{k_t}^t\}$, exactly one of which must be chosen. Agent $i$ has utility $u_i^t(a_j^t)$ if alternative $a_j^t$ is chosen for issue $t$, and utilities are additive across issues. An outcome $\mathbf{c}$ chooses one alternative for every issue. It is easy to see that if the ground set is $\cup_t A^t$, the feasibility constraints correspond to a partition matroid. We note that public decision making generalizes *private goods allocation* with additive utility [8, 23, 29] in which each private good must be allocated to exactly one agent.

Matroid constraints also capture multi-winner elections in the voting literature (see, e.g. [3]), in which voters have additive utilities over candidates, and a committee of at most $k$ candidates must be chosen. This is captured by a uniform matroid over the set of candidates.

*Matching Constraints.* In this setting, the elements are edges of an undirected graph $G(V, E)$, and the feasibility constraint is that the subset of edges chosen must form a *matching*. Matchings constraints in a bipartite graph can be seen as the intersection of two matroid constraints. Matching constraints are a special case of the more general packing constraints we consider below.

*Packing Constraints.* In this setting, we impose a set of packing constraints $A\mathbf{x} \leq \mathbf{b}$, where $x_j \in \{0, 1\}$ is the indicator denoting whether element $j$ is chosen in the outcome. Suppose $A$ is a $K \times m$ matrix, so that there are $K$ packing constraints. By scaling, we can assume $a_{kj} \in [0, 1]$ for all $k, j$. Note that even for one agent, packing constraints encode independent set. Thus, to make the problem tractable, we assume $\mathbf{b}$ is sufficiently large, in particular, $b_k = \omega(\log K)$ for all $k \in \{1, 2, \ldots, K\}$. This is in contrast to matroid and matching constraints, for which single-agent problems are polynomial time solvable. A classic measure of how easy it is to satisfy the packing constraints is the *width* $\rho$ [30]:

$$\rho = \max_{k \in [K]} \frac{\sum_{j \in [m]} a_{kj}}{b_k}. \tag{1}$$

Packing constraints capture the general KNAPSACK setting, in which there is a set of $m$ items, each item $j$ has an associated size $s_j$, and a set of items of total size at most $B$ must be selected. This setting is motivated by participatory budgeting applications [6, 10, 12, 14, 16, 17, 28], in which the items are public projects, and the sizes represents the costs of the projects. KNAPSACK uses a single packing constraint. Multiple packing constraints can arise if the projects consume several types of resources, and there is a budget constraint for each resource type. For example, consider a statewide participatory budgeting scenario where each county has a budget than can only be spent on projects affecting that county, the state has some budget that can be spent in any county, and projects might affect multiple counties. In such settings, it is natural to assume a small width, i.e., that the budget for each resource is such that a large fraction (but not all) of the projects can be funded. We note that the aforementioned multi-winner election problem is a special case of the KNAPSACK problem with unit sizes.

### 1.2 Prior Work: Fairness Properties

We define fairness desiderata for the public goods setting by generalizing appropriate desiderata from the private goods setting such as Pareto optimality, which is a weak notion of efficiency, and proportionality, which is a per-agent fair share guarantee.[1]

*Definition 1.1.* An outcome $\mathbf{c}$ satisfies **Pareto optimality** if there is no other outcome $\mathbf{c}'$ such that $u_i(\mathbf{c}') \geq u_i(\mathbf{c})$ for all agents $i \in N$, and at least one inequality is strict.

Recall that $V_i$ is the maximum possible utility agent $i$ can derive from a feasible outcome.

*Definition 1.2.* The **proportional share** of an agent $i \in N$ is $Prop_i := \frac{V_i}{n}$. For $\beta \in (0, 1]$, we say that an outcome $\mathbf{c}$ satisfies $\beta$-proportionality if $u_i(\mathbf{c}) \geq \beta \cdot Prop_i$ for all agents $i \in N$. If $\beta = 1$, we simply say that $\mathbf{c}$ satisfies proportionality.

The difficulty in our setting stems from requiring integral outcomes, and not allowing randomization. In the absence of randomization, it is reasonably straightforward to show that we cannot guarantee $\beta$-proportionality for any $\beta \in (0, 1]$. Consider a problem instance with two agents and two feasible outcomes, where each outcome gives a positive utility to a unique agent. In any feasible outcome, one agent has zero utility, which violates $\beta$-proportionality for every $\beta > 0$.

To address this issue, Conitzer et al. [9] introduced the novel relaxation of proportionality up to one issue in their public decision making framework, inspired by a similar relaxation called envy-freeness up to one good in the private goods setting [8, 23]. They say that an outcome $\mathbf{c}$ of a public decision making problem satisfies *proportionality up to one issue* if for all agents $i \in N$, there exists an outcome $\mathbf{c}'$ that differs from $\mathbf{c}$ only on a single issue and $u_i(\mathbf{c}') \geq Prop_i$. Proportionality up to one issue is a reasonable fairness guarantees only when the number of issues is larger than the number of agents; otherwise, it is vacuous and is satisfied by all outcomes. Thus, it is perfectly reasonable for some applications (e.g., three friends choosing a movie list to watch together over the course of a year), but not for others (e.g., when thousands of residents choose a handful of public projects to finance). In fact, it may produce an outcome that may be construed as unfair if it does not reflect the wishes of large groups of voters. Thus, in this work, we address the following question posed by Conitzer et al. [9]:

> *Is there a stronger fairness notion than proportionality in the public decision making framework...? Although such a notion would not be satisfiable by deterministic mechanisms,*

[1]Those familiar with the literature on fair division of private goods will note the conspicuous absence of the *envy freeness* property: that no agent should (strongly) prefer the allocation of another agent. Because we are considering public goods, envy freeness is only vacuously defined: the outcome in our setting is common to all agents.

*it may be satisfied by randomized mechanisms, or it could have novel relaxations that may be of independent interest.*

### 1.3 Summary of Contributions

Our primary contributions are twofold.

- We define a fairness notion for public goods allocation that is stronger than proportionality, ensures fair representation of groups of agents, and in particular, provides a meaningful fairness guarantee even when there are fewer goods than agents.
- We provide polynomial time algorithms for computing integer allocations that approximately satisfy this fairness guarantee for a variety of settings generalizing the public decision making framework and participatory budgeting.

### 1.4 Core and Approximate Core Outcomes

We define the notion of *core outcomes*, which has been well studied (in similar forms) as a notion of stability in economics [13, 25, 33] and computer science [10, 22] in the context of *randomized* or *fractional* allocations. Our main contribution is to study it in the context of *integer* allocations.

*Definition 1.3.* Given an outcome $\mathbf{c}$, we say that a set of agents $S \subseteq N$ form a blocking coalition if there exists an outcome $\mathbf{c}'$ such that $(|S|/n) \cdot u_i(\mathbf{c}') \geq u_i(\mathbf{c})$ for all $i \in S$ and at least one inequality is strict. We say that an outcome $\mathbf{c}$ is a **core outcome** if it admits no blocking coalitions.

Note that non-existence of blocking coalitions of size 1 is equivalent to proportionality, and non-existence of blocking coalitions of size $n$ is equivalent to Pareto optimality. Hence, a core outcome is both proportional and Pareto optimal. However, the core satisfies a stronger property of being, in a sense, Pareto optimal for coalitions of *any size*, provided we scale utilities based on the size of the coalition. Another way of thinking about the core is to view it as a fairness property that enforces a proportionality-like guarantee for coalitions: *e.g.*, if half of all agents have identical preferences, they should be able to get at least half of their maximum possible utility. It is important to note that the core provides a guarantee for every possible coalition. Hence, in satisfying the guarantee for a coalition $S$, a solution cannot simply make a single member $i \in S$ happy and ignore the rest as this would likely violate the guarantee for the coalition $S \setminus \{i\}$.

*Approximate Core.* Since a proportional outcome is not guaranteed to exist (even allowing for multiplicative approximations), the same is true for the core. However, an additive approximation to the core still provides a meaningful guarantee, even when there are fewer elements than agents because it provides a non-trivial guarantee to large coalitions of like-minded agents.

*Definition 1.4.* For $\delta, \alpha \geq 0$, an outcome $\mathbf{c}$ is a $(\boldsymbol{\delta}, \boldsymbol{\alpha})$**-core outcome** if there exists no set of agents $S \subseteq N$ and outcome $\mathbf{c}'$ such that

$$\frac{|S|}{n} \cdot u_i(\mathbf{c}') \geq (1 + \delta) \cdot u_i(\mathbf{c}) + \alpha$$

for all $i \in S$, and at least one inequality is strict.

A $(0, 0)$-core outcome is simply a core outcome. A $(\delta, 0)$-core outcome satisfies $\delta$-proportionality. Similarly, a $(0, 1)$-core outcome $\mathbf{c}$ satisfies the following relaxation of proportionality that is slightly weaker than proportionality up to one issue: for every agent $i \in N$, $u_i(\mathbf{c}) + 1 \geq Prop_i$. We note that this definition, and by extension, our algorithms satisfy scale invariance, i.e., they are invariant to scaling the utilities of any individual agent. Because we normalize utilities of the agents, the true additive guarantee is $\alpha$ times the maximum utility an agent can derive from a single element. Since an outcome can have many elements, an approximation with small $\alpha$ remains meaningful.

The advantage of an approximate core outcome is that it fairly reflects the will of a like-minded subpopulation relative to its size. An outcome satisfying approximate proportionality only looks at what *individual* agents prefer, and may or may not respect the collective preferences of subpopulations. We present such an instance in Example 2.1, in effect showing that an approximate core outcome is arguably more fair.

In our results, we will assume $\delta < 1$ to be a small constant, and focus on making $\alpha$ as small as possible. In particular, we desire guarantees on $\alpha$ that exhibit sub-linear or no dependence on $n$, $m$, or any other parameters. Deriving such bounds is the main technical focus of our work.

## 1.5 Our Results

We present algorithms to find approximate core outcomes under matroid, matching, and general packing constraints. Our first result (Section 3) is the following:

THEOREM 1.5. *If feasible outcomes are constrained to be bases of a matroid, then a $(0, 2)$-core outcome is guaranteed to exist, and for any $\epsilon > 0$, a $(0, 2 + \epsilon)$-core outcome can be computed in time polynomial in $n$, $m$, and $1/\epsilon$.*

In particular, for the public decision making framework, the private goods setting, and multi-winner elections (a.k.a. KNAPSACK with unit sizes), there is an outcome whose guarantee for *every coalition* is close to the guarantee that Conitzer et al. [9] provide to individual agents!

In Section 4, we consider matching constraints. Our result now involves a tradeoff between the multiplicative and additive guarantees.

THEOREM 1.6. *If feasible outcomes are constrained to be matchings in an undirected graph, then for constant $\delta \in (0, 1]$, a $(\delta, 8 + 6/\delta)$-core outcome can be computed in time polynomial in $n$ and $m$.*

Our final result (Section 5) is for general packing constraints. Here, our guarantee depends on the width $\rho$ from Equation (1), which captures the difficulty of satisfying the constraints. In particular, the guarantee improves if the constraints are easier to satisfy. This is the most technical result of the paper, and involves different techniques than those used in proving Theorems 1.5 and 1.6; we present an outline of the techniques in Section 5.2.

THEOREM 1.7. *For constant $\delta \in (0, 1)$, given $K$ packing constraints $A\mathbf{x} \leq \mathbf{b}$ with width $\rho$ and $b_k = \omega\left(\frac{\log K}{\delta^2}\right)$ for all $k \in [K]$, there exists a polynomial time computable $(\delta, \alpha)$-core solution, where*

$$\alpha = O\left(\frac{1}{\delta^4} \cdot \log\left(\frac{\min(V_{\max}, n, \rho) \cdot \log^* V_{\max}}{\delta}\right)\right).$$

Here, $\log^*$ is the iterated logarithm, which is the number of times the logarithm function must be iteratively applied before the result becomes less than or equal to 1. Recall that $V_{\max}$ is the maximum utility an agent can have for an outcome (thus $V_{\max} \leq m$); our additive error bound is a vanishing fraction of this quantity. Our bound is also small if the number of agents $n$ is small. Finally, the guarantee improves for small $\rho$, i.e., as the packing constraints become easier to satisfy. For instance, in participatory budgeting, if the total cost of all projects is only a constant times more than the budget, then our additive guarantee is close to a constant.

Note that $V_{\max}$ (which is bounded by $m$), $n$, and $\rho$ are all unrelated quantities. In fact, in Section 5, we state the bound more generally in terms of what we call the *maximally proportionally fair value* $R$, which informally captures the (existential) difficulty of finding a proportionally fair allocation. The quantity $\min(V_{\max}, n, \rho)$ stems from three different bounds on the value of $R$.

In the full version [11], we show that the lower bound on $\mathbf{b}$ in the above theorem is necessary: if $\mathbf{b} = O(1)$, then no non-trivial approximation to the core can be guaranteed, even when $\rho$ is a constant. Also in the full version, we consider a different (and more classical) version of the core for general packing constraints, in which a deviating coalition gets a proportional share of resources rather than a proportional share of utility. Our techniques provide a similar approximation to this version of the core, although we do not provide an efficient algorithm in this model.

### 1.6 Related Work

*Core for Public Goods.* The notion of core is borrowed from cooperative game theory and was first phrased in game theoretic terms by Scarf [33]. It has been extensively studied in public goods settings [10, 13, 25]. Most literature so far has considered the core with *fractional allocations.* Our definition of core (Definition 1.3) assumes the utility of a deviating coalition is scaled by the size of the coalition. For fractional allocations, one such core allocation coincides with the well-known notion of *proportional fairness,* the extension of the Nash bargaining solution [26]. This solution maximizes the product of the utilities of the agents, and we present the folklore proof in Section 2.2. Our main focus is on finding *integer* allocations that approximate the core, and to the best of our knowledge, this has not been studied previously.

A simpler property than the core is proportionality, which like the core, is impossible to satisfy to any multiplicative approximation using integral allocations. To address this problem, Conitzer et al. [9] defined proportionality up to one issue in the public decision making framework, inspired by related notions for private goods. This guarantee is satisfied by the integral outcome maximizing the *Nash welfare* objective, which is the *geometric* mean of the utilities to the agents. For public goods, this objective is not only NP-Hard to approximate to any multiplicative factor, but approximations to the objective also do not necessarily retain the individual fairness guarantees.

We extend the notion of additive approximate proportionality to additive approximate core outcomes, which provides meaningful guarantees even when there are fewer goods than agents. Unlike proportionality, we show in Section 2.1 that the approach of computing the optimal integral solution to the Nash welfare objective fails to provide a reasonable approximation to the core. Therefore, for our results about matroid constraints (Theorem 1.5) and matching constraints (Theorem 1.6), we slightly modify the integer Nash welfare objective and add a suitable constant term to the utility of each agent. We show that maximizing this smooth objective function achieves a good approximation to the core. However, maximizing this objective is still NP-hard [12], so we devise local search procedures that run in polynomial time and still give good approximations of the core. In effect, we make a novel connection between appropriate *local optima* of smooth Nash Welfare objectives and the core.

*Fairness on Endowments.* Classically, the core is defined in terms of endowments, not scaled utilities. In Definition 1.3, we assumed that when a subset $S$ of agents deviates, they can choose any feasible outcome; however, their utility is reduced by a factor that depends on $|S|$. A different notion of core is based on endowments [13, 33] and has been considered in the context of participatory budgeting [10] and in *proportional representation* of voters in multi-winner elections with approval voting. In this notion, a deviating coalition gets a proportional share of resources rather than a proportional share of utility. For example, if the elements have different sizes, and we need to select a subset of them with total size at most $B$, then a deviating coalition $S$ would get to choose an outcome with size at most $B|S|/n$ instead of $B$, but would not have its utility scaled down. This notion builds on the seminal work of Foley [13] on the Lindahl equilibrium, from which it can be shown that such a core outcome always exists when fractional allocations are allowed. However, it is not known how to compute such a core outcome efficiently, and it is difficult to define endowments in settings such as matroid or matching constraints. For integer allocations with packing constraints, we extend our techniques to provide approximations to the notion of core with endowments in the full version [11].

The notion of core with endowments logically implies some fairness notions considered in multi-winner election literature, such as justified representation, extended justified representation [3], and proportional justified representation [32]. Approval-based multi-winner elections are a special case of packing constraints, in which voters (agents) have binary utilities over a pool of candidates (elements), and we must select a set of at most $B$ candidates. The idea behind proportional representation is to define a notion of large cohesive groups of agents with similar preferences, and ensure that such coalitions are proportionally represented. The core on endowments represents a more general condition that holds for all coalitions of agents, not just those that are large and cohesive. Nevertheless, our local search algorithms for Theorems 1.5 and 1.6 are similar to local search algorithms for proportional approval voting (PAV) [4, 35] that achieve proportional representation. It would be interesting to explore the connection between these notions in greater depth.

*Private Goods and Envy-freeness.* Private goods are a special case of public goods with matroid constraints, and the fair allocation of private goods is well studied [15, 20, 27, 36]. A common fairness criterion for is envy-freeness: that no agent should (strongly) prefer the allocation of another agent. For integral allocations, envy-free allocations or multiplicative approximations thereof may not exist in general. Recent work has introduced envy-freeness up to one good [7, 8, 23, 29], an additive approximation of envy-freeness. The notion of envy does not extend as is to public goods, and the core can be thought of as enforcing envy-freeness across demographics. We note that in addition to resource allocation, group based fairness is also appearing as a desideratum in machine learning. Specifically, related notions may provide a tool against gerrymandered classifiers that appear fair on small samples, but not on structured subsets [19].

*Strategyproofness.* In this work, we do not consider game-theoretic incentives for manipulation for two reasons. First, even for the restricted case of private goods allocation, preventing manipulation leads to severely restricted mechanisms. For instance, Schummer [34] shows that the only strategyproof and Pareto efficient mechanisms are dictatorial, even when there are only two agents with additive utilities over divisible goods. Second, our work is motivated by public goods settings with many agents, such as participatory budgeting, wherein individual agents often have limited influence over the final outcome as formalized by notions like *strategyproofness in the large* [2].

## 2 PRELUDE: NASH SOCIAL WELFARE

Our approach to computing approximate core solutions revolves around the Nash social welfare, which is the product (or equivalently, the sum of logarithms) of agent utilities. This objective is commonly considered to be a natural tradeoff between the fairness-blind utilitarian social welfare objective (maximizing the sum of agent utilities) and the efficiency-blind egalitarian social welfare objective (maximizing the minimum agent utility). This function also has the advantage of being *scale invariant* with respect to the utility function of each agent, and in general, preferring more equal distributions of utility.

### 2.1 Integer Nash Welfare and Smooth Variants

The integer *Max Nash Welfare* (MNW) solution [8, 9] is an outcome $\mathbf{c}$ that maximizes $\sum_{i \in N} \ln u_i(\mathbf{c})$. More technically, if every integer allocation gives zero utility to at least one agent, the MNW solution first chooses a largest set $S$ of agents that can be given non-zero utility simultaneously, and maximizes the product of utilities to agents in $S$.

Conitzer et al. [9] argue that this allocation is reasonable by showing that it satisfies proportionality up to one issue for public decision making. A natural question is whether it also provides an approximation of the core. *We answer this question in the negative.* The example below shows that even for public decision making (a special case of matroid constraints), the integer MNW solution may fail to return a $(\delta, \alpha)$-core outcome, for any $\delta = o(m)$ and $\alpha = o(m)$.

*Example 2.1.* Consider an instance of public decision making [9] with $m$ issues and two alternatives per issue. Specifically, each issue $t$ has two alternatives $\{a_1^t, a_2^t\}$, and exactly one of them needs to be chosen. There are two sets of agents $X = \{1, \dots, m\}$ and $Y = \{m+1, \dots, 2m\}$. Every agent $i \in X$ has $u_i^i(a_1^i) = 1$, and utility 0 for all other alternatives. Every agent $i \in Y$ has $u_i^t(a_2^t) = 1$ and $u_i^t(a_1^t) = 1/m$ for all issues $i \in \{1, 2, \dots, m\}$. Visually, this is represented as follows.

| | $a_1^1$ | $a_2^1$ | $a_1^2$ | $a_2^2$ | $\dots$ | $a_1^m$ | $a_2^m$ |
|---|---|---|---|---|---|---|---|
| $u_{1\in X}$ | 1 | 0 | 0 | 0 | $\dots$ | 0 | 0 |
| $u_{2\in X}$ | 0 | 0 | 1 | 0 | $\dots$ | 0 | 0 |
| $\vdots$ | $\vdots$ | $\vdots$ | $\vdots$ | $\vdots$ | | $\vdots$ | $\vdots$ |
| $u_{m\in X}$ | 0 | 0 | 0 | 0 | $\dots$ | 1 | 0 |
| $u_{i\in Y}$ | $1/m$ | 1 | $1/m$ | 1 | $\dots$ | $1/m$ | 1 |

The integer MNW outcome is $\mathbf{c} = (a_1^1, a_1^2, \dots, a_1^m)$ because any other outcome gives zero utility to at least one agent. However, coalition $Y$ can deviate, choose outcome $\mathbf{c}' = (a_2^1, a_2^2, \dots, a_2^m)$, and achieve utility $m$ for each agent in $Y$. For $\mathbf{c}$ to be a $(\delta, \alpha)$-core outcome, we need

$$\exists i \in Y : (1+\delta) \cdot u_i(\mathbf{c}) + \alpha \geq \frac{|Y|}{|Y| + |X|} \cdot u_i(\mathbf{c}') \quad \Rightarrow \quad 1 + \delta + \alpha \geq \frac{m}{2}.$$

Hence, $\mathbf{c}$ is not a $(\delta, \alpha)$-core outcome for any $\delta = o(m)$ and $\alpha = o(m)$. In contrast, it is not hard to see that $\mathbf{c}'$ is a $(0, 1)$-core outcome because each agent in $X$ gets utility at most one in any outcome.

Further, note that outcome $\mathbf{c}$ gives every agent utility 1. Since $Prop_i \leq 1$ for each agent $i$, $\mathbf{c}$ satisfies proportionality, and yet fails to provide a reasonable approximation to the core. One may argue that $\mathbf{c}'$, which is a $(0, 1)$-core outcome, is indeed fairer because it respects the utility-maximizing choice of half of the population; the other half of the population cannot agree on what they want, so respecting their top choice is arguably a less fair outcome. Hence, the example also shows that outcomes satisfying proportionality (or proportionality up to one issue) can be very different from and less fair than approximate core outcomes.

*Smooth Nash Welfare.* One issue with the Nash welfare objective is that it is sensitive to agents receiving zero utility. We therefore consider the following smooth Nash welfare objective:

$$F(\mathbf{c}) := \sum_{i \in N} \ln\left(\ell + u_i(\mathbf{c})\right) \tag{2}$$

where $\ell \geq 0$ is a parameter. Note that $\ell = 0$ coincides with the Nash welfare objective. The case of $\ell = 1$ was considered by Fluschnik et al. [12], who showed it is NP-Hard to optimize. Recall that we normalized agent utilities so that each agent has a maximum utility of 1 for any element, so when we add $\ell$ to the utility of agent $i$, it is equivalent to adding $\ell \max_j u_{ij}$ to the utility of agent $i$ when utilities are not normalized.

We show that local search procedures for the smooth Nash welfare objective, for appropriate choices of $\ell$, yield a $(0, 2)$-core outcome for matroid constraints (Section 3) and a $\left(\delta, O\left(\frac{1}{\delta}\right)\right)$-core outcome for matching constraints (Section 4). For packing constraints in contrast, we show in the full version [11] that optimizing any fixed smooth Nash welfare objective cannot guarantee a good approximation to the core, even with *a single* packing constraint, motivating the need for a different algorithm.

### 2.2 Fractional Max Nash Welfare Solution

For general packing constraints, we use a fractional relaxation of the Nash welfare program. A *fractional outcome* consists of a vector $\mathbf{w}$ such that $w_j \in [0, 1]$ measures the fraction of element $j$ chosen. The utility of agent $i$ under this outcome is $u_i(\mathbf{w}) = \sum_{j=1}^{m} w_j u_{ij}$. The fractional *Max Nash Welfare* (MNW) solution is a fractional allocation that maximizes the Nash welfare objective (without any smoothing). Define the packing polytope as:

$$\mathcal{P} = \left\{\mathbf{w} \in [0,1]^m \mid \sum_{j=1}^{m} a_{kj} w_j \leq b_k, \forall k \in [K]\right\}$$

Then the fractional MNW solution is $\arg\max_{\mathbf{c}\in\mathcal{P}} \sum_i \ln u_i(\mathbf{c})$.

It is easy to show that the fractional MNW allocation lies in the core. Let $\mathbf{c}$ denote the optimal fractional allocation to the MNW program. By first order optimality, for any other allocation $\mathbf{d}$,

$$\nabla \ln \mathbf{u}(\mathbf{c}) \cdot (\mathbf{u}(\mathbf{d}) - \mathbf{u}(\mathbf{c})) \leq 0 \quad \Rightarrow \quad \sum_{i\in N} \frac{1}{u_i(\mathbf{c})} (u_i(\mathbf{d}) - u_i(\mathbf{c})) \leq 0 \quad \Rightarrow \quad \sum_{i\in N} \frac{u_i(\mathbf{d})}{u_i(\mathbf{c})} \leq n. \tag{3}$$

Suppose for contradiction that $\mathbf{c}$ is not a core outcome. Then there exists a set of agents $S \subseteq N$ and an outcome $\mathbf{d}$ such that $u_i(\mathbf{d}) \geq (n/|S|) \cdot u_i(\mathbf{c})$, and at least one inequality is tight. This implies $\sum_{i\in S} u_i(\mathbf{d})/u_i(\mathbf{c}) > n$. However, this contradicts Equation (3). Thus $\mathbf{c}$, the optimal fractional solution to the MNW program, is a core solution.

For the allocation of public goods, it can be shown that the fractional MNW outcome can be irrational despite rational inputs [1], preventing an exact algorithm. For our approximation results, a fractional solution that approximately preserves the utility to each agent would suffice, and we prove the following theorem in the full version [11].

Theorem 2.2. *For any $\epsilon, \delta > 0$, we can compute a fractional $(\delta, \epsilon)$-core outcome in time polynomial in the input size and $\log \frac{1}{\epsilon\delta}$.*

## 3 MATROID CONSTRAINTS

We now consider public goods allocation with matroid constraints. In particular, we show that when the feasibility constraints encode independent sets of a matroid $\mathcal{M}$, maximizing the smooth Nash welfare objective in Equation (2) with $\ell = 1$ yields a $(0, 2)$-core outcome. However, optimizing this objective is known to be NP-hard [12]. We also show that given $\epsilon > 0$, a local search procedure for this objective function (given below) yields a $(0, 2 + \epsilon)$-core outcome in polynomial time, which proves Theorem 1.5.

### 3.1 Algorithm

Fix $\epsilon > 0$. Let $\gamma = \frac{\epsilon}{4m}$, where $m = |W|$ is the number of elements. Recall that there are $n$ agents.

(1) Start with an arbitrary basis $\mathbf{c}$ of $\mathcal{M}$.
(2) Compute $F(\mathbf{c}) = \sum_{i\in N} \ln(1 + u_i(\mathbf{c}))$.
(3) Let a *swap* be a pair $(j, j')$ such that $j \in \mathbf{c}$, $j' \notin \mathbf{c}$, and $\mathbf{c}' = \mathbf{c} \setminus \{j\} \cup \{j'\}$ is also a basis of $\mathcal{M}$.
(4) Find a swap such that $F(\mathbf{c}') - F(\mathbf{c}) \geq \frac{n\gamma}{m}$.
   - If such a swap exists, then perform the swap, i.e., update $\mathbf{c} \leftarrow \mathbf{c}'$, and go to Step (2).
   - If no such swap exists, then output $\mathbf{c}$ as the final outcome.

### 3.2 Analysis

First, we show that the local search algorithm runs in time polynomial in $n$, $m$, and $1/\epsilon$. Note that $F(\mathbf{c}) = O(n \ln m)$ because in our normalization, each agent can have utility at most $m$. Thus, the number of iterations is $O\left(m^2 \log m/\epsilon\right)$. Finally, each iteration can be implemented in $O(n \cdot m^2)$ time by iterating over all pairs and computing the change in the smooth Nash welfare objective.

Next, let $\mathbf{c}^*$ denote the outcome maximizing the smooth Nash welfare objective with $\ell = 1$, and $\widehat{\mathbf{c}}$ denote the outcome returned by the local search algorithm. We show that $\mathbf{c}^*$ is a $(0, 2)$-core outcome, while $\widehat{\mathbf{c}}$ is a $(0, 2 + \epsilon)$-core outcome.

For outcome $\mathbf{c}$, define $F_i(\mathbf{c}) = \ln(1 + u_i(\mathbf{c}))$. Fix an arbitrary outcome $\mathbf{c}$. For an agent $i$ with $u_i(\mathbf{c}) > 0$, we have that for every element $j \in \mathbf{c}$:

$$F_i(\mathbf{c}) - F_i(\mathbf{c} \setminus \{j\}) \leq \frac{u_{ij}}{u_i(\mathbf{c}) + 1 - u_{ij}} \leq \frac{u_{ij}}{u_i(\mathbf{c})}.$$

This holds because $\ln(x + h) - \ln x \leq \frac{h}{x}$ for $x > 0$ and $h \geq 0$. Summing this over all $j \in \mathbf{c}$ gives

$$\sum_{j \in \mathbf{c}} F_i(\mathbf{c}) - F_i(\mathbf{c} \setminus \{j\}) \leq \sum_{j \in \mathbf{c}} \frac{u_{ij}}{u_i(\mathbf{c})} = \frac{u_i(\mathbf{c})}{u_i(\mathbf{c})} = 1.$$

For an agent $i$ with $u_i(\mathbf{c}) = 0$, we trivially have $\sum_{j \in \mathbf{c}} F_i(\mathbf{c}) - F_i(\mathbf{c} \setminus \{j\}) = 0$. Summing over all agents, we have that for every outcome $\mathbf{c}$:

$$\sum_{j \in \mathbf{c}} F(\mathbf{c}) - F(\mathbf{c} \setminus \{j\}) = \sum_{i \in N} \sum_{j \in \mathbf{c}} F_i(\mathbf{c}) - F_i(\mathbf{c} \setminus \{j\}) \leq n. \tag{4}$$

We now use the following result:

LEMMA 3.1 ([21]). *For every pair of bases* $\mathbf{c}$ *and* $\mathbf{c}'$ *of a matroid* $\mathcal{M}$*, there is a bijection* $f : \mathbf{c} \to \mathbf{c}'$ *such that for every* $j \in \mathbf{c}$*,* $\mathbf{c} \setminus \{j\} \cup \{f(j)\}$ *is also a basis.*

Using the above lemma, combined with the fact that $\ln(x + h) - \ln x \geq \frac{h}{x+h}$ for $x > 0$ and $h \geq 0$, we have that for all $\mathbf{c}, \mathbf{c}'$:

$$\begin{aligned}\sum_{j \in \mathbf{c}} F(\mathbf{c} \setminus \{j\} \cup \{f(j)\}) - F(\mathbf{c} \setminus \{j\}) &\geq \sum_i \sum_{j \in \mathbf{c}} \frac{u_{if(j)}}{u_i(\mathbf{c}) + 1 - u_{ij} + u_{if(j)}} \\ &\geq \sum_{i \in S} \sum_{j' \in \mathbf{c}'} \frac{u_{ij'}}{u_i(\mathbf{c}) + 2} = \sum_{i \in S} \frac{u_i(\mathbf{c}')}{u_i(\mathbf{c}) + 2}.\end{aligned} \tag{5}$$

We now provide almost similar proofs for the approximations achieved by the global optimum $\mathbf{c}^*$ and the local optimum $\widehat{\mathbf{c}}$.

*Global optimum.* Suppose for contradiction that $\mathbf{c}^*$ is not a $(0, 2)$-core outcome. Then, there exist a subset $S$ of agents and an outcome $\mathbf{c}'$ such that for all $i \in S$,

$$\frac{|S|}{n} \cdot u_i(\mathbf{c}') \geq u_i(\mathbf{c}^*) + 2,$$

and at least one inequality is strict. Rearranging the terms and summing over all $i \in S$, we obtain:

$$\sum_{i \in S} \frac{u_i(\mathbf{c}')}{u_i(\mathbf{c}^*) + 2} > \sum_{i \in S} \frac{n}{|S|} = n.$$

Combining this with Equation (5), and subtracting Equation (4) yields:

$$\sum_{j \in \mathbf{c}^*} (F(\mathbf{c}^* \setminus \{j\} \cup \{f(j)\}) - F(\mathbf{c}^*)) > 0.$$

This implies existence of a pair $(j, f(j))$ such that $F(\mathbf{c}^* \setminus \{j\} \cup \{f(j)\}) - F(\mathbf{c}^*) > 0$, which contradicts the optimality of $\mathbf{c}^*$ because $\mathbf{c}^* \setminus \{j\} \cup \{f(j)\}$ is also a basis of $\mathcal{M}$.

*Local optimum.* Similarly, suppose for contradiction that $\widehat{\mathbf{c}}$ is not a $(0, 2 + \epsilon)$-core outcome. Then, there exist a subset $S$ of agents and an outcome $\mathbf{c}'$ such that for all $i \in S$,

$$\frac{|S|}{n} \cdot u_i(\mathbf{c}') \geq u_i(\widehat{\mathbf{c}}) + 2 + \epsilon > (1 + \gamma)(u_i(\widehat{\mathbf{c}}) + 2).$$

Here, the final transition holds because $\gamma < \epsilon/(m+2) \leq \epsilon/(u_i(\widehat{\mathbf{c}})+2)$. Again, rearranging and summing over all $i \in S$, we obtain:

$$\sum_{i \in S} \frac{u_i(\mathbf{c}')}{u_i(\widehat{\mathbf{c}})+2} > (1+\gamma) \sum_{i \in S} \frac{n}{|S|} \geq n \cdot (1+\gamma).$$

Once again, combining this with Equation (5), and subtracting Equation (4) yields:

$$\sum_{j \in \widehat{\mathbf{c}}} (F(\widehat{\mathbf{c}} \setminus \{j\} \cup \{f(j)\}) - F(\widehat{\mathbf{c}})) > n\gamma.$$

This implies existence of a pair $(j, f(j))$ such that $F(\widehat{\mathbf{c}} \setminus \{j\} \cup \{f(j)\}) - F(\widehat{\mathbf{c}}) > n\gamma/m$, which violates local optimality of $\widehat{\mathbf{c}}$ because $\widehat{\mathbf{c}} \setminus \{j\} \cup \{f(j)\}$ is also a basis of $\mathcal{M}$.

*Lower Bound.* While a $(0, 2)$-core always outcome exists, we show in the following example that a $(0, 1-\epsilon)$-core outcome is not guaranteed to exist for any $\epsilon > 0$.

Lemma 3.2. *For $\epsilon > 0$ and matroid constraints, $(0, 1-\epsilon)$-core outcomes are not guaranteed to exist.*

Proof. Consider the following instance of public decision making where we have several issues and must choose a single alternative for each issue, a special case of matroid constraints. There are $n$ agents, where $n$ is even. There are $m = (n-2) + n/2$ issues. The first $n-2$ issues correspond to unit-value private goods, *i.e.*, each such issue has $n$ alternatives, and each alternative gives utility 1 to a unique agent and utility 0 to others. The remaining $n/2$ issues are "pair issues"; each such issue has $\binom{n}{2}$ alternatives, one corresponding to every pair of agents that gives both agents in the pair utility 1 and all other agents utility 0.

It is easy to see that every integer allocation gives utility at most 1 to at least two agents. Consider the deviating coalition consisting of these two agents. They can choose the alternative that gives them each utility 1 on every pair issue, and split the $n-2$ private good equally. Thus, they each get utility $n/2 + (n-2)/2 = n-1$. For the outcome to be a $(0, \alpha)$-core outcome, we need $1 + \alpha \geq (2/n) \cdot (n-1)$. As $n \to \infty$, this requires $\alpha \to 1$. Hence, for any $\epsilon > 0$, a $(0, 1-\epsilon)$-core outcome is not guaranteed to exist. □

Note that Theorem 1.5 shows existence of a $(0, 2)$-core outcome, which is therefore tight up to a unit additive relaxation. Whether a $(0, 1)$-core outcome always exists under matroid constraints remains an important open question. Interestingly, we show that such an outcome always exists for the special case of private goods allocation, and, in fact, can be achieved by maximizing the smooth Nash welfare objective. We provide a proof of this result in the full version [11].

Lemma 3.3. *For private goods allocation, maximizing the smooth Nash welfare objective with $\ell = 1$ returns a $(0, 1)$-core outcome.*

## 4 MATCHING CONSTRAINTS

We now present the algorithm proving Theorem 1.6. We show that if the elements are edges of an undirected graph $G(V, E)$, and the feasibility constraints encode a matching, then for constant $\delta \in (0, 1]$, a $(\delta, 8 + \frac{6}{\delta})$-core always exists and is efficiently computable. The idea is to again run a *local search* on the smooth Nash welfare objective in Equation (2), but this time with $\ell \approx 1 + \frac{4}{\delta}$.

*Algorithm.* Recall that there are $n$ agents. Let $|V| = r$ and $|E| = m$. Let $\kappa = \frac{2}{\delta}$. For simplicity, assume $\kappa \in \mathbb{N}$. Our algorithm is inspired by the PRAM algorithm for approximate maximum weight matchings due to Hougardy and Vinkemeier [18], and we follow their terminology. Given a matching $\mathbf{c}$, an *augmentation* with respect to $\mathbf{c}$ is a matching $T \subseteq E \setminus \mathbf{c}$. The *size* of the augmentation is $|T|$. Let $M(T)$ denote the subset of edges of $\mathbf{c}$ that have a vertex which is matched under $T$. Then, the matching $(\mathbf{c} \setminus M(T)) \cup T$ is called the *augmentation* of $\mathbf{c}$ using $T$.

(1) Start with an arbitrary matching $\mathbf{c}$ of $G$.
(2) Compute $F(\mathbf{c}) = \sum_i \ln(1 + 2\kappa + u_i(\mathbf{c}))$.
(3) Let $C$ be the set of all augmentations with respect to $\mathbf{c}$ of size at most $\kappa$.
   - If there exists $T \in C$ such that $F((\mathbf{c} \setminus M(T)) \cup T) - F(\mathbf{c}) \geq \frac{n}{\kappa r}$, perform this augmentation (i.e., let $\mathbf{c} \leftarrow (\mathbf{c} \setminus M(T)) \cup T$) and go to Step (2).
   - Otherwise, output $\mathbf{c}$ as the final outcome.

*Analysis and Lower Bound.* Since the outline of the analysis is very similar to the analysis for matroid constraints, we provide the proof of Theorem 1.6 in the full version [11]. Also in the full version, we show that for matching constraints, a $(\delta, 1 - \epsilon)$-core is not guaranteed to exist for any $\delta \geq 0$ and $\epsilon > 0$. This leaves the interesting open question of whether a $(0, 1)$-core solution always exists for matching constraints.

## 5 GENERAL PACKING CONSTRAINTS

In this section, we study approximation to the core under general packing constraints of the form $A\mathbf{x} \leq \mathbf{b}$. Recall that there are $m$ elements, $V_i$ is the maximum possible utility that agent $i$ can receive from a feasible outcome, and $V_{\max} = \max_{i \in N} V_i$. We prove a statement slightly more general than Theorem 1.7. We first need the following concept.

### 5.1 Maximal Proportionally Fair Outcome

Given an instance of public goods allocation subject to packing constraints, we define the notions of an $r$-proportionally fair ($r$-PF) outcome, a maximally proportionally fair (MPF) outcome, and the MPF value of the instance.

*Definition 5.1 (MPF Outcome).* For $r > 0$, we say that a fractional outcome $\mathbf{w}$ is *$r$-proportionally fair* ($r$-PF) if it satisfies:

$$u_i(\mathbf{w}) \geq \frac{V_i}{r} - 1, \quad \forall i \in N.$$

The *maximally proportionally fair* (MPF) value $R$ of an instance is the least value $r$ such that there exists an $r$-PF outcome. For simplicity, we say that an $R$-PF outcome is a *maximally proportionally fair* (MPF) outcome.

This concept is crucial to stating and deriving our approximation results. An $r$-PF outcome gives each agent an $r$ fraction of its maximum possible utility $V_i$ (which can be thought of as the fair share guarantee of the agent), if the agent is given 1 unit of utility for free. Thus, a smaller value of $r$ indicates a better solution. The MPF value $R$ denotes the best possible guarantee. The additive 1 in Def. 5.1 can be replaced by any positive constant; we choose 1 for simplicity. We give an upper bound for $R$ that holds for all instances. Recall from Equation (1) that $\rho$ is the *width* of the instance.

Lemma 5.2. *$R \leq \min(V_{\max}, n, \rho)$, and an MPF outcome is computable in polynomial time.*

Proof. To show that $R$ is well-defined, note that for $r = V_{\max}$, an $r$-PF outcome $\mathbf{w}$ simply requires $u_i(\mathbf{w}) \geq 0$, which is trivially achieved by every outcome. Therefore, $R$ is well-defined, and $R \leq V_{\max}$. Next, $R \leq n$ follows from the fact that there exist fractional outcomes satisfying proportionality (e.g., the outcome $\mathbf{w}$ obtained by taking the uniform convex combination of the $n$ outcomes that give optimal to each individual agent). Finally, to show $R \leq \rho$, consider the outcome $\mathbf{w}$ in which $w_j = \frac{1}{\rho}$ for each element $j$. Clearly, $u_i(\mathbf{w}) \geq \frac{V_i}{\rho}$ for all $i$. Further, $A\mathbf{w} \leq \mathbf{b}$ is satisfied trivially due to the fact that $\rho$ is the width of the packing constraints.

To compute the value of $R$ as well as an MPF outcome, we first note that the value of $V_i$ for each agent $i$ can be computed by solving a separate LP. Then, we consider the following LP:

$$\text{Maximize } \hat{r} \tag{6}$$

$$\begin{array}{rcll} \sum_{j\in W} u_{ij}w_j & \geq & V_i \cdot \hat{r} - 1 & \forall i \in [n] \\ A\mathbf{w} & \leq & \mathbf{b} & \\ w_j & \in & [0,1] & \forall j \in W \end{array}$$

Here, $A\mathbf{w} \leq \mathbf{b}$ are the packing constraints of the instance, and $\hat{r}$ is a variable representing $1/r$. Thus, maximizing $\hat{r}$ minimizes $r$, which yields an MPF outcome. This can be accomplished by solving $n+1$ linear programs, which can be done in polynomial time. □

Our main result in this section uses any $r$-PF outcome, and provides a guarantee in terms of $\log r$. Thus, we do not need to necessarily compute an exact MPF outcome. We note that an MPF outcome can be very different from a core outcome. Yet, an MPF outcome gives each agent a large fraction of its maximum possible utility, subject to a small additive relaxation. As we show below, this helps us find integral outcomes that provide good approximations of the core.

### 5.2 Result and Proof Idea

Our main result for this section (Theorem 1.7) can be stated in a refined way as follows. Recall that $\log^*$ is the iterated logarithm, which is the number of times the logarithm function must be iteratively applied before the result becomes less than or equal to 1.

THEOREM 5.3. *Fix constant $\delta \in (0,1)$. Suppose we are given a set of $K$ packing constraints $A\mathbf{x} \leq \mathbf{b}$ such that $b_k = \omega\left(\frac{\log K}{\delta^2}\right)$ for all $k \in [K]$. Let $R$ be the MPF value of this instance. Then there exists a polynomial time computable $(\delta, \alpha)$-core outcome, where*

$$\alpha = O\left(\frac{1}{\delta^4} \cdot \log\left(\frac{R \cdot \log^* V_{\max}}{\delta}\right)\right).$$

We first note that the above result cannot be obtained by maximizing the smooth Nash welfare objective as we prove in the full version of this paper [11]. To be precise, the example shows that no single value of parameter $\ell$ in the smooth Nash welfare objective can provide a polylog additive guarantee for all instances. While it may be possible to choose the value of $\ell$ based on the instance, it does not seem trivial. We take a different approach. Our idea is to start with a fractional core solution $\mathbf{x}$. Suppose it assigns utility $U_i^*$ to agent $i$. Fix $\delta > 0$, and consider the following program.

$$\text{Minimize } \alpha \tag{7}$$

$$\begin{array}{rcll} \alpha + (1+\delta) \cdot \sum_{j\in W} u_{ij}w_j & \geq & U_i^* & \forall i \in [n] \\ A\mathbf{w} & \leq & \mathbf{b} & \\ w_j & \in & \{0,1\} & \forall j \in W \\ \alpha & \geq & 0 & \end{array}$$

For the optimum value $\alpha^*$, we obtain an outcome that is $(\delta, \alpha')$-core for every $\alpha' > \alpha$. To see this, take a subset of agents $S$ and a feasible utility vector $\mathbf{U}'$ under any other (even fractional) outcome. Because $\mathbf{x}$ is a core outcome, there exists $i \in S$ such that $U_i^* \geq (|S|/n) \cdot U_i'$. For $\alpha' > \alpha$, the ILP solution implies

$$\alpha' + (1+\delta) \cdot \sum_{j\in W} u_{ij}w_j > U_i^* \geq \frac{|S|}{n} \cdot U_i',$$

which implies that the solution is $(\delta, \alpha')$-core according to Definition 1.4.

However, $\alpha^*$ obtained from this program can be rather large, as illustrated in the following example. Consider the KNAPSACK setting with $m$ unit-size projects. There is an overall budget $B = m/2$. For every feasible integral outcome $\mathbf{c}$, let there be an agent with utility 1 for every project in $\mathbf{c}$ and 0 for all other projects. Thus, there are $\binom{m}{m/2}$ agents. The fractional core outcome gives weight $1/2$ to each project, thus giving utility $V_i/2 = m/4$ to each agent $i$. However, every integral outcome gives utility 0 to at least one agent, which implies $\alpha^* = \Omega(m)$.

This example shows that when there are a large number of agents, we cannot achieve Theorem 5.3 by hoping to approximately preserve the utilities to *all* agents with respect the fractional core solution. However, note that in the above example, though there is one agent who gets very little utility, this agent has no incentive to deviate if she is given one unit of utility for free. This insight leads us to our analysis below, which is based on rounding the fractional core solution $\mathbf{x}$.

Let us apply randomized rounding to $\mathbf{x}$. Instead of using Chernoff bounds to ensure that there are no "violations" (i.e., that no agent receives utility that is too far from its utility under the core outcome $\mathbf{x}$), we hope to bound the expected number of such violations. If there are few such agents, we still have an approximate core outcome because if this small coalition of agents deviates, its utility under a new outcome will be scaled down by a large factor. Unfortunately, it can be shown that bounding the expected number of deviations by a sufficiently small number forces $\alpha = \Omega(\log V_{\max})$. This is better than $\alpha = \Omega(m)$ from our previous approach, but still *much* larger than the bound we want to achieve in Theorem 5.3 when the width $\rho$ is small.

This brings up the main technical idea. We observe that an MPF outcome, though not in the core, provides a reasonably large utility to each agent. We add a small amount of this outcome to the fractional core before applying randomized rounding. We are now ready to present our algorithm.

### 5.3 Algorithm

Fix $\delta \in (0, 1)$, and let $\gamma = \frac{\delta}{8}$.

(1) Compute the (approximate) fractional core solution $\mathbf{x}$ as in Theorem 2.2, where $x_j$ is the fraction of element $j$ chosen.
(2) Let $\mathbf{y}$ be an MPF outcome as in Definition 5.1.
(3) Let $\mathbf{z} = (1 - \gamma)\mathbf{x} + \gamma\mathbf{y}$.
(4) For each $j \in W$, choose $j$ to be in the outcome $\mathbf{c}$ independently with probability $\hat{z}_j = (1-\gamma)z_j$.

### 5.4 Analysis

We show that this algorithm yields, with at least a constant probability, a feasible outcome that satisfies the guarantee in Theorem 5.3. This directly shows the existence of such an outcome. Note that the fractional Max Nash Welfare solution $\mathbf{x}$ can be irrational, but we can compute an approximation in polynomial time (see Theorem 2.2 for details), which does not change our guarantee asymptotically. Further, $\mathbf{y}$ can be computed in polynomial time (Lemma 5.2). Hence, the algorithm runs in expected polynomial time.

We first show that the packing constraints are satisfied. Since we scale down $\mathbf{z}$ by a factor $(1-\gamma)$ before rounding, we have $A\hat{\mathbf{z}} \le (1-\gamma)\mathbf{b}$. Since $\mathbf{b} = \omega\left(\frac{\log K}{\delta^2}\right)$, a simple application of Chernoff bounds shows that with probability at least 0.99, the rounded solution $\mathbf{c}$ satisfies $A\mathbf{c} \le \mathbf{b}$. Therefore, if we show that the algorithm also yields the desired approximation of the core with at least a constant probability (1/6 to be precise), we will be done by applying union bound to the two events, feasibility and good approximation to the core.

For the ease of presentation, we suppress constants throughout the proof and use the asymptotic notation liberally. We also assume that $V_{\max} = \omega(1)$ since otherwise there is a trivial $(0, O(1))$-core outcome that chooses a null outcome, giving zero utility to each agent. For lack of space, we relegate parts of the proof to the full version of this paper [11].

*5.4.1 Grouping Agents.* In order to analyze our algorithm, we partition the agents into groups with exponentially decreasing values of $V_i$. Recall that $V_i$ is the maximum utility that agent $i$ can get from any outcome. Set $Q_0 = \log V_{\max}$, and for $\ell = 0, 1, \ldots, L-1$, define group $G_\ell$ as:

$$G_\ell = \{i \in N \mid Q_\ell \geq \log V_i \geq Q_{\ell+1}\}.$$

Here, for $\ell = 0, 1, \ldots, L-1$, we define: $Q_{\ell+1} = 2 \log Q_\ell$.

We call $G_0, \ldots, G_{L-1}$ the *heavy groups*. We choose $L$ so that $Q_L = \Theta\left(\log \frac{R \log^* V_{\max}}{\gamma^3}\right)$. This implies $L = \Omega(\log^* V_{\max}) = \omega(1)$, since $V_{\max} = \omega(1)$. For agent $i$ in a heavy group, $V_i \geq e^{Q_L} \geq \frac{2RL}{\gamma^3} > 2R$. Thus, the utility that the MPF solution provides to agent $i$ is at least $\frac{V_i}{R} - 1 \geq \frac{V_i}{2R}$.

Finally, we put the remaining agents (with a small $V_i$) in a *light group* defined as follows:

$$G_L = \{i \in N \mid \log V_i \leq Q_L\}.$$

The MPF solution may not provide any guarantee for the utility of agents in this group.

*5.4.2 Bounding Violations of Utility Preservation.* We want to bound the number of agents whose utilities are far from those under the core outcome. First, we need a specialized Chernoff bound.

Lemma 5.4. *(Proved in full version) Let $X_1, X_2, \ldots, X_q$ be independent random variables in $[0, 1]$, and let $X = \sum_{j=1}^{q} X_j$. For $\gamma \in (0, 1/2)$, suppose $\mathrm{E}[X] = (1-\gamma) \cdot A + \gamma \cdot B$ for $A, B \geq 0$. Then*

$$\Pr[X < (1-2\gamma) \cdot A] \leq e^{-\frac{\gamma^3}{2} \max(B, A/2)}$$

Recall that $\mathbf{x}$ is the fractional MNW solution, $\mathbf{y}$ is the fractional MPF solution, and our algorithm applies randomized rounding to their scaled down mixture $(1-\gamma)\mathbf{z} = (1-\gamma)^2\mathbf{x} + \gamma(1-\gamma)\mathbf{y}$. Let $\widehat{U}_i$ denote the utility of agent $i$ under the final integral outcome obtained by randomly rounding $(1-\gamma)\mathbf{z}$. Recall that $U_i^*$ is the utility of agent $i$ under the core outcome $\mathbf{x}$. We want to show that $\widehat{U}_i$ is either multiplicatively or additively close to $U_i^*$ for most agents. For a heavy group $G_\ell$, where $\ell \in \{0, 1, \ldots, L-1\}$, define

$$F_\ell = \left\{i \in G_\ell \,\middle|\, \widehat{U}_i < (1-3\gamma)U_i^*\right\}.$$

Simiarly, for the light group $G_L$, define

$$F_L = \left\{i \in G_L \,\middle|\, \widehat{U}_i < \min\left((1-3\gamma)U_i^*, U_i^* - \frac{4Q_L}{\gamma^4}\right)\right\}.$$

We will use Lemma 5.4 to bound the sizes of $F_\ell$ for $\ell \in \{0, 1, \ldots, L\}$ as follows.

Theorem 5.5. *(Proved in full version) We have that:*

*(1) With probability at least 2/3, we have $|F_\ell| \leq \frac{1}{2Le^{Q_\ell}} \cdot |G_\ell|$, $\quad \forall \ell \in \{0, 1, \ldots, L-1\}$.*

*(2) With probability at least 1/2, we have $|F_L| \leq \frac{1}{2e^{Q_L}} \cdot |G_L|$.*

*Thus, with probability at least 1/6, both the above inequalities hold simultaneously.*

*5.4.3 Approximate Core.* We showed that with probability at least 1/6, our algorithm returns a solution that satisfies conditions in both parts of Theorem 5.5. We now show that such a solution is the desired approximate core solution. The main idea is that when a set of agents deviate, the fraction of agents in a group $G_\ell$ that are in $F_\ell$ is small enough such that even if they receive their maximum possible utility, which is $e^{Q_\ell}$, their scaled down utility is at most a constant.

Theorem 5.6. *For every coalition $S$ and every possible outcome* $\mathbf{h}$, *there exists an agent $i \in S$ s.t.*

$$\frac{|S|}{n} \cdot u_i(\mathbf{h}) \leq (1+8\gamma) \cdot \widehat{U}_i + \frac{5Q_L}{\gamma^4}.$$

Proof. Let $W = N \setminus \cup_{\ell=0}^{L} F_\ell$. In other words, $W$ is the set of agents who either receive a good multiplicative approximation to their expected utility in the core (for the heavy groups), or a good additive approximation to their expected utility in the core (for the light group). In particular, for every $i \in W$, we have $\widehat{U}_i \geq \min\left((1-3\gamma) \cdot U_i^*, U_i^* - \frac{4Q_L}{\gamma^4}\right)$, which implies

$$U_i^* \leq \frac{1}{1-3\gamma} \cdot \widehat{U}_i + \frac{4Q_L}{\gamma^4}. \tag{8}$$

Consider a set of agents $S$ that may want to deviate, and let $\mathbf{h}$ be any (even fractional) outcome. There are two cases:

*Case 1.* Suppose $|S \cap W| \geq (1-\gamma) \cdot |S|$. Then, due to the fractional core optimality condition (see Section 2.2), we have:

$$\sum_{i \in S \cap W} \frac{U_i(\mathbf{h})}{U_i^*} \leq n.$$

Note that in polynomial time, Theorem 2.2 only finds an approximate solution whose utilities $\{\tilde{U}_i\}$ with $\sum_{i \in S \cap W} \frac{U_i(\mathbf{h})}{\tilde{U}_i} \leq n(1+\eta)$ for small $\eta > 0$. It is easy to check this does not alter the rest of the proof and adds a small multiplicative factor of $(1+\eta)$ to the final approximation bound. We ignore this factor for simplicity and simply assume $\{U_i^*\}$ are the optimal MNW utilities. The above implies $\frac{|S|}{n} \cdot \sum_{i \in S \cap W} \frac{u_i(\mathbf{h})}{U_i^*} \leq |S| \leq \frac{1}{1-\gamma} \cdot |S \cap W|$.

Therefore, there exists an agent $i \in S \cap W$ such that

$$\frac{|S|}{n} \cdot u_i(\mathbf{h}) \leq \frac{1}{1-\gamma} \cdot U_i^* \leq \frac{1}{1-\gamma} \cdot \left(\frac{1}{1-3\gamma} \cdot \widehat{U}_i + \frac{4Q_L}{\gamma^4}\right),$$

where the last transition is due to Equation (8) and the fact that $i \in W$. Finally, it is easy to check that for $\gamma = \delta/8 \leq 1/8$, we have $\frac{1}{(1-\gamma)\cdot(1-3\gamma)} \leq 1 + 8\gamma$ and $4/(1-\gamma) \leq 5$, which yields:

$$\frac{|S|}{n} \cdot u_i(\mathbf{h}) \leq (1+8\gamma) \cdot \widehat{U}_i + \frac{5Q_L}{\gamma^4}. \tag{9}$$

*Case 2.* Otherwise, $|S \setminus W| \geq \gamma|S|$. In this case, we want to show that there exists an agent $i \in S \setminus W$ such that $(|S|/n) \cdot u_i(\mathbf{h}) \leq 1/\gamma$. Because $\widehat{U}_i \geq 0$ and $Q_L = \omega(1)$, such an agent will also satisfy Equation (9). We show this by taking two sub-cases.

First, suppose the light group satisfies $|S \cap F_L| \geq \frac{\gamma}{2}|S|$. Then: $|S| \leq \frac{2}{\gamma} \cdot |S \cap F_L| \leq \frac{2}{\gamma} \cdot |F_L|$. Thus, for any agent $i \in F_L$, we have

$$\frac{|S|}{n} \cdot u_i(\mathbf{h}) \leq \frac{2}{\gamma n} \cdot |F_L| \cdot V_i \leq \frac{2}{\gamma n} \cdot \frac{|G_L|}{2e^{Q_L}} \cdot V_i \leq \frac{1}{\gamma}.$$

Here, the second transition follows from Theorem 5.5. To see why the third transition holds, note that $|G_L| \leq n$, and that $\log V_i \leq Q_L$ because $i \in G_L$.

Similarly, in the other sub-case, suppose $|S \cap F_L| \leq \frac{\gamma}{2}|S|$. Then, there exists a heavy group $\ell \in \{0, 1, \ldots, L-1\}$ such that $|S \cap F_\ell| \geq \frac{\gamma}{2L}|S|$. This means $|S| \leq \frac{2L}{\gamma} \cdot |S \cap F_\ell| \leq \frac{2L}{\gamma} \cdot |F_\ell|$.

Again, for an arbitrary agent $i \in F_\ell$, we have:

$$\frac{|S|}{n} \cdot u_i(\mathbf{h}) \leq \frac{2L}{\gamma n} \cdot |F_\ell| \cdot V_i \leq \frac{2L}{\gamma n} \cdot \frac{|G_\ell|}{2Le^{Q_\ell}} \cdot V_i \leq \frac{1}{\gamma}.$$

Once again, the third transition follows from Theorem 5.5, and the fourth transition holds because $|G_\ell| \leq n$ and $\log V_i \leq Q_\ell$ as $i \in G_\ell$. Putting everything together, the theorem follows. □

Since $\gamma = \frac{\delta}{8}$ and $Q_L = \Theta\left(\log \frac{R \log^* V_{max}}{\gamma}\right)$, Theorem 5.6 implies $\frac{|S|}{n} \cdot u_i(\mathbf{h}) \leq (1+\delta) \cdot \widehat{U_i} + \alpha^*$, where $\alpha^* = O\left(\frac{1}{\delta^4} \cdot \log\left(\frac{R \cdot \log^* V_{\max}}{\delta}\right)\right)$. The existence of such an agent implies that a solution satisfying Theorem 5.5 is a $(\delta, \alpha)$-core solution for every $\alpha > \alpha^*$, which completes the proof of Theorem 5.3.

## 6 CONCLUSION

We considered the problem of fairly allocating public goods. We argued that the *core*, which is a generalization of proportionality and Pareto efficiency, and approximations of the core provide reasonable fairness guarantees in this context. Given that no integral outcome may be in the core, we presented efficient algorithms to produce integral outcomes that are constant or near-constant approximations of the core, thereby also establishing the non-trivial existence of such outcomes. Note Our algorithms for matroid and matching constraints that globally optimize the smooth Nash welfare objective achieve *exact* Pareto efficiency, in addition to an approximation of the core. An interesting question is whether the same guarantee can be provided for general packing constraints.

Another natural question following our work is to tighten our upper bounds, or to establish matching lower bounds. We show the existence of a $(0, 2)$-core outcome for matroid constraints (Theorem 1.5), but our lower bound only shows that a $(0, 1 - \epsilon)$-core outcome may not exist. This leaves open the question of whether a $(0, 1)$-core outcome always exists. Existence of $(0, 1)$-core outcome is also an open question for matching constraints. For packing constraints, it is unknown if even a $(\delta, \alpha)$-core outcome exists for constant $\delta > 0$ and $\alpha = O(1)$. This also remains an open question for the endowment-based notion of core we consider in the full version of this paper [11].

At a higher level, we established connections between approximating the core in our multi-agent environment and the problem of finding the optimal (i.e., utility-maximizing) outcome for a *single* agent. For instance, given matching constraints, our algorithm uses the idea of *short* augmenting paths from fast PRAM algorithms. This hints at the possibility of a deeper connection between efficiency results and existence results.

## ACKNOWLEDGMENTS

We thank Vincent Conitzer, Rupert Freeman, Ashish Goel, and Paul Gölz for helpful comments. Brandon Fain is supported by NSF grants CCF-1637397 and IIS-1447554. Kamesh Munagala is supported by NSF grants CCF-1408784, CCF-1637397, and IIS-1447554. Nisarg Shah is supported by the Discovery Grants program from the Natural Sciences and Engineering Research Council of Canada (NSERC).

## REFERENCES

[1] S. Airiau, H. Aziz, I. Caragiannis, J. Kruger, and J. Lang. 2017. Positional Social Decision Schemes: Fair and Efficient Randomized Voting. Manuscript.

[2] E. M. Azevedo and E. Budish. 2017. *Strategy-proofness in the Large.* Technical Report. National Bureau of Economic Research.

[3] H. Aziz, M. Brill, V. Conitzer, E. Elkind, R. Freeman, and T. Walsh. 2017. Justified Representation in Approval-Based Committee Voting. *Social Choice and Welfare* 48, 2 (2017), 461–485.

[4] H. Aziz, E. Elkind, S. Huang, M. Lackner, L. Sanchez Fernandez, and P. Skowron. 2018. On the Complexity of Extended and Proportional Justified Representation. In *AAAI Conference on Artificial Intelligence.*

[5] H. Aziz and S. Mackenzie. 2016. A Discrete and Bounded Envy-Free Cake Cutting Protocol for Any Number of Agents. In *Proceedings of the 57th Symposium on Foundations of Computer Science (FOCS).* 416–427.

[6] G. Benade, S. Nath, A. D. Procaccia, and N. Shah. 2017. Preference Elicitation for Participatory Budgeting. In *Proceedings of the 31st AAAI Conference on Artificial Intelligence (AAAI).* 376–382.

[7] E. Budish. 2011. The Combinatorial Assignment Problem: Approximate Competitive Equilibrium from Equal Incomes. *Journal of Political Economy* 119, 6 (2011), 1061–1103.

[8] I. Caragiannis, D. Kurokawa, H. Moulin, A. D. Procaccia, N. Shah, and J. Wang. 2016. The Unreasonable Fairness of Maximum Nash Welfare. In *Proceedings of the 17th ACM Conference on Economics and Computation (EC)*. 305–322.

[9] V. Conitzer, R. Freeman, and N. Shah. 2017. Fair Public Decision Making. In *Proceedings of the 18th ACM Conference on Economics and Computation (EC)*. 629–646.

[10] B. Fain, A. Goel, and K. Munagala. 2016. The Core of the Participatory Budgeting Problem. In *Proceedings of the 12th Conference on Web and Internet Economics (WINE)*. 384–399.

[11] B. Fain, K. Munagala, and N. Shah. 2018. Fair Allocation of Indivisible Public Goods. *ArXiv e-prints* (May 2018). arXiv:1805.03164

[12] T. Fluschnik, P. Skowron, M. Triphaus, and K. Wilker. 2017. Fair Knapsack. arXiv:1711.04520.

[13] D. K. Foley. 1970. Lindahl's Solution and the Core of an Economy with Public Goods. *Econometrica* 38, 1 (1970), 66–72.

[14] N. Garg, V. Kamble, A. Goel, D. Marn, and K. Munagala. 2017. Collaborative Optimization for Collective Decision-making in Continuous Spaces. In *Proceedings of the 26th International World Wide Web Conference (WWW)*. 617–626.

[15] A. Ghodsi, M. Zaharia, B. Hindman, A. Konwinski, S. Shenker, and I. Stoica. 2011. Dominant Resource Fairness: Fair Allocation of Multiple Resource Types. In *Proceedings of the 8th USENIX Conference on Networked Systems Design and Implementation (NSDI)*. 24–37.

[16] A. Goel, A. K. Krishnaswamy, and S. Sakshuwong. 2016. Budget Aggregation via Knapsack Voting: Welfare-maximization and Strategy-proofness. *Collective Intelligence* (2016).

[17] A. Goel, A. K. Krishnaswamy, S. Sakshuwong, and T. Aitamurto. 2015. Knapsack voting. *Collective Intelligence* (2015).

[18] S. Hougardy and D. E. Vinkemeier. 2006. Approximating Weighted Matchings in Parallel. *Inform. Process. Lett.* 99, 3 (2006), 119 – 123.

[19] M. Kearns, S. Neel, A. Roth, and Z. S. Wu. 2017. Preventing Fairness Gerrymandering: Auditing and Learning for Subgroup Fairness. *ArXiv e-prints* (Nov. 2017). arXiv:cs.LG/1711.05144

[20] F. P Kelly, A. K Maulloo, and D. KH Tan. 1998. Rate control for communication networks: shadow prices, proportional fairness and stability. *Journal of the Operational Research society* (1998), 237–252.

[21] J. P. S. Kung. 1986. Basis-Exchange Properties. In *Theory of Matroids*, White N. (Ed.). Cambridge University Press.

[22] M. Kunjir, B. Fain, K., and S. Babu. 2017. ROBUS: Fair Cache Allocation for Data-parallel Workloads. In *Proceedings of the 2017 ACM International Conference on Management of Data (SIGMOD)*. 219–234.

[23] R. J. Lipton, E. Markakis, E. Mossel, and A. Saberi. 2004. On Approximately Fair Allocations of Indivisible Goods. In *Proceedings of the 6th ACM Conference on Economics and Computation (EC)*. 125–131.

[24] N. Luzum. 2016. Voters to Decide Fate of Durham Bond Referenda. *The Chronicle* (2016). http://www.dukechronicle.com/article/2016/10/voters-to-decide-fate-of-durham-bond-referenda

[25] T. J Muench. 1972. The Core and the Lindahl Equilibrium of an Economy with a Public Good: An Example. *Journal of Economic Theory* 4, 2 (1972), 241 – 255.

[26] J. F. Nash. 1950. The Bargaining Problem. *Econometrica* 18, 2 (1950), pp. 155–162.

[27] D. C. Parkes, A. D. Procaccia, and N. Shah. 2012. Beyond Dominant Resource Fairness: Extensions, Limitations, and Indivisibilities. In *Proceedings of the 13th ACM Conference on Electronic Commerce (EC '12)*. 808–825.

[28] PBP. 2015. Participatory Budgeting Project. Website. http://www.participatorybudgeting.org/

[29] B. Plaut and T. Roughgarden. 2018. Almost Envy-freeness with General Valuations. In *Proceedings of the 29th Annual ACM-SIAM Symposium on Discrete Algorithms (SODA)*. 2584–2603.

[30] S. A. Plotkin, D. B. Shmoys, and É. Tardos. 1995. Fast Approximation Algorithms for Fractional Packing and Covering Problems. *Math. Oper. Res.* 20, 2 (1995), 257–301.

[31] A. D. Procaccia. 2013. Cake Cutting: Not Just Child's Play. *Commun. ACM* 56, 7 (July 2013), 78–87.

[32] L. Sánchez-Fernández, E. Elkind, M. Lackner, N. Fernández, J. A. Fisteus, P. Basanta Val, and P. Skowron. 2017. Proportional Justified Representation. In *Proceedings of the 31st AAAI Conference on Artificial Intelligence (AAAI)*. 670–676.

[33] H. E. Scarf. 1967. The Core of an N Person Game. *Econometrica* 35, 1 (1967), pp. 50–69.

[34] J. Schummer. 1997. Strategy-proofness Versus Efficiency on Restricted Domains of Exchange Economies. *Social Choice and Welfare* 14 (1997), 47–56.

[35] T. N. Thiele. 1895. Om flerfoldsvalg. In *Oversigt over det Kongelige Danske Videnskabernes Selskabs Forhandlinger*. 415–441.

[36] H. R. Varian. 1976. Two problems in the theory of fairness. *Journal of Public Economics* 5, 3-4 (1976), 249–260.

# How to Make Envy Vanish Over Time

GERDUS BENADE, Carnegie Mellon University, USA
ALEKSANDR M. KAZACHKOV, Carnegie Mellon University, USA
ARIEL D. PROCACCIA, Carnegie Mellon University, USA
CHRISTOS-ALEXANDROS PSOMAS, Carnegie Mellon University, USA

We study the dynamic fair division of indivisible goods. Suppose $T$ items arrive online and must be allocated upon arrival to one of $n$ agents, each of whom has a value in $[0,1]$ for the current item. Our goal is to design allocation algorithms that minimize the maximum *envy* at time $T$, $\textsc{Envy}_T$, defined as the maximum difference between any agent's overall value for items allocated to another agent and to herself. We say that an algorithm has *vanishing envy* if the ratio of envy over time, $\textsc{Envy}_T/T$, goes to zero as $T$ goes to infinity. We design a polynomial-time, deterministic algorithm that achieves $\textsc{Envy}_T \in \tilde{O}(\sqrt{T/n})$, and show that this guarantee is asymptotically optimal. We also derive tight (in $T$) bounds for a more general setting where items arrive in batches.

## 1 INTRODUCTION

We consider the setting of fairly allocating indivisible goods when agents have additive valuations. It involves a set $[n] = \{1, \dots, n\}$ of agents, and a set of items. Each agent $i \in [n]$ assigns a normalized[1] value $v_{it} \in [0,1]$ to each item $t$; for a bundle of items $S$, the value of agent $i$ is $v_i(S) = \sum_{t \in S} v_{it}$. An *allocation* is a partition of the items into bundles $A_1, \dots, A_n$, where $A_i$ is assigned to agent $i \in [n]$.

Ideally, we would like to guarantee a fairness property called *envy-freeness* — arguably, the gold standard of fairness — which requires that each agent is at least as happy with her own allocation as the allocation of any other agent, that is, $v_i(A_i) \geq v_i(A_j)$ for any two agents $i, j \in [n]$. Envy-free solutions indeed always exist in other paradigmatic fair division settings that involve divisible goods or a numéraire, such as cake cutting [5, 14] and rent division [10, 19]. By contrast, in our context, envy is clearly unavoidable — just imagine a single (indivisible) item that is desired by two agents. That is why recent papers [7, 12] focus on the relaxed notion of *envy-freeness up to one good (EF1)*, which, when values are normalized as above, implies that $v_i(A_i) \geq v_i(A_j) - 1$ for all $i, j \in [n]$. Unlike its more stringent cousin, EF1 can always be guaranteed, and, in fact, it is quite easy to do so, e.g., by allocating the items in a round-robin fashion — each agent in her turn picks her favorite item among those that are still available.

Our point of departure is that we allow items to arrive *online*, that is, we must choose how to allocate an item when it arrives, without knowing the values of items that will arrive in the future.

[1]This assumption is made primarily for ease of exposition.

This work was partially supported by the National Science Foundation under grants IIS-1350598, IIS-1714140, CCF-1525932, and CCF-1733556; by the Office of Naval Research under grants N00014-16-1-3075 and N00014-17-1-2428; and by a Sloan Research Fellowship and a Guggenheim Fellowship.
Authors' addresses: Gerdus Benade, Carnegie Mellon University, Pittsburgh, PA, 15213, USA; Aleksandr M. Kazachkov, Carnegie Mellon University, Pittsburgh, PA, 15213, USA; Ariel D. Procaccia, Carnegie Mellon University, Pittsburgh, PA, 15213, USA; Christos-Alexandros Psomas, Carnegie Mellon University, Pittsburgh, PA, 15213, USA.


*ACM EC'18, June 18–22, 2018, Ithaca, NY, USA.* ACM ISBN 978-1-4503-5829-3/18/06....$15.00.
https://doi.org/10.1145/3219166.3219179

This setup mirrors common decision-making scenarios in humanitarian logistics. A paradigmatic example is that of food banks [1], which receive food donations, and deliver them to nonprofit organizations such as food pantries and soup kitchens. Indeed, items are often perishable, which is why allocation decisions must be made quickly, and donated items are typically leftovers, leading to lack of information about items that will arrive in the future.

Suppose, then, that at each time step an item $t$ arrives, where $t = 1, \ldots, T$. The allocation decisions made by an algorithm at each step induce an allocation $A_1, \ldots, A_n$ at the end of step $T$. For $i, j \in [n]$, let

$$\textsc{Envy}_T^{ij} = \max \left\{ v_i(A_j) - v_i(A_i), 0 \right\}$$

be the envy of $i$ for $j$. Note that this measure of cumulative envy increases by $v_{it}$ if item $t$ is allocated to $j$ (which places it in $A_j$), and decreases by $v_{it}$ if item $t$ is allocated to $i$ (which places it in $A_i$). Moreover, let

$$\textsc{Envy}_T = \max_{i,j \in [n]} \textsc{Envy}_T^{ij}$$

be the maximum envy. As noted above, in the static setting it is possible to maintain $\textsc{Envy}_T \leq 1$ for any number of items $T$, but, of course, even the round-robin allocation requires complete information about values upfront. By contrast, in the online setting, one would expect $\textsc{Envy}_T$ to inevitably grow with $T$.

Nevertheless, we can hope to control the rate at which envy grows over time. Specifically, we aim to design algorithms with *vanishing envy* — algorithms that lead to $\textsc{Envy}_T \in o(T)$, or, equivalently, we want the *average per-round envy* $\textsc{Envy}_T/T$ to go to zero as $T$ goes to infinity. Our primary research question is:

> *Are there online allocation algorithms with vanishing envy, and, if so, what is the optimal average per-round envy?*

### 1.1 Our Results

We first study randomized algorithms. The most natural candidate is the "random allocation" algorithm: allocate item $t$ to an agent chosen uniformly at random. We analyze this algorithm against an adaptive adversary that chooses the values $v_{it}$ for item $t$ after seeing the (random) allocations for items 1 through $t-1$. Our first step is showing that the optimal strategy for an adaptive adversary (against the random allocation algorithm) is in fact nonadaptive: the adversary always picks values $v_{it} = 1$. This makes the random variables for the envy between any agents $i$ and $j$ at steps $t$ and $t'$ independent, which enables us to use standard concentration inequalities for bounding the overall envy. Our result for this setting is that the random allocation algorithm has vanishing envy. Formally, Theorem 2.1 asserts that this algorithm achieves $\mathbb{E}[\textsc{Envy}_T] \in \tilde{O}(\sqrt{T/n})$.

One may hope that it would be possible to do better than allocating blindly. Surprisingly, though, we show that the random allocation algorithm is asymptotically optimal (up to logarithmic factors). Indeed, there exists an adaptive strategy for the adversary such that any allocation algorithm for $T$ items accumulates envy in $\Omega((T/n)^{r/2})$, for any $r < 1$ (Theorem 2.13). However, despite its theoretical optimality, the random allocation algorithm is intuitively unappealing. We therefore turn our attention to deterministic algorithms, only to discover that simple, greedy schemes seem to fail miserably in this setting. For example, one can construct counterexamples for natural candidates, like allocating item $t$ to minimize the maximum envy, or allocating it to the most envious agent.

Nevertheless, we prove, in Theorem 2.6, that there exists a deterministic polynomial-time algorithm with the same envy bound as the random allocation algorithm (up to logarithmic factors). The former algorithm is the result of derandomizing the latter with the method of *pessimistic estimators* [15]. Specifically, we define a potential function $\phi(t)$ that depends on the values of the first $t$ items and the allocations of the first $t-1$ items. Out algorithm allocates item $t$ in a way that $\phi(t)$ is minimized. Our proof has three main ingredients. First, the potential function is nonincreasing, i.e., $\phi(t+1) \leq \phi(t)$. Second, we prove that the potential at time $t$ is an overestimation of the probability of having large envy if in steps $t+1$ through $T$ we allocate items uniformly at random. Formally, $\phi(t) \geq \sum_{i,j\in[n]:i\neq j} \Pr[\text{Envy}_T^{ij} > \lambda]$, where $\lambda$ is the (target) performance of our derandomized algorithm. Lastly, we show that $\phi(0) < 1$. Note that characterizing the adversary's optimal strategy is not a hurdle here: since our algorithm is deterministic, adaptivity does not help. Combined, the three ingredients imply that greedily minimizing the potential function $\phi$ achieves $\text{Envy}_T \in \tilde{O}(\sqrt{T/n})$.

Having completed the picture for the setting where one item arrives at a time, in Section 3 we proceed to study a more general model. Suppose, as before, that $T$ items with adversarially chosen values arrive over time. Instead of arriving one by one, as assumed in Section 2, items arrive in *batches* of size $m$. In other words, at each time step a batch of $m$ items arrives, for a total of $T/m$ batches. To motivate this, note that in the food bank setting it is reasonable to wait until the end of the day before allocating all food donations that arrived that day. When batch $t$ arrives, the algorithm learns the values of all $m$ items for all agents, and must allocate these items immediately and irrevocably, before the next batch arrives. We use $\text{Envy}_{T,m}$ to denote the envy after the allocation of $T$ items, arriving in batches of size $m$, with the convention that $\text{Envy}_{T,1} = \text{Envy}_T$. Since the allocation algorithm is less myopic in this setting, it is natural to expect stronger performance guarantees than in the $m = 1$ case. For example, in the extreme case where $m = T$, there exist algorithms that are envy free up to one good, so $\text{Envy}_{T,T} \leq 1$.

The upper bound of Theorem 2.1 when $m = 1$ may be interpreted as the expected distance from the origin of a random walk that remains stationary with probability $1 - 2/n$, and increases or decreases by 1, each with probability $1/n$. The "step size" of 1 is the maximum change in the envy between any pair of agents after the allocation of a single item; the number of nonstationary steps is expected to be $2T/n$. This interpretation informs our approach when items arrive in batches. It is easy to find an EF1 allocation for every batch of items (round-robin suffices). Under such an allocation the maximum change in any pairwise envy due to a single batch remains 1; however, the value of an agent's bundle is likely to change with every batch. Since there are $T/m$ batches ("steps" in the random walk), we may expect a bound of the form $\text{Envy}_{T,m} \in \tilde{O}(\sqrt{T/m})$. Indeed, our main result for this setting, given in Theorem 3.3, is a deterministic algorithm that achieves this bound.

To realize this intuition, we first need to overcome a technical obstacle. Even though it is easy to find an allocation with small pairwise envy for a given batch, it is not obvious how to find allocations with low pairwise envy such that randomly outputting one of them results in an (*ex ante*) envy-free allocation. In the random walk interpretation, we need to keep the envy between agents $i$ and $j$ stationary in expectation, while at the same time maintaining a small step size. This is a crucial argument in the analysis of the one-by-one setting, in which it is trivially satisfied by allocating each item uniformly at random.

We overcome this obstacle by leveraging a result from the literature on continuous cake cutting, which allows us to show, for each batch, the existence of a fractional allocation that is entirely envy free and can be written as a convex combination of integral allocations with constant pairwise envy. We then use ideas from the derandomization of the random allocation algorithm of Section 2.2 to give a deterministic algorithm for the batch setting.[2] Finally, we prove that the lower bound for the $m = 1$ setting may be extended to show that $\text{Envy}_{T,m} \in \Omega(\sqrt{T/(mn)})$.

[2]Interestingly, we do not explicitly derandomize a specific randomized allocation algorithm as in Section 2.

### 1.2 Related Work

Conceptually our paper is related to the growing literature on *online* or *dynamic* fair division [1, 2, 9, 11, 13, 20]. In particular, motivated by applications to the food bank domain, Aleksandrov et al. [1] introduce and analyze a closely related setting where indivisible items arrive online. However, they generally assume that all values are in $\{0, 1\}$, i.e., each agent "likes" or "dislikes" every item. They introduce two simple mechanisms, LIKE and BALANCED LIKE; the former allocates the current item uniformly at random among agents who like it, whereas the latter allocates the current item uniformly at random among agents who like it and have so far received the fewest items. The analysis of these mechanisms focuses on properties such as strategyproofness, envy-freeness, and impact on welfare. Most relevant to us is the observation that BALANCED LIKE is EF1. This also highlights the technical differences between our setting and theirs, because, as noted above, with general values EF1 is impossible.

Our paper is also related to the vast body of work on *online learning* [6]. In the quintessential setting, *experts learning* (with full-information feedback), there are $T$ days, and on each day the algorithm chooses to follow the advice of one of $n$ experts. Then, the value of each expert is revealed, and the algorithm gains the value of the expert whose advice it chose to follow. The algorithm's regret is the difference between the total value accumulated by the best expert in hindsight and the value it itself has accumulated; a *no-regret learning algorithm* has the property that the ratio between regret and time goes to zero (*vanishing regret* may have been a more accurate term). Similarly, we are also interested in the difference in value accumulated over time. However, to the best of our knowledge the two problems are technically unrelated. To appreciate the difference, note that in our setting the values of the current item to all agents are known to the algorithm. But if the values of the different experts were known in the expert learning setting, the problem would be trivial — the algorithm would simply choose the expert with maximum value. Nevertheless, some of our notations were chosen to be consistent with those used in the online learning literature.

Finally, we can make a technical connection to the literature on *vector balancing games* [17]. At each time step $t \in [T]$, the adversary picks an $n$-dimensional vector with values in $[-1, 1]$, and the algorithm chooses to multiply this vector by either $-1$ or $+1$ and add it to a running partial sum vector. In one version of this game, the goal of the algorithm is to minimize the maximum entry of the partial sum vector, while the adversary wishes to maximize that quantity. For the case where $n = 2$ and items arrive one by one, our setting can be reduced to a version of vector balancing games equipped with a weaker adversary. This means that the upper bound of Spencer [17] applies to our setting (and matches our results): there exists a deterministic algorithm that guarantees envy in $O(\sqrt{T})$ when $n = 2$. Conversely, our lower bound for $n = 2$ matches the lower bound from that paper, indicating that the ostensibly weaker adversary that we consider — restricted to picking values from just one orthant — has roughly the same strength as the stronger adversary of Spencer [17]; consequently, our lower bound is significantly more involved. For more than two agents, the two problems appear unrelated, and, moreover, the batch setting has no equivalent in the vector balancing games literature.

## 2 WHEN ITEMS ARRIVE ONE BY ONE

In this section, we discuss our basic setting, in which, at each time step, exactly one item arrives. Proofs missing from this section can be found in the full version of this paper.

### 2.1 Random Allocation

A natural randomized algorithm for the case where items arrive one by one is to allocate each item to an agent selected uniformly at random; we refer to this as the *random allocation algorithm.* We analyze the random allocation algorithm by first characterizing the adversary's optimal strategy. We prove that for an adaptive adversary who maximizes $\mathbb{E}[\text{Envy}_T]$, where the expectation is with respect to the randomness of the algorithm, the optimal strategy is integral, that is, all values are in $\{0,1\}$. Using this, we show that the optimal strategy, in fact, assigns $v_{it} = 1$ for all $i \in [n], t \in [T]$. This optimal adversary strategy is nonadaptive, and therefore, since all the randomness is coming from the algorithm, the random variables for the envy between agents $i$ and $j$ at times $t$ and $t'$ are independent. Standard concentration inequalities for the envy between any pair of agents, combined with a union bound over all such pairs, gives an upper bound on the expected envy.

Theorem 2.1. *Suppose that $T \geq n \log T$, where* log *is the natural logarithm. Then the random allocation algorithm guarantees that $\mathbb{E}[\text{Envy}_T] \in O(\sqrt{T \log T/n})$.*

Note that the assumption of $T \geq n \log T$ is innocuous, otherwise we can give each agent at most $\log T$ items to achieve $\text{Envy}_T \leq \log T$.

Proof of Theorem 2.1. Consider a game tree[3] with nodes on $T+1$ levels. Every node on level $1, \ldots, T$ has $n$ outgoing arcs labeled $1, \ldots, n$. The leaf nodes on level $T+1$ are labeled by the maximum envy for the corresponding path. Let $\Omega$ be the set of all paths from the root to a leaf node, so $|\Omega| = n^T$. Equivalently, $\Omega$ is the set of all possible allocations of the $T$ items. For an allocation $\omega \in \Omega$, denote by $\omega_t \in [n]$ the agent to whom item $t \in [T]$ was allocated by $\omega$.

A fully adaptive strategy $s$ for the adversary is defined by labeling every internal node $u$ with a value vector $s(u)$, where $s(u)_i$ is the value of agent $i$ for the item corresponding to node $u$. The algorithm's strategy consists of selecting an outgoing edge, corresponding to an allocation of the item with valuation $s(u)$, at every node $u$. The adversary's strategy is allowed to depend on the allocations and valuations so far, i.e., the path from the root to $u$.

For a given adversary strategy $s$ and an allocation $\omega$, let $\text{Envy}^{ij}(s,\omega)$ denote the envy of agent $i$ for agent $j$. Denote with $\text{Envy}(s,\omega) = \max_{i,j \in [n]} \text{Envy}^{ij}(s,\omega)$ the maximum envy experienced by any agent. The objective of the adversary is to choose a strategy $s$ that maximizes the expected envy $\mathbb{E}[\text{Envy}(s,\omega)]$, where the expectation is taken over allocating every item uniformly at random.

We consider the algorithm that allocates every item uniformly at random. This is equivalent to picking a random outgoing edge at each node $u$. The following two lemmas show that the adversary labels every internal node of this tree with the vector $\mathbf{1}^n$. These lemmas are inspired by the work of Sanders [16] on load balancing.

Lemma 2.2. *The adversary has an optimal adaptive strategy that labels every internal node of the game tree with a vector in $\{0,1\}^n$.*

In a nutshell, Lemma 2.2 follows from the fact that under any allocation algorithm, for every agent's valuation of any item, it is possible to compute whether that item increases or decreases the maximum envy (in expectation). If it increases (resp. decreases) the maximum envy, the adversary benefits by increasing (resp. decreasing) the corresponding valuation to 1 (resp. to 0).

While the previous result holds for any allocation strategy, the following lemma leverages specific properties of the random allocation algorithm.

Lemma 2.3. *The adversary has an optimal adaptive strategy that labels every internal node of the game tree with the vector $\mathbf{1}^n$.*

[3]Typically we would think of an extensive-form game with nodes associated with the algorithm or the adversary, and arcs corresponding to actions (allocation of the current item in the case of the algorithm, value vector in the case of the adversary). However, because we consider a fixed algorithm here, it is more convenient to imagine an unusual, adversary-oriented game tree.

Proof. By Lemma 2.2, the adversary has an optimal strategy that labels every internal node with a vector in $\{0,1\}^n$. Let $s$ be such an optimal strategy with the smallest number of zeros, and suppose (for the sake of contradiction) that there exist internal nodes that are not labeled $\mathbf{1}^n$. Let $u$ on layer $\ell \in [T]$ be the node closest to a leaf node for which $s(u)$ contains a 0 and $s(u') = \mathbf{1}^n$ for all descendants $u'$ of $u$. Without loss of generality assume $s(u)_i = 0$, so agent $i$ has value 0 for item $\ell$ at node $u$. Define a strategy $s'$ identical to $s$ except that $s'(u)_i = 1$. Let $j(\omega) \in \arg\max_{j\in[n]} \textsc{Envy}^{ij}(s,\omega)$.

For any fixed $\omega \in \Omega$, changing $s$ to $s'$ only changes the envy of agent $i$ and only for paths that go through $u$. In particular, if $\omega_\ell \neq i$, the envy of agent $i$ toward agent $\omega_\ell$ increases by 1, which only helps the adversary. By contrast, if $\omega_\ell = i$, the envy of agent $i$ decreases by 1, toward every agent $j$ such that $\textsc{Envy}^{ij}(s,\omega) > 0$; the maximum envy, $\textsc{Envy}(s,\omega)$, is only affected if $\textsc{Envy}(s,\omega) = \textsc{Envy}^{i,j(\omega)}(s,\omega)$.

Thus, let $\omega \in \Omega$ be an arbitrary path going through $u$ with $\omega_\ell = i$ and satisfying $\textsc{Envy}(s,\omega) = \textsc{Envy}^{i,j(\omega)}(s,\omega) > 0$. Since agent $i$ may not have been the unique agent having envy equal to $\textsc{Envy}(s,\omega)$, $\textsc{Envy}(s',\omega) \geq \textsc{Envy}(s,\omega) - 1$. Now consider the path $\omega'$ that is identical to $\omega$ except that $\omega_\ell = j(\omega)$. Observe that $\textsc{Envy}(s',\omega') = \textsc{Envy}(s,\omega') + 1$. Hence, any decrease in envy due to allocating item $\ell$ to agent $i$ on $\omega$ is compensated for (in the calculation of expected envy) along $\omega'$. Since $\omega$ was picked arbitrarily and the mapping $\omega \mapsto \omega'$ is injective, it follows that the expected envy under $s'$ is at least the expected envy under $s$, and $s'$ has fewer zeros than $s$, contradicting our assumption on $s$. □

The fact that the adversary is adaptive naturally introduces a dependence in the change in any pairwise envy from one arrival to the next. The value of Lemma 2.3 lies in the fact that it allows us to circumvent this dependence as though we are dealing with a nonadaptive adversary and express any pairwise envy as the sum of independent random variables.

Specifically, given this adversary strategy, define independent random variables

$$X_t^{ij} = \begin{cases} -1, & \text{with probability } 1/n, \\ 0, & \text{with probability } 1 - 2/n, \\ 1, & \text{with probability } 1/n \end{cases}$$

for all $t \in [T]$, $i,j \in [n]$. Clearly, $\textsc{Envy}_T^{ij} = \max_{i,j\in[n]}\{\sum_{t=1}^T X_t^{ij}, 0\}$. For each $X_t^{ij}$, $\mathbb{E}[X_t^{ij}] = 0$, $\mathbb{E}[(X_t^{ij})^2] = 2/n$ and $|X_t^{ij}| \leq 1$. We use a version of Bernstein's inequality to bound the probability of having large envy between any pair of agents $i$ and $j$.

Lemma 2.4 (Bernstein 4). *Let $X_1, \ldots, X_T$ be independent variables with $\mathbb{E}[X_t] = 0$ and $|X_t| \leq M$ almost surely for all $t \in [T]$. Then, for all $\lambda > 0$,*

$$\Pr\left[\sum_{t=1}^T X_t > \lambda\right] \leq \exp\left(-\frac{\frac{1}{2}\lambda^2}{\sum_{t=1}^T \mathbb{E}\left[X_t^2\right] + \frac{1}{3}M\lambda}\right).$$

When applying this result to $\textsc{Envy}_T^{ij}$ (which equals $\sum_{t=1}^T X_t^{ij}$ when envy exists), it follows that

$$\Pr\left[\textsc{Envy}_T^{ij} \geq \lambda\right] = \Pr\left[\sum_{t=1}^T X_t^{ij} \geq \lambda\right] \leq \exp\left(-\frac{\frac{1}{2}\lambda^2}{\frac{2T}{n} + \frac{1}{3}\lambda}\right) = \exp\left(-\frac{3n\lambda^2}{12T + 2\lambda n}\right).$$

Let $\lambda = 10\sqrt{T\log T/n}$. Taking a union bound gives

$$\Pr\left[\textsc{Envy}_T \geq \lambda\right] = \Pr\left[\exists i,j \in [n] \text{ such that } \textsc{Envy}_T^{ij} \geq \lambda\right] \leq n^2 \exp\left(-\frac{300T\log T}{12T + 20\sqrt{nT\log T}}\right) \leq \frac{1}{T},$$

where the last inequality uses the assumption that $T \geq n \log T$. Since the maximum possible envy is $T$, the desired bound on expected envy directly follows. □

## 2.2 Derandomization with Pessimistic Estimators

The astute reader might have noticed that considering an adaptive adversary induces an extensive-form game of complete information between the algorithm and the adversary. In such games, randomization does not provide any benefit to either agent, as the backward induction solution is optimal [3]. This implies that there exists a deterministic algorithm with the same envy guarantee as the random allocation algorithm, i.e., $\text{Envy}_T \in \tilde{O}(\sqrt{T/n})$. However, it is *a priori* unclear whether this can be achieved in polynomial time. In fact, simple deterministic algorithms do not even lead to vanishing envy, as the following example shows.

*Example 2.5.* Consider the algorithm that at step $t$ allocates the item to the agent with the maximum envy (if she has positive value for the item, and otherwise, say, allocates to the agent with the highest value for the item). We claim that it leads to $\text{Envy}_T \in \Omega(T)$.

We construct an example where each agent envies the other by $t = 2$. For $t \geq 3$, whenever agent $i$ has maximum envy, we present an item with value $\epsilon$ for her, and value 1 for the other agent. Table 1 summarizes the analysis.

Table 1. Blindly allocating to the agent with the highest envy leads to constant per-round envy.

| $t$ | 1 | 2 | 3 | 4 | 5 | ... |
|---|---|---|---|---|---|---|
| Value of agent 1 | ($1/2$) | 1 | ($\epsilon$) | 1 | ($\epsilon$) | ... |
| Value of agent 2 | $1/2$ | ($1/4$) | 1 | ($\epsilon$) | 1 | ... |
| Envy of agent 1 | $-1/2$ | $1/2$ | $1/2 - \epsilon$ | $3/2 - \epsilon$ | $3/2 - 2\epsilon$ | ... |
| Envy of agent 2 | $1/2$ | $1/4$ | $5/4$ | $5/4 - \epsilon$ | $9/4 - \epsilon$ | ... |

For $t \geq 2$, the envy of each agent increases by 1 every two steps. Therefore, the maximum envy at step $2t$ is approximately $t$, and $\text{Envy}_T/T$ approaches $1/2$ as $T$ goes to infinity.

In the full version of this paper, we show that the average per-round envy is constant for another natural algorithm, which allocates item $t$ in a way that the maximum envy after allocation is as small as possible. These examples show that even though a simple randomized algorithm is optimal and there exists a deterministic algorithm with the same guarantee, simple deterministic algorithms are not able to provide any useful bounds.

Nevertheless, we are able to match the randomized bound of Theorem 2.1 by derandomizing the random allocation algorithm with the method of *pessimistic estimators* [15]. The outcome is an intuitively pleasing, polynomial-time, deterministic algorithm that at each step minimizes a potential function, which is essentially a penalty function exponential in each of the pairwise envy expressions.

Theorem 2.6. *Suppose that $T \geq n \log n$. Then there exists a polynomial-time, deterministic algorithm that achieves $\text{Envy}_T \in O(\sqrt{T \log n/n})$.*

The rest of this section is devoted to the proof of Theorem 2.6.

### The Algorithm

We define a potential function $\phi(t)$ that depends on $n$, $T$, the values of the first $t$ items, as well as their allocations. When item $t$ arrives, we allocate it to the agent for which the value of $\phi(t)$ is minimized. Call this algorithm $\mathcal{A}^*$. Since our algorithm is deterministic, an adversary that wants to maximize $\textsc{Envy}_T$ does not gain from being adaptive. It therefore suffices to analyze our algorithm for an arbitrary choice of item values.

Theorem 2.6 follows from choosing $\phi(t)$ in a way that satisfies three particular properties, stated in the following three lemmas. Given $t \in [T]$, let $\mathcal{A}^t$ be the algorithm that allocates, for all $\ell \in [t]$, the item $\ell$ to an agent for which $\phi(\ell)$ is minimized, and the remaining items $t+1, \ldots, T$ uniformly at random. Let $\textsc{Envy}_T^{ij}(\mathcal{A}^t)$ be the envy of agent $i$ for agent $j$ at the end of the execution of $\mathcal{A}^t$.

Lemma 2.7. $\phi(t) \geq \sum_{i,j\in[n]} \Pr\left[\textsc{Envy}_T^{ij}(\mathcal{A}^t) > 10\sqrt{T\log n/n}\right]$.

Lemma 2.8. *For all* $t \in [T-1]$, $\phi(t+1) \leq \phi(t)$.

Lemma 2.9. *For* $T \geq n\log n$, $\phi(0) < 1$.

Proof of Theorem 2.6. Notice that $\mathcal{A}^T$ is exactly the same as the algorithm $\mathcal{A}^*$. Lemmas 2.8 and 2.9 imply that $\phi(T) < 1$. Combining with Lemma 2.7, we get that for any choice of item values, and therefore for the optimal adversary strategy,

$$\Pr\left[\exists i,j \in [n] : \textsc{Envy}_T^{ij}(\mathcal{A}^T) > 10\sqrt{\frac{T\log n}{n}}\right] \leq \sum_{i,j\in[n]} \Pr\left[\textsc{Envy}_T^{ij}(\mathcal{A}^T) > 10\sqrt{\frac{T\log n}{n}}\right] \leq \phi(T) < 1.$$

Since $\mathcal{A}^T$ is deterministic — all items have been allocated after time $T$ — the inequality above implies that, for the allocation of items by $\mathcal{A}^T$, there is no $i,j \in [n]$ such that $\textsc{Envy}_T^{ij} > 10\sqrt{T\log n/n}$, and we conclude that

$$\textsc{Envy}_T = \max_{i,j\in[n]} \textsc{Envy}_T^{ij} \leq 10\sqrt{\frac{T\log n}{n}} \in O\left(\sqrt{\frac{T\log n}{n}}\right). \qquad \square$$

### Setup

We now define $\phi(t)$ and prove that it satisfies the desired properties from Lemmas 2.7, 2.8, and 2.9. For $i,j,k \in [n]$ and $t \in [T]$, let $y_{tk}^{ij}$ be a helper variable for the effect on envy between agents $i$ and $j$ when item $t$ goes to agent $k$, i.e.,

$$y_{tk}^{ij} = \begin{cases} -1, & \text{if } k = i, \\ 0, & \text{if } k \neq i,j, \\ 1, & \text{if } k = j, \end{cases}$$

and let $y_t^{ij}$ be the same but with the dependence on $k$ implicit (as $k$ is exactly determined given an allocation). Denote with $f_{ij}(t) = \sum_{\ell=1}^{t} y_\ell^{ij} v_{i\ell}$ the net value agent $i$ has for agent $j$'s allocation with respect to her own at time $t$. Notice that $\textsc{Envy}_t^{ij} = \max\{f_{ij}(t), 0\}$. Let $C = (1 + (e^s + e^{-s} - 2)/n)$, where $s$ is a damping parameter that depends only on $T$ and $n$. We use

$$s = \sqrt{2\log\left(1 + \frac{n\log n}{T}\right)},$$

and let $\lambda = 10\sqrt{T\log n/n}$ be the target maximum envy that the algorithm allows.

Define the potential function at time $t$ as $\phi(t) = \sum_{i,j\in[n]:i\neq j} \phi_{ij}(t)$, where for $i,j \in [n]$,

$$\phi_{ij}(t) = C^{T-t} \cdot \exp\left(s\left(f_{ij}(t) - \lambda\right)\right).$$

### The Proofs

Proof of Lemma 2.7. For all $\ell \in [t]$, item $\ell$ has been allocated in order to minimize $\phi(\ell)$. It suffices to show that at any time $t \leq T$, for any pair of agents $i, j$, with $\lambda = 10\sqrt{T \log n/n}$,

$$\Pr\left[f_{ij}(t) + \sum_{\ell=t+1}^{T} X_\ell^{ij} v_{i\ell} > \lambda\right] \leq \phi_{ij}(t), \tag{1}$$

where $X_\ell^{ij}$ is a random variable that takes values $-1$ and $1$ with probability $1/n$ each, and it takes value 0 with probability $1 - 2/n$. Notice that $\textsc{Envy}_T^{ij}(\mathcal{A}^t) = \max\{f_{ij}(t) + \sum_{\ell=t+1}^{T} X_\ell^{ij} v_{i\ell}, 0\}$; summing up over all pairs $i, j$ proves the lemma. Equation (1) follows from

$$\begin{aligned}
\Pr\left[f_{ij}(t) + \sum_{\ell=t+1}^{T} X_\ell^{ij} v_{i\ell} > \lambda\right] &= \Pr\left[e^{s\left(f_{ij}(t) + \sum_{\ell=t+1}^{T} X_\ell^{ij} v_{i\ell}\right)} > e^{s\lambda}\right] \\
&\leq e^{-s\lambda} \cdot \mathbb{E}\left[e^{s\left(f_{ij}(t) + \sum_{\ell=t+1}^{T} X_\ell^{ij} v_{i\ell}\right)}\right] && \text{(Markov's ineq.)} \\
&= e^{s(f_{ij}(t) - \lambda)} \cdot \mathbb{E}\left[\prod_{\ell=t+1}^{T} e^{s X_\ell^{ij} v_{i\ell}}\right] \\
&= e^{s(f_{ij}(t) - \lambda)} \prod_{\ell=t+1}^{T} \mathbb{E}\left[e^{s X_\ell^{ij} v_{i\ell}}\right] && \text{(independence)} \\
&= e^{s(f_{ij}(t) - \lambda)} \prod_{\ell=t+1}^{T} \left(1 - \frac{2}{n} + \frac{e^{s v_{i\ell}}}{n} + \frac{e^{-s v_{i\ell}}}{n}\right) \\
&\leq e^{s(f_{ij}(t) - \lambda)} \prod_{\ell=t+1}^{T} \left(1 - \frac{2}{n} + \frac{e^{s}}{n} + \frac{e^{-s}}{n}\right) \\
&= e^{s(f_{ij}(t) - \lambda)} \left(1 + \frac{e^s + e^{-s} - 2}{n}\right)^{T-t} \\
&= \phi_{ij}(t).
\end{aligned}$$

The second inequality follows from the fact that $e^x + e^{-x}$ is nondecreasing for $x \geq 0$. □

Proof of Lemma 2.8. Denote with $\phi_k(t+1)$ the potential function after giving item $t+1$ to agent $k$. We show that $(1/n) \sum_{k \in [n]} \phi_k(t+1) \leq \phi(t)$, which implies the desired result, as by definition of $\mathcal{A}^*$ we have $\phi(t+1) = \min_{k \in [n]} \phi_k(t+1)$. Recall that, for distinct $i, j, k \in [n]$, $y_{tk}^{ij}$ takes values $-1$, $1$, and 0 depending on whether item $t$ was allocated to agent $i$, $j$, or $k$. Thus, $f_{ij}(t+1) = f_{ij}(t) + y_{t+1,k}^{ij} v_{i,t+1}$.

$$\begin{aligned}
\frac{1}{n} \sum_{k \in [n]} \phi_k(t+1) &= \frac{1}{n} \sum_{k \in [n]} \sum_{i,j \in [n]: i \neq j} e^{s\left(f_{ij}(t) + y_{t+1,k}^{ij} v_{i,t+1} - \lambda\right)} C^{T-(t+1)} \\
&= \frac{1}{n} C^{T-(t+1)} \sum_{i,j \in [n]: i \neq j} e^{s(f_{ij}(t) - \lambda)} \sum_{k \in [n]} e^{s y_{t+1,k}^{ij} v_{i,t+1}} \\
&= \frac{1}{n} C^{T-(t+1)} \sum_{i,j \in [n]: i \neq j} e^{s(f_{ij}(t) - \lambda)} \left(e^{s \cdot (1) \cdot v_{i,t+1}} + e^{s \cdot (-1) \cdot v_{i,t+1}} + \sum_{k \in [n] \setminus \{i,j\}} e^{s \cdot (0) \cdot v_{i,t+1}}\right)
\end{aligned}$$

$$= \frac{1}{n} C^{T-(t+1)} \sum_{i,j \in [n]: i \neq j} e^{s(f_{ij}(t) - \lambda)} \left( e^{s v_{i,t+1}} + e^{-s v_{i,t+1}} + n - 2 \right)$$
$$\leq \frac{1}{n} C^{T-(t+1)} \sum_{i,j \in [n]: i \neq j} e^{s(f_{ij}(t) - \lambda)} \left( e^{s} + e^{-s} + n - 2 \right)$$
$$= C^{T-(t+1)} \sum_{i,j \in [n]: i \neq j} e^{s(f_{ij}(t) - \lambda)} \cdot C \; = \; \phi(t). \qquad \square$$

Proof of Lemma 2.9.

$$\phi(0) = \sum_{i,j \in [n]: i \neq j} \phi_{ij}(0) = \sum_{i,j \in [n]: i \neq j} C^T e^{s f_{ij}(0) - s\lambda} < n^2 C^T e^{-s\lambda} = e^{-s\lambda + 2\log n + T \log C}.$$

We want the above expression to be less than one, or equivalently $s\lambda - 2\log n - T\log C > 0$. Using $1 + x \leq e^x$ implies that

$$C = 1 + \frac{e^s + e^{-s} - 2}{n} \leq e^{(e^s + e^{-s} - 2)/n} = e^{2(\cosh(s) - 1)/n}.$$

Furthermore, $\cosh(x) \leq \exp\left(x^2/2\right)$, so that $C \leq \exp\left(2(\exp\left(s^2/2\right) - 1)/n\right)$. Therefore,

$$s\lambda - 2\log n - T\log C \geq s\lambda - 2\log n - \frac{2T}{n}\left(e^{s^2/2} - 1\right)$$
$$= 10\sqrt{2\log\left(1 + \frac{n\log n}{T}\right)\frac{T\log n}{n}} - 2\log n - \frac{2T}{n}\left(\frac{n\log n}{T}\right)$$
$$= \left(\frac{5}{\sqrt{2}}\sqrt{\frac{T}{n\log n}\log\left(1 + \frac{n\log n}{T}\right)} - 1\right) 4\log n.$$

We factored out $4\log n$ for convenience; it remains to show the parenthetical expression is positive. The function $\sqrt{x\log(1 + 1/x)}$ is increasing for all $x \geq 0$. Set $x = T/(n\log n)$, and note that the assumption $T \geq n\log n$ implies $x \geq 1$. Observing that $5\sqrt{\log(2)/2} > 1$ completes the proof. $\square$

## 2.3 Lower Bound

In this section, we show that an adversary can guarantee $\text{Envy}_T \in \Omega((T/n)^{r/2})$ for any $r < 1$. It follows that the deterministic algorithm we presented in Section 2.1 is optimal (up to a logarithmic factor). We first prove the bound for $n = 2$, followed by the case of an arbitrary number of agents.

### Lower Bound for Two Agents

Lemma 2.10. *For $n = 2$ and any $r < 1$, there exists an adversary strategy for setting item values such that any algorithm must have $\text{Envy}_T \in \Omega(T^{r/2})$.*

Proof. Label the agents $L$ and $R$, and let $\{v_0 = 1, v_1, v_2, \ldots\}$ be a decreasing sequence of values that we specify later, satisfying $v_d - v_{d+1} < v_{d'} - v_{d'+1}$ for all $d' < d$. The adversary keeps track of the *state* of the game, and the current state defines its strategy for choosing the agents' valuations. The adversary strategy that implies the lower bound is illustrated in Figure 1. Start in state 0, which we will also refer to as $L_0$ and $R_0$, for which the adversary sets the value of the arriving item as $(1, 1)$. To the left of state 0 are states labeled $L_1, L_2, \ldots$; in state $L_d$, the item that arrives has value $(1, v_d)$. To the right of state 0 are states labeled $R_1, R_2, \ldots$; in state $R_d$, an item will arrive with value $(v_d, 1)$. Whenever the algorithm allocates an item to agent $L$ (resp. $R$), which we will refer to as making an $L$ (resp. $R$) step, the adversary moves one state to the left (resp. right) to determine the value of the next item.

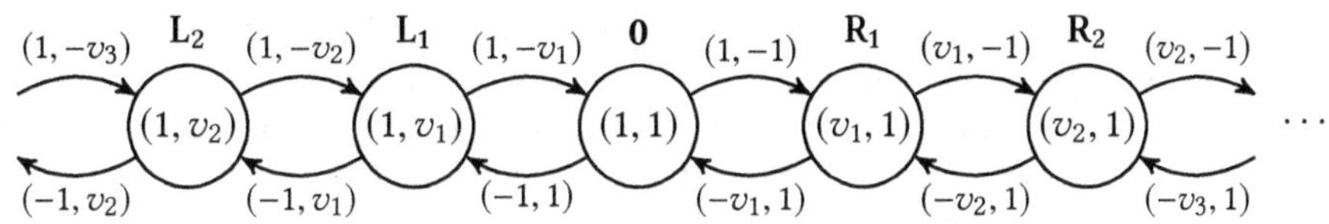


Fig. 1. Adversary strategy for two-agent lower bound. In state $L_d$, an item valued $(1, v_d)$ arrives, while in state $R_d$, an item valued $(v_d, 1)$ arrives. The arrows indicate whether agent $L$ or agent $R$ is given the item in each state. The arrows are labeled by the amount envy changes after that item is allocated.

We construct the optimal allocation algorithm against this adversary, and show that for this algorithm the envy at some time step $t \in [T]$ will be at least $\Omega(T^{r/2})$ for the given $r < 1$. This immediately implies Lemma 2.10: if the envy is sufficiently large at some time step $t$ the adversary can guarantee the same envy at time $T$ by making all future items valued at zero by both agents.

The intuition for the adversary strategy we have defined is that it forces the algorithm to avoid entering state $L_d$ or $R_d$ for high $d$, as otherwise the envy of some agent will grow to $v_0 + v_1 + \cdots + v_d$, which will be large by our choice of $\{v_d\}$. At the same time, if an $L$ step is taken at state $L_d$, followed by a later return to state $L_d$, the envy of $R$ increases by at least $v_d - v_{d+1}$; we choose $\{v_d\}$ so that this increase in envy is large enough to ensure that any algorithm which spends too many time steps close to state 0 incurs a large cost.

By the pigeonhole principle, either the states to the left or to the right of state 0 are visited for at least half the time. For the rest of this section, we assume, without loss of generality, that our optimal algorithm spends time $T' = \lceil T/2 \rceil$ in the "left" states $(L_0, L_1, \ldots)$, and that $T'$ is an even number. We prove that the envy of agent $R$ grows large at some time step $t$. We ignore any time the algorithm spends in the states $R_d$, $d \geq 1$. To see why this is without loss of generality, consider first a cycle spent in the right states that starts at $R_0$ with an item allocated to $R$ and eventually returns to $R_0$. In such a cycle, an equal number of items are allocated to both agents. All of these items have value 1 to agent $R$, yielding a net effect of 0 on agent $R$'s envy.[4] The other case is when the algorithm starts at $R_0$ but does not return to $R_0$. This scenario can only occur once, which means that the algorithm has already taken $T'$ steps on the left side; the allocation of these items does not affect our proof.

Let $K$ be an integer such that $K \leq \sqrt{T'/2}$, which we will show is without loss of generality. Denote by OPT$(K)$ the set of envy-minimizing allocation algorithms that spend the $T'$ steps in states $L_0, \ldots, L_K$ (and reach $L_K$). Note that the algorithm aims to minimize the maximum envy at any point in its execution. Let $\mathcal{A}^*(K)$ be the following algorithm, starting at $L_0$: Allocate the first $K$ items to agent $L$, thus arriving at state $L_K$. For the next $T' - 2K$ items, alternate between allocating to agents $R$ and $L$, thereby alternating between states $L_{K-1}$ and $L_K$. Allocate the remaining $K$ items to agent $R$. We show $\mathcal{A}^*(K)$ belongs to OPT$(K)$.

Lemma 2.11. $\mathcal{A}^*(K) \in \text{OPT}(K)$.

Proof. An algorithm that starts at state 0 and spends $T'$ steps in the left states can be described as a sequence of choices $s_t \in \{L, R\}$ for $t \in [T']$ such that $s_1 = L$, and at every $t \in [T']$, agent $L$ has received at least as many of the first $t$ items as agent $R$ (to avoid entering the right states). We refer to the state at time $t$ as the state *after* the algorithm choice $s_t$.

[4]We ignore agent $L$ completely, as our analysis is of the envy of agent $R$.

Consider any $\mathcal{A}(K) \in \mathsf{OPT}(K)$. We show that the corresponding sequence of allocations satisfy: (1) at time $T'$ the state is $L_0$, so agent $L$ receives the same number of items as agent $R$; and (2) there is exactly one $R$ move at states $L_1, \ldots, L_{K-1}$. This proves the lemma, since $\mathcal{A}^*(K)$ is the only algorithm that satisfies these two conditions. We utilize the fact that the envy of an allocation sequence can be calculated from the number of $L$ and $R$ moves in every state: at state $L_d$, an $L$ move increases the envy of agent $R$ by $v_d$ while an $R$ move decreases it by $v_d$.

We start with the first property: suppose that the state at time $T'$ is not 0. Let $t$ be the last index such that $s_t = L$. Allocating $s_t = R$ instead (and $s_\ell = R$ for the remaining steps $\ell > t$) reduces the envy of agent $R$ without entering state $R_1$, a contradiction.

For the second property, it suffices to show that if $s_t = L$ and $s_{t+1} = R$, then it must be that at step $t$ the state is $L_{K-1}$ (and therefore at step $t+1$ the state is $L_K$). Assume this is not the case, and we have such a $t$ where the algorithm is in state $L_{\widehat{K}-1}$, $\widehat{K} < K$. Let $\ell$ be a step in which the algorithm is in state $L_{K-1}$, which exists by the definition of $\mathcal{A}(K)$. Assume that $\ell > t+1$ (an analogous argument can be applied to the case that $\ell < t$). We divide $T'$ into three phases: (1) the first $t-1$ items, (2) the next $\ell - (t+1)$ items, and (3) the last $T' - \ell + 2$ items and consider $s' = s_1, \ldots, s_{t-1}, s_{t+2}, \ldots, s_\ell, s_t, s_{t+1}, s_{\ell+1}, \ldots, s_{T'}$. Notice that $s'$ is $s$, except the alternating allocations $L$ then $R$ are now made at state $L_{K-1}$ instead of at $L_{\widehat{K}-1}$. By construction, sequence $s'$ never goes past state $L_K$. We now prove that, using $s'$, the envy decreases with respect to $s$ at each time step after $t-1$, contradicting the assumption $\mathcal{A}(K) \in \mathsf{OPT}(K)$.

In phase (1), the envy is unchanged. For phase (2), when using $\mathcal{A}(K)$, the pair of moves $s_t$ and $s_{t+1}$ increases envy by $v_{\widehat{K}} - v_{\widehat{K}-1}$. Hence, in comparison, $s'$ has that much less envy during each time step of phase (2). At the start of phase (3) in $s'$, the alternating allocations are performed at state $L_{K-1}$, increasing envy (in $s'$) by $v_{K-1} - v_K < v_{\widehat{K}} - v_{\widehat{K}+1}$. At all remaining steps in (3), the envy is smaller in $s'$ (compared to $s$) by $(v_{\widehat{K}} - v_{\widehat{K}+1}) - (v_{K-1} - v_K)$. This completes the proof that $\mathcal{A}(K)$ must satisfy both properties; the lemma follows. □

We analyze the envy of $\mathcal{A}^*(K)$ as a function of $K$ before optimizing $K$. Agent $R$'s maximum envy is realized at step $T' - K$, right before the sequence of $R$ moves. $\textsc{Envy}_{T'-K}$ has two terms: the envy accumulated to reach state $L_K$, and the envy from alternating $R$ and $L$ moves between states $L_K$ and $L_{K-1}$, so

$$\textsc{Envy}_{T'-K} = \sum_{d=0}^{K-1} v_d + \frac{T'-2K}{2} \cdot (v_{K-1} - v_K).$$

Given $r < 1$, define $v_d = (d+1)^r - d^r$. Notice that $\sum_{d=0}^{K-1} v_d = K^r$. This validates the initial assumption that $K \le \sqrt{T'/2}$, as otherwise $\sum_{d=0}^{K-1} v_d \ge (T'/2)^{r/2} \in \Omega(T^{r/2})$.

Lemma 2.12. $v_{K-1} - v_K \ge r(1-r)K^{r-2}$.

Applying Lemma 2.12 and distributing terms yields

$$\textsc{Envy}_{T'-K} \ge K^r - r(1-r)K^{r-1} + \frac{T'}{2} r(1-r)K^{r-2} \ge \frac{1}{2}\left(K^r + T' r(1-r)K^{r-2}\right),$$

where the second inequality uses the fact that $r(1-r) \le 1/4 < 1/2$ and assumes $K > 1$ (otherwise the envy would be linear in $T'$). To optimize $K$, noting that the second derivative of the above bound is positive for $K \le \sqrt{T'/2}$, we find the critical point:

$$\frac{\partial}{\partial K}\left(K^r + T' r(1-r)K^{r-2}\right) = rK^{r-1} - T' r(1-r)(2-r)K^{r-3} = 0 \implies K = \sqrt{T'(1-r)(2-r)}.$$

Defining $C_1 = \sqrt{(1-r)(2-r)}$ and substituting into the bound on $\textsc{Envy}_{T'-K}$, we obtain

$$\textsc{Envy}_{T'-K} \geq \frac{1}{2}\left(C_1^r (T')^{r/2} + T' r(1-r) C_1^{r-2} (T')^{r/2-1}\right) \in \Omega(T^{r/2}).$$

This completes the proof of Lemma 2.10. □

### Lower Bound for Any Number of Agents

THEOREM 2.13. *For any $n \geq 2$ and $r < 1$, there exists an adversary strategy for setting item values such that any algorithm must have $\textsc{Envy}_T \in \Omega((T/n)^{r/2})$.*

PROOF. We augment the instance of Figure 1 in the following way. In addition to the first two agents, $L$ and $R$, we have $n-2$ other agents. Each of these other agents will not value *any* of the items that arrive; hence, the nonzero values remain the same as before. State transitions work as follows. If the algorithm allocates an item to agent $L$ or agent $R$, the transitions are the same as when $n = 2$. Otherwise, the adversary will remain in the same state.

Let $T_0$ be the number of items allocated to either agent $L$ or $R$. We break the analysis into two cases. First, if $T_0 \in \Omega(T/n)$, then, $\textsc{Envy}_T \in \Omega((T/n)^{r/2})$ by the analysis of Lemma 2.10. Otherwise, $T_0 \in o(T/n)$ and therefore $T - T_0 \in \Theta(T)$, i.e., agents 3 through $n$ receive many items. This implies that there exists an agent $i \in [3, n]$ that is allocated $\Omega(T/n)$ items. Without loss of generality, at least half these items were allocated in the left states, in which agent $L$ values each item at 1, so that agent $L$ has $\Omega(T/n)$ value for the items received by agent $i$. The value of agent $L$ for her own allocation is at most $O(T_0)$, i.e., $o(T/n)$. Therefore, the envy of agent $L$ for agent $i$ is at least $\Theta(T/n) - o(T/n) \in \Theta(T/n)$. □

## 3 WHEN ITEMS ARRIVE IN BATCHES

In this section, we study the more general setting where items arrive in batches of size $m$, and the values of all items in a batch are revealed simultaneously. We assume $m$ divides $T$ for convenience.

### 3.1 Upper Bound

We use the following result from the literature on the division of *divisible* goods.

LEMMA 3.1 (STROMQUIST 18). *Suppose $n$ agents have valuation functions over the interval $[0, 1]$, such that an agent's value for a subinterval is the integral of her value density function. Then there exists an envy-free division of the interval in which every agent receives a single contiguous interval.*

It will be convenient to think of the $n$ contiguous allocations as created by $n-1$ cuts on the interval $[0, 1]$. In the context of $m$ indivisible goods with additive valuations, this result implies that, if the items are placed on a line (in any order), there exists a fractional envy-free allocation in which no agent receives more than 2 fractional items. Every item corresponds to an interval of size $1/m$, and every agent's valuation in that interval is constant and proportional to her valuation for that item. Given the solution guaranteed to exist by Lemma 3.1, every agent's allocation is between at most two cuts and therefore contains no more than 2 fractional items.[5] Such a near-integral envy-free allocation is useful, since any integral allocation found by randomized rounding is guaranteed to have small envy *ex post*, as the following lemma shows.

LEMMA 3.2. *Given $m$ items, there exists an envy-free fractional allocation $A = A_1, \ldots, A_n$, such that every agent receives at most 2 fractional items. Furthermore, if $x_{i\ell} \in [0, 1]$ is the fraction of item $\ell$ allocated to agent $i$, then randomly giving each item $\ell$ to each agent $i$ with probability $x_{i\ell}$ results in an integral allocation $A'$ where for all $i, j \in [n]$, $v_i(A'_i) \geq v_i(A'_j) - 4$.*

[5] In fact only the agents who get the first and the last contiguous interval are adjacent to one cut; all other agents' allocations are between two cuts.

Proof. The first part of the statement, that there exists an allocation $A$ that is envy-free and in which each agent receives at most 2 fractional items, follows from the previous discussion. For the second part, notice that the worst-case scenario for an agent $i$ is to not get either of the fractional items allocated to her in $A$. Furthermore, some other agent $j$ might get both of her fractional items from $A$. In this scenario, the envy of agent $i$ for agent $j$ is maximized and is at most 4 (since the value for every item is at most 1). □

In Section 2, before giving a deterministic algorithm, we first analyzed the performance of the random allocation algorithm. Crucially, our analysis characterized the optimal strategy for an adaptive adversary against the random allocation algorithm, and we showed that this strategy is in fact nonadaptive. This allowed us to use standard concentration inequalities. Proving such a characterization is much trickier in the batch case. Fortunately, we can bypass this step and directly "derandomize" the algorithm that at each step outputs the (randomly-rounded) allocation of Lemma 3.2. Our main result for this setting is the following:

Theorem 3.3. *Suppose that $T \geq m \log n$. Then there exists a deterministic algorithm that achieves $\text{Envy}_{T,m} \in O(\sqrt{T \log n / m})$.*

Again, the assumption of $T \geq m \log n$ is very weak, otherwise there are at most $T/m \leq \log n$ batches, and we can use an EF1 algorithm in each to achieve $\text{Envy}_{T,m} \leq \log n$.

## The Algorithm

We define a potential function $\phi(t)$ that depends on $n$, $T$, the values of the items in the first $t$ batches, as well as their allocations. When batch $t+1$ arrives, we first find the near-integral envy-free allocation $A^{t+1}$ (of the items in batch $t+1$) guaranteed to exist by Lemma 3.2 (we address computation below). This fractional allocation is then rounded to an integral allocation in a way that $\phi(t+1)$ is minimized. Call this algorithm $\mathcal{A}^*$. Since our algorithm is deterministic, an adversary that wants to maximize $\text{Envy}_{T,m}$ does not gain from being adaptive. Therefore, there exists some optimal (for the adversary) choice of values for items 1 through $T$. We analyze our algorithm for an arbitrary choice of item values.

Similarly to our algorithm from Section 2.2, we rely on three properties of $\phi$. Given $t \in [T/m]$, let $\mathcal{A}^t$ be the algorithm that rounds $A^\ell$ (the allocation in batch $\ell$) in a way that $\phi(\ell)$ is minimized, for all $\ell \in [1, t]$, and rounds the remaining $A^\ell$ for $\ell = t+1, \ldots, T/m$ randomly. Let $\text{Envy}^{ij}_{T,m}(\mathcal{A}^t)$ be the envy of agent $i$ for agent $j$ at the end of the execution of $\mathcal{A}^t$.

Lemma 3.4. $\phi(t) \geq \sum_{i,j \in [n]} \Pr\left[\text{Envy}^{ij}_T(\mathcal{A}^t) > 100\sqrt{T \log n/m}\right]$.

Lemma 3.5. *For all $t \in [T/m - 1]$, $\phi(t+1) \leq \phi(t)$.*

Lemma 3.6. *For $T \geq m \log n$, $\phi(0) < 1$.*

Proof of Theorem 3.3. Notice that $\mathcal{A}^{T/m}$ is exactly the same as the algorithm $\mathcal{A}^*$. Lemmas 3.5 and 3.6 imply that $\phi(T) < 1$. Combining with Lemma 3.4, we get that for any item valuations,

$$\Pr\left[\exists i, j \in [n] : \text{Envy}^{ij}_T(\mathcal{A}^*) > 100\sqrt{\frac{T \log n}{m}}\right] \leq \sum_{i,j \in [n]} \Pr\left[\text{Envy}^{ij}_T(\mathcal{A}^*) > 100\sqrt{\frac{T \log n}{m}}\right] \leq \phi(T) < 1,$$

Since $\mathcal{A}^*$ is deterministic, the inequality above implies that there is no $i, j \in [n]$ such that $\text{Envy}^{ij}_T > 100\sqrt{T \log n/m}$, and we conclude that $\text{Envy}_{T,m} \leq 100\sqrt{T \log n/m} \in O(\sqrt{T \log n/m})$. □

### Setup

In batch $t$, define $A^t = A_1^t, \ldots, A_n^t$ as the envy-free fractional solution of Lemma 3.2, in which no agent receives more than 2 fractional items. Let $\hat{A}^t = \hat{A}_1^t, \ldots, \hat{A}_n^t$ be an integral rounding of $A^t$; $\hat{A}^t$ is the actual allocation used in batch $t$. Define

$$\Delta_{ij}^t(\hat{A}^t) = \left(v_i(\hat{A}_j^t) - v_i(\hat{A}_i^t)\right) + \left(v_i(A_i^t) - v_i(A_j^t)\right)$$

and let $f_{ij}(t, \hat{A}^1, \ldots, \hat{A}^t) = \sum_{\ell=1}^{t} \Delta_{ij}^t(\hat{A}^t)$. To simplify notation, we write $f_{ij}(t)$ when the allocation is clear from context. Notice that $\textsc{Envy}_{T,m}^{ij} \leq f_{ij}(T)$; this is an inequality because $\Delta_{ij}^t$ is centered to have zero mean, while $v_i(\hat{A}_j^t) - v_i(\hat{A}_i^t)$ may have mean less than zero. Also, observe that $\hat{A}^t$ is not random. However, if we were to *randomly* round $A^t$ to an integral allocation $\hat{B}^t$, then the resulting random variable $\Delta_{ij}^t(\hat{B}^t)$ has zero mean and satisfies $|\Delta_{ij}^t(\hat{B}^t)| \leq 4$, by Lemma 3.2.

Let $\lambda = 100\sqrt{T \log n/m}$ and $s = \frac{1}{4}\log(1 + \frac{\lambda m}{4T})$. For $i, j \in [n]$, define the potential function at time $t$ for $i$ with respect to $j$ as

$$\phi_{ij}(t) = \exp\left(s f_{ij}(t) - s\lambda + \left(\frac{T}{m} - t\right)\left(e^{4s} - 4s - 1\right)\right),$$

and define the overall potential function as $\phi(t) = \sum_{i,j\in[n]:i\neq j} \phi_{ij}(t)$.

### The Proofs

The proof of Lemma 3.4 is relegated to the full version of this paper. In its proof, as in the proof of Lemma 3.5, we use the following property of bounded, centered random variables (the proof of which may also be found in the full version of this paper).

Lemma 3.7. *Let $X$ be a random variable with $\mathbb{E}[X] = 0$ and $|X| \leq 4$. Then for all $v \in [0, 1]$ it holds that $\mathbb{E}\left[e^{sXv}\right] \leq \exp\left(e^{4s} - 4s - 1\right)$.*

Proof of Lemma 3.5. We prove that there exists a rounding $\hat{A}^*$ of the fractional allocation $A^{t+1}$ of batch $t+1$ so that allocating according to $\hat{A}^*$ results in $\phi(t+1) \leq \phi(t)$. Let $x_{i\ell}^{t+1}$ be the fraction of item $\ell$ in batch $t+1$ allocated to agent $i$ in $A^{t+1}$. We show that allocating every item $\ell$ to agent $i$ with probability $x_{i\ell}^{t+1}$ makes the expected value of $\phi(t+1)$ at most $\phi(t)$. We can immediately conclude that there exists an integral allocation for which $\phi(t+1) \leq \phi(t)$.

Let $\hat{B}^{t+1}$ be a possible (rounded) integral allocation, with corresponding probability $p(\hat{B}^{t+1})$, and let $D$ be the distribution where allocation $\hat{B}^{t+1}$ appears with probability $p(\hat{B}^{t+1})$. Finally, let $\phi_{\hat{B}^{t+1}}(t+1)$ be the value of the potential function after allocating batch $t+1$ according to $\hat{B}^{t+1}$. Note that $f_{ij}(t+1, \hat{A}^1, \ldots, \hat{A}^t, \hat{B}^{t+1}) = f_{ij}(t) + \Delta_{ij}^{t+1}(\hat{B}^{t+1})$.

$$\begin{aligned}
\mathbb{E}_{\hat{B}^{t+1}\sim D}\left[\phi_{\hat{B}^{t+1}}(t+1)\right] &= \sum_{\hat{B}^{t+1}} p(\hat{B}^{t+1}) \cdot \left(e^{-s\lambda} e^{(\frac{T}{m}-t-1)(e^{4s}-4s-1)} \sum_{i,j\in[n]:i\neq j} e^{sf_{ij}(t+1,\hat{A}^1,\ldots,\hat{A}^t,\hat{B}^{t+1})}\right) \\
&= \sum_{\hat{B}^{t+1}} p(\hat{B}^{t+1}) \cdot \left(e^{-s\lambda} e^{(\frac{T}{m}-t-1)(e^{4s}-4s-1)} \sum_{i,j\in[n]:i\neq j} e^{sf_{ij}(t)+s\Delta_{ij}^{t+1}(\hat{B}^{t+1})}\right) \\
&= e^{-s\lambda} e^{(\frac{T}{m}-t-1)(e^{4s}-4s-1)} \sum_{i,j\in[n]:i\neq j} \left(e^{sf_{ij}(t)} \sum_{\hat{B}^{t+1}} p(\hat{B}^{t+1})\, e^{s\Delta_{ij}^{t+1}(\hat{B}^{t+1})}\right) \\
&\leq e^{-s\lambda} e^{(\frac{T}{m}-t-1)(e^{4s}-4s-1)} \sum_{i,j\in[n]:i\neq j} \left(e^{sf_{ij}(t)}\, \mathbb{E}_{\hat{B}^{t+1}\sim D}\left[e^{s\Delta_{ij}^{t+1}(\hat{B}^{t+1})}\right]\right).
\end{aligned}$$

We notice that $\Delta_{ij}^{t+1}(\hat{B}^{t+1})$ is a random variable (since $\hat{B}^{t+1}$ is random) that satisfies the conditions of Lemma 3.7, so we get

$$\mathbb{E}_{\hat{B}^{t+1}\sim D}\left[\phi_{\hat{B}^{t+1}}(t+1)\right] \leq e^{-s\lambda}e^{(\frac{T}{m}-t-1)(e^{4s}-4s-1)} \sum_{i,j\in[n]:i\neq j} e^{sf_{ij}(t)}e^{e^{4s}-4s-1}$$
$$= e^{-s\lambda}e^{(\frac{T}{m}-t)(e^{4s}-4s-1)} \sum_{i,j\in[n]:i\neq j} e^{sf_{ij}(t)} = \phi(t). \qquad \square$$

Proof of Lemma 3.6.

$$\begin{aligned}
\phi(0) &= \sum_{i,j\in[n]:i\neq j} \phi_{ij}(0) \\
&= \sum_{i,j\in[n]:i\neq j} \exp\left(sf_{ij}(0) - s\lambda + \frac{T}{m}\left(e^{4s} - 4s - 1\right)\right) \\
&< n^2 \exp\left(-s\lambda + \frac{T}{m}\left(e^{4s} - 4s - 1\right)\right) \\
&= n^2 \exp\left(-\frac{T}{m}\left(1 + 4s + s\frac{\lambda m}{T} - e^{4s}\right)\right) \\
&= n^2 \exp\left(-\frac{T}{m}\left(1 + 4s\left(1 + \frac{\lambda m}{4T}\right) - e^{4s}\right)\right) \\
&= n^2 \exp\left(-\frac{T}{m}\left(1 + \left(1 + \frac{\lambda m}{4T}\right)\log\left(1 + \frac{\lambda m}{4T}\right) - \left(1 + \frac{\lambda m}{4T}\right)\right)\right) \\
&= n^2 \exp\left(-\frac{T}{m}\left((1+x)\log(1+x) - x\right)\right),
\end{aligned}$$

where $x = \frac{\lambda m}{4T}$. The function $h(x) = (1+x)\log(1+x) - x$ satisfies $h(x) \geq x^2/(2+2x/3)$. Therefore,

$$\phi(0) < n^2 \exp\left(-\frac{T}{m}\left(\frac{(\frac{\lambda m}{4T})^2}{2 + \frac{2(\frac{\lambda m}{4T})}{3}}\right)\right) = n^2 \exp\left(-\frac{3m\lambda^2}{96T + 8\lambda m}\right) = \exp\left(2\log n - \frac{3m\lambda^2}{96T + 8\lambda m}\right).$$

Substituting in $\lambda = 100\sqrt{T\log n/m}$ gives: $\phi(0) \leq \exp\left(2\log n - \frac{30000T\log n}{96T + 800\sqrt{Tm\log n}}\right)$, which is strictly less than 1 for $T \geq m\log n$. $\square$

## Computational Issues

Lemma 3.2, just like Lemma 3.1, is existential and leaves unanswered the question of how to find the nearly-integral envy-free allocation for every batch. We partially address this, at least from a practical point of view, by formulating a *mixed integer program (MIP)* to compute such an allocation.

Let $x_{i\ell}$ be the fraction of item $\ell$ given to agent $i$. Binary variables $x_{i\ell}^0$ and $x_{i\ell}^1$ will sum to 0 when $x_{i\ell}$ is fractional, and sum to 1 otherwise. Lemma 3.1 implies that the following MIP is feasible:

$$\sum_{\ell=1}^{m} v_{i\ell}(x_{i\ell} - x_{j\ell}) \geq 0, \qquad \text{for all } i, j \in [n] \tag{2}$$

$$\sum_{i=1}^{n} x_{i\ell} = 1, \qquad \text{for all } \ell \in [m] \tag{3}$$

$$x^0_{i\ell} \le x_{i\ell} \le 1 - x^1_{i\ell}, \qquad \text{for all } i \in [n], \ell \in [m] \tag{4}$$

$$\sum_{\ell=1}^{m}(x^0_{i\ell} + x^1_{i\ell}) \ge m - 2, \qquad \text{for all } i \in [n] \tag{5}$$

$$x_{i\ell} \in [0,1], \qquad \text{for all } i \in [n], \ell \in [m] \tag{6}$$

$$x^0_{i\ell}, x^1_{i\ell} \in \{0,1\}, \qquad \text{for all } i \in [n], \ell \in [m] \tag{7}$$

Constraint (2) ensures that the allocation is envy free, while Constraint (3) ensures every item is fully allocated. Constraint (4) ensures that $x^0_{i\ell}$ and $x^1_{i\ell}$ sum to 0 when $x_{i\ell}$ is fractional, and sum to 1 otherwise (using the fact that these variables are binary, by Constraint (7)). Constraint (5) guarantees at most 2 fractional items per agent. These constraints may be coupled with any objective function to find a near-integral fractional solution.

Unfortunately, solving a MIP is unlikely to be computationally efficient in general. Furthermore, known hardness results for related problems [8] suggest that producing an envy-free (or approximately envy-free) and contiguous fractional allocation in our setting might be a PPAD-hard problem. Such a hardness result does not rule out a polynomial time algorithm for finding an allocation with the properties of Lemma 3.2, i.e., a fractional envy-free allocation where each agent gets at most 2 fractional items.[6] In fact, we present some tractable special cases in full version of this paper. The general problem is left open.

Another step that may seem problematic (from a computational viewpoint) is rounding the fractional allocation in a way that minimizes the potential function. However, since the potential function is convex in the allocation, this can be done efficiently.

### 3.2 Lower Bound

Our last result is a lower bound for the batch setting, which is asymptotically tight in $T/m$, but, unlike the one-by-one setting, does leave a gap in terms of the dependence on the number of agents.

THEOREM 3.8. *For any $n \ge 2$ and $r < 1$, there exists an adversary strategy for setting item values such that any algorithm must have* $\text{ENVY}_T \in \Omega((\frac{T}{mn})^{r/2})$.

PROOF. The theorem follows almost directly from Theorem 2.13. Indeed, assume that in each batch there are $m - 1$ items that are worthless to all agents. In this case the batch setting reduces to the one-by-one setting, and we obtain the lower bound given by Theorem 2.13, with a total number of items equal to the number of batches, i.e., $T' = T/m$. □

## 4 DISCUSSION

We finish with a discussion of several pertinent issues that have not been addressed so far.

*Additivity assumption.* We have assumed that agents have additive valuations for bundles of items. This common assumption is typically considered strong. But for the purpose of defining envy in our online setting we consider it to be very natural. Indeed, in an online setting, the allocated items would typically be used independently of each other. Consequently, we can interpret the envy of $i$ for $j$, $\sum_{t \in A_i} v_{it} - \sum_{t \in A_j} v_{it}$, as $\sum_{t=1}^{T} v_{it}(\mathbb{I}_{t \in A_i} - \mathbb{I}_{t \in A_j})$. Notice that this is a sum over per-round envy. In other words, the additivity assumption actually amounts to envy being additive over time.

*The partial information model.* In our model the values of agents for the current item (or batch of items) are revealed before the item is allocated, and inform that decision. One can imagine a natural variant — the *partial information model* — where the values are only revealed *after* the item

[6] For our upper bound to work, even a constant number of fractional items suffices.

has been allocated. Notice that the randomized upper bound of Theorem 2.1 carries over, because the algorithm ignores the values shown to it. So does the lower bound of Theorem 2.13, because it holds *even* against more powerful algorithms. However, the game between the algorithm and the adversary is now an extensive-form game of *incomplete* information, where randomization can potentially help. This turns out to be the case, and, in fact, deterministic algorithms cannot have vanishing envy in this setting. For more details, see the full version of this paper.

*Is low envy fair enough?* We have focused with single-minded determination on a single goal – that of minimizing envy. A possible concern is that low envy, in and of itself, is not sufficient to lead to intuitively fair outcomes, as has been observed in various contexts [7, 10]. Be that as it may, even if one is interested in a combination of low envy and other properties (Pareto efficiency comes to mind), our results establish a baseline for what one could hope for, and are therefore a crucial first step in any such investigation.

## ACKNOWLEDGMENTS

We are grateful to Noga Alon for crucial pointers to the literature on derandomization and vector balancing games, and to Hervé Moulin for his help with Lemma 3.2.

## REFERENCES


[1] M. Aleksandrov, H. Aziz, S. Gaspers, and T. Walsh. 2015. Online Fair Division: Analysing a Food Bank Problem. In *Proceedings of the 24th International Joint Conference on Artificial Intelligence (IJCAI)*. 2540–2546.

[2] M. Aleksandrov and T. Walsh. 2017. Pure Nash Equilibria in Online Fair Division. In *Proceedings of the 26th International Joint Conference on Artificial Intelligence (IJCAI)*. 42–48.

[3] S. Ben-David, A. Borodin, R. Karp, G. Tardos, and A. Wigderson. 1994. On the Power of Randomization in On-line Algorithms. *Algorithmica* 11, 1 (1994), 2–14.

[4] S. Bernstein. 1946. *The Theory of Probabilities.* Gastehizdat Publishing House.

[5] S. J. Brams and A. D. Taylor. 1996. *Fair Division: From Cake-Cutting to Dispute Resolution.* Cambridge University Press.

[6] S. Bubeck and N. Cesa-Bianchi. 2012. Regret Analysis of Stochastic and Nonstochastic Multi-armed Bandit Problems. *Foundations and Trends in Machine Learning* 5, 1 (2012), 1–122.

[7] I. Caragiannis, D. Kurokawa, H. Moulin, A. D. Procaccia, N. Shah, and J. Wang. 2016. The Unreasonable Fairness of Maximum Nash Product. In *Proceedings of the 17th ACM Conference on Economics and Computation (EC)*. 305–322.

[8] X. Deng, Q. Qi, and A. Saberi. 2012. Algorithmic Solutions for Envy-Free Cake Cutting. *Operations Research* 60, 6 (2012), 1461–1476.

[9] E. Friedman, C.-A. Psomas, and S. Vardi. 2017. Controlled Dynamic Fair Division. In *Proceedings of the 18th ACM Conference on Economics and Computation (EC)*. 461–478.

[10] Y. Gal, M. Mash, A. D. Procaccia, and Y. Zick. 2017. Which Is the Fairest (Rent Division) of Them All? *Journal of the ACM* 64, 6 (2017), article 39.

[11] I. Kash, A. D. Procaccia, and N. Shah. 2014. No Agent Left Behind: Dynamic Fair Division of Multiple Resources. *Journal of Artificial Intelligence Research* 51 (2014), 579–603.

[12] R. J. Lipton, E. Markakis, E. Mossel, and A. Saberi. 2004. On Approximately Fair Allocations of Indivisible Goods. In *Proceedings of the 6th ACM Conference on Economics and Computation (EC)*. 125–131.

[13] D. C. Parkes, A. D. Procaccia, and N. Shah. 2015. Beyond Dominant Resource Fairness: Extensions, Limitations, and Indivisibilities. *ACM Transactions on Economics and Computation* 3, 1 (2015), article 3.

[14] A. D. Procaccia. 2016. Cake Cutting Algorithms. In *Handbook of Computational Social Choice*, F. Brandt, V. Conitzer, U. Endress, J. Lang, and A. D. Procaccia (Eds.). Cambridge University Press, Chapter 13.

[15] P. Raghavan. 1988. Probabilistic Construction of Deterministic Algorithms: Approximating Packing Integer Programs. *J. Comput. System Sci.* 37, 2 (1988), 130–143.

[16] P. Sanders. 1996. On the Competitive Analysis of Randomized Static Load Balancing. In *Proceedings of the 1st Workshop on Randomized Parallel Algorithms (RANDOM)*.

[17] J. Spencer. 1977. Balancing Games. *Journal of Combinatorial Theory Series B* 23, 1 (1977), 68–74.

[18] W. Stromquist. 1980. How to Cut a Cake Fairly. *Amer. Math. Monthly* 87, 8 (1980), 640–644.

[19] F. E. Su. 1999. Rental Harmony: Sperner's Lemma in Fair Division. *Amer. Math. Monthly* 106, 10 (1999), 930–942.

[20] T. Walsh. 2011. Online Cake Cutting. In *Proceedings of the 3rd International Conference on Algorithmic Decision Theory (ADT)*. 292–305.

# Redistribution through Markets

PIOTR DWORCZAK®, University of Chicago, USA
SCOTT DUKE KOMINERS®, Harvard University, USA
MOHAMMAD AKBARPOUR®, Stanford University, USA

Even when global income redistribution is not feasible, market designers can seek to mitigate inequality within individual markets. If sellers are systematically poorer than buyers, for example, they will be willing to sell at relatively low prices. Yet a designer who cares about inequality might prefer to set higher prices precisely when sellers are poor – effectively, using the market as a redistributive tool. In this paper, we seek to understand how to design goods markets optimally in the presence of persistent inequality. Using a mechanism design approach, we find that redistribution through markets can indeed be optimal. When there is substantial inequality across sides of the market, the designer uses a tax-like mechanism, introducing a wedge between the buyer and seller prices, and redistributing the resulting surplus to the poorer side of the market via lump-sum payments. When there is significant within-side inequality, meanwhile, the designer imposes price controls even though doing so induces rationing.

Full Paper: https://ssrn.com/abstract=3143887

CCS Concepts: • **Applied computing → Electronic commerce**; **Economics**;

Additional Key Words and Phrases: Optimal mechanism design, Redistribution, Inequality

---

The "®" symbol indicates that the authors' names are in certified random order, as described by Ray ® Robson (*American Economic Review*, 2018). The authors thank Benjamin Brooks, Eric Budish, Raj Chetty, Pawel Doligalski, Steven Durlauf, Abigail Fradkin, Alex Frankel, Jonathan Gould, Ravi Jagadeesan, Emir Kamenica, Paul Kominers, Moritz Lenel, Shengwu Li, Elliot Lipnowski, Giorgio Martini, Paul Milgrom, Jeff Miron, Roger Myerson, Eric Nelson, Alessandro Pavan, Canice Prendergast, Doron Ravid, Phil Reny, Marzena Rostek, Alvin Roth, Emma Rothschild, Larry Samuelson, Amartya Sen, Andy Skrzypacz, Stefanie Stantcheva, Alex Teytelboym, Marek Weretka, Bob Wilson, the referees of the Economics and Computations conference, and numerous seminar audiences for valuable feedback. All three authors thank the Becker Friedman Institute both for sparking ideas that led to this work, and for hosting the authors' collaboration. Additionally, Kominers gratefully acknowledges the support of National Science Foundation grant SES-1459912, the Ng Fund and the Mathematics in Economics Research Fund of the Harvard Center of Mathematical Sciences and Applications, and the Human Capital and Economic Opportunity Working Group sponsored by the Institute for New Economic Thinking.

Authors' addresses: Piotr Dworczak®, University of Chicago, Becker Friedman Institute, 1126 E. 59th Street, SHFE 215, Chicago, IL, 60637, USA, dworczak@uchicago.edu; Scott Duke Kominers®, Harvard University, Rock Center 219, Harvard Business School, Boston, MA, 02163, USA, kominers@fas.harvard.edu; Mohammad Akbarpour®, Stanford University, 655 Knight way, E251, Stanford, CA, 94305, USA, mohamwad@stanford.edu.

---


*ACM EC'18, June 18–22, 2018, Ithaca, NY, USA.* ACM ISBN 978-1-4503-5829-3/18/06.
https://doi.org/10.1145/3219166.3219213

# Optimal Commissions and Subscriptions in Networked Markets

JOHN BIRGE, Booth School of Business, University of Chicago, USA
OZAN CANDOGAN, Booth School of Business, University of Chicago, USA
HONGFAN CHEN, Booth School of Business, University of Chicago, USA
DANIELA SABAN, Graduate School of Business, Stanford University, USA

Full Paper: http://faculty.chicagobooth.edu/Ozan.Candogan/www/Publications_files/networkedMarkets.pdf

CCS Concepts: • **Networks** → **Network economics**;

Additional Key Words and Phrases: Revenue Management; Two-sided Market; Buyer-seller Networks;

Platforms facilitating the exchange of goods and services between individuals are prevalent: one can purchase goods from others on eBay, arrange accommodation through Airbnb, and find temporary projects/workers on online labor markets such as Upwork. The majority of these markets exhibit three key features. First, the platforms do not dictate the transaction prices, i.e., buyers and sellers determine at which price the goods/services will be exchanged. Second, not all buyers or sellers on a platform are compatible. This may be due to taste differences (a buyer may be interested only in the types of goods/services a subset of the sellers offer), geographical or import/export restrictions (e.g., being able to provide services only regionally), or other sources of mismatch (e.g., a mismatch in the desired and available skills in online labor markets). Finally, buyers/sellers are heterogeneous in their valuations for goods or services they receive/provide.

In exchange for facilitating trade, these platforms commonly obtain a commission from each transaction and/or charge subscription fees to sellers and buyers who access the platform. As such, their revenues depend both on the chosen commission/subscription fees and on the prices at which buyers/sellers transact. In settings that exhibit the aforementioned features, how should a platform design commission/subscription fees with the objective of maximizing its revenues? Is it sufficient to charge these to only one side of the market or is it necessary to charge them to both sides? What is the role of the underlying compatibility structure, and which structures are more conducive to higher revenues?

In order to answer these questions, we consider a model where potential buyers and sellers are divided into types. Not all buyer and seller types are compatible with each other, and we represent the compatibility across these types using a bipartite network: nodes on one side correspond to buyer types, nodes on the other side correspond to seller types, and edges capture compatibility between different types of buyers and sellers. Agents within each type differ in their valuation

Authors' addresses: John Birge, Booth School of Business, University of Chicago, 5807 S Woodlawn Ave, Chicago, IL, 60637, USA, john.birge@chicagobooth.edu; Ozan Candogan, Booth School of Business, University of Chicago, 5807 S Woodlawn Ave, Chicago, IL, 60637, USA, Ozan.Candogan@chicagobooth.edu; Hongfan Chen, Booth School of Business, University of Chicago, 5807 S Woodlawn Ave, Chicago, IL, 60637, USA, hongfan.chen@chicagobooth.edu; Daniela Saban, Graduate School of Business, Stanford University, 655 Knight Way, Stanford, CA, 94305, USA, dsaban@stanford.edu.


*ACM EC'18, June 18–22, 2018, Ithaca, NY, USA.* ACM ISBN 978-1-4503-5829-3/18/06.
https://doi.org/10.1145/3219166.3219216

for the goods they buy/sell. The platform chooses subscription fees, which must be paid by all agents who participate in the market. In addition, it chooses commissions, and a buyer/seller who exchanges goods/services pays a fraction of the transaction price to the platform as indicated by these commissions. The value distributions, subscription fees, and commissions are all possibly type-specific. Given the commissions/subscriptions chosen by the platform, the transaction prices and equilibrium trades are formed endogenously at a competitive equilibrium.

We establish that, in order to maximize its revenues, the platform may need to charge different commissions/subscriptions to different types, depending on their network position. In fact, we show that if the same commissions/subscriptions are employed for all agents on the same side, the revenue loss can be unbounded. We complement this worst-case result by providing a bound on the revenue loss in terms of the supply/demand imbalance across the network under homogeneous value distributions. Surprisingly, we also show that, in general, charging commissions/subscriptions to only one side of the market (i.e., only to buyers or only to sellers) leads to lower revenues than optimal, even when different types on the same side can be charged different fees. Furthermore, we characterize the impact of the network structure on the revenues of the platform. Finally, we investigate how the commissions/subscriptions chosen by the platform impact social welfare. We establish that, under mild convexity assumptions on the value distributions, the revenue-maximizing commissions/subscriptions induce at least 2/3 of the maximum achievable social welfare.

# Trading Networks With Frictions

TAMÁS FLEINER, Budapest University of Technology and Economics, Hungary and Eötvös Loránd University, Hungary
RAVI JAGADEESAN, Harvard University, United States
ZSUZSANNA JANKÓ, Corvinus University, Hungary
ALEXANDER TEYTELBOYM, University of Oxford, United Kingdom

We show how frictions and continuous transfers jointly affect equilibria in a model of matching in trading networks. Our model incorporates distortionary frictions such as transaction taxes, bargaining costs, and incomplete markets. When contracts are fully substitutable for firms, competitive equilibria exist and coincide with outcomes that satisfy a cooperative stability property called *trail stability*. In the presence of frictions, competitive equilibria might be neither stable nor (constrained) Pareto-efficient. In the absence of frictions, on the other hand, competitive equilibria are stable and in the core, even if utility is imperfectly transferable.

CCS Concepts: • **Theory of computation → Market equilibria**; Solution concepts in game theory;

Additional Key Words and Phrases: trading networks; frictions; competitive equilibrium; matching with contracts; stability; trail stability; transaction taxes; bargaining costs; incomplete financial markets; constrained suboptimality

### ACM Reference Format:

Tamás Fleiner, Ravi Jagadeesan, Zsuzsanna Jankó, and Alexander Teytelboym. 2018. Trading Networks with Frictions. In the Proceedings of 2018 ACM Conference on Economics and Computation (ACM EC'18). ACM, New York, NY, 1 page. https://doi.org/10.1145/3219166.3219171

---

A full version of this paper is available at http://sites.google.com/site/ravijagadeesan/trading-networks-frictions.pdf.
We would like to thank Samson Alva, David Delacrétaz, Battal Doğan, Laura Doval, Jeremy Fox, Daniel Gottlieb, Jens Gudmundsson, Onur Kesten, Maia King, Bettina Klaus, Scott Kominers, Shengwu Li, Michael Ostrovsky, Madhav Raghavan, Jan Christoph Schlegel, Steven Shadman, Fabien Wang, and seminar participants at Harvard, CMU/University of Pittsburgh, Oxford, and ETH for their valuable comments on this paper. Fleiner was supported by the OTKA K108383 research project and the MTA-ELTE Egerváry Research Group. Jankó was supported by the OTKA K109240 research project and the MTA-ELTE Egerváry Research Group. Part of this research was conducted while Jagadeesan was an Economic Design Fellow at the Harvard Center of Mathematical Sciences and Applications and Teytelboym was the Otto Poon Research Fellow at the Institute for New Economic Thinking.
Authors' addresses: Tamás Fleiner, Budapest University of Technology and Economics, Department of Computer Science and Information Theory, Budapest, Hungary, Eötvös Loránd University, Department of Operations Research, Budapest, Hungary, fleiner@cs.bme.hu; Ravi Jagadeesan, Harvard University, Department of Mathematics and Center of Mathematical Sciences and Applications, Cambridge, MA, United States, ravi.jagadeesan@gmail.com; Zsuzsanna Jankó, Corvinus University, Department of Operational Research and Actuarial Sciences, Budapest, Hungary, jzsuzsy@cs.elte.hu; Alexander Teytelboym, University of Oxford, Department of Economics and St. Catherine's College, Oxford, United Kingdom, alexander.teytelboym@economics.ox.ac.uk.

---


*ACM EC'18, June 18–22, 2018, Ithaca, NY, USA.* ACM ISBN 978-1-4503-5829-3/18/06.
https://doi.org/10.1145/3219166.3219171

# Chain Stability in Trading Networks

JOHN WILLIAM HATFIELD, University of Texas at Austin, USA
SCOTT DUKE KOMINERS, Harvard University, USA
ALEXANDRU NICHIFOR, University of Melbourne, Australia
MICHAEL OSTROVSKY, Stanford University, USA
ALEXANDER WESTKAMP, University of Cologne, Germany

We consider general trading networks with bilateral contracts. We show that a suitably adapted *chain stability* concept [4] is equivalent to *stability* [1, 2] if all agents' preferences are jointly fully substitutable [3] and satisfy the Laws of Aggregate Supply and Demand (a condition we call *monotone–substitutability*). We also present three examples to show that are results are sharp, demonstrating that:

- If preferences of some agents do not satisfy the Laws of Aggregate Supply and Demand, then chain stable outcomes may not be stable.
- If preferences of some agents are not fully substitutable, then chain stable outcomes may likewise not be stable.
- If blocking sets are restricted to chains that do not "cross" themselves (i.e., chains that involve each agent in at most two contracts), then an outcome that is robust to such blocks may not be robust to richer blocks.

Our results imply that in trading networks with transferable utility, an outcome is consistent with competitive equilibrium if and only if it is not blocked by any chain of contracts.

We show moreover that, from a computational perspective, checking whether an outcome is chain stable is substantially easier than checking whether that outcome is stable directly. Indeed, we show that as the size of the economy grows, the number of chains of trades (corresponding to possible blocking chains) becomes infinitely smaller than the number of general sets of trades (corresponding to possible blocking sets).

Full Paper: https://ssrn.com/abstract=3180740

We are grateful to Dave Donaldson, Alvin Roth, Alex Teytelboym, and Rakesh Vohra for helpful comments and suggestions. We thank Joseph Shayani for excellent research assistance. Kominers thanks the National Science Foundation (grants CCF-1216095 and SES-1459912, as well as a graduate research fellowship), the Harvard Milton Fund, the Yahoo! Key Scientific Challenges Program, the John M. Olin Center (a Terence M. Considine Fellowship), the Ng Fund and the Mathematics in Economics Research Fund of the Harvard Center of Mathematical Sciences and Applications, the American Mathematical Society, and the Simons Foundation for support. Nichifor received funding from the People Programme (Marie Curie Outgoing International Fellowship) of the European Union's Seventh Framework Programme (FP7/2007-2013) under REA grant agreement 625718, and thanks the Australian Research Council for financial support via a Discovery Early Career Researcher Award (DECRA). Ostrovsky thanks the Alfred P. Sloan Foundation for financial support. Westkamp received funding from the German Science Foundation and from the People Programme (Marie Curie Intra-European Fellowship) of the European Union's Seventh Framework Programme (FP7/2007-2013) under REA grant agreement 628276.

Authors' addresses: John William Hatfield, University of Texas at Austin, 2110 Speedway, B6600, Austin, TX, 78712, USA, john.hatfield@utexas.edu; Scott Duke Kominers, Harvard University, Rock Center 219, Harvard Business School, Boston, MA, 02163, USA, kominers@fas.harvard.edu; Alexandru Nichifor, University of Melbourne, 111 Barry Street, Carlton, Victoria, 3053, Australia, nichifor@unimelb.edu.au; Michael Ostrovsky, Stanford University, 655 Knight Way, Stanford, CA, 94305, USA, ostrovsky@stanford.edu; Alexander Westkamp, University of Cologne, Albertus-Magnus-Platz, 50923 Cologne, Germany, westkamp@wiso.uni-koeln.de.


*ACM EC'18, June 18–22, 2018, Ithaca, NY, USA.* ACM ISBN 978-1-4503-5829-3/18/06.
https://doi.org/10.1145/3219166.3219178

CCS Concepts: • **Applied computing** → **Electronic commerce**; **Economics**;

Additional Key Words and Phrases: Matching, Stability, Networks, Substitutability

## REFERENCES

[1] John William Hatfield and Scott Duke Kominers. 2012. Matching in Networks with Bilateral Contracts. *American Economic Journal: Microeconomics* 4 (2012), 176–208.

[2] John William Hatfield, Scott Duke Kominers, Alexandru Nichifor, Michael Ostrovsky, and Alexander Westkamp. 2013. Stability and Competitive Equilibrium in Trading Networks. *Journal of Political Economy* 121 (2013), 966–1005.

[3] John William Hatfield, Scott Duke Kominers, Alexandru Nichifor, Michael Ostrovsky, and Alexander Westkamp. 2018. Full Substitutability. (2018). Working Paper.

[4] Michael Ostrovsky. 2008. Stability in supply chain networks. *American Economic Review* 98 (2008), 897–923.

# Naive Bayesian Learning in Social Networks

JERRY ANUNROJWONG, Harvard University, USA
NAT SOTHANAPHAN, Massachusetts Institute of Technology, USA

The DeGroot model of naive social learning assumes that agents only communicate scalar opinions. In practice, agents communicate not only their opinions, but their confidence in such opinions. We propose a model that captures this aspect of communication by incorporating signal informativeness into the naive social learning scenario. Our proposed model captures aspects of both Bayesian and naive learning. Agents in our model combine their neighbors' beliefs using Bayes' rule, but the agents naively assume that their neighbors' beliefs are independent. Depending on the initial beliefs, agents in our model may not reach a consensus, but we show that the agents will reach a consensus under mild continuity and boundedness assumptions on initial beliefs. This eventual consensus can be explicitly computed in terms of each agent's centrality and signal informativeness, allowing joint effects to be precisely understood. We apply our theory to adoption of new technology. In contrast to Banerjee et al. [5], we show that information about a new technology can be seeded initially in a tightly clustered group without information loss, but only if agents can expressively communicate their beliefs.

CCS Concepts: • **Theory of computation** → **Social networks**; **Convergence and learning in games**; • **Networks** → *Network economics*;

## 1 INTRODUCTION

This paper introduces an intuitive naive social learning model that extends the DeGroot model when agents are differently informed. In standard naive learning, each agent's belief is a scalar, and each agent updates her beliefs by taking the weighted averages of her neighbors' beliefs with fixed weights. This implicitly assumes that every agent's signal quality is the same, which is often not true in practice. We propose a solution to this problem by representing each agent's belief as a probability distribution over possible states of the world. Signal quality can then be naturally communicated by using Bayes' rule to combine one's belief with the beliefs of one's neighbors. For example, if an agent has a scalar opinion $\mu$ and a scalar confidence $\tau$ indicating how sure she is of that scalar opinion, her belief can be represented by the Gaussian $\mathcal{N}(\mu, 1/\tau)$. Our model can also accommodate other forms of information. For example, an agent may believe that either one of the two values is very likely, while other values are less likely. This belief can be represented as a double-peaked distribution, but it cannot be represented in standard DeGroot models.

It is known separately in Bayesian learning and naive learning literatures that higher quality signals and more centrally located agents, respectively, have more influence in social learning. The innovation in our model is to introduce signal quality into the naive learning setting, allowing us to precisely investigate how signal quality and agent centrality interact. The two notions are

The full version of this paper is available at https://arxiv.org/abs/1805.05878 [2].

Authors' addresses: Jerry Anunrojwong, Harvard University, Department of Statistics, Cambridge, MA, 01238, USA, jerryanunroj@gmail.com; Nat Sothanaphan, Massachusetts Institute of Technology, Department of Mathematics, Cambridge, MA, 02139, USA, natsothanaphan@gmail.com.


*ACM EC'18, June 18–22, 2018, Ithaca, NY, USA.* ACM ISBN 978-1-4503-5829-3/18/06...$15.00
https://doi.org/10.1145/3219166.3219177

intertwined in the *weighted likelihood function*, where the formal expression is at equation (1) in Section 1.1. Informally, the value of this function at $\theta$ is the product of the votes of each agent, where an agent's vote is how likely the state value $\theta$ is after the agent received the signal compared to before (the signal quality part), and the number of votes is the agent's eigenvector centrality (the centrality part).

Our main theorem is that, under some conditions, long-run beliefs are concentrated near the maximizers of the weighted likelihood function. If we know the probability densities of initial beliefs, we can explicitly calculate the consensus belief. This allows us to analyze the interaction; for example, we can calculate how much more informative a signal has to be to offset the centrality disadvantage. This formula can have practical applications in the analysis of information spread in decentralized networks, such as propagation of rumors or adoption of new technologies. Practitioners interested in empirical results can also use our formula without having to fully grasp the theory in the paper. Some examples of applications are discussed in Section 7.

To the best of our knowledge, before this work, only Banerjee et al. [5] have directly tried to solve the issue of differently informed agents in DeGroot learning; they assume that each agent can either hold a scalar belief or be uninformed. While their model can capture the spread of awareness of new things, their model still has no notion of signal informativeness that our model provides.

Our model also gives a different prediction than that of Banerjee et al. [5] on how to seed a new technology for widespread adoption. Their model has a *clustered seeding* problem: there is substantial information loss if the initially informed agents ("seeds") are clustered in a small group of communities. This is a problem because a social planner who wants to maximize the impact of a newly introduced technology should seed it to centrally located opinion leaders, but these leaders are often closely connected to each other. Our model does not have this problem; the influence of each agent depends only on the agent's signal informativeness and centrality. The key modeling difference is that agents in our model can communicate confidence of their beliefs that their neighbors can take into account. Therefore, to solve the clustered seeding problem, the social planner should encourage open and expressive communication between agents.

### 1.1 Contributions

Our agents are in a social network, represented as a strongly connected directed graph. Assume that there is a true state of the world $\theta^*$. Each agent gets a signal drawn from a distribution that depends on $\theta^*$. She then forms a *belief*, the posterior probability distribution of $\theta^*$ given the signal. In each round, each agent has access to beliefs of her neighbors and naively assumes that these all come from *independent* signals. She then forms the Bayesian posterior of $\theta^*$ given the signals of her own and her neighbors as her new belief. This gives rise to an update rule that combines her belief with her neighbors' beliefs that she uses in every round.

We prove that our learning process can be viewed as follows. At every time step, each agent passes copies of signals she has to her neighbors, so copies of signals "flow" through the network. Every copy is taken as independent and no copy is discarded, so the number of copies of agent $j$'s signal that agent $i$ has at round $t$ is the number of paths from $j$ to $i$ of length $t$. Agent $i$'s belief at time $t$ is then the posterior belief conditional on these repeated signals (Prop. 4.6).

We then tackle the important question of what happens to agents' beliefs in the long run. The answer depends on the following *weighted likelihood function* $L$ (Def. 5.1). Let $f_i^{(t)}(\theta)$ be agent $i$'s belief of $\theta^*$ in round $t$ and $f_*(\theta)$ be the common prior of $\theta^*$. Then

$$L(\theta) = \prod_{i=1}^{N} \left( \frac{f_i^{(0)}(\theta)}{f_*(\theta)} \right)^{v_i}, \tag{1}$$

where $v_i$ is the eigenvector centrality of agent $i$. We show that if $L(\theta_1) < L(\theta_2)$, then as $t \longrightarrow \infty$,

$$\frac{f_i^{(t)}(\theta_1)}{f_i^{(t)}(\theta_2)} \longrightarrow 0 \tag{2}$$

(Prop. 5.3). In other words, agents' beliefs that the true parameter is $\theta_2$ are much stronger than the corresponding beliefs for $\theta_1$ as time goes on. Thus, in the long run, agents' beliefs should concentrate at values $\theta$ that maximize or nearly maximize $L$.

The form of the weighted likelihood function highlights two factors that determine the quality of learning. An agent who is more *centrally located* (high $v_i$) and has a more *informative signal* (high or low $f_i^{(0)}(\theta)/f_*(\theta)$) has more influence over the consensus belief. Note that our consensus belief is fundamentally different from that of DeGroot. In our model, the limit belief is the weighted likelihood maximizer, while in DeGroot, it is a weighted average of beliefs.

The fact that beliefs tend to converge to a point distribution agrees with the following intuition: agents take a growing number of repeated signals as independent, so they become increasingly confident in their beliefs. The fact that the limit belief is tractable and interpretable comes as a surprise, and we believe this to be an attractive feature of our model.

In spite of this intuition and much to our astonishment, the concentration previously discussed turns out not to hold in general if $\Theta$, the state space, is infinite. We discover that even with a single $\theta_{\max}$ uniquely maximizing $L$, agents' beliefs may not converge to the point distribution at $\theta_{\max}$. We resolve this difficulty by introducing an extra condition: if $\theta_{\max}$ still maximizes a "perturbed" version of $L$, then the concentration result holds. We can think of this as $\theta_{\max}$ being a sufficiently robust maximizer of $L$. This result requires careful analysis of convergences of infinite sequences, and the generalization of this idea for an arbitrary state space $\Theta$ can be found in Proposition 5.5.

When the state space $\Theta = \mathbb{R}$ is a continuum, for example in the case of Gaussian beliefs, this perturbed $L$ condition is still too strong: perturbing $L$ will almost always shift the maximizer due to the continuity of the space. The correct condition needs to allow the maximizer to shift, but not too much. Furthermore, it is insufficient to consider the density at a single point, since this tells us nothing about densities at nearby points and so cannot establish concentration. Instead, we need to show that for any neighborhood of $\theta_{\max}$, agents' beliefs that the true state lies in that neighborhood tend to 1. Our Master Theorem 5.8 pulls together all of these ideas.

With the Master Theorem 5.8, we derive a convergence theorem when the state space is a continuum, provided that the initial beliefs and priors are sufficiently continuous (Def. 6.4). Our main result in this most difficult case is Theorem 6.5. The following is a simplified version of this theorem, simplified from Corollary 6.6.

THEOREM 1.1. *Assume that the state space* $\Theta = \mathbb{R}^k$. *Suppose that the normalized beliefs* $f_i^{(0)}(\theta)/f_*(\theta)$ *are bounded continuous functions; the weighted likelihood function* $L$ *attains the maximum* $L_{\max}$ *uniquely at the point* $\theta_{\max}$*; and* $L$ *decays in the sense that there is a bounded set* $S$ *such that* $\sup_{\theta \notin S} L(\theta) < L_{\max}$. *Then, as* $t \longrightarrow \infty$, *beliefs* $f_i^{(t)}$ *converge to the point distribution at* $\theta_{\max}$.

This result states that whenever the initial beliefs are continuous functions that are bounded with respect to the prior and they decay sufficiently fast, agents' beliefs converge to the maximizer of the weighted likelihood function if this maximizer is unique. This result encompasses a wide range of probability distributions in practice. For example, the theorem applies when beliefs are multivariate Gaussian. Therefore, Theorem 1.1 is widely applicable.

The rest of the paper is organized as follows. We discuss related literature in the remaining of this section. Section 2 describes our model. Section 3 discusses mathematical preliminaries. Section 4 gives fundamental definitions, interprets the updated beliefs, and analyzes feasibility of initial conditions. Section 5 proves the "Master Theorem" that establishes concentration of beliefs near the weighted likelihood maximizers. Section 6 uses the Master Theorem to prove convergence of beliefs in the finite, infinite discrete, and $\mathbb{R}^k$ cases. Section 7 gives applications in the cases of binary, Poisson, and Gaussian beliefs.

### 1.2 Related Literature

Our paper is closely related to a growing literature on learning and belief formation in social networks [3, 4, 6, 11, 21, 22]. Much of this literature focuses on Bayesian learning [1, 7, 15, 18] and DeGroot learning [8, 12]. Comparable to Golub and Jackson [12], our model shows that centrally located agents, as measured by eigenvector centralities, have more influence on the consensus belief. However, in our model, eigenvector centralities appear as duplicate agents rather than linear weights in the limit belief.

Specifically, our paper belongs to the quasi-Bayesian social learning literature. Eyster and Rabin [9, 10] and Rahimian et al. [19] study long-run aggregation of information when agents ignore repetition. Li and Tan [14] study learning where each agent updates both her belief on the state of the world and her belief on her neighbors' beliefs. Jadbabaie et al. [13] also combine DeGroot learning with Bayesian updates. Lastly, likelihood ratios play a central role in our model; they appear in Rahimian et al. [20] and Molavi et al. [17] in a different context.

Finally, our work is related to Banerjee et al. [5]. In their model, the informedness of agents is a binary state, informed individuals hold scalar beliefs, and the learning rule is to take the average belief of informed neighbors. This contrasts with our model where informedness is a continuous attribute. Their work identifies the clustered seeding problem discussed in the introduction, which does not occur in our model. See further discussion of this problem in Section 7.3.

## 2 MODEL

We discuss the assumptions of our model in this section.

### 2.1 Social Network

Our agents are in a social network, modeled as a directed graph $G$ with $N \geq 2$ nodes, labeled $1, 2, \dots, N$ corresponding to $N$ agents. An edge from $i$ to $j$ is denoted $(i, j)$ and means that there is information flow from agent $i$ to agent $j$. Assume that $G$ is strongly connected, that is, for every $i$ and $j$ there is a path from $i$ to $j$. Suppose that there is a self-loop $(i, i)$ at every node, meaning that information flows from every agent to herself. If there is an edge $(i, j)$, we say that $i$ is an *in-neighbor* of $j$. Let $N(i)$ denote the set of in-neighbors of $i$.

### 2.2 Beliefs

Let $\Theta$ be the space of parameters $\theta$, modeled as a measure space. We model beliefs as *probability density functions* on $\Theta$: nonnegative measurable functions $f : \Theta \to \mathbb{R}_{\geq 0}$ such that the integral $\int_{\theta \in \Theta} f(\theta) = 1$. These reduce to probability mass functions in a discrete setting, i.e. when $\Theta$ is discrete with the counting measure. Note that we model beliefs as probability densities, which is a special case of general probability distributions. For example, a point distribution on $\mathbb{R}$ cannot be represented as a density, but most probability distributions in practice are densities. A *prior* on $\Theta$ is any nonnegative measurable function $f : \Theta \to \mathbb{R}_{\geq 0}$. If the integral $\int_{\theta \in \Theta} f(\theta)$ diverges, we call the prior $f$ *improper*. Note that our improper priors are not necessarily limits of proper priors, but simply densities whose integrals diverge and so cannot be normalized. An example of an improper prior is the uninformative prior, $f(\theta) \equiv 1$, where $\Theta$ is an infinite discrete set or an unbounded interval of $\mathbb{R}$.

Suppose that each agent has a common (possibly improper) prior $f_*$ for the true state of the world $\theta^*$ on $\Theta$. Assume that $f_*(\theta) > 0$ for all $\theta \in \Theta$. This assumption is important in order to state the update rule for beliefs (e.g. in Definition 2.1).

### 2.3 Belief Updates

Agents update their beliefs based on the beliefs of their in-neighbors using the following rule, which will be justified shortly.

*Definition 2.1.* The *naive Bayesian updated belief* for agent $i$ with respect to beliefs $f_1, \dots, f_N$ is the belief

$$f(\theta) = \frac{f_*(\theta) \prod_{j \in N(i)} \left(f_j(\theta)/f_*(\theta)\right)}{\int_{\theta' \in \Theta} f_*(\theta') \prod_{j \in N(i)} \left(f_j(\theta')/f_*(\theta')\right)},$$

which is well-defined whenever the integral in the denominator is nonzero and finite.

It is easily checked that this definition defines a belief. We now provide a justification for this definition. In the justification, we will assume that $f_*$ is a probability density function, but the formula in Definition 2.1 also makes sense for improper priors.

Consider the following scenario called an *underlying scenario*. Suppose that agent $i$ knows a family of probability density functions $(p_{\theta,i})_{\theta \in \Theta}$, indexed by the parameter $\theta$ and the agent $i$, over a common sample space $\Omega_i$. We make the following marginalizability assumption, which is important in order to reason consistently about marginal densities. For any integers $n_1, \dots, n_N \geq 0$, let $X_{i,1}, \dots, X_{i,n_i}$ be random variables drawn independently from $p_{\theta,i}$. We thus have a joint probability density for these random variables $p\big((X_{i,j})_{1 \leq i \leq n, 1 \leq j \leq n_i}, \theta\big) = p(\theta) \prod_{i=1}^{N} \prod_{j=1}^{n_i} p(X_{i,j}|\theta)$. Assume that this distribution can be marginalized over $\theta$ with positive density.

Agent $i$ receives a signal $X_i$ drawn from $p_{\theta^*,i}$, the distribution corresponding to the true parameter $\theta^*$, without knowing $\theta^*$. She then forms a belief $f_i(\theta)$ for $\theta^*$ conditional on the signal $X_i$. Suppose that agent $i$ learns about beliefs $f_j(\theta)$ of all her in-neighbors $j \in N(i)$, formed in the same way, and wishes to perform a Bayesian update on her own belief. The result will be the belief $f(\theta)$ for $\theta^*$ conditional on signals $X_j$ for every $j \in N(i)$. Even though the resulting density seems to depend on $X_j$, we will show in the next proposition that this update can be performed knowing only the beliefs $f_j$ but not the private signals $X_j$, with the formula as in Definition 2.1.

Proposition 2.2. *In an underlying scenario described above, the updated belief for agent i is the naive Bayesian updated belief with respect to beliefs $f_1, \dots, f_N$ as in Definition 2.1.*

Proof Sketch. Use Bayes' rule to compute the updated belief as

$$f(\theta) = p\left(\theta|(X_j)_{j \in N(i)}\right) = \frac{p(\theta) \prod_{j \in N(i)} p\left(X_j|\theta\right)}{\int_{\theta' \in \Theta} p(\theta') \prod_{j \in N(i)} p\left(X_j|\theta'\right)}.$$

Another application of Bayes' rule on $p(X_j|\theta)$ finishes the proof. □

### 2.4 Belief Dynamics

Here we describe the evolution of beliefs. Agents share a common prior $f_*$ of $\theta^*$, which may be improper, and agent $i$ starts off with *initial belief* $f_i^{(0)}$ of $\theta^*$. The functions $f_*, f_1^{(0)}, \dots, f_N^{(0)}$ are the *initial condition* of the model. The subtlety is that not all initial conditions lead to well-defined updates. Nevertheless, in Section 4.3, we will provide simple checks that guarantee the existence of updated beliefs. For $t = 0, 1, 2, \dots$, let $f_i^{(t)}$ be agent $i$'s belief of $\theta^*$ at round $t$. Agents update beliefs as follows. For $t \geq 0$, $f_i^{(t+1)}$ is the naive Bayesian updated belief (Def. 2.1) for agent $i$ with respect to beliefs $f_1^{(t)}, \dots, f_N^{(t)}$.

We call an initial condition *feasible* if the updated beliefs are well-defined in every round, that is, the integral in Definition 2.1 is nonzero and finite. Moreover, an initial condition *has an underlying scenario* if it arises from an underlying scenario in the above justification of Definition 2.1. Proposition 4.6 shows that an initial condition with an underlying scenario is always feasible.

For an initial condition with an underlying scenario, note that although the update rule is rationally justified, it is only optimal for the first round. In later rounds, an optimal update needs to take into account that the agents' beliefs are already updated at least once and so no longer independent. Still, our naive agents use the same update rule for every round. This modeling choice formalizes what we said earlier that people use Bayes' rule to learn, but they ignore repeated information.

We name our model *naive Bayesian* for two reasons. First, our model combines features from naive learning and Bayesian learning. Second, our agents assume that distributions of neighbors are independent conditional on the state, which is also the assumption made in Naive Bayes classifiers in machine learning.

## 3 MATHEMATICAL PRELIMINARIES

Here, we review Perron-Frobenius theory, which helps us determine the behavior of large powers of matrices and establish convergence of beliefs. In the full version of this paper, we also review the theory of $L^p$ spaces. That material helps us bound functions and establish feasibility of initial conditions, but it is not used after we assume feasibility, so it is omitted for lack of space.

Let $G$ be the graph of our model, and let $A$ be the adjacency matrix of $G$: $A_{ij} = 1$ if there is an edge $(i, j)$ and 0 otherwise. The Perron-Frobenius theory provides us with properties of eigenvalues and eigenvectors of $A$.

*Definition 3.1.* A square matrix $M$ is *primitive* if its entries are nonnegative and the entries of $M^k$ are positive for some $k > 0$.

Lemma 3.2. *A is a primitive matrix.*

The following theorem from Meyer [16, Chapter 8], a version of Perron-Frobenius for primitive matrices, characterizes the largest eigenvalue of a primitive matrix and the growth rate of the matrix's powers.

Theorem 3.3 (Perron-Frobenius for Primitive Matrices). *Let $M$ be a primitive matrix. Let $r = \rho(M)$ be the spectral radius of $M$, that is, the maximum absolute value of eigenvalues of $M$. Then $r$ is an eigenvalue of $M$, any other eigenvalue of $M$ has absolute value less than $r$, and there are unique vectors $v$ and $w$ with positive entries such that*

$$Mv = rv, \quad wM = rw, \quad \|v\|_1 = \|w\|_1 = 1.$$

*Note that $\|\cdot\|_1$ denotes the sum of entries. Call $v$ the* Perron vector *of $M$. Then $w$ is the Perron vector of $M^\top$.*

*Finally, the limit $\lim_{k\to\infty} M^k/r^k$ exists and is given by*

$$P := \lim_{k\to\infty} \frac{M^k}{r^k} = \frac{vw^\top}{w^\top v}.$$

*This limit $P$ is called the* Perron projection *of $M$.*

The following lemma will be useful when we reason that the entries of $A^k$ tend to infinity.

Lemma 3.4. *The spectral radius of $A$ is greater than 1, that is, $\rho(A) > 1$.*

We now define the notion of centrality alluded to in the introduction.

*Definition 3.5.* If $v$ is the Perron vector of $A$, then call $v_i$ the *eigenvector centrality* of agent $i$.

## 4 UNDERSTANDING THE MODEL

In Section 4.1, we introduce some preliminary definitions that will be useful in understanding the model in Sections 4.2 and 4.3. Then we interpret the updated beliefs in Section 4.2. Finally, we find the conditions that guarantee that an initial condition is feasible in Section 4.3.

### 4.1 Preliminary Definitions

We introduce the notion of *normalized beliefs.*

*Definition 4.1.* The *normalized belief* of agent $i$ at round $t$ is the function

$$g_i^{(t)}(\theta) := \frac{f_i^{(t)}(\theta)}{f_*(\theta)}.$$

We can interpret this as how large a a belief is compared to the prior. This quantity will appear in the weighted likelihood function in Definition 5.1 and play a central role in our analysis.

With normalized beliefs, the update rule in Definition 2.1 assumes the simpler form

$$g_i^{(t+1)}(\theta) = \frac{\prod_{j\in N(i)} g_j^{(t)}(\theta)}{\int_{\theta'\in\Theta} f_*(\theta') \prod_{j\in N(i)} g_j^{(t)}(\theta')}. \tag{3}$$

*Definition 4.2.* For nodes $i$ and $j$ of $G$ and $t \geq 0$, let $P_{ij}^{(t)}$ be the number of paths from $i$ to $j$ of length $t$. By convention, there is one path of length 0 from a node to itself and no path of length 0 from a node to a different node.

Lemma 4.3. *The numbers of paths satisfy the recurrence* $P_{ij}^{(t+1)} = \sum_{k\in N(j)} P_{ik}^{(t)}$. *Moreover,* $P_{ij}^{(t)}$ *is the* $(i, j)$ *entry of the matrix* $A^t$.

Finally, we formally define the notion of *k-feasibility* and *feasibility.*

*Definition 4.4.* For any $k \geq 1$, an initial condition $f_*, f_1, \ldots, f_N$ is *k-feasible* if the updated beliefs are well-defined up to at least round $k$. An initial condition is *feasible* if it is $k$-feasible for every $k$.

### 4.2 Interpretation of Updated Beliefs

We interpret what agents are doing in our model. Our goal is to show that each agent aggregates information where another agent's initial belief is weighted by the number of paths from that agent to the aggregating agent. This means that an agent who has many paths to other agents, i.e. an agent with high centrality, will be influential in our model. This result will lead to conditions for feasible initial conditions in Section 4.3 and show concentration of beliefs in Section 5.

Proposition 4.5. *An initial condition* $f_*, f_1^{(0)}, \ldots, f_N^{(0)}$ *is k-feasible if and only if the expression*

$$\frac{\prod_{j=1}^N g_j^{(0)}(\theta)^{P_{ji}^{(t)}}}{\int_{\theta'\in\Theta} f_*(\theta') \prod_{j=1}^N g_j^{(0)}(\theta')^{P_{ji}^{(t)}}}$$

*is well-defined for all* $i$ *and* $0 \leq t \leq k$, *and that expression is the formula for* $g_i^{(t)}(\theta)$.

Proof Sketch. Induct on $k$ and use Lemma 4.3 to get exponents into the form $P_{ji}^{(t)}$. □

Now we claim that an initial condition with an underlying scenario is feasible, as well as give an explicit formula for the updated beliefs. This is important as it gives us insight into the update process.

Proposition 4.6. *An initial condition $f_*, f_1^{(0)}, \ldots, f_N^{(0)}$ with an underlying scenario is feasible. If agent $i$ receives signal $X_i$ in the underlying scenario and $I_i^{(t)}$ is the ordered tuple consisting of $P_{ji}^{(t)}$ independent copies of $X_j$ for each $j$, then*

$$f_i^{(t)}(\theta) = p(\theta | I_i^{(t)}).$$

*In other words, the belief of agent $i$ in round $t$ for each parameter $\theta$ is the belief for that parameter conditional on the information $I_i^{(t)}$.*

Proposition 4.6 gives us an intuition of the process. At every time step, each agent passes copies of signals she has to her neighbors, so copies of signals "flow" through the network. Every copy is taken as independent and no copy is discarded, so the number of copies of agent $j$'s signal that agent $i$ has at round $t$ is the number of paths from $j$ to $i$ of length $t$. Moreover, we can interpret the normalized belief $g_i^{(t)}(\theta)$ as the amount of support that $I_i^{(t)}$ provides for $\theta$. Since $g_i^{(t)}(\theta) = p(\theta|I_i^{(t)})/p(\theta)$ by Proposition 4.6, this quantity is larger or smaller than 1 if learning $I_i^{(t)}$ increases or decreases the probability density at $\theta$, respectively.

From Proposition 4.6, we can qualitatively predict how our model behaves in the long term. Because repeated signals in $I_i^{(t)}$ are taken as independent, agents should become overconfident over time. Furthermore, because the numbers of repeated signals are the numbers of paths, agents with more paths to other agents (those with higher eigenvector centralities) should be more influential. Our results on concentration and convergence of beliefs in Sections 5 and 6 confirm these predictions.

### 4.3 Initial Conditions

In the full version of this paper, we use the theory of $L^p$ spaces to investigate containment relationships between classes of initial conditions and present simple sufficient conditions for feasibility. The only result that is used in this paper is the following sufficient condition (Corollary 4.14 in the full paper) that is easy to check in practice.

Corollary 4.7. *An initial condition $f_*, f_1^{(0)}, \ldots, f_N^{(0)}$ is feasible if the product of initial beliefs $f_1^{(0)} \ldots f_N^{(0)}$ does not vanish almost everywhere and, for every $i$, $g_i^{(0)}$ is bounded almost everywhere.*

## 5 CONCENTRATION OF BELIEFS

With the tools we have built up, we can now start seriously analyzing the model. Assume from this point onwards that the initial condition is feasible. Our goal in this section is to establish the following remarkable result about concentration of beliefs. In the long term, beliefs of agents in our model tend to concentrate at points of $\Theta$ which maximize the *weighted likelihood function* $L$ (Def. 5.1). Specifically, for a set $A \subseteq \Theta$ such that the values of $L$ on this set are dominated in some sense by $L(\theta')$ for another $\theta' \in \Theta$,

$$\int_{\theta \in A} f_i^{(t)}(\theta) \to 0$$

as $t \to \infty$. We can think of this as saying that the agents' beliefs are being concentrated more and more near the maximizer of $L$, and so the beliefs on any set that stays clear of the maximizer tend to zero. The precise statement is in the Master Theorem 5.8. Once we have this result, it will become relatively easy to show convergence of the agents' beliefs towards maximizers of $L$ in various settings; this will be done in Section 6.

### 5.1 Weighted Likelihood

We first define the weighted likelihood function mentioned in the introduction.

*Definition 5.1.* Assume that the initial condition is feasible. The *weighted likelihood function* is defined for each $\theta \in \Theta$ by

$$L(\theta) = \prod_{i=1}^{N} (g_i^{(0)}(\theta))^{v_i}.$$

Recall that $g_i^{(0)}$ is the normalized beliefs defined in Definition 4.1 and that the eigenvector centrality $v_i$ can be thought of as the influence of agent $i$. So this function aggregates the normalized beliefs of agents while being biased by the agents' influences. In the full paper, we discuss how the weighted likelihood function differs from the *unbiased* likelihood that results from optimal information aggregation. To see how this function is being "biased," the *unbiased* likelihood of each parameter $\theta$ given the initial beliefs of agents formed according to an underlying scenario (Sec. 2.3) is given by

$$L_{\text{unbiased}}(\theta) = cf_*(\theta) \prod_{i=1}^{N} g_i^{(0)}(\theta),$$

where $c$ is a normalizing constant. Under optimal information aggregation, the posterior belief is proportional to $L_{\text{unbiased}}$. To derive this, simply do the computation analogous to the one in Proposition 2.2. Notice that $L$ and $L_{\text{unbiased}}$ are different in two ways. First, each $g_i^{(0)}$ factor in $L$ is to the power of $v_i$, suggesting that $L$ is biased by the centrality of each agent as already pointed out. Second, there is an extra factor of $f_*$, the prior, in $L_{\text{unbiased}}$. This is because agents in our model become so confident in their opinions that the prior is disregarded entirely, so this factor does not appear in $L$.

We now show that the weighted likelihood function guides the convergence of the ratio of beliefs at two different points (Prop. 5.3). We can think of this as a "pointwise" concentration result. It is much weaker than the actual concentration result we seek (except when $\Theta$ is finite; see Theorem 6.2). Nonetheless, it is the basis of the proof of the Master Theorem 5.8.

The next proposition gives an explicit formula for the ratio of beliefs at two different points, highlighting the terms that become small in the limit. It is a crucial component that is used in Section 5.2 to prove the Master Theorem 5.8.

Proposition 5.2. *Let $r = \rho(A)$ be the spectral radius of $A$, and $v$ and $w$ be the Perron vectors of $A$ and $A^\top$, respectively. Then there are $\varepsilon_{i,j}^{(t)} \to 0$ as $t \to \infty$ such that for any $\theta_1, \theta_2 \in \Theta$ with $L(\theta_2) > 0$,*

$$\frac{f_i^{(t)}(\theta_1)}{f_i^{(t)}(\theta_2)} = \frac{f_*(\theta_1)}{f_*(\theta_2)} \left[ \prod_{j=1}^{N} \left( \frac{g_j^{(0)}(\theta_1)}{g_j^{(0)}(\theta_2)} \right)^{v_j + \varepsilon_{i,j}^{(t)}} \right]^{w_i r^t / w^\top v}.$$

From this proposition, we can begin to see the weighted likelihood function take shape: in the formula above, if the prior factors in front are ignored and the small terms $\varepsilon_{i,j}^{(t)}$ disregarded, what is left is the ratio $L(\theta_1)/L(\theta_2)$ raised to some power.

Proof Sketch. The proof is essentially by direct computation. Use Proposition 4.5 to get the expression for the ratio $g_i^{(t)}(\theta_1)/g_i^{(t)}(\theta_2)$. Then use Lemma 4.3 and Theorem 3.3 to transform it into the desired formula. □

We can now show the "pointwise" concentration of beliefs at maximizers of $L$. This hints at the actual concentration result in the next subsection.

Proposition 5.3. *If $\theta_1, \theta_2 \in \Theta$ are such that $L(\theta_1) < L(\theta_2)$, then as $t \to \infty$,*

$$\frac{f_i^{(t)}(\theta_1)}{f_i^{(t)}(\theta_2)} \to 0.$$

## 5.2 Master Theorem

This is a technical section; its aim is to prove the Master Theorem 5.8 which establishes concentration of beliefs in very general settings. In order to do this, subtle issues of convergence arise which can be best dealt with using ideas from measure theory (e.g. Lebesgue's dominated convergence theorem). Even in the relatively benign setting $\Theta = \mathbb{N}$, these issues are not so easy to circumnavigate. We first present the general idea of the Master Theorem. Suppose $A \subseteq \Theta$ and $\theta' \in \Theta$ are such that $L(\theta) < L(\theta')$ for all $\theta \in A$. Thus, $\theta'$ "dominates" all of $A$ in the sense of the weighted likelihood function. We hope that $\int_{\theta \in A} f_i^{(t)}(\theta) \to 0$ as $t \to \infty$. Proposition 5.3 implies the pointwise result $f_i^{(t)}(\theta)/f_i^{(t)}(\theta') \to 0$ as $t \to \infty$. We would like to aggregate this pointwise result into

$$\frac{\int_{\theta \in A} f_i^{(t)}(\theta)}{f_i^{(t)}(\theta')} \to 0 \tag{4}$$

(Prop. 5.5), so that we may conclude $\int_{\theta \in A} f_i^{(t)}(\theta) \to 0$. To do so, we need to control the convergence in Proposition 5.3; the convergence needs to be "uniform" in some way. It turns out that the correct hypothesis is that the inequality $L(\theta) < L(\theta')$ holds when the exponents in $L$ are slightly perturbed: $L(\theta)g_i^{(0)}(\theta)^{\delta_i} < L(\theta')g_i^{(0)}(\theta')^{\delta_i}$ for small $\delta_i > 0$. As explained in Section 1.1, we can think of this as $\theta'$ dominating $A$ *robustly*, i.e. the domination does not fail even if the centralities of agents are being slightly perturbed. In the full version, we offer an example where this robustness condition fails and concentration also fails, which shows that this hypothesis cannot be omitted.

After obtaining the bound (4), if $\Theta$ is discrete, i.e. $\Theta = \mathbb{N}$, then the obvious bound $f_i^{(t)}(\theta') \leq 1$ finishes the proof. But this is not so easy if $\Theta$ is continuous, i.e. $\Theta = \mathbb{R}^k$. In fact, if concentration is to be true, it is likely that $f_i^{(t)}(\theta') \to \infty$ as $t \to \infty$ if $\theta'$ maximizes $L$, and so we cannot get from (4) to the desired result directly. The second idea is to pick $\theta'$ that is *not* a maximizer of $L$ and show that $f_i^{(t)}(\theta') \to 0$ (which is likely to happen if concentration near the maximizer is to occur), which will then allow us to get the desired result. To do this, we find a set $B$ such that $L(\theta) > L(\theta')$ for all $\theta \in B$, i.e. now the set $B$ dominates $\theta'$ instead. Then if the convergence is similarly controlled, we should get

$$\frac{\int_{\theta \in B} f_i^{(t)}(\theta)}{f_i^{(t)}(\theta')} \to \infty$$

(Prop. 5.7), which implies $f_i^{(t)}(\theta') \to 0$. Putting all of this together completes the proof.

To summarize, the mechanics of the Master Theorem are a two-step domination process. Suppose that we have sets $A$ and $B$ and a point $\theta'$, such that $\theta'$ dominates $A$ and $B$ dominates $\theta'$, and both dominations are robust. Then the latter domination forces the density at $\theta'$ to go to zero, which, by the former domination, in turn forces the density on $A$ to go to zero.

In what follows, we implement the program outlined above. First we formalize the notion of this "robust domination" which allows us to control convergence. The following lemma is a purely analytical statement that contains the essential ingredients to carrying out the "$\theta'$ dominates $A$" part; then Proposition 5.5 will actually carry it out. The proof of the lemma is given in the full version.

LEMMA 5.4. *Let $S$ be a measure space. For $t \in \mathbb{Z}_{\geq 0}$ and $1 \leq i \leq N$, let $a_i, c : S \longrightarrow \mathbb{R}_{\geq 0}$ be measurable functions, $r_t > 0$ and $\varepsilon_i^{(t)} \geq -1$. As $t \longrightarrow \infty$, $r_t \longrightarrow \infty$ and, for every $i$, $\varepsilon_i^{(t)} \longrightarrow 0$. The functions $a_i$ has product $A(x) := \prod_{i=1}^N a_i(x) \leq 1$ for almost every $x \in S$. Moreover, for every $i$, there is $\delta_i > 0$ such that $A(x)a_i(x)^{\delta_i} \leq 1$ for almost every $x \in S$. Suppose that for every $t$, the integral*

$$I_t := \int_{x \in S} c(x) \left( \prod_{i=1}^N a_i(x)^{1+\varepsilon_i^{(t)}} \right)^{r_t} < \infty.$$

*Then, as $t \longrightarrow \infty$,*

$$I_t \longrightarrow \int_{A(x)=1} c(x) < \infty.$$

*In particular, if $A(x) < 1$ almost everywhere, then $I_t \longrightarrow 0$ as $t \longrightarrow \infty$.*

Note that the form of $I_t$ is reminiscent of the expression in Proposition 5.2 and indeed this is what the lemma will be used for; but this abstraction in terms of these various variables is necessary in order for the proof of the lemma to not become too large and convoluted.

Once we have Lemma 5.4, Proposition 5.5 follows immediately, although it may be a little tedious to check that all conditions are satisfied.

PROPOSITION 5.5. *Let $A \subseteq \Theta$ be a measurable set. Let $\theta' \in \Theta$ be such that $L(\theta') > 0$ and $L(\theta) \leq L(\theta')$ for almost every $\theta \in A$. Moreover, for each $i$, there is $\delta_i > 0$ such that $L(\theta)g_i^{(0)}(\theta)^{\delta_i} \leq L(\theta')g_i^{(0)}(\theta')^{\delta_i}$ for almost every $\theta \in A$. Then there is $0 \leq M < \infty$ such that, as $t \longrightarrow \infty$,*

$$\frac{\int_{\theta \in A} f_i^{(t)}(\theta)}{f_i^{(t)}(\theta')} \longrightarrow M.$$

*If the set $\{\theta \in A : L(\theta) = L(\theta')\}$ has measure zero, then $M = 0$.*

The previous proposition completes the "$\theta'$ dominates $A$" part of the program. To carry out the "$B$ dominates $\theta'$" part, we prove the following Lemma 5.6 and Proposition 5.7, which can be thought of as analogous versions of Lemma 5.4 and Proposition 5.5 but with reversed inequalities and slight changes in details. In particular, the part that changes is the final step of the lemma where here we use Fatou's lemma to conclude instead.

LEMMA 5.6. *Let $S, a_i, c, r_t, \varepsilon_i^{(t)}, A$ and $I_t$ be as in Lemma 5.4 with the following changes. The inequalities involving $A$ are reversed: $A(x) \geq 1$ for almost every $x \in S$, and for every $i$, there is $\delta_i > 0$ such that $A(x)a_i(x)^{\delta_i} \geq 1$ for almost every $x \in S$. Moreover, the integral $I_t$ may be infinite. If $A(x) = 1$ almost everywhere, then as $t \longrightarrow \infty$,*

$$I_t \longrightarrow \int_{x \in S} c(x),$$

*where the limit can be infinite. Otherwise, $I_t \longrightarrow \infty$ as $t \longrightarrow \infty$.*

One can prove the following proposition by applying Lemma 5.6 in the same way that one applies Lemma 5.4 to prove Proposition 5.5. So we omit the proof of the following proposition.

PROPOSITION 5.7. *Let $B \subseteq \Theta$ be a measurable set. Let $\theta' \in \Theta$ be such that $L(\theta') > 0$ and $L(\theta) \geq L(\theta')$ for almost every $\theta \in B$. Moreover, for each $i$, there is $\delta_i > 0$ such that $L(\theta)g_i^{(0)}(\theta)^{\delta_i} \geq L(\theta')g_i^{(0)}(\theta')^{\delta_i}$ for almost every $\theta \in B$. Then there is $0 \leq M \leq \infty$ such that, as $t \longrightarrow \infty$,*

$$\frac{\int_{\theta \in B} f_i^{(t)}(\theta)}{f_i^{(t)}(\theta')} \longrightarrow M.$$

*If $B$ has positive measure, then $M > 0$. If $\{\theta \in B : L(\theta) > L(\theta')\}$ has positive measure, then $M = \infty$.*

From here it is easy to combine Propositions 5.5 and 5.7 into the Master Theorem. Recall that the various technical hypotheses of the theorem should be intuitively read as "$\theta'$ dominates $A$, and $B$ dominates $\theta'$ robustly in the sense of the weighted likelihood function," as explained earlier in this section.

Theorem 5.8 (Master Theorem). *Let $A, B \subseteq \Theta$ be measurable sets, where $B$ has positive measure. Let $\theta' \in \Theta$ be such that $L(\theta') > 0$, $L(\theta) \leq L(\theta')$ for almost every $\theta \in A$, and $L(\theta) \geq L(\theta')$ for almost every $\theta \in B$. Moreover, for each $i$, there are $\delta_i, \delta_i' > 0$ such that $L(\theta) g_i^{(0)}(\theta)^{\delta_i} \leq L(\theta') g_i^{(0)}(\theta')^{\delta_i}$ for almost every $\theta \in A$ and $L(\theta) g_i^{(0)}(\theta)^{\delta_i'} \geq L(\theta') g_i^{(0)}(\theta')^{\delta_i'}$ for almost every $\theta \in B$. Suppose that either $\{\theta \in A : L(\theta) = L(\theta')\}$ has measure zero or $\{\theta \in B : L(\theta) > L(\theta')\}$ has positive measure. Then*

$$\int_{\theta \in A} f_i^{(t)}(\theta) \to 0.$$

Proof. By Propositions 5.5 and 5.7,

$$\frac{\int_{\theta \in A} f_i^{(t)}(\theta)}{\int_{\theta \in B} f_i^{(t)}(\theta)} \to \frac{M_1}{M_2},$$

where $M_1$ and $M_2$ are limits in the two respective propositions. Because $B$ has positive measure, $M_2 > 0$. Our final hypothesis implies that either $M_1 = 0$ or $M_2 = \infty$, so $M_1/M_2 = 0$. Then our result follows from $\int_{\theta \in B} f_i^{(t)}(\theta) \leq 1$. □

## 6 CONVERGENCE OF BELIEFS

We apply the Master Theorem 5.8 to show convergence of beliefs of agents toward a point distribution at the maximizer or near-maximizer of $L$. We establish separate results for the finite case (Sec. 6.2), the infinite discrete case (Sec. 6.3) and the $\mathbb{R}^k$ case (Sec. 6.4). Our results in the $\mathbb{R}^k$ case are the basis of Theorem 1.1. Results in this section will be used in applications in Section 7.

We first explain the general idea of this section. Recall that to use the Master Theorem, for a given set $A$, we need to find a point $\theta'$ that dominates $A$ and a set $B$ that dominates $\theta'$. What this section aims to do is the following. First, for a given set $A$, the choice of $\theta'$ and $B$ will be automated and abstracted away from the user. Second, even the choice of $A$ will be abstracted away, leaving only the conclusion that "beliefs converge to a point distribution," at least in the case of a unique maximizer. The general idea is not hard, but the details can be quite formidable.

### 6.1 Preliminaries

First we need some preliminaries. This subsection presents the technical details in carrying out the "automatically choosing $\theta'$ and $B$" part. Let $L_{\text{ess sup}} = \text{ess sup}_{\theta \in \Theta} L(\theta) \leq \infty$, that is, $L_{\text{ess sup}}$ is the smallest $M$ for which $\{\theta \in \Theta : L(\theta) > M\}$ has measure zero. Note that we can replace "ess sup" by "sup" if $\Theta$ is infinite discrete or "max" if $\Theta$ is finite. The following proposition gives sufficient conditions for beliefs to concentrate in places where $L$ is near $L_{\text{ess sup}}$.

Proposition 6.1. *Let $0 \leq M < L_{\text{ess sup}}$ and let $S = \{\theta \in \Theta : L(\theta) > M\}$. Assume that for every $i$, $g_i^{(0)}$ is bounded a.e. on $\Theta \setminus S$. Suppose that one of the following holds:*

*(1) $L$ is not constant a.e. on $S$ and for every $i$, $g_i^{(0)}$ is bounded below by a positive number a.e. on $S$;*

*(2) there is a subset $T \subseteq S$ of positive measure such that, for every $i$, $g_i^{(0)}$ is constant on $T$.*

*Then, as $t \to \infty$,*

$$\int_{\theta \in S} f_i^{(t)}(\theta) \to 1.$$

To better understand the above proposition, it will be useful to understand what roles the various hypotheses play. The "bounded" and "bounded below by a positive number" hypotheses ensure that the gaps between $A$ and $\theta'$ and $\theta'$ and $B$ are robust as needed in the Master Theorem 5.8. Now we note that $S$ dominates $\Theta \setminus S$; however, we still need to pick $\theta'$ and $B$ out of $S$. There are two ways to do this depending on the situation. First, think of $\Theta = \mathbb{R}$. In this case, if $L$ is constant on $S$, it will be hard to pick $B$ that dominates $\theta'$ robustly; but we can do this otherwise. This is condition (1) in the proposition. Second, think of $\Theta = \mathbb{N}$. In this case, even if $S$ is a single point (and so $L$ is constant on it), it will be easy to pick $\theta'$ and $B$; but this case does not satisfy (1). This is where condition (2) comes in. Putting all these details together gives us the proposition.

### 6.2 Finite Case

We now apply Proposition 6.1 to show convergence in the case where $\Theta$ is finite. The theorem in this case is quite easy and we can appeal to either case (2) of Proposition 6.1 or just Proposition 5.3.

THEOREM 6.2. *Assume that $\Theta$ is finite and the initial condition is feasible. Let $\theta_{\max}$ be the set of points that maximize $L$. Then as $t \longrightarrow \infty$,*

$$\sum_{\theta \in \theta_{\max}} f_i^{(t)}(\theta) \to 1.$$

*In particular, if $\theta_{\max}$ consists of a single point, then $f_i^{(t)}$ converges to the point distribution at that point.*

One may wonder what more can be said when $\theta_{\max}$ consists of several points. The example given in the full version shows that the behavior can greatly vary.

### 6.3 Infinite Discrete Case

We now move on to the theorem for the infinite discrete case, which follows from the second case of Proposition 6.1. This is the first nontrivial case and contains hypotheses that the the initial conditions have to verify in order for beliefs to converge.

THEOREM 6.3. *Assume that $\Theta$ is infinite discrete and the initial condition is feasible.*

*(1) Let $L$ attain the maximum $L_{\max}$ at the set of points $\theta_{\max} \neq \varnothing$. Suppose that $\sup_{\theta \notin \theta_{\max}} L(\theta) < L_{\max}$ and $g_i^{(0)}$ is bounded on $\Theta \setminus \theta_{\max}$. Then as $t \longrightarrow \infty$,*

$$\sum_{\theta \in \theta_{\max}} f_i^{(t)}(\theta) \to 1.$$

*In particular, if $\theta_{\max}$ consists of a single point, then $f_i^{(t)}$ converges to the point distribution at that point.*

*(2) If $L$ does not attain a maximum, let $L_{\sup} = \sup_{\theta \in \Theta} L(\theta)$. For any $M < L_{\sup}$, if $g_i^{(0)}$ is bounded on $\{\theta \in \Theta : L(\theta) \leq M\}$, then as $t \longrightarrow \infty$,*

$$\sum_{L(\theta) > M} f_i^{(t)}(\theta) \to 1.$$

The theorem is essentially saying the following. Note first that there are two separate cases. If maximizers of $L$ exist, then, assuming a "positive gap" condition and a "boundedness" condition, beliefs converge to those maximizers. But if maximizers of $L$ do not exist (for example, if $L(\theta)$ increases to but is never equal to a positive number), then all that we can say is that the beliefs concentrate at points where $L$ are near the supremum, with a boundedness condition similar to the first case. We give examples in the full version to show that both "positive gap" and "boundedness" conditions are necessary and not just the artifact of the proof.

### 6.4 $\mathbb{R}^k$ Case

Finally, we deal with convergence in the most difficult case, $\Theta = \mathbb{R}^k$. Convergence here depends on the topology of $\mathbb{R}^k$, so we need to work with functions that are sufficiently continuous. Concepts from real analysis will be freely used. Let $\overline{A}$ denote the closure of $A$ and $B_r(a)$ the open ball of radius $r$ around $a$.

First we introduce the notion of *piecewise continuity*. There is no universally agreed-upon definition of piecewise continuity, so we define our own in Definition 6.4. This definition is intended to rule out pathological behaviors, and should cover most densities in practice.

*Definition 6.4.* Let $\Theta \subseteq \mathbb{R}^k$. A function $f : \Theta \to \mathbb{R}_{\geq 0}$ is *piecewise continuous* if there is a countable collection of disjoint open sets $U_i \subseteq \Theta$ such that $\Theta \setminus \cup_i U_i$ has measure zero; only finitely many $U_i$'s intersect any given bounded set $V \subseteq \mathbb{R}^k$; and for each $i$, the restriction $f : U_i \to \mathbb{R}_{\geq 0}$ can be extended to a continuous function $\widetilde{f}_i : \overline{U_i} \to [0, \infty]$.

We now show convergence of beliefs when $\Theta \subseteq \mathbb{R}^k$ and $g_i^{(0)}$ is piecewise continuous. The following theorem can be regarded as the most significant result in this paper.

Theorem 6.5. *Assume that $\Theta \subseteq \mathbb{R}^k$ and the initial condition is feasible. Let $g_i^{(0)}$ be piecewise continuous. Let $L_{\text{ess sup}} = \operatorname{ess\,sup}_{\theta\in\Theta} L(\theta) \leq \infty$, and for any $M$, let $S_M = \{\theta \in \Theta : L(\theta) > M\}$. Let $\theta_{\text{ess sup}}$ be the set of all $\theta \in \overline{\Theta}$ such that for every $M < L_{\text{ess sup}}$ and $\delta > 0$, $B_\delta(\theta) \cap S_M$ has positive measure. Suppose that there is $r > 0$ such that $\operatorname{ess\,sup}_{|\theta|>r} L(\theta) < L_{\text{ess sup}}$. Moreover, there is $M' < L_{\text{ess sup}}$ such that for every $M \in (M', L_{\text{ess sup}})$, $L$ is not constant a.e. on $S_M$; $g_i^{(0)}$ is bounded a.e. on $\Theta \setminus S_M$; and $g_i^{(0)}$ is bounded below by a positive number a.e. on $S_M$. Then $\theta_{\text{ess sup}}$ is a nonempty compact set, and for any open set $U$ containing $\theta_{\text{ess sup}}$, as $t \to \infty$,*

$$\int_{\theta\in U\cap\Theta} f_i^{(t)}(\theta) \to 1.$$

*In particular, if $\theta_{\text{ess sup}}$ consists of a single point, then $f_i^{(t)}$, viewed as a density on $\mathbb{R}^k$ that vanishes outside of $\Theta$, converges to the point distribution at that point.*

The various hypotheses of the theorem fit together in the following way. First, $\theta_{\text{ess sup}}$ is supposed to be the "maximizers of $L$," except that there are two complications. One, we must not be distracted by sets of measure zero. Two, these maximizers may lie outside of $\Theta$; think $1/x^2$ with $\Theta = (0, \infty)$. The definition in the theorem that captures both of these aspects is the following: the "maximizers" are $\theta$ such that in small balls around $\theta$, the set where $L$ is near its essential supremum has positive measure. Then to show that beliefs converge to a point distribution at $\theta_{\text{ess sup}}$ (if it consists of a single point), we require $L$ to decay away at infinity, in the sense that the set where $L$ is near its essential supremum is bounded; this allows us to use compactness arguments. Then several hypotheses on nonconstancy and boundedness from above and below are required in order to use case (1) of Proposition 6.1. The conclusion is that beliefs concentrate in any open set containing $\theta_{\text{ess sup}}$, and this shows convergence in the case where $\theta_{\text{ess sup}}$ consists of a single point.

Proof Sketch. The proof is unfortunately rather technical. We will only give sketches of key steps here and refer the reader to the full version for details. The first step is to show that $\theta_{\text{ess sup}}$ is compact by showing that it is bounded (using the fact that $L$ decays away at infinity) and closed (by combining the $U_i$'s from the piecewise continuity definition judiciously). In particular, it will be important to characterize $\theta_{\text{ess sup}}$ as the set on which the continuous extensions of $L$ (in the sense of Definition 6.4) achieve $L_{\text{ess sup}}$. Next, we show that whenever $U$ is an open set containing $\theta_{\text{ess sup}}$, beliefs on $U \cap \Theta$ tend to 1. Our strategy is the following. Proposition 6.1 implies that for any

$M' < M < L_{\text{ess sup}}$, as $t \to \infty$, $\int_{\theta \in S_M} f_i^{(t)}(\theta) \to 1$. It therefore suffices to show that there is such an $M$ such that $S_M \setminus U$ has measure zero. Suppose the contrary. By restricting attention to a bounded set and a single $U_i$ and letting $M \to L_{\text{ess sup}}$, it will be possible to construct a sequence $\theta_j \in S_{M_j} \setminus U$ that tends to some $\theta \in \theta_{\text{ess sup}}$. This is a contradiction because $U$ is an open set containing $\theta$. □

Lastly, we present a simplified version of Theorem 6.5 when $\Theta = \mathbb{R}^k$ and $g_i^{(0)}$ is bounded and continuous. This version can deal with densities that are continuous on the whole of $\mathbb{R}^k$ with some mild decay conditions, and it is applicable to e.g. Gaussians and many similar densities. To prove this corollary, we directly apply Theorem 6.5, where Corollary 4.7 is used to prove that the initial condition is feasible.

Corollary 6.6. *Assume that $\Theta = \mathbb{R}^k$. Let $g_i^{(0)}$ be bounded continuous functions. Suppose that there is a bounded set $S$ such that $\sup_{\theta \notin S} L(\theta) < \sup_{\theta \in \mathbb{R}^k} L(\theta)$. Then the initial condition is feasible, $L$ attains a maximum at the set of points $\theta_{\max} \neq \varnothing$, and for any open set $U$ containing $\theta_{\max}$, as $t \to \infty$,*

$$\int_{\theta \in U} f_i^{(t)}(\theta) \to 1.$$

*In particular, if $\theta_{\max}$ consists of a single point, then $f_i^{(t)}$ converges to the point distribution at that point.*

Another (further simplified) version of Corollary 6.6 that should be useful in practice is Theorem 1.1 in the introduction.

## 7 APPLICATIONS

We now seek to apply our theoretical results to model real-world situations. One example is given for each of the cases where $\Theta$ is finite, infinite discrete, and continuous to demonstrate the use of our theorems.

### 7.1 Binary Beliefs

Suppose that the underlying state of the world is binary, $\Theta = \{0, 1\}$. For example, agents are trying to determine the truth value of a statement. At first, agent $i$ believes that the statement holds with probability $x_i$. By Theorem 6.2, we can conclude the following.

Proposition 7.1. *Let the initial belief of agent $i$ be Bernoulli distributed as* Bern$(x_i)$, $0 < x_i < 1$, *and the common prior be* Bern$(1/2)$. *Then the initial condition is feasible. If $\prod_{i=1}^n x_i^{v_i} > \prod_{i=1}^n (1-x_i)^{v_i}$, then $f_i^{(t)}$ converges to the point distribution at 1; if $\prod_{i=1}^n x_i^{v_i} < \prod_{i=1}^n (1-x_i)^{v_i}$, then $f_i^{(t)}$ converges to the point distribution at 0.*

Note that, except in the borderline case $\prod_{i=1}^n x_i^{v_i} = \prod_{i=1}^n (1-x_i)^{v_i}$, agents will reach a consensus on whether the statement is true or false. This process can be viewed as if agents cast votes on what everyone should believe: everyone will unanimously agree that the statement is true if

$$\sum_{i=1}^n v_i \log\left(\frac{x_i}{1-x_i}\right) > 0,$$

and that the statement is false if this expression is negative. Thus it is as if agent $i$ casts votes of $\log(x_i/(1-x_i))$ in support of the statement and gets $v_i$ votes. The expression $\log(x_i/(1-x_i))$, called the *log-odds*, transforms probability in $(0, 1)$ to the real line. Moreover, we can see that the strength of an agent's vote indeed comes from her confidence and her centrality.

A similar analysis holds when agents are trying to decide between a finite number of alternatives. In this case, if agent $i$ believes in alternative $j$ with probability $x_{i,j}$, then it is as if she casts votes of $\log x_{i,j}$ in support of alternative $j$. The alternative with the most votes becomes the consensus.

### 7.2 Poisson Beliefs

Now let us consider the case where there are an infinite number of alternatives, e.g. when the underlying state of the world is the number of events in a time period. The initial beliefs can be modeled by Poisson distributions.

Proposition 7.2. *Assume that the initial belief of agent i is* $\mathrm{Pois}(\lambda_i)$ *and the common prior is a flat prior, then the initial condition is feasible. Let* $\lambda^* = \prod_{i=1}^{N} \lambda_i^{v_i}$. *If* $\lambda^*$ *is not an integer, then* $f_i^{(t)}$ *converges to the point distribution at* $\lfloor \lambda^* \rfloor$. *If* $\lambda^*$ *is an integer, then* $f_i^{(t)}$ *lies in* $\{\lambda^* - 1, \lambda^*\}$ *with probability going to 1 as* $t \to \infty$.

Proof Sketch. Compute $L(\theta) \propto (\lambda^*)^{\theta}/\theta!$ and apply Theorem 6.3. □

The Poisson parameter $\lambda$ is the mean of $\mathrm{Pois}(\lambda)$ and is related to the average event rate. Our result shows that agents will reach a consensus at $\lambda^*$, the *weighted geometric mean* of the rates corresponding to agents' beliefs, where again the weight of each agent is her centrality. Note that our model indicates that Poisson rates should be combined multiplicatively rather than additively. This accords with intuition: if two connected people believe that there will be 2 and 1000 floods on average next year, respectively, then Proposition 7.2 says that they will come to believe that there will be $\lfloor \sqrt{2000} \rfloor = 44$ floods. In contrast, combining rates additively as in DeGroot leads to the counterintuitive answer of 501 floods. Thus, even though each agent carries essentially one piece of information: the event rate, by modeling the beliefs according to the actual underlying parameter space, our model leads us to a natural consensus. A similar situation is the Gaussian belief case in the next section where beliefs converge to the weighted arithmetic mean and agent $i$ also has weight $v_i$.

### 7.3 Gaussian Beliefs

Finally, we consider the interesting case of each agent carrying *two* pieces of information, her belief and her confidence. Suppose that the underlying state of the world is $\Theta = \mathbb{R}$ with the flat prior $f_* \equiv 1$. Each agent observes the true state of the world $\theta^*$ with Gaussian noise: agent $i$'s signal $\mu_i$ is drawn from the normal distribution $\mathcal{N}(\theta^*, 1/\tau_i)$, where $\tau_i$ is the *precision* known to agent $i$. Note that this is an example of an underlying scenario explained in Section 2.3, except that the prior in this case is improper. Then agent $i$'s initial belief for $\theta^*$ (conditional on the signal $\mu_i$) can be computed to be $\mathcal{N}(\mu_i, 1/\tau_i)$.

Proposition 7.3. *Assume that the initial belief of agent i is normally distributed as* $\mathcal{N}(\mu_i, 1/\tau_i)$ *and the common prior is a flat prior, then this initial condition is feasible and* $f_i^{(t)}$ *converges to the point distribution at*

$$\theta_{\max} = \sum_{i=1}^{N} c_i \mu_i, \quad c_i = \frac{v_i \tau_i}{\sum_{j=1}^{N} v_j \tau_j}.$$

Proof Sketch. The weighted likelihood function is proportional to a Gaussian with the maximum at $\theta_{\max}$. Apply Corollary 6.6. □

If we interpret the initial belief $\mathcal{N}(\mu_i, 1/\tau_i)$ as a scalar belief $\mu_i$ with confidence $\tau_i$, then the consensus belief $\theta_{\max}$ is the weighted average of agents' signals $\mu_i$ with weights $c_i$ proportional to her centrality $v_i$ and her precision $\tau_i$. Therefore, an agent who is more centrally located and has a more informative signal has more influence over the consensus belief. This phenomenon cannot be captured by the standard DeGroot model which has no notion of quality of signals.

We can evaluate quality of learning by the variance of the consensus. This works as follows. The consensus $\theta_{\max}$ is a function of the signals $\mu_i$, and the signals are random, so the consensus can be viewed as a random variable. Specifically, it is an unbiased estimator of the true state $\theta^*$, and the lower its variance, the higher the quality of learning. Since $\mu_i \sim \mathcal{N}(\theta^*, 1/\tau_i)$ are independent, $\theta_{\max} = \sum_i c_i \mu_i \sim \mathcal{N}(\theta^*, S)$ remains a Gaussian, with variance

$$S = \frac{\sum_i v_i^2 \tau_i}{(\sum_i v_i \tau_i)^2}.$$

We now investigate the effect of increasing the precision $\tau_k$ on the variance $S$. We find that, all other variables being fixed, the result depends on the threshold $V_k = 2\sum_{i \neq k} v_i^2 \tau_i / \sum_{i \neq k} v_i \tau_i$ of the centrality $v_k$. By direct computation, if $v_k \leq V_k$, then increasing $\tau_k$ always decreases $S$, while if $v_k > V_k$, then increasing $\tau_k$ decreases $S$ only if $\tau_k \geq (v_k - V_k) \sum_{i \neq k} v_i \tau_i / v_k^2$ and *increases* $S$ otherwise. Thus, increasing the precision $\tau_k$ usually decreases the variance and improves the quality of learning, *except* when the centrality $v_k$ is high and the precision $\tau_k$ is low. This result has an implication for social planners who want to encourage good learning. The social planner cannot control the network structure $v_k$ but she might be able to control the signal precision $\tau_k$. If an agent is central but relatively uninformed, increasing the precision of that agent can reduce learning quality. An intuitive explanation might be that the agent now has some confidence to use her centrality to impose her less informed opinion on the consensus. Only when that central agent is sufficiently informed will additional precision improve learning quality. Therefore, if a social planner wants to seed centrally located agents (opinion leaders) with new technologies, she must invest enough resources to make those agents well informed; otherwise, the effort can backfire.

In the full paper, we discuss the case of Gaussian beliefs with correlated initial signals. As expected, higher correlations in initial signals reduce learning quality.

Another point of interest is that our consensus does not depend on the geometry of the network beyond the eigenvector centralities; this is true for all of our analysis from Section 5 onwards and not only for this particular Gaussian case. Let us contrast this with the work of Banerjee et al. [5], which also incorporates quality of signals into DeGroot learning. In their model, the quality of signals is binary (informed/uninformed), and each agent takes the average of signals of only her informed neighbors. They identify the *clustered seeding* problem: if the initially informed agents are closely connected, some agents will "block" other agents, reducing influence of the blocked agents.

To illustrate this point, consider a social network in the shape of an undirected cycle of length $N$ and assume that only three adjacent agents $1, 2, 3$ are initially informed with the same precision. In our model, the three agents' signals have equal weights: $c_1 = c_2 = c_3 = 1/3$. But in their model, agent 2 is blocked by agents 1 and 3: $c_1 = c_3 \to 1/2$ and $c_2 \to 0$ as the number of agents $N \to \infty$. Note that all three agents do have the same centralities and the same precisions, yet the geometry of the network still allows them to block each other.

Why this occurs may be explained as follows: as the "informed segment" of the network expands, an agent who has just become newly informed will get the opinion of agent 1 or 3 first. Surely she will not be very confident because she has just heard of one opinion, but in the model of Banerjee et al. [5], her opinion counts as much as everyone else, and so the opinions of agents 1 and 3 get injected back into the informed segment and reinforce themselves to an inappropriate degree. In contrast, our model circumvents this problem by allowing agents to express their confidence. Thus, a newly informed agent is not very confident and her opinion counts less; and it turns out that this alone is enough to offset the blocking disadvantage and allows the opinion of agent 2 to come through in the consensus. We conclude that the clustered seeding problem occurs when agents can communicate whether they are informed but cannot communicate precisions of their signals. When agents can communicate precisions of signals, even if beliefs are naively updated, the problem disappears. Therefore, it is of vital importance that agents be able to communicate opinions freely and expressively, and not just state their beliefs, in order for blocking to not occur.

## ACKNOWLEDGEMENTS

We thank Ben Golub for insightful comments in the early stage of this project. We are also grateful to Nicole Immorlica and Evan Sadler for suggestions that improved the paper.

## REFERENCES

[1] Daron Acemoglu, Munther A. Dahleh, Ilan Lobel, and Asuman Ozdaglar. 2011. Bayesian Learning in Social Networks. *Review of Economic Studies* (2011).

[2] Jerry Anunrojwong and Nat Sothanaphan. 2018. Naive Bayesian Learning in Social Networks. (2018). https://arxiv.org/abs/1805.05878

[3] Venkatesh Bala and Sanjeev Goyal. 2000. A Noncooperative Model of Network Formation. *Econometrica* (2000).

[4] Abhijit V. Banerjee. 1992. A Simple Model of Herd Behavior. *The Quarterly Journal of Economics* (1992).

[5] Abhijit V. Banerjee, Emily Breza, Arun G. Chandrasekhar, and Markus Mobius. 2018. Naive Learning with Uninformed Agents. (2018).

[6] Sushil Bikhchandani, David Hirshleifer, and Ivo Welch. 1992. A Theory of Fads, Fashion, Custom, and Cultural Change as Informational Cascades. *Journal of Political Economy* (1992).

[7] Bogachan Celen and Shachar Kariv. 2004. Observational learning under imperfect information. *Games and Economic Behavior* (2004).

[8] Peter M. DeMarzo, Dimitri Vayanos, and Jeffrey Zwiebel. 2003. Persuasion Bias, Social Influence, and Unidimensional Opinions. *The Quarterly Journal of Economics* (2003).

[9] Erik Eyster and Matthew Rabin. 2010. Naive Herding in Rich-Information Settings. *American Economic Journal: Microeconomics* (2010).

[10] Erik Eyster and Matthew Rabin. 2014. Extensive Imitation is Irrational and Harmful. *The Quarterly Journal of Economics* (2014).

[11] Douglas Gale and Shachar Kariv. 2003. Bayesian Learning in Social Networks. *Games and Economic Behavior* (2003).

[12] Benjamin Golub and Matthew O. Jackson. 2010. Naive learning in social networks and the wisdom of crowds. *American Economic Journal: Microeconomics* (2010).

[13] Ali Jadbabaie, Pooya Molavi, Alvaro Sandroni, and Alireza Tahbaz-Salehi. 2012. Non-Bayesian social learning. *Games and Economic Behavior* (2012).

[14] Wei Li and Xu Tan. 2018. Learning in Local Networks. (2018).

[15] Ilan Lobel and Evan Sadler. 2015. Information diffusion in networks through social learning. *Theoretical Economics* (2015).

[16] Carl D. Meyer. 2001. *Matrix Analysis and Applied Linear Algebra.* Society for Industrial and Applied Mathematics, Philadelphia, PA.

[17] Pooya Molavi, Alireza Tahbaz-Salehi, and Ali Jadbabaie. 2018. A Theory of Non-Bayesian Social Learning. *Econometrica* (2018).

[18] Manuel Mueller-Frank. 2013. A general framework for rational learning in social networks. *Theoretical Economics* (2013).

[19] Mohammad Amin Rahimian, Pooya Molavi, and Ali Jadbabaie. 2014. (Non-)Bayesian learning without recall. *IEEE Annual Conference on Decision and Control* (2014).

[20] Mohammad Amin Rahimian, Pooya Molavi, and Ali Jadbabaie. 2015. Learning without Recall: A Case for Log-Linear Learning. *IFAC Workshop on Distributed Estimation and Control in Networked Systems* (2015).

[21] Dinah Rosenberg, Eilon Solan, and Nicolas Vieille. 2009. Informational externalities and emergence of consensus. *Games and Economic Behavior* (2009).

[22] Lones Smith and Peter Sorensen. 2000. Pathological Outcomes of Observational Learning. *Econometrica* (2000).

# Bayesian Social Learning in a Dynamic Environment

KRISHNA DASARATHA, Harvard University
BENJAMIN GOLUB, Harvard University
NIR HAK, Harvard University

Bayesian agents learn about a moving target, such as a commodity price, using private signals and their network neighbors' estimates. The weights agents place on these sources of information are endogenously determined by the precisions and correlations of the sources; the weights, in turn, determine future correlations. We study stationary equilibria—ones in which all of these quantities are constant over time. Equilibria in linear updating rules always exist, yielding a Bayesian learning model as tractable as the commonly-used DeGroot heuristic. Equilibria and the comparative statics of learning outcomes can be readily computed even in large networks. Substantively, we identify pervasive inefficiencies in Bayesian learning. In any stationary equilibrium where agents put positive weights on neighbors' actions, learning is Pareto inefficient in a generic network: agents rationally overuse social information and underuse their private signals.

Full Paper: https://arxiv.org/abs/1801.02042

Additional Key Words and Phrases: social learning; Bayesian learning; DeGroot model; information aggregation; networks; centrality

---

Authors' addresses: Krishna Dasaratha, Harvard University, Department of Economics, Cambridge, MA, 02138, dasarath@g.harvard.edu; Benjamin Golub, Harvard University, Department of Economics, Cambridge, MA, 02138, bgolub@fas.harvard.edu; Nir Hak, Harvard University, Department of Economics, Cambridge, MA, 02138, nirhak@g.harvard.edu.

---


*ACM EC'18, June 18–22, 2018, Ithaca, NY, USA.* ACM ISBN 978-1-4503-4529-3/18/06.
https://doi.org/10.1145/3219166.3219218

# Social Learning Equilibria

ELCHANAN MOSSEL, Massachusetts Institute of Technology
MANUEL MUELLER-FRANK, University of Navarra, IESE Business School
ALLAN SLY, Princeton University
OMER TAMUZ, California Institute of Technology

We consider social learning settings in which a group of agents face uncertainty regarding a state of the world, observe private signals, share the same utility function, and act in a general dynamic setting. We introduce Social Learning Equilibria, a static equilibrium concept that abstracts away from the details of the given dynamics, but nevertheless captures the corresponding asymptotic equilibrium behavior. We establish strong equilibrium properties on agreement, herding, and information aggregation.

Full Paper: http://people.hss.caltech.edu/~tamuz/papers/sle.pdf

CCS Concepts: • **Applied computing → Electronic commerce**; **Economics**;

Additional Key Words and Phrases: Consensus; Learning; Herding

Elchanan Mossel is supported by awards NSF DMS-1737944, ONR N00014-17-1-2598, and CCF 1665252. Manuel Mueller-Frank gratefully acknowledges the financial support of the Spanish Ministry of Economy and Competitiveness (Ref. ECO2015-63711-P). Omer Tamuz is supported by a grant from the Simons Foundation (#419427).

Authors' addresses: Elchanan Mossel, Massachusetts Institute of Technology , elmos@mit.edu; Manuel Mueller-Frank, University of Navarra, IESE Business School, mmuellerfrank@iese.edu; Allan Sly, Princeton University, asly@princeton.edu; Omer Tamuz, California Institute of Technology, tamuz@caltech.edu.


*ACM EC'18, June 18–22, 2018, Ithaca, NY, USA*. ACM ISBN 978-1-4503-4529-3/18/06.
https://doi.org/10.1145/3219166.3219208

# Diffusion, Seeding, and the Value of Network Information

MOHAMMAD AKBARPOUR, Stanford University, USA
SURAJ MALLADI, Stanford University, USA
AMIN SABERI, Stanford University, USA

Identifying the optimal set of individuals to first receive information ('seeds') in a social network is a widely-studied question in many settings, such as the diffusion of information, microfinance programs, and new technologies. Numerous studies have proposed various network-centrality based heuristics to choose seeds in a way that is likely to boost diffusion. Here we show that, for some frequently studied diffusion processes, randomly seeding $s + x$ individuals can prompt a larger cascade than optimally targeting the best $s$ individuals, for a small $x$. We prove our results for large classes of random networks, but also show that they hold in simulations over several real-world networks. This suggests that the returns to collecting and analyzing network information to identify the optimal seeds may not be economically significant. Given these findings, practitioners interested in communicating a message to a large number of people may wish to compare the cost of network-based targeting to that of slightly expanding initial outreach.

Full Paper: https://ssrn.com/abstract=3062830

CCS Concepts: • **Networks** → **Network economics**; • **Theory of computation** → *Social networks*;

Additional Key Words and Phrases: Diffusion, targeting, network, word-of-mouth

We thank Daron Acemolgu, Nava Ashraf, Stephane Bonhomme, Jeremy Bulow, Arun Chandrasekhar, Zoe Cullen, Darrell Duffie, Pascaline Dupas, Matthew Elliot, Ben Golub, Sanjeev Goyal, Matthew Jackson, Emir Kamenica, Alireza Khatami, Jon Kleinberg, Scott Kominers, Shengwu Li, Yucheng Liang, Greg MacNamara, Ilya Morozov, Michael Ostrovsky, Peter Reiss, Evan Sadler, Andy Skrzypacz, Alex Teytelboym, Christopher Tonetti, Carlos Varjao, Ali Yurukoglu, BREAD development economics and Network Economics seminar participants, as well as several other seminar participants, for valuable comments.

Authors' addresses: Mohammad Akbarpour, Stanford University, 655 Knight way, Stanford, CA, 94305, USA, mohamwad@stanford.edu; Suraj Malladi, Stanford University, 655 Knight way, Stanford, CA, 94305, USA, surajm@stanford.edu; Amin Saberi, Stanford University, 475 Via Ortega, 309, Stanford, CA, 94305, USA, saberi@stanford.edu.


*ACM EC'18, June 18–22, 2018, Ithaca, NY, USA.* ACM ISBN 978-1-4503-5829-3/18/06.
https://doi.org/10.1145/3219166.3219213

# On the Construction of Substitutes

ERIC BALKANSKI, Harvard University
RENATO PAES LEME, Google Research

Gross substitutability is a central concept in Economics and is connected to important notions in Discrete Convex Analysis, Number Theory and the analysis of Greedy algorithms in Computer Science. Many different characterizations are known for this class, but providing a constructive description remains a major open problem. The construction problem asks how to construct all gross substitutes from a class of simpler functions using a set of operations. Since gross substitutes are a natural generalization of matroids to real-valued functions, matroid rank functions form a desirable such class of simpler functions.

Shioura proved that a rich class of gross substitutes can be expressed as sums of matroid rank functions, but it is open whether all gross substitutes can be constructed this way. Our main result is a negative answer showing that some gross substitutes cannot be expressed as positive linear combinations of matroid rank functions. En route, we provide necessary and sufficient conditions for the sum to preserve substitutability, uncover a new operation preserving substitutability and fully describe all substitutes with at most 4 items.

Full Paper: https://arxiv.org/abs/1805.03726

CCS Concepts: • **Applied computing → Electronic commerce**; **Economics**;

Additional Key Words and Phrases: Gross substitutes; Matroids; Valuation functions.

---

Eric is supported by a Google PhD Fellowship.

Authors' addresses: Eric Balkanski, Harvard University, ericbalkanski@g.harvard.edu; Renato Paes Leme, Google Research, renatoppl@google.com.

---


*ACM EC'18, June 18–22, 2018, Ithaca, NY, USA.* ACM ISBN 978-1-4503-4529-3/18/06.
https://doi.org/10.1145/3219166.3219184

# Frugal Auction Design for Set Systems: Vertex Cover and Knapsack

MOHAMMADTAGHI HAJIAGHAYI, University of Maryland, USA
MOHAMMAD REZA KHANI, Microsoft R&D, USA
SAEED SEDDIGHIN, University of Maryland, USA

We study mechanism design for procurement auctions in which the goal is to buy a subset of items or hire a team of providers. In order to measure the efficiency of a mechanism, one defines an appropriate benchmark which denotes a reasonable expectation of the payments and defines the overpayment of a mechanism based on the benchmark. This ratio is called the *frugality ratio* of the mechanism. Procurement auctions are well-studied and benchmarks proposed for these auctions have evolved over a sequence of papers [2, 5, 8, 12, 13]. In this work, we introduce a newer benchmark, and based on that, study classic procurement auctions. Our benchmark addresses critical issues raised by the unintuitive behavior of the previous benchmarks. We show two attractive properties for our benchmark which have been lacking in the previous proposals: *monotonicity* and *smoothness*.

Based on our benchmark, we provide positive results for vertex cover and knapsack auctions. Prior to this work, Kempe *et al.* [13] propose a constant approximation mechanism for vertex cover auctions. However, their analysis suffers from an error. We give a correct analysis to the mechanism of Kempe *et al.* [13] *with respect to our benchmark*. In particular, we prove their mechanism is optimal up to a constant factor. Our analysis is different from what Kempe *et al.* [13] propose. We also study the knapsack auctions and give a truthful mechanism for such auctions with a bounded frugality ratio. We show that this is almost tight by presenting a lower bound on the frugality ratio of any truthful mechanism for such auctions. *All our results depend on both properties of the benchmark.* [1]

CCS Concepts: • **Theory of computation → Algorithmic game theory and mechanism design**;

Additional Key Words and Phrases: Frugal, Knapsack, Vertex Cover

## 1 INTRODUCTION

Suppose we want to purchase a number of different items or hire a team to accomplish certain tasks. It is quite common that the items or people are interchangeable. In other words, every task can be performed by different groups of people which naturally leads to a competition between individuals. As an example, suppose a government wishes to connect a city to another one, by building roads between intermediary cities. Constructing each road can be entrusted with a contractor at a certain

Supported in part by NSF CAREER award CCF-1053605, NSF BIGDATA grant IIS-1546108, NSF AF:Medium grant CCF-1161365, DARPA GRAPHS/AFOSR grant FA9550-12-1-0423, and another DARPA SIMPLEX grant

[1] In the interest of space, some of the proofs and results have been omitted in this version and included in the full-version.

Authors' addresses: MohammadTaghi Hajiaghayi, University of Maryland, USA, hajiagha@cd.umd.edu; Mohammad Reza Khani, Microsoft R&D, USA, rezak@microsoft.com; Saeed Seddighin, University of Maryland, USA, saeedreza.seddighin@gmail.com.


*ACM EC'18, June 18–22, 2018, Ithaca, NY, USA.* ACM ISBN 978-1-4503-5829-3/18/06...$15.00
https://doi.org/10.1145/3219166.3219229

cost. It is not natural to expect the contractors to reveal the true cost of their service since they are selfishly motivated. Therefore one of the key difficulties, especially from the government's perspective, is to find out which subset of roads to build and what the actual cost of each construction is. A very effective and commonly used approach (see *e.g.* [10, 11]) is to design a procurement auction and hope that the competition between contractors keeps the costs low enough. The goal is then to design a mechanism for the auction to (i) make the providers truthful (i.e., leave no incentive for the providers to misrepresent their costs) (ii) do not overpay by much.

Procurement auctions have been extensively studied in the literature [4, 6, 7, 10, 11, 15]. A mechanism for a procurement auction is an algorithm that receives the bids as input and specifies a subset of bidders as the winning set. In addition to the selection of the providers, the payments are also determined by the mechanism. It is shown that if the selection rule is monotonic (decreasing the bid of each provider increases his likelihood of winning), the payments are uniquely determined by Myerson's characterization of truthful mechanisms. Truthfulness makes the market transparent and reveals the actual costs. However, as a downside, the payments of a truthful mechanism are inevitably higher than the announced costs. Therefore, it is crucial to define a measure to evaluate the overpayment and as such, the efficiency of mechanisms. One natural way to define the overpayment is to compare the total payment of the auctioneer to the total cost of the cheapest option. However, this formulation becomes unbounded for all truthful mechanisms in most cases and thus can't be used to evaluate mechanisms.

One way to achieve this goal is by defining a benchmark and comparing the payments of the mechanism to the benchmark as the ratio of the overpayment. Such a benchmark receives the costs as input and maps these values to a non-negative real number. The goal then is to minimize the ratio of the mechanism's total payment to the value of the benchmark. This formulation was first defined by the pioneering work of Archer and Tardos [2] who call this ratio the *frugality* ratio of a truthful mechanism. In their work, they also propose a benchmark which is the cost of the second cheapest option. However, this measure was specifically designed to study the shortest path auction, and hence it was not extensible to general problems. Later, several attempts were made to improve the benchmark of Archer and Tardos [2], but none of the proposed benchmarks seem to be a right fit for the problem setting (see the full-version for a more detailed review). Perhaps the reason that studying frugal mechanisms is unreasonably hard or sometimes faulty is the unexpected and counterintuitive behavior of the current benchmarks.

Our main contribution is proposing a new benchmark. Our benchmark benefits from two attractive properties which have been lacking in most of the previous proposals.

- *Smoothness:* If a provider changes his bid by a small amount $\epsilon$, the benchmark changes by at most $nO(\epsilon)$ where $n$ is the number of providers.
- *Monotonicity:* If a provider decreases his bid, the benchmark does not increase.

Almost none[2] of the currently known benchmarks satisfy both of the above properties. This makes our proposal unique since both properties are naturally expected of a reasonable benchmark. We use this newer definition to show positive results for many well-studied auctions. We emphasize that the results presented in this work are based on our benchmark and thus are not direct improvements/corrections of the previous works. Nonetheless, given the justifications of our benchmark, we believe our results are strong evidence in support of the efficiency of our mechanisms.

[2]Except the proposal Karlin *et al.* [12] that has been ruled out by Elkind *et al.* [8] due to several undesired computational and non-computational properties.

### 1.1 Our Benchmark

We model an auction by a set system $(\mathcal{E}, \mathcal{F})$ where $\mathcal{E}$ denotes the set of providers and $\mathcal{F}$ is a collection of all feasible subsets of providers who can perform the task. For instance, in the case of shortest path auction, the auctioneer wishes to buy one feasible set of roads to connect the source to the destination. Therefore, every edge is a provider and every feasible set corresponds to a path from the source to the destination.

As aforementioned, our proposal is based on the price of cooperation. Suppose the auctioneer commits to a feasible set $S \in \mathcal{F}$ and asks the providers to come up with prices. Of course, the prices should be reasonable, hence, no other feasible set $T \in \mathcal{F}$ should be cheaper for the auctioneer. The maximum total payment of the auctioneer in this case is when all the winning providers collude to maximize the total payment. Therefore, we assume the providers cooperate in order to maximize the total payment of the auctioneer. Such prices can be formulated via an LP.

To formulate the above definition, let $c$ denote the true costs of the providers. We define a function $v_S^*(c)$ for an arbitrary feasible set $S$ as the solution to the following LP:

$$\begin{aligned}
\max \quad & v_S^*(c) = \textstyle\sum_{e \in S} x_e && && (1)\\
s.t. \quad & x_e = c_e && \forall e \notin S && (2)\\
& x_e \geq 0 && \forall e \in S && (3)\\
& \textstyle\sum_{e \in S} x_e \leq \sum_{e' \in T} x_{e'} && \forall T \in \mathcal{F} && (4)
\end{aligned}$$

Our proposal for the benchmark is the maximum of such values over all choices of feasible sets for the auctioneer.

**Justification of the benchmark:** Our benchmark identifies as the worst cooperative equilibrium. This explains why we take the maximum over all possible sets. Note that the previous benchmarks were defined based on the cheapest feasible set only because the corresponding LP was infeasible for the rest of the feasible sets. This is not the case for cooperative equilibria and therefore we take the maximum value over all possible feasible sets. One may think of $x_e$ as a candidate payment to provider $e$. This way, $v_S^*(c)$ formulates the smallest payment of the auctioneer subject to the winning set being a set $S$. Roughly speaking, the auctioneer has to pay at least $v_S^*(c)$ as there is no better option for him. This intuition justifies the fact that $v_S^*(c)$ is a good candidate lower bound for the payment of the auctioneer for any $S$. Therefore, we define our benchmark as

$$\mathcal{B}_{(\mathcal{E},\mathcal{F})}(c) = \max_{S \in \mathcal{F}} v_S^*(c). \tag{5}$$

Note that since the winning set is not necessarily the cheapest set, we take the maximum of $v_S^*(c)$ over all feasible sets. This is where our definition differs from that of Elkind *et al.* [8]. To capture the concept of cooperation in this benchmark, we do not enforce the candidate prices to be higher than the costs which might, in some cases, leave the LP infeasible. We provide a complete review of this benchmark, previously existing benchmarks, and their relation and properties in the full version of the paper.

### 1.2 An Overview of the Results and Techniques

Our main contribution is a novel and well-motivated benchmark for measuring the efficiency of truthful mechanisms. Our benchmark is inspired by the work of Elkind *et al.* [8] in which the authors suggest "the price of cooperation" to define the frugality ratio of mechanisms. We show that our benchmark benefits from two important properties monotonicity and smoothness both of which are naturally expected from a benchmark.

Note that, most of the previous benchmarks lack either of these properties. For instance, the benchmark of [5] ($v(c)$) is not monotone, i.e., an increase in the agents' costs might result in a decrease in the benchmark. Similarly, $\mathsf{TUMax}(c)$ and $\mathsf{TUMin}(c)$ proposed by Elkind *et al.* [8] (worst and best Nash equilibrium of a utility transferable game) satisfy neither of the properties and thus show a counterintuitive behavior in certain situations (see the full-version of the paper for more detail). We show our benchmark is easier to work with, by presenting several positive results for different set systems. Both properties of our benchmark are essential in proving all results of this paper.

*1.2.1 Vertex Cover Auctions (Section 3).* In a vertex cover auction, we are given a graph $G$ and every provider corresponds to a vertex of the graph. The goal is to hire a set of providers that cover all edges of the graph. In other words, $\mathcal{E} = V(G)$ and a set $S \in \mathcal{F}$ if and only if for every edge $(u, v) \in E(G)$ either $u \in S$ or $v \in S$ (or both).

In Section 3, we analyze the mechanism of Kempe *et al.* [13] for vertex cover auction and prove a constant competitive factor for this mechanism. Kempe *et al.* 's [13] mechanism for vertex cover is based on a spectral analysis of the graph. They define a matrix $\mathsf{WAM}(G)$ based on the adjacency matrix of the graph. $\mathsf{WAM}(G)$ is essentially the adjacency matrix of the graph except that the values are scaled based on the benchmark. Notice that the benchmark of Kempe *et al.* [13] is different from our benchmark, however replacing their benchmark with ours doesn't change the definition of $\mathsf{WAM}(G)$. $\mathsf{WAM}(G)$ only depends on the structure of the graph and is regardless of the bids or costs. Next, they define a weight $q_v$ for every vertex $v$ of the graph and later use the weights to define the winning set of their mechanism. They show the entries of the dominant eigenvector of this matrix are positive real numbers and thus formulate the weight of each vertex based on the dominant eigenvector of $\mathsf{WAM}(G)$. We denote the weights of the vertices with vector $q$ where every $q_v$ is the weight of vertex $v$.

Finally, based on the weights of the elements, they leverage a variant of the VCG mechanism to purchase the elements. We call such a mechanism a weighted VCG mechanism (WVCG). In a WVCG mechanism, every element is associated with a weight. The winning set of such auctions is the one with the minimum total weighted cost. Based on this selection rule, the prices are set according to Myerson's characterization of truthful mechanisms [14]. Therefore, every WVCG mechanism is truthful. As such, Kempe *et al.* [13]'s mechanism chooses the vertex cover with the minimum total weighted cost and computes the payments based on the Myerson's rule.

In Section 3.3, we give a correct analysis for the above mechanism and show its frugality ratio is bounded by the dominant eigenvalue of $\mathsf{WAM}(G)$. Of course, this proof is based on our benchmark $\mathcal{B}_{(\mathcal{E},\mathcal{F})}(c)$.

**Theorem** 3.5 (restated). *The frugality ratio of the vertex cover mechanism is bounded by $\alpha$ where $\alpha$ is the dominant eigenvalue of WAM(G).*

The complete proof of this theorem appears in Section 3.3.

The intuition behind the proof is that we charge the payments to the value of our benchmark. Recall that $\mathcal{B}_{(\mathcal{E},\mathcal{F})}(c) = \max_{S\in\mathcal{F}} v^*_S(c)$ and the value of function $v^*_S(c)$ for a specific set $S$ is determined by variables $x_e$'s (see LP 1). Let $S^w$ be the winning set of the mechanism and $x$ be a solution to the LP corresponding to $v^*_{S^w}(c)$ . We redistribute the value of $x_e$ for each element $e \notin S^w$ in an optimal solution of $v^*_{S^w}(c)$ in a way that guarantees the following condition: the payment to every provider is at most $\alpha$ times the value distributed to him. To this end, we leverage spectral techniques and exploit properties of the dominant eigenvector of $\mathsf{WAM}(G)$. The redistribution is essentially a double counting argument based on the payments in specific instances of the problem. Theorem 3.5 follows from the conditions of our redistribution.

Kempe *et al.* [13] also show a lower bound on the frugality ratio of any truthful mechanism for the vertex cover auction. More precisely, they show the frugality ratio of any truthful mechanism is at least $\alpha/2$ where $\alpha$ is the largest eigenvalue of $\mathsf{WAM}(G)$. We show a similar analysis works for our benchmark and hence such a lower bound holds in our setting. We extend this lower bound to randomized mechanisms as well.

**Theorem** 3.6 (restated). *No truthful randomized mechanism can get a frugality ratio better than* $\alpha/4$.

For the complete proof see Section 3.4. The above theorem along with Theorem 3.5 proves a constant competitive factor (4) for this mechanism.

One may ask how is our result different from the work of Chen *et al.* [5]? We emphasize that the result of Chen *et al.* is not constant competitive. None of the previous work provides any constant competitive analysis for any vertex cover mechanism. We present a new analysis for the mechanism of Kempe *et al.* [13] with respect to our benchmark and show it is constant competitive.

*1.2.2 Knapsack Auctions (Section 4).* Knapsack auctions have been studied in the literature of both economics and computer science [1, 3, 9, 16]. Knapsack auction captures natural economic interactions. For instance, when a company or individual aims at purchasing at least a specific amount of advertisement opportunities, the problem can be modeled via a knapsack auction. In knapsack auctions, every item has an integer volume and an auctioneer wishes to purchase a subset of items having a total volume of at least a certain number. In the knapsack auction, every element $e$ corresponds to a volume $v_e$ and every feasible set is a subset of items that has a total volume of at least $k$. All the volumes are at least 1, i.e., $v_i \geq 1$ for all items. In other words, $\mathcal{E} = \{1, 2, \ldots, |\mathcal{E}|\}$ and $\mathcal{F}$ includes every subset $S$ of $\mathcal{E}$ such that

$$\sum_{e \in S} v_e \geq k.$$

In Section 4, we present an approximately optimal mechanism for such auctions.

**Theorem** 4.3 (restated). *There exists a weighted* VCG *mechanism for the knapsack auction with a frugality ratio of at most* $\sqrt{2\mathsf{v}_{\max}}$ *where* $\mathsf{v}_{\max}$ *is an upper bound on the volume of the elements.*

Our proposal is again a WVCG mechanism described below.

- Every element $e$ has a weight $w_e = 1/\sqrt{v_e}$ and the winning set is a feasible subset of elements with the smallest total sum of the weighted costs.
- The payment to every element $e$ is set to its critical value, and as such, the mechanism is truthful.

In Section 4 we show the frugality ratio of the above mechanism is bounded by $\sqrt{2\mathsf{v}_{\max}}$. To this end, we consider an instance of the knapsack auction and run the above mechanism to specify the winning set $S^{\mathsf{w}}$ and the associated payments to the elements of $S^{\mathsf{w}}$. More precisely, for every element $e$ in the winning set, we define $p_e$ as the payment made by the auctioneer to element $e$.

Next, we provide a feasible solution for the benchmark LP. To do so, for every element $e$ in the winning set, we define $x_e = p_e/\sqrt{2\mathsf{v}_{\max}}$ and for every element $e$ outside the winning set we set $x_e = c_e$. According to Lemma 4.2, we argue that $x$ is a feasible solution for $v^*_{S^{\mathsf{w}}}(c)$ and thus the total sum of payments made by the mechanism is bounded by $\sqrt{2\mathsf{v}_{\max}}$ times the value of the benchmark. The reader can find the complete proof in Section 4. This result is followed by an almost matching lower bound.

**Theorem** 4.1 (restated). *No truthful mechanism can guarantee a frugality ratio better than* $\sqrt{\mathsf{v}_{\max}}$.

The counter-example of Theorem 4.1 is essentially equivalent to a star instance in the vertex cover auctions. We translate such an instance of the vertex cover auction into a knapsack auction by putting an item for every vertex and setting the sizes in a way that the edge constraints are implied. Theorem 4.1 along with Theorem 4.3 proves that our mechanism is optimal up to a constant factor $\sqrt{2}$.

## 2 PRELIMINARIES

A set system is a pair $(\mathcal{E}, \mathcal{F})$ where $\mathcal{E}$ denotes the set of all ground elements and $\mathcal{F} \subset 2^{\mathcal{E}}$ denotes the list of all feasible subsets of the elements. In this setting, an auctioneer wants to purchase a feasible subset of elements $S \in \mathcal{F}$, and each element $e \in \mathcal{E}$ is owned by a selfish strategic agent. For instance, in the case of shortest path auction, every element of the ground set corresponds to an edge of the graph and every feasible set in $\mathcal{F}$ is a path from the source to the target. Similarly, in a vertex cover system, every element corresponds to a vertex of the graph and every feasible set is a vertex cover of the graph.

A set system is called *monopoly-free*, if no element appears in all feasible sets ($\bigcap_{S_i \in \mathcal{F}} S_i = \emptyset$). We assume both the auctioneer and providers have the full information of the set system in advance and the auction is monopoly-free. Every provider $e \in \mathcal{E}$ has a private cost $c_e$ for the service or product he is offering. The auction proceeds as follows:

(1) Every provider submits a bid $b_e$ for his service. At this point, he is aware of the set system, the costs, and the mechanism which the auctioneer uses to run the auction.
(2) The auctioneer receives all of the bids, he will then run a predetermined mechanism $\mathcal{M}$ to select a winning set $S \in \mathcal{F}$ and assign a payment $p_e \geq b_e$ to every element $e \in S$.

A mechanism $\mathcal{M}$ for such an auction is an algorithm that receives a set system $(\mathcal{E}, \mathcal{F})$ and a vector $b = \langle b_1, \dots, b_{|\mathcal{E}|} \rangle$ of bids as input, and reports a feasible set $S \in \mathcal{F}$ and a payment $p : S \to \mathbb{R}$ to the providers such that $p_e \geq b_e$ for every $e \in S$.

A mechanism is called *truthful*, if it is in every provider's best interest to report his bid $b_e$ equal to the cost of his service $c_e$. It is known that a mechanism is truthful if and only if no losing agent can become a winner by increasing his cost and the payment of each winner is set to the highest value for which he remains in the winning set. We refer to this as the agent's critical value.

We measure the performance of a mechanism $\mathcal{M}$ by comparing the total payments of an auctioneer who uses $\mathcal{M}$ to a benchmark. Note that, since our focus is on truthful mechanisms, we assume that all of the bids are equal to the true costs and use the terms bid and cost interchangeably. For a set system $(\mathcal{E}, \mathcal{F})$ and a cost vector $c = \langle c_1, c_2, \dots, c_{|\mathcal{E}|} \rangle$, we denote our benchmark by $\mathcal{B}_{(\mathcal{E}, \mathcal{F})}(c)$ or just $\mathcal{B}(c)$ when the parameters are clear from the context. We review different benchmarks and show the properties of our benchmark in the full-version of the paper.

The frugality ratio of a mechanism $\mathcal{M}$ is formulated as

$$\mathsf{FR}(\mathcal{M}, (\mathcal{E}, \mathcal{F})) = \sup_{c} \frac{P_{\mathcal{M},(\mathcal{E},\mathcal{F})}(c)}{\mathcal{B}_{(\mathcal{E},\mathcal{F})}(c)}$$

where $P_{\mathcal{M},(\mathcal{E},\mathcal{F})}(c)$ denotes the total sum of payments when the auctioneer runs mechanism $\mathcal{M}$ on cost vector $c$ for set system $(\mathcal{E}, \mathcal{F})$. Similarly, the competitive ratio of a set system is defined as

$$\mathsf{FR}(\mathcal{E}, \mathcal{F}) = \inf_{\mathcal{M}} \mathsf{FR}(\mathcal{M}, (\mathcal{E}, \mathcal{F}))$$

where $\mathcal{M}$ is a truthful mechanism.

Finally, we say a mechanism $\mathcal{M}$ is $\kappa$-competitive for a set system $(\mathcal{E}, \mathcal{F})$ if

$$\mathsf{FR}(\mathcal{M}, (\mathcal{E}, \mathcal{F})) \leq \kappa \cdot \mathsf{FR}(\mathcal{E}, \mathcal{F}).$$

Throughout this paper, we design competitive mechanisms or mechanisms with bounded frugality ratios for classic set systems such as vertex cover and knapsack. We formally define these set systems as follows.

*Definition 2.1.* Given a connected graph $G = \langle V(G), E(G)\rangle$, a vertex cover set system is a pair $(\mathcal{E}, \mathcal{F})$ such that $\mathcal{E} = V(G)$ and $\mathcal{F}$ is the set of all vertex covers of $G$. More precisely, a subset of vertices $S$ is in $\mathcal{F}$ if and only if every edge $e \in E(G)$ is incident to at least a vertex of $S$.

We use the notation $N(u)$ to refer to the set of the neighbors of a vertex $u$ in a graph.

*Definition 2.2.* Given a collection $U$ of items, a vector $v$ specifying the volumes of the items in $U$, and an integer number $k$, a set system $(\mathcal{E}, \mathcal{F})$ is a knapsack set system, if $\mathcal{E} = U$ and $\mathcal{F}$ contains every subset of $S$ whose total sum of volumes is at least $k$. All the volumes are integer numbers greater than or equal to 1.

Finally, we define a class of truthful mechanisms for set systems. This class is a generalization of the well-known VCG mechanisms and has been used for many different auctions.

*Definition 2.3.* A WVCG mechanism $\mathcal{M}$ for a set system $(\mathcal{E}, \mathcal{F})$ is associated to a weight vector $w = \langle w_1, w_2, \ldots, w_{|\mathcal{E}|}\rangle$. For every cost vector $c$, it selects a feasible set $S \in \mathcal{F}$ with the minimum weighted sum of costs (*i.e.* $\sum_{e \in S} c_e w_e$ is minimized) . The payments are set to the critical values, and hence every WVCG mechanism is truthful.

## 3 VERTEX COVER

As mentioned before, Kempe *et al.* [13] propose a mechanism for the vertex cover auction and claim their mechanism is constant competitive with regard to their benchmark. However, the proof they provide is not entirely correct. In this section, we first explain the mechanism and show why their proof fails. Next, we provide an alternative proof for the upper bound of the mechanism with regard to our benchmark. Moreover, in Section 3.4, we show the analysis of Kempe *et al.* [13] gives the same lower bound on the frugality ratio of truthful mechanisms for our benchmark. We also extend this lower bound to all randomized truthful mechanisms. This result in addition to the upper bound given in Section 3.3 proves that the proposed mechanism is 4 competitive.

### 3.1 Mechanism

In this section, we explain the mechanism of Kempe *et al.* [13] for the vertex cover auction, namely $\mathcal{M}^{\mathsf{VC}}$. Let $G = (V, E)$ be the underlying graph and the goal be to purchase a vertex cover of $G$. Without loss of generality, we assume $V = \{1, 2, \dots, n\}$ and the cost of each vertex $u$ is $c_u$. For each node $u \in V$, let $\mathbf{1^u}$ be an $n$-dimensional vector with all indices equal to 0 except for index $u$ which is equal to 1. We define the externality of node $u$ as follows:

*Definition 3.1.* The externality of node $u$ denoted by $\beta_u$ is defined as the value of the benchmark for cost vector $\mathbf{1^u}$. In other words $\beta_u = \mathcal{B}(\mathbf{1^u})$ (recall Equation (5)).

Roughly speaking, $\beta_u$ reflects the amount of cost incurred to the auctioneer to cover all of the edges of the graph *without* buying $u$. Let $\mathsf{WAM}(G)$ be a weighted adjacency matrix of graph $G$ where the weight of an edge $(u, v)$ depends on the externality of vertex $u$. More precisely

$$\mathsf{WAM}(G)_{(u,v)} = \begin{cases} 0, & \text{if } (u, v) \notin E \\ \frac{1}{\beta_u}, & \text{if}(u, v) \in E. \end{cases}$$

We denote the dominant eignevalue of $\mathsf{WAM}(G)$ by $\alpha$ and refer to its corresponding eignevector with $q$. By the Perron-Frobenius theorem, eigenvalues of $\mathsf{WAM}(G)$ are real and indices of $q$ are non-negative real numbers. Mechanism $\mathcal{M}^{\mathsf{VC}}$ is a weighted VCG (WVCG) mechanism where the weight of every vertex $i \in V$ is $w_i = 1/q_i$. More formally $\mathcal{M}^{\mathsf{VC}}$ is defined as follows.

- The winning set is a vertex cover $S$ with the minimum total sum of weighted costs, i.e, $\sum_{i \in S} w_i c_i$ is minimized.
- The payment of every vertex $i$ is its critical value.

Since we set the payment of each node $u$ to its critical value, the mechanism is truthful.

### 3.2 Counter-Example to the Argument of Kempe *et al.* [13]

In the following, we give a counter-example to the proof of Kempe *et al.* [13] for showing that $\mathcal{M}^{\mathsf{VC}}$ has a frugality ratio of at most $\alpha$. The faulty part of their argument is for bounding the sum of the payments of $\mathcal{M}^{\mathsf{VC}}$ over their benchmark (the optimal value of LP 6 which is equal to $v(c)$). They claim that the following equation holds based on the linearity of their benchmark ($v(c)$).

$$v(c) \geq \sum_u c_u v(\mathbf{1^u}).$$

We show that this is not the case by a counter-example. Let us first formulate $v(c)$ by a linear program:

$$\begin{array}{llll} \max & v(c) = \sum_{e \in S^c} x_e & & (6) \\ s.t. & x_e = c_e & \forall e \notin S^c & \\ & x_e \geq c_e & \forall e \in S^c & \\ & \sum_{e \in S^c} x_e \leq \sum_{e \in T} x_e & \forall T \in \mathcal{F} & \end{array}$$

In the above formulation, $S^c$ denotes the cheapest feasible set. Here we give a counter-example in which the optimal solution of the above LP is smaller than $\sum_u c_u v(\mathbf{1^u})$. Kempe *et al.* [13] support their argument with the following incorrect statement: if we define $x^{(u)}$ as the optimal solution of $v(\mathbf{1^u})$ then $x = \sum_u c_u x^{(u)}$ is a feasible solution for $v(c)$. We show in the following that such a solution for $v(c)$ does not necessarily have a value of at least $\sum_u c_u v(\mathbf{1^u})$. The example is shown in Figure 1.

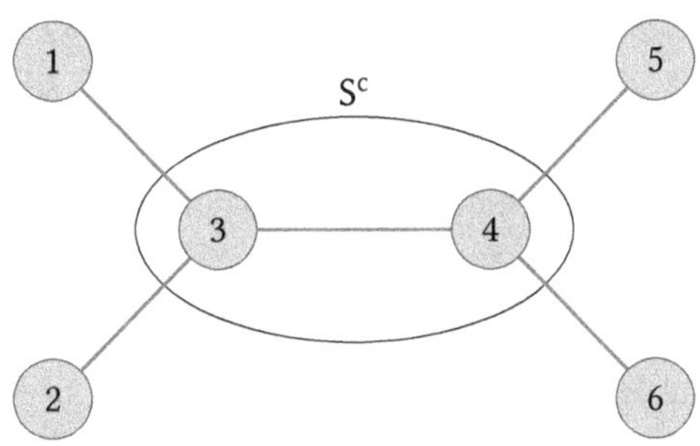


Fig. 1. The counter-example graph. Here all the costs are equal to 1 and the optimal vertex cover is shown by $S^c$.

The following table illustrates the values of vector $x$ in an optimal solution of $v(\mathbf{1^u})$ for each $u \in \{1, \ldots, 6\}$. We refer to these variables as $x^{(u)}$ for each vertex $u$.

| $v(c)$ | $x^{(u)}$ |
|---|---|
| $v(\mathbf{1^1}) = 1$ | (1, 0, 1, 0, 0, 0) |
| $v(\mathbf{1^2}) = 1$ | (0, 1, 1, 0, 0, 0) |
| $v(\mathbf{1^3}) = 1$ | (1, 0, 1, 0, 0, 0) |
| $v(\mathbf{1^4}) = 1$ | (0, 0, 0, 1, 0, 1) |
| $v(\mathbf{1^5}) = 1$ | (0, 0, 0, 1, 1, 0) |
| $v(\mathbf{1^6}) = 1$ | (0, 0, 0, 1, 0, 1) |

All costs in this example are equal to 1, i.e., $c = \langle 1, 1, 1, 1, 1, 1 \rangle$. Moreover, the cheapest feasible sets ($S^c$) are different for different $x^{(u)}$'s. For instance, when $c = \mathbf{1^1}$, one possible cheapest set is $\{3, 4\}$ whereas when $c = \mathbf{1^3}$, one cheapest set is $\{4, 1, 2\}$. Since $x = \sum_u c_u x^{(u)}$ we have $x = \langle 2, 1, 3, 3, 1, 2 \rangle$. Moreover, the objective function of LP 6 for $x$ is 6 although the optimal solution ($v(c)$) is actually 4 which can be obtained by vector $\langle 1, 1, 2, 2, 1, 1 \rangle$. This shows that they bound the total payment of $\mathcal{M}^{\text{VC}}$ by some value higher than their benchmark. The same counter-example holds even when applying their argument to our benchmark.

### 3.3 Upper Bound on the Frugality Ratio of $\mathcal{M}^{\text{VC}}$

Recall that $\alpha$ is the dominant eigenvalue of matrix $\mathsf{WAM}(G)$ corresponding to eigenvector $q$. We show that the frugality ratio of $\mathcal{M}^{\text{VC}}$ is bounded by $\alpha$ with respect to our benchmark.

The main steps for showing such an upper bound on the frugality ratio of $\mathcal{M}^{\mathrm{VC}}$ are the following: recall that the externality of a node $u$ ($\beta_u$) is defined as the value of the benchmark for cost vector $\mathbf{1}^{\mathbf{u}}$. We fix the feasible set purchased by the mechanism to be a vertex cover $S^{\mathrm{w}}$ and in Lemma 3.2 show an upper bound on the total payment of the mechanism. The upper bound follows from the fact that our mechanism buys a set $S^{\mathrm{w}}$ with the minimum total weighted costs and the payments are set according to the Myerson's characterization of the truthful mechanisms. Thus, the payment to every vertex $u \in S^{\mathrm{w}}$ is bounded by a linear expression in terms of the costs of the vertices in $N(u)$. This enables us to prove an upper bound of $(\sum_{u \notin S^{\mathrm{w}}} c_u \beta_u) \cdot \alpha$ on the total payment of the mechanism. Next, in Lemma 3.4 we show a lower bound of $\sum_{u \notin S^{\mathrm{w}}} c_u \beta_u$ for the value of the benchmark $\mathcal{B}(c)$. Notice that $\mathcal{B}(c) \geq v_S^*(c)$ for every $S \in \mathcal{F}$ and therefore $\mathcal{B}(c) \geq v_{S^{\mathrm{w}}}^*(c)$ also holds. Therefore, to show such a lower bound, it only suffices to construct a solution for $v_{S^{\mathrm{w}}}^*(c)$ that has a value of at least $\sum_{u \notin S^{\mathrm{w}}} c_u \beta_u$. The two bounds together imply that the frugality ratio of $\mathcal{M}^{\mathrm{VC}}$ is bounded by $\alpha$.

We begin by showing an upper bound on the total payment of the mechanism to the vertices of the winning set. In Lemma 3.2, we use the fact that $S^{\mathrm{w}}$ is a vertex cover with the minimum total weighted costs and that the mechanism is truthful. We denote the payment to a vertex $u \in S^{\mathrm{w}}$ by $p_u$.

Observation 3.1. *For every $u \in S^{\mathrm{w}}$, $p_u \leq \sum_{v \in (N(u) \setminus S^{\mathrm{w}})} c_v w_v / w_u$ holds.*

**Proof.** This observation follows from the fact that the payment of each provider is determined by its critical value. Recall that the critical value or payment of vertex $u$ is the minimum bid for which he remains in the winning set fixing the bids of all other bidders. Now if the critical value of $u$ ($p_u$) were higher than $\sum_{v \in N(u), v \notin S^{\mathrm{w}}} c_v w_v / w_u$ then WVCG would select all neighbors of $u$ which are not in $S^{\mathrm{w}}$ ($N(u) \setminus S^{\mathrm{w}}$) instead of $u$ since $\sum_{v \in N(u), v \notin S^{\mathrm{w}}} c_v w_v$ would be less than $p_u w_u$. □

Lemma 3.2. $\sum_{u \in S^{\mathrm{w}}} p_u \leq \left( \sum_{u \notin S^{\mathrm{w}}} c_u \beta_u \right) \cdot \alpha.$

**Proof.** This lemma follows from the following inequalities

$$\begin{aligned}
\sum_{u \in S^{\mathrm{w}}} p_u &\leq \sum_{u \in S^{\mathrm{w}}} \sum_{v \in (N(u) \setminus S^{\mathrm{w}})} c_v w_v / w_u && \text{Observation 3.1} \\
&= \sum_{v \notin S^{\mathrm{w}}} \sum_{u \in N(v)} c_v w_v / w_u && S^{\mathrm{w}} \text{ is a vertex cover} \\
&= \sum_{v \notin S^{\mathrm{w}}} \frac{c_v}{q_v} \sum_{u \in N(v)} q_u && w_u = 1/q_u \\
&= \sum_{v \notin S^{\mathrm{w}}} \frac{c_v \beta_v}{q_v} \sum_{u \in N(v)} q_u / \beta_v \\
&= \sum_{v \notin S^{\mathrm{w}}} c_v \beta_v \left(\frac{1}{q_v} \sum_{u \in N(v)} q_u / \beta_v\right) \\
&= \sum_{v \notin S^{\mathrm{w}}} \alpha c_v \beta_v && q \text{ is an eigenvector of WAM(G)} \\
& && \text{and } \alpha \text{ is its corresponding eigenvalue.}
\end{aligned}$$

□

To complement the result of Lemma 3.2, we aim to prove a lower bound on the value of the benchmark ($\mathcal{B}$). Let $S$ be a vertex cover of $G$ and $x$ be a feasible solution to $v_S^*(c)$. For each subset of nodes $U \subseteq V$, we define $x(U)$ as $\sum_{u \in U} x_u$. We state the following lemma which reinterprets the last constraint of LP 1 (the benchmark LP) for vertex cover auctions.

Lemma 3.3. *Let $\langle \mathcal{E}, \mathcal{F} \rangle$ be a vertex cover auction on graph G and $S \in \mathcal{F}$ be a vertex cover of G. A vector x is a feasible solution of LP 1 for S ($v^*_S(c)$) if and only if*

- *constraints of type (2) and (3) hold for x*
- *and for every independent set $R \subseteq S$ we have $x(R) \le x(N(R) \setminus S)$.*

**Proof. only if part.** If $x$ is a feasible solution for $v^*_S(c)$ then clearly constraints of type (2) and (3) hold. Now for every independent set $R \subseteq S$, let $T$ be equal to $(S \setminus R) \cup (N(R) \setminus S)$. $T$ is a vertex cover of $G$ since every edge with one endpoint in $R$ will be covered by either $N(R) \setminus S$ or $S \setminus R$. Moreover, the rest of the edges will be covered by $S \setminus R$. Therefore, by Constraint (4) and the fact that $R \subseteq S$ we have $x(S) = x(S \setminus R) + x(R) \le x(T)$ which can be written as $x(S \setminus R) + x(R) \le x(S \setminus R) + x(N(R) \setminus S)$ and hence $x(R) \le x(N(R) \setminus S)$.

**if part.** Let $T \in \mathcal{F}$ be an arbitrary vertex cover of $G$. $S \setminus T$ is an independent set and $N(S \setminus T)$ is a subset of $T$ since otherwise $T$ would not be a vertex cover. Moreover, let $R = S \setminus T$ be an independent set of $S$. Therefore we have

$$\begin{aligned} x(R) &\le x(N(R) \setminus S) && \text{assumption of the lemma} \\ x(R) + x(S \setminus R) &\le x(N(R) \setminus S) + x(S \setminus R) && \text{add } x(S \setminus R) \text{ to both sides} \\ x(S) &\le x(N(R) \setminus S) + x(S \setminus R) && \\ x(S) &\le x(T) && N(R) \setminus S \text{ and } S \setminus R \text{ are disjoint subsets of } T \end{aligned}$$

and thus constraints of type (4) hold for every vertex cover $T \in \mathcal{F}$ and therefore $x$ meets all constraints of LP 1. □

Now we are ready to prove the lower bound on the value of $\mathcal{B}$. Let $c$ be a vector of costs for the providers and $S^{\text{w}}$ be the set of items that $\mathcal{M}^{\text{VC}}$ buys. For every $u \notin S^{\text{w}}$, let set $\mathcal{S}^u$ be a vertex cover such that $\beta_u = \mathcal{B}(\mathbf{1^u}) = v^*_{\mathcal{S}^u}(\mathbf{1^u})$. In other words, $v^*_{\mathcal{S}^u}(\mathbf{1^u})$ is at least as large as $v^*_S(\mathbf{1^u})$ for every vertex cover $S$ of $G$. If there are multiple vertex covers that maximize $v^*_{\mathcal{S}^u}(\mathbf{1^u})$, we select the one that does not contain $u$ and if there are still more than one such vertex covers, we select one arbitrarily. In the following, we claim that $u \notin \mathcal{S}^u$ holds for all $\mathcal{S}^u$. Another way to interpret Observation 3.2 is that for every vertex $u$, there always exists a vertex cover $S$ that does not contain $u$ but maximizes $v^*_S(\mathbf{1^u})$.

Observation 3.2. *No vertex cover $\mathcal{S}^u$ contains vertex u.*

**Proof.** We consider two cases. The first case is where $\mathcal{B}(\mathbf{1^u}) = 0$. In this case for every vertex cover $S \in \mathcal{F}$ we have $v^*_S(\mathbf{1^u}) = 0$ and hence any vertex cover that does not contain $u$ is a candidate for $\mathcal{S}^u$ and thus $\mathcal{S}^u$ does not contain $u$. Next we investigate the case where $\mathcal{B}(\mathbf{1^u}) > 0$. Note that in this case if $u \in \mathcal{S}^u$ then it implies $\mathcal{B}(\mathbf{1^u}) = 0$ which is self-contradictory. □

Next, we show that $\mathcal{B}(c)$ is at least $\sum_{u \notin S^{\text{w}}} c_u \beta_u$.

Lemma 3.4. $\mathcal{B}(c) \ge \sum_{u \notin S^{\text{w}}} c_u \beta_u$.

**Proof.** To show the lemma, we construct a solution for $v^*_{S^{\text{w}}}(c)$ as follows. Let vector $x^{(u)}$ be a feasible solution that maximizes $v^*_{\mathcal{S}^u}(\mathbf{1^u})$. For every vertex $u \in S^{\text{w}}$, we set $x_u = \sum_{v \notin S^{\text{w}}} c_u x^{(u)}_v$ and for every vertex $u \notin S^{\text{w}}$ we set $x_u = c_u$.

We argue that 1) $x$ is a feasible solution for $v^*_{S^w}(c)$ and 2) the objective value of solution $x$ for $v^*_{S^w}(c)$ is equal to $\sum_{u \notin S^w} c_u \beta_u$. These two together imply that $\mathcal{B}(c) \geq v^*_{S^w}(c) \geq \sum_{u \notin S^w} c_u \beta_u$ and hence the lemma holds. We present the proof of each claim separately.

**Proof of the feasibility of $x$ for $v^*_{S^w}(c)$:** Notice that constrints of type (2) and (3) trivially hold for solution $x$. Therefore, by Lemma 3.3, it only suffices to show that for every independent set $R \subseteq S^w$ we have $x(R) \leq x(N(R) \setminus S^w)$ to complete the proof of this part. In what follows, we prove this inequality. Since $x^{(u)}$ is a feasible solution for $v^*_{S^u}(\mathbf{1^u})$, it follows from Lemma 3.3 that

$$\sum_{v \in R} x^{(u)}_v \leq x^{(u)}(N(R) \setminus S^u) = \sum_{v \in N(R) \setminus S^u} \mathbf{1^u}_v \leq 1$$

for solution $x^{(u)}$ of $v^*_{S^u}(\mathbf{1^u})$ and any independent set $R \subseteq S^u$. Morever, by scaling both sides of the inequality we get

$$\sum_{v \in R} c_u x^{(u)}_v \leq c_u \tag{7}$$

for every independent set $R \subseteq S^u$. For any $v \notin (S^u \cup \{u\})$ we have $x^{(u)}_v = 0$. This implies that if $u \notin S^w$, then $x^{(u)}_v = 0$ holds for every $v \in (S^w \setminus S^u)$. This, in addition to Inequality (7) implies that for every node $u \notin S^w$ and independent set $R \subseteq S^w$ we have

$$\sum_{v \in R} c_u x^{(u)}_v \leq c_u$$

and therefore

$$\sum_{u \in (N(R) \setminus S^w)} \sum_{v \in R} c_u x^{(u)}_v \leq \sum_{u \in (N(R) \setminus S^w)} c_u. \tag{8}$$

For an independent set $R \subseteq S^w$ and a vertex $u \notin (S^w \cup N(R))$ we have $x^{(u)}_v = 0$ for every $v \in R$ because of the following argument: If $v \notin S^u$, $x^{(u)}_v = 0$ holds by definition. Otherwise the costs of vertex $v$ and all its neighbors in $\mathbf{1^u}$ are equal to zero and if $x^{(u)}_v > 0$ for a $v \in R$ then we can replace $v$ with all of its neighbors which are not in $S^u$ and obtain a vertex cover with a smaller value. Therefore we can extend Equation (8) to

$$\left( \sum_{u \in (N(R) \setminus S^w)} \sum_{v \in R} c_u x^{(u)}_v + \sum_{u \notin (S^w \cup N(R))} \sum_{v \in R} c_u x^{(u)}_v \right) \leq \sum_{u \in (N(R) \setminus S^w)} c_u$$

Therefore we have

$$\begin{aligned}
\left( \sum_{u \in (N(R) \setminus S^w)} \sum_{v \in R} c_u x^{(u)}_v + \sum_{u \notin (S^w \cup N(R))} \sum_{v \in R} c_u x^{(u)}_v \right) &\leq \sum_{u \in (N(R) \setminus S^w)} c_u \\
\sum_{v \in R} \left( \sum_{u \in (N(R) \setminus S^w)} c_u x^{(u)}_v + \sum_{u \notin (S^w \cup N(R))} c_u x^{(u)}_v \right) &\leq \sum_{u \in (N(R) \setminus S^w)} c_u && \text{reordering} \\
\sum_{v \in R} \sum_{u \notin S^w} c_u x^{(u)}_v &\leq \sum_{u \in (N(R) \setminus S^w)} c_u \\
\sum_{v \in R} x_v &\leq \sum_{u \in (N(R) \setminus S^w)} x_u && \text{definition of } x \\
x(R) &\leq x(N(R) \setminus S^w)
\end{aligned}$$

**Proof of $\sum_{u \in S^w} x_u \geq \sum_{u \notin S^w} c_u \beta_u$:** We have

$$\begin{aligned}
\sum_{u \notin S^w} c_u \beta_u &= \sum_{u \notin S^w} \sum_{v \in S^u} c_u x_v^{(u)} \\
&= \sum_{u \notin S^w} \sum_{v \in S^w} c_u x_v^{(u)} && \text{explained below} \\
&= \sum_{v \in S^w} \sum_{u \notin S^w} c_u x_v^{(u)} && \text{reordering} \\
&= \sum_{v \in S^w} x_v && \text{definition of } x
\end{aligned}$$

The second equation follows from the fact that $x_v^{(u)}$ is equal to zero if $v$ is not in $N(u)$ and that $S^u$ contains all vertices of $N(u)$ since $u \notin S^u$. □

Finally, Lemma 3.2 along with Lemma 3.4 shows an upperbound of $\alpha$ on the frugality ratio of $\mathcal{M}^{\mathrm{VC}}$.

Theorem 3.5 (a corollary of Lemmas 3.2 and 3.4). *The frugality ratio of $\mathcal{M}^{\mathrm{VC}}$ is bounded by $\alpha$.*

### 3.4 Lower Bound

In this section we show the frugality ratio of every truthful mechanism is at least $\alpha/4$. This along with Theorem 3.5 proves the competitive factor of $\mathcal{M}^{\mathrm{VC}}$ is bounded by 4. Our proof is similar to [13] except that we extend this lower bound to all randomized mechanisms as well.

Let mechanism $\mathcal{M}$ be an arbitrary truthful randomized mechanism for a vertex cover auction $\langle \mathcal{E}, \mathcal{F} \rangle$ on graph $G$. We construct a directed graph $\overrightarrow{G}$ as follows. For any edge $(u, v) \in G$, let cost vector $c$ be $c_u = q_u$, $c_v = q_v$ and $c_i = 0$ for all $i \neq u, v$. Now if we run $\mathcal{M}$ on graph $G$ with cost vector $c$, either $u$ or $v$ appears in the winning set with probability at least $1/2$. If $u$ appears in the winning set with probability at least $1/2$ we add a directed edge from $u$ to $v$ in $\overrightarrow{G}$. Similarly if that's the case with $v$ we add a directed edge from $v$ to $u$ in $\overrightarrow{G}$. Since we iterate over all edges of $G$, for any edge $(u, v) \in E(G)$ either $u$ has a directed edge to $v$ in $\overrightarrow{G}$ or the vice versa or both.

We associate a weight to every vertex of $\overrightarrow{G}$. More precisely we set the weight of every vertex $u$ equal to $q_u$. One could show that there exists a node $v \in V(\overrightarrow{G})$ such that

$$\sum_{(u,v) \in E(\overrightarrow{G})} q_u \leq \sum_{(v,u) \in E(\overrightarrow{G})} q_u$$

(for a proof see Lemma 11 of [12]). We define a cost vector $c$ in the following way: $c_u = 0$ for all $u \neq v$ and $c_v = q_v$. Now we run $\mathcal{M}$ on graph $G$ with cost vector $c$. Note that since $\mathcal{M}$ is truthful, every node $u$ such that $(v, u) \in E(G)$ should be in the winning set. Moreover, again by truthfulness of $\mathcal{M}$, each vertex $u$ such that $(u, v) \in E(\overrightarrow{G})$ receives a payment of at least $\frac{q_u}{2}$.

The rest of the proof follows from the following inequalities that bound the total payment of $\mathcal{M}$.

$$\begin{aligned} p(\mathcal{M}) &\geq \sum_{(v,u)\in E(\overrightarrow{G})} \frac{1}{2} q_u \\ &\geq \frac{1}{4} \sum_{(v,u)\in E(G)} q_u && \text{by selection of } v \\ &= \frac{1}{4}\beta_v \sum_{(v,u)\in E(G)} \frac{1}{\beta_v} q_u \\ &= \frac{1}{4}\beta_v \alpha \cdot q_v && q \text{ is an eigenvector of WAM}(G) \end{aligned}$$

Note that the value of our benchmark for cost vector $c$ equals $q_v \cdot \beta_v$ which concludes that $\mathcal{M}$ has a frugality ratio of at least $\frac{\alpha}{4}$.

Theorem 3.6. *Every truthful mechanism (deterministic or randomized), has a frugality ratio of at least $\alpha/4$.*

## 4 KNAPSACK AUCTION

In this section, we formally define the knapsack auction and discuss the mechanism we propose for this problem. Let $\mathcal{E}$ be a set of elements, each having a volume $v_e$. In a knapsack auction, the auctioneer is willing to purchase a subset of items having a total volume of at least $k$. Therefore, every subset $S \subseteq \mathcal{E}$ is in $\mathcal{F}$ if and only if the total sum of the volumes of the elements in $S$ is at least $k$. As an example of such auction, consider a company is interested in purchasing some ad slots that guarantee a certain number of user clicks over a period of time. Moreover, we have a number of advertisement companies that offer an ad slot which is guaranteed to be clicked by a certain number of people. Now, the company wishes to run a procurement auction to purchase the ad slots.

We first show it is impossible to design any truthful mechanism for this system with a frugality ratio better than $\sqrt{\mathsf{v}_{\max}}$, where $\mathsf{v}_{\max}$ is the volume of the largest item. We then, propose a mechanism and show the frugality ratio of this mechanism is bounded by $\sqrt{2\mathsf{v}_{\max}}$.

Theorem 4.1. *Let $\mathsf{v}_{\max} = \max_{e\in\mathcal{E}} v_e$ be the volume of the largest item in $\mathcal{E}$. No truthful mechanism can guarantee a frugality ratio better than $\sqrt{\mathsf{v}_{\max}}$.*

**Proof.** Let $\mathcal{E} = \{1, 2, \ldots, \mathsf{v}_{\max} + 1\}$ contain $\mathsf{v}_{\max} + 1$ elements such that $v_i = 1$ for all $1 \leq i \leq \mathsf{v}_{\max}$ and $v_{\mathsf{v}_{\max}+1} = \mathsf{v}_{\max}$. We set $k = \mathsf{v}_{\max}$ and hence, $\mathcal{F}$ would be the union of all subsets of items whose total sum of volumes is at least $k$. We show it is impossible to design a truthful mechanism for purchasing a feasible set of items in this instance of knapsack auction that has a frugality ratio better than $\sqrt{\mathsf{v}_{\max}}$.

To this end, assume $\mathcal{M}$ is a truthful mechanism and consider a cost vector $c = \langle 1, 0, 0, \ldots, 0, \sqrt{\mathsf{v}_{\max}}\rangle$ for the elements such that $c_1 = 1$, $c_{\mathsf{v}_{\max}+1} = \sqrt{\mathsf{v}_{\max}}$, and the cost of all other elements is equal to 0. Suppose we run mechanism $\mathcal{M}$ on cost vector $c$ and end up buying a set $S$ of the elements. There are two cases for set $S$.

- $\mathsf{v}_{\max} + 1 \in S$.
- $\mathsf{v}_{\max} + 1 \notin S$ and hence $i \in S$ for all $1 \leq i \leq \mathsf{v}_{\max}$.

We show in both cases the frugality ratio of $\mathcal{M}$ cannot be less than $\sqrt{\mathsf{v}_{\max}}$. First, assume $\mathsf{v}_{\max} + 1 \in S$. Now, consider a different cost vector $c'$ in which the cost of $\mathsf{v}_{\max} + 1$ is equal to 0 and the cost of all other elements is the same as $c$. Since $\mathcal{M}$ is truthful, $\mathsf{v}_{\max} + 1$ should also be in the winning set and it should receive a payment of at least $\sqrt{\mathsf{v}_{\max}}$. Therefore, the total payment of the auctioneer in this case is at least $\sqrt{\mathsf{v}_{\max}}$. However, the benchmark $\mathcal{B}(c') = 1$ and thus, the frugality ratio of $\mathcal{M}$ is at least $\sqrt{\mathsf{v}_{\max}}$.

Next, we investigate the case where $\mathsf{v}_{\max} + 1 \notin S$. Let $c^1, c^2, c^3, \ldots, c^{\mathsf{v}_{\max}}$ be $\mathsf{v}_{\max}$ cost vectors such that $c^i_{\mathsf{v}_{\max}+1} = \sqrt{\mathsf{v}_{\max}}$ for all $1 \le i \le \mathsf{v}_{\max}$ and $c^i_i = 1$. Apart from this, all other costs in these vectors are equal to 0. With the same argument, we can conclude that running $\mathcal{M}$ on each of the cost vectors $c^1, c^2, \ldots, c^{\mathsf{v}_{\max}}$, does not lead to buying $\mathsf{v}_{\max} + 1$ unless $\mathsf{FR}(\mathcal{M}) \ge \sqrt{\mathsf{v}_{\max}}$. Now, consider a cost vector $c''$ such that $c''_{\mathsf{v}_{\max}+1} = \sqrt{\mathsf{v}_{\max}}$ and $c''_i = 0$ for all $1 \le i \le \mathsf{v}_{\max}$. Since $\mathcal{M}$ is truthful and it buys all of the elements $1, 2, \ldots, \mathsf{v}_{\max}$ for all cost vectors $c^1, c^2, \ldots, c^{\mathsf{v}_{\max}}$, it also buys all those elements for cost vector $c''$. Moreover, each item receives a payment of at least 1. Therefore, the auctioneer makes a payment of at least $\mathsf{v}_{\max}$, where $\mathcal{B}(c'') = \sqrt{\mathsf{v}_{\max}}$. Hence, $\mathsf{FR}(\mathcal{M}) \ge \sqrt{\mathsf{v}_{\max}}$. □

In the rest of this section, we propose a WVCG mechanism $\mathcal{M}^{\mathsf{K}}$ for knapsack auction and bound its frugality ratio by $\sqrt{2\mathsf{v}_{\max}}$. We first define a weight $w_e$ for every item $e$ which is equal to $\frac{\sqrt{v_e}}{v_e}$ and then define $\mathcal{M}^{\mathsf{K}}$ as follows:

- The winning set is a $S \in \mathcal{F}$ such that that minimizes the expression $\sum w_e b_e$. Ties are broken lexicographically.
- The payment of every item $e \in S$ is determined based on its critical value.

In the following, we show the frugality ratio of $\mathcal{M}^{\mathsf{K}}$ is bounded by $\sqrt{2\mathsf{v}_{\max}}$ where $\mathsf{v}_{\max} = \max_{e \in \mathcal{E}} v_e$. Before we proceed to the proof, we state an axillary lemma which we use in the proof of the theorem.

Lemma 4.2. *Let $Y = \{1, 2, \ldots, |Y|\}$ be a set of elements with volumes $v_1, v_2, \ldots, v_{|Y|}$ and costs $c_1, c_2, \ldots, c_{|Y|}$ such that $\sum v_i = b$. If $V \ge \max_{e \in Y} v_e$ and every $v_i \ge 1$ then, for any $1 \le d \le b$, there exists a subset $S$ of elements in $Y$ such that $\sum_{e \in S} v_e \ge d$ and*

$$\sum_{e \in S} c_e / \sqrt{v_e} \le \frac{\sqrt{2dV}}{b} \sum_{e \in Y} c_e.$$

**Proof.** Without loss of generality, we assume the elements are sorted in increasing order of $\frac{c_e}{v_e}$. In other words,

$$\frac{c_1}{v_1} \le \frac{c_2}{v_2} \le \ldots \le \frac{c_{|Y|}}{v_{|Y|}}.$$

Therefore for every $1 \le i \le |Y|$ we have

$$\frac{\sum_{j=1}^{i} c_j}{\sum_{j=1}^{i} v_j} \le \frac{\hat{c}}{b} \tag{9}$$

where $\hat{c}$ denotes the total cost of items in $Y$. Now let set $Q = \{1, 2, 3, \ldots, |Q|\}$ be the smallest prefix of items in $Y$ whose total sum of volumes is at least $d$. Note that, $\sum_{i=1}^{|Q|} v_i \ge d$ but $\sum_{i=1}^{|Q|-1} v_i < d$. Now, let $q$ be the total cost of all items in $Q \setminus \{|Q|\}$. In the rest of the proof we show

$$\sum_{e \in Q} c_e / \sqrt{v_e} \le \frac{\sqrt{2dV}}{b} \hat{c}.$$

Since $\min_{e \in Q \setminus \{|Q|\}} v_e \ge 1$ we have

$$\sum_{e \in W} c_e / \sqrt{v_e} \le q + c_{|Q|} / \sqrt{v_{|Q|}}. \tag{10}$$

Moreover, by Inequality (9) we have

$$q \leq \frac{(d-1)\hat{c}}{b}$$

and

$$q + c_{|Q|} \leq \frac{(d + v_{|Q|} - 1)\hat{c}}{b}.$$

Therefore (10) is maximized when $q = \frac{(d-1)\hat{c}}{b}$ and $c_{|Q|} = \frac{(v_{|Q|})\hat{c}}{b}$ and thus

$$\begin{aligned}\sum_{e \in W} c_e/\sqrt{v_e} &\leq q + c_{|Q|}/\sqrt{v_{|Q|}} \\ &\leq \frac{(d-1)\hat{c}}{b} + \frac{(v_{|Q|})/\sqrt{v_{|Q|}}\hat{c}}{b} \\ &= \frac{(d-1)\hat{c}}{b} + \frac{\sqrt{v_{|Q|}}\hat{c}}{b} \\ &\leq \frac{(d-1)\hat{c}}{b} + \frac{\sqrt{V}\hat{c}}{b} \\ &= \frac{\hat{c}}{b}(d - 1 + \sqrt{V}) \\ &= \frac{\hat{c}}{b}\sqrt{V}(1 + \frac{d-1}{\sqrt{V}}) \\ &\leq \frac{\hat{c}}{b}\sqrt{2Vd}.\end{aligned}$$

□

Next we prove $\mathsf{FR}(\mathcal{M}^{\mathsf{K}}) \leq \sqrt{2\mathsf{v}_{\max}}$.

THEOREM 4.3. *Let $(\mathcal{E}, \mathcal{F})$ be a knapsack set system and $\mathsf{v}_{\max} = \max_{e \in \mathcal{E}} v_e$. Then we have*

$$\mathsf{FR}(\mathcal{M}^{\mathsf{K}}) \leq \sqrt{2\mathsf{v}_{\max}}.$$

**Proof.** Let $(\mathcal{E}, \mathcal{F})$ be a set system and $c$ be a cost vector for the elements of $\mathcal{E}$. Suppose we run $\mathcal{M}^{\mathsf{K}}$ on the bids and determine a set $S$ as the winning set and assign a payment $p_e$ to every element $e$ in $S$. In the following we show

$$\sum_{e \in S} p_e \leq \sqrt{2\mathsf{v}_{\max}}\mathcal{B}(c).$$

By the definition, we have $\mathcal{B}(c) \geq v_S^*(c)$. Recall that $v_S^*(c)$ is equal to the objective value of the following linear program:

$$\begin{aligned} \max \quad & v_S^*(c) = \textstyle\sum_{e \in S} x_e && && (11) \\ s.t. \quad & x_e = c_e && \forall e \notin S && (12) \\ & x_e \geq 0 && \forall e \in S && (13) \\ & \textstyle\sum_{e \in S} x_e \leq \sum_{e \in T} x_e && \forall T \in \mathcal{F} && (14) \end{aligned}$$

Let $x$ be a solution of $v_S^*(c)$ in which for every $e \in S$, $x_e = p_e/\sqrt{2\mathsf{v}_{\max}}$ and for every $e \notin S$, we have $x_e = c_e$. We first show $x$ is a feasible solution of LP (11). Note that all constraints of type (12) and (13) are trivially satisfied. Now let $T$ be a feasible set for constraints of type (14). We define

$X = S \setminus T$ to be the elements of $S$ that are not in $T$ and $Y = T \setminus S$ to be the elements of $T$ that replace $X$ in $S$. Since $x_e$ is the same for both sides of constraint (14), we can rewrite the inequality as

$$\sum_{e \in X} x_e \leq \sum_{e \in Y} x_e = \sum_{e \in Y} c_e. \tag{15}$$

Now let $\sum_{e \in Y} v_e = b$ be the total volume of the elements in $Y$ and $b' = \sum_{e \in X} v_e$. Note that, since all elements of $Y$ can replace elements of $X$, then every element $e \in X$ can be replaced by some elements of $Y$ that have a total sum of volumes of at least $v_e - \max(0, b' - b)$. Since we set the price of every item in $S$ by its critical value, the payment of any item $e \in X$ that can be replaced by a subset $R_e$, (i.e., $R_e \cap S = \emptyset$) is bounded by

$$w_e p_e \leq \sum_{e' \in R_e} w_{e'} c_{e'}$$

and hence

$$p_e / \sqrt{v_e} \leq \sum_{e' \in R_e} c_{e'} / \sqrt{v_{e'}}.$$

Therefore

$$p_e \leq \sum_{e' \in R_e} \sqrt{v_e} c_{e'} / \sqrt{v_{e'}} \tag{16}$$

By applying Equation (16) to Lemma 4.2 we get

$$p_e \leq \sqrt{v_e} \frac{\sqrt{2(v_e - \max(0, b' - b))\mathsf{v}_{\max}}}{b} \sum_{e' \in Y} c'_e$$

Since $\sqrt{v_e}\sqrt{(v_e - \max(0, b' - b)} \leq v_e - \frac{\max(0, b' - b)}{2}$, we have

$$p_e \leq \sqrt{\mathsf{v}_{\max}} \frac{\sqrt{2}(v_e - \frac{\max(0, b' - b)}{2})}{b} \sum_{e' \in Y} c'_e. \tag{17}$$

We sum Equation (17) over all elements $e \in X$ and obtain

$$\sum_{e \in X} p_e \leq \sqrt{2\mathsf{v}_{\max}} \frac{\sum_{e \in X}(v_e - \frac{\max(0, b' - b)}{2})}{b} \sum_{e \in Y} c_e = \sqrt{2\mathsf{v}_{\max}} \frac{b' - |X|\frac{b' - b}{2}}{b} \sum_{e \in Y} c_e. \tag{18}$$

Note that if $|X| = 1$, (16) directly proves

$$\sum_{e \in X} p_e \leq \sqrt{2\mathsf{v}_{\max}} \sum_{e \in Y} c_e$$

otherwise $b' - |X|\frac{b' - b}{2} \leq b$ and by (18) we have

$$\sum_{e \in X} p_e \leq \sqrt{2\mathsf{v}_{\max}} \sum_{e \in Y} c_e.$$

Since we set $x_e = p_e / \sqrt{2\mathsf{v}_{\max}}$, we have

$$\sum_{e \in X} x_e \leq \sum_{e \in Y} c_e.$$

and thus all constraints of type (14) are satisfied. Since $x$ is a feasible solution of LP 11, we have

$$\mathcal{B}(c) \geq v_S^*(c) \geq \sum_{e \in S} x_e = \sum_{e \in S} p_e / \sqrt{2\mathsf{v}_{\max}}$$

and therefore $\mathsf{FR}(\mathcal{M}) \leq \sqrt{2\mathsf{v}_{\max}}$. □

## 5 ACKNOWLEDGMENT

We would like to thank Nick Gravin for having helpful discussions and his comments on an earlier version of the paper.


## REFERENCES


[1] Gagan Aggarwal and Jason D Hartline. 2006. Knapsack auctions. In *Proceedings of the seventeenth annual ACM-SIAM symposium on Discrete algorithm*. Society for Industrial and Applied Mathematics, 1083–1092.

[2] Aaron Archer and Éva Tardos. 2007. Frugal path mechanisms. *ACM Transactions on Algorithms (TALG)* 3, 1 (2007), 3.

[3] Xiaohui Bei, Ning Chen, Nick Gravin, and Pinyan Lu. 2012. Budget feasible mechanism design: from prior-free to bayesian. In *Proceedings of the forty-fourth annual ACM symposium on Theory of computing*. ACM, 449–458.

[4] Martin Bichler and Jayant R Kalagnanam. 2006. Software frameworks for advanced procurement auction markets. *Commun. ACM* 49, 12 (2006), 104–108.

[5] Ning Chen, Edith Elkind, Nick Gravin, and Fedor Petrov. 2010. Frugal mechanism design via spectral techniques. In *Foundations of Computer Science (FOCS), 2010 51st Annual IEEE Symposium on*. IEEE, 755–764.

[6] Peter Cramton, Yoav Shoham, and Richard Steinberg. 2006. Combinatorial auctions. (2006).

[7] Sudipto Dasgupta and Daniel F Spulber. 1990. Managing procurement auctions. *Information Economics and Policy* 4, 1 (1990), 5–29.

[8] Edith Elkind, Leslie Ann Goldberg, and Paul W Goldberg. 2007. Frugality ratios and improved truthful mechanisms for vertex cover. In *Proceedings of the 8th ACM conference on Electronic commerce*. ACM, 336–345.

[9] Paul W Goldberg and Antony McCabe. 2012. Commodity auctions and frugality ratios. In *Algorithmic Game Theory*. Springer, 180–191.

[10] Srabana Gupta. 2002. Competition and collusion in a government procurement auction market. *Atlantic Economic Journal* 30, 1 (2002), 13–25.

[11] Mireia Jofre-Bonet and Martin Pesendorfer. 2000. Bidding behavior in a repeated procurement auction: A summary. *European Economic Review* 44, 4 (2000), 1006–1020.

[12] Anna R. Karlin, David Kempe, and Tami Tamir. 2005. Beyond VCG: Frugality of Truthful Mechanisms. In *Proceedings of the 46th Annual IEEE Symposium on Foundations of Computer Science*. IEEE Computer Society, 615–626.

[13] David Kempe, Mahyar Salek, and Cristopher Moore. 2010. Frugal and truthful auctions for vertex covers, flows and cuts. In *Foundations of Computer Science (FOCS), 2010 51st Annual IEEE Symposium on*. IEEE, 745–754.

[14] Paul Klemperer. 2004. Auctions: theory and practice. (2004).

[15] Robert H Porter and J Douglas Zona. 1992. *Detection of bid rigging in procurement auctions*. Technical Report. National bureau of economic research.

[16] Yaron Singer. 2010. Budget feasible mechanisms. In *Foundations of Computer Science (FOCS), 2010 51st Annual IEEE Symposium on*. IEEE, 765–774.

# Matching Auctions for Search and Native Ads

RUGGIERO CAVALLO, Yahoo Research
MAXIM SVIRIDENKO, Yahoo Research
CHRISTOPHER A. WILKENS*, Facebook Research

Unit demand auctions power today's search and native ad marketplaces. Traditional implementations make an extreme "separability" assumption: the relative value of any two ad slots is the same for all advertisers. Under this assumption, the optimal assignment problem can be conveniently solved simply by sorting; without it, efficient allocation requires solving a full-blown weighted matching problem. Motivated by prior work and our own empirical evidence against separability, we abandon that assumption and tackle the algorithmic problems of assignment and pricing for general unit demand ad auctions. Instead of computing prices directly, we take a novel approach and compute bidders' full allocation curves—complete mappings from each agent's bid space to their allocation under the optimal assignment function—from which it is trivial to compute most prices of interest, like those of the Generalized Second Price (GSP) or Vickrey-Clarke-Groves (VCG) auctions. Remarkably, we show that these full allocation curves (and therefore prices) can be computed in the same asymptotic runtime required to compute the optimal matching alone.

## 1 INTRODUCTION

Consider the following auction setting that is ubiquitous in computational advertising. A set of bidders $I = \{1, \dots, n\}$ is to be matched to a set of slots $J = \{1, \dots, m\}$ (where $n \geq m$); when bidder $i \in I$ is matched to slot $j \in J$, a desired event (e.g., a click on $i$'s ad) happens with probability $\pi_{i,j}$, generating expected value $v_{i,j} \equiv v_i \pi_{i,j}$ for the bidder. The auctioneer's job is to take bids $b_i$, each purportedly representing $i$'s value $v_i$, and compute an optimal matching of bidders to slots.

Practitioners often assume the probabilities $\pi_{i,j}$ have structure that both makes them easier to learn with scalable Machine Learning methods, and also greatly simplifies the auctioning process. Specifically, it is assumed that the event-probabilities are *separable* in the following sense: there exist $\alpha = (\alpha_1, \dots, \alpha_m)$ and $\beta = (\beta_1, \dots, \beta_n)$ such that $\forall i \in I, \forall j \in J, \pi_{i,j} = \beta_i \cdot \alpha_j$; i.e., the likelihood that the event of interest (typically click) occurs when ad $i$ is placed in slot $j$ can be decomposed into the product of two terms, one depending only on the ad and one depending only on the slot.

In the separable model, the optimal allocation can be found by sorting. If $\sigma(j)$ is the ad placed into slot $j \in \{1, \dots, n\}$,[1] the optimal allocation should maximize $\sum_j \alpha_j \beta_{\sigma(j)} b_{\sigma(j)}$. Assuming WLOG that $\alpha_1 \geq \alpha_2 \cdots \geq \alpha_m$, the optimum can be computed simply by assigning the ad with highest $b_i \beta_i$ to slot 1, the ad with the second-highest $b_i \beta_i$ to slot 2, and so on — i.e. one simply needs to rank ads by $b_i \beta_i$.

The *generalized second price* (GSP) auction—so central to slot auctions since their inception in the previous decade—fits with the separability assumption like a hand in a glove. GSP sorts ads in

*Wilkens was employed by Yahoo during the time of research for this paper.
[1]To contrive a number of slots equal to the number of ads ($n$), we can tack on dummy slots with $\pi_{i,j} = 0$ as necessary.

Authors' addresses: Ruggiero Cavallo, Yahoo Research, New York, NY, cavallo@oath.com; Maxim Sviridenko, Yahoo Research, New York, NY, sviri@oath.com; Christopher A. Wilkens, Facebook Research, Menlo Park, CA, cwilkens@fb.com.


*ACM EC'18, June 18–22, 2018, Ithaca, NY, USA.* ACM ISBN 978-1-4503-5829-3/18/06...$15.00
https://doi.org/10.1145/3219166.3219191

decreasing order of $b_i\beta_i$, then charges bidder $i$ based on the next ad in the sorted list. If $\beta_{\sigma(j)} > 0$, the GSP price of ad $\sigma(j)$ is:

$$p_{\sigma(j)} = \frac{b_{\sigma(j+1)}\beta_{\sigma(j+1)}}{\beta_{\sigma(j)}}$$

Otherwise, $p_{\sigma(j)} = 0$. This price corresponds to the lowest bid that gets bidder $\sigma(j)$ his slot assignment $j$.

GSP is a workhorse of computational advertising and much research has focused on understanding its properties [7, 21]. Its elegance facilitates implementation and has led to widespread adoption, but the entire framework is critically based on the separability assumption. That assumption has always been a stretch ([8] provides good evidence against it in the case of Bing search ad auctions), and it is becoming a worse approximation as ad formats and pricing types evolve.

Consider Yahoo's Native Ads marketplace. In this setting, ads are often interspersed within a very long content stream, such that among the many ads allocated in the auction, a user will only see one or two at a time. The auction in place is GSP with the following application of separability: the slot-specific parameter $\alpha_j$ captures the probability that the user views slot $j$ (independent of which ad is shown in it), which decreases with $j$ since scrolling through the content stream is required to see ads in lower slots. Complicating matters, the "payment event" varies across ads. Advertisers can choose to pay per-impression (CPM), per-click (CPC), or in some cases even on a conversion or app-installation basis. Mapping this into the separable framework, the ad-specific parameter $\beta_i$ equals 1 for any CPM ad, while $\beta_i$ can be taken as the ad-specific "probability of click conditioned on view" for CPC ads, and similarly for other pricing types.

For CPM ads the separable model collapses to the unobjectionable assumption that whether or not an ad appears on the page is independent of the ad itself. But injecting CPC ads into the mix makes the model highly suspect; there is no a priori reason to believe that click probability conditional on view remains constant as one moves down the page. In fact empirical data strongly suggests otherwise.

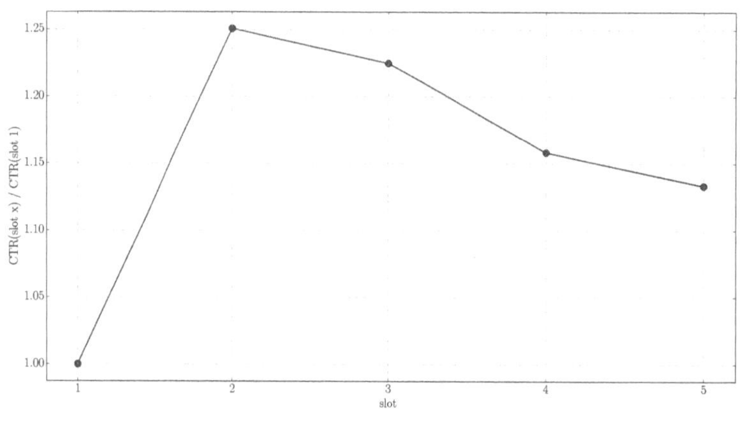


Fig. 1. Empirical click-through-rate (probability of a click conditioned on the ad being viewed) as a function of slot, aggregated over a dataset of approximately 17M pageviews with randomly selected ad impressions from Yahoo's Native Ads marketplace.

As Figure 1 demonstrates, for this Yahoo Native Ads dataset the second slot has a markedly higher click-through-rate than the first (conditioned on view), and from there on click rates slowly decline as one goes down the page. Thus, in essence, *at a minimum* different $\alpha$ vectors are called for depending on whether the ads are CPM or CPC.[2] If the two ad types are mixed, the separable model becomes a very poor fit, opening room for a more specialized model to yield efficiency improvements. A similar, if less stark, story applies in the search advertising context. Certain types of ads may hold the user's attention more consistently than others as they are moved up or down the page; a separable model precludes such effects and fails to optimize accordingly.

### 1.1 Main questions

These critical issues with the separable model motivate us to consider the following question:

> *How do we compute efficient ad allocations when click prediction does not satisfy the separability assumption?*

A natural candidate for the ad selection algorithm is to compute a maximum weighted bipartite matching in the complete bipartite graph $G = (I, J, K_{I\times J})$ with edge weights $v_{i,j} = b_i\pi_{i,j}$. This solution maximizes total advertiser value, and can be implemented in a way that meets the severe constraints on run-time inherent to the online auction domain. In our Yahoo Native Ads setting, $m \leq 21$, $n \approx 100$, and the run-time constraint is roughly a few milliseconds. The Maximum Weighted Bipartite Matching problem is a very well-studied optimization problem with a large set of algorithms to choose from. Currently, the best approximate algorithms run in almost linear time [6].[3] Run times usually depend on the number of vertices on each side ($n$ and $m$ in our case), the number of edges ($nm$ in our case), and the maximum integer weight (for cases where edge weights are integers). For our purposes the classical Hungarian algorithm extended to handle imbalanced graphs has run time $O(nm^2)$ [19] and is adequate, with empirical run time under 1ms on production instances. So far so good. This narrows our focus to the central question of this study, where our contributions lie:

> *How do we price ads that have been assigned to slots by the Maximum Weighted Bipartite Matching algorithm?*

A satisfactory pricing scheme will have desirable equilibrium properties and also be computable under the run-time constraints.

### 1.2 The VCG (Non) Solution

One attractive answer is to use externality prices as in a *Vickrey-Clarke-Groves* auction (VCG). Indeed, this is an elegant and principled solution, not to mention nearly the only solution offered in the theoretical literature. It has been the go-to implementation for new marketplaces where separability is inconceivable, and there are many methods to compute VCG prices.

Unfortunately, VCG is not a practical option for marketplaces already built on GSP, which comprise the majority of those that presently rely on some form of the separability assumption. VCG prices are quite different from GSP prices, and switching from GSP pricing to VCG pricing—a quick exercise at Yahoo calculated immediate expected revenue more than 20% lower than GSP in one of its marketplaces—would create a disruption that is likely unacceptable in terms of revenue impact, confusion, and general explainability to advertisers. Case in point: engineers at Google independently discovered VCG pricing mere months after implementing GSP in their Adwords auction, but it was already deemed too late to switch [22].

[2] It may additionally be the case that the shape of click-rate (conditioned on view) functions varies considerably amongst the CPC ads, in which case one could not effectively apply a separable model even within the subset of ads that are priced CPC.
[3] The introduction in [6] also contains a quick survey of known exact algorithms for the problem.

### 1.3 Allocation Curves

Unable to use VCG, it is natural to shift focus towards generalizing GSP. Unfortunately, what "generalizing GSP" means is itself an open question that would be impossible to address adequately in the present work. A variety of methods for generalizing GSP have been tried in the literature that have vastly different approaches and lead to substantially different prices, e.g. [4, 5, 12, 16, 24]. Fortunately, this discussion can be set aside: instead of basing our implementation on a specific definition of GSP, we show how to compute full "allocation curves" that capture what an advertiser would have achieved with an alternate bid, which can accomodate them all.

The allocation curves we want to compute are the same functions that form the foundation of most single-parameter auction theory. The allocation curve $a_i : \Re_+ \to [0, 1]$ for bidder $i$ given bids $b_{-i}$ gives $i$'s click probability in the allocation that results as a function of his submitted bid $b_i$. Possessing these curves confers substantial advantages over common auction implementations:

(1) *Flexibility and abstraction.* Explicitly computing allocation curves decouples allocation and pricing in the auction system, allowing nearly any desired pricing scheme to be implemented quickly and making it easy to refine the pricing mechanism later. For example, it is easy to compute simple GSP "threshold" prices (as we will discuss below) or more complex generalizations of GSP from [4] that limit the marginal costs associated with higher slots; it is similarly easy to start with threshold pricing and move to a more complicated method when the need arises. VCG prices can even be computed using a formula due to [17], as an area above $a_i$. Note the contrast with traditional externality pricing, which confers little or no information that would be useful for computing anything other than VCG prices.

(2) *Transparency.* By capturing counterfactual information at auction time, allocation curves aid in validation and forecasting. Advertisers often inquire about why their prices have changed and platforms often need to understand why prices are low/high in a particular auction. Additionally, advertisers often want to know how things will change if they modify their bids. In theory it is simple to compute such counterfactuals; unfortunately, real auctions are constantly evolving and, even from logged information, it is often difficult or impossible to precisely and consistently reconstruct the auction logic. Computing and logging the allocation curve explicitly obviates the need for reverse-engineering the auction and substantially facilitates ex-post analysis.

Since the allocation is deterministic, $a_i$ is characterized by the $m$ thresholds at which the advertiser moves up a position. In a separable world, computing these thresholds is again as easy as sorting — ad $i$ gets the $j$-th slot (so its event probability is $\pi_{i,j} = \beta_i \alpha_j$) when it has the $j$th-highest value of $b_i \beta_i$. Thus, we can read off $a_i$ after sorting ads by $b_i \beta_i$.

For example, consider the following setting with separable event probabilities and $\alpha_1 = 1$, $\alpha_2 = 0.9$ and $\alpha_3 = 0.1$:

| Bidder | $b_i$ | $\beta_i$ | $\pi_{i,1}$ | $\pi_{i,2}$ | $\pi_{i,3}$ |
|---|---|---|---|---|---|
| 1 | \$4 | 0.1 | $0.1 \times 1 = 0.1$ | $0.1 \times 0.9 = 0.09$ | $0.1 \times 0.1 = 0.01$ |
| 2 | \$3 | 0.2 | $0.2 \times 1 = 0.2$ | $0.2 \times 0.9 = 0.18$ | $0.2 \times 0.1 = 0.02$ |
| 3 | \$2 | 0.1 | $0.1 \times 1 = 0.1$ | $0.1 \times 0.9 = 0.09$ | $0.1 \times 0.1 = 0.01$ |

To find the allocation curve for bidder 2, we consider the $b_i \beta_i$ values $b_1 \beta_1 = 0.4$, $b_2 \beta_2 = 0.2 b_2$, and $b_3 \beta_3 = 0.2$. When $0.2 b_2 \geq 0.4$, bidder 2 will win the top slot, when $0.4 > 0.2 b_2 \geq 0.2$ it will win the second slot, and when $0.2 > 0.2 b_2$ it will win the third slot. Thus, the allocation curve for bidder 2 will be as follows:

$$a_2(b_2) = \begin{cases} 0.2 & b_2 \geq 2 \\ 0.18 & b_2 \in [1, 2) \\ 0.02 & b_2 < 1 \end{cases} .$$

Computing $a_2$ is easy because the thresholds at which the allocation changes ($b_2 = 1$ and $b_2 = 2$) can be found by inspection once we have $b_1\beta_1$ and $b_3\beta_3$ in sorted order.

However, computing allocation curves is more complicated when event probabilities lack structure. Each point on an allocation curve represents a counterfactual, and the counterfactual optima may be quite different from the true optimum. Consider the following example:

| Bidder | $b_i$ | $\pi_{i,1}$ | $\pi_{i,2}$ | $\pi_{i,3}$ |
|---|---|---|---|---|
| 1 | \$4 | 0.1 | 0.09 | 0.01 |
| 2 | \$3 | 0.1 | 0.09 | 0.01 |
| 3 | \$2 | 0.1 | 0.02 | 0.01 |

The optimal *bidder* $\longrightarrow$ *slot* allocation is $1 \longrightarrow 1$, $2 \longrightarrow 2$, $3 \longrightarrow 3$ with a total value of 0.69. optimal allocation would instead be $1 \longrightarrow 2$, $2 \longrightarrow 3$, $3 \longrightarrow 1$; not only did bidder 2 move down to slot 3 (naturally, since its bid was lowered), the relative order of bidders 1 and 3 changed. In order to compute allocation curves, we will need to find all the counterfactual optimal matchings that would result from alternative bids. The allocation curve for bidder 2 in this case will be

$$a_2(b_2) = \begin{cases} 0.1 & b_2 \geq 4 \\ 0.09 & b_2 \in [1.75, 4) \\ 0.01 & b_2 < 1.75 \end{cases}$$

One straightforward algorithm for computing $a_i$ repeatedly runs the core allocation algorithm in a binary search. The thresholds can naïvely be found in time $O(nm^3 \sum_{i \in I} \log 100b_i)$, assuming that bids are expressed to the penny. Roughly speaking, this algorithm iteratively picks counterfactual bids for bidder $i$, holding all others constant, re-runs the bipartite matching algorithm, and checks the slot that bidder $i$ receives; this is done repeatedly until the threshold bids are identified. This is sound but not fast enough in practice.

Our central result in this paper is an algorithm that computes the curves $a_i$ substantially faster, in the same $O(nm^2)$ time as the core allocation algorithm. The example above hints at the first problem we need to solve: for any bidder $x$ and slot $y$, compute the optimal matching in which $x$ is assigned to slot $y$. Given the true optimal allocation, we show that these counterfactuals can be done quickly by computing short cycles in an appropriate graph. Given these optima, we must identify the thresholds at which we transition from one optimum to another, which can be formulated as an upper envelope computation.

## 1.4 Generalizing GSP

Though what precisely a generalized GSP looks like is out of scope, we will adopt a simple definition for the sake of exposition. The following folklore definition is broadly applied for less-substantial generalizations of GSP (e.g., [12, 16]) and theoretically rationalized for general contexts in [24]: if a bidder $i$ is assigned to slot $j$, we define the GSP price as the smallest (infimum) bid it can report and still be assigned into slot $j$ or higher by the ad selection algorithm. Note that when separability holds, these prices will be the same as in a traditional GSP auction.

Perhaps the most immediately practical result of our work is a fast algorithm for computing these GSP prices. We present a simplification of our general algorithm for computing $a_i$ that computes GSP prices and runs in time $O(nm^2)$ (Theorem 3.8). In practice, our implementation of the algorithm leads to overall run time for assignment and pricing together of less than 1ms on the instances we see in production, which is more than adequate for our goals.

### 1.5 Multi-dimensional bidding

Moving from the separable model to one in which bidders can have completely idiosyncratic click probabilities across slots, as discussed above, brings a heavy dose of realism to the stylized models applied to ad auctions. But in some cases there is reason to go further yet. Even in the model we proposed above, bidders can still communicate their full valuations across slots in a single number, since the click (or impression, or conversion, etc.) probabilities are known to the auctioneer. But what if bidders' values across slots differ in ways that are known only *privately*?

Motivated by this concern, we go on to consider a more general setting where advertisers are allowed to submit separate bids for each slot. That is, we assume that bidder $i \in I$ gives us a bid $b_{i,j}$ for each $j \in J$. In this case, $i$'s (expressed) expected value for slot $j$ is defined to be $v_{i,j} = b_{i,j} \cdot \pi_{i,j}$. While this is not currently supported by major online ad publishers, we argue that such a system has the potential to significantly increase overall advertiser value in some marketplaces. Indeed, advertisers often choose the cost-per-click (CPC) payment model simply due to the ease of tracking clicks, despite clicks only being a proxy for their real "event of interest". Most advertisers actually care about *conversions*, i.e., various user actions on the advertiser's website like buying an item, downloading an app, creating an account, or just spending enough time browsing. Often conversions are observed privately by the advertiser, and thus are impossible for the auctioneer to accurately predict. If every click yields an equal probability of conversion, then a single per-click bid remains perfectly sufficient, but what about otherwise?

We examined the following hypothesis about conversion rates in Yahoo's Native Ads: users who choose to scroll down the stream are more engaged with the content and, as a result, on average clicks in lower positions will yield higher conversions than those above. In Figure 2 we plot the average rate of conversion conditioned on click for each slot position from 1 to 10 on a subset of Yahoo Native Ads data where conversions were observable. Indeed, this rate grows significantly from slot 1 to slot 8 or 9 before leveling off. An analogous and more principled study for Search ads was performed in [3].

On the other side of the equation, click-rates degrade sharply as one moves down the page, so if an advertiser is looking for wide exposure it cannot just bid for lower positions in order to reap the higher value clicks. Additionally, some advertisers (e.g., those publicizing a brand) are more or less only interested in high position slots due to their higher exposure and general viewability. This diversity of preferences across the slot positions further supports the idea that an ad marketplace with slot-specific bidding has its place in the online advertising ecosystem, or is at least worthy of further study.

Efficient allocation of bidders to slots can, again, be achieved via a maximum weighted bipartite matching algorithm here; but pricing becomes much more complex. While the generality of VCG makes it an always-ready candidate pricing mechanism, the notion of GSP-like pricing is not immediately well-defined in this context. Fortunately, we can expand our notion of allocation curves to this setting, which will allow us to recover some sensible "in spirit" generalizations of GSP. The marginal social choice function $f_i$ of bidder $i$ given bids $b_{-i}$ is a function $f_i : \mathfrak{R}_+^n \rightarrow J$ that outputs the slot $j$ that $i$ wins as a function of his bid vector $b_i \in \mathfrak{R}_+^n$. We design an algorithm to compute marginal social choice functions for all bidders with run time $O(nm^2)$ (Theorem 4.1), and discuss various options for GSP-like pricing in Section 4.

While we show that computation of the marginal social choice functions can be done efficiently, there are many practical challenges to using multiple bids per bidder. First, just carrying around a vector of many bids instead of one bid per ad creates significant challenges at the web scale. Second,

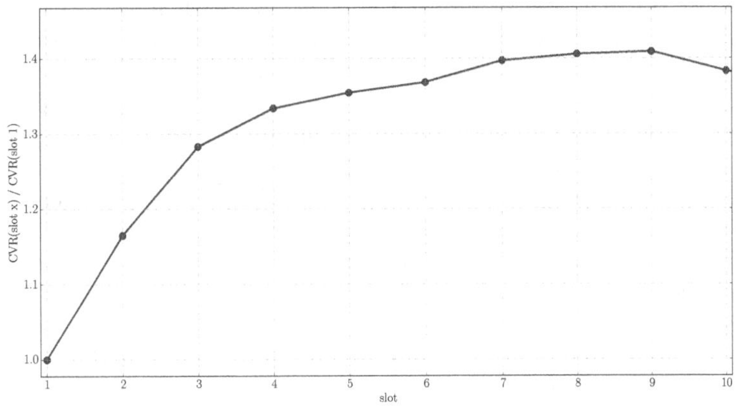


Fig. 2. Conversion-rate (probability of a conversion conditioned on the ad being clicked) as a function of slot, aggregated over all ad impressions on a set of pageviews that yielded over 300K clicks in slot 1, descending to roughly 30K clicks in slot 10.

the "equilibrium features" GSP possesses in the single-dimensional setting (e.g., local truthfulness) do not readily extend. The question of designing a GSP-like mechanism with provable equilibrium properties remains open.

## 2 RELATED LITERATURE

In computational advertising, two main research threads relate to our work: papers that analyze the separability assumption [3, 8–11] and papers that generalize GSP [1, 4, 5, 12, 16, 24]. Three natural intuitions underly the work critiquing separability. One intuition is that ads belonging to major brands benefit less from being placed in a higher slot. This is explored and generally confirmed in [8, 11]. Another idea is that user behavior follows a cascade model—a user looks at the first item, then conditionally decides whether to click or continue down the page—leading to substantial effects between ads that are not captured by an independent (separable) model; [9] estimates parameters for such a model. A third intuition is that a top slot may attract more accidental or exploratory clicks, whereas clicks on a less-prominent slot signal a stronger intent. This leads to non-separability in the conversion rate (likelihood that a click leads to a purchase, sales lead, etc.) as shown in [3].

A variety of papers use different techniques to generalize GSP, including definitions based on equilibrium properties [12], heuristic properties of the pricing scheme [16], structure of the allocation algorithm [5], or truthfulness for alternative models of advertiser preferences [1, 4, 24]; however, a definitive generalization is still an open question. Since the prices we compute as "GSP prices" can be derived as the truthful solution for preferences alternative to quasilinear utilities, our work is also related to the corresponding literature on stable matchings in the assignment model when preferences are not quasilinear. [1] builds on the Hungarian Method to design a generalized auction framework that computes a stable matching for a broad class of preferences that can include our model of GSP prices and runs in $O(nm^3)$ time. While stability is related to truthfulness, the concepts diverge in general models, so the outcome chosen by [1] would not generally be a maximum weighted matching and the outcome/prices from our auction would not generally be a stable matching. For information on stable matchings with non-quasilinear utilities, see the related work section of [1]. For an overview of the breadth of work on matching markets, see [20].

Outside advertising, our work has ties to competitive equilibria and the assignment model in matching markets. In the language of bidders and slots, letting $v_{i,j}$ be expected value to $i$ for winning slot $j$, a competitive equilibrium for quasilinear bidders is a matching with slot prices $p_j$ such that each bidder is matched to a slot that maximizes $v_{i,j} - p_j$. The minimum competitive equilibrium is always well-defined and always corresponds to VCG (a maximum weighted matching with VCG prices) [13]. Moreover, the VCG prices are the dual values associated with an optimal matching in a standard LP formulation of the assignment problem [2]. As a result, they naturally occur implicitly or explicitly in algorithms and mechanisms that have a primal-dual structure, such as the Hungarian Method and related ascending price auctions [13]. Additionally, some of our techniques are closely related to the more general literature on competitive equilibria with gross substitutes. The augmentation graph we use as a starting point for our algorithm is effectively equivalent to the exchange graph of [14], which is used as a method of computing equilibrium prices (see also [18]). We leverage the structure of this graph to identify configurations that are optimal with one fixed assignment, allowing us to recover the allocation curve.

## 3 CLASSICAL CASE: ONE BID PER BIDDER

Our main result is an algorithm that computes bidders' full allocation curves in time $O(nm^2)$, the same time required to compute a maximum weighted matching using the Hungarian Method.

We first recall our model. We have $n$ bidders $I = \{1, \dots, n\}$ who are to be matched to $m$ slots $J = \{1, \dots, m\}$. Each bidder $i \in I$ reports a bid $b_i$ and has an event probability $\pi_{i,j}$ for each $j \in J$. For convenience, we add dummy slots $\{m+1, \dots, n\}$ with $\pi_{i,j} = 0$ and call the result $J' = \{1, \dots, m, m+1, \dots, n\}$. For a matching $\sigma : J' \to I$, we write the total value as $V^\sigma = \sum_j b_i \pi_{\sigma(j),j}$. Given bids, the auction computes a maximum weighted matching $\sigma^*$ (maximizing $V^\sigma$) and we assume WLOG that bidders are labeled so that bidder $i$ is matched to slot $i$ under this matching ($\sigma^*(j) = j$). Let $x_i(b)$ denote the event probability for bidder $i$ as a function of all the bids. For a fixed bidder $i$ and bids $b_{-i}$, we say that $i$'s allocation curve is the function $a_i(b_i) = x_i(b_i, b_{-i})$. Since the allocation curve is a step function with at most $m+1$ steps we represent it as list of bid-value pairs, one for each step.

Algorithm 1 describes our main algorithm and Algorithm 2 an optimized implementation. Both algorithms implement the same logic; the second achieves better asymptotic run-time by exploiting structure. First, we apply the Hungarian Method to compute a maximal matching. From this matching, we construct a weighted graph in which the shortest cycle through edge $j \to i$ identifies the best matching that assigns bidder $i$ to slot $j$. Computing all-pairs shortest paths identifies all such cycles, from which we are able to infer the allocaiton curve for each bidder. Algorithm 1 treats dummy nodes as real slots and uses a naive implementation of the Hungarian Method for matching and the Floyd-Warshall algorithm for all-pairs shortest paths. Algorithm 2 is aware that some nodes are just dummy nodes. It uses an optimized version of the Hungarian Method and a modified version of Floyd-Warshall that exploits structure in the paths we need to compute.

Our central theorem is that these algorithms quickly compute a maximal matching as well as all $n$ allocation curves:

THEOREM 3.1. *Algorithms 1 and 2 compute a maximal matching $\sigma^*$ and one allocation curve $a_i(b_i)$ for each bidder. Algorithm 1 runs in time $O(n^3)$ and Algorithm 2 runs in time $O(nm^2)$.*

Our analysis begins with a series of claims and lemmas about matchings and paths that apply equally to Algorithms 1 and 2. The proof of Theorem 3.1 connects these claims to the algorithms. The following graph is effectively equivalent to the exchange graph of [14]. The subsequent observations

**ALGORITHM 1:** $O(n^3)$ Algorithm for Maximum Weighted Matching with Allocation Curves

**Input:** Bids $b_i$ and event probabilities $\pi_{i,j}$

**Output:** Maximum weighted matching $\sigma^*$; allocation curves $a_i(b_i)$.

1 Run the Hungarian Method to compute a maximum matching $\sigma^* : J' \to I$.
Relabel bidders so that $\sigma^*(i) = i$ and let $V^* = \sum_j b_j \pi_{j,j}$ denote the matching's value.

2 Let $G$ be a complete directed graph on vertices $J' = [n]$ with edge weights $w_{i,j} = b_j\pi_{j,j} - b_j\pi_{j,i}$.
Run Floyd-Warshall to compute all-pairs shortest path distances $d_{i,j}$ in $G$.

3 **for** $i \in I$ **do**
    **for** $j \in J'$ **do**
        Define a linear function $l_{i,j}(z) = \pi_{i,j} z + (V^* - \pi_{i,i} b_i - d_{i,j})$.
    **end**
    Compute the upper-envelope of the lines $l_{i,j}(z)$ as a sequence of segments. Call it $A_i(z)$.
    Compute $a_i(z) = \frac{dA_i}{dz}$ (i.e., one slope per segment, with the starting point of the segment). This is bidder $i$'s allocation curve.
**end**

are slightly stronger than their natural parallels in the gross substitutes literature owing to the unit-demand preferences in our setting [14, 15, 18]:

*Definition 3.2 (Augmentation Graph).* The *augmentation graph* $G^\sigma$ is a directed graph on $|J'| = n$ nodes with edge weights $w^\sigma_{i,j} = v_{\sigma(j),j} - v_{\sigma(j),i}$. When $\sigma$ is not specified we assume $\sigma = \sigma^*$ (the optimal matching chosen by the graph), so $w_{i,j} = w^{\sigma^*}_{i,j} = v_{\sigma^*(j),j} - v_{\sigma^*(j),i} = v_{j,j} - v_{j,i}$ (bidders are labeled so that $\sigma^*(j) = j$).

Observation 1. *The negative weight ($-w^\sigma_{i,j}$) is the amount the objective value would change if bidder $\sigma(j)$ were matched to slot $i$ instead of slot $j$.*

*Definition 3.3 (Augmenting Subgraph).* For two matchings $\sigma$ and $\sigma'$, the *augmenting subgraph* $H^{\sigma\to\sigma'}_v$ is a subgraph of $G^\sigma_v$. This graph has a directed edge $(i, j)$ if for some $t \in I$ the edge $(t, i)$ belongs to matching $\sigma'$ and the edge $(t, j)$ belongs to matching $\sigma$.

Observation 2. *Suppose we are given two matchings $\sigma$ and $\sigma'$ of value $V^\sigma$ and $V^{\sigma'}$ in the original bipartite graph. The total negative weight of edges in $H^{\sigma\to\sigma'}_v$ is equal to the change in objective value from $\sigma$ to $\sigma'$, i.e.,*

$$V^{\sigma'} = V^\sigma - \sum_{(i,j)\in H^{\sigma\to\sigma'}_v} w^\sigma_{i,j} \ .$$

Claim 1. *For any $\sigma$ and $\sigma'$, the connected components of $H^{\sigma\to\sigma'}_v$ are directed cycles and disconnected vertices; any subgraph $H$ of $G^\sigma_v$ consisting only of directed cycles and disconnected vertices corresponds to a matching $\sigma'$.*

Proof. First, we show that $H^{\sigma\to\sigma'}_v$ is as described. If bidder $i$ is matched to the same slot in $\sigma$ and $\sigma'$, $i$ has degree 0 in $H^{\sigma\to\sigma'}_v$ and is a disconnected vertex. For all remaining nodes, each node has exactly one incoming edge from the slot that bidder $i$ gets and exactly one outgoing edge to the bidder that gets slot $i$. A connected component whose nodes have in-degree=outdegree=1 is a cycle.

Second, we show how to construct $\sigma'$ from a given $H$: if $j$ is a disconnected vertex, leave bidder $j$ matched to slot $j$; otherwise, let $(i, j)$ denote the incoming edge to $j$ in $H$ and match bidder $j$ to slot $i$. □

**ALGORITHM 2:** $O(nm^2)$ Algorithm for Maximum Weighted Matching with Allocation Curves

**Input:** Bids $b_i$ and event probabilities $\pi_{i,j}$
**Output:** Maximum weighted matching $\sigma^*$; allocation curves $a_i(b_i)$.

1 Run the Hungarian Method to compute a maximum matching $\sigma^* : J \to I$. Assign unmatched bidders to slots $\{m+1, \ldots, n\}$ arbitrarily to get a matching $\sigma^* : J' \to I$. Relabel bidders so that $\sigma^*(i) = i$ and let $V^* = \sum_j b_j \pi_{j,j}$ denote the matching's value.

2 Let $G$ be a complete directed graph on vertices $J' = [n]$ with edge weights $w_{i,j} = b_j \pi_{j,j} - b_j \pi_{j,i}$ (do not store $G$ explicitly). Compute shortest paths $d_{i,j}$ that contain at most one node in $\{m+1, \ldots, n\}$ as follows:

/* Standard Floyd-Warshall initialization over the $i,j$ pairs we will need. */
**for** $i \in I, j \in J$ **do**

$$d_{j,i} \leftarrow \begin{cases} 0 & i = j \\ w_{i,j} & otherwise. \end{cases}$$

**end**

/* Standard Floyd-Warshall update step using only intermediate nodes in $[m]$. After this step, each $d_{i,j}$ will contain the shortest path distance from $i$ to $j$ along paths whose intermediate nodes are all in $[m]$. */
**for** $k \in \{1, \ldots, m\}, i \in I, j \in J \cup \{m+1\}$ **do**
  $d_{i,j} \leftarrow \min(d_{i,j}, d_{i,k} + d_{k,j})$
**end**

/* When $i,j \in [m]$ we do extra Floyd-Warshall style update steps to consider paths from $i$ to $j$ that contain exactly one node $k$ from $\{m+1, \ldots, n\}$. */
**for** $k \in \{m+1, \ldots, n\}, i \in \{1, \ldots, m\}, j \in J$ **do**
  $d_{i,j} \leftarrow \min(d_{i,j}, d_{i,k} + d_{k,j})$
**end**

3 **for** $i \in I$ **do**
  **for** $j \in J \cup \{m+1\}$ **do**
    Define $l_{i,j}(z) = \pi_{i,j} z + (V^* - \pi_{i,i} b_i - d_{i,j})$.
  **end**
  Compute the upper-envelope of the lines $l_{i,j}(z)$ as a sequence of segments. Call it $A_i(z)$.
  Compute $a_i(z) = \frac{dA_i}{dz}$ (i.e., one slope per segment, with the starting point of the segment). This is bidder $i$'s allocation curve.
**end**

Observation 3. *A negative weight cycle in $G_v^\sigma$ corresponds to an augmenting path in the original bipartite graph that can be used to generate a matching with a higher value.*

Observation 4. *$G_v^\sigma$ has a negative weight cycle if and only if it is not optimal.*

Claim 2. *Let $\sigma^*$ be an optimal matching for $v_{i,j}$ and fix a bidder $x$ and slot $y$. There exists $\sigma^+$ such that:*

(1) *the matching $\sigma^+$ is optimal among matchings that assign slot $y$ to bidder $x$,*
(2) *the augmentation graph $H_v^{\sigma^* \to \sigma^+}$ contains exactly one cycle $C$ if $x$ is not matched to $y$ in $\sigma^*$ ($C$ must contain the edge $(y, x)$) and contains no edges otherwise, and*
(3) *If $C$ exists then $|C \cap \{m+1, \ldots, n\}| \leq 1$, that is, at most one vertex in $C$ corresponds to a dummy slot.*

Proof. If $x$ is matched to $y$ in $\sigma^*$ we can trivially take $\sigma^+ = \sigma^*$, whose augmentation graph has no edges. Thus, assume $x$ is not matched to $y$ in $\sigma^*$.

We first show that an appropriate $\sigma^+$ exists that contains only one cycle $C$. For any constrained-optimal matching $\sigma'$ we can write

$$V^{\sigma'} = V - \sum_{(i,j)\in H_v^{\sigma^*\to\sigma'}} w_{i,j} \ .$$

Suppose that $H_v^{\sigma^*\to\sigma'}$ contains cycles $C_0, C_1, \ldots, C_k$ where $C_0$ includes the edge $(y, x)$. Let $C = \bigcup_{l=1}^k C_l$ (i.e., all edges in $H$ except the cycle $C_0$). We abuse notation and write $\sigma' - C$ as the matching implied by the augmentation graph $H_v^{\sigma^*\to\sigma'}$ with edges from $C$ removed. We can write

$$\begin{aligned} V^{\sigma'} &= V^{\sigma^*} - \sum_{(i,j)\in H_v^{\sigma^*\to\sigma'}\setminus C} w_{i,j} - \sum_{(i,j)\in C} w_{i,j} \\ &= V^{\sigma'-C} - \sum_{(i,j)\in C} w_{i,j} \ . \end{aligned}$$

If $\sum_{(i,j)\in C} w_{i,j} > 0$, then $V^{\sigma'-C} > V^{\sigma'}$. However, $\sigma' - C$ still matches $x$ to $y$, contradicting optimality of $\sigma'$. On the other hand, if $\sum_{(i,j)\in C} w_{i,j} < 0$ then we have a negative-weight-cycle in $G_v$, contradicting optimality of $\sigma^*$. Thus,

$$\sum_{(i,j)\in C} w_{i,j} = 0$$

for any cycle $C$ that does not contain the edge $(y, x)$, and

$$\begin{aligned} V^{\sigma'} &= V^{\sigma^*} - \sum_{(i,j)\in H_v^{\sigma^*\to\sigma'}} w_{i,j} \\ &= V - \sum_{(i,j)\in H_v^{\sigma^*\to\sigma'}\setminus C} w_{i,j} = V^{\sigma'-C} \ , \end{aligned}$$

implying $\sigma' - C$ is also constrained-optimal, so we take $\sigma^+ = \sigma' - C$.

Finally, we show that we can choose $C$ so that it contains at most one dummy slot. Suppose we are given a constrained-optimal $\sigma'$ with a single cycle

$$C = \{x, \ldots, w_0, z_1, w_1, \ldots, z_2, w_2, \ldots, y\}$$

where $x, \ldots, w_0 \in [m]$ and $w_2, \ldots, y \in [m]$ (possibly $x = w_0$ and/or $y = w_2$) but $z_1, z_2 \notin [m]$. Split $C$ into two cycles as follows:

$$C_0 = \{x, \ldots, w_0, z_1, w_2, \ldots, y\} \quad \text{and} \quad C_1 = \{w_1, \ldots, z_2\}$$

and call the resulting matching $\sigma''$. We have

$$V^{\sigma''} = V^{\sigma'} + v_{w_2,z_1} - v_{w_2,z_2} + v_{w_1,z_1} - v_{w_1,z_2} \ .$$

However, since $z_1$ and $z_2$ are both dummy slots we have $v_{w_2,z_1} = v_{w_2,z_2} = v_{w_1,z_1} = v_{w_1,z_2} = 0$ and so $V^{\sigma''} = V^{\sigma'}$. Now, our earlier argument says that only the cycle $C_0$ is required to construct $\sigma^+$, so we take $\sigma^+ = \sigma'' - C_1$. Remark that $C_0$ contains only one node not in $[m]$ (specifically $z_1$) as desired.

This construction for splitting $C$ works as long as $x, y \in [m]$. When $x \notin [m]$, take the cycles $C_0 = \{x, w_2, \ldots, y\}$ and $C_1 = \{w_1, \ldots, z_2\}$ instead. □

Lemma 3.4. *Fix $b$, a bidder indexed by $x$ and a slot indexed by $y \neq x$. Let $\sigma^*$ be an optimal matching (note that due to our relabelling $\sigma(x) = x$) and let $\sigma'$ be any matching that is optimal subject to the constraint that bidder $x$ is matched to slot $y$. Then,*

$$V^{\sigma^+} = V^{\sigma^*} - w_{y,x} - d_{x,y}$$

*where $d_{x,y}$ is the shortest path distance from $x$ to $y$ in $G_v^{\sigma^*}$. Moreover, there is a path from $x$ to $y$ of length $d_{x,y}$ containing at most one vertex not in $[m]$.*

Proof. Notice that all constrained-optimal matchings will have the same value. By the preceding claim, there exists a constrained-optimal matching $\sigma^+$ that has an augmenting subgraph $H_v^{\sigma^* \to \sigma'}$ consisting of a single cycle $C_0$ (and disconnected nodes), where $C_0$ contains edge $(y, x)$. We can write

$$V^{\sigma^+} = V^{\sigma^*} - \sum_{(i,j) \in C_0} w_{i,j} \; .$$

Moreover, any cycle $C$ including the edge $(y, x)$ will define a matching $\sigma'$ that assigns $x$ to $y$, so we can conclude from optimality of $\sigma^+$ that $C_0$ minimizes $\sum_{(i,j) \in C_0} w_{i,j}$ over all cycles containing $(y, x)$. (Note that $G_v^{\sigma^*}$ cannot have negative-weight cycles because $\sigma^*$ is optimal.)

Finally, given that $C_0$ minimizes $\sum_{(i,j) \in C_0} w_{i,j}$ over all cycles containing $(y, x)$, we know that

$$\sum_{(i,j) \in C_0} w_{i,j}^{\sigma^*} = w_{y,x} + d_{x,y}$$

where $d_{x,y}^{\sigma^*}$ is the shortest path from $x$ to $y$. Since we know that we can always choose $C_0$ so that it contains at most one vertex not in $[m]$, it follows that there is a shortest path containing at most one vertex not in $[m]$ and the lemma immediately follows. □

Next, we introduce the notion of configuration lines, which have been put to use in prior work [4].

*Definition 3.5.* The *configuration line* for bidder $i$ in matching $\sigma$ is a function of $b_i$ given by $l_{i,\sigma}(b_i) = \pi_{i,\sigma^{(-1)}(i)} \cdot b_i + V_{-i}^{\sigma}$, where $\sigma^{(-1)}(i)$ is the slot to which $i$ is matched in $\sigma$ and $V_{-i}^{\sigma} = \sum_{j \neq i} \pi_{j,\sigma^{(-1)}(j)} b_j$.

Claim 3. *Bidder $i$'s allocation curve can be defined as the derivative of the upper envelope of the configuration lines for all $\sigma$.*

Proof. Indeed, the upper envelope of configuration lines defines the value of the optimal matching as a function of bidders $i$ bid $b_i$. For each $b_i$ the maximum is achieved on some matching $\sigma$ and corresponding line $l_{i,\sigma}(b_i) = \pi_{i,\sigma^{(-1)}(i)} \cdot b_i + V_{-i}^{\sigma}$ is a linear function of $b_i$. The derivative at point $b_i$ has value $\pi_{i,\sigma^{(-1)}(i)}$ which is "event probability" if we allocate bidder $i$ to the spot $\sigma^{(-1)}(i)$, which matches the definition of the allocation curve. □

We can now leverage the structure of the matching problem to restrict the set of lines we need to consider when computing the upper envelope or its derivative:

Lemma 3.6. *Fix bidder $x$. For each slot $y$ define the line $l_{x,y}(z) = \pi_{x,y} \cdot z + (V^* - \pi_{x,x} b_x - d_{x,y})$. The derivative of the upper envelope of these lines is bidder $x$'s allocation curve.*

*Moreover, when $m < n$, it is sufficient to compute the upper envelope of the lines $l_{x,y}$ where $y \in \{1, \ldots, m, m+1\}$.*

Proof. All configuration lines $l_{x,\sigma}$ where $x = \sigma(y)$ will have the same slope. Thus, when computing the upper envelope, of all $\sigma$ that match $x$ to $y$, only the ones that maximize $V_{-x}^{\sigma}$ will be relevant. Consequently, it suffices, for each $y$, to find one line with maximal value of $V_{-x}^{\sigma}$.

Fixing slot $y$, maximizing $V_{-x}^{\sigma}$ is equivalent to finding the constrained-optimal matching $\sigma'$ that matches bidder $x$ to slot $y$. As shown earlier, this matching has value $V^{\sigma'} = V^{\sigma^*} - w_{y,x} - d_{x,y}$ and thus

$$\begin{aligned} V_{-x}^{\sigma'} &= V^{\sigma^*} - w_{y,x} - d_{x,y} - \pi_{x,y} b_x \\ &= V^{\sigma^*} - (\pi_{x,x} b_x - \pi_{x,y} b_x) - d_{x,y} - \pi_{x,y} b_x \\ &= V^{\sigma^*} - d_{x,y} - \pi_{x,x} b_x \ , \end{aligned}$$

from which the first part of the lemma follows.

Finally, remark that dummy slots are interchangeable, so $\pi_{x,y}$ and $d_{x,y}$ will be the same for all $y \in \{m+1, \ldots, n\}$. Thus, the lines $l_{x,y}$ will be the same and it is sufficient to take only one when computing the upper envelope (we take $y = m + 1$). □

*Proof of Theorem 3.1.* For Algorithm 1, correctness follows because the algorithm directly computes allocation as per Lemma 3.6. Steps (1) and (2) take $O(n^3)$ time due to the classical run time bounds on the Hungarian and Floyd-Warshall algorithms. Once we have computed $V^*$ and the table with all pair shortest paths, it takes $O(n^2)$ to run step (3), for an overall runtime of $O(n^3)$.

Algorithm 2 is an optimization of Algorithm 1. The Hungarian Method is easily modified to run in time $O(nm^2)$ [19]. Step (2) is simply an optimization of the Floyd-Warshall algorithm that takes into account two facts: (1) we only care about paths from $x \in I$ to $y \in J \cup \{m+1\}$ (dummy nodes are equivalent) and (2) we only care about paths that contain at most one node in $\{m+1, \ldots, n\}$ as per Lemma 3.4. The first loop in step (2) initializes the $nm$ distances we care about, the second loop computes the shortest paths where all intermediate nodes are in $\{1, \ldots, m\}$ in the same pattern as the original Floyd-Warshall algorithm, and the third loop considers paths where both endpoints are in $\{1, \ldots, m\}$ and exactly one intermediate node is in $\{m+1, \ldots, n\}$. The second and third loops run in $O(nm^2)$ time. Finally, step (3) is optimized to only use lines for $J \cup \{m+1\}$ as per Lemma 3.6 and requires $O(nm)$ time, for a total asymptotic runtime of $O(nm^2)$. □

## 3.1 GSP pricing

Our GSP prices are an important special case that can be computed with a slightly simpler algorithm (Algorithm 3). We use the following definition of GSP prices:

*Definition 3.7 ("GSP" Price).* The GSP price for bidder $i$ is defined as the minimum (infimum) bid that $i$ can submit that will maintain the slot he received.

$$p_i^{GSP} = \inf\{z \mid x_i(b_{-i}, z) \geq x_i(b)\}$$

This definition has long existed in the folklore and is commonly applied in practice. More recently, [24] justified them theoretically as being truthful for a "value maximizing" bidder who tries to maximize $x_i$ while keeping $p_i \leq b_i$ (any outcome with $p_i \leq v_i$ is preferred to any outcome with $p_i > v_i$). The following claim is a direct application of the characterization from [24]:

Claim 4. *The "GSP" price is truthful for value maximizers (almost everywhere[4]).*

If we ran Algorithm 1 we could easily compute GSP prices from the allocation curves $a_i$, but if we know we only want GSP prices we can leverage the same ideas in a simpler algorithm, shown in Algorithm 3 and proven below.

[4]Truth-telling is a best-response as long as there wouldn't be a tie under truthful bidding, which happens almost everywhere in a continuous bid space (see [24]).

Theorem 3.8. *Letting $d_{i,j}$ be the shortest path from i to j in the augmentation graph for the optimal matching $\sigma^*$, the "GSP" price for bidder i is equal to*

$$p_i^{GSP} = \max_{j|\pi_{i,j}<\pi_{i,i}} \frac{-d_{i,j}}{\pi_{i,i} - \pi_{i,j}}$$

*if there is at least one index j such that $\pi_{i,j} < \pi_{i,i}$, or equals 0 otherwise.*

*Algorithm 3 computes a maximal matching $\sigma^*$ and GSP prices $p_i^{GSP}$. It can be implemented in time $O(nm^2)$ using the same tricks as Algorithm 2.*

Proof. We want to find the smallest $b_i \geq 0$ such that the augmentation graph for $\sigma^*$ does not have a negative-weight cycle, since this is the smallest $b_i$ for which $\sigma^*$ is optimal.

When we change $b_i$, only the weights on edges incoming to node $i$ change, i.e., only $w_{j,i}$ change. If any negative cycle exists, there exists a simple negative cycle that passes through node $i$ at most once and therefore only includes one edge with a modified weight. It thus suffices to consider the edges $(i, j)$ individually to see if they are part of a negative-weight cycle.

An edge $(i, j)$ will be part of a negative-weight cycle if $d_{i,j} + w_{j,i} < 0$ where $d_{i,j}$ is the shortest path from $i$ to $j$ in the augmentation graph. Thus, to ensure no negative weight cycles we need

$$d_{i,j} \geq -w_{j,i} = -(v_{i,i} - v_{i,j}) = -b_i(\pi_{i,i} - \pi_{i,j}) \ .$$

When $\pi_{i,i} = \pi_{i,j}$ this is irrelevant. When $\pi_{i,i} > \pi_{i,j}$ this is equivalent to

$$b_i \geq \frac{-d_{i,j}}{\pi_{i,i} - \pi_{i,j}} \ ,$$

and when $\pi_{i,j} > \pi_{i,i}$ this is equivalent to

$$b_i \leq \frac{-d_{i,j}}{\pi_{i,i} - \pi_{i,j}} \ .$$

Since we want a lower-bound, we take the maximum over the lower-bounds to get the characterization of $p_i^{GSP}$ in the theorem.

The run time analysis for the Hungarian Method and Floyd-Warshall is the same as for computing allocation curves and the same tricks from Algorithm 2 can be applied to achieve $O(nm^2)$ run time (see the proof of Theorem 3.1). Computing the $n$ prices $p_i^{GSP}$ requires $O(nm)$ time. □

**ALGORITHM 3:** Algorithm for Computing Maximum Weighted Matching with GSP Prices

**Input:** Bids $b_i$ and Event Probabilities $\pi_{i,j}$
**Output:** Allocation Curves $a_i(b_i)$ as

Run the Hungarian Method to compute a maximum matching $\sigma^* : J \to I$.
Relabel bidders so that $\sigma^*(i) = i$ and let $V^* = \sum_j b_j \pi_{j,j}$ denote the matching's value.

Let $G$ be a complete directed graph on vertices $J' = [n]$ with edge weights $w_{i,j} = b_j \pi_{j,j} - b_j \pi_{j,i}$.
Run Floyd-Warshall to compute all-pairs shortest path distances $d_{i,j}$ in $G$.

**for** $i \in I$ **do**

$$p_i^{GSP} = \begin{cases} \max_{j|\pi_{i,j}<\pi_{i,i}} \frac{-d_{i,j}}{\pi_{i,i}-\pi_{i,j}} & \text{if there exists at least one } j \text{ for which } \pi_{i,j} < \pi_{i,i}, \\ 0 & \text{otherwise.} \end{cases}$$

**end**

## 4 GENERAL CASE: SEPARATE BIDS FOR EACH SLOT

While using a single bid is convenient, there is often reason to believe that bidders' values for an event may be substantially different for different slots, as discussed earlier. Allowing each bidder $i \in I$ to report a separate bid $b_{i,j}$ for each slot $j \in J$ allows them to express this. In this section we seek algorithms for this general setting that are parallel to our single bid algorithms.

We first recall our model for the general case. We have $n$ bidders $I = \{1, \ldots, n\}$ who are to be matched to $m$ slots $J = \{1, \ldots, m\}$. Each bidder $i \in I$ reports a bid $b_{i,j}$ for each slot $j \in J$ and has an event probability $\pi_{i,j}$ for each $j \in J$. For a matching $\sigma : J \to I$, we write the total value as $V^\sigma = \sum_j b_{i,j}\pi_{\sigma(j),j}$. Given bids, the auction computes a maximum weighted matching $\sigma^*$ (maximizing $V^\sigma$) and, WLOG, we assume that bidders are labeled so that $\sigma^*(j) = j$.

The allocation curve $a_i$ cannot be cleanly defined in a multi-parameter bid space. Instead, we define the *marginal social choice function* for a fixed bidder $i$ and bids $b_{-i}$ as the function $f_i : \mathfrak{R}_+^m \to J \cup \{m+1\}$ yielding the slot bidder $i$ gets when it reports bids $b_{i,j}, j \in J$. The dummy slot $m+1$ corresponds to the event when a bidder does not get any slots in $J$. The marginal social choice function can be understood as a partition of $\mathfrak{R}_+^n$ (the bid space of bidder $i$) into $m+1$ regions, one for each slot in $J \cup \{m+1\}$. Let $B_{i,j} \subseteq \mathfrak{R}_+^n$ denote the set of bid vectors $b_i \in \mathfrak{R}_+^n$ that would cause bidder $i$ to get slot $j$ (given the bids of others $b_{-i}$).

In multi-parameter settings, another useful piece of information for counterfactual analysis is the full menu of VCG prices. That is, for each slot $j \in J \cup \{m+1\}$, what would the VCG price have been if bidder $i$ had submitted bids $b_{i,j}$ such that $f_i(b_i) = j$? For reasons that we will see, the VCG price is relevant even when mechanisms do not aim to use VCG pricing.

Algorithm 4 computes a concise representation of the marginal social choice functions $f_i$, as well as the full menus of VCG prices. This all assumes that behavior in the case of ties is straightforward and/or irrelevant (e.g., if ties are broken by solving an NP-hard problem, we haven't completely recovered $f_i$). The proof of the following theorem can be found in the online version of the paper:

THEOREM 4.1. *Algorithm 4 computes an optimal matching $\sigma^*$ along with the n marginal social choice functions. It can be implemented in time $O(nm^2)$. The space required to store these functions is $O(nm)$.*

### 4.1 GSP prices

While we presented a fast algorithm to compute marginal social choice functions, the question of GSP-like pricing still stands. A natural starting point is to ask: given the optimal weighted bipartite matching where bidder $\sigma^*(j)$ is assigned to slot $j$, what would be the smallest bid that allows bidder $\sigma^*(j)$ to keep his slot in the optimal assignment? When bids are multi-parameter, even this intuition is not fully specific and lends itself to two possibilities (recall bidders are labeled such that $\sigma^*(j) = j$): (1) what is the smallest bid if $i$ strategizes over all bids $b_{i,j}, j \in J$, or (2) what is the smallest bid $b_{i,i}$ if $b_{i,j}, j \neq i$ are naively held fixed? Call the former *Weak Generalized Second Price* (WGSP) and the latter *Aggressive Generalized Second Price* (AGSP).

Unfortunately, while both WGSP and AGSP prices will be easy to compute, neither will be immediately satisfactory as a generalization of GSP, as we will discuss below. The notion that GSP prices are truthful for value maximizers offers a lens to understand why—if we insist on computing a maximum weighted matching—there will be no prices that make the auction truthful for value maximizers, suggesting that any method of generalizing GSP will sacrifice some of the elegance of a simple GSP auction. Recovering all the properties we desire may require picking a different optimization algorithm, e.g., a greedy algorithm would admit truthful prices for value maximizers [23] (inducing the stable matching computed by [1]).

**ALGORITHM 4:** Algorithm for Computing Maximum Weighted Matching with Marginal Social Choice Functions

**Input:** Bids $b_i \in \Re_+^n$ and event probabilities $\pi_{i,j}$
**Output:** Maximum weighted matching $\sigma^*$ and marginal social choice functions $f_i(b_i)$ as

1 Run the Hungarian Method to compute a maximum matching $\sigma^* : J \to I$.
Relabel bidders so that $\sigma^*(i) = i$ and let $V^* = \sum_j b_{j,j}\pi_{j,j}$ denote the matching's value.

2 Let $G$ be a complete directed graph on vertices $J' = [n]$ with edge weights $w_{i,j} = b_{j,j}\pi_{j,j} - b_{i,j}\pi_{j,i}$.
Run Floyd-Warshall to compute all-pairs shortest path distances $d_{i,j}$ in $G$. Define $V_{-i}^{-j} = V^* - v_{i,i} - d_{i,j}$.

3 **for** $i \in I$ **do**
  Compute $f_i(0) = \text{argmax}_j V_{-i}^{-j}$ breaking ties arbitrarily.
**end**

4 **for** $i \in I$ **do**
  **for** $j \in J \cup \{m+1\}$ **do**
    Define $p_{i,j}^{VCG} \cdot \pi_{i,j} = V_{-i}^{-f_i(0)} - V_{-i}^{-j} = d_{i,j} - d_{i,f_i(0)}$.
  **end**
  The marginal social choice function for $i$ is $f_i(b_i) = \text{argmax}_{j \in J \cup \{m+1\}} \{b_{i,j} \cdot \pi_{i,j} - d_{i,j}\}$.
**end**

*WGSP.* WGSP is the natural generalization of the minimum bid property we used in the single-parameter regime. Unfortunately, it turns out to be degenerate — the WGSP price is simply the VCG price:

Theorem 4.2. $p_i^{WGSP} = p_i^{VCG}$

Proof. First, observe that since the auction will maximize the sum of values, reporting $b_{i,r} = 0$ for $r \neq j$ can only reduce the minimum report $b_j$ required for bidder $i$ to be matched to slot $j$. Thus, WLOG we can fix $b_{i,r} = 0$ for $r \neq j$ and find the minimum (infimum) $b_{i,j}$ such that $i$ gets matched to slot $j$.

Recall our notation $V_{-i}^{-j}$ for the maximum total value attainable by bidders other than $i$ when they are allocated to slots other than $j$ (i.e., the maximum total value attainable by bidders other than $i$ if we fix $i$ to be matched to slot $j$). In this notation, we observe that VCG externality prices can be written as $p_{i,j}^{VCG}\pi_{i,j} = V_{-i}^{-f_i(0)} - V_{-i}^{-j}$ where $f_i$ is the marginal social choice function of bidder $i$ given $v_{-i}$.

Suppose that the mechanism assigns $i$ to a slot $k \neq j$. We know that the mechanism will get zero value from $i$ and therefore will pick the outcome that maximizes value from bidders $-i$, thus achieving an objective value of $V_{-i}^{f_i(0)}$. On the other hand, when $i$ wins slot $j$ the objective value will be $V_{-i}^{-j} + b_{i,j}\pi_{i,j}$. Thus, bidder $i$ will be assigned to slot $j$ if $V_{-i}^{-j} + b_{i,j}\pi_{i,j} > V_{-i}^{f_i(0)}$, and if $V_{-i}^{-j} + b_{i,j}\pi_{i,j} < V_{-i}^{f_i(0)}$ then it will not be assigned to slot $j$. We can thus conclude that $V_{-i}^{-j} + p_{i,j}^{WGSP}\pi_{i,j} = V_{-i}^{f_i(0)}$ and it follows that

$$p_{i,j}^{WGSP}\pi_{i,j} = V_{-i}^{-f_i(0)} - V_{-i}^{-j} = p_{i,j}^{VCG}\pi_{i,j} .$$

A detailed proof can be found in the online version of the paper. □

*AGSP.* The following theorem says that AGSP prices are easy to compute in the same manner as the GSP prices. They will generally be higher than VCG prices, which is good in that it differentiates them from VCG (unlike WGSP) but bad in that an advertiser can reduce its price simply by reducing its bid on other outcomes.

Theorem 4.3. $p_i^{AGSP} = \max\{0, \max_j \frac{b_{i,j}\pi_{i,j} - d_{i,j}}{\pi_{ii}}\}$

Proof. We want to find the smallest $b_{ii} \geq 0$ such that the augmentation graph for $\sigma^*$ does not have a negative weight cycle. Analogously to Lemma 3.7 we need to ensure that $d_{i,j} \geq -b_{i,i}\pi_{ii} + b_{i,j}\pi_{i,j}$. Therefore,

$$b_{i,i} \geq \frac{b_{i,j}\pi_{i,j} - d_{i,j}}{\pi_{ii}}.$$

□

## 5 CONCLUSION

This paper studies ad auctions when parameters may be slot-specific. The algorithms herein are simultaneously eminently practical and theoretically intriguing. From a practical perspective, our algorithms are all fast enough to be implemented under the severe run time constraints of the online advertising domain, while offering significantly more optimization power than the status quo separable model. From a theoretical perspective, our work takes a novel approach and explicitly computes bidders' allocation functions. While this may initially seem counterintuitive and excessive, it introduces a layer of abstraction between allocation and pricing that confers substantial power to the auctioneer and permits implementations that would otherwise be effectively impossible [4]. This new approach inspires a variety of questions for future work – e.g., what are other settings where allocation functions can be computed efficiently and/or practically, and what are the benefits? Is computing allocation functions provably harder than computing truthful prices in interesting settings, or provably equivalent? Given that the allocation curve is ubiquitous in proofs, the fact that the existing literature never computes it directly suggests that our approach is ripe for further study.

## REFERENCES

[1] Gagan Aggarwal, S. Muthukrishnan, Dávid Pál, and Martin Pál. 2009. General Auction Mechanism for Search Advertising. In *Proceedings of the 18th International Conference on World Wide Web (WWW '09)*. ACM, New York, NY, USA, 241–250. DOI: http://dx.doi.org/10.1145/1526709.1526742

[2] Sushil Bikhchandani and Joseph M. Ostroy. 2006. *Combinatorial Auctions.* MIT Press, Chapter From the assignment model to combinatorial auctions.

[3] Liad Blumrosen, Jason D. Hartline, and Shuzhen Nong. 2008. Position Auctions and Non-uniform Conversion Rates. In *ACM EC Workshop on Advertisement Auctions.*

[4] Ruggiero Cavallo, Prabhakar Krishnamurthy, Maxim Sviridenko, and Christopher A. Wilkens. 2017. Sponsored Search Auctions with Rich Ads. In *Proceedings of the 26th International Conference on World Wide Web (WWW '17).* International World Wide Web Conferences Steering Committee, Republic and Canton of Geneva, Switzerland, 43–51. DOI: http://dx.doi.org/10.1145/3038912.3052703

[5] Ruggiero Cavallo and Christopher A. Wilkens. 2014. *Web and Internet Economics: 10th International Conference, WINE 2014, Beijing, China, December 14-17, 2014. Proceedings.* Springer International Publishing, Cham, Chapter GSP with General Independent Click-through-Rates, 400–416. DOI: http://dx.doi.org/10.1007/978-3-319-13129-0_32

[6] Ran Duan and Seth Pettie. 2014. Linear-Time Approximation for Maximum Weight Matching. *J. ACM* 61, 1, Article 1 (Jan. 2014), 23 pages. DOI: http://dx.doi.org/10.1145/2529989

[7] Benjamin Edelman, Michael Ostrovsky, and Michael Schwarz. 2007. Internet Advertising and the Generalized Second-Price Auction: Selling Billions of Dollars Worth of Keywords. *American Economic Review* 97, 1 (2007), 242–259.

[8] Matt Goldman and Justin M. Rao. 2017. Position Auctions in Practice. (2017). DOI: http://dx.doi.org/10.2139/ssrn.2524688

[9] Renato Gomes, Nicole Immorlica, and Evangelos Markakis. 2009. Externalities in Keyword Auctions: An Empirical and Theoretical Assessment. In *Internet and Network Economics*, Stefano Leonardi (Ed.). Springer Berlin Heidelberg, Berlin, Heidelberg, 172–183.

[10] Przemyslaw Jeziorski and Sridhar Moorthy. 2017. Advertiser Prominence Effects in Search Advertising. *Management Science* 0, 0 (2017), null. DOI: http://dx.doi.org/10.1287/mnsc.2016.2677 arXiv:https://doi.org/10.1287/mnsc.2016.2677

[11] Przemyslaw Jeziorski and Ilya Segal. 2015. What Makes Them Click: Empirical Analysis of Consumer Demand for Search Advertising. *American Economic Journal: Microeconomics* 7, 3 (August 2015), 24–53. DOI: http://dx.doi.org/10.1257/mic.20100119

[12] Sébastien Lahaie and David M. Pennock. 2007. Revenue Analysis of a Family of Ranking Rules for Keyword Auctions. In *Proceedings of the 8th ACM Conference on Electronic Commerce (EC '07)*. ACM, New York, NY, USA, 50–56. DOI: http://dx.doi.org/10.1145/1250910.1250918

[13] Herman B. Leonard. 1983. Elicitation of honest preferences for the assignment of individuals to positions. *The Journal of Political Economy* 91, 3 (1983), 461–479.

[14] Kazuo Murota. 1996. Valuated Matroid Intersection I: Optimality Criteria. *SIAM J. Discrete Math.* 9 (1996), 545–561.

[15] Kazuo Murota. 1996. Valuated Matroid Intersection II: Algorithms. *SIAM J. Discret. Math.* 9, 4 (Nov. 1996), 562–576. DOI: http://dx.doi.org/10.1137/S0895480195280009

[16] S. Muthukrishnan. 2009. Bidding on Configurations in Internet Ad Auctions. In *Computing and Combinatorics*, Hung Q. Ngo (Ed.). Springer Berlin Heidelberg, Berlin, Heidelberg, 1–6.

[17] Roger B. Myerson. 1981. Optimal Auction Design. *Math. Oper. Res.* 6, 1 (Feb. 1981), 58–73. DOI: http://dx.doi.org/10.1287/moor.6.1.58

[18] Renato Paes Leme. 2017. Gross substitutability: An algorithmic survey. *Games and Economic Behavior* 106, C (2017), 294–316. https://EconPapers.repec.org/RePEc:eee:gamebe:v:106:y:2017:i:c:p:294-316

[19] Lyle Ramshaw and Robert E. Tarjan. 2012. On Minimum-Cost Assignments in Unbalanced Bipartite Graphs. (2012).

[20] Uriel G. Rothblum. 1992. Two-sided matching: A study in game-theoretic modeling and analysis: By Alvin E. Roth and Marilda A. Oliveira Sotomayor, Econometric Society Monographs, Cambridge Univ. Press, Cambridge, MA, 1990. 265 + xiii pp. *Games and Economic Behavior* 4, 1 (1992), 161–165. https://EconPapers.repec.org/RePEc:eee:gamebe:v:4:y:1992:i:1:p:161-165

[21] Hal R. Varian. 2007. Position auctions. *International Journal of Industrial Organization* 25 (2007), 1163–1178.

[22] Hal R. Varian and Christopher Harris. 2014. The VCG Auction in Theory and Practice. *American Economic Review* 104, 5 (2014), 442–45. DOI: http://dx.doi.org/10.1257/aer.104.5.442

[23] Christopher A. Wilkens, Ruggiero Cavallo, and Rad Niazadeh. 2016. Mechanism Design for Value Maximizers. *CoRR* abs/1607.04362 (2016). http://arxiv.org/abs/1607.04362

[24] Christopher A. Wilkens, Ruggiero Cavallo, and Rad Niazadeh. 2017. GSP — The Cinderella of Mechanism Design. In *Proceedings of the 26th International Conference on World Wide Web (WWW '17)*.

# The Efficiency of Resource Allocation Mechanisms for Budget-Constrained Users

IOANNIS CARAGIANNIS, University of Patras & CTI "Diophantus"
ALEXANDROS A. VOUDOURIS, University of Patras

We study the efficiency of mechanisms for allocating a divisible resource. Given scalar signals submitted by all users, such a mechanism decides the fraction of the resource that each user will receive and a payment that will be collected from her. Users are self-interested and aim to maximize their utility (defined as their value for the resource fraction they receive minus their payment). Starting with the seminal work of Johari and Tsitsiklis [8], a long list of papers studied the price of anarchy (in terms of the social welfare — the total users' value) of resource allocation mechanisms for a variety of allocation and payment rules. Here, we further assume that each user has a budget constraint that invalidates strategies that yield a payment that is higher than the user's budget. This subtle assumption, which is arguably more realistic, constitutes the traditional price of anarchy analysis meaningless as the set of equilibria may change drastically and their social welfare can be arbitrarily far from optimal. Instead, we study the price of anarchy using the liquid welfare benchmark that measures efficiency taking budget constraints into account. We show a tight bound of 2 on the liquid price of anarchy of the well-known Kelly mechanism and prove that this result is essentially best possible among all multi-user resource allocation mechanisms. This comes in sharp contrast to the no-budget setting where there are mechanisms that considerably outperform Kelly in terms of social welfare and even achieve full efficiency. In our proofs, we exploit the particular structure of worst-case games and equilibria, which also allows us to design (nearly) optimal two-player mechanisms by solving simple differential equations.

CCS Concepts: • **Theory of computation → Algorithmic game theory and mechanism design**; *Design and analysis of algorithms*;

Additional Key Words and Phrases: resource allocation; liquid welfare; price of anarchy

## 1 INTRODUCTION

Resource allocation is an ubiquitous task in computing systems and often sets algorithmic challenges to their design. As such, resource allocation problems have received much attention by the algorithmic community for decades. The recent emergence of large-scale distributed systems with non-cooperative users that compete for access to scarce resources has led to game-theoretic treatments of resource allocation.

In this paper, we study a particular simple class of *resource allocation mechanisms* that aim to distribute a divisible resource (such as bandwidth of a communication link, CPU time, storage space, etc.) by auctioning it off to different users as follows. Each user is asked to submit a scalar *signal*. Given the submitted signals, the mechanism decides the fraction of the resource that will be allocated to each user, as well as the payment that will be received from each of them. A

This work was partially supported by Caratheodory research grant E.114 from the University of Patras and by a PhD scholarship from the Onassis Foundation. We would like to thank George Christodoulou and Alkmini Sgouritsa for fruitful discussions in early stages of this work.


*ACM EC'18, June 18–22, 2018, Ithaca, NY, USA.* ACM ISBN 978-1-4503-4529-3/18/06...$15.00
https://doi.org/10.1145/3219166.3219186

typical example is a mechanism that has been proposed by Kelly [10] (henceforth called the Kelly mechanism; see also [11]), according to which the fraction of the resource allocated to each user is proportional to the user's signal, and the signal itself is her payment.

The users are self-interested. Following the standard modeling assumptions in the related literature, the value of each user for a resource fraction is given by a private *valuation function*. The above definition of resource allocation mechanisms allows the users to act strategically in the sense that the signal they select to submit is such that their utility (value for the fraction of the resource they receive minus payment) is maximized. Naturally, this behavior defines a *strategic game* among the users, who act as players. Soon after the definition of the Kelly mechanism, a series of papers studied the existence and uniqueness of *pure Nash equilibria* (snapshots of player strategies, in which the signal of each player maximizes her own utility) of the induced games [6, 13, 16] and quantified their inefficiency [8] using the notion of the *price of anarchy* [12].

In particular, Johari and Tsitsiklis [8] used the *social welfare* (i.e., the total value of the players for their received fraction of the resource) as an efficiency benchmark and proved that the social welfare at any equilibrium is at least $3/4$ times the optimal social welfare. This translates into a price of anarchy bound of $4/3$, which is tight. The paper of Johari and Tsitsiklis [8] sparked subsequent research on other resource allocation mechanisms, that use different (non-proportional) allocation rules or payments.

A first apparent question was whether improved price of anarchy bounds are possible by changing the allocation function, but keeping the simple pay-your-signal (or PYS, for short) payment rule. Sanghavi and Hajek [20] showed that no PYS mechanism has price of anarchy better than $8/7$, designed an allocation function that achieves this bound for two players, and provided strong experimental evidence that a slightly inferior bound holds for arbitrarily many players. Surprisingly, full efficiency at equilibria (i.e., a price of anarchy equal to 1) is possible via different allocation/payment functions. This discovery was made in three independent papers by Maheswaran and Basar [17], Yang and Hajek [22], and Johari and Tsitsiklis [9]. The mechanism of Maheswaran and Basar [17] uses proportional allocation (but a different payment; see Section 2 for its description), while the mechanisms of Johari and Tsitsiklis [9] and Yang and Hajek [22] are adaptations of the well-known VCG paradigm (see also the survey by Johari [7] on these results).

Our focus in the current paper is on the —arguably, more realistic— setting, in which each player has a private *budget* that constrains the payments that she can afford and, consequently, narrows her strategy space. As resource allocation mechanisms do not have direct access to budgets, budget constraints can restrict the set of equilibria so that their social welfare is extremely low compared to the optimal social welfare, which in turn is not related to player strategies, payments, or budgets. An efficiency benchmark that is suitable for budget-constrained players is known as *liquid welfare* (introduced by Dobzinski and Paes Leme [4] and, independently, by Syrgkanis and Tardos [21] who call it *effective* welfare) and is obtained by slightly changing the definition of the social welfare, taking budgets into account. Informally, the liquid welfare is the total value of the players for the resource fraction they receive, with the value of each player capped by her budget. Following the recent paper of Azar et al. [1], we use the term *liquid price of anarchy* (and abbreviate it as LPoA) to refer to the price of anarchy with respect to the liquid welfare, i.e., the ratio between the optimal liquid welfare of a game induced by a resource allocation mechanism and the worst liquid welfare over all equilibria of the game.

*Our results and techniques.* We aim to explore *all* resource allocation mechanisms and find the mechanism with the best possible LPoA. Our results suggest a drastically different picture compared to the no-budget setting. First, the analogue of full efficiency is not achievable; we show a lower bound of $2 - 1/n$ on the LPoA of any $n$-player resource allocation mechanism (under standard technical assumptions for player valuations and mechanism characteristics; see Section 2). The Kelly mechanism is proved to have an almost best possible LPoA of exactly 2. In contrast, the mechanism of Sanghavi and Hajek [20] (henceforth called SH) has an LPoA of 3. Improved bounds are possible for two players. We design the two-player PYS resource allocation mechanism E2-PYS that has an LPoA of 1.792; this bound is optimal among a very broad class of mechanisms. We also design the two-player mechanism E2-SR that achieves an almost optimal LPoA bound of at most 1.529; this mechanism uses different payments. See Table 1 for a summary of our results.

| Mechanism | LPoA | Statement | Comment |
|---|---|---|---|
| Kelly | 2 | Theorem 5.1 | Tight bound. Almost optimal among all $n$-player mechanisms (see Theorem 3.1) |
| SH | 3 | Theorem 5.2 | Tight bound (Theorem 5.3) |
| E2-PYS | 1.792 | Theorem 6.1 | Optimal among all two-player PYS mechanisms with concave allocation functions (Theorem 6.2) |
| E2-SR | 1.529 | Theorem 6.3 | Almost optimal among all two-player mechanisms (see Theorem 3.1) |

Table 1. Summary of our LPoA bounds.

Our results exploit a particular structure of worst-case (in terms of LPoA) games and their equilibria. We prove that for every resource allocation mechanism, the worst-case LPoA is obtained at instances in which players have *affine* valuation functions. In addition, all players besides one have finite budgets and play strategies that imply payments that are either zero or equal to their budget, while a single player has infinite budget and a signal that nullifies the derivative of her utility. Compared to an analogous characterization for the no-budget case (with linear valuation functions and player signals that all nullify their utility derivatives), first observed by Johari and Tsitsiklis [8] for the Kelly mechanism and later extended to all resource allocation mechanisms, the structure in our characterization is much richer and the proof is considerably more complicated. The characterization contains so much information that the LPoA bounds follow rather easily; the extreme example is the proof of our best LPoA bound of 2 for the Kelly mechanism which is only a few lines long. It can also be used in the design of new mechanisms; for example, the design and analysis of our two-player mechanisms E2-PYS and E2-SR follow by simple first-order differential equations, which would never have been identified without our characterization. And, furthermore, under assumptions about the resource allocation mechanisms (e.g., concave allocations and convex payments), the LPoA bound is automatically proved to be tight without providing any explicit lower bound instance.

*Other related work.* As an efficiency benchmark, the liquid welfare has been studied recently in different contexts such as in the design of truthful mechanisms (see [4, 14, 15]) and in the analysis of combinatorial Walrasian equilibria with budgets [5]. In the context of the price of anarchy, it was considered recently in simultaneous first price auctions by Azar et al. [1].

Caragiannis and Voudouris [2] were the first to prove that the liquid price of anarchy of the Kelly mechanism is constant. In particular, they showed LPoA upper and lower bounds of 2.78 and 2, respectively. The lower bound is essentially proved again here (see Theorem 5.1) with a completely different and more interesting technique. Christodoulou et al. [3] improved the LPoA upper bound to 2.618 and extended the results to more general settings involving multiple resources. Prior to these two papers, Syrgkanis and Tardos [21] proved that the social welfare at equilibria of the Kelly mechanism is at most a constant factor away from the optimal liquid welfare. In contrast to the analysis techniques in the current paper, the analysis of the Kelly mechanism by Caragiannis and Voudouris [2], Christodoulou et al. [3] and Syrgkanis and Tardos [21] is closer in spirit to the smoothness template (see [18, 19]) and is based on bounding the utility of each player by the utility she would have when deviating to appropriate signal strategies. Their results hold for more general equilibrium concepts such as coarse-correlated or Bayes-Nash equilibria. Our LPoA bounds in the current paper hold specifically for pure Nash equilibria, but are superior and tight.

*Roadmap.* The rest of the paper is structured as follows. We begin with definitions and notation in Section 2. Our lower bound on the LPoA of any resource allocation mechanism appears in Section 3. Section 4 is devoted to proving the structural characterization of worst-case resource allocation games and equilibria. Then, in Section 5 we present tight bounds on the liquid price of anarchy for the Kelly and SH mechanisms. In Section 6, we present our two-player mechanisms E2-PYS and E2-SR. We conclude with open problems and a discussion on possible extensions in Section 7.

## 2 DEFINITIONS, NOTATION, AND EXAMPLES

We consider a single divisible resource of unit size that is distributed among $n$ users by a *resource allocation mechanism* $M$. The mechanism $M$ consists of

- an *allocation function* $g^M : \mathbb{R}^n_{\geq 0} \to Q \cup \mathbf{0}$, where $Q = \left\{\mathbf{d} \in [0,1]^n : \sum_{i=1}^n d_i = 1\right\}$ is the unit $n$-simplex and $\mathbf{0} = (0, ..., 0)$, and
- a *payment function* $p^M : \mathbb{R}^n_{\geq 0} \to \mathbb{R}^n_{\geq 0}$,

and works as follows. Each user $i$ submits a *signal* $s_i \in \mathbb{R}_{\geq 0}$, and the mechanism $M$ allocates a fraction of $g_i^M(\mathbf{s})$ of the resource to each user $i$ and asks her for a payment of $p_i^M(\mathbf{s})$, where $\mathbf{s} = (s_1, ..., s_n)$ denotes the vector formed by all signals.

Some important properties of allocation and payment functions are as follows. First, they are *anonymous*: any permutation of the entries of the input signal vector results in the same permutation of the output. So, all users get equal resource shares and are asked for equal payments when they submit identical signals. The mechanism does not allocate any fraction and does not ask for any payment from a user that submits a zero signal. By convention, when some user is the only one with a non-zero signal, she gets the whole resource and is asked for a payment of zero. Let $(y, \mathbf{s}_{-i})$ denote the signal vector in which user $i$ has a signal of $y$ and the remaining users have their signals as in $\mathbf{s}$. Viewed as univariate functions (of variable $y$), the functions $g_i^M(y, \mathbf{s}_{-i})$ and $p_i^M(y, \mathbf{s}_{-i})$ are *increasing* and *differentiable* in $\mathbb{R}_{\geq 0}$ (with the exception of $(y, \mathbf{s}_{-i}) = \mathbf{0}$).

Each user $i$ has

- a monotone non-decreasing, concave, and differentiable[1] *valuation function* $v_i : [0,1] \to \mathbb{R}_{\geq 0}$; $v_i(x)$ represents the value that user $i$ has for a resource fraction of $x$;
- a *budget* $c_i \in \mathbb{R}_{\geq 0} \cup \{+\infty\}$, which restricts (i.e., upper-bounds) her payment to the mechanism.

Her *utility* from the mechanism is defined as the value she gets for the fraction she is given minus her payment, i.e.,

$$u_i^M(\mathbf{s}) = v_i\left(g_i^M(\mathbf{s})\right) - p_i^M(\mathbf{s}).$$

To capture the fact that budgets impose hard constraints to the users, we technically assume that $u_i^M(\mathbf{s}) = -\infty$ when $p_i^M(\mathbf{s}) > c_i$.

The users act strategically as utility maximizers and engage as players into a strategic *resource allocation game* $\mathcal{G}^M$ that is *induced* by mechanism $M$. A (pure Nash) *equilibrium* is a signal vector $\mathbf{s}$ such that, when viewed as a univariate function of variable $y$, $u_i^M(y, \mathbf{s}_{-i})$ is maximized for $y = s_i$, i.e., no player can increase her utility by unilaterally deviating to submitting a different signal.

[1]We remark that our results hold for semi-differentiable valuation functions as well. However, the proof of our characterization (Lemma 4.1) is technically more involved. So, the differentiability assumption keeps the exposition simple.

We denote by $\text{eq}(\mathcal{G}^M)$ the set of all equilibria of game $\mathcal{G}^M$. By the definition and properties of the allocation and payment functions, the signal vector $\mathbf{0}$ cannot be an equilibrium as (by the conventions mentioned above) any player has the incentive to unilaterally deviate and get the whole resource without paying anything. We use $\mathbb{X}_n$ as an abbreviation of the set $\mathbb{R}^n_{\geq 0} \setminus \{\mathbf{0}\}$.

Due to the budget constraints, we have three different cases for the strategy of player $i$ at an equilibrium $\mathbf{s} \in \text{eq}(\mathcal{G}^M)$ (assuming a non-trivial budget $c_i > 0$) and for the corresponding value of the derivative of her utility. In particular, the derivative $\left.\frac{\partial u_i^M(y,\mathbf{s}_{-i})}{\partial y}\right|_{y=s_i}$ is equal to zero in case $s_i$ is such that $0 < p_i^M(\mathbf{s}) < c_i$, non-positive in case $s_i = 0$, and non-negative in case $s_i$ is such that $p_i^M(\mathbf{s}) = c_i$. Note that nullification of the utility derivative does not necessarily imply maximization of utility.

We are interested in studying the effect of strategic behavior to the efficiency of a mechanism. An efficiency benchmark that has been used extensively in the literature is the *social welfare*. For an allocation $\mathbf{d} \in \mathcal{Q} \cup \mathbf{0}$ of a resource allocation game $\mathcal{G}^M$, the social welfare is defined as

$$\text{SW}(\mathbf{d}, \mathcal{G}^M) = \sum_{i=1}^{n} v_i(d_i),$$

where $n$ is the number of players in $\mathcal{G}^M$ and $v_i$ is the valuation function of player $i$. Then, the inefficiency of equilibria of game $\mathcal{G}^M$ can be measured by its *price of anarchy* which is defined as

$$\text{PoA}(\mathcal{G}^M) = \sup_{\mathbf{s}\in\text{eq}(\mathcal{G}^M)} \frac{\text{SW}^*(\mathcal{G}^M)}{\text{SW}(g^M(\mathbf{s}), \mathcal{G}^M)},$$

where $\text{SW}^*(\mathcal{G}^M)$ denotes the maximum social welfare over all allocations of $\mathcal{G}^M$.

However, the definition of the social welfare does not take into account the possibly finite budgets that the players may have. Therefore, we instead use the *liquid welfare* as our efficiency benchmark. The liquid welfare of an allocation $\mathbf{d}$ is defined as

$$\text{LW}(\mathbf{d}, \mathcal{G}^M) = \sum_{i=1}^{n} \min\{v_i(d_i), c_i\},$$

where $c_i$ is the budget of player $i$. Clearly, when players have no budget constraints, the liquid welfare coincides with the social welfare. The *liquid price of anarchy* of a resource allocation game $\mathcal{G}^M$ is then defined as

$$\text{LPoA}(\mathcal{G}^M) = \sup_{\mathbf{s}\in\text{eq}(\mathcal{G}^M)} \frac{\text{LW}^*(\mathcal{G}^M)}{\text{LW}(g^M(\mathbf{s}), \mathcal{G}^M)},$$

where $\text{LW}^*(\mathcal{G}^M)$ denotes the maximum liquid welfare over all allocations of game $\mathcal{G}^M$. We use the overloaded term $\text{LPoA}(M)$ to denote the liquid price of anarchy of the resource allocation mechanism $M$. This is defined as the maximum (or, more formally, the supremum) liquid price of anarchy over all games that are induced by mechanism $M$.

*Examples of resource allocation mechanisms.* Let us devote some space to the definition of some well-known mechanisms from the literature. An important class of resource allocation mechanisms is that of *pay-your-signal* mechanisms (PYS, for short). When at least two players submit non-zero signals, a PYS mechanism charges each player $i$ a payment equal to the signal $s_i$ that she submits. Otherwise, PYS mechanisms follow the general convention that we have defined at the beginning of Section 2, and do not charge any payment to any player.

The most popular PYS mechanism is the Kelly mechanism that was introduced in [10]. This mechanism allocates the resource proportionally to the players' signals (this is why it is also known as the proportional allocation mechanism in the related literature), i.e.,

$$g_i^{\text{Kelly}}(\mathbf{s}) = \frac{s_i}{\sum_{j=1}^{n} s_j}.$$

The Kelly mechanism has played a central role in the related literature; for the no-budget setting, Johari and Tsitsiklis [8] proved that its price of anarchy is 4/3. In their attempt to design the PYS mechanism with the lowest possible price of anarchy, Sanghavi and Hajek [20] defined the allocation function

$$g_i^{\text{SH}}(\mathbf{s}) = \frac{s_i}{\max_\ell\{s_\ell\}} \int_0^1 \prod_{j\neq i} \left(1 - \frac{s_j}{\max_\ell\{s_\ell\}} t\right) \,\mathrm{d}t.$$

We will refer to the PYS mechanism that uses this allocation function as SH. For two players, the allocation function has a very simple definition as $g_1^{\text{SH}}(\mathbf{s}) = \frac{s_1}{2s_2}$ when $s_1 \leq s_2$, and $g_1^{\text{SH}}(\mathbf{s}) = 1 - \frac{s_2}{2s_1}$ otherwise. Sanghavi and Hajek [20] proved that the two-player version of the SH mechanism has an optimal (among all PYS mechanisms) price of anarchy of 8/7 and provided experimental evidence that the price of anarchy of the $n$-player version is only marginally higher. As we will see later in Section 5, the comparison between Kelly and SH yields a drastically different result when players have budgets and the liquid welfare is used as the efficiency benchmark.

Other interesting classes of mechanisms use proportional allocation but different payments. Among them, a mechanism defined by Maheswaran and Basar [17] uses the class of payment functions

$$p_i^M(\mathbf{s}) = \left(\sum_{j\neq i} s_j\right) \cdot \int_0^{s_i} \frac{h^M(t + \sum_{j\neq i} s_j)}{(t + \sum_{j\neq i} s_j)^2} \,\mathrm{d}t,$$

where $h^M : \mathbb{R}_{\geq 0} \to \mathbb{R}_{\geq 0}$ is an increasing function (such as $h^M(z) = z$; Maheswaran and Basar [17] suggest several other choices for $h^M$). These mechanisms have the remarkable property of full efficiency at equilibria in the no-budget setting (i.e., they have price of anarchy equal to 1). Independently from Maheswaran and Basar [17], Johari and Tsitsiklis [9] as well as Yang and Hajek [22] presented resource allocation mechanisms that achieve full efficiency in the no-budget setting. All these mechanisms can be thought of as adaptations of the well-known VCG paradigm.

## 3 A LOWER BOUND FOR ALL MECHANISMS

The fact that the mechanisms of Maheswaran and Basar [17], Johari and Tsitsiklis [9], and Yang and Hajek [22] achieve full efficiency seems surprising, as resource allocation mechanisms do not have direct access to the valuation functions of the players. Still, the definition of these mechanisms is such that the incentives of the players are fully aligned to the global goal of maximizing the social welfare. In a sense, these mechanisms manage to achieve access to the valuation functions indirectly. In contrast, when players have budget constraints, we show below that a liquid price of anarchy equal to 1 is not possible. This means that resource allocation mechanisms fail to "mine" any kind of information about the budget values of the players, while budgets affect the strategic behavior of the players crucially.

Theorem 3.1. *Every $n$-player resource allocation mechanism has liquid price of anarchy at least $2 - 1/n$.*

Proof. Let $M$ be any $n$-player resource allocation mechanism that uses an allocation function $g^M$ and a payment function $p^M$. Let $\mathbf{s} = (s_1, ..., s_n)$ be an equilibrium of the game $\mathcal{G}_1^M$ induced by $M$ for players with valuations $v_i(x) = x$ and budgets $c_i = +\infty$, for every $i \in [n]$. Assume that the allocation returned by $M$ at this equilibrium is $\mathbf{d} = (d_1, ..., d_n)$. Since all players have the same valuation function and budget, the liquid (or social) welfare at equilibrium is optimal and, hence, $\text{LPoA}(\mathcal{G}_1^M) = 1$.

Recall that, for every signal vector $\mathbf{y} = (y_1, \ldots, y_n)$, the utility of player $i$ is defined as $u_i^M(\mathbf{y}) = v_i(g_i^M(\mathbf{y})) - p_i^M(\mathbf{y})$. Now, let $i^* = \arg\min_i d_i$ (hence, $d_{i^*} \leq 1/n$) and consider the game $\mathcal{G}_2^M$ where each player $i \neq i^*$ has the modified valuation function $\tilde{v}_i(x) = d_i + x$ and budget $\tilde{c}_i = d_i$, while player $i^*$ is as in $\mathcal{G}_1^M$ (see Figure 1). Observe that the modified utility of player $i \neq i^*$ as a function of a signal vector $\mathbf{y}$ is now $\tilde{u}_i^M(\mathbf{y}) = \tilde{v}_i(g_i^M(\mathbf{y})) - p_i^M(\mathbf{y}) = u_i^M(\mathbf{y}) + d_i$. Also, since the utility of player $i \neq i^*$ is non-negative at the equilibrium $\mathbf{s}$ of game $\mathcal{G}_1^M$, we have that $p_i^M(\mathbf{s}) \leq d_i = \tilde{c}_i$, meaning that player $i$ can also afford this payment in game $\mathcal{G}_2^M$. Hence, $\mathbf{s}$ is an equilibrium in $\mathcal{G}_2^M$ as well (and, again, $M$ returns the same allocation $\mathbf{d}$).

Its liquid welfare is $\sum_i \min\{\tilde{v}_i(d_i), \tilde{c}_i\} = \sum_i d_i = 1$ while the optimal liquid welfare is at least $1 + \sum_{i \neq i^*} d_i$, achieved at the allocation according to which the whole resource is given to player $i^*$. Hence, we conclude that the liquid price of anarchy of $M$ is $\text{LPoA}(M) \geq \text{LPoA}(\mathcal{G}_2^M) \geq 1 + \sum_{i \neq i^*} d_i = 2 - d_{i^*} \geq 2 - 1/n$, as desired. □

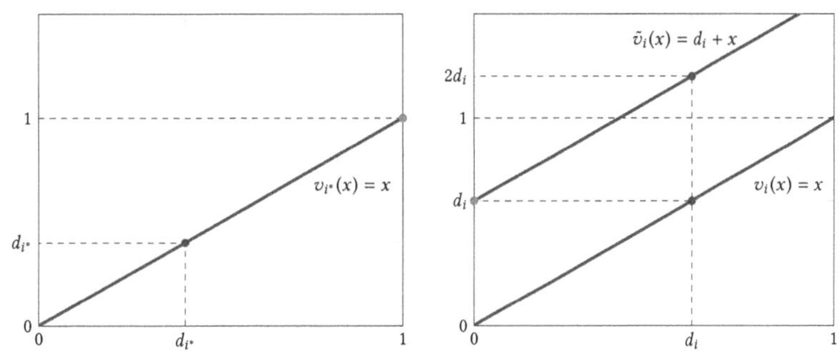


Fig. 1. A graphical representation of the games used in the proof of Theorem 3.1. The two figures depict the valuation functions of players $i^*$ and $i \neq i^*$ in games $\mathcal{G}_1^M$ and $\mathcal{G}_2^M$. The blue points (i.e., point $(d_{i^*}, d_{i^*})$ in the left figure, and points $(d_i, d_i)$ and $(d_i, 2d_i)$ in the right figure) represent the equilibrium in both games, and the optimal allocation in game $\mathcal{G}_1^M$. The optimal allocation in $\mathcal{G}_2^M$ is represented by the red points (i.e., point $(1, 1)$ in the left figure and point $(0, d_i)$ in the right one).

## 4 THE STRUCTURE OF WORST-CASE GAMES AND EQUILIBRIA

In this section, we prove our structural characterization. Given an $n$-player resource allocation mechanism $M$ (with allocation and payment functions $g^M$ and $p^M$, respectively), signal vector $\mathbf{s} \in \mathbb{X}_n$, and an integer $j \in [n]$, define the $n$-player game $\mathcal{G}^M(\mathbf{s}, j)$ as follows. Every player has the affine valuation function $\tilde{v}_i(z) = \lambda_i^M(\mathbf{s}) \cdot z + \kappa_i^M(\mathbf{s})$ and budget $\tilde{c}_i$, where

$$\lambda_i^M(\mathbf{s}) = \left( \left. \frac{\partial g_i^M(y, \mathbf{s}_{-i})}{\partial y} \right|_{y=s_i} \right)^{-1} \cdot \left. \frac{\partial p_i^M(y, \mathbf{s}_{-i})}{\partial y} \right|_{y=s_i}$$

and $\kappa_j^M(\mathbf{s}) = 0$, $\tilde{c}_j = +\infty$, and $\kappa_i^M(\mathbf{s}) = \tilde{c}_i = p_i^M(\mathbf{s})$ for every player $i \neq j$.

In the following, we show that the games defined in this way are in a sense extreme in terms of the liquid price of anarchy of mechanism $M$.

Lemma 4.1. *Let $\mathcal{G}_1^M$ be an $n$-player resource allocation game that is induced by a mechanism $M$ with $\text{LPoA}(\mathcal{G}_1^M) > 1$. Let $\mathbf{s} \in \mathbb{X}_n$ be an equilibrium of $\mathcal{G}_1^M$ of minimum liquid welfare. Then, there* *exists integer* $i^* \in [n]$ *such that*

$$\text{LPoA}(\mathcal{G}_1^M) \leq \frac{\text{LW}(\tilde{\mathbf{x}}, \mathcal{G}^M(\mathbf{s}, i^*))}{\text{LW}(g^M(\mathbf{s}), \mathcal{G}^M(\mathbf{s}, i^*))} = \frac{\sum_{i \neq i^*} p_i^M(\mathbf{s}) + \lambda_{i^*}^M(\mathbf{s})}{\sum_{i \neq i^*} p_i^M(\mathbf{s}) + \lambda_{i^*}^M(\mathbf{s}) \cdot g_{i^*}^M(\mathbf{s})},$$

*where* $\tilde{\mathbf{x}} = (\tilde{x}_1, ..., \tilde{x}_n)$ *denotes the allocation with* $\tilde{x}_{i^*} = 1$ *and* $\tilde{x}_i = 0$ *for* $i \neq i^*$.

Proof. Consider an $n$-player resource allocation game $\mathcal{G}_1^M$ that is induced by mechanism $M$. Let $v_i$ and $c_i$ be the valuation function and budget of player $i$, respectively. Let $\mathbf{s} \in \mathbb{X}_n$ be the equilibrium of game $\mathcal{G}_1^M$ of minimum liquid welfare. We denote by $\mathbf{x}$ the optimal allocation in $\mathcal{G}_1^M$. Without loss of generality, we assume that, for every player $i$, $x_i = 0$ if $v_i(0) > c_i$ and $v_i(x_i) \leq c_i$ otherwise, and we relax the allocation definition to $\sum_{i=1}^n x_i \leq 1$; this does not constrain the optimal liquid welfare which is $\text{LW}(\mathbf{x}, \mathcal{G}_1^M) = \sum_i \min\{v_i(x_i), c_i\}$. We use $d_i = g_i^M(\mathbf{s})$ for the resource fraction allocated to player $i$ in $\mathbf{s}$; let $\mathbf{d} = (d_1, ..., d_n)$.

We partition the players into the following three sets:

- Set $A$ consists of players $i$ with $v_i(d_i) < c_i$ and signal $s_i$ such that the derivative of their utility is equal to 0.
- Set $B$ consists of players $i$ with signal $s_i = 0$ (hence, $d_i = 0$) and negative utility derivative such that $v_i(0) < c_i$.
- Set $\Gamma$ consists of players $i$ with signal $s_i$ such that $v_i(d_i) \geq c_i$.

First, observe that sets $A$ and $B$ cannot be both empty, since it would then be $\text{LW}(\mathbf{d}, \mathcal{G}_1^M) = \sum_{i \in [n]} c_i \geq \text{LW}(\mathbf{x}, \mathcal{G}_1^M)$, and the liquid price of anarchy of $\mathcal{G}_1^M$ would be exactly 1, contradicting the assumption of the lemma. So, in the following, we assume that at least one of $A$ and $B$ is non-empty.

Now consider the games $\mathcal{G}^M(\mathbf{s}, j)$ for $j \in [n]$ and let $i^* = \arg\max_{j \in A \cup B}\{\lambda_j^M(\mathbf{s})\}$. We will show that

$$\text{LW}(\mathbf{d}, \mathcal{G}_1^M) \geq \text{LW}(\mathbf{d}, \mathcal{G}^M(\mathbf{s}, i^*)) \tag{1}$$

and we will furthermore show that the allocation $\tilde{\mathbf{x}}$ satisfies

$$\text{LW}(\mathbf{x}, \mathcal{G}_1^M) - \text{LW}(\tilde{\mathbf{x}}, \mathcal{G}^M(\mathbf{s}, i^*)) \leq \text{LW}(\mathbf{d}, \mathcal{G}_1^M) - \text{LW}(\mathbf{d}, \mathcal{G}^M(\mathbf{s}, i^*)). \tag{2}$$

In this way (recall that $\mathbf{s}$ is the equilibrium of minimum liquid welfare in game $\mathcal{G}_1^M$ and $\mathbf{d}$ is the resulting allocation), we will have

$$\begin{aligned}\text{LPoA}(\mathcal{G}_1^M) &= \frac{\text{LW}(\mathbf{x}, \mathcal{G}_1^M)}{\text{LW}(\mathbf{d}, \mathcal{G}_1^M)} \leq \frac{\text{LW}(\mathbf{x}, \mathcal{G}_1^M) - (\text{LW}(\mathbf{x}, \mathcal{G}_1^M) - \text{LW}(\tilde{\mathbf{x}}, \mathcal{G}^M(\mathbf{s}, i^*)))}{\text{LW}(\mathbf{d}, \mathcal{G}_1^M) - (\text{LW}(\mathbf{d}, \mathcal{G}_1^M) - \text{LW}(\mathbf{d}, \mathcal{G}^M(\mathbf{s}, i^*)))} \\ &= \frac{\text{LW}(\tilde{\mathbf{x}}, \mathcal{G}^M(\mathbf{s}, i^*))}{\text{LW}(\mathbf{d}, \mathcal{G}^M(\mathbf{s}, i^*))} = \frac{\sum_{i \neq i^*} p_i^M(\mathbf{s}) + \lambda_{i^*}^M(\mathbf{s})}{\sum_{i \neq i^*} p_i^M(\mathbf{s}) + \lambda_{i^*}^M(\mathbf{s}) \cdot g_{i^*}^M(\mathbf{s})},\end{aligned}$$

as desired. The inequality follows by (1) and (2). The last equality follows since all players in $\mathcal{G}^M(\mathbf{s}, i^*)$ besides $i^*$ have always their value capped by their budget, which is equal to their payment.

Inequality (1) is due to the fact that the contribution of each player to the liquid welfare at $\mathbf{s}$ can only decrease between the two games. Indeed, if player $i^*$ belongs to $B$, she has zero value in game $\mathcal{G}^M(\mathbf{s}, i^*)$. If she belongs to $A$, then her utility derivative is nullified and, hence, $v'_{i^*}(d_{i^*}) = \lambda_{i^*}^M(\mathbf{s})$. Due to the concavity of $v_i$, we get $v_{i^*}(d_{i^*}) \geq d_{i^*} v'_{i^*}(d_{i^*}) = d_{i^*} \lambda_{i^*}^M(\mathbf{s}) = \tilde{v}_{i^*}(d_{i^*})$. Moreover, the contribution of player $i \neq i^*$ in $\text{LW}(\mathbf{d}, \mathcal{G}^M(\mathbf{s}, i^*))$ is $\tilde{c}_i = p_i^M(\mathbf{s})$ which is at most her contribution $\min\{v_i(d_i), c_i\}$ in $\text{LW}(\mathbf{d}, \mathcal{G}_1^M)$ since the payment of player $i$ cannot exceed her budget in $\mathcal{G}_1^M$ and her utility at equilibrium $\mathbf{s}$ is non-negative. See Figure 2 for a graphical representation of valuation functions and budgets in games $\mathcal{G}_1^M$ and $\mathcal{G}^M(\mathbf{s}, i^*)$.

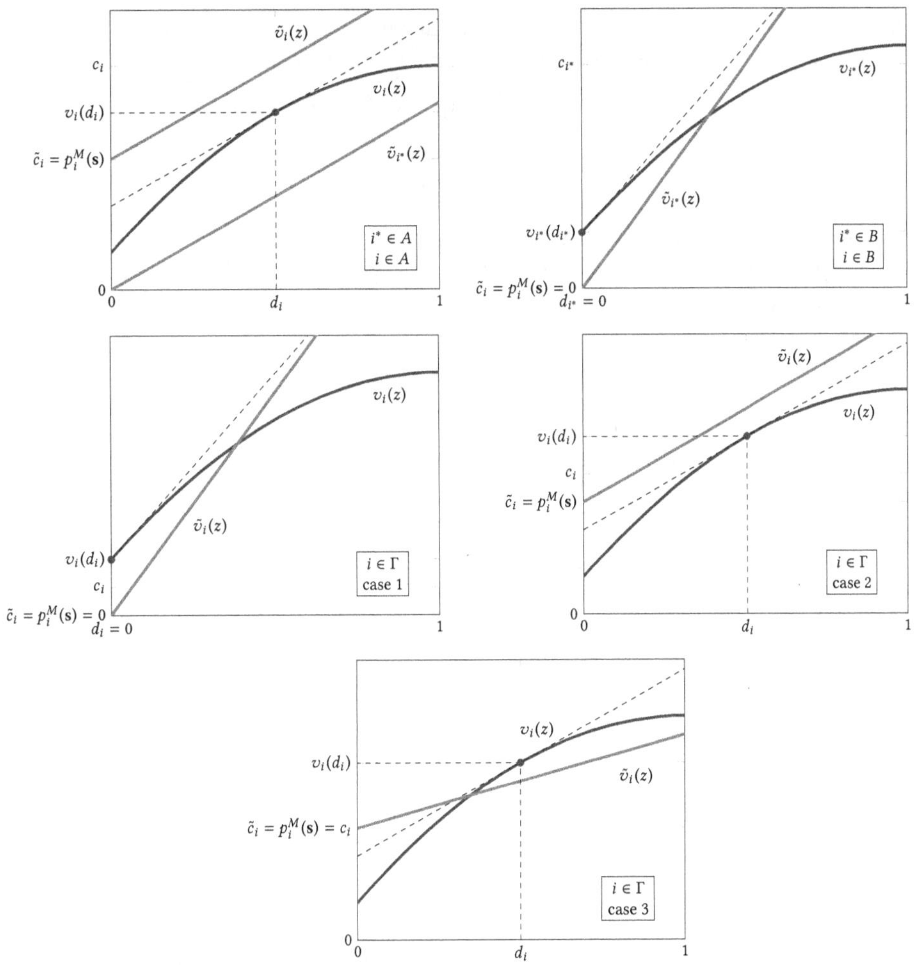


Fig. 2. Relation between the two games $\mathcal{G}_1^M$ and $\mathcal{G}^M(\mathbf{s}, i^*)$ that are used in the proof of Lemma 4.1. In the first two plots, player $i$ is different than $i^*$ and $\tilde{c}_{i^*}$ is infinite by definition. The dashed line is the tangent of $v_i$ at $d_i$. The slope $\lambda_i^M(\mathbf{s})$ of the affine valuation function of player $i$ in game $\mathcal{G}^M(\mathbf{s}, i^*)$ is greater than (upper right and middle left plots), equal to (upper left and middle right plots), or smaller than (lower plot) $v_i'(d_i)$ depending on whether the utility derivative of the player is negative, zero, or positive, respectively (in particular, these are the three cases identified in the plots for $i \in \Gamma$). This follows by the definition of games $\mathcal{G}_1^M$ and $\mathcal{G}^M(\mathbf{s}, i^*)$ and the fact that, as the utility of player $i$ in game $\mathcal{G}_1^M$ has derivative $v_i'(d_i) \left.\frac{\partial g_i^M(y,\mathbf{s}_{-i})}{\partial y}\right|_{y=s_i} - \left.\frac{\partial p_i^M(y,\mathbf{s}_{-i})}{\partial y}\right|_{y=s_i}$ at equilibrium, the sign of this derivative coincides with the sign of $v_i'(d_i) - \lambda_i^M(\mathbf{s})$.

Let

$$\delta(i) = \min\{v_i(x_i), c_i\} - \min\{\tilde{v}_i(\tilde{x}_i), \tilde{c}_i\} - \min\{v_i(d_i), c_i\} + \min\{\tilde{v}_i(d_i), \tilde{c}_i\}$$

denote the contribution of player $i$ to the expression $\mathrm{LW}(\mathbf{x}, \mathcal{G}_1^M) - \mathrm{LW}(\tilde{\mathbf{x}}, \mathcal{G}^M(\mathbf{s}, i^*)) - \mathrm{LW}(\mathbf{d}, \mathcal{G}_1^M) + \mathrm{LW}(\mathbf{d}, \mathcal{G}^M(\mathbf{s}, i^*))$. Then, in order to prove inequality (2) it suffices to prove that $\sum_i \delta(i) \leq 0$.

- For player $i^*$, we have that $v_{i^*}(d_{i^*}) < c_{i^*}$. Using the inequality $v_{i^*}(x_{i^*}) \leq v_{i^*}(d_{i^*}) + v'_{i^*}(d_{i^*})(x_{i^*} - d_{i^*})$ due to the concavity of the valuation function $v_{i^*}$ and the fact $\tilde{x}_{i^*} = 1$, we have that

$$\begin{aligned}\delta(i^*) &= \min\{v_{i^*}(x_{i^*}), c_{i^*}\} - \lambda^M_{i^*}(\mathbf{s})\tilde{x}_{i^*} - v_{i^*}(d_{i^*}) + \lambda^M_{i^*}(\mathbf{s})d_{i^*}\\ &\leq v_{i^*}(x_{i^*}) - \lambda^M_{i^*}(\mathbf{s}) - v_{i^*}(d_{i^*}) + \lambda^M_{i^*}(\mathbf{s})d_{i^*}\\ &\leq v'_{i^*}(d_{i^*})(x_{i^*} - d_{i^*}) - \lambda^M_{i^*}(\mathbf{s}) + \lambda^M_{i^*}(\mathbf{s})d_{i^*}.\end{aligned}$$

Now, we observe that (for such observations, we follow the reasoning in the caption of Figure 2) if player $i^*$ belongs to $A$, then $\lambda^M_{i^*}(\mathbf{s}) = v'_{i^*}(d_{i^*})$, while if she belongs to $B$, then $\lambda^M_{i^*}(\mathbf{s}) \geq v'_{i^*}(d_{i^*})$ and $d_{i^*} = 0$. In any case, we have that $v'_{i^*}(d_{i^*})(x_{i^*} - d_{i^*}) \leq \lambda^M_{i^*}(\mathbf{s})(x_{i^*} - d_{i^*})$, and we obtain

$$\delta(i^*) \leq \lambda^M_{i^*}(\mathbf{s})(x_{i^*} - 1). \tag{3}$$

- For all players $i \neq i^*$, observe that their value is always capped by their budget in $\mathcal{G}^M(\mathbf{s}, i^*)$. For player $i \neq i^*$ belonging to $A$ or to $B$ we have that either $\lambda^M_i(\mathbf{s}) = v'_i(d_i)$ (if $i \in A$), or $\lambda^M_i(\mathbf{s}) \geq v'_i(d_i)$ and $d_i = 0$ (if $i \in B$). Hence, using the concavity of $v_i$ and the fact that $\tilde{x}_i = 0$, we obtain that

$$\delta(i) \leq v_i(x_i) - \tilde{c}_i - v_i(d_i) + \tilde{c}_i \leq v_i(d_i) + \lambda^M_i(\mathbf{s})(x_i - d_i) - v_i(d_i) \leq \lambda^M_{i^*}(\mathbf{s})x_i, \tag{4}$$

where the last inequality follows since $\lambda^M_i(\mathbf{s}) \leq \lambda^M_{i^*}(\mathbf{s})$, due to the definition of player $i^*$. Otherwise, if $i \in \Gamma$, we have

$$\delta(i) = \min\{v_i(x_i), c_i\} - \tilde{c}_i - c_i + \tilde{c}_i \leq 0. \tag{5}$$

Hence, summing over all players, and using inequalities (3), (4) and (5) as well as the fact that $\sum_i x_i \leq 1$, we obtain $\sum_i \delta(i) \leq 0$, and the proof is complete. □

We are now ready to prove the main result of this section.

Lemma 4.2. *Let $M$ be an $n$-player resource allocation mechanism with allocation and payment functions $g^M$ and $p^M$, respectively. Then, its liquid price of anarchy is*

$$\text{LPoA}(M) \leq \sup_{\mathbf{s}\in\mathbb{X}_n}\left\{\frac{\sum_{i\geq 2}p^M_i(\mathbf{s}) + \lambda^M_1(\mathbf{s})}{\sum_{i\geq 2}p^M_i(\mathbf{s}) + \lambda^M_1(\mathbf{s})\,g^M_1(\mathbf{s})} : \lambda^M_1(\mathbf{s}) = \left(\left.\frac{\partial g^M_1(y, \mathbf{s}_{-1})}{\partial y}\right|_{y=s_1}\right)^{-1}\cdot\left.\frac{\partial p^M_1(y, \mathbf{s}_{-1})}{\partial y}\right|_{y=s_1}\right\}. \tag{6}$$

*If, in addition, $\mathbf{s} \in \mathbb{X}_n$ is always an equilibrium of game $\mathcal{G}^M(\mathbf{s}, 1)$, (6) holds with equality.*

Proof. Let $\text{weq}(\mathcal{G}^M)$ be the set of equilibria of minimum liquid welfare in game $\mathcal{G}^M$. Using the definition of the liquid price of anarchy, Lemma 4.1, and the anonymity of resource allocation mechanisms, we have

$$\begin{aligned}\text{LPoA}(M) &= \sup_{\mathcal{G}^M}\text{LPoA}(\mathcal{G}^M) = \sup_{\mathcal{G}^M}\sup_{\mathbf{s}\in\text{weq}(\mathcal{G}^M)}\frac{\text{LW}^*(\mathcal{G}^M)}{\text{LW}(g^M(\mathbf{s}), \mathcal{G}^M)} = \sup_{\mathbf{s}\in\mathbb{X}_n}\sup_{\mathcal{G}^M:\mathbf{s}\in\text{weq}(\mathcal{G}^M)}\frac{\text{LW}^*(\mathcal{G}^M)}{\text{LW}(g^M(\mathbf{s}), \mathcal{G}^M)}\\ &\leq \sup_{\mathbf{s}\in\mathbb{X}_n}\max_{i^*\in[n]}\frac{\sum_{i\neq i^*}p^M_i(\mathbf{s}) + \lambda^M_{i^*}(\mathbf{s})}{\sum_{i\neq i^*}p^M_i(\mathbf{s}) + \lambda^M_{i^*}(\mathbf{s})\,g^M_{i^*}(\mathbf{s})} = \sup_{\mathbf{s}\in\mathbb{X}_n}\frac{\sum_{i\geq 2}p^M_i(\mathbf{s}) + \lambda^M_1(\mathbf{s})}{\sum_{i\geq 2}p^M_i(\mathbf{s}) + \lambda^M_1(\mathbf{s})\,g^M_1(\mathbf{s})}.\end{aligned}$$

Now, if $\mathbf{s} \in \text{eq}(\mathcal{G}^M(\mathbf{s}, 1))$ for every $\mathbf{s} \in \mathbb{X}_n$, by just considering the games $\mathcal{G}^M(\mathbf{s}, 1)$ induced by mechanism $M$, we have

$$\text{LPoA}(M) \geq \sup_{\mathbf{s}\in\mathbb{X}_n}\text{LPoA}(\mathcal{G}^M(\mathbf{s}, 1)) \geq \sup_{\mathbf{s}\in\mathbb{X}_n}\frac{\sum_{i\geq 2}p^M_i(\mathbf{s}) + \lambda^M_1(\mathbf{s})}{\sum_{i\geq 2}p^M_i(\mathbf{s}) + \lambda^M_1(\mathbf{s})\,g^M_1(\mathbf{s})}$$

and (6) holds with equality. The last inequality follows by comparing the liquid welfare at $\mathbf{s}$ to the liquid welfare of the allocation which gives the whole resource to player 1. Recall that all players besides player 1 have always their value capped by their budget in game $\mathcal{G}^M(\mathbf{s}, 1)$. □

Lemma 4.2 is extremely powerful. It says that no game-theoretic reasoning is needed anymore for proving upper bounds on the LPoA and, instead, all we have to do is to solve the corresponding mathematical program. Furthermore, it can be used to prove lower bounds on the LPoA without providing any explicit construction. In this case, we just need to show that the condition $\mathbf{s} \in \text{eq}(\mathcal{G}^M(\mathbf{s}, 1))$ holds; then the tight lower bound follows by solving the same mathematical program.

Before we continue with the rest of our results, we define the class $C$ of mechanisms $M$ that use concave allocation functions $g^M$ and convex payment functions $p^M$. Observe that both Kelly and SH (as well as the E2-PYS mechanism presented in Section 6) are members of this class. With our next lemma, we prove that the condition $\mathbf{s} \in \text{eq}(\mathcal{G}^M(\mathbf{s}, 1))$ is satisfied for any $C$ mechanism $M$. This will allows us to prove lower bounds in the upcoming sections.

Lemma 4.3. *For any n-player resource allocation mechanism $M \in C$ and $\mathbf{s} \in \mathbb{X}_n$, $\mathbf{s} \in eq(\mathcal{G}^M(\mathbf{s}, 1))$.*

Proof. Consider any $C$ mechanism $M$ that uses a concave allocation function $g^M$ and a convex payment function $p^M$. By the definition of game $\mathcal{G}^M(\mathbf{s}, 1)$, the utility of any player $i$, as a function of her signal $y$, is $u_i^M(y, \mathbf{s}_{-i}) = \lambda_i^M(\mathbf{s}) \cdot g_i^M(y, \mathbf{s}_{-i}) + \kappa_i^M(\mathbf{s}) - p_i^M(y, \mathbf{s}_{-i})$ and its derivative is

$$\frac{\partial u_i^M(y, \mathbf{s}_{-i})}{\partial y} = \lambda_i^M(\mathbf{s})\frac{\partial g_i^M(y, \mathbf{s}_{-i})}{\partial y} - \frac{\partial p_i^M(y, \mathbf{s}_{-1})}{\partial y}.$$

Observe that, by the definition of $\lambda_i^M(\mathbf{s})$, the signal $s_i$ nullifies the utility derivative of player $i$, and since

$$\frac{\partial^2 u_i^M(y, \mathbf{s}_{-i})}{\partial y^2} = \lambda_i^M(\mathbf{s})\frac{\partial^2 g_i^M(y, \mathbf{s}_{-i})}{\partial y^2} - \frac{\partial^2 p_i^M(y, \mathbf{s}_{-1})}{\partial y^2} \le 0,$$

this signal actually maximizes the player's utility. □

## 5 PAY-YOUR-SIGNAL MECHANISMS

In this section, we will use Lemma 4.2 to prove tight bounds on the liquid price of anarchy of the Kelly and SH mechanisms. Our LPoA bounds are 2 for Kelly (Theorem 5.1) and 3 for SH (Theorems 5.2 and 5.3). Recall that both of these mechanisms belong to class $C$ and, by Lemma 4.3, the condition $\mathbf{s} \in \text{eq}(\mathcal{G}^M(\mathbf{s}, 1))$ is satisfied.

Theorem 5.1. *The liquid price of anarchy of the Kelly mechanism is* 2.

Proof. Let $\mathbf{s} \in \mathbb{X}_n$ and $C = \sum_{i\ge 2} s_i$. Since Kelly is PYS, we have that $\sum_{i\ge 2} p_i^{\text{Kelly}}(\mathbf{s}) = C$ and $\frac{\partial p_1^{\text{Kelly}}(y, \mathbf{s}_{-1})}{\partial y} = 1$. Recall that the allocation function is $g_1^{\text{Kelly}}(y, \mathbf{s}_{-1}) = \frac{y}{y+C}$, which gives $\frac{\partial g_1^{\text{Kelly}}(y, \mathbf{s}_{-1})}{\partial y} = \frac{C}{(y+C)^2}$. Also, since the mechanism belongs to class $C$, by Lemma 4.3, we have that $\mathbf{s} \in \text{eq}(\mathcal{G}^{\text{Kelly}}(\mathbf{s}, 1))$. Hence, $\lambda_1^{\text{Kelly}}(\mathbf{s}) = (s_1 + C)^2/C$ and Lemma 4.2 yields

$$\text{LPoA(Kelly)} = \sup_{s_1, C\ge 0} \frac{C + (s_1 + C)^2/C}{C + (s_1 + C)s_1/C} = \sup_{s_1, C\ge 0} \frac{2C^2 + 2s_1C + s_1^2}{C^2 + s_1C + s_1^2} = \sup_{s_1, C\ge 0} \left(2 - \frac{s_1^2}{C^2 + s_1C + s_1^2}\right) = 2,$$

as desired. □

Notice that our proof of Theorem 5.1 is surprisingly short. The proof exploits Lemma 4.2 with (6) holding with equality and, as such, it simultaneously provides a tight (upper and lower) bound. In contrast, our analysis for the SH mechanism is slightly more involved. This is mainly due to the more complicated definition of the allocation function (see Section 2), which requires to distinguish between two cases, depending on whether $s_1 < \max_\ell s_\ell$ or not. Both cases lead to inequalities that provide only an upper bound on the LPoA of the SH mechanism in the proof of Theorem 5.2. Then, in Theorem 5.3, we easily prove a matching lower bound by restricting our attention to the 2-player version of the mechanism. Actually, the proof can be thought of as providing a tight (i.e., not only lower, but also upper) bound on the LPoA of the 2-player version of the SH mechanism.

THEOREM 5.2. *The liquid price of anarchy of the SH mechanism is at most* 3.

PROOF. We will use Lemma 4.2 and upper-bound the ratio in the RHS of (6) by 3. Define $C = \sum_{i\geq 2} s_i$. First, let $\mathbf{s} \in \mathbb{X}_n$ with $s_1 < \max_\ell s_\ell$. Let $\arg\max_\ell s_\ell = i^* \neq 1$. Then, by the definition of SH and the definition of $\lambda_1^{\mathrm{SH}}(\mathbf{s})$ in (6), we have

$$\lambda_1^{\mathrm{SH}}(\mathbf{s}) = \frac{s_{i^*}}{\int_0^1 \prod_{i\geq 2}\left(1-\frac{s_i}{s_{i^*}}t\right)\,\mathrm{d}t} \tag{7}$$

and using the Bernoulli inequality stating that $1-\gamma t \geq (1-t)^\gamma$ for $t \leq 1$ and $\gamma \in [0,1]$, (7) yields

$$\lambda_1^{\mathrm{SH}}(\mathbf{s}) \leq \frac{s_{i^*}}{\int_0^1 \prod_{i\geq 2}(1-t)^{\frac{s_i}{s_{i^*}}}\,\mathrm{d}t} = \frac{s_{i^*}}{\int_0^1 (1-t)^{\frac{C}{s_{i^*}}}\,\mathrm{d}t} = s_{i^*} + C.$$

Since SH is PYS, $\sum_{i\geq 2} p_i^{\mathrm{SH}}(\mathbf{s}) = C$. Using this observation together with the last inequality, we obtain

$$\frac{\sum_{i\geq 2} p_i^{\mathrm{SH}}(\mathbf{s}) + \lambda_1^{\mathrm{SH}}(\mathbf{s})}{\sum_{i\geq 2} p_i^{\mathrm{SH}}(\mathbf{s}) + \lambda_1^{\mathrm{SH}}(\mathbf{s})\,g_1^{\mathrm{SH}}(\mathbf{s})} \leq \frac{2C + s_{i^*}}{C} \leq 3. \tag{8}$$

The inequalities follow since $\lambda_1^{\mathrm{SH}}(\mathbf{s})\,g_1^{\mathrm{SH}}(\mathbf{s}) \geq 0$, $s_1 \geq 0$, and $s_{i^*} \leq C$.

Now, let $\mathbf{s} \in \mathbb{X}_n$ with $s_1 = \max_\ell s_\ell$. In this case, $g_1^{\mathrm{SH}}(\mathbf{s})$ is defined as

$$g_1^{\mathrm{SH}}(\mathbf{s}) = \int_0^1 \prod_{i\geq 2}\left(1-\frac{s_i}{s_1}t\right)\mathrm{d}t$$

and

$$\begin{aligned}\left.\frac{\partial g_1^{\mathrm{SH}}(y,\mathbf{s}_{-1})}{\partial y}\right|_{y=s_1} &= \int_0^1 \sum_{i\geq 2}\frac{s_i}{s_1^2}t\prod_{j\neq 1,i}\left(1-\frac{s_j}{s_1}t\right)\mathrm{d}t \geq \sum_{i\geq 2}\frac{s_i}{s_1^2}\int_0^1 t\prod_{j\neq 1,i}(1-t)^{\frac{c_j}{s_1}}\,\mathrm{d}t\\ &= \sum_{i\geq 2}\frac{s_i}{s_1^2}\int_0^1 t(1-t)^{\frac{C-s_i}{s_1}}\,\mathrm{d}t = \sum_{i\geq 2}\frac{s_i}{(C-s_i+s_1)(C-s_i+2s_1)}\\ &\geq \frac{C}{(C+s_1)(C+2s_1)}.\end{aligned}$$

Using the definition of $\lambda_1^{\mathrm{SH}}(\mathbf{s})$ in (6), this last inequality implies that

$$\lambda_1^{\mathrm{SH}}(\mathbf{s}) \leq \frac{(C+s_1)(C+2s_1)}{C}. \tag{9}$$

Also, by applying the Bernoulli inequality at the RHS of the definition of $g_1^{\mathrm{SH}}(\mathbf{s})$, we obtain

$$g_1^{\mathrm{SH}}(\mathbf{s}) \geq \int_0^1 \prod_{i\geq 2}(1-t)^{\frac{s_i}{s_1}}\,\mathrm{d}t = \int_0^1 (1-t)^{\frac{C}{s_1}}\,\mathrm{d}t = \frac{s_1}{C+s_1}. \tag{10}$$

Now, we have

$$\frac{\sum_{i\geq 2} p_i^{\mathrm{SH}}(\mathbf{s}) + \lambda_1^{\mathrm{SH}}(\mathbf{s})}{\sum_{i\geq 2} p_i^{\mathrm{SH}}(\mathbf{s}) + \lambda_1^{\mathrm{SH}}(\mathbf{s})\,g_1^{\mathrm{SH}}(\mathbf{s})} \leq \frac{C^2 + (C+s_1)(C+2s_1)}{C^2 + (C+s_1)(C+2s_1)\,g_1^{\mathrm{SH}}(\mathbf{s})} \leq \frac{2C^2 + 3s_1C + 2s_1^2}{C^2 + s_1C + 2s_1^2} \leq 3. \tag{11}$$

The two first inequalities follow by (9) and (10), respectively, and the last one is obvious since $s_1, C \geq 0$.

Now, the upper bound follows by Lemma 4.2 using (8) and (11). □

THEOREM 5.3. *The liquid price of anarchy of the SH mechanism is at least* 3.

PROOF. It suffices to restrict our attention to the 2-player version of the mechanism. Let $\mathbf{s} \in \mathbb{X}_2$ with $s_1 \leq s_2$. In this case $g_1^{\text{SH}}(\mathbf{s}) = \frac{s_1}{2s_2}$ which implies that $\lambda_1^{\text{SH}}(\mathbf{s}) = 2s_2$. Since the SH mechanism belongs to class $C$, by Lemma 4.3, we have that $\mathbf{s} \in \text{eq}(\mathcal{G}^{\text{SH}}(\mathbf{s}, 1))$. Using Lemma 6, we obtain

$$\text{LPoA(SH)} \geq \sup_{\mathbf{s} \in \mathbb{X}_2 : s_1 \leq s_2} \frac{3s_2}{s_2 + s_1} = 3.$$

The proof is complete. □

## 6 TWO-PLAYER MECHANISMS

As we saw in Theorem 5.1, the Kelly mechanism has an LPoA of exactly 2 even in the case of two players. In contrast, our lower bound of 3/2 for 2-player mechanisms in Theorem 3.1 seems to leave room for improvements. Such improvements are indeed possible as we show with the mechanisms that we present in this section. Interestingly, the E2-PYS mechanism that is defined in the following is also proved to have optimal LPoA among all 2-player PYS mechanisms with concave allocation functions.

Let $\beta \approx 1.792$ be the solution of the equation $\frac{1}{\beta} - \frac{1}{\beta}\exp\left(-\frac{\beta}{\beta-1}\right) = \frac{1}{2}$ and define mechanism E2-PYS to be the PYS 2-player mechanism that uses the allocation function

$$g_i^{\text{E2-PYS}}(\mathbf{s}) = \begin{cases} \frac{1}{\beta} - \frac{1}{\beta}\exp\left(-\frac{\beta}{\beta-1} \cdot \frac{s_i}{s_{3-i}}\right) & s_i \leq s_{3-i} \\ \frac{\beta-1}{\beta} + \frac{1}{\beta}\exp\left(-\frac{\beta}{\beta-1} \cdot \frac{s_{3-i}}{s_i}\right) & s_i > s_{3-i} \end{cases}$$

for player $i \in \{1, 2\}$ and (non-zero) signal vector $\mathbf{s} = (s_1, s_2)$. Due to the definition of $\beta$, E2-PYS is a well-defined resource allocation mechanism: it is anonymous, with an increasing and differentiable allocation function, which allocates the whole resource when some player has non-zero signal. Moreover, E2-PYS belongs to class $C$: the allocation function can be seen to be concave (see also Figure 3) and the payment function is, of course, convex. The LPoA bound statement for E2-PYS follows.

THEOREM 6.1. *The liquid price of anarchy of the E2-PYS mechanism is* $\beta \approx 1.792$.

PROOF. We will prove the theorem using Lemma 4.2. Let $\mathbf{s} \in \mathbb{X}_2$. Due to Lemma 4.3, we have that $\mathbf{s} \in \text{eq}(\mathcal{G}^{\text{E2-PYS}}(\mathbf{s}, 1))$. We distinguish between two cases. First, assume that $s_1 \leq s_2$; in this case,

$$g_1^{\text{E2-PYS}}(s_1, s_2) = \frac{1}{\beta} - \frac{1}{\beta}\exp\left(-\frac{\beta}{\beta - 1} \cdot \frac{s_1}{s_2}\right)$$

and

$$\left.\frac{\partial g_1^{\text{E2-PYS}}(y, s_2)}{\partial y}\right|_{y=s_1} = \frac{1}{(\beta - 1)s_2}\exp\left(-\frac{\beta}{\beta - 1} \cdot \frac{s_1}{s_2}\right).$$

Using (6), $\lambda_1^{\text{E2-PYS}}(\mathbf{s})$ is defined as $\lambda_1^{\text{E2-PYS}}(\mathbf{s}) = (\beta - 1)s_2 \exp\left(\frac{\beta}{\beta-1} \cdot \frac{s_1}{s_2}\right)$. Then, it can be easily verified that

$$\frac{p_2^{\text{E2-PYS}}(\mathbf{s}) + \lambda_1^{\text{E2-PYS}}(\mathbf{s})}{p_2^{\text{E2-PYS}}(\mathbf{s}) + \lambda_1^{\text{E2-PYS}}(\mathbf{s})\, g_1^{\text{E2-PYS}}(\mathbf{s})} = \beta. \tag{12}$$

Now, assume that $s_1 > s_2$; in this case,

$$g_1^{\text{E2-PYS}}(s_1, s_2) = \frac{\beta - 1}{\beta} + \frac{1}{\beta}\exp\left(-\frac{\beta}{\beta - 1}\cdot\frac{s_2}{s_1}\right)$$

and

$$\left.\frac{\partial g_1^{\text{E2-PYS}}(y, s_2)}{\partial y}\right|_{y=s_1} = \frac{s_2}{(\beta-1)s_1^2}\exp\left(-\frac{\beta}{\beta-1}\cdot\frac{s_2}{s_1}\right).$$

Now, (6) yields $\lambda_1^{\text{E2-PYS}}(\mathbf{s}) = \frac{(\beta-1)s_1^2}{s_2}\exp\left(\frac{\beta}{\beta-1}\cdot\frac{s_2}{s_1}\right)$. By substituting $p_2^{\text{E2-PYS}}(\mathbf{s})$, $\lambda_1^{\text{E2-PYS}}(\mathbf{s})$, and $g_1^{\text{E2-PYS}}(\mathbf{s})$, we have

$$\frac{p_2^{\text{E2-PYS}}(\mathbf{s}) + \lambda_1^{\text{E2-PYS}}(\mathbf{s})}{p_2^{\text{E2-PYS}}(\mathbf{s}) + \lambda_1^{\text{E2-PYS}}(\mathbf{s})\,g_1^{\text{E2-PYS}}(\mathbf{s})} = \beta\frac{1 + (\beta-1)\left(\frac{s_1}{s_2}\right)^2\exp\left(\frac{\beta}{\beta-1}\cdot\frac{s_2}{s_1}\right)}{\beta + (\beta-1)^2\left(\frac{s_1}{s_2}\right)^2\exp\left(\frac{\beta}{\beta-1}\cdot\frac{s_2}{s_1}\right) + (\beta-1)\left(\frac{s_1}{s_2}\right)^2} \leq \beta. \quad (13)$$

The inequality follows since the quantity at its left is decreasing in $s_1/s_2$ (its derivative with respect to $s_1/s_2$ can be shown by tedious calculations to be non-positive for $s_1/s_2 \geq 1$) and, hence, it is upper-bounded by its value for $s_1/s_2 = 1$; this is equal to $\beta$ by its definition.

The theorem follows by Lemma 4.2 using (12) and (13). □

We remark that a preliminary analysis similar to the first half of the proof of Theorem 6.1 inspired the design of the E2-PYS mechanism (as well as that of E2-SR mechanism that is defined later) at first place. By keeping the allocation function as the unknown and requiring that the RHS of (6) is equal to some value $\alpha$ for all signal vectors $\mathbf{s} \in \mathbb{X}_2$ with $s_1 \leq s_2$ (this is essentially what (12) captures), we obtained a first-order differential equation which, using the appropriate conditions so that the resulting mechanism is valid, led to E2-PYS (for $\alpha = \beta$). Luckily, for signal vectors $\mathbf{s} \in \mathbb{X}_2$ with $s_1 > s_2$, we were able to show that the RHS of (6) is at most $\alpha$; see inequality (13).

We now show that E2-PYS has optimal LPoA among 2-player PYS mechanisms in class $C$. The proof makes use of Lemma 4.2 and a simple differential inequality that involves the allocation function.

Theorem 6.2. *Any 2-player PYS mechanism with concave allocation function has liquid price of anarchy at least $\beta \approx 1.792$.*

Proof. For the sake of contradiction, assume that there exists a PYS mechanism $M$ that has liquid price of anarchy $\beta' < \beta$. Denote by $f : \mathbb{R}_{\geq 0} \to [0, 1]$ the function defined as $f(y) = g_1^M(y, 1)$. Then, by applying Lemma 4.2 with $\mathbf{s} = (y, 1) \in \mathbb{X}_2$ to $M$ we have $\lambda_1^M(y, 1) = 1/f'(y)$ and LPoA$(M) \geq \frac{1+1/f'(y)}{1+f(y)/f'(y)}$ for every $y \in [0, 1]$. By our assumption LPoA$(M) \leq \beta'$, we get the differential inequality

$$(\beta' - 1)f'(y) + \beta' f(y) \geq 1$$

for every $y \in [0, 1]$. Using Grönwall's inequality, $f(y)$ is lower-bounded by the solution of the corresponding differential equation. Due to the condition $f(0) = 0$, this yields

$$f(y) \geq \frac{1}{\beta'} - \frac{1}{\beta'}\exp\left(-\frac{\beta'}{\beta' - 1}y\right)$$

and, hence,

$$\frac{1}{2} = f(1) \geq \frac{1}{\beta'} - \frac{1}{\beta'}\exp\left(-\frac{\beta'}{\beta'-1}\right) > \frac{1}{\beta} - \frac{1}{\beta}\exp\left(-\frac{\beta}{\beta-1}\right),$$

which contradicts the definition of $\beta$. The last inequality follows since the function $\frac{1}{z} - \frac{1}{z}\exp\left(-\frac{z}{z-1}\right)$ is decreasing in the interval $[1, 2]$. □

Let us now define a non-PYS mechanism that has considerably better LPoA than E2-PYS and almost matches the lower bound of $3/2$ from Theorem 3.1 for 2-player mechanisms. Let $\gamma \approx 1.529$ be the solution of the equation $\frac{1}{\gamma} - \frac{1}{\gamma}\exp\left(-\frac{\gamma}{2(\gamma-1)}\right) = \frac{1}{2}$ and define mechanism E2-SR to be the 2-player mechanism that uses the allocation function (see Figure 3 for a comparison of the allocation functions of Kelly, SH, E2-PYS, and E2-SR)

$$g_i^{\text{E2-SR}}(\mathbf{s}) = \begin{cases} \frac{1}{\gamma} - \frac{1}{\gamma}\exp\left(-\frac{\gamma}{2(\gamma-1)} \cdot \left(\frac{s_i}{s_{3-i}}\right)^2\right) & s_i \le s_{3-i} \\ \frac{\gamma-1}{\gamma} + \frac{1}{\gamma}\exp\left(-\frac{\gamma}{2(\gamma-1)} \cdot \left(\frac{s_{3-i}}{s_i}\right)^2\right) & s_i > s_{3-i} \end{cases}$$

and the payment function $p_i^{\text{E2-SR}}(\mathbf{s}) = s_i/s_{3-i}$ for player $i \in \{1, 2\}$ and (non-zero) signal vector $\mathbf{s} = (s_1, s_2)$. Recall that we follow the general conventions from Section 2; hence, the payments are 0 when some of the signals is equal to zero. Due to the definition of $\gamma$, E2-SR is a well-defined resource allocation mechanism. However, observe that E2-SR does not belong to class $C$ (the allocation function is not concave; see Figure 3) and the condition $\mathbf{s} \in \text{eq}(\mathcal{G}^{\text{E2-SR}}(\mathbf{s}, 1))$ is not guaranteed to be satisfied. Next, we will prove an upper bound on the LPoA of E2-SR. The proof follows in a very similar way to the proof of Theorem 6.1 with the exception that it does not provide a tight bound.

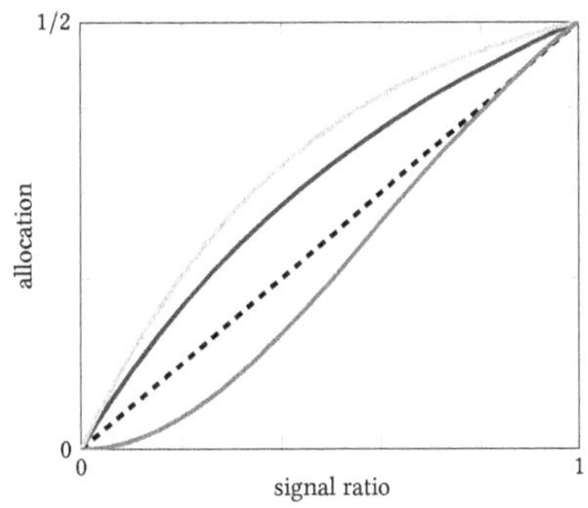


Fig. 3. A comparison of the allocation function $g_i^M$ used by E2-PYS (in green), (the 2-player version of) Kelly (in blue), SH (dashed), and E2-SR (in red) as a function of $s_i/s_{3-i}$ for $s_i \le s_{3-i}$. Among these mechanisms, E2-SR is the only one with a non-concave allocation function.

Theorem 6.3. *The liquid price of anarchy of the E2-SR mechanism is at most $\gamma \approx 1.529$.*

Proof. We will prove the theorem by mimicking the proof of Theorem 6.1. Let $\mathbf{s} \in \mathbb{X}_2$. We distinguish between two cases. First, assume that $s_1 \le s_2$; in this case

$$g_1^{\text{E2-SR}}(s_1, s_2) = \frac{1}{\gamma} - \frac{1}{\gamma}\exp\left(-\frac{\gamma}{2(\gamma-1)} \cdot \left(\frac{s_1}{s_2}\right)^2\right)$$

and

$$\left.\frac{\partial g_1^{\text{E2-SR}}(y, s_2)}{\partial y}\right|_{y=s_1} = \frac{s_1}{(\gamma-1)s_2^2}\exp\left(-\frac{\gamma}{2(\gamma-1)} \cdot \left(\frac{s_1}{s_2}\right)^2\right).$$

Also,

$$\left.\frac{\partial p_1^{\text{E2-SR}}(y, s_2)}{\partial y}\right|_{y=s_1} = \frac{1}{s_2}.$$

Using (6), $\lambda_1^{\text{E2-SR}}(\mathbf{s})$ is defined as $\lambda_1^{\text{E2-SR}}(\mathbf{s}) = (\gamma - 1)\frac{s_2}{s_1} \exp\left(\frac{\gamma}{2(\gamma-1)} \cdot \left(\frac{s_1}{s_2}\right)^2\right)$. Then, it can be easily verified that

$$\frac{p_2^{\text{E2-SR}}(\mathbf{s}) + \lambda_1^{\text{E2-SR}}(\mathbf{s})}{p_2^{\text{E2-SR}}(\mathbf{s}) + \lambda_1^{\text{E2-SR}}(\mathbf{s})\, g_1^{\text{E2-SR}}(\mathbf{s})} = \gamma. \tag{14}$$

Now, assume that $s_1 > s_2$; in this case,

$$g_1^{\text{E2-SR}}(s_1, s_2) = \frac{\gamma - 1}{\gamma} + \frac{1}{\gamma} \exp\left(-\frac{\gamma}{2(\gamma - 1)} \cdot \left(\frac{s_2}{s_1}\right)^2\right)$$

and

$$\left.\frac{\partial g_1^{\text{E2-SR}}(y, s_2)}{\partial y}\right|_{y=s_1} = \frac{s_2^2}{(\gamma - 1)s_1^3} \exp\left(-\frac{\gamma}{2(\gamma - 1)} \cdot \left(\frac{s_2}{s_1}\right)^2\right).$$

The payment derivative is again equal to $1/s_2$ and (6) yields

$$\lambda_1^{\text{E2-SR}}(\mathbf{s}) = (\gamma - 1)\left(\frac{s_1}{s_2}\right)^3 \exp\left(\frac{\gamma}{2(\gamma - 1)} \cdot \left(\frac{s_2}{s_1}\right)^2\right).$$

By substituting $p_2^{\text{E2-SR}}(\mathbf{s})$, $\lambda_1^{\text{E2-SR}}(\mathbf{s})$, and $g_1^{\text{E2-SR}}(\mathbf{s})$, we have

$$\frac{p_2^{\text{E2-SR}}(\mathbf{s}) + \lambda_1^{\text{E2-SR}}(\mathbf{s})}{p_2^{\text{E2-SR}}(\mathbf{s}) + \lambda_1^{\text{E2-SR}}(\mathbf{s})\, g_1^{\text{E2-SR}}(\mathbf{s})} = \gamma \frac{1 + (\gamma - 1)\left(\frac{s_1}{s_2}\right)^4 \exp\left(\frac{\gamma}{2(\gamma-1)} \cdot \left(\frac{s_2}{s_1}\right)^2\right)}{\gamma + (\gamma - 1)^2 \left(\frac{s_1}{s_2}\right)^4 \exp\left(\frac{\gamma}{2(\gamma-1)} \cdot \left(\frac{s_2}{s_1}\right)^2\right) + (\gamma - 1)\left(\frac{s_1}{s_2}\right)^4} \leq \gamma. \tag{15}$$

The inequality follows because the quantity at its left is decreasing in $s_1/s_2$ (its derivative with respect to $s_1/s_2$ can be shown by tedious calculations to be non-positive for $s_1/s_2 \geq 1$) and, hence, it is upper-bounded by its value for $s_1/s_2 = 1$; this is equal to $\gamma$ by its definition.

The theorem follows by Lemma 4.2 using (14) and (15). □

Interestingly, a simpler 2-player mechanism that uses the allocation function of SH and the signal-ratio payment function of E2-SR has a slightly worse LPoA of $\phi = 1.618$. In fact, this bound is tight since this particular mechanism belongs to class $C$. The proof is left as an exercise to the reader.

## 7 OPEN PROBLEMS AND EXTENSIONS

Even though we have revealed an almost complete picture on the liquid price of anarchy of resource allocation mechanisms, our work leaves an interesting open problem: is the $2-1/n$ bound achievable (as opposed to 2), preferably by a simple mechanism? In particular, is there a mechanism with proportional allocation function and appropriate non-PYS payments that achieves this LPoA bound? This question seems technically challenging even for the case of two players only.

Regarding the liquid price of anarchy over more general equilibrium concepts (e.g., correlated equilibria) or settings with incomplete information (and Bayes-Nash equilibria), is the Kelly mechanism still optimal within low-order terms? We are far from answering this question. The papers by Caragiannis and Voudouris [2] and by Christodoulou et al. [3] present LPoA bounds for Kelly, but these are not known to be tight. We conjecture that the proof of tight LPoA bounds over more general equilibrium concepts for any resource allocation mechanism should exploit the structure of worst-case games and equilibria as we did in the current paper for pure Nash equilibria. Unfortunately, extending our characterization from Section 4 to more general equilibrium concepts seems elusive at this point.

There are several interesting extensions of our setting that could be considered. *Budget-aware* mechanisms, which have access to the budget value of each player, constitute a first such extension. Of course, our analysis for mechanisms Kelly, SH, E2-PYS, and E2-SR carries over to this case. In contrast, our lower bound (Theorem 3.1) is not true anymore. The proof constructs two games, in which almost every player has different budgets. The main property we have exploited in that proof (for non-budget-aware mechanisms) is that the strategic behavior of the players results in the same set of equilibria in both games. This argument fails for budget-aware mechanisms; a small change in the budget of a single player could be enough to alter the set of equilibria. So, in principle, one might hope even for full efficiency at equilibria (i.e., LPoA equal to 1) in this case, analogously to the results of Maheswaran and Basar [17], Johari and Tsitsiklis [9], and Yang and Hajek [22] in the no-budget setting. Interestingly, our next statement rules out this possibility.

Theorem 7.1. *For $n \geq 2$, every $n$-player budget-aware resource allocation mechanism has liquid price of anarchy at least $4/3$.*

Proof. Let $M$ be any $n$-player budget-aware resource allocation mechanism that uses an allocation function $g^M$ and a payment function $p^M$. Let $\mathbf{s} = (s_1, ..., s_n)$ be an equilibrium of the game $\mathcal{G}_1^M$ induced by $M$ for players with valuations $v_i(x) = x$ for $i \in \{1, 2\}$ and $v_i(x) = 0$ for $i \geq 3$, and budgets $c_i = 1$ for every $i \in [n]$. Assume that the allocation returned by $M$ at this equilibrium is $\mathbf{d} = (d_1, ..., d_n)$. Without loss of generality, we may assume that one of the first two players (say, player 1) gets a resource share of at most $1/2$.

Recall that, for every signal vector $\mathbf{y}$, the utility of any player $i$ is defined as $u_i^M(\mathbf{y}) = v_i(g_i^M(\mathbf{y})) - p_i^M(\mathbf{y})$. Now, consider the game $\mathcal{G}_2^M$ where player 2 has the modified valuation function $\tilde{v}_2(x) = 1 + x$ while all other players are as in $\mathcal{G}_1^M$; the budgets are the same in both games and are known to the mechanism. Observe that the modified utility of player 2 is now $\tilde{u}_2^M(\mathbf{y}) = \tilde{v}_2(g_2^M(\mathbf{y})) - p_2^M(\mathbf{y}) = u_2^M(\mathbf{y}) + 1$. Hence, $\mathbf{s}$ is an equilibrium in $\mathcal{G}_2^M$ as well and $M$ returns the same allocation $\mathbf{d}$ again.

Clearly, due to the definition of the valuation functions, the contribution of players $i \geq 3$ in the liquid welfare (in any state of the game) is zero. Hence, the liquid welfare at equilibrium is $\min\{\tilde{v}_1(d_1), c_1\} + \min\{\tilde{v}_2(d_2), c_2\} = d_1 + 1 \leq 3/2$, while the optimal liquid welfare is equal to 2, achieved at the allocation according to which the whole resource is given to player 1. We conclude that the liquid price of anarchy of $M$ is $\text{LPoA}(M) \geq \text{LPoA}(\mathcal{G}_2^M) \geq 4/3$, as desired. □

In spite of the lower bound in Theorem 7.1, whether budget-aware resource allocation mechanisms can have an LPoA better than $2 - 1/n$ is an important open problem. This seems to be a technically non-trivial and extremely challenging task though.

Another possible extension of our setting could be to allow the players to declare their budgets to the mechanism in addition to their scalar signal. Taking this approach to its extreme, one could imagine resource allocation mechanisms which ask the players to submit *multi-dimensional* signals. At first glance, this seems to lead to much more powerful mechanisms than the ones we have considered here. Surprisingly, this *higher level of expressiveness* has no consequences to the LPoA at all and our lower bound of $2 - 1/n$ captures such mechanisms as well. Indeed, by inspecting the two games used in the proof of Theorem 3.1, we can verify that the same signal vector (no matter whether signals are single- or multi-dimensional) leads to the same allocation by the mechanism and the same strategic behavior of the players in both games. This observation applies to the proof of Theorem 7.1 as well.

Finally, we believe that the liquid welfare is an appropriate efficiency benchmark for auctions with budget-constrained players. The recent paper by Azar et al. [1] studies the LPoA of simultaneous first-price auctions; obtaining similar results for other auction formats (e.g., see the recent survey of Roughgarden et al. [19]) is certainly important. Needless to say, we do not expect that the liquid welfare is unique as a measure of efficiency in settings with budgets. Defining alternative efficiency benchmarks and studying the price of anarchy with respect to them would shed extra light to the strengths and weaknesses of auction mechanisms.

## REFERENCES


[1] Y. Azar, M. Feldman, N. Gravin, and A. Roytman. 2017. Liquid price of anarchy. In *Proceedings of the 10th International Symposium on Algorithmic Game Theory (SAGT)*. 3–15.

[2] I. Caragiannis and A. A. Voudouris. 2016. Welfare guarantees for proportional allocations. *Theory of Computing Systems* 59, 4 (2016), 581–599.

[3] G. Christodoulou, A. Sgouritsa, and B. Tang. 2016. On the efficiency of the proportional allocation mechanism for divisible resources. *Theory of Computing Systems* 59, 4 (2016), 600–618.

[4] S. Dobzinski and R. Paes Leme. 2014. Efficiency guarantees in auctions with budgets. In *Proceedings of the 41st International Colloquium on Automata, Languages and Programming (ICALP)*. 392–404.

[5] S. Dughmi, A. Eden, M. Feldman, A. Fiat, and S. Leonardi. 2016. Lottery pricing equilibria. In *Proceedings of the 17th ACM Conference on Economics and Computation (EC)*. 401–418.

[6] B. Hajek and G. Gopalakrishnan. 2002. Do greedy autonomous systems make for a sensible Internet? *Unpublished manuscript* (2002).

[7] R. Johari. 2007. The price of anarchy and the design of scalable resource allocation algorithms. *Chapter 21 in Algorithmic Game Theory* (2007), 543–568.

[8] R. Johari and J. N. Tsitsiklis. 2004. Efficiency loss in a network resource allocation game. *Mathematics of Operations Research* 29, 3 (2004), 407–435.

[9] R. Johari and J. N. Tsitsiklis. 2009. Efficiency of scalar-parameterized mechanisms. *Operations Research* 57, 4 (2009), 823–839.

[10] F. P. Kelly. 1997. Charging and rate control for elastic traffic. *European Transactions on Telecommunications* 8 (1997), 33–37.

[11] F. P. Kelly, A. Maulloo, and D. Tan. 1998. Rate control in communication networks: shadow prices, proportional fairness and stability. *Journal of the Operational Research Society* 49 (1998), 237–252.

[12] E. Koutsoupias and C. H. Papadimitriou. 1999. Worst-case equilibria. In *Proceedings of the 16th Symposium on Theoretical Aspects of Computer Science (STACS)*. 404–413.

[13] R. J. La and V. Anantharam. 2000. Charge-sensitive TCP and rate control in the Internet. In *Proceedings of the 19th Annual Joint Conference of the IEEE Computer and Communications Societies (INFOCOM)*. 1166–1175.

[14] P. Lu and T. Xiao. 2015. Improved efficiency guarantees in auctions with budgets. In *Proceedings of the 16th ACM Conference on Economics and Computation (EC)*. 397–413.

[15] P. Lu and T. Xiao. 2017. Liquid welfare maximization in auctions with multiple items. In *Proceedings of the 10th International Symposium on Algorithmic Game Theory (SAGT)*. 41–52.

[16] R. T. Maheswaran and T. Basar. 2003. Nash equilibrium and decentralized negotiation in auctioning divisible resources. *Group Decision and Negotiation* 12, 5 (2003), 361–395.

[17] R. T. Maheswaran and T. Basar. 2006. Efficient signal proportional allocation (ESPA) mechanisms: decentralized social welfare maximization for divisible resources. *IEEE Journal on Selected Areas in Communications* 24, 5 (2006), 1000–1009.

[18] T. Roughgarden. 2015. Intrinsic robustness of the price of anarchy. *Journal of the ACM* 62, 5 (2015), 32:1–42.

[19] T. Roughgarden, V. Syrgkanis, and E. Tardos. 2017. The price of anarchy in auctions. *Journal of Artificial Intelligence Research* 59 (2017), 59–101.

[20] S. Sanghavi and B. Hajek. 2004. Optimal allocation of a divisible good to strategic buyers. In *Proceedings of the 43rd IEEE Conference on Decision and Control (CDC)*.

[21] V. Syrgkanis and E. Tardos. 2013. Composable and efficient mechanisms. In *Proceedings of the 45th Annual ACM Symposium on Theory of Computing (STOC)*. 211–220.

[22] S. Yang and B. E. Hajek. 2007. VCG-Kelly mechanisms for allocation of divisible goods: adapting VCG mechanisms to one-dimensional signals. *IEEE Journal on Selected Areas in Communications* 25, 6 (2007), 1237–1243.

# Author Index

www.ingramcontent.com/pod-product-compliance
Lightning Source LLC
LaVergne TN
LVHW080110011026
849160LV00013B/1062